D1538516

135000 WORDS

SPELLED AND PRONOUNCED

BOOKS FOR THE HOME LIBRARY

WALKS AND TALKS IN THE GEOLOGICAL FIELD
By ALEXANDER WINCHELL, LL.D.

Late Professor of Geology and Paleontology in the University of Michigan.

Revised and edited by FREDERICK STARR, of the University of Chicago. 12mo. Cloth. Illustrated.

Price, $1.00 net; by mail, $1.13.

MEN AND MANNERS OF THE EIGHTEENTH CENTURY
By SUSAN HALE

12mo. Cloth. **Price, $1.00 net; by mail, $1.13.**

STUDIES IN AMERICAN LITERATURE
By HENRY A. BEERS

Professor of English Literature in Yale University.
12mo. Cloth. Illustrated. **Price, $1.00 net; by mail, $1.13.**

ROME AND THE MAKING OF MODERN EUROPE
By JAMES RICHARD JOY

12mo. Cloth. **Price, $1.00 net; by mail, $1.13.**

ROMAN LIFE IN PLINY'S TIME
By MAURICE PELLISON

Translated from the French by MAUD WILKINSON, and with an Introduction by FRANK J. MILLER. 12mo. Cloth. Illustrated. **Price, $1.00 net; by mail, $1.13.**

GEORGE W. JACOBS & CO., PUBLISHERS
1216 WALNUT STREET, · · PHILADELPHIA

135000 WORDS

SPELLED AND PRONOUNCED

TOGETHER WITH

VALUABLE HINTS AND ILLUSTRATIONS FOR THE USE OF CAPITALS,
ITALICS, NUMERALS, AND COMPOUND WORDS; ALSO RULES
FOR SYLLABICATION AND PUNCTUATION AND A
LARGE LIST OF HOMOPHONES

DESIGNED FOR

OFFICE, SCHOOL, AND LIBRARY USE

BY

JOHN H. BECHTEL

Author of "Handbook of Pronunciation" "Synonyms" "Slips of Speech" etc.

ROWMAN & LITTLEFIELD PUBLISHERS, INC.
Lanham • Boulder • New York • Toronto • Plymouth, UK

Published by Rowman & Littlefield
A wholly owned subsidiary of
The Rowman & Littlefield Publishing Group, Inc.
4501 Forbes Boulevard, Suite 200, Lanham, Maryland 20706
www.rowman.com

10 Thornbury Road, Plymouth PL6 7PP, United Kingdom

Copyright © 1904 by George W. Jacobs and Company
First Rowman & Littlefield paperback edition 2014

All rights reserved. No part of this book may be reproduced in any form or by any electronic or mechanical means, including information storage and retrieval systems, without written permission from the publisher, except by a reviewer who may quote passages in a review.

Library of Congress Cataloging-in-Publication Data

ISBN-13: 978-1-4422-4329-3 (pbk : alk. paper)

♾™ The paper used in this publication meets the minimum requirements of American National Standard for Information Sciences—Permanence of Paper for Printed Library Materials, ANSI/NISO Z39.48-1992.

Printed in the United States of America

LIST OF SUBJECTS

TABLE OF CONTENTS

vii

INTRODUCTION

PROVINCE OF THE DICTIONARY

The primary purpose of the lexicographer is to set forth the proper orthography, pronunciation, and definitions of the words of the language. The vast majority of persons who consult the dictionaries do so to determine questions of spelling and pronunciation much oftener than to learn the meanings of words. This is especially true of teachers and students in schools and colleges, of stenographers in professional and mercantile offices, and of business men in general.

COMPREHENSIVE VOCABULARY

By omitting definitions, and by a system of grouping which at the same time facilitates the speedy finding of the desired word, it has been made possible to bring within the compass of a single small volume a list of words almost as comprehensive and complete as that of the largest unabridged dictionaries.

SPELLING AND PRONUNCIATION

The standard authorities have been diligently compared, in order to determine the best spelling and pronunciation. In cases where several forms are in good current use, that which appears to have the greatest weight of authority has been placed first, with the variant form or forms following. All words whose pronunciation cannot be clearly and accurately set forth by the accepted orthography have been respelled to show the true pronunciation.

2   17

DIACRITICS

In the preparation of this volume, the special needs of English-speaking people and those who have a fair knowledge of the idiom of the language have been kept in view. Minor distinctions of vowel sounds, especially those occasioned by the absence of accent, have therefore been ignored. Many persons of culture, but without special training in phonetics, are in greater doubt after consulting the dictionary for pronunciation than they were before. Believing that the appearance of the printed word should be left as free as possible from foreign or extraneous signs and characters, the most limited use of diacritics consistent with the representation of the correct pronunciation of the word has been made, and only those signs that are in most general use have been selected.

SYLLABICATION AND ACCENT

Stenographers, students, business men—in short, nearly all who have occasion to write—are at times perplexed to know just where to divide a word at the end of a line. Every word of more than one syllable in the vocabulary has been divided into its syllables, and the accent properly placed. In long words, where the place of secondary accent is doubtful, it, too, has been noted.

GROUPING

In order to make it possible to include practically all the words of the most extensive unabridged dictionary within the compass of a convenient single volume, a system of grouping has been adopted which in nowise detracts from the fullest representation of the spelling and pronunciation of the words, and which, by bringing derivative and related words all under the eye at once, greatly speeds the finding of the word desired. In one of the unabridged dictionaries, the word *air*, with its related words, covers over ten columns, or nearly four pages. By grouping, these words are brought under the eye at one glance.

COMPOUND WORDS

In no other department of lexicography is there so much uncertainty as in the compounding of words. The authorities often differ with each other, and are sometimes inconsistent with themselves, their practice violating their own theories. In this volume, faithful endeavor has been made to represent the best current usage, showing what compounds are written without separation, as *breastplate*, *breastwork*, and what words should be separated by a hyphen, as *bold-faced*, *blear-eyed*. In all other cases, the words are written separately, as *bass viol*, *Bath brick*, *galvanic battery*.

CAPITALIZATION

Writers and proof-readers are much at variance in the use of capital letters. Several of the unabridged dictionaries begin all the words of the vocabulary list with capitals. The best current usage has been here set forth. All words in the vocabulary except those requiring capitals, begin with lower-case letters.

FOREIGN WORDS

Words and phrases from other languages, when first introduced into English and American books, newspapers, and magazines, are printed in italics to denote their foreign origin. In the course of time many of these, by frequent use, drop their foreign dress and become anglicized. All words and expressions in this volume that retain their foreign form and pronunciation, have been so indicated, and are italicized.

ENGLISH AND FOREIGN PLURALS

Not a little uncertainty attends the use of plurals of foreign and classical terms. In some cases, the English plural has entirely supplanted the foreign; in others, the English form is occasionally met with in the works of good writers, but the general practice is largely in favor of the classic plural. In some instances, however, good usage is quite evenly divided. In the first case, only the English plural has been given; in the second, only the classical; and in the third, both forms are presented, placing first that which seems to have the greater weight of authority.

PROPER NAMES

The names of persons and places are found in alphabetic order in the body of the work. This arrangement avoids the necessity for two distinct vocabularies. When it is remembered that we have many adjectives derived from proper names, the advantages of the plan become doubly apparent.

OBSOLETE WORDS

All obsolete, obsolescent, and archaic forms have been omitted, so that the student will know that any word found in the vocabulary of this volume is in good and current use, the purpose having been to present a thoroughly up-to-date working hand-book, and not to collect the worn-out forms of a previous age.

ORTHOGRAPHY

The words of the English language being derived from various sources, differing greatly in form and spirit, it is not surprising that they present many anomalies in their spelling and pronunciation. The carelessness and indifference of the early writers and printers also contributed to the existing irregularities, so that by the time the language began to assume a distinctive form and structure of its own, the inconsistencies of its spelling and pronunciation had become so firmly fixed that it was found impossible immediately to change them. Gradual changes are slowly going on, but the day when the English language shall become strictly phonetic—when we shall spell as we pronounce and pronounce as we spell—seems to be remote.

. The old family name of Mainwaring has shown one hundred and thirty-one variations in spelling, all drawn from authorized documents. Even as late as Shakspeare's time, much indifference was manifest, his name being written in more than thirty ways, three or four of which are still in current use. The words *aerie, aery, airy, eyry, eyrie,* still found in general use, added to *airie, aiery, ayry, ayery, eyery, eyerie,* forms found in early modern English, will serve to show some of the irregularities and inconsistencies of English spelling.

Persons who in childhood are taught to follow a certain spelling, usually adhere to that form in later life, and are sometimes intolerant of any other. The advantage of having the latest and best standard, that the child may be started aright, needs no argument.

CAUSES OF DIFFICULTY IN SPELLING

"Language," says Professor March, "is what we speak." All articulate speech is made up of words. These spoken words, in turn, are composed of sounds. An articulate, or speech, sound is the simplest element of language.

A perfect alphabet demands that there shall be as many characters, or letters, as there are elementary sounds; that each sound shall be represented by its own particular letter, and by no other; and that each letter shall represent but one sound. With such an alphabet, there could be no difficulties in spelling nor in pronunciation.

The English alphabet contains twenty-six letters. These are made to represent at least forty-seven English sounds. Three of the letters (*c, q,* and *x*) have no distinctive function, but repeat sounds represented by other letters or combinations of letters. This reduces the actual working force of the alphabet to twenty-three characters, giving an average of two sounds to each character. The work, however, is not so evenly divided. The five letters called vowels are made to bear a large part of the burden, representing no fewer than eighteen separate sounds. The consonants, too, are often used interchangeably, one sound being represented by several characters.

CLASSIFICATION OF THE LETTERS

The letters of the alphabet are divided into vowels and consonants. The vowels are *a, e, i, o, u,* and represent open vocalized sounds, with but slight obstruction in the emission of the breath. The remaining letters are called consonants. The term *consonant* seems to imply that this class of letters can be used only with vowels to form syllables; but *l* and *n* frequently represent spoken syllables without a sonant vowel. Some grammarians add *w* and *y* to the list of vowels. Strictly speaking, these are never vowels. The former often combines with *e* to represent one of the sounds of *u* (*new, pew*), and with *a* to represent one of the sounds of that letter (*saw*), and with *o* to represent long *o* (*snow*), or the diphthong *ou* (*cow*). The letter *y* is often used as a substitute for *i* (*my, happy, myrtle*), but its distinctive office is purely consonantal.

DIGRAPHS AND TRIGRAPHS

The union of two letters to represent one sound is called a digraph, and of three letters, a trigraph. The letters may be either vowels or consonants; as, *ai* in *maid; ch* in *chin; eau* in *beau; sch* in *schist.*

RULES FOR SPELLING

The best spellers are those that spell by sight rather than by rule. Many of the rules for spelling are so obvious as to require no statement, while others are attended with so many exceptions as to render the rule almost useless. Only the most important and helpful rules are here given.

DERIVATIVES

Words ending in c take k before derivative terminations beginning with *e, i,* or *y;* as, *traffic, -ficked, -ficking.*

The final consonant is doubled in forming derivatives be-ginning with a vowel, in the case of monosyllables and accented syllables ending in a single consonant (except *h* or *x*); as *plan, planned, -ning; begin, -ner, -ning.* Cases in which the vowel is preceded by *qu* (as *squat, -ted, -ting; acquit, -ted, -ter, -ting*) form no exception, as the *u* has the sound of *w*.

The final consonant is not doubled (1) when it is preceded by a vowel digraph (*need, -ed, -ing; repeat, -er, ing*); (2) when the accent falls elsewhere than on the last syllable (*profit, -ed, -ing*); (3) when the word ends in two different consonants (*affirm, -ing, -er*).

Words of two or more syllables ending chiefly in *l*, with the accent on a syllable other than the last, according to the pre-ceding rule, do not double the final consonant in taking a deriva-tive beginning with a vowel: *apparel, bevel, cancel, carol, chisel, counsel, duel, equal, imperil, label, level, libel, marshal, model, parallel, pencil, quarrel, revel, shovel, shrivel, travel, worship.* While the dictionaries are greatly at variance on this point, the International, the Century, and the Standard conform to the rule by giving the single consonant the first place, and the double con-sonant the second.

Words ending in silent c, whose derivative forms begin with a consonant, retain the *e;* as, *hate-ful, move-ment.* The most im-portant exceptions are words ending in *ge, judg-ment, acknowledg-ment, abridg-ment, lodg-ment.* The *e* in these words is retained by some authorities as a variant. When the *e* is immediately preceded by another vowel, it is usually dropped, as, *true, tru-ly, argue, argu-ment.*

Words ending in silent e, when forming derivatives beginning with a vowel, drop the *e;* as, *bridal, guidance, hoping, coming.* As a safeguard against mispronunciation and confusion, it is in some cases retained; as, *hoeing, toeing, shoeing, singeing, tinge-ing, springeing, dyeing, mileage.* To preserve the soft *c* or *g*, it is retained in *peaceable, noticeable, manageable, changeable, ad-vantageous, outrageous.*

Words ending in ie not only drop *e* upon adding *ing*, but change *i* to *y* to prevent two *i's* coming together; as, *dying, lying, vying.* Usage is divided in regard to *hying (hie-ing).*

Words ending in y preceded by a consonant, change *y* to *i* in taking an additional syllable beginning with a letter other than *i;* as, *icy, iciest, icily, tidy, tidiness.* Adjectives of one syllable in which *y* is preceded by a single consonant, usually retain *y;* as, *dryly, shyness. Drier* and *driest* are commonly written with *i.* Before the derivative suffixes *-like* and *-ship*, the *y* is retained.

Words ending in y preceded by a vowel, retain the *y* in the formation of derivatives; as, *prayed, obeying, enjoyed.* The common words *daily, laid, paid, said, saith, slain*, are exceptions· *Staid* or *stayed, gaily* or *gayly, gaiety* or *gayety*, are variable forms.

Words ending with a vowel sound retain the letters representing that sound when appending one or more syllables to form a derivative; as, *agree, -ing, -able; weigh, -ing; echo, -ed, -ing.* The third person, singular, present tense forms of verbs ending in *oo* do not add *e;* as, *coos, woos, shampoos, taboos;* but add it in the past tense and other forms; as, *cooed, wooed, wooer.*

Words ending in a double consonant usually retain both consonants on adding a prefix; as, *call, recall, tell, foretell, roll, enroll.* The weight of authority is in favor of the single *l* in *fulfil, instil.*

PLURALS

The plural of nouns is regularly formed by adding *s* to the singular. When the terminal sound is such that *s*, whether representing its own sound or that of *z*, will not combine with it, *es* is added; as, *churches, classes. Cantos, cameos, punctilios, rabbis, alkalis*, are regular. While *s* (with the sound of *z*) will readily unite with the following words, usage sanctions the *es* termination; as, *echoes, cargoes, embargoes, mottoes, potatoes. Alkalies* and *rabbies* are variants. Letters, figures, signs, etc., are pluralized by adding *s* with an apostrophe prefixed; as, *Mind your p's and q's; His 3's and 5's are well·made; He ignores the why's and wherefore's.* Some good writers omit the apostrophe; as, *I have considered the pros and cons.*

The plural of nouns ending in y preceded by a consonant, is formed by adding *es*, the *y* first being changed into *i;* as, *skies, ladies, colloquies.* The letter *u* in the last instance has the force of the consonant *w.* Proper nouns add only *s;* as, Marys, Dorothys, Timothys. Some writers use the form *Maries* as the plural of Mary, but this is apt to confound it with the plural of *Marie*, and should be discouraged. When the singular ends in *y* preceded by a vowel, the plural is regularly formed by adding *s;* as, *days, keys, moneys, monkeys, attorneys.* The forms *monies, attornies, vallies*, should be discouraged.

The plural of the following nouns ending in f, is formed by changing *f* or *fe* into *v*, and adding *es: beef, calf, elf, half, leaf, loaf, self, sheaf, shelf, thief, wolf, knife, life, wife.* Other nouns ending in *f* or *fe* form their plurals regularly: *hoofs, roofs, strifes, safes, chiefs.* The plural of *staff* is *staffs* or *staves*, according to its meaning.

The plural of nouns compounded with and ending in *-man* is *-men;* as, *firemen, workmen.* The following are not compounded, but form their plurals regularly: *Germans, Mussulmans, Ottomans, Turcomans, caymans, desmans, firmans, talismans.*

The irregular plural formations of the common words *man, men,—foot, feet,—goose, geese,* are sufficiently well known to require no discussion, but *mongoose, mongooses, Mr., Messrs., Mrs., Mesdames,* are not so well understood. *Bedouin, cannon, heathen,* are alike in both numbers. *Ethics, optics, news, politics,* and *means* (in the sense of agency) are plural in form, but, as nominatives, require verbs in the singular. The words *wages, aborigines, antipodes, pains,* and *literati,* take verbs in the plural.

The words *brother, die, pea, penny, staff,* have each two plurals, according to the meaning.

Many nouns from other languages have an English, as well as a foreign, plural: *beaus, beaux; formulas, formulæ; indexes, indices; bandits, banditti; cherubs, cherubim; seraphs, seraphim.* The English plurals are now generally preferred.

Some nouns have the same form in both numbers: *deer, sheep,*

swine, grouse, trout, Chinese, Portuguese, Tyrolese, Japanese.
Collectively, *fish* and *fowl* are plural; as individuals, *fishes* and *fowls* are the plural forms.

In certain loosely-formed hyphenated compounds, the principal word is pluralized: *courts-martial, cousins-german, knights-errant, sons-in-law.* In close compounds ending in *-ful,* the plural is formed regularly; as, *handfuls, cupfuls, spoonfuls.*

The terminations -able and -ible cause much confusion in spelling. Those adjectives from Latin words ending in *-abilis,* as well as those of English origin, take the termination *-able,* and comprise much the larger number; as, *mutable, potable, eatable, laughable,* etc. Those derived from Latin words ending in *-ibilis,* take the termination *-ible;* as, *credible, vendible, legible.* The derivative forms, as, *accessible, -ibly, -ibility, inaccessible,* etc., follow the same rule. The following short list of *-ible* terminations comprises nearly all in ordinary use. Any words not found in this list may reasonably be supposed to end in *-able*:

accessible,	convertible,	docible,	frangible,	possible,
admissible,	convincible,	edible,	fusible,	producible,
appetible,	corrigible,	effectible,	gullible,	reducible,
apprehensible,	corrosible,	eligible,	horrible,	reflexible,
audible,	corruptible,	eludible,	intelligible,	reprehensible,
cessible,	credible,	enforcible,	irascible,	resistible,
coercible,	decoctible,	evincible,	legible,	responsible,
collectible,	deducible,	expansible,	miscible,	reversible,
compatible	defeasible,	expressible,	negligible,	revertible,
competible,	defensible,	extendible,	partible,	risible,
comprehensible,	descendible,	extensible,	passible,	seducible,
compressible,	destructible,	fallible,	perceptible,	sensible,
conceptible,	digestible,	feasible,	permissible,	tangible,
contemptible,	discernible,	fencible,	persuasible,	terrible,
contractible,	distensible,	flexible,	pervertible,	transmissible,
controvertible,	divisible,	forcible,	plausible,	visible.

Derivatives from these, as, *inaccessible, infallible, illegible,* etc., also end in *-ible.*

Passible and *impassible* must be distinguished from *passable* and *impassable,*—words of different meaning.

The initial syllables em-, en-, and in- are now more definitely used than formerly. The words: *embitter, embosom, enclasp, engulf, ensnare, inclose, inquire, instil, instruct, intrust,* and a few others, still show considerable diversity of spelling. The forms having the greater weight of authority have been given in the vocabulary.

The chief points of difference between British and American spelling relate to the endings *-our* and *-ise*. The American dictionaries are, for the most part, agreed in the use of *-or*, instead of *-our*; and *-ize*, instead of *-ise*. Webster writes *Savior, glamour*, but prefers *enamor*; the Century, Standard, and Worcester, write: *Saviour*, and prefer *enamour, glamour*. With these two exceptions (enamour, glamour), the American standards agree in the suppression of the *u*.

To avoid the unsightly repetition of the *ou* digraph, many British authorities write *clamorous, humorous, laborious*, instead of *clamourous, humourous, labourious*.

While the American standards employ *-ize* in preference to the English termination *-ise*, in most words having this termination, they are generally agreed in retaining *-ise* in:

advertise,	comprise,	emprise,	improvise,	premise,
advise,	compromise,	enterprise,	incise,	reprise,
apprise (to inform),	demise,	excise,	maluprise,	revise,
chastise,	despise,	exercise,	manumise,	surmise,
circumcise,	devise,	franchise	merchandise,	surprise.
	disguise,	(af-, dis-, en-),		

The forms *catechise, criticise, exorcise*, are still in good use, with a growing preference for *catechize, criticize, exorcize*.

There is an increasing tendency to suppress silent *e* in *-ine* terminations, especially in the use of medical and chemical terms. The Century and the Standard dictionaries and the latest edition of Gould's Dictionary of Medicine represent the improved spelling, and the American Association for the Advancement of Science has recommended the new form. The words *chlorin, dentin, gelatin, glycerin, paraffin, ptyalin*, illustrate the new principle. Many chemical terms like *chloride, oxide*, etc., are now often correctly written *chlorid, oxid*.

Words ending in -er and -or occasion some confusion. The *-or* terminations constitute the larger number. No satisfactory principle of discrimination has been formulated. Nearly all terms of this class pertaining to the legal profession end in -*or.* as: *abettor, acceptor, covenantor, debtor, executor, guarantor, juror, lessor, mortgagor* or *mortgageor.*

The ending -er is generally preferred to -re; as in *theater, center.* To preserve the proper sound of *c* and *g,* the -*re* termination is retained in *acre, chancre, lucre, massacre, ogre.*

Words ending in -cion, -sion, and -tion form a large list, and are often misspelled. Those which, in their shortest form, end in -*d, -de, -ge, -mit, -rt, -se, -ss,* usually take -*sion.* Most of the others end in -*tion;* a few in -*cion.*

The letters l, f, and s, preceded by a single vowel, are doubled at the end of a monosyllable: *ball, will, bluff, cliff, class, dress.* Exceptions: *clef, if, of, as, gas, has, is, pus, this, thus, was, us, yes.* The rule does not apply to *s* when used to form the possessive case or the plural; as, *boy's, boys.*

Consonants other than l, f, s, are rarely doubled at the end of a monosyllable. The exceptions are: *abb, ebb, add, odd, rudd, egg, lamm, mumm, bunn* or *bun, inn, burr* or *bur, err, murr, parr, purr* or *pur, shirr, butt, buzz, fuzz.*

No definite rule for the spelling of words ending in -*ance, -ancy, -ant,* and of those ending in -*ence, -ency, -ent,* can be formulated. The idea of action or agency more generally pervades the former, and the idea of state or being, the latter; as, *servant, aspirant, assistant, confidant; diligent, patient, confident; defiance, resistance; excellence, confidence; buoyancy, corpulency, solvency.* The noun and adjective forms are usually in accord. If in doubt whether *transcendent* is spelled with -*ant* or -*ent,* the student may remember one of the noun forms, *transcendency, transcendence,* and this will serve to remove the doubt respecting the adjective.

The termination -*ense* is preferred to -*ence* in *defense, offense, pretense,* on the ground that *defensive, offensive, pretension,* take the *s.* The words *expense, license, recompense,* formerly spelled with *c,* have entirely dropped the old form.

O AND OH

These exclamations are often used interchangeably by careless writers. It is better to limit O to an address in the vocative, with the exclamation point at the end of the phrase, as, O my friends! It is also used as an ejaculative expression of desire or regret, as, O that I had wings like a dove! O that I should live to see this day! In trivial and colloquial speech, O is employed, as, O my! O dear! O fie! O George! O Mary!

Oh is used to denote pain or woe, or sudden emotion. Except at the beginning of a sentence, it properly takes a lower-case letter; as, She is in her grave, and oh! the difference to me.

FOREIGN WORDS

Many foreign words, like depot, debut, debris, have become so thoroughly a part of the English language as to require no accent over the vowel.

CONTRACTIONS

Abbreviated forms of spelling, as, w^h, y^e, hon^{ble}, judgm^t, once very common, especially in epistolary writing, are no longer used. In dictionaries and gazetteers; in treatises on botany, chemistry, and mathematics; in commercial tables and trades lists; and in foot-notes or very narrow columns, letters, figures, signs, and other characters are admissible, but in books, magazines, and newspapers, and in copy for the printer, as well as in ordinary correspondence, the word should be written in full. In formal legal documents, and in notes and cards for social occasions, even the day, the month, and the year are now spelled out.

The abbreviations Mr., Mrs., Messrs., Jr. or Jun., Sr. or Sen., are exceptions to the general rule. These are rarely spelled out in full; but Hon., Rev., Gen., Capt., Col., Maj., while often found in newspapers, should not be seen in books, nor in letters of a formal character. This is also true of ult., prox., and inst.

While e.g., i.e., q.v., viz., etc., may be allowed where space is limited, as in foot- or side-notes, they should be avoided in the body of the text as far as possible. Instead of the *, †, ‖, ⸸, and other marks of reference, small letters or figures are now employed by the best writers and printers, and are placed above and to the right of the word or phrase in question. The ampersand (&) is authorized in the business name of a firm or corporation, as in George W. Jacobs & Co., The Baltimore & Ohio Railroad Co., but in the text of standard books, the words are printed in full, as, Delaware and Hudson Railroad Company.

Dialect, slang, and colloquial expressions often give piquancy to a story, and may be tolerated in conversation and light description, but should not be encouraged. Ain't, hain't, are of bad form and should be avoided. Some authorities space the letters to suggest the separation between words, as, 't was, 't is, 't was n't, but most publishing houses close up the spaces. The object of abbreviation is to save space. The proper abbreviation for Pennsylvania is Pa., and for Philadelphia, Phila. The longer forms, Penn. or Penn'a, and Philada., are needless, and should be avoided.

Abbreviations like Fig. 1 or E.g. at the beginning of a sentence, even in a foot-note, are unsightly and should be avoided, although they may be perfectly admissible in the body or at the end of the sentence. In catalogues and tabulated lists, 4to, 8vo, 12mo, are used, but should never begin a sentence and should not be followed by a period.

THE DIERESIS

To prevent a combination of two vowels that must be sounded separately a dieresis is placed over the second, as, coöperate, reëlect, preëmption. If at the end of a line the first vowel is separated from the second by a hyphen, the dieresis is omitted. The hyphen is sometimes employed in other situations instead of the dieresis.

SPELLING REFORM

Among alphabetical languages the English is conceded to be the most irregular and inconsistent in its orthography. Repeated efforts have been made to correct it, but until the subject was taken in hand by the Philological Society of England and the American Philological Association, but little progress had been made.

In 1876 an International Convention for the Amendment of English Orthography was held in Philadelphia. In 1892 the Modern Language Association of America united with the Philological Societies in this movement. About 3500 words are recommended for change. The following ten rules are specially recommended by these learned bodies for general adoption:

e. Drop silent *e* when fonetically useless, as in *liv, singl, eatn, raind.* Write *er* for *re* in *theater.*

ea. Drop *a* from *ea* having the sound of short *e,* as in *fether, lether.*

o. For *o* having the sound of *u* in *but,* write *u* as in *abuv, tung.*

ou. Drop *o* from *ou* having the sound of short *u,* as in *trubl, ruf.* For *-our* write *-or,* as in *honor, labor.*

u, ue. Drop silent *u* after *g* before *a,* and also before *e* in nativ English words; and drop final *ue: gard, gest, catalog, leag.*

Dubl consonants may be simplified when fonetically useless: *bailif, batl, writn, traveler,* but not in words like *hall, call.*

d. Change *d* and *ed* final to *t* when so pronounced, as in *lookt,* etc., unless the *e* affects the preceding sound, as in *chafed.*

gh, ph. Change *gh* and *ph* to *f* when so sounded, as in *enough, laughter, phonetic* (enuf, lafter, fonetic).

s. Change *s* to *z* when so sounded, especially in distinctiv words and in *-ise: abuze, advertize.*

t. Drop *t* in *tch: catch, pitch* (cach, pich).

PRONUNCIATION

STANDARD OF PRONUNCIATION

The ultimate standard of pronunciation is the usage of the most cultured people to whom the language is vernacular. It is the province of the lexicographer to set forth this usage. The dictionary, therefore, becomes practically the standard. As usage is variable, it is not surprising that the dictionaries show much variety. The wonder is that they accord as fully as they do.

It is to be regretted that in England and America there is not some governing board or court of arbitration, something like the French Academy, to which all questions of disputed spelling and pronunciation might be referred for decision. The nearest approach to such an authoritative body is the Board appointed to determine the form of spelling of geographical names to be employed in the Government printing establishment.

There is no good reason why one standard should not serve for all the English-speaking nations throughout the world. The closer commercial relations and the increasing social intercourse between England and America make it the more desirable. While to Americans it would seem like taking a step backward to write *waggon, labour, emphasise*, and other variant spellings, to England, as the mother country, it would doubtless seem humiliating to conform to American usage. If perfect uniformity on all points of difference in spelling and pronunciation, not only between England and America, but among the American standards themselves, could be secured, scarcely any sacrifice would be too great.

In the present volume we can hope to present only the best current usage in the United States, as represented by Webster (The International), Worcester, The Century, and the Standard.

ELEMENTARY SOUNDS

The following is a table of the elementary sounds of the English language, with the diacritics employed in this volume to represent them.

VOWEL SOUNDS

Vocals

1. ă, at, apple, man, called short a.
2. ā, ate, able, made, called long a.
3. â, air, care, bear, called coalescent a.
4. ä, arm, far, alms, called Italian a.
5. ạ, all, haul, saw, called broad a.
6. à, ask, pass, chance, called intermediate a.
7. à, abide, disavow, flora, called obscure a.
8. ĕ, end, met, compel, called short e.
9. ē, evil, veto, predict, called long e.
10. ê, err, term, permit, called coalescent e.
11. ĭ, ill, mint, incur, called short i.
12. ī, ice, find, pirate, called long i.
13. ŏ, on, lot, offend, called short o.
14. ō, old, home, obey, called long o.
15. ô, orb, form, forlorn, called coalescent o.
16. ŭ, up, hunt, undone, called short u.
17. ū, use, fume, humane, called long u.
18. û, urn, curb, purloin, called coalescent u.
19. o͝o, foot, book, hoodwink, called short oo.
20. o͞o, ooze, noon, moonlight, called long oo.
21. oi, oil, coin, foible.
22. ou, out, proud, sounding.

CONSONANT SOUNDS

Subvocals

23. b, boy.
24. d, did.
25. g, gay.
26. j, judge.
27. l, land.
28. m, men.
29. n, now.
30. r, rest.
31. v, vine.
32. w, wing.
33. y, yes.
34. z, zone.
35. zh, azure.
36. th, than.
37. ng, song.

CONSONANT SOUNDS

Aspirates

38. f, fair.
39. h, hat.
40. k, kind.
41. p, pen.
42. s, sun.
43. t, tan.
44. ch, chin.
45. sh, shun.
46. th, thin.
47. wh, what.

UNUSUAL SOUNDS

48. ch, Bach.
49. ṅ, baton.
50. ü, etude.
51. ŋ, ink.

3

DIACRITICAL MARKS

The diacritics employed in the volume are: the macron, ā, ē, ī, ō, ū, ōō, used to indicate the long-vowel sounds; the breve, ă, ĕ, ĭ, ŏ, ŭ, ŏŏ, indicating the short vowels; the caret, â, ê, ô, û, designating the coalescents, and showing their blending with the sound of *r*; the dieresis, ä, a̤, ü, placed over the *a* to show what is generally called the sound of Italian *a*, and under to indicate the sound of broad *a*, and over *u* to represent French *u*; the obelisk, â, to represent intermediate *a*; and the period, ȧ, ṅ, ṇ, to represent obscure *a*, the French *n*, and the nasal *n*, sounding like *ng*. The only other marked letters are the vocal ŧħ and the German cħ.

LETTERS AND SOUNDS

It is unfortunate that the sounds and the letters that represent them are, by most persons, called by the same names, vowels and consonants. It were better to limit these terms to the characters, and find other names for the sounds, as is done by writers on phonetics and by teachers of elocution. The vowel sounds are uttered with the least obstruction or modification of the voice. They are sometimes called vocals, or tonics (tone sounds). In the utterance of the consonant sounds there is a wide range from the vowel-like openness of *l* and *r*, to the constricted mouth and throat positions for *m, p, t, g, k, th*. These sounds readily divide themselves into two classes, the first having a measure of vocality, and the second consisting of unvocalized breath. The former are called subvocals, or subtonics; the latter, aspirates, or atonics.

DIPHTHONGS AND TRIPHTHONGS

The terms diphthong and tripthong should be restricted to the sounds represented by the vowel digraphs and trigraphs. Every vowel sound which, in its utterance, requires a change of mouth position, is diphthongal. A diphthong is defined as the union of two vowel sounds pronounced in one syllable; a triphthong as the union of three vowel sounds in one syllable. The confounding of the terms diphthong and digraph, as well as triphthong and trigraph, has led to the mistaken notion that two characters are necessary to represent the diphthong, and three characters to represent the triphthong. The vowel characters *i* and *u* (high, Hugh) represent, singly, the union of two sounds, and, therefore, they are diphthongs as truly as are the sounds represented by the digraphs *oi* and *ou*. Long *a* and *o* (pay, no) are also diphthongal, although less so than *i* and *u*. The classical digraphs *æ* and *œ*, generally, but improperly, called diphthongs, are being rapidly displaced by the simple letter *e*, whose single sound, long or short, they represent: Æolian, Eolian; æsthetic, esthetic; œsophagus, esophagus.

ELEMENTARY SOUNDS

Of all the long-vowel sounds, *e* is the only one that is strictly elementary. The remaining vowel sounds, except those represented by the digraphs *oi* and *ou*, and most of the consonant sounds, may properly be regarded as elementary. The sounds represented by *j* and *ch* are capable of further analysis. The digraphs *sh*, *th*, *wh*, *ng*, represent elementary sounds. There is nothing gained by transposing *wh* to represent the pronunciation of words containing that digraph, as is done in some dictionaries.

STANDARD AND CLIPPED SOUNDS

A standard sound is one that is unmodified by its surroundings. It is the fullest form of an elementary sound. The *a* in *day* and the *p* in *cap* represent standard sounds. The *a* in *take* and the *p* in *captain* are deprived of their vanishing element and are clipped sounds. Vowel and consonant sounds alike are subject to modification by their surroundings.

COGNATES

The term cognates is applied to sounds requiring the same or nearly the same mouth positions, as *f* and *v* in *fan*, *van*; *k* and *g* in *keel*, *gale*; *p* and *b* in *pin*, *bin*; *ch* and *j* in *cheer*, *jeer*.

LONG AND SHORT VOWELS

The terms *long* and *short*, as applied to vowels, have led to much confusion. As names for certain sounds, they are· justified by long and almost universal use, but when so employed, all idea of length or quantity should be excluded. The short *a* in *mad, sang,* is longer than the long *a* in *mate, sake.*

NORMAL AND UNUSUAL SOUNDS

A table of elementary sounds should present as key words such words as afford the least opportunity for diversity of pronunciation. They should be arranged in groups under the letter or digraph that, in English usage, most commonly represents the sound which they are intended to illustrate. The five vowels, *a, e, i, o, u,* with their markings, represent eighteen sounds. The letter *a* alone represents seven sounds. It is unfortunate that in the present state of the English language one letter should be made to bear so heavy a burden, but these seven sounds are better represented by *a* than by any other letter or digraph. These sounds, then, are said to be the normal sounds of *a.* Other sounds of *a,* as in *any, what,* are better represented by other characters in the table, and are therefore unusual sounds of *a.* The normal or English sound of *ch* is heard in *chin*; its unusual sounds, in *chaise* and *chasm.*

EQUIVALENTS

Substitutes for the letters or combinations of letters usually employed to represent a sound, are called equivalents. The equivalents for short *i* are seen in the words: *E*nglish, bea*u*fin, cert*ai*n, b*ee*n, for*ei*gn, monk*ey*, carr*ia*ge, s*ie*ve, w*o*men, tort*oi*se, b*u*sy, b*ui*ld, plag*uy*, n*y*mph.

ENVIRONMENT

A full discussion of the influence of letters and sounds upon one another in their many relations as found in words, would fill a volume. Only such points as may be necessary to a better under-standing of the present work are here presented under the head of General Principles of Pronunciation. These are usually so well understood as to render the use of diacritical and other marks, in many cases, unnecessary. In the occasional, unusual, and exceptional uses of the following sounds, and in all doubtful cases, the word will be marked or respelled.

GENERAL PRINCIPLES OF PRONUNCIATION

VOWELS AND VOWEL DIGRAPHS

The vowels *a, e, i, o, u,* when forming or terminating accented syllables, are long: ā'ble, mā'ker, ē'ven, mē'ter, ī'dle, vī'tal, ō'gre, lō'cal, ū'nit, pū'pil. When they form or terminate unaccented syllables, *e, o, u,* are long, but are uttered with that diminished force and sharpness which the absence of accent always begets: el'ē ment, ap'pō site, oc'cū py.

The letter *a* when forming or terminating an unaccented syllable is obscure, and the letter *i* represents the sound of short *i*: à bout', ap'à thy, vis'ĭ ble, hap'pĭ ness. When *y* is used as a vowel, it falls under the same law as *i.*

A vowel followed by a consonant and terminal *e* in the same syllable is generally long: māte, cēde, re pīne', a lōne', pro fūse'. Many exceptions are found in the unaccented terminal syllables *-ile* and *-ine*: fertĭle, hostĭle, doctrĭne, determĭne.

A vowel followed by one or more consonants in the same syllable, but not having a terminal *e,* is short: mat, ebb, film, rob'in, sul'len.

ä.—Italian *a* is generally followed by *r,* with or without other consonants: fär, härm, cärds. In a few words it is represented by *au* followed by *n*: aunt, daunt, launch.

ạ.—Broad *a* is usually followed by *l, ll,* or silent *w*: ạl'most, fạl'ter, cạll, pạw. It is often represented by *au*: haul, maud'lin.

â.—Coalescent *a* is usually followed by *re.* It is long *a* modified by *r*: câre, dâre. In derivatives, the *e* is usually dropped on taking a suffix beginning with a vowel: shâr'ing, compâr'ing. It is often represented by *air* (pair, chair) and sometimes by *ear* (pear, bear).

â.—Intermediate *a* occurs chiefly in monosyllables ending in *ff, ft, ss, st, sk, sp, nce, nch, nt,* and in their derivatives: chậff, shâft, pậssed, chânting It is a rich, musical sound, and should not be supplanted by the less musical short *a.* In its organic formation it lies intermediate between short *a* and Italian.

à.—Obscure *a* occurs only in unaccented syllables. It may constitute or end a syllable, but it never begins one. It is sufficiently differentiated from both Italian and intermediate *a* to entitle it to a distinct and separate place in the table, and is rarely incorrectly sounded. Examples: à mong', à round', à bout', cit'à del, com'pà ny, so'fà, i de'à. When it forms or ends a syllable, and is immediately followed in the next syllable by an accented vowel, it often takes the sound of long *a*, as in ā e'ri al, chā ot'ic.

æ.—This digraph (æ) represents a single elementary sound, and not the union of two sounds. It should not therefore be called a diphthong. When it forms or terminates a syllable, it has the sound of long *e*: æ'gis, æ o'li an, Cæ'sar. When it is followed by a consonant in the same syllable, it takes the same sound that *e* would have in the same position: di *æ*r'e sis. The single *e* is gradually taking its place: *e* o'lian, *es* thet'ic. This digraph is largely used in the terminal syllables of scientific terms of classic origin: An ten'na ri'i dæ, An'dre æ a'ce æ.

ai.—The normal English sound of *ai* is long *a*: pain, maid, maintain. If followed by *r*, it becomes coalescent *a*: fair, hair, lair. In the unaccented terminal syllable -*tain*, it is equivalent to short *i*: cap'tain, foun'tain, cer'tain.

au.—The usual sound of *au* is broad *a*: haul, laud, exhaust. When followed immediately by *n*, it is usually Italian *a*: jaunt, taunt.

ay.—This digraph (ay) has the sound of long *a*: day, say, por tray'.

ê.—Coalescent *e* has been the subject of much controversy. It is always followed by terminal *r*, or by *r* with one or more different consonants following in the same syllable: err, her, term. This sound is often represented by *i*: firm, squirm. Some lexicographers confound it with *ur*, as in *burn, curl*.

ea.—The normal sound of *ea* is long *e*: meat, cheat, fear, appear.

ee.—This digraph (ee) in English words, represents the sound of long *e*: fleet, cheer.

ei.—In monosyllables and accented syllables, *ei* usually represents long *a*: rein, veil. There are many exceptions, conspicuous among them being *ei'ther, nei'ther, ceil'ing*. In unaccented syllables, the sound is usually short *i*: for'feit, sur'feit, mul'lein.

eigh.—The silent *gh* usually serves to give to the digraph *ei* the sound of long *a*: neigh, weigh, freight, inveigh.

eu.—This digraph is an equivalent for long *u*: feud, neuter, pseudonym.

ew.—These two letters combine to represent the sound of long *u*: few, new, hewn.

ey.—The digraph ey, terminating a monosyllable or an accented syllable, takes the sound of long *a*: they, obey', convey'. When unaccented, it takes the sound of short *i*: mon'ey, hon'ey.

i.—When *i* forms or terminates an accented syllable, it is long; as, i'vory, mi'ca, compli'ance. But when in. pronunciation it is made to blend with the following syllable, it becomes short; as, divi'sion, recogni'tion, ini'tial.

ie.—In monosyllables ending in *ie*, and in their derivatives, this digraph usually represents the sound of long *i*: tie, vie, hie, lied. In an unaccented terminal syllable, it becomes short *i*: bon'nie, Jen'nie.

igh.—In this combination the silent *gh* serves to give the vowel the sound of long *i*: sigh, light, plight.

-ian, -ion.—The termination *-ian* is usually sounded like *yan*, and *-ion* like *yun*: banian, bunion, minion.

ir.—This digraph has the sound of *er*: fir, firm.

oa.—The normal sound of *oa* is long *o*: boat, coat, foal, moan.

oe.—As an English termination of a syllable, it is sounded like long *o*: toe, hoe, woe, mistletoe. In words of classic origin, the letters are usually combined, and the sound is that which *e* alone would have in the same situation: œsophagus, Œdipus.

oi.—The usual sound of this digraph is that heard in oil, toil, loin, groin.

oo.—This digraph, like most of the others, represents several sounds. The most common is that of long *oo*: food, boon, loom, mood, soon.

or.—Much diversity of opinion exists relative to the proper sound of this digraph. When unmarked in this volume, it will have the sound as heard, in orb, born, storm. In unaccented terminal syllables, the sound bends toward that of *ur*: an'chor, la'bor, stu'por.

ou.—This combination represents ten or eleven different sounds. The one represented by the unmarked character in the vocabulary list is that heard in found, lounge.

-ous.—In the unaccented terminal syllable, *-ous*, the *o* is silent: en'vi ous, cal'lous, fa'mous.

ow.—This digraph represents four sounds. The most common is that heard in cow, plow, how, and is equivalent to *ou* in found. In unaccented terminal syllables, it generally takes the sound of long *o*: shad'ow, win'dow. Careless speakers give it, in such words, the sound of short *u*, as win'duh, shad'uh, mead'uh, a sound which should be carefully avoided.

u.—Long *u*, like long *i*, is a clearly defined compound vowel. Its initial element is the consonant *y*; its vanishing element is long *oo*. When preceded in the same syllable by the sound of *r*, *sh*, or *w*, it drops the *y* element and takes the sound of long *oo*: rude, shute, sure. When long *u* forms a syllable, and is immediately preceded by *r* in an accented syllable (er'u dite, vir'u lent), some authorities change *u* to long *oo*; it is better, however, to give it a shortened form of long *u*.

ur.—This digraph is often called the natural vowel. The *u* and *r* coalesce, and practically form one sound: furl, curb, murmur. It is readily differentiated from *er*, or its equivalents *ir*, *yr*.

CONSONANTS AND CONSONANT DIGRAPHS

The doubling of a consonant does not change its sound: ebb, add, staff egg, mill, crammed, pinned, sipped, purr, pass, buzz.

c.—Before *a, o, u,* the letter *c* has the sound of *k*: cat, cow, cull. Before *e, i, y,* it has the sound of *s*: cent, city, cyst.

ch.—The normal English sound of *ch* is that heard in chin, chart, chum. In words from the French, it has the sound of *sh*: chaise, charades. In words from the Greek, it has the sound of *k*: chasm, ar'chitect.

d.—The termination *-ed* following an aspirate in the same syllable, takes the sound of *t*: asked, stuffed, passed. This principle is so well understood as not to require the respelling of the word to denote its pronunciation.

g.—Like *c*, this letter before *a, o, u,* is hard, and has its own sound, as heard in gate, go, gull. Before *e, i, y,* it is usually soft, having the sound of *j*: gem, giant, gypsy. In all doubtful cases, the word or syllable will be respelled, employing the letter *g* to represent the hard, and *j* to represent the soft sound of that letter.

gh.—Before a vowel, this digraph has the sound of hard *g*: aghast, gherkin, ghostly. This combination is sometimes employed by orthoepists to represent the sound of hard *g*, as gibbous (ghib'bus). At the end of a syllable, *gh* generally represents *f*: laugh, tough, cough, enough.

n.—Before the sound of *k* in the same syllable, *n* represents the sound of *ng*: ink, sank, monk. When it terminates an accented syllable, and is immediately followed by hard *g*, *q*, or *k*, in the same word, it also takes the sound of *ng*: an'ger, an'chor, ban'quet.

ph.—The normal sound of *ph* is *f*: phase, phrensy, photograph.

qu.—This digraph represents a close combination of the sounds of *k* and *w*, and is not easily mistaken: quite, queen, quoth.

r.—While all sounds are subject to modification by their surroundings, no other consonant affects the vowel sounds to the extent that *r* does. When it follows long *a* or long *o*, it transforms these vowels at once into coalescents. When it precedes long *u*, it changes this sound into long *oo*. Before a vowel it should be trilled. In emphatic and deliberate utterance, the trill should be decided; in unaccented syllables, and in colloquial discourse, it should be less marked. The speech of most Americans would be improved by a more liberal use of the trilled *r*.

When *r* terminates a syllable having the primary accent, and is immediately followed in the next syllable by a vowel or another *r*, the vowel in the accented syllable becomes short: cär, cär'ry; hêr, hĕr'oine; sir, sĭr'up; fôr, fŏr'eign; bûr, bŭr'row. Coalescent *e* when under the secondary accent, follows the same rule: cem'e tĕr'y.

s.—The normal sound of *s* is that heard in sit, miss, insist. It is so often employed to represent the sound of *z* that in some instances it becomes almost necessary to use *c* to insure the true pronunciation of the word: profuse (-fuce′), precise (-sice′), desist (-cist′). The *z* sound of *s* is, in most situations, so well understood as to render respelling unnecessary: tubs, drags, chasm, prism, pleas, please, boxes, churches, mottoes, advise, surprise, betrays.

w.—As elsewhere remarked, the letter *w* is not a vowel. It often follows *a*, *e*, or *o*, and combines with these vowels to form new sounds: saw, new, plow.

x.—The letter *x*, like *c* and *q*, represents no sound that is not better represented by other letters. Nevertheless, it is a convenient letter, representing, as it does, two sounds in one character. Its normal sound is a combination of *ks*: tax, sex. At the beginning of a word it represents *z*: xanthine, xebec.

y.—When *y* is used as an equivalent for the vowel *i*, it is subject to all the laws governing *i*: lie, lye; grist, tryst; tapir, satyr. In verb terminations, whether accented or unaccented, it usually takes the sound of long *i*: apply, multiply, satisfy.

z.—The sound of *z* is heard in zest, topa·. While *s* often represents the sound of *z*, the latter sometimes takes the place of *s*, as in Metz, waltz.

zh.—The sound represented by this digraph is commonly called the *zh* sound. There is probably no word in the English language in which the characters *z* and *h* combine to represent the sound. In *azure, seizure*, it is represented by *z*. It is most frequently represented by *s* in the terminal syllables *-sure* and *-sion*: leisure, measure, corrosion, exclusion.

INITIAL SYLLABLES

i-, bi-, chi-, cli-, cri-, pri-, tri-.—In these initial syllables, even when not accented, the *i* is generally long: ī am′bic, bī og′ra phy, chī rop′o dist.

TERMINAL SYLLABLES

-ceous, -cious, -scious, -tious.—These syllables are pronounced -shus: cetaceous, gracious, conscious, fractious. Righteous (rī′chus) is an exceptional form In anxious (ank′shus), the *k* element of the *x* is pronounced in the first syllable, and the *s* element, which is changed to *sh* before *i*, is put into the second syllable. In *luscious* (lush′us), the *s* is lost, and *ci*, which represents *sh*, is placed in the first syllable.

-cial, -sial, -tial.—These syllables are pronounced -shal: social, controversial, partial. While the *a* sound in the -ial and -ian terminations bends toward obscure *a* or short *u*, and in the mouths of careless speakers is often omitted, yet as a standard sound, it approaches more closely to short *a* than to any other sound. When a vowel precedes -sial, -sian, -sion, the initial sound of the terminal syllable becomes *zh:* as, ambrosial, elysian, elision.

-cian, -sian, -tian.—These syllables are pronounced -shan: physician, Persian, gentian.

-cion, -sion, -t'on.—These syllables are pronounced -shun: coercion, mansion, potion. When *s* precedes the syllable -tion, this syllable is sounded -chun: exhaustion, digestion. When -sion is preceded by a vowel, it is pronounced -zhun: corrosion, delusion. A very common mistake is that of giving this sound to -sion when preceded by *r*: excursion, version.

-geous, -gious.—These syllables are pronounced -jus: courageous, contagious.

-geon, -gion.—These syllables are pronounced -jun: dungeon, legion.

-ice, -ise, -ize.—In noun and adjective forms whose accent falls upon the penult or antepenult, the *i* is usually short: lat'tice, mor'tise. In verb forms whose accent, primary or secondary, falls upon the final syllable, the *i* is long: surprise, baptize, emphasize, analyze.

-ide, -ine.—In regard to these terminations, usage is greatly varied. The Chemical Section of the American Association for the Advancement of Science, in 1889, passed a vote in favor of short *i*, and afterward voted to drop final *e* in the spelling: bromin, chlorin, iodin, iodid, chlorid, bromid.

-ile, -ite, -ive.—When not under the accent the vowel *i* in the terminations -ile and -ive is generally short, and in -ite, long: fertile, hostile, active, genitive, aconite, appetite. There are many exceptions.

-ar, -er, -ir, -or, -ur, -yr.—A loose pronunciation of these unaccented terminal syllables makes them alike. Some reputable authorities justify this. Those who have regard for the refinements of speech will make a distinction. In dignified discourse, such words as dollar, scholar, will be sounded with Italian *a*, softened by the *r*, and obscured by the absence of accent. In colloquial utterance, the *a* will lean still farther toward the dividing line between Italian *a* and coalescent *u*. The -ir and -yr terminations are identical with -er in sound: taper, tapir, satyr. In deliberate utterance, -or takes the sound of coalescent *o*, smoothly uttered and without show of effort. To pronounce *actor* with almost equal accent upon the syllables, is painfully unpleasant to the listener. In conversation, -or resembles -ur more closely. The -ur sound, often called the natural vowel, is usually pronounced correctly. Occasionally an affected effort is made to give it the lighter form of -er. The terminations -ard, -ared, -erd, -ered, -ored, -ured, -yred (drunkard, collared, shepherd, peppered, labored, murmured, martyred) follow the same law.

-any, -ary.—In *any* and *many*, the *a* takes the sound of short *e*. When the accent falls on the antepenult, the *a* forms or terminates an unaccented syllable, and, in accordance with the general rule, is obscure: botany, litany, boundary, granary. When the primary accent comes before the antepenult, the secondary accent falls upon the *a* which gives to the *a* in -any the sound of long *a*, and to the *a* in -ary the sound of coalescent *a*, with a strong leaning in both cases toward short *e*: miscellany, momentary.

ACCENT

In the English language, every word of more than one syllable is pronounced with a stress of voice upon one of its syllables. This stress is called accent. In words of three or more syllables, there is often a second stress, and in very long words, a third. The primary accent is the strongest. The lighter degrees of emphasis are called the secondary accents. An acute ear will often discover a difference in the force with which the secondary accents are given. The lightest of three varying accents might with greater propriety be called the tertiary accent.

INFLUENCE OF THE ACCENT

In monosyllables and in accented syllables the vowels are usually uttered with sharpness of outline; in unaccented syllables, with less distinctness. In all forms of dignified discourse, the sounds, consonant as well as vowel, are given a sharpness that would be quite unbefitting in colloquial speech. But the unaccented vowels must never be uttered in a careless or slovenly manner. Walker, the English lexicographer, declares that a neat pronunciation of these forms constitutes "one of the greatest beauties of speaking."

PLACE OF THE ACCENT

In nouns and adjectives of two syllables the accent usually falls upon the first, while in verbs, it occurs upon the second: al'mond, bel'lows, hap'py, cheer'ful, appear', convey'. So general is this law that the exceptions, which are quite numerous, are frequently mispronounced; as, adept', adult', research', recess', romance', finance', canine', robust', rotund', con'strue, do'nate, ran'sack, lo'cate.

DISCRIMINATIVE ACCENT

The noun and verb forms of the same word are often distinguished by change of accent; as, con'tract, contract'; es'cort, escort'. Adjectives and verbs are contrasted in like manner; as, ab'ject, abject'; ab'sent, absent'.

ANTITHETICAL ACCENT

A contrast in thought is often expressed by what is known as rhetorical or antithetical accent. The accent is transferred from its normal position to the contrasting syllable; as, He must in'-crease, but I must de'crease.

FOREIGN WORDS

VOWELS

In most of the languages of Continental Europe the letter *a* is sounded like ä, *e* like ā, and *i* like ē. The digraph *oe* is sounded nearly like *u* in burn. It is best formed by an attempt to sound ĕ with the mouth in position for ō. Long *u* is generally sounded like ōō. The French or German ü has no equivalent in English. It is fairly well represented by uttering ē through the mouth position for ōō.

CONSONANTS

The sounds of the consonant letters in foreign languages are even more irregular and unlike the English than are the vowels. These will be explained and their use in words illustrated.

The letter *r* is more strongly trilled than in English. When *m* and *n*, in French and Portuguese, occur at the end of a word or syllable, they have no distinctive sound, but simply impart nasality to the preceding vowel.

The digraph *ng* takes the English sound in most of the European tongues, but in Italian the *n* does not blend with the *g*. The sound of *th* is usually that of *t*.

OPEN AND CLOSED SYLLABLES

Syllables ending in a vowel or vowel sound are said to be open; those ending in a consonant, closed.

ACCENT

Accent, as this term is understood in English, is not so marked in the languages of Continental Europe. The stress is more evenly distributed.

Accented syllables are not struck so forcibly, and unaccented syllables are not slighted so much, as in English.

In French, the syllables are uttered with nearly equal stress. To the American ear many French words sound as if accented on the last syllable, and, to mark their proper pronunciation in English dictionaries, the primary accent is often placed upon the final syllable of such words. In the German, Hungarian, Dutch, and Swedish languages the stress is usually on the root syllable; and in the Italian, Spanish, Portuguese, and Polish, it is on the penult. In some languages the vowel quantities determine the prominence of the syllables rather than any particular stress or accent.

CHINESE

e = ā, Pe-chi-li (pā'chē'lē').
i = ē, Pe-chi-li (pā'chē'lē').
ow = ōō, Chang-Chow (chäng-chōō').
u = ōō, Chang-Cheun-Cham (chäng-chē ōōn-chäm), Aigun (ī gōōn').
sz = z, Szechuen (zä chōō ĕn').

DANISH

a = ä, Gram (gräm), Rafn (räfn).
aa = a̤, Aalborg (a̤l'bŏrg), Aarhuus (a̤r'hōōs).
e = ā when final in accented syllables; when not final it equals ĕ, Lemvig (lĕm'vĭg)   ĕ = ā̤, Zoëga (zō ā'gä).
i = ē in open accented syllables and in monosyllables, Hagi (hä'gē); in other situations = ĭ, Beelitz (bā'lĭts).
ii = ē in open accented syllables and in monosyllables; in other situations = ĭ.
o = ō when open, Altona (äl'tō nä); when closed = ŏ.
oe = û, Hoe (hû); ö has the same sound, Römer (rû'mer).
u = ōō when open, Hude (hōō'thĕ); when closed = ŏŏ, Hunte (hŏŏn'tĕ).
uu = ōō, Aarhuus (a̤r'hōōs).
c = k before a, aa, o, u; before e, i, ö, y, it is like s.
d = th when between two vowels or at the end of a syllable after a vowel, Budir (bōō thĕr'), Egvad (ĕg väth'). It is silent before t or s, Gjedsted (yĕ stĕth'), and also when final after l, n, r, t. When final it is sounded like t. When initial, d is sounded as in English.
g = g. After a vowel in monosyllables it is slightly guttural.
h = h. Before j and v it is silent, Hvam (väm).
j = y, Fjelsö (fyĕl'sû), Hjarno (yär'nō).
v = ŏŏ after s; elsewhere = v
y = ü, Nyerup (nü'er ŏŏp).

DUTCH

a   = ä in open syllables, Hals (häls), Brabant (brä bänt').

aa   = ä in open syllables, Raalte (räl'tĕ), Alkmaar (älk'mär').

au   = ou, Van Pauw (vän pow).

e   = ä when final in accented syllables, Breda (brä'dä); unaccented it = û. Before r it = â, Berkel (bâr'kĕl). Before two or more consonants it = ĕ, Delft (dĕlft).

ee   = ā when final in monosyllables and accented syllables, Eem (ām), Weeninx (wā'nĭnks). Before r it = â, Eerbeek (âr'bāk).

i   = ē in open syllables, Mieroslavski (myĕ rō släv'skē). When doubled, it has the same sound. Before a consonant in the same syllable it = ĭ, Dilsen (dĭl'sĕn).

ie   = ē, van Mieris (vän mē'rĭs).

o   = ŏ before two or more consonants, Dokkum (dŏk'kŏŏm). In open syllables it takes the sound of ō, Hodel (hō'dĕl).

oe   = ŏŏ, Doezum (dŏŏ zŏŏm').

oo   = ō in open syllables, Van Noort (vän nōrt'), Noodt (nōt), Troost (trōst).

ou   = ou, Wouverman (wow'ver män).

u   = ü in open syllables, Nuland (nü'länt). When doubled, it has the same sound. In closed syllables it is equivalent to ŭ, Jubbega (yŭb bä'gä).

uy   = oi, Enkhuysen (enk hoi'sen).

ch   = ch, Bocholz (bŏch'ŏlts).

d   = t when final, Herveld (hĕr'vĕlt); elsewhere it has the sound of English d, Bedum (bä'dŏŏm).

dt   = t, Bildt (bĭlt), Amersfoordt (ä'mers fōrt).

g   = ch or h strongly aspirated, Bergum (bĕr'hŏŏm).

j   = y, Jelsum (yĕl'sŏŏm).

sch   = sh when final before silent e; elsewhere it = sk nearly, Scheld (skĕlt), Schiedam (skē'däm).

y   = ī nearly, Mytens (mī'tĕns), Nieuwentyt (nû'vĕn tīt).

FRENCH

a   = ä when open, About (ä'bōō'); when closed, it has the sound å.

ai   = ă, Pain (păn̈).

-am, -an, -em, -en = ŏn̈, at the end of a word or syllable, Ozanam (ō zä nŏn̈'), Allemand (äl'mŏn̈'), Vieuxtemps (vyû tŏn̈'), de Montpensier (dê mōn̈ pŏn̈ sē ä').

au   = ō, Aube (ōb), Aude (ōd), Pau (pō), Quinault (kē'nō').

aux   = o, *faux pas* (fō på).

e = ā when open, Sablé (sä blä'). e = ě when closed, Mettray
(mě trā'); when final and unaccented it is silent, Scarpe (skärp).
Before r when not followed by a second consonant, it is sounded
like â, Perdu (pâr'dü').

eau = ō, Beaune (bōn), Eauze (ōz), *chateau* (shä tō').

eaux = ō, Meaux (mō).

ee = ā, Seez (sā).

ei = â before r, Pereire (pě'râr').

ens = ăṅ, Amiens (ä'mē ăṅ). When accented it takes the sound of
ŏṅ, Perrens (pâ rŏṅ').

ent In the third person plural of verbs, *ent* is silent.

esmes = ām, Solesmes (sō läm').

esnes = ān, Fresnes (frān).

i = ē when open, Picot (pē'kō'), Ribot (rě'bō'). i = ĭ when closed,
Finisterre (fĭn is târ').

ie = ē, Marie (mä'rē').

ier = ē ā, Garnier (gär nē ā').

-im, -in, -ym, -yn, -aim, -ain, -eim, -ein = ăṅ, at the end of a word
or syllable, timbre (tăṅ'br), Poussin (pōō'săṅ'), Nymphe
(năṅf), syntaxe (săṅ'tăks).

o = ō when open, Amero (ä'mä'rō). o = ŏ when closed, Postel
(pŏs'těl).

oi, ois, oix = wä, Noire (nwä'rā'), Blois (blwä), Agénois (ä zhā nwä'),
Foix (fwä).

on = ōṅ, Conte (kōṅ'tä'), Pons (pōṅ).

ou = ōō, Dɪ̇ioude (brō ōōd'), Agincourt (ä zhăṅ kōōr'), de la Noue
(dě lä nōō').

u = ü when open, *étude* (ā tüd').

-um, -un = ŭṅ at the end of a word or syllable, *humble* (ŭṅ'bl) *chacon*
(shăk'ŭṅ).

c = s before e, i, y. Before a, o, u, it = k. ç has the sound of s
before all vowels.

ch = sh, Auch (ōsh), Chauvin (shō'văṅ'). Before a consonant in the
same syllable it has the sound of k.

cq = k, Flobecq (flō běk'), Roncq (rōnk).

d, g, n, s, t, x, and z when final are usually silent, and leave the syllable
open, Nord (nōr), Flers (flâr), Gannat (găn'nă'), Géant
(zhā'ŏṅ'), Carmaux (kär'mō'). In proper names, *d*, when
final, is generally sounded, Boyard (bō'yärd'). Before a vowel
beginning the next word it has the sound of t.

de = dê, de Tocqueville (dě tŏk'vĭl).

g = zh before e, i, y, Bergerac (bâr zhā räk'), Agen (ä zhŏṅ'); before a, o, u, it has the sound of English g, Guerande (gä rŏṅd'), Guise (gēz). When final it is usually silent, Troplong (trŏ'lŏṅ').

gn = ny, Mignet (mēn'yä'), Persigny (pĕr'sēn'yē').

gue = gä, Guerande (gä rŏṅd').

gui = gē, Guise (gēz).

h Generally silent, St. Haro (st. ä'rō), St. Hautmont (st. ŏ'mŏṅ'), Heric (ä'rēk').

j = zh, Anjou (ŏṅ zhōō').

ll = y or ly, Pouillet (pōō'yä' or pōō'lyä').

n See d.

pt = t, Sept-Isles (sĕt ēl').

q and qu = k, Alquier (äl kē ä'), Quost (kōst).

ques, quet, quette = kä, Quesnel (kä'nĕl'), Hecquet (ä'kä').

s = z when between two vowels, Lisieux (lē'zĭ'û'), Rémusat (rä'mû'zä'). When final it is often silent, Paris (pä'rē'), Serres (sâr).

t When final is usually silent, Guyot (gē'ō'), Thibaut (tē'bō').

x = z before a vowel, Auxerre (ō zär'). See d.

y = ē, Gretry (grä'trē'), Oudry (ōō'drē').

z final is silent, Nez Percés (nä'pâr'sä'). See d.

GERMAN

a = ä, Abresch (ä'brĕsh), Kalk (kälk). ä = ĕ, Wächter (vĕch'ter).

aa = ä, Saale (sä'lĕ).

ai = ī, Nicolai (nē'kō lī).

au = ou, Pausa (pow'sa), Haupt (houpt), Rau (row), Strauss (strous).

e = ā in accented open syllables, Schlegel (shlä'gĕl). Before r, or two consonants, or a double consonant = ĕ, Hersfeld (hĕrs'-fĕlt). When final = ê, Reiske (rīs'kê).

ee = ā, Schneeberg (shnä'bĕrg).

ei = ī, Eider (ī'der).

eu = oi, Beuthen (boi'ten), Creuzburg (kroits'bōōrg).

ey = ī, Pleyel (plī'ĕl).

i = ē in open syllables or before a single consonant, Henrici (hen-rĭt'sē). In closed syllables it equals ĭ, Fritz (frĭts).

ie = ē, Siegen (sē'gĕn). The g has a slightly guttural quality.

o = ŏ before two consonants or a double consonant, Morhof (mŏr'hŏf). In other situations it = ō, Zollikofer (tsŏl'ē kō fer).

u = ōō when open, Kuty (kōō'tē). In closed syllables it has the sound of ŏŏ, Luckau (lŏŏk'ow).

ui = wē, pfui (pfwē).

b = p when final or immediately before a final consonant, Abt (äpt).

c   = k before a, o, u, Cassel (käs'sĕl), Coblenz (kō'blents). Before
       ä, e, i, y = ts, Peucer (poit'ser).
ch   = ćh, Bach (bäćh). When initial it = k, Chemnitz (kĕm'nits).
d   = t when final or immediately before a final consonant, Crefeld
       (krä'fĕlt), Burscheid (bōōr'shīt).
dt   = t, Mundt (mᴏᴏnt), Schmidt (shmĭt).
g   = g, Siegen (sē'gen). It sometimes takes a guttural quality. When
       followed by t it is equivalent to ćh, Vogt (fōćht).
j   = y, Jena (yä'nä), Jacobi (yä kō'bē).
s   = z when initial or after a consonant other than b, p, or ch, Reinesius
       (rī nä'zē ᴏᴏs), von Riedesel (fŏn rē'dē zĕl).
sch = sh, Schaumburg (shoum'bᴏᴏrg).
sz   = s, flusz (flᴏᴏs), gusz (gᴏᴏs).
th   = t, Beuthen (boi'tĕn).
ti   = ts in the terminal syllable -tion, nation (nằt sĭ ōn').
z   = ts, Brenz (brĕnts), Bregenz (brä'gĕnts).

HINDUSTANI—BRITISH INDIA

a   = ä, Rajapur (räj ä pōōr'), Rajkot (räj kōt').
aa   = ä, Raat (rät).
ai   = ī, Raipur (rī'pōōr'), Dainhat (dīn hät').
i   = ē, Riwari (rē wä rē'), Darjiling (där jēl'ing).
dh   = th, Pandharpur (pän thär pōōr').
pur = pōōr, Mirpur (mĕr pōōr'), Nagpur (näg pōōr').

HUNGARIAN

a   = ŏ, Baja (bŏ yŏ'), Krasso (krŏsh'shō). á = ä, Bács (Bäch).
aa   = ä, Raab (räb).
e   = ĕ, Breukelen (brĕ'kĕl en). é = ā, Széchenyi (sā'chĕn yĕ).
i   = ĭ, Dimrich (dĭm'rĭch). í = ē.
o   = ō softened, Losoncz (lō'shŏnts'). ó = ō sharp, Bagyon (bŏd yōn').
u   = ᴏᴏ, Ujfalvy (ᴏᴏ'ē fŏlv). û = ōō or ᴏᴏ, Lugos (lōō gōsh'), Mun-
       kacsy (mᴏᴏn kä'chē).
c   = ts, Popovec (pō pō vĕts').
cs   = ch, Bács (bäch), Becse (bĕt'chĕ), Csik (chĭk), Sztanicsics (stä nē-
       chĭch').
cz   = ts, Brestovacz (brĕs tō'väts), Petrovacz (pä trō väts'), Czegled
       (tsä'glĕd).
ds and dy = j, Mindszent (minj sĕnt').
g   = g, Bogat (bō gät').
gj and gy = j.
    4

gh = g, Ghimes (gē'mĕs).

gy = dy, Gyoma (dyō'mä), Magyar (mŏd yŏr').

j = y when used as a consonant, Jankovacz (yŏn'kō'väts'). When employed as a vowel it is equivalent to ē, Ujfalvy (ōō'ē fŏlv).

rz = zh, Brzezany (bzhā zhä'nĕ).

s = sh, Almas (äl mäsh'), Borsod (bŏr shŏd'), Szentes (sĕn tĕsh'), Saros (shä'rŏsh).

sz = s, Paszto (päs'tō), Sztanicsics (stä nē chĭch').

ts and ty = ch, Hertkovtsi (hĕrt kŏv'chē), Brettyo (brĕt'chō).

y = ē when used as a vowel, Gyalu (gē ä'lōō).

zs = zh, Uzsok (ōō zhŏk').

ITALIAN

au = oû, Aula (ou'lä).

e = ā in open syllables, Amadeo (ä mä dā'ō). In closed syllables it equals ĕ, Pecci (pĕt'chē), Bettola (bĕt tō'lä).

er = ĕr, Perrone (pĕr rō'nä).

i = ē, Almici (äl mē'chē), Altissimo (äl tēs'ē mō).

o = ō when open, Allori (äl lō'rē). When closed it equals ŏ, de Ponte (dä pŏn'tā).

oi = ō ē, Goito (gō'ē tō).

on = ŏn, Conti (kŏn'tē).

u = ōō, Amelunghi (ä mä lōōn'gē).

c = ch before e and i, Paceco (pä chä'kō), Portici (pōr'tē chē).

cc = k before a, o, u, Lecco (lĕk'kō). Before e and i it = tch, Castelluccio (käs tĕl lōōt'chō), Pecci (pĕt'chē), Ricci (rēt'chē), Riccio (rēt'chō), Peccioli (pĕt'chō lē).

ch = k before e and i, Cherubini (kā rōō bē'nē), Chiusa (kē ōō'sä). cch = k, Lamporecchio (läm pō rĕk'kē ō).

g = j before e and i, Agira (ä jē'rä).

gg = dj, Buggiano (bōōd jä'nō), Caravaggio (kä rä väd'jō).

gh = g, Alghisi (äl gē'zē).

gl = ly, Ceglie (chäl'yä), Ronciglione (rŏn chēl yō'nä).

gn = ny, Bagnara (bän yä'rä), Bagni (bän'yē).

h Generally silent, Borghetto (bŏr gät'tō).

j = y, Ajaccio (ä yät'chō), Bojano (bō yä'nō).

ng n does not blend with g, Angri (än'grē).

qu = kw, Querini (kwä rē'nē).

s = z when between two vowels, Alvisi (äl vē'zē), Paisiello (pī zē ĕl'lō).

sc = sh before e and i, Bisceglie (bē shäl'yä), Scicli (shēk'lē), Sciglio (shēl'yō). Before a, o, u, it equals sk, Scarpa (skär'pä).

sch = sk, Schio (skē'ō).

z   = ts, Luzzara (!o͞ot sä′rä), Levantzo (lä vänt′sō). When initial or
      after a consonant it equals dz, Zanchi (dzän′kē), Brienza
      (brē ĕn′dzä).
zz = ts, Arezzo (ä rĕt′sō).

NORWEGIAN

The sounds are, for the most part, like those of the Danish.

d   = t when final in many nouns and adjectives, Tonstad (tŏn′stät).
g   = y before ä, e, i, ö, y, Vigerö (vē yä′rû).
j   = y, Fjeld (fyĕld).
sk = sh, Skjergehavn (shyĕr′yä hävn).
y   = ü, Trydal (trü′däl).

POLISH

o   = ō when unaccented, Bulkov (bŏŏl′kōv). When accented it has
      the sound of ŏŏ, Dobra (dŏŏ′brä).
ow = ov, Mczconow (mshă zō′nŏv), Pinczow (pĭn′chŏv).
c   = ts, Dzialoszice (dzē ä lŏ shē′tsä), Potocki (pō tŏts′kē).
ch = ch. When initial it equals k, Checiny (kĕt sēn′yē), Chelm
      (kĕlm).
cz = ch, Czentochow (chĕns tō′kŏv), Pinczow (pĭn′chŏv).
dz = j, Bodzetyn (bō jĕ′tēn).
j   = y, Zamojski (zä moy′skē).
rz = zh, Brzezyn (bzhă′zĭn).
sc = ts nearly, Brzesc (bzhāts).
sz = ch, Naruszevitch (nä rōō shĕ′vĭch).
w   = v, Poniatowski (pō nē·ä tŏv′skē).
y   = ü nearly, Pulawy (pōō lä′wü).

PORTUGUESE

a   = à when final, Braga (brä′gà).
am = ouṅ, Azambuja (ä zouṅ bōō′zhä).
ão = ouṅ, Bissão (bĭs souṅ′).
o   = ō when open, Minho (mēn′yō). In closed syllables it has a
      softened or relaxed form of the same sound.
ou = ō nearly, Vouga (vō′gä).
ç   = s, Alcobaça (äl kō bä′sä).
cc = kk before a, o, u. Before e, i, y, it equals ks.
ch = sh, Chanza (shän′zä).
g   = j before e, i, y, Angeja (än jä′zhä).
gue = gā, Agueda (ä gä′dä).
gui = gē, Aguiar (ä gē är′).

h	Often silent, Asinhal (ä sē näl').
j	= zh, Alemtejo (ä lĕṅ tä'zhō).
lh	= ly, Velho (väl'yō).
m	= ṅ when final or when following *e*, Almairim (äl mä'ē rēṅ).
n	= ṅ when final or when following *e*, Almendra (äl mäṅ'drä).
nh	= ny, Banho (bän'yō).
qu	= k before e and i, Alemquer (ä lĕṅ kăr'). Before a and o it equals kw.
s	= z when between two vowels, Areosa (ä rä ō'zä).
x	= sh generally, Caxaria (kä shä rē'ä).
z	= s when final, Aviz (ä vēs').

RUSSIAN

a	= ä, Susdal (sōōs'däl'), Sviaga (svē ä'gä).
au	= ou, Chaussy (chou'sē).
ev	= ĕf, Balashev (bä lä shĕf').
i	= ē, Svir (svēr), Styr (stēr).
ch	= k, Chotyn (kō tēn').
sch	= sh, Schavli (shäv'lē), Schklov (shklŏv).
w	= v, Narew (nä'rĕv).
y	= ē, Chotyn (kō tēn').

SPANISH

Words ending in a consonant usually take the accent on the last syllable; those ending in a vowel, on the penult.

ai	= ī, Daimiel (dī mē ĕl').
au	= ou, Alcaudete (äl kou dä'tä).
ue	= wä, Cienfuegos (sē ĕn fwä'gōs).
b	= v between two vowels, Ribera (rē vä'rä), Cordoba (kor dō'vä).
c	= th before e and i, Albacete (äl bä thä'tä), Alcira (äl thē'rä). When final or before a, o, u, l, r, it equals k.
ch	= k before a vowel having the circumflex accent. In other situations it is sounded like the English ch, except in the province of Catalonia, where it has the sound of k.
d	= th when final, or when between vowels, Mellid (mĕl lēth'), Adajo (ä thä'hō).
de	= dā, de Toledo (dā tō lä'dō).
g	= ch *or* y before e and i, Puente de Genil (pwĕn tä dä chä nēl'). Before a, o, u, l, r, it has the sound of English g.
gua	= gwä, Guadalquiver (gwä däl kē vēr').
gue	= gā, Guedeja (gā dä'hä). **güe** = gwä, güepil (gwä pēl').
gui	= gē, Aguilas (ä'gē läs). **güi** = gwē.

guo = gwō.

h Silent, except before ue, when it has a nasal sound, Brihuega (brē wä′gä).

j = ch nearly, or h strongly aspirated. Badajos (bäd ä hōs′), Loja (lō hä′).

ll = ly, Montilla (mōn tēl′yä), Tafalla (tä fäl′yä).

ñ = ny, Alcañiz (äl kän yēth′), cañon (kǎn′yon).

qu = k, Barranquilla (bär rän kēl′yä).

y = ē when standing alone or when final or after a vowel followed by a consonant. Orozco y Berra (ō rŏs′kō ē bĕr′rä). Before a vowel in the same syllable, or between two vowels, it has the sound of j.

z = th, Alcañiz (äl kän yēth′), Azuaga (ä thōō ä′gä).

SWEDISH

In Swedish words the accent falls on the root syllable.

a = ä, von Wrangel (fŏn vräng′ĕl). **ä** = ā.

aa = ạ, Kaai (kạ′ē).

e = ā when accented, Wener (vä′ner).

i = ē, Kisa (kē′sä).

o = ō when final, Orno (ŏŏr′nō); elsewhere it = ŏŏ. **ö** = û, Nordenskjöld (nôr′dĕn shûld), Ulfö (ŏŏl′fû).

c — k before a, o, u, and aa, Calmar (käl′mär). Before e, i, y, ä, and ö it has the sound of s, Cimbrishamm (sĕm brē′shäm).

ch = k before a, o, u, and aa. When initial, it takes the sound of English ch.

dt = t, Zetterstedt (zĕt′ter stĕt).

f = v when final, Anderslöf (än′der slûv); **fv** = v, Afvaudden (ä vou′dĕn).

g = y before e, i, ä, ö, y, Gefleborg (yĕv lä bōōrg′). When it ends a syllable following another consonant it takes a sound resembling ch or g strongly aspirated, Taberg (tä′bĕrch, or tä′bĕrg). Elsewhere as English g, Berga (bĕr′gä).

h = h English. It is silent before j and v.

j = y, Jemtland (yĕmt′länt), Björnstjerna (byûrn styĕr′nä), Hjelmar (hyĕl′mär).

k = ch before ä, e, i, ö, y, Kengis (chän′yēs); elsewhere like English k, Kull (kŏŏl). It is sounded before n, Knaby (knä′bē).

kj = ch, Kjoping (chō′pēng).

skj = sh, Nordenskjöld (nŏŏr′dĕn shûld).

tj = ch, Tjorn (chŏŏrn).

y = ü, Yngaren (ün′gä rĕn).

CAPITALS

The use of capitals as a means of distinction, like the use of italic, has been carried to excess. The custom of the best proofreaders of to-day is to allow no capital where a lower-case letter will serve. The chief difficulty attending the use of capitals grows out of the fact that a word may demand a capital in one situation, and a lower-case in another. In headings and titles, even a preposition or conjunction may be so important as to require a capital. In writing, full-sized capitals are indicated by three parallel lines drawn under the letter or letters; small capitals, by two lines. The following suggestions and cautions will prove helpful:

SENTENCES

Every sentence must begin with a capital letter. To this rule there is probably no exception unless it be in quoting from an illiterate writer to show that he began his sentence improperly.

POETRY

Every line in poetry must begin with a capital letter. This does not apply to an incomplete line carried over by reason of a narrow measure or page.

PROPER NAMES

Among the rules for the use of capitals, none greets the ear of the schoolboy more frequently than that which says, "Every proper name must begin with a capital letter." But while the letter of the rule is familiar, its spirit is commonly misunderstood. Such words as Government, Administration, State, Constitution,

Cabinet, Capitol, Committee, are proper names in one situation, and common in another. The line of distinction is sometimes so fine that even the teacher who reprimands his pupil for neglect of the rule is at times uncertain how to decide.

PREFIXES TO PROPER NAMES

Von, in German, Van, in Dutch, De or D' in French, and Da, De, Della, or Di, in Italian, when used to introduce a foreign proper name, usually take a capital; as, D'Aubigne, De Mille, Van der Meer, Von Wallenstein. When preceded by a title or by the baptismal name, the lower-case letter is most generally used in French and German; as, M. de Tocqueville, Ludwig van Beethoven. In the Italian language, usage is somewhat divided.

Proper nouns and adjectives preceded by pre- are written with lower-case and a hyphen: pre-adamite, pre-mosaic, pre-raphaelite.

ADJECTIVES

Words like Senatorial, Congressional, Presidential, Gubernatorial, Councilmanic, referring to a definite person or office, are capitalized.

Many qualifying adjectives derived from proper names, and compounded with prefixes or suffixes, as, herculean, plutonian, tropical, hyperborean, are not capitalized.

DEITY

All names and appellations of the Deity, as God, Jehovah, Almighty, Father, Creator, Son, Holy Ghost, Saviour, Jesus Christ, Divine Sprit, Divine Benefactor, must begin with a capital.

In the Bible the pronouns He, His, Him, Thou, Thy, Thine, Thee, referring to the Deity, are set in lower-case, but in hymn-books, and manuals of devotion, and in newspapers, magazines, and epistolary correspondence, they are capitalized.

BIBLE

Capitals are employed in naming the Bible or parts thereof, and in the important divisions of the Book of Common Prayer; as, The Scriptures, Gospels, Epistles, Psalms, Pentateuch, Collects, Litany, etc.

SATAN

Satan and Beelzebub are written with capitals. Devil, and Evil Spirit, when used with a strongly emphasized individuality, take a capital; when used in general terms, they often are written in lower-case.

HADES

Poetical and mythological terms relating to the place of future abode, as Hades, Valhalla, are capitalized; but hell, purgatory, paradise, and similar words commonly have lower-case initials.

TITLES OF OFFICE AND HONOR

When titles of distinction precede a name, they are capitalized; as, Secretary Knox, Corporal Jones, Engineer Smith, Officer Brown. In the use of military titles, some writers use lower-case for non-commissioned officers up to corporal and midshipman. Terms employed to denote ordinary vocations, as, barber Jones, coachman Kelly, are also written lower-case. When the title follows the name, the first letter need not be capitalized, as:

Hon. John Hay, secretary of State.

Hon. Boies Penrose, senator from Pennsylvania.

When abbreviated titles of honor immediately follow a name, they are capitalized:

W. T. Harris, Ph.D., LL.D.

Joseph Spencer Kennard, Ph.D., D.C.L.

Henry C. McCook, D.D., Sc.D.

James Thompson, Esq.

A short name in lower-case, followed by a long list of titles in large capitals, is not pleasant to the eye. Small capitals give a neater appearance to the page.

The words Judge and Justice should always be capitalized when applied to the official holding that name.

A title of office when used instead of the name of the incumbent is capitalized, as:

He called upon the Governor.

Mr. Speaker, I rise to a point of order.

Good morning, Senator.

The Queen drove to the palace.

The Vice-president and the Lieutenant-colonel called at the Secretary's office.

COMPOUND TITLES

But one capital is required in a compound title, as, Ex-president Harrison, Major-general Stewart, Chief-justice Marshall, Vice-president Morton, Governor-general Brown, Rear-admiral Greene. By some, the form ex-President is preferred.

SOCIETIES AND CORPORATIONS

The principal words of the titles of societies and corporations begin with a capital letter; as, The Society for the Protection of Children; The Senate and House of Representatives of the State of Pennsylvania. Such expressions as, the Club, the House, the Assembly, are often employed for brevity, and are capitalized. When not designed to specify any particular organization or association they are written with lower-case; as, a state, a government, a company; but when used as a proper noun, require a capital; as, the State, the Government, the Company, the Union, the Parliament, the Convention. It will be observed that those written with a capital usually take the article *the* before them.

DENOMINATIONS, PARTIES

The names of religious denominations and political parties are capitalized. The word Church is capitalized when it refers

to a denomination, and also the word State as applied to a system
of government or to one of the United States.

CEREMONIAL FORMS

In formal letters or addresses to dignitaries, such terms as
Your Honor, Your Majesty, Your Reverence, are often employed
instead of the name.   In the third person, when Her Grace, His
Royal Highness, and similar forms are used, the pronoun as well
as the noun should be capitalized.   When reference is made to
a special person, the office with a capital letter is usually employed; as, the President, the Governor, the Senator, the Pope,
the Sultan.   When the title has no application to a definite
individual, a lower-case initial must be used.

Complimentary salutations occurring within the body of a
sentence or paragraph, as *sir*, *madam*, *my lord*, do not require a
capital.

TITLES OF BOOKS, PERIODICALS, PLAYS

The title of every book, periodical, play, or picture mentioned
in the text begins with a capital letter, and every important word
of the title is usually capitalized, as:

Robins' Romances of Early America.

Kennard's Some Early Printers.

Sheridan's School for Scandal.

In lengthy titles, the important words, as nouns, verbs, participles, and adjectives, should be capitalized; the articles, conjunctions, and prepositions rarely or never.   Usage is somewhat
divided in regard to titles, some excellent proof-readers limiting
the use of capitals to nouns and important verbs, and setting the
rest of the title in lower-case.

Mr. F. Horace Teall, who has made this and other points in
writing a subject of close study, says that the best rule for capital-
ization in headings seems to be to capitalize all the important or
emphatic words.   He then declares that the best practice under
this rule would be the avoidance of strenuous effort toward in-

flexible application of it, remarking that most rules are better and more satisfactory in their result if not applied too minutely.

When reference is made in the text to the name of a newspaper or periodical, the article *the* is not capitalized, as, It appeared in the Tribune; but in the naming of a book, it takes a capital, as, Have you read The Taming of the Shrew?

TABLES OF CONTENTS

The same rule that governs the use of capitals in book titles may be applied to tables of contents, summaries of chapters, running titles, and similar work. Use capitals for nouns and important verbs, always; for pronouns, adjectives, participles, and adverbs, seldom; for articles, prepositions, conjunctions, and interjections, rarely or never.

PERSONIFICATION

Abstract qualities, when personified in vocative address, are capitalized, as:

O Freedom! thou art not as poets dream.

O Liberty! what crimes are committed in thy name!

When such words as war, slavery, intemperance, riot, fortune, fame, fate, are not employed as synonyms of personified forces, they should not be capitalized.

I AND O

In English composition, the pronoun I and the interjection O always take the capital. The interjection *oh* is written with a lower-case letter, except at the beginning of a sentence.

DAYS, MONTHS, HOLIDAYS

The names of the days and months begin with capitals. Feast- and fast-days, festivals and holidays, follow the same rule; as, Arbor Day, Decoration Day, Good Friday, Christmas, Easter, Thanksgiving. Days of special historic interest, as Black Friday, are also capitalized.

GEOGRAPHICAL NAMES

Regions or sections of the world, used as proper nouns, take a capital, as, the Orient, the Occident, the Levant, the Tropics.

Geographical terms used as nouns or adjectives, in the vocabulary of trade and commerce, are usually written with lower-case letters, as china, morocco, castile soap, india rubber, prussian blue, turkey red. Custom sanctions the use of the capital in the words, French, German, Spanish, Italian, when used as qualifiers, and the dictionaries endorse the custom, but the catalogues of manufacturers, merchants, and auctioneers, and the usage of some reputable writers, ignore the custom, and use the lower-case letter. The words anglicized, americanized, romanized, germanized, and frenchified, like roman, italic, and arabic, in the terminology of the printer's sanctum, are gradually winning their way with the lower-case initial.

EAST, WEST

When used as nouns to particularize and define sections of the country, the terms East, West, North, South, and the compounds Northeast, Southwest, etc., are capitalized. When used to denote direction only, they are not capitalized:

And fresh from the west is the free wind's breath.

The wind was north-northwest.

Geographical and other terms indicative of place, as, river, lake, island, mountain, valley, road, street, avenue, when qualified by another descriptive word or phrase, are capitalized, as:

Bay of Biscay	Arlington Heights
Long Island Sound	Lafayette Place
Blackwell's Island	Fall River
Lancaster County	Rocky Mountains

When the general name precedes the particular, as, "In the county of Chester, state of Pennsylvania," or, "In the city of San Juan, on the island of Porto Rico," only the specific name is capitalized.

LEGAL DOCUMENTS

In legal documents and in all formal writings, and also in cases where displayed typography is desired, capital letters are used for the general as well as for the specific name.

HISTORIC EVENTS

The principal words in the names of historic events are capitalized, as:

the Captivity	the Civil War
the Restoration	the Peace of Utrecht
the Deluge	the Council of Nice
the Middle Ages	the Diet of Worms
the Renaissance	the Age of Pericles

QUOTATIONS

A complete sentence when quoted should begin with a capital. Words, phrases, and broken parts of a sentence, occurring within the body of the text, should be inclosed by quotation marks, but not capitalized.

DISPLAY

In newspapers and magazines, in circulars and other forms of advertising, in job-work, and wherever display is desirable, capitals may be used more freely than in book-work. No definite rule can be laid down. In case of doubt, it is safer to use lower-case. The style of an author is often impaired by an excessive use of capitals. Mr. Theodore Low De Vinne says that a projecting capital in a text is like a rock in the current, for it diverts the eye and interrupts an even stream of attention.

EMPHASIS

An initial capital is sometimes used as a form of emphasis to call attention to a word. In some kinds of descriptive writing, this use of the capital may be permissible, but if the word is repeated, it is better to use a lower-case after the first instance.

THE, O', AND A. M.

The definite article is often capitalized when it should be written with a small letter: the Public Ledger, the New York Herald, the Dark Ages, the Thirty Years' War.

In expressions like Tam o' Shanter, John o'Groat's, six o'clock, *o* is set in lower-case, with the apostrophe following. In proper names the *o* is separated from the word following by a short space.

The abbreviations a. m. and p. m. are generally written with lower-case letters.

SMALL CAPITALS

Two lines drawn under one or more words indicate that such parts of the manuscript are to be set in small capitals. The uses of small capitals are many and important, but, like large capitals, they should not be employed to excess. Coming between capital and lower-case, they afford a pleasing variety on a title-page, and are of advantage for the side-headings of short articles or separate paragraphs, for running titles, and whenever variety or display is desired.

They are often selected for the first word of a new chapter following a heavy-faced or ornamental initial. If the first word is very short, the second, and sometimes the third, word is set in small capitals.

When the chapter begins with the name of a person, each part of the name is set in capitals, the first letter of each part of the name taking a large capital, as:

OLIVER WENDELL HOLMES was one of the most genial of American writers.

The signature of a writer or an editor, or the credit given to an author may be set in capitals and small capitals at the end of an article or paragraph. Italic lower-case is preferred by some good proof-readers. When book and author are named, the name may be set in small capitals and the title of the book in italic.

The dedication of a book is usually set in small capitals. For purposes of emphasis, small capitals, as well as italic, must be used sparingly.

ITALICS

PROPER USE OF ITALICS

An excessive use of italic in print, like repeated emphasis in oratory, or profuse underscoring in writing, defeats the purpose for which it is intended. Where everything is made striking, nothing impresses. While the use of italic has been carried to excess, however, it has its proper place, and cannot be dispensed with. Its most important office is that of marking words and phrases that need to be distinguished in the text. It is also employed for running titles, for the headings of tables, and for subheadings. In the names of vessels, as the *Merrimac*, the *Illinois*, italic is generally employed.

EMPHASIS

The use of italics for emphasis, formerly quite common, is now almost wholly discontinued, and is confined chiefly to inexperienced writers. The modern type-setting machine makes no adequate provision for italicizing, and this, too, has encouraged the disuse of italics. Italics are rarely seen in the text of the reading-matter of the leading newspapers. The commingling of upright with inclined letters is displeasing to the eye, and if too freely employed, is confusing. A roman letter with a slightly bolder face is, by the better printing establishments, made to take the place of the italic.

FOREIGN WORDS

Foreign words and phrases are not italicized to so great a degree as formerly. Many of the best proof-readers use roman letters for every foreign word or phrase which appears as English in any approved English dictionary. A few suggestive examples are herewith given: ad valorem, alias, alibi, chapeau, charge d' affaires, debris, debut, ennui, facsimile, fete, naive, patois, per annum, per capita, post-mortem, pro rata, regime, rendezvous, role, savants, sobriquet, ultimatum, verbatim, vice versa, viva voce.

The expressions pro tem and per cent, contractions of pro tempore and per centum, may be said to have become so fully a part of the English language as to require neither italic nor the period.

Unusual foreign expressions employed to convey precise description, should be printed in italic in the first instance, but repetitions of the word may be put in roman. The omission of the French accents in such words as debris, regime, role, is also common.

SCIENTIFIC TERMS

Names of diseases, as angina pectoris, diabetes insipidus, and of remedies, as nux vomica, require neither italics nor initial capitals.

Geological terms do not take italics nor capitals except when derived from proper names, in which case capitals must be used; as, Devonian trilobites, Jurassic period.

In zoology and botany, latinized names composed of two words are written in italic. The first word usually denotes the genus, and begins with a capital; as, *Rana esculenta, Arvicula amphibius.* If the second name is derived from that of a person or place, it too should begin with a capital; as, Darlingtonia Californica; otherwise it begins with a lower-case letter. When first used, all such words should be italicized. When repeated in the same article, the names of species continue in italics, but all the larger divisions are set in roman.

Writers on scientific subjects differ concerning the use of italics, but the above suggestions are supported by a majority of the best authorities.

AUTHOR AND BOOK

In the text of a book, pamphlet, or newspaper, in which reference is made to a writer and his work, roman is used for the name of the author and italic for the title of the book; as, George Eliot, *The Mill on the Floss.*

FOOT-NOTES

In foot-notes, and in a quotation that makes a full paragraph, the better form is to put the name of author and book in roman lower-case. At the end of a paragraph or foot-note in making reference to a book, the author's name is put in roman and the book in italic. If the book alone is given, use italic.

When reference is made in the body of the text or in foot-notes, to a newspaper or magazine, use roman lower-case, without quotation marks; as, the New York Herald. If placed at the end of a paragraph as a credit, use italics.

VARIANT USAGE

Some phrases, when used as adverbs, may be set in italics; when used as qualifiers of nouns, they are set in roman.

The Vice-president is, *ex officio*, the chairman.

An ex-officio member of the committee.

The evidence is, *prima facie*, conclusive.

Prima-facie evidence.

RUNNING COMMENTS

These are usually bracketed in the text and do not require to be italicized.

QUOTATION

Extracts and quotations that make two or more lines should be given a separate place or paragraph. If in the same type as the text, they should be set off by quotation marks; if in smaller type, with blank before and after, no quotation marks are needed.

One line with the pen drawn under the word or phrase indicates to the printer that the parts thus underlined are to be set in italic.

5

NUMERALS

BOOKS, NEWSPAPERS, AND CORRESPONDENCE

In books, magazines, and newspapers, and in general correspondence, figures and numbers should be avoided as much as possible. In dates, catalogues, trades lists, and wherever economy of space is important, they may be used. In commercial printing they are largely employed. In legal documents, and in all kinds of formal writing where great precision of statement is desired, figures and abbreviations should not be used. In social correspondence, except in dates, street numbers, etc., figures should be avoided.

QUANTITIES AND VALUES

Figures must not begin a sentence. Quantities are properly written in words, while values are expressed in figures, especially if the value involves fractions; as, ten yards of calico at 7½ cents a yard. Degrees of temperature, records of votes or of time in a race, are usually expressed in figures, this custom being sanctioned by the best authorities, as:

The highest temperature last summer was 98 degrees.

The specific gravity of gold is 19.

The vote stood 50 yeas to 76 nays.

His best time was a mile in 2 minutes, 36½ seconds.

The form $500 is better than $500.00. In tables containing columns for dollars and cents, the two ciphers are written to occupy what would otherwise be an unsightly vacant space.

FIGURES AND WORDS

A combination of figures and words is displeasing to the eye. The forms *a ten-foot pole, a twelve-story building,* are more sightly than *a* 10-*foot pole, a* 12-*story building.* Where frequent repetition or comparison is necessary, figures make the subject more clear, and are usually preferred; as, 4-penny, 6-penny, and 10-penny nails; 8-point, 12-point, 24-point type.

DATES

When the day is placed before the month, retain the *st, d, th*; as, 10th May, 22d June; when placed after the month, omit these endings, as, May 10, 1896. The shorter forms 2d, 3d, are preferred to 2nd, 3rd.

LARGE NUMBERS

In the expression of large numbers consisting of four, five, six or more figures, it is an assistance to the eye to separate the number by commas into groups of three figures each. A number of four figures standing alone, as 7584, is better without a comma. A date, as 1776, should never be written with a comma.

HOUSE AND STREET NUMBERS

To distinguish between the number of the house and that of the street, the former is usually written in figures and the latter in words; as, 55 Fifth Street. If the street were indicated by a figure, it might be mistaken for 555th Street. The English custom of placing a comma after the house number is not observed in the United States. Where a distinction must be made between street and avenue, the avenue is written in words, and the street in figures; as, Third Avenue and 132d Street.

HOURS OF THE DAY

Two o'clock, half-past seven, or fifteen minutes before eight are more sightly than 2 o'clock, 7.30, 7.45. When figures are used, hours are separated from minutes by a period, and not by a colon. The forms o'clk, o'cl'k, and o'c should be avoided except where space absolutely prevents the use of the entire word.

DYNASTIES AND RULERS

Centuries, dynasties, and rulers are now usually expressed in words; as, the twentieth century, the sixteenth dynasty, Henry the Eighth, instead of, the XXth century, the XVIth dynasty, and Henry VIII.

PUNCTUATION

The roman numerals XX, VIII, XC, are not abbreviations any more than are 20, 8, 90, and do not require a period as a mark of abbreviation.

SYLLABICATION

There is no system of syllabication so perfect as to command universal adoption. Many English writers are governed by the junction of the constituent parts of consolidated words: geo logy, dia meter, pro position, typo graphic, cata strophe. This system is logical and etymological. Another system authorizes the division of a word after the vowel, when not inconsistent with pronunciation. This leads to such strained divisions as re co gnize, pre fe rence, cata stro phe, ca pa ci ty, com pa ti bi li ty. The orthoepical division separates the words into parts, with a view to bringing out the accented and unaccented syllables in conformity with the accepted forms of pronunciation. While this system is most widely followed in the United States, it is not without some disadvantages.

The compositor usually follows the dictionary used in his office, but the author or the proof-reader sometimes differs with the lexicographer, and the compositor is discomfited. The dictionaries unfortunately differ with one another and are not always consistent in their own practice.

PURPOSE OF DIVISION

Outside of dictionaries and spelling books, words are rarely divided except at the end of a line, where lack of space prevents the completion of a word. The author, copyist, and typewriter encounter no special difficulty, since they are not required to observe a right-hand margin. They may complete a word at the end of a line or carry it over bodily to the next. The compositor, on the other hand, must make his lines of even length. His measure may not admit of more than a fourth or a half of a word. To carry all of the word over to the next line, especially if the word be lengthy or the measure narrow, would necessitate such wide spacing between the remaining words as to appear unsightly. To crowd all the word into the line would often make the line itself look like one long word. A division therefore becomes unavoidable.

PRINCIPLES OF DIVISION

When the division of a word become necessary, it should be made in accordance with recognized principles, so far as they are discoverable. The best general rule is that a word should be broken in writing or printing as it is divided in speaking. The American dictionaries aim to carry out this rule, and yet there are many differences among them.

TYPOGRAPHICAL DIVISIONS

The typographer's division aims to please the eye, as well as to satisfy the ear. It becomes apparent at the outset, therefore, that the speaker and the typographer will each have specific rules that will not apply to the other. The speaker utters every word by syllables. In ordinary book and newspaper composition, the typographer divides no word in the line, except, in some cases, the last, unless he encounters a chance hyphenated compound.

MONOSYLLABLES

Words of one syllable, even though they are long and the measure narrow, must not be divided. When words like *through, ground, brought,* occur in narrow columns, they often occasion trouble to the compositor.

SHORT SYLLABLES

Some good proof-readers, in order to prevent the carrying over or the leaving behind of a syllable consisting of one or two letters, forbid the division of such words as fasten, given, often, moisten, prayer, eleven, soften, listen, heaven. Many printing-houses follow the rule that in a measure of eighteen ems or more, a noun of one syllable which forms its plural by adding *s* (voices, verses, horses) must not be divided. In very narrow measure, this rule cannot be followed.

DIVISION BETWEEN CONSONANTS

When two consonants meet between two vowels, the division is generally made between the consonants: mar ket, mil lion, moun tain, for tune. When three consonants come together, the two that form the closer union in pronunciation are usually coupled: ac tress, pitch er, chil dren, trench er.

INFLUENCE OF ACCENT

A change of accent is often attended with a change in the division of a word: commend' able, commen da'tion; prod' uct, pro duc'tion; pro cure'ment, proc ura'tion.

DOUBLE CONSONANT

When the final consonant is doubled on taking a suffix, the separation occurs between the consonants: admit ted, concurrence; but if a double consonant ends the stem, the consonants are not divided: add ing, ebb ing, call ing, spell ing.

PREFIXES AND SUFFIXES

A prefix or a suffix forms a loose juncture with the stem to which it is attached, and usually affords a desirable point for division: dis appoint ment, equi ponder ance, un answer able; but if such separation misrepresents the pronunciation, the word is differently divided: big amy, prov idence, trim eter.

-able, -al, -ant, -ent, -ive, -or, -ory, -ure.—These suffixes usually follow the rule laid down for -ed, -er, -ing.

-ar, -er.—In the coalescents *ar* and *er*, the *r* must not be separated from the vowel: par ent, fair est, gener al, aver age.

-cian, -sian, -tian.—These terminal syllables are not divided in printing and writing, and there is good authority for an unbroken syllable in pronunciation: magi cian, opti cian, physi cian, A sian, Per sian, Chris tian, gen tian. When *elysian* is pronounced with four syllables, it forms an exception.

-cial, -sial, -tial.—These suffixes are not divided: gla cial, spe cial, so cial, cru cial, offi cial, ambro sial, ini tial, pruden tial, nup tial. Some authorities divide *tial* in *bes ti al i ty*.

-cion, -sion, -tion.—In English words these terminal syllables are never divided: coer cion, suspi cion, inva sion, cohe sion, vaca tion, ora tion. With a view of preserving the sound of short *i*, many persons improperly place *s* in the ultimate in such words as deci sion, eli sion, deri sion, revi sion. The dictionaries (International, Standard, Worcester), while divided on many points, are unanimous in the division of words in this class. The Century does not show the division of the printed or written word.

-ceous, -cious, -scious, -tious.—These suffixes are long, and in the setting up of narrow measure, the compositor may find it difficult to avoid breaking them; but in printing, as in pronunciation, they should not be divided: ceta ceous, herba ceous, spa cious, deli cious, con scious, fac tious, cau tious.

-ed, -er, -ing.—The dictionaries are much at variance regarding the suffixes of verbs ending in silent *e*. The practice of the Standard is the most uniform, most consistent with its principles, and most easily followed; but is probably least in accord with current usage. According to this authority, nearly all verbs of this class join the terminal consonant or consonants with the suffix, as: bi-ter, ting; deba-ted, -ting, -tor, -table; ag'ita-ted, -ting, -tive, -tor.

Webster's rule, if not quite so simple, is more in accordance with the best current usage, and his practice is seldom at variance with his principles. Worcester's division is, in the main, in accord with the International.

Many verbs of one, two, three, four, or more syllables end in silent *e*. In monosyllables and in dissyllables of this class which have the accent on the ultimate, the *e* is dropped on taking the suffixes -ed, -er, -ing, the consonant remaining with the stem: dat′ ed, quot′ ed, comput′ ed, recit′ ed, bit′ ing, dot′ ing, adher′ ing, implor′ ing, smit′ er, debat′ er. While the primary accent remains unchanged, most of the other suffixes follow the same division: comput′ able, recit′ al, dot′ ish. But with a change of accent, the consonant is carried over with the suffix, as: dis′pu tant, rep′u table, com′pa rable.

When the accent falls upon the penult or antepenult, the consonant is carried over to the suffix: contrib′u ted, -ting, -ter, -table, -tor, -tory; illus′tra ted, -ting, -tive, -tor, -tory; antic′ipa ted, -ting, -tive, -tor, -tory.

-ee, -or.—Usage is greatly divided regarding the spelling of legal terms with the above endings. The consonant generally goes with the suffix: lega tee′, les see′, mortga gee′, do′ nor, guar′-an tor. Exceptions are found in assign ee′, consign ee′, grant ee′, for reasons which are obivous.

-geous, -gious, -geon, -gion.—The words coura geous, gorgeous, conta gious, sacrile gious, gud geon, sur geon, conta gion, re gion, illustrate the general use of these suffixes. The dictionaries are greatly at variance in the case of several words having such terminations. The Standard divides widge on, pig eon, gudg eon, relig ion, relig ious, litig ious, thus breaking the general rule. Worcester makes the same division, except in widg eon. The International preserves the suffixes unbroken, except in widg eon, bludg eon, where, in accordance with the general rule, every reason seems to point to the division between the two consonants: dun geon, sur geon, stur geon. If it be argued that the accented vowel would suffer a change by dividing, as in reli gion, pi geon, reli gious, liti gious, the reply is that the *g* sound would be more likely to suffer a change if transferred to the penult. The accented vowel is in no greater danger in the above words than it is in scores of others whose division is never questioned, as: na tional, spe cial, judi cial, offi cial, suspi cious, nutri tious.

-le.—When the terminal *-le* is preceded by a single consonant or consonant digraph, the dictionaries are much at variance regarding the division of the word. The International writes trou ble, spec kle, tic kle, buc kle, cou ple; the Standard makes the division before the *l*, as, troub le, speck le, etc. The compositor will find the former division a convenience, especially in narrow measure, but the latter is more in harmony with pronunciation.

SHORT AFFIXES

Other short prefixes, as in-, en-, ex-, ad-, af-, on-, de-, and suffixes, as, -al, -an, -on, -ly, should not be separated from the stem. This is especially true of -ed when it is sounded with the main part of the word in one syllable, as, looked, slaked, tacked, passed. Some good proof-readers protest against separating the suffixes -ed, -er, and -ing when preceded by a double consonant, as, combat ted, -ting; fit ter, -test; glad der, -dest.

BASIS OF DIVISION

In writing, there is little occasion for the division of words except when they are very long. In printing, custom, taste, and convenience alike require that the right, as well as the left margin shall be observed. Custom requires also that words shall be broken according to certain principles. The most general principle is that the printed word shall be divided according to its syllabication in speech. But the material substance of spoken words is sound—fleeting, volatile, difficult to grasp, and more difficult to harness—hence the diversity of usage among those who syllabize according to pronunciation.

SPACING

The beauty of a printed page depends, in no small degree, upon the spaces between its words. In a wide column or page it is an easy matter for the compositor to adjust his spaces without violation of the principles of division; but in narrow measure it is often a question whether good taste is not better conserved by an equalization of the spaces than by a strict adherence to the rules of division of the word at the end of the line.

In the present unsettled usage, the compositor might be pardoned for dividing the word according to his space; as, trou ble or troub le, buc kle or buck le, reli gion or relig ion. Since many words admit of two spellings or two forms of pronunciation, he may, with the greater propriety, claim such privilege. Different divisions of the same word, however, should not occur in the same paragraph or page.

WIDE MEASURE

In wide measure, the taste and judgment must determine, in a large degree, where to break the word. Some authors claim that the first part of a broken word must always be long enough to suggest the word. This is not practicable in narrow measure, and would be found inconsistent with good spacing even in wide measure. But one or two letters should not be separated from the rest of the word either at the beginning or at the end. Such words as eleven, given, heaven, horses, often, striven, voices, verses, over, able, avow, amen, and many others, should not be separated when it is possible to avoid it.

GOOD JUDGMENT

Despite all that has been said regarding the division of words, it is impossible to construct rules that will cover all cases. The junction between a prefix or suffix and the stem is less close than between the syllables of the stem itself, and will often serve as the best place for division. Dis infect, dis organize, dis avow, disagree, in humanity, un able, service able, are better divisions than disin fect, disor ganize, disa vow, disa gree, inhu manity, una ble, servicea ble.

COMPOUND WORDS

Compound words, whether hyphenated or consolidated, when occurring at the end of a line, should be broken between the elements of the compound, and not between the syllables of one of their parts; as, twenty-one, fellow-creatures, apple-tree, cotton-seed; not twen-tyone, fel-lowcreature, ap-pletree, cot-tonseed.

PROPER NAMES

Proper names should not be divided when it is possible to avoid it. The setting of Theo- at the end of a line, or even the whole word Theodore, does not look so well as the full name Theodore Roosevelt on one line; but in the adjustment of such a matter, the author's assistance may be necessary. A word may have to be added or omitted to bring the two parts of the name on the same line.

NUMBERS

Like proper names, numbers, when broken at the end of a line, are awkward. Dates must never be broken (1492, 1776, 1904), and are read in hundreds. Large numbers other than dates are pointed off in groups of three figures, and when divided at the end of a line, must be separated between the groups, as, 4, 396, 718,-425. Decimals are pointed off from the decimal point toward the right, and should be divided in the same way as whole numbers. A number consisting of less than six figures should not be divided.

DISPLAY LINES

In the title-page, words of bold display should not be divided. Subtitles and summaries in small capitals may be divided. In eccentric composition, as in the setting of a square or rectangular title, a word is often divided in the middle of a syllable, even without the formality of a hyphen.

A subheading of two lines should not break a word if it is possible to throw the full word into the second line.

COMPOUND WORDS

GUIDING PRINCIPLES

The absence of any satisfactory guiding principles in the compounding of words is apparent to all who have sought information in this department. Mr. F. Horace Teall has probably made a more careful and exhaustive study of the subject than any other writer. To illustrate a fundamental principle in compounding, he uses the following: an *iron fence* is a fence made of iron; an *iron-saw* is a saw intended to cut or saw iron; and *ironwood* is the name of a tree whose wood is intensely hard. The manner of combining these words brings out the distinction in meaning, and shows how clearness of thought is often dependent upon a proper compounding of words. In like manner *Aaron's beard* signifies the beard of Aaron, while *Aaron's-beard* is the name of a plant.

When railroads and steamboats first came into use, *rail* and *road, steam* and *boat,* were written as separate words. After a time they were combined with a hyphen; later they were consolidated. Many compounds, both hyphenated and consolidated, have undergone, and others are now undergoing, a similar change.

Usage is the law of language. When it is uniform and fully established, there is no appeal. But usage should be founded on principle. Where it is greatly varied, the principle should be applied, and the best usage secured and made general. In several of the later dictionaries, an attempt has been made, in all cases of unsettled usage, to establish a guiding principle, and to make the varying forms employed by printers, proof-readers, stenographers, and writers conform to it. The best current usage is represented in the body of this work. The following suggestions will prove helpful.

POINTS OF THE COMPASS

Points of the compass, as, northeast, southeast, are better written without a hyphen. When the first part is repeated, the hyphen is required, as in south-southeast.

NUMERALS

Fractions and numerals, as, one half, two thirds, ten thousand, need no hyphen unless combined to qualify a noun; as, one-half interest. If the fraction is complex, as in five sixty-thirds, one hundred and twelve ten-thousandths, the hyphen is needed, also in the specification of numbered streets, as Seventy-fifth Street, One-hundred-and-twenty-eighth Street. Compounds with half, quarter, etc., are generally joined with a hyphen, as, half-crown, half yearly, quarter-dollar, quarter-section. Numerals of one syllable prefixed to fold, penny, pence, score, are consolidated, as in fourfold, halfpence, sixpenny; but if the numeral contains two or more syllables, it is written as a separate word, as thirty fold, fifteen pence, twenty score. When used as an adjective qualifier, as in fourteen-penny tax, the hyphen may be used. First-rate, second-rate, and similar terms, are compounded. First-lieutenant, second-mate, when used as adjective qualifiers, are compounded; as, Second-lieutenant Brown. Numerals helping to form adjective qualifiers are followed with the hyphen; as, a four-story house, a ten-acre lot.

KINDRED

Words of kinship in frequent use, if short and closely united in thought, are consolidated; as, grandfather, godmother, stepson. Longer forms and those in less common use take the hyphen;

as, foster-brother, great-grandfather, mother-in-law, great-aunt, second-cousin, grand-uncle.

TITLES

Military and civil tltıes require the hyphen; as, Major-general, Lieutenant-colonel, Vice-president. Viceroy and Viceregent are consolidated.

DESCRIPTIVE COMPOUNDS

Brief descriptive compounds, as long-haired, blue-eyed, broad-shouldered, sharp-nosed, require the hyphen.

COLORS

Silver-gray, olive-green, and similar compounds, take the hyphen; but reddish brown, yellowish white, etc., are separate words.

POSSESSIVE CASE

Forms like crow's-nest, bird's-eye, jew's-harp, have good authority; but the tendency of the best writers and printers is toward the unbroken word; as, ratsbane, beeswax, townspeople.

SCHOOL

As the initial word, school is consolidated in schoolboy, schoolmate, schoolmistress. It is hyphenated in school-bred, school-teaching, when used to qualify a noun. It is a separate word in school children, school teacher, school days, school district.

As the second word of the compound, the word school is generally written separately, as Normal School, High School. In Sabbath-school and Sunday-school, usage varies, some authorities writing the words separately.

SHORT WORDS

Compounds whose constituent parts are short, especially if in common use, are usually consolidated.

out-, over-, under-.—These prefixes are usually written without the hyphen, unless the second part consists of two or more syllables.

extra-, non-, sub-, semi-, demi-.—These are compounded without a hyphen unless the combination is unusual.

above-, ill-, so-, well-.—When these prefixes precede a participle, and the compound is used as a qualifier, the hyphen is usually employed; as, above-named, ill-bred, well-formed, so-called.

self-.—Most compounds beginning with self- require the hyphen; as, self-assertion, self-conceit, self-conscious. Those ending with -self are consolidated; as, myself, itself, oneself.

mid-.—Words in common use beginning with mid- require no hyphen; as midday, midnight, midsummer. Those in less common use take the hyphen; as, mid-heaven, mid-ocean.

pre-, re-.—When followed by a word beginning with *e*, the hyphen instead of the dieresis is often employed; as, pre-empt, pre-engage, re-enter, re-echo. To distinguish between words of different meaning, as in rec ollect, re-collect, rec ommend, re-com-mend, the hyphen must be employed. Pre-adamite, pre-raphaelite, pre-occupy pre-historic, and similar expressions take the hyphen.

-like.—Compounds ending in -like, especially if short or in common use, are written as one word, as lifelike, childlike. To avoid an unpleasant combination of letters, a hyphen is employed in the words bell-like, shell-like, etc.

-fish, -bird.—A convenient rule for compounds ending in -fish, -bird, and one on which careful writers are generally agreed, is to consolidate when the first part consists of only one syllable, and to hyphenate when it consists of two or more syllables; as, dogfish, bluefish, swordfish, harvest-fish, ribbon-fish, blackbird, bluebird, reedbird, humming-bird, tailor-bird. In rare and unusual compounds, the hyphen is employed even when the parts are monosyllables.

-tree, -wort.—Words compounded with -tree usually take the hyphen; those with -wort omit the hyphen: apple-tree, lemon-tree, pear-tree, milkwort, thoroughwort.

-man, -woman.—Compound words ending in -man or -woman are generally consolidated; as in warehouseman, workingman, marketwoman, needlewoman.

any, every.—These words are usually consolidated; as, *anybody, anything, everywhere,* but *any one, every one,* are written as separate words.

T rail, T square, U bolt, U tube, V gage, V gear, and similar expressions are usually written as separate words.

PHRASES

After a while, by and by, it may be, by the bye, ever to be remembered, in no wise, in the meantime, long looked for, uncalled for, and many similar phrases are best written as separate words. *Good day, good night, good by,* are also written as separate words, except when used as adjective qualifiers; as, *a good-night kiss, a good-day greeting.*

PUNCTUATION

PRIMARY PURPOSE

The student of punctuation will not have proceeded far in his studies without discovering that this branch of learning has not yet reached the condition of an exact science. Different writers interpret and apply the rules differently. Nor can these rules be applied strictly alike to all kinds of writing. Poems and trades lists, sermons and market reports, cannot be punctuated by the same codes. Different systems prevail in different publishing houses. Authors, editors, and proof-readers have opinions of their own, and do not always defer to the grammarians, and the lot of the compositor is often a trying one.

Remembering that the primary purpose of punctuation is to make the meaning more clear, it is a safe general rule to omit any marks whose use will not promote this purpose. A sentence may be long and yet so clear as to require no points. Another, though comparatively short, may be so involved as to require a number of them. Some writers punctuate very closely and precisely, while others write carelessly and with great lack of uniformity in regard to punctuation.

GENERAL TENDENCY

The general tendency is toward the use of fewer points than were formerly considered necessary, especially in ordinary descriptive writing, but in composition of legal and ecclesiastical matter, and in precise composition of every kind, the strictest rules of punctuation must be observed. By the careless insertion of a comma instead of a hyphen in the official printing of an enactment of Congress, certain articles which should have paid duty were imported free, with a resulting loss of thousands of dollars to the Government.

A careful observance of the usage of good writers and proofreaders, as illustrated in well-edited books, magazines, and newspapers, will prove a valuable study in punctuation.

DUTY OF THE COMPOSITOR

All persons who prepare copy for the press should understand and apply the rules of punctuation. But so long as manuscripts are presented without comma or period, or with the dash used indiscriminately for every other mark, there will be something for the compositor to do. It is his duty, in every case, to try to make composition intelligible, so far as it can be done by the proper use of points.

GRAMMAR AND PUNCTUATION

The use of points is so largely dependent upon a knowledge of sentence-structure, that the study of grammar should precede that of punctuation. Just as the book is made up of chapters, sections, paragraphs, and sentences, so the sentence is composed of members or clauses, phrases, and words.

6

The purpose of this volume forbids an extended discussion of the grammatical principles underlying the structure of the sentence, but a few simple definitions with illustrations are herewith presented.

SENTENCES

A sentence is a combination of words so arranged as to make complete sense.

1 The wise man throws himself on the side of his assailants.
2 Are the stars mere decorations of the night?
3 How often does an unseen hand shift the scenes of life!
4 Consider the sad consequences of a misspent life.

These four sentences are called respectively, Declarative, Interrogative, Exclamatory, Imperative.

According to their structure, sentences are classified as Simple, Complex, and Compound. A simple sentence represents a single statement, and contains one subject and one predicate. The foregoing are examples of the simple sentence.

A compound sentence consists of two or more simple sentences connected. The parts are called members and are independent of each other.

1 Columbus discovered a new world, and Americus Vespucius gave it a name.
2 The wind blew furiously, and the waves dashed high.
3 To err is human; to forgive, divine.

These are examples of a compound sentence. By some grammarians, the members are called independent clauses.

A complex sentence is one composed of a principal clause and one or more dependent clauses. Examples:

1 Fools rush in *where angels fear to tread.*
2 *When the morning dawned,* all doubts were dispelled.
3 Hannibal was the deadliest foe *that Rome ever had.*

The subordinate or dependent clauses are in italics. It will be observed that each member or clause has a subject and a predicate.

A phrase is a group of two or more words which usually perform the office of an adjective or an adverb.

1 All men admire an act *of heroism.*
2 Dewey won a great victory *at Manila.*
3 He writes *with great rapidity.*

COMPOUND SENTENCES

1 John learned a trade and Henry went to college.
2 The wind blew furiously, and the waves dashed high.
3 The policeman ran swiftly, but the thief escaped.

In the first of the foregoing sentences, no comma is needed because the members are short, of equal rank, and independent. In each of the others, the second statement follows as a consequence of a condition expressed in the first, and a comma is employed.

RESTRICTIVE CLAUSES

1 The diamond that I lost was a Christmas gift.
2 The diamond, which is pure carbon, is a brilliant gem.
3 No thought, of which good sense is not the groundwork, can be just.

In the first sentence, the clause *that I lost* restricts *diamond* to the one lost, and requires no comma. In the second, the subordinate clause is non-restrictive, and must be set off by commas. When the subordinate clause, even if restrictive, is introduced by *of which* or *of whom,* the comma is necessary.

ADJECTIVE AND ADVERB CLAUSES

When these clauses are restrictive, they follow the rule for restrictive clauses.

1 I plucked the peaches that were ripe.
2 I plucked the peaches, which were ripe.
3 Youth is the time when character is formed.
4 Solomon, who built the temple, was the son of David.

In the first sentence, only the ripe peaches were plucked; in the second, all were ripe and all were plucked. It will be observed that the junction of the non-restrictive, or supplementary, clauses in the second and fourth sentences is not so close as that of the restrictive clauses in the first and third.

PHRASES

1 The guide standing on the rock is looking toward us.
2 The guide, standing on the rock, reached out his hand to save us.
3 The old baron sat, on one cold night, in a small room, before the empty grate.
4 We went from Philadelphia to New York in two hours.

Participial phrases, when not restrictive, are set off with commas. When more than two adverb phrases modify the same word, they are pointed off with commas; but, if the phrases are short and the sentence clear, as in the fourth example, no comma is required.

SERIES

Words, phrases, and clauses, alike in character or construction, and arranged in a series, are separated by commas.

1 Industry, honesty, and temperance are essential to happiness.
2 Industry, honesty, temperance, are cardinal virtues.
3 Alfred the Great was a grave, pious, and patriotic prince.
4 The address was eloquently, forcibly, and beautifully delivered.
5 Beauty is seen alike in leaf, in bud, in flower, in fruit, in tree.
6 It is education that enlarges our minds, that corrects our opinions, that broadens our views, and that renders us more useful.
7 A beautiful white lily grew in the garden.
8 Long, difficult, pious pilgrimages were made to Mecca.

Many persons make the mistake of omitting the comma before *and* which connects the last two words of the series; as in the first, third, and fourth sentences. In the second sentence, the omission of *and* makes it necessary to use the comma before the verb. The adjective modifiers in the seventh sentence require no comma of separation because they are not in the same construction. The word *white* modifies *lily*, and *beautiful* modifies the expression *white lily*. Compare this with the eighth sentence.

PAIRS

Words or phrases arranged in pairs take a comma after each pair.

1 Poverty and distress, desolation and ruin, anarchy and confusion, follow civil war.
2 He shot or hanged, imprisoned or exiled, the troublesome insurgents.
3 Cotton grows in Egypt and in India, in Brazil and in the United States.

INTERJECTED EXPRESSIONS

Such expressions as *however, indeed, perhaps, therefore, in fact, in truth, by the way, according to his own statement,* when interjected between the parts of a sentence, are somewhat parenthetical in character, and are usually set off by commas.

1 He promised, however, to reform at once.
2 The whole town, in fact, was aroused by the noise.
3 This book is, generally speaking, better than the other.

INTRODUCTORY EXPRESSIONS

Introductory expressions, which show a connection between the sentence and something preceding, are set off by commas, as:

1 Moreover, he hath left you all his walks.
2 Lastly, what lay you to their charge?

The words *whereas* and *resolved*, used in connection with a series of resolutions, are generally, but needlessly, set off by commas.

ELLIPSIS

The comma is often employed to denote the omission of a word.

1 The stern and rigid Puritans worshiped here.
2 The stern, rigid Puritans worshiped here.
3 The sun and the moon and the stars revolve.
4 The sun, the moon, and the stars revolve.
5 The sun, the moon, the stars, revolve.
6 From law arises security; from security, inquiry; from inquiry, knowledge.
7 From law arises security; from security inquiry; from inquiry knowledge.
8 Homer was the greater genius; Virgil the better artist.

9 Reading maketh a full man; conference a ready man; writing an exact man.

While the sixth sentence illustrates the rule, and is in accord with former usage, the closeness of construction, as exemplified in the last three sentences, justifies the omission of the comma, and illustrates the practice of many good writers and proofreaders of today.

INVERSION

Words and phrases out of their natural order are set off by commas.

1 Abraham Lincoln was our first martyred president.
2 Garfield, James A., was our second martyred president.
3 Heaven hides the book of fate from all creatures.
4 Heaven, from all creatures, hides the book of fate.
5 In the dead of night, with a chosen band, under cover of a truce, he approached.
6 Between the two mountains lies a fertile valley.
7 He who leads the most pious life preaches most eloquently.
8 He preaches most eloquently, who leads the most pious life.

When the connection is close, and there is no break in the thought, as in the sixth sentence, no comma is needed.

NOUNS INDEPENDENT, APPOSITIVE, OR VOCATIVE

1 Henry, will you close the door?
2 Paul the Apostle was a man of energy.
3 Paul, the great Apostle of the Gentiles, was a prolific writer.
4 Noah Porter, D.D., LL.D., was an eminent scholar.
5 They elected him Governor of Ohio.
6 I rise, Mr. President, to a point of order.
7 The puma, or American lion, inhabits South America.

The noun independent, as in the first sentence, requires a comma. When the appositive noun stands in close relation to the noun to which it belongs, as in the second sentence, no comma is required. Titles, as in the fourth sentence, are usually considered as part of the name, but are really nouns in apposition and are separated by commas.

CLEARNESS

A comma should be used whenever the sense would not be clear without it.

1 They landed and killed fifty Indians.
2 They landed, and killed fifty Indians.
3 Elizabeth's favorite Raleigh was beheaded.
4 Elizabeth's favorite, Raleigh, was beheaded.
5 Bennett's daughter Mary attended college.
6 Bennett's daughter, Mary, attended college.
7 He went skating because he was told to go.
8 He did not go skating, because he was not told to go.
9 The prisoner said the witness was a notorious burglar.
10 The prisoner, said the witness, was a notorious burglar.
11 That the Governor of this great State of Illinois should make this unworthy appeal to the passions and prejudices of the foreign-born citizens of the nation must always be a cause of mortification to every lover of his country.
12 It remains, perhaps, to be said, that, if any lesson at all, as to these delicate matters, is needed, in this period, it is not so much a lesson, ...

An examination of the first ten sentences will show the difference in meaning produced by the presence of the comma. The eleventh illustrates the fact that a long nominative does not always require a comma after it. The twelfth is an example of a sentence greatly overburdened by commas; a better punctuation would retain the comma after *that, period,* and *lesson,* and omit the rest.

QUOTATIONS

A short quotation, or a sentence resembling a quotation, is usually preceded by a comma.

1 Patrick Henry began his celebrated speech by saying, "It is natural to indulge in the illusions of hope."
2 A good rule in education is, Learn to be slow in forming your opinions.
3 Nathan said to David, "Thou art the man."
4 Nathan's words to David were these: "Thou art the man."
5 Cain asked, "Am I my brother's keeper?"
6 Cain asked whether he was his brother's keeper.

THE COMMA

The most frequently used, and probably the most abused mark of punctuation, is the comma. Dean Alford declares that it is the great enemy to understanding anything printed in our lan·guage. He condemns the unthinking, mechanical use of this point by compositors, and expresses satisfaction in the reflection that, in the course of editing the Greek text of the New Testament, he destroyed more than a thousand commas which, if allowed to remain, would have prevented the text from being properly understood.

SEMICOLON

The semicolon marks a more decided break in the sentence than that indicated by a comma. It serves also to prevent a repetition of the comma when the divisions are numerous and somewhat similar in character. It is usually found in long sentences, but may be needed in short ones.

LOOSE JUNCTION

Parts of a sentence loosely connected in meaning are separated by semicolons.

1 Wisdom is the principal thing; therefore get wisdom; and with all thy getting, get understanding.
2 Everything grows old; everything passes away; everything disappears.

MAJOR AND MINOR DIVISIONS

When the comma is used for the small divisions, the larger generally require the semicolon.

1 And now abideth faith, hope, charity; but the greatest of these is charity.
2 It may cost treasure, and it may cost blood; but it will stand, and it will richly compensate for both.

COMMON DEPENDENCE

Clauses or phrases having a common dependence upon some other clause or word are separated from each other by a semicolon.

1 Here let us resolve that they shall not have died in vain; that this nation shall, under God, have a new birth of freedom; and that government of the people, by the people, and for the people, shall not perish from the earth.

2 Philosophers assert, that Nature is unlimited in her operations; that she has inexhaustible treasures in reserve; that knowledge will always be progressive; and that all future generations will continue to make discoveries.

3 That Nature is unlimited in her operations; that she has inexhaustible treasures in reserve; that knowledge will always be progressive; and that all future generations will continue to make discoveries: these are among the assertions of philosophers.

The formal structure of the third sentence requires the colon near the close.

EXPLANATION

When a member of a sentence is added for the sake of contrast, inference, or explanation, the semicolon is used to separate it from the preceding member.

1 The world will little note nor long remember what we say here; but it can never forget what they did here.

2 Apply yourself to study; for it will redound to your honor.

3 The ground is wet; it must have rained last night.

PARTICULARS

When such expressions as *namely, as, viz., i. e., that is,* precede an example or a specification of particulars, the semicolon is usually placed before the introductory word and the comma after.

1 Five great enemies are constantly harassing us; namely, ambition, avarice, anger, envy, and pride.

2 Some words are spelled in two ways; as, inquire, enquire; skeptic, sceptic; bazar, bazaar.

3 Adjective pronouns are divided into three classes; distributive, demonstrative, and indefinite.

4 Adjective pronouns are divided into three classes: first, the distributive, which are four in number; second, the demonstrative, which are also four in number; and third, the indefinite, of which there are nine.

5 The following officers were elected: Henry Brown, President; John
  Jones, Vice-president; Samuel Smith, Secretary; and Thomas Reed,
  Treasurer.
6 Wisdom hath builded her house; she hath hewn out her seven pillars;
  she hath killed her beasts; she hath mingled her wine; she hath furnished her table.
7 Wisdom hath builded her house, hewn out her seven pillars, killed her
  beasts, mingled her wine, and furnished her table.

The introductory word is sometimes omitted, as in the third
example. When the parts are somewhat formally introduced,
or contain commas, the colon follows the general statement, and
the semicolon separates the particulars, as in the fourth and fifth
sentences. The close connection of the parts in the seventh
sentence justifies the use of the comma.

If the particulars or illustrations introduced by *as* are given a
separate line, many good writers and proof-readers place a comma
before *as* and a colon after, as:

I eat to live; you live to eat.

But if *as* is followed by *in*, the closer connection justifies the
use of the comma alone, as in,

To err is human; to forgive, divine.

THE COLON

When the minor divisions of a sentence are separated by semicolons, the greater division requires the colon.

1 Art has been to me its own exceeding great reward: it has soothed my
  afflictions; it has refined my enjoyments; it has endeared solitude;
  and it has given me the habit of wishing to discover the good and
  the beautiful in all that surrounds me.
2 Among those present were: Charles Wright, who made an address;
  Silas Carey, with his wife and daughters; and James Brown, Secretary
  of the Association.
3 Among those present were Charles Wright, Silas Carey, and James
  Brown.

The colon serves as the hinge upon which the sentence turns.

INFERENCE

A clause, complete in itself, and followed by some remark, inference, or illustration, not connected with the clause by a conjunction, requires a colon.

1 Avoid affectation: it is a contemptible weakness.
2 Avoid affectation; for it is a contemptible weakness.

A colon is sometimes used before a direct quotation, when incorporated in the body of the sentence.

1 Holmes says: Sin has many tools, but a lie is the handle that fits them all.

The quotation marks, although often employed in such sentences, are unnecessary here.

TITLE-PAGES

1 English Grammar: An Exposition of the Principles of the English Language.
2 English Grammar; or An Exposition of the Principles of the English Language.
3 Philadelphia: George W. Jacobs and Company, 1904.

The subtitle, when connected with the main title by *or*, is usually preceded by a semicolon; when *or* is omitted, the colon is used. Modern taste forbids, on a title-page, the use of any points that can possibly be omitted. The principles of punctuation, as applied to the text of a book, are almost wholly disregarded here.

SALUTATION

It is customary to put a colon after the complimentary salutation in a letter or an address, as:

Dear Sir: My dear Madam: Gentlemen:

The use of this mark is the most logical, and is preferable to the semicolon or to the comma followed by the dash.

FORMAL INTRODUCTORY WORDS

The more formal introductory words, *to wit, as follows, the*

following, for example, this, and *these,* are usually followed by
the colon.

THE PERIOD

The period should follow every declarative and imperative
sentence, and every abbreviation. It separates whole numbers
from their decimal fractions, and is now generally employed
instead of the colon, to separate hours from minutes in the time-
tables and railway guides.

It should follow a signature to a letter or other document, and
a name when standing alone; but names printed in columns
require no punctuation.

The period is not needed after a figure or figures used at the
beginning of paragraphs, or to number verses or other subdivisions
in poetry.

Usage is divided regarding the roman numerals in chapters of
books and in kingly titles.   The later custom omits the period
after the numeral, and many good writers and proof-readers
omit the word *chapter.*

William I made many mistakes.
Louis II ascended the throne at the age of fifty.

Unless care is exercised in the writing, the first might be read:
William, I made many mistakes; the second: Louis, the eleventh,
ascended the throne at the age of fifty.

THE DASH

While this mark has been much overworked, and has been
made a convenient cover for ignorance, it has its legitimate sphere,
which should be understood.

ABRUPT CHANGE IN STATEMENT

A sudden break in a statement is usually marked by a dash.

1 Thus the plot thickens—but I weary you.
2 He had no malice in his mind—no ruffles on his shirt.

3 You have given the command to a person of illustrious birth, of ancient family, of innumerable statues—but of no experience.
4 They yield—they break—they fly—
They faint—they fall—they die.

The third and fourth sentences illustrate a break that is more largely elocutionary than one of grammatical construction.

CONCLUDING CLAUSE

A concluding clause upon which several other expressions depend is usually preceded by a dash.

1 He was witty, learned, industrious, plausible—everything but honest.
2 The great men of Rome, her beautiful legends, her history, the height to which she rose, and the depth to which she fell—these make up one-half of a student's ideal world.

PARENTHESIS

Parenthetical expressions are sometimes included between dashes.

1 The smile of a child—always so ready when there is no distress, and so soon returning when the distress has passed—is like an opening of the sky, showing heaven beyond.
2 The ideal forms of things without—if not in a metaphysical sense, yet in a moral sense—exist within us.
3 Religion—who can doubt it?—is the noblest theme for contemplation.

The reason for using the interrogation point with the dash in the third sentence is apparent.

OMISSION

The omission of letters or figures is indicated by a dash, as:
He was minister to B—a, 1900–1904.

ITERATION

The rhetorical repetition of an expression requires the employment of a dash, as in,
Shall I, who was born in the tent of my father, amid the roar and din of battle—shall I, the conqueror of Spain and Gaul—shall I compare myself with this half-year captain?
This form of speech is called the *Echo*.

SIDE-HEADS

The dash is often placed between the period following the side-head, and the text, when both occur on the same line. It serves also to connect the text with the name of the writer, at the close. Some good proof-readers now omit it in both cases.

THE INTERROGATION

A direct question is followed by the interrogation point. An indirect question is one that is merely mentioned or spoken of, and does not require an answer.

1 Why do you punctuate in this manner?
2 He asked why you punctuate in this manner.
3 He asked, Why do you punctuate in this manner?
4 Shall a man obtain the favor of heaven by impiety? by murder? by falsehood? by theft?
5 A man cannot obtain the favor of heaven by impiety, by murder, by falsehood, by theft.
6 Where be your gibes now; your gambols; your songs; your flashes of merriment, that were wont to set the table in a roar?
7 Where be now those things of yours that were wont to set the table in a roar?—your gibes? your gambols? your songs? your flashes of merriment?
8 You will grant my request?
9 He asked, May I go to college, and met with his father's refusal.

When the interrogation point marks a degree of separation equal to a period, it must be followed by a capital letter. In a series of questions, as in the fourth example, where no reply intervenes, a lower-case letter follows. By changing the interrogation to an affirmation, as in the fifth sentence, the separative value of the interrogation point may be determined.

When several questions have a common dependence upon a concluding clause, but one question mark is employed; but if the particulars come last, each question requires a sign, as in the seventh sentence.

A sentence, declarative in form but interrogative in spirit, takes the question mark; as in the eighth example.   In the last sentence, many writers would place a question mark after the word *college*, but as the words are simply descriptive, the comma is sufficient.   If the clause were lengthy or involved, quotation marks might be necessary.

THE EXCLAMATION

In point of separation, this mark is usually equivalent to a period; but, like the interrogation, it may be equivalent to a comma, a semicolon, or a colon.   Like the dash, it is much over-worked.   Its purpose is to express surprise, emotion, ardent wish, admiration, or contempt.   It usually follows an interjection.

1 What a piece of work is man! how noble in reason! how infinite in
  faculties! in form and moving how express and admirable! in action
  how like an angel! in apprehension how like a god!
2 Alas, poor Yoric!
3 Behold the daughter of Innocence!
4 Down, soothless insulter! I trust not the tale.
5 Charge, Chester, charge! on, Stanley, on!
6 When, O my countrymen! will you begin to exert your power?
7 Bah! that's the third umbrella gone since Christmas.
8 Fie, fie, fie! how silly you are!
9 You thought you would not be found out, eh?
10 That man virtuous!!   You might as well try to tell me of the virtue of
  Judas Iscariot!!
11 O men of Athens! my honor prompts me to speak.
12 Oh, the bloodiest picture in the book of time!

The position of the exclamation is sometimes a matter of doubt. It should be placed at the end of the exclamatory word or phrase; but if the exclamatory idea extends through the sentence, it is placed at the end of the sentence.

When an interjection is repeated, a comma usually occurs between them, and the exclamation is placed after the last.   The interjections *eh* and *hey* often take the form of a question, and should be followed by the interrogation.   To illustrate intense emotion, the double exclamation is employed.

Many good writers limit O to the vocative address, placing the exclamation after the phrase which it introduces, and employ *oh* to express emotion.

Properly used, the exclamation point imparts life and force to language; when used to excess, it transforms pathos into bombast, and admiration into ridicule.

THE APOSTROPHE

The chief use of the apostrophe is to indicate the possessive case of nouns, and to denote the contraction of words.   To form the possessive, the apostrophe is placed before the *s* except in the case of nouns whose plural is formed by adding *s* or *es* to the singular.   Contractions are formed in a variety of ways.

1 A man's hat. A boy's cap. A wolf's den. The men's hats. Five boys' caps. The wolves' dens. James's coat. Brooks's store. For conscience' sake. Hughes's farm. Moses's law. Moses' law.
2 I'll go, for I've purchased my tickets.
3 He'll tell 'em 't was 'twixt two an' four.
4 They were filled with the spirit of '76.
5 Dot your i's and cross your t's.
6 Make your 5's and 8's more distinct.

To avoid the unpleasant sibilant, many writers omit *s* after the apostrophe in *Moses' law, for conscience' sake, for goodness' sake,* and similar cases.

The apostrophe must not be used to form the possessive of the personal pronouns.   Such errors as *her's, it's, our's, your's, their's,* are sometimes seen in the letters of inexperienced stenographers.

The possessive of *company* should rarely be abbreviated.   The form *Co's* may be tolerated in narrow measure, but *Company's* is preferable.

TWO POINTS

There is seldom need to use two points together.   The greater covers the less.   The combination is usually offensive to the eye. If, in any case, the meaning should be obscured by the omission of the inferior mark, appearance must be sacrificed to clearness.

1 He reached the station at 6 p.m. but the train had gone.
2 He reached the station at 6 p.m., but the train had gone.
3 Greece, Carthage, Rome—where are they?
4 Greece, Carthage, Rome,—where are they?

A comma may follow, but should not precede, a mark of parenthesis. When a complete sentence is enclosed, the period is placed before the closing mark of parenthesis. If only a few words are enclosed at the end of the sentence, the period should come after the last mark of parenthesis.

A comparison of the late with the early editions of the English classics shows the growing tendency to use fewer points.

QUOTATION MARKS

Marks of quotation are employed to separate the exact words of another when embodied within the text of a sentence. This does not apply to the many phrases from the Bible, and from Shakspeare, Milton, and other famous writers, which, by their terseness and frequent use, have become a part of the coinage of the English language.

When the quoted extract consists of several paragraphs, the initial quote-mark is placed at the beginning of each paragraph, but the closing mark is used only at the end of the extract. If the several paragraphs are taken from different parts of the book or essay, each paragraph should begin and end with quote-marks. If the quotation is made up of several detached portions, the fact that the extracts are not continuous is indicated by the insertion of four or five successive periods separated by spaces between the several extracts.

The former custom of placing the initial quote-mark at the beginning of each line in a lengthy quotation is sometimes seen in the columns of newspapers, but is no longer employed in good book-work. The limit or extent of the extract is made manifest to the eye by narrower measure, by smaller type, or by less space between the lines. When smaller type or narrower measure or both are employed, the use of quote-marks is unnecessary.

7

The single quote-mark, consisting of an inverted comma at the beginning and an apostrophe at the close, is used to mark a single word or phrase, or to note a quotation within a quotation.

The fact that no quote-marks are employed in the Bible goes far to prove that their use is not so essential to clearness as has been supposed. Writers, printers, and stenographers are sometimes in doubt whether to place a closing quote-mark before or after a comma, semicolon, or period. The mark must enclose the quoted parts only. If a complete sentence is quoted, the period is placed within the quote-mark; if the quoted words end with a comma, semicolon, or colon, these points usually follow the quote-marks; but if the sentence is a question or an exclamation, the interrogation or exclamation point is enclosed within the marks of quotation.

Quote-marks within quote-marks are sometimes necessary, but these should be avoided so far as possible, especially when several quotations culminate at the close of a sentence. Double quote-marks are usually employed for the first, and single marks for the inclosed quotations.

1 The command, "Thou shalt not kill", forbids many crimes besides that of murder.
2 Some one has said, "What an argument for prayer is contained in the words, 'Our Father which art in heaven'!"
3 "I will mention only such as are the same parts of speech; thus, 'sun' and 'son'; 'reign', 'rain', and 'rein'; 'hair' and 'hare'; 'plate' and 'plait'; 'moat' and 'mote'; 'pair' and 'pear'; 'air' and 'heir'; 'ark' and 'arc'; 'mite' and 'might'; 'pour' and 'pore'; 'veil' and 'vale'; 'knight' and 'night'; 'knave' and 'nave'; 'pier' and 'peer'; 'rite' and 'right'; 'site' and 'sight'; 'aisle' and 'isle'; 'concent' and 'consent'; 'signet' and 'cygnet'."

The third example, from Trench, *English Past and Present*, illustrates the overuse of quotation marks. All of the single quote-marks might safely be omitted. Theodore Low De Vinne, in *The Practice of Typography*, says: "To read line after line bristling with these points is as irritating as a walk through briar-bushes."

FOREIGN WORDS

Foreign words and phrases are usually set in italics, and do not require the quote-marks to indicate their origin. When the foreign words make one or more sentences, it is better to set them in roman with quote-marks.

SEPARATION AND SPACING

When several abbreviated titles as A.M., LL.D., occur at the end of a line, one title may be separated from the rest, but the parts of the same title must not be divided. No space other than that required by the period is necessary.

The form "pages 136, 137" is preferable to "pages 136-7", and the form "pages 139 to 160" is preferred to "pp. 139–160." A period of time covering two successive years may be expressed 1903–4. When the years are not consecutive, write in full, thus: 1897, 1900, 1904. The use of the apostrophe, as '97, '99, '04, is unsightly in books and should be avoided.

ABBREVIATIONS EMPLOYED IN THIS BOOK

Afr. . . . . . . Africa, -can	Carth. . . . . . Carthaginian
Alas. . . . . . . Alaska, -kan	chem. . . . . . . chemist, -istry
Amer. . . . . . America, -can	chron. . . . . . chronicle, -icler
Arab. . . . . . . Arabia, -bian	co. . . . . county
archæol. . . . . archæology, -ogist	Colom. . . . . . Colombia, -bian
Archi. . . . . . Archipelago	conch. . . . . . conchology, -ogist
Arg. Rep. . . . . Argentine Republic	Cors. . . . . . . Corsica, -sican
Ariz. . . . . . . Arizona	coun. . . . . . . country
astron. . . . . . astronomer, -omy	
Aust. . . . . . Austria, -rian	Den. . . . . . . Denmark
Austral. . . . . Australia, -lian	dept. . . . . . . department
auth. . . . . . . author	dipl. . . . . . . diplomat, -matist
Balto. . . . . . . Baltimore	dist. . . . . . . district
Bav. . . . . . . Bavaria, -rian	dram. . . . . . . drama, -atist
Belg. . . . . . . Belgium, -gian	Egyptol. . . . . Egyptology, -ogist
Bohem. . . . . . Bohemia, -mian	embryol. . . . . embryology, -ogist
bot. . . . . . . Botany, -nist	entom. . . . . . entomology, -ogist
Braz. . . . . . . Brazil, -zilian	
c. . . . . city	fem. . . . . . . feminine
Can. . . . . . . Canada, -dian	Fr. . . . . France, French

Gen.	General
geol.	geology, -ogist
geom.	geometer, -etry
Ger.	German, -many
Gr.	Greece, Grecian
gram.	grammar, -marian
herpet.	herpetology, -ogist
Hind.	Hindustan
hist.	history, -torian
Hung.	Hungary, -garian
Ia.	Iowa
ichth.	ichthyology, -ogist
Ida.	Idaho
Ill.	Illinois
Ire.	Ireland
isl.	island
It.	Italy, Italian
l.	lake
lexicog.	lexicographer, -phy
litt.	litterateur
Maced.	Macedonia, -nian
masc.	masculine
math.	mathematics, -tician
mech.	mechanician
Medit.	Mediterranean
meteor.	meteorology, -ogist
mfr.	manufacturer
mineral.	mineralogy, -ogist
Mont.	Montana
mts.	mountains
mus.	music, -cian
nat.	naturalist
nav.	navigator
N. D.	North Dakota
Neth.	Netherlands
N. Mex.	New Mexico
Norw.	Norway
N. S.	Nova Scotia
O.	Ohio
orient.	orientalist
ornith.	ornithology, -ogist
Pac. Oc.	Pacific Ocean
paleon.	paleontology, -ogist
Para.	Paraguay
Pata.	Patagonia
pathol.	pathology, -ogist
pen.	peninsula
Pers.	Persia, -sian
philan.	philanthropist

philol.	philology, -ogist
philos.	philosophy, -opher
physiol.	physiology, -ogist
Pol.	Poland, -lish
Port.	Portugal, -guese
pos.	possessive
P. R.	Porto Rico, P. Rican
pro.	pronoun
pros.	prosody
prov.	province
Prus.	Prussia, -sian
psychol.	psychology, -ogist
Que.	Quebec
r.	river
Repub.	Republic
Rev.	Revolution, -ary
R. I.	Rhode Island
Roum.	Roumania
Russ.	Russia, -sian
S. Amer.	South America
Sax.	Saxony
schol.	scholar
sci.	science, -entist
Scot.	Scotland, Scotch
sculp.	sculptor, -ture
Serv.	Servia, -vian
Shak.	Shakspeare
Sib.	Siberia, -rian
Sp.	Spain, Spanish
Sw.	Sweden, Swedish
Switz.	Switzerland, Swiss
Syr.	Syria, -ian
teratol.	teratology, -ogist
Test.	Testament
theol.	theology, -ogian
therap.	therapeutics
topog.	topography
toxicol.	toxicology, -ogist
trag.	tragedian, -edy
trav.	traveller
Turk.	Turkey, Turkish
twp.	township
typog.	typography
Uru.	Uruguay
U. S.	United States
Venez.	Venezuela, -elan
vil.	village
volc.	volcano
zoöl.	zoölogy, -ogist

135,000 WORDS

CORRECTLY SPELLED AND PRONOUNCED

A

Aa'chen (ä'chen *or* ä'ken), prov. and c. Prus.
aal (äl).
Aal'börg (al'-), seaport of Den.
aam (awm *or* äm) or *ähm.*
Aar (är), r. Switz., aar, an eagle.
aard'vark (ärd'-), *aard'wolf.*
Aa'ron (âr'on *or* ä'ron), *Bib.*, -ron'-ic, -ic al, Aa'ron ite, -it'ic, Aa'-ron's-beard, -rod, aa'ron, a plant.
ab'a.
ab'a ca or *-ka.*
ab'a cay.
ab a cis'cus, ab'a cist.
a back'.
A'ba co (ä'bä cō), *Geog.*
ab ac'ti nal.
ab ac'ti o (-shĭ o), -ac'tion, -ac'tor.
ab'a cus, *pl.* ab'a cī *or* -a cus'es, *a bac' u lus.*
A bad'don, the angel of the bottomless pit.
a bâft'.
a bâi'ser, *a bais sé'* (a bä sä'), *a-baissed'* (-bäst').
ab äl'ien ate (-yen-), - ā ted, -ā'tion.
ab a lö'nē.
ab a mü'rus.
a ban'don, -doned (-dŭnd), -doned-ly, -don er, -don ment, -don ee', *a ban don'* (ä bän doń').
a băn'ga.
a bap tis'ton, pl. *-tis'ta.*
ab ar tic u lä'tion.

à bas' (ä bä'), down with.   a bäs', a coin.   ä'bas, a disease.
a base', -ment, -based', -băs'ing, -bās'er.
a bash', -ment, -bashed'.
a bate', -ment, -băt'a ble, -bāt'er *or* -or.
ab'a tis *or* ab'at tis (-tis *or* -tĕ'), -tised (-tist).
a bat'-jour' (ä bä'zhoor') or *a bat-jour'* (ä bä zhoor').
à băt toir' (-twor'), pl. *-toirs'.*
a bat-voix (a bä'vwŏ').
ab ax'i al *or* -ax'ĭle.
abb.
ab'ba, father; Ab'ba, the Heavenly Father.
ab bac'i nate (-bas'-), -nā'tion.
ab'ba cy.
Ab bad'o na, a fallen angel.
äb băn dō nä tä men'te.
ab bas'ĭ or *à băs'sĭ* or *-sĭs.*
äb bä' te.
ab bä'tial.
ab bé' (á bā'), ab'bess.
Ab'be ville, co. S. C.
Abbe ville' (äb vēl'), t. Fr.
ab'bey (-by), *pl.* -beys, ab'bey-coun'ter, -laird, -land, -lub'ber.
ab'bot, -ship, -gen'er al.
ab boz'zo (-bot'so).
ab bre'vi ate, -ā ted, ā- ting, -ā tor, -to'ry, -ā'tion,   *ab bre vi a'ti o plac i to'rum* (-ä'shĭ o plas-).

---

fāte, făt, fär, fạll, fâre, făst, sofà, mēte, mĕt, hêr, īce, ĭn, nōte, nŏt, nôr, ūse, ŭp, ûrn, etüde, fōōd, fŏŏt, aṅger, boṅmot, thus, Bach.

abb'-wool.
ab cä'ree.
ab cha'sian (-kä'shan *or* -zhan).
ab da la'vi *or* ab de la'vi (-lä'vē).
Abd-el-Kä'dir (äbd-) *or* Ab dul-
   Ka'dir, *Biog.*
Ab de'ri an, Ab'de rite.
ab'dest.
Ab dev'en ham.
ab'di cate, -cä ted, -cä ting, -ca tor,
   -cant, -cä'tion.
ab do'men (*or* ab'-), -dom'i nal,
   -nal ly, -i nous, -i nos'co py.
ab du'cens, -cent.
ab duct', -duc'tor, -duc'tion.
Ab dul-A ziz' (äb'dŏol ä zēz'),
   Biog.
Ab dul-Ha'mid (äb'dŏol hä'mid),
   Biog.
Ab dul Me jid' (äb'dŏol me jeed'),
   Biog.
a beam'.
ă be ce dä'ri an, -ri ʮm, *pl.* -ri a,
   -ce'da ry, A be ce da'ri an, one
   of a religious sect.
a bed'.
A bĕd'ne go, *Bib.*
a bee'.
Ab'e lard, *Biog.*
a bele'.
A bel'i an (ā bĕl'ĭ an *or* -yan),
   A'bel ite, A'bel o'ni an.
A'bel mos'chus (-kus), ä'bel-
   mosk.
ä'bel-tree.
a be ne pla'ci to (ä bä'nē plä'chē-
   to).
Ab e o'na, *Myth.*
Ab'er crom bie (-krŭm bĭ), *Biog.*
ab'er de vine'.
ab ĕr'rance, -ran cy, -rant, rä'tion,
   -tion al.
ab e run'ca tor (-ruṇ'-).
a bet', -ted, -ting, -ter *or* -tor, -ment.
ab e vac u a'tion.
ab ex'tra.
a bey'ance (-bä'-), -an cy, -ant.
ab'hăl or *-hel* or *-hul.*
ab hôr', -horred', -hŏr'ring, -hŏr'-
   rence, -rent, -rent ly, -rer.
A bī'a, *Bib.*
A bī'a saph, *Bib.*
A bī'a thar, *Bib.*

A'bib.
a bide', -bīd'ing, -ing ly, a bīd'ing-
   place.
A'bĭ el, *Bib.*
ab'i ē tĕne, -ē tin, -et'ic, -e tin'ic.
ab'i ē tīte.
a big'e at (-bij'-).
A bī'hu, *Bib.*
A bī'jah, *Bib.*
Ab'i lĕ'nĕ, *Bib.*
A bim'e lech (-lĕk), *Bib.*
ab in i'ti o (-ish'i o), *ab in'tra.*
ab in tes'tate.
ab'i o gen'e sis, -e sist, -ge net'-
   ic, -ic al ly, -og'e nist (-ŏj'-),
   -og'e nous, -e ny.
ab i o log'ic al (-lŏj'-), -al ly.
ab ir'ri tate, -ri tant, -tā tive, -tā'-
   tion.
A bī'ud, *Bib.*
ab'ject, -ly, -ness, -ject'ive, -jec'tion.
ab jŭ dĭ ca'tion.
ab jure', -jured', -jūr'ing, -er *or* -or,
   -jŭ'ra to ry, -rä'tion.
ab'kar, ab kä'ri *or* -ry.
Ab khä'sian (-zhan).
ab lac ta'tion.
a blas te m'ic, -blas'tous.
ab la'tion, -la ti'tious (-tish'us).
ab'la tive, -tī'val.
ab'laut (äb'lout *or* Ger. äp'lout).
a blaze'.
a'ble, -bler, -blest, -bly, a bil'i ty,
   a'ble-bod'ied, -mind'ed.
ab'le gate, -gä'tion.
a'ble whack'ets.
ab'lo cate, -cä ted, -ting, -cä'tion.
a bloom'.
ab lu'tion, -a ry, ab'lu ent.
ab'ne gate, -gä ted, -ting, -tor, -gä'-
   tion.
ab nerv'al.
ab'net.
ab nor'mal, -ly, -nor'mi ty, -mous,
   -mal'i ty.
a board'.
a bode'.
ä bō gä'dō.
a boi'deau (-dō *or* -dō'), -teau (-tō).
a bol'ish, -ing, -a ble, -er, -ment,
   -ished.
ab o li'tion (-lĭsh'un), -al, -a ry,
   -ism, -ist, -ize, -ized, -ī zing.

---

fāte, făt, fär, fạll, fâre, făst sofȧ, mēte, mĕt, hêr, īce ĭn, nōte,

a bol'la, pl. *-læ.*

a bo'ma.

ab o ma'sum, pl. *-sa, ab o ma'sus*, pl. *-sī.*

Ab'o mey' (-mā'), t. Afr.

a bom'i na ble, -ness, -na bly, -i nāte, -na ted, -ting, -tor, -nā'tion.

a boon'.

ab o'ral, -ly.

a bord'age.

ab o rig'i nal (-rĭj'-), -nal ly, -na ry, -nal'i ty, *-rig'i ne*, pl. -nes (-nēz).

a bort', -ed, -bor'ti cide, -tient, -ti-fā'cient.

a bor'tion, -al, -ist, -bor'tive, -ly, -ness, *a bor'tus.*

a bound', -ed, -ing.

a bout', -sledge.

a bove', -board, -deck, -ground.

ab ō'vō.

a box'.

ä'bra.

ab'ra ca dab'ra.

a brac'a lam

a brä'chi a (-kĭ a), -chi us.

ab rade', -ra'dant.

A'bra ham, -ite, -it'ic, -ic al, -ham'-ic, -i dæ, A'bra ham-man *or* A'bram-man.

A bran'chi a (-bran̩'kĭ a), *-chi ä'ta*, chi ate, -chi an.

ab rase' (-rāz *or* -rās), -rased', -rās'-ing.

ab ra'sion (-zhŭn), -sĭve.

ab'raum (ab'rawm *or* Ger. äp'roum).

A brax'as or Ab'ra sax.

ab'ra zite, -zit'ic.

a breast'.

a'breu'voir' (a'brê'vwor').

a'brid.

a bridge', -bridged', -bridg'ing, -er, -ed ly, -ment.

ā'brin (*or* ăb'rin).

a broach'.

a broad'.

ab'ro gate, -gā ted, -ting, -tor, -tive, -ga ble, -gā'tion.

ab rot'a noid.

ab rot'a num.

ab rupt', -ly, -ness, -rup'tion.

A bruz'zo (ä brōōt'so), dept. It.

ab'scess, -scessed, ab'scess-root.

ab scind', -ed, -ing.

ab scise' (-sīz'), -scised', -scis'ing.

ab scis'sa, *pl.* -sas *or* -sæ.

ab scis'si o in ʃĭ nĭ'tĭ (ab sĭsh'-).

ab scis'sion (-sĭzh'un).

ab sconce'.

ab scond', -ed, -er, -ing.

ab'sent, *a.*, ab sent', *v.*, -ed, -ing, -sen tā'tion, -sen tee', -tee'ism, -tee'ship, -sen'ter, ab'sence, -sent-ness, ab'sent-mĭnd'ed, -mind'ed-ly, -mind'ed ness.

ab'sinth *or* -sinthe, -sin'thate, -thi al, -thi an, -thic, -thin, -thĭne, -thi um, -thi ate, *v.*, -ä'ted, -a'ting, -sin'-thism (*or* ab'-).

ab'sit ō'men.

ab'so lute, -ly, -ness, -lu tism, -lu-tist, -tis'tic, -sol'u to ry, -so lu'-tion.

ab solve', *v.*, -solv'er, -ing, -i tor, -a to ry *or* -i to ry, -a ble.

ab sorb', -ing, -ing ly, -a ble, -a bil'-i ty, -ed ly, -ed ness, -en cy, -ent, -er, -e fā'cient.

ab sorp ti om'e ter (-shĭ om'-).

ab sorp'tion, -tive, -tive ness, -tiv'-i ty, ab sorp'tion bands, a. lines, a. spec'trum.

abs'que hoc, abs'quē tă'lĭ cau'sa.

ab stain', -ing, -er, -ment, -stained'.

ab ste'mi ous, -ly, -ness.

ab sten'tion, -ist, -tious.

ab ster'gent, -ster'sion, -sive, -sive-ness.

ab'sti nence, -nen cy, -nent, -nent ly.

ab'stract, *a.* and *n.*, ab stract', *v.*, -ing, -ed, -ed ly, -ed ness, -er, -strac'tion, -tion al, -tion ist, -strac'tive, -tive ly, -tive ness, ab'-stract ly, -stract ness.

ab struse', -ly, -ness.

ab surd', -i ty, -ly, -ness.

Abt (äpt), Ger. mus.

ab ter'mi nal.

ab'thāin, -ry.

ā buc'co (-bŏŏk'-).

ā bu'li ä (-bōō'-), *-lo mä'ni a.*

ab um'bral, -brel'lar.

a bu'na (-bōō'-).

a bun'dance, -dant, -dant ly.

ab ur'be con'di ta.

a bur'ton.

a buse' (-būz'), *v.*, -būsed, -būs'ing,

-bu'sive (-sĭv), -sive ly, -sive ness,
a buse' (-būs'), *n.*

a but', -tal, -ter, -ment, a but'ment
crane'.

a buzz'.

a bysm' (-bĭzm'), -bys'mal (-bĭz'-),
-mal ly, a byss' al (-bĭs'-).

Ab ys sin'i a, coun. E. Afr., -i an.

a ca'cia (-sha *or* -shi a), a ca'cia-
tree.

ac'a cin *or* -cĭne.

A ca'ci us (-shĭ us), Bishop of
Cæsarea, -cians (-shans).

a cad'e my, -e mist, ac a de'mi al,
-dem'ic, -ic al, -al ly, -i cism,
Ac'a deme, -dem'ics, A căd'e mist.

A că'dĭ a, Nova Scotia; co. La.,
-di an.

a ca'di al ite.

ac'a jou (-zhōō).

ac'a lĕph *or* -lĕphe, -lĕ'phan, -lĕ'-
phoid.

a cal'y cal, -y cĭne, ac a lyc'i nous
(-lĭs'-), -lyc'u late (-lĭk'-).

a camp'si a *or* -sy.

ac a na'ceous.

ä căn del li e're (-ā're).

a can'tha, pl. *-thæ,* -can'thĭne, -can'-
thoid, ac an thā'ceous (-shŭs),
-thā'ri an.

a can'tho pod, -pō'di ous.

a can'thus, *n.*, *pl.* -thus es (-ĕz) *or*
-thī, -thous, *a.*

ä că pel'lä or *căp pĕl'-.*

a cap'su lar.

A ca pul'co (ä kä pool'ko), t. Mex.

a car'di a, -di ac, -di us, ac ar di'-
a cus, *pl.* -cī.

A ca ri' (ä kä rē'), t. Peru.

a ca'ri an.

ac a ri'a sis.

ac'a rid, a căr'i cīde, -i no'sis.

ac'a roid gum.

a car'pous, -pel ous.

a cat a lec'tic.

a cat'a lep sy, -lep'tic.

a cat'a pha'si a (-fā'zĭ a *or* -zhĭ-).

a cau'date.

a cau'les (-lēz), ac au les' cence,
-cent.

Ac'cad, -ca'di an, language of early
Babylon.

ac ce'das ad cu'ri am.

ac cede', -cēd'ed, -er, -ence, -ing.

ac cel er an'do.

ac cel'er ate, -a ted, -ted ly, -ting,
-tive, -a tor, -to ry, -ā'tion, ac cel-
er ā'tion-di a gram.

ac cend'i ble, -i bil'i ty.

ac cen'di tē.

ac cen'sion, -sor.

ac'cent, *n.*, ac cent', *v.*, -ed, -ing,
-cen'tor, -tu al, -al ly, -tu ate,
-ā ted, -ā'tion, -al'i ty.

ac cept', -er *or* -or, -ed, -ed ly, -ing,
-a ble, -ble ness, -a bly, -bil'i ty,
-ance, -an cy, -ant, -cep tā'tion.

ac cep'ti late, -la ted, -ting, -la'tion.

ac'cess (*or* -ses'), ac ces'sa ry (*or*
ac'-), -si ble, -i bly, -bil'i ty, -ces'-
sion, -sion al, -sive, -so'ri al, -ces'-
so ri ly, -ces'so ry (*or* ac'-).

ac ciac ca tu'ra (ät chäk kä tōō'rä).

ac'ci dence, -dent, -den ted, -den'-
tal, -tal ism, -tal ist, -tal ly, -tal-
ness, -tal'i ty.

ac cip'i ter, pl. *-tres* (-trēz), -i tral,
-i trĭne.

ac cis'mus (-sĭz'-).

ac claim', -claimed', -claim'ing,
-cla ma'tion, -clam'a to ry.

ac clī'mate, -ma ted, -ma ting, -clī-
mā'tion, -clī'ma tize, -tĭ za ble,
-ti zer, -tĭ zā'tion.

ac cli'nal, ac'cli nate.

ac cliv'i ty, -i tous, -clī'vous.

ac co lāde' (*or* -lăd').

ac'co la ted.

ac col lé' (ăk ol lā').

ac com'mo date, -dā ted, -dā ting,
-ting ly, -da ble, -da tive, -tive ness,
-da tor, -dā'tion, ac com mo dā'-
tion bill, a. cramp, a. lad der, a.
lands, a. road, a. train, a. works.

ac com'pa ny (-kŭm'-), -ing, -pa-
nĭed, -nist.

ac com'plice (-kŏm'plĭs).

ac cŏm'plish, -ing, -a ble, -er,
ment, -plished.

ac cord', -ed, -ing, -ing ly, -ance,
-an cy, -ant, -ant ly, -er.

ac cor'di on, -ist, ac cor'di on-
play'er.

ac cost', -ed, -ing, -a ble.

ac couche'ment (-kōōsh'moṅ), *ac cou-
cheur'* (-shêr'), *-cheuse* (-shêz').

ac count', -ed, -ing, -a ble, -ble ness,
-a bly, -bil'i ty, -ant, -an cy, -ant-
ship, ac count'-book, -day, account'ant-gen'er al.
ac cou'ter *or* -tre (-ko͞o'-), -ment.
ac cred'it, -ed, -ing.
ac'cre men ti'tial (-tĭsh'al), -ti'-
tion.
ac cres'cence, -cres'cent.
ac cres ci men'to (-kresh ĭ-), *ac cres-
cen'do.*
ac crete', -crēt'ed, -crēt'ing, -cre'-
tive, -tion.
ac crue', -ment, -cru'ing, -cru'er,
-crued'.
ac cul tu ra'tion.
ac cum'bent.
ac cu'mu late, -lā ted, -la ting,
-lā tive, -tive ly, -tive ness, -la tor,
-lā'tion.
ac'cu rate, -ly, -ness, -ra cy.
ac curse', -curs'ing, -cursed' *or*
-curs'ed, *a.*, -curs'ed ly, -ed ness,
ac curst'.
ac cuse', -cus'ing (-kūz'-), -ing ly,
-al, -a ble, -er, -a tive, -tive-
ly, -cused', -cu'sa to ry, -sa'tion
(-za'-)
ac cus'tom (-tŭm), -a ble, -a bly,
-a ry, -a ri ly, -ing, -tomed,
-tomed ness.
ace, -point.
a ce'di a.
A cel'da ma.
a cen su a'da (a thän'so͞o ä'tha),
-a *dor'* (-a thor').
a cen'tric.
A ceph'a la, ac'e phal (ăs'e făl),
-ceph'a lan, -a lous.
A ceph'a li, -a lite, -a list.
a ce'qui a (ä sä'kē ä).
ac'er ate (ăs'-).
a cerb', -ic, -i ty, a cerb'ate *or*
ac'er bate (as'-).
a cĕr'ic.
ac'er ose (as'er ōs), -er ous.
a cer'ra.
a cer'vate, -vate ly, -va tive,
-vu lĭne, -vu lus, ac'er vā'tion
(as'-).
a ces'cence, -cen cy, -ces'cent.
ac e tab'u lum (as-), pl. *-u la,* -u lar,
-u li form, -u lif'er ous.

ac'e tal (as'- *or* a cē'-).
a cet'a mid *or* -mĭde (*or* ac'et ăm'-).
ac'e ta ry (as'-), -ta'ri ous, -e tate,
-ta ted, -tā'tion.
a cet'ic *or* -cē'tic, -cet'i din, -i fy,
-fy ing, -fied, -fī er, -fī cā'tion.
ac e tim'e ter (as-) *or* -tom'-, -tim'-
e try, a cet i met'ric al.
ac'e tin (as'-), -e tone, -ton'ic,
-to nē'mi a.
ac'e tous (as'-) *or* a ce'tous, ac'e tose
(-tōs), *a ce'tum.*
ac'e tyl (as'-), -tyl'ic, -i zā'tion,
a cet'y lene *or* ac'e-.
Ach æ me'ni an (ăk e mē'-).
a chæ'no carp (a ke'-).
A chā'ia (a kā'ya), *Bib.*; Greece.
-ian (-yan).
A'chan (-kan), *Bib.*
a cha'ne (-kä'-).
a char'.
a charne'ment (ä sharn'mŏn *or* -shar'-
nĕ-).
A cha' tes (-kā'tēz), companion of
Æneas.
ache (āk), -less, ached (ākt), ach'ing,
ache'weed.
A che'an *or* A chæ'an (-kē'-).
Ach'en bǎch (ăch'en bǎch *or* ä'ken-
bäk).
a che'ni um (-kē'-), *pl.* -ni a, a chene'
(-kēn'), -che'ni al.
Ach'e ron (ăk'-), *Myth.*, -rŏn'tic.
a che val'.
a chieve', -ment, -chieved', -chiev'-
ing, -a ble, -er.
a chi'la ry (-kĭl'-).
A chil'les (-kĭl'lēz), a legendary Gr.
hero, Ach'il lē'an (ăk'-), -lē'id,
-lē'is, A chil'les' ten'don.
Ach i nese' (-nēs' *or* -nēz').
a chi o'te (ä chē o'tā).
a chi'ra (a chē'-).
A chit'o phel (-kit').
a chlam'y date (-klăm'ĭ-), ach la-
myd'e ous (ăk-).
a chō'li a (-kō'-), ach'o lous (ăk'-).
ach'or or *a'chor* (ăk'- *or* ā'kor), pl.
a cho'res (-rēz). A'chor (-kor),
Bib.
ach'ro ite (ăk'-).
ach ro mat'ic (ăk-), -al ly.
a chro'ma tize, -tized, -ti zing,

-tĭ za'tion, -ma tin, -ma tous,
or a chro'mous, -ma tism, -ma-
top sy, -to'sis.
a chron'ic, -ic al.
ach'root (atch'-).
a chy'lous (-kĭ'-).
a cic'u la (-sĭk'-), pl. *-læ* (-lē), -u lar,
-lar ly, -u late, -lā ted, -u lid,
-u li form, -u lĭne, -u lus, *pl.* -u lĭ,
ac'i form (as'-).
ac'id (as'-), a cid'ic, -i ty, -cid' i fy,
-i fi a ble, -fi er, -fĭ ca'tion, ac id-
if'er ous, -if'ic, -im'e ter, -e try,
-i met'ric al, -om'e ter, ac'id-
pump, ac'id green, a. ma gen'ta,
a. yel'low.
a cid'u late, -la ted, -la ting, -u lent,
-u lous.
ac'i er ate (ăs'-), -er age, -er ā'tion.
a cil'i ate, -a ted.
ac i na'ceous (ăs-), -na'ri ous.
a cin'a ces (-sēz).
ac i nac'i form (ăs i năs'- *or* a cin'-).
ac i net'i form (ăs-).
ac'i noŭs (ăs'-), -nōse (-nōs), a cin'-
i form.
ac i pen'se rid (ăs-), -se rĭne, -se-
roid.
ack'er.
ac knowl'edge (-nŏl'ĕj), -edged,
-edg ing, -edg er, -edg ment.
a clas'tic.
ac'me.
ac'mite *or* ak'-.
ac'ne.
ac nes'tis, *pl.* -ti des (-dēz).
ac'node, -no'dal.
a col'o gy, ac'o log'ic.
a co'loŭs.
ac'ŏ lyte, -o lyth *or* -lythe (-lĭth),
-lyth'ic al, a col'y thate.
a'con (*or* ăc'on).
A con cä'gua (ä-), Andes mts.
a con'dy lous *or* -lose (-lōs).
a cone'.
ac'o nite (ăk'-), -o nī'tal, -nĭt'ic,
a con'i tate, a con'i tin *or* -tĭne.
a con'ti um (-shĭ um), pl. *-ti a.*
a cop'ic.
a'cor.
a'corn (-korn *or* -kurn), -corned,
a'corn-cup, -duck, -moth, -oil,
-shell, -wee'vil (-vl), -worm.

a cos' mism (-kŏz'mĭzm), -mist,
-mis'tic.
a cot y lē' don, -lē' do nous   (*or*
-lĕd'o nous).
a cou'chi, -res'in (a kōō'shĭ rĕz'in).
a cou'chy (a kōō'shē).
a cou' me ter (-kow'- *or* -kōō'-),
-me try, -cou sim'e ter, a cous-
mat'ic (-kous- *or* -kōōs-).
a cous'tic (-kous'- *or* -kōōs'-), -tic al,
-al ly, -tics, -ac'ous ti'cian (-tĭsh'-
an).
ac quaint', -ed, -ing, -ance, -ance-
ship, -ed ness.
ac que reur' (ak kā rêr').
ac qui esce', -ment, -esced', -es'cing,
-cing ly, -cence, -cen cy, -cent,
-cent ly.
ac quire', -ment, -quired', -quir'ing,
-er.
ac qui si'tion (-zĭsh'un), -quis'i-
tive, -tive ly, -tive ness, -i tor.
ac quit', -quit'ted, -ting,- tal, -tance,
-ment, ac quit'tance-roll.
a cra'ni a, -ni al.
a crā'si a (-zhĭ a *or* -zĭ a), excess;
intemperance.   A cra'si a (-zhi a),
Spenser's *Faerie Queen.*
a cras'pe dote.
a cra'ti a (-shĭ a), debility; impotence.
a'cre (-ker), -a ble, -age, -cred
(-kerd), a'cre-dale, A'cre (ä'ker *or*
ä'-), c. Syr.
a cre cen'ci a (ä kra sän'sē a *or* -thän'-
thē a).
ac rem bol'ic.
A'cri (ä'krē), t. It.
ac'rid, -rid ly, -ness, -rid'i ty (*or*
a crid'-).
a ri doph'a gus.
ac'ri mo ny, -mo'ni ous,   -ous ly,
-ous ness.
a cris'i a (-krĭs'-), ac'ri sy.
a crit'ic al.
ac'ri to chro'ma cy, -mat'ic.
ac ro ā'ma, *pl.* -am'a ta, -a mat'ic,
-ic al, -ics.
ac ro a'sis, -at'ic, -at'ics.
ac'ro bat, -ism, -bat'ic, -ic al ly.
ac'ro blåst.
Ac'ro ce rau'ni an.
ac ro chi ris'mus (-kĭ ris'-).

ac'ro chord, -chor'did.
ac ro chor'don, *pl.* -dō'nes (-nēz).
ac'ro dŏnt.
ac ro dyn'i a.
ac'ro gen, -gen'ic,-rog'e nous (-roj'-).
a crog'ra phy (*or* ac rog'-).
a cro'le in.
ac'ro lith, -lith'ic, -crol'i than.
a crol'o gy, ac ro log'ic, -ic al, -al ly,
   ac'ro logue.
a crom'e ter.
a cro'mi on, -mi al, -cro'mi o cla vic'-
   u lar.
ac'ro mon'o gram mat'ic.
ac'ro nar cot'ic.
a crŏn'yc *or* -ych, -yc al, -al ly,
   ac ro nyc'toŭs.
a crop'e tal, -tal ly.
a croph'o ny, ac'ro pho net'ic.
ac ro po'di um, pl. *-po'di a.*
a crop'o lis, ac'ro pol'i tan.
ac ro sar'cum.
ac ro sau'rus, *pl.* -sau'rī.
ac'ro spire.
ac'ro spore, -spōr'ous (*or* a cros'-
   po rous).
a cross'.
a cros'tic, -al, -al ly, -ti cism.
ac ro sto'li um, *pl.* -li a.
ac ro tar'si um, -si al.
ac'ro te leu'tic.
ac ro te'ri um, pl. *-te'ri a,* -ri al, -te'-
   ral, ac'ro ter.
ac ro thym' i on *or* -i um, *pl.*
   -thym'i a.
a crot'ic.
ac'ro tism.
a crot'o mous.
act, -ed, -ing, -a ble, ac'tive, -tive ly,
   -tiv'i ty, ac'tor, -tress, act'-drop.
Ac tæ'on (-tē'-), *Myth.*
Ac'ti an (-shi an), A. games.
ac tin'i o chrome.
ac'tin ism, -tĭn'ic, -tin'o graph, -ti-
   nol'o gy, -ti nom'e ter, -nom'e try,
   -no met'ric.
ac'tion, -a ble, -a bly, -al, -a ry, -ist,
   -ize, -less, ac'tion-ser mon.
ac'tu al, -ism, -ist, -al ly, -al'i ty.
ac'tu al ize, -ized, -i zing, -I za'tion.
ac'tu a ry, -a'ri al.
ac'tu ate, -a ted, -a ting, -a'tion.
ac'u ate, a cu'i ty.

ä cu er'do (ä kōō âr'dō).
a cu'le us, pl. *-le ī,* -le ous, *a.,* -le o-
   late, -le i form, -lē ate.
a cu'men, -mi nate, -mi nose (-nōs),
   -mi nous, -na'tion.
ac'u press, -pres'sion, -pres'sure (*or*
   ac'-).
ac'u punc'ture (*or* ac'-), -tured,
   -tu ra tor.
a'cus, *pl.* a'cus.
a cute', -ly, -ness, -cu'tate, -ti fo'li-
   ate, -tilo'bate, acute'-an'gled, -an'-
   gu lar *or* a cût'an'gu lar.
ac'u te nac'u lum, pl. *-u la.*
a cu'tĭ plan'tar.
ä cu yä'ri-wood (-kōō-) *or* a. wood.
a cy'a no blep'si a *or* -blep'sy
   (a cī').
a cyc'lic (-sik'lik).
ac'y rol'o gy (as-).
a dăc'tyl, -tyl ous, -tyl ism.
ad'age.
a dä'gio (-jō), *a dä giet'to* (-jět'to).
Ad'am, -ist, -ite, -ĭt'ic, -ic al, -i tism,
   A dam'ic, -ic al, -al ly, Ad'am's-
   flan nel, -nee dle, Ad am's ale, A.
   ap ple.
ad'a mant, -man'tĭne, -man'toid,
   -man tĕ'an, ad a man'tĭne lay er,
   a. spar.
ad'a man'to blâst.
Ad'a mas'tor, *Spirit of the Stormy
   Cape.*
ad am bu lä'cral.
Ad'an so'ni a.
a dapt', -ed, -ed ness, -er, -ing, -a ble,
   -ble ness, -ive, -ive ly, -ive ness,
   -dap'tion al, -ti tude, ad'ap ta'-
   tion.
A'dar.
a dar'ce.
a dar'kon.
ad'a tĭ or *-tis.*
a daw'let *or* -lut.
ad cap tan'dum.
add, -ed, -er, -ing, -a ble, -a bil' i ty
   or -i bil'i ty, add'ing-ma chine'.
ad'da.
ad'dax.
ad den'dum, pl., *-da.*
ad'der, -bēad, -bolt, -fish, -fly, -gem,
   -grăss, -pike, -spit, -stone.
ad'der's-fern, -flow er, -meat,

-mouth, -spear, -tongue, -vi′o let,
-wort, *or* ad′de wort.
ad dict′, -ed, -ed ness, -ing, -dic′-
tion.
ad dī′em.
ad di′tion, -al, -al ly, -a ry, -dit′ a-
ment, -men′ta ry, ad′di tive, -tive-
ly, -di tor.
ad′dle, -dled, -dling, ad′dle brain,
-head, -pate, -plot, ad′dle-brained,
-head′ed, -pa′ted, -pa′ted ness,
-pool.
ad dress′, *n.* and *v.,* -ing, -er, -ful,
ad′dress ee′, -dressed′, ad dress′-
ing-ma chine.
ad duce′, -du′cing, -cent, -cer, -ci-
ble *or* ad duce′a ble, -duced′, -duc′-
tive, -duc′tor, -duc′tion.
ad duct′, -ed, -ing, -duc′tion, -tive,
-tor.
a deem′.
a de lan ta dil′lo (ä dä län tä dēl′ yō).
a de lan ta′do (ä′dä län tä′dō).
ad e las′ter.
ä′del fisch.
a de′lo pod *or* -pōde (*or* -del′o-).
a del′phous.
a demp′tion.
A′den (ä′den *or* ā′-), Brit. seaport,
Arab.
ad e nal′gi a.
a de′ni a, A de′ni a, *Zool. genus.*
ad e nī′tis, -den′ i form.
a den′ko.
ad′e no car′ci no′ma, *pl.* -ma ta.
ad e nog′ra phy, -no graph′ic.
ad′ e noid, -noid′al.
ad e nol′ o gy, -log′ ic al.
ad e no′ ma, *pl.,* -nō′ma ta, -nom′-
a tous.
ad e noṇ′cus, *pl.* -non′cī (-sī).
ad e nop′a thy.
ad′e no phăr′yn gī′tis (-jī′-).
a den′o phore, ad e noph′o rous.
ad′e nos.
ad e no sar co′ma, *pl.* -ma ta.
ad′e nose (-nōs) *or* -nous.
ad e not′o my, -no tom′ic.
ad e pha′gi a, -deph′a gous.
ad′eps.
a dept′, -ness, -ship.
ad′e quate, -ly, -ness, -qua cy.
Ad es se na′ri an.

ad e un′dem.
ad ex tre′mum.
ad fi′nem.
ad gus′tum.
ad here′, -hēred′, -hēr′ing, -ence,
-ent, -ent ly.
ad he′sive (-sĭv), -ly, -ness, -he′sion
(-zhun), ad he′sion-car.
ad hib′it, -hi bī′tion (-bish′un).
ad hoc.
ad hom′i nem.
ad′i a bat′ic, -al ly.
ad′i ac tin′ic.
ad i aph o re′sis *or* -ro′sis, -ret′ic.
ad i aph′o rism, -o rist, -ris′tic,
-aph′o rite, -o rous, -o *ron,* pl. -o *ra,*
-o ro′sis.
ad′i a ther′man cy (*or* a dī′-), -ther′-
mic, -ma nous.
ad′i a thet′ic (*or* a dī′-).
a dic′i ty (-dĭs′-).
a dieu′ (a dū), *pl.* a dieus′.
ad in def′i nī′tum.
ad in′fi ni′tum.
ad in′qui ren′dum.
ad in′ter im.
a di′os (ä′dyōs′ *or* ä dē′ōs).
a dip′ic, ad i pes′cent.
ad′i po cere′, -poc′er ate (-pŏs′-),
-er ite, -er ous, -a′tion, -po cĕr′i-
form.
ad′i po-fī bro′ma.
ad′i pog′e nous (-pŏj-).
ad′i po lyt′ic.
ad′i po′ma, -pom′a tous.
ad′i pose (-pōs) *or* pous, -pō′sis,
-pŏs′i ty, -pog′e nous (-poj′-).
a dip′si a *or* ad′ip sy, -dip′sous.
ad′it, -lev el.
ad ja′cent, -ly, -ja′cence, -cen cy.
ad′jag.
ad′jec tive, -ly, -tī′val (*or* ad′jec tĭv.
al), -tī′val ly.
ad′jī ger.
ad join′, -ing, -joined′.
ad joûrn′, -ing, -joûrned′, -joûrn′al,
joûrn′ment.
ad judge′, -judged′, -judg′-ing, -er,
-judg′ment *or* -judge′ment,
-judge′a ble.
ad ju′di ca taire′.
ad ju′di cate, -ca′ted, -ca tive, -ca-
ting, -tor, -ca′tion, -cà ture′.

ad'junct, -ly, -junc'tive, -tive ly,
-tion.
ad ju'ra re'gis.
adjure', -jūr'er, -ju'ra to ry, -ra'tion.
ad just', -ed, -ing, -a ble, -a bly,
-er, -or, -ment, ad just'ing-cone,
-srcew, -tool.
ad'ju tant, -ship, -tan cy, ad'ju tant-
bird, -crane, -gen er al, -stork.
ad'ju vant (*or* -ju'-).
Ad'lai (-lā), *Bib.*
ad le ga'tion.
ad lib'i tum.
ad man u en'sis, *pl.* -en'ses (-sēz).
ad max'il la ry.
ad meas'ure, -ment, -ured, -ur ing,
-ur er.
ad me'di an, -di al.
ad mi nic'u lum, *pl.* -la, -u lar,
u la'ry, ad min'i cle.
ad min'is ter, -ing, -tered, -is tra-
ble, -is trant, -is te'ri al, -tra'tion,
-tion al, min'is trate, -tra tive,
-tive ly, -tra'tor, -tor ship, -tra'-
tress, -tra'trix.
ad mi'ni stra dor' (ad mē nē strä-
dōr' *or* -thōr').
ad'mi ra ble, -ness, -ra bly.
ad'mi ral, ty, ad'mi ral-shell.
ad mire', -mired', -mir'ing, -ing ly,
-er, -mi ra'tion.
ad mis'si ble, -ness, -si bly, -si bil'-
i ty, -mis'sive, -so ry.
ad mit', -ted, -ted ly, -ting, -ta ble
or -ti ble, -tance, -ter, *ad mit ta'tur.*
ad mix', -ing, -mixed', -mix'ture.
ad mo'dum.
ad mŏn'ish, -ing, -ing ly, -er, -ished,
-mon'i tor, -to ry, -to ri ly, -to'ri al,
-mō ni'tion, Ad mo ni'tion ist.
ad nas'cence, -cent.
ad'nate, -nā'tion, -nā'ta.
ad nau'se am.
ad nerv'al.
ad nexed'.
ad nom'i nal, -ly, -i na'tion.
a do' (-dōō').
a do'be (a dō'bä).
ad o les'cent, -cence, -cen cy.
ad'o lode.
Ad o nā'ĭ (or a dō'nī), A do'nist.
Ad'o na'is, Shelley's poem.
A do'ni a.

Ad'o nī'jah, *Bib.*
Ad'o nī'ram, *Bib.*
A do'nis, *Myth.*, -ni a, -don'ic, Ad o-
ne'an *or* A do'ni an, a do'nis, a wig.
a dopt', -ant, -ed, -er, -ing, -ive,
-ive ly, -a ble, -bil'i ty.
a dop'tion, -al, -al ism, -al ist.
ad o'ral, -ly.
a dore', -dored', -dōr'a ble, -a bly,
-a bil'i ty, -dōr'ing, -ing ly, -dōr'er,
ăd'o rā'tion.
a dorn', -ment, -ing, -ing ly, -er,
-dorned'.
ad os'cu la'tion.
a down'.
ad'ox a'ceous.
ad'pao (-pou).
ad pā'tres (-trēz).
ad quod dam'num.
ad ra'di al, -ly.
ad'ra gant, -gan'thin.
Ad'ra myt'ti um, *Bib.*
a dras'.
ad rec'tal.
ad ref er en'dum.
ad rem.
ad re'nal.
A'dri an Īte, -an ist.
Ad'ri an o'ple (ăd-), c. Turk.
Ad'ri at'ic (*or* ā'-), Gulf of Venice.
a drift'.
a drip'.
ad'ro gate, -ga ted, -ga ting, -ga tor,
-gā'tion.
a droit', -ly, -ness.
ad ros'tral.
ad sci ti'tious (-tish'ŭs), -ly.
ad'script, -script'ed, -scrip'tive,
-tion, -ti'tious (-tish'us).
ad sorp'tion.
ad stip'u late, -la ted, -la ting, -la-
tor, -la'tion.
ad strict', -stric'tion, stric'to ry.
ad'sum.
ad ter'mi nal.
ad u la'ri a.
ad'u late, -lā ted, -ting -la tor, -to'-
ry, -tress, -la'tion.
A dul'lam, Cave of; A dul'lam ite.
a dult', -ness.
a dul'ter ate, -ly, -ness, -a ted,
-a ting, -ant, -ter er, -ter ess *or*
-tress, -ter Ine, -ous, -ous ly, -ter y.

ad um′brate, -brā ted, -brā ting, -tive, -tive ly, -bral, -bra′tion.

ad um brel′lar.

ad′u na′tion.

ad un̤′cate, -cā ted, -ting, -cal, -cous, a dun′ci ty.

ad un̤′guem.

ad va lo′rem.

ad vânce′, -a ble, -ment, -vanced′, van′cing, -cing ly, -cer, ad vance′- bill, -guard, -note.

ad van′tage, -taged, -ta ging, -ta′- geous, -geous ly, -geous ness, ad- van′tage-ground.

ad′vent, -ven ti′tious (-tish′us), -tious ly, -tious ness, -ti′tion.

Ad′vent, -vent ist.

ad ven′ture, -some, -some ness, -tured, tūr ing, -er, -ess, -ous, -ous- ly, -ous ness.

ad′verb, -ver′bi al, -al ize, -al ized, -i zing, -al ly, -al′ i ty.

ad ver sa′ri a.

ad′ver sa ry.

ad ver′sa tive, -ly.

ad′verse, -ly, -ness, -ver′si ty.

ad ver si fo′li ate, -fo′ li ous.

ad vert′, -ed, -ing, -ence, -en cy, -ent, -ent ly.

ad ver tise′ or -tize′, -tised′, tis′ing, -tis′er (or ad′-), ad ver′tise ment (-tĭz-) or -tize′ment.

ad vice′, n., -boat.

ad vise′, v., -ment, -vised′, -vis′ing, -a ble, -a bly, -a ble ness, -a bil′i ty, -vis′er, -vis′ed ly, -ed ness, -vī′- so ry.

ad vī′vum.

ad′vo cate, -ship, -cā ted, -ting, -tor, -to ry, -tress, -ca cy, -ca′tion.

ad vo ca′tus Dē′ĭ, a. dĭ ab′o lĭ.

ad vow′son (-zn).

ad y na′mi a, -nam′ic, -dyn′a my.

ad′y tum, pl. *-ta.*

adz or adze, -plane.

æ′des (ē′dēz).

æ dic′u la, pl. *-læ.*

æ dil′i ty.

æ dœ ot′ o my.

Æ′ga des (ē′ga dēz), isl. near Sicily.

Æ ge′an or E ge′an.

Æ ge′ri a, -ri an.

æ ge′ri id, æ ge′ri an.

Æ gī′na, an island, -gĭ ne′tan, -net′- ic.

Æ′gi pan (ē′jĭ-), *Myth.*

æ′gi rīte, -rīne.

æ′gis (ē′jis). See *egis.*

Æ′glē (ē′glee).

æ goph′o ny, -go phon′ic.

æ gro′tans, *pl.* -tan′ tes (-tēz), -gro′- tant, *-tat.*

Æ ne′as, of Troy. Æ′ne as, of Cor- inth.

a ē′ne ous.

Æ o′li an, -ol′ic, æ ol′i pile, æ′o lism.

æ o′li an, *Meteor.; Geol.,* -o li′na.

æ o lot′ro py, -lo trop′ic.

Æ′o lus, *Myth.; Entom.,* æ′o lus, an instrument for renewing air in rooms.

Æ o′ni an.

æ quŏ′re al.

ă′er.

æ ra′ri um, pl. *-ri a,* -ri an.

a′er ate, -a ted, -a ting, -a tor, -a′- tion.

ă e′ri al, -ly, -ness, -ri an, -ri al′i ty.

A e′ri an (ā e′-).

æ′rie or æ ry (ē′ry or â′ry or ā′ry or ā′e ry), *pl.* æ′ries, æ′ry-light.

a′er i fy′, -ing, -fīed, -i form, -i fac′- tion, -if′er ous, -i fi ca′tion.

a′e rŏbe, -rob′ic, -ic al ly, -ro′bi a, -bi an, -bi ous, *-bĭ o′sis,* -bĭ ot′ic.

a′er o bran̤′chi ate.

a′er o cli′no scope.

a′er o cyst.

a′er o drome.

a′er o dy nam′ic, -ics (-dĭ-).

a er og′ra pher, -ra phy, -o graph′ic, -ic al.

a′er o hy′dro dy nam′ic, (-hĭ dro- dĭ-), -hy′drous.

a′er o lite, -lith, -lit′ic, -li thol′o gy.

a er′ol′o gy, -o gist, -o log′ic, -ic al.

a′er o man′cy, -man cer, -man′tic.

a er om′e try, -e ter, -o met′ric.

a′er o naut, -ism, -naut′ic, -ic al, -ics.

a′er o phane.

a′er o pho′bia or a′er o pho′by (or -oph′-).

a′er o phone, -phore, -phytẹ, -plane.

a′er o scep′sy (-skep-), -scep′sis.

ā′er o scope, -scŏp′ic, -os′co py.
æ′rose (ē′rōs), a′er o sid′er ite, -sid′-
er o lite (or -si dē′ro-).
ā′er o sphere, -o stat, -stat′ic, -ic al,
-ics, -sta′tion, -ther a peū′tics,
-ther′mal, -to nom′e ter, -ot′ro-
pism, -o trop′ic.
æ ru′go, -ru′gi nous (-ji-).
æs (ēz).
æ′sa lon. Æ′sa lon, Ornith. genus.
Æs′chi les (ĕs′kĭ lēz), Gr. orator.
Æs′chy lus (ĕs′kĭ lus), Gr. poet,
-le′an.
æs′chy nite (es′kĭ nīt).
Æs cu la′pi us. See Esculapius.
-pi an.
Æ′sir (ā′ser or ē′ser).
Æ′sop, Gr. fabulist, -so′pi an, -sop′-
ic.
Æ so′pus, Rom. trag.
æs ta′tes (-tēz).
æs′tha cyte.
æs the′ma tol′o gy.
æs the′si a or es-, æs the′sis or es-.
æs the′si o gen, -si og′ra phy, -ol′o-
gy, -o ma′ni a.
æ′tho gen (ē′tho jen or ĕth′-).
æth′ri o scope (ĕth′- or ē′thri-).
A e′ti an (ā ē′shi an).
æ ti ol′o gy or e ti-, -o gist, -o log′-
ic al, -al ly.
A e′ti us (ā ē′shĭ us), Rom gen.
Æt′na or Et′na, -ne′an.
Æ to′li an.
a far′.
a feb′rĭle.
A′fer, the southwest wind.
af′fa or ŏf′fa.
af′fa ble, -ness, -fa bly, -bĭl′i ty.
af fair′.
af fäl′.
af fect′, -ed, -ed ly, -ed ness, -ing,
-ing ly, -i bil′i ty, -fec ta′tion,
-tion ist, -fec′tion, -tion al, -ate,
-ate ly, -ate ness.
Af′fen tha ler (äf′fen tä ler), wine.
af′fe rent.
äf fet tu o′so (-tōō-).
af fi′ance, -anced, -an cing, -an cer,
-ant.
af fiche′ (ä fēsh′).
af fi dā′vit.
af fil′i ate, -i a ted, -i a ble, -i ā′tion.

af fin′i ty, pl. -ties (-tĭz), -fī′nal,
-fin′i ta tive, -tive ly, -fin′i tive.
af firm′, -ing, -er, -a ble, -a bly,
-ance, -ant, -a tive, -tive ly, -to ry,
-firmed′, -fir ma′tion.
af fix′, -ing, -fixed′.
af flā′tus, -flā′tion.
af fleu ré′ (a flê rā′).
af flict′, -ed, -ed ness, -er, -ing,
-ing ly, -ive, -ive ly, -flic′tion.
af′flu ence, -en cy, -ent, -ent ly,
-ent ness.
af′flux, -flux′ion (-fluk′shun).
af ford,′ -ed, -ing, -a ble.
af for′est, -ment, -es ta′tion.
af form′a tive.
af fran′chise (-chĭz or -chīz), -ment.
af fray′.
af freight′, (-frāt), -er, -ment.
af fric′a tive.
af fright′, -ed, -ed ly, -en, -er, -ing,
-ful, -ment.
af front′ (-frŭnt′), -ed, -ed ly, -er,
-ing, -ing ly, -ive, -fron tee′, af-
fron té′ (-frŭn tā′).
af fu′sion.
Af′ghan.
Af ghan is tan′ (äf gän′is tän′),
Geog.
a field′, a fire′, a flame′, a flaunt′,
a float′, a flow′, a foam′, a foot′,
a foul′, a front′.
a fore′, -go ing, -hand, -men tioned,
-named, -said, -thought, -time.
a for ti o′ri (-shĭ o′rī).
a fraid′.
a fresh′.
Af′ri can, -can ism, -can ize, -īzed,
-i za′tion, -can′der or -kan′-.
à froid′ (ä frwŏ′).
âft, -most, -ward, -wards, âft′-gate.
af′ta ba.
âft′er, -birth, -brain, -clap, -come,
-crop, -feed, -game, -glow, -grâss,
-growth, -guard, -math, -most,
-noon, -piece, -shâft, -thought,
-ward, -wards, -wash, -wort.
aft′er-act, -a′ges, -blow, -bod′y,
-câst, -course, -damp, -egg, -eye,
-game, -gland, -hold, -hood,
-hours, -im′age, -men′tioned,
-note, -pains, -proof, -rake, -run,
-sea′son, -shine, -stuff, -song,

-stud y, -swell, -taste, -time, -wale,
-wise, -wit, -wit ted, -years, aft'er-
noon-la'dies, a. plant, aft'er wash-
cis'tern.
a ga or *a gha* (ä'ga *or* a gä' *or* ä'-
ga).
Ag'a ba, *Bib.*
ag a bä'nee.
ag a cel'la.
a gain' (-gen'), a gainst' (-genst').
ä'gal-ä'gal.
ag a lac'ti a, -tous.
ag'a lax y.
a gal'ma, *pl.* -ma ta. *Zoöl. genus.*
ag al mat'o lite.
Ag a mem'non.
ăg'a mĭ, a bird.
ag'a mo'bi um, pl. *bi a.*
a gam'o spore.
ăg'a my, non-recognition of marriage, -a mist, -a mous, a gam'ic,
-ic al ly, -ag'a mo gen' esis, -ge-
net'ic, -ic al ly.
a gaŋ'glĭ ŏn'ic.
a gape' (-gäp' *or* -gāp'), adv. *or* a.,
ag'a pe, n., pl. *-pæ.*
Ag a pem'o nĕ, -o nīte, -pe mo'ni-
an.
ag'a phite (-fīt).
ä'gar-ä'gar.
ăg'a ric (*or* a găr'ic), -gar'i ci form,
-gar'i cin, -i coid.
A'gas siz (ăg'a sē), naturalist.
a găs'tric.
ag'ate, ag'a ti form, -a tĭne, -a tize,
-tized, -ti zing, -a ty, -tif'er ous,
ag'ate-glăss, -shell, -snail, -ware.
ag'a thism, -a thist.
ag'a tho cac'o log'ic al, -tho dæ'-
mon, -mon'ic, -tho poi et'ic.
A gă'vĕ.
a gaze'.
age, aged, *v.,* a'ged, *a.,* a'ged ly,
-ged ness, age-less, a'ging (-jing),
age'-prayer.
A gen' (ä'zhŏň'), t. Fr.
a'gen cy, a'gent, -gen'tial.
a gen'dum, pl. *-da* (-jen'-).
a gen'e sis, ag e nes'ic, -ne'si a (-sĭ a).
a gen nē'sis (aj-), -ne'si a, -nes'ic,
-net'ic.
A gé nois (ä'zhä'nwä').
a'ger (-jer).

A ger'a tum (-jĕr'- *or* ăj'er ä'tum),
Bot. genus, a ger'a tum, a plant.
A ges i lä'us (-jes'-), King of Sparta.
a geus'ti a or *-geu'si a* or *-geu'sis*
(-gū'-).
ag glom'er ate, -a ted, -a ting,
-a tive, -at'ic, -a'tion.
ag glu'ti nate, -nă ted, -nă ting,
-na tive, -nant, -na'tion, -tion ist.
ag grade', -grad'ed, -ing, -gra da'-
tion.
ag'gran dize, -dized, -di zing, -di-
za ble, -di zer, -gran'dĭze ment (*or*
ag'gran dīze'ment).
ag'grav ate, -vāted, -vating, -ting-
ly, -va tive, -va tor, -va'tion.
ag'gre gate, -ly, -gă ted, -ga ting,
-gă tive, -ga tor, -gant, -ga'tion.
ag gres'sion, -ist, -gres'sive, -sive ly,
-sive ness, -sor.
ag grieve', -grieved', -griev'ing.
ag group', -ing, -ment, -grouped'.
ag'gry or *-gri,* -beads.
â ghä'nee (*or* ăg hä'nĕ).
a ghâst'.
ag'i la-wood (ăg'-).
ag'Ile (aj'-), -ness, -ile ly, a gil'i ty.
A gin court (ăj'in kŏrt *or* ă zhăn-
kōōr').
ag'i o (ăj'- *or* ä'jĭ ō), -o tage.
a gior' no (ä jōr'no).
a gist' (-jist'), -age, -gist'or *or* -er,
-ment.
ag'i tate, -tā ted, -ted ly, -tä ting,
-ta tive, -ta tor, -ta to'ri al, -ta'-
tion, -tion al.
a gi ta'to (ä jĭ tä'to).
a glare'.
ag'leaf.
a gleam'.
a glee' *or* a gley' (-glā').
ag'let *or* äig'let.
a glim'mer.
ag lo bu'li a, a glob'u lism.
a glos'sal, -sate.
a glow'.
ag lu ti'tion.
a glyph'o dŏnt.
ag ma tol'o gy.
ag'men, *pl.* -mĭ na.
ag'mi nate, -nä ted.
ag'nail.
ag'name, -named.

---

fāte, făt, fär, fặll, fâre, fặst, sofâ, mēte, mĕt, hêr, īce, ĭn, nōte,

ag'nate, -na'tĭ, -nat'ic, -al ly, -na'-
tion.
ag nă'thi a, ag'na thous, -nath'ic.
ag'nel, a coin.
ag nœ'a.
Ag no ē'tæ, Ag'no ēte *or* -īte, ag-
no e'tism, ag noi ol'o gy.
ag no'men, pl. *-nom'i na,* -nom'ic al,
-nom'in al, -i na'tion.
ag nos'tic, -tic al ly, -ti cism.
ag'nus, pl. *ag'nus es* or *ag'nĭ. Ag'-
nus,* Entom. and Ichth. genus,
*Ag'nus De'ĭ, A. cas'tus, A. Scyth'-
i cus.*
a go', a gŏne'.
a gog'.
a gom'e ter.
a gom phī'a sis.
a gon'ic, -gon'id, ag'o nal, -o noid.
ag'o nist, -nis'tic, -tic al, -al ly,
-nis'tics, -nis'tarch (-tark). .
ag'o nize, -nized, -nī zing, -zing ly,
-nī'zant, -ō ny.
a go'no thete, -thet'ic.
ag'o ra, -ra nome'.
ag'o ra pho'bi a
A gos'ta (ä gŏs'ta), c. It.
a go sta de'ro (ä gō stä dä'rō *or* -thä'-
ro).
a gou a'ra (ä gōō ä'rä).
a gou'me nŏs (-gōō-).
a gou'ta (-gōō-).
a gou'ti (-gōō'tĭ).
A'gra (ä'gra), prov. India.
a graffe' (-grăf').
A gra man'te (ä grä män'tä), Ag'-
ra mant.
a gram'ma tism.
a graph'i a, -graph'ic.
a gra'rian, -ism, -ize -ized -I zing.
a gree', -ing, -a ble, -ble ness, -a bly,
-a bil'i ty, -gree'ment, -greed'.
a gre'non.
a gres'tial (-chal).
ag'ri a.
A gri ca'ne (ä grē kä'nä), Ag'ri can.
ag'ri cul ture, -cul'tur al, -al ly, -al-
ist, -tur ism, -tur ist, a gric'o lous.
à griffes (ä grēf').
ag ri men'sor, pl. *-so'res* (-rēz).
ag'ri mo ny.
a grin'.
ag ri ol'o gy, -o gist, -o log'ic al.

a grip'pa, *pl.* -pæ.
A grip pin'i an.
ag ro dol'ce (ag ro dōl'chē).
ag'rom (*or* ä'grom).
a gron'o my, -o mist, ag'ro nome,
-no'mi al, -nom'ic, -ic al, -ics.
a grope'.
ag'ros tog'ra phy, -ra pher, a gros'-
to graph'ic, -ic al.
ag'ros tol'o gy, -o gist, a gros' to-
log'ic, -ic al.
a ground'.
a gryp'ni a, -gryp'node, -gryp not'ic.
ä'gua, -toad.
ä' gua cä' te (-tä).
a gua ji' (ä'gua hē').
a guä'ra.
a guar'di en'te (-gwär'-).
ä gua vi'na (-vē'-).
ä'gue, -gu ey, -gu ish, -ish ness, a'gue
weed.
a'gue-bark, -cake, -drop, -face, -fit,
-grăss, -poi'son, -proof, -root,
-spell, -tree.
A gui lar' (ä gē lar'), Eng. authoress.
A'gui las (ä'gē läs), t. Sp.
a gu'ja (ä gōō'ha).
ag'y na ry (ăj'-), -y nous, a gyn'ic.
a gy'rate (-ji'-).
äh, ä hä'.
a head', a heap', a hem', a hoy'.
ähm. See *äam.*
äh'na, -tree.
a'hu (ä'hōō).
a'hu at le (ä'ōō at l).
a hun'gered.
A'I, *Bib.*; ä'I, a sloth, *pl.* ä'is (-ĭz); ai
(ī) *or* äh'yŭ, a fish.
A I'ah (*or* ä'yah), *Bib.*
ai ai'a (ī ī'ä) *or* aj aj'a (ī ī'ä) or ai ai'-
ai (ī ī'ĭ).
äib'lins.
Aich met'al *or* Aitch's met'al.
aid, -ed, -ing, -ance, -ant, -er, -less,
aid'-ma'jor, -prayer.
aid'-dē-cămp (*or* äd'dê kän'), *or*
aide-, *pl.* aids- *or* aides-.
A i dc' (ä'ĕ'dä'), Eng. poet.
Ai din' (ī dēn'), t. Turk.
Ai do'ne (ī do'nä), t. It.
äig'let. See *aglet.*
äi' gre more (ä'ger-).
äi'gret *or* -grette'.

---

nŏt, nôr, ūse, ŭp, ûrn, etüde, fōōd, fŏŏt, aŋger, boṅmot, thus, Bach.

8

aigue-ma rine' (āg-ma reen').
ai gui ère' (ā gĭ air').
ai guille' (ā gweel'), ai guil lesque'
(-lesk').
ai gui se' (ā gwē zā').
ăi'gû let, -guĭl lette'.
ăi'kin Īte.
ail, -ing, -ment, -ailed, ail' weed.
ăi lette'.
Ail sa-cock (ail'za-).
aim, -ing, -er, -ful, -ful ly, -less,
-less ly, -less ness, aimed, aim'ing-
drill, -stand.
Ain (ăṅ), dept. Fr.; Ain (ăṅ), r. Fr.;
A'in, *Bib.*
Ai nad' (ĭ'näd'), t. Arab.
ain'hum.
Ai'no (ĭ'no) *or* Ai'nu (-nōō).
ain't, an inelegant contraction of
am not or *are not;* it is often incorrectly used for *is not.* It is
sometimes written *an't.*
air, -ing, -er, -i fied, -i ly, -i ness,
-less, -om'e ter, -ward *or* -wards,
-way, -y, aired, air'o hy'dro gen.
air'-bag, -bal loon', -bath, -bed,
-blad'der, -blast, -bone, -box,
-brake, -brāv'ing, -breath'er,
-brick, -bridge, -brush, -buck'et,
-buf'fer, -bug, -built, -cam'el,
-cane, -car'bu ret er, -cās'ing.
air'-cas'tle, -cav'i ty, -cell, -chăm'-
ber, -cham'bered, -cock, -com-
press'or, -cone, -cool'er, -course,
-cross'ing, -cush'ion, -cyl'in der,
-dew, -drain, -drawn, -dried,
-drill, -drum, -duct, -end'way,
-en'gine, -e'qual i zer, -es cape',
-ex haust'er, -fau'cet, -fil'ter,
-flue, -foun'tain, -fun'nel, -fur'-
nace, -gas, -gage, -gate, -gos'sa-
mer, -gov'ern or, -grāt'ing, -gun,
-hĕad'ing, -heat'er, -hoist,
-hold'er, -hole, -in ject'or, -jack'-
et, -lev'el, -line, -lock, -lo co-
mo'tive, -logged, -ma chine, -ma-
nom'e ter, -me'ter, -ov'en.
air'-pas'sage, -pipe, -pit, -plant,
-poise, -port, -pres'sure, -proof,
-pump, -py rom'e ter, -re cep'-
ta cle, -reg'u la tor, -res'er voir,
-sac, -scut'tle, -set'ting, -shăft,
-slāked, -so'lar, -space, -spring,

-stack, -stove, -strake, -ther-
mom' e ter, -thread, -tight, -trap,
-trunk, -tube, -tum'bler, -tur'-
bine, -valve, -ves'i cle, -ves'sel,
-wash'ings, -wood, air'ing-stage.
aisle (īl), *n.*, -less, aisled (īld).
ais le' (ā lā'), *a.*
Aisne (ān), r. and dept. Fr.
aitch, -bone, -piece.
Aix-la-Cha pelle' (āks lä shä pĕl'),
c. Prus.
Aix-les-Bains' (āks lā băṅ'), t. Fr.
A jac'cio (ä yät'chō), c. Corsica.
a jar'.
a jee' *or* a gee' (-je').
a jou'pa (-jōō'-).
à jour (ä'zhōōr').
a jou ré' (a zhōō rā').
aj'ow an or *-ou an* (ăj'ōō an).
aj'u tage.
a kä'la.
a ka matsu (ä ka măts').
a kaz'ga.
ak'beer.
a kee'.
A'ken (ä'-), t. Prus.
ak'ey (ăk'ā).
a kim'bo.
a kin'.
ak i ne'si a or *-ne'sis,* -ne'sic, -net'ic.
ak'o.
äl.
ä'la, pl. *-læ.*
Al a bä'ma, state and r. U. S., -bä'-
mi an.
al a ban'dĭne, -dīte.
al'a barch (-bark) *or* ar'a-.
al'a bâs ter, -bas'tri an, -trīne, -trī'-
tes (-tēz).
al a bas'trum, pl. *tra,* -bas'tos.
à la carte' (ä lä kärt').
a lack', -a day.
a lac'ri ty, -ri tous, -ri ous, -ous ly.
à la cuisse' (ä lä kwēs').
A lad'din, -din ist, -din ize, -ized.
al ad ja' (al a jä').
al'a gai (al'a gī).
à-la-grecque' or *à-la-grec'* (ä lä-
grĕk').
Al a hânce'.
ä laï'.
a lai sé' (a lä zā').
a la'li a.

al′ a līte.
A la me′da (ä lä mä′da), co. and c.
   Cal.; *a la me′da.*
a′la mo (ä′lä mō).
äl′a mode′ or *à la mode*′ (ä lä-
   mōd′), according to the fashion.
äl′a mode′ (*or* -mōd′), a thin silk
   fabric.
al a mort′ or *à la mort*′ (ä lä môr′).
al′and, a fish.
a länd′, on land.
a lan′dier.
al′ant cam′phor.
A la pur′ (ä′lä pōͅōr′), t. India.
ä′lar.
a larm′, -ing, -ing ly, -a ble, -ed ly,
   -ist, -larmed′.
a larm′-bell, -bird, -clock, -com′-
   pass, -fun′nel, -gage, -gun, -lock,
   -post, -watch.
a lär′um (*or* -lär′-), -bell.
ä′la ry.
a läs′.
A las′can, one of a religious sect,
   -kan, pertaining to Alaska.
a las′ka ite, *Chem.*
a lat cha′ (ä lä chä′).
ā lat′ē rē.
al′a tern, *-ter′nus.*
â la′tion.
a lat ti ci′ni o (ä lät ti chē′ni o).
alb, Alb Sun day.
al′ba.
Al ba ce′te (äl bä thä′tä), prov. Sp.
al ba dä′ra.
Al ba nen′ses (-sēz), -nen′si an.
Al ba′ni an.
al ba rel′lo.
al ba′ri um.
al bä′ta.
Al bä′tI.
al′ba tross, -cloth.
al bē′do.
al bē′it.
al ber′ca.
Al′bert cloth, A. cōal.
Al ber′tI ·bäss.
Al′ber tIne tracts.
Al′bert ist.
al′bert ite.
Al′bert Ny an′za (nī-), l. Afr.
al′ber type.
al bes′cence, -cent.

al′bi cans, *pl.* -can ti a (-shI a), -cant,
   -ca′tion, -bI flo′rous.
Al bi gen′ses (-sēz), -gen′sI an (*or*
   -shan).
Al′bin, a name applied to Scotland;
   al′bin, a mineral.
Al bI′na, c. Ore.
äl bI′no (*or* -bē′nō), *pl.* -nos (-nōz),
   -bi′ness, al′bi nism *or* -bi′no ism,
   -bI nis′tic *or* -not′ic.
Al′bi on, Great Britain. al′bi on-
   met′al.
al bi ŏ′ne.
äl′bite, -bit′ic.
al′bo-car′bon (*or* -car′-).
al′bo lith *or* -līte.
Al′bright (al′-).
al′brŏnze (*or* -brōnz).
al bu gin′e a (-jin-), -e an, -e ous
   or -bu′gi nous, -gi nI′tis.
al bu′go.
Al′bu la (äl′bo͝o la), mt. pass, Switz.
al′bum, *al′bum græ′cum.*
al bū′men, the white of an egg,
   -ize, -ized, -i zing.
al bū′min, -mi nate, -mi nif′er ous,
   -mi nim′e ter, -mi nin, -mi nip′a-
   rous, -mi noid, -noid al, -mi nose
   (-nōs) *or* -nous, -mi nŏne, -mi no′-
   sis, al bu′min beer, a. pa per.
al bu mi nu′ri a, -nu′ric.
al′bu mose (-mōs), -paper.
Al bu quer′que (äl bo͞o kâr′kä),
   t. N. Mex.; t. Sp.
al′burn, -bur′nous.
al bur′num.
Al cæ′us (-sē′-), a Gr. lyric poet,
   Al cä′ic, al cä′ic verse.
al cāid′ *or* *-cāyde*′.
äl cäl′dō (*or* äl käl′dä).
Al′cä mo (äl′-), t. It.
al can′na.
Al can′ta rIne.
al car rä′za.
al′ca tras.
Al′cä träz Is′land (äl′-), Cal.
al ca vä′la or -bä′la.
al ca zär′ (*or* -kä′- *or* äl kä thär′).
Al ceste′ (äl säst′), Molière's comedy.
al′che my, -mist, -mis′tic, -tic al,
   -chem′ic, -ic al, -al ly.
al cho cho′den (-kō kŏ′-).

---

nŏt, nôr, ūse, ŭp, ûrn, etüde, fo͞od, fo͝ot, aŋger, boṅmot, thus, Bach.

Al ci bī'a des (-dēz), Athenian.
Al ci'na (ăl che'na).
Al ci'ra (äl thē'rà).
Alc ma'ni an.
al'co.
al'co gene.
al'cŏ hol, -hol ate, -hol'a ture, -hol'-
 ic, -ic al, -al ly, -hol ic'i ty, al'-
 co hol-en'gine, -me'ter.
al'co hol ize, -ized, -i zing, -ī zā'-
 tion, -hol ism, -hol om'e ter, -e try,
 -o met'ric, -ric al, -al ly.
Al'cor.
Al'co ran (*or* al co rän'), -ish, -ist,
 -ran'ic.
al cor no'que (äl kor nō'kä) or *-no'co.*
Al'cott (awl'-), Amos Bronson,
 philos. Louisa May, daughter of
 A. B. A., Amer. writer.
al'cove (*or* al cove').
Al cy'o nē (-sī'-), *Myth.,* al'cy on'ic,
 -on'i form.
al'de hyde, -hy'dic (*or* al'-).
ạl'der, -buck'thorn.
ạl'der man, *pl.* -men, -man ate,
 -man cy, -man ly, -man ry, -man-
 ship, -man'ic, -i ty, al'der man-
 liz ard.
Al'di bo ron'ti phos' co phŏr'ni o,
 a character in Carey's burlesque
 tragedy.
Al'dīne (ăl'- *or* -dĭn *or* awl'dīn).
al'dose (-dōs).
ale, -ber ry, -wife, ale'-bench,
 -brew'er, -con'ner, -cost, -dra'per,
 -drink'ing, -fed, -gar'land, -gill
 (-jĭl), -house, -pot, -sil'ver,
 -tāst'er, -vat, -washed, -yard.
a lēak'.
al e at'i co.
ā'le a to'ry.
ā'lec, ăl'e cize, -cized, -cī'zing.
a lec' tŏ rŏ morph, -morph'ous.
a lec try om'a chy (-ky) *or* -to-
 rom'a chy.
a lec'try o man'cy.
Al'e do, c. Ill.
al'e gar (*or* ā'le-).
al'em.
A le man'nic *or* Al le-, -man'ni an.
a lemb'dar (-lem'-).
a lem'bic, a lem'broth.
A lem quer' (ä lĕñ kär'), t. Port.

A lem te'jo (ä lĕñ tā' zhō), prov.
 Port.
A len çon' (ä'lŏñ'sōñ'), c. Fr.
ā'lĕph.
a lep'i dote.
A lep'po, c. Turk., -lep'pĭne. a lep'-
 po, a. e'vil.
a lerce', -tree.
a lert', -ly, -lert'ness.
a ler'ta (-lär'tä).
a le'thi ol'o gy.
a lĕ'tho scope.
a lette' or *al lette'.*
a leū'ro man cy.
al eū rom'e ter.
a leū'rŏne, -ron'ic.
A leu'tian (*or* à lū'shĭ an *or* ăl e-
 ōō'shĭ an), Alas. Isl., -leū'tic.
al'e vin.
al ex an'ders *or* al i san'ders (ăl-
 ĕgz-).
al ex an'dra, a fly, or bait.
Al ex an'dri an (ăl ĕgz-), -ism *or*
 -drin ism, -an'drĭne.
al ex an'drīte.
Al ex än drō'pŏl (äl egz-), t. Russ.
a lex'i a.
a lex'in.
a lex i phar'mic, -mic al.
a lex'i py ret'ic (-pī-).
a lex i ter'ic, -ic al.
ä le zän'.
al'ja, -grăss.
al fal'fa.
al ja qui' (-kē').
al'fe nĭd *or* -nīde.
al'fet.
Al fi e'ri (äl fē ā'rē), It. statesman.
al fon'sin, a fish.
Al'ford (awl'-), Eng. poet and divine.
al jor'ja.
äl jres'co.
Al fur' (-fōōr'), Al fu rese' (-fōō-
 rēs' *or* -rēz'), -fu'ro (-fōō'-).
al'ga, pl. -gæ (-jē), a plant of the
 class *Algæ.* al'gal, -gist, -goid,
 -gous, -gol'o gist, -o gy, -go log'-
 ic al, al'gal fun'gus.
Al'gæ (-jē), a division of crypto-
 gams.
al'ga rŏt *or* -rŏth.

---

al gar ro'ba or *-ga ro'ba*, *-gar ro bil'la*
  or *-ga vil'la.*
al ga zel' (*or* ăl'-).
Al'ge bar (-je-).
al'ge bra, -brä'ic, -ic al, -al ly,
  -brä ize, -brä ist *or* -brist.
Al ge ci'ras (-sē'ras), t. Sp.
al ge'do (-jē').
al ge fa'cient (-shent)
Al'ger (ăl'jer), Amer. auth.
Al ge' ri an, -ge rine' (-reen').
al'ger īte.
al'gid, -gid'i ty, -gif'ic, *al'gor.*
al gom'e ter, -e try.
Al gon'quin *or* -kin, -gon'ki an.
al'gŏ rism (-rĭzm) *or*- rithm, -ris'-
  mic (-rĭz'-) *or* -rith'-, al'go rist,
  -ris'tic.
al guä zil' (-zeel').
al'gum *or* al'mug.
al ha ce'na (äl ä thä'nä).
Al ham'bra, -bra'ic, -bresque'
  (-bresk').
al hen'na.
ă'li as, *pl.* -as es.
al'i bī.
al'i ble, -bil'i ty.
al'i cant.
Al i can'te (ä lē kän'tä), prov. Sp.
al'i chel (-shel).
al'ic tī'sal (-tī'zal).
a lic'u la.
al'i dade.
ăl'ien (āl'yen), -ism, -ist, -or, -ee',
  al'ien-house.
ăl'ien ate, -a'ted, -ā'ting, -a ble,
  -age, -a'tor, -a'tion, -a bil'i ty, ăl'-
  ien ig'e nate (-ij'-), āl ien a'tion-
  of'fice.
ăl i eth'moid, -moid'al.
al'i form, a lif'er ous, a lig'er ous
  (-lij'-).
a light', -ed, -ing.
a lign' (-lĭn'), -ing, -ment, -ligned'.
a like'.
a'lim (ä'leem).
al'i ment, -men'tal, -tal ly, -ta ry,
  -ta ri ness, -men'ta tive, -tive ness,
  -ta'tion, -men'tic.
al'i mo ny.
al i na'sal (-zal).
a line', -ment, -lined', -lĭn'ing, -lĭn'-
  er, -lĭn' e ate, -a'tion *or* al lĭn'-.

Also spelled *align* and sometimes
  alline.
al'i nit.
al'i ped.
al'i phat'ic.
al'i quänt.
al'i quŏt.
al'i sep'tal.
al is ma'ceous, a lis'mad, -lis'mal,
  -lis'moid.
al i sphe'noid, -noid'al.
a list'.
al'i trunk.
ă li un'de.
a live'.
al i zä'rĭ.
ȧ liz'a rin (*or* al i zä'rin), -a rate,
  -i zăr'ic.
ălk, -gum.
al'ka hest *or* -ca hest, -hes'tic, -tic al.
al kal'a mĭde (*or* al'kal am'ĭd).
al'ka lĭ (*or* -lĭ), *pl.* -lis (-lĭz) *or* -lies
  (-lĭz), -ka les'cence, -cen cy, -cent,
  al'ka lĭ-grăss, -stiff.
al'ka li fy (-fī), -ing, -fied, -fi' a ble,
  -ka lif'er ous, -lig'e nous (-lij'-).
al'ka lim'e ter, -e try, -li met'ric,
  -ric al, -al ly.
al'ka līne (*or* -lĭne), -lin' i ty, -lin ize,
  -ized, -ī zing.
al'ka lize, -lized, -lĭ zing, -ka lĭ'za-
  ble, -lĭ zate, -za'ted, -za'ting, -za'-
  tion, -ka loid, -loid'al.
al kar'sin *or* -sīne.
al ke ken'gĭ (-jĭ).
al ken'na.
al ker'mes (-mēz).
Al'ko răn (*or* -rän'), -ran'ic, -ran'-
  ish, -ran'ist.
all, all'bone, -good, a plant, -heal,
  a plant, -mouth, a fish, -ness,
  -seed, a plant, -whith'er, all-fired',
  -fired'ly, -fours', a game, -glo'ri-
  ous, -hail', *v.*, -mer'ci ful, -one,
  -o'ver -pit'i less, -round, -sorts, a
  beverage, -ups.
ăl'lä bre've (brä'vä).
al la bu'ta.
ăl'lä cä pel'lä.
al'la gite (-jĭt).
al'la go ste'mo nous.
Al'lah.
Al lä hä bäd', div. India.

al'lan īte.
al lan'to is, -to'ic, -lan'toid, -toid'al,
-toid'i an.
al lan to tox'i cum.
ăl'lä pri'ma (prē'mä), *a. te des'ca*
(tā dās'ka).
al las so ton'ic.
al lay', -ing, -er, -ment, -layed'.
al'le cret.
Al'le ga'ny, co. Md.; co. and vil.
N. Y.
al lege' (-lĕj'), -a ble, -lĕged', -lĕg'-
ing, -lĕg'er *or* le ga'tor, -le gā'-
tion.
Al'le ghä'ny, co. N. C.; co. Va.,
A. Moun'tains, A. vine.
Al'le ghe'ny (-gä-), co., riv., and c.
Pa.; a township in Blair, in Butler,
and in Westmoreland Counties,
Pa.
al le'giance (-jans *or* -ji ans),
-giant (*or* -ji ant). •
al'le go ry, -gŏr'ic, -ic al, -al ly, -al-
ness, al'le gō rist, -go rize', -rīzed,
-rī'zing, -rī'zer, -gŏr i za'tion.
al le gret'to (ăl lā gret'to), *al le'gro*
(*or* ăl lā'gro).
al le lu'ia (-lōo'ya) *or* -iah.
al'le mănde'.
Al le man'nic. See *Alemannic.*
al le mon'tite.
al'len, pasture land.
al len'ar ly.
ạl'ler-float, -trout.
al le'ri on.
al le'vi ate, -ā'ted, -a ting, -a tive,
-a tor, -to'ry, ā'tion.
al'ley, *pl.* -leys, -leyed (-lĭd), al'ley
way, -ley-taw. As a playing
marble, it is sometimes spelled
ally.
All'-Fa'ther, -hal'low,-saints,-souls.
All hal'low e'en, -low mas, -low-
tide.
al li a'ceous.
al li'ance, -li'a ble.
al'lĭce *or* -lis, -shad.
al li ga'tion.
al'li ga tor, -ap'ple, -fish, -pear,
-ter'ra pin, -tor'toise (-tiss), -tree,
-tur tle, -wood. Some authorities write the following compounds
as separate words: al'li ga tor

for'ceps *or* -for ceps, a. wrench *or*
-wrench.
al lign' *or* -line'. See *aline.*
al lit'er ate, -a ted, -a ting, -a tive,
-tive ly, -tive ness, -tor, -a'tion,
-er al.
Al'li um.
Al lo brog'ic al (-broj'-).
al'lo cate, -ca ted, -ting, -ca'tion, *al-
lo ca'tur.*
al lo chi'ri a (-kī'-) *or -chei'- (-kī'-).*
al lo chro'ic, -loch'ro ite (*or* -lo-
chro'), -ro ous, -chro mat'ic.
al'lo cryp'tic.
'al lo cu'tion.
al lo'di a, -di al, -al ism, -al ist, -al ly,
-al'i ty, -lo'di a ry, -di um, -lod'i-
fi ca'tion, al'lod.
al log'a my, -a mous.
al'lo ge ne'i ty, -ge'ne ous, -gen'ic.
al'lo grǎph.
al lom'er ism, -er ous.
al'lo morph, -mor'phic, -phism,
-phīte.
al longe' (-lunj').
al'lo nym, -lon'y mous.
al'lo path, -path'ic, -ic al ly, -lop' a-
thist, -a thy.
al'lo phane, -phan'ic, -loph'a nate.
al'lo phyle (-fīl), -phyl'ic, -phyl'i an.
al loph'y toid.
al'lo plǎst.
al lo'qui al, -ism.
al'lo the ism.
al lot rio ph'a gy, -lo troph'ic.
al lot'ri ous.
al'lo trope, -trop'ic, -ic al, -ally,
-tro pic'i ty, -lot'ro pism, -pize,
-pized, -pī'zing, -py.
al low', -low'ing, -a ble, -ble ness,
-bly, -ance, -ed ly, -er, -lowed'.
al loy', *n.* and *v.*, -ing, -age, -loyed',
al loy'-bal'ance.
al lo zo'oid.
all'spice.
al lŭde', -lŭd'ed, -lud'ing, -lu'sive,
-sive ly, -sive ness, -so ry, -lu'sion
(-zhun).
al lu mette' (-lōo-).
al lūre', -ment, -lūred', -lur'ing, -ing-
ly, -ing ness, -lūr'er.

---

fāte, făt, fär, fạll, fâre, fȧst, sofȧ, mēte, mĕt, hêr, īce, ĭn, nōte,

al lu′vi um, *pl.* -vi ums *or* -vi a,
-vi al, -vi on, -vi ous.
al ly′, *pl.* -lies (-līz), al ly′, *v.*, -ing,
-lied′.
al′ma *or* -mah.
äl′mä cen′ (-sän′ *or* -thän′).
al ma di′a (-dē′a) *or al′ma die.*
Al′ma gest (-jest).
al mä′gra (*or* -mä′-).
Al′main, -riv′et.
al′ma ma′ter.
al′ma nac.
äl′man din *or* -dĭne, -man dite.
Al man′zor.
Al ma-Ta de′ma (äl′mä tä dä′mä
or tä′-), Belg. painter.
al me′na.
al might′y, -i ly, -i ness, -y ship.
Al might′y, the deity.
al mi′qui (awl mē′kē).
al mi′rah (-mē′rä).
Al mo do′var (al-), Span. dipl.
Al′mond (äl′-), tp. and vil. N. Y.
alm′ond *or* al′mond (ä′mund *or*
äl′-), älm′ond-cake, -eyed, -fur′-
nace, -oil, -tree, a. paste.
äl′mon er *or* alm′ner (äm′-), äl′-
mon er ship, -mon ry.
al′most,
alms (ämz), -giv er, -giv ing, -house,
-man.
alms′-bag, -ba sin, -box, -chest,
-deed, -dish, -drink, -fee, -folk,
-gate, -pot.
al mu can′tar *or* -ter, -stáff.
al′mûce. See *amice.*
al mud′ or -mude′ (-mōōd′ *or* -mūd′).
al′mug.
al′mund.
al′nage, -na ger (-jer), -ger ship.
al nas′char ism (-kar-).
Aln′wick (än′nik), t. Eng.
al′o dy.
äl′oe (-ō), *pl.* -oes (-ōz), -ōed, -o et′-
ic, -ic al, Al′ō ē, *Bot. genus,* äl′ōe-
tree, äl′oes-wood.
al o e′da ry, -da′ri um.
a lŏft′.
A lo′gi an, *pl.* Al′o gī.
a logic, -ic al.
al o got′ro phy.
al′o in.
al′o man cy.

A lom brä′do. See *Alumbrado.*
a lone′, -ness.
a long′, -shore, -shore man, -side.
a loof′, -ness.
al o pe′coid (*or* lop′e-).
A lo′pi as.
a lose′ (-lōs′).
al ou ǎtte′ or *al′ou äte* (-ōō-).
a lou′chĭ or *-lu′-* (-lōō′-).
a loud′.
à l′ou trance′ (ä lōō troħs′).
alp, al pes′tri an, -trine, al′pĭne (*or*
pĭn), -pĭne ry, -pĭn ist, alp′-horn,
al′pen glow, -horn, -stock. When
used as a proper adjective, "alp"
is capitalized.
al pac′a.
al′pha.
al′pha bet, -bet′ic, -ic al, -al ly,
-bet′ics, -be ta′ri an, al′pha bet ize,
-ized, ī zing, -ism.
Al phæ′us *or* -phē′us, *Bib.*
al phen′ic.
Al phe′us, *Myth.* Al′phe us, Chr.
name.
al′phi to mor′phous.
Al phon′sĭne, pertaining to Alphonso; al phon′sin, a forceps.
al pho′sis.
al′phus.
al′pist *or* al′pi a, bird-seed.
Alps, Al′pĭne, Al′pĭ mä′lāy an.
al′quier (-keer).
al′qui fou (-kä fōō) or *-qui fore.*
Al Ra kim′ (äl rä kēm′).
al rĕad′y.
al′-root.
al ru′na.
Al′sace (äl′säs), tp. Pa.
Al sace′ (äl′säs′), prov. Fr.
Al sace′-Lŏr′räine′ (äl säs′-), prov.
Ger.
Al sa′tian (-shän).
al seg′no (äl sän′yo).
al si na′ceous.
al′so.
Al sto′ni a bark.
al′ston īte.
ält, -horn.
äl′tä.
Al tai′ (äl tī′), mts. Asia.
Al tä′ian (-yan), -ta′ic, al ta′ite.
äl tair′.

Al'ta ma hạ', r. Ga.
al tam bour' (-boor').
ạl'tar, -age, -ist, -piece, -wise, al'tar-
board, -bread, -card, -car pet,
-cav i ty, -chime, -cloth, -cross,
-curtain, -cush ion, -desk, -dues,
-fire, -fron tal, -lan tern, -ledge,
-light, -pro tec'tor, -rail, -screen,
-side, -slab, -stairs, -stole, -stone,
-ta ble, -thane, -tomb, -tray,
-vase, -ves sel, -wall, -wine.
alt az'i muth.
ạl'ter, -tered, -ter ing, -a ble, -ble-
ness, -a bly, -bil'i ty, -ant, -a tive,
-ä'tion.
ăl'ter cate, -ca'tion.
ăl'ter ĕ'go.
al'ter ĭ'dem.
al'tern.
al ter nat' (-nä').
al ter'nate, a. and n., al'ter nate
(or -ter'-) v., -na ted, -na ting,
-ter'nate ly, -nate ness, -na tive,
-tive ly̆, -tive ness, -nant, -na'tion,
al'ter na'tor.
Al thæ'a, Myth., -thæ'a or -the'-,
Bot. genus, al thæ'a, Rose of
Sharon.
al thĕ'in or -Ine.
Al'thing (-ting or -thing), -man.
ạl though'.
al tic'o mous.
al tim'e ter, -et ry.
al'tin.
al tin' car.
al'ti scope.
al tis'o nant, -o nous.
al tis'si mo.
al'ti tude, -tu'di nal, -di na'ri an.
ăl'tŏ (or äl'-), a part in music,
-rĕ liĕ'vŏ, ăl'to-ri lie'vo (-rĕ lyă'-
vŏ).
al trop'a thy.
al'tru ism, -ist, -is'tic, -tic al ly.
al'u del, -fur nace.
al'u la, pl. -læ, -lar, -let.
al'um, -bat'ter y, -earth, -rock,
-root, -stone.
a lu'mi na, -mi nate, -mi nif'er ous,
-min'i form, -min'ic, -min'i um,
-lu'min ite, -mi nize, -nous, -nose
(-nōs), -mi num, al'u min or
-mĭne.

a lum'na, fem., pl. -næ, -nal, -ni-
ate.
a lum'nus, masc., pl. -nĭ.
al'u nite.
ăl'ure.
a lu'no gen.
a lu'ta, -ta'ceous.
al'va ma rĭ'na.
Al vä rä'do (äl-), c. Tex.; r. Mex.
al've a ry, -a ted.
al've o lar (or -vĕ'-), -la ry, al've o-
lar in'dex, a. pas'sa ges, a. point,
a. proc'ess es (prŏs'-).
al ve'o lus, -o late, -la'ted, -lā'tion,
-lar'i form, -o lo den'tal, -o lo lā'-
bi al.
al've us, pl. -ve ĭ, -vĭne (or -vīne).
ạl'way, -ways.
al'ysm (-izm).
A lys'sum, a lys'son.
Al'zey (äl'tsī), t. Ger
ä'ma.
am a crat'ic.
am'a crĭne.
Am'a da vat'. Sometimes spelled
av'a- or -du väde'.
am a del'phous.
am'a dou (-dōō)
am'ah or ä'mah.
A mai'mon or -may-.
a main'.
am'al dar or -il-.
Am'a lĕk ĭte, Bib.
A mal'fi tan.
a mal'gam, -ga ma.
a mal'ga mate, -ma ted, -mä'ting,
-ma ble, -ma tive, -ma tor, -ga-
mist, -ga ma'tion.
a mal'tas.
am'an.
a mând'.
am'an din or a man'dĭne.
am'a nĭ'ta.
a man'i tin or -tĭne.
am'a nous.
a man u en'sis, pl. -ses (-sēz).
am'a ranth, -ran'thĭne, or -tin,
-thoid, am'a ranth-feath'ers, Am-
a ran'thus or -tus.
ä mar go'so-bark.
am a ryl'lis, -ryl' li da'ceous, -lid'e-
ous, Am a ryl'lis, Bot. genus.
Am'a sa, Bib.

a mȧss', -massed', -mass'ing, -a ble,
-er, -ment.
ă'mäs'sette' or *ăm a zette'.*
am'as then'ic.
am a teur' (-ter' *or* am'a tūr *or*
-tūr'), -ish, -ish ly, -ish ness, -ism,
-ship.
am a ti'to (-tee'-).
ä mä to'ri o, pl. *-to'ri i* (-rē ē).
ăm' a to ry, -to'ri al, -al ly, am'a-
tive, -tive ness.
am au ro'sis, -rot'ic.
a mau'sīte.
a maze', -ment, -mazed', -māz'ing,
-ing ly, -māz'ed ly, -ed ness.
Am'a zon, r. Braz.; *Myth.,* a female
Scythian warrior; -zō'ni an, Am'a-
zon-ant *or* A. ant, A. stone.
am'a zon, a quarrelsome 'woman; a
species of parrot; -zon īte, mineral.
am'bage, pl. *-ba ges* (-jĕz *or* -bā'jēz)
-bag'i nous (-baj'-) *or* -ba'gious
(-jus), -gious ly, -gious ness.
am'ban.
am'ba rĭ, a covered howdah.
am bar va'li a.
am'ba ry, a plant.
am'bash.
am bas'sa dor *or* em-, -dor ship,
-do'ri al, -bas'sa dress.
am'bē.
am'ber, -fish *or* a. fish, -seed *or* a.
seed, -tree *or* a. tree.
am'ber gris (-grēs).
am bi dex'ter, -tral, -trous, -trous-
ly, -trous ness, -ter'i ty.
am'bi ens, *pl.* -en'tes (-tēz).
am'bi ent.
am'bi gen *or* -gēne, -big'e nal
(-bij'-), -e nous.
am bi gu'i ty, -big'u ous, -ous ly,
-ous ness.
am bip'a rous.
am'bit, -al, *am'bĭ tus.*
am bi'tious (-bĭsh'us), -ly, -ness,
-bi'tion, -tion less.
am'ble, -bled, -bler, -bling, -bling ly.
am blo'sis, -blot'ic.
am bly ă'phi a.
am bly o'pi a, am'bly o'py, -op'ic.
am'bo, pl. *-bos* or *-bo'nes* (-bōz *or*
-bō'nēz), *am'bon.*
am bol'ic.

Am boy'na but'ton, A. pine, A.
wood.
Am boy nese' (-nēs' *or* nēz').
am bre ă'da.
am'bre in, -bre'ic.
am brette'.
am'brite.
am brol'o gy.
am bro'sia *or* -si a (-zha *or* -zhĭ a),
am bro'si ac (-zĭ- *or* zhĭ-), -si a'-
ceous (-zĭ-), -sial (-zhal *or* zhi al),
-sial ly, Am bro'sia, *Bot. genus.*
Am bro'sian. Relating to St. Am-
brose.
am bro si'no (-zē'no) *or* am'brō sin.
am'bro type.
am'bry.
am'bu lance, -lant, -late, -la'ted,
-la ting, -la tive, -la tor, -to'ry,
-to'ri al, -la'tion.
am'bur y. See *anbury.*
am bus cade', -cād'ed, -cād'ing.
am'bush, -ing, -er, -ment, -bushed.
a meer' *or* -mir' (-mēr'), -ship.
am'el-corn *or* am'el corn.
a mĕl'i a.
a mel'i fi ca'tion.
a mĕl'io rate (-yo-), -ra ted, -ra-
ting, -ra ble, -ra tive, -ra tor, -ra'-
tion.
am'e lus, *pl.* -lī.
ă'men'. In singing, ä'men'.
a me'na ble, -na bly, -ble ness, -bil'-
i ty.
a mend', -ed, -ing, -a ble, -ble ness,
-a to'ry, -er, -ment, -mends,
a mend'ment-mon'ger.
a mĕnde' (*or* ä mänd'), *a. hon o rä'-*
ble.
a men'i ty.
a men'o ma'ni a or *a mœ'no-.*
a men'sa et tho'ro.
am'ent, *a men'tum,* pl. *-ta,* -men'tal,
-ti form.
am en ta'ceous, -tif'er ous.
a men'ti a (-shi a).
a merce', -a ble, -ment, -merced',
-mer'cing, -mer'cer.
A mer'i can, -ism, -ist, -ize, -ized,
-i zing, -ĭ zā'tion.
am e ris'tic.
am'e thyst, -thys'tĭne.
am e tro'pi a, -trop'ic, -trom'e ter.

---

nŏt, nôr, ūse, ŭp, ûrn, etüde, fōōd, fŏŏt, aŋger, boṅmot, ᵺus, Bach.

am'garn.
Am hăr'ic.
Am'herst (-erst), *Geog.*
a'mi a ble, -ble ness, -a bly, bil'i ty,
  am i an'tus *or* -thus, -an'ti form,
  -an'tĭne, -an'toid, -toid'al.
am'i ca ble, -ble ness, -bly, -bil'i ty.
am'ice (-ĭs) *or* ăl'mūce.
am'i crŏb'ic (*or* -crŏ'bic).
a mic'tus, a cloak; A mic'tus, *Entom. genus.*
a mi'cus cu'ri æ.
a mid', -ships, a midst'.
Am'ĭ das (ăm'-), Eng. nav.
a mid'u lin.
A'mi ens (ä'mĭ ăn'), t. Fr.
ä mi'go (-mē'-), pl. *-gos* (-gŏz).
am'il, -il dar.
a mim'i a.
a mir'. See *ameer.*
Am'ish *or* Om'ish.
a miss'.
A mĭt'tai (-tä), *Bib.*
am'i ty.
am'ma.
am'man *or* -mant.
Am'man ite.
am'me ter.
am'mĭte.
am'mo chryse (-krĭs).
Am'mon, -mo'ni an, relating to
  Ammon.
am mo'ni a, -ni ăc, -ni'a cal, -ni' a-
  cum, -ni al'um, -mo'ni ate, -a ted,
  -mo'nic (*or* -mon'ic), -mo ni e'mi a,
  -mon'i fi ca'tion, am mo'ni a-me'-
  ter.
am'mon ite, -mon'i tid,- mo ni tif'-
  er ous.
am mo'ni um, -nī'u ret, -ret ed *or*
  -ret ted.
am mu ni'tion, -chest, am mu ni'-
  tion bread, a. shoes, a. stock'ings.
am ne mon'ic.
am ne'si a (*or* -ne'zĭ a), -ne'sic, -nes'-
  tic, Am ne'si a, *Entom. genus.*
am'nes ty.
a mo'lē (*or* -lä).
a mong' (-mung'), -mongst'.
a mon til la'do (ä mŏn til yä'dō).
am o ret'to, pl. -tĭ.
am o ri'no (ăm o rē'- *or* ä mō-), pl. *-ri-
ni* (-rē'nē).

am'or ist, -o rous, -rous ly, -rous-
  ness
am o ro'sa, masc. *am o ro'so.*
a mor'phism, -phic, -phous, -phous-
  ly, -phous ness.
A mor pho zo'a, -zo'ic, -zo'ous.
a mort'.
a mor'tĭze *or* -tĭse, -tized, -ti zing,
  -tize mĕnt, -tĭ za'tion.
a mount', -ed, -ing.
a mour' (-moor'), *a. prō pre* (prŏ'-
  pr).
ä'mou'rette' (-ōō-).
A moy' (ä moi'), seaport China.
am'pac.
am pä'ro.
am'pas sy.
am'pe lite, -lit'ic.
am pere' (-pâre') -per'age, -pe rom'-
  e ter, am pere'-foot, -hour, -me-
  ter, -min ute, -sec ond, -turn,
  -volt, -wind ing, Am pe'ri an *or*
  -re an.
am'per sand, am'pas sy.
am'per y.
am'phi ar thro'sis, -thro'di al.
Am'phi as ter, a genus of starfishes.
  am'phi as ter, *Embryol.*
am phib'a lus, *pl.* -a lī, -a lum,
  pl. -a la.
am phib'i a, -i al, -i an, -i ous, -ous ly,
  -ous ness, *-i um,* pl. *-ums,* or *-i a,*
  -i on, -i ol'o gy, -o log'ic al, Am-
  phib'i a, *Zoöl. genus.*
am'phi bŏle, -bol'ic, -bo lif'er ous,
  -phib'o lĭne, -o līte, -o loid.
am phi bol'o gy, -o gism, -bol'ic,
  -phi bo log'ic al, -al ly, -phib'o-
  lous, -o ly.
am phi chro'ic, -chro mat'ic.
am phic' ty on, *pl.* -ons. Often
  capitalized. -ty o ny, *pl.* -o nies,
  -on'ic.
am'phi ge'an.
am phig'o ny, -o nous *or* -phi gon'ic.
am'phi go ry, -gor'ic.
am phil'o gy, -o gism.
am phim'a cer.
Am phi'on, *Myth.*
am'phi pro'style (*or* -fĭp'rŏ-), -sty'-
  lar.
am phis bæ'na, -bæ'ni an, -nic, -nid,
  -nous, Am *phis bæ'na,* Zoöl genus.

am phis'ci i (-fish'ĭ ĭ), -phis'cians (-fish'anz).
am phi sty'lic.
am phi the'a ter *or* -tre, -a tral, -at'ric, -ric al, -al ly.
am phith'y ra (-fĭth'ĭ rà).
Am phi trī'te, *Myth.*
am phit'ro pous *or* -pal.
am phit'ry on, Am phit'ry on, *Zoöl. genus.*
am'phi type.
am'pho phil'ic.
am'pho ra, pl. *-ræ*, -ral, -pho ric'i ty, -phor'ic, -roph'o ny.
am pho ter'ic.
am pho'tis, *pl.* -phot'i des (-dēz), Am pho'tis, *Entom. genus.*
am'ple, -ness, am'ply, -pli tude.
am plex'i cau'date.
am plex'i caul, -i fo'li ate.
am'pli a tive.
am'pli fy, -fied, -fy ing, -fi er, -fi ca tive (*or* -plif'-), -ca tor, -to ry, (*or* -plif'-), -ca'tion.
am pongue' (-pŏng').
am pul'la, pl. *-læ*, -li form, am'pul lar (*or* -pul'-), -la ry, -late, -la ted (*or* -pul'-), -la'ceous, -lin'u la, -los'i ty, am pul'ling-cloth
am'pu tate, -tā ted, -tor, -ting, -ta'tion, -tion al, am'pu ta ting-knife, -saw.
am'pyx, pl. *-pyx ĕs* or *-py ces* (-sēz).
am.ri'ta (-rē' *or* -rit'-).
am shas'pand.
Am'stel pŏrce'lain (-lĭn), A. pot'ter y.
åmt (*or* ămt), *pl.* åmts *or* ämt'er, amt'man, *pl.* -men.
a muck'.
am'u la, *pl.* las *or* læ (-läz *or* lē).
am'u let, -let'ic.
A mur' *or* A moor' (ä moor'), r. Asia; prov. Siberia.
a muse' (-mūz'), -ment, -mused', -mus'ing, -ing ly, -er, -mu'sive (-zĭv *or* -sĭv), -ly.
am u sette' (zĕt').
Am y clæ'an.
a myc'tic.
a myg'da la, pl. *-læ*, -la'ceous, -dal'ic, -da lif'er ous, -da late, -dule, -da lin, -lĭne, -da lī'tis, -da loid, -loid'-

al, -da lot'o my, am'yg dal'ic, A *myg'da lus*, *Bot. genus.*
am'yl *or* -ule, *Chem.*, am'yl am'in, am'yl ate, -ene, -yl'ic, am'yl al'co hol, a. ni'trite, a. hy'drid.
am'yl, *starch*, am'y la'ceous, -lif'er ous, am'y lin, a myl'o gen (-jen), am'y lo gen'e sis, -gen'ic, -y lom'e ter.
am'y o sthe'ni a (*or* a mĭ'o-), -sthen'ic.
am y ot'ro phy, a my'o troph'ic (mĭ'-), am'y ous.
Am y ral'dĭsm, -dist.
a'my-root.
a myzt'lĭ (-mist-).
am'zel *or* -sel.
an'a (*or* ā'na).
an a ban'tid, -toid.
an a bap'tism, -bap tis'tic, -tic al, -al ly, an a bap tize', -tized', -ti'zing, An a bap'tist.
An'a bas, an ab'a mous, an a ban'tid, -ban'toid.
a nab'a sis, pl. *-ses* (-sēz), A nab'a sis, Xenophon's account of a Persian campaign.
an a basse'.
an ab'a ta, -a bat'ic.
an'a bĭ ot'ic.
an ab'o le, an ab'o lism, -a bol'ic.
an'a brânch.
a'na ca hui'te *or* -ta (ăn'a kä hwē'tē *or* ä nä kä wē'tä), -wood.
an a camp'tic, -al ly.
an'a canth, -can'thĭne, -thous.
an'a card, -car'dic, -di a'ceous.
an'a ca thar'sis, -thar'tic.
an ach' ro nism, -an a chron'ic, -ic al, -ach'ro nĭst, -ro nis'tic *or* -tic al, an ach'ro nize, -nized, -ni zing, -ro nous, -nous ly.
an ac'la sis, *Pros.*, an a clas'tic, -clas'tics.
an'a cli'nal.
an ac'li sis, *Med.*
an'a cœ no'sis.
an'a co lu'thi a, -lu'thic, -al ly, *-lu'thon*, pl. *-tha.*
an a con'da.
an a cos'ta, a Dutch textile fabric; an' a cos' ti a, a French textile fabric.

A năc′re on, Gr. lyric poet, -on′-tic.
a nac′ro tism, an a crot′ic.
an a cru′sis, -crus′tic.
an a cu′sis.
an′a dĭ plo′sis.
an′a dip′si a, -dip′sic.
an′a drom, a nad′ro mous.
an æ′ti o log′ic al (-ē′tĭ-).
an a gen ne′sis.
an′ a glyph, -glyph′ic *or* -glyp′tic,
-glyph′ics *or* -glyp′tics, -glyph′ic al,
-o scope, -glyp′to grâph, -graph′ic,
-glyp tog′ra ph y, -glyp′ton, an ag′-
ly phy.
an′ag nor′i sis.
an′ag nŏst.
an a go′ge *or* an′a go gy (-jy), -go-
get′ic al (-jet′-), -gog′ic (-gŏj′-),
-ic al, -al ly.
an′ a gram, -gram mat′ic, -ic al,
-al ly, -gram′ma tize *or* -tise, -tized,
-ti zing, -tist.
an a′gua (-ä′gwa).
A na huac′ (ä nä wäk′), Mex.
plateau.
an′a kan.
ă′nal.
an′a lav.
an′a lect, *pl.* -lects, *-lec′ta,* -lec′tic.
an a lep′sis or *-si a,* *or* an′a lep sy,
-lep′tic.
an al ge′si a *or* -al′gi a, -get′ic *or*
-ges′ic (-jet′- *or* -jes′-).
a nal′gid.
an′al lag mat′ic.
a nal′o gy, *pl.* -gies (-jĭz), an a log′ic,
-ic al, -al ly, -al ness, *a nal′o gon,*
a nal′o gize (-jīz) *or* -gise, -gized,
-gi zing, -gous, -gous ly, -gist
(-jĭst), -gis′tic.
an al′pha bet, -be′tic.
a nal′y sis, -an′a lyze (-līz), -lyzed,
-ly zing, -ly zer, -ly za ble, -ble-
ness, -ly za′tion, an′a lyst, -lyt′ic,
-ics, -ic al, -al ly.
A năm′ *or* An năm′, div. China,
An a mese′ *or* An na- (-mēs′ *or*
-mēz′), An′a mite.
a nam′e site.
an am ne′sis, -nes′tic.
an a mor′pho sis, -mor′phism, -pho-
scope, -phose (-fōs), -pho sy,
-phous.

a nā′nas (*or* -nä′- *or* -năn′-), A na′-
nas, *Bot. genus.*
an an′drous.
An a nī′as, *Bib.*
an an′ther ous, *-ther um,* -an′thus.
an′a peĭ rat′ic.
an′a pest *or* -pæst, -pes′tic, -tic al,
-al ly.
an a phal an ti′a sis.
an aph′o ra, pl. *-ræ.*
an aph ro dis′i a (-diz′-), -dis′i ac,
-ro dit′ic, -dī′tous.
an′a plas ty, -plas′tic, an′a plâst.
an′a ple ro′sis, -rot′ic.
an ap′no grâph, -nom′e ter.
an ap o dic′tic.
an ap′ty chus (-kus), pl. *-chi* (-kī).
an′arch y (-ark-), -arch ism, -ist,
-ist′ic, -arch ize, -ized, -i zing,
an′arch, an ar′chic (-kik), -chal
or -chi al *or* -chic al (-kăl *or* -kī al
or -kĭk al).
an ar′thri a, -thric, -throus.
An ar throp′o da, an ar throp′o dous.
A′nas.
an a sar′ca, -sar′cous.
an a seïs′mic.
An as ta′si us (-zhĭ us *or* -shĭ-)
an′a state, -stat′ic.
an as′tig mat′ic.
an′a sto me.
a nas′ to mose (-mōz), -mosed
(-mōzd), -mot′ic.
a nas′tro phe.
a nas′trous.
a nath′ e ma, *pl.* -mas (-maz),
-e ma tize, -tized, -ti zing, -ti zer,
-ma ti za′tion, -mat′ic, -ic al, -al ly,
a nath′e mize, -e mized, -mi zing.
A nat′i fa, pl. *-fæ,* a nat′i fer, an a-
tif′er ous.
An a to′li an, -tol′ic.
a nat′ o mize, -mized, -mi zing,
-mĭ zer, -o mism, -o mist, -o my,
an a tom′ic, -ic al, -al ly.
a nat′o pism.
an a trep′tic, refuting.
an a trip′sis, -trip sol′o gy, -trĭp′-
tic, pertaining to massage.
an′a tron.
a nat′ro pal, -ro pous.
a nat′to. See *Arnatto.*

An ax ag′o ras, Gr. philos., -o re′an.
an ax′i al.
An ax i man′ der, Gr. philos.,
-man′dri an.
An ax o′ni a, an ax o′ni al.
a′nay (ä′nī).
an′bur y. Sometimes am′bu ry and
an′ber ry.
an′ces tor, -ces try, -ces′tral *or*
-tri al, -tral ly, -to′ri al, -al ly,
an′ces tor-wor ship.
aṇ′chi lops (-kĭ-).
An chi′ses (-kī′sēz), *Myth*.
an′chor, -ing, -a ble, -age, -ate, -less,
-chored, an′chor-ball, -bolt, -buoy,
-chock, -drag, -gate, -hold, -hoy,
-ice, -lift, -lĭn ing, -ov en, -plate,
-ring, -rock et, -shac kle, -shot,
-stock, -trip per, -watch, -well.
a. light.
aṇ′cho ret *or* -rīte, -cho ress *or*
-rĭ tess, -ret′ic *or* -rit′ic, -ic al,
-ret ish, -ret ism.
an cho′ vy (-chō′-), *pl.* -vies, an-
cho′vy-pear.
ăn′cient (-shent), -cient ly, -cient-
ness, -cient ry.
an cī′le, pl. *-cil′i a*.
an′cil la ry.
an cip′i tal, -i tate, -i tous.
aṇ′con *or* -*cone*, pl. -*co′nes* (-nēz),
-co nad, -co nal, -cö′ne al, -ne ous,
aṇ co ne′us, pl. -*ne′i*, aṇ′co noid.
aṇ′co ra, pl. -*ræ*, -ral.
aṇ′crée (ang′krä), an′cred (-kerd).
an cy′roid *or* an ky′roid.
An da lu′si a (-shi a *or* än dä lōō-
thē′ä), div. Sp., -lu′sian (-zhan),
an da lu′sīte.
An′da man ese′ (-ēz′).
än dän′te (-tä *or* ăn dăn′tē), -*ti′no*
(-tē′-).
an′da rac.
an′da ze.
An′des (-dēz), mts. S. Amer., -dē′an,
-dĭne (*or* -dīn).
an′dē sin *or* -sĭne (-zin), -site (-zīt),
-sit′ic (-zit′-).
an di′ra-guä ca (-dē-).
and′i ron (-urn).
An dor′ra, a small repub. in Europe,
-dor′ran.
an′douille (äṅ′dōō′y′).

An′do′ver, t. Mass.; t. N. H.; bor.
Eng.
an′dra.
an′dra dite.
An′ dras sy (on′ drä she), Hung.
statesman.
An′dré (-drä *or* -drĭ), Major, Eng.
spy.
An′ dre a Fer rä′ ra.
an′dre o līte.
an dro ceph′a lous.
an drog′ y ny (-droj′I-), -y nal,- nal-
ly, -y nism, -y nos, -y nous, an′-
dro gyne (-jĭn), -gy ne′i ty, -gyn′i a.
an′droid *or an droï′des* (-dēz).
an′dro lep′si a, an′dro lep′sy.
An drŏm′a che (-kē), *Myth*.
an dro ma′ni a.
An drom′e da, *Myth., Astron.*, an′-
dro med *or* -mēde.
an dro mor′phous.
an′dron, -dro nĭ′tis.
An′dro nī′cus, *Bib*.
an dro pet′a lous.
an droph′a gus, pl. -*gi* (-jĭ), -a-
gous.
an′dro pho′bi a.
an′dro phore, -droph′o rous.
an′ dro sphinx.
an′ dro spore.
an drot′o my, -o mous.
a near′.
an′ec dote, -do′tal, -do′tist, -dŏt′ic,
-ic al, -al ly.
an e lec′ tric, -trode, -tro ton′ ic,
-*trot′o nus*.
an el′ y trous.
a ne′mi a or -næ′-, a nem′ic, -ne′-
mĭed, a ne′ma to′sis.
a nem′o chord.
a nem′o gram, -o grăph, -grăph′ic,
an e mog′ra phy, -mol′o gy, -mo-
log′ic al, -mom′c ter, -e try, -mo-
met′ric, -ric al, -mo met′ro grăph,
-graph′ic, a nĕm′o scope.
a nem′o ne *or* a nem′o ny, *pl.* -o nies
(-nēz), an e mon′ic, an e moph′-
i lous, A nem′o ne, *Bot. genus*.
an en ceph′a lus, pl. -*lĭ*, -*ce pha′li c,*
-phal′ic (*or* -sef′a lik), -ceph′a loid,
-a lous, -a ly, -a lo tro′phi a.
a nent′ *or* -nenst′.
an en′te rous.

---

an e pig'ra phous.
an ep i thym'i a.
an'e roid.
an er y throp'si a.
an'e sis.
an es the'si a (or -zhi a) or an æs-,
-si ant, -sis, -thet'ic, -ic al ly, -i za'-
tion, an es'the tize *or* -tise, -tized,
-ti zing, -the tist.
a net'ic.
an'eū rism, -ris'mal (-riz'-), -mal-
ly, -mat'ic, *a neu'ri a.*
a new'.
an frac'tu ose (-ōs), -ous, -ous-
ness, -os'i ty.
aṇ ga'ri a.
aṇ'ge kok (-ge-) *or* -ga- (ang'-).
ăn'gel, ăn gel'ic, -ic al, -al ly, -al-
ness, *ān gel ol'a try, -ol'o gy, -oph'-
a ny,* an' gel hood, an' gel-fish,
-light, -shot, -wa ter, an'gel's-eyes,
-trum'pets.
ăn gel'i ca, An gel'i ca, *Bot. genus.*
-tree, an gel'i co, ăn'ge lin.
An gel'i cals (ăn-).
An gel'i can (ăn-).
ăn gel'i cate.
An gel'i cī (ăn-).
An ge'lique' (ăṅ zhā lēk'), an ge-
lique' (-lēk'), a tree.
an'ge li'to (än hā lē'to).
ăn'gel ize (-jel-).
Ang'eln (äng'-), dist. Prus.
An'ge lo.
ăn'ge lot (-jē-).
ăn'ge lus.
aṇ'ger, -ing, -gered.
An gers' (ŏṅ'zhā'), c. Fr.
An'ge vin *or* -vīne.
an'gi li-wood *or* an'gel y-.
an gi'na (or an'-), an'gi nal, -noid,
-nose (-nōs), -nous.
an'gi o car'pi an, -pous.
an'gi o mon'o sper'mous.
an'gi o neu ro'sis, -rot'ic.
an'gi o pa ral'y sis, -par'e sis.
an'gi o sar co'ma, *pl.* -co'ma ta.
an'gi o scope.
an gi o'sis.
an'gi o spasm.
an'gi o sperm, -sper'mal, -mous,
-ma tous, -os'po rous.
an gi o sto'ma tous, -os'to mous.

an gi ot'o my.
aṇ'gle -gled (-gld), -gling, -gler,
an'gle wise, -worm.
aṇ'gle-bar, -bead, -beam, -bev'el,
-block, -brace, -brack'et, -brick,
-cap'i tal, -chuck, -cock, -dog,
-float, -i ron, -me'ter, -mo dil'-
lion, -plane, -pod, -raft'er, -shades,
-splice, -stäff, -tie, -valve, aṇ'gler-
fish.
Aṇ'gle, *pl.* An'gles.   One of an
early Teutonic tribe, -gli an, -glic.
Aṇ'gli can, -ism, Aṇ'gli can chănt.
An'gli ce (-sē).
Aṇ'gli cize *or* -cise, -cized, -ci zing,
-cism, -ci za'tion.   Frequently,
an'gli cize.
Aṇ'gli fy, -fy ing, -fied, -gli form,
-fi ca'tion.
Aṇ'glo-A mer'i can, -A'sian, -A si-
at'ic, -Cath'o lic, -Ca thol'i cism,
-Chi nese', -Dän'ish, -French,
-In'di an, -I'rish, -Jap a nese',
-Nor'man, -Sax'on, -Sax'on dom,
-Sax on'ic, -Sax'on ism.
Aṇ glo gæ' a (-jē'), -gæ'an.
Aṇ glo ma'ni a, -ma'ni ac, Aṇ'glo-
phobe, -phō'bist, -phō'bi a, -phō'-
bic.
Aṇ go'la cat, A. pea, A. seed, A.
weed.
aṇ'gor.
aṇ go'ra, light wool fabric.
Aṇ go'ra cat, A. goat, A. wool.
Aṇ gos tu' ra (äṇ gŏs tōō'ra), t.
Venez.
aṇ gos tu'ra bark (äng gŏs tōō'ra).
aṇ'gry, -gri ly, -gri ness.
aṇ guic'u læ, -u lar.
Aṇ'gui fer.
aṇ'gui form.
aṇ guil'li form, -guil'lid, -guil'lous.
aṇ guil'lule, -guil'lu lid, -lu loid.
aṇ'guīne, -guin'e al, -e ous.
aṇ'gui ped *or* -pēde.
aṇ'guish (-gwish), -guished.
aṇ'gu lar, -lar ly, -lar ness, -lăr'i ty,
aṇ'gu lose (-lōs), -gu lous, -los'i ty.
aṇ'gu late, -la'ted, -la ting, -late ly,
-la'tion.
aṇ' gu lā' to-gib' bous, -sin' u ous,
an' gu lo-den' tate, aṇ gu lo' so-
gib'bous.

---

fāte, făt, fär, fạll, fâre, făst, sofà, mēte, mĕt, hêr, īce, ĭn, nōte,

aṇ gu lif'er ous.
aṇ'gu li nerved.
aṇ gu lo m'e ter.
aṇ'gu lus, pl. *lī, Anat.*, Aṇ'gu lus.
Zoöl. genus.
aṇ gus'tate, -ta'tion.
aṇ gus'ti clave, -ti fo'li ate, -ti ros'-
trate.
an gwän ti'bo (-tē'-).
an har mon'ic.
an he'dron, *pl.* -drons *or* -dra, -dral.
an he la'tion.
an hĭ dro'sis *or* an i-, -drot'ic.
an'hĭ ma, An'hĭ ma, *Ornith. genus*.
an hiṇ'ga.
an his'tous.
an hy'drate, -dra'tion, -dre'mi a *or*
-dræ-, -drid *or* -drĭde (*or* -drĭde),
-drous.
a'ni (ä'nē).
an i el'lid, -loid.
an'il, a plant, a nĭl'la.
an'Ĭle (*or* -ile), feeble, a nil'i ty.
an'i lĭne, -i lĭde (*or* -lĭde), a nil'i a,
-nil'ic.
an'i ma, pl. *-mæ*, -mal ly.
an'i mad vert', -vert'ed, -vert'ing,
-vert'er, -ver'sive, -sive ness, -ver'-
sion.
an'i mal, -ness, ism, -ist, -is'tic,
-mal'i ty, -i cul'ture, *-mal'cu la*,
-cu læ, -cu lar, -cule, -cu lĭne, -cu-
lism, -cu list, *-cu lum*, pl. *-cu la*,
an'i mal-clutch, -flow er, -trap.
an'i ma liv'o rous.
an'i mal ize, -ized, -i zing, -ī za'tion.
an i mas'tic.
an'i mate, -ness, -ma ted, -ted ly,
-ma ting, -ting ly, -tive, -tor, -ma-
ter, -ma'tion.
an'i me.
an'i min *or* -mĭne.
an'i mism, -mist, -mis'tic.
an i mos'i ty, an'i mose (-mōs), an'-
i mus.
an i rid'i a.
an'Ĭse, -i säte, -i so'ic, a nis'ic, an'i-
seed *or* an'ise-seed, *an i sette'*, an'-
ise-cam phor, -tree.
an'i so co'ri a.
a nĭ so dac'tyl *or* -tyle (-tĭl), -tyl'ic,
-dac'ty lous.
a nĭ'so dŏnt *or* an'i-.

an ĭ sog'na thous.
an ĭ sog'y nous (-soj'-).
a nĭ'so mĕr'ic.
an i som'er ous.
a nĭ'so met'ric (*or* an'-).
a nĭ'so me tro'pi a, -trop'ic.
a nĭ so pet'a lous (*or* an'-), -soph'-
yl lous *or* -so phyl'lous.
a nĭ so pleu'ral, -rous.
a nĭ so pog'o nous.
an ĭ sop'ter ous.
a nĭ so stem'o nous (*or* an'-).
a nĭ so sthen'ic (*or* an'-).
an ĭ sot'ro py, -ro pous, a nĭ'so-
trope, -trop'ic.
an i trog'e nous (-troj'-).
an i u'ma.
an jee'la.
An jou' (ŏṅ'zhoō'), former Fr. prov.
aṇ'ker, -īte.
aṇkh.
aṇ'kle, -klet, -kled (-kld), aṇ'kle-
bone, -boot, -clo'nus, -deep,
-jack, -jerk, -joint, -re'flex, -tie.
aṇ'kus or kush.
aṇ'ky lose (-lōs), -lō'sis, -lot'ic, -lot'-
o mus, -kyl'o tome.
an'laut (än lout).
an'na, a coin; an'na, an animal;
An'na, a proper name.
an'nal, -nals, -nal ist, -is'tic.
An na mese' *or* A nam ese' (*or*
-mēz), An'nam ite *or* A'nam.
an'nat *or* -nate.
an nat'to. See *arnatto*.
an neal' *or* a neal', -er, -ing, -nealed',
an neal'ing-arch, -box, -col'or,
-fur'nace, -lamp, -ov'en, -pot.
an nec'tent.
an'ne lid *or* -lĭde, -lism, -loid, -nel'i-
dan, -nel'i dous, -ne-lid'i an.
an nex', -nexed, -nex ing, -a'tion,
-tion al, -tion ist, an nex', *n.* (*or*
an'-), *pl.* -nex es.
an'ni cut *or* an'i-.
an nĭ'hĭ late, -la ted, -la ting, -tive,
-tor, -to ry, -la ble, -la'tion, -tion-
ism, -tion ist.
an ni ver'sa ry.
an'no da ted.
an'no Dom'i nĭ.
an'no heg'i ræ or *hej'*- (hĕj'ĭ- or hē-
jĭ'-), *a. mun'dĭ, a. ur'bis con'di tæ*.

an nom i na'tion.
an'no tate, -ta ted, -ta ting, -ta tor,
 -ta'tion, -no'ta to ry.
an'no tĭne, -not'i nous.
an not'to. See *arnotto.*
an nounce', -ment, -nounced',
 -noun'cing, -cer.
an noy', -ing, -ing ly, -ing ness,
 -noy'er, -ance, -ment, -noyed'.
an nū aire' (-air').
an'nu al, -al ist, -al ly, -a ry, an nu'-
 i ty, -i tant.
an nul', -nulled', -nul'ling, -ment.
an'nu lar, -lar ly, -la ry, -lăr'i ty,
 an'nu lar gear.
an'nu late, -la ted, -la'tion.
an'nu let.
an'nu lus, pl. *-lī.*
an nun'ci ate (-shĭ- *or* -sĭ-), -a ted,
 -a ting, -a tor, -to ry, -a'tion, an-
 nun ci a'tion li'ly.   An nun ci a'-
 tion, a religious festival.
an'nus de lib er an'dī, a. mĭ rab'i lis.
an o car'pous.
an'o ca thar'tic.
an'ode, -o dal, a nod'ic, an'o don,
 An'o don, *Zoöl. genus.*
an'o dyne, a nod'y nous.
an o ĕ'ma.
an o et'ic.
an o gen'ic.
a noint', -ed, -ing, -er, -ment.
a nom'a list, -a lism, -lis'tic, -tic al,
 -al ly.
a nom'a lo ceph'a lus.
a nom'a lous, -lous ly, -lous ness,
 a nom'a ly.
An o mœ'an *or* -me'an, -me'an ism.
a nŏn'.
a non'y mous, -ly, -ness, -muŋ'cūle,
 an'o nym.
an o'pi a.
an'op sy.
an o rex'i a *or* an'o rex y, -rec'tous,
 -rec'tic.
an or'ga na, -ga nism, -gan'ic, -ga-
 nog'no sy, -nog'ra phy, -ga nol'-
 o gy.
a nor'mal, -mal'i ty.
an or'thic, -or'thīte, -thit'ic.
a nor'tho clase.
an or tho'pi a, -or'tho scope.
a nor'tho sīte.

an os'mi a, -os mat'ic.
an oth'er (-ŭth'-).
a not'ta.   See *arnotto.*
an ox ĕ'mi a *or* -æ'mi a.
an'sa, pl. *-sæ,* an'sāte, -sā ted, -sa'-
 tion.
an'sar, -sa'ri an.
An'ser, -ser a'nas, *An'se res* (-rēz),
 an'se ra ted, -ser ĭne, -ser ous.
an'swer (ăn'- *or* ăn'ser), -er, -ing,
 -ing ly, -a ble, -a ble ness, -a bly,
 -less, -less ly, -swered.
ănt, ănt-bear, -bird, -catch er, -cow,
 -eat er, -egg, -hill, -hil lock, -king,
 -li on, -shrike, -thrush, -tree, -wart,
 -worm, -wren, ant's-wood.
an'ta, pl. *-tæ.*
ant ac'id (-as'sid), -ac'rid.
ant ad'i form.
Antæ'us, *Myth.*
an tag'o nize, -nized, -ni zing,
 -o nism, -o nist, -nis'tic, -tic al,
 -al ly, -ni za'tion.
an'tal.
an tal'gic.
ant al'ka lĭ (*or* -lĭ), -ka lĭne (*or*
 -līne).
ant am bu la'cral.
ant an ac'la sis (*or* -cla'sis).
ant'aph ro dis'i ac (-diz'i ak), *or*
 an ti aph-ro dit'ic.
ant ap o plec'tic.
Ant arc tă'li an.
ant arc'tic.
An ta'res (-rēz).
ant ar thrit'ic *or* an ti ar-.
ant asth mat'ic (-ast- *or* -as- *or*
 -az-).
ant a troph'ic (-trŏf'-).
an'te, -chăm'ber, -chap'el, -choir,
 -church, -com mūn' ion, -cox' al,
 -cur'sor, -curv'a ture, -date, -da-
 ted, -da ting, -dĭ lu'vi al, -vi an,
 -dor'sal, -fix, *pl.* fix es, -flec'ted,
 -flec'tion, -flexed, -grade, -lo ca'-
 tion, *-ju ra men'tum,* -lu'can, -me-
 rid'i an, -mun'dane, -mu'ral, -na'-
 ri al, -na'tal, -nave, -nup'tial, -oc'-
 u lar, -or'bit al, -pag'ment, -pas'-
 chal (-kal), -pec'tus, *-pen'di um,*
 pl. *-di a,* -port, -po si'tion (-zish'-
 un), -pran'di al, -pre dic'a ment,
 -pre ton'ic, -pros'tate, -pros tăt'ic,

---

fāte, făt, fär, fạll, fâre, fạ̈st, sofȧ, mēte, mĕt, hệr, īce, ĭn, nōte,

-ro lat′er al, -room, -ro pa rī′e tal,
-ro pos te′ri or, -ster′num, -stom′-
ach (-stum′ak), -tem′ple, -type,
-vēn′ient, ver′sion, -vert, -vert′ed.
an′te-act, *-nā′tĭ,* -Nĭ′cēne.
*an′te bel′lum, a. lu′cem, a. me rid′i-
em, a. mor′tem.*
⸳**an′te brā′chi al** *or* an tĭ brach′i al
(-brăk′-).
an te cēde′, -cēd′ed, -cēd′ing, -cēd′-
ence, -en cy, -ent, -ent ly, -ces′sor.
an te′cians *or* an tœ′- (-shanz).
an′te lope, -lo pĭne, -lo′pi an.
ant e met′ic.
an ten′na, *pl.* -næ, -ten′nal, -na ry,
-nate, -ni form, -nule, -nu la, *pl.*
-læ, -lar, -la ry, -nif′er ous.
an′te pe nult′ (*or* -pe′nult), -nul′ti-
mate, *-nul′ti ma.*
ant eph ĭ ăl′tic.
ant′ep i lep′tic, -tic al.
an te′ri or, -or ly, -ŏr′i ty.
ant he′li on (*or* an the′- *or* -hēl′-
yun), *pl.* -li a.
ant′he lix (*or* an′the-), *pl.* ant hel-
i ces (ant hel′- *or* an thel′i sēz).
an thel min′tic *or* -thic.
an′the m, -wise.
an the′mi on, pl. *-mi a,* -frieze (-frēz),
-mold ing.
ant′hem or rhag′ic (-răj′-).
an′ther, -al, -ĭd, -oid, -the rid′i al,
-rid′i an, *-t ŭm,* pl. *-i a,* -ther it′-
er ous, -thĕr′i form *or* an′-, -ther-
og′e nous (-oj′), -o zo′id, -zo′oid.
An thes tē′ri on, -te′ri a.
an tho cy′a nin *or* -nĭne, -tho-
cy′an.
an thog′ra phy.
an′thoid.
an thol′o gy, -o gist, *-y sis,* -tho log′-
ic al.
an′tho rism, -ris′mus (-riz′-).
an′thra cĭte, -ci′ tous, -cit′ic, -cif′-
er ous.
an′thra co man′cy.
an thra com′e ter, -co met′ric.
an thrac′o nĭte *or* -o līte.
an′thra pur′pu rin.
an′thrax, *pl.* -thra ces (-sēz), -thra-
coid, -thrac′ic (-thras′-), An′thrax,
Entom.
an′thro po cen′tric.

an′ thro po gen′ e sis, -ge net′ ic,
-gen′ic, -pog′e nist (-poj′-), -e ny.
an′thro po glot.
an thro pog′ra phy.
an′thro poid, -poid′al.
an thro pol′a try.
an throp′o līte, -thro po lith′ic.
an thro pol′o gy, -o gist, -po log′-
ic, -ic al.
an′thro po man′cy.
an thro pom′e try, -e ter, -po met′-
ric, -ric al, -al ly.
An′thro po mor′pha, an′thro po mor′-
phic, -phic al, -al ly, -po mor′-
phism, -mor′ phist, -mor′phous,
-mor′phite, -phit′ic, -ic al, -mor′
phit ism.
an′ thro po mor′ phize, -phized,
-phī zing, -mor phol′o gy, -pho′sis,
-pho the′ist.
an thro pon′o my, -po nom′ic al.
an thro pop′ a thy, -po path′ ic,
-ic al, -al ly, -pop′a thism, -a thīte.
an thro poph′a gus, pl. *-gi* (-jī), -po-
phag′ic (-făj′-), -ic al, -poph a-
gin′i an, -poph′a gism (-jizm),
-a gy, -a gite, -a gous (-gus).
an thro pos′o phy, -o phist, -pot′-
o my, -o mist, -po tom′ic al.
ant hyp not′ic.
ant′hyp o chon′dri ac.
ant hy poph′o ra (*or* an thy-).
ant hys tĕr′ic.
an′ti-. This Greek prefix, signify-
ing *opposed to, against, answering
to, equal to,* and *over against,* is
used with many words. an′ti al-
bu′mate, -bab y lo′ni an ism,
-bac′chic (-kĭk), -bac chī′us, *pl.*
-chī′i, -bac te′ri al, -ba sil′i can
(-zil′-), -bil′ious, -ti bĭ ot′ic, -car-
niv′o rous, -ca tar′rhal, -cau sod′-
ic, -cau sot′ic, -caus′tĭc, -chris′-
tian, -clas′tic, -clī′max, -cli′nal,
-clīne, -con ta′gious, -con vul′sive,
-cor ro′sive (-cĭv), -cos met′ic
(-kŏz-), -cy′ clone, -cy clon′ic, -cy-
clon′ ic al ly, -dac tyl, -dem o-
crat′ ic, -dem o crat′ ic al, -dys-
en tĕr′ic, -dy sū′ric.
an′tĭ fat, -feb′rĭle (*or* -fē′-), -feb′-
rĭne (*or* -fē′-), -fed′er al, -fer′ment,
-fer ment′a tive, -foul′ing, -fric′-

nŏt, nôr, ūse, ŭp, ûrn, etüde, fōōd, fŏŏt, aŋger, boṅmot,· ᵺus, Baᴄh.

9

tion, -ga lac′tic, -he lix, -hem or-
rhag′ic (-răj′-), -hy′lō ist, -hyp-
not′ic, -hyp o chon′dri ac (-kŏn′-),
-hy poph′o ra, -hys těr′ic, -lī bra′-
tion, -lith′ic, -lœ′mic, -log′a rithm
(or -rithm), -log a rith′mic, -lu-
et′ic, -lys′sic, -lyt′ic, -ma nī′a cal,
-ma′son ry, -mes′mer ist (-měz′-),
-mne mon′ic, -mo nar′chic (-kik),
-mo nar′chic al, -mon′arch ist,
-mo nop′o ly, -mo nop′o list, -mŏr′-
al ist, -my cot′ic, -nat′u ral, -neph-
rit′ic.

an tĭ pa′pal, -pa pis′tic al, -pär′-
al lel, -pär′a lyt′ic, -pär′a lyt′ic al,
-par a sit′ic, -pa thet′ic, -pa thet′-
ic al, -pā tri ot′ic (or -păt-), -pe-
duŋ′cu lar, -pep′tone, -pe ri od′ic,
-pes ti len′tial, -pet′a lous, -phlo-
gis′tian (-chan), -phlo gis′tic,
-pho net′ic, -phon′ic, -phon′ic al,
-pho to gen′ic, -phthis′ic, -phys′ic,
-phys′ic al, -poi′son (-zn), -pole,
-pope, -prī′mer, -pru rit′ic, -pu-
tre fac′tive, -pu tres′cent, -ra′cer,
-re mon′ strant, -rent′, -rent′er,
-sab ba ta′ri an, -scrip′tur al,
-slāv′er y, -slāv′er y ism, -so′cial,
-so′cial ist, -so′lar, -spas mod′ic
(-spaz-), -trust, -type, -typ′ic, An′-
ti christ, An ti ma′son, -ma son′-
ic.

an′ti-ac′id, -al bu′mose (-mōs), -an-
ar′chic (-kik), -aph ro dis′i ac
(-dĭz′-), -ar thrit′ic, -asth mat′ic
(-ast- or as- or az-), -at tri′tion,
-e met′ic, -en thu si as′tic (-zi-),
-eph i al′tic, -ep i lep′tic, -e pis′-
co pal, -ev an gel′i cal (or -ē van-),
-gal′li can, -ic těr′ic, -in′crus ta′-
tor, -in duc′tion, -Jac′o bin, -Jac′-
o bin ism, -Le comp′ton, -ma-
chine, -Ne bras′ka, -or gas′tic,
-trade or an′ti trade′, An ti-
Fed er al, -Fed er al ism, -Fed er-
al ist, -Sem′ite, -Sem′it ic, -Sem′i-
tism.

an′ti ar, -ti a rin or -rĭne.
An′ti burgh er.
an′tic, -ness.
an′ti ca chec′tic (-kĕk′-).
an ti car′di um, -di ac.
an tich′thon (-tik′-), pl. *-thō nes* (-nēz).

an tic′i pate (-tis′-), -pa ted, -pa-
ting, -pa tive, -tive ly, -pa tor,
-to′ry, -i pant, -i pa′tion.
an tĭ′cum, pl. *-ca,* -tĭ′coŭs.
An′ti dic o mā′ri an īte.
An ti dor′cas.
an ti do′ron.
an′ ti dōte, -ism, -do′tal, -tal ly,
-do′ta ry, -dot′ic al, -al ly.
an tig′e ny (-tij′-).
An ti gna′na (än teen yä′nä).
An tig′o ne, *Myth.*
An tig′o nus, Maced. gen.
an tig′ŏ rīte.
an′ti grâph, -tig′ra phy.
an ti grop′e lŏs (or -lōz).
An ti′gua (än tē′ga), isl. and prov.
Brit. W. I.
an ti gug′gler.
an′ti le gom′e na.
An til les (än til′lēz or ŏṅ′tēl′),
isl. W. I., -til le′an.
an ti lo′bi um.
an til′o gy, *pl.* -gies (-jĭz), -o gous.
An til′o pe, an til′o pīne.
an′ti ma cas′sar.
an′ti mâsk.
an ti men′si um.
an′ti měre, -měr′ic, an tim′e rism.
an ti me′ri a.
an′ti me tab′o le, -me tath′e sis.
an ti mo′ni al, -mo′ni ate, -ni a′-
ted.
an′ti mon soon′.
an′ti mo ny, -mo nĭde or -nīde,
-mo nīte, -mo nous, -mon′ic, -mo-
nif′er ous, -mo′ni ous, -mo nĭ′u-
ret, -u ret ed or -u ret ted, an′ti-
mo ny-blěnde′, -blōōm′, -fur′nace,
-glânce′.
an′ti node.
an tin′o my, -o mist, -ti no′mi an,
-an ism, -nom′ic, -ic al.
An′ti o chī′a (-kī′a), *Bib.*
An tī′o chis (-kis), *Bib.*
An tī′o chus (-kŭs), King of Syr.,
-ti ŏ′chi an (-kī-), -an ism.
an′ti o dŏnt, -don tal′gic.
an′ti păr′a be′ma, *pl.* -ma ta.
An′ti pasch (-pask).
An tĭp′a ter, *Bib.*
an tip′a thy.
an ti pa′tri arch (-ark).

an′ti pe ris′ta sis, -per i stal′sis, -i stal′-
tic, -i stat′ic.
An tiph′o lus, Shak.
an′ti phon *or* -phŏne, -tiph′o nal,
-nal ly, -o na ry, -o ny, *pl.* -o nies,
-o non, *pl.* -o na. An′ti phon, Gr.
orator.
an tiph′ra sis, -ti phras′tic, -tic al,
-al ly.
an ti plăs′tic.
an′ti pode, *pl.* an tip′o des (-dēz *or*
an′ti podes), an tip′o dal, -o dism,
-o dist, -o de′an, -ti pod′ic, -ic al.
an′ti point.
an′ti prism.
an ti pros′tate, -tat′ic.
an tip to′sis.
an ti py′rin *or* -rĭne, py ret′ic (-pī′-).
an ti qua′ri an, -an ism, -ri um, *pl.*
-ri a, an′ti qua ry.
an′ ti quate, -qua′ ted, -ted ness,
qua′tion, tiq′ui ty (-tĭk′-).
an tique′ (-teek′), -ly, -ness, -tiqued′
(-teekt).
an ti rab′ic.
an′ti scŏr bu′tic, -tic al.
an ti sep′a lous.
an ti sep′sis, -sep′tic, -tic al ly, -sep′-
ti cist, -sep′ti cize, -cized, ci zing,
-sep′tion.
an′ti spast, -spas′tic.
an ti sple net′ic *or* -splen′e tic.
an tis′ta sis.
An tis′the nes (-nēz), Gr. philos.
an tis′tro phe, -tro phal, -ti stroph′ic,
-ic al ly.
an tis′tro phon.
an ti stru′mous, -mat′ic.
an′ti syph i lit′ic.
an tith′e sis, -ti thet′ic, -ic al, -al ly.
an′ti trin i ta′ri an, -ism.
an′ti type, -ty′ pal, -typ′ic, -ic al,
-al ly, an tit′y py.
an′ti vac ci na′tion ist, -vac′cin ist.
an′ti va rī′o lous.
an ti ve′lum, *pl.* -la, -ve′lar.
an ti zym′ic, -zy mot′ic (-zī-).
ant′ler, -lered, ant′ler-moth.
ant oc′u lar.
an′to no ma′si a (-mā′zhĬ a), -mas′-
tic, -tic al, -al ly
an′to nym.
ant or′bi tal.

An to si an′dri an.
an trorse′, -trorse′ly, -tror′si form.
an′trum, pl. *-tra,* -tral.
an trus′ti on, -ship.
A nu′bis, an Egyptian deity.   a nū′-
bis, a baboon.
A nu′ra or *-nou′ra,* a nu′ran.
a nu′ri a, an u re′sis, -ret′ic, a nu′-
rous, an′u ry.
a′nus.   A′nus, *Bib.*
an′vil, an′vil-block, -cup′per, -dross,
-vīse (-vĭs).
anx i′ e ty (ang zī′ e ty), anx′ious
(ank′shus), -ious ly, -ious ness.
a′ny (ĕ′ny), -bod′y, -how, -thing,
-way, -ways, -where, -whith er,
-wise, a′ny one, -thing a′ri an,
-thing a′ri an ism.
A o′ni an (ā ō′-).
ā′o rist, -ris′tic, -tic al ly.
â ôr′ta, *pl.* -tæ, -tal, -tic, -tī′tis.
â us′mic.
A os′ta (ä ōs′tä), t. It.
a′ou dad (ä′ōō dăd).
a′oul (ä′ōōl).
à ou trance′ (ä ōō trŏns′).
a pace′.
A pa′ che (ä pä′ chä), *pl.* -ches
(-chäz), A pä′ chĕ, co. Ariz,
A pach′e-plume (*or* ä pä′chä-).
a pa e si (ä pä ā′zē)
ap a go′ ge (-jē), -gog′ic (-gŏj′-),
-ic al.
a pan′thro py.
ap′ar *or* ap′a ra.
a pa re′jo (ä pä rā′hō).
ap a rith me′sis.
a part′, -ment, -men′tal, -ness,
a part′ment-house.
a par′te an′te.
a par′te post.
ap ar thro′sis, -thro′di al.
ap as′tron.
ap′a tet′ ic.
ap′a thy, -thist, -thet′ic,   -ic al,
-al ly.
ap′a tite.
Ap a tu′ri a.
ape, -dom, -hood, -let, aped, āp′ing,
-ish, -ish ly, -ish ness, -er, -er y,
ape′ -bab oon′, -man, apes′- on-
horse′back, a plant.
a pĕak′.

A pel'les (-lēz), Gr. painter; *Bib.*
a pel'lous.
Ap e man'tus, Shak.
Ap'en nīne.
a pep'si a *or* a pep'sy.
a per çu' (å'pâr'so͞o').
ap e re'a.
a pe'ri ent, a pĕr'i tive.
a pe'ri od'ic.
a pĕr'i sper'mic, -sper'mous.
ap er tom'e ter.
ap'er ture.
a pet'a lous, -ness.
ā'pex, *pl.* a'pex ĕs *or* ap'i ces (-sēz),
-beat.
a pha'gi a.
aph'a nīte, -nit'ic, -nis'tic, a phan'i-
tism.
aph a noz'y gous.
aph a ryn'ge al.
a pha'si a (-zhi a), a phā'sic (-zik),
-si ac (-zi ak).
aph e lex'i a.
a phe'li on (*or* -fēl'yun), *pl.* -li a,
-li an.
a phe'li o trop'ic, -ic al ly, -ot'ro-
pism.
a phe'mi a, -phĕm'ic.
a phen'ge scope (-je-).
a phĕr'e sis *or* -phær'-, aph e ret'ic,
-ic al ly.
aph'e sis.
aph'e ta, a phet'ic, -ic al, -al ly, aph'-
e tize, -tized, -tī zing, -tism.
A phi'ah, *Bib.*
aph'id, aph'i did, a phid'i an, -i ous,
aph i diph'a gous (-dif'-), -i div'-
o rous, a'phis-fly, -li'on, -su gar.
aph lo gis'tic.
a pho' nia, -phon'ic, aph' o nous,
-o ny.
a pho'ri a.
aph'o rism, -o rist, -ris'tic, -tic al,
-al ly, aph'o ris mat'ic (-riz-),
-ris'mic, aph'o rīze, -rized, -rī zing.
A ph ro dī'te, Myth. As a variety of
meerschaum, and as a chemical
term, it is notcapitalized. Aph ro-
dis'i a (-dīz'-), *Myth.,* aph ro-
dis'i a, *Med.,* -i ac, -i an, -dī'tous.
aph thar'to do ce'tæ, -ce'tism.
aph'thong, -thon'gal.
a phyl'lŏŭs (*or* ăf'il-).

A'pi a (ä'pē a), harbor Samoa.
a pi a ce're (ä pē ä chä'rā).
a'pi a ry, -a rist, -pi cul ture, -tur ist,
-pi ol'o gy, -o gist, a'pi an, a pi a'-
ri an, a piv'o rous.
ăp'i cal, -cal ly, -ca ted, ap i cil'la ry.
A pi'cian (-pish'an).
a pic'u late, -la ted, *-u lus,* pl. *-u lī.*
a piĕce'.
a pil'a ry.
ap'i noid.
ap'i oid.
ap'i ol (*or* ā'pĭ-).
A'pis, *Egypt. Myth.; Entom. genus,*
Ap'i dæ.
a pish'a more.
a pla'si a (*or* -zhi a), -plas'tic.
a pla tis seur' (-tē ser').
ap'līte.
a' plomb' (å plŏṅ').
ap lus'trē (*or* -ter).
a pob'a tes (-tēz), pl. *-tæ.*
ap'o blâst.
a poc'a lypse, -lyp'tist, -tic, -tic al,
-al ly, -ti cism.
ap o car'pous.
ap'o ca tas'ta sis.
ap o chro mat'ic, -chro'ma tism.
a poc'o pate, -pa ted, -pa'tion.
a poc'o pe, A *poc'o pe,* Zoöl. genus.
ap o cren'ic.
A poc're ŏs.
ap o cris'i a ry *or* a poc'ri sa ry.
a poc'ry pha. As a collection of the
fourteen books subjoined to the
Old Testament it is capitalized.
-ry phal, -phal ist, -phal ly, -phal-
ness.
ap'ŏd *or* -ōde, -o dal, -o dan, -o dous.
ap o dĭc'tic *or* -deīc'tic, -tic al, -al ly,
ap o dix'is.
a pod'o sis.
ap'o dy te' ri um (*or* a pŏd'y-), pl.
-te'ri a.
a pog'a my, -a mous, -mous ly, ap o-
gam'ic.
ap'o gee (-jē), -ge'al, -ge'an, -ge'-
ic.
ap'o ge o trop'ic, -ge ot'ro pism.
ap'o grâph.
ap'o jove.
a po'lar.
ap o lạus'tic.

A pol′lo, -pol′line, -li′no (-lē′no),
-li na′ri aṇ, -an ism, -na′rist, Ap-
ol lo′ni aṇ, -lin′ic, -lon′ic.
A pŏll′yon (*or* a pol′ly on).
ap′o logue.
a pol′o gy, -o gist, -o gīze, -gized,
-gi zing, -gi zer, -get′ic, -ic al,
-al ly, -get′ics.
ap′o me com′e try, -com′e ter.
ap o neū rŏ′sis, -rŏt′ic, -rot′o my.
ap o pemp′tic.
ap o phan′tic.
a poph′a sis.
a poph′y ge.
a poph′y sis, pl. *y ses* (-sēz), -y sa′ry,
-y sate, ap o phys′i al (-fĭz′).
ap′o plex y, -plec′tic, -tic al, -plec′-
ti form.
a po′ri a, pl. *-ri æ.*
Ap o ro′sa, ap′o rose (-rōs).
a port′.
ap′o sī o pe′sis, -pet′ic.
ap o sit′i a, -sit′ic.
a pos′ta sy, -tate, -ta tize, -tized,
-ti zing, ap′o stat′ic al.
a pos te ri ō′rī.
a pos′tĭl *or* -tĭlle.
a pos′tle (-pos′l), -ship, -to late,
ap os tol′ic, -ic al, -al ly, -al ness,
-tol′I cĭsm, -to lic′ĭ ty, apostle-
mug, -spoon.
Ap os to′li an, A pos′tu lĭne.
a pos′tro phe, -tro phīze, -phized,
-phi zing, ap o stroph′ic *or* -os-
troph′ic.
Ap o tac′tite, -tac′tic.
a poth′e ca ry.
ap′o thegm (-thĕm), -theg mat′ic,
-ic al, -theg′ma tize, -tized, -ti zing,
-ma tist.
ap′o thĕm *or* -thēme, a poth′e ma.
ap o the′o sis, *pl.* -ses (-sēz), -the′o-
size, -sized, -si zing.
a poth′e sis.
a pot′o me, -o my.
ap′o tro pa′ion (-pa′yŏn), pl. *-pa′ia*
(-ya).
a pox y om′e nos, pl. *-om′e noi.*
ap pạl′ *or* -pạll′, -palled, -pall ing,
-ing ly.
Ap pa la′chi an (*or* -lăch′i an).
ap′pa nāge *or* ap′pen age.
ap pa rā′tus. This form is gener-

ally used for both numbers;
rarely apparatuses.
ap păr′el, -par′eled *or* -elled, -el ing
or -el ling.
ap pâr′ent, -ent ly, -ent ness.
ap pa ri′tion (-rish′un), -tion al.
ap păr′i tor.
ap pau mée′ (ȧ′po mā′).
ap peal′, -ing ly, -ing ness, -a ble,
-peal′er, -pealed′.
ap pear′, -ing, -ance, -peared′.
ap pease′, -ment, -peased′, -peas′-
ing, -er, -ive, -peas′a ble, -a ble-
ness.
ap pel′ (*or* ȧ pāl′).
ap pel′la ble, -lan cy, -lant, -late,
-la tive, -tive ly, -tive ness, -la to ry,
-la bil′i ty, -la′tion, -pel′lor *or* -lor′,
ap pel lee′.
ap pend′, -ed, -ing, -age, -aged,
-ance, -ant.
ap pen′dix, *pl.* -dix es *or* -dĭ ces
(-sēz), -pen dĭ ci′tis.
ap pen′tĭce.
ap per ceive′, -ceived′, -cep′tive,
-cep′tion.
ap per tain′, -ing, -tained′.
ap′pe tence, -ten cy, -tent.
ap′pe tĭtc, -tĭ ble, -tĭ bil′i ty, -pet′-
i tive (*or* ap′pe tī′tĭve), ap′pe tize,
-tized, -ti zing, -ti zer.
Ap′phi a (ăf′fĭ a), *Bib.*
Ap′phus (ăf′fŭs), *Bib.*
Ap′pi an.
ap′pla nate.
ap plaud′, -ed, -ing, -er, ap plause′,
-plau′sĭve.
ap′ple, -ber′ry, -jack, -bud, -cor er,
-cur cu′li o, -green, -head ed,
-john, -mint, -moth, -pâr er, -pie,
a plant, -pulp, -scoop, -seed,
-shell, -snail, -tree, ap′ple bran dy,
a. but ter, a. pie, a pic.
ap pli que′ (ăp′lē′kā′).
ap ply′, -ing, -pli′ance, -er, -plied′,
ap′pli ca ble, -ble ness, -bly, -bil′-
i ty, ap′pli ca′tive, -ca tor, -cant,
-ca′tion.
ap pog gia′to (ȧ pod jä′to), *ap pog-
gia tu′ra* (ȧ pod jä tōō′rä).
ap point′, -ed, -ing, -a ble, -er, -ive,
-ment, -point ee′, -point or′ (*or*
-poin′tor).

ap poin té' (å poin tä').
Ap'po mat'tox, r. and co. Va.
Ap po quin'i mink, tp. Del.
ap por'tion, -ing, -er, -ment, -tioned.
ap pose', -pōs'ing, -pos'a ble, -posed.
ap'po site (-zĭt), -site ly, -site ness,
   -si'tion (-zish'un), -tion al, -al ly,
   -pos'i tive.
ap pos i to'ri um.
ap praise', -ment, -praised, -prais'-
   ing, -al, -er.
ap pre'ci ate (-shĭ āte), -a'ted,
   -a ting, -ting ly, -a tive', -tive-
   ness, -a'tor, -to'ry, -to'ri ly, -ci a-
   ble, -ci ant, -ci a'tion.
ap pred'i cate.
ap pre hend', -ed, -ing -hen'si ble,
   -si-bil'i ty, -hen'sion, -sive, -sive ly,
   sive ness.
appren'tĭce, -ticed, -ti cing, -tice-
   ship, ap pren'tice-box.
ap pressed'.
ap prê teur (å prä ter').
ap prise' (-prīz'), to inform, -prised',
   -pris'ing.
ap prize', to value, -prized, -priz'ing,
   -priz'er, -prize'ment.
ap proach', -ing, -er, -less, -a ble,
   -a ble ness, -a bil'i ty, -proached'.
ap'probate, -ba ted, -ba ting, -ba'-
   tive, -tive ness, -ba tor, -to ry,
   -ba'tion.
ap pro'pri ate, -a ted, -a ting, -ate-
   ly, -ate ness, -a tive, -tive ness,
   -a tor, -a'tion.
ap prove', -ment, -proved, -prov'-
   ing, -ing ly, -al, -a ble, -a ble ness,
   -ed ly, -er.
ap prox'i mate, -ma ted, -ma ting,
   -mate ly, -ma tive, -tive ly, -tive-
   ness, -ma tor, -ma'tion.
ap pui' or *-puy'* (åp pwē'), *point
d'appui'* (pwän dap pwē').
ap'pŭlse (*or* -pulse'), -pul'sion, -sive,
   -sive ly.
ap pur'te nance, -nant.
a prax'i a.
a'pri cot.
A'pril.
ā prĭ o'rĭ (*or* -prī-), -o'rism, -o'rist,
   -rist'ic, -ŏr'i ty.
a'pron (-prŭn *or* -purn), -lĭn'ing,
   -man, -piece, -roll, -string.

ap ro pos (ap rō pō' *or* ap'-).
ap'ro sex'i a.
ap ro tĕr'o dŏnt.
aps, white-poplar wood.
apse, a recess, ap'si dal, -dal ly,
   -sid'i ole, apse'-aisle, -chapel.
ap' sis, pl. *-si des* (-dēz).
apt, -ly, -ness. Apt (äpt), t. Fr.
ap'ter al, -ter an.
ap te'ri um, pl. *-ri a,* -ri al, ap'ter ous,
   -ter oid.
ap'ti tude, -tu'di nal, -nal ly.
ap to so chro'ma tism.
ap'tŏte, -tot'ic.
ap ty'a lism.
ap'ty chus (-kus), pl. *-chi* (-kī).
A pu'li a (a pōō'le a), dept. It.,
   -pu'li an.
ap y rex'i a, -rex'i al, -ret'ic, ap'y-
   rex y.
a py'ro type.
a py'rous.
ā'qua, -ma rine' (-reen'), -punc'ture,
   -pult, -tint, -tin'ta, -tint'er, -tint'-
   ing, a'que ous, -ous ness, *ăq ua-
relle',* -rel'list, a'qua-me'ter, *a qua
am mo'ni æ, a. for'tis, a. ma rī na,
a. re'gi a, a. vi'tæ,* a. To fä'na.
ā'quăge.
ā'qua ma nĭ'le, ā quæ ma nā'l·, pl.
   -li a.
a qua'ri um, *pl.* -ri ums *or* -ri a,
   -ri al, -ri an, A qua'ri us, ā'qua-
   ri cul'ture.
a quar'ter (-kwôr').
a quar ti e'ri (ä kwär tē ā'rĭ).
a quăt'ic, -ic al.
ā' qua vi va'ri um, pl. *ri a.*
aq'ue duct.
ā'qui cul ture, -cul' tur al.
A'qui fo'li ā'ce æ, a'qui fo li a'ceous.
ā'qui form, -quif'er ous.
Aq'ui la (ăk'wĭ la), Translator of
   Old Testament.
A'qui la (ä'kwe lä), Ger. theol.;
   prov. and c. It.
Aq'ui la, Ornith.; Astron. aq'ui la, a
   reading desk.
A quĭl'nas, It. schol.
Aq ui tä'ni an.
a quom'e ter.
a quos'i ty.
A'ra (ā'ra).

Ar'ab (ăr'ab).
a rä'ba or ar'ba, a Turkish wagon.
ăr'a ba, a kind of monkey.
ăr'a besque' (-besk').
A ra'bi a, -bi an, Ar'a bic, -a bize,
-bist, -bism, A rab'i cize, -cized,
-ci zing, ar'a bic, Bot.
ä'rab'ji' (-jě').
ăr'a ble, -bil'i ty.
ar a caŋ'ga or ar'a ra caŋ'ga.
ar a cä'ri (or ä rä cä'rĕ).
A rach'ne (-rak'-), Myth.
A rach'ni da, a rach'nid, -ni dan.
a rach'noid, -noid'al, -noi'de an.
ar'ach nol'o gy, -o gist, -no log'-
ic al.
a rä'do.
är'a go disk.
Ar'a gon (ăr'-), Sp., -go nese' (or
-nēz').
A ra'gua (ä rä'gwa), t. Venez.
ăr a gua'to (or ä rä-).
A ra guay' (ä rä gwi'), r. Braz.
a rai gnée' (å rä nyä').
a rake'.
ar'a kĭ.
Ar a mä'ic, -me'an or -mæ'an, -an-
ism.
Ar'ä mism.
a ra ne ol'o gy, -o gist.
a ra'ne ose (-ōs), -ne ous.
a raŋ'ga.
a raŋ'go, pl. -goes.
A rap'a hŏe, pl. -hoes (-hōz).
a ra paï'ma.
ar a puŋ'ga.
ä rä'rä.
ar'a ram bo'ya.
Ar'a rat (ăr'-), Bib.
ar a rau'na.
ar a ro'ba.
är'ar-tree.
a rä'trum ter'ræ.
Ar au ca'ni an, A rau'can.
a rä'u ha (-ōō ä).
A ray'at (ä rī'ät), t. Luzon, P. I.
ar bac'cio (är bäch'yo).
ar'ba list or -lest, -list er or
-lest-.
ar'bi ter, -bi tress, -bi trage, -tra ger,
-bi tral, -bit'ra ment, ar bi tra-
geur' (-zhêr').
ar'bi tra ry, -ri ly, -ri ness.

ar'bi trate, -tra'ted, -tra ting, -tra'-
tive, -tra tor, -tor ship, -tra trix,
pl. -tra trī'ces (-sēz), -tra'tion,
-tra'tion al.
ar'bor, -bored, -bo're al, -re ous,
-bo ra'ceous, -bo resce' (-res'),
-resced (-rest), -res'cing, -cent,
-cence, ar'bo ret, -re'tum, ar'bor-
chuck, -day, -vine, -vi'tæ or arbor vi'tæ.
ar'bor ize, -ized, -i zing, -i form,
-i za'tion, -bor ist, -bŏr'i cole, -bo-
ric'o lous, -ric'o lĭne, -bor i cul'-
ture, -cul'tur al, -tur ist, ar'bor-
ol'a try.
ar'brĭ er.
ar'bus cle, -bus'cu lar, -bus'cule.
ar bus'tum, pl. -tums or -ta.
ar'bu tin.
ar bu'tus, -bu'te an, ar'bute, Ar bu'-
tus (or ar'bu-), Bot. genus.
Arc, Jeanne d' (zhän därk), Joan of
Arc.
arc, -ta'tion, arc-co se'cant, -co'sīne,
-co tan'gent, -light, -piece, -se-
cant, -sine, -tan'gent.
ar'ca, pl. ar'cæ (-sē), Ar'ca, Zoöl.
genus.
ar ca bu ce'ro (är'kä lxx) thä'rō).
ar cade', -cad'ed.
Ar ca'di an, -an ism, -ca'dic.
ar ca'num, pl. -ca'na.
ar'ca ture.
Ar ce'vi a (ar chä'vē a), t. It.
arch, -ly, -ing, -ness, arched.
arch'ab'bot, -bish'op, -bish'op ric,
-but'ler, -cham'ber lain, -chan'cel-
lor, -chap'lain, -count, -dap'i fer,
-dea'con, -dea'con ate, -dea'con-
ry, -dea'con ship, -dean', -dean'-
er y, -di'o cēse, -dru'id, -du'cal,
-duch'ess, -duch'y, -duke, -duke'-
dom, -lutc, -ma gi'cian, -mar'shal,
-pil'lar, -po'et, -pol i ti'cian (-tish'-
an), -prel'ate, -pres'by ter (-prĕz'-),
-priest', -pri'mate, -proph'et,
-prot' es tant, -pro'to pope, -trai'-
tor, -treas'ur er, -type, -vil'lain,
-vil'lain y, -way, -wise, Arch-
ar'chi tect.
arch'-a pos'tate, -a pos'tle, -band
or arch'band, -bar, -board, -brick
or a. brick, -but' tress, -con'fra-

ter'ni ty, -en'e my, -mold'ing, -see, -so dal'i ty, -stone.
ar chæ'an (ke'-).
ar chæ og'ra phy (-ke-), -o graph'-ic al.
ar chæ ol'o gy *or* ar che- (-ke-), -o gist, -o lo'gi an, -o log'ic, -ic al, -al ly, ar'chæ o logue.
ar cha'ic (-ka'-), -ic al, -al ly, -i cism, ar'chä ism, -ist, -is'tic, -ize, -ized, -i zer, -i zing.
ar cham'phĭ as'ter (-kam'fi-).
arch'ăn'gel (ark'-), -ăn gel'ic.
ar chĕ' (ar shä').
Ar'che lä'us (-ke-), *Bib.*
ar'che o zo'ic (-kē-).
arch'er, -er ship, -er y, arch'er-fish.
ar'che spore (-ke-).
ar ches thet'ic (-kes-), -thet'i cism *or* -ches'the tism (-kes-).
ar chet'to (-ket'-).
ar'che type (-ke-), -ty pal, -ty pist, -typ'ic, -ic al, -al ly.
ar'chi am'phi as'ter (-ki-).
ar chi ä'ter (-kĭ-).
ar'chi blăst (-kĭ-), -blăs'tic, *-blas'-tu la*, pl. *-tu læ.*
ar'chi dĭ ac'o nate, -o nal.
ar'chi e pis'co pa cy (-kĭ-), -co-pate, -co pal, -co pal'i ty.
ar chi'e rey (-kĭ'e ry).
ar chi gen'e sis (-ki jen'-).
ar'chil (-kil). Sometimes or'chal *or* or'chil.
Ar chil'o chus (-kil'o kus), Gr. poet, -chi lo'chi an (-kĭ lŏ'kĭ-).
ar'chi mäge (-kĭ-), *-ma'gus*, pl. *-gi* (-jĭ).
Ar chi mä'go (-kĭ-), Spenser.
ar chi man'drĭte (-ki-), -dri täte.
Ar'chi me'des (-dēz), Gr. math., -me'de an (*or* -me de'an).
ar chi pel'a go (-kĭ-), -pe la'gi an, -pe lag'ic (-lăj'-).
ar chip'pus (-kip'-), a butterfly. Ar chip'pus, *Bib.*
ar'chi tect (-kĭ-), -tec tive, -tec-ton'ic, -ic al, -al ly, -ton'ics.
ar'chi tec ture (-tec'tur al, -al ly, -al ist.
ar chi ton nerre' (ar shi ton ner'-).
ar'chi trave (-ki-), -traved.
ar'chi ty pog'ra pher (-kĭ tĭ-).

ar'chive (-kĭv), -chī'val (*or* ar'kĭ-), ar'chĭ vist, -vŏlt.
ar chol'o gy (-kol'-).
ar'chon (-kon), -ship, -tate, -chon'-tic.
arch'y, -flect ed.
ar'cĭ form, -ci fin'i ous.
Ar cīte' (*or* Ar'-), Chaucer.
arc'o grâph (*or* ar'co-).
ar co so'li um, *pl.* -li a.
Arc ta mer'i ca, -i can.
Arc'tic (ark'tik), -ti'cian (-tish'an), arc'tic-bird, arc'tic grăss.
Arc'tos.
Arc tu'rus.
ar'cu ate, -a ted, -ate ly, -cu al, -a'tion.
ar'cu lum, pl. *-la.*
ar'cus.
ar'dash, *ar das sine'* (-sēn').
ar'deb.
Ar dennes' (ar'den'), dept. Fr.
ar'dent, -ly, -ness, -den cy.
ar dil'la (-dēl'ya).
ar'dish.
Ard'ĭtes, *Bib.*
ard'luke.
ard maer' (-mèr').
ar dois' sys'tem (ar'dwä').
ar'dor.
ar drigh' (-drĕ').
ar'du ous, -ly, -ness.
are (är). From the verb *to be.* are (air *or* är). A term used in metric system. a-re (ä'rä'). A musical term.
a're a, *pl.* -as, -re al, a're a-sneak.
ăr'e ca, -nut. *Ar'e ca* (*or* -rē'-), *Bot. genus.*
a re'na.
ăr e na'ceous (-shus), ăr e na'ce o-cal ca're ous.
ăr e na'tion, -na'ri ous, ăr'e na-ted.
a ren'da lĭte.
a reng' or *a reṇ'ga*, A reṇ'ga, *Bot. genus.*
ăr'e nose (-nōs), -e nous.
ä're o cen'tric, -o graph'ic, -og'ra-phy, -ol'o gy.
a re'o la, *pl.* -o læ, -o lar, -o late, -la ted, -la'tion, ăr'e ōle (*or* ä're-), a re'o let (*or* ăr'e o let).

a're om'e try (*or* ăr e-), -e ter,
-o met'ric, -ric al.
Ar e op'a gus, -op'a gist (*or* -jist),
-a gite (*or* -jīt), ar e op a git'ic
(*or* -jit'-).
ä re'o style, a re'o sys'tyle.
A re qui'pa   (ä rä ke̅'pa),   dept.
Peru.
A'res (-rēz), *Myth.*
ăr e ta'ics.
Ar'e tas (ăr'-), *Bib.*
a rête' (a räte').
A re thu' sa, *Myth.*
a re ti cel'li (ä rä te chel'lē).
Ar'e tĭne, -tin ist, -tin'i an.
A rez'zo (ä ret'sō), prov. It.
arf'ved son ĭte (ar'ved-).
ar'gal, ar'ga lĭ, a sheep.
ar'ga la, a bird.
Ar ga li'a (-lē'a), Bojardo.
Ar gän', Molière.
ar'gan-oil, -tree.
Ar'gand lamp.
Ar gän'tĕs, Tasso.
Ar ge'an.
ar'gel or *-ghel.*
ar'ge ma (-je-), *pl.* -gem'a ta, Ar'-
ge ma, *Zoöl. genus.*
ar'gent, -gen tan, gen tate, -gen-
tĭne, -gen tĭte, -gen'tal, -gen'tic,
-gen'tous, -tif'er ous, -gen ta'tion.
Ar gen teuil' (ar'zhŏṅ'twēl'), t. Fr.;
co. Quebec.
ar gen'te us, *pl.* -te ĭ.
Ar gen ti e'ra (ar jen tē ä'ra), isl. in
Ægean Sea.
ar gen til'la.
ar gen tī'na, ar gen'ti nid, -ti noid,
Ar gen tī'na, *Ichth. genus.*
ar gen'to type.
ar gen'tum, -gen to bis'mu tĭte
(-biz'-), ar gen tom'e ter.
ar gho̅o̅l'.
ar'gil (-jil), -gil la'ceous, -gil lif'er-
ous, ar'gil līte, -lit'ic, -gil'lo, -lo ar-
e na'ceous, -lo cal ca're ous, -cal'-
cīte, -lo fer ru'gi nous, -gil'loid,
-gil'lous.
Ar'gĭve (-gĭv).
Ar'go, Myth. and *Astron.* ar'go,
Zoöl.
ar'gol.
Ar'go lis, t. Gr., -gol'ic.

Ar'go naut, *Myth.,* -naut'ic, -nau'-
tid. ar'go naut, a cuttlefish.
ar'go sy, *pl.* -sies (-siz).
ar got (ar'go *or* ar'got *or* ar gō').
ar'gue, -gūed, -gu ing, -gu a ble,
-gu er.
ar'gu ment, -men'tal, -men'ta tive,
-tive ly, -tive ness, -ta'tion.
ar gu men'tum, pl. *-ta.*
Ar'gus, Myth.; Ornith. genus, -eyed,
ar'gus-pheas'ant (-fĕz-), -shell.
ar gute', -ly, -gute'ness.
Ar gyll' (-gīl'), t. N. Y.
ar hap'e dan.
Ar'hat, -han, ar'hat ship.
a rhi'zal, -zous, a rhyth'mic (-rith'-
mik).
a'ri a (ä'rĭ a *or* ä'-), *ä ri et'ta,*
ŏ ri ette'.
Ar i ad'ne (*or* ä rĭ-), *Myth.*
A'ri an, pertaining to Arius, -an ĭsm,
-an ize, -ized, -i zing, -ĭ zer.
Ar'i ca bark.
ăr'id, -ness, a rid'i ty.
ar'i das.
a ridge'.
A'ri el, a spirit; Shak.; *Myth.* a'ri el,
Ornith.; Zoöl.
A'ri es (-ēz), Astron., ar i et'i form,
ar'i e tĭne.
a right'.
Ar'i masp, *Myth.,* -mas'pi an.
A ri'on, *Myth.*
a ri o'so (ä re-), ăr'ĭ ose (-ōs).
A ri os'to (ä rē os'to), It. poet.
a rise' (-rīz'), a rose', a ris'ing,
a rĭs'en.
ar'ish.
Ar is tar'chus (-kus), Gr. gram.
ar'is tarch (-tark), tar'chy, -tar'-
chi an.
a ris'tate *or* -ris'tu late.
Ar is tī'des (dēz), Gr. statesman.
Ar is tip'pus, Gr. philos.
Ar'is to bŭ'lus, *Bib.*
ar is toc'ra cy, a ris'to crat (*or* ar'-
is-), ar'is to crat'ic, -ic al, -al ly,
-al ness, ar'is to crat'ism (*or*
ar is toc'ra tism), -toc'ra tize,
-tized, -ti zing, ar'is to de moc'-
ra cy, -to dem o crat'ic al.
ar is tol'o gy, -o gist, -to log'ic al.
Ar'is toph'a nes (-nēz), Gr. comic

poet; -to phan'ic, ar is to phan'ic,
Gram.
Ar'is tot le, Gr. philos., -to te'li an
(*or* -tĕl'ian) *or* -tot e le'an, -te'li
an ism, -tĕl'ic.
a ris'to type, a ris'to pa per.
a ris'tu late.
ar'ith man cy, -man'ti cal, a rith'-
mo man cy.
a rith'me tic, ăr'ith met'ic al, -al ly,
-mom'e ter, a rith'mo grăph, -me
ti'cian, a rith'mo-pla nim'e ter,
ar ith met'i co-ge o met'ric al.
à ri tor'te (ä rē-).
A rī'us (*or* ä'rĭ), Gr. patriarch.
ark, -net, -shell.
Ar kan sas (ar'kan saw *or* ar kan'-
zas), one of U. S.; co. in Ark.
Ar kan'sas (-zas), mt. and r.
U. S.
ar'kan sĭte (*or* -kan'-).
ar kose' (-kōs) *or* -cose'.
ark'su tĭte.
arles (ärlz).
ar'li e nan'se (är'li ä nän'sā).
arm, -ing, -ful, -chair, -hole, -less,
-let, -er, -pit, armed, ar mif'er ous,
arm'-band, -board, -bone, -chest,
-guards, -rack, -rest, -saw, -scye
(-sī), -sling, -span, -sweep, arm's-
end, -length, -reach.
arm'ing-buc'kle, -doub'let, -point,
-press, -spear, -sword.
ar mă'da (*or* -mä'-).
ar ma dil'lo, *pl.* -los (-lōz).
ar'ma ment.
ar'ma ture.
Ar me'ni an, Ar me'no-Turk'ish.
armes' par lantes' (arm'par'länt').
ar'met.
arm'iak (-yak).
Ar mi'da (-mē'-), Tasso.
ar'mi ger, -mig'er al (-mij-), *-mig'-
e ro,* -mig'er ous.
ar'mil.
ar mi lau'sa.
ar mil'la, pl. *-las* or *-læ,* ar'mil la ry,
-mil late, -la ted.
Ar min'i an, -an ism, -an ize, -ized,
-i zing.
ar'mis tice (-tis).
ar moire' (-mwŏr').
ar'mor, -mored, -mor er, -mor y,

pl. -ies, -mo ried, -mor ist, -mo'-
ri al, ar'mor clad, *n.*, ar'mor-
beâr'er, -clad, *a.*, -grāt ing,
-plate, -plāt'ed, -shelf.
ar mo zeen' *or* -zine' (-zēn').
Arm'strong gun.
ar'mure.
ar'my, -cloth, -corps (-kōr), -list,
-worm.
arn.
ar'na.
ar nat'to *or* -nŏt'to.
Ar naut' (-nout').
ar'nee or *ar'ni* (-nē).
ar'ni ca, ar'ni cin *or* -cĭne, Ar'ni ca,
Bot. genus.
ar nil'lo.
Ar nolph', Molière.
ar'nŭt *or* ar'nŏt.
a ro'ba.
ăr o ei'ra (-ā'ra).
Ar'o er (ăr'-), *or* A ro'er (ă-), *Bib.*
a ro'li um, *pl.* -a.
a rol'la.
a ro'ma, *pl.* -mas (-maz), ar o-
mat'ic, -ic al, -al ly, a ro'ma tĭte,
-ma tize, -tized, -ti zing, -ti zer,
-ma tous, -ma ti za'tion.
A rōōs'took, r. and co. Me.
ä ro tel'le.
a round'.
a rouse' (-rouz'), -roused', rous'ing,
-rous'al.
ar peg'gio (är ped'jo), -gi a'tion.
ar'pent.
ar'que bus *or* -buse (-bus), -bus-
ade', -bus ier' (-ēr').
ar'qui foux (-kĭ fōō).
ar ra cach'a (ăr a catch'a).
ar ra ché' (ar ra shā').
ar'rack.
ar'rah.
ar raign', -ing, -ment, -er, -raigned'.
ar range', -a ble, -ment, -ranged',
-ran'ging, -rān'ger.
ar'rant, -ly.
ar'ras, -rased (-rast), ar'ras wise.
ar'ra sēne (*or* -răs ene).
är räs'trē (*or* -trä) or *-trä.*
är rä'tel.
ar ray', -ing, -al, -er, -ment, -rayed.
ar rear', -age.
ăr'rel.

ar ren da'tion, ar'ren da'tor, ar-
rent', -ren ta'tion.
ar rest', -ed, -er, -ing, -ive, -or,
-a ble, -ment, ar res ta'tion, -res-
tee'.
ar'rha, pl. -rhæ, -rhal.
Ar rhe pho'ri a, ar'rhe phore.
ar rhi'zal, -rhi'zous.
ar rhyth'mi a, -mic, -mic al, -mous.
ar rière' (ăr rēr'), -bras' (-brä'), -jee,
-fiē], -peň sée' (-poň sä'), -vas'sal,
-vous sure' (-vōō sūr').
ar ri e'ro (ä rē ä'rō).
ar'ris, -wise, -fil'let, -gut'ter, -piece,
-rail.
ar rive', -rived', -rīv'ing, -rīv'al.
ar ro'ba.
ăr'ro gance, -gan cy, -gant, -gant-
ly, -gant ness.
ăr'ro gate, -ga'ted, -ga ting, -ga-
tive, -ga'tion.
ar ron'dĭ or -dee.
ar ron disse'ment (ä rŏň dēs'moň).
ar rope'.
ar'rōw, -y, ar'row head, a plant,
-leaf, a plant, -let, -root, -wood,
a plant, -head, head of an arrow,
-head'ed, -poi son, -shaped, -stone,
-tie, -wood, wood for arrows,
-worm, -grass or a. grass, a.
snake.
ăr ro)'o, pl. -os (-ōz).
Ar' sa ces (ar'sa sēz or -sä'sēz),
founder of Parthia.
arse, -foot, -smart.
ar'se nal.
Ar se'ni an.
ar'se nic, n., -se nate, -se nĭde (or
-nīde), -se nīte, ar'sĭne, -sen'ic, a.,
-ic al, -al ĭze, -ized, -ĭ zing, -sen'i-
cate, -sen'i cize, -cized, -cī zing,
-cism, ar sen'o blăst, -o līte, ar se'-
nĭ ate, -nĭ ous, -se nĭ'u ret or -sen'-
u ret, -ret ed, -se nĭ'a sis, -se no-
py'rīte, -se nif'er ous, -sen i coph'-
a gy, ar' se nic-black, -fur'nace,
-glăss.
ar se nil'lo.
ar shin' or -shine' or -sheen' (-shēn').
Ar sin'ō ē, Daughter of Ptolemy I.
ar'sis, pl. -ses (-sēz).
ar'son.
art, -ful, -ful ly, -ful ness, -less,

-less ly, -less ness, art-ūn ion,
-worm.
ar'ta ba.
Ar tax erx'es (-ēz), King of Pers.
Ar'te gal, Milton.
Ar te'mi a, Zoöl. genus.
Ar'te mis, Myth.
Ar te mis'i a (-mish'i a), Queen of
Halicarnassus.
ar'te mŏd.
ar'ter in.
ar'ter y, -te'ri ole, -ri al, -al ly, -al-
ize, -ized, -ĭ zing, -ĭ za'tion, ar te'-
ri o cap'il la ry, -ri o coc cyg'e al
(-kok sij'-), -o scle ro'sis, -o ve'-
nous, -o gram, -o tome, -ri og'-
ra phy, -ri ol'o gy, -ri ot'o my,
ar te rī'tis, ar'ter y-for ceps.
Ar te'sian (-zhan), ar te'sian well.
ar'the mis.
ar thrī'tis, -thrit'ic, -ic al.
ar thro'di a, -di al, -throd'ic.
ar'thro gas'tran.
ar throg'ra phy, -throl'o gy, -throp'-
a thy, ar'thro phragm (-fram).
ar'thro mere, -mer'ic.
ar thro'sis, pl. -ses (-sēz).
ar'thro stome.
ar'thro tome, -throt'o my.
Ar thu'ri an.
ar'ti choke.
ar'ti cle, -ti cled, -ti cling.
ar tic'u late, -ness, -ly, -la ted,
-la ting, -la tive, -la tor, -to'ry,
-la'tion, ar tic'u lus, pl. -lī.
ar'ti fact or ar'te fact.
ar'ti fĭce, -tif'i cer, -ti fĭ'cial (-fish'-
al), -cial ly, -cial ness, -fĭ'ci al'i ty.
ar til'ler y, -ler ist, -ler y man, -ship,
ar til'ler y-căr'riage, -lev'ĕl, -plănt.
ar ti mor an ti'co (-tē'ko).
ar'ti san (-zan).
ar'tist, -tis'tic, -tic al, -al ly, ar'tis-
try (or art'ist ry), ar tiste' (-tēst'),
ar tist-like.
Ar'ti um Bac ca lau're us (ar'tĭ-),
A. Ma gis'ter.
Ar tois' (ar'twä'), dept. Fr.
ar'to le.
ar to pho'ri on, pl. -ri a.
ar'to type, -ty py (-tī-).
Ar to ty'rīte.
ar'tus, pl. ar'tus.

Ar un děl'ian.
ar un dif'er ous, -din'e ous, a run-
di na'ceous, -di nose (-nōs).
a ru'ra.
a rus'pex or *-pĭce,* pl. *-pĭ ces* (-sēz),
a rus'pi cy.
ar'val *or* -vel.
ar vic'o lĭne, -o lous.
Ar'yan (är'- *or* är'-) *or* Ar'i an (är'ĭ-),
Ar'yan ize, -ized, -ī zing, -yan'dic.
ăr y bal'lus, *pl.* -lī.
a ryt'e noid (*or* ăr y te'noid), -noid'-
al, -noid'e us, ar'y ep i glot'tic,
-glot tid'e an.
as (ăz), *adv., conj., pro.* As (ăss),
Myth., pl. Æ'sir (ā'ser). *as* (ăss),
a coin; a weight, *pl. ass'es,* as'-
duc'at.
ăs'a (*or* ä'sä).
as a dul'cis.
as a fet'i da *or* -fœt'i da.
as'a phĭ'a.
A saph'ic.
ä'sar.
ä sä'ua (-wä).
as bes'tos *or* -tus, -bes'tic, -bes'ti-
form, -tĭne, -tin īte, -toid, -tous,
as bes'tos-stove.
As'ca part.
as cend', -ed, -ing, -a ble *or* -i ble,
-en cy *or* -an cy, -ence *or* -ance,
-ent *or* -ant, -er, as cen'sion, -sion-
al, -cen'sive, as cent'.
As cen'sion day.
as cer tain', -a ble, -er, -ment.
as cet'ic, -ic al, -al ly, -i cism, -cet'-
er y.
Asch (äsh), t. Bohem.
As'cham (-kam), Eng. teacher.
as'cham, a cupboard.
As'che (äs'chě), t. Belg.
as'cian (ash'yan *or* ăsk-).
as cid'i an, -ĭ ate, -i id, -i oid, *-i um,*
pl. *-i a, -i a'ri um,* pl. *-a'ri a,*
-i form, -i ol'o gy, -i o zo'an,
-zo'oid, as'ci dic'o lous.
as cif'er ous, -cig'er ous (-sij'-).
as ci'tes (-tēz), -cit'ic, -ic al, -ci ti'-
tious (-tish'us).
As cle pĭ'a des (-dēz), Gr. phys.,
-pi ad'ic, -cle'pi ads, as cle'pi ad,
-pi a da'ceous.
as'con, pl. *-cons* or *-co'nes* (-nēz).

as cribe', -cribed', -crīb'ing, -crīb'-
a ble, -crip' tion, -crip ti' tious
(-tish'us).
as'cu la, pl. *-læ.*
as'cus, *pl.* -ci (-sī), as'can.
as'cy phous.
a sea'.
a seel'.
a seĭs mat'ic.
a se'i ty.
a se'mi a.
a sep'ti cize, -cized, -ci zing, *-sep'-*
sis, -sep'ta, -sep'tic, -tic'i ty,
a sep'tŏl.
a sex'u al, -al ly.
As'gard, *Myth.*
ash, -y, -en (-n *or* -en), -er y, *pl.*
-ies, ash'weed, ash'-bar'ber ry,
-bar rel, -bead, -bin, -cake, -can'-
dles, -col'or, -col'ored, -fire, -fly,
-fur'nace, -hole, -key, -leach, -pit,
-plate, -shoot, Ash Wednes'day.
a shame', -shamed', -shām'ed ly,
-ed ness.
A shan'tee *or* -ti (-te *or* ash'ante').
A she'rah, pl. -rahs or *-rim.*
ash'et.
a shĭne'.
Ash ke naz'im, -naz'ic.
ash ko'ko.
ash'ler *or* -lar, -ler ing.
a shore'.
ash raf'ĭ.
Ash'to reth, a female divinity. *pl.*
-ta rŏth. Sometimes spelled As'-
to reth.
Ash'u ra.
A'si a (a'shĭ a *or* a'sha *or* āzh'ya),
A'sian (ā'shan *or* āsh'yan *or* āzh'-
yan), A si an'ic, A'sian ism, -si
arch (-ark), -si at'ic, -at'i cism,
-at'i cize, -cized, -cī zing, -cĭ za'-
tion.
a side'.
a sĭd'er īte.
As'i na'rĭ ī.
as'i nĭne (*or* -nĭn), -nin'i ty, as'i-
nus.
As'i nus, *Zoöl. subgenus.*
a si'ti a (-sish'i a).
ăsk, -ing, asked.
as'ka.

---

fāte, făt, fär, fạll, fâre, fạ̈st, sofà, mēte, mĕt, hêr, īce, ĭn, nōte,

a skånce', a skånt'.
a skew'.
as'kos.
as'la.
as lä'nĭ.
a slånt'.
a sleep'.
a slope'.
as'man īte.
As manns häu'ser (äs mänz hoi'-
zer).
As mo de'us (or az-).
As mo ne'an.
As ni ères (äs nē air'), t. Fr.
ä'sō.
ås'or.
åsp, -ish.
as pal'a thus, a shrub. As pal'a-
thus, Bot. genus.

as pår'a gus, -a gi (-jī or -gī),
-pa rag'ic (-råj'-), -rag'i nous,
-par'a gin or -gĭne, -par'a mĭde,
-pär gin'ic, -par'mate, -par'täte,
-par'tic, as par'a gus-bēan, -bee'-
tle, -stone, -tongs.
As pa'si a (-zhĭ- or -shi-), a noted
Grecian woman.
As pa'ti a (-shi a), a character in
Beaumont and Fletcher.
as'pect, -pect'ant, -pect'ing.
as'pĕn.
as'per, as'per a, -per ate, -a'tion,
-per'u lous, as'per-ar'ter y.
as per gil'lus (-jil), pl. -lī, as per-
gil'lum, pl. -la, -gil'li form.
as per'i ty.
as per'ma tism, -ma tous, -per'-
mous, -per'mi a.
as perse', -persed', -pers'ing, -pers-
er, -ive, -ive ly, -per'sion.
as per so'ri um, pl. -ri a, -per'so ry,
as per soir' (-swor').
as'phält (or -fält'), n., as phalt', v.,
-ed, -ing, -phäl'ter, -tite, -tus,
-tum, -to type, as phal'tum-fur-
nace.
as'pho del, -pho dĕl'ian.
as phyx'i a, -i al, -i ant, -i ate, -a ted,
-a ting, -a tive, -a'tion, -phyc'tic,
as phyx'y.
as'pic, -a spic'u late, -u lous.
as'pi rate, -ra ted, -ra ting, -tor,
-ra'tion, as pīr'a to ry.

as pire', -pired', -pīr'ing, -ing ly,
-pīr er, -ant.
as'pis. As'pis, Entom. genus.
a spo'rous.
as pri'no (ås prē'-).
a squat' (-skwŏt').
a squint'.
a squirm'.
åss, a quadruped, -ish, äss, ashes;
a unit of weight. ass-ear, -head,
ass's-ear, -foot.
as'sa cu (-kōō).
as'sa gaī or as'se-, -wood.
as sa'i (ås sä' I), a musical term.
as sai' (-si'), a tree, -palm.
as sail', -ing, -a ble, -ant, -er, -ment,
-sailed'.
As'säm', prov. Brit. India.
as'sa mar.
as sart'.
as sas'sin, -ate, -a ted, -a ting,
-a tor, -a tive, -si na'tion.
as sault', -ed, -ing, -a ble, -ant,
-er.
as say', n. and v., -ing, -a ble, -er,
-sayed', as say'-bal'ance, -fur'-
nace, -mås'ter.
As saye' (ås sī'), t. Hind.
asse (åss or åss).
as sem'ble, -bled (-bld), -blage,
-bler, -bling, -bly, -bly man, -bly-
men, as sem'bly-room.
as sent', n. and v., -ed, -ing, -ing ly,
-er, -or, -sen'tient (-shent).
as sert', -ed, -ing, -a ble or -i ble,
-a tive, -er, -or, -ive, -ive ly, -ive-
ness, -ser'tion, -to ry, -to'ri al,
-al ly, -tŏr'ic, -ic al.
as sess', -ing, -a ble, -a bly, -ment,
-or, -or ship, -ses so'ri al, -sessed'.
as'set, pl. -sets.
as sev'er ate, -a ted, -a ting, -a tive,
-a to'ry, -a'tion.
as sib'i late, -la ted, -la ting, -la'-
tion.
As si de'an.
as'si dent.
as sid'er a'tion.
as si du'i ty, -sid'u ous, -ous ly,
-ous ness.
as si en'to, -en'tist.
as sign', -ment, -ing, -er, -a ble,
-a bly, -a bil'i ty, -sign ee' (-sī nē'),

-or', -signed', as sig na'tion (-sig-),
as sign', *n.*, *pl.* -signs'.
as'sig nat (*or* å se nyä').
as'si lag.
as sim'i late, -la ted, -la ting, -la-
tive, -la to'ry, -la ble, -la bil'i ty,
-la'tion.
as'sis.
as sist', -ed, -ing, -ance, -ant, -ant-
ship, -er, -ful, -ive, -less, -or.
as size', -ment, -sīz'er, -or, as size'
ser'mon.
as so'ci ate (-shĭ-), -a ted, -a tor,
-a ting, -a tive, -tive ness, -a'tion
(-sĭ ā'shun *or* -shĭ-), -tion al, -tion-
ism, -tion ist, -ci a ble (-shĭ-),
-ble ness, -a bil'ĭ ty, -ateship.
as'so nance, -nanced, -nant, -nan'-
tal, -nan'tic, as'so nate, -na ted,
-na ting.
as sort', -ed, -ing, -ment.
as suage', -ment, -suaged', -suā'-
ging, -sua'ger, -sua'sive.
as sume', -sumed', -sūm'ing, -ing ly,
-a ble, -a bly, -ed ly, -er, -sump'-
tion, -tive, -tive ly, *as sump'sit.*
As sur' (äs'sōōr'), t. Afr.
as sure' (å shōōr'), -sured', -sur'ing,
-ing ly, -a ble, -ance, -ed ly, -ed-
ness, -er.
as sur'gent.
As syr'i an, -syr'i o lŏgue, -ol'o gy,
-o gist, -o log'ic al.
a star'board.
a stare'.
As tar'te, Myth.
a stat'ic, -ic al ly, -i cism, as'ta tize,
-tized, -ti zing, -ti zer.
äs tät'ki (-kē),
a stay'.
as te a to'sis, -to'des (-dēz).
as'te ism.
as'tel.
as'ter, -wort, As'ter, *Bot. genus.*
as te'ri a.
As te'ri as, Zoöl. genus. as te'ri as,
Ornith.
as'ter isk.
as'ter ism.
a stern', -ster'nal.
as'ter oid, -oid'al.
As ter'o pe, Myth.
as'the nol'o gy.

asth'ma (ast'ma *or* as'- *or* az'-),
-mat'ic, -ic al, -al ly.
as'ti chous (-kus).
as tig mat'ic, -ma'tion, a stig'ma-
tism, as tig'mism, as tig mom'e-
ter, -e try.
a stir'.
as ton'ish, -ing, -ing ly, -ment,
-ished.
As'to reth. See *Ash'to reth.*
as tound', -ed, -ing, -ing ly.
a strad'dle.
As træ'a, Myth.
as'tra gal, -trag'a lar, -a lus, pl. -li,
as'tra gal-plane, -tool.
as'tra khăn (*or* -khăn'), -ite. As-
trä khän' (äs-), dist. Russ.
as'tral, -ism.
a strand'.
as tra pho'bi a.
a stray'.
a stride'.
as trin'gent, -ly, -gen cy.
as trog'no sy, -trog'o ny, -trog'ra-
phy, -tro gon'ic.
as'troid.
as'tro ite, as'trīte.
as'tro labe.
as trol'a try.
as'tro li thol'ogy.
as trol'o ger, -tro log'ic, -ic al, -al ly,
-trol'o gize, -gized, -gī zing, -o gy.
as'tro man cy.
as trom'e try, -e ter, as'tro me'te-
or ol'o gy, -ol'o gist, -o log'ic al.
as tron'o my, -o mer, -o mize
-mized, -mi zing, -tro nom'ic,
-ic al, -al ly, -nom'ics.
As'tro phel, Sidney.
as tro pho tog'ra phy, -pho tom'-
e ter, -e try, -pho to met'ric al.
as tro phys'ic al, -phys'ics.
as'tro scope.
as'tro the ol'o gy.
as tu'cious, -ly, -tu'ci ty.
As'tur, *Ornith. genus,* as'tu rĭne.
As tu'ri as (äs tōō'rē äs), prov. Sp.,
-tū'rĭ an.
as tute', -ly, -ness.
a sty'lar, -sty'lic.
A sun ci on' (ä sŏŏn sē ōn'), c. Para.
a sun'der.
as'ū ra (*or* å sōō'-), *Myth.*

---

as'wail.
a sy'lum.
a sym bo'li a.
a sym met'ric, -ric al, -al ly, a sym'-
me try.
a sym'phy note.
as'ymp tote (-im tŏt), -tot'ic, -ic al,
-al ly.
a syn'ar tete, -tet'ic.
a syn'chro nism, -chro nous.
a syn'de ton, as yn det'ic, -ic al ly,
-yn tac'tic.
as'y ner'gi a.
a sys'tŏ lĕ, -to lism, -tol'ic.
a syz'y get'ic (-jet-)
at'a bal.
a tac'a mīte.
a tac'tic.
a ta'jo (ä tä'hō).
at'ak.
At'a la.
at'a man.
at a mas'co *or* -mos'co, -lil'y *or* a.
lil y.
at a rax'i a, at'a rax y.
a täunt', a täun'to.
at'a vism, -vis'tic, -tic al ly, a tav'ic.
a tax'a pha'si a (-fa'zhi a).
a tax'i a, -tax'ic, a tax'y (*or* at'ax y)
At bä'rä (ät-), r. Afr.
Atch af a lay'a Bay'ou (atch af'a-
li'a bi'ōō), r. La.
at'che.
atch'i son, a coin.
āte. See *eat.* A'tē, *Myth.*
a tech'nic (-tek'-), -nic al, a tech'ny.
a'tees (-tēs).
ä'tef, -crown.
at e lec'ta sis, -lec tat'ic.
a te lier (ä tē lyä').
at'e līne, -līte.
A tel'lan, -läne.
ä tem'po, ä tem'po pri'mo (prē'-).
ä tem'po gius'to (jōōs'to).
Ath a bas'kan *or* -can.
Ath'a lie (at'a le *or* ä'tä'lē'), Racine.
ath a nä'si a (-se a *or* -shi- *or* -zhi a),
a than'a sy.
Ath a na'si us (-shĭ us), Gr. father
of the church, -na'sian (-shan *or*
-zhan), -ism, -ist.
ath'a nor.

a'the ism, -ist, -ist' ic, -ic al, -al ly,
-al ness, a'the ize, -ized, -ī' zer,
-ī' zing.
ath'el ing.
A the'na, A the'nē, *Myth.*
Ath e nag'o ras, Gr. philos.
Ath e ne'um *or* -næ'um.
A the'ni an.
a the o log'ic al, -al ly.
a ther'man cy, -ma nous, a ther'-
mous.
ath e ro'ma, pl. -ro'ma ta, -ma tous,
ath'e rome.
ath e to'sis, ath' e toid.
a thirst'.
ath'lēte, -let'ic, -ic al ly, -let' i cism,
-let'ics, ath'le tism.
Ath'os, mt. Turk.
a threp'si a.
a throb'.
a thwart', -ships.
A thy' (ä thī'), t. Ire.
at'i my.
a tin'ga.
at'ka fish.
at lan'tad, -lan'tal.
at lan'tes (-tēz).
At lan'tic.
At lan'tis, -lan te'an *or* -lan'ti an,
-ti des (dēz).
at'las, a book of maps. At'las, *Myth.*
at'lee.
at mi'a try.
at'mid al'bu mose (-mōs).
at mi dom'e ter, -e try.
at mol'o gy, -o gist, -mo log'ic al.
at'mo lyze, -lyzed, -ly zer, -ly zing
(-lī'-), -ly za'tion (-lĭ-), -mol'y sis.
at mom'e ter.
at'mos phere, -phĕr'ic, -ic al, -al ly.
a to'cha, -grass.
a tok'.
a to'le (-lä).
a tŏll' (*or* at'ol).
at'om, -o mat'ic, -o mi'cian (-mish'-
an), -mic'i ty, at'om ism, -om ist,
-o mis'tic, -tic al, -al ly, a tom'ic,
-ic al, -al ly, at'om y, -om ol'o gy.
at'o me chan'ics (-kan-).
at'om ize, -ized, -i zing, -i zer, -ĭ za'-
tion.
a tone', -ment, -toned, -tōn'ing,
-tōn'a ble, -tōn'er.

at′o ny, a tŏn′ic.
a top′.
at′ra bi la′ri an, -ri ous, -bil′i ar,
  -bil′ia ry, -bil′ious.
a tra′che ate (-ke-), -che′li ate.
at′ra ment, -men ta′ri ous, -men′-
  tous.
A′trĕ us or A′treus (-trōōs), Myth.
A′tri (ä′trē), prov. It.
A trī′dæ, Myth.
a′tri o ven tric′u lar.
a trip′.
a′tri um, pl. -tri a, -tri al.
at ro ce ru′le ous.
a trŏ′cious (-shus), -ly, -ness,
  a troc′i ty (-trŏs′-).
at′ro phy, -phĭed, -phy′ing (-fĭ-),
  a trŏph′ic.
At′ro pos, Myth.
at′ro pous.
a try′.
ăt tăc′ că, -cō.
at tach′, -a ble, -ing, -ment, -tached′,
  at tach′ment-screw.
at ta ché (ăt tă shā′).
at tack′, -ing, -a ble, -er, -tacked′.
at tac′o lite.
At′tai (-tā), Bib.
at tain′, -ing, -a ble, -a ble ness,
  -a bil′i ty, -tain′der, -tain′ment,
  -tained′.
at taint′, -ed, -ing.
At′ta lī′a, Bib.
at tal′i ca.
at′tap.
at′tar or ot′tar.
at tem′per, -tem′per ate, -ā′ted,
  -ā′ting, -a′tion, -per ment or -per-
  a ment.
at tempt′, -ed, -ing, -a ble, -a bil′i ty,
  -tempt′er.
at tend′, -ed, -er, -ing, -ing ly, -ance,
  -ant, -ten′tion, -ten′tive, -tive ly,
  -tive ness.
at ten′u ate, -a ted, -a ting, -u ant,
  -a′tion.
at test′, -ed, -ing, -a tive, -er, -or,
  -test′ive, at′tes ta′tor, -ta′tion.
At′tic, relating to Attica or Athens,
  -ti cize or -cise, -cized, -ci zing,
  -cism, -cist, at′tic.
at ti haw′meg.
At′tĭ la, King of the Huns.

at tire′, -tired, -tir′ing, -tir′er, at tire′
  wom′an.
at′ti tude, -tu′di nal, -di na′ri an,
  -an ism, -tu′di nize, -nized, -nī-
  zing, -ni zer.
at′tle.
ăt to′le (-lä).
at tor′ney (-tur′-), -ism, -ship, -gen′-
  er al, -gen′er al ship.
at tract′, -ed, -ing, -ing ly, -a ble, -er,
  -or, -ĭle, -ive, -ive ly, -ive ness,
  -a bil′i ty, -trac′tion, -tiv′i ty.
at trib′ute, -u ted, -u ting, -u tive,
  -tive ly, -u ta ble, at′tri bute, n.
  -bu′tion.
at trī′tion, at trīte′, -trī′tus, at tri′-
  tion-mill.
at tune′, -tuned′, -tūn′ing.
at typ′ic, -ic al, -al ly.
a tum′ble.
a typ′ic, -ic al, -al ly.
a′u a (ä′ōō a).
au bade (ō băd′).
au bain (ō bān′ or ō băṅ′), au baine′
  (-bān′).
Aube (ōb), r. Fr.
Aube nas′ (ōb′nä′), t. Fr.
au berge (ō bârzh′ or a̤′berj), au′ber-
  gist.
a̤u′ber gĭne.
au′ber′nage′ (ō bare näzh′).
au bin (a̤′bin or ō băṅ′).
au′burn.
Auch (ōsh), t. Fr.
auch′let (auch′-).
au cou rant′ (ō kōō rŏṅ′).
a̤uc′tion, -a ry, -eer′, auc′tion pitch,
  a. pool.
a̤uc to′ri al.
au′cu ba. Au′cu ba, Bot. genus.
au dā′cious, -ly, -ness, -dac′ i ty
  (-dăs′-).
Aude (ōd), r. and dept. Fr.
Au′di an, -ism.
au′di ble, -ness, -di bly, -di bil′i ty,
  -di ent, -ence, -di tive, -to ry, au′-
  dile, -di′tion, au′di ence-cham′ber,
  -court.
a̤u di en′do et ter mi nan′do.
au di om′e ter, -e try, -o met′ric,
  -di phone.
au′dit, -ed, -ing, -di tor, -tor ship,
  -to′ri al, au′dit-ale, -house, -of′fice.

---

fāte, făt, fär, fạll, fâre, făst, sofȧ, mēte, mĕt, hêr, īce, ĭn, nōte,

au dĭ′ta que re′la.
au di to′ri um, *pl.* -ri ums *or* -ri a.
Au′drey (-drĭ), Shak.
Au′du bon (ō′dōō bŏn), co. Iowa.
Au′du bon, Amer. ornith.
Au′er bach (ou′er bäch *or* -bäk),
  Ger. novelist; t. Sax.
au fait′ (ō′fä′), *au fond′* (ō′fŏn′).
au′ge (ou′gĕ), pl. *-gen.*
Au ge′an, *Myth.*
au′ger, a tool, -bit, -fau′cet, -gage,
  -hole, -māk′ing, -shell, -stem,
  -twist′er.
au get (ạ jet′ *or* ō′zhä′).
augh *or* ach (aw *or* ạch).
aught (ạwt).
au′gite (-jĭt), -git′ic.
aug′ment, *n.*, -ment′, *v.*, -ment′ed,
  -er, -ing, -a ble, -ment′a tive,
  -tive ly, -men ta′tion.
au gra tin′ (ō grä tan′).
Augs′burg (ougz′ bōōrg *or* ouchs′-
  bōōrch), c. Bav., A. Con fes′sion.
au′gûr, -ing, -ship, -gū ral, -gū ry,
  -gū rate, -gū′ri al, -gûred.
au gust′, -ly, -ness.
Au′gust.
au gus′ta, a tree.
au gus′tal, ta′lis, *pl.* les (lēz).
Au gus′tan.
Au gus′tĭn *or* -tĭne (*or* au′-), -tin′-
  i an, -an ism.
Au gus to′vo (ou gōōs tō′vō), t.
  Russ.
ạuk, -let.
ạuld, ạuld′ lăng syne′.
au le′tes (-tēz), *pl.* -tai (-tĭ), -let′ic,
  -le′tris, *pl.* -tri des (-dēz).
au′lic, -lic al, -li cism.
au′lin, -scout′y.
ạum.
Au male′ (ō′mäl′), t. Alg.
Au male′, d' (dō′mäl′), Duc.
ạu′mil, -mil dar.
aune (ōn).
äunt, -y, -ie, -hood.
ạu′ra, -ral.
au′ra mĭn *or* -mĭne, -ran′ti a
  (-shi a).
au′rate, -ra ted.
au re′ (ō rā′).
au′re ate, -re ous, -re′i ty.
au re′o la, au′re ole, -oled, -ōl ing.

au re′o lin.
au re′o sin.
au re voir (ō re vwor′).
au′ri-ar gen tif′er ous.
au′ri cle, -cled (-kld), -ri lave, -ric′u-
  lar, -lar ly.
au′ri fy, -fied, -fy ing, -ri form,
  -rif′er ous, -rif′ic.
Au rĭ′ga, Astron. au rī′ga, *Med.*
Au ril lac′ (ō′rē′yäk′), t. Fr.
au′rin *or* -rĭne.
au ri phryg′i a (-frij′-), -i ate.
au ri pig′ment.
au′ris, pl. *-res* (-rēz).   Au′ris,
  Conch. genus.
au′rist, -ri scalp, -ri scope, -ris′co-
  py.
au′rochs (-rŏks).
au ro′ra, -ro′ral, -ral ly, -re an, au-
  ro′ra-shell, a. bo re ä′lis, a. glo′ry,
  Au ro′ra, *Myth.*
au′rum, au′rous, -ric, -ric′o mous,
  -rif′ic, -rig′er ous (-rij′-), -rig′ra-
  phy, -riv′o rous.
Au Sa′ble (aw sä′bl), r. Mich.
Au sa′ble (ō sạ′bl), tp. and chasm
  N. Y.
ạus′cul tate, -tā′ted, -tā′ting, -tā′tor,
  -tor ship, -cul′ta tive, -ta to′ry,
  -ta′tion.
aus′laut (ous′lout).
Au so′ni an.
ạus′pex, *pl.* -pi ces (-sēz), -pi cate,
  -ca ted, -ca ting, -ca tor, -to′ry.
aus′pĭce, *pl.* -pi ces (-sēz), aus pi′-
  cious, -ly, -ness.
aus′ter. When specialized, it should
  be capitalized. -land, aus′tral.
aus tere′, -ly, -ness, -tĕr′i ty.
Aus′tin.   Same as Augustinian.
Aus tra′li a, -tra′li an (*or* -trāl′yan),
  -la′sia (-sha *or* -zha), -la′sian.
Aus tra′li oid *or* -tra loid.
Aus′tri a, -tri an, -tra′sian (-shan).
aus′trin ger (-jer).
Aus′tro co lum′bi a, -bi an.
Aus tro gæ′a, -gæ′an, -tro ma lā′ya,
  -lā′yan.
aus′tro man cy.
au tan tit′y py.
au te′cious.
au′ter droit′ (ō′ter drwŏ *or* -droi).
au′ter foits′ (ō ter fwŏ′ *or* -foi).

nŏt, nôr, ūse, ŭp, ûrn, etüde, fōōd, fŏŏt, ạnger, bonmot, thus, Bach.

10

au'ter vie (o'ter vē).
au then'tic, -tic al, -al ly, -al ness,
-ti cate, -ca ted, -ca ting, -ca'tion,
-tic'i ty, -then'tics.
au'thor, -cråft, -hood, -like, -ess,
au tho'ri al, au'thor-card, -cat a-
logue, -en try, -head ing, -mark,
-ta ble.
au thŏr'i ty, -i ta tive, -tive ly,
-tive ness, -i ta'ri an.
au'thor ize, -ized, -i zer, -i zing,
-i'za ble, -ĭ zā'tion.
au'tho type.
au'tō (ou'-), a Spanish play; **au'tō,**
a prefix.
au'to bī og'ra phy, -ra pher, -o-
graph'ic, -ic al, -al ly.
au to chrŏn'o grăph (*or* -krŏ'-
no-).
au toch'thon, *pl.* -thons *or* -tho-
nes (-nēz), -tho nal, -tho nism,
-tho nous, -nous ly, -tho ny,
-thon'ic.
au to clas'tic.
au'to clave.
au'to crat, -ship, -crat'ic, -ic al,
-al ly, au toc'ra cy.
au'to di ag no'sis.
au to di ges'tion.
au to dy nam'ic (*or* -dĭ-).
au' to grăph, -ism, -om' e ter,
-graph'ic, -ic al, -al ly, -tog'ra-
phy.
au'to harp'.
au to hyp'no tism.
au'to kī ne'sis, -net'ic.
au to la ryn'go scope, -lăr yn gos'-
co py.
au tol'o gy, -tol a try.
Au tol'y cus, Shak.
au to mat'ic, -ic al, -al ly, -ma tic'-
i ty, -tom'a tism, -a tist, -a tize,
-tized, -ti zing, -a ton, *pl.* -a tons
or -a ta.
au tom'e try, -to met'ric.
au to mo'bīle.
au to mor'phic, -al ly -phism.
au to mo'tor.
au ton'o my, -o mist, -o mous, -to-
nom'ic, -ic al ly.
au'to nym.
au'to phon, -toph'o ny.
au toph thal'mo scope.

au to pol'y grăph.
au'top sy, -top'sic, -sic al, -al ly,
-top'tic, -tic al, -al ly, -tic'i ty.
au to sche'di asm (-skē'-), -di as'-
tic, -tic al, -sche'di aze, -azed,
-a zing.
au'to scope, -tos'co py, -to scŏp'ic.
au'to site, -sit'ic, -si ta'ri us, *pl.*
-rĭ ī.
au to sty'lic (*or* -stīl'ic).
au'to sug ges'tion.
au'to the ism, -the ist.
au'to tox æ'mi a, -tox i ca'tion, -tox'ic.
au'to trans form'er.
au'to type, -typed, -typ'ing (-tīp'-),
-typ'ic, -ty pog'ra phy (-tī-),
-tot'y py.
au'tre fois' (ŏ'tr fwä').
au'tumn, -tum'nal, au tumn-bells.
Au tun' (ŏ'tuṅ'), c. Fr.
Au vergne (ŏ vârn'), mts. and
former prov. Fr., au ver gnat'
(ŏ vâr nyä').
Au vergne', d' (dŏ'vârn'), Pierre.
aux'a nom'e ter.
Au xerre' (ŏ'sâr' *or* ŏ'zâr'), c. Fr.
aux e'sis, -et'ic, -ic al ly.
aux il'ia ry (awg zil'ya ry), -iar ly.
aux il'i um (awg zil'-).
aux ol'o gy (awks ŏl'-), -om'e ter.
Aux onne' (ŏ'sŏṅ'), t. Fr.
aux'o spore.
Aux vasse' (ŏ'văs'), tp. Mo.
ă'va, a drink. ă'va, a bird. a va'
(a va̧'), Scotch, *of all.*
a vail', -ing, -ing ly, -a ble, -a bly,
-a bil'i ty, -vailed'.
ă'val, ·av'i tal, relating to grand-
parents. *a val',* suretyship.
av'a lånche (*or* -lănch).
av'a līte.
A val lon' (ä'väl'lŏṅ'), t. Fr.
a vă'nĕh.
a vă'ni a (*or* ä vä nē'a), -ni ous.
a vant'-bras (a voṅ'-brä), -cou'ri er
(-kŏō'-), -fos sé' (-fos sā'), -gärde.
av'a rīce, -ri'cious (-rish'us), -cious-
ly, -ness.
a vāst' (*or* -väst').
av a tar' (*or* av'-), *Myth.* -a tä'ra.
a väunt' (*or* -va̧unt').
A've (ä'vē *or* ä'vā), salutation for
the Virgin Mary, a've (ä'vē *or*

ä'vä), a welcoming, *or* a farewell salutation.

Ave'bur y *or* **A'bur y** (ä'bĕr ĭ), vil. Eng.

av'el, -el er.

a vel'läne *or* -lan (*or* av'-).

A've Ma ri'a (ä'vä mä̇ rē'a), **A've Ma'ry** (ä'vē mä'ry).

A ve'na, av e na'ceous, a ve'ni form, -ve'nin.

av'e nage, -e ner.

A venches' (ä'vŏnsh'), t. Switz.

a venge', -venged', -ven'ging, -ger.

a ve'nous, -ni ous.

Av'en tĭne.

a ven'tu rin *or* -rĭne.

av'e nue.

a ver', *v.,* -ring, -ment, -ra ble, -verred'.

av'er age, -aged, -a ging, av'er age-ad just'er, -stāt'er, -tak'er.

av e rä'no.

a ver'dant.

A ver'nus, -ni an.

Av er ro'ism *or* -rho', -ro ist, -is'tic.

av'er ruŋ ca'tor (*or* -ca'tor).

a ver'sant.

a verse', -ly, -ness, -ver'sion.

a vert', -ing, -er, -i ble.

A'ves (-vēz), ā'vi an, -vīne, -vi a ry, a'vi cul'ture, -vi form.

A ves'ta, -tan.

a' ves truz' (-trōōz').

a'vi a'do (ä'vē ä'thō), *av'i a dor'.*

a vic'u la, -u lar, -*la'ri um,* pl. -*ri a,* -ri an, A vic'u la, *Conch. genus.*

a vid'i ty, av'id, -id ly, a vid'i ous ly.

ä vi ʃau'na, pl. -*næ,* -nal.

A'vig'non' (ä'vĕn'yŏn'), c. Fr.; A. ber'ry.

A'vi la (ä'vē lä), prov. Sp.

A'vĭtes (ā'-), *Bib.*

av i vage' (-väzh').

av i zan'dum *or* -san'-.

A vize' (-vēz').

av o cä'do or -*to.*

av o cat' (-ō kä').

av o ca'tion.

av'o cet *or* -set.

a void', -ed, -ing, -a ble, -a bly, -ance, -er, -less.

av'oir du pois' (-poiz').

a vo'li (ä vo'lē).

A'von (ā'von *or* ăv'on), r. Eng.; vil. N. Y.; vil. O.

Av'on dale, t. Ala.; vil. O.

a vouch', -ing, -a ble, -er, -ment, -vouched'.

a vou é' (a vōō ā').

a vow', -a ble, -a bly, -al, -ance, -ant, -ed ly, -er, -ry, -ing, a vowed'.

A vranches' (ä'vrŏnsh'), t. Fr.

A vran chin (ä'vrŏn shăn'), dept. Fr.

a vuŋ'cu lar.

ä'wä, a fish. a wä', Scotch for *away.*

a wa̧'bi (-bē).

a wait', -ed, -er, -ing.

a wake', -ment -waked', -wak'ing, -en, -en ing, -en ing ly, -en à ble, -en er, a woke'.

a wane'.

a ward', -er, ed-, -ing.

a ware', -ness.

a wash' (wŏsh').

away', -go ing.

awe, -less, -some, -strick'en, -struck, awed, aw'ing, -ful, -ful ly, -ful ness.

a wea'ry, -wea'rĭed.

a weel'.

a weigh'.

a we'to (ä wä'tō).

a while'.

a wing'.

awk'ward, -ly, -ness.

awl, -wort, -bird, -clip, -shaped, -tree.

awn, -er, -less, awn'y, awned.

awn'ing, -block.

a wry' (-rī').

ax *or* axe, *pl.* ax'es, ax'man *or* axe-, *pl.* -men, ax' mas ter, -grind er, -han dle, -head, -helve, -mäk er, -shaped, -stone, a. break er.

ax'il, *n.,* ax iʃ'er ous.

ax'Ile, a., *ax iʃ'la,* pl. *læ,* -iʃ'lant, ax'-il lar, -la ry.

ax'i lem'ma.

ax'ĭn, *Chem.,* -in'ic.

ax'ĭne (-ĭn), pertaining to deer.

ax'in o man'cy (*or* ax in'-).

ax'i o lĭte, -lit'ic.

ax'i o m, -o mat'ic, -ic al, -al ly.

ax'is, *pl.* ax'es (-ēz), ax'i al, -al ly, -i oid, -i oid' e an, -i om'e ter, -i sym met'ric, -if' u gal, Ax'is,

Zoöl. genus, ax' is-cyl' in der,
-deer.
ax'le, ax'led (ax'ld), -le tree, **ax'le-**
ad jus'ter, -arm, -bar, -block,
-box, -clip, -col'lar, -gage, -guard,
-hook, -mak ing, -nut, -pack'ing,
-pin, -sad dle, -seat, -set ting,
-skein, -sleeve, -tooth, -yoke, ax'le-
tree-clamp.
Ax'min ster car'pet.
ax'ode.
ax'o lotl.
ax om'e ter.
ax'on, pl. *-o nes* (-nēz).
ax o nom'e try *or* ax i nom'-.
ax o sper'mous.
ax ot'o mous.
ax'unge (-ŭnj), -un'gi ous (-ji-).
ay *or* aye (ā), ever, always. ay *or*
aye (ā), an exclamation of surprise
or regret. aye *or* ay (ī), yes, yea,
truly. aye *or* ay (ī), an affirma-
tive vote. Ay (ā), a wine. **äy'-**
green *or* äye'-.
ä'yah.
ä yä pä'nä.
aye'-aye (ī'ī .
ä ye nee'.
äy'let.
ay'ni-wood (ī nǐ-).
ayr (air), a gravelly point of land.
Ayr (air), co. Scot.
a yu dan'te (ä yōō thän'tä).
ä yŭn'tä mi en'to.
A yut'hi a (ä yōōt'hē'ä), former
cap. of Siam.

A za'le a, *Bot. genus.* a za'le a, a
species of plants.
a zän'.
az'a rin.
az'a rŏle.
A za'zel, Milton.
a zed'a rach (-răk).
az'iam (-yam *or* -ī am).
A'zǐ el (ā'-), *Bib.*
az'i mŭth, -muth'al, -al ly, az'i-
muth cir'cle.
a zi o'la (ä tsē o'la).
az o ben'zēne, -ben'zōl.
az'o-blue, -e ryth'rin, az o dī phen'-
yl.
a zo'gue (ä thō'gä *or* -so'gä).
a zo'ic.
a zon'ic.
a zo o sperm'a tism, -sperm'i a.
ä'zor.
A zores' (-zōrz'), Portu. Isl., -zo'-
ri an.
a zo te'a (ä'thō tā'a *or* ä so-).
az'o tize, -tized, -ti zing, -o tǐde (*or*
-tīd), -o tin, -o tom'e ter.
Az'ra el *or* -il.
Az'tec, -tec an.
a zu le'jo (ä thōō lä' ho).
a zum' bre (ä thoom'brä).
az'ure (ăzh' ûr *or* ăzh' ûr), a'zure
(ā'zhūr *or* ā'zhûr), -stone.
az'u rǐne (azh'-), -u rite, -u ry.
az'y gos, -y gous, -gous ly.
az'ym *or* -yme (-ǐm), a zym'ic, az'y-
mous, Az'y mǐte.
az zi mi'na (ät se mē'na).

B

baa (bä).
Bä'al, -ism, -ist, -īte.
Bäal'bĕc', t. Syr.
Ba'al-pe'or, *Bib.*
bab, a tassel or cockade; a bob.
Bäb, a Babist, Bäb'ism.
bä bä', a cake.
Bä'ba, a title of respect
Ba'ba, A'li (ä'lē bä'bä).
bä bä kŏ'to.
bab'ber.
bab'bit ting, -jig, Bab'bitt met'al.

bab'ble, -bled (-bld), -bling, -bling-
ly, -bler, -ble ment.
Bä'bel, *Bib.* Bä'bel *or* bä-, confusion; disorder.
bab'il lard.
Bab'ing ton's-curse, a plant.
bab i rus'sa or *-rous'sa* (-rōōs'-) *or*
bab y-.
băb'läh.
Bä'ble (-blä).
bab oon', -er y, -ish, bab ū ī'na.
ba boosh'.

Ba bou'vism (-bōō'-), -vist.
ba bu' (-bōō') or *bōō'*.
bâ bul' *or* -bool (-bōōl' *or* bä'-).
Bä'bu yän' (-boo-), isl. Pacific.
bä'by, -ish, -ish ly, -ish ness, -ism,
-hood, -ship, -ol'o try, ba'by-car'-
riage (-rĭj), -clothes, -farm,
-farm'er, -farm'ing, -house,
-jump'er, -pin, -walk'er.
Bab y lo'ni an, -lon'ic, -ic al, -lo'-
nish, Bab'y lon īte.
ba cä'ba, -palm (-päm).
bä'ca lä'o.
bac ca lau're ate, -re an.
Bac ca när'ist.
bac ca rat' (-rä'), or *-rä'*, a game.
Bäc'cä'rat' (-rä'), t. Fr.
bac'cha nal (-ka-), -nä'li a, -li an,
-an ism, -an ly, bac'chant (-kant),
bac chante (bäk'kant *or* -kant' *or*
-kan'te), *pl.* bac'chantes (-kant) *or*
-chan'tes (-kan'tēz), -chan'tic.
Bac'chus, *Myth.*, -chic (-kĭk).
Bach (bäch), Ger. composer.
Bach'a rach *or* -rack (bäk'a räk).
Bache (bāch), Amer. philos.
bach'el (bäk'-).
bach'e lor, -hood, -lor ism, -ship,
bach'c lor's-but'tons.
ba ci'le (-chē'lä), pl. *-ci'li* (-chē'lē).
ba cil'lus, pl. *-li,* ba cil'lar *or* bac'-
(bas'-), bac'il la'ry, -cil'li form,
-li an, -li cīde, -cĭd'ic, -cil'li cul'-
ture, Ba cil'lus, *Bot. genus.*
ba ci'no (ba chē'no), pl. *-ci'ni* (-nē).
back, -er, ings, backed, back'bite,
-bīt er, -bīt ing, -ing ly, back'bone,
-boned, -cap, -down, -fall,
-ground, -hand, -hand ed, -ed ly,
-ed ness, -hand er, -head, -house,
-lash, -less, -log, -most, -piece,
-plate, -rope, -set, -side, -slide,
-slīd er, -slid ing, -ing ness, -stay,
-ster, -stitch, -stone, -ward, -wards,
-ward ly, -ward ness, -wa'ter,
-wood, -woods, -woods man,
-worm, -wort.
back'-ac'tion, -bal'ance, -band,
-bar, -block, -bond, -bone, bone of
the back, -cas'ing, -cast, -cen'ter,
-chain, -cloth, -comb, -end, -fil'-
let, -flap, -frame,· -game, -gear,
-joint, -lin'ing, -link, -lye, -mill,

-mold, -o'ver man, -paint'ing,
-pres'sure, -rack et, -rak'ing,
-rent, -rest, -re turn, -saw,
-scra'per, -scratch'er, -set'tler,
-shift, -sight, -skin, -slang, -spear,
-speed, -speer, -splint ing, -spring,
-staff, -stair, *a.*, -stairs, *a.*, -stall,
-step, -stop, -strap, -strapped,
-stream, -string, -stroke, -swim'-
mer, -sword, -tack, -tool, -trick,
-washed, -wound ing.
back door, b. look, b. room, b.
stair, *n.*, b. stairs, *n.*
back'ache (-āk), back'ache-brake,
-root.
back'et.
back gam'mon (*or* back'-), back-
gam'mon-board, -play ing.
back'ing, -boards, -deals, -ham-
mer, -i'ron, -met'al, -pan.
back'sheesh or *bak'shish* (-shēsh).
Ba'con, -ism, -co'ni an.
ba'con (-kn *or* -kon), -ize, -ized,
-i zing, -con y, -con weed, ba'con-
bee'tle.
bäc'täl.
bac te'ri a, -ri al, -ri an, -ri cī'dal,
-ri cide, -ri form, -ri oid, -ri ol'o gy,
-o gist, -o log'ic al, -o scop'ic, -os'-
co py, -o ther a peu'tic, -ther'a py,
-te rit'ic, Bac te'ri a, *Entom. genus.*
Bac'tri an, B. cam'el.
Bac'tris.
Bäd a joz' (-hōs'), prov. Sp.
bad'ak-tap'a.
ba dä'neh.
bä'daud' (-dō)'.
bad'dam.
bad'der locks.
bad'dock.
bade (bäd). See *bid.*
Bä'den, state Ger.
badge, -less, -man.
badg'er, -ing, -er, -ly, -ered, badg'er-
bait'ing, -dog, -hound, -legged,
-plane, -er's-bane.
bäd'gir (-geer).
bad i ä'ga.
ba dĭ'geon (-jun).
bad i nage (-näzh' *or* bad'ĭ näj).
Ba din guet' (-dăn'gä').
bad'min ton *or* Bad'-.
ba e ta (bä ā tä).

bœ'tu lus, pl. *-li.*
bæ'tyl, -tyl us.
baf'fle, -fled (-fld) -fling, -fling ly, -fling ness, -fle ment, -fler, baf'fle-plate.
baf'ta.
bag, -ful, -ger, -ging, -gy, -gi ness, bagged.
bag'man, -nut, -pipe, -pīp'er, -wig-ged.
bag-clåsp, -fast' en er, -fill er, -fil'-ter, -fox, -frame, -hold'er, -lock, -ma chine', -pud'ding, -reef, -room, -tie, -weigh er, -worm, bag'ging-time, bag' press, b. pump, b. trou sers, b. wig.
ba gä'nä.
ba gasse', -fur nace.
bag a telle', -board, -play ing, -ta'ble.
bag at ti'no (båg åt tē'no), pl. *-ni* (-nē).
Bäg däd', t. Turk.
bag'gage, -man, -çar, -check, -mås'-ter, -truck.
bag'ga la, bag'lo.
bag'git.
bagn'io (băn'yo).
Bag'no a Ri'po li (bän'yō' ä rē'-pō lē), t. It.
Bag no'li an.
băg'rě (or bä'grä).
ba gui'o (-gē'-).
bäh.
ba hạ'dur (-dōor).
Ba hä'ma Banks, B. chan'nel, B. Is'lands, B. gråss, B. sponge.
ba här'.
Ba ha'wal pur (bä hä'wal'pōor), state India.
Ba hi'a (bä ē'ä), state Braz., *bä hi'a* (-ē'a), a bay.
bah rain'ga (bä rīŋ'ga).
ba hut' (-hōot').
Bä'ian ism.
bai'dak (bī'däk).
bai'dar (bī'-).
Baï'e ra.
baign oire' (bä nwŏr').
bail, -ing, -er, -a ble, -age, -ment, bailed, bails'man, bail ee', bail or'.
bail-bond, -dock, -piece, -scoop, bail'ing-ma chine'.

ba'i le (bä'ë lä).
bail'iff, -iff ship, -i wick.
bäil'lie-brush'kie.
bail lon' (bäl yoṅ'), *bail lo né* (bäl-yo nä').
bä'i lo.
bain, *bain-ma rie'* (băṅ ma rē').
Bai räm (bī'- *or* -räm').
Bai'reuth (bī'roit), c. Ger.
bairn, -li ness, -time, -wort.
bait, -ing, -er, -ed, bait-box, -fish'-ing, -house, -mill, -poke, -rod.
bäize.
Ba ja (bŏ'yŏ'), t. Hung.—(bä'yä), t. It.
Ba jar'do (-yär'-).
ba'jo na'do (bä'hō nä'tho).
bake, bak'ing, -er, -er y, bake' board, -house, -stone, baked, baked-apple, -meat, bāk'ing-pow'der.
bak'er-foot, -kneed, -legged.
bak'shish or băkh'shish or back'shish or -sheesh or bŭk'shish (-sheesh).
Bä'ku' (-koo'), prov. Russ.
bak'u fu (-ŏŏ fōō).
bạl.
Bä'laam, *Bib.*, -ite, -it'ic al, ba'-laam, -bås'ket, -box.
bal'a chong *or* -chan.
bal'a jo.
bal'a hŏŏ *or* bal'la-.
Bäl'ä klä'vä, t. Russ.
bal a laï'ka.
bal'ance, -ment, -an cing, -an cer, -anced.
bal'ance-bar, -ba rom'e ter, -beam, -bob, -book, -bridge, -crane, -dy-na mom'e ter, -e lec trom'e ter, -en'gine, -fish, -frame, -gate, -knife, -lev'el, -pit, -plow, -reef, -rud'der, -rynd, -sec'tions, -sheet, -step, -ther mom'e ter, -valve, -vise, -wheel.
ba lan'dra.
ba lä'o.
bal'a ta, -gum, -tree.
bal'a trŏn *or* -trŏŏn, -tron'ic.
ba lạus'ta, -laus'tin.
bal a yeuse' (-à yêz').
bạl-boy, -cap'taiṅ.
Bal brig'gan.
bal'bu sard.
bal bu'ti es (-shĭ ēz).

bal'co ny, -nĭed, -net'.
bạld, -head, a person, -ly, -mon'ey,
-ness, -pate, -rib.
bald'-coot, -faced, -head'ed, -pāt'ed.
bal'da chin (-kin), -chi'no (-kē'-).
bạl'der dash.
bal'di coot.
bạl'dric, -wise.
bale, -ful, -ful ly, -ful ness, -less,
bāl'ing, bāl'er, baled, bale-fire,
-hook, -tie, bāl'ing-ma chine,
-press.
Bǎl e ǎr'ic, isl. Medit., -ā'ri an,
-ǎr'i ca, bal e ar'ic an.
ba leen', -knife.
ba leine' (-lān'), a platform.
ba li'ki (-lē'ke).
ba line' (-lēn'), a coarse canvas.
Ba lis'tes (-tēz).
bal is tra'ri a.
ba lize' or -lise' (-lēz), a sea-mark.
Bä lize' (-lēz'), c. and r. Cen.
Amer.
balk (bawk), -ing, -er, -y, balked,
balk-line, -stäff.
Bäl kän' (or bạl'kan), mts. Europe.
Bäl'kis.
ball, -er, -ing, balled, ball'room.
ball-bear' ing, -block, -cal' i bcr,
-car'tridge, -cǎst'er, -cov er, -field,
-flow'er, -game, -i'ron stone,
-joint, -lĕv'er, -mine, -play ing,
-proof or -proof, -rack, -screw,
-seat er, -stock, -train, -trim'mer,
-trol ley, -turn ing, ball blue, b.
cock, b. grind'er, b. gud'geon
(-jŭn), b. mount'ing, b. so'da, b.
valve, b. vein.
ball'ing-fur'nace, -gun, -i'ron, -ma-
chine', -tool.
bǎl'lǎ.
bal'lad, -er, -ism, -ist, -ize, -ized,
-i zing, -ling, -mak'er, -me ter,
-mon'ger (-mŭng-) or b. moŋ'ger,
-op'e ra, -sing'er.
bal'la hou (-hoō).
bal'lam.
bal'lan, b. wrasse (răs').
bal'last, -ed, -ing, -age, bal'last-
en'gine, -fin, -get ter, -ham'mer,
-heav'er, -hole, -light'er, -line,
-mǎs ter, -plant, -port, -shov el,
-trim.

bal la toon'.
bal le ri'na (bäl lä rē'nä), pl. -nas
or -ne (-näz or -nä).
bal'let' (-lä or -lĕt), a dance. bǎl'let,
Her.
bal lis'mus (-lĭz'- or -lis'-).
bal lis'ta, pl. -tæ, -lis'tic, -tics, -tīte.
bal loon', -er, -ing, -ist, -ry, balloon'-fish or b. fish, -jib, -net,
-sail, -vine, bal loon' boil'er, b.
frame, bal loon'ing spi'der.
bal'lot, -ed, -er, -ing, -age, -ist,
bal'lot-box, -stuff'ing.
bal'lo tade' (-täd' or -tād'), or
bal'o-.
bal'lotte'ment' (-mäŋ' or -lot'mĕnt).
balm (bäm), -y, -i ly, -i ness, balm-
ap ple, -crick'et, -oil.
bạl'maid'en.
Bal mŏr'al, a garment; a boot.
Bǎl'mung (-moŏng).
bal'ne al, -ne a ry, -a'tion, -ne og'-
ra phy, -ol'o gy, -o log'ic al.
ba lŏ'ghi a (-gĭ-).
ba lo'ne a.
Bǎl'rǎm pur' (-poōr'), t. India.
bạl'sam, -y, -a'tion, -ĭne, -ous,
-sam'ic (or bǎl-), -ic al, -i na'-
ceous, if'er ous, sam ize, bal'-
sam root, a plant, -weed, bal'sam-
ap'ple, -bog, -fir, -herb, -pop'lar,
-tree.
bal'sa mo den'dron.
Bạl'tic.
Bạl'ti more bird, B. o'rǐ ole.
Bä lu chis tan' (-loo'chis tän'), or
Bĕl oō'chǐs tän', Asia.
bǎl'us ter, -tered, -träde (or -träde'),
-tra'ded, -ding, bal'us ter-shǎft,
-stem.
Bal zac', de (dĕ bäl'zäk'), Fr. novelist.
bǎl za rine' (-rēn').
bǎm, -ming, bammed.
bam'a lip, -lip'ton, bam'ba ra.
bǎm bi'no (-bē'- or bǎm-).
bam boc'ci äde (or -boch'-).
bam boō', -bri'er, -palm, -par'-
tridge, -rat, -reed.
bam boo'zle, -zled, -zling, -zler.
bam bou'la (-boō'-).
Bam bu'sa, -sa'ceous.
bǎ'mi a.

ban, _v._, -ning, banned. _bǎn_, a
  fabric.
_bä na bä'_ (-vä').
Ban'ā ī'as, _Bib._
ban'al, ba nal'i ty, _pl._ -i tĭes.
ba nä'na (_or_ ba năn'a), ban'a niv'-
  o rous, ba nä'na-bird, -eat er, -fish,
  -peel, -plant, -quit, -skin.
Bä näng', t. P. I.
Bä nät,' t. Hung.
ban'at _or_ -āte.
bănc.
bäŋ'ca.
ban'co.
band, -ed, -e let _or_ band'let, -ing,
  -age, -a ging, -a ger, band'fish,
  band'-ax'is, -bird, -brake, -coup'-
  ling, -cut' ting, -driv'er, -lāc'ing,
  -lin en, -mas'ter _or_ band'mas'ter,
  -mount'ing, -nip'pers, -pul'ley,
  -rob in, -saw, -set'ter, -string,
  -wheel, -work, bands'man, band'
  spec' trum.
ban dä'la.
ban dan'na _or_ -dan'a.
band'box.
ban dě' (boṅ dā').
ban'deau (-dō _or_ -dŏ'), pl. -_deaux_
  (-dōz).
Bän de'rä (-dā'-), co. Tex.
ban'der et.
ban de ril'la (-rĕl'ya), -_ril le'ro_ (-rĕl-
  yā'ro).
band'e role _or_ -rŏl _or_ band'rŏl.
ban'di coot.
band'ing-ma chine', -plane _or_ b.
  plane, -ring.
ban'dit, _pl._ -dits _or_ -dit'tĭ.
ban'dle.
băn'do, pl. -_dos_ (-dōz).
ban'dog.
ban do leer' _or_ -lier', -fruit.
ban'do lĭne.
ban'dore (_or_ -dore').
ban'dy, -ing, ban'died, ban'dy man,
  ban'dy-ball, -jig, -legged.
bane, -ber ry, -ful, -ful ly, -ful ness,
  -wort.
Banff (bămf), co. Scot.
bang, -er, -ing, banged, bang'-
  beg gar, -pitch er, -straw, -up.
bang'al'ay (-ăl'ī).
baŋ'ga lŏw.

baŋ'ghy (bang'gy), -post, -wal'-
  lah.
Băng kŏk' _or_ Baŋ-, c. Siam.
baŋ'gle, -ear, -eared.
ban ian _or_ -yan (ban'yan _or_ -yan'),
  -tree.
ban'ish, -ing, -er, -ment, -ished.
ban'is ter _or_ -nis ter, -cross.
ban'jo, -ist, -rine' (rĕn'), -frame,
  -play er, -string.
bank, -a ble, -er, -ing, -less, -side,
  banked.
bank'-ac count', -bait, -bill _or_ b.
  bill, -book _or_ b. book, -cred'it,
  -game, -head, -hol'i day, -hook,
  -lev'el, -mar'tin, -note _or_ b. note,
  -plate, -post, -pro tect or, -shot,
  -stock, -swal'low _or_ b. swal'low,
  -work, bank dis count, b. fence.
bank'ing-file, -pin, -wax.
băŋ ket'.
bank'rupt, -ed, -ing, -cy.
băn'li eue (-lē û) _or_ _ban'lieue_ (-lū)
ban'ner, -et, -ŏl, -less, -man, -nered,
  ban ner-plant, -roll, -stone, -vane.
ban'nock, -fluke.
banns _or_ bans.
baŋ'quet, -er, -ing, ban'quet-hall,
  -house, baŋ'quet ing-hall, -house,
  -room.
baŋ quette' (bang ket' _or_ bŏng ket'),
  b. slope, b. tread.
Baŋ'quo.
bân sä lä' gue (-gā).
ban'shee _or_ -shiē.
ban'stic kle.
Bän'täm', prov. Java.
ban'tam, Ban'tam-work _or_ B. work.
ban'teng.
ban'ter, -ing, -er, -tered.
ban'ting, -ism.
bant'ling.
băn'tu (-tōō), _pl._ -tus (-tōōz).
ban'yan. See _banian._
ba'o bab (_or_ bä'-).
Baph'o met, -met'ic.
Bap ti'si a (-tĭzh'i a).
bap'tism, -tis'mal (-tiz'-), -mal ly,
  -tist, -tis ter y _or_ -tis try, -tis'tic,
  -tic al.
bap tize', -tized', -tiz'ing, -er, -a-
  ble.
ba quet' (-kā').

bar, barred, bar'ring, bar'keep er,
-man, -maid, -mâs'ter, -room,
-tend'er, -way, -wise, -wood, bar-
cut ter, -dig gings, -fee, -fish,
-frame, -gown, -i'ron, -lâthe,
-lift, -lock, -loom, -mag'nate,
-min'ing, -net, -plow, -post,
-pump, -roll, -shear, -shoe, -shoot'-
ing, -shot, -sight, -tailed, -weir,
bar hive.
bâr'ad.
bar a nee'.
bar a the'a-cloth.
bar'a thrum, pl. *-thra.*
barb, -ing, barbed, barb'-bolt,
-fĕath ers, -pi geon, barbed bolt,
b. shot, b. wire.
Bar ba'dos *or* -does (-dōz), isl. W.
I., -ba'di an, Bar ba'dos-pride, B.
cher'ry, B. leg, B. nut, B. tar.
bar'ba ra, a term in logic. Bar'ba-
ra, Chr. name.
bar ba'ri an, -an ism, -bâr'ic, -ic ally, -i ty, bar'ba rize *or* -rise, -rized,
-ri zing, -ba rous, -rous ly, -rous-
ness, -ba rism.
Bar'ba ry, B. ape, B. gum, B. horse.
bar'bate, -ba ted.
barbe.
bar'be cue, -cued, -cu ing.
bar'bel, -beled *or* -belled.
bar'bel late, -bel'lu late.
bar'ber, -ing, -bered, bar'ber-boat,
-fish *or* b. fish, -sur'geon, -sur'-
ger y.
bar'ber'ry, *pl.* -ries, bar'ber'ry-
fuŋ'gus.
bar'bet.
bar bette', -car'riage, b. bat ter y,
b. gun, b. ship.
bar'bi can *or* -ba can.
bar big'er ous (-bij'-).
bar'bi on.
bar'bi ton or *-bi tos.*
bar bo'ne (-nä).
bar'bo tīne.
bar'bu (-bōō), *-bu'do* (-boo'thō).
bar'bule.
bar'ca, a fish. Bar'ca, dist. N.
Afr., -can.
bar'ca role *or* -rŏlle.
bar'ce nīte.
Bar'clay, *Biog.,* -an, -ite.

bar'con *or* -co'ne.
bar'coo', b. grâss.
bard, a poet, -ic, -ish, -ism, -ling,
-let, -ship.
bärd *or* bärde, defensive armor, a
term in cookery. bard'ed.
bar'do cu cul'lus.
bare, -back, -backed, -boned, -faced,
-faced ly, -faced ness, -foot, -foot'-
ed, -hand ed, -head ed, -head ed-
ness, bared, bâr'ing, bare'ly, bare-
legged, -necked, -ness, bare'-
picked, -pump, -ribbed, -worm.
ba rege' (-räzh').
Bä reil'ly (-rä'lē), dist. India.
bare'sark.
bâr'es the'si om'e ter, -o met'ric.
bar'gan, a weapon.
bar'gaĭn (*or* -gĕn *or* -gän), -ing, -er,
-ee', -gained, bar'gain man, bar'-
gain-chop, -coun ter, -work, b.
day.
barge, -man, -mâs'ter, -mate, -raf'-
ter, -stone, barge-board, -cou ple,
-course.
bar'ghest *or* -guest (-gest).
bä'ri (-rē), a slate. Bä'ri, a wine.
ba ril'la.
bär'il let.
bâr'is, *pl.* bâr'es (-ēz). Bar'is,
Entom.
bär'i tone. See *barytone.*
bä'ri um, ba'rite, ba'ri um chro'-
mate, b. hy'drate, b. nī'trate, b.
ox'id, b. sul'phate.
bark, *v.,* -ing,, -er, barked.
bark *or* barque, a vessel. bark'an-
tine *or* -en tine (-tēn).
bark, *n.,* -er y, -less, -om'e ter,
-stone, bark'y, bark-bed, -bound,
-cloth, -feed'er, -galled, -louse,
-mill, -pa'per, -pit, -plān'ing,
-stove, -tanned, bark' bee'tle, b.
path, b. walk.
Bark er's mill.
bark'ing-ax, -bill, -bird, -i'ron,
-mal'let, -ma chine, -tools.
bark'lak.
bar'ley, -corn, -hood, -bigg, -bird,
-brake *or* -break, -bree *or* -broo,
-broth, -fe'ver, -fork, -is land,
-meal, -mill, -sick, -su'gar,
-wa'ter, -wine.

---

nŏt, nôr, ūse, ŭp, ûrn, etüde, fōōd, fŏŏt, aŋger, boŋmot, thus, Bach.

barm, -brack, barm′y, barm-cloth, barm′y-brained.
Bar′me cide *or* -ma-, -ci dal.
bar mil′ian.
bar′mote.
barn, -floor, -ful, -man, -storm er, -storm ing, -door, -gal lon, -gråss, -owl, -swal low (-swŏl-), -yard.
bar′na bee.
Bar′na bite.
Bar′na by-bright, B. day.
bar′na cle, -eat′er, -goose, -scale.
Barn′burn er.
bar′ney, -pit.
barn′hardt ite.
ba roc′co, *Arch.* See *baroque*.
ba rō′co *or* -ro′ko, *Logic.*
bǎr′o grâph, -graph′ic, -o gram.
bǎr′o lite.
ba rol′o gy.
bǎr o ma crom′e ter.
ba rom′e ter, -e try, bar o met′ric, -al ly, -met′ro grâph, -rog′ra phy, ba rom′e ter-flow′ers, -gage.
bǎr′o metz.
bǎr′o mo tor.
bǎr′on, -age, -ess, -et, -ism, -on y, *pl.* -on ies, -et age, -et cy, ba ro′ni al, bar on nette′, bar′on-court.
ba rong′.
ba roque′ (-rōk′) *or* *ba roc′co* *or* *ba ro′co*, *Arch.*, ba roque′-pearl.
bǎr′o scope, -scop′ic, -ic al.
bǎr o sel′e nite.
bǎr′o tax′is.
bar′o ther′mo graph.
ba rouche′ (-rōōsh′), -rou chet′ (-rōō shä′).
ba rox′y ton.
barque. See *bark*.
bǎr′ra can.
bǎr′rack, -mås ter.
bǎr′ra clade.
bǎr ra coon′.
bǎr ra cu′da *or* -cou′ta (-kōō′).
bar′ra gan.
bǎr′rage.
bǎr ra gu′do (-goo′-).
bǎr ran′ca *or* -*co.*
Bär rän quil′la (-kēl′yä), prov. Colom.

bǎr′ra tor, -trous, -tro us ly, -ra try.
bǎr re′ (-rä′). Bǎr′rē, tp. and vil. Mass.; tp. and vil. Vt.
bärred, -owl.
bar′rel, -reled *or* -relled, -rel ing *or* -ling, bar′rel-bay′o net, -bel′lĭed, -bōlt, -bulk, -fill′er, -fish, -gage, -head, -hooks, -hoop, -hoop ing, -lift′er, -māk ing, -plate, -roll er, -saw, -screw, -set′ter, -shaped, -vise (vīs), -wash er, -work, bar′rel curb, b. drain, b. loom, b. or gan, b. pen, b. pier, b. pro cess, b. vault.
bǎr′ren, -ly, -ness, -wort, -spir′-it ed.
bǎr′ret, -cap.
bär re te′ro (-tä′-).
bär′rette′.
bǎr ri cåde′, -cåd′ed, -cåd′ing, -cåd′er, -cä′do.
bǎr ri′co (-rē′-).
bǎr′ri er, -gate, b. reef, b. sys′tem, b. trea′ty.
bar ri gu′do (-gōō′-).
bär′ri o, pl. -*ri os* (-rē ōz).
bǎr′ris.
bǎr′ris ter, -ter ship, -te′ri al.
bǎr′row, -man, -way, -coat, -pig, -pump, -tram, -truck.
Bar′row ist.
bǎr′ru let, -ru ly, -ru let ty, -ru lée′ (-lä′).
Bar′sac.
barse.
bars′-gem′el (bärz′-jem′el).
bar′ter, -ing, -er, -tered.
barth.
Bär thol′di (-tōl′de *or* -tol′dē′), Fr. sculp.
Bar thol′o mew-tide, B. day, B. fair.
Bar thol′o mite.
Bar′tĭ mæ′us (-mē′-), *Bib.*
bar′ti zan, -zåned.
Bart′lett.
Bå′ruch (-rŭk), *Bib.*
bǎr′u tine.
bar y cen′tric.
ba ryph′o ny, bar y pho′ni a.
ba ry′ta, -ry′tes (-tēz), -ryt′ic, bǎr′y tīne.

---

fāte, făt, fär, fall, fâre, fåst, sofá, mēte, mĕt, hêr, īce, ĭn, nōte,

băr′y tōne *or* -ĭ tone.
ba ry′tum.
bā′sal, -nerved.
ba sạlt′, -ic, -i form, -salt′oid.
bas′a nīte (*or* baz′-).
bas-bleu′ or *b. bleu′* (bä blê′).
bas′ci net *or* bas′i-.
bas cu la′tion.
bas′cūle, b. bridge.
base, -ly, -less, -less ness, -man, -ness, -ball, based, bā′sic.
base′-bag, -board, -born, -bred, -bul lion, -burn′er, -burn′ing, -court, -dânce, -heart ed, -hit, -lev′el, -line, -mind′ed, -mind- ed ly, -mold′ing, -plate, -ring, -rock er, -rock et, -run′ning, -run′ner, -spir it ed, base broom, b. fee, b. ten ure.
Bä′sel-Land (-zel-) *or* Bâle- (bäl), *or* Basle (bäl), prov. Switz.
base′ment, sto′ry.
ba se ol′o gy.
Bä′shan, *Bib.*
ba shaw′.
bash′ful, -ly, -ful ness.
bash′i-ba zouk′ (-zo͞ok′).
bash′lyk or *-lik.*
ba′ɑi-al vc′o lɑr.
ba sic′i ty (-sis′-).
ba′sic slag.
ha sid′i um.
ba′ si fixed, -sif′u gal.
ba′ si fy, -ing, -fi er, -fied, -fĭ ca′- tion.
Bä′sĭl *or* -sil′ius, *Biog.*, -sil′i an (*or* -yan).
bas′il (baz′-), -ing, -ĭled, bas′il- weed, bas′il-oil, -thyme.
bas′i lar (baz′-), -la ry.
ba sil′ic, a portico or hall, -ic al, -i can, *-i con,* bas i lis′cĭne.
Ba sil′i ca, a code of laws, -sil′ics.
Bas i lid′i an, -an, ism.
Bas′i lis′co.
bas′i lisk.
ba′sin (-sn), -sined, ba′sin-cock, -grate, -plug, -stop per, -trap, -waste, -wrench, ba′ sin ing- cloth.
bas′i net *or* bas′net. See *bascinet.*
ba′si on.

ba′sis, *pl.* -ses (-sēz).
bâsk, -ing, -basked.
bâs′ket, -ful, -ket ry, -wood, a plant, -work, -ball, -bea′gle, -cloth, -fern, -fish, -han dle, -hare, -hilt′ed, -hood, -hoop, -liz′ard, -māk ing, -oak, -palm, -shell, -ur′chin, -weave, -wĭthe, -wood, -worm, bas ket-of-gold, bas ket boat, b. but ton, b. car riage, b. couch ing, b. grate, b. hilt, b. rack.
bas′lard.
bä′so phīle *or* -phĭl, -phĭl′ic, -soph′i lous.
Bâsque, a language; a people.
bâsque, bâsqued, bâs quine′ (-keen′).
bas qui′na (-kē′nya), *-quine′* (-kēn′).
bas′-re lief′ (bä′-) *or* băss-.
bâss, a fish; a tree; a mat, bâss′- wood, bâss′-rope.
bâss, a part in music; a term in mining, bäss′-bar, b. clar′ i net, b. clef, b. cor′net, b. drum, b. horn, b. stâff, b. string, b. vi′ ol, b. voice.
Bâss′ goose.
băs sā′lĭ a, -li an.
Bâs sä′nĭ ō.
bas′set, -ing, bas′set horn, b. hound.
bas′si net.
bâs′so, -buf′fo, *-con ti′nu o* (-tē′- no͞o ō), *-di-can′e ra* (-dē-), *-os ti nä′to, -pro jon′do* or *-fun′-, -ri lie′vo* (-rē lyä′vo) *or* -re lie′vo (băs′so rē lē′vo).
bas soon′, -ist, *bas soṅ′.*
bast, -palm, -tree.
bäs′tä, an interjection. bäs′ta, a term in cards.
bas′tard, -ize, -ized, -i zing, -tar dy, bas′tard tur′bot, b. type, b. wheel, b. wing.
bâste, bäst′ing, -ed, -er, bäst′ing- ma chine.
bas ter′na.
bâs tide′ (-tēd′ *or* bas′tĭd).
bâs tile *or* -tille (bâs teel′ *or* bâs′-).
bas′ti na′do, *pl.* -does (-dōz), -nâde′.

---

nŏt, nôr, ūse, ŭp, ûrn, etüde, fo͞od, fo͝ot, aŋger, boṅmot, thus, Bach.

băs′tion (-chun), -tioned, -tion et.
băs′to.
ba su′tos (-sōō′tŏz).
băs′yl *or* -yle (*or* bä′-), -y lous.
bat, -ted, -ting, -ty, -ter, -let,
-fish, -man, bats′man, bat-bolt,
-fowl er, -mon ey, -print ing,
-shell, -tick, bat's-wing.
ba tä′ra.
ba tar deau′, pl. *-deaux′* (-dōz′).
ba tä′tăs or *ba tä′ta,* Bå tä′ta,
Bot. genus.
Ba ta′vi an.
batch.
bate, -ment, -stone, băt′ed, -ing,
bate′ment-light.
bat′e a.
ba teau′ or *băt teau′* (-tō′), *pl.*
-teaux′ (-tōz′), ba teau′-bridge.
bat′e leur (-lêr).
bâth, *pl.* baths (båthz), bath′room,
-tub, -wort, -chops, -cock, -fur-
nace, -heat er, -house, -kol,
-sponge, -spring, băth, a measure.
Bâth brick, B. bun, B. chair, B.
met′al, B. note, B. ō′ō līte, B.
stone.
bâtńe, bäth′ing, -er, bathed.
ba thet′ic.
bath′ic.
băth′ing-box, -dress, -house, -ma-
chine′, -suit, -tub.
băth′mic, bath′mism.
bath′mo dŏnt.
bath′o līth or -līte.
ba thom′e ter.
bat′horse.
bä′thŏs.
Băth shē′ba (*or* băth′-), *Bib.*
ba thyb′i us, -i al, -i an, -an′ ic.
bath′ y lim net′ ic.
ba thym′ e try, bath′ y met′ ric,
-ric al.
bath′ y pe lag′ ic (-lăj′-).
ba tiste′ (-tēst′).
ba tol′o gist.
bat′on (*or* bä toṅ′), bat′on-cross.
Băt′on Rouge (rōōzh), c. La.
Ba tra′chi a (-kĭ-), ba tra′chi an.
bat′ta.
bat tage′ (-täzh′).
bat tal′ion (-yun), -ioned, bat-
tal′ion drill.

bat′tel, -er.
bat′ten, -ing, -tened, bat′ten door,
b. floor.
bat′ter, -ing, -er, -tered, -ter y,
bat′ter-head, -lev el, -rule.
bat′ter ing-charge, -gun, -piece,
-ram, -rule, -train.
bat′ter y, -box, -brush, -gun,
-head, -shoot′ing, -wag′on.
bat′ting, -block, -ma chine, -stăff.
bat′tle, -tled, -tling, -tle ment,
-ment ed, bat′tle-ax *or* -axe,
-bolt, -brand, -club, -cry, -field,
-flag, -ground, -lan tern, -mace,
-piece, -scarred, -shout, -song.
bat′tle dore *or* -door.
bat tol′o gy, -o gize, -o gist, -to-
log′ic al.
bat′tue (*or* -tue′).
bat ture′ (*or* bat′-).
băt tu′ta (-tōō′-).
băt′ūle (*or* bå tōōl′), bat toule′-
board (-tōōl′-).
bătz (*or* bäts), *pl.* bătz′en (*or*
bät′sn).
bau′ble.
Bau′cis and Phĭ lē′mon.
bau′de kin *or* baud′kin.
bauge (bōzh).
bau′le a.
bau′lite.
Bau′ mé′s′ scale (bō′māz′).
baun′scheidt ism (boun′shīt izm).
bau′son, -sond, bau′son-faced.
Bau tain′ (bō′tăn′), Fr. theol.
bå var dage′ (-dăzh′).
Ba va′ri a, Ger., -ri an.
ba vette′ (-vĕt).
ba vière′ (bå vyâr′).
baw bee′ *or* bau-.
bawd, -y, -i ly, -i ness, -mon′ey,
-ry, bawd′ship, bawd′y-house.
bawl, -er, -ing, bawled.
bax′ter.
Bax′ter, -te′ri an, -an ism.
bay, -ing, -ber ry, -man, bayed,
bay′-ant ler, -birds, -bolt,
-breast′ed, -cod, -gall, -goose,
-leaf, -ma hog′a ny, -o′l, -por-
poise (-pus), -salt, -stall, -tree,
-winged, -wood, -yarn, b. rum,
b. win′dow, bay′ber ry-tal low.
bä′ya, -bird.

---

fāte, făt, fär, fạll, fâre, fåst, sofå, mēte, mĕt, hêr, īce, ĭn, nōte,

ba yăd' or *-yătte'*.
bä ya dĕre' *or* -deer'.
bä'yal.
bä yä'mo. Bä yä'mō, t. Cuba.
bäy'ard.
Bay'ard (bī'ard). Amer. statesman.
Bay'ard, de (dĕ bä'ard), Chevalier, Fr. warrior.
Bäy'ard, Rinaldo's famous steed.
Ba yeux' (bä'yŭ'), *Geog.*, B. tap'es try.
Bay of Nī'pe (nē'pä), Cuba.
Bay of Quīnte, Can.
bay'o net, -ed, -ing, bay'o netcatch, -clǎsp, -scab bard, b. clutch, b. joint.
bay'ou (bī'oo), *pl.* -ous (-ōōz).
ba zaar' *or* -zar' (-zär'), -maund.
ba zä'ras.
bdel lat'o my (dĕl-), -lom'e ter.
bdel'li um (*or* del'yum).
be, -ing, -ing less, -ing ness, Be'ing, the Supreme Being. be'-all.
beach, -ing, -y, -man, -mǎs ter, beached, beach-birds, -clam, -comb er (-kōm er), -flea, -grǎss, -pea, -plum, -wag on.
bea'con, -age, -less, bea'con-blaze, -fire, -tow er.
Bēa'cons field (*or* bĕk'-), Benjamin Disraeli, Eng. statesman.
bead, -ed, -er, -ing, -y, -wom'an, -work, -house *or* bede'house, bead'man *or* beads- *or* bedes-.
bead'-fur nace, -loom, -mold, -mold'ing, -plane, -proof, -roll, -sight, -snake, -stuff, -tool, -tree, bead'work-lathe.
bea'dle, -dom, -ism, -ry, -ship.
bea'gle, -gling.
beak, -er, beak'head, -i'ron, beaked, beak-rush, -sheath, beak'er-cells, beak'ing-joint.
bēal, a drink; bēal (*or* bāl), a narrow pass.
beam, -ing, -ing ly, -ful, -y, -i ly, -i ness, -less, -let, -age, -ster, beamed, beam-bird, -board, -cal'i per, -cen ter, -com pass, -en gīne, -fĕath er, -fill'ing, -gud'geon (-jŭn), -hook, -knife,

-light, -line, -plat'form, -roll, -room, -trawl, -tree, -truss, beam'-ing-ma chine'.
bean, -y, bean'-brush, -cake, -ca'-per, -cod, -crake, -curd, -dol'-phin, -feast, -fed, -fly, -goose, -har'vest er, -har'vest ing, -king, -meal, -mill, -pole, -shell'er, -shoot er, -shot, -stalk, -tree, -tre foil, -wee vil.
bear (bâr), -er, -ing, -ish, -ishness, -a ble, -a bly, -ance, -bane, -ber ry, -bine *or* -bind, -herd, -skin, -ward, -wood, -wort.
bear - an i mal' cule, -bait'ing, -cat'er pil'lar, -cloth, -dog, -gar'-den, -grǎss, -hound, -lead'er, -moss, -mouse, -oak, -pig, -pit, -whelp.
beard, -ing, -less, -less ness, -let ed, -ling, -y, beard'tongue, a plant, beard'-grǎss, -moss, beard'ing-line.
bear er-bar, -pin.
bear'ing-bin'na cle, -cloth, -feel'-er, -neck, -note, -rein, -robe.
bear's-bed, -bil'ber ry, -breech, -ear, -foot, -gar'lic, -grape, -weed.
boaot, -hood, -like, -ly, -li ness, beast'-hide, beast's-bane.
beat, -en, -er, -ing.
beat'er-press.
beat'ing-brack'et, -en'gīne, -hammer, -ma chine'.
be a tif'ic, -ic al, -al ly, -at'i fy, -i fied, -fi ca'tion, -i tude.
Bē'a trīce.
Beat'tie (bē'ty *or* bā'-), Scotch poet.
be at'tle.
beau (bō), *pl.* beaus *or* beaux (bōz), -ish, -ship, beau'-i de'al, -*mŏnde*, -pŏt.
Beau Brŭm'mel (bō-).
Beau'champ (bee'cham), de, Eng. gen.
Beau champs' (bō'shŏn'), Fr. astron.
Beau'clerk (bō'clärk), Eng. schol.
Beau court', de (dĕ bō'kōōr'), Fr. hist.
beau'fet (bō'-).
beau'fin (bō'- *or* bĭf'-).

Beaū'fort, Eng. cardinal; t. S. C.

Beau'fort (bō'fŏrt), t. N .C.— (bō for'), t. Fr.

Beau'fort's scale (bū'-).

Beau har nais', de (dĕ bō'är'nā'), Alexandre, Vicomte.

Beau har nois' (bō'är'nwä'), co. Que.

beau'mont ite.

Beaune (bōn), t. Fr.; a wine.

Beau're gard (bō'rē gard), Confed. gen.

beau sé ant' (bō sä än' *or* bō'-).

Beau temps'-Beau pré' (bo'tŏn'-bō'prā'), Fr. scientist.

beau'ty (bū'-), -te ous, -ous ly, -ous ness, -ti fy, -fy ing, -fied, -fi er, -fi ca'tion, -ful, -ful ly, -ti less.

beau'ty-sleep, -spot, -wash, -of-the-night, a plant.

Beau'vais' (bō vā'), c. Fr.

beaux'ite (bōz'-).

bea'ver, -vered, -ver teen, bea'ver-root, a plant, -tongue, a plant, bea ver-poi'son, -rat, -tree.

be bĭ za'tion.

be blub'ber, -bered.

be'bung (bā'-).

be cälm', -ing, -ment, -cälmed.

be came'.

be cap', -ping, -capped.

bec'ard.

be cässe', -cas sine' (-sēn').

be cause'.

bec ca buŋ'ga.

bêch'a mel (besh'-).

be chânce'.

bêche (bāsh).

bêche-de-mer (bāsh'dê mâr').

be'chic (-kik).

Bech u ä'nas (bĕch'ŏͦ-).

beck, -ing, becked, beck'-i'ron.

beck'er.

beck'et.

beck'on (-n), -ing, -er, -oned.

be cloud', -ed, -ing.

be come' (-kŭm'), -com'ing, -ing-ly, -ing ness, -came'.

bec quê' (bĕ kā').

becque'rel' rays (bĕk'-).

Bec'se (bĕt'che), t. Hung.

be cui'ba-nut (-kwē'-).

be cu'na (*or* bā kōō'na).

bed, -ded, -der, -ding, -bug, -cham'ber, -clothes, -cord, -cov'er (-kuv'-), -fåst, -fel low, -gown, -māk'er, -mate, -plate, -piece, -post, -quilt, -rid den, -room, -side, -sprĕad, -stĕad, -stock, -stone, -straw, -tick, -tick ing, -time, -way, -work.

bed-ale, -board, -bolt, -bot tom, -chair, -clip, -fåst'en er, -frame, -hang ings, -key, -lāthe, -lin en, -lounge, -mold ing, -pan, -press-er, -right, -rite, -rock, -sack ing, -screw, -sore, -spring, -steps, -thrall, -tool, -vein, -wrench.

bed'ding-mold ing, -plant, -stone.

be dab'ble, -bled, -bling.

bed'a gåt.

be dash', -dashed', -dash'ing.

be d̪aub', -ing, -daubed.

be daz'zle, -zled, -zling, -zling-ly.

be deck', -ing, -decked.

bed'e gar or *-guar* (-gär).

Be dĕ'iah (-yah), *Bib.*

be'del *or* -dell', -ry.

be dew', -er, -ing, -ment, -dewed'.

bed'ger y.

be dight'.

be dim', -ming, -dimmed'.

Bed'i vĕre, Sir.

be dĭz'en (*or* -dī'zen), -ment.

bed'lam, -īte, -ism.

Bed'ou ĭn (-ōō ĭn *or* -ēn), -ism.

be drab'ble, -bling, -bled.

be drag'gle, -gling, -gled.

be dye', -dyed', -dye'ing.

bee, -hive, -house, -keep er, -keep-ing, -mås ter, bees'wax, -wing, -winged.

bee'-bird, -block, -bread, -cul ture, -eat er, -feed, -feed er, -fu'mi ga tor, -flow er, -fly, -gar den, -glue, -gum, -hawk, -herd, -kill er, -king, -line, -louse, -mar tin, -moth, -net tle, -or'chis (-kis), -par a site, -scap, -skep, -tree, -wolf, -worm, b. lark'spur.

bee'bee.

beech, -en, -y, beech'drops, -nut, -coal, -fern, -finch, -fuŋ'gus,

-gall, -hop per, -mar'ten, -măst, -oil, -owl.

beef, *pl.* beeves, beef'y, -ish, -i ness, -steak, -wood, -brained, -cat'tle, -eat er, -head ed, -herd, -kid, -mēa sle, -wit ted, beef tea.

beef'steăk-fuŋ gus, -plant, beef'-su'et-tree.

Be el'ze bub, -ze bŭl.

been (bin).

beer, -y, -i ness, -stone, beer'-bar rel, -brew er, -drink ing, -en'gĭne, -fau cet, -float, -fountain, -gar'den, -glăss, -hop per, -house, -ma chine, -meas ure, -mon'ey, -pre serv'er (-zerv'-), -pull, -pump, -sa loon', -sell ing, -shop, -swill er, -vat.

Bē'er, *Bib.*

Bē er she' ba (*or* bē er' she ba), *Bib.*

beet, -chards, -fly, -măs ter, -mis ter, -press, -rad ish, -rave, -root.

Bee'tho ven, van (vän bā'tō ven), Prus. composer.

bee'tle, -tled, -tling, bee'tle head, a person; a bird, -stone, -brow, -browed (-broud), head ed, -mite, -stock, bee'tling-ma chine'.

be fall', -en, -ing, -fell'.

be jä'na, a gift. *Be jä'na,* a fairy.

be fit', -ted, -ting, -ting ly.

be fool', -ing, -fooled'.

be fore', -hand -time.

be foul', -ing, -fouled'.

be friend', -ed, -er, -ing.

be frill', -ing, -frilled'.

be fud'dle, -dled, -dling.

beg, -ging, -gar, -gar ly, -li ness, -gar hood, -gar ism, -gar dom, -gar y, begged, beg' gar weed, beg'gar-my-neigh'bor, beg'gar's-băs'ket, -lice, -nee dle, -ticks.

be get', -ting, -got'ten, -got'.

Beg'hard *or* Be guard'.

be gin', -ning, -ner, -gan', -gun'.

be gird', -ed, -ing, -girt', -gir'dle.

beg'ler beg' (*or* bā'ler bā'), *or* bey'-ler bey (bā'-).

be gŏne'.

be gŏ'ni a, a plant, -a'ceous (-shus). Be go'ni a, *Bot. genus.*

be grime', -grimed', -grīm'er, -grīm'ing.

be grudge', -grudged', -grudg'ing, -ing ly.

be guile' (-gīl'), -ment, -guiled', -guil'ing, -ing ly, guil'er.

Be guin or *-guine* (beg'in *or* bā-găn' *or* beg'win), *be'gui'nage'* (bā gē năzh').

bě'gum (*or* bā'-).

be half' (-häf').

be hăve', -hāved', -hāv'ing, -hāv'-ior (-yur).

be hěad', -ed, -ing.

be'he moth (*or* -he'-). Bē'he-moth, *Bib.*

be'hen *or* běhn.

be hest'.

be hind', -hand.

be hold', -en, -ing, -er, -held'.

be hōof', -hōove', -hooved', -hoov'ing.

beige (bāzh).

bei gnet' (bā nyā').

Bei'rut *or* Bey'root (bā'rōot), t. Syr.

be'jan *or* -jant.

be jew' el, -eled *or* -elled, -el ing *or* -ling.

be ju'co (ba hōo'ko).

be jum'ble, -bled.

bě'kah.

be knot'ted, -ness.

bel, a tree. Bel, a Babylonish god.

be la'bor, -ing, -bored.

be late', -lāt'ed, -lāt'ing.

be lay', -ing, -laid' *or* -layed', be lay'ing-bitt, -pin.

belch, -ing, belched.

bel'dăm *or* -dāme (*or* -dăm).

bel du'que (-doo'kā).

be lea'guer (-le'ger), -er, -ing, -ment, -guered.

bě'lem nite (*or* běl'em-), -nit'ic.

bel - es prit' (-pre'), pl. *beaux-es prits'* (bōz es prē').

Běl'făst, c. Me.—(-făst'), c. Ire.

bel'fry, *pl.* -frĭes, -frĭed, bel fry-owl, -tŭr'ret.

Bel'gi um, -gĭ an, -gic.

Bel gra'vi a, -vi an.

Bē'lĭ al (*or* běl'yal).

be lie', -lied', -ly'ing.
bĕ lĭēve', -lieved', -liev'a ble,
-a ble ness, -liev'er, -ing, -ing ly.
be like'.
be lit'tle, -tled, -tling.
bell, -flow er, -man, -mouth, v.,
-wort, belled.
bell'-an'i mal, -an i mal' cule,
-bind, -bird, -bloom, -bot tle,
-boy, -buoy (-bwoi), -cage, -call,
-can o py, -chăm ber, -chuck,
-cord, -cote, -crank, -found er,
-found ry, -ga ble, -gam ba,
-gas'tru la, -hang er, -mag nate,
-mag pie, -mare, -met al, -met'-
ro nome, -mouth, n., mouth of a
bell, -mouthed, -nosed, -pep per,
-pol yp, -pull, -punch, -ring er,
-rope, -rose, -shaped, -sound,
-tow er, -tŭr'ret, -weth er, -work.
bell bear'er, b. glăss, b. harp,
b. jar, b. mouth, n., a mouth-
piece of bell shape, b. pump,
b. roof, b. screw, b. tel'e graph,
b. trap.
bel'la don'na, -nĭn or -nĭne.
bel'lar mĭne.
Bel lä'ry, dist. India.
bel la sŏm'bra.
belle.
bel leek'-ware.
Bĕlle'fŏn'tāine, t. O.
Bĕlle Isle' (-il'), isl. in Atlantic.
Bel lĕr'o phon.
Bel lē'rus.
belles-let'tres (bel-let'tr), -let trist,
-tris'tic, -tic al.
bel'li cose, -cose ly (-kōs-), -cos'-
i ty.
bel lig'er ent (-lij'-), -ent ly, -ence,
-en cy, -lip'o tent.
Bel'lis.
Bel lo'na, Myth. bel lo'na, Herpet.
bel lo'ni on.
bel'low, -ing, -er, -lowed.
bel'lows (-lŭs or -lōz), -cam e ra,
-fish, -pump, -sound.
bel'ly, pl. -lies (-liz), bel'lied,
-ly ing, -ly ache, -ful, bel'ly-band,
-boards, -bound, -brace, -but-
ton, -churl, -doŭb'let, -god,
-guy, -piece, -pinched, -pipe,
-rail, -roll, -slave, -stay, -tim-

ber, -ven geance (jăns or -jens),
-wash, -worm.
bel' o man cy.
be lŏng', -ing, -lŏnged'.
bel'o nite, -o noid.
Bel oo'che or -chee.
be loved', -lov'ed, p. a.
be low'.
Bel phœ'be (-fē'-).
belt, -ed, -ing, belt'-clamp, -clăsp,
-coŭp'ling, -cut ter, -la cing,
-mold ing, -pipe, -punch,
-punch ing, -rail, -saw, -screw,
-shift er, -ship'per, -speed'er,
-splĭ'cing, -stretch'er, -tight'-
en er, -tool, -weav ing.
Bel'tane.
be lū'ga (or bel'ōō-), a sturgeon.
Be lu'ga, a genus of whales.
Be'lus.
bel ve dĕre', -dered'.
Bel vi dē'ra.
bel'ze buth.
be'ma, pl. -ma ta, -ma tist.
be moan', -ing, -er, -a ble,
-moaned'.
be mourn', -ing, -mourned'.
be mud'dle, -dled, -dling.
be muf'fle, -fled, -fling.
bĕn, -kit, -nut, -oil, -teak.
Bĕ nä'iah (-yah), Bib.
bench, -er, -ing, benched, bench
măs ter.
bench'-clamp, -drill, -forge,
-ham'mer, -hook, -lāthe, -lev el,
-mark, -plane, -reel, -screw,
-shears, -stop, -strip, -ta ble,
-vise, -war rant, bench show.
ben chu'cha (-chōō'cha).
bend, -ed, -ing, -er, -a ble, -let,
-wise, bent, bent'y, bent'ing-
time, bend'-lĕath'er, bent-grăss,
bend ing-ma chine, -strake.
ben'dy, -tree, ben'dy bar'ry, b.
pa'ly.
be neath' (or -nēth').
Ben'e dic, -dic'i tē (dis'-), a hymn.
-dic'tus, ben e dic'i te, an invocation.
ben'e dick or -dict.
Ben e dic'tĭne.
ben e dic'tion, -al, -a ry, -dic'tive,
-dic'to ry.

be'në dis ces'sit, b. ex'e at.
ben e fac'tion, -fac'tor, -tress.
ben'e fĭce, -less, -fĭced.
be nef'i cence, -cen cy, -cent,
-cent ly, -cen'tial, -nef'ic.
ben'e fit, -ed, -ing, -er, -fi cial
(-fish'al), -cial ly, -cial ness,
-fi'ci a ry (-fish'i a ry *or* fish'a-
ry), -fi'ci ate (fish'), -a ted,
-a ting, -a'tion.
bē'ne plac'i to (*or* bä nä plä chē tō).
be nev'o lence, -lent, -lent ly.
Ben gạl', prov. India, -gal'ee *or*
-gạl i' (-gạl'ē *or* -gạl ē'), -gạl ese'
(-ēz'). bengạl', a fabric.
Ben gạl' grảss, B. light, B.
quince, B. root, B. stripes, B.
ti'ger.
ben go'la.
Bĕn gue'lä (-gä'-), coun. Afr.
Ben'-hä'dad, *Bib.*
Ben'-Hur (*or* Bĕn'-hur'), *Bib.*
Be ni' (bä nē'), r. S. A.
be night', -ed, -ing, -ment.
be nign' (-nīn'), -ly, -nig'nan cy,
-nig'nant, -nant ly, -nig'ni ty.
be nish' (nēsh').
ben'i son (-zn).
bĕ nĭ'tier (bä nĕ'tyä)
Ben'ja min, -ja mīte.
ben'ja min, -bush, -tree.
ben'jy.
Ben-Lo'mond, mt. Scot.
ben'ne.
ben'net.
Ben nū'ī, *Bib.*
Ben ŏ'nĭ, *Bib.*
ben'sel.
Ben'tham (-tam *or* -tham), Eng.
writer, -tham ism, -tham ĭte,
-tham'ic.
ben'thŏs.
be numb' (-nŭm'), -ing, -ment,
-numbed', -numbed'ness.
ben'zĕne (*or* -zēn').
ben'zĭle (*or* -zīle), -zil'ic.
ben'zĭn *or* -zĭne (*or* -zēn').
ben'zo ate, -a'ted.
ben'zo in (*or* -zoin'), a gum,
-zoin'a ted.
ben'zol *or* -zōle', -zo lin *or* -lĭne,
-zo lize, -lized, -lī zing.
Bĕ'o wulf (-wōŏlf *or* bä'-).

be queath', -ing, -al, -er, -a ble,
-ment, -queathed'.
be quest'.
Bĕr'ā ī'ah, *Bib.*
Bé ran ger', de (dĕh bä'rŏn'zhä'),
Fr. poet.
be rate', -rāt'ed, -ing.
berbe.
Ber'ber.
Be re'an.
be reave', -ment, -reav'ing,
-reaved, -reft.
Ber en ga'ri an, -an ism.
Ber e nĭ'cĕ, -ni'cĕ's locks, B.
hair. Bĕr'ĕn ī'cē, c. Egypt.
be ret' (bä rä').
berg, berg'y.
Ber'ga măsk *or* -go măsk.
ber'ga mot, -oil.
Ber'ge rac (*or* berzh răk').
berg'man īte.
berg'măs'ter.
berg'mēal *or* -mehl (-mäl).
bĕrg'schrund (-shrŏŏnt), *berg'stŏck.*
ber'i ber i or *be'rĭ be rĭ* (bä'-).
bĕr'ī gŏr'a.
Be rī'ītes, *Bib.*
Bĕ'rītes, *Bib.*
Bĕrke'ley, -ism, -le'ian.
ber'ko vets, -ko witz (-vĭts).
Ber'lin (*or* -lin'), cap. Prus., B.
wool, B. work.
ber'lin (*or* -lin'), a carriage; a
glove.
Ber li oz' (bĕr le ōz'), Fr. composer.
berm *or* berme.
ber mil'lians.
Ber mu'da, an isl., -mu'di an,
Ber mu'da grảss.
Bĕr na dŏttc' (*or* bĕr-), Fr. marshal.
ber'na fly.
Ber'nar dĭne.
Bĕrne, t. Switz. Bĕr nese' (-nēz').
Ber nī'ce, *Bib.*
ber'ni cle, -goose.
be roon'.
bĕr ret'ta. See *bĭ ret'ta.*
ber'ru găte.
ber'ry, -ing, -ried.
ber'sa glie're (bâr'sä lyä'rä), *pl.*
-ri (rē).

nŏt, nôr, ūse, ŭp, ûrn, etüde, fōōd, fŏŏt, aŋger, boṅmot, thus, Bach.

ber'serk *or* -ser ker.
berth, -age, -ing, berthed. berth'-
brace, -deck, -latch, -room, berth'-
ing-rail.
Ber'tha, Chr. name.
ber'tha, a drapery.
Ber'til'lon' sys'tem (bär tē yôn').
Bĕr ti'ni (-tē'nē), Fr. composer.
bĕr'tram *or* bar'-.
bĕr'yl, -līne, -loid, be ryl'li um.
bē'sa.
bes'a bol.
Be sant' (-sănt' *or* -zănt' *or* bĕz'-
ant), Eng. auth.
be seech', -ing, -ing ly, -ing ness,
-seech'ment, be sought.
be set', -ting, -ter, -set'ment.
be'sha.
besh'lik.
besh'met.
be show' (*or* -shou'), a fish.
be shroud', -ed, -ing.
bes i clom'e ter.
be side', -sides'.
be siĕge', -ment, -sieg'ing, -ing ly,
-er, -sieged'.
be smear', -ing, -er, -smeared'.
be smirch', -ing, -smirched'.
be'som (-zum).
be sot', -ted, -ted ly, -ted ness,
-ting, -ting ly.
be span'gle, -gled, -gling.
be spat'ter, -ing, -tered.
be speak', -ing, -spoke', -spō'ken.
be sprin'kle, -kler, -kling, -kled.
Bes sel'ian *or* -sel'li an.
Bes'se mer, -ize, -ized, -ī zing, B.
con vert'er, B. i ron, B. prŏ'cess,
B. steel.
be stĕad'.
bes'tial (-chal *or* best'yal), -ize,
-ized, -ī zing, -tial ly, -tial'i ty.
bes'ti a ry, a treatise on beasts.
be stir', -ring, -stirred'.
be stow', -ing, -er, -al, -ment,
-a ble, -stowed'.
be strad'dle, -dled, dling.
be strew' *or* be strōw', -strew'ing,
-strewed', -strewn'.
be strīde', -strode', -strīd'den,
-strīd'ing.
be stud', -ded, -ding.
be su'go (bä sōō'-).

Be'ta, Bot., be'ta (*or* bä-), a Greek
letter, -cism.
bête (bät), *bête noire* (nwär).
be'tel, -box, -pep'per, be'tel-nut
or be'tel nut.
Bet'el guese (-gēz).
Bĕth'-ăb'a ra, *Bib.*
beth ab'a ra wood.
Be thĕs'da (-thez'-), *Bib.*
Beth'-gā'der, *Bib.*
be think', -ing, -thought'.
Beth'le hem, -ite *or* -lem ite.
Beth'-pe'or, *Bib.*
Beth'pha ge (-fa jē *or* fāj), *Bib.*
Beth'sa'i da, *Bib.*
Be thū'el, *Bib.*
Beth'u lī'a, *Bib.*
be thumb', -thumbed'.
Be thune (-thōōn' *or* -thūn'),
Amer. poet.
Bé thune' (bā'tûn'), t. Fr.
be tide', -tīd'ed, -tīd'ing.
be times'.
be to'ken, -ing, -kened.
be'tōl.
bé ton' (bā ton' *or* bĕt'ŏn).
bet'o ny, be ton'i ca.
be tray', -al, -er, -ing, -trayed'.
be trŏth' (*or* -trōth'), -al, -ment,
-ing, -trothed'.
bet'ter, -ment, -most, -ness.
be tween', -twixt', be tween'-
decks.
beur ré' (bûr rā').
bev'el, -eled *or* -elled, -el ment,
-el ing *or* -ling.
bev'el-gear, -hub, -jack, -joint,
-plāt'er, -pro trac'tor, -rest,
-square, -tool, -ways, -wheel,
-wise.
bev'el ing-board, -edge, -frame,
-ma chine'.
bev'er age.
be vūe'.
bev'y, *pl.* -ies.
be wail', -ing, -er, -a ble, -ment,
-wailed'.
be ware'.
be wil'der, -ing, -ing ly, -ment,
-dered, -dered ness.
bew'it *or* -et (bū'-).
be witch', -ing, -ing ly, -ing ness,
-er, -er y, -ment, -witched.

fāte, făt, fär, fạll, fâre, fặst, sofà, mēte, mĕt, hêr, īce, ĭn, nōte,

Be xar' (bā här'), co. Tex.
bey (bā), -lic *or* -lik, -ship.
be yond', -sea.
Bē'zai (-zā), *Bib*.
Be zăl'ē ĕl, *Bib*.
bez'an.
be zant' *or* bĕz'-, be zan'ty.
bez an tée' *or* -te' (-tā').
bez-ant'ler.
bez'ĕl, -eled *or* -elled, -el ing *or*
  -ling.
be zet'ta.
Bé ziers' (bā zyā').
be zique' *or* ba- (-zēk').
be'zoar, bĕz o ar'dic *or* -tic, be'-
  zoar-goat.
be zo'ni an.
be zu'go (bā sōō'-).
bhäng *or* bäng.
bhees'ty *or* -tĭe, bhis'tēe *or* -tĭ
  (bĕs'-).
Bhil (bĕl).
bho'gai (bō'gī).
bhun'der (bŏŏn'-).
Bhu tan ese' (bōō tan ēs' *or* -ēz').
bĭ ac'id.
Bi an'ca (bē-).
bĭ aŋ'gu lar, -late, -la'ted.
bĭ an'nu al, -al ly.
bĭ an ther if'er ous.
Biar'mi an (byar'-) *or* Bĭ ar'-.
Bi ar ritz' (bē är rēts'), t Fr,
  bi ar ritz', cloth.
bĭ ar tic'u late.
bĭ'as, *pl.* -as es (-ĕz), -ing *or* -sing,
  -ăsed *or* -assed, bi'as-draw ing.
bĭ au ric'u lar.
bĭ au ric'u late.
bĭ ax'al *or* -i al.
bi'az (bē'ăz).
bib, -cock.
bĭ bac'ĭ ty (-bas'-), ba'cious, -ba'-
  tion, bib'a tive ness, -a to ry,
  bib'u lous, -lous ly.
bĭ ba'sic.
bĭb'ber.
bibe'lot (bĭb'lō).
bĭbe'ron (bĭb-).
Bi'ble, -clerk, -oath, Bib'li cism,
  -cist. Bib'list, -li ol'a ter.
bi'ble, bib'lic, -lic al, -al ly, -li-
  cal'i ty, -li o clast, -li o graph,
  -og'ra pher, -ra phy, -o graph'ic,

-ic al, -al ly, -ol'a try, -a trist,
  -ol'o gy, -o log'ic al, bib'li o-
  man cy, -ma'ni a, -ni ac, -nĭ'-
  ac al, -li og'nōst, -og nos'tic,
  bi'ble-press.
bib li op'e gy, -e gist, -gis'tic,
  -o peg'ic (-pej'-).
bib'li o phīle, -oph'i lism, -i list,
  -o pho'bi a.
bib'li o pole, -op'o lar, -o lism,
  -o list, -lis'tic, -o pol'ic.
bib'li o taph, -ot'a phist.
bib'li o thec, *-the'ca*, -the'cal.
bibs, a cloth. bibbs, timber.
bĭ cap'i tate, -ta ted.
bĭ cap'su lar.
bĭ car'bon ate.
bĭ car' bu ret ed *or* -ret ted.
bĭ cau'dal, -date.
bĭce *or* bĭse.
bĭ cen'te na ry, -ten'ni al.
bĭ ce phal'ic (*or* -ceph'-), -a lous.
bĭ'ceps.
bĭ ces'sis.
bi chir' (bē shēr').
bĭ chlo'rid *or* -rĭde.
bi'cho (bē'chō).
bĭ'chord (-kórd).
bĭ chro'māte, -mat'ic, -chro'mic,
  -ma tize, -tized, -ti zing.
bich'y.
bĭ cir'cu lar, -cir'cloid.
bick'er, -ing, -er, -ered.
bick'ern, bick'i ron.
bĭ cla'vate.
bĭ col lat'er al.
bĭ col'li gate.
bĭ'col'or, -ored.
bi con'cave.
bĭ con'dy lar (-dĭ-).
bĭ con so nan'tal.
bĭ con'vex.
bĭ'corn, -corned, -cor'nous, -cor'-
  nu ate.
bĭ cor'po ral, -po rate.
bĭ cres cen'tic.
bĭ cus'pid, -al, -ate, bi cus'pid
  valve.
bĭ'cy cle (-cĭ-), -cled (-kld) -cling,
  -clism, -clist, bi cyc'lic, -cyc'u lar.
bid, -ding, -der, -da ble, -dance,
  -den, băde, bid-hook, -stand.
bĭ dac'tyl.

bid a go'va.
bid'der y-ware.
bid'ding-prayer (-prâr).
Bid'dy, a domestic. bid'dy, a hen.
bid'dy bid.
bīde, bīd'ing.
bī'dent, -den'tal, -tate, -tial, -tic'-
u late.
bī den'tal, pl., *ta'li a.*
bī det' (*or* bē dā'), -pan.
bid'rĭ, -ware, -work.
bid'u ous.
Biĕ'la's com'et.
Biĕ'lĭd.
bī en'nĭ al, -ly.
biĕr, -right.
biĕst *or* beest, -ings.
biĕ'tle.
bī fā'cial.
bif'a ra.
bif'fin.
bī'fĭd, bif'i date, -da ted, bī fĭd'i ty.
bī fī'lar (*or* bĭf'i-), -ly.
bī fĭs'tu lar, -tu lous.
bī flec'nŏde.
bī'flex.
bī flo'rate, -rous.
bī fo'cal.
bī'fold.
bi fo'li ate, -li o late, -*li um*, pl.
-*li a.*
bī fo'rāte (*or* bif'o-), -fo'rous,
bif'o rĭne.
bī'fôrked.
bī'form, -formed, -form'i ty.
bī'frŏns, -front (-frŭnt), -front ed.
big, -ger, -gest, -ly, -ness, big'eye,
a fish, -foot, a bird, -head, a
person; a fish, -horn, a sheep,
-mouth, a fish, -root, a vine, -wig,
a person.
big-bel'lĭed, -boned, -en'di an,
-eyed, -sound ing.
bī'ga.
big'a my, -a mist, -a mous.
big'a rāde.
big a roon', -ar reau' (-ro').
bī gas'ter.
bī'ge ner (-je-), -nĕr'ic.
big'gin.
big'gon, -go net.
big'ha (bē'ga).
bight.

bī glan'du lar.
Big no'ni a, -*ni ā'ce æ*, big no ni a'-
ceous.
big'ot, -ot ed, -ed ly, -ot ry.
Bi got' (be'gō'), Fr. auth.
big'root, b. tree.
bī hour'ly.
bī-il'i ac.
bi jou' (bē zhōō'), *pl. bi joux*
(-zhōōz'), -jou'try.
bī ju'gate, -gous, -gal (*or* bĭj'-).
bīke.
bĭkh.
bī'kos, *pl.* -koi.
bik'shu, -shu ni (-nē).
bī'ku kŭl'la.
bil, a fish.
bī lä'lo.
bī lam'el late, -la ted, -lam'i nar,
-i nate.
bil'an der (*or* bī'lan-).
bī lat'er al, -ism, -ly, -al ness,
-al'i ty.
Bĭl bä'o, c. Sp.
bil'ber ry.
bil'bŏ, *pl.* -boes *or* -bos (-bōz).
bil'bō quet (-ket *or* -ka').
bil'cock.
bild'stein.
bīle, -stone, bī'lic, bile-cyst, -duct,
-pig'ment.
bĭlge, -ways, bil'gy, bilge'-board,
-coad, -free, -keel, -keel son,
-piece, -plank, -pump, -wa'ter.
Bil har'zī a.
bil'i a ry, -i a'tion, bī lif'er ous.
bī lin'e ar, -e ate, -a ted.
bī liŋ'gual, -ly, -ism, -guar, -guist,
-guous (-gwus).
bil'ious (-yus), -ness.
bī lit'er al, -al ism.
bilk, -ing, bilked.
bill, -ing, billed, bill' bee tle, -bug,
-fish, -board, -book, -bro ker,
-cham ber, -hawk, -head, -hook,
-post'er, -scale, -stick er.
bil'la long' *or* bil'ly-.
bil'lard.
bil'let, -ing, -ed, bil'let-ca ble,
-head, -mås ter, -mold ing, bil'let-
ing-roll, *bil let-doux'* (bil'lā dōō'),
pl. -lets-doux (-la-dōōz').
bil'liard (-yard), -liards, -liard ist,

bil liard-ball, -cloth, -cue, -mark-
er, -play er, -room, -ta ble.
bil'ling.
bil'lings gate.
bil'lion (-yŭn), -aire, -ism, -lionth.
bill'man, *pl.* -men.
bĭl'lon' (*or* bē yoṅ').
bil'lot.
bil low, -y, -lowed.
bil'ly, *pl.* lies (lĭz), -boy, -cock,
bil'ly-bīt er, -gate, -goat, -piĕc er,
-rŏll er, -web.
bī'lobed, -lo'bate (*or* bī'-).
bī lo ca'tion, -loc'u lar, -u late.
bī lo cel'late.
bī loph'o dŏnt.
bī lŏ'qui al, bil'o quist.
bil'sah.
bil'sted.
bil'tŏng or *-tongue.*
bī mac'u late, -la ted.
Bim'a na (*or* bī'ma-), bĭm'a nous,
bi man'u al.
bī mar'gin ate.
bī mäs' tism, -mas'tic, -mas'toid.
bim'bo.
bī mē' di al.
bī mem'bral.
bī mes'tri al.
bī me tal' lic, -met'al lism, -list,
-lis'tic
Bī'mi ni (be'me ne).
bī month'ly.
bī mus'cu lar.
bi'na (bē'-).
bī'na ry.
bī'nate.
bin au'ral (*or* bī nau').
bīnd, -er, -er y, -ing, -ing ly, -ing-
ness, bound, bind' web, -weed,
-with, -wood, a plant, bind-rail.
bīnd'er-frame, bīnd'ing-cloth,
-guide, -joist, -piece, -post,
-raft'er, -screw, -strakes, -wire.
bī nerv'ate.
bing'stĕad, bing-hole, -ore.
biṇk.
bin'na cle, b. list.
bin'ny.
bin'o cle, bĭn oc'u lar (*or* bī noc'-),
-lar ly, -lăr'i ty, -oc'u late.
bī'node, -nŏd'al.
bī no'mi al, -ism, -ist, -mi al ly.

bī nor'mal.
bī no'tate, -ta ted.
bī not'o nous.
bī'nous.
bin'tu rong.
bī o cen'tric.
bī o chem' is try (kem'-), -chem' ic.
bī'od, -o dy nam'ic (-dī-), -ic al,
-nam' ics.
bī' o gen, -ge na' tion, -gen' e sis,
-e sist, -ge net'ic, -ic al ly, -og'e-
nist (-oj'-), -e ny.
bī og'ra phy, -ra pher, -ra phist,
bī'o graph, -o graph' ic, -ic al,
-al ly.
bī'o ki net'ics.
bī ol'o gy, -o gist, -o log'ic, -ic al,
-al ly.
bī ol'y sis, -o lyt'ic.
bī o mag'net ism, -net'ic.
bī om'e try.
bī'o phor *or* -phore.
bī'o phys i og'ra phy, -i ol'o gy,
-o gist, -o log'ic al.
bī'o plasm, -plas'mic (-plaz'-),
-plast, -plas'tic.
bī or'di nal.
bī or'gan.
bī'os.
bī'o scope.
bī o stat'ics, -stat'ic al, -sta tis'tics.
bī'o tax y.
bī ot'ics, -ot'ic, -ic al.
bī ot'o nus.
bī pal'mate.
bī păr'a sit'ic.
bī pā ri'e tal.
bip'a rous.
bī part'ed, -part'ĭ ble, -par'tient,
-par'tīle.
bip'ar tītc (*or* bī par'-), bī par ti'-
tion (-tish'un).
bī pas'chal (-kal).
bī pec'ti nate, -na ted.
bī'ped, bip'e dal (*or* bī pe'-),
-dal'i ty.
bī pen' nate, -nā ted, -ni form,
-nat'i fid.
bī pen'nis, pl. *-nes* (-nēz).
bī pet'a lous.
bī pin'nate, -ly, -na ted, -nat'i fid,
-i form.
bī'plane, -plä'nar.

---

nŏt, nôr, ūse, ŭp, ûrn, etüde, fo͞od, fo͝ot, aṅger, boṅmot, t͟hus, Bac͟h.

bip'li cate (*or* bĭ'plĭ-), bī plic'i ty.
bī po'lar, -lăr'i ty.
Bī'pont, -pon'tĭne.
bī'prism.
bī pul'mo na ry.
bī puṇc'tate, -tu al.
bī pu'pil late.
bī py ram'i dal (-pĭ-).
bī quad'rate, -rat'ic (-kwŏd-).
bī quar'ter ly.
bī'quartz.
bī'qua ter'ni on.
bī ra'di ate, -a ted, -ra'di al, -al ly.
bī ram'bĭ.
bī ra'mose (-mōs), -ra'mous.
bī ra'tion al (-rash'un-).
birch, -en, -ing, birched, birch'-
wort, birch-cam phor, -bark, -oil,
-wa ter, birch broom, b. wine.
bird, -ie, -gāz'er, -i kin, -ing, -let,
-like, -lime, -ling, -man, bird-bait'-
ing, -bolt, -cage, -call, -catch'er,
-dog, -duf fer, -eye, -eyed, -fan'-
ci er, -fau na, -foot, -house, -louse,
-net, -or'gan, -pep'per, -piece,
-plant, -seed, -shot, -spi'der, -tick,
-trap, -wit ted, bird's-bread, -eye,
-foot, -mouth, - nest, *a.*, -nest ing,
-tares, -tongue, bird's nest, *n.*
bī rec taṇ'gu lar.
bī re frin'gence, -gent.
bī'reme.
Bi re'ṇọ (be rā'no).
bī ret'ta *or* bir ret'- *or* ber ret'-.
bī rhom boid'al.
bī'rī mose' (-mōs).
birk.
bir'kie.
birl.
birn.
Bĭr'on.
bī ros'trate, -tra ted.
bī ro ta'tion, -ro'ta to ry.
bĭr'o tĭne.
bī rŏ'tu late.
birr.
bir'rus, *pl.* -rī.
birse.
birth, -day, -land, -less, -mark,
-night, -place, -right, -root, a
plant, -wort.
birth'-child, -hour, -rate, -sin,
-song, -stran'gled.

bis.
bi'sa *or* -za (bē'za), bi sa an'telope.
bī sac'cate.
bĭs cä'cha or *biz-.*
Bis câỵ'an.
Bis ceg lie (bē shāl'yā), t. It.
bis coc'ti form.
bis'cro ma.
bis'cuit (-kĭt), -co tin, bis'cuit-
ov'en (-ŭv'-), -root.
bis'dĭ a pā'son (*or* -zn).
bise (bēz).
bise (bīs).
bi sect', -ed, -ing, -sec'tor, -sec'-
tion, -tion al, -al ly, -sec'trix, *pl.*
-trī'ces (-sēz).
bī seg'ment, -men'tal.
bī sep'tate.
bī se'ri al, -al ly, -ri ate, -ate ly.
bī sĕr'rate.
bĭ sette' (-zet').
bī'sexed, -sex'u al.
bish'op (-ŭp), -dom, -like, -ly, -ric,
-hood, -ship, -weed, bish'op-
bird, -ray, -sleeve, bish'op's-cap,
-el der, -hat, -leaves, -mi ter, -ring,
-weed, bish op's length.
bĭs il'i ac.
bī sil'i cate.
bī sil'i quous (-kwus).
bī sin'u ate, -a'tion.
bisk *or* bisque, a soup; ice-
cream.
bis'mer *or* -mar, -pund (-pŏŏnd).
bis mil'lah.
bis'muth (biz'-), -al, -ic, -id, -ous,
-ite *or* -mut ite (*or* -mū tite),
-muth yl, -al, -in *or* -ĭne, -if'er-
ous, bis'muth-blende, -fur nace,
-glănce.
bĭs'oc-plow.
bī'son, -tĭne.
bī'so nant.
bī sphĕr'ic al.
bī spi'nose (-nos), -nous.
bī spī'ral.
bī'spŏre, -spō'roŭs.
bisque (bisk), a soup; unglazed
porcelain.
bisque (bisk), a term in tennis and
croquet.
bis sex'tĭle.

bis′ter *or* -tre, -tered *or* -tred.
bĭ stip′uled, -u late.
bis′tort.
bis′tou ry, -tour nage.
bis tŭr′ris, *pl.* -res (-rēz).
bĭ sul′cate.
bĭ sul′phate, -phĭd, -phīte, -phu-
ret.
bis u nique′ (-nēk′).
bĭ syl lab′ic, -syl′la bism.
bĭ sym′me try, -met′ric al.
bit, -less, bit-brace, -key, -pin′cers,
-stock, -strap.
bĭ tan′gent, -gen′tial (-shal).
bitch, -wood.
bite, -less, bīt′er, bīt′ing, -ly, -ness,
bĭt, bit′ten, bĭt′ing-drag′on.
bĭ tem′po ral.
bĭ ter′min al.
bĭ ter′nate.
bi′ti (bē′tē).
Bĭt′lis′ (-lēs′), t. Turk.
bit no′ben.
bi′to (bē′-), -tree.
bitt, -head, -pin, -stop′per, bitts.
bit′ter, -ish, -ing, -ness, -ter ly,
-ters, bit′ter bark, -blain, -bloom,
a plant, -bush, a plant, -head, a
fish, -nut, a tree, -root, a plant,
-stem, a plant, -stick, a plant,
-sweet, a plant, -weed, -wood, a
tree, -wort.
bit′ter-end, a nautical term, -grăss,
-herb, -king, -spar, -sweet, bit′ter
earth, b. end, b. salt, b. vetch.
bit′ter ling.
bit′tern.
bit′ting, -har′ness, -rig′ging.
bitt′lin.
bit′tock.
bĭ tū′men, -mĭ nate, -na ted,
-na ting, -mi noid, -mi nous,
-mĭ nize, -nized, -nĭ zing, -nĭ za′-
tion, -nif′er ous.
bĭ ū′ni ty, -ni al.
bĭv′a lent *or* bī′-, -lence, -len cy.
bĭ′välve, -valved, -val′vous, -val′-
vu lar, -*val′vi a.*
bĭ vas′cu lar.
bĭ vault′ed.
bĭ vec′tor.
bĭ ven′ter, -tral.
bĭ′verb, -ver′bal.

bĭ vit′tate.
biv′i um.
bĭ vo′cal, -ized.
biv′ouac (-wăk *or* -ōō ak), -ouacked
(-wăkt), -ouack ing.
bi′wa (bē′-).
bĭ′week ly (*or* -week′-).
bĭ zärre′, -zär′re riē.
bi zet′ (bē-).
bĭ zy go mat′ic (-zī-).
bjel′kīte (byĕl′-).
Björn son (byêrn′son *or* bē yurn′-),
Norw. auth.
blab, -bing, -ber, blabbed.
black, -en, -en er, -en ing, -ened,
-er, -ish, -ly, -ness, -y *or* -ey,
blacked, black′a moor, -a vīsed.
black′back, a bird; a fish, -ball,
v., -band, -bel′ly, a fish, -ber′ry,
-ber′ry ing, -bird, -board, -bon-
net, a bird, -boy, a tree, -breast,
a bird, -bur, a plant, -butt, -cap,
a bird; a plant, -coat, a person,
-cock, -fin, a fish, -fish, -fish′er,
-foot, a person, -guard, -guard-
ism, -guard ly, -head, a duck;
a fish, -heart, a cherry, -lĕad, *v.*,
-leg, a person, -list, *v.*, -mail,
-meat, mouth, a person, nob,
-pole, -root, a plant, -seed, a
plant, -size, *v.*, -smith, -snake,
-tail, a fish; a deer, -thorn, a
plant, -wall, -wood, a tree, -work,
-wort. black′lead ing-ma chine′,
black′y-top.
black′-bee′tle, -browed, -brush,
-cat -drăught, -drop, -duck,
-dye, -ex′tract, -flea, -fly, -fox,
a bird, -grăss, -gum, -heart′ed,
-horse, a fish, -jack, -knot,
-liq′uor, -mack, -match, -moss,
-mouthed, -pig′ment, -pot,
-quar′ter, -rod, a person, -salt′er,
-samp′son, -shell, -spaul, -spot,
-strap, -stripe, -tongue, a disease,
-wad (wŏd), -ward, -wash, -wạ′-
ter. black′-eyed Su′san, black-
var nish tree.
black′ing-box, -brush, -case.
black băss, b. cat′tle, b. damp,
b. fri ar, b. hel′met, b. hole,
b. lĕad, *n.*, b. let′ter, b. list, *n.*,
b. mul′let, b. plate, b. pud′ding,

b. salts, b. tur'peth, b. vom'it,
b. whale.
Black Flags, B. Fri'day, B.
Hand, B. Ma ri' a, B. Mon'day,
B. Rod.
blad'der, -fish, -nose, a seal, -nut,
a plant, -pod, a plant, -snout, a
plant, -wort, blad'der y. blad'der-
blight, -brand, -cam'pi on, -fern,
-gas'tru la, -green, -herb, -kelp,
-ket'mi a, -nosed, -sen na,
-worm, -wrack.
blade, -let, blād'ed, -er, -ing, -y,
blade'fish, blade'-bone, -met'al,
-mill, -ore, -spring.
blæ (blä *or* blē), -ber ry, -lin en.
blæ'si tas (blĕ-').
blaf'fert.
blague.
blain.
blake, -ling.
blame, blām'a ble, -ble ness,
-a bly, blame'ful, -ful ly, -ful-
ness, -less, -less ly, -less ness,
-wor thy, -thi ness.
blanc (blangk *or* blŏṅ), blanc-
mange' (blä mäṅzh'), -man ger'
(-mäṅ zhä').
blaṇ'card (blang'-).
blânch, -er, -ing, -im'e ter,
blănched, blanch'-farm, -hold-
ing, blanch'ing-liq uor.
blaṇ'co.
bland, -ly, -ness, blan'dish,
-dish er, -dish ment, -dil'o-
quence, -dil'o quous, (-kwŭs),
-di lo'qui ous.
blan'du ril'la.
blaṇk, -ly, -ness, blank'-book,
printed forms, blank book, a
book that is blank, blank'ing-
press.
blaṇ'ket, -ed, -ing, -y, -eer', -leaf,
a plant. blan'ket-bar, -clause,
-de pos'it, -piece, -sluice, -wash er.
b. bal'lot, b. mort'gage (môr-),
b. sheet.
Blanque'fort (bloṅk'-).
blan quette' (bloṅ ket').
blan quil'lo (blăng kēl'yō).
blare, blâr'ing, blâred.
blar'ney, -ing, -neyed (-nid).
blă sé' (-zā').

blash, -y.
blăs phe me', -phemed', -phēm'ing,
-er, blăs'phe mous, -mous ly,
-phe my.
blâst, -ed, -er, -ing, -y, -ment.
blâst'-box, -en'gine, -fur'nace,
-gate, -heärth, -hole, -lamp,
-ma chine', -me'ter, -noz'zle,
-ŏr'i fice, -pipe, -re cord'er, -reg'-
u la tor.
blâst'ing-car'tridge, -fuse (-fuz),
-gel'a tin (-jel'-), -mix'ture,
-nee'dle, -oil, -pow'der, -tools,
-tube.
blăs te'ma, pl. -*ma ta,* -mal, -mat'ic.
blas'tĭde (*or* -tīd), -tid.
blas to car'pous.
blăs'to cele.
blăs'to derm, -der'ma, -der'mal,
-ma ta, -mic, -mat'ic.
blas'to disc, -to col'la.
blas'toid, -*toid'e a.*
blăs'to mĕre, -mĕr'ic.
blăs'to phore, -tŏph'o ral, -to-
phŏr'ic, -to pore, -to pŏr'ic, -to-
po'ral.
blas'to sphere.
blas'to style.
blăs'tu la, -tule, -tu la spore, -tu-
la'tion.
blas'tus, n., pl. -*tĭ,* -toŭs, *a.*
blā'tant, -ly, -tan cy.
blaṭṭ'er, -y, -skīte.
blat'ta, -ti form.
blat'ter, -ing, -er, -tered, -ter ā'-
tion.
blau'bok (blou'-), -fish (blaw'-).
blā'wort *or* blāe'-.
blay, -ber ry, -lin en.
blaze, -less, blazed, blāz'ing, -ing-
ly, -er, blāz'ing-star, a plant.
blā'zon (-zn), -er, -ing, -ment, -ry.
blea, -ber ry.
bleach, -er, -er y, bleached,
bleach-field.
bleach'ing, -flu id, -liq uid,
-pow'der.
blĕak, -ish, -ly, -ness.
blĕar, bleared, -ness (*or* blear'ed-
ness), blear'i ness, -y, -eye, a
disease, -eyed, -wit ted.
bleat, -ed, -er, -ing.
bleb, -by.

bleed, -er, -ing, bled, bleed′ing-
heart, a plant, -tooth, -valve.
blel′lum.
blem′ish, -ing, -less, -ment, -ished.
blem′ma trope.
blench, -er, -ing, blenched.
blend, -ed, *or* blent, blend′er,
-ing, blend′-corn, -wa ter.
blĕnde, *Mineral.* blend′ous, -y.
Blen′heim (-im), B. or′ange, B.
span′iel, B. wig.
blen nog′e noŭs (-nŏj′-), blen′-
noid.
blen′nor rhe′a, -rhe′al.
blen′ny.
blens.
bleph a rī′tis.
bles′bok or *bless′-*.
bless, -ĕd, -ed ly, -ed ness, -ing,
blessed, bless′ed-herb, a plant,
b. this′tle (-l).
blet, -ted, -ting.
blet′on ism (*or* blĕ′ton-), -on ist.
blĕ′wart.
blew′its (blо̄о̄′-).
blick.
blick′ey.
Blĭ′fil.
bligh′i a (blĭ′ĭ a).
blight, -ed, -ing, -ing ly, *pl.*
blights, blight-bird.
blīnd, -ed, -ed ly, -ing, -ing ly,
-ly, -ness, -age, -er, blind′ball,
-fish, -fold, -fold′ed, -fold′ing,
-man, -snake, -stitch, *v.*, -worm.
blind′-ball, -born, -făst, -Har ry,
-ink, -lift, -of′fi cer, -op′e ra tor,
a machine, -pull, -slat, -style,
-sto ry, -tool ing, blind′age-
frame, blind a′re a, blind man's
ball, b. man's bel′lows (-lus),
b. man's buff, b. man's hol′i-
day.
blink, -er, -ing, -ing ly, -y, -ard,
blinked, blink′-beer, -eyed, blink′-
ing chick′weed.
blirt, -y.
bliss, -ful, -ful ly, -ful ness, -less.
blis′ter, -ing, -y, -tered, blis′ter-
bee′tle, -cop per, -fly, -plas ter,
-steel.
blīte.
blīthe (*or* blīth), -ful, -ful ly, -ly,

-ness, -some, -some ly, -some-
ness.
bliz′zard.
blŏat, -ed, -ed ness, -er, -ing.
blob, -by, blob′-kite.
blo cage′ (-kȧzh′).
block, -age, -an, -er, -ish, -ish ly,
-ish ness, -y, -i ness, -ade′,
blocked, block′ head, -house,
-like.
block′-bond, -book, -col′ors, -fur′-
nace, -hole, -ma chine′, -mȧk′-
-ing, -plane, -print′ing, -ship,
trail, -truck, block ade ′-run ner,
block coal, b. tin.
block′ing, -course, -ham′mer, -ket′-
tle, -ma chine′, -press.
bloke *or* bloak.
blŏnd *or* blŏnde, *a.*, -ness.
blŏnd *or* blŏnde, *n.* *blonde* is
sometimes used as the feminine
of *blond.* blond′-lace, -met al.
blood (blŭd), -ed, -y, -i ly, -i ness,
-less, -less ly, -less ness.
blood′-bap′tism, -be spot′ ted,
-bought, -cell, -con sūm′ing,
-cor′pus cle, -cups, -curd ling,
-disk, -dri er, -finch, -fine,
-guilt y, -guilt less, -guilt′i ness,
-heat, -horse, -hot, -leech, -mare,
-mon ey, -or ange, -phĕas ănt,
-plaque (-plăk), -plate, -poi′son-
ing, -red, -re la′tion, -re la′tion-
ship, -sac′ri fice, -sound, -spav-
in, -spill er, -stain, -stäunch,
-stick, -stone, -strange, -stroke,
-suck er, that which sucks blood,
-suck ing, -swell ing, -tree, -vas′-
cu lar, -ves sel, -warm, -wite,
blood pud ding.
blood′ drop, -flow er, a plant,
-hound, -let, *v.*, -root, a plant,
-shed, -shed′der, -shed′ing, -shot,
-suck′er, a lizard, -thirst y,
-thirst′i ness, -wood, a tree,
-worm, -wort.
blood′y-bones, -eyed, -faced,
-fluxed, -mīnd ed, -red, -war-
rior, a plant, -man's-fin ger, a
plant.
blо̄о̄m, -ing, -ing ly, -ing ness,
-er, -er y, -y, -less.
bloom′-hook, -tŏngs, bloom′er-pit,

bloom'ing-mill, -sal ly or Sal-, a plant.

blos'som, -less, -y, -somed, blos'-som-bill, -head, -peck er, -ri fler.

blot, -ted, -ting, -ting ly, -ter, -ty, -less, blot'ting-book, -pad, -pa'-per.

blotch, -y, blotched.

blot tesque', -ly.

Blou ët' (bloō'ā'), Paul, "Max O'Rell," Fr. writer.

blouse (blouz), bloused.

blout.

blŏw, -ing, -er, blown, blew, blow'fish, -out, -pipe, blow-ball, -cock, -fly, -gun, -hole, -milk, -off, -o'ver, -point, -through, -tube, -up, -valve, -well.

blow'ing-ad der, -charge, -cyl'in-der, -en'gĭne, -fan, -fur'nace, -house, -i'ron, -ma chine', -pipe, -pot, -snake, -tube.

blowze (blouz), blowz'y, blowzed.

blub'ber, -ing, -ing ly, -er, -ous, -y, -bered, blub'ber-chain, -fork, -guy, -hook, -knife, -lip, -lipped, -spade, -tac kle.

Blü'cher, von (fon bloō'ker or blücher), Prus. field-marshal.

blu'cher (bloō'cher or blü'ker).

blud'geon (-jŭn).

blūe, -ness, -ling, -ly, blued, blu'-ing, -er, -est, -ish, -ey.

blue'back, -beard, -bell, -ber'ry, -bill, -bird, -bon'net, -bot'tle, a fly; a flower, -breast, -buck, -bush, -but'tons, -cap, -coat, -fin, -fish, -gown, -head, a fish, -hearts, -jack, -jack'et, -leg, -man-tle, -mope, -nose, -pod, -point, point er, -poll, a fish, -sides, -start, -stem, -stock'ing, n., -stock ing ism, -stone, -tail, -throat, -tongue, -weed, -wing, -wood.

blue'-ball, -bil ly, -black, -blāz'er, -blind, -chat, -curls, -dis ease', -eyed, -grăss, -gum, -haf'it, -hot, -john, -laws, -mold, -oak, -pai'dle, -pa per, -pe ter, a bird, -pi geon, -pipe, -pōk er, -pot, -print, -print'ing, -rib bon ism, -rib bon ist, -sit, a bird, -spar,

-stock ing, a., -tan gle, -eyed-Ma ry, a plant.

blue' book, b. but ter, b. cod, b. creep er, b. devils, b. glede, b. hawk, b. jay, b. kite, b. lake, b. light, b. măss, b. o cher, (-ker), b. oint ment, b. pear' main, b. perch, b. pe ter, a signal flag, b. pie, a bird, b. pike, b. pill, b. pox, b. pro cess, b. ra cer, b. rib bon, b. rob in, b. rock, b. ru'in, b. snap'per, b. this tle, b. wa ter.

bluff, -er, -ing, -ness, -ly, -y, bluffed, bluff'-bowed (-boud), -head ed.

blun'der, -er, -ing, -ing ly, -dered, blun'der buss, -head, -head ed, -head ed ness.

blunge, blun'ger, -ging.

blunk, -er.

blunt, -ed, -ing, -ness, -ly, -ish, -ish ness, blunt'head, blunt'-wit ted.

blur, -ring, -ry, blurred.

blurt, -ed, -ing.

blush, -ing, -ing ly, -er, -ful, -ful ly, -less, -y, blushed, blush'-wort, -rose.

blus'ter, -er, -ing, -ing ly, -ous, -y, -ter a'tion, -tered, blus'trous.

bo'a, -con stric'tor.

bo'a lee.

Bo'a ner'ges (-jēz), Bib., -ner'-gism (-jĭzm).

boar, -ish, -ish ly, -ish ness, boar'-fish, -spear, -stag, boar's tusk.

board, -ed, -er, -ing, -a ble, board' school, board'-clip, -cut-ter, -meas ure, -rack, -rule, -scale, -wa ges, board'ing-clerk, -gage, -house, -joist, -knife, -ma-chine, -net ting, -of'fi cer, -pike, -school.

boast, -ed, -ing, -ing ly, -er, -ful, -ful ly, -ful ness, -less, boast'ing-chis'el.

boat, -ed, -ing, -er, -a ble, -age, -bill, -ful, -man, -man ship, -swāin (or bō'sn), -tail, -wom an, -wright, boats'man.

boat'-build er, -car, -chock, -dav-it, -fly, -hook, -house, -in' sect,

-keep er, -low er ing, -race, -rā-
cing, -rope, -shaped, -shell, -skid,
-sŏng, -tailed, -yoke, boat
bridge, boat's gripes, boat'-
swain's chair.
bob, -ber, -bing, bobbed, bob'cat,
-stay, -tail, -tailed, bob'-cher ry,
-fish ing, -fly, -je rom, -lin coln
(-kn), -sled, -sleigh, -white,
-wing, bob'stay-piece, bob'tail-
wig, bob veal.
bŏ'bac (*or* bŏb'ac).
Bob'a dil, -ism, -dil'ian.
bob'bin, -net', -wīnd'er, -work,
bob bi net'.
bŏ'ca, bō'cal.
bŏ car'do *or* -kar'-.
boc'a sĭne.
boc'ca, -rel'la.
Boc cac'io (bŏk kät'chō), It.
novelist. boc cac'cio, a fish.
boc cä'le.
bock, -pot, b. beer.
bŏck'ey.
bŏck'ing.
bō'co-wood.
bō cŏn', pl. *-co'nes* (-kō'nās).
bō dark'.
bŏde, -ful, bŏd'ed, ing, ing ly.
bō de'ga.
Bŏ'den heī'mer.
Bŏ'dhi sat (-dĭ-), -ship, -satt'va,
bo'dhi-tree.
bŏ'di an.
bod'Ice, -Iced (-ist). ·
bo'dĭ ē'ron.
bod'kin, -work.
bō'dle (*or* bŏd'l).
Bod lēi'an (*or* bod'-).
bo dŏck'.
bod-worm.
bod'y, *pl.* -ies (-iz), -like, bod'Ied,
-i less, -i li ness, -i ly.
bod'y-bag, -bol ster, -brace, -cav'-
i ty, -clŏth, -clŏthes, -coat,
-col or, -guard, -hoop, -horse,
-knee, -log, -loop, -louse, -oil,
-plan, -post, -serv'ant, -snatch-
er, -tran som, -var nish, -wall,
-whorl, b. cor'por ate, b. pol i tic.
Boêh'men ism, -men ist.
Bœ o'ti a (bē ō'shĭ a), -tian (-shan),
-ot'ic, bœ o'tarch (-tark).

Boer (bōōr) *or* Boor.
Bœuf, Front de (frôn de bûf).
bog, -gish, -gy, -gi ness, -gler, -let.
bog'house, -jump er, -suck er,
-trot, -wort.
bog-as'pho del, -bil'ber ry, -bean,
-ber ry, -bird, -blit'ter, -bluit er
(-blōōt-), -bull, -bump er, -but-
ter, -cut ting, -earth, -glede,
-i ron, -land, -man'gan ese,
-moss, -myr tle, -oak, -on ion,
-or ange, -or'chis (-kis), -ore,
-rush, -spav in, -trot ter, -vi'o let,
-wood.
bŏ'ga.
bŏ'gie *or* -gey *or* -gy (-gy), bō'gle,
bo'gie-bar row, -car riage, -en'
gine.
bog'o mile.
bo'gŏng.
Bŏ gŏ tä', c. S. Amer.
bŏgue.
bō'gus.
bo hēa'.
Bo hĕ' mi a, -mi an, -an ism,
Bo he' mi an Breth'ren, B. glass.
bŏ hi'o (bō ē'o).
bŏ'hôr.
Bohun u'pas.
bo iar (bō yar' *or* boi'ar).
boil, -er y, boiled.
boil'er, -a larm', -brace, -clamp,
-feed er, -fer rule, -float, -fur'-
nace, -house, -i ron, -keel'son,
-māk ing, -me ter, -plate, -pro-
tec'tor, -prov er (-prōōv-),
-shell, -shop, -smith, -tube,
-wag on.
boil'ing, -fur nace, -point.
bois (bwŏ), *-brû lē'* (-brōō lä'),
-chêne (-shän), *-dur ci'* (-dōōr-
sē'), *b. d'arc'.*
Boi'sé (-zä), co. Ida.
Bois Guil'bert', Bri an' de (brē-
än' de bwä gĕl bāre').
bois seau' (bwŏ sō').
bois'ter ous, -ous ly, -ous ness.
bo jŏ'bĭ.
bo'ka dam' (*or* bŏk'a-).
bo'kark.
boke.
Bŏk ha'ra (-ä'rä), Turkestan.
bo'lar.

---

nŏt, nôr, ūse, ŭp, ûrn, etüde, fōōd, fŏŏt, anger, bonmot, thus, Bach.

bŏ lar'go.
bo'las.
bold, -er, -est, -en, -ened, -ly,
-ness, -face, a person.
bold'-face, *a.*, a type, -faced,
-spĭr'it ed.
bŏl'do.
bole.
bo lec'tion, -tioned.
bo le'ro (-lā'-).
Bo le'tus, bo let'ic.
Bol'eyn (bŏŏl'in), Anne, wife of
Henry VIII.
bo'lĭde (*or* -lĭd).
bo'lis.
bo li'ta (-lē'-).
Bŏl'i var, a liberator of Bolivia.
bol'i var, a coin.
Bo liv'ian, B. bark, bo liv i ä'no
(*or* -lē vē-).
bŏll, -ing, bolled, boll'man, -rot,
-worm.
Bol'land ist.
bol'lard, -tim'ber.
bŏl li'to (-lē'-).
bol'lock-block.
bŏ'lo.
Bo lo'gna (-lō'nya *or* -lō'na), c.
and prov. It., -lo'gnese' (-nyēz'
or -nēz), -lo'gnian (-lo'nyan *or*
-lo'ni an).
Bo lo'gna phos'phor us, B. sau'-
sage, B. stone, B. vi al.
bo lom'e ter, -lo met'ric.
bŏl'sa.
bŏl'son.
bol'ster, -er, -ing, -stered, bol'ster-
plate, -spring, -work.
bŏlt, -ed, -ing, -er, -less.
bolt'-au ger, -blank, -boat, -chis-
el, -clip per, -cut ter, -die, -dog,
-ex tract or, -feed er, -head, -head-
er, -hold er, -hole, -hook, -knife,
-māk'er, -rope, -saw ing, -screw-
ing, -strake, -thrĕad er, bolt'er-
cloth.
bolt'ing-chest, -cloth, -cord, -house,
-hutch, -mill, -mill stone, -reel,
-tub.
bŏl'tant.
bŏl'tel.
bŏl'tĭ.
bŏl'ton Ĭte.

bŏl'ty.
bŏ'lus, *pl.* -lus es.
bŏm.
bŏ'mah-nut.
bŏ mā're a.
bomb (bŏm *or* bŭm), -shell, bomb'-
chest, -fuse, -gun, -har poon',
-ketch, -lance, -proof, -ves sel.
bom'ba cā'ce æ, -ca'ceous (-shus).
bŏm ba'ceous (-shus).
bom'bard, *n.*, bŏm bard' (*or*
bŭm-), *v.*, -ed, -ing, -ment,
-bar dier', *-bar'don,* bom bar-
diēr'-bee'tle.
bŏm'bâst (*or* bŭm'-), -bast ry,
-bas'tic, -tic al, -al ly.
Bŏm bǎs'tes Fu ri o'so (-tēz fŏŏ-).
Bom'bax.
Bŏm bay', c. India, B. duck, B.
shell.
bŏm'ba zet' *or* -zette' (*or* bŭm'-).
bŏm'ba zine' *or* -sine' (bŏm ba-
zēn' *or* bŭm-).
bŏm'bic.
bŏm'bi late, -lā'tion, -bi nate,
-na'tion.
bom bil'la (-bil'ya).
bom'bo lo, *pl.* -loes.
bŏm'bou (*or* bŭm'-).
bŏm'bus, a buzzing noise. Bŏm'-
bus, a genus of bees.
bŏm byc'i nous (-bĭs'-), -i form.
bon (bŏṅ), *b. jour* (zhŏŏr), *b. mot*
(mō), pl. *bons mots* (bŏṅ mōz),
b. soir (swôr), *b. tôṅ, b. vi vant'*
(vē väṅ). *boṅmot* is often written
as one word.
bo'na ci' (-sē').
bŏ'na fĭ'de, bo'na-fĭ'de, *a., bo'na
nō ta bil'i a, b. pĕr ĭ tu'ra, b. ro'ba.*
bŏ nang'.
bŏ nan'za.
Bŏ' na parte, -part'ism, -part'ist,
-part'e an.
bo nä'sus *or* -näs'sus.
bôn'bôn', -niēre' (-nyâr').
bŏnce.
Bon'-chrĕ'tien' (bôṅ krāt'yǎṅ').
bon'ci late *or* -si-.
bond, -ed, -ing, -er, -age, -folk,
-hold er, -land, -less, -maid,
-man, -wom'an. bonds'man,
-wom an.

bond'-coop er, -cred'it or, -debt,
-pa per, -serv ant, -serv ice,
-slave, -stone, -ten ant, -tim ber.
bon'duc, -seeds.

bone, -less, -fish, -flow er, -set,
bōned, bōn'ing, -y, -i ness, bōn'y
tail.

bōne'-ace, -ache (-āk), -ash, -bed,
-bind er, -black, -breāk'er,
-brec cia (-bretch ya), -brown,
-car'ti lage, -cave, -cell, -char
coal, -cor pus cle, -dog, -dust,
-earth, -eat er, el'e va'tor, -fe ver,
-flour, -gel a tin, -glåss, -glue,
-heap, -lace, -laced, -ma nure',
-meal, -mill, -năph tha (or
-năp-), -nip pers, -oil, -phos
phate, -porce lain, -pot, -saw,
-set ter, -shark, -spav in, -spīr it,
-tur quoise (-koiz'), -waste,
-whale, -yard, bōn'ing-rod.

bon'fire.
bon'gar.
bong-bong'.
bong'ga.

Bon heur' (bŏn'er'), Rosa, Fr.
painter.

bon'ho mie' or -hom mie' (bŏn ŏ-
mē').

Bon'homme', Jacques (zhäk
bŏ nŏm').

Bŏn'i fåce, -fa'cial.

bŏn'i fy, -ing, -fied, -i fi cā'tion,
-i form.

bon'i tä'ri an, bon' i ta ry.

bō ni'to (-nē'-).

Bon nat' (-nä'), Fr. painter.

bonne (bŏn), b. bouche (bōōsh), pl.
bonnes bouches (bŏn' bōōsh').

bon'net, -ed, -less, -head, a fish.

bon'net-block, -fluke, -gråss,
-laird, -lim pet, -må cåque',
-måk ing, -mon key, -pep per,
-piece, -rouge (-rōōzh), -shark,
-shell, -stack, -string, -worm.

bŏn'ny or -nie, -ni ly, -ni ness,
bon'ny-dame.

bon'ny clab'ber.

bo no'te (-tä).

bŏn'si late.

Bon'temps', Ro ger' (rō'zhä'
bôn tän').

bŏn'zē or bŏnze, bon'zi an.

bōō'bōōk.

bōō'by, -ish, -ism, -al'la, -hatch,
-hut, -hutch, -prize.

Bōōdh or Bōō'dha, -ism, -ist.
See Buddha.

bōō'dle, -dler.

bōōf.

bōō'hōō', -hōōed'.

book, -ful, -ing, -ish, -ish ly, -ish
ness, -less, -let, -lung, -y.

book'-ac count, -back, -buy er,
-clamp, -cov er, -crab, -debt,
-edge, -fair, -fold ing, -formed,
-han dler, -hold er, -hunt er,
-ink, -knowl'edge (-nŏl'-),
-learned (or -learn'ed), -learn
ing, -lore, -louse, -lov er, -mad
ness, -māk'er, -mark, -mus lin
(-mŭz-), -name, -no tīce, -num
ber, -oath, -plate, -pōst, -rack,
-room, -scor'pi on, -sew ing
(-sō-), -shop, -slide, -stall,
-stamp, -stand, -stone, -trade,
-tray, -trim mer, -work.

book'bind er, -er y, book'case,
-craft, -keep er, -keep ing, -land,
-man, -mate, -mon ger, -sell er,
-sell ing, -shelf, -store, -worm,
-wright.

book'ing-clerk, -ma chine', -of'-
fice.

boom, -er, -ing, -kin, boomed,
boom'slang'e, boom'-boat, -cov er,
-i ron, -jig ger, -main sail,
-tac kle.

boom'das.

boom'er ang (or -e rang).

boon, -worm.

boon'gå ry.

bōōnk.

bōōr, -ish, -ish ly, -ish ness.

bōōst, -ed, -er, -ing.

bōōt, -ed, -ing, -ee', -less, -less ly,
-less ness, -bill, -black, -jack,
-lick, -māk er, boots.

bōōt'-but ton er, -calk (-kạk),
-catch er, -chan'nel ling, -clamp,
-clos er (-klōz-), -crimp, -crimp
ing, -cuff, -edge, -groov ing,
-heel, -hold er, -hook, -hose,
-lace, -last, -leg, -pat'tern, -pow'
der, -rack, -seam, -shank, -spat
tern, -stock ing, -stretch'er, -top,

---

nŏt, nôr, ūse, ŭp, ûrn, etüde, fōōd, fŏŏt, aŋger, boṅmot, thus, Bach.

-top ping, -tree, -ven'ti la tor,
boot'ing-corn.
Bo o' tes (bō ō'tēz), Astron.
bōōth (or booth), -age.
bōō'ty, -tĭed.
bōōze, booz'er, -ing, -y, boozed.
bo-peep'.
bŏ'ra, a dry wind; an aboriginal
rite. bō'ra, Meteor.
bo rac'ic (-răs'ik), bo'ric, -rĭde
(or -rīd), bo'ra cīte, -ra coŭs,
-ra cif'er ous.
bor'age (bŭr'-), -wort, bo rag'i-
na'ceous (-răj i nā shus), bō'ra-
gin'e ous (-jin-).
bo ras'co.
bo'rax, -rate, bo'rax-bead.
bord, -land, -lode, -serv ice.
bord'age.
bord'ar.
Bor deaux' (-dō'), c. Fr.; tp. S. C.
B. mix'ture, Bor'de lais' (-lā').
bor'der, -ing, -er, -dered, bor'der-
knife, -land, -lights, -plane,
-shears, -stone, -war rant
(-wŏr'-), bor'der ruf'fian (-yan),
b. tow'er, bor'der ing-wax.
bor'de reau' (-rō'), pl. -reaux (-rō').
bor'dure.
bore, -dom, -ism, bored, bōr'er,
bore-bit, -hole, -log, -meal, -rod,
-tree, -worm.
Bo're as, Myth., -re ad, bo're al,
-re an.
bŏre'côle.
bŏr'ee', a dance; bo ree', a tree.
bŏ reen'.
bŏr'e gat.
bŏr'e le.
Bŏr get'to, t. Sicily.
Bŏr ghet'to (-gāt'to), t. Lom-
bardy.
Bor'gia (-jä), Lucrezia, Duchess
of Ferrara.
bŏr'ing, -an'chor (-kŭr), -bar,
-bench, -bit, -block, -col'lar,
-dust, -gage, -hĕad, -lāthe, -ma-
chine', -mill, -rod, -sponge, -ta'-
ble, -tool.
Bŏr'jä.
bor'lase (-lās).
bŏr'ley.
bor'ling.

bôrn, borne.
bor né' (bôr nā').
bor'nĕ ĕne, -ne ōl.
Bor'ne o, isl. Malay Archi.,
-ne an, Bor'ne o cam'phor.
bor'nĭne, -nīte.
Bŏr ō di'no (-dē'-), t. Russ.
bŏ'ron, bo ro cal'cīte, -ro glyc'er-
ĭde (or -ide), -glyc'er in (-glĭs'-).
bor'ough (bŭr'-), -mås'ter, -mon'-
ger, -mon'ger ing, -ship, bor'-
ough-court, -Eŋ glish, -hold er,
-reeve, -ses sions, -town.
bŏr ras'ca (or -räs'-).
Bŏr'rel ist.
Bŏr rŏ me' ŏ (-mā'o), Carlo, It.
cardinal.
bŏr rŏ' tŏ.
bŏr'row, -ing, -er, -rowed, bor'row-
head, bor'row ing-days.
bôr sel'la.
bort.
Bŏs.
bos'cage or -kage.
Bos'ca wen, Eng. admiral.
bosh.
bosh'bok, or bosch'-, -vark.
Bos'jes man (bosh'ez- or boš'yes-),
pl. -mans or -men.
bŏsk, bos'kage, -ket or -quet (-ket).
bosk'y, -i ness.
bos'om (bŏŏz'um or bōō'zum),
-ing, -y, -omed.
bos'om-board, -spring, -ståff.
bŏss, pl. -es, bossed, v., boss'ing,
-ism, -i ness, -age.
bŏs'se la'ted.
Bŏs suet' (-swā'), Fr. orator.
bos'sy, n., a cow or calf. boss'y, a.,
studded with bosses; domineering.
bos tan'jĭ.
Bos'ton, c. Mass. bos'ton, a game
of cards.
bos'try choid (-trĭ koid), -choid'al.
bos'tryx.
Bos'well (bŏz'-), Eng. writer,
-well ism, -well īze, -ized, ī zing,
-well'li an.
Bos'wort (boz'-), Eng. philol.
bŏt, bots, bot'-fly.
bot'a ny, -a nize, -nized, -ni zing,
-ni zer, -nist, bo tan'ic, -ic al,
-al ly.

bo tar'go *or* -ga.
botch, -er, -er y, -y, -i ly,
 botched.
bot'ĕ rŏl *or* -rŏll.
Bŏt'e toûrt, co. Va.
bŏth, -hand'ed, -hand'ed ness,
 -sīd ed, -sid'ed ness.
botħ'er, -er ing, -ment, -some,
 -a'tion, -ered.
Bŏth'ni a, -ni an, -nic.
bŏth ren'chy ma (-kĭ-).
both'rĭ um, pl. *-ri a.*
Bŏth'well (botħ'-), James Hep-
 burn, *Biog.*
bo'to cu'dos (-kōō'dōz).
bŏ tōn', pl. *-to'nes* (-tō'năs).
bo'-tree.
bot'ry o gen (-jen).
bot'ry oid, -oid'al, -al ly.
bot'ry o lite.
bot'ry ose (-ōs).
bots.
bott'ha m'mer.
Bot ti cel'li (-tē chĕl'lē), It. painter.
bot tine' (-teen').
bot'ting.
bot'tle, -tled, -tler, -tling, bot'tle-
 flow'er, -head, -nose.
bot'tle - bel lied, -bird, -boot,
 -brush, -brush ing, -bump, -căr'-
 ri er, -case, -char'ger, -chart,
 -clip, -coast er, -cod, -com pan'-
 ion, -con'jur er (-kŭn'-), -drop-
 sy, -fạu'cet, -fill er, -fish,
 -friend, -glăss, -gōurd, -grăss,
 -green, -hold er, -imp, -jack,
 -mold, -mold ing, -nosed, -ore,
 -pump, -rack, -screw, -stand,
 -stoop, -stop per, -tit, -tom,
 -track, -tree, -wash er, -wax,
 bot tle nose-oil.
bot'tling-ma chine, -room.
bot'tom, -ing, -less, -less ness,
 -most, -ry, -tomed.
bot'tom-cap'taīn, -fish, -fish ing,
 -glade, -grăss, -heat, -ice, -land,
 -lift, -plate, -tool, bot'tom ing-
 hole, -tap.
bot'ton y.
bot'u li form.
bot u lin'ic.
bou charde (bōō shard').

bouche (bōōsh).
bou chée' (bōō shā'), pl. *-chées'*
 (-shā').
bou'cher ize (bōō'sher-), -ized, -ī-
 zing.
bou chette' (bōō shĕt').
bou'ching (bōō'shing), -bit.
Bou ci cault' (bōō'sẽ'kō'), Irish
 dram.
Bou'di not (bōō'de not), Amer.
 patriot.
bou'doir (bōō'dwôr).
bouf fant' (bōō fŏn').
bouffe (bōōf).
bouf'fons (bōō'fonz).
bouge (bōōj).
bou'get (bōō'jet *or* -zhā').
bough (bou), -y, bough'-pot.
bou gie (bōō'jĭ *or* -zhē').
bou'gong (bōō'-).
Bougue reau' (bōōg'rō'), Fr. painter.
bouil li (bōō'yē' *or* bōōl'yē'),
 bouil lon (bōōl'yŏn' *or* bōō'yŏn').
bouk *or* bowk.
boul *or* bool (bōōl).
Bou lan ger' (bōō'lŏn'zhā'), Fr.
 gen.
bou lan'ger īte (bōō lăn'jer ĭt).
bŏul'der, -y, boul'der-belt, -clay,
 -crack ing, -fans, -hĕad, -pave-
 ment, -pav'ing, -stone, -train,
 boul'der ing-stone.
boule (bōōl), same as buhl;
 bou'le (bōō'lē).
bou let' (bōō lā'), -lĕtte'.
bou'le vard (bōō'-), *-var diẽr'* (*or*
 bōōl'var'dyā').
bou'lon (bōō'-).
bounce, -a ble, bounced, boun'-
 cing, -cing ly, -cer, boun'cing-
 bet.
bound, -a ble, -ed, -er, -ing, -less,
 -less ly, -less ness, bound bail'iff.
bound'a ry, *pl.* -a ries (-rĭz).
boun'ty, -te ous, -ous ly, -ous ness,
 -ti ful, -ful ly, -ful ness, boun'ty-
 jump'er.
Bou pho'ni a (bōō-).
bou quet' (bōō kā'), -hold er, *bou-*
 quet ier' (bōō kā teer').
bou que tin' (bōō kā tăn').
bou rasque' (bōō rask').

---

nŏt, nôr, ūse, ŭp, ûrn, etüde, fōōd, fŏŏt, aŋger, boṅmot, tħus, Bacħ.

Bour′bon (boor′-), -ism, -ist, Bour′-
bon palm, B. whis key.
Bour da loue′ (boor′dä′loo′), Fr.
preacher.
bour′don (boor′-).
bour don né′ (boor don nā′).
Bourg (boorg), a wine; *bourg*, a
borough.
bour gäde′ (boor-).
bour geois′ *or* bur- (bur jois′), a
size of printing type, *bour geois′*
(boor zhwä′), a burgher, *bour-
geoi sie′* (-zhwä zē′).
bour′geon (bur′jun).
Bourges (boorzh), c. Fr.
Bour′get′ (boor′zhā′), l. Fr.
Bour guig non′ (boor gē nyoṅ′).
bou′ri (boo′rĕ).
Bou rign′ian (boo rĭn′yan), -ian-
ism, -rign′on ist (-yon ist).
bŏurn *or* bŏurne, a stream.
bŏurn *or* bourne (boorn), a boundary.
Bŏurne′moŭth, t. Eng.
bour′non īte (boor′-).
bour rée′ (boor rā′).
bourse (boorse).
bour′-tree (boor-).
bouse *or* bowse (bous), *v*., boused,
bous′ing, to haul with tackle;
bouse′ (bous *or* boos), *n*., impure
ore. bouse′-tĕam.
bou stro phe′don (boo-), -don′ic,
-stroph′ic.
bou′ton (boo′-), *bou′ton′nière′* (boo-
ton nyâr′).
bouts-ri més′ (boo rē mä′).
Bou var′di a (boo-).
Bou vier′ (boo′vyä′), Fr. physician.
Bou vier′ (boo veer′), Amer.
writer.
Bou′zy (boo′-).
bŏ′vate.
bŏ′vĭne *or* -vīne, bo′vid, -vi form.
bŏ′void.
bŏw, -er, -ing, -bell, -bent, -fin,
-less, -man, -men, -pot, -spirit,
-stãff, *pl*. -staves, -spring, -string,
-wood, bowed.
bŏw′-arm, -backed, -beâr er,
-billed, -boy, -brace, -case,
-cla vi er, -com pass (-kum-),

-drill, -hand, -harp′si chord,
-head, -head ed, -in′stru ment,
-i ron, -kail, -knot, -leg′ged *or*
-legged, -net, -pen, -pen cil,
-pin, -saw, -shot, -wise, bow′-
man's-root, bŏw win dow.
Bŏw′-bell, -bells, -dye.
bow (bou), -ing, -ing ly, -man, *pl*.
-men, bowed.
bow′-chas′er, -fast, -grace, -oar,
-piece, -tim bers.
Bow′dich (bou′-), Eng. trav.
Bow′ditch, Amer. schol.
Bŏwd′ler ism (*or* boud′-), -ler ize,
-ized, -ī zing, -ī ză′tion.
Bow′doin (bŏ′dn), Amer. statesman.
Bow′doin ham (bou′dn am), t.
Me.
bŏw′el, -eled *or* -elled.
bŏw′en īte.
bŏw′er, -ing, -er y, -ered, bow′er-
aṇ′chor, -bird, -eaves, -maid,
-thane, -wom an.
bow′ess, bow′et.
bow′ie (bou′-), a wooden bowl.
bŏw′ie-knife (*or* bŏŏ′-).
bŏwl, -er, bowls, bowl′-ma chine′,
-spĭr it.
bŏw′lĭne (*or* -lĭn), -bri′dle, -criṇ′-
gle, -knot.
bŏwl′ing, -al ley, -crease, -green,
-ground.
Bŏw′ling Green, c. Ky.; vil. Mo.;
vil. O.
bŏw′string-bridge, -gird er.
bow′wow′.
bŏw′yer.
box, -ing, -er, boxed, box′bĕr ry,
-fish, -haul, -haul ing, -wood,
Box′er, a Chinese insurgent.
box′-chro nom e ter, -coat, -coup-
ling, -crab, -day, -el der, -hook,
-i ron, -keep er, -key, -lob by,
-lock, -māk ing, -met al, -mon′-
ey, -of fice, -oys ter, -o′pen er,
-pack ing, -plãit ing, -re lay,
-room, -scrãp er, -sēat, -set,
-set ter, -slãt er, -sta ple, -stew,
-strap, -thorn, -tor′toise (-tis),
-turn ing, -tur tle, box′-and-tap′.
box bãr′row, b. bĕam, b. bed,
b. bridge, b. cage, b. car, b.

---

fāte, făt, fär, fạll, fâre, făst, sofà, mēte, mĕt, hêr, īce, ĭn, nōte,

churn, b. coil, b. drain, b.
frame, b. gird er, b. pläit, b.
slip, b. snuf'fers, b. stall, b.
steps, b. stairs, b. trap, b.
vălve.
box'ing-glove, -ma chine', -match,
-night, b. off, Box'ing-day, -time.
boy, -hood, -ish, -ish ly, -ish ness,
boy bish op, boy's-love, a plant,
boy's play.
boy'ar, -ard, -ard ism.
boy au (bwä'yō *or* -yō' *or* boi'ō).
boy'cott, -ed, -er, -ing, -ism.
boy'la.
boyn.
boy u'na (-ōō'na *or* bō yū'-).
bŏ'za.
Bōze'man, t. Mont.
bŏ'zon.
Boz zar'is *or* Bot'zar is (bŏz zăr'is
or bŏt'sä rēs), Gr. patriot.
Bra ban çon' (bra bŏn sŏń'), -çonne
(-sŏn'), -ban'ter, -ban'tĭne.
brăb'ble, -ment, -bled, -bling.
bră'cæ (-sē), brăc'cæ (brăk'se).
brac'cate.
brac ci ä'le (brak sĭ-).
brac'cio (brăt'chō), pl. -cia
(-cha).
brace, -let, braced, bra'cer, -cing,
-cing ly, -cing ness.
brace'-drill, -hĕad, -kēy, -mōld,
-pend'ant, -stake, bra'cing-chain.
brach'i al (brăk'- *or* brä'ki al),
-i ate, -i um, pl. -i a.
brach'i og'a noid (brăk'-), -noid'-
ē ĭ, -i o lä'ri a.
brach'i o pod (brăk'-), -i op'o da.
brach'y car'di a (brăk-), -y dī ag'-
o nal, -y dōme, -y dŏnt, -y el'y-
trŏus.
brach'y ce phal'ic (brăk-), -y-
ceph'a lous, -a ly, -a lism.
bra chyc'er al (-kĭs'-), -er ous.
bra chyg'ra pher (-kĭg'-), -ra phy,
-chyl'o gy (-kil'o jy), -chyp'te ra
(-kĭp'-), -tє res (-rēz), -ter ous,
-chys'to chrone (-kis'to krōn).
bra chyp'o doŭs (-kip'-).
brach'y prism (brăk'-), -y pyr'a mid.
brach'y tin'a coid (brăk'-), brach'-
y ty'pous (*or* bra kit'i pus), -y ŭ'-
ra, -u'ral, -u'ran, -u'rous.

brack.
brack'en, -clock.
brack'et, -ed, -ing, brack'et-cock,
-crab, -trail.
brack'ish, -ish ness.
brac'o nid.
bract, -ed, -less, -let, brac'te al,
-te ate, -te ĭ form, -te o late, -te ole.
brad, -awl, -drīv'er, -set ter.
Bra da man'te (brä dä män'tä).
brae (brā).
brag, -gart, -gart ly, -ger, -ging,
-ging ly, -ga do'cio (-shŏ or -shyŏ),
bragged.
Brag'mar'do', Ja'no'tus' de (zhä'-
nō'tŏŏs' de brăg'mar'dō').
bră gue'ro (-gä'ro).
Brahe (brä *or* brä), Dan. astron.
Bräh'ma, -mä'ic, -man *or* -min,
-ma na, -ma nee, -man ess,
-man i (-ē), -man'ic, -ic al,
-man ism, -man ist, -mo ism,
Brähm, Bräh'mo-So mäj'. bräh'-
ma, a hen.
Bräh'ma pu'tra (-pōō'-), r. India.
braid, -ed, -er, -ing, -ist, braid'-
comb, -pol'ish ing, -siz'ing,
braid'ing-ma chine'.
brail, *Naut.*
braille (brāl) or *brail lé* (brā'lyā'),
printing.
brain, -ing, -y, -less, -less ness,
brained, brain'pan, -sand, -sick,
-sick ness, -stone.
brain'-blad'der, -box, -case,
-cav'i ty, -fag, -mag'got, -rack-
ing, -stem, -throb, -tu'mor,
-wave, -work, -worm, b. cŏr'al,
b. fe'ver, brain'stone cor'al.
brăi'ro.
brăise *or* brăize, brais'er, *brais sé'*
(brä zā'), braiz'ing-ket tle, -pan.
brăit.
brake, -age, brăk'y, brake'man,
brakes'man, brake'-band, -bar,
-beam, -block, -cyl in der, -dog,
-fin ger, -hang'er, -head, -hop'-
per, -hose, -lĕath'er, -pipe, -rod,
-rub ber, -shăft, -shoe, -sĭeve,
-spool, -strap, -van, -wheel,
brake'ing-ma chine.
Brä'ma. See *Brahma.* Brä'ma,
Brä'mah lock, B. press.

---

nŏt, nôr, ūse, ŭp, ûrn, etüde, fōōd, fŏŏt, aŋger, boŋmot, thus, Bach.

12

Brä man tesque', brä'man tip (*or*
-man'-).
bram'ble, -bled, -bling, -bly, -ber-
ry, bram'ble-bond, -bush, -finch,
-net, -rose, -worm.
bran, -ny, -tail, -drench, -dust er,
-new. See *brand-new.* bran
bread.
bran'card.
brânch, -er, -er y, -ing, -i ness,
-less, -let, -y, -stand, branched,
branch'-block, -chuck, -her-
ring, -leaf, -pi lot, -pipe, -point.
bran̯'chi al (-kĭ-), -chi ate.
bran chic'o lous (-kĭk'-), bran̯'-
chi o mēre' (-kĭ-), -chi rēme.
bran̯'chi o pod (-kĭ-).
brand, -ed, -er, -ing.
brand'-book, -goose, -i ron,
-mark, -new *or* bran'-, -spore,
brand'ing-chute, -hel met, -i ron.
Brän'den burg (-bŏŏrg), prov.
Prus., B. porce'laĭn. brăn'den-
bûrg, a button; an ornament.
bran'der, -ing.
bran'dish, -er, -ing, -dished.
brand'ling *or* -lin.
bran'dy, *pl.* -dies (-diz), -dĭed,
bran'dy-bot tle, -faced, -fruit, b.
paw'nee, b. smash, b. snap.
brank'ur sĭne.
branle (bränl).
bran'lin.
brant, -bird, -coot, -fox, -goose,
-snipe.
bra se'ro (-sä'-).
brash, -y.
brä'sier. See *brazier.*
brăsque.
brâss, -y, -i ly, -i ness, brass'back,
a bird, -black ing, -col or,
-fin'ish er, -foil, -found er, -fur-
nace, -leaf, -paved, -pow der,
-smith, -vis aged (-viz-), -ware,
-wind, b. bass.
brâs'sage.
brâs'sart *or* -sard.
brâsse, a fish.
Bras'si ca, bras'si ca'ceous.
bratch'et.
brät'sche.
brat'tach (-tăk).
brăt'tĭce, -cloth.

brat'tle, -tled, -tling.
brau'lid, -loid.
brau'na.
Brau ne ber'ger (brou ne bâr'-
ger).
braun'ĭte (broun'-).
bra vä'do, *pl.* -does (-dōz).
brave, -ly, -ness, brāv'ing, -ing ly,
-er y, braved.
brä'vo (*or* brä'-), *pl.* -vos *or* -voes
(-vōz), -vis'si mo.
brä vu'ra (-vōō'-).
braw, -ly.
brawl, -er, -ing, -ing ly, brawled.
brawn, -y, -i ness.
brax'y.
bray, -er, -ing, brayed.
brä'za (brä'tha).
braze, brazed, brāz'ing, braz'ing-
tongs.
brä'zen (-zn), -ing, -ly, -ness,
-face, *n.*
bra'zen-browed (-broud), -faced,
-fist ed, b. age, b. sea.
bra'zier *or* -sier (-zhêr).
Bra zil', -zil'ian, Bra zil'-nut,
-root, B. tea, B. wax.
bra zil'-wood.
braz'i let'to.
bre a (brä' à).
breach, -ing, -y, breached, breach'-
ing-bat'ter y.
brĕad, -less, -ber ry, -fruit, -meal,
-nut, -root, -stuff, -win ner.
bread'-barge, -bås'ket, -corn,
-crumb, -knife, -māk ing, -rasp,
-room, -sli cer, -tray, -tree,
-weight, bread'fruit-tree.
brĕadt͡h, -less, -ways, -wise.
brĕak, -ing, -age, -a ble, -er,
-a way, broke, bro'ken (-kn),
break'ax, -bones, -cir'cuit (-kĭt),
-down, -neck, -share, -stâff, -stone,
-wa ter.
brĕak'-back, -club, -in, -i ron,
-joint, -lät͡he, -line, -ŏff, -prom-
ise, -sig nal, -up, -van.
brĕak'ing-crew, -dī am'e ter, -en'-
gine, -frame, -ma chine, -weight.
brĕak'fast, -ed, -ing, brĕak'fast-
cap, -dish es, -set, -ta ble, -time.
brĕam, -ing, breamed, bream'-
flat.

brĕast, -ed, -ing, -pin, -plate, -weed, -wise, -work.
brĕast'-back'stay, -band, -beam, -board, -bone, -chains, -col lar, -deep, -drill, -fåst, -gas'ket, -har'ness, -height, -high, -hook, -knee, -knot, -line, -mold ing, -pāin, -pang, -plow, -pump, -rail, -strap, -sum mer, -wall, -wheel, -wood, brĕast'ing-knife.
brĕath, -less, -less ness, -y, breath'-sound.
brĕathe, brĕath'er, -ing, -a ble, -a ble ness.
brĕath'ing-hole, -mark, -place, -pore, -sound, -space, -spell, -time, -tube, -while.
brec'cia (brĕt'cha), -ci a ted (-chĭ-ā ted *or* brĕk'shĭ-), -ci ā'tion.
brĕech (*or* brĭch), -ing, -less, breeched.
brĕech-band, -băr'row, -block, -cloth, -clout, -load er, -load ing, -mech'an ism (-mĕk'-), -piece, -pin, -plug, -screw, -sight, -wrench.
breech es (britch'ĕz), -buoy (-bwoi *or* boi), -flue, -pipe.
breech'ing-bolt, -hook, -loop, -strap.
breed, -ing, -er, brĕd.
breed'ing-cage, -ground, -pen, -place, -pond, -sea son.
breeks.
breeze, -less, breez'y, -i ly, -i ness, breeze'-fly, -ov en (-ŭv-).
breg'ma, pl. *-ma ta,* -mat'ic.
breĭt'haup tĭte (-houp-).
Breĭt'mann, Häns, Amer. humorist.
breĭt'o līne.
brĕ lan' (-län').
bre loque' (-lŏk').
Brĕm'en, c. Ger.
brent, -fox, -goose.
bren'ta.
bren'te.
brĕq'uĕt-chain.
Bres'ci a (brĕsh'ē a), prov. It.
Brĕs'lau (-lou), c. Prus.
bres'son.
Bre tagne' (brĕ tänye'), prov. Fr.
breth'ren.
Brĕt'on (*or* brĭt'-).

brett.
brĕve.
bre vet', -ted, -ting, -cy.
brē'vi a ry (*or* brĕv'i a ry *or* brĕv'-ya ry).
brev i cau'date, -fō'li ate, -i liṇ'-gual, -i pen'nate, -i ros'tral, -ros'-trate.
brē vier' (-veer').
brev'i ty.
brew, -ing, -age, -er, -er y, brewed, brew'-house, -ket tle, -wife.
brews'ter ĭte.
Brī ā're us, *Myth.,* -ā're an.
brībe, bribed, brīb'ing, -a ble, -er, bribe'-bro ker, -pan der, -tāk er.
brīb'er y, -oath.
bric'-à-brac.
brick, -bat, -field er, -lay er, -māk-er, -nog, -nog ging, -stone, -wise, -work.
brick'-ax, -băr'row, -built, -clamp, -clay, -dri er, -dust, -earth, -el'e va tor, -field, -fur'nace, -kiln (-kĭl), -ma chine, -ma son, -mold, -oil, -pane, -press, -tile, -trim'mer, -truck, -yard, brick tea.
brĭ côle'.
bride, -groom, -groom ship, -hood, -maid, -man, -ship, -stake, -wain, -well, -wort.
bride'-ale, -bed, -bowl, -cake, -chäm ber, -day, brides'-la ces.
brides'maid, brides'man, brī'dal-wreath, brī'dal trip.
bridge, -less, -wa ter, bridged, bridge'pot.
bridge'-bar, -board, -crane, -deck, -head, -is'let (-ĭ'let), -pile, -pit, -rail, -stone, -tow er, -train, -tree, -truss, -ward.
bridg'ing, -floor, -joist, -piece.
brī'dle, -less, -wise, -dled, -dling, -dler. . brī'dle-bit, -ca'ble, -chains, -hand, -i ron, -path, -port, -rein, -road, -rod, b. strict ure.
brī doon'.
brie'cheese (brē-).
brĭĕf, -ly, -less, -less ness, -less ly, -ness.

brī′er _or_ -ar, -er y, bri′er-bird,
-root, -rose, -wood.
briĕve.
brĭ gåde′, -ma jor.
brig a diĕr′, -gen er al.
brig′a low.
brĭg′and, -age, -ish, -ism, -an-
dīne (_or_ -dĭn), -an tīne (_or_ -tĭn).
Bri ghĕl′la (brē-).
bright, -en, -en ing, -ish, -ly,
-ness, -some, -work, bright′-cut,
-eyed, -har nessed.
Brign oles′ (brĕn yŏl′), t. Fr.
brill.
bril lan′te (brĕl län′tä).
bril′liant   (-yant),   -ly,   -ness,
-liance, -lian cy.
bril′lian tine (-yan tēn).
brills.
brim, -ful, -ful ness, -less, -mer,
-ming, -ming ly, -stone, -stone-
wort, brimmed.
brin′ded.
Brin′di si (brēn′dē sē), c. It.
brin′dle, -dled, brin′dle-moth.
brine, brīn′y, -i ness, -ish, -ish-
ness.
brine′-e vap′o ra tor, -fly, -gage,
-pan, -pit, -pump, -shrimp,
-spring, -valve, -worm.
bring, -ing, -er, brought.
brin′jạl _or_ -jaul.
brin jar′ree or _brin ja′ree′_ or _-jar′ry._
brink.
brĭ′o (brē′o).
bri oche′ (bre ŏsh′).
bri′o lette′ (brē-), _or_ brī′o let.
brĭ quet′   (-ket′   _or_   brĭk′-)   _or_
bri quette′, a block of stone or
coal.
brĭ quet′ (-ket′ _or_ brē kä′), _Her._
brīse (brīz), fallow ground.
bri sé′ (brē zä′), broken, as music.
brise′ment (brēz′-).
brĭ sĭn′goid.
brisk, -ly, -ness.
bris′ket.
bris′ling, a fish.
bris′tle (-l), -tled, -tling, -tlings.
-tly, -tli ness, bris′tle tail, -wort.
bris′tle-fern, -bird, -grăss, -hĕr′ring,
-like, -moss, -point′ed, -rat,
-shaped.

Bris′tol, -board, B. brick, B.
di a mond (_or_ dī′mond), B. milk,
B. pa per, B. porce′laĭn, B. potter y, B. red,⁻ B. stone.
bris′ure (brĭz′- _or_ brē zur′).
brit _or_ britt.
Brit′ain-crown.
Bri tan′nĭ a, Great Britain, -tan′-
nic, bri tan′ni a, a metal.
Brit′ish, -ish er, -i cism, Brit′on.
Brit o mar′tis _or_ Brit′o mart.
brit′ter worts.
brit′tle, -ness, -worts, b. star.
britz′ska _or_ brits′ka.
brŏach, -er, -ing, broached.
brŏach-post, -turn er, broach′ing-
press.
brŏad, -en, -er, -cst, -ly, -ness,
-ish, -cast, -side, -wise, -ax _or_
-axe, -bill, -brim, -cloth, -horn
-leaf, -mouth, -stone, -sword,
-tail, -throat.
broad-backed, -bāsed, -billed,
-brimmed, -chest ed, -church,
-church man, -eyed, -front ed,
-gāge, _a._, -gaged, -horned,
-leaved, -piece, -seal, _v._, -shoul-
dered, -sight ed, -spo ken,
-sprĕad, -spread ing, -trĕad,
broad′leaf-tree.
broad ar′row, b. gage, _n._, b.
lig′a ment, b. seal, b. tool,
Broad Church.
brob.
Brob′ding nag, -nag′i an.
bro cåde′, -cåd′ed, -cåd′ing, bro-
cade′-shell.
brŏc′ard, brō car′dic.
brŏ′ca tel _or_ -telle (_or_ brŏc′-) -tel′lo.
brŏc′co lĭ.
broch (brŏk _or_ brŭk).
brŏch′an.
brŏ′chant (-shant).
brō chan′tīte (brō shăn′tīte _or_
brŏk′-).
brō′chate (-kāte).
bro chĕ′ (brō shā′),   brocaded;
stitched.
bro chet′ (brō shā′), a fish.
brō chette′ (-shĕt′), a skewer.
bro chid′o drone (-kĭd′-).
brō chure′ (-shōōr′).
brŏck, -faced.

---

brock'age.
Broc'ken spec'ter (-kn).
brock'et.
brŏd, -dle.
brō'gan (or -gan').
brög'ger ĭte (brêg'-).
Brog'lie, de (dĕ brō'y), Fr. statesman.
brŏgue.
broid'er, -ing, -er, -ered, -er y,
pl. -er ies.
broil, -er, -ing, broiled.
brŏke, brō'ken (-kn), -ken ly, -ken-
ness.
brō'ken-backed, -bod ied, -down,
-heärt'ed, -kneed, -wĭnd'ed, b.
brĕast, b. cord, b. coal, b. line,
b. vict uals.
brō'ker, -age.
brō'ma, -mal, -mate, -ma loin,
-ma tog'ra phy, -ma tol'o gy,
-o gist.
brome-grȧss or brŏm-.
Bro me'li a, bro me'li ā'ceous.
brō'me lin.
Bro'mi an.
brō'mĭne, -mic, -mĭde (or -mīd),
-mi na ted, -min ism, -mism,
mīte, mīsc, misɔd, mī sing,
-mo gel'a tin, -mog'ra phy, -mū-
ret, -ret ed, -my rīte, brome.
brom'ming.
bro mog'ra phy.
broŋ'cho (-kō) or -co.
broŋ'chus (-kus), pl. -chi (-kī),
-chi a (-kī-), -chi al, -chic, -cho-
cele, -cho tome, bron chit'ic
(-kĭt'-), -chī'tis, -coph'o ny, -chot'-
o my.
Brŏn'tĕ, Charlotte, Eng. novelist.
bron tol'o gy, -tom'e ter, bron'tograph.
bron to sạu'rus, -to the'ri um, -to-
zo'um.
brŏnze, bronzed, bronz'ing, -ĭne,
-ist, -īte, -y, bronze'wing.
bronze'-back'er, -gold, -lĭq uĭd,
-lĭq uor, -paint, -pow der, bronz'-
ing-ma chine', -salt.
Brŏn zō mär'tĕ.
brooch (brōch or brōōch), a breast-
pin.

brōōd, -ed, -ing, -er, -y, brood'-
bud, -cap'sule, -cav'i ty, -cell,
-comb, -food, -mare, -pouch,
-space.
brood'-spi'oen (brōd'-spē un).
brōŏk, -ing, -let, -y, -ite, brooked,
brook'fish, a killifish, -lime, -side,
-weed.
brook'-fish, -bet' o ny, -lam prey,
-mint, -moss, -ou zel, -pick'er el,
-runner, -trout.
Brōŏk'lĭne, t. Mass.
brōōm, -y, -ster, -stȧff, -stick,
-weed.
brōōm'-brush, -bush, -corn,
-crow'ber ry, -grȧss, -han dle,
-hĕad, -man, -pälm, -pine,
-rape, -root, -sedge, -sew'ing
(-sō'-), -tree, -vise (-vīs).
brōse (brōz), brō'sy.
brot'an, -a ny.
brŏth.
brŏth'el.
broth'er (brŭth'-), -hood, -less,
-like, -ly, -li ness, -tail, -ship,
-wort, broth'er-in-law, b. ger man,
b. of'fi cer.
brough (brŏk or brŭf).
Brough'am (brōō'am or broōm),
Brit. statesman, brough'am, a
carriage.
brought (brawt).
brow (brou), -beat, -beat er, -ing,
brow'-a gue, -ant ler, -band,
-bound, -post, -snag, -spot,
-tran som.
brown, -er, -est, -ish, -ness, -ing,
-back, -bill, -ie, -tail, -stone, -wort,
browned.
brown'-backed, -bess, -crops,
-george, -lee mer, -spar, brown
blaze, b. coal, b. mix ture, b.
stout, b. stud y, b. thrash er, b.
thrush.
Brown'i an, Brown ism, -ist, -ist ic,
-ic al.
Brown-Sé quard' (-sā'kär'), Fr.
physiol.
browse (brouz), browsed, brows'-
ing, -er, browse'-wood.
bru'ang (or -ang').
bru'bru.
bru'chid (-kĭd).

Brŭ′ges (brū′jĕz *or* brōōzh′-), c. Belg.

bruh (brōō), a monkey.

bru′ĭn.

bruise, -wort, bruis′er, -ing, bruised, bruis′ing-ma chine, -mill.

bruit.

Bru′lé (brōō′lā), co. S. Dak.

brû′lée (brōō′lā).

bru′mal, bru′mous, *Bru maire′.*

brum′by.

Brŭm′mel, Beau Brum mel, Eng. fop.

Bru′ne hild (brōō′nĕ hĭlt) *or* **Bru′-nĕ hil′dĕ.**

bru nĕtte′.

bru nis sure′ (broo′nĕ′sōor′).

brun′ner ite (brōōn-).

Bruns′wick, co. N. C.; co. Va.; c. Ga., B. black, B. green; bruns′wick, a lady's coat.

brunt.

brush, -er, -ing, -ful, -y, -i ness, -īte, -let, -man, -ment, -wood, brushed.

brush′-bird, -burn, -chĕr ry, -harrow, -hat, -hoŏk, -jack, -monkey, -ore, -plow, -pull er, -rat, -tailed, -tongued, -tur key, -wheel, brush′ing-ma chine′.

brŭsk *or* brusque (brōōsk), -ness, brus′que rie (brōōs′kĕ rē).

Brus′sels, c. Belg., B. car′pet, B. lace, B. point, B. sprouts.

brut.

Bru′ta.

bru′tal, -ize, -ized, -ī zing, -ī zā′tion, -ly, -tal′i ty.

brute, -hood, -ness, bru′ti fy, -fy ing, -fied, bru′tish, -ly, -ness, -tism.

bru′tum ful′men.

Brū′tus, *Biog.*; bru′tus, a wig.

bru yère′ (-yâr′).

Bry ā′ce æ, bry a′ceous (-shus).

Bry′an ĭte.

Bryce (brīs), Eng. writer.

bryg′mus.

bry ol′o gy (brī-), -o gist, -o log′ic-al (-lŏj′-).

Bry o zo′a (brī′-), bry o zo′an, -zo′-id, -zo′um.

Brze za′ny (bzhā zhä′nĕ), t. Aust.

Brze′zyn (bzhā′zĭn), t. Pol.

bu an su′ah (bōō an sōō′a).

bu′at (bōō′-).

bu′āze, -fi′ber.

bub′ble, -bled, -bler, -bling, -bly.

bub′ble-shell, -tri er, bub′bling-fish.

bū′bo, *Med.,* -bon′ic, -bon′o cĕle, Bu′bo, *Ornith.*

bu′bu lin.

buc′an *or* -can.

bu′ca ro (bōō′kä rō).

buc′ca, pl. -*cæ* (-sē), -cate, -cal, *-cu-la.*

buc′ca neer′ *or* buc a- *or* -nier, -neer′ish.

buc che′ro (bōōk kä′-).

buc′ci na, pl. -*ci næ,* -ci nal, *-ci-na′tor,* -na′to ry.

Buc ci′no (bōōt chē′no), t. It.

bu cen′taur.

Bu ceph′a lus.

Bŭ chan′an (-kăn′-) (*or* bŭk an′-an), *Biog.* and *Geog.*

Bū′cha rest′ (-ka-), c. Roum.

bū′chŭ (-kū).

buck, -er, -ish, -ism, bucked, buck′board, -eye, -finch, -pot, -shot, -skin, -thorn, -wash, -wash-ing, -wheat, Buck′tail.

buck-a gue, -băs ket, -bean, -eyed, -fe ver, -fly, -hound, -jump er, -log, -mack′er el, -moth, -plate, -rake, -saw, -stall, -tooth, -wag on, buck-and-ball, buck's-beard, -horn.

buck′et, -ful, -en gine, -hook, -lift, -māk ing, -pitch, -pump, -rod, -shop, -valve, -wheel.

buck′horn, -sight.

buck′ie *or* -y.

buck′ing, -i ron, -kier *or* -keir, -plate, -stool, -strap, -ta ble.

buc′kle, -kled, -kling, -kler.

buc′kle-beg gar, -chape, -horns.

buc′kler-fern, -fish, -head ed, -mus tard.

buck′ling, a fish.

buc′kling-cŏmb.

buck′ra.

buck′ra m.

bū col′ic, -ic al, -al ly.

bu crā′ni um, pl. -*ni a,* bu crane′ (*or* bu′-).

Bu'czacz (bōō'chäch), t. Aust.
bud, -ded, -ding, -let, bud'-cell,
-finch, bud'ding-knife.
Bud'dha (bōō'da), -dhism, -dhist,
-dhist'ic, -ic al.
bud'dle.
Būde burn'er, B. light.
budge, budg'er, -ing, -y, budge'-
bär'rel.
budg'er ee gah' or -er i gar'.
budg'e ro or -row (or buj'rō).
budg'et.
bud'la.
bud'mash.
Būe'na Vīs'ta, co. Io.; t. Col.;
(bwä nä vēs'tä), t. Mex.
Bue'nos Ay'res (bō'nus ā'riz or
bwä'nōs i'res), prov. Arg. Rep.
bŭff, -y, buff'-coat, -laced, -lĕath-
er, -stick, -tip, -ware, -wheel,
h. jer kin.
buf'ja (bōōf'a).
buf'fa lo, pl. -loes or -los, buf'-
fa lo-bĕr'ry, -bird, -bug, -chips,
-clo'ver, -cod, -fish, -fly, -gnat,
-grăss, -hide, -hunt, -hunt ing,
-jack, -moth, -nut, -perch,
-range, -robe, -skin, -wal low.
buf'fer, -arm, -bar, -beam, -block,
-head, -spring, -thim ble.
buf'fet, v., -ed, -ing, -er.
bŭf'fet, n. (or bōō fā'), -car,
-stool.
buf'fing, -block, -lāthe, -ma chine',
-spring, -wheel.
buf'jo (or bŏŏf'-).
buf foon', -ish, -ism, -ly, -er y.
Bū'fo, -fon īte, -fon id, -oid, -fon' i-
form.
bug, -ger, -gy, -gi ness, bug'bane,
-beâr, -eye, -fish, -head, -seed,
-wort, -shad.
bug'a bōō (or -bōō').
bug'ger y.
bug'gy, pl. -gies, bug'gy-boat, b.
cul'ti va tor, b. plow.
bu'gis (bōō'jis).
bū'gle, -gled, -gler, -gling, bu'gle-
weed, -wort, -call, -cap, -horn,
-ród.
bū'gloss.
bū'gong.
bū'gor.

bŭ'hach (-hatch).
bŭhl (or bōōhl), -work, -saw.
buhr (bur), -stone, -dress er,
-driv er.
build, -ed, -ing, -er, buĭlt.
build'ing-block, -i ron, -mov er,
-slip, -stance, -wax, b. lease,
buĭlt-up, a.
buire (bwēr) or bu ire (bōō ēr').
buis son' (bwē sôň').
bu'ke (bōō'kä).
buk'kum, -wood.
buk'shee.
Bul.
Bu la can' (bōō'lä kän'), prov.
P. I.
bulb, -ar, -el, -let, -ous, -i form,
-ule, -y, bul bif'er ous, -ba'ceous,
bul'bo-tu ber.
bul'ber ry.
bul bil'la.
bul'bul (bŏŏl'bŏŏl).
Bul'gar, -gā'ri an, -gär'ic.
bŭlge, -ways, bulged, bul'gy (-jĭ),
-ging, -ger.
bū lim'i a, -lim'ic, -lim'i ous.
bulk, -ing, -er, -y, -i ness, bulked,
bulk'head.
bull (bŏŏl), -ish, -ish ly, -bat,
-beg'gar, -ber ry, -bri'er, -comb'-
er, -dog, -doze, -dozed, -doz er,
-doz ing, -finch, -fish, -fist, -fly,
-frog, -head, a fish, -hoof, -huss,
-jub, -knob, -nose, -nut, -pout,
-weed, -wort.
bull-bāit'ing, -bay, -bee, -beef,
-bird, -boat, -calf, a person,
-dance, -faced, -feast, -fight,
-fight er, -fronts, -head, a.,
-head ed, -hide, -neck, -necked,
-net, -pine, -pŏll, -pout, -pump,
-ring, -roar'er, -rope, -rout,
-segg, -snake, -spink, -stag,
-stang, -ter'ri er, -trout, -voiced,
-wal lop er, -whack, -whack er,
-wheel, -whip, bull'head-plov er
(-plŭv-), bulls-and-cows, bull's-
eye, -foot, -mouth, -nose, b.
calf.
bŭl'lāce.
bŭl'late, -la ted, -la'tion, -lous,
-les'cence.
bul'len (bŏŏl-), -bul'len, -nail.

bul'let (bŏŏl'-), -head, a person,
-bag, -com pass es, -ex tract'or,
-head, a round head, -head ed,
-hook, -lā'dle, -ma chine, -māk'-
ing, -mold, -mōld'ing, -probe,
-proof, -screw, -shell, -tree,
-wood.
bul'le tĭn (bŏŏl'-), -tin ist, -board.
bul'ling (bŏŏl'-), -shov'el (-shuv'-)
bul'lion (bŏŏl'yon), -ism, -ist,
bul'lion-bar, -fringe, -point,
-van.
bul'lock (bŏŏl'-), -shell, bul'lock's-
eye, -heart.
bul'ly (bŏŏl'-), *pl.* -lies, -lĭed,
-ly ing, bul'ly rag, bul'ly-beef,
-boy, -cod, -head, -rock, -ruf-
fian, -tree.
Bu'low, von (fon bü'lō), Prus.
gen.
bul ree'dy (bŏŏl-).
bul'rush (bŏŏl'-), -y.
bŭlse.
bŭlt, bul'tow (bŏŏl'tō).
bŭl'tong or *bĭl'-.*
bul'wark (bŏŏl'-).
Bul'wer (bŏŏl'-), William Henry
Lytton Earle, Eng. auth.
Bul'wer-Lyt'ton, Edward George
Earle Lytton, Brit. novelist.
Bul'wer-Lyt'ton, Edward Robert,
Eng. poet.
bum, -mer, -ming, bummed,
bum'bail iff, -bar rel, -boat,
-clock, -wood.
bū mas'tus.
bum'ble bee, bum'ble ber ry,
-dom, -foot, a disease of fowls,
-kite, -pup py, -pup pist, -foot,
-foot ed, -stăff.
Bū mě'li a.
bum' ick y.
bum'kin, a beam or spar.
bum'ma lo.
bump, -er, -ing, -tious, -tious ness,
-y, bumped.
bump'er-tim ber, bump'ing-post.
bump'kin, a rustic, -ly.
bun *or* bunn.
bunch, -ing, -y, -i ness, bunch'-
back, -backed, -ber ry, -flow er,
-fish, -grăss, -oys ter, -whale.
buņ'co *or* -ko, -ing, -coed (-kōd),

buņ'co-game, -joint, -man,
-steer'er.
buņ'combe (-kum), *or* buņ'kum.
bŭnd, an embankment.
bund (bŏŏnd), a league.
bŭn'der, -boat.
Bun'des rath or *-rat* (bŏŏn'des rät).
bun'dle, -dled, -dling, bun'dle-
pil lar, -sheath, bun'dling-ma
chine, -press.
bun'do bust.
bung, -ing, bunged, bung'buck'et,
-bor er, -cut ter, -draw er, -hole,
-lāthe, -plug, -seat, -start er,
-stave, -vent.
bun'găll.
buņ'ga lŏw.
buņ'ga rum.
buņ'gle, -some, -gled, -gling,
-gling ly, -gler.
buņ'go, -tree.
bun'ion *or* -yon.
buņk, buņ'ker.
buņ'ker, a sand hole; bunk'er, a
fish.
bun'nings.
bun'ny.
bū'nō dŏnt.
Bun'sen (bŏŏn'-), Ger. chem.
Bun'sen burn er (bŏŏn'-), B.
bat'ter y, B. cell, B. fil ter-
pump.
bun'sen ĭte (bŏŏn'-).
bunt, -box, -y, bun'ter, -ted, bunt-
ear, -gas'ket, -jig ger, -whip.
bun'ting, -crow, -finch, -i ron,
-lark.
bunt'lĭne, -cloth.
bun'tons.
bun'ya, -bun'ya.
bun'yĭp.
buoy (bwoi *or* boy *or* bŏŏ'y),
-age, -ance, -an cy, -ant, -ant ly,
-ant ness, buoy'-rope, -safe.
bur *or* burr, -rish, -ry, bur'fish,
-stone, -bark, -brick, -chis el,
-cut ter, -dress er, -drill, -drīv er,
-gage, a drill gage, -grăss, -mar
i gold, -mill stone, -nip per,
-oak, -pars ley, -pump, -reed,
-this tle, -tree.
bu'ran (bŏŏ'-).
bu rat ti'no (bŏŏ rät tē'no).

bur'bark.
bur'bot, -bolt, bur'bot-eel.
bur'da läne *or* -lõne.
bur'de kin.
bur'den *or* -then, -ing, -er, -some,
  -some ly, -some ness, -dened,
  bur'den-bear'er.
Bur dett'-Coutts' (-kõõts'), Eng.
  philanthropist.
bur'dock, -grãss.
bü'reau (-rõ), *pl.* -reaus, bu'reau-
  crat, -crat'ic, -ic al, -al ly,
  -reau'cra cy, -cra tist.
bu re'o (bõõ rä'o).
bü rětte'.
burg, bur gen'sic (-jen-), burg'grave
  or bur'-, -gra'vi ate.
burg'age, -ten'ant, -ten'e ment.
bur'gall.
bur'ga net *or* -go net.
bur'gee (-je).
bur'geon (-jun).
bur'gess, -dom, -ship, bur'gess
  list, b. oath, b. roll.
burgh, -al, -er, -er mãs'ter, -er-
  ship, burgh'mãs ter, bur'go-
  mãs'ter.
bur'glar, -ize, -ized, -i zing, -gla-
  ry, -gla'ri ous, -ous ly.
bur'glar-a larm, -proof.
bur'goo.
Bur goyne', Eng. gen., bur goyne',
  an implement.
Bur'gundy, B. pitch.
bur'hel *or* -rhel (*or* bõõr'-).
bur'i al (běr'-), -aisle, -case,
  -clothes, -ground, -hill, -mound,
  -place, -robe, -vault, bur'i al
  serv ice, b. so ci e ty.
bü'ri-nut.
bü'rin, -ist.
bü'ri on.
bü ri ti' (-tee').
bur'ka.
burke, burked, burk'ing, -er,
  -ism.
burl, -ing, -er, burled, burl'ing-
  i ron, -ma chine.
bur'lace.
bur'lap.
bur lesque', -ly, -ness, -lesqued'
  (-leskt'), -les'quer, -lesqu'ing
  (-lesk'ing).

bur let'ta.
Bur'lin game, Amer. dipl.
bur'ly, -li ly, -li ness, bur'ly-
  boned, -head ed.
Bur'man, *pl.* -mans (-manz).
Bur man'ni a.
Bur mese' (-mês' *or* -mēz').
burn, -er, -ing, -ing ly, -a ble,
  burned, burnt, burn'bake, -gate,
  -side, -stic kle, -wood, -beat,
  -fish ing, -mouth, -trout.
burn'ing-bush, -flu'id, -glãss,
  -house, -lens, -mĭr'ror, -point.
bur'net, -moth, -rose.
bur'nish, -a ble, -er, -ing,
  -ment, -nished, -ing-ma chine.
burn'-nose' bark.
bur'nõõse *or* -nous' (-nõõs).
burnt, -ear, -stone, b. of'fer ing,
  b. sac'ri fice, b. sĭ en na, b.
  um ber.
bŭr'ra mun'dĭ.
bur'ra wang.
bŭr'rel, -fly, -shot.
bûr'ring, -ma chine, -saw, -wheel.
bur ri'to (bõõr re'-).
bŭr'ro, a donkey.
Bŭr'rõughs (-rõz), Amer. auth.
bŭr'row, -er, -ing, -rowed, bur'-
  row-duck, bur'row ing owl.
bur'sa, pl. *sæ,* -sal.
bur sä'lis, -sal'o gy.
bur'sar, -ship, -sa ry, -sa'ri al.
bursch (bõõrsh), pl. *bursch'en.*
burse, bur sic'u late, bur'si form,
  bur sĭ'tis, burse'hold er.
Bur'se ra, bur'se ra'ceous (-shus).
Burs'lem põrce'laĭn, B. pot ter y.
burst, -er, -ing, burst'wort, burst'-
  ing-charge.
bur'then. See *burden.*
bur'ton.
bur'y (běr'ry), -ied, -y ing, bur'-
  i er.
bur'y ing-bee tle, -ground, -place.
bus *or* buss, an omnibus.
bus'-bars, -rods, -wires.
bus'by (bŭz'-), -bag.
bus'cõn, pl. *-cõ'nes.*
bush (bõõsh), -ing, -y, -i ly,
  -i ness, bushed, bush'boy, -buck,
  -cat, -chat, -man, -mãs'ter,
  -rän'ger, -whack er.

bush'-bab'bler, -bean, -beat er,
-block, -chirp'er, -cor al, -cow,
-creep'er, -dog, -ex tract'or,
-fight ing, -goat, -hăm'mer,
-hăr'row, -hawk, -hog, -hook,
-lark, -law'yer, -met'al, -ov'en,
-quail, -rope, -scythe, -shrike,
-tailed, -tit.
bush'ĕl (boŏsh'-), -el age, -el er *or*
-ler, -el ing *or* -ling, -man,
-wom an, -bar rel, -oys ters.
busi'ness (bĭz-), -like.
busk, -ing, busked.
bus'kin, -kĭned.
bus'su-pälm (boŏs'soō-päm).
bust.
bus'tard.
bus'tic.
bus'tle (-l), -tled, -tling, -tler.
bus'y (bĭz'-), -bod'y, *pl.* -ies,
bus'i ly.
butch'er (boŏch'-), -dom, -ly, -li-
ness, -y, -ing, -ered, butch'er-
bird, -crow, -knife, -meat,
butch'er's-broōm, -prick wood.
Bu'te a.
bū'tēne.
but'ler, -y, -age, -dom, -ship.
bū' to mad.
but'ment, -cheek.
butt, -wom an, -bolt, -chain, -end,
-hinge, -how el, -joint, -shăft,
-strap, -weld, but ting-joint, -ma-
chine, -ring, -saw, butt lĕath er,
butt and butt, butts and bounds,
butt's length.
Butte (būt), co. Cal.; co. S. Dak.
butte (būt *or* boŏt).
but'ter, -ing, -y, -tered, but'ter
ball, a duck, -bump, a bird, -cup,
-flip, -flow er, -fly, -man, -milk,
-munk, -nut, -weed, -wife,
-wom an, -wort.
but'ter-ale, -ball, -bean, -bird,
-boat, -bowl, -box, -burr, -car-
ri er, -col or, -cow, -crock,
-dai ry, -dai sy, -dock, -duck,
-ex tract or, -fin'gered, -fin gers,
-fir'kin (-fer'-), -fish, -knife,
-la dle, -māk'ing, -mold, -pad-
dle, -pat, -plate, -pot, -print,
-ra tions, -scotch, -shag, -snipe,
-stamp, -store, -tŏngs, -tooth,

-tree, -tri er, -tub, -work er,
but'ter-and-eggs, a plant.
but'ter fly-fish, -gur'nard, -lil y,
-nose, -or chis (-kis), -pea,
-plant, -ray, -shaped, -shell,
-weed, b. cock, b. damp er, b.
valve.
but'ter y-bar, -book, -hatch.
but'ter in *or* -ĭne.
but'tock, -er, -tock-line.
but'ton (-tn), -ing, -er, -y, -toned,
but'ton flow er, -hole, -weed,
-wood.
but'ton-ball, -blank, -brace, -bush,
-cau ter y, -ear, -eared, -fas'-
ten er (-fas' n er), -hook, -lăthe,
-loom, -mold, -nosed, -piece,
-quail, -riv et ing, -shell, -sol-
der, -sol'der ing, -su ture, -tool,
-tree, but' ton hole-ma chine.
but'ton hole, *v.,* -holed, -hōl ing,
-hōl er.
but'tress, -ing, -tressed, -tress-
tow er.
but'ty, -col'lier, -gang.
bux'om, -ly, -ness.
Bux'us.
buy, -er, -ing, -a ble, bought.
buzz, -er, -ing, -ing ly, -y, buzzed,
buzz'wig, a person, buzz'-saw,
-wig, a wig.
buz'zard, -clock, -hawk, -moth,
buz'zard dol lar.
by, -gŏne, -play, -stand er, -wa ter,
-way, -word.
by'-aim, -al tar, -ball, -bid der,
-blow, -book, -busi ness, -cause,
-com ment, -cor ner, -dwell er,
-e lec'tion, -end, -lane, -law,
-mat ter, -mo tive, -name, -note,
-pass, -pas sage, -pass er, -păst,
-păth, -place, -plot, -prod'uct,
-pur'pose, -road, -room, -speech,
-street, -stroke, -talk, -term,
-view, -walk, -wash.
by'ard.
by the by, by and by.
by-by *or* bye-bye, farewell.
bye'-ball.
byn'e des'tin.
by'nĭn.
byre.
byr'law, -man, -court.

---

fāte, făt, fär, fạll, fâre, fâst, sofà, mēte, mĕt, hêr, īce, ĭn, nōte,

byr'nie (ber'ny).
By'ron, Brit. poet, -ism, -ro'ni an,
-ron'ic, -ic al, -al ly.
bys'sal, -sā'ceous, -sif'er ous, -so-
lite.

bys'sus, pl. -*sĭ*, -sĭn *or* -sĭne,
-sog'e nous (-soj'-).
Byz'an tĭne *or* By zan'-, -zan'tian
(-shan), -zan'tin ism. by zan'-
tĭne (bĭ-), a coin.

C

C string.
caa'ing-whale (caw'-).
cäa'ma.
căb, -man, -men, -stand.
ca băl', -bălled', -băl'ling, -er,
cab'a list, -lis'tic, -tic al, -tic-
al ly.
cab'a la *or* kab'-.
cab a let'ta.
căb'al lä'ri a or *ca bal le ri'a* (kä'-
văl yä rē'a), *ca'bal le'ro* (kä'bä-
lyä'rō *or* kä'văl-), cab'al lĭne.
ca bal'lo (kȧ văl'yo).
ca ban' (*or* -vän').
cab as (kăb'a *or* ka bä').
cab as set'.
ca bas'sou (-sōō).
cab'băge, -baged, -ba ging.
cab'băge-bug, -but'ter fly, -flea,
-fly, -mag'got, -moth, -oil, -pälm,
-păl met'to, -rose, -tree, -wood,
-worm.
cab'ble, -bled, -bling, -bler.
cab'by, *pl.* -bies (-bĭz).
ca be'ça (ka bä'sa) or *ca bĕsse'.*
cä'ber.
Ca bĕ'rĕ a.
ca bes'tro (-vās'-).
cab'e zon' (*or* kä'bä thōn').
căb'ĭn, -ined, căb'in-boy, -mate.
cab'i net, -măk'er, -mak'ing,
-work.
Cab i rē'an.
ca bĭ'rĭ, -bĭr'ic, -bĭr'i an, cab i-
rit'ic.
ca'ble, -gram, -way, -bled, -bling,
-blet.
ca'ble-bend, -buoy (-bwoi), -căr'-
rĭ er, -cŭr'rent, -drill ing, -grip'-
per, -hŏŏk, -laid, -lock er,
-mold ing, -nip'per, -rail road,
-road, -screw, -shac kle, -stop'-
per, -tiĕr, -tools, ca'ble's length.

ca bŏb' *or* ka bŏb', -bing, -bobbed.
cab o ceer'.
ca bŏched' (-bosht') *or* -boshed.
ca bo choň' (-shoň').
ca boc'le (-bŏk'l).
Ca bom'ba.
ca bōō'dle.
ca bōōse'.
Căb'ot, Eng. nav.
ca bot' (-bō'), a dry measure.
cab'o tăge.
ca bou'ja (-bōō'ya) *or* ca bu'ya
(-bōō'-).
ca brē (-brä'), *Heraldry.*
ca brée (-brä'), an antelope.
ca brĭl'la (*or* -brēl'ya).
cab'ri o let' (-lä').
căb'rit (*or* ca brē'), an antelope.
cab'rĭte, a lizard.
cab rou'et (-rōō'-).
ca cä'ĭn *or* Ine.
ca'ca jao' (kä'kȧ zhoung').
ca cä'o, -but ter, -nut.
Ca'ce res (kä'thä rĕs), prov. Sp.
cach'a lot (kăsh'- *or* katch'-).
Cache (kăsh), co. Utah.
căche (*or* kăsh), n., -*pot'* (-pō'),
cached, cach'ing.
ca chĕ'mi a (-kē'-), -chē'mic.
ca chet' (-shä' *or* kăsh'ä).
ca chex'i a (-kĕk'si a), -chex'y,
-chec'tic.
cach'i bou (kash'i bōō *or* kȧ'-
shē bōō').
cach'in na'tion (kăk'-), ca chin'-
na to ry (-kin'-).
ca chi'ri (ka shē're).
cach'o long (kăsh'-).
ca chou' (-shōō').
ca chu'cha (-chōō'cha).
ca chun'de (-chōōn'dä).
ca cique' (-sēk').
cac'kle, -kled, -kling, -kler.

ca cŏ'.
cac o cho'li a, -o chyl'i a (-kil'-),
-o chym'i a, -chym'ic, -ic al.
cac'o dē'mon, -de mo'ni al, -de'-
mon ize, -ized, -i zing.
cac'o dox'y, pl. -dox'ies, -dox'-
ic al.
cac'o ep y, -o ē'thes (-thēz),
-o gas'tric, -o gen'e sis, -o graph'-
ic, -ic al, ca cog'ra phy.
cac'o let (-o lā).
cac'o nym, -nym'ic, ca con'y-
my.
ca cōōn'.
ca coph'o ny, cac'o phon'ic, -ic al,
-coph'o nous, -o phō'ni ous.
cac'o plas'tic, -o prā'gi a, -o sŏ'-
mi um, -o thym'i a, ca coth'y my,
-cot'ro phy.
cac ta'ceous.
cac'tus, pl. -tus es or -tī, -tal,
-tĭn or -tīne, cac'tus-wren.
ca cū'men, pl. -mi na, -mi nal.
cad, -dish, -bait.
ca das'ter or -tre, -das'tral, cad'as-
tra'tion.
ca dăv'er or -dā'ver, -dav'er ic,
-ĭn or -īne, -er ous, -ous ly, -ous-
ness.
cad'dis or -dĭce, -fly, -shrimp,
-worm.
cad'dle.
cad'dy or -die, pl. -dies.
cade, -lamb, -oil, -worm.
ca dĕlle'.
cad'e nas.
ca'dence, -denced, -den cing, -den-
cy, -dent, -den'za.
ca dēne'.
Ca dē'nus, Swift.
ca det', -ship.
cadge, cadg'ing, -er, -y, -i ly,
-i ness.
ca'di or ka'di (kä'dĭ or kä'dē).
Căd'il lac', t. Mich.
ca dil'lac (or kad'il lăk'), a pear.
Cä'diz, prov. Sp., C. lace.—(kăd'-
iz), t. O.
Cad mē'an.
cad'mi a.
cad'mi um, cad'mic, -mif'er ous,
cad'mi um red, c. yel low.
cad'rans.

cä'dre (-dr).
ca dū'ce us, -ce an, -ci a ry (-shĭ),
-ci branch (-braṇk), -braṇ'chi-
ate.
ca du'ci ty, -du'cous, -du'ci corn.
ca'dus, pl. -dī.
Căd wal'a der (-wŏl'-), Amer.
gen.
cæ'ca (sē'ka), ce'cal, -cal ly.
Cæ'ci as or Cē-.
cæ'cum, pl. -cums or -ca.
Cæd'mon (kĕd'- or kăd'-), poet.
cæ lom'e ter (sē-).
Caeṇ (kŏṅ), c. Fr.
Cæ no gæ'a (se no je'a), cæ no-
gæ'an, -gen'e sis, -ge net'ic.
Cæ'no zo'ic or Ce-.
Cä'en stone.
Cæ'sar (sē'zar), -ism, -sa'rē an
or -rĭ an (-za'-).
Cæs'a rē'a (sĕs'-), C. Phĭ lĭp'pī,
Bib., -re'an.
cæ'si um (-zi um).
cæ su'ra (se zu'- or -su'-). See
cesura.
ca'jé (ka'fä'), ca'je tal (kä'fä täl),
căf fē'ic, -fe'ine, -fe'in ism, -fē'one,
-fe tan'nic, c. chan tant (shŏṅ'-
tŏṅ'), c. noir (nwor).
ca fe cil'lo (kä fä sēl'yo).
căf'fa.
ca fis'so.
caf'tan (or -tan').
Cä gay än' (-gī-), prov. Luzon,
P. I.
cage, -ling, caged, cä'ging, cage'-
bird, -guides, -seat, -shuts.
cä'git (-jit).
Ca glio'stro (kăl yō'stro), a literary imposter.
Ca'got' (-gŏ').
Ca hens'ly ism.
ca hier' (kä'yä').
ca hiṇ'ca-root.
ca hiz' (cä ēth'), -hiz a da (-e thä'-
da).
ca hoot'.
Cä'ia phas (kā'ya fas), Bib.
cail cĕd'ra (kĭl-), -ced'rin.
cail lette' (kä let' or kăl yet').
cail lou' (kă yōō'), -lou tage
(-yōō täzh').
cai'ma cam' (kī'ma käm').

Cāi′man, *Herpet. genus.* cāi′man, an alligator. See *cayman.*

cai mi′to (kī mē′to).

Cain′-and-A′bel, a plant.

Cāin′īte.

ca ique′ (kä ēk′).

Ça i ra′ (sä′ē rä′).

Čaï rēne′ (kī-).

cairn, -gorm, -y, cairned, cairntan gle *or* cärn-.

Cai′ro (kī′ro), c. Egypt.—(kā′ro), t. Ill.; t. N. Y.

cais′son (käs′-), -dis ease′

cāi′tiff.

căj′e pŭt.

ca ji′ (-hĕ′) *or* -*xi* (-hĕ′).

ca jole′, -ment, -joled′, -jōl′ing, -er, -er y, -er ies.

ca jon′ (-hōn′).

cǎ′jŭn, of Acadian descent.

ca jun′ (-hōōn′), a plant.

cake, -al′um, -băk′er, -băs′ket, -brĕad, -cop′per, -cut′ter, -lake, -mix′er, -steam′er, -ur′chin, -walk.

cal′a ba, -ba zil′la *or* -cil′la (-sĕl′-ya).

Cal′a bar, C. bean, c. skin.

cal′a bar ïn *or* -ine (*or* bär′).

cal′a bash, -tree.

cal′a bä zil′la (-sĕl′ya).

cal′a bōōse′.

cal′a bra sel′la.

Ca lä′bri a, prov. It., -bri an.

cal′a bur-tree.

ca lāde′.

Ca lä′di um, Bot. genus.

Ca lais′ (kä′lä′), t. Fr.—(kăl′is), t. Me.

cal′ă īte (*or* -ă-).

cal′a maŋ′co.

cal′a man′der-wood.

Cal′a mū′ri a, cal a mă′rĭ an.

cal′a ma ry.

cal′am bac, -am bour (-bōōr), -bŭ′co.

cal′a mif′er ous, ca lam′i form (*or* kăl′-).

cal′a mĭn *or* -mïne.

cal′a mint.

cal′a mis′trum, pl. -*tra.*

ca lam′i ty, -i tous, -tous ly, -tous-ness.

cal′a mog′ra pher.

cal′a mus, *pl.* -a mī.

ca lan′chĭ.

ca lăn′do.

ca lan′dra, -drid, -droid.

cal an drō′ne.

ca laŋ′gāy.

cal′a pĭtte.

ca lăsh′.

ca lä′ta.

cal′a thus, pl. -*thĭ,* ca lath′i form (*or* kal′-).

cä la vē′rīte (*or* kal-).

cal câire′.

cal ca′ne um, pl. -*ne ums* or -*ne a,* -ne al, -ne an.

cal′car, a furnace.

cal′car, pl. -*ca′ri a,* Bot.; Zoöl.; Anat., -ca rate, -ra′ted.

cal ca′re o-ar gil la′ceous, -bi tu′-mi nous, -si li′cious.

cal ca′re ous, -ness, -căr′i form, -ca rif′er ous, cal′ca rĭne.

cal ca rō′ne.

cal′ce a men′tum, pl. -*ta.*

cǎlced.

cal ced′o ny, -ce don, -don′ic, -do′ni an. See *chalcedony.*

cal′ces (-sēz), -cĭc (-sĭk), -ci cole, -ci form, -cif′er ous, -cif′u gous, -cig′e nous (-sij′-), -cig er ous.

cal cid′e ra.

cal′ci fy, -ing, -ci fied, -ci fi ca′-tion.

cal′ci grade.

cal′ci mĭne (*or* -mĭn), -mined, -mĭn′ing, -mi ner, -ci mu′rite, -cim′e ter.

cal′cĭne (*or* -cīne′), -cined, -cining, -cin a ble, -cin er, -cin ize, -cin′a to ry, -ci na′tion.

cal ciph′o roŭs.

cal′cīte, -ci trant, -ci trate, -ci um, -cit′ic, -civ′o rous, -coph′o rous.

cal cog′ra phy, -ra pher -co-graph′ic, -ic al.

calc′-sin′ter, -spar, -tu′fa, -tuff.

cal′cu late, -la ted, -ting, -la ble, -la tive, -la tor, -to ry, -la′tion, cal′cu la ting-ma chine′.

cal′cu lus, *n.,* *pl.* -li, -cu lous, *a.*

cal de′ra (-dā′ra), *cal dā′ri um,* pl. -*ri a.*

Cal de rä'rĭ.
cạl'dron.
cặle.
cale can'non *or* cole-.
ca lèche' (-lāsh').
Cal'e do'ni a, -ni an, C. brown.
ca led'o nīte *or* cal'e-.
cal e fa'cient, -fac'tion, -fac'tive, -fac'tor, -to ry.
cal'em bour' (-bōor').
cal'en dar, an almanac, a table of days, -dared (-dêrd), -dar ing, -dar-clock, cal'ends, cal en dog'ra pher, ca len'dric, -dric al.
cal'en der, a smoothing machine, -dered, -der ing, -en drer, cal'en der ing-rub'ber.
Cal'en der *or* Kal'-, a dervish.
ca len'du lin.
cal'en ture.
ca le sa (kä lä' sä), -le sin (-lä sēn').
ca les'cence.
cặlf, *pl.* calves (kävz), calf'kill, -skin.
calf-bone, -lick, -like, -love, -snout, -ward.
calf's-foot, -head.
Cặl houn' (-hōōn'), Amer. statesman.
Cä'li or *Kä'li* (-lē).
cal'i a tour-wood (-tōōr-).
Cal'i ban, Shak., *Tempest.*
cal'i ber *or* -bre, c. gặge, c. rule, c. square.
cal i bo'gus.
cal'i brate, -brā'ted, -ting, -brā'tion.
cal'ĭce.
ca li'che (-lē'che *or* -chä).
cal'i cle.
cal'i co, -back, -bặss, -bush, -print er, -print ing, -wood.
ca lic'u la, pl. -*læ,* -u lar, -u late.
cal'i da'ri um, pl. -*ri a.*
Cal'i dore, Spenser, *Faerie Queene.*
ca'lif *or* -liph, -ship.
cal'i fate *or* -phate.
Cal'i for'ni a, C. cof'fee, C. con'dor, C. jack.
cal'i ga, *pl.* -i gæ (-jē).
cal'i ga'ted.
ca lig'ra phy. See *calligraphy.*
Ca lig'u la, Rom. Emperor;

Entom. ca lig'u la, *pl.* -læ, *Ornith.*
cā'lin.
cal i ol'o gy, -o log'ic al.
cal i pash' (*or* cal'-).
cal i pee' (*or* cal'-).
cal'i pers.
Ca lip'o lis, Shak., *Henry IV.*
Cal'i sä'ya bark.
Ca lis'ta, Rowe, *Fair Penitent.*
cal'is the'ne um, -then'ic, -then'ics.
Ca lix'tĭne.
calk *or* caulk (kawk), -ing, -er, calked, calk'-swage, calk'ing-i'ron, -mal'let.
call, -ing, -er, called, call'-bell, -bird, -box, -boy, -but'ton, -chặn'ges, -loan, -note.
call'ing-crab, -dorp, -hare, -wire.
cặl'la.
Cặl lä'ŏ (*or* -yä'o), t. Peru.
cal'le (käl'yä *or* -lä).
cal lig'ra phy, -ra phist, -ra pher, -li graph'ic, -ic al, -al ly.
cal'li mus, *Mineral.* Cal'li mus, *Entom.*
Cal lī'o pe, *Myth.* cal lī'o pe, a steam organ.
cal'li op'sis.
cal'li thump'i an.
cal lo'sum, -lo'sal.
cal'lot.
cal'lous, *a.,* -ly, -ness, -beaked, cal los'i ty.
cal'lŏw.
cal'lus, *n.,* *pl.* -lī.
cặlm, -er, -ly, -ness, -ing, -a tive, calmed, calm-belt, -lat'i tude.
cal'muck, *pl.* -mucks.
cal'o mel.
Cal'o phyl'lum.
ca lor'ic, -lor'i duct, -i fā'cient, -i-fere, -i fi'ant, -i fi'cient (-fish'ent), -fi ca'tion, -i met'ric, -ric al, -al ly, -i mo'tor, -cal'o ry, -o rie, -o rist, -o res'cence, -o ric'i ty, -o rif'ic, -o rim'e ter, -e try, ca lor'ic par'a dox.
ca lotte' *or* cal'lot, -lot'tist.
cal'o type, -o ty'pist.
ca loy'er (*or* cal'oy er).
cal'pac *or* -pack, -packed.
cal'par.

---

fāte, fặt, fär, fạll, fâre, fảst, sofả, mēte, mĕt, hêr, īce, ĭn, nōte,

cǎlpe, Cal'pe, *Entom. genus.*
cal te tep'on.
ca lum'ba.
ca lum'bin.
cal'u met.
ca lum'ni ate, -a ted, -a ting, -a tor, -to ry, -ni ous, -ous ly, -ous ness, -ni ā'tion, cal'um ny.
cal va'ri a, -ri an.
Cal'va ry, cal-, a shrine.
calve (käv), calved, calv'ing, calves'-snout, -tongue.
cal'ver.
Cal'vin, -ism, -ist, -is'tic, -tic al, -vin īze, -ized, -ī'zing, -vin'i an.
cal vi'ti es (-vish'ī ēz).
calx, *pl.* -es *or* cal'ces (-sēz).
cal'y bīte.
cal y can'the mous, -can'the my, -y flo'rate, -flo'rous, ca lyc'i form (-lĭs'-), -i nal.
cal'y cīne, -y clc, -y cled (-kld).
Cal y co zo'a, cal'y co zo'an, -zo'ic, ca lyc'u lar, -u late, -u la'ted.
ca lym'na.
Ca lyp'so, Homer, *Odyssey.*
ca lyp'to blas'tic, -to crin'id, -to-me'rous.
ca lyp'tra, -trate, -tri form, -tri-mor'phous, -tro gen.
cǎ'lyx, *pl.* -es *or* cal'y ces (-sēz), cal'y cate, -y cif'er ous, -y coid, -coid'e ous.
cal za'da (kǎl sä'tha *or* -thä tha).
cam, -cut'ter, -loom, -pump, -shǎft, -wheel, -yoke, cam'wood.
cä'mǎ gōn'.
ca mǎil'.
Ca mǎl'do lǐ, -do lese' (-lēz' *or* lēs').
cä mä lig (-lēg').
cam'a ra, -wood.
cam a rǎde riē' (*or* kǎ'mǎ rǎ'dc-rē').
cam a ril'la (*or* -rēl'ya).
cä'mǎ rōn'.
ca mau'rum, *pl.* -ra.
Cam'ba lu, a city in Cathay.
cam'bee.
cam'ber, -bered, -ber ing, cam'-ber-keeled, -slip, -win'dow, cam'ber ing-ma chine'.
cam'bi o, -bist, -bist ry.

Cam bon (kŏn'bōn'), Fr. revolutionist.
cam'bra sĭne (*or* -zēn).
Cam'bri a, -bri an.
cǎm'bric, -grǎss, -mus'lin.
Cam'bro-Brit'on, -Si lu'ri an.
cam bu'ca.
Cam'bus can (*or* -can'), Chaucer, *Squire's Tale.*
Cam by'ses (-bī'sēz), King of Persia.
cam'el, -ry, -backed, -bird, -crick'et, -driv'er, -grǎss, -in'-sect, -lo'cust, -necked, camel's-hair, -thorn.
Ca mel'li a (*or* -mel'ya), ca mel'-lin.
ca mel'o pard (*or* kam'e lo-).
Cam'e lot, parish in Somersetshire.
Ca me'nǣ.
cam'en es (-ēz).
cam'e o, *pl.* -os (-ōz), -type.
cam'e o-conch (-konk), -glǎss, -press, -shell, -ware.
cam'e ra, *pl.* -ras (-raz), -lens, -stand, *c. lu'ci da, c. ob scu'ra.*
cam'e ra lis'tic, -tics.
cam e ra'ri us, pl. -rī ī.
cam'e rīne.
cam'e ri tě'lous.
cam er lin'go.
Cam e ro'ni an.
ca mes'tres (-trēz).
Ca mil'la, Virgil, *Æneid.*
Ca mille' (-mēl'), Dumas.
ca mi'no (-mē'-).
cam'ion.
ca mi'sa (-mē'-), ca mise' (-mēs').
Cam'i sard (-zärd).
cam'i sōle.
cam'let, -ed, -een'.
cam'ma rón.
cam'mock.
Cǎm'o ens, Port. poet.
cam'o mile *or* cham'- (kam'-).
Ca mor'ra, -mor'rism, -rist.
ca mō'te (-tä).
ca mou'flet (-mōō'flä).
camp, -ing, -er, -shed, -sheet, -sheet'-ing, -shot, camped, camp-ceil'-ing, -chair, -drill, -fight, -fire, -fol'low er, -ket'tle, -meet ing, -sheath'ing, -stool, -vin'e gar.
Cam pa'gna (-pän'ya).

cam'pa'gnol' (kän på nyol').
cam'pa gus, pl. *-gi* (-jī).
cam paign' (-pān'), -er, -ing.
cam pă'na.
cam păne', -pāned'.
cam'pa ne'ro (-nä'ro).
cam pan'i form, -pa nil'i form,
-pan'u late, -pa nol'o gy, -o gist,
cam pan u la'ri an.
cam'pa ni'le (-nē'lä), -pa nist.
Camp'bell ite (kăm'el īte *or* -bel-).
Cam peach'y wood.
Cäm pe'che (-pä'chä), state and
bay Mex.
cam pes'tral, -tri an.
cam'phene (*or* -fēn'), a substance
resembling camphor, -phī lēne.
cam phine' (-fēn'), rectified oil.
cam'pho gen.
cam'phor, -phor ate, -ā' ted, -phyl,
-phol, -phol'ic, -phor'ic, -pho-
ra'ceous, -pho ron'ic.
cam'phor-lạu'rel, -oil, -tree,
-wood, -wood oil.
cäm pi' lăn (-pē'-).
cam'pi on.
cam'po, *pl.* -pos (-pōz), -po de'-
i form, -po'de oid.
cam poi'.
camp tē'ri um, pl. *-ri a.*
camp'to drome, cam'py lo drome'.
cam'pus.
cam'py lite.
cam'py lom'e ter.
cam'py lo sper'mous,   -lot'ro-
pous.
căn, -ning, -ful, canned, can-
bot'tle, -buoy, -cart, -frame,
-hook, -o'pen er, -rov ing, -sol'-
der ing.
cä'nä, a measure; Cä'na, *Bib.*
Că'naan (-năn), *Bib..* -ite, -i tish.
ca na' da (kan yä'da), a small
cañon.
ca nä'da, a liquid measure.
Can'a da, *Geog.,* C. bạl'sam, C.
rice.
Ca na'di an, C. em broid'er y.
ca năi'gre (-ger).
ca naille' (-nāl').
Can'a jō hăr'ie, t. N. Y.
can'a jong.
ca nal', can a lic' u lar, -u late,

-u la ted, *-u lus, -u lī,* -a lif'er ous,
ca nal i ros'trate.
ca nal'-boat, -lift, -lock.
ca nal'ize, -ized, -i zing.
ca nam'.
Căn'an dāi'gua, t. N. Y.
ca nard' (*or* -nar').
can'a rĭn *or* -rĭne.
ca na'ry, -bird, -creep'er, -finch,
-grăss, -moss, -seed, -stone,
-weed, -wood.
ca nas'ter.
can a til'lo (-tĕl'yo).
can'can.
can'cel, -celed *or* -celled, -cel ing
or -cel ling, -cel lous, -cel late,
-la ted, -la'tion.
can'cel ing-press, -stamp.
can cel'lī.
Can'cer, *Astron.; Zoöl.; Geog.*
can'cer, -cer ate, -cer ous, -ous ly,
-ous ness, -cer ite, -cer a'tion,
can'cer root, -weed, -wort.
can'cer-band age, -cell, -juice,
-mush'room.
cạn'crid, -cri form, -crĭne, -cri-
so'cial, -cri zans, -croid, -croid'e-
an, -croph'a gous, -criv'o rous.
cạn'crum, *pl.* -cra.
cănd.
Căn'da ce, *Bib.*
can'da reen'.
can de lā'brum,   *pl.* -bra *or*
-brums.
can'de rŏs.
can des'cence, -des'cent.
can'did, -ly, -ness.
can'di date, -ship, -da cy, -da-
ting, -da ture.
Căn'dide' (-dēd'), Voltaire.
căn dil' (-dēl').
Can'di ot *or* -ote.
can'dīte.
can di teer'.
can'dle, -ber ry, -nut, -stick,
-wood.
can'dle-bal'ance, -beam, -bear er,
-bomb, -case, -coal, -dip'ping,
-end, -fir, -fish, -flame, -fly,
-hold'er, -light, -mine, -mold,
-pow er, -rush, -tree, -wāst er,
-wick, -myr'tle, -tree.
Can'dle mas, -bell.

can'dŏ.
can'dock.
can'dor.
can'droy.
can'duc.
can'dy, -ing, -tuft, -dĭed, *can'dy*, a weight.
can'dy-pull, -pull ing, -su gar.
cane, caned, căn'ing, -y.
cane'-bŏr'er, -brake, -col'ored, -har'vest er, -hole, -juice, -kill'-er, -knife, -mill, -rush, -pol'ish-ing, -press, -scrăp'er, -split'ter, -strip'per, -su'gar, -trash, -work'-ing, c. gun.
ca nel'la, -wood. *Ca nel'la*, Bot. genus.
ca nelle'-brown.
Ca neph'o rus, masc., pl. -*rĭ*, -*o ra*, fem., pl. -*ræ*, can'e phore.
ca nes'cence, -nes'cent.
că'net.
ca nette'.
can'e va.
can'field Ite.
caṇ'ga.
caṇ'gan *or* kaṇ'-.
cangue (kăng).
Ca nic'u la *or* can'i cule, ca nic'-u lar.
ca nĭne', -ni'nal, -nĭn'i form, -nin'-i ty.
can'ion (-yun).
Cā'nis, C. Ma'jor, C. Mi'nor.
can'is ter, -shot.
ca ni'ti es (-nish'i ēz).
can'jar.
caṇ'ker, -ing, -ous, -y, -ker ber'ry, -root, -weed, -kered.
caṇ'ker-bird, -bit, -bloom, -blos'-som, -dort, -fly, -nail, -rash, -worm.
can'na, a grass; a measure; *Can'-na*, Bot. and Entom. genus.
Căn'ne (-nā), t. It.
cănne (kăn), a measure.
can'nel, -coal.
can'nel la ted, -ne lŭre, -lured.
can'ne quin (-kĭn).
can'ner, -y.
Cannes (kän), t. Fr.
can'ni bal, -bal ly, -bal ism, -ba lis'tic.

can'ni kin.
can'noid.
can'non, *pl.* -nons *or* -non, -non-ade', -non eer', -eer'ing, -non ry.
can'non-ball, -bit, -bone, -cast-ing, -lock, -met'al, -pin'ion, -proof, -range, -shot, -stove.
can'not.
can'nu la, -lar, -late, -la ted, -la ting.
can'ny *or* -nie, -ni ly, -ni ness.
ca noe' (-nōō'), -noe'ing, -noe'ist, -noe'man, -wood, -birch, -ce dar.
can'on, -ess, -ist, -is'tic, -ize, -ized, -i zing, -i za'tion, -ic'i ty, -on ry, -ship, ca non'ic, -ic al, -al ly, -al ness, -ic als, -i cate.
cañ'on, or can'yon (-yun), *cañ on-ci'to* (-yun sē'to), cañ'on-wren.
ca non'i zant.
Ca nŏ'pus, Egyp. god of water; a star.
can'o py, *pl.* -pĭes, -pĭed, -py ing.
ca nŏ'ræ, -rous, -rous ness, -rous ly.
cănt, -ed, -ing, cant'-block, -board, -bod y, -chis el, -dog, -fall, -file, -frames, -hook, -mold'ing, -piece, -pur'chase, -rail, -rob'in, -spar, -tim'ber, cant'ing-coin, -wheel.
căn't, shortened form of *cannot*.
Can'tab.
căn tä'bi le (-bē lā).
Can tä'bri an.
Can'ta brig'i an (-brĭj'-).
can'ta lev'er *or* -ti-.
can'ta loup *or* -loupe *or* -leup (-lōōp).
can taṇ'ker ous, -ly, -ness, -os'i ty.
can'tar, -*tä'rō*.
căn'tä rä.
căn tä'tä.
Can tä'tē.
can'ta trice (-trēs) *or* -tri'ce (*or* kăn'tä trē'chä).
can teen'.
can'ter, -ing, -tered.
Can'ter bur y, C. gal'lop, C. tale.
can'ter bur y, a stand for holding music; -bell, a plant.
Can'tha ris, *pl.* -thăr'i des (-dēz), can thar'i dal, -i din, -tha rid'-i an, -rid'ic.

nŏt, nôr, ūse, ŭp, ûrn, etüde, fōōd, fŏŏt, aṇger, boṅmot, thus, Bach.

13

can'tha rus, pl. *-rī.*
can'tho plas ty, -plas'tic.
can'thus, pl. *-thī,* -thī'tis.
can'ti cle.
can'ti coy.
can'ti cum, pl. *-ca.*
can'ti le'na.
can'til late, -la ted, -til la to ry, -la'tion.
can'ti nière' (kăn'tēn yâr').
căn ti'no (-tē'-).
can'tle.
cant'let.
cant'ling.
can'to, *pl.* -tos (-tōz), *căn'to ĭer'mo, c.* fĭg u ra'to (fig ōō rä'to).
Can ton', c. China. Can'ton, c. O.; tp. Ct. Can'ton crape, C. flan nel.
can'ton, a dist. in Switz. or Fr., -ment, -ize, -ized, -i zing, -toned.
can to nē' (-nä').
can'ton ite.
can tōōn'.
can'tor, -tor al, -to'ris.
can'trap *or* -trip.
can'trĕd.
can'tus.
can'ty.
Ca nuck' *or* Ka-.
can'u la, -lar, -la ted.
ca nŭte'.
ca nu til'lo (-nōō tēl'yo).
can'vas, *n.,* a strong, heavy fabric; *a.,* made of canvas; *v.,* to cover with canvas. can'vased *or* -vassed, -vas ing *or* -vas sing, can'vas-cut ter, -stretch er, -work, can'vas back.
can'vass, *n.,* solicitation; official scrutiny; *v.,* to solicit trade or votes, -vassed, -vass ing, -vass-er.
can zo'ne or *-zo'na* (kăn tsō'nä *or* -nä), can'zo net' *or* -nette'.
ca ouane' *or* -ouanne' (kä wän').
caout'chĭn *or* -chīne *or* -chēne (kōō'-), -chou cin *or* -cine (kōō'-chōō sĭn).
caout'chouc (-chŏŏk).
cap, -ping, -ful, -peak, -stone, capped, cap-pa per, -piece, -pot, -pud ding, -rock, -screw, -scut-

tle, -sheaf, -shore, -sill, -square, cap'ping-plane.
cä'pa.
ca'pa ble, -ble ness, -pa bly, -bil'-i ty.
ca pā'cious (-shŭs), -ly, -ness.
ca pac'i ty, -i tate, -tā' ted, -tā' ting.
cap a piĕ'.
ca par'i son, -ing, -soned (-sŭnd).
ca pär'ra or *-re* (-rä) or *-ro.*
cape, caped, cāp'ing, cape'net. cape'weed.
ca pe'a dor' (kå pā'å thōr' *or* -ä'dor).
Cape A gul'has (ä gōōl'yäs), Afr.
Cape Brĕt'on (*or* brĭt'-), isl. N. S.
Cape Cä tō'che (-chä), Yucatan.
Cape Cŏm'o rin, India.
Cape Fin is tere' *or* -terre' (fē nēs-târ'), headland Fr.
Cape Găs'pé (*or* gäs pā'), head-land, Can.
Cape Gra'ci as-a-Di'os (grä'sē äs-ä-dē'ōs), Cent. Amer.
Cape Guar da fui (gwar'da fwē'), Afr.
ca'pĕl *or* -ple.
căpe'lin (*or* kăp'e lĭn) *or* căp'e lan.
ca'pe line' (kå'pe lēn') *or* căp' el lĭne.
ca pel'la.
ca pel'le (-lä).
cap'el let.
ca pel li'na (kä pel yē'nä).
cå pell'meĭs'ter.
ca'pêr, -ing, -pêred, ca'per-weed, -ber ry, -bush, -cut ting, -plant, -sauce, -spurge, -tea, -tree.
Ca per'na um, -na īte, -it'ic, -ic al, -al ly.
Cape Sän Juan (-hōō än' *or* săn jū'an), Porto Rico.
Ca pē'tian.
Cape Trăf'al gär', Sp.
cap e u'na (-e ōō'-).
caph *or* kaph (kăf).
caph'ar.
ca'pi as.
ca'pi bä'ra (-pē-).
cap'id gi (-jī).
cap'il lâire'.
cap'il la rim'e ter.
cap'il la ry (*or* -pil'-), -la ri ness, -lăr'i ty, ca pil'li, -li fo'li ous, -li-form, *-li'ti um* (-lĭsh'i um), pl.

-*ums* or -*a*, cap'il lōse (-lōs),
-la'ceous.
cap'i rōte.
ca pis'trum, pl. -*tra*, ca pis'trate.
cap'i tal, -ist, -is'tic, -ism, -tal ly.
cap'i tal ize, -ized, -i zing, -ĭ za'-
tion.
ca pi tan'-pa sha' *or* -cha' (kä'-
pē tän'-på shä').
cap'i tate, -ta'tim, -ta'tion.
cap i tā'tum, pl. -*ta*.
cap'i tē.
cap i tel'late, -lar, -li form.
cap i tel'lum, pl. -*la*.
cap'i tol, -to'li an, -to līne.
cap'i to ped'al.
ca pit'u late, -la ted, -ting, -tor,
-to ry, -la'tion.
ca pit'u lum, pl. -*la*, -pit'u lar,
-lar ly, -la ry, -u li form.
ca pi'vi (-pē've).
Cap noi'des (-dēz).
cap'no măn cy.
cap'oc.
ca'pon, -ize, -ized, -i zing, ca'-
pon's-fĕath er.
cap o niere' *or* -on niere' (-nēr').
ca pot', -ted, -ting.
cä'po täs'to.
ca pote'.
ca pouch' (-pōōch').
cap'pa dĭne.
cä'pra.
cap'rate.
ca prē'o lus, pl. -*lĭ*, -o līne (*or*
cap'-), cap're o late, -o lar, -o la-
ry, cap'ric, ca pro'ic.
Cä'pri (-prē), isl. Bay of Naples.
ca pric'cio (kä prēt'cho), -*cio'so*
(-chō'sō).
ca price' (-prēs') -pri'cious
(-prĭsh'us), -ly, -ness.
Cap'ri corn, *Astron.*, cap'ri corn.
cap'ri fig, -ri fi'cus.
cap'ri fō'li um, -fo'li ā'ceous, -ri-
foil.
cap'ri form, ca prig'e nous (-prij'-),
cap'rĭne, -ri ped.
cap'ri fy, -fy ing, -fīed, -fi cate,
-fi ca'tion.
cap'ri ōle.
cap'ri zant.
cap'ro ate.

cap'sal.
Cap'si cum, cap'si cĭn *or* -cĭne.
cap size', -sized, -sīz'ing.
cap'stan, -bar, -băr rel, -swift er.
cap'stone.
cap'sule, -su lar, -la ry, -late,
-la ted, -suled, -su lif'er ous,
-lig'er ous (-lij'-), -lot'o my,
-sü lī'tis.
cap'taĭn, -cy, -ship.
cap'tain-gen'er al, -gen'er al cy,
-pa shä', cap'tain cy-gen'er al.
cap'tion.
cap'tious, -ly, -ness.
cap'ti vate, -va ted, -va ting,
-ting ly, -va'tion.
cap'tĭve, -tiv'i ty.
cap'ture, -tured, -tur ing, -tur a-
ble, -tor, -to'ri al.
Cap'u an.
Cap u chin (-ū sheen' *or* cap'u-
chin), a member of a religious
order. cap u chin, a pigeon;
a monkey; a crow; a cloak or
hood.
cap'u cĭne.
cap'u let.
cap'u lin.
ca'put (*or* cap'-), pl. *cap'i ta*.
ca pu'ti um (-shĭ um), pl. -*ti a*
(-shĭ a).
cä'py bä'ra.
car, -ax le, -bås ket, -brake, -buf-
fer, -bump er, -coup ling, -drĭv-
er, -heat er, -horse, -in'di ca tor,
-jack, -lamp, -lan'tern, -load,
-lounge, -taŋ gle, -re plāc'er,
-seal, -seat, -spring, -stand'ard,
-stake, -start'er, -stove, -swal'-
low, -track, -truck, -truss,
-wheel, -win'dow.
cä'rä bä'o.
cär'a bĭd.
cär'a boid.
cär'a cal.
cär a cär'a (*or* cä'ra cä'ra).
Cä rä'cäs, dist. Venez.
Car ac cesque' *or* Car rac- (kå-
rä chesk').
cär'ack *or* cär'rack.
cär'a cole, *en car a cole'* (äṅ' kå'-
rä kōl').
car'a col'y *or* -col ĭ.

căr'a cŏre *or* -co'ra.
ca răje' or *-răffe'.*
car a i' pi (kăr a ē'pe) *or* ca raï'-
pi (-pe).
căr a jä'rä *or* -ju'ra.
ca ram'ba, -ram'bo la (*or* -bō'la).
căr'a mel, -īze, -īzed, -i zing,
-ĭ za'tion.
car'a mote.
cä räng'.
căr'ap, -oil, -wood.
Căr'a pa.
căr'a pace, -a pax, -pa'cial.
ca rä'pō.
căr'at *or* kăr'-.
ca rạu'na *or* -ran'na.
căr'a van (*or* -van'), -eer', -van'-
sa ry.
căr'a vel.
căr'a way.
car'bĭd *or* -bīde, -bi mĭde.
car'bīne, -bi neer', car'bīne-
thim'ble.
car'bi nŏl.
car'bo hy'drate, -hy'drĭde, -hy'-
drous.
car'bol'ize, -ized, -i zing, -bo la-
ted, -bo lu'ri a, -bol'ic.
car'bon, -ate, -a ted, -ĭde, -bo na'-
ceous, -bon'ic, -if'er ous, -ize,
-ized, -i zing, -i zer, -ĭ za'tion,
-o hy'drous, -om'e ter, car'bo-
nous, -bon yl.
car'bon-black, -bronze, -but ton,
-pa per, -point, -print, -print ing,
car'bon i zing-fur nace, -i za'-
tion-bed.
Car bo nä'ro, *pl.* -rī, -nä'rism.
car'bo ne'ro (-nä'-).
car'bo run'dum.
car'boy.
car'buṇ cle, -buṇ cled (-kld),
-buṇ'cu lar, -cu late, -cu la'tion.
car'bu ret, -ed *or* -ted, -ret ing
or -ret ting, -ret er *or* -ret or.
car'bu rize, -rized, -ri zing, -rĭ za'-
tion, -rom'e ter.
car'ca jou (-jōō).
car'ca net.
car'cass *or* -case.
Car ca vel'hos (kär'ka väl'yŏs).
Car cel' lamp.
car'ce rule, -cer'u lar.

car cha ri'nus (-ka-), car char'o-
dŏnt (-kăr'-).
car che'si um (-ke-).
car'ci nol'o gy, -o gist, -no log'ic al,
-noid.
car ci no'ma, pl. -ma ta, -nom'a-
tous.
car'ci nus, pl. -nī, -ci no'sis, -ci no-
mor'phic.
card, -ed, -er, -ing, -i form,
-board, -bas ket, -case, -cloth-
ing, -cut ter, -grind er, -mak er,
-match, -par ty, -play er, -rack,
-press, -print ing, -set ting,
-sharp er, -ta ble, -tray, c.
cat a logue, card'ing-engĭne, -ma-
chine.
Car'da mīne (*or* -dam'i nē *or*
-da mī'ne).
car'da mom.
car dan'ic.
car'del.
car'de nal'.
car'der, a jackdaw. card'er, one
who cards, car'der-bee.
car'di a, -di ac, -dī'ac al, car'di ac-
pŭl mon'ic.
car'di al'gi a, -di al'gy (*or* car'-)
-di a nas'tro phe, -di asth'ma
(-ast- *or* -as'-), -di a tro'phi a,
-di ec'ta sis.
car'di gan, c. jack et.
car'dĭ ĭd.
car'di nal, -ate, -ist, -ize, -ized,
-ship, -bird, -fish, -flow'er, -red.
car'di oid, -di om'e try.
car'di o in hib'i to ry, -di ol'o gy,
-di o ma lā'ci a (-shĭ a), -di o-
pal'mus, -o per i car'dī'tis,
-o pneu mat'ic (-o nū-), -o pul'-
mo na ry, -o py lŏr'ic, -o rhex'is,
-o sphyg'mo graph, -o ste nō'sis,
-ot'o my, -ot'ro mus, car dī'tis.
car'do, pl. -di nes (-nēz).
car doon'.
care, -ful, -ful ly, -ful ness, -less,
-less ness, -less ly, -tāk er, cared,
câr'ing, care'-crazed, -kill ing,
-lined, -tuned, -worn, Care Sun-
day.
ca reen', -ing, -age, -reened'.
ca reer', -ing, -reered'.
ca ress', -ing, -ing ly, -ressed'.

că'ret (*or* căr'et), a printer's mark. *pl.* -goes, -block, -book.

car'go, *pl.* -goes, -block, -book.

car'gŏose, *pl.* -geese.

căr'i a cou (-ko͞o) *or* cär'ja cou.

cä'ri ä'ma or *ça ri-* (sä'rē-).

Căr'ib *or* -ib bee, -ib be'an.

căr'i be (*or* ka rē'bā).

căr'i bou *or* -bo͞o (-bo͞o).

car'i ca ture, -tured, -tur ing, -tu'rist, car'i ca ture-plant.

căr'i cĭn *or* -cĭne.

car i cog'ra phy, -col'o gy, -o gist.

car'i co͝us.

ca'ri es (-ēz).

căr'il lon.

ca rĭ'na, pl. *-næ,* -rī'nal, -rĭn'i-form, -rī'no lat'er al.

căr'i nate, -na ted.

căr'i ŏle.

ca'ri ous, -ness, -ri os'i ty.

cark, -ing.

carl, -cat, -crab, -hemp.

car'let.

car'lie.

car'line (*or* -lĭn).

car li'no (-lē').

Cär lisle' (-lĭl'), Sir Anthony, Eng. surgeon, John G., Amer. states-man.

Carl'ist, -ism.

car'lock.

Car lo vin'gi an.

Carls'bad twins (-bät).

Car lyle', -ly'li an *or* -ly'le an, -ly lese', -lyl'ism (-lĭl-).

car'ma'gnole' (kär ma nyŏl').

Car'mel ite, -mel in.

car'min ate, -mi na ted, -min'a-tive, -min'ic.

car'mĭne (*or* -mĭne), -min'ic.

car'mot.

car'nage.

car'nal, -ly, -ism, -ist, -ize, -ized, -i zing, -nal'i ty, car'nate, -ne-ous, -nic, car'nal-mĭnd'ed, -mĭnd'-ed ness.

car na'tion, -na'tioned, car na'-tion-grass.

car nau'ba (-nou'- *or* -nä o͞o'-).

car nĕl'ian *or* cor-.

car'ni jex.

car'ni fy, -fied, -fy ing, -fĭ ca'tion.

car'ni val, -val esque' (-esk).

Car niv'o ra, car'ni vōre, -niv'o-rous, -rous ly, -rous ness, -o ral, -niv'o rac'i ty.

car nos'i ty, car'no͝us *or* -nōse' (-nōs').

Cär'not' (-nō'), Hippolyte Lazare, Fr. writer; Marie Francois Sadi, Pres. Fr.

carn-taŋ'gle.

căr'ob, -bean.

căr'ol, -ŏled *or* -ŏlled, -ol ing *or* -ol ling, -ol er.

căr'o la.

car'o lin, a coin.

Căr'o lī'na, C. bark, C. pink, Car o lin'i an.

car o lit'ic *or* -lyt'-.

Car'o lus, *pl.* -lus es *or* -lī.

căr'om *or* car'rom.

Ca ron'de let (-lā), tp. Mo.

car o tel' *or* -teel'.

ca rot'id, -id al, i co tym pan'ic, ca rō'tis, *pl.* -rot'i des (-dēz).

ca rŏtte'.

ca rouse', -roused', -rous'ing, -ing-ly, -rous'er, -rous'al.

carp, -ing, carped, carp'-bream, -suck er.

car pa dē'li um, *pl.* -li a.

car'pal, c. aŋ gle.

car pä'le, pl. *-li a.*

Car pa'thi an.

car'pe dī'em.

car'pel, -pel la ry.

car'pen ter, -ing, -pen try, car'-pen ter-ant, -bee, -bird, -moth, -ter's-herb.

car'pet, -ed, -ing, -less, -bag, -bag'ger, -mon'ger, -weed.

car'pet-beat'er, -bed'ding, -bee-tle, -broom, -brush, -clean er, -dănce, -fas ten er (-n-), -friend, -knight, -līn ing, -loom, -moth, -rod, -sew er (-sō-), -snake, -strain er, -stretch er, -sweep er, -tack, -thrēad, -worst ed.

car phol'o gy.

car'pid, -pid'i um, *pl.* -i a.

car pin'cho.

car'pin te'ro (-pēn tā'-).

car po băl'sa mum.

Car'po crä'tian.

car pol'o gy, -o gist, -po log'ic al,
-po lite.
car' po mä'ni a.
car'po met a car'pal, -po ped'al.
car'po phore, -po phyl, -po phyte.
car pop'o dite, -dit'ic.
car'po spore, -spŏr'ic, -po stome,
-po sperm.
car' pus, pl. *-pī.*
car quaise' (-käz').
cärr.
căr'ra geen *or* -rha- *or* -ri- (-gēn).
Cär rä'rä, c. It.
Car räs'co, Cervantes.
car ré' (ka rä').
car reau', *pl.* -reaux' (-rō', -rōz').
cär'rel.
cär'rel age (or kär're låzh').
cär re'ta (-rä'-).
cär' re tōn' (-rä-).
cär'rĭage, -a ble, -way, -bōlt,
-brake, -bridge, -coŭp ling, -free,
-guärd, -jack, -lock, -piece,
-shac'kle, -spring, -top, -wheel.
cär'rick, -bend, -bitt *or* -bitts.
cär'ri on, -bee'tle, -buz'zard, -crow,
-feed'er, -flow'er, -hawk, -vul'-
ture.
car'ritch.
cär'ro.
cär roc'cio (-rŏt'cho), pl. *-roc'ci*
(-rŏt'chē), cär'roch.
car'roll ite.
car ron åde'.
cär'ron-oil.
cär rōōn'.
cär'rot, -y, -i ness, -tree.
car'rou sel (-rōō zel) *or* car'ou sal
or -sel.
car'row.
cär'rub, a fish.
cär'ry, -ing, -all, -ri a ble, -ri er,
-rĭed.
car sack'ie.
carse.
cart, -ed, -ing, -age, -er, -ful,
-man, -way, -wright, -bod y,
-bote, -horse, -jade, -lad der,
-load, -sad dle, -tail.
Cär ta ge'na (-je'-) *or* -tha-, c. Sp.;
c. Colom.
cärte, -de-vi sité' (-dä-vē zēt'), pl.
cartes-. c. *blanche'* (blänsh').

Car taph'i lus, the Wandering
Jew.
car'ta ret.
car tel' (*or* car'-), -ship.
Car te'sian (-zhan), -ism.
Car tha gin'i an.
car'tha min *or* -mĭne, -tham'ic.
Car thu'sian (-zhan).
Car'tier' (-tyā'), Fr. nav.
car'ti lage, -lag'i nous (-laj'-),
-i noid, -la gin'e ous, -gin'i fi-
ca'tion.
Cart'ist.
car tog'ra phy, -ra pher, -to-
graph'ic, -ic al ly.
car'to man'cy.
car'ton, car tôn'-pâte' (-pät'),
-pierre (-pyâre').
car'ton nage (*or* -nåzh').
car toon', -ist.
car touch' *or* -touche' (-tōōsh' *or*
-tōōch'), *pl.* -es (-ĕz).
car'tridge, -bag, -belt, -block,
-box, -cap per, -case, -fill er,
-gåge, -load er, -pa per, -pouch,
-prīm'er, -re tract'or, -wire.
car'tu la ry, *pl.* -ries.
cär'u cate *or* -ru-.
ca ruŋ'cu la, -cu lar, -cu lous, -cu-
late, la'ted, car'uŋ cle.
ca'rus.
ca ru'to.
car'val.
carve, carved, carv'ing, -er.
car'vel, -built, -joint, -work.
carv'ing-chis el, -fork, -knife,
-lâthe, -ma chine', -ta ble.
cär'y at'id, -at'ic, *-at'i des* (-dēz),
-i de'an.
cär'y ĭn *or* -Ine.
cär'y o phyl lä'ceous (-shus),
-y oph'yl lous, -yl lin (*or* -ō fil'-).
cär'y op'sis.
cä'sa (*or* kä'-), -sal.
cas'ban.
cas'ca bel.
cas cade'.
cås cäl'ho (-yō).
cas căn' *or* -cäne'.
câs'câ râ.
cas'ca ril'la, c. bark.
cas'chrom (-krom).
cäs'co (*or* cäs-).

case, -man, -weed, cased, cās'ing, -er.

case-bay, -bear er, -bear ing, -bind ing, -bot tle, -char, -end- ing, -hard en, -hard ened, -knife, -lock, -māk er, -pa per, -rack, -shot, -work, -worm.

că'se ate, -se a ted, -a ting, -a'tion, -se fied, -se ic, -se in or -īne, -in'o gen, -se ous, -ose, -se um.

Ca sel'la, Dante.

case'mate, -ma'ted, case'mate- car riage, -gun, -truck.

case'ment, -ment ed.

că'sern (-zern or -zern').

cash, -ing, cashed, cash'-book, -box, -boy, -car ri er, -cred it, -day, -girl, -keep er, -note, c. account.

cash'er-box.

ca shew', -bird, -nut, -tree.

cash ier', -ier'er.

cash'mēre, c. shawl, cash' me- rette'.

Cash me'ri an.

ca si'no (-sē'-).

câsk, căs'ket.

casque (căsk), a helmet.

Cac oa gnac', de (dĕ kä'sän'yäk'), Fr. journalist.

cas'sa reep or -si reepe.

cas sa'tion.

cas sä'va, -wood.

cas sē'na, a plant.

casse'-pa'per or cas'sc-, -tête (kăs-tät').

cas'se role, -fish.

cas sette'.

Cas'sia (căsh'a), Bot. genus, -bark, -buds, -lig'ne a, -oil, -pulp, -wheel.

cas'si can.

cas sīd'e ous.

cas'si mēre.

cas sine' (-sēn').

cas si nette'.

Cas sin'i an, C. o'val.

cas'si noid.

Cas'si o (kash'ĭ ō), Shak., Othello.

cas'si o ber'ry (kăs'-).

Cas'si o pe'ia (-ya).

Cas'si us Lon gi'nus (kăsh'e us lŏn jī'nus), Rom. patriot.

cas'sius (kash'yus or kas'-), a pig- ment.

cas'sock, -socked.

cas'so lette (or -lette').

cas'son ade'.

cas soon'.

cas soum'ba (-sōōm'-).

cas'so wa ry.

cas'su mu'nar, -mu'ni ar.

câst, -ing, -er, -gate, -i ron, a., -net, -off, a., -steel, a., cast'- i ron, n., c. knit ting, c. shad ow, c. steel, n.

cas'ta'gnole' (kăs tăn yōl').

Cas tā'li a, a fountain, Myth., Cas tā'li an, Myth., Cas tā'li a, Zoöl. and Entom. genus.

Cas ta'ne a.

cas tā'ne ous.

cas'ta net, -nets.

câst'a way.

câste.

cas'tel lan, -tel la ny, -lar, -let, -la ted, -la'tion.

Cas tel lane', de (dĕ käs'tĕl'län'), Fr. marshal.

cas'ter, -wheel.

cas'ti gate, -ga ted, -ga ting, -ga- tor, -to' ry, -ga'tion.

Cas ti glio'ne (käs tēl yō'nä), t. It.

Cas tile' (käs tēl'), prov. Sp.

cas'tile soap (tēl or -tēl').

Cas til'ian (-yan).

câst'ing-bot tle, -box, -glăss, -la dle, -net, -pit, -pot, -press, -slab, -ta ble, -weight, c. vote.

căs'tle (kăs'l), -tled (-ld), -tling, -tlet, -tle ry.

căs'tle wick, -wise, -build er, -guard -stĕad, -town, -ward.

cas'tor, a beaver; a hat; a kind of cloth. cast'or, a small wheel. Cas'tor, Zoöl. genus.

Cas'tor and Pol'lux.

cas'tor-bean, -oil.

cas'to rin or -rĭne.

cas'tra me ta'tion.

cas'trate, -tra ted, -tra ting, -tra'- tion, -trä'to.

cas'trum, pl. -tra, -tren'sial, -tren'- sian.

cas'u al (kăzh'-), -ism, -ist, -ly, -ness, -ty.

cas′u ist (kăzh′-), -ist ry, -is′tic,
-tic al, -tics.
cas′u la.
ca′sus bel′lī.
cat, -bird, -bill, -brain, -bri er,
-call, -fish, -gut, -head, v., -like,
-mint, -nip, -nut, -skin, -stitch,
-tail, a plant.
cat′-back, -beam, -block, -boat,
-cas tle, -chop, -eyed, -foot ed,
-fall, -gold, -hammed, -har pin,
-haws, -head, n., -hole, -hook,
-ice, -lap, -nap, -owl, -pipe,
-rake, -raked, -rig, -rigged,
-rope, -rush, -salt, -shark, -sil-
ver, -squir rel, -stane, -stick,
-stop per, -tac kle, -thrash er.
cat′s-brains, -claw, -cra dle, -ear,
-eye, -foot, -head, -milk, -purr,
-tail, cat-in-clo ver, cat-o′-
moun taĭn, cat-o′-nine-tails.
ca tab′a sis, pl. -ses (-sēz).
cat′a bĭ ot′ic.
ca tab′o lism, cat a bol′ic.
cat′a caus′tic.
cat′a chre′sis (-krē′-), pl. -ses
(-sēz), -chres′tic, -tic al, -al ly.
cat ach thon′ic (kăt ăk-).
cat′a clĭ′nal.
cat′a clysm (-klĭzm), -clys′mal,
-mic, -mist, -a clasm, -a clas′tic.
cat′a comb (-kōm).
cat′a co rol′la.
cat′a cous′tics (or -kōōs′-).
cat a crot′ic, ca tac′ro tism.
cat′a di op′tric, -tric al, -trics.
cat′a drome, ca tad′ro moŭs.
cat′a falque′ (-fălk).
cat′ag mat′ic, -ic al.
Cat′a lan.
cat a lec′tic, -lec′ti cant.
cat′a lep sy, -sis, -lep′tic, -ti form,
-lep′tize, -tized, -ti zing, -lep′-
toid.
cat a lex′is.
ca′ta li nē′ta (kä tă lē nā′ta).
cat al lac′tics.
cat′a logue, -lŏgued, -logu er,
-logu ing (-lŏg′ing).
Cat a lo′ni an.
ca tăl′pa.
ca tal′y sis, pl. -y ses (-sēz),
cat′a lyt′ic, -ic al, -al ly.

cat a lys′o type.
cat′a ma ran′.
cat a mē′ni a, -ni al.
cat′a mīte.
cat′a mount.
cat a pan′.
cat′a pasm.
cat′a pet′al ous.
cat a phă′si a (-zhĭ a).
cat′a phĕbe (-fēb).
cat′a phon′ic, -ics.
cat a phor′ic, -a pho rē′sis.
cat′a phract, -ed, -phrac′tic.
cat a phyl′lum, pl. -la.
cat a phys′ic, -ic al.
ca tap′la sis.
cat′a plasm.
cat′a plex y.
cat′a pŭlt, -pul′tic, -pul tiĕr′.
cat′a ract, -for′ceps, -knife, -nee′-
dle, -spoon.
ca tarrh′ (-tar′), -tarrh′al, -ous,
-ish.
cat′ar rhĭne (or -rīn).
cat′a sar′ca.
cat′a stăl′tic.
ca tas′ta sis, cat a stat′ic.
ca tas′ter ism.
ca tas′to mid, -to moid.
ca tas′tro phe, -tro phism, -tro-
phist, cat′a stroph′ic.
Ca taw′ba.
cătch, -er, -ing, -a ble, -y, -all,
-pen ny, -pŏll, -wą ter, -weed,
-word, -work.
catch′-bar, -ba sin (-bā′sn), -bŏlt,
-club, -drain, -feed′er, -fly, -hoŏk,
-land, -lĕv′er (or -lē′ver), -line,
-match, -mĕad ow, -weight,
catch′ment-ba′sin.
catch′up or ketch′up or cat′sup.
cat e chet′ic (-ket′-), -ic al, -al ly,
-chet′ics.
cat′e chin or -chine (-chĭn).
cat′e chize or -chise (-kĭz),
-chized, -chĭ zing, -chi zer,
-chĭ za′tion, -chist, -chism, -chis′-
tic, -tic al, -al ly, -chis′mal.
cat′e chol (-kŏl or -chōl).
cat′e chu (-chōō or -kū), -chu′ic,
-chu′in.
cat e chu′men (-ku′-), -men al,
-men ate, -men ist, -men′ic al.

cat'e go rem, -go rē'ma, pl. -ma ta,
-gor e mat'ic, -ic al, -al ly.

cat'e go ry, -go rist, -gor'ĭc al,
-al ly, -al ness, -gor i za'tion.

cat e lec'trōde, -tro ton'ic, -trot'-
o nus.

ca tē'na, pl. -næ, cat'e nate, -na ted,
-na ting, -na'tion.

ca ten'u late.

cā'ter, -ing, -er, -ess, -têred,
cā'ter-cor'nered (or căt'er-),
-cous in (-kŭz n), -cous in ship.

căt'er pil lar, -catch'er, -eat'er,
-fuṇ'gus, -hunt'er.

cat'er waṇul, -ing, -wauled.

cātes.

Cath'a rī, -rism, -ris'tic.

cath'a rine-wheel or -e rine-.

Cath'a rist.

cath'a rīze, -rized, -ri zing, -rism.

ca thar'ma.

ca thar'sis, -thar'tate, -tic, -tic al,
-al ly, -al ness, -tin, -to gen'ic,
-to man'nit.

Ca thay'.

cath'e dra (or ka thē'), -thē'dral,
-dral'ic.

cath e ret'ic.

oath'c ter, -ize, -ized, -i zing, -ism,
-i za'tion.

cath'e tus, pl. -tī, -e tal, -e tom'e-
ter.

ca this'ma (-thiz'-), pl. -ma ta.

cath'ode, -o dal, ca thod'ic, -thod'-
o graph.

cath'o lic, -ly, -ness, -lic'i ty
(-lis'-), ca thol'i cal, -i cism,
-i cize, -cized, -ci zing, -i con,.
-i cos or -i cus.

Cat'i līne, Rom. conspirator. -li-
na'ri an.

cat'i on or kat-.

cat'kin.

cat'lin īte.

cat'nar.

cat'o ca thar'tic.

cat'o dŏnt.

Ca to'ni an.

ca tōōse', -toosed'.

ca top'ter, -top'tric, -tric al,
-trics, -top'tro man cy.

ca tos'to mid, -to moid.

cat ti man'dōō or kat-.

cat'tle, -men, -beet, -bell, -cab-
bage, -chain, -farm, -feed er,
-guard, -hĕr on, -lēad er, -louse,
-mar ket, -mark ing, -pen,
-plāgue, -pump, -ranch, -rānge,
-run, -show, -stall, -tie, -trade,
-trough.

cat'ty.

Cau ca'sian (-shan or -căsh'yan).

caṇu'cus, -er, -ing or -sing, -cused
or -cussed.

caṇu'da, pl. -dæ, -dad, -dal, -dal ly,
-date, -da ted, -da'tal, -dex, pl.
-dex'es or -di ces' (-sēz), -di cle,
-dic'u la, -di trunk, -do tib'i al,
-i ā'lis.

cau'dle, -dled, -dling, cau'dle-cup,
Cau'dle lec'ture.

caṇuf, -ward.

caught.

caṇuk, -er, -ing, -y.

caul.

caṇuld.

cau'li cle, -li cole, -li cūle, -lic'o-
loŭs, -lif'er ous, -lig'e nous (-lij'-),
cau'li form, -li na ry, -lĭne.

cau'li flow'er.

caulk (kawk). See calk.

cŭ u ong (kŭ' ōō ŏng).

cause, -ful, -less, -less ly, -less-
ness, caus'a ble, -al, -al ly, -al ty,
-a tive, tive ly, cau sal'i ty
(-zal'-), -sa'tion, -tion ist, cause-
rie (kōz rē' or kōz'-).

cau'seuse' (kō'sêz').

cause'way.

cau'si a.

cau'sid.

cau sid'i cal.

caus'tic, -tic al, -al ly, -ness, -tic'-
i ty (-tĭs'-), caus'tic-vine.

cau'sus, Med., Cau'sus, Herpet.

cau'ter īze, -ized, -i zing, -I za'-
tion, -ter ant, -ism, -y, cau'-
ter y-e lec'trōde.

cau'ting-i'ron.

cau'tion, -a ry, -er, -ing, -ry,
-tious, -tious ly, -tious ness,
-tioned, cau'tion-mon'ey.

Ca vai gnac' (kä'vän'yäk'), Fr.
gen.

cav al cade' (or cav'-).

cav a lier', -ish, -ism, -ly, -ness,

Cav a lier', belonging to the party of Charles I of England.
ca väl'la.
cav al lard' (-al yard').
ca val le'ri a (kä väl yā'rē ä).
cav'al ry, -man.
cav a si'na (*or* kä va sē'na).
ca vass' *or* ka-.
cåv a ti'na (-tē'-).
cave, -man, caved, cāv'ing, ca va'-tion.
cave'-bear, -crick et, -dwell er, -fish, -hy e na, -keep er, -li on, -pī ca, -swal low, -ti ger, cāv'ing-rake.
cā've a, pl. *-ve æ.*
ca vĕach'.
cā've ŭt, -ā tor, -a ting.
Cav e lier (käv'lē ā' *or* -vêl yā'), Fr. sculp.
cav'en dish.
cav'ern, -ous, -er nose (-nōs), -erned, -er nic'o loŭs, -er nule, ca ver'nu lous.
cav'es son *or* -e zon.
ca vet'to.
cav i är' (*or* cav'-).
cav'i corn, *Cav'i cor'ni a.*
cav'Il, -Iled *or* -illed, -il ing *or* -il ling, -ing ly *or* -ling ly, -il er *or* -il ler.
ca vin'na-wood.
cav'i ta ry.
Cä vi te' (-vē tā'), prov. Luzon.
cav'i ty, -i tIed.
cä'vo-re liĕ'vo *or* *-ri lie'vo* (-rē-lyā'vo).
ca vort', -ed, -ing.
cā'vum, pl. *-va.*
cǎ'vy, *pl.* -vies.
caw, -ing, cawed.
caw'ney *or* -ny.
Cąwn'pur' (-pōōr'), c. India.
caw'quaw.
cax'on (-n).
Cax'ton.
cä'yä.
Cäy enne' (*or* kī-), C. pep per, C. rose, cay enned'.
Cäy'lĕy an, Cay'ley's the'o rem.
cǎy'man.
cä'yō.
Cä yu'gas.

cay use' (kī-).
ca̧'zI *or* cau'-.
ca zi'mi (-zē'-).
ca zique' (-zēk') *or* -cique (-sĕk').
cä'zo (-tho *or* -so).
cease, -less, -less ly, -less ness, ceased, ceas'ing.
Cĕ bï'næ, cē'bīne, -boid.
Cec chet'ti (chĕk kĕt'tē), It. hist.
Cec'chi (chĕk'kē), It. poet.
Cec co'ni (chĕk kŏ'ne), It. writer.
Cech *or* **Czech** (chĕk), Bohem. poet.
ce cid' i um, pl. *-i a.*
Cec'il (sĕs'il *or* sĭs'-), Eng. states-man.
cĕ'cils.
cĕ'co graph.
ce'co morph, -mor'phic.
cĕ'dar, -dared, -darn, ce'dar-ap ple, -bird, -gum, -lark, -oil, -pine, -tree, -wood.
cĕde, cēd'ed, -ing.
ce dil'la.
cĕ'drăte *or* -drăt, -drēne, -drĭn *or* -drĭne, -dri um.
Ced'ric (ked'- *or* sed'-), Scott, *Ivanhoe.*
cĕ'dron.
cĕd'u la.
ce'i ba (sā'I bä *or* sā'e vä).
ceil, -ing, cĕiled, ceil'ing-boards, -joist, -plate.
ce'ja (sā'ha).
cel'a don.
Ce læ'no (-lē'-).
cel'an dĭne.
cĕ lā'rent.
cĕ las'trin *or* -trĭne.
ce lā'tion, cel'a tive.
Cĕl'e bes (-bĕz), isl. Malay Archi-pel.
cel'e brate, -bra ted, -ting, -tor *or* -ter, -bra'tion.
ce leb'ri ty.
cel e min' (thĕl ā mĕn'), cĕl'el-minth (*or* sē lel'-).
cel'e o morph, -mor'phic.
ce lĕ'ri ac (*or* -lĕr'i-).
ce lĕr'i ty.
cel'er y, -pine.
cĕ lĕste'.
ce les'tial (-chal), -ize, -ly, -ness,

cel'es tĭne, -tīte, Cel'es tin i' an
or -tine.
Cĕ'li a (or sēl'ya), Shak., As You
Like It.
cĕ'li ac.
cel'i ba cy (or ce lib'-), -bate.
Cĕ'li'mène' (sā lē mān'), Molière.
cell, cĕlled, cel lif'er ous, cel'lu lar,
-lule, -lu lif'er ous.
cell'-an i mal, -cap'sule, -de vel
op ment, -en am'el, -mem brane,
-mouth, -par a site, -pro to
plasm, -sap, -space, -sub stance.
cel'la, pl. -læ.
cel'lar, -age, -er, -ing, -ist, -man,
pl. -men, -ous.
cel'lar-book, -flap, -rat, -snail.
cel'lar et (or -et').
cel la ri'no (chĕl lä rē'no).
Cel li'ni (chĕl lē'ne), It. artist.
cel'lo (chel'lo), cel'list (chĕl'-).
cel'lu late, -la ted, -la'tion.
cel lu lĭ'tis.
cel'lu loid.
cel'lu lose (-lōs), -lō'sic.
ce los'to my.
ce lot'o my.
cel'sĭ an (or -shĭ-).
Cel'si us, C. ther mom'e ter,
Celt or Kelt, Celt i bē'ri an, Celt'-
ic, -i cize, -i cism, -ish, -ism,
-ĭst, -o ma'ni a, Cel'to-Ro'man.
cem'ba lo (or chăm'-), -bal ist.
ce ment' (or cem'-), n., -a to ry,
-al.
ce ment'-cop'per, -duct, -gland,
-mill, -stone.
ce ment', v., -ed, -ing, -er, cem'-
en tā'tion.
ce ment'ing-fur'nace, -ov'en, cem-
en tā'tion-box, -fur'nace.
cem'e ter y.
ce nan'thy.
Cen'ci, Be a tri'ce (bā ä trē'chä
chĕn'chē), Rom. beauty.
cen'o bīte (or cĕ'-), -bit'ic, -ic al,
cen'o bĭ tism (or cĕ'nō bĭ-).
cĕ nō'bi um, pl. -bi a, cĕn'o by (or
sē'-).
ce nog'a my, -a mous, -o nous,
cen'o gen'e sis, -o ge net'ic.
cen'o tăph.
ce'no zo'ic, -zo ol'o gy.

cens (sän or säns), cĕn'sive, cen'-
so (sän'so or thän'so).
cense, cen'ser, a vase.
cen'sor, a critic, -ship, -ate, -so'-
ri al, -ri an, -ri ous, -ous ly, -ous-
ness.
cen'su al (-shu-).
cen'sure (shōŏr), -sured, -sur a-
ble, -ble ness, -a bly, -er.
cen'sus, -pa per.
cent, -age.
cen'tal.
cen'tare.
cen'taur, -tau rom'a chy (-ky).
cen tä'vo (then- or sän-).
cen te nä'ri us, pl. -rĭ ĭ.
cen'te na ry, -na'ri an, -ten'ni al,
-al ly, -ni um.
cen'ter or -tre, -tered or -tred,
-ter ing or -tring, -ter board,
-piece.
cen'ter-bar, -bit, -block, -chis el,
-chuck, -drill, -fire, -gage,
-guide, -lāthe, -mold, -pin,
-plate, -punch, -rail, -saw, -sec'-
ond, -ta'ble, -tools, -valve, -ve'-
lic, -wheel.
cen'ter ing or -tring-gāge, -ma
chine', -tool.
cen tes'i mal, -mal ly, -i mate,
-ma ted, -ma ting, -ma'tion.
cen tes'i mo (or chĕn-).
cen tē'sis.
cen'ti are.
cen'ti grade.
cen'ti gram or -grămme.
cen'ti li'ter or -tre (-lē'tr or
-til'-).
cen'time' (sän'tēm').
cen'ti me'ter or -tre (or -tim'-),
-ti nor'mal.
cen tin'o dy.
cen' tĭ nor' mal.
cen'ti pĕd, -ti pĕd'al.
cen'ti stĕre.
cent'ner.
cen'to, pl. -tos (-tōz), -to ist, -to-
nism.
cen to'ne (chĕn-).
cen'trad.
cen'tral, -ism, -ist, -ize, -i zing,
-i zer, -ly, -ness, -tral'i ty, -ĭ za'-
tion.

cen tral' (săn träl' *or* thän-), a
  sugar mill.
cen trax ŏ'ni a, -ni al.
cen'tric, -al, -al ly, -tric'i ty
  (-tris'-), -tri cip'i tal.
cen trif'u gal, -ly, cen'tri fuge.
cen trip'e tal, -ly, -ism, -e tence,
  -ten cy.
cen tris'coid.
Cen'trist.
cen'trode, -troid, -tro sōme.
cen'tro sphere, -tro sym'me try.
cen'trum, pl. *-trums* or *-tra.*
cen'tum.
cen tum'vir, pl. *-virs* or *-vi ri,*
  -vi ral, -vi rate.
cen'tu ple, -pled (-pld), -pling,
  -tu'pli cate, -ca ted, -ca ting.
cen'tu ry, -ried, -tu'ri on, cen'-
  tu ry-plant.
ce pā'ceous.
ceph'a lad.
ceph a lag'ra, *-lal'gi a,* -lal'gic,
  ceph'a lal gy.
ceph'a late, ce phal'ic.
ceph a lĕ'tron.
ceph'a lī'tis.
ceph'a lize, -lized, -li zing, -lĭ za'-
  tion.
ceph'a lo braņ'chi ate (-ki-), -lo-
  cau'dal, -lo cele, -lo cer'cal, -lo-
  chord -chord'al, -lo cone, -con'-
  ic, -lo'dĭne, -lo dyn'i a, -lo gen'-
  e sis, -lo ge net'ic, -log'ra phy,
  -lo hu'mer al, -lol'o gy, -lo men-
  in gī'tis (-ji'-), -lom'e ter, -e try,
  -lo met'ric, -lo man cy *or* -lon'o-
  man cy, -lop'a thy, -lo pode,
  -pod'ic, -lop'o dan, -o dous,
  -lop'ter id, -ter oid, -ter ous,
  -lo tho'rax, -tho rac'ic (-ras'-),
  -lo tome, -lot'o my, -lo trībe,
  -lo trip sy, -lo troch' (-trŏk'),
  -lot'ro chal, -lo troch'ic (-trŏk'-),
  -lot'ro chous (-kus).
ceph'a loid, -a lont, ce phal'o-
  phĭne, -o phore, ceph'a lo-
  phragm (-fram), -lo pod, -a lous,
  -lop'o da, -lop'te ra, -lot'ro cha
  (-ka).
Ceph a lo'ni a (sef- *or* chĕf-), isl.
  Medit. Sea.
Ce'pheus (-fūs), *Astron.*

cep'o lid, -o loid.
ce ram'ic *or* ke-, -ram'ics, cer'a-
  mist.
cer a mog'ra phy, -mo graph'ic.
cĕr'a sin, -a site, ce ras'i nous.
cĕ'rate, -ra ted, -rig'er ous (-rij'-),
  ce'roŭs.
cer'a to blast.
Cer'a to braņ'chi a (-kĭ-), cer'a to-
  braņ'chi al, -chi ate.
ce rā'tum.
ce raụ'nic, -nics, -nīte, -no scope.
Cer'be rus, -bĕ're an.
cer'ca, pl. *-cæ,* cer'cal.
cer'clé (-klā).
cer'cus, pl. *-ci.*
cere, cered, cēr'ing.
cĕ're al, -re a lin *or* -lĭne.
Ce re ā'li a, -a'li an.
cer'e bel'lum, *pl.* -lums *or* -la,
  -bel'lar, -bel'lous, -bel lī'tis,
  -bel lo spi'nal.
cĕr'e bral, -ism, -ist, -ize, -ized,
  -i zing.
cĕr'e brate, -bra ted, -bra ting,
  -brā'tion.
ce rĕb'ri form, -form ly, cer e-
  brif'u gal.
cer'e brĭn *or* -brĭne, -e brize,
  -brized, -brī zing, *-brī'tis.*
cer'e bro gaņ'gli on, -on'ic, -bro-
  me dul'la ry, -brop'a thy, -bros'-
  co py, -bros'i ty.
cĕr'e brŏ sĭde (*or* -sĭd).
cer'e bro spī'nal, c. ax'is, c. fe'ver,
  c. men in gī'tis.
cĕr'e brum, pl. *-brums* or *-bra.*
cere'cloth.
cere'ment.
cĕr'e mo ny, -mo'ni al, -al ism,
  -al ly, -al ness, -al'i ty, -mo'ni-
  ous, -ous ly, -ous ness.
Cĕ'res (-rēz), *Myth.; Astron.*
cĕr'e sin (*or* cĕ're-).
ce're ous, like wax.
Cē're us, Bot. genus.
cĕr'e vis.
ce'rĭn *or* -rĭne, -ric, -rif'er ous.
Ce rin'thi an.
cĕr'iph *or* sĕr'if *or* sĕr'iph.
ce rise' (-rēz').
cĕ'rīte.
ce rith'i oid.

cē'ri um, -ric.
cern, -ing, cerned.
cer'nu ous.
cē'ro (or sā'-), -graph, -graph'ic,
-ic al, -rog'ra phy, -ra phist,
-ro'le in, -ro līte, -ro'ma, -ro-
man cy, -ro mel, -ro plas'tic,
-ro plas'tics, -ro plas'ty, -ro sĭn
or -sĭne, -ro tate, -rot'ic.
ce rōōn'. See seroon.
cĕr'ris, -ri al.
cer'taĭn, -ly, -ness, -ty.
cer tif'i cate, -ca ted, -ca ting.
cer'ti fy, -ing, -fied, -fi er, -fī ca'-
tion.
cer'ti o rā'rī (-shĭ o-).
cer'ti tude.
cert'-mon ey.
cer to'sä (chĕr-), -to si'na-work
(cher tō sē'nä-).
ce rū'le an, -le in, -le um, cer u-
les'cent, -u lif'ic.
ce ru'men, -min ous, -mi nif'er ous,
-mi nip'a rous.
cē'ruse (-rōōs), -rused, -ru sīte or
-rŭs site.
Cer van'tes (-tĕs or -tĕz or -tēz),
Sp. novelist, -van'tist, -tic.
cer'van tite (or -van'-).
Cer vä'ro (chĕr-), t. It.
cer ve lière' (-lyâr' or sâr-).
Cer ve'ra (thĕr vä'rä), t. Sp.; Sp.
admiral.
cĕr'vi cal, -vi ci plex, -vi ci car'-
di ac, -vi ci spī'nal, -vi cī'tis.
cer vi cap'rĭne, -vi cīde, -vi corn,
cer'vĭne, -vid, -void.
cer vi co bra'chi al (-ki-), -braŋ'-
chi ate, -vi co dyn'i a, -co fā'cial
(-shal).
cer vic'u late, cer'vix, pl. -vix ĕs
or -vi ces (-sēz).
Cer'vus.
ce'ryl, -ryl'ic.
cē'sa re (-za rē).
Ce sa're an or -ri an (-zā'-). See
Cæsarean.
Ces no'la (ches nō'la), It. archæol.
Ces'pe des (thes'pä des or thäs-
pä ĭhäs), Cuban revolutionist.
ces'pi tose (-tōs), -toŭs, -pit'u lose.
ces sā'tion.
ces sā'vit.

ces'si o bo nō'rum (sĕsh'-).
ces'sion, -a ry.
cess'pool, -pit, -pipe.
ces'tode, -toid, -toid'e an, -e ous.
Ces'trum, Bot. genus. ces'trum,
pl. -tra.
ces'tus, a girdle, pl. -tī; ces'tus
or cæs' (ses'-), a gauntlet, pl.
ces'tus or cæs'tus.
ce su'ra or cæ- (sē zū'ra or -su'-),
pl. cē su'ras (-raz) or cæ su'ræ
(-re), -su'ral, -su'ric.
Ce tā'ce a (or -she a), ce ta'cean
(-shan), -ceous.
cē'tate.
Cē'tē, Zoöl., cē'tēne, -tic, -tĭn or
-tīne.
cet'e rach (-rak).
cet'e ris păr'i bus.
Cete wä'yō or Cety wä'yō or Ket-
chwä'yo (Ketch wä'yō) or Cet'-
ti- or Cet'ty- (sĕt'tĭ-), Zulu king.
ce tol'o gy, -o gist, -to log'ic al,
-to mor'phic.
Cette (set), t. Fr.
Cet tin'jé (chĕt'tēn'yä or chä'-),
t. Montenegro.
cē'tus, a whale; Cē'tus,. a constellation.
cē'tyl, -tyl ene, -tyl'ic.
Ceu'ta (su'ta), t. Sp.
Cey lŏn' (sē-), -lon ese' (-ēs' or
-ēz'), cey'lon īte or -lan- (or
-lon'-, -lan'-), Cey lon' moss,
C. stone.
Cha blis' (sha blē').
cha bouk' or -buk' (cha bōōk' or
sha-).
cha'ca (kā'- or chä'-), Cha'ca,
Zoöl. genus.
chăck, -stone.
chăc'ma.
chăc'o.
cha cŏnne' or -cone' (shä-).
cha cu'ru (-kōō'-).
Chad or Tchad or Tschad (chäd),
l. Afr.
chad, -an, -ding, -lock, -pen'ny.
chæ nich'thy id (kē nĭk'thĭ ĭd).
Chær o ne'a (kĕr-), c. Gr.
chæ'ta (kē'-), pl. -tæ, -tif'er ous
or -toph'o rous.
chæ'to dŏnt (kē'-), -don'tid, -toid.

chæ'to tax'y (kē'-).
chafe, chafed, chāf'ing, chāf'er,
one who chafes; -er y, chā'fer,
a beetle; chafe'weed, chāf'ing-
board, -check, -dish, -gear, -plate.
châff, -ing, -er, -er er, -er ing,
-less, -y, chaffed, châff'seed,
-wax, -weed, -cut'ter, -en'gine,
-flow'er, -hal'ter.
chaf'finch.
cha gi'gah (ha gē'gä).
Chä'grĕs, t. Colom.
cha grin' (sha grin' or -grēn'),
-ing, -grĭned.
cha gul' (-gōōl').
châin, -ing, -less, -let, -man,
-smith, -wise, -work, chained.
chain'-ball, -bear'er, -bit, -boat,
-bolt, -chest, -coŭp'ling, -fas'ten-
ing, -fern, -gang, -gēar, -grate,
-guard, -hook, -in cli nom'e ter,
-knot, -lift'er, -lock, -lock'er,
-loom, -mold'ing, -pier, -pin,
-pipe, -plate, -pul'ley, -pump,
-rule, -saw, -shot, -snake,
-stitch, -stop'per, -tim'ber, -tow'-
ing, -wale, -well, -wheel.
chain' bond, c. bridge, c. ca'ble, c.
cŏr'al, c. light'ning, c. mail, c.
syl'lo gism.
chair, -man, -man ship.
chair'-arm, -back, -beâr'er, -bed,
-bolt, -days, -leg, -māk'er, -or'-
gan, -rail, -seat, -spring, -web.
chaise (shāz).
chait'ya (chĭt'yä).
chä'ja (-hä or -jä).
chä'kĭ.
chăk'ra.
cha las'tic (ka-).
cha lä'za (ka-), pl. -zas or -zæ,
-la'zal, -laze', -lä'zi on or -zi um,
pl. -zi a, chal a zif'er ous (kal-).
Chal ce'don (kal-), -do'ni an.
chal ced'o ny (kal sed'- or kal'se-),
-ced'o nyx, -o nus, -ce don'ic,
-do'ni an.
chăl'chi huitl' (-chē wētl').
chal cid'i an (kal-), chal'cid,
chalcid fly.
Chal cid'i an (kal-), pertaining to
Chalcis, Chal cid'ic.
chal cid'i cum, pl. -i ca.

chal'cĭ dĭne (kal'-), -cid'i form.
chal'co cite (kal'-), -co dite.
chal'co graph (kal'-), -co graph'ic,
-ic al, -cog'ra pher, -ra phist,
-ra phy.
Chal'dee (kăl'dee or -dee'), -de'an,
-da'ic, Chal'da ism, -dæ ism.
chạl'der, a measure; a rudder-
band.
chal'drich or -drick (chawl'dritch
or kăl'drĭk).
chăl'dron (or chawl'-).
cha let' (shä lā').
chal'Ice, -Iced, chal'ice-case, -cells,
-pall, -spoon, -veil.
chal i co'sis (kal-).
cha lil' (ha lēl').
chal'i noid (kal'-).
chalk (chawk), -ing, -i ness, -y,
-stone, chalked, chalk'-box, -cut'-
ter, -draw'ing, -en grāv'ing, -line,
-mark, -pit.
chal'lenge, -a ble, -len ger, -len-
ging, -lenged.
chal'lis (shal'lĬ) or shal'li.
Chal lons' (shäl'lŏn'), t. Fr.
chal u meau' (shal u mō').
chä'ly.
Cha lyb'e an (ka- or kal i be'-),
pertaining to the Chalybes.
cha lyb'e ate (ka-), -e ous, -e an,
chal'y bīte (kal-).
cha made' (sha mäd' or -mād').
cham'æ ce phal'ic (kam-), -ceph'-
a ly.
cha mæ'rops (ka mē'-).
cha'mal (kä'mäl).
chạ mär'.
chăm'ber, -ing, -let, -maid, -laĭn,
-lain ship.
chăm'ber-coun'cil, -coun'sel,
-coun'sel lor, -fel'low, -gäge,
-hang'ings, -kiln, -mås'ter,
-mu'sic, -or'gan, -piece, -prac'-
tice, -sto'ry.
Cham ber tin' (shäṅ'bĕr tăṅ').
Cham bord, de (dĕ shŏṅ'bor'), Fr.
polit.
cham branle' (sham branl').
Cham bray, de (dĕ shŏṅ'brä'), Fr.
hist.
cham'bray (sham'-).
cha mĕck' (shä- or chä-).

cha mē'lĕ on (ka-), -on ize, -on-
fly, -moth.
cham'fer, -ing, -fered, -fret, -fret-
ing, -fron.
cham'id (kam'-), -oid.
chăm'i sal.
chăm'i so.
cham'ois (shăm'my *or* shå moi'
or sham'wŏ).
cham'o mīle (kam'-). See *camomile.*
Cha mou ni' (shä'mōō nĕ'), val.
Fr.
chămp, -er, -ing, champed.
Cham pagne' (shŏń pän' *or* shăm-
pän'), prov. Fr.   cham pagne'
(shăm pän'), a wine.
Cham paign' (shăm pän'), co., tp.,
and c. Ill.; co. O.   cham paign'
(shăm pän'), a plain.
cham'pak *or* -pac.
cham pa'na (shäń pä'na).
cham'per tor, -per ty, -per tous,
cham'part' (shäń pär').
cham pi'gnon (shăm pĭn'yon).
cham'pi on, -ing, -ess, -ship, -pi-
oned.
champ le vĕ' (shamp lē vä').
chä'na.
chănce, chanced, chan'cing,
chance'-med'ley.
chan'cel, -aisle, -arch, -rail,
-screw, -ta'ble.
chan'cel lor, -ship.
chan'cer y.
chan'cre (shăń'ker), -croid, -crous.
chan dä'lä *or* -daul'.
chan de lier' (shan'dē lēr'), -tree.
chand'la.
chan'dler, -y.
chan dōō'.
chan'frĭn (*or* shan'-), -fron.
chang.
chănge, -a ble, -a ble ness, -a bly,
-a bil'i ty, -ful, -ful ly, -ful ness,
-less, -less ly, -less ness, -ling,
chăn'ging, -ger, -ger wife.
change'-house, -pump, -ra'ti o,
-ring'ing, -wheel, chan'ging-
house.
chănk, -shell.
chan'nel, -neled *or* -nelled, -nel-
ing *or* -nel ling, -nel bill, a bird.

chan'nel-bar, -băss, -board,
-bone, -cat, -duck, -goose,
-i'ron, -leaved, -plate, -stone,
-wale, chan'nel ing-ma chine'.
Cha'nos (kā'nŏs), cha'nī (kā'-).
chan'son (shăn'-), -nette'.
chănt, -ed, -ing, -er, -ey, -ress,
chan'tant' (shäń'täń').
chan'tage' (shäń täzh' *or* chănt'āj).
chan'te rĕlle' (shäń-).
chan'ti cleer.
chan'tier' (shäń'tyä').
Chan'til'ly' (shŏń tēl yĕ' *or* -tĕ'-
yĕ'), t. Fr., C. lace, C. porce'-
lain.
chant'lāte.
chân'try.
cha'nu ca (hä'nōō-).
chā'os (kā'-), -ot'ic, -ic al ly.
chao'-ting' (chou'-ting').
chăp, *n.,* a cleft or crack; a
fellow.
chap (chŏp), *n., pl.* chaps (chŏps),
the jaws or mouth.
chăp, *v.,* to crack; to strike.
-ping, chapped.
chä'pa.
chä pä pō'te (-tä)
chä'pä rä'jos (-hŏs), *-pa re'ras* (-ra'-
räs).
chä'par răl' (*or* chä'păr răl'), -cock.
chap'book.
chāpe, less
cha'peau' (shä'pō'), *pl.* -peaux'
(-pōz'), c. bras (brä).
chap'el, -ry, -et, -ine, -lage.
chap'el-cart, -clerk, -măs'ter,
cha pel'-dĕ-fĕr' (sha-).
chap'er ŏn (shăp'-), -age, -ing,
-ŏned.
chap'fall en (chŏp'-).
chä'pin.
chap'lain, -cy, -ship.
chăp'let.
chä pō'te (-tä).
chăp paul'.
chap pĕ' (sha pä') or *chappe* (shap).
chăp'pie *or* -py, a little chap.
chăp'py, chăpped.
chap'ter, -ing, -al, -tered, chap'ter-
head, -head'ing, -house, -lands.
chap'trel.
cha que'ta (chä kā'-).

chär, to burn or blacken, -ring,
-ry, charred, chär'-ov'en.
chär *or* châre, a job or chore,
-wom'an, -work.
Cha'ra (kā'-).
char'-a-bancs' (shär'-à-bäṅ').
char'ac ter (kăr'-), -ize, -ized,
-i zing, -ism, -less, -is'tic, -tic al,
-al ly, -ĭ zā'tion.
cha rāde' (sha-).
char'bŏn (shar'-).
chär'co.
char'coal, -black, -burn'er, -cool'-
er, -draw ing, -fil'ter, -fur'nace,
-i'ron, -pa'per, -pen'cil, -pit,
-plates, -tree.
Char'cot' (shär kō'), Fr. neurolo-
gist.
chard.
Char'don (shar'-), vil. O.
charge, -a ble, -a ble ness, -a bly,
-less, charged, char'ging, charge'-
sheet.
char gé d' aj faires' (shär zhā'dâf'-
fâr'), char gé' ship (shär zhā'-).
char'ger, -pit.
char'i nid (kăr'-), -i noid.
chăr'i ot, -ee', -eer', -eer'ing,
chăr'i ot-man, -race.
char'ism (kăr'- *or* kā-'), -is mat'ic,
cha ris'ma (-riz'-), pl. *-ma ta.*
chăr'i ta ble, -ble ness, -ta bly.
chăr'i ty, c. boy, c. child, c. girl,
c. school.
cha ri'va ri' (shä rē vå rē' *or* shär-
ĭ văr'i).
chark.
char'ka.
char'la tan (shar'-), -ism, -ry,
-tan'ic, -ic al, -al ly.
Char le boix', de (dĕ shär'lĕ bwä'),
Jesuit missionary.
Char'le magne (shär'le măn), Fr.
king.
Charles's Wain, C. law.
char'lin.
char'lock.
char'lŏtte (shar'-), a delicate dish.
c. russe' (rōōs').
char'ly-muf'tĭ.
charm, -er, -ing, -ing ly, -ing ness,
-less, -ful, charmed.
char'nel, -house.

Cha'ron (kā'-), *Myth.*
char'pie (shar'py).
char'poy.
char'que (-kē).
char ri ère' (shä rĭ âr').
chart, -ed, -ing, -less, -room.
char tă'ceous (kar-).
char'ta (kar'-), pl. *-tæ.*
Charte (shärt).
char'ter, -ing, -er, -ist, -a ble,
-age, -tered.
char'ter-land, -mås'ter, -par'ty.
Char'ter house, -ter ist *or* Chart'-
ist, -ter ism, Charter boy, C.
broth'er.
Char ti er' (shär'tē ā' *or* shär tyā'),
Fr. poet.
Chär'tiĕrs', tp. Pa.
char tog'ra pher (kär-), *or* car-,
-ra phy, -to graph'ic, -ic al, -al ly,
-to man'cy, -tom'e ter.
Char tres, de (dĕ shärtr), Fr.
prince.
Char'tres (shär'tr), c. Fr.
char'treuse' (shar'trēz'), *-treux'*
(-trē').
char'tu la ry (kar'-).
chär'y (*or* chä'ry).
Cha ryb'dis (kå-).
Cha rytch' (chä rĭch'), r. Siberia.
chase, chased, chas'ing, -er, chase'-
gun, -mor'tĭse, -port, -ring.
Chas'i dim (kăs'- *or* chas-).
chās'ing-chis'el, -ham'mer, -lāthe,
-tool.
Chasle'si an (shäl'zi an).
chasm (kăzm), chasmed, chas'my
(kăz'-).
chas'ma (kăz'-).
chas mog'a my (kăz-), -a mous.
chasse (shäs), a shrine. *chasse*
(shås), a drink.
chas sé' (shăs sā'), *chas séd'* (-sād'),
chas sé'ing (shăs sā'ing).
chas'se las (shăs'-).
chasse'pot' (shås pō'), *chasse'-
ma rée* (-mǎ'rā'), *-ca'jé* (-kǎ'-
fā').
chas'seur' (shås'sêr').
chăs'sĭs (*or* shäs-).
chāste, -ly, -ness, -eyed, -tree,
chăs'ti ty.
chast'en (chā'sn), -er, -ing, -ened.

fāte, făt, fär, fạll, fâre, fạst, sofà, mēte, mĕt, hêr, īce, ĭn, nōte,

chas tise' (-tīz'), -tis'a ble (-tīz'-),
-tis'er, -tis'ing, chas'tise ment
(-tĭz-).
chas'u ble (or chaz'-).
chăt, -ted, -ting, -ty, -some, -roll'er,
-thrush, -wood.
cha'teau' (shä tō'), pl. -teaux' (-tōz').
Cha teau bri and', de (dĕ shä'-
tō'brē'ŏn'), Fr. auth.
Cha teau bri ant' (shä'tō'brē'ŏn'),
t. Fr.
Chat eau gay' (shăt o gā'), t. N. Y.
chat'e lāin (shăt'-), a keeper of a
castle.
chat'e lāine (shăt'-), a clasp or
brooch.
Chat e let' (shät lā' or -tĕ lā'), t.
Belg.
cha'ti' (shä tē').
cha ton' (sha tôn').
cha toy'ant (sha-), -an cy, -toy'-
ment.
chat'tah or -ta, an umbrella.
chat'tel (-tĕl or -tl), -ize, -ized,
-i zing, -ism, -hood.
chat'ter, -ing, -er, -a'tion, -tered,
chat'ter box, -bǎs'ket, -pīe, -wa'-
ter.
chau (chou).
Chạu'cer, -ism, -ce'ri an.
chạud'-med'ley.
chạuf'fer (shạf'-), a small furnace.
chauf feur' (shō fer').
chaus (chouse), a trick; a trick-
ster.
cha'us (kā'-), a lynx.
Cha'us (kā'-), Zoöl. genus.
chaus sée' (shō sā').
chaus'ses (shō'sĕz or shōs).
chaus'sure' (shōs sōōr').
Chau tau'qua (sha tạ'-), vil. and
l. N. Y.
Chau veau' (shō'vō'), Can. statesman.
Chau ve net' (shō'vĕ nā' or shō'-),
Amer. math.
Chau vin' (shō'vǎn'), Fr. refugee,
chau vin' (shō'vǎn'), a wild en-
thusiast, -ism, -ist, -ist'ic.
Chav'i ca (kǎv'-), Bot. genus.
chǎv'i cha (chǎv'i cha), a fish.
chay (shā).
cha zan' or chaz zan' (kä zän').

cheap, -ness, -ly.
chĕap'en (-n), -er, -ing, -ened.
chēat, -a ble, -ble ness, -er, -ing,
-ing ly, -ed.
Che bac'co-boat (or shē-).
chē'bec (or shē'-), a boat; a xebec.
che bec', a bird.
Che ci'ny (kĕt sēn'yē), t. Pol.
check, -age, -er, -ered, -less, -mate,
-mat'ed, -mat'ing, -y, checked.
check'-book, -bridge, -chain, -clerk,
-cord, -end, -hook, -key, -line,
-list, -lock, -nut, -rail, -rein, -roll,
-rope, -row'er, -stop, -strap,
-string, -tāk'er, -valve.
check'er, -ers, -ered, -er ber'ry,
-wise, -work.
check'er-board, -roll, -tree, check'-
ing-file.
Ched'dar, C. cheese.
chee'cha.
chee'chee.
cheek, -y, cheeked, cheek'-band,
-blade, -block, -bone, -piece,
-pouch, -strap, -tooth.
chee'la or che'-, -ship.
cheep, -ing, -er, -y, cheeped.
cheer, -er, -ful, -ful ly, -ful ness,
-i ly, -i ness, -ing, -ing ly, -less,
-less ly, -less ness, -y.
cheese (chēz), chees'y, -i ness, -lip
or -lep, mak'er, a plant; -mon'-
ger, -pâr'ing, -wood.
cheese'-cake, -ce ment', -cloth,
-cut'ter, -fly, -hoōp, -mag'got,
-māk'er, -mite, -mold, -pale,
-press, -ren net, -room, -run'-
ning, -scoop, -shelf, -tāst'er,
-tōast'er, -turn'er, -vat.
cheet.
chee'tah. See chetah.
chef (shĕf or shäf), -d'œuvre
(-dèvr'), pl. chefs- (shā-).
chef'ford.
cheg'ŏe.
Chei lan'thes (kī lăn'thēz).
cheir (kīr).
che ki' (-kē').
chĕk'mǎk.
che'la (kē'-), a claw, pl. -læ, -late,
che'la (chä'), a novice.
chel'i fer (kel'-), -i form (or kē'-),
che lif'er ous (ke-).

nŏt, nôr, ūse, ŭp, ûrn, etüde, fōōd, fŏŏt, aŋger, boṅmot, thus, Bach.

14

che'li ped (kē'-).
chel'o dine (kel'-).
Che lo'ne (ke-).
chel'ys (kel'is), a lyre. Chel'ys,
Zoöl. genus.
che'me (kē'me).
chem'ic (kem'-), -ic al, -al ly.
chem'i co-al ge bra'ic (kem'-),
-e lec'tric, -gal van'ic, -tech'nic-
al.
che min' de ronde' (she măn' de
rônd').
che mise' (she mēz'), chem i sette'
(shem ĭ zet').
chem'ism, chem'ist, -is try, -i type,
-i typy (-i tī'py).
Chem'nitz (kĕm'nits), t. Ger.;
Ger. divine.
che'mŏsh (kē'-).
chem'o tax'is (kem-).
che mot'ro pism.
Che mung' (she-), co. N. Y.
chē'na.
chĕng.
che nille' (shē nēl'), -ma chine',
-nee'dle.
cheque (chĕk). Sometimes used instead of *check*, as an order on a
bank.
che ras'sĭ.
Cher bourg (sher'burg *or* shĕr-
bōōr'), naval arsenal Fr.
Cher bu li ez' (shĕr'bōō lē ā'), Fr.
auth.
cher if (shĕr'-). See *sherif.*
cher'i moy'er.
chĕr'ish, -ing, -er, -ished.
cher'ma ny.
cher'na (*or* chĕr'-), -*ne*, -*nĕtte'.*
cher'no zen.
Chĕr'o kees' (-kēz').
che root' (she- *or* che-).
chĕr'ry, -bird, -blight, -blos'som,
-chop'per, -coal, -cob, -cof'fee,
-col'ored, -finch, -gum, -lạu'rel,
-net, -oil, -pep'per, -pit, -plum,
-snipe, -stick, -stone, -stŏn'er,
-tree.
cher'ry bounce, c. bran'dy, c.
cor'dial, c. pie, c. rum, c. wine.
cher'si an (ker'-), -sid, -sīte.
cher'so nese (ker'so nēs *or* -nēz).
chert, -y.

Chert'sey (chĕs'se *or* chert'sy), t.
Eng.
Che'rub (kē'rub), a city, *Bib.*
chĕr'ub, *pl.* -ubs *or* -u bim, -u bim'-
ic, che ru'bic, -bic al.
Che ru bi'ni (kā rōō bē'ne), It.
mus.
cher'vil.
Ches'a peake, a bay.
chess, -man, *pl.* -men, -board,
-ap'ple, -play'er, -rook, -tree,
-type.
ches'sel, a vat.
chess'es.
ches'sil (-sl), gravel.
chest, -ed, -bel'lows (-lus), -foun'-
der, -lock, -meas'ure, -reg'is ter,
-rope, -saw, -tone, -voice.
Chĕs'te (-tā), t. Spain.
Ches'ter field, Eng. earl, -field'i an,
ches'ter field, a top coat.
ches'ter līte.
chest'nut (ches'-), -ting, -brown,
-bur, -meal, -oak, -tree, c. coal.
chē'tah *or* chee'- *or* chee'ta.
chĕt ve rĭk', chet'vert, -ver tăk,
-vert'ka.
chê văl' (shê-), pl. -*vaux'* (-vō'),
chê văl'-glăss, -screen.
chê văl'-de-frise' (-de-frēz'), pl.
che vaux'-de- (shê vō'-).
che vale'ment (shê văl'moṅ).
chev'a let (shev'a lā)
Che va li er' (shĕ vä'lē ā' *or* -văl'-
yā'), Fr. economist.
chev'a liĕr' (shev-).
chev e lure' (shev loor' *or* shĕv'e-
loor).
che vet' (shê vā').
che ville' (shê vēl').
Chev'i ot, a breed of sheep; chev'-
i ot, a woolen fabric.
chev'ron (shev'-) *or* chev'e ron,
-roned, -ro né (-rō nä'), chev'ro-
nel, -ron ways, -ron wise.
chev'ron-bone, -mold'ing, -work.
chev'ro tāin (shev'-).
chĕv'y, -chase.
chew (chōō *or* chū), -er, chewed,
chew'-stick.
chē wagh' (-wä').
chew'ing, -ball, -gum.
chē wink'.

Chey enne' (shī ĕn'), co. Col.; co. Kan.; co. Neb.; c. Wyo.

Chey enne' (shē ĕn'), *pl.* -ennes' (-enz'), a tribe of Indians.

che yo'te (chā yō'tā), *-yo til'la* (-yo-tēl'yä).

chan'das (chăn'dås).

chī, a fish; (chē) a magistrate; (kī *or* kē *or* hē) a Greek letter.

chi'a (chē'a).

Chi'an (kī'an), C. earth, C. tur'-pen tine.

chi ăn'ti (kē-).

chiar'os cu'ro (kyär ŏs kōō'ro) *or chi-a'ro-os cu'ro* (kē ä'rō-ŏs kōō'rō), -ros cu'rist.

chi'asm *or* *-as'ma* (kī'azm *or* kī az'ma), -as'mal, *-as'mus*, -as'tic.

chi as'to līte (kī-).

chi as to neū'ral (kī as-), -neu'-rous.

chi bouk' *or* *-bouque'* or -buk' (chī bōōk').

chic (shēk).

chi'ca (chē'ka).

Chi ca'go (shī kä'go *or* shē kạ'go), c. Ill.

chi ca lo'te (chē kä lō'tā).

chi cane' (shī-), -căn'er, -er y.

chich (chĭtch).

chi'cha (chē'-).

chi chär'ro (chē-).

chich'e ree.

Chĭch'es ter, c. Eng.

chĭck, -a ber'ry, -a bid'dy, -a dee, -a ree, -stone, -weed, -house, -pea.

chick ă'ra.

Chick'a saw, C. plum.

chick'een.

chick'en, -y, -weed, -bird, -breast'-ed, -chol'er a, -coop, -corn, -feed'-er, -grape, -hal'i but, -hawk, -heärt, -pox, -tor'tolse, chick'-en's-meat.

chic'le, -gum.

chi'co (chē'-), Chi'co, c. Cal.

chic'o lar'.

chic'o ry.

chi'cot (chē'kō).

chide, chīd'ed, -ing, -ing ly, -er.

chiēf, -less, -ly, -ry, -ship, -taln, -taln cy, -taln ship, chief-jus'tice-ship, -rent, c. jus'tice.

chiēl.

chiff'châff *or* chiff-.

chif'jŏn (shĭf'- *or* shē'fôṅ'), -work.

chif'fo niēr' *or* chef- (shĭf- *or* shĕf-).

chi'gnon (shĭn'yon *or* shē'nyôṅ).

chig'ŏe.

chih (chē).

chĭ kä'ra, an antelope; chĭk'a ra, a stringed instrument.

chil'blain.

chīld, *pl.* chil'dren, child'bed, -birth, -like, -like ness, -hood, -ish, -ish ly, -ish ness, -less, -less-ness.

child'-beâr'ing, -crōw'ing, c. bish'-op, c. wife, child'ish-mind'ed, -mind'ed ness.

Chil'der mas, C. day.

Chi'le (chē'lā *or* chĭl'e), rep. S. Amer.; Chĭl'i (-ē), prov. China; Chĭl'ĭ, tp. N. Y.; Chil'e an *or* -i an.

chil'i ad (kĭl'-), -i a gon, -i a hē'-dron, -i arch (-ark), -arch y (-ark-y), -i asm -i ast, -as'tic.

chill, -i ness, -ing, -ish, -ness, -y, -har'den ing.

chĭl'lĭ *or* -e *or* -i *or* -ly, the pod of the Guinea pepper. -coy'o te (-kĭ'ō tē), -pep'per.

chil'lo.

chil'lum, -chee.

chi'log nath (kī'-), -log'na than, -nath o mor'phous, -log'na thous, -lo'ma, *pl.* -ma ta, -lo plas ty, -lo pod, -pod'i form, -pod o mor'-phous, lop'o dan, -o dous, -lo-stom'a tous, -los'to moŭs.

Chil'tern Hun'dreds.

chil'ver.

chi măn'go (shē- *or* kī-).

Chim bo rä'zo, mt. S. A.

chime, chimed, chĭm'ing, -er, chime'-băr'rel, -bell, -ring'ing, chĭm'ing-ma chine'.

chi me'ra *or* -mæ'- (kī-), an idle fancy, -mĕr'ic, -ic al, -al ly.

chi mere' *or* -me'ra (shī-), an outer robe.

chĭm'ming.

chim'ney, *pl.* -neys (-nĭz), -neyed (-nĭd), -ney board, -piece.

chim'ney-brĕast, -can, -cap, -col'-
lar, -cor'ner, -head, -hook, -jack,
-jamb, -mon'ey, -pot, -shăft,
-stack, -stạlk, -swal'low, -sweep,
-sweep'er, -swift, -top, -valve,
-work.
chim pan'zee (*or* -zee').
chimp'ings.
chin, -band, -cloth, -jerk, -piece,
-scab, -strap, -welk.
Chī'na, -nēse' (-nēs' *or*- nēz'), -na-
man, C. as'ter, C. bark, C. blue.
chī'na, -ware, -ale, -clay, -grăss,
-root, -shell, -shop, -stone, -to'-
ken, -tree, -wĭthe.
chĭ nar', -tree.
chinch, -bug.
chin'chĕ *or* -chä.
chin chil'la, an animal; fur used
for muffs, etc ; a thick cloth.
Chin chil'la, *Zoöl. genus.*
Chin cholle' (shăn'shōl'), Fr. writer.
chīne, chined, chīn'ing, chine'-
hōōp.
chi ne' (shē nä').
Chin gach'gŏŏk (-gäk'-), Cooper,
Leather Stocking Tales.
chink, -y, -ing.
chiṇ'ka.
chĭṇ'ka pĭn *or* -ca- *or* -qua-,
-perch.
chiṇ kä'ra.
chink'ie, a chinaman.
Chin'ne reth (kin'-), *Bib.*
Chin'ne roth (kin'-), *Bib.*
chi'noi'ser ie' (shē nwä ze rē').
chin'o lĭne (kĭn'-).
Chĭ nŏŏk'.
chin'qua pin. See *chinkapin.*
chin'quis.
chinse (chince), chinsed, chins'ing.
chins'ing-i'ron.
chintz, cotton cloth.
Chi ob'be (chē ŏb'bā), c. China.
Chi og'gia (kē od'jä), t. It.
chi'o lĭte (kĭ'-).
chip, -per, -py, chipped, chip'chop,
n., -chop, *a.*
chip'muṇk.
chip'pen dale.
chip'ping, -bird, -chis'el, -knife,
-ma chine', -piece, c. spar'row, c.
squir'rel, c. up.

chi ret'ta (*or* kī-).
Chi ri qui' (chē rē kē'), r. Colom.
chi'ri vi'ta (chē'rē vē'ta).
chirk.
chirm.
chi'ro (chē'-).
chi rog'no my (kī-), -nom'ic, -ro-
graph, -rog'ra pher, -ra phy, -ra-
phist, -ro graph'ic, -ic al, -grapho
o soph'ic, -ro gym'nast.
chi rol'o gy (kī-), -o gist, -ro lō'-
gi a, -log'ic al, -ro man'cy, -man-
eer, -ro mant, -man'tic, -tic al,
-man'tist, -ron'o my, -o mer, -ro-
nom'ic.
chi'ro nym (kī'-), -ro plase (-plāz),
-ro plast, -ro pod, -rop'o dy, -o-
dist, -o dous.
chi rop'ter (kī-), -ter an, -ter ous,
-te ryg'i an (-rĭj'-), -i ous.
chi ros'o phy (kī-), -o phist, -ro-
soph'ic al, -ro thē'ca, -rot'o ny.
chirp, -ing, -ing ly, -er, chirped.
chirr.
chĭr'rup, -ing, -y, -rŭped.
chi rur'geon (kī rur'jun), -ly, -rur'-
gic.
chis'el (chĭz'-), -eled *or* -elled
-el ing *or* -el ling.
chis'el-drăft, -edge-point, -shaped,
-tooth.
Chis'holm (chĭz'om), Eng. philanthropist
Chis'wick (chĭz'ik), t. Eng.
chĭt, the germ of a seed; a short
writing; -ty, chit'-book, -chat.
chi tai (chē'tĭ').
chit'al.
chit'a ra.
chi'tĭn *or* -tĭne (kĭ-), -ti nized,
-nĭ zā'tion, -ti nous, -nog'e nous
(-nŏj'-), -no cal că're ous, -no-
-ăr e nā'ceous (-shus).
chi'ton (kī'-), -to nid.
chit'ra or -*tra*, a deer. *Chit'ra*,
Zoöl. genus.
chit'tack.
chit'ta gong, -wood.
chit'ta m-wood.
chit'ter lings.
Chĭt'tim (kĭt'-), *Bib.*
chit'ty, *n.* In the East Indies, a
short letter or writing.

chiv′al ry (shiv′-), -al ric (*or* shl-val′-), -al rous, -rous ly, -rous-ness, -al resque′.

chi vär′räs or *-rōs* (chē-).

chĪve *or* cive, -gar′lic.

Chi vil co y (chē vēl kō′ ē), t. Arg. Rep.

chlad′nĪte (klad′-).

chlæ′na, *pl.* -næ.

chlak (klak).

chlam′y date (klam′-), -y dō spore, -y phore, chla myd′e ous (-mĬd′-).

chlä′mys (klä′- *or* klăm′-), pl. *-y des* (-dēz).

chlo an′thĪte.

chlo as′ma (klō az′-).

Chlŏ′e (klō′-), one of a pair of Greek lovers.

chlŏ′ral, -ism, -ist, -ize, -ized, -i zing, -am′Ĭde, -rac′e tate (-ras′-), -ra cet′ic (*or* -sē′-), -ra gog′ic (-goj′-), -ral′o in.

chlo′rate, -ric, -rĬd *or* -rĬde, -ri-date, -rid′ic, -rid ize, -ized, -i-zing, -rim′e ter.

chlo′rĬn *or* -rĬne, -rin ate, -ri na-ted, -na′tion, -rin ize, -ized, -i-zing.

chlo′rĪte, -rit′ic, -ri toid, -rĬze, -rized, -ri zing, chlor′meth′āne.

chlo ro cal′cĪte, -ro car bon′ic, -ro-chrous (-krus), -ro cy an′ic (-cĪ-).

chlo′ro form, -formed, -form ing, -for′mic, -mi za′tion, -ro fu′cine, -ro gen′ate, -gen′ic, -gen′in, -ro-hy′dric (-hĪ′-), chlo′roid.

chlo rom′e ter, -e try, -ro met′ric.

chlo′ro phyl *or* -phyll, -ro phăne, -ro phyl la′ceous (-shus), -phyl′-lan, -phyl′li an, -phyl lif′er ous, -lig′e nous (-lij′-), -lig′er ous (-lij′-), -phyl′lĪte, -phyl′loid (*or* -rof′-), phyl′lous (*or* -rof′-).

chlo ro′sis, -ro sperm, -sperm′a tous, -sper′mous, -ros′po rous, -rot′ic, -ro tĪle, -rous.

Chmi el′ nik (chmē ĕl′nĭk), t. Russ.

chŏ′a na, pl. *-næ*, -a nate, -a nĪte, -a no cyte (-cĪte), -cy′tal (-cĪ′-), -no flag′el late (-flaj′-).

cho′a noid, -noid′e us, -a noph′o-roŭs, -a no sōme, -no so′mal.

Chŏate, Amer. jurist.

choat′y.

chob′dar.

cho′card.

chŏ′chō or -co.

chŏck, -block, -full, -a-block, -and-block.

choc′o late, -house, -root, -tree.

Choc′taws.

chœ ro′di an.

choice, -ly, -less, -ness, -note.

choil, a term used in cutlery; choile, to overreach.

choir (kwĪr), -man, -mås ter, -boy, -of′fice, -or′gan, -pitch, -rul′er, -screen, -serv′ice, -tip′pet.

choke, choked, chōk′age, -ing, -er, -y *or* -ey, -ber′ry, -weed, -wort, -bore, -cher′ry, -damp, -peâr, -pond′weed, -strap.

cho′ki dar.

Chok′mah (hok′-)

cho læ′mi a (kō lē′-), -læ′mic.

chol′a gogue (kol′-), -a gog′ic (-goj′-), cho lan′gi o i′tis (-jĬ-).

cho′la-plant (kō′-).

chol′ate (kol′-), -e ate, -e cyst, -cys′tic, -*cys′tis*, -cys tĪ′tis, -cys-tot′o my.

chol′e doch (kol′e dok), cho led′-o chous (-kus), chol e dog′ra phy, -dol′o gy, chol′e ic (*or* cho le′-), -e in.

chol′er (kŏl′-), -er ic, -ic ly.

chol′er a (kol′-), -a′ic, -er i form, -er ig′e nous (-ij-), -er Ĭne, -er i-za′tion, -er oid, -er o pho′bi a, cho lĕr′o phone.

cho′li ah (kō′-).

cho′li amb (kō′-), -am′bic.

chol′oid (kŏl′-), -oi din′ic, cho-loid′ic (*or* -lo id′ic).

chŏl′try *or* chŏul′-.

cho′mage′ (shō′măzh′).

chō′mer.

chon′dral (kon′-), -dral′gi a, -drar′-se nĪte.

chon dren′chyme (kon dren′kĬm), -chym′a toŭs (-kĬm′-).

chon′dri fy (kon′dri fĪ), -ing, -fied, -fĪ ca′tion.

chon′dri gen (kon′-), -drig′e nous (-drij′-), -dri glu′cose (-kōs).

chon′drĬn *or* -drĬne (kon′-), -drĪte,

-drĭt′ic, -drĭ′tis, -dro crä′ni um,
pl. -ni a, -ni al, -dro dīte, -dro-
gan′oid, -dro gen (-jen), -gen′e-
sis, -ge net′ic, -drog′e ny (-droj′-),
-e nous, -dro glos′sus, -glos′sal,
-drog′ra phy, -dro graph′ic, -drol′-
o gy, -dro log′ic (-loj′-).
chon′dro blast (kŏn′-), -dro cos′-
tal.
chon dro′i tin (kŏn-), -dro it′ic,
-dro mu′coid, -dro sin, -dro skel′-
e ton.
chon′dro phŏre (kŏn′-), -droph′o-
rous, -dro plast, -drop te ryg′i an
(-rij′-), -ryg′i ous, -dro sar co′ma,
-com′a tous, -dro′sis, -dros′te ous,
-drot′o my, -dro tome.
chone (kōn).
chōōch′kĭe.
choose, chōse, chŏ′sen (zn), choos′-
a ble, -er, -ing, choos′ing-stick.
chop, -ping, -per, ' -py, chopped,
chop-boat, -cher′ry, -dol′lar,
-ham′mer, -house, -log′ic (-loj′-),
-nut, -sticks. chop′ping-block,
-board, -knife, -mill, -note,
-tray, chop′per-cot.
chope.
Cho pin′ (sho′pǎṅ′), Pol. mus.;
chŏp′in *or* -pin, a liquid measure.
chŏ pine′ (-pēn′) *or* chŏ pin′, a clog.
cho quette′ (shō kĕt′).
cho rā′gus (kō-) or *-rē′gus*, pl.
-rā′gī or *-rē′gī*, -rag′ic (-raj′-),
chŏr′a gy *or* -e gy.
chŏr′al (ko′-), -ist, -ly, -rā′le on,
-rau′la, cho′ric, chŏ′ral-book.
Cho rā′zin (ko-), *Bib.*
chord (kôrd), chor′dal, -dom′e ter,
-do tō′nal.
chor′da (kor′-), *pl.* -dæ, *Chor′da,*
Bot. genus.
Chor dā′ta (kor-), chôr′dāte (kor′-).
chor dau lo′di on (kor-).
chor′del (kor′-).
chŏre, -wom′an.
chŏ rē′a (ko-), -re′al, -re′ic, -re′i-
form, -re′oid.
chŏ′ree (ko′-).
cho re og′ra phy (kō-) *or* -reg′ra-
phy *or* -rog′-, -re o graph, -graph′-
ic, -ic al, -al ly.
cho′re pis′co pus, -co pal.

cho rē′us (ko-).
cho′ri am′bus (ko-), *pl.* -bus es *or*
-bī, -ri amb, *pl.* -ambs, -am′bic.
cho′ri on (ko′-), pl. *-ri a,* -on′ic,
-o ret i nī′tis.
chor′is ter (kŏr′-).
cho ris′to pod (kō-), -top′o dous.
cho′ro dĭ das′ca lus (kō-), *pl.* -ca-
li.
cho′roid, -roid′al.
cho′rok.
cho rol′o gy (ko-), -o gist, -ro
log′ic al (-loj′-), cho rom′e try.
chŏ′rus, -rused *or* -russed, -rus ing
or -sing, cho′rus-mâs′ter.
chose (shōz), n., pl. *cho′ses* (shŏ′sĕz),
chōse, *v.* See *choose.*
chŏ tei′ (-tā′).
chou (shōō), pl. *choux* (shōō).
Chou′an (shōō′-), -an′ne riē.
chou ca′ri (chōō kä′rĭ).
Chou et′ (shōō′ä′), Swiss philos.
chough (chuf).
chourt′kä (chōōrt′-), Chourt′ka,
Ornith. genus.
chouse, choused, chous ing.
chou′sing ha.
chout.
chŏ′vy, *pl.* -vĭes.
chow′chow *or* chow-chow.
chow′der, -beer, -head ed.
chow′ry.
chre′ma tis′tics (krē-).
chres tom′a thy, -to math′ic, -ic al.
Chriem′hild (krēm′hilt) *or* Kriem′-,
a German heroine of rare beauty.
chrism, chris′mal, -ma′ri um, *pl.*
-ri a, -ma′tion, -ma to ry, chrism′-
child.
chris′mon (krĭz′-).
Chrĭst, -hood, -less, -like, -li ness,
-ly, -chĭld, Christ′s-thorn.
Chrĭs′ta del′phi an.
Chris′te e le′i son (kris′tē e lā′i-
son).
chris′ten (-n), -ing, -tened.
Chris′ten dom (-n-).
Chris′tian (-chan *or* krist′yan),
-ti an′i ty (*or* -chǎn′i ty), *v.,* -tian-
īze, -ized, -i zing, -ĭ zā′tion.
chris′tian, a coin; -ti ä′na, a coin;
-tian īte, a mineral.
Christ′mas (krĭs′-), -tide.

---

fāte, făt, fär, fạll, fâre, fȧst, sofȧ, mēte, mĕt, hêr, īce, ĭn, nōte,

Chris to cen'tric, -tol'a try, -tol'o-
gy, -to log'ic al, -to lyte, -toph'-
a ny.
chris to'fi a, -to phīte.
chro mam'e ter, -ma scope.
chrō'mate, -mat'ic, -ics, -ic al ly,
-ma tin.
chrō'ma tize, -tized, -ti zing, -tism.
chro mat'o graph, -ma tog'ra phy,
-tog'e nous   (-toj'-),   -tol'o gy,
-tom'e ter, -to path'i a, -path'ic,
-to phile, -to phore, -toph'o rous,
-top'si a, -top sy, -to scope (or
chro mat'-), -tos'co py, -to'sis, -to-
sphĕr'ic, -ma trope or -mo-, -ma-
tu'ri a, -ma type, -mat'y py.
chrōme, -al'um, -col'or, -i'ron,
-i'ron stone, -mī'ca, -ō'chre
(-ker), -ox'īde, c. black, c. green,
c. or'ange, c. red, c. yel'low.
chrō'mic, -mid, -mid'i um, pl. -i a,
-mi dro'sis, -mif'er ous.
chrō'mi om'e ter, -mi um.
chrō mo crin'i a, -mo blast, -mo-
col'lo graph, -graph'ic, -log'ra-
phy, -mo cy'clo graph (-cī'-), -col'-
lo type, -mo cy tom'e ter (-cī-),
-mo gen, -gen'ic, -mog'e nous
(-moj'-), mo graph, -moid, -mo-
leū'cite, -mo lith, -lith'ic, -lith'o-
grăph, -graph'ic, -li thog'ra pher,
-ra phy, -mo mere
chrō'mo phan or -phane, -mo-
phĭle (or -fīl), -moph'i lous,
-moph'o rous, -mo pho'to grăph,
-to graph'ic, -tog'ra phy, -mo-
plasm, -plas'mic (-plaz'-), -mo-
plas'tid, -prō'te id, -mop tom'e-
ter, -to met'ric al, -mo trope,
-mop'si a, -mop'sy, -mo sphere,
-sphĕr'ic.
chrō'mo type, -typ'ic, -ty pog'-
ra phy (-ti-), -mo ty'py (-tī'-),
-mo xy'lo graph (-zī'-), -mo xy-
log'ra phy (-zī-).
chron'ic, -ic al, -al ly, chro nic'i ty
(-nis'-).
chron'i cle, -i cled (-kld), -i cling,
-i cler, -i con.
chron'o ba rom'e ter, -o gram,
-gram mat'ic, -ic al, -al ly, -gram'-
ma tist, -o graph, -graph'ic,
chro nog'ra pher, -ra phy, -nol'-

o ger, -o gist, -o gy, chrŏn o log'-
ic al (-loj'-), -al ly, chrō nol'o-
gize, -gized, -gi zing, chron'o ĭ'-
so ther'mal, -o pho'to grăph,
chro nom'e ter, -e try, chrŏn o-
met'ric al, -o pher, -o scope,
-o ther mom'e ter, chrō nos'co py,
-nos'te al, -nos'te on, pl. -te a.
Chrō'nŏn hō'tŏn thŏl'ō gŏs, hero
in Carey's burlesque tragedy.
chro sper'ma.
chrō'tic.
chrys'a lis, pl. -lis es or chry sal'-
i des (-dēz), chrys'a lid, -a līne,
-a loid, chrys'a lis-shell.
chrys'a mīne or -am'- (chrĭs'-),
-am'mic, -am min'ic, -a nis'ic.
chrys am'pho ra (chrĭs-).
chrys an'the mum, Chrys an'the-
mum, Bot. genus.
chrys'a zin (chrĭs'-), chrys'in.
Chry sē'is (krī-), Homer, Iliad.
chrys'o bĕr yl, -o chlore, -o chlŏr'-
ous, -o chrous, -o col'la, -o gen,
-o grăph, chry sog'ra phy (krī-),
chrys'oid, -oi'dīne (or -ō'ī dīne),
-o lep'ic, -o lin, -o līte, -o lith,
-o lit'ic.
chrys'o car'poŭs (krĭs'-).
chry soph'e nin (krī sŏf'-).
chrys'o po et'ic.
chrys'o prase (-prāz), -o tan'nin,
-o tīle, -o to lu'i dīne, -o type.
Chrys'ŏs tŏm (krĭs'- or krĭs os'-),
Gr. theol.
chrys'ūre.
chtho'ni an (thō'-), -noph'a gy (-jī),
chthŏn'ic, chthon o phā'gi a.
chub, -by, -bi ness, chub'-cheeked,
-mack'er el, -suck'er.
chuck, -er, -ing, chucked, chuck'-
a bid'dy.
chuck'-far'thing, -full, -lăthe, -a-
by, chuck'ing-ma chine', chuck'-
will's-wid'ow.
chuc'kle, -kled, -kling, chuc'kle-
head, a person; -head, a head;
-head'ed.
chud'da or -dah.
chud'der or -dar.
Chū'di, -dic.
Chu e'ta (chōō ā'-), pl. -tas.
chū'fa.

chuff, chuf'fy, -fi ly, -fi ness.
chug, -ger, -ging.
chu'lan.
chum, -ming, -my, -ship, chummed.
chump, -end.
chu nam'.
chunk, -y, -head, -block -yard.
chu'pa or *-pah* (chσσ'-).
chu pä ro'sa (chσσ-).
chu pat'ty.
chu pras'sy.
Chu qui sa'ca   (chσσ kē sä'kä),
    dept. Boliv.
church, -dom, -go er, -go ing, -ism,
    -less, -like, -ly, -li ness, -man,
    -man like, -men, -man ly, -man-
    ship, -ship, -war'den, -war'den-
    ship, -way, -wom'an, -y, -yard.
church'-ale, -bread, -bug, -gang,
    -garth, -haw, -hay, -house, -land,
    -lit'ten, -loaf, -mem'ber, -mouse,
    -owl, -quack, -rate, -scot, -town,
    -wake, -work, -writ, c. dues, c.
    trus tee'.
church'ite.
chu'ri a (chσσ'-).
churl, -ish, -ish ly, -ish ness, -y,
    churl's-hĕad, -trĕa'cle.
churn, -ing, churned, churn'-
    dash'er, -drill, -jump'er, -milk,
    -owl, -pow'er, -stäff.
churr, -worm.
chur ro' (chσσ-).
chŭr'rŭs or *-ras.*
Chu ru bus'co (chσσ rσσ bσσs' ō),
    t. Mex.
Chu san' (chσσ'sän'), China.
chu'sīte (chσσ'-).
chute (shσσt).
chut'ney.
chu'va (chσσ'-).
chyle (kīl), chy la'ceous (kī la'-
    shus), -la'que ous, -li fy (-fī),
    -fied, -lif'er ous, -lif'ic, -lif'i-
    ca to ry, -loŭs, chyl i fac'tion (kīl'-
    I- or kī'lĭ-), -fac'tive, -i fi ca'tion.
chyle-blad'der, -cor'pus cle, -in-
    tes'tĭne, -space, -stom'ach.
chy'lo cyst (kī'-), -cys'tic, -lo gas'-
    ter, -gas'tric, *-lo-poi e'sis,* -lo poi-
    et'ic, *-lo'sis, -lu'ri a.*
chyme (kīm), chym'i fy (kīm'- or
    kī'-), -fy ing, -fied, -fī cā'tion,

chy mif'er ous (kī-), -mous, -mä'-
    que ous, -mo sin, -mo sin'o gen
    (-jen), -om'e ter, chyme-măss.
chypre (shēpr).
chyt'rid i ä'lēs (kit-).
cī ba'ri ous, -ri al, -ri an, -ba'tion.
cib'ol.
ci bō'ri um, *pl.* -ri a.
ci cä'da, *pl.* -das (-daz) *or* -dæ,
    cic'ad.
ci ca'la (sĭ kä'la *or* chē kä'la).
cic'a trīce (sik'-), *pl.* -trī'ces (-sēz),
    -tri'cial (-trish'-), -tri cose (-kōs),
    -tric'u la, *pl.* -læ, -trī'sĭve, *cic'a-*
    trix (*or* -cä'-), pl. *cĭc a trī'ces*
    (-sēz), cic'a trize, -trized, -tri'-
    zing, -trī'zant, -trĭ zä'tion, -a-
    trose (-trōs).
cic'e ly (sĭs'-).
Cic'e ro (sis'-), Rom. orator, -ro'-
    ni an, -an ism, -an ist. cic'e ro,
    a printer's type.
cic e rō'ne (*or* chē chä rō'nä).
cich'lid (sik'-), -loid, -lo mor'phic.
Ci co'gna (chē kōn'yä), It. writer.
cic'o nine (sik'o nīn *or* -nĭn).
cic'u tox'in.
Cid (sid).
cid'a ris, pl. *-res* (rēz).
cī'der, -ap ple, -mill, -press, -tree,
    c. bran'dy, c. vin'e gar.
ci-de vant' (sē'-dĕ vän').
ci e nä'ga (sē- *or* sē ä'na ga).
Ci en fue'gos (sē ĕn'fwä'gōs),   t.
    Cuba.
cierge (syârzh).
Ci e za (thē ä'thä), t. Sp.
ci gar', -bun'dler, -case, -fish,
    -hold'er, -light'er, -ma chine',
    -mäk'er, -plant, -press, -steam'er,
    -store, -tree, -tube.
cĭg'a rette', -fill'er, -ma chine',
    -pa'per, c. bee'tle.
Ci gna ro'li (chēn yä rō'lē),   It.
    painter.
ci'gua te'ra (sē'gwä tä'ra *or* thē-).
cil'i a.
cĭl'i ate, -ly, -a ted, -a ting, -a ry
    (*or* -ya ry) -a'tion.
cil'īce, *-i um,* pl. *-i a, -i el'la,* pl.
    -læ.
Ci li'cian (-lish'-).
ci lic'i um (-lish'i-), *pl.* -lic'i a.

cĭ lif′er ous *or* cil′ĭ if′-, cil′i form,
-i o brā′chi ate (-brā′kĭ- *or*
-brăk′-), -i o flag′el late (-flăj′-),
-i o grade, -i o late, -i o spī′nal,
ci lĭ′o lum, pl. *-la*.
cĭl′lo, *-lo′sis*, -lot′ic.
ci mär rŏn′ (sē-).
cim′bi a, *pl.* -æ, -bi al.
Cim′bri an, -bric.
ci mē′li um, *pl.* -li a.
cĭm′i cĭne, -i cif′u gin (-jin), -i-
coid.
cim′lĭne.
Cim mē′ri an.
cim′o lĭte, ci mo′li an.
cinch.
Ciṇ cho′na (-ko′-), ciṇ′cho nate,
-cho nĭne, -nin′ic, -na′ceous,
-cho′ni a, *-nid′i a*, -chon′a mĭne,
-chon′i cĭne, -i dĭne, -i dī′na,
-chon′ic, -cho nize, -nized, -nī-
zing, -nism, -cho tan′nic, ciṇ cho′-
na-tree.
Cin cin nă′tus, Rom. dictator.
ciṇ′clis, *pl.* -cli des (-dēz), -clid.
ciṇc′ture (sink′-), -tured.
cin′der, -y, -bed, -cone, -fall,
-frame, -notch, -sift′er, -tub,
-wench, -wom′aṇ, -wool, c.
päth, c. pig.
cin′e mat′o graph.
cĭ nē′mo graph.
cin e rā′ri um, pl. *-ri a*.
ci nē′re a, -re al, -re ous, cin e rā′-
ceous, -e rā′tion, -e res′cent, -e ri′-
tious (-rish′-), -e ra ry.
Ciṇ′ga lēse′ (*or* -lēz′) *or* Sin gha-.
ciṇ′gu lar.
ciṇ′gu lum, pl. *-la*, -gu late, -la ted.
cin′na bar, -băr′ic, -bär ĭne, -bar-
green.
cin′na mate, -na mēne, -na mic
(*or* -nam′-), -na mŏ′me ous,
-mom′ic.
cin′na mon, ′-brown, -fern, -oil,
-stone, -su′et, -wa′ter.
cin′no lĭne *or* -lin.
cinq′-trou (sink′-trōō).
cinque (sink), -foil, -pace, Cinque
Ports.
cin que-cen′tist (ching′kwe-chen′-
tist), *-cen′to* (-chen′to), *cin qui′-
no* (ching kwē′nō).

cin quième′ (saṇ kyām′).
Cĭ nū′ra, ci nū′rous.
cĭ o′no crā′ni al, -nor rhā′phi a,
-on′o tome, -o not′o my.
cĭ′pher, -ing, -er, -hood, -phered,
ci′pher-key, -tun′nel, cĭ′pher ing-
-book, -slate.
cip′o lin, *-ol li′no* (-o lē′no).
cip′pus, pl. *-pĭ*.
Cĭ pri a′ni (chē prē ä′nē), It.
painter.
cir car′.
Cir cas′si a (-kash′ĭ a), -sian
(-shan), -sic.
cir cas si enne′.
Cir′ce, -ce′an.
cir cen′sian (-shan), -sial.
cir′ci nal.
Cir′ci nus.
cir′cle, -cled, -cling, -cler, -clet,
cir′cle-cut′ter, -i′ron, -read′ing,
-squar′er.
cir con dä′ri o (chēr-).
cir′cuit (-kĭt), -cu′i tous, -tous ly,
-tous ness, -cu′i ty.
cir′cuit-break′er, -clōs′er, -rĭd′er.
cir′cu lar, -cu lant, -lăr′i ty, -lar-
ize, -ized, -i zing, -ly.
cir′cu late, -la ted, -la tĭng, -la to′-
ry.
cir′cu lā′tion, -coil, -stove.
cir′cu lus, *pl.* -li.
cir cum am′bi ent, -ence, -en cy.
cir cum am′bu late, -la ted, -la-
ting, -la tor, -la′tion.
Cir cum cel′lion (-sel′yun).
cir′cum cen′ter, -cen′tral, -cum-
cir′cle.
cir′cum cise, -cised, -ci ser, -ci-
sing, -ci′ sion (sĭzh′un).
cir′cum cŏne, -con′ic, -cu′bic,
-cres′cent, -cum de nu dā′tion,
-cum duct′, -duc′tion, -duc′to ry,
-cum e so pha′ge al.
cir cum′fer ence, -fer ent, -fer-
en′tial, -tial ly, -en′tor.
cir′cum flect (*or* -flect′), -cum flex,
-flex′ion (-flek′shun) *or* -flec′tion,
-flex′us.
cir cum′flu ence, -ent, -flu ous,
-fo rā′ne an, -ne ous.
cir cum fuse′, -fused, -fūs′ing, -fu′-
sion.

cir cum gy'rate (-jĭ'-), -rā'ted, -rā'-
ting, -ra to'ry, -ra'tion.
cir'cum in ces'sion, -in'su lar.
cir cum jä'cent, -jä'cence, -cen cy,
-jo'vi al, -vi an.
cir cum li'tion (-lish'un), -lit'-
to ral.
cir cum lo cū'tion, -tion al, -tion-
a ry, -loc'u to ry, -cum me rid'-
i an.
cir'cum nav'i gate, -ga ted, -ga-
ting, -ga ble, -ga tor, -ga'tion.
cir cum nu'tate, -nu'ta ted, -ta-
ting, -ta tor y, -ta'tion, -nu'clear, -oc'u lar, -o'ral, -pal'li al,
-par'al lel'o gram, -pen'ta gon.
cir cum pŏ'lar, -pol'y gon, -po si'-
tion, -ra'di us, pl. -ra dĭ ī, -re'-
nal.
cir cum rŏ'tate, -ta ted, -ta ting,
-ta ry, -ta to'ry, -ta'tion, -scis'-
sĭle.
cir cum scribe', -scribed', -scrīb'-
ing, -scrīb'er, -scrīb'a ble,
-scrip'tion, -tive, -tive ly, -sep'-
ted, -so'lar.
cir'cum spect, -ly, -ness, -spec'tion.
cir'cum stance, -stanced, -stan-
cing, -stan'tial, -tial ly, -ti al'i ty
(-shi al'-), -stan'ti ate, ⁚ti a'tion,
-cum tor'sion, -cum trĭ'aŋ gle,
-cum trop'ic al.
cir cum val'late, -la ted, -la ting,
-la'tion.
cir cum vent', -vent'ed, -ing, -ive,
-or, -ven'tion, -cum'vo lant, -vo-
lu'tion.
cir'cus, -ring.
cire per due' (sēr per dü').
cirl-bun'ting.
cirque (serk).
cĭr'rāte, -ra ted.
cĭr rhŏ'sis, -rhŏt'ic, -rhŏn'o sus, -ri-
braŋ'chi ate (-kĭ-).
cĭr ro-cu'mu lus, -strā'tus, -vē'-
lum.
cĭr'ro pŏd or -pōde, -rop'o dous.
cĭr'rōse (-rōs), -ro stom'a tous,
-ros'to mous, -roŭs.
cĭr'rus, pl. -rī, -rus-sac, -sheath.
cir'so cĕle (ser'-), cir'soid, -som'-
pha lös, -soph thal'mi a, -thal'-
my, cir'so tome, -sot'o my.

cis ăl'pĭne, -at lan'tic, -leï'than
(or -tan), -mon'tāne, -o ce an'ic
(-she-), -pā'dāne, -sä hăr'ic.
cis'co.
cise'leur (sēz'ler), -lŭre.
cis'sing.
cis'soid, -soid al (or -soid'-).
cist, -ed.
Cis ter'cian (-shan).
cis'tern, -ba rom'e ter.
cis toph'o rus, pl. -o rī, -to phor'ic,
-to phore.
cis'tu la, pl. -læ, Cis'tu la, Zoöl.
genus.
cit, a citizen; Cit (chit), a Spirit.
cit'a del.
cīte, cīt'ed, -ing, -er, -a ble, cī ta'-
tion.
cith'a ra, -a rist, -ris'tic.
cith'er or -ern or cit'tern.
cit'i grade, -finch.
cit'i zen (-zn), -ry, -ship.
cit'rate, -ra con'ic, -re an, -rene,
-re ous, -ric.
cit'ril, -finch.
cit'rīne, -rin ous, -ri na'tion, cĭ-
trom'e ter.
cit'ron, -ro na'tion, -ro nel'la.
cit'ron-oil, -tree, -wa'ter, -wood,
-yel'low.
cit'rus, -fruits, -tree. Cit'rus, Bot.
genus.
cit'y, pl. -ies, cit'y ful, -ward.
cīve.
civ'et, -cat.
civ'ic, -ics, -i cism.
civ i ere' (-âr').
civ'il, -ist, -ly, cĭ vil'ian, -vil'i ty,
civ'il-suit ed.
civ'i lize, -lized, -lī zer, -li zing,
-lī'za ble, -lī za'tion.
clab'ber, -y.
clach, -an.
clack, -ing, -er, clacked, clack-box,
-dish, -door, -goose, -mill, -piece,
-seat, -valve.
clad.
clag, -gy.
claim, -ing, -a ble, -ant, -er, -less,
claimed, claim'-no'tice.
clâir ạu'di ence, -di ent, -voy'-
ance, -voy'ant, -ob scure'.
claire'-cole.

clam, -ming, -my, -mi ly, -mi ness, clammed, clam'bake, -cod, -crack'-er, -scrăp'er, -shell, -tongs, -worm, clam'ming-ma chine'.
clă'mant (*or* clăm'-), -ly.
clam'ber, -ing, -bered.
clam jam'phrïe *or* -jam'fe ry.
clam'mer, -ming.
clam'or, -ing, -er, -ous, -ous ly, -ous ness, -some, -ored.
clamp, -ing, -er, clamped, clamp'-cell, -con nec'tion, -coŭp'ling, -dog, -i'ron, -kiln, -nail, -screw.
clan, -nish, -nish ly, -nish ness, -ship, clans'man, *pl.* -men.
clan des'tïne, -ly, -ness.
clang, -ing, clanged, clang'-col'or, -tint.
claņ'gor, -ous.
clank, -ing, -less, clanked.
clap, -ping, clapped, clap'match, -trap, -brĕad, -dish, -net, -sill, -stick.
clap'board (klăb'bord), -gäge.
clape.
clap'per, -ing, -pered, -per bill, -claw, -stay, -valve.
clăque (klăk), *cla'queur'* (-kêr').
Clar'chen (klĕr'chen *or* -kyen), Goethe.
clăr'ence, a carriage.
Clăr'en ceux *or* -cieux (-shōō *or* -sū).
clăr'en don, a printer's type.
clăr'et, -cup, -red.
clăr i bel'la, clăr'i chord, -i cym'-bal, clar'i bel-flute.
clăr'i fy (-fï), -ing, -fied, -fi er, -fi-cā'tion.
clar i gā'tion.
cla ri né' (-rē nä').
clăr'i net (*or* -net') *or* -i o net', -net'tïst, clä rin' (-rĕn'), cla ri'-no (-rē'-).
clăr'i on.
Cla risse' (-rēs'), an order of nuns.
clăr'i ty.
clä'ro-ob scu'ro (-skōō'-).
clärt, -y.
clä'ry, -wa'ter.
clash, -ing, -ing ly, clashed.
clâsp, -ing, -er, -ered, clasped, clasp'-hook, -knife, -lock, -nail.

clâss, -a ble *or* -i ble, -ing, -man, -mate, -room, classed, class'-day, -fel'low, -lēad'er, -shoot'ing.
clăs'sic, -al, -al ly, -al ism, -al ist, -al ness, -si cal'i ty, -si cism, -si-cist.
clas'si fy, -ing, -fi'a ble, -fi er, -fied, -fi ca'to ry (*or* -sif'-), -sif'-ic, -si fi cā'tion.
clăs'sis, *pl.* -ses (-sēz).
clas'tic.
clăth'rate, -rose (-rōs), -roid.
clat'ter, -ing, -ing ly, -er, -tered, -ter-goose.
Claude glâss, C. Lor rain' mir'ror.
Clau'di o, Shak., *Measure for Measure.*
Claụ'di us, -di an.
claụse, clau'su lar (-zu-), clause'-rolls.
claus'thal ite.
claụs'tral
claụs tro pho'bi a, -tro pho'bic.
claụs'trum, pl. -tra.
clä'va, pl. -væ, -val, Clä'va, *Zoöl. genus.*
clä'vate, -ly, -va ted, -va'tion, clav'-el late, -la ted.
cla veau' (-vō').
clav'e cin, -cin ist.
clăv'i chord, -i a tur' (-tōōr'), -i a-ture, i ole, -i cyl'in der.
clăv'i cle, *cla vic'u la,* pl. -læ, -u-lar, -u late, -u lus, *pl.* -lï.
clav'i corn, -cor'nate.
clä'vi er (*or* -vĕr'), -er ist.
clav'i form.
clav'i ger, cla vig'er ous (-vij'-).
Cla vi le'no A li ge'ro (klä vē lä'-nyo ä lē hä'rō), a wooden horse.
clä'vis, pl. -ves (-vēz).
clä'vism.
clä'vo.
clăv'o la, pl. -læ, -o let.
clav'u la, pl. -læ, -ule.
clä'vus, pl. -vï.
clâw, -ing, -less, clawed, claw'-back, -ham'mer, a coat; -bạlk, -bar, -foot, -ham'mer, a hammer; -hand, -joint, -sick, -wrench.
clawk'er.
clay, -ey, -ish, -band, -bĕad, -brained, -built, -clot, -cold,

-course, -kiln, -mill, -pit, -pul'-
ver i zer,   -screen'ing,   -stone,
-yel'low, clay'ing-bar.
clay'more.
Clay to'ni a.
clĕach'ing-net.
clead'ing.
clean, -er, -ness, -skins, -cut,
-hand'ed, -limbed, -up.
clean'ing, -hy'drant (-hī'-), -ma-
chine', -valve.
clĕan'ly, *a.*, habitually clean.   -li-
ly, -li ness.
clĕan'ly, *adv.*, in a clean manner.
clĕanse, clĕansed, cleans'er.
clĕans'ing, -days, -round, -square,
-vat, -week.
Cle ante' (klä'änt'), Molière.
clĕar, -age, -ance, -er, -ly, -ness,
-starch, -starch'er, -sto'ry, -weed,
-wing, cleared, clear'-cole, -cut,
-eyed, -head'ed, -head'ed ness,
-melt'ing, -seer, clear'er-bar.
clear'ing, -bat'ter y, -beck, -house,
-nut, -pan, -plough, -ring, -sale,
-screw, -stone.
clĕat.
cleav'age, -cav i ty, -cell, -glob ule,
-mass, -nu'cle us.
clĕave, cleav'er, -a ble, -a bil'i ty,
cleaved *or* cleft.
cleave'land ĭte.
cleav'ing, -knife, -saw
clé'ché' (klä'shä')
cledge, cledg'y.
clee.
clĕf.
cleft, -foot'ed, -grăft, -grăft'ing.
cleī'do man'cy.
clĕik *or* cleek.
cleīs'to carp. See *clistocarp.*
Clé lie' (klä'lĕ'), heroine of an his-
torical romance.
clem.
clem'a tis, a plant.   Clem'a tis,
Bot. genus.
clem'en cy, -ent, -ent ly.
Clem'en tĭne (*or* -tīne).
clench.   See *clinch.*   clench'-bolt,
-nail, -ring.
Cle o mā'che an (-kē-).
Cle o pā'tra, Queen of Egypt.
Cle'o pā'tra's nee'dle, an obelisk.

clep'sy dra (-sĭ-), *pl.* -dras.
clep to ma'ni a. See *kleptomania.*
Clerc (clăre), Fr. hist.
cler'gy, -man.
clĕr'ic, -al, -al ism, -i cal'i ty, -i-
cism.
clĕr'i go.
clĕrk, -ing, -ly, -ship, clerked.
clĕr'o man cy (*or* clĕ'-).
clĕ'ruch (-rōŏk *or* -rŭk), -ru'chi al,
-ru chic (-kik), -ru chy, *pl.* -chies
(-kĭz).
cleuch *or* cleugh (klōōćh *or* klŏŏk).
cleve'īte.
clĕv'er, -ly, -ness.
clĕv'is, *pl.* -is ĕs (-ĕz), *or* clev'y,
pl. ies, clev'is-bolt.
clew *or* clue.
clich (klitch).
cli ché (kle shā').
Cli chy' (klē shē'), t. Fr.
click, -er, -et, -y, clicked, click'-
bee'tle, -pul'ley, -wheel.
clī'do man cy, -mas'toid, -do ster'-
nal.
clī'ent, -age, -ship, cli'en cy, -en'-
tal, -en'te lage, -te la ry, -en tĕle'
(*or* clī'-).
cliff, -brake, -lime'stone, -swal'low.
clift, -ed, -y.
clif'ton īte.
clī'ma.
clī mac'ter, -mac'ter ic (*or* clĭm'-
ac tĕr'ic), -ic al.
clī'mat (klē'mä).
clī'mate, -mat'ic, -ic al, -al ly,
-ma tic'i ty,   -tog'ra phy,   -to-
graph'ic al,   -tol'o gy,   -o gist,
-to log'ic al, -al ly, -tom'e ter,
-ma tize, -tized, -ti zing, -tar'-
chic (-kik).
clī'max, -mac'tic.
climb (klīm), -a ble, -er, climbed.
climb'ing, -fish, -i'rons, -perch,
c. boy, c. fern.
clime.
clĭmp.
clī nā'men, pl. *-nā'mĭ na.*
clī'nant.
clinch *or* clench.   These two terms
are used somewhat synonymously.
In nautical and mechanical uses,
and in colloquial discourse, the

---

former is more generally employed. clinch'er, clinch'ing
clinched, clinch-built, clinch'er-
built, -plāt'ing, -work.

cling, -ing, -fish, -stone, clung.

clin'ic, -al, -al ly, -i cist, cli ni'cian
(-nĭsh'an), -nique (-nēk').

clĭ nid'i um, pl. *-i a.*

clink, -ing, -stone, clinked, clink'-
shell.

clink'er, -bar, -built, -plāt'ing,
clĭnk'um-bell.

clĭ no ceph'a ly, -ce phal'ic, -no-
chlore, -node, -no dĭ ag'o nal, -no-
dōme, -no graph'ic, -no hē'drĭte,
-no hū'mĭte, -noid, -no log'ic,
-nol'o gy, -no met'ric (*or* clĭn-),
-ric al, -nom'e try, clĭ'no-ax'is.

clĭ no m'e ter, -lev'el.

clĭ no pin'a coid, -coid'al, -no-
prism, -no pyr'a mid, -no rhom'-
bic.

clin'quant (klĭn'kant).

clin'ton ĭte, *Clin tŏ'ni a.*

Clī'o (*or* klē'o).

clip, -ping, -per, clipped, clip'-
chair, -can'dle stick, -finch, -hook,
-plate, -pul'ley, -swage, -yoke,
clip'per-built, -ship, -ping-ma-
chine', -shears, -time.

clip'fish *or* clipp-.

clique (klēk), *n.,* clique, *v.,* cli'quish
(klē'kish), -quish ness, -quism.

clis e om'e ter.

clish'ma clash, -ma clā'ver, clish'-
clash.

clĭs'to carp, -car'poŭs, -to gam'ic,
-tog'a mous, -a my, -to gene, -tog'-
e noŭs (-toj'-), -tog'e ny.

cli tel'lum, pl. *-la, -tel'lus,* pl. *-lĭ.*

clĭth rid'i ate.

clĭ'to ris (*or* klĭt-), -to rid'e an, -to-
ri dec'to my, -to rism, -to rī'tis

clit'ter-clat'ter.

clives.

clī'vus, *pl.* -vī.

clŏ ā'ca, pl. *-cas* (-kaz) *or -cæ* (-se),
-a'cal.

cloak, -ing, -room, cloaked,
cloak'-a nem'o ne, -bag, -fern.

clŏam *or* clōme.

clŏck, -bird, -like, -wise, -work,
clocked, -a larm', -bee'tle, -case,

-face, -māk'er, -move'ment, -oil,
-pil'lar, -set'ter, -spring, -star,
-stock'ing, -tow'er, -tŭr'ret,
-watch.

clod, -dish, -dish ness, -dy, -hop-
per, -hop ping, -pate, -pāt'ed,
-poll, -breāk'er, -crush'er, -fish'-
ing.

clŏff *or* clough (klŏf), a rebate.

clog, -ging, -gi ness, -gy, clogged,
clog'head, -weed, -ạl'ma nac,
-bur nish er, -dănce, -dan'cer,
-horn'pipe, -pack.

cloi'son (-zn), -son nage, *-son né*
(-nä' *or* klwä zō na').

clois'ter, -tered, -ter er, -tral, clois'-
ter-garth, c. vault.

clo'nus, -nic'i ty (-nis'-), clon'ic,
-ism (*or* klō'-).

cloop.

cloot, Clōō'tĭe.

Clŏ'quet' (-kā'), Fr. surgeon.

close (klōz), *v.,* closed, clŏs'ing,
-ed ness, clō'sure (-zhur).

close (klōs), *a.,* -ly, -ness, clŏs'er,
-est, clos'er (klŏz'-), *n.,* close'-
fist ed, -hand ed.

close'-band'ed (klōs'-), -bärred,
-bod'ied, -fights, -hug, -pent,
-plane, -point, -quar'ters, bulk-
heads; -sea'son, -stool, -time,
-wing, -work, c. quar'ters, clōs'-
ing-ham'mer, -ma chine'.

clos'et (klŏz'-), -ed, -ing.

closh-hook.

Clos Vou geot' (klŏ vōō zhō').

clot, -ted, -ting, -ty, clot'bur, -weed.

clŏth (*or* klawth), *pl.* clŏths.

cloth'-creas'er, -dress'ing, -dry'-
ing, -fin'ish ing, -fold'ing, hall,
-lap'per, -mĕas'ure, -meas'ur ing,
-pa'per, -plate, -press, -prov'er
(-prōōv-), -shear'er, -shop,
-spon'ger (-spunj'-), -stitch,
-stitch'er, -teaz'ler, -test'er,
-var'nish ing, -wheel, -work'er,
-yard.

clŏthe, clŏthed *or* clad, clŏth'ing,
-ier, clŏthes.

clŏthes'-bȧs'ket, -brush, -dri'er,
-horse, -line, -moth, -pin, -press,
-sprin'kler, -wring'er.

Clŏ'tho. *Myth.*

clo'ture' (-tōōr').
cloud, -ed, -ing, -y, -i ly, -i ness,
-less, -less ly, -let, -land, -ber'ry,
-burst, -scape.
cloud'-bank, -born, -capped, -com-
pel'ler, -drift, -kissed, -rack,
-ring, -topped.
clou é' (klōō ā').
clough (klŏf), a rebate. See *cloff.*
clough (klŭf *or* klou), a sluice,
-arch (klŭf-).
clour (klōōr).
clout, -ed, -ing, -nail, -shoot ing.
clŏve, *v.,* clō'ven (-vn), clo'ven-
ber'ry, -foot'ed, -hoofed.
clove, *n.,* -wort, -bark, -cin'na mon,
-gil'ly flow er, -hitch, -hook, -nut'-
meg, -or'ange, -pink.
clo'ver, -y, -vered, clo'ver-grăss,
-hull'er, -leaf, -sick, -wee'vil (-vl),
clown, -ish, -ish ly, -ish ness, -ist,
-hēal, clown's-mus'tard, -trēa'cle.
cloy, -ing, -less, cloyed.
club, -bing, -ber, -bish, -bist, -fist,
-fist'ed, -foot, -foot'ed, -hand,
-hạul, -house, -man, one who
uses a club; -room, -root, clubbed.
club'-ball, -com'pass es, -grăss,
-law, -man, a member of a
club; -măs'ter, -moss, -pälm,
-rush, -shaped, -skate, -top sail.
clŭck, -ing, -ing-hen, clucked.
clūe. See *clew.*   clue'-gar'net,
-i'ron, -jig'ger, -line, -net.
clum'ber.
clump, -ing, -y, clumps, clump'-
block, -boot.
clum'sy (-zy), -si ly, -si ness, -boots,
-cleat.
clunch, -y.
Clu'ni ac.
clunk.
Clu'ny lace, C. gui gūre' (gē-).
clu'pe id, -pe i form, -pe oid.
clŭ'pe in.
clus'ter, -ing, -ing ly, -ter y, -tered,
-ter-cups, -pine, -spring.
clutch, -ing, clutched, clutch'tail,
-drill, -lamp.
clut'ter, -ing, -ment, -tered.
clyp e as'troid, -e ate, -e i form,
-e o front'al, -e ole, cly pe'o la
(klī-), -o lar, -o late.

clys'mi an (klĭz-), -mic.
clys'ter, -ize, -ized, -i zing, -pipe.
Cly tem nes'tra (klī- *or* klĭt-),
wife of Agamemnon.
Cly'ti e (klī'tĭ e *or* klĭt'- *or* klĭsh'i e),
a sea nymph.
cne'mis (nē-), *pl.* -mi des (-dēz),
-mi al, -ma poph'y sis, -mid'i um,
pl. -i a.
cnī'cĭn (nī'-).
cnic'nŏde (nĭk-), cnic'trŏpe.
Cni'cus (nī'-).
cnī'da (nī'-), pl. -dæ, cnī'do blast,
-do cell, -do cil, -do phore.
Cnī'dus (nī'-), *Bib.*
Cnos'si an (nŏs'-).
coach, -ful, -ing, -let, -bell, -fel'low,
-māk'er, -man, -măs'ter, -whip, a
snake; a pennant; -wood, coached.
coach'-bit, -box, -col'ors, -cŭr'ri er,
-dog, -found'er, -horse, -leaves,
-ŏf'fice, -screw, -stand, -trim'-
mer, -wheel, -whip, coach'whip-
snake.
co act', to compel, -ac'tion, -ac'-
tive, -tive ly.
co-act', to act together, -ac'tive,
-ac tiv'i ty, -ac'tor.
co ad ja'cent, -cence.
co ad just', -ment.
co ad jute', -ju'tive, -ju'tor, -tor-
ship, -ju'tress *or* -trix, -ad'ju tant.
co ad'ju vant, -van cy.
co'ad min'is tra'tor, -tra'trix.
co ad'u nate, -na'tion.
co a'gent, -gen cy.
co ag'u late, -la ted, -la ting, -tive,
-tor, -to ry, -u la ble, -la bil'i ty,
-la'tion, -u lum, *pl.* -la.
co aī'ta.
cŏak.
co'a kum.
cŏal, -ing, -fish, -man, -măs'ter.
cŏal'-back'er, -barge, -ba'sin
(-sn), -bed, -bin, -black, -bŏr'ing,
-box, -brand, -brăss, -breăk'er,
-buṇ'ker, -car, -căr'ri er, -cart,
-chute (-shoot), -cut'ting, -drop,
-dump'ing, -dust, -field, -fit'ter,
-gas, -goose, -hēav'er, -hod,
-hole, -hood, -hulk, -mĕas'ures,
-me'ter, -mine, -min'er, -mouse,
-note, -oil.

---

fāte, făt, fär, fạll, fâre, făst, sofȧ, mēte, mĕt, hêr, īce, ĭn, nōte,

cŏal'-pass'er, -pipe, -pit, -plant, -sack, -screen, -scut'tle, -ship, -slack, -sledge, -smut, -staith, -stone, -stove, -tar, -tit, -tŏngs, -trim'mer, -view'er, -whip'per, -work'ings, -works, coal'y, -hood.

co a lĕsce', -lesced (-lĕst), -les cing, -cence, -cent.

co a li'tion (-lish'un), -er, -ist.

co-al ly'(-lĭ'), *pl.* -lïes'.

cŏam'ings.

co apt', -ap tate, -ap ta'tion, co'-ap ta'tor.

co'arb (*or* -arb') *or* co'marb.

co arc'tate, -ta'tion.

cŏarse, -ly, -ness, -grained.

co ar tic'u la ted, -la'tion.

cŏast, -al, -ed, -er, -ing, -wise, -ward, -wards.

coast'-guärd, -ice, -līne, -pï'lot, -rat, -wäit'er.

cŏat, -ed, -ing, -less, -ar'mor, -but'-ton, -col'lar, -link, -mon'ey, -pock'et, -sleeve, -tail.

coat ee'.

cŏ ä'ti (-tē *or* -ä'tĭ).

coax, -er, -ing, -ing ly, coaxed.

co ax'al *or* -ax'i al, -al ly.

cob, -bing, -by, cobbed, cob'coal, -head, -nut, -stone, -swan, -web, -web'bing, -web'by, -webbed, -worm, -horse, -i'ron, -joe, -loaf, -poke, -stack'er, c. house, c. wall.

cŏ bä'do.

cŏ'balt (*or* -bŏlt), -ine, -ite, -balt'ic (*or* co'-), -ous, -if'er ous, -i cy'a-nĭde, -bal tom'e nite.

cŏ'balt-broom, -brŏnze, -crust, -glänce, -o'chre (-ker), -vit'ri ol, c. blue, c. green, c. yel'low.

cŏ'bang *or* ko-.

co bä'ya.

cob'ble, -bled (-bld) -bling, -bler, -bler y, -bly, -ble stone, -bler-fish.

cŏ be zou'tĭ ant (-zōō'-), -zou'toid.

co'bĭ a, cob'i tid, -i toid.

Cŏ'blenz *or* Kŏ'- (-blents), c. Ger.

cob'ler.

cŏ'bra, -bric, -bri form, co'bra-de-ca pel'lo, -mŏn'il.

Co'bûrg *or* -bourg (-bōörg).

co'ca, -ca ïne, -in ism, -in ïze, -ized, -i zing, -ï za'tion.

Cŏc agne' (-än').

coc'a lon.

co cärde'.

Coc ce'jus *or* -ius (kŏk tsä'yŏŏs), Dutch theol.   -ce'ian (-yan), -ian ism.

coc'ci form, -cif'er ous, -coid, -cid.

coc cin'e an, -e ous, -ci nĭn, -nel'-lid, -nel'lïne, *Coc'ci nel'la.*

coc'co.

coc'co līte, -co lith, -co sphere.

Coc cos'te us.

coc cu lif'er ous.

coc'cus, pl. *-ci,* -cous, -cule.

coc'cy go morph, -mor'phic.

coc'cyx, pl. *-cy'ges* (-sĭ'jēz), -cyg'e al (-sĭj'-), -e us, -ē ï, -i an, -cy gĭne' (-sĭ-), -cy go dyn'i a (-dĭn'-) *or* -cy o dyn'i a.

cŏ'chin.

Cŏ'chin Chī'na, *Geog.*   cŏ'chin-chï'na, a fowl.

coch'i nĕal (*or* -nēl'), c. fig.

co chi'no (-chē'-).

coch'le a, pl. *-le æ* (kŏk'-), -le an, -le ar, -ar'i form, -le'i form, -a-ïy, -ate, -a ted, -le ŏld, -le ous, -ä're, *pl.* -a'ri a.

co ci ne'ra (kŏ thï nä'ra).

cŏ'ci nin, -ci nate, -cin'ic.

cock, -ing, cocked, cock'bill, -boat, -chä'fer, -crow, -crow ing, -eye, -eyed, -gräss -head, -horse, -loft, -mate, -pit, -roach, -rob'in, -spur, -stone, -tail, -up, a fish; -web, -weed.

cock'-ale, -bead, -brässs, -bread, -brŏth, -fĕath'er, -fight, -fight'er, -gar'den, -hedge, -laird, -mäs'ter, -match, -met'al, -nest,- pen'ny, -schnăp'per, -spär'row, -sure, -up, a., -wa'ter, c. lob'ster.

cock'-a-hoop, -and-bull, cocked-hat, cock'ie-leek'ie, cock'ing-main, cock'spur-grass.

cock ade', -äd'ed.

Cock aigne' (-än'), an imaginary country of idleness and luxury.

cock'a ma rŏŏ'.

cock'a teel.

cock'a tŏŏ', -bush, c. fence.

cock'a trice (-trĭs or -trīs).
Cock'burn (kō'burn), Eng. jurist.
cock ee'.
cock'er el.
cock'er megs.
coc'kle, -boat, -brained, -bril lion,
-bur, -gar'den, -hat, -oast, -sauce,
-shell, -stair, -stove, -wife.
cock'ney, -neys (-nĭz), -ney dom,
-ney fy (-fī), -ney ish, -ney ism.
cocks'comb, -grăss, -oys'ter,
cocks'foot-grăss, cocks'head, a
plant.
cock'swain or cox'-.
cock'y ol'ly-bird.
cŏ'coa (-kō) or co'co, -nut, -nut-
crab, -nut-oil, -nut-tree.
cŏ'coa-oil, -plum, -pow'der, -tree.
co co bŏ'lo or -bo'las.
co co-de-mer (-mâr), -wood or
co'cus-.
co coi'.
co cōōn', -er y, -ing, coc'u lon.
co'co rīte.
coc'tĭle, -tĭve.
co cui'sa or -za (-kwē'sa)
co'cum-but'ter, -oil.
cŏ cyt'i nid, -i noid.
cod, -ded, -ding, -der, cod-fish'er,
-fish'er y, -glove, -line, -liv'er,
-piece, -pole, -sound, -worm.
cŏ'da, co det'ta.
cod'dle, -dled, -dling.
cod'dy, -mod'dy.
cŏde.
co'dex, pl. cod'i ces (-sēz), cod'i cal.
cod'fish, c. ball, c. cake.
cod'ger.
cod'i cil, -i cil'la ry.
cod'i fy, -fied, -fi er, -fy ing, -fĭ ca'-
tion.
co dil'la.
co dĭlle'.
cod'ling, -moth.
cod'lins-and-cream.
cŏ'do.
cŏ'don.
co do nos'to ma, pl. -mas.
cŏ ef fi'cient (-fĭsh'-), -ly, -cien cy.
coe'horn.
coel'a canth (sĕl'- or sē'-).
cœ lā'ri um (sē-), pl. -ri a.
Cœ'lebs (sē'-), hero of Hannah

More's novel, Cælebs in Search of
a Wife. cœ'lebs.
Cœ'lel mĭn'tha (sē'lel- or sĕl'el-) or
-min'thes (-thēz), cœ'lel minth,
-min'thic.
Cœ len'te ra (sē-), -te ron.
co el'ho (-āl'yo).
cœ'li a (sē'-), pl. -li æ, -li ac, -li an.
cœ li ag'ra (sē-), -li al'gi a.
cœ'li ot'o my.
cœ lo blas'tu la (sē- or sĕl-), -lo gas'-
tru la.
cœ'lo dŏnt (sē'-).
cœ lo neū'ral (sē-), -lo-nav'i gā'-
tion.
cœ lo plan'u la (or sĕl- or -pla nu'-
la), -no gen'e sis (or sĕn'o-), -no
ge net'ic, -no sīte (or sĕn'o-)
cœ ru'le in.
cœ'lo sperm, -sper'mous (or sel-).
cœ'lum (sē'-), pl. -la.
cœ lū'rid (sē-).
co en'doo or -dou (-dōō).
cœn es thē'sis (sĕn-), -thē'si a.
cœn'o bīte (or sē'-).
cœ nŏ'bi um, pl. -bi a.
cœ'no blast (sē'-), -blas'tic.
cœ nog'a my.
cœ nos'te um, -te al.
cœ'no type (sē'-), -typ'ic.
cœ'nure, -nu'rus.
co e'qual, -qual ly, -qual ness,
-qual'i ty (-kwŏl'-).
co erce', -erced, -er'cing, -cion,
-ci ble, -ble ness -cive, -cive ly,
-cive ness.
cœr'e bīne (sĕr'-).
co'es sen'tial, -ly, -ti al'ĭ ty.
co e ter'nal, -ly.
cœur (kêr).
Cœur de Li on' (kōōr dĕ lē on'
or kûr dĕ li'on), Richard I of
England.
cŏ ē'val.
co ex ist' (-eg zist'), -ence, -ent,
-ing.
co ex ten'sive, -sive ly, -sive ness,
-ten'sion.
cŏ-feoff'ee (-fĕf'-).
cŏf'fee, -bean, -ber ry, -big'gin,
-blight, -bor'er, -bug, -clean'er,
-corn, -cup, -grīnd'ing, -house,
-hull'er, -māk'ing, -man, -mill,

-nib, -nut, -pol'ish er, -pot,
-pulp'er, -roast'er, -room, -sage,
-shop, -stand, -tree.

cof'fer, -ing, -fer work, -dam,
-fish.

cŏf'fin, -less, cof'fin-boat, -bone,
-căr'ri er, -fish.

cŏf'fle.

cof'fre-fort (-fr-), cof'fret.

cog, -ging, -ger, cogged, cog'ware,
-wood, -bells, -rail, -wheel.

cŏ'gent, -ly, -gen cy.

cog'ger.

cog'gle, -gled, -gling, -gle dy, -gly.

cog'i tate (kŏj'-), -ta ted, -ta ting,
-ta ble, -ta bil'i ty, -ta bun'di ty,
-ta tive, -tive ly, -tiv'i ty, -tā'tion.

cog'i to er'go sum (kŏj'-).

Co'gnac' (kōn'yäk'), t. Fr., C. pot'-
ter y. cō'gnac (kōn'yäk).

cog'nate, -ness, *-nā'lī*, -na'tion,
-nat'ic.

cog'ni tum, pl. *-ni ta*, -ni tive, -ni'-
tion (-nish'un).

cog'nize, -nized, -ni zing, -ni za-
ble, -za bly, -zance, -zant, -zee',
-zor'.

cog nŏ'men, -nom'i nal, -i nate,
-na ted, -ting, -i ne, -na'tion.

cog nosce' (-nŏs'), -nosced (-nŏst')
-nos cing, -nos cence, -ci ble,
-ci bil'i ty, -no'vit, *-nos cen'te*, pl.
-ti.

cŏ gŏn', *-go näl'*, pl. *-nä'les* (-läs).

co gre'di ent.

co hab'it, -ed, -ing, -ant, -an cy,
-i ta'tion.

co heir' (-air'), -ess, -ship.

co here', -hered', -hēr'ing, -hēr'er,
-ence, -cn cy, -ent, -ent ly.

cŏ hē'sion (-zhun), -sive, -sive ly,
-sive ness.

co'hŏ bate, -ba ted, -ting, -tor,
-ba'tion.

Co hoes' (kō hōz'), c. N. Y.

cŏ hōes', a salmon.

co'hog.

co'hort.

co hort'a tive.

co'hŏsh (*or* -hosh').

co hune' (-hōōn').

coif, -fure, *-jeur'* (kwŏf'fēr'), coifed,
coif fette' (kwŏf fet').

coiffe'-de-jer (kwŏf'-dê-fĕr), *-de-*
mailles' (-mäl').

coign *or* coigne (koin), coign'y.

coil, -ing, coiled, coil'-plate.

Cŏ'i la, dist. Scot.

coin, -a ble, -age, -ing, -er, -less,
coined, coin'-as sort'er, -bal'-
ance, -count'er, -sil'ver, -weigh'-
ing, coin'ing-press.

cŏ in cide', -cīd'ing, -ed, -er, -in'-
ci dence, -den cy, -dent, -dent ly,
-den'tal, -tal ly.

cŏ in'di cant, -di ca'tion.

cŏ in hēre', -hcred', -hēr'ing,
-hĕr'i tance, -i tor.

cŏ in sure', -sured, -sūr'ing.

cŏ in verse'.

coir *or* coire (koir *or* kīr).

co i'tion (-ish'un).

cō'i tus.

cŏke, -băr'row, -fur'nace, -māk'-
ing, -om'ni bus, -ov'en, -tow'er,
cōk'ing-kiln, -ov'en.

cŏl, a mountain pass.

cŏ'la, -nut, -seed. *Co'la*, Bot.
genus.

col'an der (kŭl'-) *or* cul'len der,
-shov'el.

col är'co.

Cŏl'burn, Amer. math.

col can'non.

col'chi cĭn (-kĭ *or* -chĭ-) *or* -cine
(-sĭn *or* -sēn).

Col'chi cum (-kĭ- *or* -chĭ-), *Bot.
genus.*

Cŏl'chis (-kĭs), prov. Russ.

cŏl'col.

col'co thar.

cŏld, -ly, -ness, -blood'ed, -drawn,
-chis'el, -cream, -ham'mer,
-kind, -mov'ing, -pale, -sheet,
-short, -shot, -sore, -stōk'ing,
-swĕat'ing, -tank'ard, -tin'ning.

cole, -mouse, -perch, -wort, -rape,
-seed, -slaw, -tit.

co lec'to my.

cŏl'e ŏ phyl, -phyl'lous.

Cŏ'le op'te ra (*or* col'-), cŏ'le op'-
ter, -op'ter al, -ter an, -ter ous,
-ter ist, -tĭle, *-le o rhī'za*, -le pid.

cōle'pix y.

co-les see', -les sor'.

Co'le us.

---

nŏt, nôr, ūse, ŭp, ûrn, etüde, fōōd, fŏŏt, aŋger, boṅmot, thus, Baċh.

15

Cŏl'fax, V. Pres., U. S.
co li'bri (-lĕ'brē *or* kŏl'ĭ brĭ).
cŏl'ic, -al, -ick y, -wort, -ic-root.
cŏl'ie. See *coly*.
cŏl'i form.
Co li gny *or* -gni, de (dĕ kŏ'lĕn'yē'
or -lēn'-), Fr. admiral.
cŏl'in.
col in'de ry, *pl.* -ries.
col'i o mor'phic.
Col i sē'um. See *Colosseum*.
co lĭ'tis.
col lab'o rate, -ra ted, -ting, -tor,
-ra teur' (-ter'), -ra'tion.
col'la gen (-jen), -lag'e nous (-lăj'-).
See *collogen*.
col lăpse', -lapsed, -laps ing, -laps'-
i ble *or* -a ble.
col'lar, -age, -ing, -bags, -lared,
-lar et *or* -ette'.
col'lar-awl, -bēam, -bird, -block,
-bōlt, -bone, -box, -but'ton,
-cell, -check, -har'ness, -läun'-
der, -nail, -plate, -swage, -tool,
-work.
col'lards.
col lă'rē, *pl.* -ri a.
col late', -lāt'ed, -ing, -a ble, -lā'-
tion, -tive, -tor.
col lat'er al, -al ly, -al ness.
col'lēague, -ship.
col lect', -ed, -ed ly, -ed ness, -a ble
or -i ble, -ive, -ive ly, -ive ness,
-or, -or ate, -or ship, -lec'tion,
-tion al.
col lect'ing, -bot'tle, -cane, -net,
col lect'or mag'is trate.
col lect'iv ism, -ist, -lec tiv'i ty.
col'leen (*or* -lēn').
col'lēge, -leg er, -lē'gi al, -al ism,
-gi an, -gi ate, *-gi um*, pl. *-gi a*.
Col le'gi ant.
col le'gno (cŏl lā'nyo).
Col lem'bo la, col'lem bōle, -bŏl'ic,
-lem'bo loŭs.
col lē'me ĭne, -le'moid.
col len'chy ma (-kĭ-), -chym'a tous
(-kĭm'-), -len'chyme (-kĭm).
col'len cyte (-sīte), -cy'tal (-sī'-).
col'ler y-stick.
col'let.
col le tē'ri um, pl. *-ri a*, -ri al, -lĕ'-
ter, -let'ic, -le to cys'to phore.

col'let in.
col lide', -lĭd'ed -ing, -li'sion
(-lĭzh'un), -li'sion al, -lĭ'sive.
cŏl'li dĭne.
col'lĭe, a dog, -shang'ĭe, -brand.
col'lier (-yer), -y, *pl.* -ies, -a'phis.
cŏl'li form.
col'li gate, -ga ted, -ga ting, -gā'-
tion.
col li loŋ'gus, *pl.* -gi (-jĭ).
col'li mate, -ma ted, -ma ting, -ma-
tor, -ma'tion.
col'lin.
col lin'e ate, -e ar, -e ā'tion.
col lin'ic.
col'li quate, -qua ted, -qua ting,
-qua'tion, -liq'ua ble (-lĭk'wa-),
-ua tive, -tive ness, -ue fac'tion.
col'lish.
col'lo cate, -ca ted, -ca ting, -ca'-
tion.
col lō'di on, -ize, -ized, -i zing,
-di o type, -di um.
col'lo gen (-jen) *or* -la-, -lo gen'ic,
-log'e nous (-loj'-).
col'lo grăph, -graph'ic, -log'ra phy.
col'loid, -loid'al, -loi dal'i ty.
col'lop.
col'lo phore.
col lo'qui al, -al ism, -al ize, -ized,
-i zing, -lo quist, -lo quy, *pl.*
-quies, *-lo'qui um*, pl. *-qui a*.
col'lo type (-tīpe).
col lude', -lūd'ed, -ing, -er.
col'lum, pl. *-la*.
col lŭ'sion (-zhun), -lu'sĭve, -sive-
ly, -sive ness, -so ry.
col'lu to ry, -tō'ri um, *pl.* -ri a.
col lŭ'vi al.
col'ly bos, *pl.* -ba.
col'ly bus, *pl.* -bĭ.
col lyr'i um, *pl.* -ums *or* -i a.
col'mar.
co lŏ'bi on, -bi um, pl. *-bi a*.
col o bō'ma, pl. *-ma ta*.
col o ceph'a loŭs.
col o cō'lo.
col'o cynth, -cyn'thē in, -thin, -thi-
tin.
Cŏ lo'gna (kō lōn'yä), t. It.
Cŏ logne' (-lōn'), t. Ger., C. earth,
C. glue, C. ware, co logne'.
col'o līte.

co lom'bin.
co lom'e try.
cŏ'lon, a mark of punctuation.
co lon', a coin. Co'lon, t. Panama.
co lŏ'nate.
colo'nel (kur'nl), -cy, -ship.
co lŏ'ni al, -ize, -ized, -i zing, -al-
ly, -al ism, col'o nist, -o nize,
-nized, -ni zing, -ni zer, -o nĭ-
za'tion, -tion ist, -o ny, *pl.* -nies,
co lo'ni al goose'.
col o nĭ'tis.
col on nade'.
co lŏnne', col on nette'.
co lŏ'nus, *pl.* -nī.
col'o phon, -pho'ni an.
col'o phŏ'ny (*or* ko lŏf'-), -o-
phon'ic.
col'or (kŭl'-), -a ble, -ble ness,
-a bly, -ant, -ing, -ine, -ist, -less,
-less ness, -a ture, -a'tion, -if'ic,
-im'e ter, -e try, -I met'ric, -or-
man, -ored.
col'or-bear'er, -blind, -blind'ness,
-box, -chart, -cir'cle, -com bi-
nā'tion, -com'pa ra tor, -cône,
-con'trast, -cyl'in der, -di'a-
gram, -doc'tor, -e qua'tion,
-guard, -lake, -line, -par'ty,
-print'ing, -re ac'tion, -sen sa'-
tion, -sense, -ser'geant (-sär'-
jent), -strīk'er, -trī'an gle, -va ri-
a'tion, -va ri'e ty, col'or ing-
mat'ter.
Col'o rä'do, state and r. U. S.;
co. and t. Tex. C. bee'tle, C.
group, col o rä'do īte.
cŏ lŏs'sal.
Co lŏs'se *or* -sæ, *Bib.*
Col os sē'um *or* Col'i se'um.
Co los'sian (-los'yan), pertaining
to Colossæ.
Co lŏs'sĭ ans (*or* -lŏsh'i anz *or*
-lŏsh'anz), a book of the Bible.
co los'sus, *pl.* -sī *or* -sus es, -sus-
wise.
co los'trum, -los'trŏŭs, -los'tric, col-
os tra'tion.
co lot'o my.
col pen'chy ma (-kĭ-).
col peû ryn'ter.
col pī'tis.

col'por'tage, -por ter *or* -teur.
Colqu houn' (kŏ hōōn'), Brit. explorer.
col'rake.
cŏlt, -ish, -ish ly, -ish ness, -ale,
-e'vil, -like, -pix'y, colts'foot,
a plant; colt's-tail, a plant; colt's
tooth.
cŏl'ter *or* coul'ter, -neb.
Col'u ber, col'u brĭd *or* -brĭde, -u-
brīne, -broid, co lū'bri form.
col'u bris.
co lum'ba, *Co lum'ba,* pl. -bæ,
Ornith. genus, col um ba'ceous,
-bā'ri um, pl. -ri a, -ba ry, co-
lum'bid, -boid.
co lum'bate.
Col um bel'la.
Co lum'bi a, -bi an.
co lum'bi ad.
co lum'bi er.
co lum'bĭn.
col'um bīne.
co lum'bi um.
col'u mel, -mel'la, *pl.* -mel'læ,
-lar, -li form.
col'umn (-um), co lum'nar, -na-
ted, -ni a'tion, -nu la, *pl.* -læ,
col'um nâr'i ty, -umned (-ŭmd),
-um nif'er ous, col' umn-lathe,
-rule, -skulls.
co lūre', *pl.* -lūres'.
cŏl'y (*or* cō'-) *or* col'ie, a bird; *pl.*
col'ies.
co lym'bi on.
cŏl'za, -oil.
cō'ma, -mal, -mate, -ma tōse (-tōs),
-toŭs.
Co man'che (*or* -chä), *pl.* -ches
(-chĕz *or* -chäz).
cō'marb, -ship. See *coarb.*
Co mat'u la, co mat'u lid.
cŏmb (kōm), -er, -ing, -less,
combed, comb'-bear'er, -brōach,
-brush, -cap, -cut'ter, -frame,
-hon'ey, -jel'ly, -pa'per, -pot,
-rat, -saw, -ing-ma chine'.
cŏm'bat (*or* kŭm-), -ant, -er, -ive,
-ive ness, -a ble (*or* -bat'-).
com'bat'tant' (kŏn bä tän').
Combe (kōōm *or* kōm), Scot.
physiol.
Combes (kŏnb), Fr. writer.

com bīne', -bined, -bīn'ed ly,
-bīn'er, -bīn'ing, -bīn'a ble, -ble-
ness, -bǐ na'tion, -bī'nant (*or*
kom'-), -bīn'a tive, -a to ry, -a-
to'ri al.

com bus'ti ble, -ble ness, -tive,
-tion (-chun), -ti bil'i ty.

come (kum), -at-a ble, -at-a bil'i ty,
-down, -ŏff, com'er, com'ing,
-floor, -in.

cŏm'e dy, *pl.* -dies, co me'di an,
-*mé di enne'* (kō mā'dǐ ĕn'), *cō-
mĕ'dǐ ĕt'ta.*

come'ly (kum'-), -li ness.

cŏ mĕn'ic.

co meph'o rid.

co'mes (-mēz), pl. com'i tes (-tēz).

co mes'ti ble.

com'et, -e ta ry, -e tā'ri um, pl.
-ri a, -et og'ra phy, -ra pher,
-ol'o gy, co met'ic, com'et-find'-
er, -seek'er.

com'fit (kum'-), -fi ture.

com'fort (kum'-), -ed, -ing, -er,
-a ble, -ble ness, -bly, -less, -less-
ly, -less ness.

com'frey (kum'fry).

com'ic, -ic al, -al ly, -al ness, -i cal'-
i ty, -ique' (-ēk').

co mi'da (kō mē'da).

com i tā'li a.

com i tā'tus.

co mǐ'ti um (-mǐsh'i-), pl. -ti a, -mi'-
tial (-mish'al).

cō'mi ti'va (-mē tē'-).

com'i ty.

cŏm'ma, *pl.* -mas (-mäz), -mat'ic,
-ic al, -ma tism, -ma-tipped.

com mând', -ed, -ing, -ing ly,
-a ble, -er ship, -er y, -ment,
-mǎn dänt', -mǎn'do.

com mând'er, -in-chief, -man-
deer'.

com mas'see.

comme il faut (kŏm ēl fō).

com mem'o rate, -ra ted, -ting,
-ble, -tive, -tor, -to ry, -ra'tion.

com mence', -ment, -menced',
-men'cing.

com mend', -ed, -ing, -a ble, -ble-
ness, -a bly, -a tor, -to ry, -men-
da'tion.

com men'dam.

com men'sal, -sal ism, -sal'i ty.

com men'su rate, -ly, -ness, -ra-
ted, -ting, -ble, -bly, -bil'i ty,
-ra'tion.

com'ment, *n.* com'ment (*or*
-ment'), *v.*, -ed, -ing, -er *or* -or,
-ment'a tive, -men ta'tion.

com'men ta'tor, -ship, -ta to'ri al.

com'merce, -mer'cial, -cial ism,
-cial ly.

com mi na'tion, -min'a to ry.

com min'gle, -gled, -gling.

com'mi nute, -nu ted, -nu ting,
-nu'tion.

com'mis' (kō mē').

com mis'er ate (-miz'-), -a ted,
-a ting, -a tive, -a tor, -a ble,
-a'tion.

com'mis sa ry, -ship, -sa'ri at,
-ri al, com'mis sa ry-court, -gen'-
er al, -ser'geant (-sär'jent).

com mis'sion (-mǐsh'un), -er, -er-
ship, -sioned, -sion ing, -sion al,
-a ry, -aire', -ship, c. a'gent, c.
mer'chant.

com'mis sure (-shoor *or* -mǐsh'-),
-su'ra, pl. -ræ, -mis'su ral
(-mish'-).

com mit', -ted, -ting, -tal, -ta ble,
-ter, -tor, -ment.

com mit'tee, -man, -room.

com mix', -mixed, -mix'ing, -mix'-
tion (-chun), -ture.

com'mo dā'tum, pl. -ta.

com mode'.

com mŏ'di ous, -ous ly, -ous ness.

com mod'i ty.

com'mo dore.

Com'mo dus, Rom. Emperor.

com'mon, -age, -a ble, -al ty, -er,
-ish, -ly, -ness, -place, -place-
ness, -weal, -wealth, com'mons,
-mon-sense, *a.*, -mon place-book.

com'mo rant, -rance, -ran cy.

cŏm'mos, *pl.* -moi.

com mo'tion.

com'mu nal, -ism, -ist, -is'tic.

com'mune, *n.*, -mu nard, -mu-
ner, *com mū'ne bŏ'num.*

com mune', *v.*, -muned', -mūn'-
ing, -mun'er.

com mu'ni cate, -cant, -ca ble,
-ble ness, -ca bly, -ca tive, -tive ly,

-tive ness, -ca tor, -to ry, -ca ted,
-ting, -can'tes (-tēz).
com mu ni ca'tion, -plate, -valve.
com mu'ni o.
com mūn'ion, -cloth, -cup, -rail,
-ta'ble.
com'mu nism, -nist, -nis'tic, -tic
al ly.
com mu'ni ty, -ni ta'ri an.
com mu ta'tion, c. tick'et.
com mute', -mūt'ed, -mūt'ing,
-mūt'er, -mūt'a ble, -ble ness,
-mūt a bil'i ty, com'mu tate, -ta
ted, -ta ting.
cŏ'moid.
Cŏ'mon fort, Pres. Mexico.
cŏ'mose (-mŏs), -moŭs.
cŏm pä'chŏ.
com'pact, *n.,* -pact', *a.* and *v.,*
-ed, -ed ly, -ed ness, -er, -i ble,
-ly, -ness.
com pāge', -pā'ges (-jez).
Cŏm pa gno'ni (-pan yō'nē), It.
auth.
cŏm pan'ion, -a ble, -ble ness,
-a bly, -less, -ship, -way, -lad'der.
com'pa ny (kŭm'-).
cŏm pare', -pared', -pâr'ing, -pâr'
er, -pa ra ble, -ble ness, -pa rate,
-pâr'a tive, -tive ly, -pa ra tor
(*or* -pâr'-), -pâr'i son.
com part'ment, *-par ti men'to.*
com'pass (kŭm'-), -passed, -pass
ing, -a ble, -less.
com'pass-bar (kŭm'-), -board,
-bowl, -box, -brick, -card, -dī'-
al, -hĕad'ed, -joint, -nee'dle,
-plane, -plant, -saw, -sig'nal,
-tim'ber, -win'dow, c. rŏŏf.
cŏm pas'sion (-pash'un), -ate,
-a ted, -a ting, -ate ly, -ate ness.
cŏm pat'i ble, -ble ness, -bly,
-bil'i ty.
cŏm pā'tri ot, -ot ism.
cŏm pĕar', to appear in court; -er,
-ance.
com peer', an equal.
com pel', -ling, -ling ly, -ler, -la
bly, -la to ry, -pelled'.
com pel'la tive, -pel la'tion.
cŏm'pend, -pen'di oŭs, -ous ly,
-ous ness, -di um.
com'pen sate (*or* -pen'-), -pen'sa-

tive, -tive ness, -sa to ry, com'-
pen sa tor.
com pen sä'tion, c. bal'ance, c.
bars, c. pen'du lum.
com pēte', -pēt'ed, -pēt'ing, -pĕt'-
i tive, -i tor, -to ry, -pe ti'tion
(-tish un).
cŏm'pe tent, -ly, -tence, -ten cy.
com'pe ten'tes (-tēz).
com pile', -pīled, -pīl'ing, -pīl'er,
-pĭ lā'tion.
cŏm pi tā'li a.
cŏm plā'cent, -cence, -cen cy,
-cent ly.
cŏm plāin', -er, -ing, -ing ly,
-plained', -plaint'.
cŏm'plai sance (-plā zăns *or*
-zăns), -sant, -sant ly, -sant ness,
com pla nä'tion.
cŏm'ple ment, -men'tal, -men'-
ta ry.
com plete', -ly, -ness, -plēt'ed,
-ed ness, -ing, -ple'tive, -plē'tion,
-ple to'ri um, pl. -ri a.
com'plex, -ly, -ness, -plex'i ty,
-plex'us.
com plex'ion (-plĕk'shun), -ist,
-al, -ioned.
com pli'ance, -an cy, -ant, -ant ly.
com'plĭ cate, -ly, -ness, -cà cy,
-cà tive, -cant, -cā'tion.
com plic'i ty (-plĭs'-).
cŏm'plĭ mĕnt, -ed, -ing, -er, -men'-
ta ry, -ta ri ly.
com'plin *or* -plĭne.
cŏm'plot, *n.,* -plot', *v.,* -ted, -ting,
-ting ly, -ter, -ment.
com plu'vi um, pl. *-vi a.*
com pō'nĕ, -pōned'.
cŏm pō'nent, -nen cy, -nen'tal.
cŏm port', -ed, -ing, -a ble, -ment.
com pose', -posed, -pōs'ed ly, -ed
ness, -er, -pŏs'i tive, -i tor,
-pō sĭ'tion (-zish'-), -pō'sure.
com pŏs'ing, -frame, -ma chine',
-room, -rule, -stand, -stick.
Com pos'i tæ.
com pos'Ite, -i tous.
cŏm'pos men'tis.
cŏm'pŏst.
cŏm'pōte, com po ti er' (-pō te ā').
com'pound, *n.* and *a.,* -pound',
v., -ed, -ing, -er, -a ble.

comprador 230 concitato

cŏm prä dōr'.

com pre hend', -ed, -ing, -er, i ble, -hen'si ble, -ble ness, -bly, -bil'- i ty, -hen'sive, -sive ly, -sive- ness, -hen'sion.

cŏm'press, *n.*, -press', *v.*, -ing, -ive, -i ble, -ble ness, -i bil'i ty, -or, -pres'sure, -sion, -pressed', com pres' sion -cǎst' ing, -cock, -ma chine'.

com prīse', -prised', -prīs'ing.

cŏm'prŏ mise, -mised, -mī sing, -mī ser, c. wheel.

compt'o graph (kount'o-), cŏmp- tom'e ter.

comp trŏl'ler (kŏm-), -gen'er al. See *controller.*

com pul'sion, -sive, -sive ly, -ness.

com pul'so ry, -so ri ly, -ri ness.

com puṇc'tion, -less, -tious, -tious- ly.

com'pur ga tor, -to'ri al, -ga'tion.

cŏm pūte', -pūt'ed, -pūt'ing, -pūt'- er, -a ble, -a bil'i ty, -pu ta'tion, -ta'tion al.

cŏm'rǎde (*or* -rǎd *or* kŭm'rǎd *or* -rǎd), -ship.

comte (kôṅt), the French title for Count.

Comte (kôṅt), Fr. philos. Com'ti- an (kŏm'ti an *or* kôṅ'-), Comt'- ism (kŏmt'izm *or* kôṅt'-), -ist.

Cŏ'mus.

cŏn, -ning, -ner, conned, con'ning- tow er.

cŏn ǎj fĕt'tō, con ä mō're, con bri'o (brē'-).

con am'a rin.

cō nā'ri um, pl. *-ri a,* -ri al.

co na'tion, *-nā'tus,* co'na tive.

cŏn ax'i al.

con cam'er ate, -ā' ted, -ā' ting, -a'tion.

con cat'e nate, -nā' ted, -nā' ting, -na'tion.

con cǎu les'cence, -les'cent.

coṇ'cave (*or* kon-), -ly, -ness, -cav'i ty, -ca va'tion.

con cǎ'vo-con'cave, -con'vex.

con cĕal', -ed ly, -ed ness, -er, -ing, -ment, -a ble, -cealed.

con cede', -cēd'ed, -ed ly, -er, -cēd'- ing.

con cĕit', -ed, -ed ly, -ed ness.

con cĕive', -ceiv'a ble, -ble ness, -a bly, -er, -ing, -a bil'i ty.

con cen'ter *or* -tre, -tered *or* -tred, -ter ing *or* -tring.

con cen'trate (*or* con'-), -tra ted, -tra ting, -tra tive, -tive ness, -tra'tion, con'cen trā'to.

con cen'tric, -al, -al ly, -tric'i ty.

con cen'tus.

con'cept, -ism.

con cep'ta cle, -tac'u lum, *pl.* -u la, -u lar.

con cep'tion, -ist, -al, -al ist, -cep'tive, -tu al, -al ism, -al ist, -is'tic.

con cern', -ed ly, -ed ness, -ing, -ment, -cerned'.

con'cert, *n.*, -cert', *v.*, -ed, -ed ly, -mǎs'ter, c. grand, c. mū'sic, c. piece, c. pitch.

con cer tän'te (-chär-).

con cer ti'na (-tē'-), *-cer ti'no* (*or* -chär tē'-).

con cer'to (*or* -chär'-), *pl.* -tos (tōz).

con ces'sion, -ist, -ces sive, -sive ly, -so ry.

con cet'to (*or* -chät'-), pl. *-cet'ti.*

conch (kŏnk), *coṇ'cha* (kŏṇ'ka), pl. *-chæ,* -chal (-kal), -chate (-kāt), -chǐt'ic, -choid, -choid'al, coṇch'-shell.

Con chif'e ra (-kǐf'-), coṇ'chi fer (-kǐ-), -chif'er ous, -chi form.

coṇ chin'a mǐne (-kin'-), coṇ'chi- nǐne.

Cŏn'chŏ, r. Tex., coṇ'cho-grǎss.

con chol'o gy (-kol'-), -o gist, -chom'e ter, -e try, -cho spī'ral.

coṇ'chus (-kus), pl. *-chi* (-kī), -chy- la'ceous *or* -chyl i a'ceous, -chyl'- i a ted, -chy lif'er ous, -chyl'- iom'e ter, -e try, -i o mor'phite, -chyl'i ous, *-i um,* pl. *-i a.*

con'cierge (kôṅ'syârzh'), *-cierge'riē.*

con cil'i ate, -a ted, -a ting, -a ble, -a tive, -a tor, -to ry, -a'tion.

con cil'i um, *pl.* -i a, -i ar, -a ry.

con cin'ni ty.

con cīse', -ly, -ness, -cis'ion (-sizh'- un).

con ci ta'to (-chē tä'-).

fāte, fǎt, fär, fᶏll, fâre, fᶏst, sofᶏ, mēte, mĕt, hêr, īce, ǐn, nōte,

con'clave (*or* kon'-), -cla vist.
con clude', -clūd'ed, -clūd'ing, -er,
 -i ble, -clū'sive, -sive ly, -sive-
 ness, -sion (-zhun).
con coct', -ed, -ing, -er, -ive, -coc'-
 tion.
con col'or (-kŭl'-), -or ate, -or ous.
con com'i tant, -tant ly, -tance,
 -tan cy.
con'cord, -cord'an cy, -ant, -ant-
 ly, -ist, -cor'dat.
con cor'po rate, -ra'tion.
con cos'tate.
con cours' (kôn'kōōr').
con'course.
con crĕsce', -cresced', -cres'cing,
 -cres'cence, -cres'ci ble.
con'crete, *n*., con'crete (*or* kon'-
 or -krēt'), *a*., con crete', *v*., -ly,
 -ness, -crēt'ed, -crēt'ing, -cre'-
 tion, -tion al, -a ry, -tive, -tive-
 ly, -tor, con'crete-press.
con'cu bīne, -cu'bi nage, -bi nal,
 -bi na ry, -na'ri an.
con'cu la, *pl*. -læ.
con cu'pis cence, -cent, -ci ble,
 -ble ness.
con cur', -curred', -cur'ring, -rence,
 -ren cy, -rent, -rent ly, -ness,
con cur'so.
con cuss', -cus'sive, -sion, -sion-
 fuse.
con cu'ti ent (-shĭ-).
con cyc'lic (-sĭk'-).
Con dé', dĕ (dĕ kôn'dā'), Fr.
 prince.
con del i ca tez'za (dä lē kä tĕt'sa),
 con de li'ri o (dä lē'rē o).
con demn', -demned', -dem'ning
 (*or* -dem'ing), -dem'na ble, -na-
 to ry, -ned ly, -ner (*or* -dem'er),
 -na'tion.
con dense', -densed', -dens'ing,
 -er, -er y, -den'sa ble, -sa bil'i ty,
 -sate, -sa tive, -sa'tion, -dens'er-
 gāge, -ing-coil.
con de scend', -ed, -ing, -ing ly,
 -ence, -scen'sion.
con dic'tion.
con dign' (-dīn'), -ly, -dĭg'ni ty.
con'di ment, -men'tal.
con di'tion (-dish'un), -al, -al ly,
 -al'i ty, -ate, -dĭ'tioned, -dĭ ti o-

nā'tum, -tion ing-house, con di'-
 ti o sĭ'nē quä non (kon dish'i o).
con dōl'.
con dole', -doled', -dōl'er, -ing,
 -do'la to ry, -do'lence.
con do min'i um, -dom'i nate.
con dōne', -doned', -dōn'ing, -do-
 na'tion.
con'dor.
con'dot tie're (-tyä'rā).
con duce', -duced', -dū'cing, -ci-
 ble, -ble ness, -bil'i ty, -cive,
 -cive ness.
con'duct, *n*., -duct', *v*., -ed, -ing,
 -ance, -i ble, -bil'i ty, -ive, -or,
 -o ry, -duc'tion, -duc tiv'i ty,
 -duc tom'e ter, con'duct-mon'ey,
 -duct'or-head.
con'duit (kon'dĭt *or* kŭn'-).
con dū'pli cate, -ca ted, -ca ting,
 -cant, -ca'tion.
con dur'rīte.
con'dyle (-dĭl *or* -dīl), -dy lar (-dĭ-),
 -dy loid, -lōme, -lus, *pl*. -lī,
 -lo'ma, -lŏm'a tous, -dyl'i an,
 -dyl'o pod, -dy lop'o dous (-dĭ-),
 con'dy loid joint.
cōne, cō'noid, -noid'al, -noid'ic,
 -ic al, cone'flow'er, -bear ing,
 -billed, -gam'ba, -gear, -gran'-
 ule, -in-cone, -joint, -nose,
 -plate, -seat, -shell, -valve, c.
 bit, c. clutch, c. pul'ley, c. wheel.
co ne'jo (-nā'hŏ).
co nen'chy ma (-kĭ-).
cō'ne patl, -pätl (*or* -pätl).
con'fab, -fab'u late, -u lar, -u la-
 tor, -to ry, -la'tion.
con fär're ate, -re a'tion.
con fec'tion, -a ry, -er, -er y, -pan.
con fed'er ate, -er a cy, -al, -a tive,
 -a'tion.
con fer', -ferred', -fer'ring, -ra ble,
 -ral, -rer, -fer ee', con'fer ence.
con fer ru'mi nate, -na ted.
Con fer'va, *pl*. -væ, -fer vä'les (-lēz)
 con fer'void, -vous, -vīte, -va'
 ceous.
con fess', -ed ly, -er, -or, -or ship,
 -ing, -fes'sion, -sion al, -al ism,
 -a ry, -ist, -fessed', -fes'sion-
 chair.
con fet'to, *pl*. -tĭ.

con fīde', -fīd'ed, -er, -ing, -ing ly,
-ing ness, con'fi dence, -dent,
-dent ly, -dent ness, -den'tial,
-tial ly, -fi dănt', *fem.* -dănte'.
con fig u ra'tion.
con'fīne, *n.*, -fīne', *v.*, -ment,
-fīned', -fīn'ing, -fīn'er.
con firm', -ing, -ing ly, -a ble,
-ance, -a tive, -tive ly, -a to ry,
-ed ly, -ed ness, -er, -fir mee',
-ma'tion, con'fir mā'tor, -firmed'.
con'fis cate (*or* -fis'-), -ca ted,
-ting, -tor, -fis'ca to ry, -fis'ca-
ble, -ca'tion.
con'fla grā'tion.
con flate', -flāt'ed, -flāt'ing, -fla'-
tion.
con'flict, *n.*, -flict', *v.*, -ed, -ing,
-ive.
con'flu ence, -ent, -ent ly.
con'flux, -flux'i ble, -ble ness.
con fō'cal.
con form', -ing, -a ble, -ble ness,
-bly, -bil'i ty, -form'er, -ist, -i ty,
-for mā'tion, -formed'.
cŏn' for'za (fôr'tsä).
con found', -ed, -ed ly, -ed ness,
-ing, -er.
con frac'tion, -to'ri um.
con fra ter'ni ty.
cŏn frère' (or kôn'frâr').
con front' (-frunt'), -er, -ment,
con'fron'té (kôn'frôn'tā').
Con fū'cian (-shan), -ism, -ist.
con fuo'co (fwō'ko).
con fuse' (-fuz'), -fused', -fus'ed ly,
-ed ness, -ing, -ing ly, -fu'sive
(-sĭv), -sion.
con fute', -fūt'ed, -ing, -er, -a ble,
-ant, -a tive, -fu ta'tion.
con'gé' (kôn zhā' *or* kŏn'jē), *n.*,
cŏn'gē, *v.*, -ge a ble, -ing, -geed.
con gēal', -a ble, -a ble ness, -ed-
ness, -ment, -ing, -gealed', -ge-
la'tion.
cŏn'gee (*or* kŭn'jē), *n.*, leave-
taking. con gee', *n.*, boiled rice;
a jail. con'gee, *v.*, -ing, -geed,
-gee-house, -wa'ter.
cŏn'gē ner, -ge nĕr'ic, -ic al, -net'-
ic.
con gē'ni al, -al ly, -al ness, -al'-
i ty

con gen'i tal, -tal ly, -i ture.
con'ger, -ee', -ger-doust, -eel.
con gĕ'ri es (-jē rĭ ēz).
con gest', -ed, -ive, -ing, -ges'tion
(-jes'chun).
con'gi a ry, *pl.* -a rĭes.
con'gi us, pl. -gĭ ĭ.
con glō'bate (*or* con'-), -ly, -ba'tion.
con glom'er ate, -er it'ic, -ā'tion.
con glu'tĭn *or* -tĭne, -ti nant, -ti
nate, -na ted, -ting, -tive, -tor,
-ti nous, -nous ly, -na'tion.
Coņ'go, C. pea, C. red, C. snake.
coņ'go, a dance, coņ'go-eel'.
con gon'ha (-ya).
coņ'gou (-gōō).
con grat'u late, -la ted, -la ting,
-la tor, -to'ry, -la ble, -lant, -la'-
tion.
coņ'gre gate, -ga ted, -ga ting,
-ga'tion, -tion al, -al ly, -al ism.
Coņ gre ga'tion al ist, -al ism.
coņ'gress, a meeting or assembly.
Coņ'gress, the national legislature
of U. S. con gres'sion al, coņ'-
gress man (*or* Coņ'-).
coņ'grēve, Con'greve rock'et.
coņ'grid, -groid.
coņ'gru ence, -en cy, -ent, -ent ly,
-ous, -ous ly, -ous ness, -ist, -is-
tic, -grū'i ty.
con hy'drĭne (-hĭ'-).
co nĭ'a (or kō'nĭ a).
cŏn'ic, -ic al, -al ly, -al ness, -i cal'-
i ty, -i cle, -i co cy lin'dric al
(-sĭ-), -i coid, -ics, -ic-a cute',
-ō'vate.
con'id, *co nid'i um*, pl. -*i a*, -i al,
-nid ĭ if'er ous, -nid'i oid, -i o-
phore, -i oph'o rous, -o spore.
cō'ni fer, -ni form, -nif'er ous,
con'i o sper'moŭs, *Co nif'e ræ.*
co nif'er in, co'nĭne, -nĭte.
con'i ma.
con'i o cyst.
cō ni ros' ter, -ros'tral, *Co'ni ros'tres*
(-trēz).
co nis'tra.
con jec'ture, -tūr a ble, -al, -al ly,
-al ist, -al'i ty, -tūr er, -ing,
-tured.
con join', -ing, -ed ly, -joint',
-joint'ly, -joined'.

---

fāte, făt, fär, fạll, fâre, fȧst, sofȧ, mēte, mĕt, hêr, īce ĭn, nōte,

con'ju gal, -ly, -ga cy, -ju'gi al (-jĭ-).
con'ju gate, -ga ted, -ga tive, -ga'-
tion, -tion al, -al ly, con ju ga'-
tion-bod'y, -cell, -nū'cle us.
con juṇct', -ly, -juṇc'tion, -tion al,
-al ly, -tive, -tive ly, -tive ness,
-ture, -ti vī'tis.
con juṇc tī'va, -tī'val.
con'jûre (kŭn-), to effect by magic,
-jûr er, -jûr ing, -jûr y, -jûred,
-jûr ing-cup.
cŏn jûre', to adjure, -ment, -ing,
-er, -jūred'.
coṇk.
con mō'to.
cŏn'nate (*or* -nāt'), -nā'tion, -nā'-
tion al, -nate-per fō'li ate.
con nat' u ral, -ly, -ness, -nā'ture.
con'naught, a cotton fabric. Con'-
naught, prov. Ire.
Cŏn'ne aut', t. O.
con nect', -ed, -ed ly, -ing, -ive,
-ive ly, -or, -nec'tion, con nect'-
ing-cell, -link, -rod.
con nel'lĭte.
con'ner (kun'-), a fish.
cŏn'nex, -nex'i ty, -ī'vum, *pl.* -va.
con ṇīve', -nived', -nĭv'ing, -ance,
-ent, -er.
cŏn nois seur' (-nis sûr' *or* -sûr'
or -sōōr'), -ship.
con'no tate, -ta ted, -ting, -ta'tion,
con note', -nōt'ed, -ing, -a tive,
-tive ly.
con nū'bi al, -ly, -al'i ty.
con nu tri'tious (-trish'us).
co'nŏ dŏnt.
cō'no scope.
coṇ'quer (-ker), -a ble, -ble ness,
-ing, -ing ly, -or, -quered, -quest.
coṇ quet' (-kwet').
con quis'ta dor (*or* -kis tä dôr').
con saṇ guin'i ty, -guin'c al, -c an,
-e ous, -saṇ'guine.
con'science (-shens), -less, -smit-
ten.
con sci en'tious (-shĭ en'shus), -ly,
-ness, -scion a ble, -ble ness.
con'scious (-shus), -ly, -ness.
con'script, *a.* and *n.*, -script', *v.*,
-ed, -ing, -scrip'tion, -tion al.
con'se crate, -cra tor, -to ry, -cra'-
tion, -crā'tion-cross.

con'se cu'tion.
con sec'u tive, -ly, -ness.
con sen'sus, -su al (-shōō-).
con sent', -ed, -er, -ing, -ing ly,
-a ble, -sen ta'ne ous, -ous ly,
-ous ness.
con sen'tience, -tient (-shent).
con'se quent, -ly, -quen'tial, -tial-
ly, -tial ness, -se quence.
con serv'a tive, -ly, -ness, -serv'-
a ble, -ant, -an cy, -a tism, -a tory, -ser va'tion, -tion al, -va'tor.
con'ser'va toire (*or* -twor').
con serve', -served', -serv'ing,
-serv'er.
con sid'er, -a ble, -a bly, -ing,
-ing ly, -a'tion.
con sid'er ate, -ly, -ness.
con sign' (-sīn'), -ing, -or (*or*
-sĭ nor') *or* -er, -signed', -sig'na-
to ry, -na ture, -na'tion.
con sĭl'i a ry, -i ence, -i ent.
con sist', -ed, -ing, -ence, -en cy,
-ent, -ent ly, *-sis ten'tes* (-tēz).
con sis'to ry, -to'ri al, -ri an.
con'so brī'nal.
con so'ci ate, -a ted, -a ting, -a'-
tion, -tion al, -tion ism.
Con so lä'to del Mü're.
con sole', -soled, -sōl'ing, -sōl'a-
ble, -ble ness, -sōl'a to ry, -sō-
la'tor, -la'tion.
con'sole, *n.*, -ta'ble.
con sŏl'i date, -da ted, -da ting,
-da tive, -da'tion.
con'sŏls (*or* -sōlz').
con som mé (-sŏ mā' *or* kôṅ-).
con'so nant, -ly, -ness, -ism, -ize,
-nance, -nan cy, -nan'tal, -so-
noŭs.
con sor di'ni (-dē'nē), *c. spi'ri to*
(spē'rē to).
con sort', -ed, -ing, -a ble. con'-
sort, *n.*, -ism, -ship, -sor'ti um
(-shĭ-).
con spec'tus.
con sperse'.
con spic'u ous, -ly, -ness.
con spire', -spīr'ing, -ing ly,
-spīr'er, -ant, -spĭr'a tor, -a cy.
con'spur cate.
con'sta ble (kŭn-), -ship, cŏn-
stab'u la ry.

nŏt, nôr, ūse, ŭp, ûrn, etüde, fōōd, fŏŏt, aṇger, boṅmot, thus, Bach.

Con′stans′ (kŏn′stŏṅ′), Fr. politician. Cŏn′stans (-stanz), Rom.
Emperor.
con′stant, -ly, -ness, -stan cy.
Con stan′ti a (-shĭ-).
Cŏn′stan tīne, Rom. Emperor.
Con stan′ti nŏ′ple, c. Turk., -no-
pol′i tan.
con′stat.
con state′, -stăt′ed, -ing.
con stel la′tion, -stel′late (*or*
kon′-), -stel′la to ry.
con ster na′tion.
con′sti pate, -pa ted, -pa ting,
-pa′tion.
con stit′u ent, -en cy.
con′sti tute, -tu ted, -ting, -tive,
-tive ly, -ter, -tor, -tu′tion, -tion-
ist, -tion al, -al ism, -al ist, -al ly,
-al ize, -ized, -i zing, -al′i ty.
con strain′, -ing, -er, -ed ly, -a ble,
-strained′, -straint′.
con strict′, -ed, -ing, -ive, -or,
-stric′tion.
con strin′gent.
con struct′, -ed, -ing, -or *or* -er,
-ive, -ive ly, -ive ness, -struc′-
tion, -tion al, -al ly, -ist, -tion-way.
con′strue (*rarely* -strŏō′), -strued,
-stru ing.
con′sub stan′tial, -ism, -ist, -ly,
-ti ate, -ti al′i ty, -ti a′tion.
Con su e lo (-ā′lo *or* kŏṅ′sŏō′ā′-
lŏ′), George Sand.
con sue tū′di na ry (-swe-).
con′sul, -age, -ship, -su lar, -late,
-sul-gen′er al, -su late-gen′er al.
con sult′, -ed, -ing, -er, -ive, -a ry,
-a tive, -a to ry, -sul ta′tion.
con′sum ah *or* -ar.
con sume′, -sumed′, -sūm′ing,
-ing ly, -er, -sump′tion, -sump′-
tive, -tive ly, -tive ness.
con sum′mate, *a.,* -ly, -ma tive.
con sum′mate (*or* kon′-), *v.,* -ma-
ted, -ma ting.
con sūte′.
con ta bes′cence, -cent.
con′tact, -tac′tu al, -tact-breăk′er,
-lev′el, -lĕv′er.
con tä di′no (-dē′-), pl. *-di′ni* (-dē′-
nē), fem. *-di′na* (-dē′nä), pl.
-di′ne (-dē nä) *or* *-di′nas* (-näz).

con tä′gion (-jun), -ist, -gious
(-jus), -gious ly, -ness, *-ta′gi um,*
-gioned (-jund).
con tāin′, -er, -ing, -a ble, -ment,
-tained′.
con tam′i nate, -na ted, -na ting,
-na tive, -na′tion.
con tan′go, *pl.* -goes.
Con té (kŏṅ′tā′), Fr. painter.
con temn′, -temned (-temd′),
-tem′ning (*or* -tem′ing), -ner (*or*
-er).
con tem′plate (*or* kon′-), -plă ted,
-ting, -tive, -tive ly, -tive ness,
-plă′tion.
con tem′po ra′ne ous, -ly, -ness,
-ra ne′i ty.
con tem′po ra ry, -ri ness.
con tempt′, -i ble, -ble ness, -bly,
-bil′i ty, -temp′tu ous, -ous ly,
-ous ness.
con tend′, -ed, -ing, -er.
con ten′e ment.
con′tent, *n.,* that which is contained; the contents; -less, -tents
(*or* -tents′).
con tent′, *a., n.,* and *v.,* -ed, -ed ly,
-ed ness, -ment.
con ten′tion, -tious (-shus), -ly,
-ness.
con ter′mi nal, -na ble, -nant,
-nous.
con test′, *v.,* -ed, -ing, -ing ly,
-a ble, -ant, -tes ta′tion, con′-
test, *n.*
con′text, -tex′tū al, -al ly, -tūr al,
-tūre
Cŏn′ti (-tē), It. poet.
con tig′u ous, -ly, -ness, -ti gu′i ty.
con′ti nent, *n.,* -nen′tal, -tal ist,
-tal ism. con′ti nent, *a.,* -ly,
-nence *or* -nen cy.
con tin′gent, -ly, -ness, -tin′gence,
-gen cy.
con tin′ue, -ued, -u ed ly (*or* -ūd-
ly), -u er, -u ing, -ing ly, -u ous,
-ous ly, -u al, -al ly, -al ness,
-u ance, -ant, -u a tive, -tive ly,
-a tor, -a′tion, -ti nu′i ty.
cŏn tĭn′ū ō (*or* -tē′nŏō-).
cŏnt-līne (*or* -lĭn), -splice
con′to.
con tor′ni ate.

con tort', -ed, -ing -tor'tion, -tion-
ist, -tor'tive, -tor tu'pli cate.
con tour' (-tōōr' *or* kŏn'-), -ing,
-tour'-fĕath'er, -hair, -line.
con tour né (-nä')
con'tra band, -ism, -ist.
con'tra băss (*or* -bäs') -băs'so,
-tra oc'tave.
con'tra bŏ'nos mŏ'res (-rēz).
con'tract, *n.*, con tract', *v.* -ed,
-ed ly, -ed ness, -i ble, -ble ness
-Ile, -ive, -or, -ant, -i bil'i ty,
-trac'tion, -ture, -til'i ty, -tion-
rule.
con'tra-dánce.
con tra dict', -ed, -ing, -er, -a ble,
-ive, -ive ly, -o ry, -ri ly, -ri ness,
-dic'tion, -tion al, -tious, -tious-
ness.
con'tra dis tinc'tion,   -tinc'tive,
-tin'guish.
con'trä fă gŏt'to.
con'tra fis'sure (-fish- *or* -fish'-).
con tra grē'di ent.
con trăl'to.
con tra'ri ant.
con'tra ry, -tra ri ly, -ri ness, -ri-
wise', -rī'e ty, -tra ry-mind'ed.
con'trăst, *n.*, -trăst', *v.*, -ed, -ing,
-ive, con'trast-di'a gram.
con'tra stim'u lant.
con'trate, -wheel.
con'tra ten'or.
con'tra val lā'tion.
con tra vēne', -vened', -vēn'ing,
-vēn'er, -vēn'tion.
con'tra yer'va.
con'tre fort (-tr-), *-tre temps'* (-täṅ'),
con'tre-coup (-kōō), *-vair', -er'-
mine, -let'tre.*
Cŏn tre'ras (-trä'-), t. Mex.
con trib'ute, -u ted, -ting, -tive,
-tor, -to ry, -tri bu'tion, -tion al.
con'trīte, -ly, -ness, -tri'tion
(-trĭsh'un).
con trit'u rate, -ra ted, -ra ting.
con trive', -trived', -trīv'a ble,
-ance, -er.
con trŏl', -ling, -la ble, -ble ness,
-bil'i ty, -ment, -ler ship, -ler *or*
comp-, -trolled', con trol'-ex per'-
i ment, -trol'ler-gen'er al, -trol'-
ling-noz'zle.

con'tro ver sy, -ver'sial, -sial ist,
-sial ly.
con tro vert' (*or* kon'-), -ed, -ing,
-er, -i ble, -i bly, -ist.
con'tu ma cy, -mā'cious (-shus),
-cious ly, -ness.
con'tu me ly, -me'li ous (*or* -mēl'-
yus), -ous ly, -ous ness.
con tuse' (-tūz), -tused, -tūs'ing,
-tū'sive (-siv), -tu'sion.
cŏ nŭn'drum.
co nure' (*or* kon'-).
cŏ'nus, pl. *-nī;* Cŏ'nus, *Conch. genus.*
con va lesce', -lĕsced' (lĕst), -les'-
cing, -cence, -cen cy, -c e n t,
-cent ly.
Con'val lā'ri a.
con va nesce', -nesced' (-nest'),
-nes'cing, -nes'ci ble.
con vec'tion, -vec'tive, -tive ly.
con vene', -vened', -vēn'ing, -vēn'-
a ble, -vēn'er.
con vēn'ience, -ien cy, -ieṅt, -ient-
ly.
con'vent, -ven'ti cal, -ven'tu al,
Con ven'tu al, a member of a
religious sect.
con ven'ti cle, -ti cler.
con ven'tion, -al, -al ism, -al ist,
-al ize, -ized, -i zing, -I za'tion,
-al ly, -al'i ty, -a ry, con ven'tion
coin, c. dol'lar.
con verge', -verged', -ver'ging,
-gence, -gen cy, -gent, -ges'cence.
con'ver sant, -sant ly.
con ver sa'tion, -al, -al ist, -al ly,
-ism, -ist, -tion-tube, *con'ver sa'-
zi o'ne* (kŏṅ'ver sä'tsē ō'nä *or*
kōn-), pl. *-o ni* (-nē).
con verse', -versed' (-vŭrst), -vers'-
ing, -er, -a ble, -ble ness, -bly.
con'verse, *n.* and *a.*, -ly, -vers'i-
ble.
con vert', -ed, -ing, -er, -i ble, -ble-
ness, -i bly, -i bil'i ty, -ver'sive,
-ver'si ble, -ver'sion, -vert'ing-
fur'nace.
con'vert, *n.*, -ver tend'.
con'vex, -ly, -ness, -vexed', -vex'-
ed ly, -ed ness, -i ty, -vex'o-
con'cave, -con'vex, -plane.
con vey' (-vā'), -a ble, -ance, -an-
cer, -an cing, -er *or* -or, -veyed'.

nŏt, nôr, ūse, ŭp, ûrn, etüde, fōōd, fŏŏt, aṅger, boṅmot, thus, Bach.

con'vict, *n.*, -ism, -vict', *v.*, -ed,
-ing, -ive, -ive ly, -ive ness, -vic'-
tion.
con vĭnce', -vinced', -vin'cer,
-cing, -cing ly, -cing ness, -ci ble,
-vic'tion.
con viv'i al, -ist, -ly, -al'i ty
con voke', -voked', -vōk'ing, -vo-
ca'tion, -tion al, -al ist.
con'vo lute, -lū'ted, -tive, -lū'tion.
con volve', -volved', -volv'ing,
-volv'ent.
Con vol'vu lus, *pl.* -lŭs es *or* -vu lī,
-*vu la'ce æ*, con vol vu la'ceous.
con'voy, *n.*, -voy', *v* -voyed',
-voy'ing.
con vulse', -vulsed' (-vŭlst), -vul'-
sant, -sing, -sive, -sive ly, -sion,
-sion al, -sion a ry, -sion ist.
cŏ'ny (*or* kŭn'y), *pl.* cō'nĭes, cŏ'-
ney, *pl.* -neys (kŏ'nĭz *or* kŭn'iz),
cŏ'ny-bŭr'row, -fish, -wŏŏl.
coo (kōō), -ing, -ing ly, -ey, -ee',
cooed, cōō'-in-new'.
cōō'bä.
co ob lĭ gŏr'.
cōō'ey *or* -ee *or* -ie.
coof (kŏŏf).
cōō'ja.
cŏŏk, -ing, -y *or* -ey *or* -ie, -er y,
-maid, -room, -shop, -ish,
cooked, cook'-book, -con'ner,
-house, -wrasse (-răss), -ing-rānge,
-stove.
cōōl, -ing, -er, -ish, -ish ly, -ish-
ness, -ly, cooled, cool'weed,
-wort, -cup, -hĕad'ed, -tănk'ard,
cool'ing-cup, -floor.
cōōl'a man.
coo'li bah (-le bä).
cōō'lĭe *or* cōō'ly, *pl.* -lies (lĭz).
cōōm.
coomb (kōōm).
cōō'mie.
cōōn, -skin, -bear, -heel, -oys'ter.
cōōn'da-oil.
coon'tee, a harrow.
coon'tĭe *or* -ty, a plant.
cōōp, -ing, cooped.
coop'er, -age, -ing, -y, -er's-wood.
co op'er ate, -er a tive, -a tor,
-ant, -a'tion, -tion ist.
co op'ta tive.

co or dain', -ing, -dained', -or'di-
nance.
co or'di nate, -ly, -ness, -na ted,
-na ting, -tive, -to ry, -na'tion.
coor'gee.
cōō'rong.
Cŏ ŏs', co. N. H.—(cōōs), co. Ore.
—(kŏ'ŏs), *Bib.*
coot, -foot, a bird, -foot'ed, -grebe.
coot'er.
cooth.
coo thay'.
cop, -frame, -spin ning, -tube,
-wind'er.
cŏ'pa.
co păi'ba *or* -va, -pai'vic, -ba-oil.
co pai'yé-wood (-pä'yä-).
co'pal, -pal ĭn *or* -ĭne, -if'er ous,
-ĭte.
co pal'che *or* -chĭ.
cŏ'pälm.
co par'ce ner, -ce ny, -ce na ry.
co part'ner, -ner ship, -ner y.
co pä'trĭ ot.
cope, coped, cŏp'ing, -er, cope'-
stone, -chis'el.
cŏ'peck *or* ko'-.
Co'pen hä'gen, c. Den.
co pen hä'gen, a drink; a game.
Co per'nĭ cus, Pol. astron., -nĭ-
can.
Co phet'u a, Tennyson's *The
Beggar Maid.*
cŏ'pi a *or* bō'rum.
cŏ'pi ous, -ness.
cŏp pé (-pä').
Cŏp pée (-pä'), Fr. poet.
cop'per, -ing, -ish, -ize, -ized,
-i'zing, -y, -pered, cop'per bell,
-bel ly, -head, -nose, -plate,
-smith, -wing, -work.
cop'per-bit, -bot'tomed, -col' ored,
-faced, -făs'tened, -fur'nace,
-glănce, -laced, -nick'el, -pow'-
der, -rose, -wall, -works, -worm,
c. cap'tain.
cop'per as.
cŏp'pĭce.
cŏp'pin.
cŏp'ping-plate, -rail.
cŏp'ple, -pled, -ple-crown, -crowned.
cŏp'po, *pl.* -pĭ.
cŏ'pra (*or* kŏp'-).

co prē'mi a or *-præ'-*, -prem'e sis,
-prē'mic.
cop'ro līte, -lĭt'ic.
co prol'o gy, -proph'a gy, -proph'-
i loŭs.
co proph'a gan, -a gous.
cŏpse, -wood, cops'y.
cop'stick.
Cŏpt, Cop'tic.
cop'u la, *pl.* -las *or* -læ, -u lar.
cop'u late, -lā ted, -lā ting, -lā-
tive, -tive ly, -là to'ry, -la'-
tion.
cop'y, *pl.* -ies, -ĭed, -y ing, -i er,
-y ist, -y grăph, -hold, -hold'er,
-right, -book, -hold'er, -mon'ey.
cop'y ing-ink, -lāthe, -ma chine',
-pa'per, -pen'cil, -press, -rib'bon.
coque (kŏk).
Coque'lin' (kŏk'lăṅ'), Fr. actor.
coque'li quot (kŏk'lĭ kō).
co quet', *v.*, -ted, -ting, -ry (*or*
co'-), -tish, -tish ly, -quette', *n.*
co quil lage' (kō kēl yäzh').
co quil'la-nut (-kēl'ya-), *co quil'lo*
(-kēl'yo).
cŏ quille' (-kēl').
co quim'bīte (*or* -kĭm'-).
Cŏ quim'bŏ (-kēm'-), prov. Chile.
co quim'bo (-kim'-), an owl.
co qui'na (-kē'-).
co qui'to (-kē'-), -oil.
cŏr'a cle.
cŏr'a coid, -coid'al.
co rad'i cate.
cŏ'rah.
cŏr'al, -let, -lĭne, -līte, -lit'ic, -al-
loid, -loid'al, -la'ceous, -lif'er-
ous, -lig'e nous (-lij'-), -lig'er-
ous, -aled, co ral'li form, *co ral'-
lum.*
cor'al ber'ry, -root, -wort, -fish,
-in'sect, -mud, -plant, -pol'yp,
-rag, -snake, -stitch, -tree,
-wood, -zone.
co rä'mĭ.
*co'ram ju'dĭ cē, c. nŏ'bis, c. non ju'-
di cē, c. pǎr'i dus, c. pop'u lo.*
corb, cor'ban.
cor'beil (-bel).
cor'bel, -beled *or* -belled, -bel ing
or -bel ling, cor'bel-piece, -steps,
-ta'ble.

cor bic'u lum, pl. *-u la,* Cor bic'u la,
Zoöl. genus.
cor'cass.
cŏrd, -age, -al, -ed, -ing, -wain,
-wain er, -grăss, -leaf, -ma-
chine', -sling, -stitch, -wood,
-work.
cor'date, -di form, cor'date-lan'ce-
o late, -ob'long, -sag'it tate
(-saj'-).
cor'dax, -dac'tes (-tēz).
cor-de-chasse' (-shăs').
cor del' (kor dăl').
Cor dē'li a (*or* -dēl'ya), Shak.,
King Lear.
Cor de liĕr'.
cŏr de lière' (-dēl yâr').
cor'dĕlle (*or* -del').
cor'dial (-jal *or* kord'yal), -ly,
-ness, -dial'i ty.
cor'dĭ es (-ēz).
cor dil'las (-läz).
cor dil'ler a (*or* -dĭl yā'ra).
cord'īte.
Cŏr'dŏ ba *or* -va, prov. Sp. Cŏr'-
dŏ vä, prov. Arg. Rep.; t. Mex.
cor'don, -do nette', -*don net* (-nä').
cor don nier' (-dōn nyä').
cor'do van.
cor dua soy' (-dwą soi').
cŏre, -less, cored, cor'ing, -er,
core'-băr'rel, -box, -lĭft'er, -piece,
-print, -valve, -wheel.
co rec'ta sis.
co rec'tŏme, -to my, cŏr ĕc tŏ'-
mi a, -tŏ'pi a, -e dī al'y sis.
co-rē'gent.
co rel'la.
Co re op'sis.
cŏr'e plas ty, -plas'tic.
co-re sid'u al (-zĭd'-).
co-re spond'ent *or* co re-.
corf, corves, corf'-house.
Cor'fĭ ōte *or* -fūte.
co'ri ā'ceous.
co'ri an'der, -seed.
Co rinne' (-rēn'), Madam De
Staël.
co'rĭnne' (*or* -rēn'). A quadruped;
a bird.
Cŏr'inth, Co rin'thi ac, -thi an.
Co'rĭ ō lā'nus, Rom. hero.

cō′ri um.
cork, -age, -er, -ing, -y, -i ness,
 corked, cork′brain, -screw, -wood.
cork′-bark, -black, -board,
 -brained, -clasp, -cut′ter, -fas′-
 ten er, -fau′cet, -fos′sil -lĕath′er,
 -ma chine′, -oak, -press, -press′er,
 -pull, -pull′er, -tree, cork′ing-
 ma chine′.
corm, -el, -oid.
corme.
Cor mid′i um, pl. *-i a*
cor moph′y ly.
cor′mo rant.
cor′mus, pl. *-mī.*
corn, -bells, -bīnd, -bot′tle, -brash,
 -cob, -crake, -crib, -field, -flow′er,
 -shell′er, -shuck, -stalk, -starch,
 -stone, -y, corned.
corn′-bad′ger, -bee′tle, -chan′dler,
 -clean′er, -coc′kle, -cov′er er,
 -crack′er, -cul′ti va tor, -cut′ter,
 -drill, -eat′er, -fac′tor, -fed, -flag,
 -floor, -fly, -goose, -grāt′er,
 -grōw′ing, -harp, -har′vest er,
 -hook, -hull′er, -husk, -husk′er,
corn′-juice, -knife, -land, -law,
 -lift, -loft, -măr′i gold, -me′ter,
 -mill, -mint, -moth, -mull′er,
 -oys′ter, -pars′ley, -pipe, -plant′-
 er, -plăs′ter, -plow, -pop′per,
 -pop′py, -rent, -rig, -rose, -rōw,
 -sal′ad, -saw′fly, -shuck′ing,
 -snake, -strip′ping, -thrips, -van,
 -vi′o let, -wee′vil, -worm, corn′-
 ing-house.
corn ball, c. bread, c. cake, c.
 dod′ger, c. ex change′, c. frit′ter,
 c. pone.
cor′ne a, -ne al, -ne i′tis, -ne ule,
 cor′ne a-lens, -re′flex.
Cor neille′ (-nāl′), Fr. poet.
cor′ne in.
cor′nel, -tree.
cor′ner, -er, -ing, -wise, -nered,
 cor′ner-chis′el, -cut′ter, -drill,
 -piece, -plate, -punch, -saw,
 -stone, -tooth, -valve, cor′ner-
 ing-ma chine′.
cor′net, -y, -er, -tist *or* cor′nist,
 cor′net-stop
cor ne′ta (-nā′-).
cor nette′.

cor′nic.
cor′nĭce, -nĭced (-nĭst), -nice-hook,
 -plane, -ring.
cor nic′u lum, pl. *-la,* -u late.
cor′ni fy, -ing, -fied, -nif′ic, -nif′-
 er ous, -ni form, -ni fi ca′tion,
 -nic′ u late, -nig′er ous (-nij′-).
cor′nin *or* -nīne.
cor′ni plume.
Cor′nish, -man.
cor′no di băs sĕt′to (dē), pl. *cor′ni*
 (-nē), *cor′no In gle′se* (ĕn glā′zā).
cor′nu, pl. *-nu a,* -nu al, -nute′,
 -nūt′ed, -ny.
cor nu co′pi a.
cor′nu pēte.
cŏr′o cōre.
cŏ rol′la, cor′ol, -ol list, -ol late,
 -la ted, -la′ceous, -lif′er ous,
 co rol′li form, -rol′lĭne (*or* cor′-),
 -li flō′ral, -flō′rous, *co rol′lu la,*
 pl. *-læ.*
cor′ol la ry, *pl.* -rĭes.
Cor′o man′del, *Geog.* C. wood.
co rō′na, *pl.* -năs *or* -næ, cor′o nal,
 -nal ly, -o na ry, -o nate, -na′-
 ted, co ro′ni um.
cor′o nach *or* -a nach (-năk).
cō rō nä′do (-nä′thō).
cŏr o nä′men.
cŏr o nä′tion, -oath, -roll.
co rō′ne, -rŏn′i form, cŏr′o nūle.
cŏr′o ner.
cŏr′o net, -ed.
Cŏr o nil′la, *Bot. genus.*
cō rō nil′la (-nēl′ya), a coin.
co rō′ni um.
co rō′nis.
cŏr′o noid.
co ro′zo (-thō) *or* -*ros′so* (-rō′-
 sō).
cor′phun.
cor′po ral, -ly, -ral ship, -ral′i ty,
 -ral-case, -cloth, -cup.
cor′po rate, -ly, -ness, -ra tor,
 -ra ture, -ra′tion, -tion stop.
cor pŏ′re al, -ism, -ist, -ly, -ness,
 -re′i ty, -re al′i ty, -pŏ′re al ize,
 -ized, -i zing, -ĭ zā′tion, -po ros′-
 i ty.
cor′po sant (-zant).
corps (kōr), *pl.* corps (kōrz),
 corps d′ar mée (kōr′där′mä′).

corpse, -can'dle, -cool'er, -gate,
-light, -plant, -pre serv'er, -sheet.
cor'pu lent, -ly, -lence, -len cy.
cor'pus, pl. *-po ra.*
cor'pus cle (-l), -pus'cu lar, -la-
ted, -cu loŭs, -cu la'ri an, *-cu lum*,
pl. *-la.*
cŏr răl', *n.* and *v.*, -rălled' (*or*
räld), -ral'ling.
cor ră'sion (-zhun).
cŏr're al.
cor rect', -ed, -ing, -a ble *or*
-i ble, -ly, -ness, -or, -o ry, -rec'-
tion, -tion al, -rect'ive, -rect'ing-
plate. .
Cor reg'gio (kŏr rĕd'jō), t. It.
Cor reg'gio, da (dä kŏr rĕd'jō),
It. painter.
cor reg'i dor (-rej'-), *-reg'i mi en'to.*
cor re late' (*or* cor'-), *v.*, -lät'ed,
-lät'ing, -la'tion, cor're late, *a.*
and *n.*, -rel'a tive, -tive ly, -tive-
ness, -tiv'i ty.
cŏr re'ō (-rä'o).
cor re spond', -ed, -ence, -en cy,
-ent, -ent ly, -ing, -ing ly, -spon'-
sive, -sive ly.
cŏr'ri dor.
cor'ri gen'dum (jen'-), pl. *-gen'da.*
cŏr'ri gent.
cŏr'ri gi ble, -ness, -bil'i ty.
cŏr rŏb'o rate, -ra ted, -ting,
-rant, -ra tĭve, -ra to'ry, -ră'tion.
cor rob o ree' (*or* -rob'-) *or* -rob'-
o ry.
cor rode', -rŏd'ed, -rŏd'ing, -i ble,
-ro'di bil'i ty, -ro'sion.
cŏr'roi.
cŏr rŏ'sive (-siv), -ly, -ness, -si ble,
-ble ness, -bil'i ty.
cŏr'ro val, -val Ine (*or* -rŏ'-).
cŏr'ru gate, -ga ted, -ga ting,
-ga tor, -gant, -gā'tion.
cor rupt', -ed, -er, -i ble, -ble ness,
-bly, -bil'i ty, -ing, -ing ly, -ive,
-ive ly, -less, -ness, -rup'tion,
-tion ist.
cor'sage (*or* -säzh').
cor'sair.
cor'sak *or* -sac.
côrse.
corse'let.
cor sesque' (-sesk').

cor'set, -ed, -ing, cor'set-māk'er.
Cor'sĭ can.
cor'sĭte.
cor'tège' (-täzh').
Cor te re al' (kor tä rä äl'), Port.
nav.
Cor'tĕs *or* -tĕz, Sp. conqueror.
Cor'tes, the national legislature
of Sp. or Port.
cor'tex, pl. *-tĭ ces* (-sēz), -ti cal, -ti-
cate, -ca'ted, -ca ting, -ca'tion,
-tic'i fer (-tis'-), -i form, -ti cif'-
er ous, -ti cine, -cin'ic, -ti cole,
-cose, -cous, -tic'o lĭne, -o lous.
cor'tĭle (*or* -tē'le).
Côr tôn'.
Co ru'ña (kō rōōn'yä), prov. Sp.
co run'dum, *pl.* -dums, -run-
doph'i lĭte, -dum-point, -tool.
Co rŭn'na, c. Mich.
cŏr'us cate (*or* ko rus'-), -ca ted,
-ca ting, -ca'tion.
cor'vée' (-vǎ' *or* -vē').
cor vette'.
cor vet'to.
cor vi'na (*or* -vē'-).
cor'vĭne (*or* -vīn), -vi form, -void.
cŏr'y bant (-ĭ-), *pl.* -bants *or*
-ban'tes (-tĕz), -ban'tic, -ban'ti-
asm, -bant'ism.
Cŏr'y don, Virgil.
Cŏ'ry ĕll' (-rĭ-), co. Tex.
cŏr'y lĭn (-ĭ lin).
cŏr'ymb (-ĭmb *or* -ĭm), -ymbed,
-ym bif'er ous, co rym'bi ate, -bi-
a ted, -rym'bose (-bōs), -bose ly,
-bous, -bu lose (-lōs), -bu lous,
-rym'bus, *pl.* -bī.
cŏr'y phæ'noid (-fē'-).
co'ry'phēe' (kō rē fā'), cŏr'y phē'us,
pl. -us es *or* -phē'i.
cŏr'y phene.
Co ryph'o don, co ryph'o dŏnt.
cŏr ys tē'ri um, *pl.* -ri a.
cō ry'za (-rī'-).
cos cin'o man'cy (*or* cos'ci no-).
cos'co ro'ba (*or* cos cor'-).
co sē'cant.
co seĭs'mal, -seĭs'mic.
co sen'tient (-shent).
cŏsh'er, -ered, -er ing, -er er, -er y.
Cŏ'si *or* Kŏ'- (kŏ'sē), r. Ind.
co sig'na to ry.

---

co'sĭne.
cos'mēte.
cos met'ic (kŏz-), -ic al, -me tol'-o gy.
cos'mic (kŏz'-), -mic al, -al ly, -mism.
cos mog'o ny (kŏz-), -o nal, -o ner, -o nist, -mo gon'ic, -ic al.
cos mog'ra phy (kŏz-), -ra pher, -ra phist, -mo graph'ic, -ic al, -al ly.
cos'mo lăbe (kŏz'-).
cos mol'a try (kŏz-).
cos'mo lĭne (kŏz'-).
cos mol'o gy (kŏz-), -o gist, -mo log'ic al, -al ly, -mom'e try, -mo plas'tic.
cos mop'o lite, -mo pol'i tan, -tan ism, -po lit'ic al.
cos mo rä'ma (or -rä'-), -răm'ic.
cos'mos (kŏz'-), -mo scope, -mo sphere, -mo the ism, -thet'ic, -mo poi et'ic.
Cosne (kōn), a wine.
cŏss.
Cos'sack.
cos'sas (-săz or -sᶏz).
cos'see.
cos'set.
cos sette'.
cos'sum.
cos'sy rīte.
cŏst, -ing, -less, -ly, -li ness, cost'-book, -free, -sheet.
cŏs'ta, pl. -tæ, -tal, -tal ly, -tate, -tă' ted, -tă' to vĕ'nose (-nōs), -tel'late, -tel'lum, pl. -la, -tif'er ous, -ti form, -ti spi'nal, -to cla vic'u lar, -to col'ic, -to cŏr'a coid, -to scap'u lar, -u lä'ris, -to ster'-nal, -to tome, -to trans verse', -to ver'te bral, -to xiph'oid (-zif'-), cos'tal-nerved.
cos tēan', -ing, -tean'-pit.
cos'ter, -mon'ger, -boy.
cŏs'tive, -ly, -ness.
cŏst'ma ry.
cos'tume (or -tume'), n., cos tume', v., -tumed', -tūm'ing, -tūm'er (or cos'tūm'-).
cos'tus-root.
cot, -bet'ty, -roll er, -town, cot'tar-town.

co tan'gent.
cōte.
co teau' (-tō'), pl. -teaux (-tōz').
co'te lé (kō'te lā).
co te line' (-lēn').
co tem'po rä'ne ous, -ly, -ness. -tem'po ra ry.
cō te riē (or -rē').
co ter'mi noŭs.
Cōte'-ro tiĕ'.
Co tē'sian (-zhan).
cŏ'thon.
co thurn', -thur'nate, -na ted, -nal, -nus, pl. -nĭ.
cŏt i cé (-sä').
co tic'u lar.
co tĭd'al.
co ti gnac' (-tēn yak').
co til'lion (-yun).
co tĭn'ga.
cŏ'to, Cŏ'to bark.
cŏ tŏ'ne a.
co'trŭs tee'.
cots'wŏld.
cot'ta, pl. -tas or -tæ.
cot'ta bus.
cot'tage, -taged, -ta ger.
cot'ter, -tered, -ter el, -ter-drill, -file, -plate.
cot'tĭse, -tĭsed (-tĭst).
cot'tle.
cot'toid.
cot'to lene.
cot'ton (-n), -ade' (or cot'-), -ee', -ous, -y, -ize, -ized, -i zing, -mouth, -tail, -weed, -wood.
cot'ton-bale, -blue, -bro'ker, -brush, -cake, -chop'per, -clean'-er, -el'e va tor, -fi'ber, -float'er, -gin (-jin), -grăss, -hŏŏk, -lord, -ma chine', -man u fac'to ry, -man u fac'ture, -mill, -o'pen er, -pick'er, -plant, -plant'er, -plan ta'tion, -pow'der, -press, -rat, -rush, -scrăp'er, -sedge, -shrub, -stain'er, -sweep, -this'tle (-l), -top'per, -tree, -waste, -wool.
Cot tŏ'ni an.
cot'ton seed, -clean'er, -mill, -oil.
cot'y lĕ, -y loid, -loid'al, -y lig'-er ous (-lij'-), co tyl'i form.
cŏt'y lē'don, -lĕd'on al (or -lē'-), -on ar, -on a ry, -on ous, -on oid,

---

fāte, făt, fär, fᶏll, fâre, fᶏst, sofᶏ, mēte, mĕt, hêr, īce, ĭn, nōte,

-y loph'o roŭs, *Cot'y lē'don*, Bot.
genus.
cou'a (kōō'ä), Cou'a, *Ornith.*
genus. cou'cal (kōō'-).
couch, -ing, -er, -ant, -an cy, -less,
couched, couch'-fel'low, -grăss,
-ing-nee'dle.
cou dĕ' (kōō dā'), bent at right angles. *cou di ère'* (kōō dĭ âr').
cou'dée (kōō'dā), a measure.
Coues (kowz), Amer. naturalist.
cou'gar (kōō'-).
cough (kawf), -ing, -er, -wort,
coughed.
coug'nar. (kōōg'-).
could (kŏŏd).
cou lé (kōō lā').
cou'lée' (kōō'lā').
cou'leur' (kōō'ler').
cou lisse' (kōō lēs').
cou loir' (kōō lwạr').
cou'lomb' (kōō'lom' *or* -lomb' *or*
-lôn'), -me'ter.
cou'lūre' (kōō'lōōr').
cou'ma rou (kōō'ma rōō).
coun'cil, -or *or* -lor, -man, -board,
-book, -chăm'ber, -house, -ta'-
ble.
coun'sel, -sĕled *or* -selled, -sel ing
or -sel ling, -sel or *or* -lor, -or-
ship, -sel-keep'er.
count, -ed, -ing, -a ble, -er, -less,
-fish, -ship, -out, -wheel, count'-
ing-house, -rōōm.
coun'te nance, -nanced, -nan-
cing, -nan cer.
coun'ter, -act', -act'ed, -act'ing,
-act'ive, -ive ly, -ac'tion, -a'gent,
-bal'ance, -anced, -an cing,
-blăst', -bracc', *n.,* -brace', *v.,*
-braced', -bra'cing, -buff', *n.,*
-buff', *v.,* -buffed', -buff'ing,
-change', *n.,* change', *v.,*
-changed', -chăn'ging, -charge',
n., -charge', *v.,* -charged',
-char'ging, -charm', *n.,* -charm',
v., -charmed', -charm'ing,
-check', *n.,* -check', *v.,* -checked',
-check'ing, -draw', -draw'ing,
-drawn', -faced', -foil', -force',
-fort', -gage', -glow'.
coun'ter mănd, *n.* -mănd', *v.,*
-ed, -ing, -a ble, -march', *n.,*

-march', *v.,* -marched', -march'-
ing, -mark', *n.,* -mark', *v.,*
-marked', -mark'ing, -mine', *n.,*
-mine', *v.,* -mined', -mĭn'ing,
-move', *n.,* -move', *v.,* -moved',
-mov'ing, -mūre', *n.,* -mure' *v.,*
-mured', -mūr'ing, -paled', -pā'-
ly, -pane', -păr'ry, *v.,* -par'rĭed
-păr'ry ing, -part', -pĕd'al, -plēad',
-ed, -ing, -er, -plot', *n.,* -plot',
v., -plot'ted, -ting, -point', -poise',ˈ
n., -poise', *v.,* -poised', -pois'-
ing, -pon'der ate, -a ted, -a ting,
-prove', -proved', -prov'ing.
coun'ter scarp', -seal', *v.,* -sealed',
-seal'ing, -sīgn', *n.,* -sign', *v.,*
-signed', -sign'ing, -sig'nal,
-sink', *n.,* -sink', *v.,* -sink'ing,
-sunk', -stock', -turn', -vail', *n.,*
-vail', *v.,* -vailed', -vail'ing, -view',
-weight', -wheel', -wheeled',
-wheel'ing, -work', *n.,* -work',
v., -worked', -work'ing.
coun'ter-ap peal', -ap pel'lant,
-ap proach', -arch', -at tired',
-at trac'tion, -at tract'ive, -bat'-
ter y, -bat'tled, -beam', -bond',
-brand', -camp', -cärte', -chev'-
ron ny (-shev'-), -claim', -clock'-
wise, -col'ored, -com pō'ny,
-couch'ant, -cou'ränt (*or* -ränt'),
-cŭr'rent, -deed', -dis tinc'tion,
-drain', -earth', -em bat'tled,
-em bōwed', -en am'el, -er'mĭne,
-es cal'loped (-kŏl'-), -ev'i dence,
-ex ten'sion, -fạll'er, -force,
-gear', -guärd', -hurt'er, -in'flu-
ence, -Ir'ri tant, -ir ri ta'tion,
-jump'er, -līght', -lode'.
coun'ter-mo'tion, -mo'tive,
-move'ment, -nâi'ant, -neb'u lé
(-lä), -ne go ti ā'tion (-shi ä'-),
-noise', -o'pen ing, -pace', -păr'-
a dox, -pa rōl', -păr'ry, *n.,* -pas'-
sant, -pend'ent, -pis'ton, -plēa',
-plot', *n.,* -poi'son (-zn), -po'-
tent, -prac'tice, -pres'sure,
-prŏj'ect, -proof', -punch',
-quar'tered, -rag ūled', -rail,
-ram'pant, -re flect'ed, -rev o-
lu'tion, -rev o lu'tion a ry, -rev-
o lu'tion ist, -round, -scuf'fle,
-sea', -seal', *n.,* -shăft', -sig'na-

---

nŏt, nôr, ūse, ŭp, ûrn, etüde, fōōd, fŏŏt, aŋger, boṅmot, thus, Bach.

ture, -slope', -stand', -state'-
ment, -stat'ute -step', -stroke',
-sub'ject, -sure'ty, -sway', -tal'-
ly, -ten'den cy, -ten'or, -term',
-tide, -tiĕrce', -tim'ber, -time',
-trac'tion, -trench', -trip'pant,
-trip'ping, -turn, -type', -vâir',
-vair'y.

coun'ter feĭt, *a.*, *n.*, and *v.*, -ed,
-ing, -er, -ly, -ness.

'count'ess, *pl.* -ess es (-ĕz).

coŭn'try, -tri fy (-fĭ), -fy ing,
-fied, -man, -side, -wom'an,
-base, -bred, -dånce, -rock,
-seat.

coun'ty, -seat.

coup (ko͞o), *n.*, *coup' de gråce'*,
coup' de măĭn', *c. d. sō leil'*
(-lål'), *c. d'é tat'* (dä tä'), *c.
d'œil'* (-dĕl' *or* -dêy).

cou pé (ko͞o pä'), a carriage.

cou pee' (ko͞o pē' *or* -pä'), a motion
in dancing; cou pée (ko͞o pä'),
a term in heraldry; couped
(ko͞opt).

coupe'-gorge' (ko͞op'-gŏrzh').

cou'per (ko͞o'-).

cou'ple (kŭ'pl), -pled (-pld),
coup'ler, coup'let, cou'ple-close
(-klŏs).

coŭp'ling, -box, -link, -pin, -pole,
-strap, -valve.

cou'pon (ko͞o'-), c. bond, c.
tick'et.

cou pūre' (ko͞o-).

coŭr'age, -a'geous (-jus), -geous ly,
-geous ness.

cou'rant (ko͞o'rănt *or* -ränt'), *a.*
and *n.*, a term in heraldry.

cou rånt' (ko͞o-), *n.*, a dance; a
kind of music.

cou'rant (ko͞o'ränt *or* -rănt'), a
newspaper.

cou răp' (ko͞o-).

cour'ba ril (ko͞or'-).

cour çon' (ko͞or'sŏn').

courge (ko͞orzh).

cou'ri er (ko͞o'-).

cou'ril (ko͞o'-).

cour'lan (ko͞or'-).

cour'lett (ko͞or'-).

cour'mĭ (ko͞or'-) *or* -cûr'-.

cou'rol (ko͞o'-).

---

còu ron né' (ko͞o rŏn nä').

cou'rou cou (ko͞o'ro͞o ko͞o).

cŏurse, coursed, cours'er.

cours'ing, -hat, -joint, -tri'al.

cŏurt, -ed, -ing, -er, -ier (-yer),
-ier ly, -like, -ly, -li ness, -ling,
-craft, -ship, -yard.

court'-băr'on, -bred, -card, -day,
-dress'er, -hand, -house, -lands,
-leet, -mar'shal, a marshal at
court; -mar'tial, *v.*, to arraign;
-plås'ter, -rolls, -shift, -ten'nis,
c. chap'laĭn, c. dress, c. fa'vor,
c. fool, c. guide, c. mar'tial, *n.*,
a trial; c. mourn'ing, c. sword.

cour'te sy (kur'-), *pl.* -te sies (-sĭz),
courte'sy (kurt'sy), -sĭed, -sy ing.

cour' te zan *or* -san (kur'-), -ship.

cou'ry (kow'-).

cous'-cous (ko͞os'-ko͞os) *or* cous'-
cou sou' (-ko͞o so͞o'), a favorite
African dish.

cous'cous (ko͞os'ko͞os), *Zoöl.*

cou'se ran ĭte (ko͞o'ze-).

Cou sin' (ko͞o'zăṅ'), Jean, Fr.
painter; Victor, Fr. philos.

cous'in (kŭz'n), -hood, -ly, -ry,
-ship.

cous' si net' (ko͞o'sĭ net' *or*- sĕ nä').

cou sū' (ko͞o-).

cou teau' (ko͞o tō'), *pl.* -teaux
(-tōz').

cou'til (ko͞o'- *or* -til').

cou'väde' (ko͞o'-).

cou verte' (ko͞o vĕrt').

cou veuse' (ko͞o vêz').

cou'vre-nuque (ko͞o'vr-nūk).

cou'xi a (ko͞o'shĭ a), -*xi o* (-shĭ o).

co vä'do.

co vä'ri ant.

cŏve, coved, cove'-brack'et ing,
-plane.

co vel'lĭne *or* -lĭte (*or* cŏv'el-).

cov'e nant (kŭv'-), -ed, -ing, -er,
one who makes a covenant; -or
and -nan tee', in law, parties to
a contract.   Cov'e nan ter, a
religious body.

Cov'en try (kŭv'-), t. Eng.   C.
Act, C. blue, cov'en try-bell,
-rape.

cov'er (kŭv'-), -ered, -er er, -er-
ing, -er let, -er lid, -er-cloth,

---

fāte făt, fär, fạll, fâre, fặst, sofȧ, mēte, mĕt, hêr, īce, ĭn, nōte,

-glȧss, -point, -side, -slip, -er-
ing-board, -strap.
co-versed' sïne.
cov'ert (kŭv'-), -ly, -er ture,
cov'ert-bȧr'on, -fĕath'er, -way.
cov'et (kŭv'-), -a ble, -ed, -er, -ing,
-ous, -ous ly, -ous ness, -ive-
ness.
co vet'ta.
cov'ey (kŭv'y), pl. -eys.
cŏ'vid.
cŏv'ing.
cow, -ing, cowed, cow'bane, -ber'-
ry, -bind, -bird, -boy, -catch'er,
-fish, -herd, -hide, -lick, -like,
-pock, -pox, -quakes, -slip,
-weed.
cow'-beck, -bell, -black'bird,
-blakes, -bun'ting, -cher'vil,
-cress, -doc'tor, -feed'er, -gate,
-grȧss, -heel, -herb, -hitch,
-hocked, -horn, -house, -keep'er,
-kill'er, -leech, -leech'ing, -man,
-oak, -pars'ley, -pars'nip, -pȧth,
-pea, -pi'lot, -plant, -poi'son,
-po'ny, -shark, -stone, -tree,
-troop'i al, -wheat, c. calf, cow'-
pen-bird.
cow'ard, -ice (-Iɜɜ), -ly, -li nɛss.
cow'die-gum.
cow'er, -ing, -ered.
cow'hage (-āj).
cowl, -mus'cle.
cowle (koul).
Cow'per (or kōō'-), Eng. poet,
Cow pë'ri an, -ri an glands.
cow'rie-pine or -ry-.
cow'ry.
cox'a, pl. -æ, -al, -al'gy, -al'gĭ a,
-al'gic.
cox'cŏmb (-kŏm), -comb'ic al
(-kŏm'-), -al ly, -comb ry.
cox en'dix, pl. -di ces.
cox'swain. See cockswain.
cox'y.
coy, -ish, -ly, -ness.
coy'ŏ tĕ (kī'-) or -ōte or cŏ yŏ'te.
coy'pou or -pu (-pōō).
coz (kŭz).
co zä'rĭ.
coz'en (kŭz'n), -age, -er, -ing.
cŏ'zy, -zi ly, -zi ness.
crab, -ber, -bing, -ber y, -catch'er,

a bird; -eat'er, a fish; -sï'dle,
-stick, -stock, -stone.
crab'-ap'ple, -catch'er, a person;
-eat'er, a person; -farm'ing,
-grȧss, -lob'ster, -louse, -oil,
-pot, -roll'er, -spï'der, -tree,
-winch, -wood, -yaws, crab's-
claw, -eyes.
crab'bed, -ness.
crack, -ing, -er, 'cracked, crack'-
skull, -tryst, cracks'man, crack'-
brained, -wil'low, -er-bāk'er.
crac'kle, -kled, -kling, c. chï'na,
c. glȧss, c. porce'laĭn, c. ware.
crack'nel.
crack'y.
Cra cŏ'vi an.
cra co'vi ĕnne'.
crä'dle, -dled, -dling, -dle-bar,
-cap, -clŏthes, -hole, -rock'er,
-scythe, c. vȧult.
crȧft, -i ly, -i ness, -less, -y,
crȧfts'man, -man ship.
crag, -ged, -ged ness, -gi ness, -gy,
crags'man.
crag'gan.
crȧig, -fluke, c. floun'der.
crȧil'-cä'pon.
crȧi'sey (-zy) or -zey.
crȧke, craked, crȧk'ing, crake'-
ber'ry, -hĕr'ring, -nee'dles.
crȧm, -ming, -mer, crammed.
crȧm bȧm'bŭ lĭ or -lee.
crȧm'bŏ, -cliṇk, -jiṇ'gle.
cramp, -ing, -y. -fish, cramped,
cramp'-bark, -bone, -drill, -i ron,
-joint, -ray, -ring, -stone.
cram'pet or -pit.
cram'pon or -pōōn', -po nee'.
cran'ber ry, -gȧth'er er, -tree.
crȧnch. See craunch.
cran'dall.
crane, craned, crȧn'er, -ing, -age.
crane'-fly, -lä'dle, -line, -necked,
-post, -shȧft, -stȧlk, cranes'bill,
a plant.
cra'ni um, pl. -ni a, -ni al, -ni a-
crŏ'mi al, -ni o fä'cial, -o clasm,
-o clȧst, -o graph, -ol'o gy, -o-
gist, -o log'ic al, -om'e try,
-o met'ric, -ric al, -os'co py,
-co pist, -ot'o my.
cranḳ, -i ness, -y, -bird, cranked.

cran̲k'-ax'le, -brace, -hatch'es,
-hook, -pin, -plane, -pull'er,
-shăft, -sĭd'ed, -wheel.
cran'nog or -noge (-nŏj).
cran'ny, -nĭed, -ny ing.
cran'ock.
cran'ta ra (or -tā'ra or -tä'ra).
crap'au dĭne.
crape, craped, crăp'ing, -y,
crape'-cloth, -fish, -hair, -myr'-
tle, crăp'ing-ma chine'.
crăp'ple or crap'et.
crăp'pit-hĕad.
crăps.
crap'u lence, -u lent.
crăsh, -ing, crashed.
crä'sis.
cras ped'o drŏme.
crăss, -ness, -ly.
cras'sĭ lin̲'gual.
cras su lä'ce ous.
crate, crāt'ed, -ing.
crä'ter, -al, -ter let, -ter ous, -tĕr'-
i form.
cräunch or crănch, -ing, craunched.
cra vat', -ted, -vat'-goose.
crave, craved, crăv'ing, -ing ly,
-ing ness, -er.
crä'ven (-vn).
crä'vo.
craw, -fish or cray'fish.
crawl, -er, -ing, -ing ly, -y, crawled,
crawl'-a-bot'tom.
craw'ley, -root.
crăy'on, -ŏned, -on ing, -on-board,
-draw'ing.
crăze, crazed, crăz'ing, -ed ness,
cra'zy, -zi ly, -zi ness, -zy weed,
cra'zy-bone, -quilt, -work.
creak. -ing, -ing ly, -y, creaked.
cream, -er, -er y, -i ness, -y,
-cups, a plant; -fruit, -cake,
-col'ored, -faced, -freez'er, -jug,
-laid, -nut, -pan, -pitch'er, -pot,
-slice, -white, -wove, c. cheese,
c. ware, cream'ing-pan.
crease, creased, creas'er, -ing, -y,
-ing-ham'mer, -tool.
crē'ăt.
crē ate', -a'ted, -a'ting, -a'tive,
-a tive ness, -a' tor, -tor ship,
-a'tion, -tion al, -tion ism.
cre a toph'a goŭs.

crĕa'tūre, -ship.
cre'brĭ cos'tate, -bri sul'cate.
crèche (krāsh).
Cré'cy (krĕs'sĭ or krā sē'), t. Fr.
crē'dence, -den'dum, pl. -da,
-dent, -dence-ta'ble.
cre den'tial.
crĕd'i ble, -i bly, -i bil'i ty.
crĕd'it, -ed, -ing, -or, -a ble, -ble-
ness, -a bly, cred'it-ūn'ion.
crē'dit' jon'cier' (krā'dĕ' fôn'syä'),
Cre dit' Mo'bi'lier' (mō'bēl'yä').
crē'do, -du'li ty, crĕd'u lous, -lous-
ly, -lous ness.
Cree, pl. Crees, a tribe of Indians.
cree, to soften by boiling; cree'ing,
creed.
creed, -less, creeds'man.
crĕek, -y, -fish, -duck. Creeks, a
tribe of Indians.
crĕel, -frame.
creep, -er, -y, -i ness, -hole, -mouse.
creep'ing, -ly, -disk, -jack, -jen'-
ny, -sail'or, -sheet, -sick'ness.
creese, a sword.
Cre'feld (krā'felt), t. Ger.
crē'mail'lère' (krā'māl'yär').
crē mas'ter, crem'as tĕr'ic.
cre'mate (or -mate'), -ma'tor,
-ma'tion, -tion ist, crĕm'a to ry
(or crē'-), -to'ri um, pl. -ums.
crem'ba lum, pl. -ba la.
crême (krām or krâm).
crĕm'o carp.
Crē mŏ'na, -mo nese' (or -nēz'),
-mo'ni an.
crē'na, pl. -næ, cren'u la, pl. -læ.
crē'nate, -ly, -na ted, -nä'tion,
crĕn'a ture (or krē'-), cren'u-
late, -la'ted -la'tion.
cren'el ate or -late (or krē'-),
-a ted or -la ted, -a ting or -la-
ting, -ā'tion or -la'tion.
cre nĕlle' or -nel', -nelled'.
crē'nic, -nit'ic.
crē'ole.
crē'o lin.
cre oph'a goŭs.
crē'ŏ sŏl (or -sŏl).
crē'o sōte, -bush, -wa'ter.
crē'pance or -pāne.
crêpe (krāp), -lisse' (-lēs').
crep'e ra, pl. -ræ.

crep'i da, *pl.* -dæ.
cre pi dŏ'ma, *pl.* -ma ta.
crep'i tac'u lum, pl. *-la.*
crep'i tate, -tā'ted, -tā'ting, -tā'-
tive, -i tant, *-i tus*, -i tā'tion.
crē'pon (krep'- *or* krē'- *or* krā'pŏn').
cre pus'cle *or* -cūle, -cu lar, -cu-
lous, -cu lum.
cres cen'do (*or* krĕ shen'do).
cres'cent, -ed, -cen toid, -cen'tic,
-tic al ly, -ti form, -cent wise,
-cent-shaped.
cres'hawk.
crĕ'sŏl (*or* -sŏl).
crĕ sŏt'ic.
cress, -y, -rock'et.
cres selle'.
cres'set, -light, -stone.
crest, -ed, -ing, -less, -fall'en,
cres tol'a try, crest'-tile.
crĕ syl'ic.
crĕ tā'ceous (-shus), -ceous ly,
-tac'ic (-tas'-).
Crēte, isl. Med. Crĕ'tan, -tic, -ti-
cism, -tism.
crête (krāt).
Crē'ti ans (-shǐ anz *or* -shanz),
Bib.
crĕ'ti fy, -ing, -fied, -fac'tion, -fi-
ca'tion, cre'tose (-tōs).
crĕ'tin, -ism, -tin ous.
crĕ'tion.
orc tŏnne'.
creut'zer (kroit'ser). See *kreutzer.*
creux (krê).
crĕ vässe' (*or* krĕv ăs'), -vassed',
-vasse'-stop'per.
crève'cœur' (krāv'ker')
crev'et.
crev'ĭce, -ĭced, -in.
cre visse' (-vēs').
crew (krōō).
Crewe (krōō), t. Eng.
crew'el (krōō'-), -stitch, -work.
Crey'ton (krā'-), pen name of J.
T. Trowbridge.
crib, -bing, -ber, cribbed, crib'-
work, -bǐt'er, -dam, -muz'zle,
-strap.
crib'bage, -board, -play'er.
crib'ble, -bled, -bling, -ble-brĕad.
crĭ bel'lum, pl. *-la.*
cri blé' (krĕ blä').

crib'rate, -ri form, rose (-rōs),
-rum, -rate, -puṇc'tate.
cric (krǐk).
Crich'ton (krī'-), Scotch schol.
crick (krǐk).
crick'et, -er, -ings, -ball, -bat,
-bird, -club, -field, -frog, -game,
-ground, -i'ron, -play'er, -shoes.
crī'coid, cri co pha ryn'geal, -co-
thy'roid (-thī'-) -roid'e an, -e us.
crīed, crī'er.
crǐm, -ming, crimmed.
crīme, crǐm'i nal, -nal ly, -nal ist,
-nal ness, -nal'i ty.
crǐm'i nate, -na ted, -na ting,
-tive, -tor, -to ry, -nā'tion, -nol'
o gy, o gist.
crimp, -age, -er, -ing, crimped,
crimp'-press, crimp'ing-board,
-fit, -house, -i'ron, -ma chine'.
crim'son (-zn), -son ing, -soned
(-znd), -son-warm.
crī'nal, -nate, -na ted, crǐn'a to ry
(*or* krī'-).
crǐnge, cringed, crin'ging, -ging ly,
-ger.
criṇ'gle.
crǐn ière' (-yâr').
crī'nite, crǐn'i to ry (*or* krī'-),
cri nif'er ous, -nig'er ous (-nij'-).
crǐṇ'kle, -kled, -kling, -kly, -kle-
root.
crǐ'noid (*or* crǐn'-), -noid'al,
-noid'e an.
crin'o līne (*or* -lin).
crī o ceph'a lus, *pl.* -a lǐ, -a lous,
-*o sphinx.*
crip'ple, -pled, -pler, -pling, -ply.
crī'sis, *pl.* -ses (-sēz).
crisp, -er, -ly, -ness, -y, crisp'ing-
i'ron, -pin.
cris'pate, -pa ted, -pa ture, -pa'-
tion.
Cris'pi (krēs'pē), It. statesman.
Cris'pin.
cris'sal.
criss'cross', -crossed, -cross-crow.
cris'sum, pl. *-sa.*
cris'ta, *pl.* -tæ, -tate, -ta ted,
-ti form, -tim'a nous.
cris to bal'īte.
crī tē'ri on, *pl.* -ri a.
crǐth, -o man cy.

crit′ic, -ic al, -al ly, -al ness, -ic-
as′ter, -i cal′i ty.
crit′i cīze *or* -cise, -cized, -ci zing,
-ci za ble, -ci zer, -cist, -cism,
crĭ tique′ (-tēk′).
criz′zle, *v.*, -zled, -zling.
criz′zle *or* -zel, *n.*
crŏak, -er, -ing, -y, croaked.
Crŏ′at, -a′tian (-shan).
croc.
croche (krŏch).
cro chet′ (-shā′), -cheted′ (-shād′),
-chet ing (-shā′ing), cro chet′-
-hook, -lace, -nee′dle, -type,
-work.
crock, -er y, -y, crock′-saw.
croc′o dīle, -dil′i an *or* -e an,
-dile-bird.
cro cō′ta, *pl.* -tæ.
crŏ′cus.
Crœ′sus (krē′-), King of Lydia.
crŏft, -er, -ing, -land.
crŏ′hol.
crŏ′ma.
Crom′ar ty, co. Scot.
crŏme.
crom′lech (-lĕk).
cro mor′na.
Crŏm′well (*or* krŭm′-), Oliver,
Protector Eng.
crŏne, -bane.
crŏ′nel, -net.
crŏnk.
Crŏn′stadt (-stät), t. Russ.
cron′stedt ite (krŏn′stĕt īt).
crŏ′ny, *pl.* -nies.
crŏŏk, -ed, *a.* -ed ly, -ed ness,
crooked, *v.* crook′back, -backed,
-bill, -neck, -rāft′er, crook′ed-
backed.
crŏŏkes′īte.
Crŏŏkes′ tube *or* Crookes′s tube.
crŏŏl.
crŏŏn, -er, -ing, crooned.
crop, -per, -ping, -ful, -py, -fish,
-weed, cropped.
crop′-ear, -eared, -hide, -ore,
crop′ple-crown.
crŏ quant′ (-kȧṅ′).
cro quet′ (-kā′), -queted′ (-kād′),
-quet′ing (-kā′-), -quet′-ball,
-ground, -mal′let, -play′er.
cro quette′ (-kĕt′).

crō quis′ (-kē′).
crŏre.
cro′sier (-zher). See *crozier*.
crŏss, -ing, crossed, cross′beak,
-bill, a bird; -bōw, -bōw′man,
-cut, *v.*, -fish, -flow, -flow′er,
-grained, -lĕgged, -piece, -roads,
-tree, -wort.
cross-ac′tion, -aisle (-īl), -armed,
-ax′le, -ban′is ter, -bar, -beam,
-beâr′er, -bear′ings, -bed′ding,
-belt, -bill, in law; -birth, -bit,
-bond, -bone, -breed, -bun,
-but′tock, -chock, -cloth, -clout,
-coun′try, -course, -curve, -cut,
n. and *a.*, -days, -ex am′ine,
-eye, -eyed, -fer′til ize, -file,
-fire, -fox, -frog, -fur′row,
-gar′net, -guard, -hair, -hatch′-
ing, -head, -hilt, -in ter rog′a-
to ry.
cross′-jack, -lode, -loop, -mar′-
ria ges, -mouth, -mul ti pli ca′-
tion, -nerv′ure, -pawl, -pile,
-piled, -pol li na′tion, -pur′pose,
-quar′ters, -ques′tion, -read′ing,
-ref′er ence, -road, -row, -ruff,
-rule, -sec′tion, -set, -shed, -sill,
-spī′der, -spring′er, -stȧff,
-stitch, -stone, -sum′mer, -tail,
-tie, -tim′ber, -tīn′ing, -valve,
-vault′ing, -vein, -vine, -way,
-weav′ing, -web′bing, -week,
-wire.
crŏsse.
crŏs′set, -sette′.
crŏss′īte.
Crot′a lä′ri a (*or* krō-), crŏt′a līne,
-a lin, -a lid.
crot′a lo, -a lum.
Crot′a lus (*or* krō′-).
crō′ta phe (*or* krŏt′-), crot′a phīte,
-phit′ic, cro taph′ic.
crotch, -et, -et ed, -et y, -et i ness,
-et eer′.
cro′ton, -ate, -in *or* -īne, -ton′ic,
-ton′y lēne, cro′ton-bug, -oil,
Cro′ton, *Bot. genus.*
crouch, -ing, -back, crouched,
crouch′-clay, -ware.
croup (krŏŏp), -al, -i ness, -ous,
-y.
crou pāde′ (krŏŏ-).

crou'pi er (kro͞o'-).
crou pi ère' (kro͞o pi âr').
crou'städe' (kro͞o'-).
crŏw, -ing, -bar, -bells, -ber'ry,
-flow'er, -foot, -stone, -toe.
crŏw'-bait, -black'bird, -corn,
-flight, -nee'dles, -nest, -net,
-quill, -roost, -shrike, -silk,
-steps, crow's-bill, -foot, -nest,
crow'foot -hal'yard.
crowd (kroud), -ed, -ing.
crow'dy *or* -die (krou'-), -time.
crowl (kroul), -ing.
crown, -ing, -er, -land, a province;
-less, -let, crowned, crown'beard,
-piece, a strap; -work.
crown'-ant'ler, -arch, -badge,
-bar, -crane, -face, -gate,
-gråft'ing, -head, -im pe'ri al, a
plant; -net, -palm, -pa'per, -pi'-
geon, -post, -saw, -scab, -sheet,
-shell, -spăr'row, -sum'mit,
-this'tle, -tile, -valve, -wheel.
crown' glåss, c. land, land owned
by the crown; c. piece, a coin;
c. prince.
croy'don.
croyl'stone.
croze, cro'zer, -zing, crozed, crŏ'-
zing-ma chine'.
cro'zĭer (-zher) *or* -sier (-zher),
-ziered.
croz'zle, -zled, -zling.
cru'cial (-shal).
cru'cian (-shan), c. carp.
cru'ci ate-com'pli cate (-shĭ-), -in-
cum'bent.
cru'ci ble, -mold, -ov'en, -tongs.
cru'ci fer.
cru'ci fix, -ci fix'ion (-fĭk'shun),
-ci form, -cig'er ous (-sij'-).
cru'ci fy, -ing, -fied, -fi er.
crude (krood), -ly, -ness, cru'di ty.
crue'-her'ring.
cru'ĕl, -ly, -ty.
cru'et, -stand.
Cruik'shank (kro͝ok'-), Eng. artist.
cruise (kro͞oz), cruised, cruis'er, -ing.
crŭl'ler.
crumb (krŭm), -ing, crumbed,
crum'my *or* crumb'y, crumb'-
brush, -cloth, -knife, -re mov'er,
-tray.

crum'ble, -bled, -bling, -bly.
cru'men.
crum'pet.
crum'ple, -pled, -pler, -pling, -ply.
crunch, -ing, crunched.
cru'nŏde, -no'dal.
cru'or, -o rĭn *or* -rĭne.
crup'per, -ing, -pered, -per-chain.
cru re'us or *-ræ-.*
crus, pl. *cru'ra,* cru'ral.
cru sade', -sãd'ed, -er, -ing.
cru sä'do *or* -zä'-.
cruse (kro͞os), cru'set.
crush, -er, -ing, crushed, crush'-
-hat, -room, crush'er-gage,
crush'ing-ma chine'.
cru'so cre at'i nĭn.
crust, -ed, -ing, -y, -i ly, -i ness,
crus'ta ted, -ta'tion, crust-hunt,
-hunt'er, -liz'ard.
crus'ta, pl. *-tæ.*
Crus tā'ce a (-shē a *or* -sē a), crus-
tā'cean (-shan), -ceous, -ceous
ness, -ce ol'o gy, -o gist, -o log'-
ic al.
crus tal'o gy, -o gist, -ta log'ic al.
crut.
crutch, crutched, crutch'-han'dle,
-han'dled, -pal'sy.
crutch'et.
crux, pl. *-es* or *cru'ces* (kro͞o'sēz),
c. an sa'ta.
Cruys hau tem (krois how'-) t. Belg.
cry, -ing, crī'er, cried, cry'ing-bird.
cry'er (krī'-), a bird.
cry mo dyn'i a (krī mo dĭn'-).
cry oc'o nīte (krī-).
cry'o gen (krī'-), -o hy'drate (-hī'-),
-o lite *or* kry'-, -oph'o rus,
-o phŏr ic, -o phyl'līte, os'co py,
-o scop'ic.
cry om'e ter (krī-).
crypt (krĭpt), *cryp'ta* (krĭp'-), pl.
-tæ, -tal, -tic, -tic al, -al ly, -ti-
dīne.
Cryp'to gā'mi a, cryp to gā'mi an,
-gam'ic, -tog'a mous, -a mist,
-a my.
cryp'to gram, -to graph, -graph'ic,
-ic al, -tog'ra phal, -ra pher, -ra-
phist, -ra phy.
cryp'to līte, -tol'o gy.
cryp'to nym.

cryp'to pĭne, -perth'īte, -to phyte,
-tō'pi a.
cryp to por'ti cus, -to scope, -tos'-
co py.
Cryp tŭ'rī.
crys'al.
crys'tal, -tal'lic, -lif'er ous, -lig'-
er ous (-lĭj'-), -tal lĭn, n., -tal-
lĭne (or -lĭn), a. and n., -lin'i ty,
-līte, -lī'tis.
crys'tal līze, -līzed, -lī zing, -zer,
-za ble, -lĭ za'tion, -tal lod,
-lo gen'ic, -log'e ny (-loj'-),
log'ra pher, -lo graph'ic, -ic al,
-al ly, -log'ra phy, -tal loid,
-loid'al, -lol'o gy, -lo mag net'ic,
-lo man cy, -lom'e try, -lo type,
-lur gy, -tal wort.
Csik (chĭk), co. Hung.
cte nid'i um (te nid'-), pl. -i a,
-i al, -i o braŋ'chi ate (-kĭ-).
cten'o branch (ten'o brăŋk or
tē'no-), -bran'chi ate.
Cte noid'e ĭ (tē-), -noph'o ra, cte-
noph'o ral, -o ran, -o rous,
cten'o phore, -phor'ic.
cua'dra (kwä'-).
cuär'ta (kwär'-).
cuar'tas (kwär'täs).
cuär til'la (-tēl'ya), -til'lo (-tēl'yo).
cuär'to.
cub, -hood, -less.
cu'ban īte.
cub'bridge-heads.
cŭb'by, pl. -bies, -by hole, -house,
-yew.
cube, cubed, cūb'ing, -age, -an'gle,
-a ture, -i form, cu'boid, -boid'-
al, -boi'des (-dēz), cube'-spar,
c. ore, c. powder.
cŭ'beb, -beb in, -beb'ic, cū'beb-
pep'per.
cŭ'bic, -al, -al ly, -al ness, -bi cite,
-bi cone, -bi con tra vā'ri ant, -bi-
co vā'ri ant.
cu bic'u lar.
cū bic'u lum, pl. -u la.
cu'bit, -bit al, -bit ed -bit-bone,
-fash'ion.
cu'bi ti dig'it al (-dij'-).
cu'bi to-car'pal, -ra'di al.
cu bi tus, pl. -lĭ.
cub'la.

cŭb'oc ta hĕ'dral, -oc ta hē'dron.
cu'bo-cŭbe, -cū'nē ĭ form, -do dec-
a hĕ'dral, -oc'ta hĕ'dral, -oc'ta-
hĕ'dron, cu'bo-cu'bo-cūbe, cu bo-
cu'bic.
cu'ca (kōō'-), -ca īne.
cŭck'hold.
cŭck'ing-stool.
cŭck'ōld, -old ize, -ized, -old ly,
-old ry, -ol dom, -old-măk'er,
cuck'old's-neck, -old's knot.
cuck'oo (kŏŏk'ōō), -ale, -bee,
-dove, -fish, -flow'er, -fly, -grăss,
-gur'nard, -pint, -shell, -shrike,
-spit, cuck'oo's-bread, -eye,
-maid, -mate, -meat.
cu cu'jo (kŏŏ kōō'hō or ku'ku jō),
a beetle.
cu cul'lis, pl. -lĭ, cu'cul late (or
-kul'-), -la ted, -cul'li form.
cŭ'cu loid, -cu li form, -cu lĭne.
cu'cum ber, cu cū'mi form (or
cū'cu-), -cum ber-bee'tle, -oil,
-root, -tree.
cŭ'cŭ pha.
cu cur'bit or -bĭte, -bi tal, -bi-
tĭn or -tīne, -bi tive, bi tā'ceous
(-shus).
cu cu'yo (kōō kōō'yō), a fish.
cŭd, -bear, -weed.
cud'dle, -dled, -dling.
cŭd'dy, pl. -dies, -dy-legs.
cudg'el, -eled or -elled, -el er or
-el ler, -el ing or -el ling,
cudg'el-play, -proof.
cudg'er ie.
cue, -ball, -but'ton, -owl, -rack, -tip.
Cuen'ca (kwĕn'-), prov. Sp.
cuer'dä (kwer'- or kōō âr'dä).
cuer'po (kwer'-).
Cuesmes (kwäm), t. Belg.
cues'ta (kwäs'ta).
cuff, -ing, cuffed, cuff'-but'ton,
-frame.
Cŭf'fy.
Cū'fic.
cui bŏ'nō (kī or kē).
cuin'age (kwĭn'-).
cui rass' (kwē răs' or kwē'-),
-răssed, -ras sier' (-sēr').
cuir'tan (kwer'-).
cuish (kwĭsh or kwĭs), -es.
cui'sine' (kwē'zēn').

cu'lâsse' (ko͞o'-).
Cul'dee (or -dē').
cul-de-jour' (ko͞ol'-de-fo͞or' or kul'-), pl. culs-de-jour', -de-lampe' (-lŏmp'), -de-sâc'.
cŭ'let.
cŭ'le us, pl. -le i.
Cū'lex, cu lic'i form (-lĭs'-), -i fuge.
cŭ'li cĭd.
cŭ'li na ry, -na ri ly.
cull, -ing, -er, culled.
cul'len der. See colander.
cul'len gey.
cul'lion (-yun).
cul'lis, pl. -lis es.
culls.
cul'ly, -ing, -lied.
culm (kŭlm), cul mic'o lŏŭs, -mif'-er oŭs, -mig'e nous (-mĭj'-), culm-bar.
cul'men.
cul'mi nate, -na ted, -na ting, -nal, -nant, -mi nā'tion.
cŭ'lot (-lō).
cu lot'tic, -lot'ism.
cul'pa ble, -ness, -pa bly, -bil'i ty, -pa to ry.
cul'prit.
cul'rage.
cult, -ism, -ist.
cultch.
cul tel lā'ri us, pl. -rĭ ĭ.
cul tel lā'tion.
cul tel'lus, pl. -lĭ.
Cul'ti ros'tres (-trēz), -ros'tral.
cul'ti vate, -va ted, -va ting, -va-ble, -va'ta ble, -va tor, -va'tion.
cul'trate, -tra ted, -tri form, -tri-ros'tral.
cul'ture, -less, -tūred, -tūr al, -tūr a ble, -tūr ist, -ture-bulb, -cell, -flu'id, -me'di um, -ov'en, -tube.
cul'tus, -cod.
cul'ver, -house, -tail, -wort.
cul'ver in, -in eer'.
cul'ver key.
cul'vert, -age.
cum'ber, -ing, -er, -some, -some-ly, -some ness, -brous, -brous ly, -brous ness, -bered.
cum'bly.
cŭm'in or cum'min, -in'ic.

cum'mer bund.
cum'ming.
cum'ming ton īte.
cum'ŏl (or -ōl).
cum'quat (-kwŏt) or kum'-.
cum'shaw or kum'-.
cŭ'mu lant.
cu'mu late, -la ted, -la ting, -la-tive, -tive ly, -la'tion.
cŭ'mu līte.
cŭ'mŭ lo-cĭr'ro-strā'tus, cu'mŭ-lo-cĭr'rus, -nim'bus, -stra'tus.
cŭ'mŭ lus, pl. -lĭ, -mu lose (-lōs), -loŭs.
cū nab'u lar.
cun du răn'go.
cŭ'ne ate, -ly, -a ted, -a tor, -ne-al, -at'ic.
cŭ nĕtte'.
cŭ'ne us, pl. -ne ĭ, -ne'i form or cŭ'ni-.
cu nic'u lus, pl. -lĭ, -u lar, -u late, Cu nic'u los, Zoöl. genus.
cun'ner.
cun'ning, -ly, -ness.
cup, -per, -py, cupped, cup'board, -cŏr al, -ful, -man, -rose, -séed, -an'vil, -bear'er, -cake, -gall, -guard, -hilt'ed, -land, -leath'er, -li'chen (-ken), -moss, -mush'-room, -plant, -purse, -shaped, -shrimp, -sponge, cup-and-cone, cup'-and-sau'cer, cup guard, c. purse, c. valve.
cŭ pee'.
cŭ'pel, n., cŭ pel', v. -pelled', -pel'ling, -pel la'tion, cu'pel-dust.
Cŭ'pid, cu pid'i ty, -i noŭs.
cŭ'pi dŏne.
cŭ'po la, -fur'nace.
cup'pa.
cup'ping, -glâss, -ma chine', -tool.
cŭ'pram.
cŭ'prate.
cŭ'pre a-bark, cŭ'pre īne, -pre-oŭs.
cŭ'pric, -prif'er ous, -prīte, -proid, -prum.
cŭ'pule, -pu late, -pu lar -li form, -pu lif'er ous.
cur, -rish, -rish ly, -rish ness, -ship, c. dog.
cu ra çoa' (ko͞o ra sō' or -so'a) or

nŏt, nôr, ūse, ŭp, ûrn, etüde, fo͞od, fŏŏt, aŋger, boṅmot, thus, Bach.

-çao' (-sŏ'), cu ra çao'-bird, Cu ra çao, isl. W. I.

cŭ rä'rĕ or -rä'rĭ or -rä'rä (or kōō rä'-), cŭ rä'rĭn or -rĭne (or kōō rä'-), -ra rize, -rĭ za'tion.

cŭ răs'sŏw.

cŭ'rate, -ship, -ra cy.

cŭ rä'tor, -ship, cu'ra to ry.

curb, -ing, -less, curbed, curb'-stone, -bit, -chain, -key, -pin, -plate, -send'er, c. roof.

cur cŭ'li o, -li on'i doŭs, -li o-trap.

curd, -y, -i ness, -less, cur'dle, -dled, -dling, curd'-break'er, -cut'ter, -mill.

cure, -less, cŭr'a ble, -ble ness, -bil'i ty, -a tive, -tive ly, -er, -ing, cured, cure-all, cŭr'ing-house.

cu rē (kōō rä').

cŭ rette' (or kŏŏ-), -ret'ted, ret'ting.

cur'few, -bell.

cŭ ri a, pl. -æ, -ri al -al ism -ri-ate, -a lis'tic.

cŭ'ri o, pl. -ri os (-ōz), -o log'ic (-lŏj'-).

cŭr ri os'i ty, -shop.

cŭ'ri ous, -ly, -ness, -ri o'so, pl. -sos (-sōz) or -si (-sē).

curl, er, -ing, -ing ly, -ed ness, -y, -i ness, curled, curl'-cloud, -pate, curl'y-pate, -hĕad'ed, -ing-i'ron, -stone, -tongs.

cur'lew, -ber'ry, -jack, -knot.

curl'i cue or -y cue.

cur'lĭe wur'lie.

cur mud'geon (-jun), -ly.

cŭr'rant, -bōr er, -clear'wing, -gall, -mŏth, -tree, -worm.

cŭr'rent, -ly, -ness, -ren cy, -rent-breāk'er, -fend'er, -gage, -me'-ter, -mill, -reg'u la tor, -sail'ing, -wheel.

cŭr'ri cle, -ri cled, -ri cling.

cŭr ric'u lum, pl. -lums or -la.

cŭr'ry, -ri er, -ri er y, -ry ing, -ried, -ry cōmb, -ry-card, -leaf, -pow'der, -ry ing-glove.

curse, curs'er, -ing, cursed, v., curs'ed, a., -ed ly, -ed ness.

cur'si tor.

cur'sive, -sive ly.

Cur sō'res (-rēz).

cur'so ry, -so ri ly, -ri ness, -so'-ri al, -ri ous.

cur'sus.

curt, -ly, -ness.

cur tail', -ing, -er, -ment, -tailed'.

cur'tail-step, c. dog.

cur'taĭn, -less, -tained, -tain-an'gle, -lec'ture, -pa'per, -wall.

cur'tate, -ta'tion.

Cur tä tŏ'ne (kōōr'- -nä), t. It.

cur tein' (-tān') or -tā'na.

cu'ru ba (kōō'rōō bä).

cu'ru cu'cu (kōō'rōō kōō'kōō).

cŭ'rule.

cu ru'ro (kōō rōō'ro).

curve, curved, curv'ing, -ed ness, -al, -ant, -ate, -a ted, -a tive, -a ture, cur va'tion.

cur'vet (or -vet'), -ed or -ted, -ing or -ting.

cur'vi cau'date, -cos'tate, -den'-tate, -fo'li ate, -lin'e ad, -lin'e al, -e ar, -ar ly, -ăr'i ty, -vi ros'tral, -vi ner'vate, -se'ri al, cur'vi-form, -vi nerved, -vi ty, -vo-grăph, -vu late.

Cur'vi ros'tres (-trēz).

Cus'co bark, C. chī'na, cus'co-cin'cho nĭn (-kō-).

cus'cus, -grăss, -oil, Cus'cus, Zoöl. genus.

cŭsh.

cush'at (kŏŏsh-).

cŭsh'ew-bird (-ōō-).

cush'ion (kŏŏsh'un), -ing, -less, -y, -ioned, -ion et, -ion-cap'i tal, -căr'om, -dănce, -pink, -răft'er, -scale, -star, -stitch.

Cŭsh'īte, Bib.

cŭsk, -eel.

cŭsp, cus'pa ted, cus'pis, pl. cus'-pi des (-dēz).

cus'pid, -pi dal, -pi date, -da'ted.

cus'pi dor.

Cus set (küs sä'), t. France.

cus'so (kŭs'- or kōōs'- or kūs'-).

cus'tard, -ap'ple, -cups, a plant.

cus'to dy, -tōde, -to dee', -to'di al, -di am, -di an, -an ship, cus'tos, pl. -to'des (-dēz).

cus'tom, -a ry, -a ri ly, -ri ness, -er, cus'tom-house, cus'toms du'ty, c. ŭn'ion.

---

fāte, făt, fär, fąll, fâre, fåst, sofå, mēte, mĕt, hêr, īce, ĭn, nōte,

cut, cut′a way, cut′purse, -throat, -wa′ter, -weed, -worm, -a gainst (-genst), -chŭn′doo, -grăss, -lips, -lugged, -mark, -off, -out, -pile, -splay, -toothed, -work, c. drop.

cū tā′ne ous, -ous ly.

cutch, -er, -er y.

cute, -ly, -ness.

cū′ti cle, -tic′u la, pl. -læ, -u lar, -lar ize, -ized, i zing, ĭ zā′tion, -u lum, cū′ti fy, -fied, -fy ing, -fĭ ca′tion, cū′tin, -tin ize, -ĭ za′- tion, cū′tis, -ti pŭnc′tor, -ti sec′- tor.

cut′las or -lass, -fish.

cut′ler, -ler y.

cut′let.

cut′lins.

cut′nĭ.

cū′tose (-tōs).

cut′ter, -bar, -grĭnd′er, -head, -stock.

cut′ting, -board, -box, -com′pass (-kum′-), -en′gine, -file, -gage, -line, -lip′per, -nip′pers, -off, -out, -plane, -pli′ers, -press, -punch, -shoe, -spade, -thrust, -tool.

cut′tle, -bone, -fish, -fish-bone.

cut′to.

cut′tōō-plate (or -tōō′-).

cut′ty, -gun, -quean, -stool, -wren.

cut′wạl.

cū vette′.

Cu vi er′ (kōō′vē ā′), Fr. natural- ist.

Cuy a hŏ′ga (kĭ-), co. O.

Cuz′co (kōōs′-), dept. Peru.

Cwm′du (kōōm′dĕ), t. Wales.

cy′an am′ĭd or -ĭde (or sĭ′-).

cy′a nate (sĭ′-), -ā′ne an, -an′ic, -an au′rate.

cy′an hem′a tin (sĭ′-), -an hy′dric (-hĭ′-).

cy′a nĭd or -nĭde (sĭ′-), -a nĭne, -a nĭte, -an′o gen (-jen).

cy′a no hem′o glŏ′bin (sĭ′-).

cy a nom′e ter (sĭ-), -e try, -nop′- a thy.

cy′a no phyc′e æ (sĭ′a no fis′-), -phy′- ceous (-fish′us).

cy an′o phyl or -phyll (sĭ-), cy a noph′i loŭs.

cy a nŏ′sis (sĭ-), -a nosed (-nŏst), -an′o site, -o type, -a not′ic.

cy an′u ret (sĭ-), -a nu′rate, a- nu′ric, -an u ram′ĭde.

Cy ath′e a (sĭ-), cy′a thoid, -a tho- zŏ′oid.

cy ath′i form (sĭ-), -ath′o lĭth, -a tho phyl′loid.

cy′a thus (sĭ′-), pl. -a thĭ.

Cyb′ē lĕ, *Myth.*

Cy′cas (sĭ′-), cy′cad, cyc a dā′- ceous (sĭk-).

Cyc′la men, *Bot. genus,* cyc′la- min, *Chem.*

cyc′las (or sĭ′-).

cy′cle, -cled, -cler, -cling, -clist, -clide, cyc′lic (or sĭ-), -lic al.

Cy′clo braŋ′chi a (sĭ klo brang′- kĭ a), -chi ā′ta, cy clo braŋ′chi ate (-kĭ-), -clo ceph′a lus, *pl.* -lĭ, -ce phal′ic.

cy′clo cæ′lic (sĭ klo sē′lik).

cy′cloid, -cloid′al, -cloid′e an, -clo grăph.

cy′clo lĭth.

cy clom′e ter (sĭ-), -e try, -clo- met′ric.

cy′clone, -clo nal, -clon′ic, -ic al- ly, -clo′no scope.

cy′clŏ neū′ral, -neu′roŭs.

cy′clo pē′di a or -pæ′-, -pē′dic (or -pĕd′-), -dĭc al, -pe′dist.

Cy′clops, -clop′ic, -clo′pi a.

cy clop′ter id (sĭ-), -ter ĭne, -ter- oid.

cy′clo rä′ma (or -rā′-), -ram′ic.

cy′clo scope.

cy clo′sis (sĭ-).

cy′clo style, -sty′lar.

cy clot′o my (sĭ-), -clo tom′ic.

cy dăr′i form (sĭ-).

cyg′net, -ne ous, -nĭne.

cyl′in der, -in drā′ceous, -dric′i ty, -droid, cy lin′dric, -dric al, -al ly, -dri form, -dro met′ric, cyl′in der- ax′is, -bit, -bore, -cock, -cov′er, -face, -grĭnd′er, -mill, -mill′ing, -port, -pow′er, -snail, -snake, -stăff, -tape, -wrench, c. car, c. desk, c. en′gine, c. es cape′ment, c. gage, c. glăss, c. press.

cyl′in dreŋ′chy ma (-kĭ-).

Cyl lē′ni an.

---

cy'ma (sī'ma *or* kĕ'ma), pl. *-mæ,*
  -ma'ti um (-shi um), pl. *-ti a.*
cy'ma graph (sī'-), -ma phen.
cy mat'o līte (sī-).
cym'bal, -er *or* -ler, -baled *or*
  -balled, cym'bal-doc'tor.
cym'bate,   -be ce phal'ic   (*or*
  -sef'-), -bi form,   -bo ce phal'ic
  (*or* -sef'-), -bo ceph'a ly.
Cym'be līne (*or* -lĭn), Shak.
cyme,   -let, cy mif'er ous   (sī-),
  cy'moid, -mose (-mōs), -mose ly,
  -moŭs, -mule, -mu lose.
cy'mĕne (sī'-), -mol.
cy'mic (sī'-).
cy'mĭ dīne.
cym'lin *or* -blin, *or* -ling *or* -bling.
cy'mo gene.
cy'mo phane (*or* sĭm'-), -moph'a-
  nous.
cy mot'rĭ chous (sī-, -kŭs).
Cym'ry (kĭm'-) *or* Kym'ry, -ric.
cy nan'che (sĭ nang'ke).
cy năn'thro py (sī-).
cyn'arc tŏm'a chy (-kĭ).
cyn hy e'na (-hī-).
cyn'i at'rics.
cyn'ic,   -ic al,   -al ly,   -al ness,
  -i cism.
cyn'i pid, -i poid, -pid'e ous, cy-
  nip'i dous (sī-), Cyn'ips (*or* sī-).
cyn o ceph'a lous, -ce phal'ic (*or*
  -sef'-), Cyn'o ceph'a lus (*or* sī'-
  no-).
cy'noid (*or* sĭn'-), -noi'de a, -no-
  lys'sa, -no su'ral (-shōō'-), -no-
  morph'ic, -no phre nol'o gy, -no-
  pĭ the'coid.
cyn'o phŏbi a   (*or*   sī-).
cy nop'o dous (sī-).
cy'no sure (-shoor *or* sĭn-), -su'-
  ral.
Cyn'thi a, *Myth., Entom. genus.*
Cy pe'rus (*or* sĭp'-), cy'pe rog'ra-
  pher, -rol'o gist.
cy'phel, -phel'la, -phel'late, -phel'-
  læ form.
cy'pho nau'tes (-tēz *or* sĭf'-).
cy'pho nism   (*or* sif'-).
cy pho'sis (sī-).
cy præ'id (sī prē'-), -præ'oid.
cy'press, -knee, -moss, -root,
  -tree, -vine.

cyp'rĭne, -ri ot, -ri noid.
Cy'pris.
Cy'prus, isl. Med.   Cyp'ri an, cy'-
  prus-bird, -lawn, C. tur'pen tine.
Cyp'se lĭ,   -se līne,   -loid,   -lo-
  morph, -morph'ic, -sel'i form (*or*
  cyp'se-).
Cy re'nĕ (sī-), -ni an, Cyr'e na'ic,
  -na'i cism.
cyr'to līte (sêr'-).
cyr tom'e ter.
cyr tŏ'sis.
cyr'to style (sêr'-).
cyst, -ed, -ic, -e in, cys tal'gi a,
  cys'tel minth, -ti cle, cys'tous.
cys teņ'chy ma   (-kĭ-),   cys't e n-
  chyme (-kī m), -chym'a tous
  (-kĭm'-).
cys ti cer'cus, -cer'coid.
cys'ti tome.
cys'to carp, -carp'ic.
cys'to cele.
cys to coc'coid.
cys'to cyte, -to scope.
cys'to lith, -lith'ic, -li thī'a sis.
cys to'ma,   pl.   -ma ta, -to mor'-
  phoŭs, -to pa ral'y sis.
cy'tăs ter (*or* sĭ tas'-).
cyte (sīt).
Cyth e re'a, -re'an.
cyt'i sin.
Cyt'i sus.
cy'to chy lē'ma (sī'to kī-), -to clā'-
  sis (*or* -tŏc'la-), -clas'tic, -to-
  derm, -to glŏ'bin, -tol'o gy, -tol'-
  y sis, -to lymph, -to prŏct, -to-
  re tic'u lum,   -to sĭn, -to sōme,
  -to tax'is, -toth'e sis, -tot'ro pism.
cy to coc'cus (sī-).
cy to gen'e sis (sī to jen'-), -gen'-
  ic, -ge net'ic, -tog'e nous (-toj'-),
  -tog'e ny.
cy'toid.
cy'to stŏme, -tos'to mous.
cy'var (kĕ'-), cy've lin (kĕ'-).
Czai kov'ski (chī kŏv'skĕ), Pol.
  novelist.
czar (zar), *or* tzar *or* tsar (tsar),
  -e vitch *or* -o vitch *or* -o witz,
  czä rev'na, -ri'na (-rĕ'-), -rit'za
  or -sa.
Czar to rys'ki (chär tō ris'ke), Pol.
  statesman.

---

fāte, făt, fär, fạll, fâre, fặst, sofá, mēte, mĕt, hêr, īce, ĭn, nōte,

Czech (chĕk), -ic.
Czer'no witz (chĕr'no vits), t. Aust.

Czer'ny (chĕr'ne), Aust. composer.
Czu'czor' (tsōō'tsor'), Hung. writer.

D

D links, D string, D valve.
daal'der (däl'-).
dä'än.
dab, -ber, -bing, dabbed, -bing ma chine'.
dab'ble, -bled, -bling, -bling ly.
dab'chick, -wash.
dab'er lack.
dab'i tis.
da boy'a or *-boi'a.*
dä ca pel'la, dä cä'po, dä chie'sa (kyä'-).
dace.
dä'cey (-sĭ).
dachs'hund (dächs'hŏŏnt or däks-).
dä'cian (-shan).
dack'er, -ered, -er ing.
da coit', -koit or -coit'y.
dac'ry o līte or -līth.
dac'tyl or -tyle (-tĭl), -ty lar, -tyl'ic, -tyl ist.
Dac'ty lī, *Myth.*
dac tyl'i o glyph, -i og'ly phy̆, -og'ra phy, -ol'o gy, -o man'cy.
dac'tyl on'o my, -op'ter ous, -tyl o zo'oid.
dad'dle, -dled, -dling.
dad'dy or -die, -dy-long'legs.
dä'do (or dä'-), *pl.* -does, -do-plane.
dæ'dal, -däl'ian (-yan).
Dæd'a lus (ded'-), *Myth.*
daf'fo dil, -dil'ly, -fo down dil'ly.
dâft, -ly, -ness.
dag'gar, a fish.
dag'ger, -fi'ber, -knee, -knife, -moth, -plant, -thrust.
dag'gett.
D'A gin'court' (dä'zhăn'kōōr'), Fr. archæol.
dag'lock.
dä'go or Dä'go.
da gö'ba (or dag'-).
Dä'gon, an idol; dä'gon, an ox.
dägue.
Dä'guerre' (-gêr'), Fr. inventor, Da guĕr're an, da guerre'o type

(-tĭp), -o typed, -o ty'ping, -ty'-per, -ty'pist, -ty'py, -typ'ic (-tĭp'-).
dä hä bē'ah or *-hä bi'yeh* (-bē'ĕ).
Däh'lia (-lya or däl'ya), *pl.* -lias (-yåz).
Dä hŏ'mey (-mä), king W. Afr.
da hōōn'.
däi'ly.
däi'men.
Dai'mi o (dī'mĭ o or dīm'yo).
däin'ty, -ti ly, -ti ness.
daï'ri (-rē), *-sä'mä.*
däi'ry, *pl.* -ries, -ry ing, -ry maid, -man, -wom'an, -farm.
dä'is.
däi'sy (-zy), *pl.* -sies, -sied, -sy bush, -cut'ter.
daj'aksch (dī'aksh).
da'ker-hen.
Da kŏ'ta, -tan.
dāl.
dāle, -land, -land'er.
dales'man.
dālle.
dalles (dălz).
dal'ly, -li ance, -li er, -lĭed, -ly ing, -ing ly.
dal mat'ic or -i ca.
dăl'rĭ pa.
dāl se'gno (sän'yo).
Dạl'ton, Amer. physiol.
Dạl'tŏ'ni an, dạl'ton ism.
dam, -head, -plate, -stone.
dam'age, -a ble, -aged, -a ging.
dä'man.
Dăm'as cēne, *n.* and *a.*
dăm as cēne', *v.,* -cened', -cēn'ing, dam'as cene, *n.,* a plum.
Dam'a scenes', *Bib.*
Da mas'cus, a city. da măs'cus, a kind of sword.
dăm'ask, -ing, -asked, -ask-loom.
dam as keen' (or dam'-), -ing, -keened'.
da mas sé' (dă măs sä'), dam as sin'.

dam'brŏd.
dame, -wort, -school.
Dă'mĭ an ĭte, -an ist.
Da'mis' (dă'mē'), Molière.
dam'mar, -gum, -pine, -pitch,
  -res'in (-rez'-).
damn (dăm), damned, dam'na-
  ble, -ble ness, -na bly, -na bil'-
  i ty, -na to ry, -na'tion, -ning
  (or -ing), -nif'ic, -nif'i ca ble,
  -ni fi ca'tion, dam'num, pl. -na.
dä mŏ'.
Dam'o cles (-klēz), -cle'an.
Da mœ'tas, Virgil.
Dă'mon, friend of Pythias.
da mouch' (-mōōch').
da mour'ĭte (-mōōr'-).
damp, -ing, -en, -en er, -er, -ish,
  -ish ly, -ish ness, -ly, -ness,
  damped, damp'er-pĕd'al.
Däm'rosch (-rŏsh or -rōsh), Prus.
  mus.
dam'sel (-zel), -fly.
Dan, -ĭte, Bib.
dan.
Dan'ă ē, Myth.
dă'na ĭd, -ĭde.
Dă'na is or -us, Dăn ā'i des
  (-dēz), Dä'na id'e an (or dăn'-).
dä'na ĭte, -na lĭte.
dan'bur ĭte.
dănce, dănced, dan'cer, dance'-
  mu'sic.
dan cette', -cet té' (-sĕt tā'), -cet'-
  ty.
dăn'cing, -dis ease', -girls, a
  plant; -măs'ter, -room, -school,
  d. girls, dan seuse' (doṅ sêz').
dan'da.
dan'de lĭ on.
dan'der, -der ing.
dän'di (-dē).
dan'di prat or -dy prat.
dan'dle, -dled, -dling, -dler.
dan'druff or -driff.
dan'dy, -ish, -ism, -ize, -ized, -ling,
  -di fy, -fy ing, -fied, dan'dy-brush,
  -cock, -fe'ver, -hen, -horse, -note,
  -rig, -rŏll'er.
Dane, Dä'ni cism, Dăn'ish, -ism,
  Dăns'ker, -ker man, dane'flow'-
  er, -weed, -wort, dänes'blood.
Dăne'geld or -gelt, Dane'law.

dä'neq (-nĕk).
dăn'ger, -ous, -ous ly, -ous ness,
  -sig'nal.
daṇ'gle, -gled, -gling, -gler, -gle-
  ber'ry.
daṇk, -ish, -ness.
Dan'ne brog or Dan'e-.
Dăn'te (or dän'tā), It. poet, Dan'-
  te an (or -te'an), -tesque', -tist,
  -toph'i list.
dant'su (-sōō).
Dănt'zic or Dän'zig (-tsig), c.
  Ger., D. beer, D. wa ter.
dap, -ping, dapped.
Daph'nĕ, Myth.; Bot. genus.
  daph'nē.
Daph'ni a, daph'net in, -ni ā'-
  ceous, -ni ad, -nin, -no man'cy.
dap'per, -per ling.
dap'ple, -pled, -pling, -ple-bay,
  -gray.
Dar'by, -ism, -ĭtes, dar'by, a
  plasterer's tool.
Dar'da nĕlles', strait bet. Europe
  and Asia.
Dar dĕnne', tp. Mo.
dare, dared, dâr'ing, -ing ly, -ing-
  ness, dare'dev il, -il try.
dăr'ic.
dä'rĭ I.
dä'ri ole.
Da rī'us, Bib.; king of Persia.
dark, -en, -ened, -en er, -en ing,
  -ly, -ness, dark'-arch es, -slide.
dar'kle, -kled, -kling, -kling-bee'tle.
dar'ky or -key.
dar'ling.
darn, -ing, -er, darned, darn'ing-
  ball, -last, -nee'dle, -stitch.
dar'nel.
da ro'ga or -gha.
da rōō'-tree.
dăr'ri ba.
dart, -ed, -ing, -ing ly, -er, dart'-
  moth, -sack, -snake, -er-fish.
dar'tars.
dar'tŏs.
dar'tre (-tr), -trous.
Dar win'i an, -ism, -win ism, -ist,
  -ize, -ized.
dash, -ing, -ing ly, -er, -y, dashed,
  dash'board, -guard, -lamp, -pot,
  -rule, -wheel, -er-block.

---

fāte, făt, fär, fạll, fâre, fạst, sofà, mēte, mĕt, hêr, ice, ĭn nōte,

das'sy.
das'tard, -ly, -li ness.
das tu'rĭ (-tōō'-).
da sym'e ter.
date, -less, dāt'ed, -er, -a ble,
-ing, date'-line, -mark, -palm,
-plum, -shell, -sug'ar, -tree, d.
wine.
dä te ä'tro (tā ä'-), *dä ti rar'si*
(tē rär'sē).
da tĭ'sĭ.
dā'tive, -ly, -ness.
dä'tŏ *or* -tu (tōō) *or* dăt'tō.
dä'tum, pl. *-ta*, -line, -plane.
dąub, -er, -ing, -y, daubed.
Daub (doup), Ger. theol.
Daube'ny (dōb'ny *or* dąu'be ny),
Eng. chemist.
D'Au'bi'gne' (dō'bē'nyä'), Fr.
hist.
Dau'bi'gny' (dō'bē'nyē'), Fr.
painter.
dąu bree'lĭte, -brē'īte.
dąud.
Dau'det' (dō'dā'), Fr. auth.
dąugh'ter, -less, -li ness, -ly, -in-
law.
dąunt, -ed, -ing, -er, -less, -less ly,
-less ness.
dąu'phin, -ess, -phine (-fēn).
dauw (dąw).
dăv'en port, a desk.
dăv'ĭt (*or* dā'-), -fall, -hook.
dā'vīte.
dā'vyne (-vīne), -vy um.
daw, -ish, -fish, -pate, -dress'ing.
daw'dle, -dled, -dler, -dling.
dawk.
dawm.
dawn, -ing, dawned.
daw'son Ite.
day, -ber'ry, -break, -flow'er,
-man, -mare, -shine, -sight,
-spring, -time, -wom'an, -blind'-
ness, -book, -coal, -dream,
-feed'er, -fly, -hole, -house, -la'-
bor, -lev'el, -lil'y, -nurse, -nur'-
ser y, -owl, -peep, -room, -rule,
-schol'ar, -school, -star, -tale,
-work, -writ, days'man.
dā'yal.
daze, dazed, dāz'ing, -ed ly, -ed-
ness.

daz'zle, -zled, -zling, -zling ly,
-zler.
dēa'con, -ess, -hood, -ry, -ship,
-seat.
dĕad, -en, -en er, -en ing, -ened,
-ly, -li ness, -ness, -eye, -fall,
-head, a person; -light, -lock,
-man, a log; -an'gle, -beat,
-born, -cen'ter, -clothes, -col'or-
ing, -dip'ping, -door, -file, -flat,
-ground, -hand, -head, a term
used in machinery; -house,
-latch, -line, -lock, a door-lock;
-march, -neap, -net'tle, -oil,
-plate, -pledge, -point, -reck'on-
ing, -rise, -sheave, -shore,
-spin'dle, -stroke, -tongue, -wa'-
ter, -weight, -well, -wĭnd,
-wood, -wool, -work, -works, d.
load, d. rope, d. set.
dead'-man's-hand, a plant;
-men's-bells, a plant; -men's-
fin'gers, a plant; -men's-lines, a
plant; dĕad'ly-hand'ed, -live'ly.
dĕaf (*or* dĕf), -en, -en ing, -ly,
-ness, -ad'der, -dumb'ness,
-mute, -mute'ness, -mūt ism.
dĕal, -ing, -er, dĕalt, deal'fish,
-frame, -tree.
De A mi'cis (dā ä mē'chēs), It.
auth.
dĕan, -er y, -ship.
dĕar, -ly, -ness, -y *or* -ie, -bought,
-loved.
dĕar'born.
dĕarn.
dĕarth, -ful.
dĕa'sil (-shēl).
dĕath, -ful, -ful ness, -less, -less-
ness, -like, -ly, -li ness, -ward,
-bed, -blow, -watch, a beetle;
-ad'der, -ag'o ny, -bell, -bird,
-cord, -damp, -dănce, -day,
-fire, -grap'ple, -hunt'er, -măsk,
-point, -rate, -rat'tle, -stroke,
-struck, -thrŏe, -tick, -to'ken,
-trănce, -trap, -war'rant, -watch,
a watcher; -wound, death's-
head, -herb.
dĕ bă'cle (*or* -băk'- *or* -bä'kl).
de bar', -ment, -ring, -barred'.
de bark', -ing, -barked', -bar kā'-
tion.

de base', -ment, -based', -bās'er,
-bās'ing, -ing ly.
de bate', -bāt'a ble, -bāt'ing, -ing-
ly, -er, -ed.
de bạuch', -ment, -ed ly, -ed ness,
-er, -er y, -ing, -bauched', deb'-
au chee' (-ō shē' *or* dā'bŏ'-
shā').
de beige' (-bāzh').
dĕ ben'ture, -tured.
de bĭl'i tate, -ta ted, -ta ting, -ta'-
tion, -i ty.
dĕb'it, -ed, -ing.
dĕ bĭ tū'min ize, -min Ĭ za'tion.
dé blai' (dā blā').
dĕb'o nâir', -ly, -ness.
de bouch' (-bōōsh'), -ment.
dé'bou'ché' (dā'bōō'shā'), *-bou'-
chure'* (-shŏŏr').
dé bride'ment (dā brēd'mŏṅ).
dé'bris' (dā'brē').
dĕ bruised'.
debt (dĕt), debt'or, -ee', -less, -let.
de'bu scope (dā'bŏŏ-).
dé'but' (dā'bōō'), *-bu'tant'* (-tŏṅ'),
-tante' (-tŏṅt').
dĕc'a chord, -chor'don, -a cū'mi-
na'ted.
dec'ăde *or* ad, -a dal, -a da'tion.
dĕ că'dence, -den cy, -dent.
dec'a gon, -a gram *or* -gramme,
-a gyn (-jin), -gyn'i an, de cag'o-
nal, -cag'y nous (-kaj'-).
dec a hĕ'dron, -he'dral.
de cal'ci fy (-fĭ), -ing, -er, -fied,
-fĭ ca'tion.
dĕ cal'co mā'ni a.
dec'a let.
dec'a li'ter *or* -tre (-lē'ter *or*
de kal'-), *-li'ron*, pl. *-ra.*
dec'a logue, de cal'o gist.
De cam'e ron'ic.
dec'a mĕ ter *or* -tre, de cam'er ous.
de camp', -ing, -ment, -camped'.
dec'a nal, *dē că'nĭ.*
dec'a nate.
de can'drous, -can'dri an, -can'der.
dec ạn'gu lar.
de cant', -ed, -er, -ing, -can ta'tion.
dec'a pet'a lous, -a phyl'lous (*or*
de caph'-).
de cap'i tate, -ta ted, -ta ting, -ta'-
tion.

De cap'o da, de cap'o dal, -o dous,
dec'a pod, -a pod'i form.
de car'bon ize, -ized, -i zing,
-i zer, -bon ate, -a ted, -bu rize,
-rized, -rĭ za'tion, -bon i zing-
fur'nace.
dĕc âre' (*or* dĕk'-), dec'a stēre (*or*
-stare).
dec a sĕ'mic.
dec'a stich (-stĭk), -a style (-stĭle),
-a syl lab'ic, -a tō'ic.
de cạu'date, -da ted, -da ting.
de cay', -a ble, -er, -ed ness (*or*
-cayed'ness), -ing.
de cease', -ceased', -ceas'ing, -ce'-
dent.
de ceit', -ful, -ful ly, -ful ness, -less.
de cĕive', -ceived', -ceiv'ing, -er,
-a ble, -ble ness, -bly.
De cem'ber, -ber ly, -brist.
dĕ cem cos'tate, -cem den'tate,
-cem'fid, -cem loc'u lar, -cem-
ped'al (*or* -cem'pe-), -cem pen'-
nate.
de cem'vir, pl. -virs *or* -vĭ rī,
-vi ral, -vi rate, -vir ship.
de cen'na ry, -ni al, *-ni um*, pl.
-ums or *-a*, -no val.
de'cent, -ly, -ness, -cen cy.
de cen'tral ize, -ized, -i zing,
-Ĭ za'tion.
de ceph'a lize, -lized, -li zing, -lĬ-
za'tion.
de cep'tive, -ly, -ness, -cep'tion.
dé chaus sé' (dā shō sā').
dech'en Ĭte.
dec iare' (dĕs yâr').
de cide', -cīd'ed, -ed ly, -er, -ing.
de cid'u a, -u al, -u ate, -u ous,
-ous ness.
dec'i gram *or* -gramme (dĕs'-),
-i li'ter *or* -tre (-lē'ter *or* dĕ sil'-),
dec'Ĭl *or* -Ĭle.
de cil'lion, -lionth.
dec'i mal (des'-), -ize, -ized,
-i zing, -Ĭ za'tion, -mal ism,
-mal ly, -i mate, -ma tor, -ma'-
tion, -i ma, pl. -mæ, *de cime'*
(dā sēm').
dec'i me'ter *or* -tre (dĕs'- *or*
de cim'-).
dec'i mo (dĕs'-), -sex'to.
dec'i mole (des'-).

de ci'pher, -a ble, -ing, -ment,
-phered.
de ci'sïve, -ly, -ness, -cis'ion.
dec'i stēre (des'i stēr *or* -stär').
deck, -ing, -er, decked, deck'-
head, -beam, -bridge, -car'go,
-car'lïne, -cleat, -col'lar, -curb,
-fĕath'er, -feed, -flat, -hand,
-hook, -house, -light, -load,
-mold'ing, -nail, -pas'sage,
-pas'sen ger, -pipe, -plank'ing,
-plate, -pump, -sheet, -stop'per,
-tac'kle, -tran'som.
dec'kle *or* deck'el, dec'kle-edged,
-strap.
dē clāim', -ing, -er, -claimed',
-clăm'a to ry, dec'la mā'tion.
de clare', -clared', -clâr'ing, -ed ly,
-ed ness, -er, -a ble, -ant,
-clăr'a tive, -tive ly, -a to ry,
-to ri ly, dec'la ra'tor, -rā'tion.
de clen'sion, -al.
de clīne', -clined', -clïn'ing, -a ble,
-al -a to ry (*or* -klïn'-), -a ture,
-ous, dec'li nate, -na'tion, -na'-
tor, -nom'e ter.
de cliv'i ty, -i tous, -clï'vous, dec'-
li vent, -li vate, -vant.
de coct', -ed, -ing, -ive, -i ble,
-coc'tion.
de col'late, -la ted, -la ting, -la'-
tion, *dé'col'le té'* (dä'kŏl'lā tā'),
-*tée*, n. fem.
de col'or, -ant, -ate, -ize, -ized,
-i zing, -ï zā'tion *or* -a'tion.
de com pose', -posed', -pōs'ing,
-pōs'a ble, -pōs'er, -pŏs'ite -po-
si'tion (-zish'un), -pos'ing-fur'-
nace.
de'com pound', -ed, -ing, -a ble.
dec'o rate, -ra ted, -ra ting, -ra-
tive, -tive ness, -ra tor, -rā'tion.
de cŏ'rous (*or* dĕk'-), -ly, -ness,
-cŏ'rum.
de cor'ti cate, -ca ted, -ting, -tor,
-cā'tion.
dé cou plé' (dä kōō plä').
de coy', -ing, -er, -coyed'.
de coy', d. bird, d. duck.
de crease', -creased', -creas'ing,
-ing ly.
de cree', -a ble, -ing, -crē'er,
-crē'tal, -crē'tist, -tive.

dec're ment.
de crep'it, -i tate, -ta ted, -ta ting,
-i tude, -i tā'tion.
dē crĕs cen'dō (*or* dä krä shen'do).
de cres'cent, -pin'nate.
dec're to ry, -ri ly.
de crus tā'tion.
de cry', -ing, -crï'al, -crï'er,
-cried'.
dec'u man.
de cum'bent, -ly, -bence, -ben cy.
de cŭ'ri on, -on ate.
de cŭr'rent, -ly, -ren cy.
de cûr'sive, -sive ly.
de curve', -curved', -cur'va ture,
-va'tion.
dec'u ry.
de cus'sate, -ly, -sa ted, -tive,
-tive ly, -sā'tion.
de cus'sis, *pl.* -ses (-sēz).
de cus sŏ'ri um, *pl.* -ri a.
dē'cyl (-sïl *or* dĕs'sïl), -cyl'ic.
dē'dal *or* dæ'-, dāl'ian (-yan),
ded'a lous.
de dans' (dĕ dän' *or* dē'dăns).
dē'dĕs.
ded'i cate, -i cant, -ca ted, -ca-
ting, -ca tor, -to ry, -to'ri al,
-i cā'tion.
ded'i mus.
dé dit' (dā dē').
de'do (dā'-).
ded o lā'tion.
de duce', -duced', -du'cing, -ci-
ble, -ble ness, -bly, -bil'i ty,
-cive.
de duct', -ed, -ing, -i ble, -ive,
-ive ly, -duc'tion, *-duc'tor.*
deed, -ful, -less, -y, -box.
deem, -ing, deemed.
deem'ster.
deep, -en, -ly, -ness, -laid,
-mouthed, -sea, *a.*, -waist'ed.
deer, -let, -ber'ry, -herd, -hound,
-skin, -fold, -gråss, -hair, -lick,
-mouse, -neck, -stalk'er, -ti'ger,
deer's-hair, -tongue.
deese (dēz).
de face', -ment, -faced', -fa'cer,
-fa'cing.
dē fac'to.
de făl'cate, -ca ted, -ca ting, -ca'-
tion, def'al ca'tor.

nŏt, nôr, ūse, ŭp, ûrn, etüde, fōōd, fŏŏt, aṅger, boṅmot, thus, Bach.

17

de fame', -famed', -fām'ing, -ing-
ly, -er, -făm'a to ry, def'a ma'-
tion.
de fault', -ed, -ing, -er.
de fea'sance (-zans), -sanced,
-fea'si ble, -ble ness.
de feat', -ed, -ing.
def'e cate, -ca ted, -ca ting, -ca-
tor, -ca'tion.
de fect', -ive, -ive ly, -ive ness,
-less, -fec'tion.
de fend', -ed, -ing, -er, -a ble, -ant.
de fense', -less, -less ly, -less ness,
-fen'si ble, -ble ness, -sive, -sive-
ly, -sor, -so ry, -si bil'i ty.
de fer', -ring, -rer, -ment, -ferred',
def'er ence, -er ent, -en'tial
(-shal), -tial ly.
de fi'ance, -ant, -ant ly, -ant ness.
de fi'cien cy (-fish'en-), -fi'cient,
-cient ly, def'i cit.
dē fī'dē.
def i lade' (or dē'fī-), -lād'ing.
de file', v., -ment, -fil'er, -ing,
-filed', -file' (or dē'-), n.
de fine', -fined', fīn'ing, -fīn'a ble,
-a bly, -er, def i ni'tion (-nish'-
un).
def'i nīte, -ly, -ness.
dē fin'i tive, -ly, -ness, -i tude,
děf i nī'tum.
def'la grate, -gra ted, -ting, -tor,
-gra ble, -bil'i ty, -grā'tion.
de flā'tion.
de flect', -ed, -ing, -or, -a ble,
-flec'tion, -tion ize, -I zā'tion.
de flex', -flexed', -flex'ion (-flek'-
shun), -flex'ure (fleks'-).
de flō'rate, def lo ra'tion.
de fō'li ate, -a ted, -a tor, -a'tion.
de force', -ment, -forced'.
de for'ciant (-shant), -for ci a'-
tion (-shī-).
de fŏr'est, -es ta'tion.
de form', -er, -ing, -i ty, -a ble,
-ed ly, -ed ness, -a bil'i ty, def-
or ma'tion.
de fraud', -ed, -ing, -er.
de fray', -al, -er, -ment, -ing,
-frayed'.
deft, -ly, -ness.
def'ter dar.
de funct'.

de fy' (-fī'), -ing, -fīed', -fī'er.
deg, -ger, -ging, degged, deg'ging-
ma chine'.
dé ga gé' (dā gä zhā').
de gen'er ate, -ly, -ness, -a cy,
-a tive, -a'tion, -tion ist.
de ger'mi na tor.
de glu'ti nate, -na ted, -na ting,
-ti to ry, deg'lu ti'tion (-tǐsh'un).
de gote'.
de grade', -grād'ed, -ing, -ing ly,
deg ra dā'tion, -tion al.
dé gras' (dā grä')
de gree'.
de'gu (dā'gōō or děg'-).
deg'us ta'tion.
dé ha ché' (dā hǎ shā').
de hisce', -hisced' (-hǐst'), -his'-
cence, -cent.
dē horn', -ing, -horned'.
de hors' (-hôrz' or -hôr').
dē hū'man ize, -ized, -i zing,
-I za'tion.
dē hy'drate (-hī'-).
de hy'dro gen ize, ized, ī'zing,
ī zā'tion.
Dē'ī a nī'ra, wife of Hercules.
deīc'tic, -al ly.
dē'i fy, -ing, -fied, -fi er, -form,
-if'ic, -ic al, -i fi ca'tion.
deign (dān), -ing, deigned.
Dē ī grā'ti a (-shī a), Dē ī ju di'-
ci um (-dish'i um).
Deī'mŏs, Astron.
Deīp nos'o phist.
dē īp'o tent.
dē'ism, -ist, -is'tic, -tic al, -al ly
-al ness, de'i ty.
de ject', -ed, -ed ly, -ing, -er, -jec'ta,
-tion, -to ry, -ture.
dé'jeu'ner' (dā'zhê'nā').
dē jū'rē.
děk'a drachm (-drăm), a gram.
De Kălb', Ger. gen.
děk'ass.
dē lāine'.
de lam i nā'tion.
de lay', -ing, -ing ly, -er, -a ble,
-layed'.
děl crěd'er e.
dē'lē, de lēte', -le'ted, -le'ting,
-lē'tion, -lē'tive, del'e to ry,
-e ti' tious (-tǐsh'-).

de lec'ta ble, -ness, -ta bly, -bil'-
i ty, -lec tā'tion.
del'e gate, -e gant, -ga ted, -ting,
-ga'tion.
de len'da.
del e tē'ri ous, -ly, -ness.
delf *or* delft, -ware.
Del'hi (děl'lē *or* děl'hī), Brit.
Ind.—(děl'hī), tp. N. Y.; tp. O.
Dě'li an.
de lib'er ate, -ly, -ness, -a ted, -ting,
-tive, -tive ly, -a ter *or* -a tor,
-a'tion.
del'i cate, -ly, -ness, -ca cy.
del'i ca tesse' (-těs'), -ca tes'sen.
de li'cious (-lish'us), -ly, -ness.
de lic'tum, pl. *-ta.*
del'i gate, -gā'tion.
de light', -ed, -ed ly, -ing, -er,
-a ble, -ful, -ful ly, -ful ness,
-some, -some ly, -some ness,
-less.
De lī'lah, *Bib.*
de lim'it, -ed, -ing, -i tā'tion.
de lin'e ate, -a ted, -ting, -tor,
-to ry, -a ture, -a ble, -a ment,
-a'tion.
de lin'quent, -ly, -quen cy.
del'i quesce', -quesced' (-kwest'),
-ques'cing, -cence, -cent.
de lir'i um, -i ant, -i ous, -ous ly,
-ous ness, -i fā'cient.
De'Litzsch (dä'lich), Ger. theol.
de liv'er, -a ble, -ance, -er, -ered.
de liv'er y, -roll'er, -valve.
dell, -bird.
Del'la Crus'ca, -Crus'can, D.
Rob'bi a ware.
Del Nor'te (-tā), co. Cal.
de lō'cal ize, -ized, -i zing, -I za'-
tion.
de lōō' (*or* dā'lō).
Del'phi an, -phic, del'phin *or*
-phīne.
Del'särte' sys'tem.
del'ta, -ta'ic, *-tid'i um,* pl. *-i a,*
-to hē'dron, -toid, -toi'des (-děz),
-ta-met'al.
de lu'brum, pl. *-bra.*
de lude', -lūd'ed, -ing, -er.
del'ūge, -uged, -u ging (-jing).
de lun'dung.
de lū'sive (-sĭv), -ly, -ness, -lu'so ry,

-lu'sion (-zhun), -sion al, -sion-
ist.
del vaux'ene (-vō'zēne), -vaux'ite
(-vō'zīt).
delve, delved, delv'er, -ing.
de mag'net ize, -ized, -i zing,
-I za'tion.
dem'a gŏgue, -gog ism, -gog'ic
(-goj'-), -ic al, -gog'y (-gŏj ĭ).
de mānd', -ed, -ing, -a ble, -ant, -er.
de man'toid.
de mar'cate, -ca'tion, de mark', *v.*
de'march (-mark), *n.*
děme.
de mēan', -or, -ing, -meaned'.
de ment'ed, -men'tate, *-men'ti a*
(-shĭ a), -men tā'tion.
de meph'i tize, -tized, -ti zing,
-tĭ zā'tion.
de měr'it.
de mersed', -mer'sion.
de mesne' (-mēn').
De mē'ter, *Myth.*
De mē'trĭ us, Gr. orator.
dem'i cir'cle, -I far'thing, -I god,
-I john, -I rep, -I sem'i quā'ver.
dem'i-gaunt'let, -mŏnde' (*or*
-mŏńd'), *-ri lie'vo* (-rē lyā'vŏ),
-vŏlt, -wolf.
de mil'i ta rize, -rized, -ri zing.
de mise' (-mīz'), -mis'a ble (-mīz'-),
-a bil'i ty.
dem'i urge, -ur'gic.
de mŏb'i lize, -lized, -li zing,
-lĭ za'tion.
dem'o crat, -crat'ic, -ic al, -al ly,
de moc'ra cy, -ra tism, -ra tist.
De moc'ri tē'an, Dem o crit'ic,
-ic al.
De'mo gor'gon (*or* děm-).
de mog'ra phy, -ra pher, dem o-
graph'ic.
dem oi sello' (děm wŏ zěl').
de mol'ish, -ing, -er, -ished,
dem o li'tion (-lish'un), -tion ist.
de'mon, -ism, -ist, -ize, -ized,
-i zing, -ship, -mon'ic, -mon'i-
fuge, -mon oc'ra cy, -og'ra pher,
-ol a ter, -a try, -ol'o gy, -o gist,
-o log'ic al, -o man'cy, -o ma'-
ni a, -op'a thy, *-o pho'bi a,* -mo'-
ni ac, -ni'a cism, dem o nī'a cal,
-cal ly.

---

nŏt, nôr, ūse, ŭp, ûrn, etüde, fōōd, fŏŏt, aŋger, boṅmot, thus, Bach.

de mon'e tize, -tized, -ti zing,
-tĭ zā'tion.

de mon'strate (or dem'-), -stra-
ble, -ble ness, -bly, -ted, -ting,
-tive, -tive ly, -tive ness, dem'-
on strā'tor, -tor ship, -strā'tion.

de mŏr'al ize, -ized, -i zing, -ĭ za'-
tion.

dĕ'mŏs.

De mos'the nes (-nēz), Dem os-
thē'ni an or -ne an, -then'ic.

dĕ mot'ic.

de mul'cent.

de mûr', -ra ble, -rage, -ral, -rer,
-ring, -murred'.

de mūre', -ly, -ness.

dĕ my' (-mĭ'), pl. -mies' (-mīz'),
dĕ my'ship (-mĭ'-).

den, -tree.

de nar'co tize, -tized, -ti zing,
-tĭ za'tion.

dĕ nā'ri us, pl. -rĭ ĭ, de na'ro
(dā nä'-).

den'a ry.

de na'tion al ize (-nash'-), -ized,
-i zing, -ĭ za'tion.

de nat'u ral ize, -ized, -i zing.

den'dra chate (-kāt).

den dran thro pol'o gy.

den'drīte, -drit'ic, -ic al, -al ly,
-dri form.

dene'-hole.

den'gue (dĕŋ'gā).

dĕ nĭ'al, -nĭ'a ble, -nĭ'er.

dĕ nier' (-nēr') n. (-nyā') v.

den'im.

dĕ nĭ'trate, -trā'tion, -tri fy, -fy-
ing, -fīed, -fi ca'tor, -fi cā'tion.

den'i zen (-zn), -ship, -i zā'tion.

den'net.

de nom'i nate, -i nant, -na ble,
-na ted, -ting, -tive, -tive ly,
-tor.

de nom i nā'tion, -al, -al ism,
-al ist, -al ly.

de note', -nōt'ed, -ing, -ive,
-nōt'a ble, -a tive, -tive ly, -no-
tā'tion.

dĕ'noue'ment (dā'nōō'mŏn or
-mäṅ').

de nounce', -nounced', -noun'cing,
-cer.

dĕ nō'vo.

dens (dĕnz), pl. dĕn'tes (-tēz).

dense, -ly, -ness, den'si ty.

den'sher or -shire (-shĕr).

den sim'e ter.

dent, -ed, -ing.

den'tal, -tal'i ty, -tag'ra, -tal īte,
-tal'ĭ ĭd, -tal i za'tion, -ta ry,
-tā'ta, -ti cle, -tic'u late, -la'ted,
-late ly, -la'tion, den'ti fac'tor,
-ti form, -ti frice (-frĭs), -tig'er-
ous (-tij'-).

den'tate, -ly, -tate-cil i ate, -sĕr'-
rate, -sin'u ate.

den telle'.

den'ti cĭne.

den'ti cule, -tic'u lus, pl. -lī.

den'tĭl or -tĕl.

den tĭ lā'bi al, -ti liŋ'gual or den'-
to-, -til'o quy, -o quist, den ti-
na'sal or den'to-.

den'ti la'ted, -ti la'tion, -tĭle.

den'tĭn or -tĭne, -ti nal, -ti phone.

den ti ros'ter, -ros'tral, -trate.

den'tist, -ry, -ti scǎlp, -toid, -ture,
-ti'tion (-tish'un).

de nude', -nūd'ed, -ing, den'u-
dā'tion.

de nū'mer ant, -mer ā'tion.

de nun'ci a (dā nōōn'thĭ ä), -ci a-
mi en'to (-mē än'tō).

de nun'ci ate (-shĭ'-), -ā'ted,
-ā'ting, -ă tive, -a'tor, -to'ry,
-ă ble, -ant, -ā'tion.

dĕ nu tri'tion (-trish'- or den u-).

de ny (-nĭ'), -ing, -ing ly, -nied'.

dĕ'o dand.

de o dar'.

de o'dor ize, -ized, -i zer, -i zing,
-ĭ zā'tion, -dor ant.

Dĕ'ō jā vĕn'tĕ, Dĕ'ō grā'ti as
(-shĭ'-), Dĕ'o vō lĕn'tĕ.

dĕ on tol'o gy, -o gist, -to log'ic al
(-loj'-).

dĕ ŏ per'cu late, -la ted, -la ting.

dĕ os'si fy, -ing, -si fied, -fĭ cā'-
tion.

dĕ ox'i dize, -dized, -di zer, -zing,
-dĭ zā'tion, -i dā'tion.

dĕ ox'y gen ize, -ized, -i zing,
-gen ā'tion.

dĕ ŏ'zon ize, -ized, -i zing.

de part', -ed, -ing, -er, -par'ture.

de part'ment, -men'tal, -tal ly.

dĕp'as.
de pạu'per ate, -a ted, -a ting,
-per ize, -ized, -ĭ za'tion.
de pend', -ed, -a ble, -ble ness,
-ence, -en cy, -er, -ing, -ing ly.
de pend'ent or -ant, n. de pend'-
ent, a., -ent ly.
dep'hal.
de phleg'mate, -ma ted, -ting,
-tor, -to ry, -ma'tion.
de phos'phor ize, -ized, -i zing,
-ĭ za'tion.
de pict', -ed, -ing, -er, -pic'tion,
-pic'ture, -tured, -tur ing.
dep'i late, -la ted, -ting, -tor, -la'-
tion, de pil'a to ry.
dep'la mate (or dē plā'-).
de plā'no.
de plete', -plēt'ed, -ing, -ple'tive,
-to ry, -tion.
de plore', -plored', -plor'ing, -er,
-a ble, -ble ness, -bly, -bil'i ty.
de ploy', -ing, -er, -ment, -ployed'.
de plume', -plumed', -plūm'ing,
-plū'mate, dep'lu mā'tion.
de pō'lar ize, -ized, -i zing, -i zer,
-ĭ zā'tion.
de pō'nent.
de pop'u late, -la ted, -la ting,
-la tor, -lā'tion.
de port', -ed, -ing, -er, -ment,
-por tā'tion.
de pose', -posed', -pōs'ing, -pōs'er,
-pōs'a ble, dep o si'tion (-zish'-
un).
de pos'it, -ed, -ing, -i tā'tion, -i tive,
-i tor, de pos'it-re ceipt', -it ing-
dock.
de pos'i ta ry, a. and n., -i to ry,
n. As nouns these words are,
to some extent, used interchangeably. The better usage limits
depositary to the person, and depository to the place.
de'pot (dē'pō or dĕp ō' or dā pō').
de prave', -praved', -prāv'ed ly,
-ed ness, -er, -ing, -ing ly,
-prăv'i ty.
dep're cate, -ca ted, -ca ting,
-ting ly, -ca tive, -tive ly, -ca'tor,
-to'ry, -cā'tion.
de prē'ci ate (-shĭ-), -ci a'tive,
-tive ly, -tor, -to'ry, -ci ā'tion.

dep're date, -dā'ted, -dā'ting, -dā'-
tor, -to ry, -dā'tion.
de press', -ing, -ing ly, -ive,
-ive ness, -i ble, -or, -ant, -pres'-
sion.
dep're ter.
de prive', -prived', -prīv'ing, -er,
-a ble, dep'ri vā'tion.
dē prō fŭn'dĭs.
depth, -less, -gage.
de pulp'er.
dep'u rate, -ra ted, -ting, -tive,
-tor, -rant, -rā'tion.
de pute', -pūt'ed, -ing, dep'u table, -u tize, -tized, -ti zing, -ty,
-tā'tion.
de rail', -er, -ing, -ment, -railed'.
de range', -a ble, -ment, -ranged',
-ran'ging, -rān'ger.
de ray'.
Der'bē, Entom. genus.
der'bend.
der'boun (-boon).
Der'by (-bĭ), tp. Conn.; tp. and
vil. Vt.; (dêr'by or där'-), co.
Eng.
Der'by, Eng. earl; a horse race.
D. day.
der'by, a float; a hat.
Der'by shīre, D. drop, D. neck,
D. spar.
de re'cho (dā rā'-).
dĕr'e lict, -lic'tion.
dĕr'ham (-am).
dĕr'ic, a.
de rīde', -rīd'ed, -ing, -ing ly, -er,
-rī'sive, -sive ly, -sive ness, -so-
ry, -ri'sion (-rĭzh'un).
dĕ ri'gueur' (rē'ger').
dĕr'i vant (or dē rī'-).
de rive', -rived', -rīv'a ble, -a bly,
-a bil'i ty, -rīv'a tive, -tive ly,
-tive ness, der i vā'tion, -tion al,
-tion ist.
dêr'ma, -mad, -mal, -mal'gi a,
derm'-skel'e ton.
der map'ter an, -ter ous, -mat'ic,
-ma tī'tis, -ma tog'ra phy, -ma-
toid, -tol'o gy, -o gist, -tol'y sis,
-to my co'sis (-mī-), -ma ton'o-
sis.
der'ma to phyte (-fīt), -phyt'ic
(-fĭt'-), -top'a thy, -to plas'ty,

-ma tŏr rhe′a, -ma tō′sis, -to skel′-
e ton.
Der mes′tes (-tēz), der mes′tid,
-mes′toid.
der′mis, -mic.
der mo braŋ′chi ate (-kĭ-), -mo-
gas′tric, -mo he′mal, -mo hē′-
mi a, -mo hŭ′mer al, -hu me rā′-
lis, -moid, -mo mus′cu lar, -mo-
neū′ral, -mo os′se ous, -os′si fy,
-fy ing, -fied, -fĭ cā′tion, -mo-
path′ic, -mop′a thy.
der′mop tēre, -mop′tēr an, -ter-
ous.
der′nĭ er (*or* dĕr′nyā′).
dĕr′o gate, -ga ted, -ga ting, -gā′-
tion, de rog′a tive, -tive ly, -to-
ry, -to ri ly, -ri ness.
dĕr′o treme, -trĕm′a tous, -trē′-
mous.
Dé′rou′lède′ (dā′rōō′lād′), Fr.
poet.
dĕr′rick, -car, -crane.
dĕr′ries.
dĕr′rin ger.
dĕr′ry.
der′vish.
Des′brosses′ (dā′brŏs′), Fr.
painter.
des′ca mi sa′do (dās′kà mē sä′do *or*
-tho).
des′cant, *n.,* -cant′, *v.,* -ed, -ing,
-er, des′cant-vi ol.
Des′cartes′ (dā′kärt′), Fr. philos.
de scend′, -ed, -ing, -ing ly, -er,
-i ble, -i bil′i ty.
de scend′ant, *n.* de scend′ent, *a.,*
-scen den′tal ism, -tal ist.
de scent′, -scen′sion, -sion al,
-scen′sive.
Des champs′ (dā′shŏǹ′), Fr.
painter.
de scribe′, -scribed′, -scrīb′ing,
-er, -ent, -scrip′tion, -tive, -tive-
ly, -tive ness.
de scry′ (*or* des cry′), -ing,
-scried′, -scrī′er.
Des′de mō′na (dĕz′-), Shak.,
Othello.
des′e crate, -cra ted, -ting, -ter
or -tor, -cra′tion.
de seg′ment ed, -men ta′tion.
de sert′ (-zert′), *v.,* -ed, -ing, -er.

des′ert (dĕz′-), *n.,* -chough
(-chuff), -fal′con (-fạ′kn), -hare,
-mouse, -palm, -pea, -snake.
de serve′, -served′, -serv′ed ly, -er,
-ing, -ing ly.
des′ic cate, -ca ted, -ca ting, -cant
(*or* de sic′-), -ca tive (*or* de sic′-),
-ca tor, -cā′tion.
de sid′er ate, -a ted, -a ting, -a-
tive, -*e ra′tum,* pl. -*ra′ta.*
de sign′ (-zīn′ *or* -sīn′), -ing, -er,
-a ble, -ed ly, -ed ness, -less,
-less ly, -signed′.
des′ig nate (dĕs′-), -na ble, -na-
ted, -ting, -tive, -tor, -to ry,
-na′tion.
de sil′i ca ted, -si lic′ ida′tion (-lĭs′-),
-lic′i fi cā′tion, -lic′i fy, -fy ing,
-fied, -sil′i cized, -sil′i con ize,
-ized, -i zing.
de sil′ver, -vered, -ver ize, -ized,
-i zing, -ĭ za′tion.
des′i nence.
de sire′ (-zīr′), -less, -sīr′a ble,
-ble ness, -a bly, -er, -ous, -ous-
ly, -ous ness, -ing, -a bil′i ty,
-sired′.
de sist′ (*or* -zist′), -ed, -ing, -ance.
Des′jar′dins′ (dā′zhär′dăǹ′), Fr.
hist.
desk, -cloth, -knife, -māk′er,
-room, -work.
des′ma, pl. -*mas* (-màz) *or* -*ma ta,*
-ma chy′ma tous (-kĭ′-), -ma-
chyme, -ma cyte (-sĭt).
des′man.
des mid i ol′o gy, -ol′o gist.
des′mīne.
des mī′tis.
Des′mou′lins′ (dā′mōō′lăǹ′), Fr.
revolutionist.
des′o late, -ly, -ness, -la ted, -la-
ting, -la ter *or* -tor, -la′tion.
De Sō′tō (dā), Sp. explorer.
des ox′a late, -ox al′ic.
de spair′ (*or* dĕs-), -ing, -ing ly,
-ing ness, -spaired′.
des patch′ (*or* de-) *or* dis-, -er, -ing,
-patched′, -patch′-boat, -box,
-tube.
des′per ate, -ly, -ness, -ā′do, -a′-
tion.
des′pi ca ble, -ness, -bly.

---

fāte, făt, fär, fạll, fâre, fåst, sofà, mēte, mĕt, hêr, īce, ĭn, nōte,

de spise' (*or* des-), -spised',
-spīs'ing, -ing ly, -er.
dĕ spīte' (*or* dĕs-), -ful, -ful ly,
-ful ness.
Des Plaines' (dā plān'), r. Wis.
dĕ spoil' (*or* dĕs-), -er, -ing, -ment,
-spoiled', -spō li a'tion.
des pond' (*or* dē-), -ed, -ence,
-en cy, -ent, -ent ly, -er, -ing,
-ing ly.
des'pot, -ism, -ist, -ize, -ized,
-i zing, -pot'ic, -ic al, -al ly,
-al ness.
Des'pres' (dā'prā'), Fr. littérateur.
des'pu mate (*or* de spu'-), -ma-
ted, -ting, -mā'tion.
des'qua mate (*or* -kwā'-), -ma'-
tion, de squăm'a tive, -a to ry.
dess.
Des' saix' (dā'sā'), Fr. soldier.
Des'sa'lines' (dā'sä'lēn'), ruler of
Hayti.
des sert' (dĕz zert'), -spoon.
dĕs'sia tĭne (-ya-).
des sus' (dĕs sōō').
D'Es taing' (dĕs'tăṅ'), Fr. admiral.
des'tĭne, -tĭned, -tĭn ing, tĭ ny,
-ti na'tion.
des'tĭ tute, -ly, -ness, -tū'tion.
des'to (*or* dās'-).
des'trä mä'nō.
des troy' (*or* de), -ing er, a ble,
-troyed'.
de struct'i ble, -ness, -bil'i ty,
-struc'tive, -tive ly, -tive ness,
-tor, -tion, -tion ist.
des'u dā'tion.
des'ue tūde (-wē-).
de sul'phur, -ing, -phûred, -phū-
rate, -ra'tion, -phûr ize, -ized,
-i zing, -ĭ za'tion, -phū ret ed *or*
-ret ted, -phûr ĭ zing-fur'nace.
des'ul to ry, -to ri ly, -ri ness.
de'syn on'y mize, -y mi za'tion.
de tach', -a ble, -ed ly, -ing,
-ment, -a bil'i ty, -tăched',
-tach'ing-hook.
de tail', *v.*, -ing, -er, -tailed';
de tāil' (*or* dĕ'-), *n.*
de tain', -ing, -er, -tained', -ten'-
tion, -ten'tive, -tent', -tent'-joint.
de tect', -ed, -ing, -ive, -a ble *or*

-i ble -or *or* -er, -tec'tion,
-tect'or-lock.
de têr', -ment, -rent, -ring,
-terred'.
de terge', -terged', -ter'gent,
-gence, -gen cy, -gi ble.
de te'ri o rate, -ra ted, -ra ting,
-ra'tion.
de ter'ma.
de ter'mi nate, -ly, -ness, -na-
tive, -na'tion.
de ter'mine, -mined, -mĭn ed ly,
-mĭn er, -mĭn ism, -min ist,
-min is'tic, -mĭn ing -mi na ble,
-ble ness, -bil'i ty, -mi nance,
-nant.
de ter'sive, -sive ly, -sive ness,
-sion.
de test', -ed, -er, -ing, -a ble,
-ble ness, -bly, -bil'i ty, dĕt'es-
ta'tion (*or* dĕ tes-).
de throne', -ment, -thrōned',
-thrōn'ing, -er.
det'i net, -i nue.
det'o nate, -na ted, -ting, -tive,
-tor, -na ble, -na'tion, -na ting-
fuse, -tube.
det'o nize, -nized, -ni zing, -nĭ-
za'tion.
de tour' (-tōōr').
de tract', -ed, -ing, -ing ly, -or
or -er, -o ry, -trac'tion.
det'ri ment, -men'tal, -tal ly, -tal-
ness.
de trīte', -trī'tal, -trī'ted, -trī'tus,
-tri'tion (-trĭsh'un).
dĕ trop (trō).
de trude', -trūd'ed, -ing.
de trun'cate, -ca ted, -ca ting,
-ca'tion.
dĕ'tûr (*or* dā'tōŏr).
Deü cã'li on, *Myth.*
deüce, deü'ced, -ced ly.
Deü ĕl', co. Neb.; co. Dak.
Dē'us mis'er e a'tur (miz'-).
deü'ter o ca non'ic al, -ter og'a-
my, -a mist, -ter o gen'ic,
-o mē'sal, -op'a thy, -o path'ic,
-os'co py, -*os'to ma*, -o stom'a-
toŭs, -o zo'oid.
Deü'ter on'o my, -o mist, -mis'-
tic, -o nom'ic, -ic al.
Deutsch (doich), Ger. scholar.

nŏt, nôr, ūse, ŭp, ûrn, etüde, fōōd, fŏŏt, aṅger, boṅmot, thus, Bach.

Deutz (doits), t. Prus.
Deut'zi a (doit'sĭ a *or* dūt'sĭ a).
deux'-temps' (dê'-tŏň').
dĕv (*or* dāv) *or* *de'va* (dā'-), pl.
   de'vas.
de vap o ra'tion.
dev'as tate, -ta ted, -ting, -tor,
   -ta'tion, *-ta'vit.*
de vel'ŏp (*or* -up), -ing, -er, -a ble,
   -ment, -men'tal, -tal ly, -ment-
   ist, -oped.
de ver'soir (-swŏr).
dĕ'vi ate, -a ted, -ting, -tor,
   -a'tion.
de vice'.
dev'il (-l), -iled *or* -illed (-ld), -il ing
   or -il ling, -ish, -ish ly, -ish ness,
   -kin, -ment, -ry, -ship, -try, -fish,
   -wood, -bean, -bird, -bolt,
   -car'riage, -screech'er, -tree,
   -wor'ship.
dev'il's-ap'ple, -a'pron, -bird, -bit,
   -claw, -club, -cot'ton, -cow, -dust,
   -ear, -fig, -fiŋ'ger, -horse, -milk,
   -shoe'string.
dev'il-in-a-bush, a plant; dev'il-
   may-care.
dĕ'vi o scope.
dĕ'vi ous, -ly, -ness.
de vis'cer ate, -a ted, -a ting, -a tion.
de vīse' (-vīz'), -vised', -vīs'ing,
   -vīs'a ble, -vīs'al.
de vīs'er, one who invents; de-
   vīs'or, one who bequeaths; dev'-
   i see' (-zē').
de vī'tal ize, -ized, -i zing, -ĭ zā'-
   tion.
de vit'ri fy, -ing, -fied, -fi cā'tion.
de vŏ'cal ize, -ized, -i zing, -ĭ zā'-
   tion.
de void'.
de voir' (dĕ vwôr').
de volve', -volved', -volv'ing.
Dev'on, co. Eng., De vo'ni an,
   -von'ic.
Dev'on shĭre col'ic, D. lace.
de vote', -vōt'ed, -ed ly, -ed ness,
   -er, -ing, dev o tee', -tee'ism.
de vŏ'tion, -al, -al ist, -al ly.
de vour', -a ble, -er, -ing, -ing ly,
   -ment, -voured'.
de vout', -less, -less ly, -less ness,
   -ly, -ness.

dew, -y, -i ness, dew'ber'ry, -drop,
   fall, -lap, -stone, -worm.
dew'-beat'er, -be sprent, -claw,
   -cup, -drink, -grăss, -plant,
   -point, -shoe.
dĕ waṇ', -wạ'nĭ.
dex i o trop'ic.
dex'ter ous *or* dex'trous, -ly,
   -ness, dex ter'i ty, dex'trad, -tral,
   -tral ly, -tral'i ty.
dex'trīne, -tro rŏ'ta to ry, -trorse'
   (*or* dex'-), -tror'sal.
dex'trŏse (-trŏs), -tron'ic, -trot'-
   ro pous.
dey (dā).
de ziṇc'i fy, -ĭ fi ca'tion.
de zy'mo tize (-zī'-), -tized, -ti-
   zing.
dhabḅ (dăb).
dhā'di um.
dhak.
dhăl'ee.
dhăm'noͦo.
dhăn.
dhar.
dhăr'ma.
dhăr'rĭ.
Dhau'la gi'ri (dou'lä gē'rē) *or*
   Dha wal a ghi'ri (dȧ wŏl a gêr'ē),
   mt. peak India.
dhau'rĭ.
dhŏ'bĭe or -by, -bie man.
dhōle.
dhŏ'tee *or* -ty.
dhow (dou).
Dhu leep' Singh (doͦo leep' sĭng),
   Indian prince.
dhun'chee.
Dhŭr'rŭm pur' (-poͦor'), Rajput
   state, India.
dhur'ry.
dĭ'a băse, -bā'sic, -ba te'ri al,
   -ban'tīte, -a base-por'phy rite.
dĭ'a bē'tes (-tēz), -bĕt'ic, -ic al.
Di'a'ble, Le (lê dĕ'ä'bl), Satan.
dĭ'a bol'ic, -ic al, -al ly, -al ness,
   -ab'o lism, -o lus, Di ab'o lus,
   Zoöl. genus.
dĭ a brot'ic, -a ca thol'i con, -a-
   cạus'tic, -a ce'tin, *-a che'ni um*
   (-kē'-), pl. *-ni a,* -a cho'ri al,
   -ach'y lon or *-y lum* (-ăk'-),
   -ach'y ma, -ac'id, *-a clā'sis* (*or*

dī ăk'-), -clī'nal, -*a cŏ'di um,
-a cœ'li a.*

dī ac'o nate, -o nal, -*a con'i ca,
-i con* or -*i̇ cum.*

dī̇ ac'o pe, Dī̇ ac'o pe, Ichth. and
Entom. genus.

dī a cous'tic (-kōōs'- or -kous'-),
-tics, -a cran tē'ri an, -a cris i-
og'ra phy.

dī a crit'ic, -ic al.

dī ac'tīne, -ti nal, -tin'ic.

dī'a dem, -dĕmed, -dem'a tid,
-dem-le'mur, -spī'der.

dī a dex'is.

di'a dŏ'chi an (-kĭ-).

dī ær'e sis. See *dieresis.*

dī'a ge o trop'ic, -ge ot'ro pism.

dī'a glyph, -ic or -glyp'tic.

dī'ag nose' (-nōs'), -nosed'
(-nōst'), -nōs'ing, -nō'sis, dī'-
ag nost, nōs'tic, -tics, -ti cate,
-ca ted, -ca ting, -ti cian (-tish'-).

dī a gom'e ter.

dī ag'o nal, -ly, -nal-built.

dī'a gram, -gram mat'ic, -ic al,
-al ly, -gram'ma tize, -tized, -ti-
zing, -gram'me ter.

dī'a grăph, -graph'ic, -ic al, -ics.

dī a gryd'i ate, -i um.

dī a gy'l os (-jĭ'-).

dī a he'lĭ o trop'ic, -li ot'ro pism.

dī'al, -bird, -lock, -plate, -re sist'-
ance, -tel'e graph, -wheel, -work.

dī'a lect, -lec'tal, -tal ly, -tic,
-tic al, -al ly, -ti cian (-tish'an),
-ti cism, -tics, -tol'o gy, -o ger,
-o gist, -to log'ic al.

dī'al er or -ler, -al ing or -ling,
-al ist.

dī̇ al'la ge (-je), Rhet., dī'al lage,
Mineral.

dī al lĕ'lon, *pl.* -le'la, -le'lous, *a.,*
-le'lus, *n., pl.* -le'lĭ.

dī'a lŏgue, -log'ic (-loj'-), -ic al, -al-
ly, -al'o gism, -o gist, -gis'tic, -tic-
al, -al ly, -al'o gize, -gized, -gi zing.

dī'a lyze, -lyzed, -ly'zing (-lī'-), -zer,
-lyz'a ble (-līz'-), -ly zā'tion (-lĭ-).

dī'a mag net'ic, -ic al ly, -mag'-
net ism, -net i za'tion, -mag ne-
tom'e ter.

dī am'e ter, -e tral, -tral ly,
-a met'ric, -ric al, -al ly.

dī am'ĭd or -ĭde, -am'in or -ĭne
(or dī'-)

dī'a mond (-a mund or dī'mund),
-ed, -mond back, -backed, -bee'-
tle, -bird, -break'er, -cut'ter,
-drăft, -drill, -dust, -finch,
-floun'der, -gage, -knot, -mor'-
tar, -plăice, -plate, -point,
-pow'der, -set'ter, -shaped,
-snake, -spar, -truck, -wee'vil,
-wheel, -work.

dī'a mo tŏ'sis.

Dī an'a (or dī ā'na), *Bib.*

Dī an'a (or -ā'na), *Myth.; Ichth.
genus.* dī an'a, a kind of silver;
a species of monkey.

di an cis'tron.

Dī̇ an'dri a, di an'der, -an'dri an,
-an'drous.

dī a nŏ'dal, -a nome.

di a no ct'ic, -a noi al'o gy.

dī a pă'son (zon or -son).

dī'a ped.

dī'a pe dĕ'sis, -pe det'ic.

dī̇ a pen'te.

dī'a per, -pêred, -pêr ing, -per-
work.

dī aph'o noŭs, -nous ly, -nous-
ness.

dī aph'o ny, -a phon'ic, -ic al,
-phon'ics.

dī'a pho rĕ'sis, -pho ret'ic, -ic al.

dī'a phragm (-frăm), -phrag'mal
(-frăg'-), -mal'gi a, -mal gy, -mat'-
ic, dī'a phragm-fạu'cet, -plate,
-pump, -valve.

dī ap no'ic, -not'ic.

dī'a po re'sis.

dī'a pos'i tive.

dī'arch y (-ark-).

dī'ar rhĕ'a or -rhœ'a, -rhĕ'al,
-rhĕ'ic, -rhet'ic.

dī̇ ar thrŏ'sis, pl. -*ses* (-sēz),
-thrŏ'di al.

dī'a ry, -a rist, -a rize, -rized,
-ri zing, -a'ri al, -ri an.

dī'a schis'ma (-skĭz'-).

dī ă'si a (-sĭ-).

dī'a skeŭ'a sis, -skeŭ'ast.

dī̇ as'po ra.

dī'a spŏre.

dī a stal'tic.

dī'a stăse, -as'ta sis.

dĭ a stim′e ter.
dĭ as′tō lē, -as tol′ic.
di as′tro phism, -as troph′ic.
di′a style.
dĭ a tes′sa ron.
dĭ a ther′ma nous, -ther′mal, -man-
  cy, -man ism, -mic, -mom′e ter.
dĭ ath′e sis, -a thet′ic, -ic al ly.
dĭ at′o min *or* -mĭne, -o mist,
  -o mĭte, -o moŭs, -a tom′o scope.
dĭ a ton′ic, -ic al ly, -at′o noŭs.
dĭ′a tribe, -at′ri bist (*or* -a trī′-).
dĭ qu′lŏs.
dĭ ax′on, -ō′ni a.
dĭ ăz′o tize.
dĭ a zeŭx′is, -zeŭc′tic *or* -zeŭ′tic.
dĭ a zō′ma, pl. *-ma ta, -zon′al.*
dib, -bing, -ber, dibbed, dib′-
  stone, -hole.
dib′ble, -bling, -bler, -bled, -bling-
  ma chine′.
dĭ blas′tu la, pl. *-læ.*
dĭ′brach (-brăk).
dĭ braŋ′chi ate (-kĭ-).
dibs.
dĭ cæ ol′o gy (-sē-).
dĭ cal′cic, dĭ car bon′ic.
dĭ′cast.
dĭ cat a lex′is, -a lec′tic.
dice, dĭ′cer, dice′-box, -coal,
  -play′er, dĭ′cing-house.
dĭ cel′late.
Dĭ cen′tra, Bot. genus; di cen′tra,
  a plant.
dĭ cĕr′i on, dic′er ous (dis′-).
dĭ′chas (-kas).
dĭ chā′si um (-kā′sĭ- *or* -kā′zĭ-), pl.
  si a, -si al.
dĭ chog′a my (-kog′-), -a mous,
  -cho gam′ic.
dĭ chop′tic (-kŏp′-).
dĭ′chord.
dĭ chot′o mize (-kŏt′-), -mized,
  -mi zing, -mĭ za′tion, -chot′o-
  mal, -o mous, -mous ly, -o my,
  -cho tom′ic, -ic al ly.
dĭ′chro ism (-kro-), -chro is′tic,
  -chro ĭte, -it′ic.
dĭ chro′mate, -ma tism, -mat′ic,
  -chro′mic.
dĭ′chro nous, -chro scope, -scop′ic.
dick′er, -ing, -er, dick′ered.

dick′y, a donkey, *pl.* -ĭes.
dick′y, *pl.* -ies, *or* dick′ey, *pl.*
  -eys, an apron or bib; a shirt
  front or collar; a carriage-seat.
dick′y-bird.
dĭ clin′ic, dĭ′clin ate, -clin ism,
  dic′li nous (*or* dĭ klĭ′-).
dĭ cot y lĕ′don, *pl.* -dons, -lĕd′-
  on ous (*or* -lē′-), dĭ co tyl′i-
  form.
dĭ crot′ic, -crō′tal, dic′ro tism,
  -ro tous (*or* dĭ′krō-).
dic′tate, -ta ted, -ta ting, -tā′tion,
  -tā′tor, -to′ri al, -al ly, -al ness,
  -ta′tor ship.
dic′tion, -a ry.
dic′tum, pl. *-ta* or *-tums.*
did, didn′t, didst′, *rarely* did′dest.
dĭ dac′tic (*or* dĭ-), -tics, -tic al,
  -al ly, -ti cism, -ti′cian (-tish′-).
did′ap per (*or* dĭ′dap-) *or* -op per.
did′dle, -dled, -dling, -dler.
Dide′rot′ (dēd′rō′), Fr. philos.
dĭ′do, Di′do, Queen of Carthage.
dĭ dō′dec a hē′dral, -dron.
Di dot′ (dē′dō′), Fr. printer.
dĭ′drachm (-drăm), -drach′ma
  (-drăk′-), -drach′mon.
dĭe, *v.,* dĭed, dy′ing (dī′-), -ing ly,
  -ing ness.
dĭe, *n.,* a cube, *pl.* dĭce. die,
  general pl., dies.
die′-a way′, -back, -hold′er,
  -sink′er, -stock, -work.
dieb (dēb).
dĭ ē′cian *or* di œ′-, -e′cious.
di e′do (dē ā′dō).
dĭ′e gē′sis.
dĭ e lec′tric.
Di eppe′ (dē ĕp′), t. Fr.
dĭ er′e sis *or* dĭ ær′-.
dĭ e ret′ic.
Dĭ′es I′ræ (dī′ēz ī′rē), *dĭ′es
  ju rid′i cus.*
Diest (dēste), t. Belg.
dĭ′et, -ed, -ing, -er, -et a ry, -ĭne,
  -ist, dĭ′e ta′ri an, -e tet′ic, -ic al,
  -al ly, -tet′ics, -tet′ist, -et′ic,
  -ic al, dĭ′et-brĕad, -drink,
  -kitch′en.
Die′trich (dē′trĭch *or* -trĭk), Ger.
  painter.
Diez (deets), Ger. philol.; t. Ger.

dĭ e zeŭg'me non.

dif'fer, -ing, -ent, -ent ly, -en'ti a
(-shĭ a), pl. -ti æ, -en'tial, -tial-
ly, -ti ate, -a ted, -a ting, -a tor,
-a'tion, -en'ti ant (-shĭ ant).

dif'fer ence, -en'gine, -e qua'tion,
-gage.

dif'fi cult, -cul ty.

dif'fi dent, -ly, -dence.

dĭf'flu ent, -flu ence.

dif'form, -for'mi ty.

dif fract', -ed, -ing, -frac'tive,
-tive ly.

dif frac'tion, d. grāt'ing, d. spec'-
trum.

dif fran'gi ble, -gi bil'i ty.

dif fuse' (-fūz'), v., -fused', -fūs'-
ed ly, -ed ness, -er, -ing, -i ble,
-ble ness, -bil'i ty, -fu si om'e-
ter.

dif fuse' (-fūs'), a., -ly, -ness,
-fu'sive, -sive ly, -sive ness.

dif fū'sion (-zhun), -os'mose
(-ŏz'mōs), -tube, -vol'ume.

dig, dug or digged, dig'ging, -ger,
-ger-pine, -wash, -ging-machine'.

dĭ gal'lic.

dĭ gam'ma, -gam'mate, -ma ted.

dĭ gas'tric.

dig'by, pl. -bles.

dĭ gen'e sis, -ge net'ic, dig'e nous
(dĭj'-).

dĭ gest', v., -ed, -ed ly, -ing, er,
-i ble, -ble ness, -bil'i ty, -ive,
-ive ly, -ges'tion (-chun), di'gest, n.

dĭght, -ly.

dig'it (dĭj'-), -i tal, -tal in or -ĭne,
-tā'li a, -tăl'ic, -tăl'i form, Dig i-
tā'lis.

dig'i tate (dĭj'-), -ly, -ta ted, -ta'-
tion, -i ti form, -ti grade, -grā-
dism, -ti nerved, -ti par'tĭte.

dig i tō'ri um, pl. -ri a, -i tox'in
or -ĭne, -i tule, -i tus, pl. -tĭ.

dĭ'glot, -glot'tic.

dĭ'glyph.

Digne (dēn), t. Fr.

dig'ni fy, -ing, -fied, -fied ly,
-ni ta ry, -ni ty.

dĭ go neū'tic, -neū'tism, -go nop'o-
rous, dig'o nous (or dĭ'-).

di grä'do (dē grä'dō).

dĭ'grȧph, -graph'ic, dĭ'gram.

dĭ gress' (or dī-), -gressed', -gres'-
sing, -sive, -sive ly, -gres'sion
(-gresh'un), -sion al.

dī'gyn, -gyn'i an (-jĭn'-), dig'y-
nous (dĭj'-).

dĭ hē'dron, -hē'dral, -hex ag'o nal,
-hex a hē'dral, -hē'dron, dĭ hy'-
drīte (-hī'-).

dĭ I amb', pl. -ambs', or -am'bus,
pl. -bī.

Dĭ'jon' (dē'zhŏṅ'), c. Fr.

di'ka (dē'- or dī'-), dī'ka-bread,
-fat.

dĭk a măl'ĭ.

dīke, -let, diked, dīk'ing, dīk'er,
dīke'-grave, -reeve.

dĭ kē'tone.

dĭ lamb'dŏ dŏnt.

dĭ lap'i date, -da ted, -ting, -tor,
-da'tion.

dĭ late' (or dī-), -lāt'a ble, -bil'i-
ty, -ed, -ed ly, -er or -or, -ing,
-ive, -la'tant, -tan cy, -la'tate,
-la'tion, dil'a ta'tor, -a ta'tion.

dil'a to ry, -to ri ly, -ri ness.

dĭ lem'ma (or dī-), -lem'mist,
-lem mat'ic.

dĭl'et tănt', a., -tănt', n., dĭl'ĕt-
tăn'te (-tā or dĕ'lät tän'tā)
-tănt'ish or -tan'te ish, -tănt'ism
or -tan'te ism.

dil'i gent, -ly, -gence.

dill, -weed.

dil'ly, -dal'ly.

dil'o gy.

di'lu en'do (dē'lōō än'do).

dĭ lute', -lūt'ed, -ed ly, -ing, -er,
-lu'tion, -lute'ness, dil'u ent.

dĭ lū'vi al (or dī-), -ist, -vi an,
-an ism, -vi on, -vi um, pl.
-ums or -a.

dim, -ly, -ming, -mer, -mish,
-ness, dimmed, dim'-sight'ed,
-sight'ed ness.

dim'a ris or -a tis.

dīme.

dĭ men'sion, -sion al, -al'i ty,
-sion less, -men'sum.

dĭ me tal'lic.

dim'e ter, dī met'ric.

dĭ meth'yl, -y lan'i lĭn or -lĭne.

dĭ mid'i ate, -ā'ted, -ā'ting,
-a'tion.

dĭ min'ish, -a ble, -er, -ing, -ing-
ly, -ished, -min'u ent, -u en'do,
dim'i nū'tion, dĭ min'ish ing-rule,
-scale, -stuff.
dĭ min'u tive, -ly, -ness, -u tī'val
(*or* -min'u tĭv-).
dĭ min'u tize, -tized, -ti zing.
dim'is so ry, -so'ri al.
dĭ mit', -ted, -ting.
dim'i ty.
di mŏl'tō (dē).
dĭ'morph, -mor'phic, -phism,
-phous.
dim'ple, -pled, -pling, -ply.
dimp'sy.
Dim'y a, -y ā'ri a, dim'y a ry,
-ā'ri an.
din, -ning, dinned.
Di naj pur' (dē näj pōōr'), t. India.
di nan'de rie (dē nŏn'dê rē).
di nar' (dē- *or* dī'-).
din'din.
dīne, dined, dīn'ing, -er, -er-out,
-ing-room.
di ne'ro (dē nā'ro).
ding, -ing, dinged (dĭngd), ding'-
dong.
din'gar.
din'gey *or* -ghy (ding'gy).
din'gle, -gled, -gling, -gle-dan'gle.
din'go.
din'gy (-jĭ), -gi ly, -gi ness.
din'i cal.
dĭ nī'tro cel'lū lose (-lōs).
din'ner, -less, -ly, -y, *dĭ nette'*,
din'ner-bell, -hour, -ta'ble,
-time, -wag'on.
dĭ nom'ic.
dī'nŏs, pl. *-nī.*
dĭ'no saur, -sau'ri an.
Dĭ no thē'ri um, dī'no thēre.
dint, -less.
dī'nus.
dĭ ŏb'ol.
dī'o cēse, *pl.* -cēs ĕs, -oc'e san
(-os' *or* dī'o sē'-).
dī'ock.
dĭ oc ta hē'dral.
dī'o dŏnt.
Dĭ o dŏ'rus, Rom. hist.
dĭ œ'cian (-ē'shan), -cious, -cious-
ly, -cious ness, dī'e cism. See
diecian.

Dĭ og'e nes (-ŏj'e nēz), Gr.
philos., -o gen'ic, -e nes-crab,
-cup.
dī'o nym, -on'y mal.
Dĭ ŏ nys'i us (-nish'i us), tyrant
of Syracuse; Gr. hist.; Rom.
abbot; *Bib.*
Dĭ ŏ ny' sus (-nī'-), *Myth.*, *-nys'-
i a* (-nĭs'-), -nys'i ac, -nys'i an.
Dĭ ŏ phăn'tus, Gr. arithmetician,
-phan'tĭne.
dĭ op'sĭde (*or* -sīd), -op'tase, -op'-
ter, -op'trate.
dĭ op'tric, -al, -al ly, -trics, -tron,
pl. -tra, -try (-trĭ).
dĭ o rä'ma (*or* -rä'-), -răm'ic.
dī'o rīte, -rit'ic.
dĭ or thŏ'sis, -thot'ic.
dĭ os cŏ're in, -re ā'ceous.
Dĭ os cū'rĭ, -cū'ri an.
dĭ os'mŏse, -mŏ'sis, -mot'ic.
Dĭ ŏt're phes (-fēz), *Bib.*
dip, -per, -per ful, -ping, dipped,
dip'-buck'et, -cir'cle, -head,
-net, -pipe, -reg'u la tor, -rod,
-roll'er, -sec'tor, -splint, -tray,
-tube, -per-clam.
di pä' (dē pä').
dĭ pet'a lous.
di pet'to (dē).
diph thē'ri a (dif- *or* dip-), -the-
rit'ic, -ic al ly, -rī'tis.
diph'thong (dif'- *or* dip'-), -ize,
-ized, -i zing, -thong'ic, -thoņ'-
gal, -gal ize, -ized, -gal ly, -ga'-
tion.
diph y cer'cal, diph'y cer cy.
dĭ phyl'lous (*or* dĭph'-), diph'y-
o dŏnt (-I-), -o zō'oid *or* -y zō'-
oid.
dip'la cū'sis.
dĭ plă'si on (-sĭ-), -plăs'ic.
dĭ'ple.
dĭ plē'gi a, -pleg'ic (-plej'-).
dĭ pleī'do scope.
dĭ'plex.
dĭ plŏ'ma, -cy, -ma tism, -tist,
-tize, -tized, -ti zing, dip'lo mat,
-mat'ic, -ic al, -al ly, -mat'ics.
dĭ plŏ'pi a, -plop'ic.
dip neū'mo nous.
dī'pŏde, -pod'ic, dip'o dy.

dĭ pō'lar.
dip'ping-com'pass, -frame, -house,
-lĭq'uor, -nee'dle, -pan, -tube,
-vat, wheel.
dip'sas. Dip'sas, *Zoöl.* and *Entom.*
genus.
dip'sey (-sĭ) *or* -sy, -line.
dip so mā'ni a, -ni ac, -nī'a cal.
dip sop'a thy, -sō'sis.
dip'ter, -ad, -al, -an, -ist, -ol'o gist,
-o gy, -o log'ic al.
dip'tote.
dip'tych (-tĭk).
dĭ py'gus (-pī'-), *pl.* -gi (-jī).
dip'y lon (-ĭ-), *pl.* -la.
dĭ py rē'nous (-pī-).
Dir cæ'an.
dīre, -ful, -ful ly, -ful ness.
dĭ rect', -ed, -ing, -ive, -ive ly,
-ness, -or, -o rate, -o ry, -or-
ship, -ress *or* -rix, -rec tō'ri al,
-rec'tion, -rect'-ac'tion, -draught,
-ing-cir'cle.
dirge, -ful.
dĭr'i gi ble, -i gent, -i go, -i go-
mo'tor.
dirk (derk), -knife.
dirl (derl).
dirt, -y, -i ly, -i ness, dirt'-bed,
-bŏard, -cheap, -eat'ing, -scrăp'-
er, dirt'y-al'len.
dis ă'ble, -ment, -bled, -bling,
-bil'i ty.
dis a buse' (-būz'), -bused', -būs'-
ing.
dis ac cord', -ed, -ing, -ant.
dis ac cus'tom, -ing, -tomed.
dis'ad van'tage, -taged, -ta'geous,
-geous ly, -geous ness.
dis'af fect', -ed, -ed ly, -ed ness,
-fec'tion.
dis af firm', -ing, -ance, -firmed',
-fir ma'tion.
dis af fŏr'est, -ed, -ing, -ment,
-es ta'tion.
dis ag'gre gate, -ga ted, -ga ting,
-ga'tion.
dis a gree', -a ble, -ble ness, -bly,
-ment, -greed'.
dis'al low', -a ble, -ble ness, -ance.
dis al ly' (-lī'), -ing, -al lied'.
dis an nul', -ler, -ment, -ling,
-nulled'.

dis ap păr'el, -eled *or* -elled, -el-
ing *or* -el ling.
dis ap pear', -ance, -ing, -peared'.
dis ap point', -ed, -ing, -ment.
dis ap'pro ba'to ry, -ba'tion.
dis ap pro'pri ate, -pri ā'tion.
dis ap prove' (-prōōv'), -proved',
-prov'er, -prov'ing, -ing ly.
dis arm', -ing, -er, -a ment,
-armed'.
dis ăr rānge', -ment, -ranged',
-răn'ging.
dis ăr rāy', -ing, -ment, -rayed'.
dis'as sō'ci ate (-shĭ-). See *dis-
sociate.*
dis as'ter (dĭz ăs'ter *or* dĭs ăs'-),
-as'trous, -trous ly, -trous ness.
dis a vow', -al, -er, -ing, -ment,
-vowed'.
dis band', -ed, -ing, -ment.
dis bar', -ring, -ment, -barred'.
dis be lieve', -liev'er, -lieved',
-lief'.
dis bur'den (-dn), -ing, -dened.
dis burse', -ment, -burs'er, -ing,
-bursed'.
disc, dis'coŭs, -cal. See *disk.*
dis calced' (-kalst').
dis card', -ed, -ing.
dis case', -cased', -cās'ing.
dis cern' (dĭz zern'), -er, -i ble,
-ble ness, -ing, -ing ly, -ment,
-cerned'.
dis charge', -char'ger, -ging,
-charged', -charge'-valve, -dis-
char'ging-arch, -gear, -rod,
-tongs.
dis church', -churched'.
dis'ci flō'ral, -flō'rous, dis'ci form,
-cif'er ous.
dis cī'ple, -ship, -pled, -pling, -cip'-
u lar.
dis'cĭ plĭne, -plĭned, -plĭn'ing, -er,
-a ble, -ble ness, -plĭ nā'ry,
-nā'ri an, -ri um, *pl.* -ri a.
dis cis'sion (-sish'-).
dis clăim', -er, -ing, -claimed'.
dis close' (-klōz'), -closed', -clōs'-
er, -ing, -clō'sure (-zhoor).
dis cob'o lus, pl. *-li.*
dis'co carp, -car'pi um, *pl.* -pi a,
-car'pous.
dis'coid, -coid'al.

dis'co lĭth.

dis col'or, -ored, -or ing, -or a'tion.

dis com'fit (-kŭm'-), -ed, -ing, -fi ture.

dis com'fort (-kŭm'furt), -ed, -ing, -a ble, -ble ness.

dis com mode', -mŏd'ed, -ing, -mō'di ous, -ous ly, -ous ness.

dis com pose' (-pōz'), -posed', -pōs'ing, -ed ly, -ed ness, -pō'-sure.

dis con cert', -ed, -ing, -ment.

dis con nect', -ed, -ed ly, -er, -ing, -nec'tion.

dis con'so late, -ly, -ness.

dis con tent', -ment, -ed, -ed ly, -ed ness.

dis'con tin'ue, -tin'ued, -u ing, -u ance, -u or, -u ous, -ous ly, -u ee', -u ā'tion, -con'tĭ nū'i ty.

dis'cord, -cord'ance, -an cy, -ant, -ant ly, -ant ness.

dis'count, n., dis'count (or -count'), v., -ed, -ing, dis'count'er, -count'-a ble, dis'count brō'ker.

dis coun'te nance, -nanced, -nan'-cing, -nan'cer.

dis coŭr'age, -ment, -a ble, -aged, -a ging, -ging ly, -a ger.

dis côurse', n. and v., -coursed', -cours'er.

dis coûr'te ous, -ly, -ness, -te sy.

dis cov'er, -a ble, -er, -ing, -y, -ered, -y-claim.

dis cred'it, -ed, -ing, -or, -a ble, -a bly.

dis creet', prudent; -ly, -ness, -cre'tion (-krĕsh'-), -tion al, -al-ly, -a ry, -a ri ly.

dis crep'ance, -an cy, -ant (or dis'cre-).

dis crete', disconnected; -ly, -ness, -cre'tive, -tive ly.

dis crim'i nate, -ly, -ness, -na-ted, -ting, -ting ly, -tive, -tive ly, -tor, -to'ry, -nal, -nant, -nant'al, -na'tion, -i noid, -noid'al.

dis crown', -ing, -crowned'.

di͞ cur'sive, -ly, -ness, -cur'sus.

dis'cus, pl. -cus es (-ĕz) or -ci (-sī).

dis cuss', -a ble, -er, -ing, -cussed', -cus'sive, -sion, -sion al.

dis cū'tient (-shent).

dis dain' (or diz-), -ful, -ful ly, -ful ness, -ing, -dained.

dis ease' (dĭz ēz'), -eased.

dis em bark', -ing, -ment, -barked', -bar ca'tion.

dis em băr'rass, -ment, -rassed.

dis em bat'tled.

dis em bit'ter, -ing, -tered.

dis em bod'y, -bod'ied, -bod'i-ment.

dis em bogue' (-bōg'), -ment, -bōgu'ing.

dis em bow'el, -ing, -ment, -eled or -elled.

dis em broil', -ing, -broiled'.

dĭ sē'mic.

dis en chânt', -ed, -er, -ing, -ment.

dis en cum'ber, -ing, -ment, -bered, -brance.

dis en dow', -ing, -ment, -dowed'.

dis en gage', -ment, -gāged', -gā'-ged ness, -gā'ging, -gā'ging-gēar.

dis en nō'ble, -bled, -bling.

dis en shroud', -ed, -ing.

dis en tâil', -ing, -tāiled'.

dis en tan'gle, -ment, -gled, -gling.

dis en thrạll', -ing, -ment, -thrạlled'.

dis en tī'tle, -tled, -tling.

dis en tomb' (-tōōm'), -tombed'.

dis en trânce', -ment, -trânced', -trân'cing.

dis en twine', -twīned', -twīn'ing.

dĭ sep'a lous.

dis es tab'lish, -ing, -ment, -lished.

dis es teem', -ing, -teemed'.

dis fā'vor, -ing -er, -vored.

dis fēa'ture, -tured, -tūr'ing.

dis fel'low ship, -ing, -shiped or -shipped.

dis fig'ure, -ment, -ur ing, -ured, -u rā'tion.

dis fŏr'est, -ed, -ing.

dis fran'chise (-chĭz or -chīz), -ment, -chised, -chis ing.

dis gôrge', -ment, -gorged', -gor'-ging, -ger.

dis grace', -ful, -ful ly, -ful ness, -graced', -gra'cer, -gra'cing.

dis grun'tle, -tled, -tling.

dis guise' (-gīz'), -guised', -guis'-
ed ly, -ed ness, -er, -ing.
dis gust', -ful, -ful ness, -ing,
-ing ly, -ing ness.
dish, -ing, dished, dish'ful,
-wash'er, -wa'ter, -catch,
-cloth, -clout, -faced, -heat'er,
-hold'er, -rack, -rag, -tow'el.
dis'ha bille' (-a bĭl' or -bēl').
dis hal'low, -ing, -lowed.
dis har'mo nize, -nized, -ni zing,
-mo ny, -mo'ni ous, -mon'ic.
dis heärt'en, -ing, -ment, -ened.
dis helm', -helmed'.
dĭ shev'el (-l), -ment, -eled or
-elled, -el ing or -el ling.
dis hon'est (or dĭz-), -ly, -es ty.
dis hon'or (or dĭz-), -a ble, -ble-
ness, -bly, -er, -ing, -ored.
dis hôrn', -ing, -hôrned'.
dis'il lu'sion (-zhun), -ing, -ment,
-ize, -ized.
dis'in cline', -clined', -clīn'ing,
-clĭ nā'tion.
dis'in close', -closed', -clōs'ing.
dis'in côr'po rate, -ra'ted, -ra'-
ting, -ra'tion.
dis'in crus'tant.
dis'in fect', -ed, -ing, -ant, -or,
-fec'tion.
dis'in gĕn'u ous, -ly, -ness.
dis'in hĕr'it, -ed, -ing, ance.
dis in'te grate, -gra ted, -ting,
-tive, -tor, -gra'tion.
dis in tĕr', -ment, -ring, -têrred'.
dis in'ter est ed, -ly, -ness.
dis in vig'or ate, -a ted, -a ting.
dĭ sip'pus.
dis ject', -ed, -ing.
dis join', -ing, -joined.
dis joint', -ed, -ed ly, -ed ness, -ing.
dis juŋct', -juŋc'tive, -tive ly, -tion,
-ture, -tor.
disk or disc, -less, disk-gas'tru la,
-owl, -shell, -wheel, d. ar'mature, d. clutch, d. dy'na mo
(dĭ'-), d. har'row, d. tel'e graph,
d. valve.
dis like', -liked', -līk'ing, -līk'a-
ble.
dis'lo cate, -ca ted, -ting, -ca'tion.
dis lodge', -lodged', -lodg'ing,
-lodg'ment.

dis loy'al, -al ly, -al ty.
dis'mal (dĭz'-), -ly, -ness.
dis man'tle, -tled, -tling.
dis mâst', -ed, -ing, -ment.
dis may', -ful, -ing, -mayed'.
dis mem'ber, -er, -ing, -ment,
-bered.
dis mem'bra tor.
dis miss', -al, -ing, -ive, -missed',
-mis'sion (-mish'-), -mis'so ry.
dis mount', -ed, -ing.
dis ō bē'di ent, -ly, -ence.
dis o bey' (-bā'), -ing, -er, -beyed'.
dis o blige', -ment, -bliged', -blī'ger,
-blī'ging, -ging ly, -ging ness.
dĭ sō'ma tous.
Di son' (dē'zŏṅ'), vil. Belg.
dis or'der, -ly, -li ness, -dered,
-dered ness.
dis or'gan ize, -ized, -i zing, -i zer.
dis ōwn' (or diz-), -ing, -ment,
-owned'.
dis pär'age, -ment, -a ger, -a ging,
-ging ly.
dis'pa rate, -ly, -ness.
dis pär'i ty.
dis part', -sight.
dis pas'sion ate (-păsh'-), -ate ly,
-sioned.
dis pau'per ize, -ized, -i zing.
dis pel', -ler, -ling, -pelled'.
dis pen'sa ble, -ness, -sa ry, -sa-
tive, -tive ly, -sa tor, -to'ry,
-to'ri ly, -sā'tion, -tion al, -sa-
bil'i ty.
dis pense', -pensed', -pens'er, -ing.
dis pēo'ple, -pled, -pling, -pler.
dĭ sper'mous, -ma tous.
dĭ sperm'y, -sperm'ic.
dis perse', -persed', -pers'ed ly,
-ed ness, -er, -ing, -ive, -ive ly,
-ive ness, -per'sion.
dĭ sphē'noid.
dis pĭr'it, -ed, -ed ly, -ed ness,
-it ment.
dis plâce', -a ble, -ment, -placed',
-pla'cer, -pla'cing, -place'ment-
dī'a gram.
dis plant', -ed, -ing, -er, -plan ta'-
tion.
dis play', -er, -ing, -played',
-play'-let'ter, -line, -stand, -type.
dis plēase', -plēased', -plēas'ed ly,

-ed ness, -er, -ing, -ing ly, -ing-
ness, -pleas'ure (-plĕzh'-), -ur a-
ble.
dĭ spon'dee, -spon dā'ic, -spon dē'-
us.
dis port', -ed, -ing, -er, -ment.
dis pose' (-pōz'), -pos'al (-pōz'-),
-pōs'a ble, -pōsed', -pōs'ed ly,
-pōs'er, -pōs'ing, -ing ly, -po si'-
tion (-zish'un), -tion al.
dis'pos sess' (-pŏz zĕs' *or* -pŏs-
ses'), -sessed', -sess'or, -sess'ing,
-ses'sion.
dis praise' (-prāz'), -praised',
-prais'ing, -ing ly.
dis pro por'tion, -a ble, -al, -al ly,
-al'i ty, -ate, -ate ly, -ate ness,
-tioned.
dis prove' (-proov'), -prov'al, -a ble,
-er, -proof'.
dis pute', -less, dis'pū ta'ble (*or*
-pūt'à-), -ble ness, dis'pu tant,
-tā'tion, -tā'tious, -tious ly, -tious-
ness, -pūt'a tive, -er, -ing, -ed.
dis qual'i fy (-kwŏl'-), -ing, -fied,
-fī ca'tion.
dis quī'et, -ed, -ing, -er, -ly, -ness,
-e tude.
dis qui si'tion (-zish'un), -al,
-a ry, -quis'i tive, -i to ry, -to'-
ri al.
Dis ra'el i (dĭz rā'ĕl ĭ *or* -rā'lē *or*
-rē'le), Eng. statesman.
dis rate', -rāt'ed, -rāt'ing.
dis re gard', -ed, -ing, -er, -ful,
-ful ly.
dis rel'ish, -ing, -ished.
dis re pâir'.
dis re pute', -rep'u ta ble, -ta bly.
dis re spect', -ed, -ing, -ful, -ful ly,
-ful ness.
dis robe', -robed', -rōb'er, -rōb'ing.
dis rupt', -ed, -ing, -ive, -ive ness,
-rup'tion, -rup'ture.
diss.
dis sat'is fy, -ing, -fied, -is fac'-
to ry, -to ri ness, -fac'tion.
dis sect', -ed, -ing, -i ble, -sec'-
tor, -sec'tion, -sect'ing-for'ceps,
-knife, -mi cro scope.
dis sēize, -seized', -seiz'ing, -sēi'-
zor, -sēi zee', -sēi'zin, -sēi'zure
(-zhoor).

dis sem'ble, -bled, -bling, -bling-
ly, -bler.
dis sem'i nate, -na ted, -ting,
-tive, -tor, -na'tion.
dis sent', -ed, -ing, -er, -sen'sion,
-sen ta'ne ous, -sen'tient (-shent),
-tious, -tious ly.
dis sep'i ment, -men'tal.
dis'ser ta'tion, -al, -ist.
dis serv'īce, -a ble, -ble ness, -bly.
dis sev'er, -ing, -ance, -ment,
-ered.
dis'si dence, -si dent.
dis sil'i ent, -i ence, -i en cy.
dis sim'i lar, -ly, -lăr'i ty.
dis sim i la'tion, -sim'i la tive,
-si mil'i tude.
dis sim'u late, -la ted, -ting, -tor,
-la'tion.
dis'si pate, -pa ted, -ting, -tive,
-pa'tion.
dis so'cial (-shal), -so'cia ble
(-sha-), -bil'i ty.
dis so'ci ate (-shĭ-) *or* **dis as so'-**
ci ate, -a ted, -ting, -tive, -a'tion.
dis'so lū ble, -ness -lu bil'i ty (*or*
-sol'-).
dis'so lute, -ly, -ness.
dis solve' (dĭz zŏlv'), -solved',
-solv'ing, -ing ly, -er, -ent,
-a ble, -ble ness, -a bil'i ty, dis'-
sō lu'tion (dis'sō-).
dis'so nant, -so nance.
dis suade' (-swād'), -suād'ed, -ing,
-er, -suā'sive (-sĭv), -sive ly,
-so ry, -sua'sion (-zhun).
dis syl'la ble, -lab'ic, -lab'i fy,
-fy ing, -fied, -fi ca'tion, -syl'la-
bize, -bized, -bī'zing, -la bism.
dis sym'me try, -sym met'ric, -ric-
al.
dis'tad.
dis'tâff, *pl.* -tăffs, *rarely* -taves.
dis'tal, -ly.
dis'tance, -tanced, -tan cing,
-tant, -tant ly, -tance-block,
-judge, -piece, -post, -sig'nal.
dis tāste, -ful, -ful ly, -ful ness.
dĭ stē'mo nous.
dis tem'per, -ing, -ate ly, -pered,
-per-brush, -ground.
dis tend', -ed, -ing, -er, -ten'si ble,
-bil'i ty, -sive, -ten'tion.

---

fāte, făt, fär, fạll, fâre, fȧst, sofȧ, mēte, mĕt, hêr, īce, ĭn, nōte,

dis'tich (-tĭk), -ti chous (-kŭs), -chous ly, -ti chĭ'a sis (-kĭ'-).

dis til' *or* -till', -tilled', -til'ling, -la ble, -late, -la to ry, -ler, -ler y, -lā'tion, -ler y-fed'.

dis tiṇct', -ly, -ness, -tiṇc'tive, -tive ly, -tive ness, -tion.

dis tiṇ'guish, -a ble, -ble ne ss, -a bly, -er, -ing, -ing ly, -guished.

dis tôrt', -ed, -ed ly, -er, -ing, -ive, -tor'tion.

dis tract', -ed, -ed ly, -ed ness, -er, -i ble, -ile, -ing, -ive, -ive ly, -trac'tion.

dis train', -a ble, -er *or* -or, -ment, -ing, -trained', -traint'.

dis trait' (-trā').

dis traught' (-trȧt').

dis tress', -ful, -ful ly, -ing, -ing-ly, -ed ness, -tressed'.

dis trib'ute, -u ted, -u ting, -u ter, -u tȧ ble, -u tȧ ry, -u tive, -tive-ly, -tor, -tee', -tri bū'tion, -tion al.

dis'trict, -ed, -ing.

dis triṇ'gas.

dis'trix.

dis trust', -ed, -ing, -ing ly, -er, -ful, -ful ly, -ful ness, -less.

dis turb', -ance, -er, -ing, -turbed'.

dis'tyle.

dĭ sul'phate, -sul'phid, -sul phu'ric.

dis ūn'ion, -ist, -u nīte', -nīt'ed, -ing, -er, -ū'ni ty.

dis use' (-ūz'), *v.*, -used', -ūs'ing, -us'age.

dis use' (-ūs'), *n.*

dis ū'til ize, -ized, -i zing, -til'i ty.

dis wĕap'on (-n), -oned.

dĭ syn'thĕme.

dis yoke', -yōked', -yōk'ing.

dĭt'al.

ditch, -er, -ing, ditched, ditch'-bur, -dog, -fern, -grȧss, -wa'ter, -ing-ma chine', -plow, -tools.

dī'te trag'o nal.

dĭ thĕ'cal, -thĕ'cous.

dī'the ism, -the ist, -is'tic, -tic al.

dĭth'er, -ing, -ered, -ing-grȧss.

dĭth i on'ic.

dith'y ramb (*or* -ram), -ram'bic, -ram'bus.

dit'o koŭs (*or* dī-).

dī'tōne.

dī'trī glyph, -trig'o nal.

dī trō'chee (-kē), -che an.

dĭt'tay.

dit'to, -gram, graph, -tog'ra phy, -tol'o gy, dit'to-suit.

dit tob'o lo.

dit'ty, -bag, -box.

dĭ ū rē'sis, -ret'ic, -ic al.

dī ur'nal, -ly, -ness, -na'tion.

dī'va (dē'-).

dī'va gate, -ga'ted, -ga'ting, -ga'-tion.

dī'va lent (*or* dĭv'-).

dī van'.

dī vap o ra'tion, -ri za'tion.

dī vȧr'i cate, -ly, -ca ted, -ting, -ca tor, -ca'tion.

dive, dived, dīv'ing, dīv'er, dīv'ing-bell, -dress, -net, -stone, d. bee'tle, d. bird, d. buck, d. spi'der.

dī ver'bi um, pl. *-bi a.*

dī verge', -verged', -ver'ging, -ging ly, -gence, -gen cy, -gent.

dī'vers, *a.*

dī verse' (*or* dī'-), -ly.

dī ver'si fy, -ing, -fied, -fi'a ble, -si form, -si fi ca'tion, -si flo'rous, -si fo'li ous, -ver'si ty.

dī vert', -ed, -er, -ing, -ing ly, -ing ness, -i ble, -ver'sion (-shun) -vert'ise ment (-ĭz-).

dī'ver tic'u lum (*or* dĭv'-), pl. *-u la,* -tic'u lar, -u la ted.

dī vest', -ed, -ing, -i ble, -i ture.

dī vīde', -vīd'ed, -ed ly, -er, -a ble, -ing, div'i dend, di vīd'ing-en'-gine, -i ron, -ma chine'.

dī vīne', -ly, -ness, -vīned', -vīn'-ing, -vīn'er, -vĭn'a to ry, -vĭn'-i ty, div'i na tor, -na'tion, di-vīn'ing-rod, -stȧff.

di vi'si (dē vē'zē).

di vi'sion (-vĭzh'un), -al, -a ry, -vis'i ble (-viz'-), -ble ness, -bly, -bil'i ty, -vī'sive (-siv), -sive ly, -sive ness, -vī'sor (-zor), di vi'-sion-board, -mark, -plate.

di vorce', -a ble *or* di vor'ci ble, -less, -ment, -vor'cing, -cer, -cee'.

dī vort'.

div'ot, -spade.

di vo'to (dē-).

---

dĭ **vulge′,** -vulged′, -vul′ging,
-vul′ger.

di **vul′sor,** -sion.

dix (dēs).

diz′en (-n *or* dĭ′zn).

diz′zy, -zi ly, -zi ness.

Dnie′per (nē′-), r. Russ.

Dnies′ter (nēs′-), r. Russ.

do (dōō), -ing, did, does (dŭz),
done (dŭn), do-all.

dŏ, a syllable in music.

dŏab, a dark clay.

dŏ′ăb (*or* -äb) or *doo* (dōō), a tract
of country.

dŏ′băsh *or* -bhash *or* du băsh′
(dōō-).

dob′bin.

dob′by, -ma chine′.

dŏ′bla, *do blŏn′.*

dŏ′bra.

doch′mĕ (dŏk′-).

doch′mi us (dŏk′-), pl. *-mĭ ĭ, -mĭ′a-
sis.*

doc′ile (dŏs′il *or* dŏ′sil), doc i-
bil′i ty (dŏs-), dŏ cil′i ty.

dock, -age, -er, -ing, -măs′ter,
-yard, -docked, dock′-block,
-char′ges, -cress, -dues, -rent,
-war′rant.

dock′et, -ed, -ing.

doc′tor, -al, -ate, -ing, -ship,
-tored, doc′tor-box, -fish, -gum.

doc′trĭne, -tri nal, -nal ly, -na′ri-
an, -an ism, *-nâire′.*

doc′u ment, -men′tal, -ta ry.

dod *or* dodd, dod′ded.

Dŏd′a nim, *Bib.*

dod′der, -dered, dod′der-grăss,
-lau′rel, -seed.

dod′dy.

do dec′a gon, -a gyn (-jin), -gyn′-
i an, -a he′dron, -de cag′o nal,
-cag′y nous (-kaj′-), -de cam′er-
ous, -de can′der, -can′dri an,
-can′drous.

dŏ′dec a sĕ′mic.

dŏ′dec a style (*or* -dek′-).

do′dec a syl′la ble (*or* -dek′-),
-syl lab′ic.

dodge, dodged, dodg′ing, -er, -y.

dŏ′dŏ, *pl.* -does (-dŏz).

dŏe, *pl.* does (dōz), -skin, doe-bird.

doe′gan (dŏ′-).

dŏff, -ing, -er, doffed, doff′er-
rŏll, doff′ing-cyl′in der, -knife.

dŏg, *v.*, -ging, dŏgged, dŏg′ged, *a.*,
-ged ly, -ged ness.

dog, *n.*, -gish, -gish ly, -gish ness,
-gy, -bane, -ber ry, -blow, -bri er,
-fish, -hood, -like, -rose, -shore,
-skin, -tooth, a shell; -wood,
dog′-belt, -bis cuĭt, -cart,
-catch′er, -cheap, -cher′ry, -col′-
lar, -dai′sy, -days, -draw,
-eared, -faced, -fan′ci er, -fen′-
nel, -fly, -grăss, -grate, -head,
-house, -ken′nel, -Lat′in,
-leech, -let′ter, -li′chen, -muz′-
zle, -nail, -nose, -pars′ley,
-pow′der, -pow′er, -ray, -sălm′on,
-shark, -show, -sleep, -star,
-tent, -tooth, -tree, -trick,
-vane, -watch, -wea′ry, -wheat,
-whelk, -whip′per, -wor′ship, dog
ape, d. bee, d. fox, dog′wood-
bark, -oil, -tree.

dog′s-bane, -chop, -ear, -fennel,
-grăss, -nose, -tongue, dog′s meat.

dŏ gä′na.

doge (dŏj), -ship, dŏ′gal, -gate *or*
doge′ate, dŏ ga res′sa.

dŏg′ger, a fishing vessel, a mineral;
-man.

dŏg′ger el.

dog′ma, *pl.* -mas *or* -ma ta,
-mat′ic, -ics, -ic al, -al ly, -al-
ness, -ma tism, -tist, -tize,
-tized, -ti zing, -ti zer.

doi′ly.

doit, -kin.

dŏkh′ma or *-meh.*

dŏ lä′bra, pl. *-brœ,* -lä′brate, -lăb′-
ri form.

dŏ′läng.

dŏl′ce (dŏl′chä *or* dŏl′-).

dŏl′ce far ni en′te (dŏl′chä fär
ne än′tä), *dŏl′ce men′te* (-chä-
män′tä), *dol ci′no* (-chē′no) or
-ci ä′no or *-ci′na* (-chē′nä).

dŏl′drums.

dŏle, -ful, -ful ly, -ful ness, -some
(-sum), -some ly, -some ness,
dŏled, dŏl′ing, dole′stone, -fish,
-mĕad′ow.

dŏ len tis′sĭ mo.

dŏl′er ĭte, -it′ic, -e roph′a nīte.

Dŏl′gŏ rou′ki (-rōō′kē), Russ. princess.

Dol′go ru′ki (-rōō′kē), Russ. soldier.

dŏ′lĭ cā′pax (-paks).

dŏl′i chu′rus (-kū′-), -chu′ric.

dŏll, dol′ly, Dol′ly Var′den, *Fiction*; a gown; a fish. dol′ly-bar, -shop, -tub.

dŏl′lar, -bird, -fish, -mark.

dŏl′lee-wood.

dŏl′ma.

dŏl′man, a garment, *pl.* -mans.

dŏl′men, a stone, *pl.* -mens, -men′ic.

dŏl′o mīte, -o mize, -mized, -mizing, -mĭ za′tion *or* -mit i za′tion, -mit′ic.

dŏl′or ous, -ly, -ness, -or if′er ous, -if′ic, -ic al, *dō lō rō′sō.*

dŏ′lose (-lōs).

dol′phin, -flow′er, -fly, -strīk′er.

dŏlt, -ish, -ish ly, -ish ness.

dŏm, a title; a term used in cards. dŏm pē′dro, a game.

dō māin′, -mā′ni al.

dŏm′ba.

dōme, dō′mal, dō′mic al (*or* dŏm′i cal), -cal ly, dome′-cov′er, -head.

dō mes′tic, -al, -al ly.

dō mes′ti cate, -cā′ted, -ting, -cā′tive, -cā′tion, -mes′ ti ci ze, -cized, ci′zing, -tic′i ty.

dŏm′ett.

dō mey′kīte (-mā′- *or* dō′mĭ-).

dŏm′i cĭl *or* -cĭle, -cĭled, -cĭl′ing, -cil′i a ry (*or* -sĭl′ya ry), -i ate, -a ted, -ting, -a′tion.

dŏm′i nant, -ly, -nance, -nan cy, -nate, -na′ted, -ting, -tive, -tor, -na′tion.

dō′mĭ ne (*or* dŏm′-), a clergyman; a fish. See *dominie.*

dom i neer′, -ing, -ing ly, -neered′.

dō min′ic al, *do min′i cā′lē.*

Dō min′i can, dŏm′i nie (*or* dō′-).

dŏm i nie (*or* dō′-), a schoolmaster; a clergyman.

dō min′ion, *-min′i um.*

dŏm′i nŏ, a garment; a person; a mask. *pl.* -nos (-nōz).

dŏm′i noes (-nōz), a game; the pieces used in the game. Some authorities prefer *dominoes* as the plural of *domino* in every sense.

dō mi no tier′ (dō mē nō tyā′).

dŏm′i nus, pl. *-nĭ.*

dŏ′mīte, -mit′ic.

dŏn, *v.*, -ning, donned.

dŏn, *n.*, an important personage; a fellow of an English university. Don, a title in Spain and Italy corresponding to Sir in England.

do′na (dōn′ya), *fem.* of don.

dō′nä nō′bis.

dō′nate, -na ted, -ting, *-na′tor*, -na′tion, dŏn′a tive, -a to ry, dō′nor, -nee′, dō nā′tion par′ty.

Dō nä′ti (-tē), It. astron.

Dŏn′a tist, -a tism, -tis′tic, -tic al.

do′naught (dōō′-), do′noth ing, -ing ness.

dō′nax, *Dō′nax*, Conch. genus.

dŏn cel′la (*or* dŏn thāl′ya).

done (dŭn).

Dŏn e gạl′, co. Ire.

dŏng.

don′ga.

Dŏṇ′gŏ la, prov. Afr.

dō′nĭ.

Do ni zet′ti (-nē dzĕt′te), It. mus.

don′jon (dŭn′jŭn *or* dŏn′jŏn), *dŏn jŏn né* (-nā′).

Dŏn Jū′an, Byron's *Don Juan.*

dŏṇ′key (dŏn′kĭ *or* dŭng′ky), -en gine, -pump, -rest.

dŏn′na, a lady. Don′na, a title of respect, for It., Sp., and Port. ladies, corresponding to Span. Doña.

don′nee′ (dŏ′nā′).

Don Quix′ōte (Sp. pron. dōn kē hō′tä), Cervantes.

don′sky.

dōōd, -wal′lah (-wŏl′-).

dōō′dle, -sack, -dled, -dling.

dōōk.

dōō′ly *or* -lee.

dōōm, -ful, doomed, dooms′day, Dooms′day Book *or* Domes′day, doom-palm.

dōōn.

dooṇ′ga.

door (dōr), -case, -check, -keep′er, -less, -nail, -plate, -post, -sill, -stĕad, -step, -stone, -stop, -way,

-weed, -yard, -a larm′, -bell,
-fas′ten er, -frame, -guard,
-hang′er, -jamb, -knob, -knock′-
er, -latch, -lock, -mat, -piece,
-pin, -pull, -roll′er, -shaft,
-spring, -strap, -strip.
doorn (dōrn).
dōōr′shĕk.
dōō sōō′tee.
dŏp, -chick′en, dop′per-bird.
dope, doped, dōp′ing, -ey.
dop′pia (-ya), -piet′ta (-yet′ta).
dop′pler īte.
dō put′ta.
dôr *or* dôrr, -bee′tle, -bug, -fly,
-hawk.
Dŏ′räṅte′, Molière.
Dor dogne′ (-dōn′), dept. Fr.
Do′ré′ (dō′rā′), Fr. artist.
dŏ′ri a.
Do′rine′ (-rēn′), Molière.
Dŏ′ris, ancient Gr. city; -ri an,
Dŏr′ic, -i cism, -i cize, *Dŏ′ris,*
Conch. genus.
dôr′king.
dôr′mant, -man cy, -mi tive, -mi-
to′ry, dorm.
dôr′mer, -mered, -mer-win′dow.
dôr′mouse, *pl.* -mice.
dôr′my.
dôr′nick *or* -nock.
dor′sal, -ly, -sad, -sad′i form.
dorse.
dôr si cum′bent, dor′si fixed, -si-
grade, -sig′er ous (-sij′-), -si-
lat′er al, -sip′a rous, -si spī′nal,
-si ven′tral, -tral ly.
dôr sō cau′dal, -so cer′vic al, -so-
dyn′i a, -so lat′er al, -so lum′-
bar.
dō′ruck.
dō′ry, *pl.* -rīes, a fish; a boat.
dŏs, *dos′-a-dos′* (dō′-zà-dō′).
dose (dōs), dōs′age, -ing, dosed,
do sim′e ter, -sol′o gy *or* -si ol′o gy.
dō′sĕh.
dō shal′la.
dō sim′e try, -e trist.
dŏs′sal *or* -sel, a woven fabric.
dŏs′ser.
dŏss-house.
dos′sier′ (dō′syā′ *or* dŏs′si er),
dos′sière (dō′syâr′).

dŏs′sil *or* -sel, a spigot; a wisp
of hay; a bit of lint; a cloth.
dot, -ted, -ting, -ter, dot′-punch,
-stitch, -wheel, -ting-pen.
dō′tage, -tard, -tard ly, -tish.
dō′tal.
dotch′in.
dote, dōt′ed, -ing, -ing ly, -y.
doth (dŭth).
dō′ti (-tē).
dou ane′ (dōō ăn′) ,-a nier′ (-à′nyā′).
dou′ar (dōō′-).
dou′ble (dŭb′l), -ness, -bled,
-bler, -bly, -ble tree, -act′ing,
-bank, -banked, -băr′reled,
-băss, -benched, -bīt′ing, -bitt,
-bod′Ied, --breast′ed, -brēath′er,
-charge, -coṅ′cave, -cone, -con′-
vex, -crown, -dēal′er, -deck′er,
-dye′ing, -ea′gle, -edged, -end′er,
-face, -faced, -first, -flow′ered,
-foot′ed.
dou′ble-gēar, -gild, -h a n d′ e d,
-head′ed, -hĕad′er, -hung, -lock,
-man, -manned, -mean′ing,
-milled, -mīnd′ed, -na′tured,
-nos′triled, -quick, -rip′per, -ruff,
-run′ner, -shade, -shīn′ing, -shot,
-snipe, -stop, -struck, -time,
--tongue, -tongued -top′sail,
-touch, -trou′ble, -worked.
dou′ble d′or (dōō′bl dôr), *d. en ten′*
dre (ŏṅ tŏṅ′dr).
doŭb′let.
dou′bling, -frame, -nail.
doŭb lōōn′.
dou′blure′ (dōō′blōōr′).
doubt (dout), -ed, -er, -ful, -ful ly,
-ful ness, -ing, -ing ly, -less,
-less ly.
douc (dōōk).
douce (dous), *dou′ceur′* (dōō′ser′).
douche (dōōsh).
dou cine (dōō sēn′ *or* dōō′-).
dough (dō), -y, -i ness, -face, a
person; -nut, -baked, -balls,
-bird, -brake, -knēad′er, -māk′-
er, -mix′er, -rais′er, -trough.
dough′ty (dou′-), -ti ly, -ti ness,
-ty-hand′ed.
doup, -weav′ing.
doupe (dōōp).
dour (dōōr), -ness.

dou′ree (d⊙ō′-).
Dou′ro (d⊙ō′-), r. Sp.
dou rou cou′li (d⊙ō r⊙ō c⊙ō′lĭ).
douse *or* dowse, doused, dous′ing,
-er, dous′ing-chock, -rod.
dou′zain′ (d⊙ō′zăn′), a piece of
verse.
dou′zaine′ (d⊙ō′zān′), a dozen
men.
dove (dŭv), -kĭe, -let, -like, -ling,
-ship.
dove′-col′or, -cote, -dock, -eyed,
-house, -plant, -wood. ·
dove′tail, -tailed′, -tail′ing, -tail-
box, -cut′ter, -fish, -mark′er,
-plane, -saw, d. joint, d. mold′-
ing, d. plates.
Dŏ′vre fiĕld *or* -fjeld′ (-fyĕld′),
mts. Norw.
dow′a ger, -ism.
dow′dy, -ish, -di ly, -ness.
dow′el, -ĕled *or* -elled, -el ing *or*
-ĕl ling, dow′ĕl-bit, -joint, -pin,
-point′er, -ĕl ling-ma chine′.
dow′er, -less, -ered, -er-house.
dowl.
dow′las *or* -lass.
down, -y, -i ness, downed, down′-
bear, -cȧst, -come, -draw, -fall,
haul, -heart′ed, -hill, -land,
-looked, -ly′ing, -pȯur, -right,
-rush, -set, -sit′ting, -take,
-throw, -trod′den, -ward, -wards,
-weed, -weigh.
down′-beard, -by, -drought, -east,
a., -east′er, -share, -stairs,
-stream, -town, d. bed. The
Downs, a roadstead in Eng.
dow′ry.
dox ol′o gy, -o gize, -gized, -gi-
zing, dox′o log′ic al (-loj′-)
dox′y, *pl.* -ies.
doy′en′ (dwä′yän′).
doze, dozed, doz′ing, -er, -y,
-i ness.
doz′en (dŭz′-).
drab.
drab′bets.
drab′ble, -bled, -bler, -bling.
Drä′chen fels (*or* -kĕn fels′), mt.
Prus.
drachm (drăm), drach′ma
(dräk′-), *pl.* -mas *or* -mæ.

Drä′co, -co′ni an, -cŏn′ic, -ic al ly.
drac′o nin (dräk′- *or* dra cō′-),
drä′cin *or* -cĭne, -cī′na.
drȧff, -ish, -y.
drȧft *or* draught (drȧft), -y
-i ness, drȧfts′man, -man ship,
drȧft′-an′i mal, -bar, -box,
-cat′tle, -com′pass es (-kum′-),
-en′gine, -e′qual i zer, -eye,
-fur′nace, -hole, -hook, -horse,
-net, -ox, -reg′u la tor, -rod,
-spring, -tree, -tug.
drag, -ging, dragged, drag′man,
pl. -men, drags′man, *pl.* -men.
drag′-an′chor, -bar, -bench, -bolt,
-chain, -drĭv′er, -hook, -hound,
-hunt, -link, -net, -rake, -rope,
-sail, -saw, -seine, -sheet,
-spring, -stȧff, -twist, -wash′er.
dra gan′tin.
dra gée (-zhā′).
drag′gle, -gled, -gling, -gly.
drag′o man, *pl.* -mans.
drag′on, -ess, -et, -ish, -on root,
-wort, -beam, -fish, -fly, -leech,
-piece, -shell, -stand′ard, -tree,
-wa ter, -on′s-blood, -eye, -head,
-tail.
drag on ade′ *or* -on nade′.
drȧg′on né′ (-nā′).
dra gŏōn′, -ing, -gooned′, -goon′-
bird.
drȧil.
drȧin, -a ble, -er, -ing, -pipe,
-tile, -trap, drained, drain′-cap,
-cock, -curb, -gȧge, -gate, -well.
drȧin′age, -way, -ba′sin, -tube.
drain′ing-au′ger, -en′gine, -ma-
chine′, -plow, -pot, -pump, -tile,
-vat.
drai sine′ (drā zēn′).
drake, -stone, -fly.
dram, -sell′er, -shop.
drä′ma (*or* drā′-), drȧ mat′ic, -ic-
al, -al ly, drȧm′a tize, -tized,
-ti zing, -ti za ble, -tĭ za′tion,
-a tist, -a turge, -tur′gy, -tur′-
gist, -tur′gic.
drank. See *drink*.
drap′ d′été′ (drä′ dā tā′).
drape, drȧped, drä′ping, -per,
-per y, *pl.* -per ies.
dras′tic.

draught (dråft), -board, draughts'-
man, *pl.* -men, draughts'man-
ship. The older form *draught* is
giving way to the shorter form
draft.
draughts, the game of checkers.
Dra vid'i an, -vid'ic.
draw, drew, drawn, draw'a ble,
-back, -bore, *v.,* -bridge, -er,
-ee', -file, *v.,* -glove, a game;
-shave.
draw-bar, -bays, -bench, -bōlt,
-bore, *n.,* -boy, -cut, -gate,
-gēar, -glove, a glove; -head,
-horse, -kiln, -knife, -lid, -link,
-loom, -net, -plate, -point,
-pŏk'er, -rod, -spring, -stop,
-ta'per, -tim'ber, -tongs, -tube,
-well, drawn'-work.
draw'ing, -awl, -bench, -block,
-board, -book, -com'pass, -en'-
gine, -frame, -glove, -hook,
-knife, -lift, -ma chine', -mas'-
ter, -ma te'ri als, -pa'per, -pen,
-pen'cil, -pin, -point, -press,
-rōlls, -room, -ta'ble, d. in.
drạwl, -er, -ing, -ing ly, -ing ness.
dray, -age, -man, *pl.* -men, dray'-
cart, -horse.
drĕad, -ed, -ing, -er, -ful, -ful ly,
-ful ness, -less, -less ness.
drĕad'nạught *or* -nought.
drĕam, -er, -ful, -ful ly, -y, -i ly,
-i ness, -ing, -ing ly, -less, -less-
ly, -land, drēamed *or* drĕamt,
dream'-hole, -while, -world.
drĕar, -y, -i ly, -i ness.
drĕdge, -man *or* dredg'er man, *pl.*
-men, dredg'er, dredge'-boat,
-box, -net.
dredg'ing, -box, -ma chine'.
Dred Scot case.
dregs, dreg'gy, -gi ness, -gish.
drei'bund' (drī'bo͝ont').
drench, -er, -ing, drenched, -ing-
horn.
Dres'den (*or* drĕz'-), c. Ger.;
(drĕz'-), t. Ohio; D. ware, D.
point-lace.
dress, -er, -y, -i ness, dressed,
dress'māk'er, -māk'ing, -cir'cle,
-goods, -guard, -spur, d. coat,
d. pa rade,' d. u'ni form.

dress'ing, -bench, -case, -floor,
-frame, -gown, -jack'et, -knife,
-ma chine', -room, -sack, -ta'ble.
dres'soir' (-swär').
Drey'fus īte (drī'-).
drib'ble, -bled, -bler, -bling, -let
or -blet·
drid'dle, -dled, -dling.
drī'er, drī'est, drī'ly. See *dry.*
drift, -ed, -ing, -y, -age, -bolt,
-less, -piece, -pin, -way, -weed,
-wĭnd, -wood, -aŋ'chor (-kur),
-cŭr'rent, -ice, -land, -lĕad,
-mīn'ing, -net, -net'ter, -sail.
drill, -er, -mȧs'ter, -stock, -băr'-
row, -bit, -bōw, -chuck, -clamp,
-ex tract'or, -gage, -hăr'row,
-hold'er, -hus'band ry, -jar,
-pin, -plate, -plow, -press, -rod,
-ser'geant, -spin'dle, -tongs.
drill'ing, -jig, -lāthe, -ma chine'.
driŋk, drăŋk, drŭŋk drink'a ble,
-ble ness, -er, -ing, -less, -mon'-
ey, -of'fer ing, drink'-a-pen'ny,
drink'er-moth, -ing-bout, -foun'-
taĭn, -horn.
drip, -ping, -stone, dripped, drip-
joint, -pipe, -pump, -stick,
-tray, -ping-pan.
drive, drove, drĭv'en, drĭv'er,
drive'pipe, -way, drive'-boat,
-bolt, -wheel, drĭv'er-ant, -boom.
drĭv'ing, -ax'le, -band, -bolt, -box,
-cap, -chis'el, -gēar, -gloves, -rein,
-shȧft, -spring, -wheel.
driz'zle, -zled, -zling, -zly.
drŏ'ger *or* -gher.
Drŏ'gī ŏ (-jī o), Zeno's imaginary
land.
drŏgue.
dro guet' (-gā').
droit (*or* drwä).
drōll, -er y, -ing ly, -ish, droll'y.
drom'e da ry (drŭm'-), -da rist,
-da'ri an.
dro'mo graph, -mo scope, mom'e-
ter.
drŏm'os (or drŏ'-), pl. -oi, drom'ic,
-ic al.
drōne, -pipe, drŏn'ish, -ish ly,
-ish ness, -ing, drōned, drone'-
bȧss, -bee, -bee'tle, -cell, -comb,
-fly, -trap.

dron'go, -cuck'oo, -shrike.
drŏn'te.
droo'ge veld (drō'gĕ fĕlt).
drōōl.
drōōp, -er, -ing, -ing ly.
drop, -per, -ping, -ping ly, -let,
-light, -stone, -wort.
drop'-bar, -black, -bot'tom, -box,
-curls, -cur'tain, -drill, -el'bōw,
-fin'gers, -flue, -fly, -fŏr'ging,
-glâss, -ham'mer, -han'dle,
-keel, -let'ter, -me'ter, -net,
-press, -ripe, -roll'er, -scene,
-shut'ter, -ta'ble, -tee, -tin,
-worm, drop-the-hand'ker chief,
drop'ping-bot'tle, -tube, drop'-
seed-grâss.
drop'sy, -si cal, -cal ness.
drŏsh'ky or drŏs'ky, pl. -kies.
drŏ som'e ter.
drŏss, -less, -y, -i ness.
droud.
drought (drout) or drouth, -y,
-i ness.
Drou ot' (drōō'ō'), Fr. gen.
drŏve, drŏ'ver, -ving.
drown, -ing, drowned.
drowse (drouz), drowsed, drow'-
si ly, -si ness, -sy, -sy head,
ay-hĕad'ed.
drub, -ber, -bing, drubbed.
drudge, drudged, drudg'er, -er y,
-ing, -ing ly.
drug, -ging, -gist, drugged, drug'-
bee'tle, -mill, -sift'er, -store.
drug'get.
dru'id, -ish, -ism, -id'ic, -ic al,
dru'id-stone.
druk (drōōk), -ker.
drum, -mer, -ming, -beat, -fish,
-head, -stick, -wood, drummed.
drum'-call, -corps, -curb, -cyl'-
in der, -guard, -ma'jor, -saw,
-sieve, -skin, -wheel, d. ar'mature, drum'ming-log.
drum'mock.
Drum'mond light.
drunk, -ard, -en, -en ly, -en ness,
-en ship, -wort. See *drink*.
drupe, -let, dru pâ'ceous, -pel,
-pe ole, -pe'tum, pl. -pe'ta.
Druse (drōōz), a religious sect.
Dru'si an (-zi an), pertaining to

the Druses. Dru'si an (-si an),
relating to Drusus.
drux'y or -ey.
dry, -ing, -ly, -ness, dried, drī'er,
drī'est, d. wash.
dry'-blow'ing, -boned, -câst'ing,
-câs'tor, -cup, -cup'ping, -cure,
-eyed, -gild'ing, -goods, -grīnd'ing,
-house, -mul'ture, -nurse, n.,
-pipe, -point, -press, -rent, -rot,
-rub, -salt, -sand, v., -stone,
-stove, d. dock.
dry'ing-box (drī'-), -case, -chãm'-
ber, -floor, -house, -ma chine',
-ov'en, -plate, -room, -stove,
-tube, d. off.
dry'nurse, v., -nursed.
dry'salt er, -er y.
dŭ'ad, -ad'ic.
dŭ'al, -ism, -ist, -is'tic, -al'i ty.
dŭ'al in.
dŭ'an.
du'arch y (-ark-).
dub, -ber, -bing, dubbed, dub'-
bing-tool.
dub'-a-dub'.
dubb, a bear.
dŭ'bi ous, -ly, -ness, -bi os'i ty,
-bi'e ty, -bi ta ble, -ta'tion.
dŭ'cal, -ly.
dŭ'cape.
dŭc'at, duc a toon'.
dŭ'ces tē'cum (-sēz).
Du Chail'lu' (dü shä'yü'), Fr.-
Amer. traveler.
Du ché (dü shä'), chaplain First
Cont. Congress.
duch'ess, duch'y, pl. -ies, duch'y-
cõurt.
du chesse' d'An'gou'leme' (dōō,
shäs' dän'gōō'lãm'), a kind of
pear.
duck, -er, ducked, duck'bill, a
quadruped; -ling, -meat, -weed,
-ant, -bar'na cle, -billed, -hawk,
-legged, -mole, -oak, -shot,
-snipe, -weight.
duck'ing, -gun, -sink, -stool,
duck's-bill, -egg, -foot, -meat.
duct, -less, *duc'tus*.
duc'tile, -ly, -til'i ty, -ti lim'e ter.
duc'tor-roll'er.

---

dud′dy *or* -die, dud′der y, dud′-
man, *pl.* -men.
dŭde, dŭd′ish, -ish ness, -ism,
-ine′ (-een′), du di nette′.
du deen′.
du′du (dōō′dōō).
dudg′eon, -tree.
dŭe, -bill, dŭ′ly.
dŭ′e (dōō′ā), mus. term. *du′e*
cor′de (kôr′dā).
dŭ′el, -ing *or* -ling, -ist *or* -list,
-el′lo.
dŭ en′na (*or* dōō ä′nya), pl. *-nas.*
dŭ et′, *-et ti′no* (dōō′ĕt tē′no), *-et′-*
to (-āt′to), dŭ′o.
Dü′faure′ (-fōr′), Fr. statesman.
duff, -day.
duf′fa dar′ (*or* -fä′dar).
duf′fel *or* -fle.
duf′fer.
duf′fing.
dŭ′foil.
dug, -way. See *dig.*
dŭ′gong.
dug′out.
duke, -dom, -ling, -ly, -ship,
duke′s-meat.
Du kho bort′si (dōō kō-).
duk′n (dōōk′n).
dul ca mä′ra, -rin.
dulce, sweet; sweet wine; dul′cet,
-cet ness.
dul′ci ăn′a.
dul′ci fy, -ing, -fied, -fi ca′tion.
dul′ci mer.
dŭ′ledge.
dŭ li′a.
du lil′ī (dōō-).
dull, -er, -ing, -ish, -ard -ness *or*
dul′-, -head, dul′ly, dulled, dull′-
brained, -browed, -eyed, -sight′-
ed, -wit′ted.
dulse, a seaweed.
dŭ′mal, du′me tose, du′mōse *or*
-moŭs.
Du′mas′ (dü′mä′), Fr. novelist.
Du Mau′ri er′ (dü mō′rē ä′), Fr.
artist and writer.
dumb (dum), -ly, -ness, dumb′-
bell, -bid′ding, -bird, -cake,
-cane, -chạl′der, -cräft, -plate,
-wäit′er, d. show, d. spin′et.
dum′ble, -dore.

dum′dum bul′let.
dum′found′ *or* dumb′-, -ed, -er,
-ing.
dum′my, -ing, -ism, -mĭed.
Du′ Mont′ (dü′ mōṅ′), Augustin
Alexandre, Fr. sculp.; Pierre
Etienne Louis, Swiss scholar.
dump, -age, -ing, -er, dumped,
dump′-bōlt, -car, -cart, dump′-
ing-buck′et, -car, -cart, -ground,
-reel, -sled, -wag′on.
dum′ple, -pled, -pling, -pling-
duck.
dump′ling, a pudding.
dump′y, dump′ish, -ish ly, -ish-
ness, -y-lev′el.
dun, -ning, -ner, -nish, -bird, -fish,
dunned, dun-cow, -dīv′er.
duṇ′can.
dunce, -dom, -pōll, dun′cer y,
-ci cal, dunce′-ta′ble.
dun′der, -bolt, -funk, -head,
-head′ed, -pate, -pōll.
Dŭn ferm′line (-fer′lĭn *or* -ferm′-
or dum fer′-), t. Scot.
dung, -hill, -y.
duṇ ga ree′.
dun′geon (-jun), -er.
duṇ′gi yah.
dun′īte.
Duṇ′ker *or* -kard *or* Tuṇ′ker.
dun′lop.
dun′nage, -naged, -na ging, -nage-
grāt′ings.
dun′ning, curing fish.
dun′nock.
dun′pic kle.
dun′rob in.
Dŭn′sĭ nāne′, hill Scot.
dun′sta ble, a woven fabric.
dŭnt.
dŭ ŏ dec a hē′dron, -hē′dral, -de-
cen′ni al, -dec′i mo (-dĕs′-),
-i mole, -i mal, -mal ly, -de cin′-
i fid, -dec′u pole, -den′a ry.
dŭ′o dĕne, -de′nal.
dŭ o dē′num, pl. *-dē′na,* -dē′nal,
-de nī′tis, -de nos′to my.
dŭ o drä′ma, -o lit′er al, -o lŏgue.
dŭ om′a chy (-ky).
duo′mo (dwō′-).
dŭ′o pod.
dup (düp).

dŭpe, dūp'a ble, -er, -ing, -a bil'-
i ty, dūped.
dŭ'pi on.
Du'ples'sis'   (dü'plä'sē'),   Fr.
painter.
dŭ'plex, -ing, -plexed.
dŭ'pli cate, -cā'ted, -ting, -tive,
-tor, -ture, -cand, -ca'tion.
du plic'i dent (-plis'-), -pli ci den'-
tate, -ci pen'nate.
dŭ plic'i ty (-plĭs'-).
dŭ pon'di us, -dĭ ĭ.
Du'quesne' (dü'kān'), Fr. naval
commander.
dur (dōōr).
dŭ'ra, -ral, dŭ'ra mā'ter.
dŭ'ra ble, -ness, -bly, -bil'i ty.
du rā'men.
dŭr'ance, -an cy, dū ra'tion.
Dū rănd', Amer. painter.
Du'rand' (dü'rŏn'), Fr. architect.
Du ran'te (dōō rän'tä), It. composer.
dŭ ran'té bě ně plac'i to   (-plas'-),
d. vĭ'ta.
Du raz'zo (dōō rät'so), t. Turk.
dur'bar.
dŭ'rēne.
Du'rer (dü'rer), Ger. painter.
dŭ'ress (or -ress'), n., -ress', v.,
-ress'or.
Dur'ga (dōōr'-).
Dur'ham (-am), co. Eng.; a breed
of cattle.
dŭr'ing.
dur'jee.
dur'mȧst.
durn or durns.
du'ro (dōō'-).
dŭ rom'e ter.
dûr'ra (or dōōr'-).
dŭ'sack.
dusk, -y, -i ly, -i ness, -ish, -ish-
ly, -ish ness.
Düs'sĕl-dŏrf', c. Prus.
dust, -ed, -er, -less, -y, -i ness,
-brush, -man, -pan, -ward, -ball,
-bin, -brand, -cart, -chăm'ber,
-col'lar, -fĕath'er, -guard, -hole,
-prig, -shot, -storm, -whirl,
dust'y-mil'ler, a plant.
dust'ing, -brush, -col'ors.
dus toor' (-tōōr'), -toor'y.

Dutch, a. and n., D. gold, D.
lace, D. liq'uid, D. met'al, D.
ov'en, D. roll'er, D. school.
dutch, v., -ing, dutched.
Dutch'man, pl. -men, -man's-
breech'es (-brĭch'ĕz), a plant;
-pipe, a plant.
dŭ'ty, pl. -ties, -te ous, -ous ly,
-ous ness, -tĭed, -ti a ble, -ti-
ful, -ful ly, -ful ness, du'ty-free.
dū ŭm'vir, pl. -virs or -vĭ rĭ, -vi-
ral, -vi rate.
du vet' (dōō vä').
dux, pl. dŭ'ces (-sēz).
Duyck'inck   (dĭ'kĭŋk),   Amer.
writer.
duy'ker or -ker bŏk (dĭ'-).
du'yong.
Dvor'ak (dvŏr'zhäk), Bohem. mus.
dwăle.
dwalm (dwäm).
dwang.
dwarf, -ish, -ish ly, -ish ness, -ing,
-ling, dwarfed.
dwell, -er, -ing, dwelt or dwelled,
dwell'ing-house, -place.
Dwen'dĭ (dwän'-).
dwi (dwē).
Dwi'na (dwē'-), r. Russ.
dwin'dle, -ment, -dled, -dling.
dy'ad (dĭ'-), -ad'ic, dy'ad-dēme
(dĭ'-).
Dy'ak (dĭ'-).
dy'arch y (dĭ'arch y or -ark y).
Dy'as (dĭ'-), -as'sic.
dye (dĭ), -ing, -stone, -stuff, -ware,
-weed, -wood, dy'er, dyed.
dye'-băth, -beck, -house, -ket'tle,
-pine, -pot, -tri'al, -vat, -works,
dy'er's-broom   (dĭ'-),   -green'-
weed, -moss, -weed, dye'wood-
cut'ter.
dy'go gram (dĭ'-).
dy'ing (dĭ'-), -ly, -ness. See die.
dy nac tĭ nom'e ter (dĭ-), dy'na-
grăph (dĭ'-).
dy nam'ic (dĭ-), -al, -al ly, -ics,
dy'nam (dĭ'-), -nam'e ter, -na-
met'ric, -ric al, -na mism, -na-
mist, -mist'ic, -na mi tard'.
dy'na mĭte (dĭ'-), -mĭ'ted, -ting,
-ter, -tism, -mit'ic al, -al ly,
dy'na mĭte-gun (dĭ'-).

nŏt, nôr, ūse, ŭp, ûrn, etüde, fōōd, fŏŏt, aŋger, boṅmot, thus, Bach.

dy′na mize (dĭ′-), -mized, -mi-
zing, -mĭ za′tion.
dy′na mo-e lec′tric (dĭ′-), -e lec′-
tric al.
dy nam′o gen (dī-), -na mog′e ny
(-mŏj′-), -mo gen′ic, -gen′e sis,
-nam′o grȧph, -na mo met′a mor′-
phism, -mor′phosed (-fŏst), -na-
mom′e ter, -mo met′ric, -ric al,
-mom′e try, -mo′tor.
dy′nas ty (dĭ′-), *pl.* -tĭes, -nast,
-nas′tic, -ti cism.
dyne (dīn).
dy′o phy sit′ic (dī′o fĭ zĭt′-), -o-
the ism, -oth′e lism, -oth′e līte.
dys al′bu mose′ (-mōs′).
dys an′a lyte (-lĭt).
dys ar′thri a, -ar′thric, -*ar thro′sis.*
dys cra′si a (-zhĭ a *or* -sĭ a),
-cras′ic.
dys′en ter y, -ter′ic, -ic al.
dys lă′li a, *dys lex′i a*, dys′lo gy,
-lo gis′tic, -tic al ly.

dys′no my.
dys′o dŏnt.
dys ŏ′pi a, -op′si a, -op′sy,
-o rex′i a, -rex y.
dys pep′si a *or* -pep′sy, -pep′tic,
-tic al, -pep′tone.
dys phā′gi a or dys′pha gy, -phag′ic
(-făj′-).
dys phā′si a (*or* -fā′zhĭ a).
dys pho′ni a or dys′pho ny.
dys phŏ′ri a.
dysp nœ′a (disp ne′a), -nœ′al
-nœ′ic.
dys tel′e ol′o gy, -o gist, -o log′-
ic al.
dys thy′mĭ a (-thĭ′-), -thym′ic
(-thĭm′-).
dys′tōme, -to moŭs, -tom′ic.
dys′tro phy, -troph′ic.
dzĕ′ren *or* -ron.
Dzi a lo szi′ce (dzĕ ä lō shĕ′tsä),
t. Pol.
dzig′ge tai (-ge tī).

E

E string.
E′a cles (ē′a klēz), *Entom. genus.*
Eads (ēdz), Amer. eng.
ĕa′ger, -ly, -ness.
ĕa′gle, -stone, -wood, -glet,
ĕa′gle-bird, -eyed, -flīght′ed,
-hawk, -owl, -ray, -sight′ed,
-vul′ture.
ear, -ing, -less, -ache, -bob, -drop,
-drum, -lap, -lid, -lock, -mark,
-marked, -pick, -reach, -ring,
-shot, -wax, -wit′ness, -wort,
eared.
ear′-bone, -brush, -cap, -conch
(-koŋk), -cor′net, -cough, -dust,
-flap, -gland, -hole, -lap′pet,
-lift′er, -lobe, -net, -pend′ant,
-piece, -pier′cer, -pock′et, -riv′-
et, -sand, -shell, -snail, -split′-
ting, -string, -syr′inge (-sĭr′-),
-worm, ear-drop tree, ear′ing-
criŋ′gle.
ĕarl, -dom, -duck, -mar′shal.
ĕar′ly, -li er, -li est, -li ness.
ĕarn, -ing, ĕarned, ĕarn′ing-grass.

ĕar′nest, -ly, -ness, -mon′ey.
earth, -en, -en ware, -i ness, -li-
ness, -ly, -bag, -bank, -board,
-born, -bred, -drake, -fall, -fork,
-kin, -nut, -pea, -shock, -star,
-ward, -wards, -wolf, -work,
-worm, -y.
ĕarth-au′ger, -ball, -bath, -bat′-
ter y, -bōr′er, -car, -chest′nut,
-clos′et, -crab, -cŭr′rent, -eat′er,
-fast, -flax, -flea, -fly, -foam,
-gall, -hog, -house, -in duct′or,
-louse, -moss, -oil, -pea, -pig,
-pit, -plate, -pul sa′tion, -shine,
-smoke, -stop′per, -ta′ble, -tilt′-
ing, -tongue, -treat′ment, -tre′-
mor, -wire.
ĕarth′ly-mīnd′ed, earth′nut-pea.
earth′quake, -a larm′, -shad′ow,
-shock.
ĕar′wig, -ging, -wigged.
ease, -ful, -ful ly, -ful ness, -ment,
eased, eas′ing, -i ly, -i ness,
ease′-off, eas′ing-spar′row, -swal′-
low.

fāte, făt, fär, fạll, fâre, fȧst, sofȧ, mēte, mĕt, hêr, īce, ĭn, nōte,

east, -er ly, -er ling, -ern, -ern er, -ern most, -ing, -ward, -ward ly, the East, the Orient; the East′ern Empire.

Eas′ter, -tide, -flow′er.

East-In′di an, -In′dia man.

eas′y, eas′i er, -i est, eas′y-go′ing, e. chair.

ĕat, ate *or* ĕat, -en, -ing, -a ble, -age, -er, -ing-bat, -house.

eau (ō), pl. *eaux* (ōz), *eau′-dê- Cō logne′* (-lŏn′), *eau′-de-vie′* (-vē′), *eau′ ce leste′* (ō′ sā′lĕst′), *eau′ forte′* (fôrt′).

Eau′claire′ (ō′klâr′), co. and г. Wis.

Eaux Vives (ō vĕv), vil. Switz.

Eauze (ōz), t. Fr.

ĕaves, -drop, *v.*, -drop′ping, -per, -dropped, eaves′-board, -catch, -drip, -drop, *n.*, -lȧth, -swal′- low, -trough.

é bau choir′ (ā bō shwŏr′).

ebb, -ing, ebbed, ebb′-an′chor, -tide.

E′bers (ā′bers), Ger. novelist.

E′bĭ on īte, -on it′ic, -on ism *or* -o nī′tism.

Eb′lis (-lēz), a fallen angel.

ĕ′bŏe, -light, -torch′wood, -tree.

ĕb′on, -ist, -īte, -īzc, -ized, -i zing, -y.

é boule′ment (ā bōōl′mŏn̄).

é bril lade′ (ā brēl yäd′).

e bul′lient, -lience, -lien cy, -lio- scope (-yō-), eb ul li′tion (-lish′-).

eb′u rĭn *or* -rīne, -rīte, e bur′na- ted (*or* eb′ur-), -ne an, -ne ous, -ni fi ca′tion, eb ur na′tion.

é cail lé (ā′kāl′yā′), -work.

é car té (ā′kar′tä′).

ec′ba sis, -bat′ic.

ec′bo lē, -bo lĭne, -bol′ic.

Ec′cĕ Hō′mō or *ec′cĕ hō′mō*, *ec′cē sig′num*.

ec cen′tric, -al, -al ly, -tric′i ty, ec cen′tric-gĕar, -hoop, -rod, -strap.

ec clē′si a (-zĭ a), pl. *-si æ* or *-sĭ as*, -si an, -si arch (-zĭ ark), -si ast, -si as′tic, -tic al, -al ly, -as′ti- cism, -si og′ra phy, -si ol′o gy, -o gist, -o log′ic al (-loj′-).

Ec clē si as′tes (-zĭ as′tez), -as′ti- cus.

ech′e lon (esh′-), -lens.

e chid′nĭne (-kid′-).

ech′i nate (ek′-), -na ted.

ĕ chi′no derm (-kĭ′-), -der′mal, -der′ma toŭs.

e chi′nus (-kĭ′-), pl. *-nĭ*, -chĭ′noid, -chin′u late (-kĭn′-).

ech′o (ĕk′o), *pl.* -oes (-ōz), -er, -ic, -ing, -ism, -less, -scope, ech′oed, ech′o-or′gan, -stop.

ĕ chom′e ter (-kŏm′-), -e try.

E′ci ja (ā′thē chä), t. Sp.

é clair (ā′klâr′), -clair′cize, -cized, -ci zing, *-cisse ment* (-sis ment *or* -sēs mŏn̄′).

é clat′ (ē klä′ *or* ā-).

ec lec′tic, -al ly, -ti cism.

ec lim′e ter.

e clipse′, -clipsed′, -clips′ing, -clip′tic.

ec′lŏgue.

ec′ly sis (ek′lĭ-).

ec mne′si a (ek nē′-).

ec′o nŏme.

e con′o mize, -mized, -mi zing, -mi zer, -o mist, -o my, ē co- nom′ic (*or* ĕc o-), -ic al, -al ly, -nom′ics.

é cor chê (ā′kŏr′shä′).

É cos saise′ (ā kŏs säz′) or *é cos-*.

ó coute (ā′kōōt′).

ec pho ne′sis, pl. *-ses* (-sēz).

é cra seur′ (ā′krä′zêr′), *-crase ment′* (-krȧz′mŏn̄′).

é cru′ (ā′krōō′).

ec′sta sy, -stat′ic, -ic al.

ec′ta sis.

ec trop′ic.

ec tro pom′e ter.

é cu′ (ā kū′ *or* ā′-).

Ec ua dor′ (ĕk wȧ dŏr′), rep. S. Amer., -dō′ri an *or* -dōr′an.

ec u men′ic, -ic al, -al ly, -me- nic′i ty (-nis′-).

ec′ze ma, -zem′a tous.

e dā′cious, -ly, -ness, -dac′i ty (-das′-).

Ed′da, -dic *or* -da′ic.

ed′dish.

ed′dy, *pl.* -dies, -dy ing, ed′died, -dy-wa′ter, -wind.

---

e'del weïss (ā'dl vīs *or* ĕd'el wīs).
E'den, -den'ic.
e den'tate, -den'tu late, -tu lous,
-tā'tion.
Edes, Amer. antiq.
ed es'tin.
edge, -less, -shot, -ways, -wise,
edg'er, -y, edged, *v.*, edged *or*
edg'ed, *a.*
edge'-bolt, -coals, -cut'ting, -joint,
-key, -mail, -mill, -mold'ing,
-plane, -play, -rail, -roll, -set'-
ter, -stitch, -stone, -tool, -trim'-
mer, -wheel.
edg'ing, -i'ron, -ma chine', -saw,
-shears, -tile.
ed'i ble, -ness, -bil'i ty.
ē'dict, -dic'tal (*or* ē'-).
ed'i fīce, -fi'cial (-fish'al).
ed'i fy, -ing, -ing ly, -fied, -fī cā'-
tion.
ē'dīle, -ship, -dil'i an.
E dī'na, poetic for Edinburgh.
Ed'in burg, t. Ind.
Ed'in burgh (-bŭr'rō), c. Scot.
Ed'i son, Amer. elec.
Ed'is to, r. S. C.
ed'it, -ed, -ing, -i tor, -to'ri al,
-al ly, -tor ship, e di'tion (-dish'-).
é di tion' de luxe' (ā'dē'syôn' dê
lōōx').
ē di'ti o prin'ceps (-dĭsh'ĭ o).
ed'u cate, -ca ted, -ting, -tive,
-tor, -ca ble, -bil'i ty, -ca'tion,
-tion al, -tion ist.
e dūce', -duced', -du'cing, -du'ci-
ble, -duc'tion, -duc'tive, -tion-
pipe, -port, -valve.
e dul'co rate, -ra ted, -ting, -tive,
-tor, -rant, -ra'tion.
eel, -buck, -er, -er y, -y, -fare,
-grăss, -pot, -pout, -skin,
-spear.
eel'-bås'ket, -fish, -fly, -fork, -gig,
-hook, -moth'er, -oil, -pump, -set,
-shaped, -shark, -trap, -worm.
e'en (ēn).
e'er (air).
ee'ry *or* -rie, -ri ly, -ri ness.
ef face', -a ble, -ment, -fa'cing,
-faced'.
ef fect', -ed, -ing, -er, -i ble, -ive,
-ive ly, -ive ness, -less, -less ly,

-fec'tion, -fec'tu al, -al ly, -al-
ness, -tu ate, -a ted, -a ting,
-a'tion.
ef fem'i nate, -ly, -ness, -i na cy.
ef fen'dĭ, pl. *-dis* or *-dies* (-dĭz).
ef'fer ent.
ef fer vesce', -vesced' (-vest'), -ves'-
cing, -cence, -cen cy, -cent, -ci ble,
-cĭve.
ef fête', -ness.
ef'fi ca cy, -fi cā'cious, -cious ly,
-cious ness.
ef fi'cient (-fish'-), -ly, -cien cy.
ef'fi gy, *pl.* -gies, -mound.
ef fla'tion.
ef'fleu rage' (ef'flōō räzh').
ef flo resce' (-rĕs'), -resced' (-rest'),
-res'cing, -res'cence, -cen cy, -cent.
ef'flu ence, -en cy, -ent.
ef flu'vi um, *pl.* -vi a, -vi al.
ef'flux, -flux'ion (-flŭk'shun).
ef'fort (-furt), -less.
ef fray'ant, ef frä yé' (-yä').
ef front'er y.
ef fŭl'gent, -ly, -gence.
ef fuse' (-fūz'), *v.*, -fused', -fūs'-
ing, -fū'sion (-zhun).
ef fuse' (-fūs'), *a.*, -fū'sive, -sive-
ly, -sive ness.
eft.
E gĕ'ri a, *Myth.*
Eg'er ton (ĕj'-), Eng. statesman.
e gest', -ed, -ing, -ges'ta, -ges'tive,
-ges'tion (-chun).
egg, -er, -er y, -ing, -fish, -hot,
-ler, -nog, -plant, -shell, -wife,
egged.
egg'-al bu'min, -an'i mal, -ap pa-
rā'tus, -ap'ple, -as sort'er, -bag,
-bald, -bås'ket, -bēat'er, -bird,
-blow'er, -boil'er, -born, -căr'-
ri er, -case, -cell, -clēav'age,
-coc'kle, -co coon', -cup, -dance,
-de tect'er, -de vel'op ment,
-drill, -end'ed, -flip, -for'ceps,
-glåss, -glue, -hatch'ing, -lay'ing,
-light'er, -mem'brane, -mite.
egg'-pär'a site, -pie, -pod, -pop,
-pouch, -sac, -shaped, -shell,
-slice, -spoon, -squash, -suck'er,
-syr'inge (-sĭr'-), -test'er, -tĭm'er,
-tongs, -tooth, -trot, -tube,
-ur'chin. eggs-and-ba con, a

plant; eggs-and-col′lops, a plant;
egg′sauce, e. nu′cle us.
Eg′gles ton (ĕg′glz-), Amer. writer.
e′gi′gi′ (ā′hē′hē′).
ĕ′gis *or* æ′-.
e glan′du lar, -du lose, -dŭ loŭs.
eg′lan tīne (*or* -tĭn).
ĕ′go (*or* ĕg′o), -ism, -ist, -is′tic,
-tic al, -al ly, -go′i ty, -go the′-
ism, -go tism, -go tist, -tist′ic,
-ic al, -al ly.
e grē′gious (-jus), -ly, -ness.
ĕ′gress.
ĕ′gret (*or* ĕg′ret) *or* e grĕtte′.
ĕ′gri ot.
E gyp′tian (-shan), -tol′o gy,
-o gist, -o ger, -to log′ic al.
Eh′ren breĭt′steĭn (ā′ren-), t. Prus.
Eh′ret (ā′ret), Ger. painter.
Eich′bĕrg (īch′-), Ger. mus.
El′der, r. Ger.
eĭ′der, -down, -duck, -goose,
-yarn.
eĭ′do grȧph, -do scope, -do trope,
-do lol′o gy, -do′lon, pl. -la.
eĭ dŏ′lŏ scŏpe.
eĭ dou ra′ni on (-dōō-).
Ei′fel (ī′fel), mt. Ger.
Eif′fel (ī′fel *or* ĕf′fĕl′), Fr. eng.;
the Eiffel tower.
eight (āt), -een′ (ā′teen′), -een mo,
-eenth, -foil, -fold, -score, -i eth,
-y, eighth, eighth′ly, eighth
note, e. rest.
eĭ′kon, pl. -ko nes (-nēz), ei kon′ic.
Eil′don (ēl′-), hills Scot.
eĭ′len burg (ī′len bŏŏrg), t. Ger.
eĭ′mer.
El′sen äch, t. Ger.
El′sen bĕrg, t. Ger.
El′sen burg (ī′zen bŏŏrg), co. Hung.
eĭ′sen rahm (-zn räm).
Ei′sen stadt′ (ī′zen stät′), t. Hung.
Eis′le′ben (īs′lā′-), t. Ger.
eis tedd′fod (ī stetħ′vŏd), pl.
-fod′au (-vŏd′ou).
eĭs′-wōōl.
ei′ther (ē′ther *or* ī′-).
e jac′u late, -la ted, -ting, -tor,
-to′ry, -la′tion.
e ject′, -ed, -ing, -ment, -or,
-jec′tive, -tive ly, -tion, -ta, -or-
con dens′er.

e ji′do (ā hē′do).
ē′joo (-jōō).
ēke, ēked, ēk′ing.
ĕ′kĭ ä (*or* ĕk′-).
e lab′o rate, -ly, -ness, -ra ted,
-ting, -tor, -to′ry, -ra′tion.
el æ om′e ter *or* ē lāi om′-, -op′-
tēne, -o sac′cha rĭne (-ka-).
E laine′ (-lān′), Tennyson.
é lan′ (ā lŏñ′).
ĕ′land (*or* ĕl′-).
e lapse′, -lapsed′, -laps′ing.
e las′tic, -al ly, -ti cian (-tish′an),
-tic′i ty.
e lāte′, -lāt′ed, -ed ly, -ed ness,
-la′tion.
e lat′er ist, -er īte, -e rom′e ter,
el a trom′e ter.
Elbe (ĕlb), r. Ger.
el′bōw, -ing, -board, -chair, -room,
-bōwed, el′bow-cuff, -gaunt′let,
-grease, -guard, -joint, -piece,
-plate, -rail, -scis′sors, -shāk′er,
-shield, -sleeve, -tŏngs.
El′bruz′ (-brōōz′), mts. Pers.
eld′er, -er ly, -er ness, -er ship,
eld′est.
el′der, a plant, -bĕr′ry, -wort,
-tree, e. gun, e. wine.
El Do rä′do *or* El do rä′do (*or*
-rä′do).
El e at′ic (*or* ē le-), -at′i cism.
el′o oam panc′.
e lect′, -ed, -ing, -ive, -ive ly, -or,
-or al, -or ate, -or ship, e lec′-
tion, -tion eer′, -eer′er, -eer′ing.
e lec′tric, -al, -al ly, -al ness,
-tric′i ty, -tri′cian (-trish′an),
-tri fy (-fī), -fy ing, -fied, -fi′a-
ble, -fī ca′tion, -trĭne, -tri′tion
(-trish′un), -trize, -trized, -trī′-
zer, -trī′zing, -trĭ za′tion, -trep′-
e ter, e. wave.
e lec′tro, -bal lis′tic, -bal lis′tics,
-bath, -bĭ ol′o gy, -bĭ ol′o gist,
-bi os′co py, -cap′il la ry, -cap′il-
lȧr′i ty, -chem′ic al, -chem′is try,
-chrŏn′o grȧph, -chron′o graph′ic,
-cul′ture, -dy nam′ic (-dī-), -dy-
nam′ic al (-dī-), -dy nam′ics
(-dī-), -dy′na mom′e ter (-dī′-),
-gild′ing, -gilt, -kĭ net′ic, -kĭ-
net′ics.

e lec'tro mag'net, -m a g net'ic,
-mag'net ism, -met'al lur'gy, -mo'-
tion, mo'tive, -mus'cu lar, -neg'a-
tive, -phys i ol'o gy, -phys ĭ ō-
log'ic al, -pō'lar, -pos'i tive,
-puṇc'ture, -stē're o type (or
-stĕr-), -te leg'ra phy, -tel'e-
graph'ic, -thĕr'a peŭ'tics, -thĕr'-
a py, -ther'man cy, -vī'tal, -vī'-
tal ism.
e lec'tro cute or -tri cute, -cū'ted,
-ting, -cū'tion.
e lec'trŏde, -tro gen'ic, -gen'e sis,
-trog'e ny (-trŏj'-), -tro grăph,
-tro liĕr', -trol'o gy, -trol'y sis,
-tro lyte (-līt), -lyt'ic (-lĭt'-),
-ic al, -lyze, -lyzed, -ly'zing
(-lī'-), -ly zā'tion (-lĭ-), -tro-
poi'on, -tech'nics (-tek'-), -tech'-
nic al.
e lec'tro-en grăv'ing, -etch'ing,
-op'tic, -op'tics.
e'lec trom'e ter, -e try, -tro met'-
ric, -ric al, -tro mo'tor, -trop'a-
thy, -tro phone, -troph'o rus,
-tro plate, -pla'ted, -ting, -ter.
e lec'tro scope, -scop'ic, -stat'ic,
-stat'ics, -tro tint, -tro ton'ic,
-tro to nic'i ty (-nĭs'-), -trot'o-
nize, -o nous, -o nus.
e lec'tro type (-tĭp), -typed, -ty'-
ping, -ty'per, -ty'py, -typ'ic
(-tĭp'-).
el ee mos'y na ry, -na ri ly, -ri-
ness.
el'e gant, -ly, -gance, -gan cy.
e lē'gi ac (or ĕl'e jĭ'ak), -gi ast,
el'e gī'a cal.
el'ĕ gy, pl. -gies (-jĭz), -e gize,
-gized, -gist.
el'e mē or -e mĭ.
el'e ment, -men'tal, -tal ism, -tal-
ly, -tal'i ty, -ta ry, -ri ness.
el'e phant, -phan'ter, -phan'tid,
-tĭne, -toid or -toid'al.
el'e phant-ap'ple, -bee'tle, -bird,
-creep'er, -fish, -grăss, -mouse,
-seal, -shrew, el'e phant's-ear,
a plant, -foot, -tusk, a mollusk.
el'e phan tī'a sis, -phan'ti ac.
El eŭ sin'i a, -i an.
el'e vate, -va ted, -ted ness, -va-
ting, -tor, -to ry, -va'tion.

ĕ lĕv'en (-n), -enth.
elf, pl. elves, -in, -ish or elv'-,
-ish ly, -ish ness, -kin, -land,
-lock.
elf'-ăr'row, -bolt, -child, -dart,
-dock, -fire, -king, -queen,
-shot, -stone.
Elgg (ĕlk), t. Switz.
El'gin mar'bles.
E'lĭ a, Charles Lamb.
E lī'ab, Bib.
E lī'a kim, Bib.
E lī'am, Bib.
e lic'it (-lĭs'-), -ed, -ing.
ĕ līde', -līd'ed, -ing, -lis'ion
(-lizh'un).
E'lĭ el, Bib.
E'lĭ ē'zer, Bib.
el'i gi ble, -ness, -bly, -bil'i ty.
E lī'hu, Bib.
e lim'i nate, -na ted, -ting, -tive,
-tor, -to'ry, -na ble, -nant, -na'-
tion.
E lĭph'a let, Bib.
el'i quate, -qua ted, -ting, -qua'-
tion, e liq'ua ment (-lĭk'-).
E'lis, anc. Gr. city. E'li ac.
é'līte' (ā'lēt').
E lī'u, Bib.
E lī'ud, Bib.
e līx'ir (-er).
E liz'a bĕth'an (or -bĕth'-).
elk, -nut, a plant; -wood, a tree;
elk-tree.
El kä'nah (or el'-), Bib.
ĕll, a measure; a wing of a house;
an elbow of a pipe or tube.
el'la chick.
el'le bo rin or -rĭne.
el lipse', -lip'so grăph, -soid,
-soid'al, -lip'tic, -tic al, -al ly,
-tic'i ty, -to graph, -toid.
el lip'sis, pl. -ses (sēz).
elm, -y, -bee'tle, -bōr'er, -but'ter-
fly, -moth, -saw'fly, -wood.
El'nă than, Bib.
el o cu'tion, -a ry, -ist.
ĕl'od.
e lō'di an (or el o'-).
é'loge' (ā'lōzh').
e lon'gate, -ga'ted, -ting, -ga'tion.
e lōpe', -ment, -loped', -lōp'ing,
-er.

el'o quent, -ly, -quence.
El Pä'sŏ, co. Col. and Tex.; c. Ill.
else, -where.
e lū'ci date, -da ted, -ting, -tive,
-tor, -da'tion.
e lude', -lūd'ed, -ing, -i ble, -lū'-
sion (-zhun), -lū'sive, -sive ly,
-ness, -lū'so ry, -so ri ness.
e lu'tri ate, -a ted, -ting, -a'tion.
el'van, -īte, -it'ic.
E lys'i um (-lizh'i um or -liz'i um
or -lizh'yum), E lys'ian (-lizh'-
yan or -liz'yan or -lizh'an).
el'y trum (-ĭ-) or -tron, pl. -tra,
-trig'er ous (-trĭj'-), e lyt'ri form.
El'ze vir (-ver), Dutch printer;
-vi'ran (-vē'-) or -vĭr'i an.
em, pl. ems, Typog.
e ma'ci ate (-shĭ-), -ā'ted, -ting,
-a'tion.
em'a nate, -na'ted, -ting, -tive,
-tive ly, -to'ry, -nant, -na'tion.
e man'ci pate, -pa'ted, -ting, -tor,
-to'ry, -pa'tion, -tion ist, -ci pist.
e mar'gi nate, -ly, -na'ted, -na'-
tion.
e mas'cu late, -la'ted, -ting, -tor,
-to'ry, -la'tion.
em bälm' (-bäm'); -ing, -er, -ment,
-balmed'.
em bank', -ing, -ment, -banked'.
em bar'go, -gŏed, -go ing.
em bark', ing, ment, -barked',
-bar ka'tion.
em băr'rass, -ing, -ing ly, -ment,
-rassed, -rassed ly.
em'bas sy, pl. -sĭes.
em ba tē'ri on, pl. -ri a.
em bat'tle, -ment, -tled, -tling.
em bel'lish, -ing, -ing ly, -er,
-ment.
em'ber, -tide, -bēred, em'ber-
days, -eve, -făst, -goose, -week.
em bez'zle, -ment, -zled, -zling,
-zler.
em bit'ter or im-, -ing, -er,
-ment, -tered.
em blaze', -blazed', -blāz'ing.
em blā'zon, -ing, -er. -ment, -ry,
-zoned.
em'blem, -at'ic, -ic al, -al ly,
-blem'a tize, -tized, -ti zing,
-tist, -blē'ma, pl. -ma ta.

em'ble ment.
em bod'y, -ing, -bod'i er, -i ment,
-ĭed.
em bog', -ging, -bogged'.
em bŏld'en (-n), -ened, -en ing,
-en er.
em'bo lism, -lis'mal (-lĭz'-), -lis-
mat'ic, -ic al, -lis'mic, -mic al,
-lis'mus.
em'bo lite.
em'bo lon or -lum, pl. -la.
em'bo lo phā'si a (-fā'zĭ a).
em bon point' (ŏṅ'bŏṅ'pwăṅ').
em bor'der, -ing, -dered.
em bŏss', -ing, -er, -ment,
-bossed', -ing-i'ron, -ma chine',
-press.
em bou chure' (ŏṅ'bōō'shōōr').
em bow'er, -ing, -ered.
em brăce', -ment, -brăced', -bră'-
cing, -cer, -cer y.
em brănch'ment.
em brā'sure (-zhūr).
em'bro cate, -ca ted -ting, -ca'-
tion.
em broid'er, -er, -ing, -y, -ered,
em broid'er y-frame, -nee'dle,
-păste.
em broil', -er, -ing, -ment,
-broiled'.
em brown', -ing, -browned'.
em'bry ŏ (-brĭ-), -gen'ic, -og'e ny
(-ŏj'-), -og'o ny, -og'ra phy,
-o grăph, -graph'ic, -ol'o gy,
-o gist, -o log'ic (-loj'-), -ic al,
-al ly, -bry o nal, -o nate, -na'-
ted, -on'ic, -ic al ly, -o plas'tic,
-o scope, -scŏp'ic, -ot'o my,
-ot'ic, em'bry ŏ-sac (-brĭ-).
Em e lye' (-lē'), Chaucer.
e mend', -ed, -ing, -er, -a ble,
-a to'ry, em'en da'tor, -dā'tion.
em'er ald, -ĭne, -ald-fĭsh, -moth.
e merge', -merged', -mer'gen cy,
-gence, -gent, -mer'sion.
e mĕr'i tus.
Em'er son, Amer. philos.; -sō'ni an.
ĕm'er y, -bag, -board, -cake,
-cloth, -pa'per, -pow'der, -rī'fle,
-stick, -stone, -wheel.
e met'ic, -ic al ly, em'e sis, -e tol'-
o gy.
é'meute' (ā'mūt' or -mêt').

nŏt, nôr, ūse, ŭp, ûrn, etūde, fōōd, fŏŏt, aṅger, boṅmot, thus, Bach.

em'i grate, -gra'ted, -gra'ting, -grant, -gra'tion, -tion al, -tionist, *é mi gré* (ā'mē'grā').

E'mile' (ā'mēl'), Rousseau.
E mil'ian (-yan).

em'i nent, -ly, -nence.

e mir' (ē mēr' *or* ē'mêr), e mir'ate, -mir'ship.

em'is sa ry, -ship.

e mit', -ted, -ting, -ta ble, e mis'sive, -si ble, -mis'sion (-mish'-).

em'met, an ant. Em'met, Irish insurrectionist.

em'me trope, -trō'pi a, -trop'ic.

e mol'lient (-yent *or* -lĭ ent).

e mŏl'u ment.

e mŏ'tion, -al, -al ism, -al ist, -al'i ty, -mo'tive, -tive ly.

em pale'. See *impale*.

em pan'el, -ing, -ment, -ĕled.

em'per or, -ship, -press.

em'pha size, -sized, -si'zing, -sis, -phat'ic, -ic al ly.

em'pïre, -ship, -per y.

em pïr'ic, -al, -al ly, -i cism, -i cist, Em pïr'ic, one of an ancient Greek sect.

em plas'tic.

em plec'tum *or* -ton.

em ploy', -ing, -er, -ment, -a ble, -ployed', -ploy'ed ness, em ployee' (*or* -ploy'-), *ĕm'ploy'é'* (-ā' *or* ŏn plwŏ yā').

em plume', -plumed', -plum'ing.

em pŏ'ri um.

em pow'er, -ing, -ered.

em prise', (-prïz').

emp'ty, -ing, -ti er, -ti ness, -tĭed, -ty-hand'ed.

em pur'ple, -pled, -pling.

em pyr'e al (-pĭr'e al *or* -pĭ rē'al), -py rē'an.

ē'mu.

em'u late, -la'ted, -ting, -tive, -tive ly, -tor, -to'ry, -la'tion.

em'u lous, -ly, -ness.

e mul'si fy (-fī), -ing, -fïed, -fĭ ca'tion, -mul'sic, -sive, -sion, -sionize, -ized, -i'zing.

en ā'ble, -bled, -bling.

en act', -ed, -ing, -ive, -ment, -or.

en al'la ge (*or* ē nal'-).

en am'el, -eled *or* -elled, -el ing

or -ĕl ling, -el er *or* -el ler, -elist *or* -el list.

en am'el-blue, -cells, -col'umns, -cu'ti cle, -fï'bers, -germ, -kiln, -mem'brane, -or'gan, -paint'ing, -pa'per, -prisms, -rods, en am'el ing-fur'nace, -lamp.

en am'or *or* -our, -ing, -ment, -ored.

en arched', *en ar chē* (-shā').

en' bloc' (ŏn' blŏk').

en ca chette' (ŏn kå shĕt').

en cage', -caged', -ca'ging.

en cal'en dar.

en camp', -ing, -ment, -camped'.

en case'. See *incase*.

en caus'tic.

en ceinte' (ŏn sănt').

en chāin', -ing, -ment, -chained'.

en chânt', -ed, -ing, -ing ly, -er, -ment, -ress.

en chase', -chased', -chās'er, -ing.

en cïnc'ture (-sink'-), -tured -tūring.

en cir'cle, -cled, -cling.

en clâsp', -ing, -clăsped'.

en clois'ter, -ing, -tered.

en close'. See *inclose*.

en cœur (ŏn kêr).

en cof'fin, -ing, -fïned.

en coi gnure' (ŏn kwŏ nyür').

en co'mĭ um, *pl.* -ums, -mi ast, -as'tic, -tic al, -al ly.

en com'pass (-kum'-), -ing, -ment, -passed.

en co quille' (ŏn kō kēl').

en core' (ŏn kōr'), -cored, -cor'ing.

en coun'ter, -ing, -er, -tered.

en coûr'age, -ment, -aged, -a ging, -ging ly.

en crim'son (-zn), -ing, -soned.

en croach', -er, -ing, -ing ly, -ment, -croached'.

en crust', -ed, -ing, -ment.

en cum'ber, -ing, -ing ly, -bered, -brance, -bran cer.

en cyc'lic (-sik'-), -al.

en cy'clo pe'di a (-sĭ'-) *or* -pæ'-, -pe'dic (*or* -pĕd'-), -dic al, -pē'dism, -pē'dist.

en cyst', -ed, -ing, -ment, -cysta'tion.

end, -ed, -ing, -a ble, -less, -less-
ly, -less ness, -most, -ways,
-wise, end-all, -ar'ter y, -bulb,
-game, -i'ron, -leaf, -man, -on',
-pa'per, -piece, -plate, -p l a y,
-prod'uct, -shake, -stone.
en dăn'ger, -ing, -ment, -gered.
en dĕar', -ing, -ing ly, -ed ly, -ed-
ness, -ment, -deared'.
en dĕav'or, -ing, -er, -ored.
en dem'ic, -al, -al ly, -de mic'i ty,
-mi ol'o gy.
en'dĭve.
en dog'a my, -a mous.
en'do gen, -do ge net'ic, -dog'e-
nous (-doj'-), -nous ly.
en dŏme', -dŏmed', -dŏm'ing.
en doph'a gy (-dof'a jĭ), -a goŭs.
en dow', -ing, -er, -ment, -dowed'.
en dŭe', -ment, -dūed', -dū'ing.
en dūre', -dûr'a ble, -ble ness,
-bly, -bil'i ty, -dûr'ance, -er,
-ing, -ing ly, -ing ness, -dured'.
En dym'i on (-dĭm'-), Myth.
en é chelle' (ŏṅ ā shĕl').
ĕn'e ma (or ē nē'ma), pl. -mas
or -ma ta.
en'e my.
en er get'ic (-jĕt'-), -al ly, -al-
ness, -ics, en'er gize, -gĭzed, -gĭ-
zing, -gi zer, -gy, pl. -gies.
ĕ ner'vate (or en'er-), -va ted,
-ting, en'er vā'tion.
en fa mille' (ŏṅ fä mēl').
en fee'ble, -ment, -bled, -bling,
-bler.
en feoff' (-fĕf'), -ing, -ment,
-feoffed' (-fĕft').
en fī lăde', -lăd'ed, -lăd'ing.
en fold', -ed, -ing.
en force', -ment, -a ble or -for'-
ci ble, -forced, -for'cing, -cer.
en fŏr'est, -ed, -ing.
en fran'chise (-chĭz or -chīz),
-ment, -chised, -chis er, -ing.
en gage', -ment, -gaged', -ga'ged-
ly, -ged ness, -ga'ger, -ging,
-ging ly, -ging ness.
en gen'der, -ing, -er, -dered.
en'gĭne, -ry, -man, -gi neer',
-neered', -neer'ing, en'gine-
bear'er, -count'er, -drīv'er, -fur'-
nace, -house, -lāthe, -plane,

-room, -run'ner, -shăft, -turned,
-turn'ing.
en gird', -ed, -ing, -gir'dle, -dled,
-dling.
Eng'land (ing'gland), -lish
(-glish), -lish man, -wom'an.
en gŏbe'.
en gorge', -ment, -gorged', -gor'-
ging.
en grăil', -ing, -ment, -grailed'.
en grave', -ment, -graved', -grăv'-
ing, -er.
en grŏss', -er, -ing, -ment,
-grossed'.
en gulf', -ing, -ment, -gulfed'.
en'gy scŏpe (-jĭ-).
en hănce', -ment, -hănced', -han'-
cer, -cing.
en har mon'ic, -al, -al ly.
en hy'drīte (-hī'-), -hy'droŭs.
en hy pos'ta tĭze (-hī-), -tized,
ti zing, -po stat'ic.
e nig'ma, pl. -mas, -mat'ic, -ic al,
-al ly, -ma tize, -tized, -ti zing,
-tist, -tog'ra phy, -tol'o gy.
en join', -ing, -er, -joined'.
en joy', -a ble, -ble ness, -er,
-ing, -ment, -joyed'.
en kin'dle, -dled, -dling.
en lace', -ment, -laced'.
en large', -ment, -larged', -lar'-
ged ly, -ged ness, -ger, -ging.
en lau'rel, -reled or -relled, -rel-
ing or -rel ling.
en light'en (-n), -er, -ment, -ened.
en list', -ed, -ing, -ment.
en līv'en (-n), -er, -ing, -ment,
-ened.
en man ché (ŏṅ mŏṅ shā').
en masse' (ŏṅ mȧs').
en mesh', -ing, -ment, -meshed'.
en'mĭ ty.
en nŏ'ble, -ment, -bled, -bling,
-bler.
en nui' (ŏṅ nwē'), en nuy é (ŏṅ-
nwē ā'), -nuy'ée' (-nwē'ā').
e nŏd'al, -ly, -nŏd'ous.
e nol'o gy.
e nor'mi ty, -nor'mous, -mous ly.
en or'tho trope.
e nough' (-nŭf').
e nounce', -ment, -noun'cing,
-nounced'.

---

nŏt, nôr, ūse, ŭp, ûrn, etüde, fōōd, fŏŏt, aṅger, boṅmot, thus, Bach.
19

en pas sant' (ŏṅ păs sŏṅ').
en pied (ŏṅ pyā).
en prince (ŏṅ prăṅs).
en rage', -raged', -rā'ging.
en rap port' (ŏṅ răp pôr').
en răpt', -rap'ture, -tured, -tūr ing.
en règ'le (ŏṅ reg'l).
en rich', -er, -ing, -ment, -riched'.
en rōbe', -ment, -rōbed', -rōb'ing.
en rōll' *or* -rōl', -rōll'er, -rōl'ment
    or -roll'-.
en' route' (ŏṅ' rōōt').
en sam'ple.
en saṅ'guine   (-gwin),   -gwĭned,
    -guin ing.
Ens che'de (ens chā'de), t. Neth.
en scŏnce', -sconced', -scon'cing.
en sem'ble (ŏṅ sŏm'bl).
en shrīne', -shrīned,' -shrīn'ing.
en shroud', -ed, -ing.
en'sign (-sīn),   *n.,*   -cy,   -ship,
    -bear'er.
en sīgn' (*or* en'-), *v.,* -ing, -signed'.
en'sĭ lage, -laged, -la'ging, en'-
    sīle, -sīled, -sīl'ing, -sĭ list.
en slāve', -ment, -slaved', -slāv'-
    ing, -ed ness, -er.
en snare', -snared', -snar'er, -ing,
    -ing ly.
en sūe', -sued', -sū'ing.
en suite' (ŏṅ swēt'), *en tab li er'*
    (ŏṅ tăb lĭ ā').
en tab'la ture.
en tāil', -ing, -er, -ment, -tailed'.
en taṅ'gle, -ment, -gled, -gling,
    -gler.
en tente' cor di ale' (ŏṅ tŏṅt' kôr-
    dĭ ăl').
en'ter,   -ing,   -er,   -tered,   -ing-
    chis'el, -file, -port.
en te rī'tis, -tĕr'ic, -te rit'ic.
en'ter prise   (-prīz),   -prīs'ing,
    -ing ly.
en ter tāin', -er, -ing, -ing ly,
    -ing ness, -ment, -tained'.
en thrạll', -ing, -ment, -thrạlled'.
en thrŏne',   -ment,   -thrŏned',
    -thrŏn'ing, -ize, -ized, -i zing.
en thū'si asm   (-zĭ azm),   -si ast,
    -as'tic, -tic al, -al ly.
en tĭce', -a ble, -ment, -ticed',
    -tĭ'cing, -cing ly, -cer.
en tīre', -ly, -ness, -ty.

en tī'tle, -tled, -tling.
en'ti ty,   *pl.*   -ti ties,   -ti ta'tive,
    -tive ly.
en'to cele.
en tomb' (-tōōm'), -ing, -ment,
    -tombed'.
en to mol'o gy,   -o gize,   -gized,
    -gi zing, -gist, -mo log'ic, -ic al,
    -al ly, -mom'e ter.
en tou rage' (ŏṅ'tōō'răzh').
en'tr'acte' (ŏṅ'tr act' *or* ŏṅ'trăct').
en'trails.
en'trance,   *n.,*   -way,   -trant,
    -trance-hall.   en trănce',   *v.,*
    -ment, -tranced', -tran'cing.
en trap', -ment, -trapped', -trap'-
    ping, -ping ly.
en trēat', -ed, -ing, -ing ly, -er,
    -a ble, -y.
en trée' (ŏṅ trā').
en tre mets' (ŏṅ tr mā').
en trench'. See *intrench.*
en'tre nous (ŏṅ'tr nōō).
en'tre pas (ŏṅ'tr pä).
en'tre pôt (ŏṅ'tr pō).
en tre pre neur' (ŏṅ tr prê nêr').
En'tre Ri'os (en'trā rē'ŏs), prov.
    Arg. Rep.
en'tre sol (ŏṅ'tr sŏl *or* ĕn'-).
en trust' *or* in-, -ed, -ing.
en'try,   *pl.* -trīes, -try man, -way.
en twine', *or* in-, -ment, -twined',
    -twīn'ing.
en twist', -ed, -ing.
e nu'cle ate,   -a ted,   -a ting,
    -a'tion, -a ter, one who enu-
    cleates; -a tor, a bird; E nu'cle-
    a tō'res (-rēz), the parrots.
e nū'mer ate, -a ted, -ting, -tive,
    -tor, -ā'tion.
e nun'ci ate (-shĭ-), -a'ted, -ting,
    -tive, -tive ly, -tor, -to'ry, -a ble,
    -bil'i ty.
en u rē'sis.
en vel'op (-up)   *or*   -ōpe,   *v.,*
    -oped (-ŭpt), -op ing, -op ment.
en'vel ōpe (*or* -vel'- *or* ŏṅ'vê lōpe)
    or -vel'op (-up), *n.,* en'vel ope-
    ma chine'.
en ven'om (-um), -ing, -omed.
en vī'ron, -ing, -ment, -men'tal,
    -tal ly, -roned (rund), -vī'rons
    (*or* ĕn'vĭ rons).

---

fāte, făt, fär, fạll, fâre, făst, sofà, mēte, mĕt, hêr, īce, ĭn, nōte,

en vis'age (-vĭz'-), -ment, -aged, -a ging.

en'voy, -ship.

en'vy, -ing, -vi a ble, -ble ness, -bly, -vi er, -vi ous, -ous ly.

en wrap', -ping, -wrapped'.

en wreathe', -wreathed', -wreath'-ing.

en zo ot'ic.

ě'ŏ lā'tion.

e'on or **æ'on,** -o nist, -ō'ni an, -ŏn'ic.

E'os, Myth.

ě ŏ zŏ'ic.

e'pact (or **ĕp'act**).

ep a gŏ'ge, -gog'ic (-gŏj'-).

E pam'ĭ non'das, Theban gen.

ep'arch (-ark), -arch y.

ep'au let or -lette, -let ed or -let-ted, **é pau lière'** (ā pō lyâr').

e pergne' (-pêrn').

E per nǎy' (ā per-), t. Fr.

e'phah or -pha (ē'fä).

eph'ebe (ĕf'ēb), **-e bē'um,** pl. -be'a, e phē'bic.

e phem'e ra, pl. -ras or -ræ, -e ral, -ral'i ty.

e phem'e ris, pl. eph e mĕr'i des (-dēz), e phem'er ist, -er ous, eph e mē'ri us.

Eph'e sus (ĕf'-), anc. city. E phē'sian (-zhan) or Eph'e-sĭne. E phe'sians, Bib.

ĕph'od.

é pi' (ā pē').

ep'ic, -al, -al ly.

ep i car'di um, -di al, -di ac.

ep'i cen ter.

Ep'ic tě'tus, Rom. philos. -tē'-tian (-shan).

ep'i cure, -cûr ize, -ized, -i zing, -ism.

Ep'i cū'rus, Gr. philos., -cu rē'an, -an ism.

ep'i cy cle (-sī-), -cy'cloid (-sī'-), -cloid'al, -cyc'lic (-sĭk'-).

ep i dem'ic, -al, -al ly, -dĕ mĕ og'-ra phy, -mi ol'o gy, -o gist, -o log'ic al, -al ly.

ep i der'mis, ep'i derm, -der'mal, -der'mic, mic al, -mi za'tion.

ep i dic'tic or -deĭc'tic, -tic al.

ep i gas'tric.

ep i glot'tis, pl. -ti des (-dez), -glot'tic, -tid'e an.

E pig'o nus, pl. -o nĭ.

ep'i gram, -ist or -gram mist, -gram mat'ic, -ic al, -al ly, -gram'ma tize, -tized, -ti zing, -ti zer, -tist, -tism, tā'ri an.

ep'i graph, -graph'ic, -ic al, -al ly, -ics, e pig'ra phy, -ra phist, -ra-pher.

ep'i lep sy, -lep'tic, -tic al, -al ly, -ti form, -to gen'ic, -tog'e nous (-tŏj'-).

ep'i lŏgue, -log'ic (-lŏj'-), -ic al, -lo gis'tic, -lo gize, -gized, -gi-zing.

Ep ĭ měn'ĭ des (-dēz), Cretan poet.

e piph'a ny (-pĭf'-), an appear-ance. E piph'a ny, a Christian festival.

E pī'rus, -pī'rōte or -rŏt, Ep i-rot'ic.

e pis'co pa cy, -co pal, -pal ism, -pāl'ian ism, -păl ly, -co pate, -co pize, -pized, -pi zing.

E pis'co pal, relating to the Epis-copal Church, -co pā'li an (or -pāl'yan), -an ism.

ep'i sŏde, -so dal, -so'di al, -sod'ic, -ic al, -al ly.

e pis'tle (-l), -to la ry, -to lē'an, -tol'ic, -ic al, -to lĭ zer, -to lo-graph'ic, -log'ra phy.

E pis'tle, in liturgics.

ep'i style (-stĭl), -sty'lar.

ep'i taph, -er, -ist, -taph'ic.

ep'i tha lǎ'mĭ um or -mĭ on, pl. -mi ums or -mi a, -thal'a mize, -mized, -mi zing.

e pith'e sis.

ep'i thet, -thet'ic, -ic al, -al ly.

ep'ĭ thyme (-tīm).

e pit'o me, pl. -mes (-mēz), -o mist, -o mize -mized, -mi-zing, -mi zer.

e pit'ro pe.

ep i zŏ'o ty, -zo ot'ic.

e plu'ri bus ū'num.

ep'och (ĕp'ok or ē'pok), ep'o-chal (-kal), ep'och-māk'ing.

ep'o nym (-nĭm), -nym'ic, e pon'-y mal, -y mist -y mous, -y my.

ē'qual, -ly, -ness, ē'qua ble (or
ĕk'wa-), -ble ness, -bly, e quăled
or e quălled, e qual ing or -ling,
e qual'i ty (-kwăl'-), e'qual-
end'ed, -fall'ing.
e'qual ize, -ized, -i zing, -i zer,
-ĭ zā'tion, -i zer-spring, -i zing-
bar, -file, e'qual ĭ'zing cur'rent.
e qua nim'i ty.
e quă'tion.
e quā'tor, -tō'ri al -al ly
eq uer ry or -ue ry (ĕk'wĕr ry or
ē kwĕr'e).
e'ques (ē'kwēz), pl. eq'ui tes (ĕk'-
wĭ tēz), Rom. antiq.
e ques'tri an, -ism, -tri enne'.
ē'qui an'gled, -aŋ'gu lar.
ē quĭ dis'tance, -tant, -tant ly.
ē'quĭ form.
ē quĭ lat'er al, -al ly.
ē quĭ lib'ri um, pl. -ums or -a,
-lib'ri ous, -ous ly, -ri ty, ē quĭ-
li'brate, -bra ted, -ting, -to ry,
-bra'tion, -lĭ'brism, -lĭ'brist (or
-quĭl'i brist), -lib'ri um-s c a l e,
-valve.
ē'quĭne (or -kwīn).
ē'quĭ nox, -noc'tial (-nŏk'shal),
-tial ly.
ē quip', -ping, -ment, -quipped'.
eq'ui page (ĕk'wĭ-).
ē'quĭ poise.
ē quĭ pon'der ate, -a ted, -ting,
-ant, -ance, -an cy.
eq'ui ta ble (ĕk'-), -ble ness, -bly.
eq'ui tes (ĕk'wĭ tēz). See eques.
eq'ui ty (ĕk'wĭ ty), pl. -tĭes.
e quiv'a lent, -ly, -a lence, -len cy.
e quiv'o cal, -ly, -ness, -cant.
e quiv'o cate, -ca'ted, -ting, -tor,
-to'ry, -ca'tion.
E'quus (ē'kwŭs), e quiv'o rous.
ē'ra, pl. -ras (-răz).
e rā dĭ ā'tion.
e rad'i cate, -ca'ted, -ting, -tive,
-ca ble, -ca'tor, -to'ry, -ca'tion.
e rase' (-rās'), -rased', -rās'ing,
-rās'er, -a ble or -i ble, -ra'sion
(-zhun), -ra'sure (-zhūr or
-zhûr).
E ras'mus (-răz'-), Dutch schol.
Er'a to (ĕr'-), Myth.
ere (âr), ere'long', ere'while'.

Er'e bus (ĕr'-).
e rect', -ed, -ing, -a ble, -er, -ĭle,
-ive, -ly, -ness, -rec'tion, -rec-
til'i ty, -rec'tor.
ĕr'e mīte, -mīt ish, -mīt'ism,
-mit'ic, -ic al.
Er'furt (ĕr'fŏŏrt), c. Prus.
er'ga tan'droŭs, -ga tog'y n o u s
(-tŏj'-), -ga toid.
êr'go.
er'go grăph, -gom'e ter, -go met'-
ric.
ĕr'got, -got ed, -got'ic.
ĕrg'-ten.
Er'ics son (ĕr'ĭk son), Sw. eng.
E rid'a nus.
E rĭn'ys (or -rī'-), pl. -rĭn'y es
(-ĭ ēz), Myth.
Er'läng en (ĕr'-), t. Ger.
erl'king.
er'mĭne, -mĭned, -mĭn ing, er'-
mine-moth.
e rode', -rōd'ed, -ing, -ent, -i ble,
-rō'sion (-zhun), -sion ist, -ro'-
sive (-sĭv).
E'ros, Myth. e rot'ic, -ic al.
e rōse' (-rōs').
êrr, êrred, êrr'ing (or ĕr'ing),
-ing ly, ĕr'ra ble, -ble ness, -ro'-
ne ous, -ous ly, -ous ness, ĕr'ror,
er'ran cy.
ĕr'rand.
ĕr'rant, -ry.
ĕr rat'ic, -al, -al ly, -al ness.
ĕr rā'tum, pl. -ta.
êrs (êrs), a plant.
Erse (êrs), a language.
êrst, -while'.
ĕr ŭ bes'cent, -cence, -cen cy.
e ruc'tate, -ta'ted, -ting, -tā'tion.
ĕr'ŭ dite (or ĕr'ŏŏ-), -ly, -ness,
-di'tion (-dish'-).
e rupt', -ed, -ing, -rup'tion, -tion-
al, -tive.
ĕr'y sip'e las (er'ĭ-), -sip'e lous.
es ca lade', -lād'ed, -ing, -er.
es'ca lā'tor.
es cal'ier-lace (-kal'yā-).
es cal'lop or -cal'op (-kŏl'-),
-loped, -lop-shell.
es cape', -ment, -caped', -căp'ing,
-ca pāde', -cape'-valve, -wheel.
es carp', -ment.

es *car te lé'* (-tē lā'),   or   *-car'te lée*, -car'tēled.

es **chĕat'**, -ed, -ing, -a ble, -age, -or, -or ship.

es **chew'** (-cho͞o' *or* -chū'), -al, -ance, -er, -ment.

es *clŭt té'* (-tā').

es *cōl'ta, -cōl'tar.*

es **co pet'**, *-pette'.*

es *cō'ri al*, a mine; Es co'ri al *or* Es cu'ri al, a palace.

es'**cort**, *n.*, es cort', *v.*, -ed, -ing.

es'**crĭ toire'** *or* -toir' (-twŏr'), -to'- ri al.

es *cu'dō* (-ko͞o'do *or* -tho͞o).

Es'**cu lă'pi us** *or* Æs cu la'pi us, -pi an.

es'**cu lent.**

Es **cu ri al'** (ĕs ko͞o rē äl'), t. Sp.

es **cutch'eon** (-un), -eoned.

Es'**kĭ mo,** *pl.* -mos (-mōz) *or* -qui mau (-ke mo̊), *pl.* -qui- maux (-ke mŏz).

es'**me ral'da.**

e **soph'a gus** *or* œ soph'-, -a ge'al, (*or* -sō făj'e al), -a gism.

es'**o tĕr'ic,** -ic al, -al ly, -ter'ics, -i cism, -ter'ist, -ter y.

es *pa'da* (-pä'tha).

es *pä gno lette'* (-nyo lĕt').

es **pal'ier** (-yer).

es *par'to*, -grăss.

es **pe'cial** (pĕsh'al), -ly.

es **plà nàde'.**

es **plees'** (-plēz').

es **pouse'** (-pouz'), -ment, -pous'al, -ing, -er, -poused'.

es *pres si'vo* (-sē'vō).

es *prit'* (-prē').

es **py'** (-pī'), -ing, -pied', -pī'al, -pī'er, es'pĭ o nage (*or* -näzh').

es **quire'.**

es'**say**, *n.*, -ish, -ist, -is'tic, -say- ette', es say', *v.*, -er, -ing, -say ed'.

es'**sence**, -senced, -sen cing.

Es **senes'** (-sēnz'), a community of Jews, -sē'ni an, -sē'nism (*or* es'-).

es **sen'tial** (-shal), -ly, -ness, -ti al'i ty (-shĭ al'-).

Es'**sonnes'** (-sŏn'), vil. Fr.

es **tab'lish**, -ing, -er, -ment, -lished.

es *ta cāde'* (*or* -kåd').

es *tä däl'.*

es *ta jet'* or *-jette'.*

Es'**taing',** d' (dĕs'tăn'), Fr. ad- miral.

es **tam'in.**

es *ta'mi net'* (-mē nā').

es *tan'ci a* (-tăn'thĕ à),   *-ci e'ro* (-thĕ ā'rō).

es *tän'co.*

es **tàte'.**

es **teem'**, -ing, -er, -teemed'.

Es'**ter ha'zy** (ĕs'ter hä'ze), Hung. nobleman.

es *thĕ'si a* or *æs-.*

es'**thete** *or* æs'-, -thet'ic, -ic al, -al ly, -ics, -the ti'cian (-tish'an), -thet'i cize, -cized, -cī'zing.

es'**tĭ mate**, -ma'ted, -ting, -tive, -tor, -má ble, -ble ness, -bly, -ma'tion.

es *tin'to* (-tēn'-).

es'**ti vage.**

es'**tĭ val** (*or* -tī'-) *or* æs-, -ti vate, -va ted, -va ting, -va'tion.

es *toile'* (ās twäl').

es **top'**, -ping, -pel, -topped'.

es *tou jāde'* (-to͞o-).

es **tràde'.**

Es **tra ē'lon,** plain in Palestine.

es **trànge'**, -ment, -trànged', -trăn'ging, -ged ness, -ger.

es **tra pàde'.**

es **tray'.**

es **trĕat'**, -ed, -ing.

es **trepe'**, -ment, -trēped', -trĕp'- ing.

es'**tu a ry**, -a rĭne, -ā'ri an.

es *tu'ja* (-to͞o'-), pl. *-jas.*

é *ta gère* (ā tà zhâr').

Et'**a min,** a star.   et'a mĭne, a textile fabric.

e *tàpe'* (*or* ā'tăp').

é *tat'-ma jor'* (ā tä'-mä zhôr').

ĕt *cĕt'e ra* or *et cĕt'e ra* or *et cæt'e ra.*

etch, -er, -ing, etched, etch'- grain, -ing-em broid'er y, -ground, -nee'dle, -point, -var'nish.

e **ter'nal**, -ist, -ly, -ni ty, -nize', -nized, -nī'zing, -nĭ za'tion, -nal'- i ty.

e **tĕ'sian** (-zhan).

---

nŏt, nôr, ūse, ŭp, ûrn, etüde, fo͞od, fo͝ot, aṅger, boṅmot, thus, Bach.

e'ther, e the're ous, -re al, -al ly,
-al ness, -al ism, -al ize, -ized,
-i'zing, -I za'tion, -al'i ty.

ē'ther ize, -ized, -i'zing, -i'zer,
-I zā'tion, ē thĕr'ic, -ic al, ē'ther-
i fy' (-fī'), -fy ing, -fied, -form.

ĕth'ics, eth'ic, -ic al, -al ly, eth'i-
cist, -i cize, -cized, -cī'zing.

E'thĭ op, -op'ic, -ō'pi an.

eth'narch (-nark), -y.

eth'nic, -al, -al ly, -ni cism, -nog'-
e ny (-noj'-), -no gen'ic, -nog'-
ra phy, -ra pher, -ra phist, -no-
graph'ic, -ic al, -al ly, -nol'o gy,
-o ger, -o gist, -no log'ic (-lŏj'-),
-ic al, -al ly.

eth'no psy chol'o gy   (-sī kŏl'-),
-chō log'ic al (-lŏj'-).

e thog'ra phy, -thol'o gy, -o gist,
ĕth o log'ic (-lŏj'-), -al.

e'thos.

ĕth'yl, -y la'ted (-I lā'-), e thyl'ic
(-thĭl'-), ĕth'yl-blue.

ĕth'y lēne (-I-), -blue.

E'tienne' (ā'tyĕn'), Fr. writer.
Et In cär nä'tus, Et Res ur rĕx'it.

ē'tĭ o late, -la'ted, -lā'tion.

et'i quette (-ket or -ket').

Et'na, vol. Sic., -nē'an, et'na, a
vessel for heating water.

é toile' (ā twŏl').

é tou pille' (ā tōō pēl').

Et'o wah, co. Ala.

E tru'ri an, -trus'can.

é tude' (ā tüd').

é tui' (ā twē').

et y mol'o gy (-I-), -o gist, -o gize,
-gized, -gi'zing, -mo log'ic (-loj'-),
-ic al, -al ly.

Eu bœ'a   (ū bē'a),   isl.   Med.,
-bœ'an.

Eu ca lyp'tus, Bot. genus; eu'ca-
lyp tog'ra phy.

eū'cha rist (-ka-), -ris'tic.

eū'chre (-ker), -chred (-kerd),
-chring, eu'chre-deck, -pack.

Eū clid ē'an or -clid'i an.

Eū fąu'la, c. Ala.

Eu gé nie' (ü'zhā'nē'), Fr. empress.

Eu'ler (u'ler or oi'ler), Swiss
math.

eu lo'gi a, pl. -æ.

eū'lo gize, -gized, -gi'zing, -gist,
-gis'tic al, -al ly, -lo gy, pl. -gīes,
-lō'gi um, pl. -ums.

Eu'me nes (ū'mē nez), Bib.

Eu men'i des (-dēz).

Eu'nice (u'nis or u nī'ce), Bib.

eū'nuch (-nŭk).

eū'phe mism, -mis'tic, -tic al,
-al ly, -mize, -mized, -mi'zing.

eū phō'nĕ, -phō'ni ad.

eū phŏn'ic, -al, -phō'ni ous, -ous-
ly, -ni um, eu'phō nize, -nized,
-ni'zing, -pho noŭs, -pho ny.

Eu phrŏs'y nē (-frŏs'I-), Myth.

Eu'phu es (ū'fū ēz), Fiction.

eū'phŭ ism, -phu ist, -is'tic, -tic-
al ly, -phu ize, -ized, -i'zing.

Eu rā'sia (-rāsh'ya or -sha), -rā'-
sian (-shan or -zhan).

eū rē'ka.

Eu rip'i des (-dēz), Gr. poet.

Eū roc'ly don (-lĭ-), Bib.

Eū rō pē'an, -ism, -an ize, -ized,
-i'zing, -I zā'tion.

Eu ryd'i ce (-rĭd'-), Myth.

Eu sē'bĭ ŭs, Father of Church
History; -bi an.

Eū stā'chi an (-kĭ-).

Eū ter'pe, Myth., -pe an.

eū tha nā'si a (-zhĭ a or -zi a).

eū thym'i a (-thĭm'-).

eū'trŏ phy, -trŏph'ic.

Eu'ty chus (ū'tĭ kŭs), Bib.

Eūx'Ine.

e vac'u ate, -a ted, -ting, -tive,
-tor, -ant, -a'tion.

ē vāde', -vād'ed, -ing, -a ble or
-i ble, -vā'sive, -sive ly, -sive-
ness, -sion (-zhun).

E vǎd'nĕ, Beaumont and Fletcher.

ĕv a nesce', -nesced' (-nest'), -nes'-
cing, -nes'cence, -cent, -cent ly,
-ci ble.

ē van'gel, -ism, -ist, -is tic, -ize,
-ized, -i'zer, -i'zing, -I zā'tion.

ev'an gel'ic (or ē'van-), -al, -al ly,
-al ness, -al ism, -gel'i cism.

E vǎn'ge lĭne (or -lĭn), Longfellow.

e vap'o rate, -ra'ted, -ting, -tive,
-ra ble, -ra'tion, -rom'e ter or
-rim'-, e vap'o ra ting-cone, -dish,
-fur'nace, -pan, -ra'tion-gage.

ēve, -churr.
ē'ven (-vn), *v*., -er, e'ven ing,
making even; -ly, -ness, -vened,
e'ven-fall, -hand'ed, -hand'ed-
ness, -mind'ed, -tem'pered,
-song, e. down.
eve'ning (*or* ē'vn ing), the close
of the day; -tide, -flow er, -gros-
beak, -prim rose, -song, e. star.
e vent', -ful, -less, -ven'tu al,
-al ly, -al'i ty, -tu ate, -a'ted,
-ting, -a'tion.
ev'er, -last'ing, -ing ly, -ing ness,
-er glade, -green, -more, -bloom'-
er, -dūr'ing, -liv'ing.
ē ver'sion (-shun), -vẹr'si ble.
eve'ry (ĕv'ry *or* ĕv'er y), -bŏd'y,
-thing, -where, -ry-day, *a*.
e vict', -ed, -ing, -or, -vic'tion.
ev'i dent, -ly, -ness, -dence,
-denced, -den'cing, -den'tial
(-shal), -tial ly.
ē'vil (-vl), -ly, -ness, -vil-dis-
posed', -do'er, -eyed, -mind'ed,
-starred.
E'vil Mĕr'ō dach (-dăk *or* e'vil-
me rō'dach), *Bib*.
e vince', -ment, -vinced', -vin'-
cing, -vin'ci ble, -ci bly.
e vis'cer ate, -a ted, -ting, -a'tion.
e vōke', -voked', -vōk'ing, ĕv'o-
ca ble, -ca tor, -ca'tion.
ĕv o lū'tion, -al, -a ry, -ism, -ist,
is'tic, -o lute, -lu'tive.
e vōlve', -ment, -volved', -vŏlv'a-
ble, -ing, -ent, -er.
E'wald (ä'vält), Ger. critic.
ewe (ū), -cheese, -lease, -neck,
-necked.
Ew'ell (ū'el), Confed. gen.
ew'er (ū'er), -y, *pl.* -les.
ex ac'er bate (ĕgz ăs'-), -ba'ted,
-ba'ting, -bes'cence.
ex act' (ĕgz akt', -ed, -ing, -ing-
ness, -ly, -ness, -ac'tion.
ex act'er (ĕgz-), in general, one
who exacts. ex act'or, specific-
ally, an officer.
ex ag'ger ate (ĕgz aj'-), -a'ted,
-ted ly, -a'ting, -tive, -tive ly,
-tor, -to'ry, -a'tion.
ex ạlt' (ĕgz-), -ed, -ed ly, -ed-
ness, -ing, -er, -ạl ta'tion.

ex am'ine (ĕgz-), -ined, -in ing,
-i nȧ ble -nȧ bil'i ty, -nant,
-nate, -na'tion, -tion al, -tion-
ism, -i nee', -in er, -er ship,
-i nā'tion-pa'per.
ex am'ple (ĕgz-).
ex'a ris'tate.
ex as'per ate (ĕgz-), -a ted, -a-
ting, -a ter, -ā'tion.
ex'ca văte, -vā ted, -ting, -tor,
-vā'tion.
ex ceed', -ed, -er, -ing, -ing ly.
ex cel', -celled', -cel'ling.
ex'cel lent, -ly, -lence, -len cy.
ex cel'sĭ or, *n*., *ex cel'si or*, ever
upward.
ex cept', -ed, -ing, -er, -cep'tion,
-tion a ble, -ble ness, -a bly,
-tion al, -al ly, -al ness, -al'i ty,
-tion less, -cep'tive, -tor.
ex cerpt', -ed, -ing, -cerp'tive, -tor,
cerp'ta.
ex cess', -ive, -ive ly, -ive ness.
ex chānge', -a ble, -a bly, -a bil'-
i ty, -changed', -chăn'ging, -ger.
ex chĕq'uer (-chĕk'er).
ex cise' (-sīz'), -man, *pl.* -men,
-cised', -cī'sing (-zing), -ci'sion
(-sĭzh'un).
ex cīte', -ment, -ful, -cīt'ed, -ing,
-ing ly, -a ble, -a bil'i ty, -cīt'ant,
-a tive, -ive, -or, -cīt'a to ry, ex'-
ci ta'tor, -ci ta'tion.
ex clāim', -er, -ing, -claimed',
-clăm'a tive, -tive ly, -a to'ry,
-to'ri ly, -cla mā'tion, -mā'tion-
mark, -point.
ex clūde', -clūd'ed, -ing, -er, -clū'-
sion (-zhun), -sion ism, -sion ist,
-clū'sive (-sĭv), -sive ly, -sive-
ness, -siv ism, -siv ist, -so ry.
ex cog'i tate (-kŏj'-), -i tā'tion.
ex com mū'ni cate, -ca'ted, -ting,
-cȧ ble, -cā'tor, -to'ry, -cant, -cā'-
tion.
ex con ces'so.
ex cŏ'ri ate, -a ted, -ting, -a ble,
-ā'tion.
ex'cre ment, -men'tal, -men'ta ry,
-men ti'tial (-tish'al), -ti'tious
(-tish'us).
ex cres'cence, -cen cy, -cent,
-cen'tial.

---

nŏt, nôr, ūse, ŭp, ûrn, etüde, fōōd, fŏŏt, aŋger, boṅmot, thus, Bach.

ex crēte′, -crēt′ed, -ing, -crē′tive
(*or* ex′-), ex′cre to ry (*or* -crē′-).
ex cre′ta, -cre′tal (*or* ex′-), -crē′-
tion.

ex cru′ci ate (-shĭ ate),   -a′ted,
-ting, -ting ly, -ā′tion.
ex cu′bi tŏ′ri um, pl. *-ri a.*

ex cul′pate, -pa ted, -ting, -to′ry,
-pa ble, -pā′tion.
ex cū′ri a.

ex cur′sion (-shun), -al, -ist.

ex cur′sĭve, -ly, -ness, *ex cur′sus.*

ex cuse′ (-kŭz′),   *v.,*   -cused′,
-cūs′ing,   -cūs′a ble,   -ble ness,
-a bly, -a to′ry, -er.

ex cuse′ (-kūs′), *n.,* -less.

ex′e crate, -cra′ted, -ting, -crà-
ble, -bly, -tive, -tive ly, · -to′ry,
-crā′tion.

ex′e cute, -cu′ted, -ting, -ta ble,
-cu′ter, -cū′tion, -tion er.

ex ec′u tive (ĕgz-), -tive ly, -u tant,
-tor,   -tor ship,   -to′ry,   -tŏ′ri al,
-u trix *or* -tress, *ex ê cu toire′* (egz-
ā kōō twŏr′).

ex e gē′sis,   -get′ic,   -ic al,   -al ly,
-ics,   ex′e gēte, -gē′tist.

ex em′plar (ĕgz-),   ex′em pla′ry
(ĕgz′- *or* ĕks′-), -ri ly, -ri ness.

ex em′pli fy (egz-), -ing, -fied,
-fī′a ble, -fī′er, -fĭ cā′tion.
ex em′pli gra′ti a (egz em′plĭ grā′-
shĭ a).

ex empt′ (ĕgz-), -ed, -ing, -i ble,
-emp′tion.
ex′e quā′tur.

ex′e quy, -e′quĭ al.

ex′er cise (-sĭz), -cised, -cī′sing,
-cī′sa ble, -ser, -ci tā′tion.

ex er′cĭ tor (ĕgz-), -tŏ′ri al.

ex ert′ (ĕgz-), -ed, -ing, -ive,
-er′tion.
ĕx′ē ŭnt.

ex hale′, -haled′, -hāl′ing, -a ble,
-ant, -ha lā′tion.

ex haust′ (ĕgz aust′ *or* -hạust′),
-ed, -ing, -ing ly, -er, -i ble,
-i bil′i ty, -ive, -ive ly, -less,
-haus′tion (-chun),   ex haust′-
chăm′ber, -dràught, -fan, -noz′zle,
-pal′let, -pipe, -port, -pu′ri fi er,
-reg′u la tor,   -steam,   -syr′inge
(-sĭr′-), -valve.

ex hib′it (egz ĭb′it *or* eks hib′it),
-ed, -ing, -er, -ant, -ive, -ive ly,
-or,   -o′ry,   ex hi bi′tion (eks hĭ-
bish′un), -tion al, -tion er.

ex hil′a rate (egz il′-),   -ra′ted,
-ting,   -ting ly,   -a rant′,   -a rā′-
tion.

ex hort′ (egz ort′), -ed, -ing, -er,
-hor′ta tive, -ta to′ry, ex hor ta′-
tion (eks′hor-).

ex hume′, -humed′, -hūm′ing, -hu-
mā′tion.

ex′i gen cy, -gence, -gent, -gi ble.

ex ig′u ous (egz ig′- *or* eks ig′-),
-ness.

ex′ĭle (eks-), -iled, -ĭl′ing.

ex ist′ (egz-),   -ed,   -ing,   -ence,
-en cy, -ent, -i ble, -bil′i ty.

ex′it, ex i′tial (egz ish′al),   -i′tious
(-ish′us).
ex le′ge (eks lē′je).
ex lī′bris.

ex′o dus, ex′ode, -od′ic.
ex oj fi′ci o (-fĭsh′ĭ ō).

ex og′a my,   -a mous,   -o gam′ic,
-ga mit′ic.

ex′o gen,   -ge net′ic,   -og′e nous
(-ŏj′-).

ex on′er ate (ĕgz-), -a′ted, -ting,
-tive, -tor, -ā′tion.

ex′o ra ble (ĕks′-).

ex or′bi tant (egz-),   -ly,   -tance,
-tan cy.

ex′or cise, -cised, -cī′sing (-zing),
-ci′ser, -cism, -cis′mal   (-sĭz′-),
-cist.

ex or′di um (egz-),   pl. -ums *or*
-*a,* -di al.

ex os′cu late (*or* egz-),   -la′ted,
-ting, -lā′tion.

ex′os mose′ (-mōs′ *or* ex′ŏs′-), -os′-
mic *or* -os mot′ic, -mō′sis.

ex o tĕr′ic,   -al,   -al ly,   -i cism,
-ics.

ex ot′ic (egz- *or* eks-), -ic al, -al-
ness, -i cism.

ex pand′, -ed, -ing, -er, -panse′,
-pan′si ble, -ble ness, -bly, -bil′-
i ty, -pan′sĭle, -pan′sive, -sive ly,
-sive ness.

ex pan′sion, -ist, -sion-can, -coûp′-
ling, -curb, -curve, -drum, -en′-
gine, -gēar, -joint, -valve.

---

ex par′te, adv., *ex-par′te*, a.

ex pā′ti ate (-shĭ-), -a′ted, -ting, -tor, -to′ry, -ā′tion.

ex pā′trĭ ate, -a′ted, -ting, -ā′tion.

ex pect′, -ed, -ed ly, -ing, -ing ly, -a ble, -ance, -an cy, -ant, -ant- ly, -a tive, -pec tā′tion.

ex pec′to rate, -ra′ted, -ting, -tive, -rant, -rā′tion.

ex pē′di ent, -ly, -di en cy, -en′- tial, -tial ly.

ex′pe dīte, -ly, -dĭ′ted, -ting, -dĭ′- tious (-dish′us), -tious ly, -tious- ness.

ex pe dĭ′tion (-dish′un), -a ry, -er.

ex pel′, -ling, -la ble, -lant, -ler, -pelled′, -pul′sive, -sive ness, -pul′sion.

ex pend′, -ed, -ing, -er, -a ble, -i tor, -i ture.

ex pense′, -pen′sive, -sive ly, -sive ness.

ex per′ge fac′tion (-jĕ-).

ex pē′ri ence, -enced, -en cing, -en cer, -en′tial, -tial ism, -tial- ist.

ex pĕr′i ment, -ed, -ing, -men′ter, -tist, -men′tal, -tal ist, -tal ize, -tal ly, -men tā′tion.

ex pert′, a., -ly, -ness. ex′pert (*or* -pert′), *n.*

ex′pĭ ate, -a ted, -ting, -tor, -to′ry, -a ble, -ā′tion, -tion al.

ex pīre′, -pired′, -pīr′ing, -a ble, -ant, -a to′ry, -pĭ rā′tion.

ex plāin′, -ing, -er, -a ble, -plained′, -plăn′a tivc, -a to′ry, -to ri ly, -ri ness, -pla nā′tion.

ex′ple ment.

ex′ple tĭve, -tivc ly, to′ry.

ex′pli cate, -ca′ted, -ting, -ca ble, -ble ness, -tive, -tor, -to ry, -cand′, -cā′tion.

ex plic′it (-plĭs′-), -ly, -ness.

ex plŏde′, -plŏd′ed, -ing, -ent, -er, -plŏ′si ble, -sive (-sĭv), -sive ly, -sive ness, -sion (-zhun).

ex ploit′, -ed, -ing, -er, -ploi′ture, -ploi tā′tion.

ex plōre′, -plōred′, -plōr′ing, -plōr′a ble, -a tive, -to′ry, -er, -plo ra′tion.

ex pō′nent, -nen′tial.

ex′port, *n.,* ex port′, *v.,* -ed, -ing, -a ble, -a bil′i ty, -er, -por tā′- tion.

ex pose′ (-pōz′), -pōsed′, -pos′ed- ness, -pos′er, -al, -ing, -pō′sure (-zhūr), -po si′tion (-zish′un).

ex po sé′ (eks′pō′zā′).

ex pos′i tor (-pŏz′-), -i to′ry, -i tive.

ex pŏst fac′to.

ex pos′tu late, -la′ted, -ting, -tor, -to′ry, -lā′tion.

ex pound′, -ed, -ing, -er.

ex press′, -age, -ing, -er, -i ble, -i bly, -ive, -ive ly, -ive ness, -ly, -ness, -pressed′, -press′man, -press′-bul′let, -car, -ri′fle, -train, -wag′on.

ex pres′sion (-presh′un), -al, -less, -sion-mark, -point, -stop.

ex prō′pri ate, -a′ted, -ting.

ex punge′, -punged′, -pun′ging, -pun′ger.

ex′pur gate (*or* -pur′-), -ga tor, -pur′ga to ry, -to′ri al, -gā′tion.

ex′qui site (-zĭt), -ly, -ness.

ex sect′, -ed, -ing, -sec′tion.

ex sert′ed *or* -sert′, a., -ser′tĭle, -ser′tion.

ex′sic cate (*or* -sic′-), -ca′ted, -ca′ting, -ca′tor, -sic′ca tive, -cā′tion.

ex′tănt (*or* -tănt′).

ex tem po rā′ne ous, -ly, -ness, -tem′po ra ry, -ra′ri ly, -tem′- po rē.

ex tem′po rize, -rized, -rī′zer, -ri′zing, -rĭ zā′tion.

ex tend′, -ed, -ed ly, -ant, -er, ing, -i ble, -i bil′i ty, -ten′sĭ ble, -ble ness, -bil′i ty, -sĭle, -sion al, -sive, -sive ly, -sor, *pl.* -sors *or* -so′res (-rēz), -som′e ter, ex tent′.

ex ten′sion, -pĕd′al, -tā′ble.

ex ten′u ate, -a′ted, ting-, -ting ly, -tive, -tor, -to′ry, -ā′tion.

ex tē′ri or, -ly, -ize, -ized, -ĭ′zing, -ĭ zā′tion, -or′i ty.

ex ter′mĭ nate, -na′ted, -ting, -tor, -to′ry, -nā′tion.

ex ter′nal, -ly, -ism, -ize, -ized, -ĭ′zing, -ĭ za′tion, -is′tic, -nal′i ty, ex′tern *or* -terne′.

---

nŏt, nôr, ūse, ŭp, ûrn, etüde, fōōd, fŏŏt, aŋger, bon̑mot, thus, Bach.

ex tinct', -tinc'tion.
ex tin'guish, -a ble, -er, -ing,
-ment.
ex'tir pāte (or -ter'-), -pa'ted,
-ting, -tive, -tor, -tir'pa to'ry,
-pā'tion.
ex tŏl' (or -tōl'), -ling, -ler,
-tolled'.
ex tŏrt', -ed, -ing, -er, -tor'tion,
-tion a ry, -ate, -er, -ist.
ex'trả.
ex'tract, n., ex tract', v., -ed, -ing,
-a ble or -i ble, -ive, -or,
-trac'tion.
ex'tra dīte, -dī'ted, -dī'ting, -dī'-
ta ble (or -dī'-), -dī'tion (-dish'-
un).
ex trả'dŏs, -dŏsed.
ex'tra-es sen'tial.
ex'tra haz'ard ous, -ju di'cial
(-dish'al), -cial ly, -mun'dāne,
-mū'ral.
ex trả'ne ous, -ly.
ex traor'di na ry (-trôr'-), -na-
ri ly, -ri ness.
ex trav'a gant, -ly, -gance, -gan'za,
-gan'zist.
ex trēme', -ly, -ness, -trēm'ist,
-trēm'ism, -trēm'i ty.
ex'tri cate, -ca ted, -ting, -cā'tion.
ex trin'sic (-sĭk), -al, -al ly, -al-
ness, -si cal'i ty.

ex trôrse', -ly, -tror'sal.
ex trude' (-trōōd'), -trūd'ed,
-trūd'ing, -tru'so ry, -tru'sion
(-zhun).
ex ū'ber ance (or egz-), -an cy,
-ber ant, -ant ly.
ex ūde', -ūd'ed, -ūd'ing, -ūd'a-
tive, -u dā'tion.
ex ult' (ĕgz-), -ance, -an cy, -ant,
-ing, -ing ly, -ed, -ul tā'tion
(eks'-).
ex ū'vi ate (or ĕgz-), -a ted, -ting,
-vĭ al, -a ble, -a bil'i ty, -ā'tion.
eye (ī), eyed, ey'ing or eye'ing,
eye'less, -bait, -ball, -bar, -beam,
-bŏlt, -bright, -brow, -cup,
-drop, -flap, -glănce, -glăss,
-hole, -lash, -let, -let eer', -lid,
-piece, -reach, -sälve, -serv'ant,
-serv'er, -serv'ice, -shot, -sight,
-sore, -stalk, -stone, -string,
-tooth, -wash, -wa'ter, -wink,
-wink'er, -wit'ness, -wort.
eye'-ag'ate, -bone, -bright'en ing,
-case, -doc'tor, -dot'ter, -for-
ceps, -in'stru ment, -lens, -line,
-lobe, -mem'o ry, -mĭnd'ed,
-o'pen er, -pit, -point, -pro tect'-
or, -shade, -spec'u lum, -splice,
-spot, -spot'ted.
ey'ra (ī'ra).
eyre (air).

F

f-hole, F-pan el, F clef.
fä, a musical syllable.
fạ', contraction of fall.
fā'ber, a fish. Fä'ber, Eng. divine.
Fä'ber, Ger. divine.
fā'ble, -bled, -bling, -bler, -ble-
mon'ger (-mŭn'-).
făb'ric, -ri cate, -ca'ted, -ting,
-tor, -cant, -cā'tion.
Fa bri'ci us (fà brĭsh'i us), Rom.
gen. and statesman.
Fa bri'ci us (fä brĭt'sē ŏŏs), Ger.
critic.
fab'u lous, -ly, -ness, -u list, -u lize,
-lized, -lī'zing.

ja çade' (-säd' or -säd').
fåce, faced, fā'cer, fā'cing, face'-
a ble, fā'cial, -cial ly, -ci es
(-shĭ ēz).
face-ache, -a'gue, -card, -cloth,
-cov'er, -guard, -ham'mer, -joint,
-lāthe, -mite, -mold, -paint'er,
-piece, -plan, -plate, -pow'der,
-wall, -wheel, f. val'ue.
fac'et (fas'-), -ed, -ing.
fa cē'tious (-shus), -ly, -ness,
-cē'ti æ (-shĭ ē).
fac'ile (făs'-), -ly, fac'i le prin'ceps.
fa cil'i tate, -ta'ted, -ting, -cil'i ty,
-ĭ tā'tion.

---

fāte, făt, fär, fạll, fâre, făst, sofạ̄, mēte, mĕt, hêr, īce, ĭn, nōte,

fā'cing-brick, -ma chine', -sand.
fäck'el tanz (-l tänts).
fac sim'i le (făk-), *pl.* -i les (-lēz), -i list.
fact.
fac'tion, -al, -tion ist, -tious, -tious-ly, -tious ness.
fac ti'tious (-tish'us), -ly, -ness.
fac'ti tive, -ti tude.
fac'tor, -age, -tor ize, -ized, -ī'zing, -tor ship, -to ry, -to'ri al.
fac tō'tum, *pl.* -tums.
fac'ul ty, -ul ta'tive, -tive ly.
fad, -dish, -dish ness, -dist.
ja daise' (-dāz').
fade, -less, -less ly, fād'ed, -ed ly, -ing, -ing ly, -ing ness.
jæ'ces (fē'sēz). See *jeces.*
Faed (fād), Scot. artist.
jæx pop'u li (feks).
fag, -ging, fagged, fag-end, -măs'-ter.
fag'ot, -ed, -ing, fag'ot-i'ron, -vote, -vōt'er.
ja got'to.
Fah'ren heit (fä'- *or* fär'-), the name of the thermometer and its inventor.
Fai dherbe' (fā'dêrb'), Fr. gen.
ja ionco' (fü yŏńs').
fāil, -ing, -ure, fāiled.
jaille (fä'y' *or* fāl).
Fail lon' (fä'yōń'), Fr. auth.
fain, -ness.
Fai né ant', Le Noir (lê nwär fā'nä'ŏń'), Scott, *Ivanhoe.*
jai né ant' (fā nä ŏń'), fāin'e ănce.
Fai né ants', Les Rois (lä rwä fā'nä'ŏń'), *Fiction.*
faint, -ed, -ing, -ish, -ish ness, -ly, -ness, -heärt, -heart'ed, -heart ed ly, -heart ed ness.
fâir, -ly, -ness, -way, -con di'-tioned, -faced, -fin'ished, -ground, -hair, -haired, -lead'er, -maid, a fish; -mīnd'ed, -mind-ed ness, -na'tured, -seem'ing, -spō'ken, -wěath'er, *a.,* fair-maids-of-Feb'ru a ry, a plant; fair-maids-of-France, a flower.
Fair Gěr'al dine.
fâir'y, -land, -like, -ism, fair i ly, fair'y-bird, -but'ter, -cups.

-fiŋ'gers, -loaf, -mar'tin, -purs'es, -shrimp, -stone.
jait ac com'pli (fāt ac cóń'plē).
faith, -ful, -ful ly, -ful ness, -less, -less ly, -less ness, -cure, -doc'tor, -heal'er.
Fai za'bad' (fī zä'bäd'), div. and t. Brit. India.
fake, -ment, faked, fāk'ing, fāk'ing-box.
fā'ker, a surfman; a street vender; one who originates a fake; a pickpocket. Sometimes spelled fā'kir.
fā'kir (fā'kêr *or* -kêr'), a Mo-hammedan mendicant; -kir'ism.
făl căde'.
făl'cate, -ca ted, -cā'tion.
fạl'chion (-chun).
Fäl cŏn', state Venez.
fal'con (fạ'kn *or* fặl'kon), -con er (fạ'kn er), -con ry, fặl'co net, fal'con-bill, -eyed, -gen'tle, -shaped.
Fal'con er (fawk'ner *or* faw'kon-er), Scot. poet; Scot. scientist.
fặl det'ta.
Fa ler'no, -ler'ni an.
fạll, fell, fall'ing, -en (-n), -er, fall'-fish, -way.
fall'-block, -board, -cloud, -gate, -rope, -trap, -un'der.
fall'ing-door, -sickness, fall'ing off, f. out, f. star, fall'en-star, a plant; fall'er-wire.
fal lā'cious (-shus), -ly, -ness, fal'la cy, *pl.* -cies.
fặl'low, -ness, -chat, -crop, -dun, -finch, f. deer.
false, -hood, -ly, -ness, -faced, -heart'ed, -heart'ed ness, -hoofed.
fạl set'to, *pl.* -tos (-tōz).
fạl'si fy, -ing, -fied, -fi'a ble, -fi er, -fī ca'tor, -cā'tion, fal'-si ty.
Fạl'ståff, -ståf'fi an.
fạl'ter, -ing, -ing ly, -tered.
fä lu'ä (-lōō'-).
jalx (fălks), pl. *fặl'ces* (-sēz).
fāme, -less, famed, fām'ing.
ja meuse' (-mūz' *or* -mêz').
fa mil'iar (-yar), -ly, -ness, -mil i ăr'i ty (*or* -mil yăr'-).

fa mil'iar ize (-yar-), -ized, -i zing, -ĭ zā'tion.

făm'i ly.

Fa min' (fä'măṅ'), Fr. publicist.

făm'ĭne, -brĕad.

făm'ish, -ing, -ished.

fā'moŭs, -ly.

făm'u lus, pl. *-lī,* -u list.

fan, -ner, -ning, fanned, fan'fish, -foot, -light, -tail, -wise, fan'-blăst, -blow'er, -cŏr'al, -crest, -crest'ed, -crick'et, -frame, -gov'ern or, -jet, -lace, -palm, -shell, -tailed, -tan, -train'ing, -veined, -ven'ti la tor, -wheel, -winged, f. struc'ture, f. tra'-cer y, f. win'dow, fan'ning-ma-chine', -mill, f. out.

fā'năl'.

ja näm'.

fa năt'ic, -al, -al ly, -al ness, -i cism, -cize, -cized, -cī'zing.

făn'cy, -ing, -ci er, -ci ful, -ful ly, -ful ness, -ci less, fan'cy-free, -line, -mon'ger, -sick, -store, -work.

fan daṇ'gle.

fan daṇ'go.

fāne.

fă ne'ga (-nä'-).

Fan'euil (făn'el or fŭn'el), founder of Faneuil Hall in Boston.

fan'fare, -făr o nāde'.

fang, -er, -ing, -less, fanged, fang'ing-pipes.

faṇ'gle.

faṇ'got.

făn'ion.

fan tas'tic, -al, -al ly, -al ness, -ti cal'i ty, fan tasque' (-task').

fan'ta sy, -ing, -ta sĭed, făn tä'-si a (-zĭ a).

jan toc ci'ni (făn'tōt chē'nē).

far, -ness, -a way', *a.,* -fetched, -off, -reach'ing, -see'ing, -sight, -sight'ed, -sought. See *farther.*

Făr'a day, Eng. scientist; -dā'ic, făr a dā'ic, pertaining to elec-tricity, făr'ad, -ad'ic, -a dism, -a dize, -dized, -dī'zing, -zer, -dĭ zā'tion.

jar al lon' (fär äl yōn').

ja ran dole' or *-ran'do la.*

farce, fär'cĭ cal, -cal ly, -cal ness, -cal'i ty, *-ceur'* (sêr').

far'cy-bud.

far'da.

far'dage (*or* -dăzh').

far'del, -bound.

far'ding-bag.

fâre, fared, fâr'ing, fare well', fare'-box, -in'di ca tor, -wick'et.

Fa ri bault' (fä'rē bō'), Can. anti-quarian.

Far'i bault' (făr'ē bō'), co. and c. Minn.

fa ri'na (-rĕ'- *or* -rī'-), făr'i nā'-ceous, -ceous ly, -i nose (-nōs), -nose ly, fa ri'na-boil'er.

Fa ri na'ta de'gli U ber'ti (fä-rē nä'ta dā'lyē ŏŏ bĕr'tē), Dante, *Inferno.*

far'leû.

farm, -ing, -er, -a ble, -house, -stead, -yard, -bail'iff, -build'ing, -hand, -meal, -of'fice, -place, -vil'lage.

fä'ro, a game, -bank, -box.

fä'rŏ, a Belgian beer.

Fä'rŏ, t. Port. (fä'rōō), isl. Baltic sea.

Fa'roe (fä'rō *or* -rōō e), -rō ēse' (*or* -ēz').

Far'quhar (fär'kwär), Irish dram.

făr rā'go.

Fär'rar, Eng. divine.

făr'ri er, -er y.

făr'rŏw, -ing, -rŏwed.

far'ther, -most, -thest, fur'ther, -thest. Some writers limit *far-ther* and *farthest* to distance in time or space, and *further* and *furthest* to quantity or degree. This distinction is not sustained by the dictionaries.

far'thing.

far'thiṇ gale.

fas'ces (-sēz).

fas'cet.

fas'ci a (făsh'i a), pl. *-ci æ,* -ci al, -ci ate, -a ted, -ate ly, -a'tion, fas'ci a-board.

fas'ci cle, -cled, -ci cule, -cic'u-lar, -lar ly, *-u lus,* pl. *-u lĭ,* -u late, -la'ted, -late ly, -lā'tion.

---

fāte, făt, fär, fᾳll, fâre, fᾰst, sofá, mēte, mĕt, hêr, īce, ĭn, nōte,

fas'ci nate, -na'ted, -ting, -ting-
ly, -tor, -nä'tion.
fas cine' (-sēn'), -cined', -cin'ing
(-sēn' ing), fas cine'-dwell'er,
-dwell'ing.
fash, -er y.
fash'ion (-un), -ing, -a ble, -a bly,
-a ble ness, -er, -less, -ioned.
fash'ion-mon'ger, -piece, -plate,
-tim'ber, fash'ion ing-nee'dle.
Fäs quelle' (-kĕl'), Fr. auth.
fåst, -ed, -ing, -er, -ness, -land,
-day, -hand'ed, -shot, fast'ing-
day.
fas'ten (făs'n), -ing, -er, -tened
(-nd).
fas tid'i ous, -ly, -ness.
fas tig'i ate (-tĭj'-), -ly, -a ted,
-i um, pl. -i a.
fåt, -ted, -ting, -ling, -ly, -ness,
fat'ten (-n), -tened, -ten er,
-ten ing, -ty, -ti ness, -back, a
fish; -head, a fish.
fat'-bird, the sandpiper; -brained,
-cell, -fāced, -hĕad'ed, -hen, a
plant; -lean, -lute, fat'ting-
knife.
få'tal, -ly, -ness, -ism, -ist, -ist'ic,
-tal'i ty.
få'tä Mŏr gä'nä.
fate, -ful, -ful ly, -ful ness, fāt'ed,
fate'-like.
fä'ther, -ing, -hood, -less, -less-
ness, -ly, -li ness, -land, -ship,
-in-law.
Fä'ther, the Supreme Being; a
title.
fåth'om (-um), -ing, -a ble, -er,
-less, -omed, -om-line, -wood.
fa tid'ic, -ic al, -al ly.
fa tigue' (-tēg'), -tigued', -tigu'-
ing (-tēg'ing), -ing ly, -tigue'-
some, -call, -cap, -dress, -du'ty,
-par'ty.
Fä'ti mä (-tē-), daughter of
Mohammed.
Fåt'Ĭ ma, Fiction.
Fåt'Ĭ mĭte or -mĭde.
fa tis'cence, -cent.
fat'trels.
fåt'u ous, fa tū'i tous, -i ty.
fau'bourg (fō'bŏŏrg or fō'bŏŏr').
fau'ces (-sēz), fau'cal

fau'cet, -bit, -fil'ter, -joint, -key,
-valve.
fau'chard (fō'shard).
Fau cher' (fō'shā'), Fr. economist.
Fau gère' (fō'zhêr'), Fr. littérateur.
Fau'glia (foul'yä), vil. It.
fåult, -y, -i ly, -i ness, -less, -less-
ly, -less ness, -fĭnd'er, -fĭnd'ing,
-block, -es carp'ment, -rock.
faun.
fau'na, pl. -næ or -nas, -nal,
-nä'li a, -nist, -nist'ic, -nol'o gy,
-no log'ic al, -nule.
Fau'nus, Myth. fau'nus, pl. -nĭ,
Entom.
Faust (foust), Ger. necromancer.
Faus'tus, Fiction.
fau'teuil' (fō'tĕl').
faux jour (fō' zhŏŏr'), faux' pas'
(pä').
fa vě'o late, -o lus, pl. -lĭ, fa-
vōse'.
fa vil'lous.
fa vis'sa, pl. -sæ.
Fa vō'ni us, Myth., -ni an.
fa'vor, -ing, -ing ly, -a ble, -bly,
-ble ness, -Ĭte, -it ism, -ize, -ized,
-ĭ'zing, -less, -vored, -vored ly,
-vored ness.
Favre (fävr), Fr. politician.
fawn, -er, -ing, -ing ly, -ing ness,
fawned, fawn'-col'ored.
fay, -ing, fayed.
Fay al' (fī al'), Azores isl.
fē'al ty.
fēar, -ing, -er, -ful, -ful ly, -ful-
ness, -less, -less ly, -less ness,
-naught, -some, -some ly,
feared.
fea'si ble (fē'zĭ-), -ble ness, -bly,
-bil'i ty.
fēast, -er, -ing, -ful, -ed, feast'-
day.
fēat.
fĕath'er, -ing, -y, -i ness, -less,
-let, -few, -foil, -head, -top, -bone,
-brain, -weight, a person; -wing,
a moth; feath'ered.
fĕath'er-al'um, -bear'er, -bed,
a bird; -bird -board'ing,
-brained, -cloth, -curl er, -drĭv-
er -edge -fish er, -grass, -joint,

-māk er,　-man,　-moss,　-ore,
-pälm,　-poke,　-ren'o va tor,
-shot,　-spray,　-spring,　-star,
-stitch,　-tract,　-veined,　-weight,
a weight; -work, f. bed, a bed.
fĕa'ture, -less, -ly, -li ness, -tured,
-tur ing.
fĕ'brĭle　(_or_　feb'-),　-bril'i ty,
-brif'er ous,　-brif'ic,　-brif'u gal,
feb'ri fuge,　-ri fā'cient.
Feb'ru a ry.
Feb'ru ŭs, _Myth._, feb ru ā'tion.
fĕ'ces (-sēz) or _fæ'ces_, fe'cal.
Fech'ner (fĕćh'ner), Ger. naturalist.
Fech'ter (fĕćh'ter), Fr. actor.
fĕ'cit.
fec'u lence, -len cy, -lent.
fĕc'und, -un date, -dā'ted, -da tor,
-dā'tion, fe cun'di ty.
fed'dan.
fed'er al, -ism, -ist, -ize, -ized,
-ī'zing, -ĭ zā'tion.
fed'er ate,　-a ted,　-ting,　-tive,
-tive ly, -ā'tion, -ā'tion ist.
Fe de rí'ci　(fā dā rē'chē),　It.
dram.
fe dŏ'ra.
fee, -a ble, -ing, feed, fee'-es tate,
-farm, -fund, -grief.
fee'ble,　-ness,　fee'bly,　-ble-
mind'ed, -mind'ed ness.
feed, -ing, -er, fed, feed'-a pron
(-ā'purn), -bag, -cloth, -cut ter,
-door, -hand, -head, -heat er,
-mo tion, -pipe, -pump, -rack,
-reg'u la tor, -roll, -screw,
-trough, -wa ter, -wheel, -wire.
feed'ing-bot tle, -en'gine, -ground,
-head, -plat'form.
Fee jee'an. See _Fijian._
feel, -er, -ing, -ing ly, felt.
feer, -ing, feered.
feign (fān), -ing, -ing ly, -er, -ed,
-ed ly, -ed ness, feigned.
feint (fānt).
Feith (fīt), Dutch poet.
fĕld'spar.
Fe li'ce (fā lē'chā), It. auth.
fe lic'i tate　(-lis'-), -i tous, -tous-
ly,　-tous ness,　-i ty,　-i ta ted
-ting, -ta'tion.
fĕ'lĭne, -lĭn'i ty, -lit'o mist, -o my.

Fĕ'lix, a Bishop of Rome.
Fé lix' (fā lēs'), Fr. preacher.
fell,　-a ble,　-er,　-ing,　-ness,
felled,　fell'ing-ax,　-ma chine',
-saw, -wedge.
fel'low,　-less, fel'low-crăft, -feel,
-feel'ing, -like, -wheel.
fel'low be'ing,　f. cit'i zen,　f.
com'mon er,　f. coun'try man,　f.
crea'ture,　f. gen'er a tor,　f. heir,
f. help'er,　f. man,　f. mor'tal,
f. sub'ject.
fel'low ship, -ping, -shipped.
fel'ly　or　fel'loe,　_pl._　fel'lies, fel'-
loes (-lōz),　fel'ly-au'ger,　-bend'-
ing, -bōr'ing, -coŭp'ling, -dress'-
er, -ma chine', -plate, -saw'ing.
fel'on,　-y,　-ry,　-wood,　-wort,
fe lo'ni ous,　-ous ly,　-ous ness,
fel'on-grăss, -herb, -weed.
felt, -ed, -ing, -y, -māk'er, -work,
-cloth, -grain, felt'ing-ma chine'.
Fĕl'tre (-trā), t. It.
fe luc'ca.
fĕ'male, -mal'i ty.
feme, femme (fĕm).
fem'er ell _or_ -el _or_ -al.
fem'ĭ nĭne,　-ly,　-ness,　-nĭn'ĭ ty,
-ĭ cīde, -nal'ĭ ty.
femmé'-de-cham'bre (făm'-dê-shoṅ'-
br).
fĕ'mur, _pl._ -murs _or_ fĕm'o ra.
fen,　-nish,　-ny,　-ber ry,　-man,
fen-boat, -crick et, -duck, -fire,
-fowl,　-goose,　-land,　-or'chis
(-kis), -thrush.
fence, -ful, -less, fen'cing, -cer,
-ci ble, fenced.
fence'-jack,　-lizard,　-month,
-play,　-post,　-rail,　-time,
-view er,　fen'cing-gāge,　-ma-
chine', -nail, -school.
fend, -ed, -ing, -er, fen'der-beam,
-board, -bōlt, -pile, -pose, -stop.
fen dil lé (fŏṅ'dēl'yā').
fen du' (fŏṅ dü').
Fé'ne lon' (fā'nĕ lŏṅ' _or_ fān'lŏṅ'),
Fr. prelate.
fe nes'tral, -trāte, -trā'ted, fen-
es tra'tion.
fen'gite (-jīt).
Fe'ni an, -ism.
fen'nel, -flow er, -seed, -wa ter.

---

fāte, făt, fär, fₐll, fâre, fₐst, sofȧ, mēte, mĕt, hêr, īce, ĭn, nōte,

Fe'o dor (fā'ŏ dôr), Czar of Russ.
feoff (fĕf), -ment, feoffed, feof'-
  fing, feof'for *or* -fer.
fē'ral, fē'rĭne, -rĭne ly, -rĭne ness,
  fĕr'i ty.
Fe rǎ'li a.
fer'ment, *n.*, -oil, -or'gan ism,
  -se cre'tion.
fer ment', *v.*, -ed, -ing, -a ble,
  -a bil'i ty, -a tive, -tive ness,
  -men tive, -ta'tion, fer ment'ing-
  square, -vat.
fer'me ture.
fĕrn, -gale, -leaf, -shaw, -y,
  fĕr'ner y, fern'-bird, -owl, -palm,
  -seed, -tree.
Fer nǎn'dĕz, Sp. navigator.
fe ro'cious, -ly, -ness, -roc'i ty
  (-rŏs'-).
Fĕr rä'rä, prov. It.; -rä resc' (-rēs'
  or -rēz').
fĕr'ret, -ed, -er, -ing.
fĕr'ric, fĕr'rous, -ru'gi na ted, -gi-
  nous, -gin'e ous (-jĭn-).
fĕr'ro type, -ty per (-tī'-).
fĕr'rule (fĕr'rĭl *or* -rōōl), a ring
  or cap of metal; -ruled.
fĕr'ry, *n.*, -man, -boat, -bridge,
  -mǎs'ter.
fer'ry, *v.*, -ing, -rĭed, -ri age.
fĕr'tĭle, -ly, -ness, -til'i ty.
fĕr'ti lize, -lized, -li'zing, -li zer,
  -lĭ zā'tion, tion-tube.
fĕr'ule (-ōōl *or* -ĭl), a rod, cane
  or ruler; -uled, -ul ing.
fĕr'vent, -ly, -ven cy.
fĕr'vid, -ly, -ness, -vor, -ves'cent,
  -vid'i ty.
fĕs'tal, -ly.
fĕs'ter, -ing, -tered.
fĕs'ti val, -tive, -tive ly, -tiv'i ty.
fĕs'ton.
fĕs tōōn', -er, -ing, -y, -tooned',
  fes toon'-blind.
fetch, -er, -ing, fetch'-can'dle,
  -light.
fête (fât), -day, *fête cham pê'tre*
  (shŏṅ pä'tr).
fĕt'id, -ness, fe'tor.
fē'tish *or* -tich (-tish), -ism, -ist,
  -is'tic, -man, -snake.
fĕt'lock, -locked, -lock-boot, -joint.
fet'lŏw.

fet'ter, -ing, -er, -less, -lock,
  -tered, -ter-bone, -bush.
fet'tle, -tled, -tling.
feūd, -ist, feū'dal, -dal ism, -dal ist,
  -is'tic, -dal'i ty, -dal ize, -ized,
  -ĭ'zing, -ĭ zā'tion, feū'da ry, -da-
  to'ry *or* -ta ry.
jeu de joie (fê dê zhwŏ).
Feu'er bach (foi'er bäċh),   Ger.
  philos.
Feuil'let' (fê'yā'), Fr. auth.
fē'ver, -ish, -ish ly, -ish ness,
  -ous, -few, -bush, -nut, -root,
  -twig, -weed, -wort, -bark,
  -blis ter, -heat, -sore, -tree.
few, -ness.
few'trils.
fez, *pl.* fez zes (-ĕz).
Fĕz'zän', N. Afr.
fi ǎ'cre (fē ä'kr *or* fyǎ'kr).
fi an cé, fem. -cée (fē ŏṅ sā').
fias chet'ta (fyǎs kĕt'tä), -chi no
  (-kê'nŏ), pl. -chi'ni (-kē'nē).
fi as'co (fē äs'ko), pl. -coes or -cos
  (-kŏz).
fī'at.
fi au'i (fē a̧'ĕ).
fib, -ber, -bing, fibbed.
fī'ber *or* -bre, -bered, -ber less,
  -brous, fī'ber-cross, -faced, -gun,
  -plant, -stitch.
fī'bril, -bril'la, pl. -læ, fī'bril lar,
  -late, -la ted, -la'tion, -lĭf'er ous,
  -bril lose (-lōs), -lous.
fī'brin, -bri nous, -bri na'tion.
Fich'te (fĭċh'tĕ), Ger. philos.
fi chu' (fē shōō' *or* fĭsh'ōō).
fic'kle (-l), -ness.
fi'co (fē'kō), fī'coid, -coid'al.
fic'tĭle, -ness, -til'i a, -til'i ty, -tor.
fic'tion, -al, -ist.
fic ti'tious (-tish'us), -ly, -ness.
fid, -ded, -ding.
Fi däl'gŏ (fē-), harbor Alas.
fid'dle, -dled, -dling, -dler, -dle-
  stick, -wood, a tree.
fid'dle-bee tle, -block, -bow,
  -de-dee', -fad dle, -fish, -head,
  -shaped, -string, -wood, wood
  used in making fiddles; fid'dler-
  crab.
fid'dley.
Fī dĕ'lĕ, Shak., *Cymbeline.*

---

nŏt, nôr, ūse, ŭp, ûrn, etüde, fōōd, fŏŏt, aṅger, boṅmot, thus, Baċh.

fĭ del'i ty.
fĭd'get, -ed, -ing, -y, -iness.
fĭ du'ci a ry (-shi-), -du'cial (-shal).
fīe.
fĭĕf.
fiēld, -ed, -ing, -er, -fare.
field'-ale, -ar til'ler y, -bat'ter y, -bean, -bed, -bird, -book, -bug, -căr'riage, -col'ors, -cor'net, -crick'et, -day, -dĕr rick, -ĕq'ui page (-ĕk'wĭ-), -glăss, -gun, -hand, -hos'pi tal, -house, -lark, -lens, -lore, -mad'der, -mag'net, -măr'i gold, -mar shal, -mar tin, -mouse, -night, -notes, -of'fi cer, -park, -piece, -plov'er (-plŭv'-), -preach'er, -rŏll'er, -serv'ice, -spăr'row, -sports, -stăff, -tel'e grăph, -train, -vole, -work, -works.
fiĕnd, -ish, -ish ly, -ish ness, -like.
Fi'e ra bras' (fĕ'ä rä brä'), *Fiction.*
fiĕrce, -ly, -ness.
fĭ'e rĭ fā'ci as (-shĭ-).
fĭ'er y (*or* fī'ry), -flare, -foot ed, -hot, -new, -short.
Fies'o le (fyes'ō lä), t. It.
fĭ es'ta (fe ĕs'ta).
fĭfe, fifed, fif'ing, fĭf'er, fife ma'jor, -rail.
fif'teen', -teenth.
fifth, -ly.
fif'ty, -ti eth, -ty-fold.
fig, -ging, -gy, fig'eat er, a beetle; -feed'er, an insect; -wort.
fig-ap ple, -ba nä'na, -blue, -cake, -dust, -eat er, a person; -faun, -gnat, -leaf, -măr'i gold, -moth, -shell, -tree, -wart, -worm.
Fi'ga'ro' (fĕ'gȧ'rō'), *Fiction.*
fight, -er, -ing, fought (fạwt), fight'ing-fish, -sand'pi per, -stop'-per, f. cock.
fig'ment.
Fi gui er' (fē gē ā'), Fr. auth.
fig'u late, -la ted, -lĭne.
fig'ure, -ur al, -ur a ble, -a bil'-i ty, -ured, -ur ing, -ur ism, -u rine' (-rēn'), -u rant, *fem.* -rante', -ur ate, -ā'ted, -a ting, -ȧ tive', -tive ly, -tive ness, -u ra'-tion, fig'ure head.

fig'ure-câst'ing, -dȧnce, -māk'er, -stone.
Fi'ji an (fē'jē an *or* -je'-) *or* Fee'jee an (*or* -jee'-).
fĭ lā'ceous (-shus).
fil'a ment, -ed, -men'ta ry, -tous, -tif'er ous.
fĭ lăn'der.
fĭ'lar, fil'a ture.
fĭ lasse' (-läs').
fil'a tor.
fil'bert, -gall, -tree.
filch, -er, -ing, -ing ly, filched.
file, -fish, fīl'er, -ing, filed, file'-blank, -card, -căr'ri er, -chis'el, -clean'er, -clos'er (-klōz'-), -cloth, -cut'ter, -fin'ish ing, -fīr'ing, -grīnd'ing, -guard, -lēad'er, -march'ing -mark, -sharp'en ing, -shell, -strip'per, -tem'per ing.
fĭl'ing-block, -board, -ma chine', fil'ings-sep'a ra tor.
fĭ let' (fē lā').
fĭl'ial (-yal), -ly, fil'i ate, -a ted, -ting, -ā'tion.
fĭl'i beg.
fĭl'i bus ter, -er, -ing, -ism, -tered.
fĭl iere' (fēl yâr').
fil'i form, -formed, fĭ lif'er ous, fĭ'lose (-lōs), fil o selle' (-zel' *or* fil'o sel *or* -sel').
fil'i gree, -glăss, -point, -work.
Fil i o'que.
Fil i pi'no (-pē'-), *pl.* -nos (-nōz), *fem.,* -pi'na, *pl.* -nas (-năz).
fill, -er, -ing, filled, fill'er-box.
fill'ing-can, -en gine, -pile, -post, -thread, -tim bers.
fil'let, -ed, -ing, -cut ter, -plane.
fil'lip, -ing, -lĭped.
fil'ly.
film, film'y (*or* fil'my), film'i ness (*or* fil'mi-)
fĭls (fēs).
fil'ter, -er, -ing, -tered, fil'ter-bed, -fạu cet, -gal ler y, -pa per, -press, -pump.
fil'ter ing-bag, -ba'sin (-sn), -box, -cup, -fun'nel, -hy'drant (-hī'-), -pa'per, -press, -stone, -tank.

filth, -y, -i ly, -i ness.
fil'trate, -tra ted, -ting, -tra'tion.
fim'ble, -hemp.
fim'brĭ ate, -a ted, -ting, -a'tion.
fim'e tā'ri ous.
fin, -ning, -ny, finned, fin'back, -fish, -foot, a bird; -tock, -weed.
fin'-chain, -fold, -foot, foot of a bĭrd; -pike, -ray, -spine, -told, -whale, -winged, fin'back-calf.
fi'nal, -ly, -nal'i ty, *fĭ na'le* (fe nä'lä).
fĭ nance', -nan'cial, -cial ly, -nan cier', -cier'ing, -ciered'.
finch, finched, finch'-backed, -fal'con (-fä'kn), -tan'a ger.
find, -a ble, -er, -ing, found, find'-spot, find'ing-list, -store.
fine, -ly, -ness, fin'a ble, fin'er, -er y, fine'spun, fine-arch, -cut, -fin'gered, -rolls, -still, -spo ken (-kn), -fine'top-grass.
fin'ing, -forge, -pot, -roll er.
fine'drąw, -er, -ing, -drawn, -drew, -drawn, *a.*
fĭ nesse' (-něs'), -nessed', -nes'-sing.
fin'ger, -er, -ing, -ling, -gered, fin'ger breadth, -flow er, a plant
fin'ger, -al'pha bet, -bar, -board, -bowl, -brush, -cŏr al, -count ing, -cym bals, -fern, -glȧss, -grȧss, -grip, -guard, -hole, -key, -mark, -mĭr ror, -nut, -plate, -point, -post, -puff, -read ing, -ring, -shell, -shield, -sponge, -stall, -steel, -tip.
fin'i al.
fin'i cal, -ly, -ness, -cal'i ty, -ick ing, -ick y.
fin'i kin.
fi'nis.
fin'ish, -er, -ing, -ished, fin'ish ing-card, -drill, -ham mer, -press, -rolls, -tool, fin'ish-turn.
fi'nīte, -ly, -ness, fin'i tude.
Finn, Fin'land'er, Finn'ic, -ish.
fi'nos (fē'nōz).
fin'ta.
fiord or *fjord* (fyôrd).
fĭp'pence, -pen ny.
fir (fêr), -ry, fir-pȧr rot, -tree, -wood, -wool.

fire, fired, fir'ing, fi'er y, fire'arm, -back, -board, -bod y, -brand, -bug, -crack er, -crest, a bird; -drake, -flare, -flirt, -fly, -light, -lock, a gun; -man, -place, -proof, *v.,* -side, -tail, an insect; a bird; -weed, -works.
fire-a larm, -an ni'hi la tor, -ant, -ar row, -backed, -ball, -bal loon, -bar, -bȧr rel, -bȧs ket, -bea con, -bell, -bill, -bird, -blȧst, -blight, -boast, -boom, -bote, -box, -brick, -bridge, -bri gade,' -brush, -buck et, -cage, -chãm'ber, -clay, -cock, -com'pa ny, -cross, -damp, -dog, -door, -dress, -eat er, -en gine, -es cape, -ex tiṇ'guish er, -eye, a bird.
fire'-fan, -feed er, -fiend, -finch, -fish ing, -flag, -fork, -gild ing, -gilt, -god, -grate, -guard, -hold er, -hole, -hook, -house, -hunt, -hunt ing, -hy drant, -in sur'ance (-shōōr'-), -i'ron, -kiln (-kil), -lad der, -leaves, -light er, -lock, a lock; -mace, -main, -mar ble, -mȧs ter.
fire'-new, -of fice, -o pal, -or'-de al, -pan, -pike, -pink, -plȧt'-ing, -plug, -point, -pol'i cy, -pot, -proof, *a.,* -quar ters,' -rȧft, -rais ing, -red, -reg'u la tor, -roll, -room, -screen, -set, -set ting, -shield, -ship, -shov el, -sil'ver ing, -spĭr it, -spot, -steel, -stick, -stone, -stop, -sur face, -swab, -tel'e graph, -tow er, -trap, -tree, -tube, -ward, -war den, -wa ter, -wood, -worm, -wor ship, fire de part'-ment.
fir'ing-i ron, -ma chine', -par ty, -pin, -point.
fir'kin (fêr'-).
fir'lot (fêr'-).
firm, -er, -est, -ly, -ness, firm'-foot'ed, -hoofed, firm'er-chis'el, firm name.
fir'ma ment, -men'tal.
fir'man (fêr'- *or* -män').
firme (ferm).
firn (fêrn).

---

first, -ly, -ling, first'-be got'ten,
-clåss, -foot, -fruit, -hand, -rate.
fis'cal, fisc, fis'cus.
fīse'-dog.
fish, *pl.* fish, collectively; fish'es,
individually; fished, fish'ing, -er,
-er y, -a ble, -y, -i ness, fish'-
ber'ry, -mon ger, -moth, -tail,
an insect; -way, -wife, -wom an,
-worm, fish'er man, -er folk, -er-
boat.
fish'-back, -backed, -bait, -ball,
-bar, -bås ket, -beam, -bed,
-block, -bolt, -book, -boom,
-breed er, -cake, -can, -car,
-carv er, -chum, -coop, -creel,
-crow, -cul ture, -cul'tur ist,
-dåv it, -day, -driv er, -duck,
-fag, -fall, -farm, -farm er,
-flake, -flour, -food, -fork,
-freez er, -front, -fun gus,
-garth, -gig, -globe, -glue, -god,
-gua'no (-gwä'-), -hawk, -hook,
-hus'band ry.
fish'-joint, -ket tle, -knife, -lad der,
-line, -mar ket, -maw, -meal, -net,
-oil, -owl, -pack ing, -pearl, -plate,
-poi son, -pom ace (-pum-), -pond,
-pool, -pot, -pre serve', -prong,
-rēf'use, -roe, -sauce, -scale,
-scrap, -show, -skin, -slice,
-slide, -smoth er, -sound, -spear,
-stage, -store, -sto ry, -strain er,
-tac kle, -tail, tail of a fish;
-tongue, -tor pe'do, -trap, -trow-
el, -van, -war den, -wēir, -wood,
-work er, -works, f. chow der,
f. pie.
fish'ing-banks, -boat, -duck,
-ēa'gle, -float, -frog, -ground,
-hawk, -line, -net, -place, -rod,
-room, -smack, -sta'tion, -swiv'-
el, -tac'kle, -tube, f. out.
fis'sion (fish'un), fis'sate, -sīle,
-sil'i ty, -si lin'gual.
fis'si ped, -al (*or* -sip'e dal), -si-
ros'tral.
fis'sure (fish'-), -less, -s u r a l
(-shŏŏr-), -su ra'tion, -sured, fis'-
sure-nee dle, -vein.
fist, -ic, -i cuff, -cuff er, -ing,
-i an'a, fist'-ball, -law, -mate.
fis tu'ca.

fis'tu la, -tu lar, -lâr y, -late,
-lā'ted, -lōse (-lōs), -lous.
fit, -ted, -ting, -ting ly, -ting ness,
-ter, -ful, -ly, -ment, -ness,
-ful ly, -ful ness, fit weed, -root,
a plant; -rod, fit ting-shop.
fitch, -brush.
five, five'fin'ger, a plant; -fin gers,
a starfish; -leaf, a plant;
-mouth, a parasite; -pence,
-penny.
five'-boat er, -fin gered, -spot,
-square, -twen ty, -fin ger-tied,
fives-court.
Fives (fēv), vil. Fr.
fix, -a ble, -ate, -a tive, -a ture,
-a'tion, -ed ly, -ed ness, -er, -ing,
-i ty, -ture, fixed, fixed-eyed,
fix'ing-båth.
Fi'zen' (fē'zĕn'), prov. Japan.
fizz, -ing, fizzed, fiz'gig.
fiz'zle, -zled, -zling.
fjeld (fyĕld).
fjord. See *fiord.*
flab'by, -bi ly, -bi ness.
flac'cid, -ly, -ness, -cid'i ty.
flag, -man, -pole, -ståff, -stone,
-worm, -ging, -ging ly, flagged.
flag-bear er, -cap tain, -fĕath er,
-lieu ten'ant, -of'fi cer, -root,
-share, -ship, -sta tion, f. side,
flag'ging-i ron.
flag'el late (flaj'), -lā'ted, -ting,
-tor, -lant, -la'tion.
fla gel'lum, pl. *-lums* or *-la.*
flag'eo let (flăj'ō-), -tones.
fla gi'tious (-jish-), -ly, -ness.
flag'on.
flå'grant, -ly, -gran cy.
flå'grum.
flail, -stone.
flake, flaked, flāk'ing, -er, -y,
-i ness.
flake'-fĕath er, -room, -stand,
-white, -yard, flāk'ing-ham'mer.
flam bage' (-bäzh').
flam bé (flŏn bā').
flăm'beau (-bō), *pl.* -beaux *or*
-beaus (-bōz).
flam boy'ant, -ly, -an cy.
flame, -less, flām'ing, -ing ly,
flām'y, flăm'mule, flāmed,
flame'flow er, a plant.

flame'-bear er, -bed, -bridge,
-cell, -chām ber, -col or, -col-
ored, -en gine, -re ac'tion, -stop,
-tree, -of-the-woods, a plant.
flā'men, *pl.* -mens *or* flăm'i nes
(-nēz), -men ship, fla min'e ous,
-min'i cal.
fla min'go, -plant.
flăn, a flaw; a sudden gust of wind.
flan (flŏn), a piece of metal.
flănch, flanched.
flå neur' (-nêr'), -ne rie' (-rē').
flange, flanged, flan'ging, flange'-
gāge, -joint, -lip, -pipe, -rail,
-turn ing, -wheel, flan'ging-
ma chine, -press.
flank, -er, -ing, flanked.
flan'nel, -let, -nĕled, flan nel-
flow er, -mouthed, -plant, f. cake.
flan'ning.
flap, -per, -ping, flapped, flap'-
drag on, -jack, -tail, a monkey;
-door, -eared, -keep er, -tile,
-valve, flap'per-skate.
flare, flared, flâr'ing, -ing ly,
flare'-tin, -up.
flash, -er, -ing, -y, -i ly, -i ness,
flash'board, -man.
flash'-flue, -house, -light, -pan,
-pipe, -point, -test, -torch,
-wheel, flash'ing-board, -bot tle,
-fur nace, -point.
flask, -board, -clamp, -shaped.
flat, -ly, -ness, flat'bill, a bird;
-boat, -fish, -long, -top, a plant;
-wise, -worm, Flat'head, an
Indian.
flat'-bot tomed, -clam, -house,
-i ron, -or'chil (-kil), -press,
v., -rod, -tool, -ware, f. car.
flat'ten, -er, -ing, -tened.
flat'ten ing-fur nace, -heârth,
-mill, -ov en, -plate, -stone,
-tool.
flat'ter, -a ble, -er, -ing, -ing ly, -y.
flat'ting, -coat, -fur nace, -heârth,
-mill, -plate, -stone, -tool.
flat'u lent, -ly, -lence, -len cy,
-u ous, -ous ness, flā'tus.
Flau'bert' (flō'bêr'), Fr. novelist.
flăunt, -er, -ing, -ing ly, -y.
flau'to (flou'to), *flau tän'do*, *-tä'to,
-ti'no* (-te'-), *-to'nē.*

fla van'i line.
fla vē'do.
flăv'in, flav'i cant, fla ves'cent.
flā'vor, -ing, -less, -ous, -vored.
flaw, -less, -less ly, -y, flaw'-piece.
flax, -en, -y, flax'seed, -weed,
-bird, -brake, -bush, -comb,
-cot ton, -cut tiñg, -dress er,
-mill, -plant, -pull er, -scutch er,
-thresh er, flax'seed-mill.
flay, -er, -ing, flayed.
flea, -bane, a plant; -bite, -bit ten,
-seed, a plant; -wort, -bee tle,
-bug, -glăss, -louse.
fleam, -tooth.
flèche (flāsh).
fleck, -er, -less, -y, -i ness,
flecked.
flec'node.
flec'tion *or* flex'ion (flĕk'shun),
-al, -less.
fledge, fledged, fledg'ling *or*
fledge'ling, fledg'y.
flee, -ing, fle'er, fled.
fleece, fleeced, flee cer, -cy, -cing,
fleece-fold er, -wool.
fleer, -ing, -ing ly, -er, fleered.
fleet, -ing, -ing ly, -ing ness, -ly,
-ness, fleet'-dike, -foot, -foot ed,
-milk.
fleg.
Flei'scher (flī'sher), Ger. orientalist.
Flĕm'ing, Flem'ish, Flem'ish
bond, F. brick, F. coil, F.
di'a monds, F. point-lace, F.
stitch.
Flers (flâr), t. Fr.
flesh, -er, -ful, -y, -i ness, -less,
-ly, -li ness, -mon ger.
flesh'-ax, -brush, -clogged, -col or,
-crow, -eat er, -flea, -fly, -fork,
-hook, -hoop, -juice, -knife,
-meat, -pot, -red, -spic ule,
-tint, -tooth, -worm, -wound,
f. broth, flesh'ing-knife, flesh'ly-
mind ed.
fletch, -er, -ing, fletched.
fleur-de-lis' (flêr-de-lē'), pl. *fleurs-*
(flêr-), *-vo lant'* (flêr-vŏ lŏn').
fleu'ret (flōō'-), *fleu ron'* (flê rŏn').
flewed, flews (flōōz).
flex, -ing, flexed.

flex'i ble, -ness, -Ĭ bly, -Ĭ bil'i ty, -Ĭle.
flex'ion. See *flection*.
flex'ure (flĕk'sho͝or), -u ral, -u ose, -u ous, -or, *pl.* -ors *or* -o'res (-rēz).
flick, -ing, flicked.
flick'er, -ing, -ing ly, -ered.
flī'er *or* fly'er. Some authorities prefer *flyer* in certain cases. flī'er-lathe.
flight, -y, -i ly, -i ness, -less, flight'-ăr'row, -fĕath'er, -goose, -shăft, -shoot ing, -shot.
flim'flam.
flim'sy (-zy), -si ly, -si ness.
flinch, -er, -ing, -ing ly, flinched.
flin'der, -ders.
fling, -er, -ing, flung, fling'ing-tree.
flint, -y, -i ness, flint'lock, a gun; -stone, -ware, -wood, -heart ed, -knack er, -knap per, -lock, a lock; -mill, -pâr ing, -rope, -sponge, f. glass.
flip, -ping, flipped, flip'flap, -jack, -dog.
flip'pant, -ly, -ness.
flip'per.
flird (flêrd).
flirt, -ed, -ing, -ing ly, -i gig.
flisk, -ing, -y, -ma hoy, flisked.
flis'sa.
flit, -ted, -ting, -ting ly, -ter, -ty.
flitch, -beam.
float, -age, -ed, -er, -ing, -y, -stone, -board, -case, -cop per, -file, -grăss, -min er al, -ore, -valve.
float'ing-board, -heart, -is land, -lĕv er, -plate, -screed.
floc'cus, pl. *-cī,* floc'cose (-kōs), -cu lar, -cule, -cu lence, -cu-lent, -cu lose, *-cu lus,* pl. *-lī.*
flock, -ling, -ing, -y, flocked, flock'man, -măs ter, -cut ter, -duck, -grīnd ing, -o pen er, -pa per, -pow der, -print ing, f. bed, flock'ing-fowl, -ma chine.
flo coon'.
floe, -berg, -ice, -ṛat.
flog, -ger, -ging, flogged, flog'-măs'ter, flog'ging-chis el, -ham-mer.

Floi rac' (flwŏ răk').
flong.
flood (flŭd), -age, -ed, -ing, -er, -gate, -aṇ chor, -cock, -fence, -flaṇk ing, -mark, -tide.
floor, -age, -er, -ing, -less, -chis el, -cloth, -cramp, -frame, -guide, -hang er, -hĕad, -hol low, -light, -pan, -plan, -plate, -tim ber, -walk er, floor'ing-clamp.
flop, -per, -ping, -py, -wing, -damp er.
Flō'ra, Goddess of flowers; name of a person.
flo'ra, *Bot.,* flō'ral, -ral ly, -rist, -ra scope, -re a ted, -res'cence, -res'cent, flo'ret, -ri cul'ture, -cul'tur ist, -tur al.
Flo ré al' (flō rā ăl').
Flōr'en tīne (*or* -tēn *or* -tīn).
flō'res (-rēz).
flŏr'id, -ly, -ness, -u lent, flō rid'-i ty, -rif'er ous, -ri form, flō-roon'.
Flŏr'i da, F. bark, F. wood, Flō rid'i an.
flo rid'e ous.
flŏ rid'i a-green, -red.
flŏr'in.
flosh, -hole, -silk.
floss, -y, floss-em broid er y, -hole, -silk, -yarn.
flŏ til'la, flo'tant, -ta'tion.
Flo'tow (flō'tō), Ger. mus. com-poser.
flots.
flot'sam.
flounce, flounced, floun'cing.
floun'der, -er, -ing, -dered, -der-lan tern.
flour, -y, flour-băr rel, -bee tle, -bolt, -box, -cool er, -dredge, -dredg er, -dress er, -em'er y, -gold, -mill, -mite, -pack er, -sift er, -worm, flour'ing-mill.
floŭr'ish, -er, -ing, -ing ly, -ished, flour'ish ing-thrĕad.
flout, -ed, -ing, -ing ly, -er, -ing-stock.
flow, -age, -ing, flowed, flow-bog, -lines, -moss, flow'ing-fur nace.
flow'er, -age, -er, -et, -y, -i ness, -ing, -less, -less ness.

flow'er-an i mals, -bell, -bird,
-bug, -clus ter, -fence, a plant;
-fly, -gen tle, a plant; -head,
-peck er, a bird; -piece, -pot,
-pride, a plant; -stalk, -wa ter,
-work, -de-luce, f. clock.
flu'can.
fluc'tu ate, -a ted, -a ting, -ant,
-ā'tion.
flue, flu'ey, flued, flue'-boil er,
-bridge, -brush, -cin der, -clean-
er, -ham mer, -plate, -scrāp er,
-stop, -sur face, -work.
flu'ent, -ly, -ness, -en cy.
fluff, -y, -i ness, -i er, -i est,
fluff-gib.
Flü'gel (flü'gel), Ger. orientalist.
flü'gel, -horn, -man.
flu'id, -al, -ness, -id'ic, -id'i ty,
-i fy, -fy ing, -fied, -fī ca'tion,
flu'id ize, -ized, -i'zing.
flu'id-com pass, -lens, -me ter.
flūke (*or* flōōk), flūk'y, flukc'-
wort, -chain, -rope, -spade,
-worm.
flūme, -car.
flŭm'mer y.
flunk, -ing, flunked.
flunk'y *or* -ey, -dom, -ism.
flu o res'cence, -res'cent.
flū'or o scope, -scŏp'ic, -os'co py.
flŭr'ry, -ing, -ried.
flush, -er, -ing, -ing ly, -ness,
flushed, flush'board, -box,
-decked, -pot, -tank, -wheel,
flush'ing-box, -rim.
flus'ter, -ing, -tered.
flute, flūt'ed, -er, -ing, -ist, -y,
flute'mouth, -bird, -bit, -or gan,
-pipe, -play er, -shrike, -stop,
-work.
flūt'ing-cyl'in der, -i ron, -lāthe,
-ma chine, -plane, -scis sors.
flu ti'na (-tē'-).
flut'ter, -er, -ing, -ing ly, -y,
flut'ter-wheel.
flu'vi al, -ist, -a tīle, -at'ic, -vī o-
grāph, -om'e ter.
flux, -ing, -i ble, -ble ness, -i bil'-
i ty, -ā'tion, -ion (flŭk'shun),
-ion al, -ion a ry, -ion ist, -ure.
flux'weed, flux'-root, -spoon, flux'-
ing-bed, flux'ion-struc ture.

fly, *n., pl.* flies. Plural of *fly*, a
light carriage, is *flys*.
fly, *v.*, flew, flown.
fly'a way, fly'bane, -blow, -blown,
-boat, -catch er, a bird; -fish,
-man, -snap per, a bird; -tail,
a net; -wort.
fly'-a gar'ic, -bait, -bit ten, -blis-
ter, -block, -board, -book, -boy,
-brush, -bug, -cap, -case,
-cāst er, -catch er, -catch ing,
-clip, -dress ing, -drill, -fin ish-
er, -fish er, -flap, -flap per,
-frame, -fringe, -gal ler y, -gov-
ern or, -hon ey suc kle, -hook,
-leaf, -line, -māk'er, -mix ture,
-net, -nut, -oil, -or chis (-kis),
-pa per, -pen ning, -poi son,
-pow der, -press, -punch ing,
-rail, -reed, -rod, -sheet, -shut-
tle, -specked, -tac kle, -tāk er,
-tent, -tī'er, -tip, -trap, -wa ter,
-wee vil, -wheel.
fly'ing-fěath er, -ma chine, -watch-
man.
fly'ing cat, f. drag on, f. fish, f.
fox, f. frog, f. geck o, f. gurnard, f. hook, f. le mur, f.
liz ard, f. mar mot, f. pha lan'-
ger, f. rob in, f. shot, f. squid,
f. squir rel (skwêr-), f. torch,
f. watch man, fly'er-lāthe, fly a-
way-grāss, fly-up-the-crēek, a
bird; a person.
fōal, -foot, a plant; -teeth.
foam, -ing, -ing ly, -less, -y,
-bōw, -cock, -col lect'or, -spar,
-wreath.
fob, -bing, fobbed, fob'-chain,
-watch.
fō'cus, *pl.* -cus es *or* -ci (-sī),
-cus ing *or* -cus sing, -cused *or*
-cussed, -cal, -cal ize, -ized,
-ī'zing, -ī zā'tion, fo cim'e try.
fo'cus ing-cloth, -frame, -glass.
fod'der, -ing, -er, -dered, fod'der-
grāss, -plant.
foe, -man.
foehn (fēn).
fog, -ging, -gy, -gi er, -gi est,
-gi ness, -gi ly, -less, fogged,
fog'fruit, a plant; fog'-a larm',
-bank, -bell, -bound, -bōw,

-cheese, -dog, -eat er, -gun,
-horn, -ring, -sig nal, -smoke,
-trum pet, -whis tle (-l), fog'gy-
bee.
Fog'gia (fŏd'jä), prov. It.
Fog gi'ni (fŏd jē'nē), It. archæol.
Jo gli et'to (fōl yĭ ĕt'tō).
fŏ'gy, *pl.* -gies (-gĭz), -gy dom,
-gy ish, -gy ism.
Fŏh, -ism, -ist.
fŏh, an exclamation.
foi'ble.
foil, -a ble, -er, -ing, foiled,
foil'-căr'ri er, -stone.
foist, -ed, -ing, -er.
Foix (fwä), t. Fr.
fold, -ed, -ing, er, -age, -less, fold'-
garth, -net, -yard, fold'ing-
boards, -ma chine.
Jo li'a.
fo'li age, -aged, -li ar, -li ate,
-ā'ted, -a'tion, -a'ceous, fo'li-
ous, -li um, *pl.* -ums *or* -a,
fo'li age-plant, -tree.
fol'io (*or* fō'lĭ o), fo'li ose (-ōs),
-os'i ty. .
folk (fōk), -land, -moot, -free,
-lore, -psy chol'o gy, -right, -song,
-speech, -sto ry.
Fŏl'kĕ thing (-ting).
fŏl'li cle, -lic'u lar, -u late, -lā'ted,
-u lose, -u lous.
fŏl'lŏw, -er, -ing, fol'low-board,
-low er-plate, -low ing-time.
fo ment', -ed, -er, -ing, -men ta'-
tion.
fon'dle, -dled, -dler, -dling,
caressing; fond'ling, a person;
fond'ly, -ness.
fon'don.
Jŏṅ dü', *a.,* blended; softened.
Jŏṅ due' (-dü'), a pudding.
font, -al.
fōōd, -less, -stuff, -fish, -lamp,
-yolk (-yōk).
fōō'-fōō.
fool, -er y, -har'dy, -har'di hood,
-di ly, -di ness, -ish, -ish ly,
-ish ness, -fish, -stones, a plant;
-born, -duck, -faṅ gle, -hen,
-kill er, -trap, fools'cap, a
paper; fool's cap, a cap; fool's-
coat, -pars ley.

fōōt, -ed, -ing, -er, -less, -ling,
-ball, -boy, -fall, -hold, -hook,
-lights, -man, -mark, -pace, -pad,
a person; -print, -set, -stalk,
-stall, -step, -way.
foot'-ar til'ler y, -band, -baṅk,
-băr'racks, -base, -băth, -bel-
lows (-us), -bench, -blow er,
-board, -brĕadth, -bridge, -brig,
-cloth, -cush ion, -fight, -folk,
-gear, -grain, -guard, -halt,
-ham mer, -hand ed, -hawk er,
-hedge, -hill, -hot, -i ron, -jaw,
-joint, -key, -lāthe, -lev el,
-line, -loose, -muff, -note.
foot-pad, a padding; -page, -pas-
sen ger, -păth, -pave ment,
-pick er, -plate, -plow, -po et,
-post, -pound, -pound al,
-press, -race, -rail, -rat, -rest,
-rope, -scent, -screw, -se cre tion,
-sol dier, -sore, -stick, -stove,
-stump, -ton, -tub, -tu ber cle,
-valve, -vise, -wāl ing, -walk,
-wall, -warm er, -wash ing,
-worn.
foot'ing-beam, foot man-moth,
foot rule, foot-space rail.
fop, -pish, -pish ly, -pish ness, -ling,
-per y.
fŏr'age, -aged, -a ging, -a ger,
for'age-cap, -guard, -măs ter,
for'a ging-cap.
for'as much'.
fŏr'ăy, -er.
for beâr', -ance, -er, -ing, -ing ly,
-bore, -borne.
for bid', -den, -den ly, -der, -ding,
-ding ly, -ding ness, -băde'.
force, -ful, -ful ly, -ful ness,. -less,
-a ble, that may be forced; for'-
ci ble, vigorous; -ble ness, -ci bly,
-cing, force'meat, forced.
force'-di'a gram, -func'tion, -piece,
-pump, for'cing-house,-pit, -pump.
for'ceps, -can'dle stick, -tail.
ford, -a ble, -a ble ness.
fore, fore'arm, *n.,* fore arm', *v.,*
-armed', -arm'ing.
fore'bay, -beam, -bod'y, -brace,
-brain.
fore bode', -bōd'er, -bod'ing,
-ing ly.

fore'câst, *n.*, -câst', *v.*, -câst'er,
-câst'ing.
fore'cas tle (-kăs l), -man.
fore close', -closed', -clos'ing,
-clo'sure (-zhūr).
fore date', -dāt'ed, -dāt'ing.
fore dōōm', -ing, -doomed'.
fore'fath er, -fin ger, -foot, the
fore part of a foot; -front, -girth,
-gleam, -glimpse.
fore go', -er, -ing, -gone', -went'.
fore'ground, -ham mer, -hand'ed,
-hard, -head (fŏr'ed), -heärth,
-hold, -hook.
for'eign (-in *or* -en), -er, -ism,
-ize, -ized, -ī'zing, -ness.
fore judge', -judged', -judg'ing,
-judg'er.
fore knŏw', -a ble, -er, -ing,
-ing ly, -knew', -known'.
fore'land, -lock, -man, *pl.* -men,
-man ship, -măst, -mast man,
-most, -moth er, -name, -named,
-night, fore'noon'.
fŏ ren'sic, -al.
fore or dâin', -ing, -dained', -or di-
nā'tion.
fore'peak, -plan, -post.
fore run', -ner, -ning, -ran'.
fore'sâll.
fore see', -ing, -ing ly, -sē'er,
saw', -seen'.
fore shad'ow, -er, -ing, -owed'.
fore'shâft, -ship, -shore, -shot,
-side.
fore short'en, -ing, -ened.
fore show', -er, -ing, -showed',
-shown'.
fore'sight, -ed, -sketch, -skin,
-sleeve.
fŏr'est, -ed, -ing, -age, -al, -er,
-ry, -less, -bug, -court, -fly,
-folk, -liz ard, -mar ble, -ox,
-peat, -tree.
fore stall', -er, -ing, -stalled'.
fore'stay, -sail, -stick, -stone,
-sum mer.
fo ret' (fō rā').
fore'tâste, *n.*, -taste', *v.*, -tâst'er,
-tâst'ing, -tâst'ed.
fore tell', -er, -ing, -told'.
fore'thought, -time.
fore'tŏ ken, *n.*, -tō'ken (-kn), *v.*

fore'top, -man, -măst.
for ev'er, -more.
fore warn', -ing, -er, -warned'.
fore'wind, -wom an, -word, -yard.
fore'-bank, -boom, -căr'rĭage,
-choir, -cī'ted, -deck, -door,
-gaff, -gift, -loop er, -pas sage,
-piece, -plane, -plate, -rake,
-room, -sheet, -stâff, -stall,
-star ling.
fore end, f. foot, the front foot;
fŏre'head-cloth (fŏr'ĕd-) fore'-
lock-bōlt, fore lock-hook, fore'-
part, fore'-part i ron, fore'
teeth, fore' wing, fore'yard-arm.
for'felt, -ed, -ing, -er, -a ble,
-fei ture.
for gath'er, -ing, -ered.
forge, -a ble, -a bil'i ty, -măs ter,
-man, forged, for'ger, -ger y,
-ging, forge'-roll, -scale, -train,
-wa ter, for'ging-ham mer, -ma-
chine, -press.
for get', -a ble *or* -ta ble, -ble ness,
-ful, -ful ly, -ful ness, -ter, -ting,
-ting ly, -got', -got'ten, for get'-
me-not, a plant.
for gĭve', -ness, -gĭv'a ble, -giv'er,
-ing, -ing ly, -ing ness, -gave',
-giv'en.
for go'. This spelling has been
almost entirely superseded by
forego.
fork, -ing, -er, -ed, -ed ly, -ed ness,
-less, -y, -i ness, forked, fork'-
beard, a fish; -tail, a fish; a
bird; -beam, -moss, -rest,
-tailed, forked'-beard, forks-
and-knives, a moss; fork' chuck,
f. head, f. wrench.
for lorn', -ly, -ness.
form, -a ble, -al, -al ly, -al ism,
-al ist, -al ize, -ized, -ī'zing,
-a tive, -tive ly, form'less, -less-
ly, -less ness, for mal'i ty, -ma'-
tion, form-board, -el'e ment,
-ge nus, -spe cies, -word, form'-
ing-cyl in der, -i ron, -ma chine.
for'mal, *n.*
for mat' (-măt *or* -mä' *or* -mät').
for'mer, *a.*, -ly, form'er, *n.*
For'mes (-měs), Ger. vocalist.
for'mic, -mi cate, -ca ry, -câ'tion.

for'mi da ble, -ness, -bly, -bil'i ty.
for'mu la, *pl.* -las *or* -læ, -mu lar,
-la ry, -la ris'tic, -lar ize, -ized,
-i'zing, -ĭ zā'tion.
for'mu late, -lā'ted, -ting, -to'ry,
-la'tion.
for'mu lize, -lized, lĭ'zing, -lism,
-lĭ' zā'tion.
for'ni cate, -cā'ted, -ting, -tor,
-tress, -cā'tive, -nĭc'i form
(-nĭs'-).
for'nix, pl. *-ni ces* (-nĭ sēz), -nĭ-
cal.
for sake', -sāk'ing, -sāk'en (-n),
-sāk'er, -sook'.
for sōōth'.
for spēak', -spoke', -spo'ken.
for spend'.
for sweâr', -er, -ing, -swore',
-sworn'.
For syth' (-sīth'), co. Ga.; co.
N. C.; Amer. statesman.
fort, -a lĭce, -let, -ad'ju tant.
fôrte, that in which one excels;
part of a sword.
for'te (-tā), Mus., *for'te-pi a'no*
(-pē ä'no), *for tis'si mo.*
For'tes cue, Eng. jurist.
Fort Gra'ti ot (grăsh'ĭ ot), c. Mich.
forth, -com'ing, -go'ing, -put'ting,
-right, -with' (*or* -wĭth'), -is'su-
ing (-ish'ōō), -push ing.
for'ti fy, -ing, -fied, -fī'a ble,
-fī er, -fī cā'tion, -ca'tion-
ag'ate.
For'tĭn bräs, Shak., *Hamlet.*
for'ti tude.
fort'nĭght (*or* -nĭt), -ly.
for'tress, -tressed.
for tŭ'i tous, -ly, -ness, -tu'i ty.
For tū'na, *Myth.; Astron.*
for'tu nate, -ly, -ness.
For'tu nā'tus, *Bib.*
for'tune, -less, -tuned, for'tune-
book, -hunt'er, -tell er.
for'ty, -ti eth, for'ty-five, -knot,
-nin'er, -spot.
fŏr'u la, *pl.* -læ.
fō'rum, *pl.* -rums *or* -ra.
for'ward, -er, -ed, -ing, -ly, -ness.
for zan'do (for tsän'dō), *for za'to*
(-tsä'tō).
fŏss, -way.

fos'sa, pl. *-sæ.* Fos'sa, *Zoöl.*
genus.
fos sette'.
fos'sil, -ism, -ist, -ize, -ized,
-i'zing, -ĭ zā'tion, -if'er ous,
-sĭled.
fos'sor, pl. *-so'res* (-rēz), -so'ri al.
fos'ter, -age, -er, -ing, -hood,
-ling, -ship, -tered.
fos'ter-babe, -broth er, -child,
-dam, -daugh ter, -earth, -fath-
er, -land, -moth er, -nurse,
-pâr ent, -sis ter, -son.
Fou cauld' (fōō'kō'), Fr. philos.
Fou cault' cur'rents (fōō kōl').
Fou ché (fōō'shā'), Fr. officer.
Fou cher' (fōō'shā'), Fr. jurist.
Fou geres' (fōō'zhâr'), t. Fr.
Fou ge rolles' (fōō'zhe rōl'), dept.
Fr.
foul, -ing, -ly, -ness, fouled, foul-
brōōd, a disease of bees; -faced,
-mouthed, -tongued.
fou lard' (fōō lärd' *or* -lär'), -lar-
dine' (-dēn').
found, -ed, -ing, -er, *n.*
foun da'tion, -al, -less, -chain,
-mus lin, -net, -school, -square,
-stone.
foun'der, *v.*, -ing, -dered.
found'ling.
found'ry *or* -er y, -man.
foun'tain, -less, -let, -head,
-tained, fount, foun'tain-fish,
-shell, f. ink'stand, f. pen, f.
pump.
four, -fold, -pence, -pen ny,
-score, -square, -wings, a bird;
-boat er, -cant, -cen tered, -cor-
ners, a game; -horse, -joint er,
-o'clock, a plant; -part; -post er,
-pound er, -way, -wheel er, -in-
hand, -lane-end.
four chette' (fōōr shĕt').
Fou'ri er (fōō're er *or* -re ā'), Fr.
socialist.
Four mies' (fōōr'mē'), vil. Fr.
Four ni er' (fōōr'nē ā'), Fr. littérateur.
fourth, -ly, fourth-clâss, -rate,
four'teen', four'teenth'.
fowl, -er, -er y, -ing, fowl'-
chol'er a, fowl'ing-net, -piece.

fox, -y, -i ness, -ing, -ish, -er y,
foxed, fox'bane, a plant; -ber ry,
a plant; -fire, -fish, -glove, a
plant; -hound, -tail, a grass;
-tongue, a plant; -wood.

fox-bat, -bolt, -brush, -case,
-chase, -earth, -e vil, -finch,
-goose, -grape, -hunt, -hunt er,
-moth, -nosed, -shark, -sleep,
-snake, -spar row, -squir'rel,
-trap, -trot, -wedge, -wolf,
Fox-type, fox'glove-pug, a moth,
fox'tail-gråss, -pine.

joy'er' (fwŏ'yä').

frå'cas.

frache (fräsh).

frac'tion, -al, -al ly, -a ry, -ate,
-ā'ted, -ā'ting, -a'tion, -tious,
-tious ly, -tious ness.

frac'ture, -tured, -tūr ing, -tūr al,
-tū os'i ty, frac'ture-box.

Frä Di a'vo lo (dē ä'vō lō).

frag'ile (fräj'ĭl), -ly, -ness, fra-
gil'i ty.

frag'ment, -men ta'ry, -ta'ri ly,
-ri ness, -men'tal, -men ta'tion.

frå'grănt, -ly, -ness, -grance,
-gran cy.

fråil, -ly, -ness, -ty.

fraise, n., frāise, *v.,* fraised.

frame, framed, frām'ing, frām'er,
frame'work, a structure; -break-
er, -di'a gram, -hel met, -house,
a house in which framing is done;
-knit ting, -lev el, -saw, -tim ber,
-work, fancy-work done on a
frame; frām'ing-chis el, -ta ble,
frame bridge, f. house.

frănc, *-ar cher'* (frŏŋk'-är shä').

fran çaise' (frŏñ säz').

Fran ces'ca da Ri'mi ni (frän-
chĕs'ka dà rē'mē nē), *Fiction.*

fran'chise (-chĭz *or* -chĭz), -ment,
-chised, -chis er, -chis ing.

Franck (frŏñk), Fr. philos.

Franc'ke (fräng'kĕ), Ger. divine.

francke'ĭte (fränk'-).

Fran'co-Chĭ nese' (-nēz' *or* -nēs'),
-Prus'sian   (-Prush'ăn   *or*
-Prōōsh').

Fran'cœur'   (frŏñ'kêr'),   Fr.
geometer.

fran'co lin.

Fran cuc'ci   (frän kōōt'chē),   It.
painter.

fran'gi ble, -ness, -bil'i ty.

Frank, *n.,* fraŋk, *a.,* -ly, -ness,
frank, *v.,* -ing, -er, franked.

frank'-bank, -chase, -fee, -ferm,
-heärt ed,   -law,   -mår riage,
-pledge,   -serv ice,   -ten ant,
-ten e ment.

Frank'en stein,' *Fiction.*

frånk furt'er (-fŏŏrt'-).

frank'in cense.

Frank'lin, -ism, -lin'ic, -lin'i an.

fran'tic, -al ly.

frap pé' (fräp pā').

frass.

frä'te (-tä), pl. *-ti* (-tē).

frå ter'nal, -ly,   -ni ty,   frăt'er-
nize,   -nized,   -nĭ zing,   -nĭ zer,
-nĭ zā'tion.

frat'rĭ cide, -cĭ'dal.

frau (frou), pl. *frau'en,* *fräu'lein*
(froi'-).   As titles, capitalized.

frṣud, -ful, -ful ly, -less, -less ly,
-less ness,   -u lence,   -len cy,
-lent, -lent ly.

fray, -ing, frayed.

frĕak, -ish, -ish ly, -ish ness, -y,
-i ness.

frec'kle, -kled, -kled ness, -kling,
-kly, frec'kle-faced.

free, -ing, -ly, -ness, fre'er, fre'-
est, free'man, -mar tin, -ma son,
-stone, a peach; a brownstone;
-think er,   -war ren,   -wom an,
freed, freed'man, freed'wom an.

free-bench, -board, -born, -bor-
ough, -chase, -foot ed, -hand,
-hand ed, -lance, -liv er, -lov er,
-mill ing, -soil, *a.,* -swim mer,
-trade, *a.,* -trăd'er, -will, *a.,*
-writ er, Free'-soil'er, -soil'ism,
free'ma son's-cup.

free love, f. soil, f. trade.

freeze, freez'a ble, -er, -ing,
-ing ly, froze, fro'zen, freez'-
ing-box,   -liq uid,   -mix ture,
-point.

fre gia tu'ra (frä jä tōō'rä).

Freī'bĕrg, t. Sax.

Freī'burg (-bŏŏrg), dist. and c.
Baden.

---

nŏt, nôr, ūse, ŭp, ûrn, etüde, fōōd, fŏŏt, aŋger, boñmot, thus, Bach.

freight (frāt), -age, -er, -ing, -less, -car, -en gine, -house, -lo co mo'tive, -train.
frei'hĕrr (frī'-).
Frei'schutz (frī'shŏŏts).
Frē'ling huy sen (-hī zn), Amer. statesman.
Fré' mi et' (frä'mē ä'), Fr. sculp.
Fre mŏnt', Amer. gen.
French, -i fy, -fy ing, -i fīed, -i ness, -man, -wom an.
fre net'ic, -al, -al ly.
fren'zy, -zied, -zied ly.
frē'quent, *a.*, -ly, -ness, -quen cy.
fre quent', *v.*, -ed, -ing, -er, -a ble, -quen tā'tion.
Frère (frâr), Fr. painter.
Frere (freer), Eng. baronet.
fres'co, *n.*, *pl.* -coes *or* -cos (-kŏz), fres'co, *v.*, -ing, -er, -coed.
fres'co-paint er, -paint ing.
fresh, -er, -est, -ly, -ness, fresh'-blown, -col ored, -wa ter, *a.*
fresh'en, -ing, -er, -ened.
fresh'man, -hood, -ship, -man'ic, fresh'wom an.
Fres nel' (frä'nĕl'), Fr. optician.
Fresnes (frän), t. Fr.
fret, -ted, -ting, -ter, -ful, -ful ly, -ful ness.
frette (fret), fret'tage, fret'ted, fret'ty, fret'work, fret'-saw.
Freu'den stadt (froi'den stät'), t. Ger.
Freu'den thal (froi'den täl'), t. Aust.
Freud'wei ler (froit'vī ler), Swiss painter.
Freund (froint), Ger. lexicog-rapher.
Frey (frī), Frey'a, *Myth.*
Frey (frī), Swiss engraver.
Frey ci net', de (dĕ frä'sē'nä'), Fr. statesman.
Frey'stad tel (frī'stĕt tel), t. Hung.
Frey'tag (frī'täg), Ger. orientalist; Ger. auth.
frī'a ble, -ness, -bil'i ty.
frī'ar, -y, fri'ar-bird, -skate, fri ar's-cap, -cowl, -crown, -lan tern, -this tle.
frib'ble, -bler, -bled, -bling.

fric an deau' (-dō'), pl. *-deaux'* (-dōz'), *-an delle'*.
fric as see', -ing, -seed'.
fric'tion, -al, -al ly, -less, fric'a-tive, fri cā'tion.
fric'tion-balls, -brake, -brec cia (-brĕt cha), -card, -clutch, -cones, -coŭp ling, -gēar, -match, -plate, -pow der, -prī'-mer, -sound, -tight, -tube, -wheel.
Fri'day.
Frie'de mann (frē'dĕ män), Ger. teacher.
Fried'land (frēt'länt), t. Hung.; t. Ger.
Fried'län der (frēt'lĕn der), Ger. writer.
Fried'rich (frēd'rĭch), Ger. theol.
friĕnd, -less, -less ness, -like, -ly, -li ly, -li ness, -ship.
Friese (frēz), Frie'sian (frē'zhan) *or* Fris'ian (frĭz'yan), Friĕs'ic (frēz'-), -ish.
friĕze, friezed, friez'ing, friez'er, frieze'-pan'el, -rail, friez'ing-ma chine.
frig'ate, -bird, -built, -mack'er el, -pel'i can.
Frigg, Frig'ga *or* Frig'a, *Myth.*
frīght, -ed, -ing, -en, -ened, -en a ble, -ful, -ful ly, -ness.
frĭg'id (frĭj'-), -ly, -ness, *-i da'ri-um*, pl. *-da'ri a*, fri gid'i ty, frig o rif'ic (frig-), -rif'ic al.
fri jole' (frē hōl'), *fri jo lil'lo* (frē-hō lēl'lō).
frill, -ing, frilled, frill'back, -liz ard.
Fri maire' (frē'mâr').
frim'sel.
fringe, -less, -let, frin'ging, -gy, fringed, fringe'pod, -backed, -like, -tree.
Fri'o (frē'ō), co. Tex.
frip'per, -er, -y.
fri seur' (frē zĕr'), fris'let (friz'-), *fri sure'* (frē'zŏŏr').
frisk, -er, -ing, -ing ly, -ful, -y, -i ly, -i ness, frisked.
frit, -ted, -ting, -ter.
frith, -borg, -gild, -so ken, -splot, -stool.

fāte, făt, fär, fạll, fâre, făst, sofá, mēte, mĕt, hêr, īce, ĭn, nōte,

frit'ter, -er, -ing, -tered, frit'ting-
fur nace.

frĭ vol'i ty, friv'o lous, -ly, -ness.

frizz or friz, frizzed, friz'zy,
friz'zing-ma chine.

friz'zle, -zled, -zling, -zler, -zly,
friz'zling-i ron.

fro.

Frŏb'ish er, inlet Brit. N. A.

frock, -ing, -less, frocked, frock'-
coat.

Froe'bel (frê'-), Ger. educational-
ist; -ism, -bĕl'i an.

frog, -ging, -ger, -ger y, -gy, -gi-
ness, -gish, -ling, frogged, frog'-
bit, -fish, -foot, a plant; -hop-
per, an insect; -mouth, a bird;
-stool.

frog-cheese, -clock, -crab, -eat er,
-fish ing, -fly, -grăss, -mouthed,
-or chis (-kis), -plate, -shell,
-spawn, -spit, -spit'tle, frog's-
bit, frog's march.

Frois'sart (frois'ärt or frwä sär'),
Fr. writer.

frol'ic, -icked, -ick ing, -ick y,
-ic some, -some ly, -some ness.

Fro'ment' (-mŏn'), Fr. painter.

frŏnd, -age, -ed, -let, fron da'tion,
fron desce', -desced' (-dest), -des'-
cing, -des'cence, -des'cent, -dif'er-
ous, fron'dose (-dōs), -dose ly,
-dous.

Frŏnde, Fr. hist.

front (frŭnt), -age, -a ger, -ed,
-ing, -let, -wise, frŏn'tal.

Frŏn'te näc', co. Ont.

frŏn'tiĕr (or -tēr'), -tiers man or
-tier man.

Fron ti gnan' (frŏn tē nyŏn') or
Frŏn ti niac' (-tē nyăk').

frŏn'tis piece.

frost, -ed, -ing, -y, -i ly, -i ness,
-less, -fish, -root, -weed, -work,
-wort.

frost-bear er, -bird, -bite, -blite,
a plant; -bound, -but ter flies,
-line, -mist, -nail, -smoke,
-valve.

froth, -ing, -y, -i ly, -i ness, -less,
-fly, -in sect, -spit, -worm.

frot té' (frŏt tā').

frot'to la.

Froude (frōōd), Eng. hist.

frou'-frou (frōō'-frōō).

frŏ'ward, -ly, -ness.

frown, -er, -ing, -ing ly, frowned.

frow'zy, -zi ly.

frŏ'zen (-zn), -ness. See freeze.

Fruc ti dôr'.

fruc'ti fy, -ing, -fied, -fi'a ble,
-ti cist, -tif'er ous, -tes'cence,
-tu a ry, -tule, -tu a'tion.

fru'gal, -ly, -ness, -gal'i ty,
-giv'o rous (-jiv'-).

fruit, -age, -ed, -er, -er er, -er y,
-ful, -ful ly, -ful ness, -ing, -y,
-i ness, -less, -less ly, -less ness,
-let, fru i'tion (-ish'un).

fruit-al co hol, -bat, -bear er,
-bud, -cake, -car, -crow, -cul-
ture, -dot, -dri er, -fly, -gath-
er er, -house, -jar, -knife, -loft,
-pick er, -piece, -pi geon,
-press, -stand, -store, -su gar,
-tree, -trench er, -worm.

fru men ta'ceous, -ta'ri ous, -tā'-
tion, -men'tum, -men ty.

frus'trate, -trā'ted, -ting, -trā'tion.

frus'tum, pl. -tums or -ta.

fru tes'cent, -cence.

fry, -er, -ing, fried, fry'ing-pan.

Fu cec'chi o (fōō chĕk'kē ŏ), t.
It.

Fu'chau (fōō'chow), c. China.

Fuch'si a (fū'shĭ a or -shɑ), pl.
Fuch'sias or -si æ (-shăz or
-shĭ ē), a genus of plants;
fuch'si a, a species of plants.

fuch'sin or -sīne (fōōk'sin), -site.

fud.

fud'dle, -dled, -dling, -dler.

fudge, -wheel.

fü'el, -e con'o mi zer, -feed er, -gas.

fu gā'cious, -ness, -gac'i ty (-găs'-).

fu'gi tive, -ly, -ness, -tiv ism.

fū'gle man, pl. -men.

fūgue, fu'gal, fu gä'rä (fōō-),
fu ga'to (fōō gä'tō), fu ghet'to
(-gĕt'-), fügued, fū'guing (-ging),
-guist (-gist).

Fu'ki en (fōō'kē ĕn), prov. China.

Fu ku'i (fōō kōō'ē), t. Japan.

fŭl'crum, pl. -crums or -cra,
-cra'ceous.

Ful'da (fōōl'dä), r. and t. Ger.

ful fil′ _or_ -fill′, -filled′, -fil′ling,
-fil′ment _or_ -fill′ment.
fŭl′gent, -ly, -gen cy.
ful′gu rite, -gu rous.
fū lig′i nous (-lĭj′-), -ly, -nos′i ty.
full, _a._, -er, -est, -ness, ful ly,
full′-armed, -blood ed, -bloomed,
-blown, -born, -bot tom, -bot-
tomed, -bound, -bril liant, -cen-
tered, -charged, -dress, -eyed.
full′-face, -faced, -fed, -fleshed,
-flow ing, -for tuned, -gorged,
-grown, -hand ed, -heart ed,
-length, -mouth, -mouthed,
-orbed, -rōed, -sailed, -souled,
-summed, -tide, -toned, -tuned,
-voiced, -winged.
full, _v._, -ing, -er, -er y, fulled,
full′er′s-tea zel, -this tle, -weed,
full′ing-mill, -soap.
full′-back, -bīnd′ing.
fŭl′mi nate, -nā′ted, -ting, -nant,
-na to′ry, -na′tion.
fŭl′mĭne, -mĭned, -mĭn ing, -min′-
e ous, -min′ic.
fŭl′some, -ly, -ness.
fŭl′vid, fŭl′vous.
fŭm′ble, -bled, -bler, -bling,
-bling ly.
fūme, fumed, fūm′ing, -ing ly, -y,
-i ly, fume′wort, fūm′ing-box, -pot.
_fu′mē′_ (fü′mā′).
fū mette′.
fū′mi gate, -gā′ted, -ting, -tor,
-tō′ry, -gā′tion, -ga tō′ri um.
fun, -ning, -ny, -ni ly, -ni ness,
fun′ny-bone, f. man.
Fun chal′ (fōōn shäl′), t. Madeira
Isl.
func′tion, -al, -al ly, -al′i ty, -al-
ize, -ized, -ĭ′zing, -a ry, -less.
fund, -ed, -ing, -er, -a ble, -less,
-hold er, -mon ger.
fun da men′tal, -ly, -ness.
Fu′nen (fü′nen), isl. Baltic sea.
fu′ner al, -ne′re al, -al ly.
Fünf′haus (fünf′hous), t. Aust.
fun′gus, _pl._ fun′gī (-jī) _or_ -gus es,
-goŭs, -gos′i ty, fun′gus-bee tle,
-cel lu lose, -foot, -gnat, -midge,
-stone, -tin der.
fū′ni cle, -nic′u lar, _-nic′u lus_, pl.
_-lĭ._

fun′nel, -neled _or_ -nelled, -nel-
form, -nel-like, -shaped, -top.
fū′nor.
fûr, -ring, -ri er, -er y, -ry, -ri ly,
furred, fur-bear ing, -moth,
-seal.
fûr′be low, -lowed.
fûr′bish, -a ble, -er, -ing, -bished.
fur′cal, fur cel′late.
fū′ri ous, -ly, -ness, _fū rĭ ō′sō._
fûrl, -ing, -er, furled, furl′ing-line.
fûr′long.
fûr′lough (-lō), -ing, -loughed
(-lōd).
fûr′nace, -man, -bar, -bridge,
-burn ing.
Fur′ness, Amer. writer.
fûr′nish, -er, -ing, -ment, -nished.
fûr′nĭ ture, -plush, -print, -store,
-stop, an organ-stop.
fū′ror.
fûr′rōw, -ing, -y, -rōwed, fur′row-
drain, -faced, -slice, -weed,
fur′row ing-ma chine.
Fûr′ry-day.
furst (fōōrst _or_ fürst), pl. _furst′en._
fûr′ther, -ance, -er, -ing, -more,
-most, -thered, -thest. See
farther.
fûr′tive, -ly.
fur′wà (fōōr′-).
fū′ry, _pl._ -ríes.
fûrze, fûrz′y, furze′chat, -chirp er,
-chit ter, -hack er, -wren.
fūse (fūz), fused, fūs′ing, fu′si ble,
-si bil′i ty, -si form, -sion (-zhun)
-sion ism, -sion ist, -sion′less,
fuse′-au′ger, -ex tract or, -gāge,
-hole, -mal let, -plug, -set ter,
-wheel, -wire, -wrench, fūs′ing-
disk, -point.
fu see′ (-ze′), -en gine.
fū′sel (-zel), -oil.
fū′sil (-zil), -sil eer′ _or_ -ier′, -sil-
lāde′, -lād′ed, -lād′ing, fū′sil-
mor tar.
fuss, -y, -i ly, -i ness.
fus′tian (-chan), -ist.
fus′tic.
fus′ti gate, -gā′ted, -ting, -ga′tion.
fus′ty, -ti ness.
fū′tĭle, -ly, -til′i ty, -i tā′ri an.
fŭt′tah.

Füt teh pur' (-pōōr'), dist. Brit. India.
fut'tock, -band, -hoop, -plates, -shrouds, -stäff, -stave, -timbers.
fū'ture, -less, -tūr ist, -tū'ri ty.

Fu'zes' Gyar'math' (fü'zĕsh' dyŏr'mät'), t. Hung.
fŭzz, -y, fuz'zi ly, -zi ness, fuzz'-ball.
fyke (fīk), -fish er man, -net.
Fy'vie (fi'vē), parish Scot.

G

G string.
gab, -bing, gabbed, gab'-lĕv er, -lift'er.
gab'ar dine' *or* -er- (-dēn').
Găb'ba tha, *Bib.*
gab ble, -bled, -bling, -bler.
gä'bel.
gä'bi (-bē).
gä'bi on, -age, -oned, -on ade'.
gä'ble, -bled, ga'ble-board, -end'ed, -pole, -win'dow, g. end, g. roof.
Gä bŏ ri au' (-rē ŏ'), Fr. novelist.
gad, -ded, -der, -ding, -ding ly, -dish, -dish ness, -a bout, -fly, -wall, -bush, -steel, -stick, -whip, gad'ding-car, -ma chine', gads'man.
Găd'a ra, -a rēnes', *Bib.*
Găd dänes'.
Gael (gāl), -ic.
Ga'e ta (gä'ā tä), c. It.
găff, -er, -ing, gaffed, gaffs'man, gaff-hook, -top sail.
gag, -ger, -ging, gagged, gag root, a plant; gag'-law, -rein, -runner.
gage *or* **gäuge,** gaged *or* gäuged, gä'ging *or* gäu'ging, gä'ger *or* gau'ger.
gag'gle, -gled, -gling, -gler.
gäi'e ty *or* gäy'e ty, gäi'ly *or* gay'ly. See *gay.*
gain, -a ble, -er, -ful, -ful ly, -fulness, -ing, -less, -less ness, -ly, gained, gain'ing-ma chine', -twist.
gain say', -ing, -er, -said' (-sed').
Gains'bor ough, Eng. painter.
gait.
gäit'er.
Gä'ius (-yus), *Bib.*
gä'la, -day, -dress.

gä'lah (*or* gä'-).
ga lan'gal.
gal'an tine.
gal a pä'go.
Ga läp'a gŏs, isl. Pacific ocean; Gal a pä'gi an.
Gal a tē'a, *Myth.*
Ga lä'tian (-shan).
Ga lä'tians (-shanz), *Bib.*
Gal'ax y, *Astron.;* gal'ax y, *pl.* -ax ies.
gale, -beer, -day.
Gä'len, Rom. physician; -ism, -ist, -lē'ni an, -len'ic, -ic al.
Ga lē'na, c. Kan.; tp. Mo.; mt. Col.
ga lē'na, -len'ic, -ic al, -if'er ous.
ga lĕtte'.
Ga'li'bis' (gä'lē'bē').
Ga li'ci a (ga lish'i a), prov. Aust.; -li'cian (-lish'yan).
Ga lig na'ni (gä lēn yä'nē), Eng. journalist.
Gal'i lee, *Bib.;* -i lē'an.
gal'i lee, a chapel; -porch.
găll, -ing, -ing ly, -ing ness, galled, gall'nut, -wort, -ap ple, -bee tle, -blad der, -cyst, -duct, -fly, -gnat, -in sect, -louse, -maker, -midge, -mite, -moth, -pipe, -sick ness, -stone, -wasp.
gal'lant, *adv.,* -ly, -ness, -ry.
gal lant', *v.,* -ed, -ing.
gal lant', *a.,* courtly, polite, attentive to ladies.
gal lant', *n.,* one who is attentive to ladies.
Găl lau dĕt', Amer. clergyman.
găl'le in.
găl'le on.
gal'ler y, -ler ied, -ler y-fur nace, g. pic ture, g. road.

---

nŏt, nôr, ūse, ŭp, ûrn, etüde, fōōd, fŏŏt, aŋger, boṅmot, thus, Bach.

gal'let, -ted, -ting.
gal le'ta-gráss (găl lā'tä-).
găl'ley, -balk, -bird, -cab i net,
-fire, -man, -news, -proof, -punt,
-rack, -rest, -slave, -work, -yarn.
găl'liard (-yard).
găl'lic, -li can, -can ism, -li cism,
-li cize, -cized, -cī'zing.
găl'lic, g. ac'id
gal li gas'kins.
găl'li nip per.
găl'li pot.
gal li'to (găl yē'tō).
Gal'lit zin, t. Pa.
găl li vant', -ed, -ing.
găl'lon.
găl lōōn', -looned'.
gal'lop (-lup), -er, -ing, gal loped,
-lo pāde', -pād'ed, -pād'ing.
gal'lop er-gun.
găl'lo way.
găl'low gláss.
gal'lows (-lus or -lōz), pl. -lows es
(-lus es) or -lows, gal lows-bird,
-bitts, -faced, -frame, -free,
-locks, -ripe, -stan chions, -top,
-tree.
ga lŏche' or -lŏshe' or -lŏsh'
(ga lŏsh').
gal'op (or găl'ō or ga lō').
ga lŏre'.
Gäl vä'ni (-nē), It. inventor.
gal van'ic, -al.
gal'van ize, -ized, -ī'zing, -ī'zer,
-ist, -ism, -ĭ zā'tion.
gal'va nom'e ter, -e try, -van o-
met'ric, -ric al, -van'o scope,
-scop'ic, gal'van o-ther mom'e-
ter.
gam, -ming, gammed.
Ga'ma, da (dä gä'mä), Port.
navigator.
gä'ma-grass.
Ga mä'lĭ el, Bib.
gam bade', -bä'do.
gam'bit.
gam'ble, -bled, -bling, -bler,
-bling-house.
gam'bŏ.
gam boge' (-bōj' or -bōōj'), -bo'-
gi an, -bo'gic (-jik).
gam'bol, -boled or -bolled, -bol-
ing or -bol ling.

gam'brel, -ing or -ling, -breled
or -brelled, gam'brel roof.
gam brōōn'.
gäme, -less, -ly, -ness, -some,
-some ly, -some ness, -ster,
gām'ing, gām'y or -ey.
game'keep er, -bag, -bird, -cock,
-egg, -fish, -fowl, -hawk, -law,
-pre serve', -pre serv'er, gām'-
ing-house, -room, -ta ble.
găm'in (or ga măn').
gam'ma, -moth.
gam'ma cism, -cis'mus (-sĭz'-).
gam'mon, -ing, -moned, gam'-
mon-plate, -shac'kles, gam'mon-
ing-hole.
gamp.
gam'ut.
ganch.
gan'der, -par ty, -pull, -pull ing.
gan dou'ra (-dōō'-)
gang, -board, -flow er, -măs ter,
-plank, -way, gangs'man.
gang'-bŏr'ing, -by (-bĭ), -cash,
-cul'ti va tor, -day, -drill, -edg-
er, -plow, -press, -punch, -rīd'er,
-saw, -tide, -week, gang'way-
lad der.
gan'ging (-jing), -line.
gaṇ'gli on, pl. -gli ons or -gli a,
-gli al, -gli ar, -gli ate, -ā'ted,
-gli form, -gli on a ry, -on ā'ted,
-on ic, -glĭ ous, gaṇ'gli on-cell,
-cor pus cle, -glob ule.
gaṇ'grene, -grened, -grēn ing,
-gre nous, -gre nes'cent.
găngue.
gan'jah.
gan'nen.
gan'net.
Gans (gänss), Ger. jurist.
Găn'se bōōrt, Amer. officer.
găn'ta.
gant'let, a military punishment.
Gan'y mede, Myth.
gä ou'es (-ōō'äs).
găp, -ping, -per, gapped, gap-
lathe, -toothed, -win dow.
gäpe (or gäpe), gap'er, -ing,
-ing ly, gaped, gape'mouth, a
fish; -seed, -eyed, -gaze, gap'-
ing-stock.
gar.

---

găr'an cin, _ga ran ceux'_ (ga rŏn-sê').

garb, -ing, garbed.

gar'bage.

gar'bel.

gar'bill.

gar'ble, -bled, -bler, -bling.

gar'board-plank, -strake.

garce.

Gar ci'as, Pe'dro (pä'dro gär-thē'as), _Fiction._

gär çon' (-sôn').

gar'dant.

gärde' bräs' (-brä), **-nuque** (-nŏŏk).

gar'den (-dn), -ing, -er, -esque', -less, -dened.

gar'den-balm, -bạl sam, -bee tle, -bird, -bond, -dor mouse, -en gine, -flea, -gate, a plant; -glăss, -house, -mite, -mold, -net, -par ty, -plot, -pump, -snail, -spi der, -squint, -stand, -stuff, -sweep, -war bler.

gare, -fowl.

Găr'eth, Knight of the Round Table.

gar'fish.

Gar ga nelle', _Fiction._

Gar gan'tu a, _Fiction._

gar'ga rïsm.

gar'get.

gar'gil.

gar'gle, -gled, -gling.

gar'goyle.

Găr ï băl'dï, It. patriot; -băl'di-an; **găr ï băl'dï,** a garment; a fish.

gâr'ish _or_ gâir'ish, -ly, -ness.

gär'land, -ed, -ing, -less, -ry, -land-flow er.

gar'lic, -wort, -lick y, -lic-eat er, -mus tard, -shrub.

gar'ment, -less.

gar'ner, -ing, -nered.

gar'net, -if'er ous, -ber ry, -work, -blende, -hinge, -rock.

gar'nish, -ing, -er, -ee', -ee'ing, -eed', -ment, -nished, gar'nish-bolt.

Gä rŏnne', r. Sp.

ga rŏŏ'kŭh.

găr'ran.

găr'ret, -eer'.

găr'ri son, -ing, -soned, -son-ar til'ler y.

gar'rot, a duck; a bandage.

găr rōte', -rōt'ed, -rōt'ing, -rōt'er.

găr'ru lous, -ly, -ness, -ru'li ty.

Găr'ru lus.

gar'ter, -ing, -tered, gar'ter-fish, -plate, -ring, -snake.

Gar'ter king, Order of the Gar ter.

garth, -man.

gä'rum, ga'rous.

găs, _n., pl._ găs'es (-ĕz), găs, _v.,_ gassed, gas'sy, gas'light, gas'e ous.

gas'-a larm, -an'a lyz er, -ap pa rä'tus, -bag, -băth, -bat ter y, -bel'lows (-lus), -black, -bleach-ing, -blow pipe, -boil er, -brack et, -buoy, -burn er, -car bon, -check, -coal, -com press'or, -con dens'er, -drain, -drip, -en gine, -field, -fit ter, -fix ture, -flame, -fur nace, -gage, -gen'-er a tor, -globe, -gov'ern or,.-gun.

gas'-heat'er, -hold er, -house, -in'di ca tor, -jet, -lamp, -light-ing, -lime, -liq uor, -ma chine, -main, -man, -me ter, -mo tor, -ov en, -pipe, -plant, -plate, -plot, -pore, -port, -pu'ri fi er, -range, -reg is ter, -reg'u la tor, -re tort, -ring, -sand, -sock et, -stove, -ta ble, -tank, -tar, -trap, -tube, -valve, -wash er, -wa ter, -well, -works.

gas con ade', -ād'ed, -ād'ing, -ād'er.

Gas'con y, prov. Fr.; Gas'con.

gash, -ing, gashed, gash-vein.

gas'i fy, -ing, -fied, -fi ca'tion, -form.

gas'ket.

gas'kin.

gas'king.

gas'o lïne _or_ -lene, -o lier' _or_ -a lier', gas om'e ter, -e try, -o met'ric, -o scope.

găsp, -ing, -ing ly, găsped.

Găs pe' (-pä'), dist. Que.

gas'sing, -frame.

gas soul' (-sōōl').

gas'tric, -trī'tis.

---

gas'tro grâph, -tro soph.
gas tron'o my,   -o mist,   -o mer,
-tro nom'ic, -ic al.
gas tros'to mize,   -mized,   -mi-
zing,   -tros'to my,   -trot'o my,
-tro tom'ic.
gä tä'.
gate, -less, -house, -keep'er, -man,
-post, -ward, -way, -wise.
gate-bill,   -chăm'ber,   -chan'nel,
-end, -fine, -hook, -meet'ing,
-mon'ey, -post, -road, -saw,
-shut'ter, -tow'er, -valve, -vein.
gatĥ'er,   -a ble,   -er,   -ing,   -ered,
gatĥ'er ing-board, -coal, -hoop,
-i ron, -note, -pal'let, -peat,
-rod, -string, -thread.
găt'tĭe.
gat tine' (-tēn').
gauche (gōsh), -rie' (-rē').
Gau cher' (gō shä'), Fr. writer.
Gau'cho   (gou'chō),   pl.   -chos
(-chōz).
Gau cin' (gou thēn' or -sēn'), t.
Sp.
gạud,   -y,   -i ly,   -i ness,   -er y.
gau de ä'mus (or gou'dä ä'mus).
găuge,   -a ble,   gauged,   gău'ging,
gău'ger, -ger ship. See gage.
găuge'-bar,   -block,   -box,   -cock,
-con cus'sion,   -door,   -glăss,
-knife, -lad der, -lathe, -pin,
-play,   -point,   -saw,   -stuff,
-wheel,   gău'ging-cal'i per,   -rod,
-rule, -thread.
Gaul ti er' (gō tē ä'), Fr. educa-
tor.
Gaul tier (goul'teer), Leonhard,
Ger. engraver.
gạum, -less, -y, gaum'-like.
găunt, -ly, -ness.
găunt'let,   -ed,   -ing,   gäunt'let-
guard, -pipe, -shield, -sword.
gauss (gous).
Gau'ta ma   (gạu'ta ma),   Indian
philos.
Gau ti er' (gō tē ä'), Fr. novelist.
gạuze,   gạuz'y,   -i ness,   gạuze'-
dress er, -tree, -winged.
ga vage' (-väzh').
Ga vaz'zi   (gä vät'sē),   It.   politician.
găv'el, -er, -et, -eled.

găv'ot or ga vŏtte'.
gạwk, -y, -i ness.
gạwp, -ing, gạwped.
gay, gai'ly or gay'ly, gai'e ty or
gay'e ty,   gay'ness,   gay'some,
gay'fĕatĥ er, a plant.
gay'-you (gī'-ū).
găze,   gazed,   găz'ing,   gaze'hound,
gäz'ing-stock.
ga zĕlle or ga zel'.
ga zĕtte',   -zet'ted,   -zet'ting,   gaz'-
et teer'.
gaz zet'ta (gât set'ta).
gēan (gēn).
gear (gēr), -ing, geared, gear-box,
-cut ter,   -wheel,   gēar'ing-chain,
-wheel.
Gea'ry (gē'ry or gä'-), co. Kan.
Gea'ry   (gä'ry or gē'ry),   Amer.
gen.
geat (jēt).
Ge au'ga (jē ạ'gä), co. O.
geb'bĭe.
Gĕ'ber (gĕ'-), Bib.
Ge'bir (jĕ'-), Fiction.
geck'o.
gee'bung (jĕ'-).
geen.
Gef'le (yĕv'lä), t. Sw.
Ge hä'zĭ, Bib.
Ge hen'na (ge-), Bib.
Gei'kie (gee'kĭ), Eng. auth.
Geĭ'sen heĭ mer.
Geiŝ (gäsh), mt. Afr.
gei'sha (gä'-).
geit'je (gīt'yĕ).
ge la'sian (jē la'shan).
gel'a tin or -tĭne (jĕl'-), -tin ate,
-tin'i form,   -tin if'er ous, ge lat'i-
nate,   -na ted,   -na ting,   -na'tion,
ge lat'i nize, -nized, -i nous, -nous-
ly, -nous ness.
ge leem' (gē-).
ge los'co py (je-).
gem (jem), -cut ting, -en grav'ing,
-peg,   -ring,   -sculp'ture,   -stick,
-stone, gem'my.
gem'el (jem'-), -ring, -win dow.
gem'i nate   (jem'-),   -ly,   -na tive,
-nä'tion.
Gem'i nĭ (jem'-), -i nid.
gems'bok (gĕmz'-), gems'horn.
ge nappe' (je nap').

gen darme' (jen därm' *or* zhŏń'-
därm'), pl. *gen'darmes'* (zhŏń'-
därm'), *-darm'er ie* or *-er y.*
gen'der, -less.
gen'e al'o gy (jĕn'-), -o gist, -o gize,
-gized, -gī'zing, -a log'ic, -ic al,
-al ly.
gen'er al, -ize, -ized, -ī'zer, -ī'zing,
-ī'za ble, -I za'tion, -al ly, -al'i ty.
gen'er ate, -ā'ted, -ting, -tive,
-tor, -åble, -a bil'i ty, -ā'tion.
ge nĕr'ic, -ic al, -al ly, -al ness.
gen'er ous, -ly, -ness, -os'i ty.
Gen e see' (jĕn-), co. Mich.; co.
N. Y.
Gen e sĕ'o, c. Ill.; vil. N. Y.
gen'e sis, *pl.* -ses (-sēz), ge net'ic,
-ic al, -al ly.
Gen'e sis, *Bib.*
Ge ne'va, G. ar bi tra'tion, G.
a ward', G. Bi ble, G. con-
ven'tion, G. cross, G. gown.
Gen e vieve' (jĕn e vēv'), heroine of
a ballad by Coleridge.
Ge nev'ra, in *Orlando Furioso.*
gen e vrette' (jen-).
Gen'ghis Khan (jĕn'gĭs kän),
Asiatic conqueror.
gĕ'nĭl al (*or* jēn'ial), -ly, -ness,
-al'i ty.
Gé nin' (zhā năń'), Fr. philol.
gen'i tive, -i tī'val (*or* jen'i tiv al).
gen'ius (jĕn'yus *or* gĕ'nĭl us), *pl.*
-es (ĕz).
gĕ'nĭl us, a spirit; *pl.* gĕ'nĭl ī.
ge'ni us lo cī.
Gen nĕs'a ret (gen-), *Bib.*
Gen'o a (jen-), prov. It.; t. N. Y.
-o ese' (*or* -ēz').
gen'o type (jen'-).
Ge noude' (zhĕ nōōd'), Fr. jour.
gen're (zhäń'r).
gens (jenz), pl. *gĕn'tes* (-tēz).
Gen'ser ic (jen'-), King of the Van-
dals.
gent, gen teel', -teel'ly, -teel'ness.
gen'tian (jen'shan), -wort, -bit'-
ter, -spĭr'it.
Gen'tĭle, *Bib.* Gen'tĭle *or* gen'-
tĭle, among the Mormons, one
who is not of their church.
gen'tĭle (*or* -tĭl), -tĭl ism.
Gen til ly' (zhŏń tē yē'), t. Fr.

gen'tle, -ness, -tly, -try, -tle folk,
-tle hood, -tle man, -man hood,
-man like, -man ly, -li ness, -man-
ship, -wom an, -heart ed.
gĕn u flect' (jen-), -ed, -ing, -flec'-
tion *or* -flex'ion.
gen'u ĭne, -ine ly, -ine ness.
gĕ'nus, *pl.* gen'e ra.
gĕ'ŏde, -o des'ic, -ic al, -od'e sist,
-e sy, -o det'ic, -ic al, -al ly,
-det'ics.
Geof'frey (jĕf'ry), Eng. chron.
Geof froy' (zhō frwä'), Fr. painter.
ge og'e ny (-ŏj'-), -e nous, -o-
gen'ic.
ge og'no sy, -nos'tic, -tic al, -al ly.
ge og'ra phy, -ra pher, -o graph'-
ic, -ic al, -al ly.
ge ol'o gy, -o gist, -o gize, -gized,
-gī'zing, -o log'ic, -ic al, -al ly.
gĕ'o man cy, -man cer, -man'tic,
-tic al, -al ly.
ge om'e try, -om'e trize, -trized,
-trī'zing, -o met'ric, -ric al, -al-
ly, -om e tri'cian (-trish'an).
ge'o mor'phy, -mor'phic, -mor-
phol'o gy.
Ge'orgs wal de (gā'ŏrgs väl dĕ), t.
Aust.
Ge'ra (gā'rä), t. Ger. Gē'ra, *Bib.*
ge'rah (gē'-).
ge rä'ni um.
gerbe (jeɪb).
ger'fal'con (jer'fạ'kn) *or* gyɪ'-.
Ger'ge sēnes' (ger'gē-), *Bib.*
Ger'ge sĭtes (ger'gē-), *Bib.*
Gĕr'i zim (gĕr'-), *Bib.*
germ, -ule, -ā're a, -cell, -cup,
-dis ease, -disk, -form, -gland,
-his to ry, -lay er, -mem brane,
-plas ma (-plăz-), -pore, -shield,
-stock, -tube, -ves i cle.
ger'man, closely related; a term
used in dancing.
Ger'man, pertaining to Germany,
-man ism, -man ist, -man ize,
-ized, -ī'zing, -I zā'tion, -man'ic,
-man o phobe, -o pho'bi a.
ger man'der.
ger måne'.
ger'man town, a carriage.
ger'mĭ cide, -cī'dal, -mi cul ture,
-cul'tur ist.

---

nŏt, nôr, ūse, ŭp, ûrn, etüde, fōōd, fŏŏt, aŋger, bońmot, thus, Bach.
21

ger'mi nate, -nā'ted, -nā'ting, -nant, -nal, -na tor, -na'tion.
Ge ron'i mo, Indian chief.
Gé ronte' (zhā rôṅt'), a character in Molière's comedy.
Gĕr'ry, Vice-pres. U. S.
ger'ry man der (ger'-), -der ing, -dered.
gĕr'und (jĕr'-), ge run'di al, -al ly, -run'di val, -run'dive, -dive ly.
Ger vi'nus (gĕr vē'nŏŏs), Ger. hist.
ger yg'o ne (jer ig'-).
Ge se'ni us (gē sē'nĭ ŭs), Ger. orientalist.
Gĕsh'u rites (gesh'-), Bib.
Gess'ler (gĕs'ler), Aust. tyrant.
ges'so (jes'-).
ges tate' (jes-), -tā'ted, ta'ting, -ta to'ry, -to'ri al.
ges tic'u late (jes-), -lā'ted, -ting, -tive, -tor, -tō'ry, -lā'tion.
ges'ture (jĕs'-), -tured, -tūr ing, -tūr er, -tūr al, -ture less, ges'-ture-laŋ guage, -speech.
get, -ter, -ting, got, got'ten, get'-noth ing, -up, get'ting-rock.
Geth sem'a nē, Bib.
Ge va'ert (hā vä'ĕrt), Belg. composer.
gew'gaw (gū'gạ), -gawed.
gey'ser (gī'-), -ic, -ser ite.
ghast'ly (gȧst'-), -li ness.
ghạt or ghạut.
ghä wä'zee.
Ghe'ber (gē'ber or gā'-) or Gue'-ber.
ghee (gē), a liquid butter.
gher'kin (gêr'-).
Ghet to (gĕt'to or gät'o), pl. Ghet'tĭ or -tos (-tōz).
ghor, a valley.
ghŏst, -like, -ly, -li ness, -fish, -land, -ship, -can'dle, -coal, -de'-mon, -flow'er, -moth, -plant, -seer, -show, -soul, -sto ry, -train, -word.
ghoul (gōōl), -ish, -ish ly.
ghŭr ry.
Gia co mel'li (jä kō mĕl'lē) Fr. painter.
Giam'schid (zhäm'shĭd), Pers. Myth.

gī'ant, -ess, -ant ish, -ship, gi'ant-ket tle, -kill er, -quell er, g. pop'py, g. pow der, giant's stride.
giaour (jour).
Giar're (jär'rā), t. It.
gib (jib), -bing, gibbed, gib'staff.
gib (gib), -ber, -ber ish, -bing, -bered, gib-cat, -fish, -keel er, -tub.
gi bä'ro (or hē'bä rō), pl. -ros (-rōz).
gib'bet (jib'-), -ed, -ing, gib'bet-tree.
gib'bon.
gib'bous, -ly, -ness, -bos'i ty.
gibe (jīb), gibed, gīb'ing, gīb'er.
Gīb'e a, Bib.
gib'let (jĭb'-), -check, -cheek.
gi'bus (jī'bus or zhē'bü).
gĭd'dy, -di ly, -di ness, -dy-head, -head ed, -paced, -pate, -pāt'ed.
gies (gēs), mats of bark.
gift, -ed, -ed ness, gift'-en'ter-prise, -horse, -rope.
gig, -ger, -ging, gigged, gig'man, gigs'man.
gig'-lamp, -ma chine', -mill, -sad dle, -saw, -tree, gig'ging-ma chine'.
gi gan'tic (jī-), -gan'te an, -gan-tesque'.
gig'gle, -gled, -gling, -gler.
Gig noux' (zhēn yōō'), Fr. painter.
Gi goux' (zhē gōō'), Fr. painter.
gigue (zhēg).
Gī'hŏn, Bib.
Gi'la (hē'la), r. Col.; co. Ariz. G. mon'ster.
gil'bert, a magnetic unit.
Gil Blȧs (zhĕl bläs), hero of the romance by Le Sage.
Gil bŏ'a, Bib.
gild, -ed, -ing, -er, gild'ing-press, -size, -tool, -wax.
Giles (jīlz), Amer. clergyman.
gi let' (zhē lā').
Gĭl'gặl, Bib.
gil'guy (gĭl'gī), -hoot er.
gill (gĭl), -ing, -er, gilled, gill'-arch, -bar, -box, -breath er, -cav'i ty, -chăm'ber, -cleft, -comb, -cov er, -fil'a ment, -fish ing, -flap, -frame, -hoot er,

-lid, -ma chine', -mem'brane, -net, -net ter, -net ting, -o pen- ing, -plate, -plume, -rāk'er, -sac, -slit.
gill (jĭl), -beer, -house.
Gil les'ple (gĭl-), Amer. engineer.
Gil'lott (gĭl'lot), Eng. manfr. of steel pens.
gil'ly flow'er (jĭl'-), -flow'er-ap'- ple.
gil răv'age (gĭl-).
gilt, -head, a fish; -pōll, -tail, -brŏnze, -edged.
gim'bal (jĭm'-), -bals, gim'bal- jawed.
gim'crack (jĭm'-), -er y.
gīme.
gim'let, -ed or -ted, -ing or -ting, gim'let-eye, -eyed.
gimp, -ing, -y, gimp'-nail.
gin (jin), -ner, -ning, ginned, gin'- block, -horse, -house, -mill, -pal'ace, -race, -ring, -saw, -shop, -tac'kle, -wheel, gin fizz, g. sling.
ginge (ginj).
gin'ger (jin'jer), -ade, -bread, -ly, -nut, -ous, -snap, -wort, -grăss, -pine, ginger ale, g. beer, g. pop, g. wine, gin'ger bread- palm, -plum, -tree, -work.
ging'ham (ging'am).
ging'ko (ging'-), -tree.
gin'seng (jĭn'-).
gio co'so (jō kō'sō).
Gior da'no (jŏr dä'nō), It. painter.
Gior gio'ne (jŏr jō'nä), It. painter.
Giot'to (jŏt'to), It. painter; Giot tesque' (jŏt tesk').
Gio van'ni (jō vän'nē), It. philos.
Gip'sy or Gyp'sy (jip'-), n.
gip'sy, v., -ing, -dom, -ism, -ry, -wort, -sĭed, gip'sy-cart, -herb, -hĕr ring, -moth, -winch, g. rose.
gi raffe' (jĭ răf').
gir'an dole (jĭr'-).
Gi rard' (zhē rär'), Fr. philol.
Gi rard', Stephen (jē rard'), founder of Girard College.
gird, -ed, -ing, -er.
gird'er, -age, -bridge, gird'ing- beam, -hook.

gir'dle, -dled, -dling, -dler, gir'- dle-belt, -bone, -knife, -swiv'el, -wheel.
Gir'ga shīte or -sīte (ger'-), Bib.
girl, -ie, -ish, -ish ly, -ish ness, -hood.
gi'ro (jē'rō).
Gi ronde' (jĭ rŏnd'), -ron'dist, -ron'din.
gir'ouette' (zhēr'wet').
girt, -line.
girth, -ing, girthed.
gist (jĭst).
gi tä'no (jĭ-), fem. -tä'na.
Giu glia'no (jōol yä'nō), t. It.
Giu li a no'va (jōo lē ä nō'vä), t. It.
gius'to (jōōs'tō).
give, gave, giv'en, giv'ing, giv'er.
Gi vet' (zhē vä'), t. Fr.
gi vre (zhē'vr).
giz'zard, -fall'en, -shad, -trout.
gla bres'cent.
gla cé (gla sā').
glā'cial (-shal or -shi ăl), -ist, -ly, -ci ate (-shĭ ät), -ā'ted, -a ting, -ā'tion.
gla'cier (-sher) or gla'ci er (glăs'ĭ er), -et, -ci ol'o gy (-shĭ-), -o gist, -o log'ic al (-loj'-), -om'e- ter, -ci ère' (glăs i âr').
glā'cis.
gla çure' (glä sōōr').
glad, -der, -dest, -den, -dened, -den ing, -ly, -ness, -some, -some ly, -some ness, glad'-eye, a bird.
glāde, -net.
glăd'i a tor, -ism, -ship, -tō'ri al, -ri an.
gla dī'o lus, glad'i ōle.
Glad'stōne, -stō'ni an.
glair, -in, -ing, -e ous, -y, glaired.
glăm'our (or glä'mur), -ous, ous- ly, -ly.
glănce, glanced, glăn'cing, -cing- ly, glance'-coal, -fish, -pitch.
gland, -box, -cock, glan'du lar, -lar ly, -dule, -du lif'er ous, -du lous.
glan dă'ceous, -dā'ri ous, -dif'er- ous, -di form.
glan'der, -ous, -ders.
glāre, glared, glăr'ing, -ing ly, -ing ness, -y, -i ness.

glâss, -y, -i ly, -i ness, -ful, -chord, -eye, a bird; a fish; -man, -ware, -work, -wort.

glâss'-ar'go naut, -blow er, -cav'- i ty, -ce ment, -cloth, -col or ing, -crab, -cut ter, -dust, -en am'el, -en grāv'ing, -eyed, -fur nace, -gall, -gāz'ing, -grind er, -hard, -house, where glass is made; -mãk'er, -met al, -mold, -mount- er.

glass'-ov en, -paint er, -pa per, -pot, -press, -rōll'ing, -rope, -shell, -shrimp, -sil ver ing, -snail, -snake, -soap, -sol'der- ing, -spin ning, -sponge, -stain- er, -tin ner, -tongs, -weld ing, -work er, -works, g. coach, glass'ing-jack, -ma chine.

Glau'ber (glou'ber), Ger. chem.; G. salt, glau'ber īte.

glau'cous, of a greenish color.

Glau'cus, *Ichth.* and *Conch.* *genus;* glau'cus.

glave *or* glāive, glaved.

glaze, glazed, glāz'ing, -y, glaze- kiln, -wheel, glāz'ing-bãr'rel, -ma- chine, -pan el, -tool, -wheel.

gla'zer, one who or that which glazes; gla'zier (-zher), one who sets window glass.

glēam, -ing, -y, gleamed.

glean, -er, -ing, gleaned.

glēbe, -less, glebe-house, -land.

glede.

gledge (glĕj), gledged, gledg'ing.

glee, -ful, -ful ly, -some, -man, -club.

gleek, -ing, gleeked.

gleet.

Gleig (glĕg), Scot. divine.

Gleim (glīm), Ger. poet.

glen.

Glen'dower (-dōōr), Welsh chief- tain.

glen găr'ry, a cap.

glib, -ly, -ness.

glide, -wort, glīd'ed, -er, -ing, -ing ly, glīd'ing-plane.

glim'mer, -ing, -ing ly, -mered.

glimpse, glimps'ing, glimpsed.

glis sāde', -san'do (glēs sån'dō), glĭs'sant.

glis'ten (-n), -ing, -tened.

glit'ter, -ing, -ing ly, -y, -tered.

glōam, -ing.

glōat, -ed, -ing.

globe, glo'bate, -bā'ted, -bose, (-bōs'), -bose'ly, -bŏs'i ty, globe'wise, -fish, -flow'er, glŏb'y.

globe'-am'a ranth, -an i mal, -dai sy, -ra nuṇ'cu lus, -run ner, -sight, -sla'ter, -this tle, -trot'- ter, -tube, -tu'lip, g. cock, g. light'ning, g. valve.

glŏb'ûle, -u lar, -lar ly, -lar ness, -u let, -u lin, -u lism, -u list, -u lite, -u lit'ic, -u loid, -u lose, -u lous, -lous ness.

glo'chis (-kis).

glōōm, -ing, -y, -i ly, -i ness, gloomed.

glō'ri fy, -ing, -fi er, -fīed, -fī ca'- tion.

glō'ry, -ri ous, -ous ly, -ous ness, glo'ry-flow er, -hole, -pea, -vine.

glŏss, -ing, -ing ly, -er, -less, -y, -i ly, -i ness, glossed.

glŏs'sa ry, -rist, -sā'ri al, -ri an, glos'sate.

glos'so grâph, -sog'ra pher, -ra- phy, -graph'ic al.

glos sol'o gy, -o gist, -so log'ic al (-lŏj'-).

Glos'ter *or* Glou'ces ter (glŏs'ter), a kind of cheese.

glŏt'tis, *pl.* -tī des (-dēz), -tal, -tic, -tid, -tid'e an.

Glou'ces ter (glŏs'ter), t. N. J.; t. Mass.; t. Eng.

glove (glŭv), glov'er, -ing, gloved, glove-band, -but'ton er, -cälf, -clãsp, -fight, -hŏōk, -lĕath er, -mãk'er, -mon ey, -sheep, -shiēld, -sil'ver, -sponge, -stretch'er.

glōw, -ing, -ing ly, glowed, glow'- worm, -lamp.

glow'er (glour), -ing, -ered.

gloze, glozed, glōz'ing.

Glück, Ger. jurist.

glu com'e ter.

glu'cose (-kōs), -co sĭd *or* sīde, -cos'ic.

glue, glued, glū'ing, -er, -ey, -ey ness, -ish, -tin ous, -ous ness, -ti nos'i ty.

glue'-boil er, -can, -dri er, -plant,
-pot, -size, -stock, glū'ing-ma-
chine', -press.
glum, -ly, -ness.
glume, glu'mous, -mel'la, -mel'lu la,
-mif'er ous, -mi flō rous.
glut, -ted, -ting, glut'-hĕr'ring.
glu'ten, -bread, -cā'se in, -fī'brin.
glu'tin ize, -ized, -ī'zing.
glŭt'ton (-tn), -ish, -ize, -ized,
-ī'zing, -ous, -ous ly, -ous ness, -y.
glyc'er in or -īne (glĭs'-), -er ize,
-ized, -ī'zing.
glyph (glĭf), -ic.
glyph'o grâph, -graph'ic, gly-
phog'ra pher, -ra phy.
glyp'tic, -tics, -to grâph, -graph'ic,
-tog'ra pher, -ra phy.
Gmel'i na (mĕl'-).
gnarl, -ing, -y, gnarled, gnarl'ing-
tool.
gnash, -ing, -ing ly, gnashed.
gnat, -ling, -catch'er, -flow'er,
-hawk, -worm.
gnat'ter, -ing, -tered.
gnaw, -a ble, -ing, -er, gnawed.
gneiss (nīs), gneis'sic, -soid, -sose
(-sōs).
Gneist, Ger. publicist.
gnome (nōm), gnomed, gnōm'ic
(or nŏm'-), -ic al, -al ly, -ist,
gnome-owl.
gnŏ'mon, ist, -mon'ic, -ic al,
-al ly, -mon'ics, -mon ol'o gy.
gnŏ'sis (nō'-), gnos'tic, -tic al,
-al ly, -ti cize, -cized, -cī'zing.
Gnos'tic, -ti cism.
gnu (nū).
go, -er, -ing, went, gōes, gŏne,
go'-a head', a., -a hĕad'a tive, -a-
head'a tive ness, -be tween', -by,
-cart, -down, -har vest, gō'ing-
băr'rel, -fu see' (-zē'), -wheel,
go'ings-on, go-to-bed-at-n o o n,
a plant; go-to-meet'ing, a.
gŏad, -ed, -ing, -ster, goads'man,
goad'-spur.
gŏal, -keep'er, -post.
gŏat, -ish, -ish ly, -ish ness,
-beard, a plant; -chā'fer, a
beetle; -fish, -head, a bird;
-herd, -land, -skin, -stone,
-suck'er, a bird; -weed.

goat'-an'te lope, -bush, -lĕath'er,
-mar'jo ram, -milk'er, -m o t h,
-owl, goat's'-bane, -beard, -foot,
-horn, -rue, -thorn, goat'weed-
but'ter fly.
gob, -bing, gobbed, gob'-line,
-road.
go bang'.
gob'ble, -bled, -bler, -bling.
Gŏb'e lĭn (or gŏb'lăn'), Fr. dyer.
gŏ'bĕ lĭng (or gŏb'- or gō bê-
lăn').
gŏb'let, -cell, -shaped.
gŏb'lin.
go bôr'ro.
go bur'ra.
god, -child, -daugh'ter, -dess,
-fä ther, -hood, -less, -less ly,
-less ness, -like, -like ness, -ly,
-li ly, -li ness, -moth'er, -send,
-ship, -son, -wit, a bird; god-
māk'er, -tree.
God, -head, -ward, -fear ing, -for-
sāk'en, -speed, God's'-a'cre.
Go dī'va, title of a poem by Tennyson.
Goen toer' (gōōn tōōr'), vol. Java.
Goes (hōōs), t. Neth.
Goe the' (gwĕt tē'), tp. S. C.
Goe'the (gē'tĕ), Ger. auth.
gŏ'e ty, -e tic.
gof'fer, -ing, -fered, gof'fer ing-
i'ron, -press, -tool.
gog'gle, -gled, -gling, -gler, -gly,
gog'gle nose, -gle-eye, -eyed.
goi'ter or -tre, -tered, -trous, -tral,
goi'ter-stick.
Go'i to (gō'ē tō), vil. It.
gold, -en, -bås ket, a plant;
-breast, a bird; -crest, a bird;
-cup, a plant; -dust, a plant;
-finch, -fin'ny, -fish, -ham'mer,
a bird; -sin ny, a fish; -smith,
-spink, -stone, -tail, a moth;
-thread, a plant; -wasp, -worm.
gold'-bank, -bear'ing, -beat'er,
-block'ing, -book, -bound,
-cush'ion, -dig'ger, -dust, -fern,
-field, -filled, -find'er, -foil, -fur'-
nace, -ham'mer, -hunt'er, -knife,
-leaf, -lil'y, -mine, -min'ing,
-mole, -note, -paint, -pow'der,
-proof, -shell, -size, -stick,

-wash'er, -of-pleas ure, a plant;
gold'smith-bee'tle.
gold'en back, a bird; -en bough,
a plant; -en bug, a bird; -en-
chain, a plant; -en club, a
plant; -en ear, a moth; -en eye,
a duck; a fish; an insect; -en-
head, a duck; -en knap, a bird;
-en maid, a fish; -en pert, a
plant; -en rod, a plant; -en seal,
a plant.
gold'en-cheeked, -flow'er, -spoon,
a tree; -swift, a moth; gold'en-
rod-tree.
golf, -er, -ing, golf-club, -stick,
golf'ing-ground, golf arm.
Gŏl'gŏ thä, Bib.
gŏ'li a.
gŏ'li ard, -y, -ar der y, -ar'dic.
gŏ lĭ'ath, -bee'tle. Gŏ lĭ'ath, Bib.
Gŏ mŏr'rah, Bib.
gon'do la, -do let, -do liēr'.
gone. See go.
Gon'er il, daughter of King Lear.
gon'fa lon, -fa lon iēr'.
gŏng, -bell, -ham'mer, -met'al,
-stand.
go nĭ om'e ter, -e try, -o met'ric,
-ric al.
gon or rhe'a or -rhœ'- (-rē'-),
-rhe'al.
gŏŏd, -ish, -like, -ly, -li ness, -ness,
-y, -man, -wife, -sire.
good'-by or -bye, -con di'tioned,
-day, n., -e ven, n., -e'ven ing,
n., -morn ing, n., -mor'row, n.,
-night, n., -will, of a business;
g. will.
goods-en gine, -shed, -train,
-truck, -van, -wag'on.
good'y-bread, -good, -good'y,
-good'y ism.
gŏŏr.
goose, pl. geese, goose'bēak, a
fish; -ber'ry, -fish, -flesh, -foot,
a plant; -herd, -neck, -tongue,
a plant; goos'y.
goose'-bird, -brant, -corn, -egg,
-foot'ed, -gräss, -green, -gull,
-house, -mus'sel, -pim'ples,
-quill, -skin, -step, -tan'sy,
-wing, goose'ber'ry-bush, -moth,
goos'ey-gan'der.

gŏŏ'tŏŏ.
gŏpe, goped, gŏp'ing.
gŏ'pher, -root, a shrub; -wood, a
tree; go'pher-man, -snake, -wood,
the yellow-wood.
go'pu ra (-pŏŏ-).
gôr'-crow.
Gŏr'di an.
gŏre, gored, gŏr'ing, -y, gore'bill,
a fish; gore'-strake.
gorge, gorged, gor'ging, -ger,
gorge-cur'tain, -hook.
gor'geous (-jus), -ly, -ness.
gŏr'get (-jet).
Gor'gi o (-gĭ-).
gor'gon, -go'ne an or -ni an,
-go nei'on, -gon esque', gor'gon's-
head.
gŏ ril'la.
gôr'mand or gour'- (gŏŏr'-), -ize,
-ized, -ĭ'zer, -ĭ'zing.
gŏr'ri on.
gorse, gors'y, gorse'hatch, a bird;
-hop'per, a bird; -duck.
gos'hawk.
Gŏ'shen, Bib.
gŏ'shen īte.
gos'ling (gŏz'-), gos let, -ling-
green.
gŏs'pel, -er, -ize, -ized, -ĭ'zing, gos'-
pel-list, -oak, -oath, -tree.
gos'sa mer, -y.
gos'sip, -er, -ing or -ping, -siped
or -sipped, -y, -mon'ger.
gos sŏŏn'.
gos'sy pĭne, -sy pose (-pŏs).
gŏ'ta.
Gŏth, -ic, -ĭ'cism, -ĭ'cize, -cized,
-cĭ'zing, -i cist.
Gŏ'tham, t. Eng., a name applied
to New York city; -ist, -ite.
Gŏtt'schälk, Amer. composer.
gouache (gwäsh).
gou a ree' (gŏŏ a rē').
gouge (gouj), gouged, gou'ging
(-jing), gou'ger, gouge-bit,
-chis'el, -fŭr'row, -slip.
Gough (gŏf), Amer. temperance
reformer.
gou'jon (gŏŏ'-).
gou'lard (gŏŏ'-).
gou'lâsh (gŏŏ'-).
Gou'nod' (gŏŏ'nŏ'), Fr. composer.

fāte, făt, fär, fąll, fâre, fȧst, sofȧ, mēte, mĕt, hêr, ice, ĭn, nŏte,

gŏurd, -y, -i ness, -mouth, a fish;
-worm, -mel'on, -shaped, -shell,
-tree, gourd'seed-suck'er, a fish.
gour met' (gōōr mä' or gōōr'met).
gou'rou-nut (gōō'rōō-).
gout, -ish, -y, -i ly, -i ness, -weed,
-wort, -stone, gout'y-gall.
Gouv er neur' (gōōv er nōōr'),
vil. N. Y.
gov'ern (guv'-), -a ble, -ble ness,
-bil'i ty, -erned, -ern ing, -ess,
-ment, -men'tal, -or ship.
gov'ern or, -block, -gen'er al,
-valve, gou'ver nänte' (gōō'-).
gown, -ing, -boy, -man, gowned,
gown-piece.
grab, -bing, -ber, grabbed, grab-
all, -bag, -game, -hook, -i ron,
-line.
grab'ble, -bled, -bling.
Grac'chus (grăk'us), Rom. statesman.
grace, -ful, -ful ly, -ful ness, -less,
-less ly, -less ness, graced, gra'-
cing, the Graces, Myth.; grace'-
hoop, -note, -stroke, -term, -wife.
grac'ile (grăs'il), gra cil'i ty.
grā ci ō'sō.
grā'cious, -ly, -ness.
grā'date, -dā'ted, -ting, -da'tim,
-da'tion, -tion al, grăd'a to ry.
grade, grād'ed, -ing, -er, grā'di-
ent, grăd'ing-in stru ment, -plow,
-scrāp'er, -shov'el.
gra di'no (grä dē'nō) pl. -nos
(-nōz).
grä'dō.
grad'u al, -ly, -ness, -ist, -al'i ty.
grad'u ate, -ship, -ā'ted, -a ting,
-and', -ā'tor, -to'ry, -ā'tion,
-tion-en'gine.
Græme (grām), Scotch poet.
grāf.
grăff, -age.
grăft, -age, -ed, -er, -ing, grăft'-hy'-
brid, -hy brid i zā'tion (-hī-).
graft'ing-chis'el, -knife, -saw,
-tool, -wax.
Grā'ham (-am), a diet reformer;
-ize, -ized, -i'zing, -ism, -īte, G.
bread.
grāil, a cup or chalice.
grail or graille, a file.

grain, -age, -er, -ing, -y, -fields,
grained, grains'man.
grain'-al'co hol, -bin, -bīnd'er,
-bruis'er, -car, -clean'er, -cra'-
dle, -damp'er, -door, -dri'er or
-dry'er, -farm, -fork, -gage
-har'vest er, -hull'er, -lĕath'er,
-me'ter, -mill, -mois'ten er,
-moth, -oil, -rake, -sack'er,
-scale, -scour'er, -screen, -sep'-
a ra tor, -shov'el, -soap, -stăff,
-test'er, -tin, -tree, -wee'vil,
-wheel.
grain'ing-board, -col'ors, -plate,
-tool.
gram or gramme, -cen'ti me ter,
-dē gree', -me'ter.
grä'ma-grăss.
gram'mar, -ma'ri an, -an ism,
-mar less, -mat'ic, -ic al, -al ly,
-al ness, -mat'i cism, -cize,
cized, ci'zing, ma tol'a try.
gram'o phone.
gram'pus.
grăn'a ry, -bee'tle.
grand, -ly, -ness, -aunt, -child,
-daugh'ter, -fa'ther, -ther ly,
-mä, -măm mä' or -mä mä' (or
-mä'mä), -moth'er, -er ly,
-neph'ew (-nĕf'- or -nĕv'-),
-nièce, -pä or -pa pa (-pä pä' or
-pä'pä), -par'ent, -ent age, -sire,
-son, -un'cle, -père' (grŏń'pâr').
grand'-du'cal, -duke, an owl;
-guard, armor; -piece, armor;
grand'fä'ther-long-legs, Grand'
Bank'er, g. duke.
gran'dăm or -dāme.
gran dee', -ship.
gran'deûr.
gran dil'o quent, -ly, -quence,
-quous (-kwŭs).
gran di ose' (-ōs'), -ly, -ō'so,
-os'i ty.
Grand pré', de (dĕ grŏń prä'), Fr.
navigator.
gran'drills.
grănge, grăn'ger, -ger ism, -ger-
īte, -ize, -ized, -ī'zer, -ī'zing.
grăn'īte, gra nit'ic, -ic al, -nit'i fy,
-fy ing, -fied, -fī ca'tion, -i form,
gran'īte ware, -ax, -por'phy ry.
gra niv'o rous.

grăn′ny, -knot *or* grăn′ny's knot. *grä′no,* pl. *-ni* (-nē).

grănt, -ed, -ing, -er, -a ble. In law, grant′or and gran tee′.

gran′u la, *pl.* -læ, -u lar, -lar ly, -lăr′i ty, -u late, -lā′ted, -lā′ting, -lā′tive, -lā′tor, -lā′tion, gran′ulā′ting-ma chine′.

gran′ule, -u lif′er ous, -u lose (-lōs), -u lous, gran′ule-cells.

gran′u līte, -lit′ic.

gran′u lize, -lized, -lī′zing.

grăn′za, *pl.* -zas (-zàz).

grape, -less, -let, -flow′er, a plant; -fruit, a tree and its fruit; -stone, -vine, grăp′y, -er y.

grape-cure, -fern, -hy′a cinth, -juice, -louse, -mil′dew, -root, -rot, -shot, -su′gar, -tree, -trel′lis.

graph′ic, -al, -al ly, -al ness, -ics.

graph′īte, gra phit′ic.

gra phol′o gy, -o gist, graph olog′ic al (-loj′-), -o met′ic, -ic al, -met′rics, gra phom′e ter.

graph′o phone, -phon′ic, -o scope, -o spasm, -o type, -typ′ic.

grap′nel, -plant.

grap′ple, -pled, -pler, -pling, grap′ple-plant, -shot, grap′pling-i ron, -line, -tŏngs.

grăsp, -a ble, -er, -ing, -ing ly, -ing ness, -less.

grăss, -er, -ing, -y, -i ness, -less, -chat, a bird; -finch, -man, -nut, -quit, a bird.

grăss′-bar, -băss, -bird, -bleach′-ing, -cloth, -cut ter, -drake, -em broid′er y, -green, -grown, -hand, -har′vest er, -land, -like, -lin en, -moth, -oil, -par′ra keet, -pink, -plot, -plov′er, -seed, -snake, -snipe, -spi′der, -sponge, -ta ble, -tree, -vetch, -war′bler, -wid′ow, -wid′ow er, -worm, -wrack. Grass′-week.

Grasse (grås), t. Fr.

grăss′hop per, -beam, -en′gine, -lark, -mouse, -spar row, -warbler.

grate, grăt′ed, -ing, -ing ly, -er, grate′-bar, -room, -sur′face.

grate′ful, -ly, -ness, grăt′i tude.

Gra ti a′no (grä she ä′nō), one of Shakspeare's characters.

grat′i cule, gra tic u lā′tion.

grat′i fy, -ing, -ing ly, -fied, -fi′er, -fĭ cā′tion.

gra tin′ (-tăṅ′), grat′i nate, -nā′ted, -nā′ting.

Gra′ti ot (grăsh′ĭ ot), co. Mich.

grā′tis.

gra tu′i tous, -ly, -ness, -i ty.

grat′u la to′ry, -lā′tion.

gra vā′men, pl. *-vā′mens* or *-văm′-i na.*

grave, -less, -ly, -ness, -stone, -yard, -clothes, -dig′ger, -robber.

grave, *v.,* graved, grăv′ing, -er, grave′-dock, -piece.

grav′el, -ing *or* -ling, -ly, -root, a plant; -blind, -car, -mine, -pit, -plant, -stone, -weed.

Grave lot′ (gräv lō′), Fr. engraver.

graves *or* greaves, refuse; sediment.

Graves (grăv), a wine.

grav′i tate, -tā′ted, -ting, -tive, -tā′tion, -tion al, -al ly.

grav′i ty, -bat′ter y, -fault, -rail′-road, -so lu′tion.

grā′vure.

grā′vy, -boat.

gray *or* grey, -ish, -ish ness, -ly, -ness, -back, a person; a duck; -beard, a person; -bird, -coat, a person; -fish, -head, a person; -lord, a fish; -stone, -wăck′e (*or* -wăk), -weth′er, -bear, a spider; -fly, -wash′ing, -whăl′er.

graze, grăz′er, -ing, gra′zier (-zher), grazed, grăz′ing-ground.

gra′zi o′so (grä′tsē ō′sō).

grease (grēs), *n.,* -wood, a plant; -box, -cock, -cup, -jack, -pot.

grease (grēz *or* grēs), *v.,* greased, greas′ing, -y, -i ly, -i ness, -er. Greas′er *or* greas′er, a Mexican.

greăt, -ly, -ness, -coat, -head, a duck; -aunt, -eyed, -fruit′ed, -grand′fa ther, -heart′ed, -uṅ cle, -great-grand son.

grēaves, greaved.

grēbe, -cloth.

Grē′cize *or* -cian ize, -ized, -i′zing.

Gre′co-Bac′tri an, -Lat′in -Ro′-man, -Turk′ish, Gre col′a try.

grecque (grĕk).

Grē′cian, G. bend, G. fire, G. horse, G. knot, G. leath er, G. net′ting, Greek.

greed, -y, -i ly, -i ness.

gree′gree.

green, -er y, -ing, -ish, -ish ness, -let, -ness, -bane, a fish; -bird, -bone, a fish; -bri′er, -broom, a plant; -cha′fer, an insect; -finch, -fish, -fly, -gill, an oyster; -gro′cer, -hĕad, a bird; -heärt, a tree; -horn, a person; -house, -room, a room in a theater; -sand, a sandstone; -sauce, a plant; -shank, a bird; -sick, -sick′ness, -stone, -sward, -weed, -wing, a duck; -withe, a plant; -wood, a forest.

green′-bag, -beard′ed, -coat, -cod, a fish; -corn, the egg-capsules of a mollusk; -la′ver, a seaweed; -rot, -snake, -stall, -stick, -tail.

green băss, g. book, g. cheese, g. cloth, g. corn, g. sir′up, g. stur′geon, g. ta′ble, g. tar, g. wa ter.

green′back, Green′back er, -back-ism.

Green′wich, vil. Ct.; tp. N. J.; tp. N. Y. (Grĕn′ij); t. Eng.

greet, -ed, -er, -ing.

greeve, -ship.

gre gā′ri an, -ism, -ri ous, -ous ly, -ous ness.

grei′sen (-sn).

gre lot′ (-lō′).

gre nāde′, -nā′do, gren a diĕr′.

gren′a din.

gren a dine′ (-dēn′).

grès (grā *or* grà).

gres sō′ri al, -ri ous.

Gré′vy′ (grā′vē′), Pres. Fr. repub.

grey′hound (grā′-).

grid′dle, -dled, -dler, -dling, -cake.

grīde, grid′ed, -ing.

grid′i ron.

grief, -mus′cle, -shot.

Gries (grē), mt. Switz.

griēve, grieved, griev′ing, -ing ly, -er, -ous, -ous ly, -ous ness.

griff, a piece of machinery; a rocky glen.

griff *or* gri′ffe, a mulatto.

griffe (grĭf), a term used in architecture and in wine making.

grif′fin, *Myth.;* -age, -fin ish, -fin ism, grif′fin-male, -vul′ture.

Grif′fon, a person; grif′fon, a dog.

grif′fon age (*or* -äzh′).

grĭll, -ing, grilled, gril lade′, -lage, grill′-room.

grille (grĭl *or* grēl).

gril lé′ (gre lyā′).

grĭlse.

grim, -mer, -mest, -ly, -ness, -grib-ber.

grĭ măce′, -maced′.

grĭ măl′kin (*or* -măl′-).

grime, grimed, grīm′ing, -y, -i ly, -i ness.

grin, -ning, grinned, grin′ning-mus′cle.

grĭnd, -ing, -ing ly, -er, -er y, -stone, ground.

grind′ing-bed, -bench, -block, -clamp, -frame, -lāthe, -ma-chine′, -mill, -plate, -roll, -slip, -spheres, -tooth, -vat, -wheel, grind′stone-grit.

grĭŋ′go.

grĭ otto′.

grip, -ping, -per, gripped, grip′-man, -sack, -car, -grăss, -pul′-ley, -yard, grip′ping-wheel.

grīpe, griped, grīp′ing, -ing ly, -er.

grippe (grĭp), an influenza.

Grī′qua (grē′-), *pl.* -quas.

gri saille′ (grē zāl′ *or* -zā′y′).

grīse (grīs).

Grĭ sĕl′da, one of Chaucer's characters.

grĭ sette′ (-zĕt′).

gris′ly (grĭz′-), -li ness.

grĭ′son, a monkey.

Gri sons′ (grē zung′ *or* grē′zŏn′).

grist, -mill.

gris′tle (-l), -tled, -tly, -tli ness.

Gris′wold (griz′ŭld), Amer. auth.

grit, -ted, -ting, -ty, -ti ness, -stone, -cell, -rock.

---

nŏt, nôr, ūse, ŭp, ûrn, etüde, fōōd, fŏŏt, aŋger, boṅmot, thus, Bach.

griz'zle (-zl), -zled, -zling, -zly.
grōan, -er, -ing, groaned, groan'-
ing-malt.
grōat, a coin.
grōats, hulled oats.
grō'cer, -y, -y man, -y-store.
grog, -ger y, -gy, -gi ly, -gi ness,
grog'-blos'som, -shop.
grŏg'ram, -yarn.
groin, -er y, -ing, groined, groin-
arch, -cen'ter ing, -point, -rib.
grŏm'met or -et, g. wad (wŏd).
grōōm, -er, -ing, groomed,
grooms'man, groom-grub'ber,
-por'ter.
grōōve, grooved, grōōv'er, -ing,
-y, groove'-board, -fel'low, -ram,
-roll'er, groov'ing-plane.
grōpe, groped, grŏp'er, -ing,
-ing ly.
gros (grō), g. de Tours (grō dè
tōōr), gros'grāin (grō'-).
grŏs'bĕak.
gro'schen (-shen or grŏsh'en).
grōss, -ly, -ness, -hĕad'ed.
Gros Ven'tres (grō vän'tr).
grō tesque' (-tĕsk'), -ly, -ness.
Gro'ti us (-shĭ-), Dutch jurist;
-ti an (-shĭ an).
Grot'te (grŏt'tā), vil. It.
grŏt'to, pl. -toes (-toz), grŏt,
grot'to-work.
Grou'chy', de (dĕ grōō'she'), Fr.
gen.; grouch'y, sulky.
ground, -age, -ed, -ed ly, -er, -ing,
-less, -less ly, -less ness, -ling,
-ber'ry, -nut, -sill, -ways, -work.
ground'-aŋ'gling, -an'nu al, -ash,
-au'ger, -bai'liff, -bait, -beam,
-bee'tle, -bird, -chĕr'ry, -cis tus,
-cloth, -cock, -cuck'oo, -cy'-
press, -dove, -down, n., -fäst,
-feed er, -finch, -fir, -fish,
-game, -gru, -gud'geon, -hem'-
lock, -hog, -hold, -horn'bill,
-ice, -i vy, -joint, -joist, -keep'-
er, -lay'er, -line, -liv'er wort,
-liz'ard, -mail, -mark'er, -mäss,
-mold, -mul'let.
ground'nest, -net, -niche (-nich),
-par ra keet', -pea, -pearl, -pig,
-pĭ'geon, -pine, -plan, -plane,
-plate, -plot, -plum, -rat, -rent,

-rob'in, -roll'er, -rope, -scrāp'er,
-scratch'er, -sea, -seat, -shark,
-sloth, -sluice, -snake, -spar'-
row, -squir'rel, -star'ling, -strake,
-swell, -ta'ble, -tac'kle, -throw,
-thrush, -tim'bers, -wheel,
ground'ing-tool, ground'sel-tree,
ground floor, g. form.
group (grōōp), -age, -er, -ing,
grouped, group'-spring.
grouse, -pĭ'geon.
grout, -er, -ing, -head, a person;
-ale, -hĕad'ed.
grŏv'el (-l), -eled or -elled, -el ing
or -el ling, -el er or -el ler.
grōw, -a ble, -er, -ing, -ing ly,
grew, grown, grown'-up, grow'-
ing-cell, -slide.
growl, -er, -ing, -ing ly, growled.
grōwth, -ful, growth-form.
gro'zing-i ron.
grub, -ber, -ber y, -bing, grubbed,
grub'worm, -ax, -hook, -plank,
-saw, -stake, -time, Grub street,
grub'bing-ax, -hoe.
grudge, grudged, grudg'er, -er y,
-ing, -ing ly, -ing ness.
gru'el.
gru e'so (-ā'sō).
grue'some or grew'-, -ness.
gruff, -ly, -ness.
gru'-gru, g. pälm, g. worm.
grum, -ness.
grum'ble, -bled, -bler, -bling,
-bling ly.
grump'y, grump'i ly, -i ness, -ish.
grun'dy, a metal; Grun'dy, a
critic of society; -di fied, -dy ism.
grunt, -ed, -er, -ing, -ing ly,
-ling, grunt'ing ox.
grup'po (grōōp'pō).
Guä dä lä jä'rä (-lä hä'rä), prov.
Sp.; c. Mex.
Guä däl cä zär' (-kä sär'), t. Mex.
Guä däl qui vir' (-kē vēr'), r. Sp.
Gua da lupe' (gạ da loop'), co.
Tex.; mt. Sp.; t. Uruguay.
Gua de loupe' (gạ da loop'), Fr.
West India colony.
Guä di ana (gwä dĕ ä'nä), r. Sp.
Gua'na (gwä'nä), isl. W. I.
guä'nä, a lizard; a cloth.
guä nä'cŏ.

---

fāte, făt, fär, fạll, fâre, fâst, sofâ, mēte, mĕt, hêr, ĭce, ĭn, nōte,

Gua na jay' (gwä nä hǐ'), t. Cuba.
Gua na jua'to (gwä nä hwä'tō), state Mex.
guä'nǒ, *pl.* -nos (-nōz), gua'nize, -nized, -nǐ'zing, gua'no-mix'er, -sow'er.
guä'ō.
guä rä'chä.
guǎr an tee', *pl.* -tees' (-tēz'), one who receives a guaranty, guǎr'-an tor, -an ty, a warrant, *pl.* -ties (-tǐz), guǎr an tee', *v.*, -teed', -tee'ing.
guä rä'po.
guä rau'nä.
guärd, -ed, -ed ly, -ed ness, -ing, -a ble, -ant, -less, -ship, protection, -fish, guards'man.
guärd-boat, -book, -brush, -cell, -chain, -chäm'ber, -du ty, -fin-ger, -flag, -house, -i'rons, -lock, -mount'ing, -pile, -plate, -rail, -rein, -ring, -room, -ship, a vessel; -tent.
guard'i an (*or* -yan), -less, -ship, -cell, g. än'gel.
Gua tē mä'la (ga-), Cent. Amer.; -mä'lan *or* -lǐ an.
guä'va.
Gua vi a're (gwä vē ä'rä), r. Colombia, S. A.
guä'yä.
Guay a can' (gwī ä kän'), vil. Chile.
Guay a'ma (gwī ä'mä), t. Porto Rico.
Guay a quil' (gwī ä kēl'), c. Ecuador.
gu'bat.
gǔ'ber na tō'ri al.
gud'geon (-jun).
Gue'ber (gē'-). See *Gheber.*
Guelf *or* Guelph, -ic, -ism.
gue'lis (gwä'lēs).
Guelph (gwĕlf), c. Ontario.
guer'don (ger'-), -a ble, -er, -ing, -less, -doned.
Gué rin (gä rǎṅ'), Fr. surgeon.
gué rite (gä rēt' *or* gĕr'ǐt).
guern'sey (gern'zy), a garment.
Guern'sey (gern'zy), isl. Eng.; co. O.; G. blue, G. cow, G. ear-shell, G. lil'y.

guer ril'la (gêr-).
Gues clin' (gä klǎṅ'), Fr. officer.
guess (gĕs), -a ble, -er, -ing, -ing ly, -work, guessed, guess'-rope, -warp.
guest, -ling, -ănt, -chäm'ber, -fly, -moth, -room, -rope, -wasp.
Gueux (gê).
guf faw', -ing, -fawed'.
Gug liel'mi (gōōl yĕl'mē), It. composer.
gui'da (gē'dä).
guide (gīd), guid'a ble, -ance, -er, -ing, -ing ly, guide'crǎft, -less, -way, -bar, -block, -book, -eye, -fĕath'er, -flag, -pile, -post, -pul'ley, -rail, -roll'er, -ropes, -screw, -tube, -yoke.
Gui'di (gwē'dē), It. poet.
Gui'do (gwē'dō), It. gen.; -dō'ni an.
Gui'do Re'ni (gwē'dō rā'nē), It. painter.
guï'don.
Guignes, de (dĕ gēn'), Fr. orientalist.
guild, -hall, -house, -ale, -broth'-er, -rent.
guil'der (gil'-).
guile (gil), -ful, -ful ly, -ful ness, -less, -less ly, -less ness.
guil laume' (gēl yōm'), a tool.
Guil'laume' (gē'yōm'), Fr. painter.
Guil'lau'met' (gē'yō'mä'), Fr. painter.
Guil'le met' (gē'yĕ mä'), Fr. artist.
Guil'le min' (gē'yĕ mǎṅ' *or* gĕl'-mǎṅ'), Fr. scientist.
guil'le mot (gǐl'-).
guil'loche' (gē'yōsh' *or* gǐl lŏsh').
Guil'lon' (gē'yōṅ'), Fr. auth.
guil'lo tine (gǐl'lo tēn), *n.*, -tine' (-tēn'), *v.*, -tined', -tin'ing, -tine'ment.
guills (gǐlz).
guilt (gilt), -y, -i ly, -i ness, -less, -less ly, -less ness, guilt'-sick.
guimp (gǐmp).
gui nä'ra (gē-).
guin'ea (gǐn'ē), -boat, -cock, -corn, -drop per, -edge, -fowl, -goose, -grains, -grǎss, -green, -hen, -pig, -worm.

Guin'ea (gĭn'ē), Afr., -man, a ship; -e an, Guin'ea-cloth, G. hog, G. peach, G. pep'per, G. plum.

Guin'e vĕre (gwin'-), Queen to King Arthur.

gui pŭre' (gē-).

gui'ra (gwē-).

Guise, de (dĕ gwēz'), Fr. states-man.

Guise (gēz), t. Fr.

guise (gīz), guised, guis'er, -ing.

guĭ tär', -ist, -play'er, -string.

Gui'zot' (gē'zō' or gwē'zō'), Fr. hist.

gū'la, pl. -læ or -lås (-låz), -lar.

gulch.

gul'den (gŏŏl'-), -head.

gūles, gūl'y.

gulf, -y, -weed.

gul'gul.

gull, -er, -er y, gull'-billed, -catch'er, a bird; -chäs'er, a bird.

gul'let, -er, -ing, -lar val, -saw, gul'let ing-file, -press, -stick.

gul'lĭ ble, -bil'i ty.

gul'ly, -ing, -lĭed, gul'ly mouth, a pitcher; -drain, -hunt'er, -răk'er, -squall, -wĭnd.

gu'loc (gŏŏ'-).

gulp, -er, -ing, gulped.

gum, -mer, -ming, -mous, -my, -mi ness, gummed, gum'wood, a tree; gum'-an'i mal, -boil, -cis'tus, -drop, -game, -plant, -pot, -rash, -stick, -tree, -wa'-ter, -wood, wood of the gum tree; g. dy'na mīte (dī'-), g. res'in, gum'-top tree.

Gum'mer e, Amer. math.

gun', -ning, -ner, -ner y, -boat, -cot ton, -mäk er, -man, -pow-der, -shot, -smith.

gun'-bar'rel, -bat'ter y, -brig, -cap tain, -car riage, -case, -deck, -fire, -flint, -gear, -har poon', -i ron, -lift, -lock, -met al, -mon ey, -pen'du lum, -pit, -port, -reach, -room, -search'er, -shy, -slide, -sling, -stick, -stock, -stock'er, -tac kle, -wad, -wad ding, -work.

gun'ner-fluke, gun'ner y-licu ten'-ant, -ship.

gun'ning-boat, gun'pow der-man-u fac'tory, -mill, -pa'per, -press, -van.

gun'ny-cloth, g. bags.

Gun'ter's chain, G. line, G. quad rant, G. scale.

Gun'ther (gün'ter), Gr. philos.

gun'wăle.

gur'gle, -gled, -glet, -gling, -gling ly, -gi tä'tion (-jĭ-).

gur'let.

gur'nard.

Gu row'ski (gŏŏ rŏv'skē), Polish patriot.

gŭr'rah.

gŭr'ry, -ing, -rĭed, gur'ry-bait, -butt, -fish, -ground, -shark.

gu'ru (gŏŏ'rŏŏ), -nut.

gush, -er, -ing, -ing ly, -y, gushed.

gus'set, -nee'dle, -plate, -stay.

gust, -y.

gust'a tive, -a to'ry.

gŭs'to, -to'so.

gut, -ted, -ting, -wort, gut'-formed, -hook, -length, -scrăp'er -weed.

Gu'ten berg (gŏŏ'ten bĕrg), Ger. inventor of printing.

gut'ta-per'cha, -pu'tih (-pŏŏ'tĭ), -ram'bong, -shĕ'ä, -sing'ga rip, -sun'dek, -tä'ban, -trap.

gut ta'lim.

gut'ter, -y, -ing, -tered, gut'ter-blood, -board'ing, -cock. -flag, -hole, -ledge, -man, -snipe, -spout, -stick, -tee'tan.

gut'tu la, pl. -læ, -tu late.

guy (gī), -er, -ing, guyed, guy'-rope.

Guy an dotte' (gī an dŏt'), r. W. Va.

Guy'on (gī'on), Fr. authoress.

Guy'ot' (gē'ō'), Swiss naturalist.

Guz man'-Blan'co (gŏŏth män'-blän'kō), Pres. Venezuela.

guz'zle, -zled, -zler, -zling.

guz'zy.

Gy'ges (jī'jēz), King of Lydia.

gym nä'si um (-zĭ um or -zhĭ-um), -si al, -si arch (-zĭ ark), -si ast, gym'nast, -nast'ic, -ic al,

-al ly, -nas'ti cize, -cized, -cī'-
zing, -nas'tics.

gyn e col'o gy   (jin-),   -o gist,
-co log'ic al, -cō nǐ'tis, -cop'a thy,
-co păth'ic.

Gyo'ma (dyō'mŏ), vil. Hung.

Gyon'gyos' (dyên'dyêsh'), t. Hung.

Gyon'gyo sy (dyên'dyê shē), Hung.
poet.

Gyp'sey (jǐp'-). , See Gipsy.

gyp'sum (jǐp'-), gyp'sous, gyp'sum-
fur'nace.

Gyp'sy. See Gipsy.

gy'rate   (jī'-),   -rā'ted,   -rā'ting,
-ral,   -ra tō'ry, -rā'tion, -tion al,
gyr'o man cy (jǐr'-).

gyre'-car'lin (gīr'-).

gyr'fal'con (jêr'fạ'kn).   See gerfalcon.

gy'ro scope (jī'-), -scŏp'ic.

gy'ro stat (jī'-), -stat'ic.

Gy'ro wetz (gē'rŏ vĕts),   Bohem.
composer.

Gyu'la (dyō͞o'lŏ), t. Hung.

Gyu'lai (dyō͞o'lī), Hung. gen.

gyve (jīv), pl. gyves.

H

H-brånch, -drill, -piece.

Ha băk'kuk (or hăb'-), Bib.
hä'be as cor'pus.

hab'er dash er, -y.

ha bīl'i ment, -ed.

ha bil'i tate, -tā'ted, -tā'ting, -tā'-
tor, -tā'tion.

hab'it, -ed, -ing, -i tude, -a ble,
-a ble ness,   -a bil'i ty,   -ant,
hab'i tat, -tā'tion, ha bit'u al,
-al ly, -al ness, -u ate, -ā'ted,
-ā'ting, -ā'tion, ha bi tu ṡ' (habit'u ā' or ȧ be tō͞o ā').

hab'it-cloth, -māk'er, -shirt.
hä'cǐ ĕn'da (or ä'thē ãn'da).

hack, -er, -ing, hacked, hack'-
ber'ry, -bolt,   a   bird; -man,
-băr'row, -file, -ham'mer, -i ron,
-trap, -watch, hack'ing-seat.

hack'a more.

hack'but.

hack'ee.

hack'er y.

hac'kle,   -kled,   -kling,   -kler,
hac'kle-bar,   -fĕath'er,   -fly,
hac'kling-ma chine'.

hack'ma tack.

hack'ney, -man, -ing, -neyed (-nid),
hack'ney-coach.

Hă'dad, Bib.

had'do.

had'dock, -er, -dock-tea.

Hă'des (-dēz).

Hăd'ith.

Hăd'lăi (or -lä ǐ), Bib.

Hä'fiz.

hâft, -ed, -er, -ing, hâft'-pipe.

hag, -ging, -gish, -gish ly, hagged,
hag'her'ry, -fish, -weed, -gull,
-mouth, -rid'den, -stăff, -ta per,
-tracks, -worm, hag's-tooth.

Hä'gen, Fiction.

Hăg'gă I, Bib.

hag'gard, -ly, -ness.

hag'gle, -gled, -gler, -gling.

hă'gi ar chy   (-ji-),   -gi oc'ra cy,
-gi o graph,   -og'ra phal,   -ra-
pher, -ra phy, -o graph'ic, -ol'a-
try, -ol'o gy, -ogist, -o log'ic, -ic al.

Hague'nau' (äg'nō'), t. Ger.

hä'-hä', laughter; hä'hä' (or hä'hä'),
a fence or ditch.

Hai dee' (hī-),   a character in
Byron's Don Juan.

haik (hīk).

hai'kwän' (hī'-).

hâil, -ing, hailed, hail'stone, -fel'-
low, -storm.

Hai năn' (hī-), isl. China.

Hai'naut' (hä'nō'), prov. Belg.

hâir, -y, -i ness, -less, haired,
hair'brained, -breadth, -cloth,
-pin, -streak, a butterfly; -tail,
a fish; -worm.

hâir'-bird,   -brack'et,   -brush,
-bulb, -cell, -clam, -com'pass es,
-dress, -dress'er, -dye, -eel,
-fĕath'er, -fol'li cle, -gland,
-grăss, -knob, -lace, -li'chen
(-ken), -line, -net, -oil, -pick'er,

nŏt, nôr, ūse, ŭp, ûrn, etüde, fō͞od, fŏŏt, aŋger, boṅmot, thus, Bach.

-pow'der, -quag, -sack, -salt,
-seal, -shaped, -sheath, -space,
-split'ter, -spring, -star, -stroke,
-trig'ger, -weav'ing, -work.

hâir'branch-tree, hair'cap-moss,
hair'cup-plow, hair'trig ger-
flow er, hair'y bait, a worm;
-y crown, a bird; -y head, a
bird; hair's breadth.

hake, haked, hāk'ing, hakes'dame,
a fish, hake's-tooth.

Ha'las' (hŏ'lŏsh'), t. Hung.

hăl'berd (or hŏl'-), -ier', -man,
-head'ed, -shaped, -weed.

hal'cy on (-sĭ-), -on'ic, -ō nĭne',
-ō nīte', -ō noid'.

Hal cy'o ne (-sī'-), Myth.

hāle, -ness, -wort, hāl'ing, haled.

half (häf), -beak, a fish; -bill, a
bird; a fish; -pen'ny.

half-ape, -back, -baked, -belt,
-bent, -bind'ing, -blood, -bloom,
-board, -board'er, -boot, -box,
-breed, -bril'liant, -broth'er,
-câste, -cent, -cheek, -chess,
-cock, -crown, -deck, -dime,
-dol'lar, -ea'gle, -face, -far'-
thing, -fĕath'er, -guin'ea, -hitch,
-hol'i day, -hose, -hour, -hour'-
ly, -length, -line.

half.mâsk, -mâst, -meas'ure,
-moon, -mount'ing, -mourn'ing,
-pace, -pay, a., -pike, -port,
-price, a. and adv., -prin'ci pal,
-re lief', -round, -roy'al, -shell,
-sis'ter, -sole, -sov'er eign, -stitch,
-stop, -stuff, -tan'gent, -thought,
-throw, -tide, -tim'ber, -tint,
-tone, -tongue, -trap, -trav'el,
-truth, -vir'tue, -way, -wit,
-yard, -yarn, -year, -year'ly.

hälf'-and-hälf', hälf'-seas-o ver,
hälf' dis'tance, h. note, h. pay,
n., h. price, n., h. rest, h. step.

hal'i but (hŏl'-), -broom, -slime.

hall, -way, -house, -mark, h.
Bi ble.

hal'la ba lōō'. See hullabaloo.

Häl'lĕ, c. Prus.

hăl le lu'iah or -jah (-lōō'ya).

Hăl lŏ'esh, Bib.

hăl lōō' or hĕl lō' or hŏl'lō (or -lō')
or hŭl lō', hăl lōō'ing, -lōōed'.

hăl'lōw, -ing, -lōwed.

Hăl low e'en', Hal low-eve', -fair,
-tide.

hal lū'cĭ nā tor, -to'ry, -nā'tion.

hă'lo, pl. -los (-lōz).

halt, -ed, -er, -ing, -ing ly.

hal'ter, -ing, -tered, hal'ter-
breāk.

hälve (häv), halved, hälv'ing,
hälve-net, hälv'ing-belt.

hăl'yard, -rack.

Ham, Bib., -īte, -it'ic. Ham
(ŏñ), vil. Fr.

ham, -string, n., -bee'tle, -knife.

ham'a dry'ad, pl. -ads or -dry'-
a des (-dēz).

Ha ma mat su' (hä mä mät sōō'),
t. Japan.

Hā'man, Bib.

hăme, -fas'ten er, -lock, -ring,
-strap.

Ha mĭl'car, Carth. gen.

ham'let, Ham'let, in Shakspeare.

ham'mer, -ing, -er, -mered,
ham'mer head, a fish; a bird;
-man, -wort.

ham'mer-ax, -beam, -blow, -cap,
-catch'er, -cloth, -dressed, -fish,
-hard'en, -head, the head of a
hammer; -helve, -joint, -mark,
-nail, -oys'ter, -pick, -pike,
-scale, -sedge, -shell, -spring,
-stone, -tail, -tongs, -wrought.

Häm'mer fĕst, t. Norw.

hăm'mock, -bat'ten, -cloth,
-clues, -net'tings, -rack.

Hăm'o nah (or ha mō'-), Bib.

ham'per, -ing, -pered.

ham'shac'kle, -kled, -kling.

ham'ster.

ham'string, v., -ing, -strung or
-stringed.

Ha nan'e el (or hăn'a neel), Bib.

Ha nă'nĭ (or hăn'-), Bib.

han'a ster.

Hä'nau (-nou), t. Prus.

hănd, -ed, -ing, -er, -ful, -less,
hand'ball, -bill, a circular,
-book, -brĕadth, -cuff, -fish,
-hold, -līn'ing, -locked, -maid,
-maid'en, -screw, -spike, -spike'-
man, -spring, -stâff, -while,
-worm, -wrist, -write, -wrīt'ing.

---

fāte, făt, fär, făll, fâre, fâst, sofå, mēte, mĕt, hêr, īce, ĭn, nōte,

hǎnd'-an'vil, -bag, -bag'gage, -bǎr'row, -bell, -bill, an implement; -bŏr'row, -bōw, -brace, -bridge, -buc kler, -can non, -car, -cart, -claw, -di rec'tor, -drop, -flail, -float, -fly, -foot'-ed, -fork, -frame, -gal lop, -gear, -glǎss, -gout, -gre nade', -grip, -gripe, -guard, -guide, -gyve (-jīv), -ham'mer, -har-mon'i ca, -heat, -hole, -hook.

hand'-i'ron, -lan'guage, -lāthe, -lĕad, -let ter, -lĕv'er, -line, -list, -loom, -made, -mill, -mĭr ror, -mold, -mon'ey, -mor'tar, -or'-chis (-kis), -or'gan, -pa'per, -plant, -play, -plow, -post, -pot, -press, -prom'ise, -pump, -punch, -quill, -rail, -run'ning, -sail, -sale, -saw, -screen, -shake, -spear, -strap, -tar get, -taut, -ten nis, -tight, -vise, -waled, -warm er, -wheel, -work, -wrought.

hǎnd'flow er-tree, hand'maid-moth, hand'saw-fish, hand-to-hand, a., hand-to-mouth, a., hand's breadth, hand's turn.

hand'ker chief (haŋ'ker chĭf).

han'dle, -dled, dling, dler, han'dle-net.

hand'some (hǎn'sum), -ly, -ness, -som er, -som est.

han'dy, -di er, -di est, han'dy-bil'ly, -dan'dy, han'dy man.

Hǎ'nes (-nēz), *Bib.*

hang, -ing, -er, -a ble, hung *or* hanged, hang'bird, -dog, a., -man, -nail, -nest, a bird.

hang'-choice, -nest, a nest, -worm, hang'er-board, -on.

hang'ing-bird, -guard, -ma chine', -moss, -nee'dle, -peǎr, -post, -stile, -tie, -tool.

haŋ'gle.

ha nif' (hä nēf'), hǎn'if it ism.

haŋk, -worst'ed (-wōōst'ed).

han'ker, -ing, -ing ly, -kered.

Hä nŏ'i (-nō'ē), c. Indo-China.

hǎnse, han se at'ic, hanse-house.

Hǎnse, Hanse towns, Han se at'ic league.

hǎn'som (-sum), h. cab.

hǎp, -ping, -less, -less ly, happed, hap-warm.

hap'haz'ard.

hap'pen (-pn), -ing, -pened.

hap'py, -pi ly, -pi ness, hap py-go-luck y.

ha pu'ku (hä pōō'kōō).

hä'rä-ki'ri (-kē'rĭ).

Hǎ'ran, *Bib.*

ha rangue' (-rang'), -rangued', -rangu'ing (-rang'ing), -rangue'-ful, -rangu'er (-rang'er).

hǎr'ass, -er, -ing, -ment, -assed.

har'bin ger (-jer), -ing, -gered, har'bin ger-of-spring, a plant.

har'bor, -age, -er, -less, -ing, -bored.

har'bor-dues, -gas'ket, -light, -log, -mǎs'ter, -reach, -seal, -watch.

hard, -er, -est, -ly, -ness, -bake, a sweetmeat; -beam, a tree; -bill, a bird; -hack, a plant; -hay, a plant; -head, a coin; a fish; -mouth, a fish; -ship, -tack, a duck; -biscuit; -tail, a fish; -ware, -ware man, -wood, a tree.

hard'-bit'ted, -fa'vored, -fea'-tured, -fern, -fish, -fist'ed, -fought, -grǎss, -hand ed, -head ed, -heart'ed, -pan, -pear, a tree; -port, a., -shell, -vis'aged, -wood, a., hard fin'ish, h. met'al, h. wood, a solid wood.

hard'en (-n), -er, -ing, -ened, hard'en ing-fur'nace, -kiln, -ma-chine', -skin.

har'dy, -di ly, -di ness, -di hood.

hȧre, -brain, a person; -brained, -foot, a plant; -hound, -lip, a fish; a divided lip; -stane.

hȧre'-eyed, -foot, like a hare's foot; -kan ga rōō', -this'tle.

hȧre's'-bane, -beard, -cole wort, -ear, -foot, -let'tuce (-lĕt'tis), -pal'ace, -pars'ley, -tail.

Har hǎ'iah (-ya *or* -hä ī'ah), *Bib.*

hǎr'i cot, -bean.

hark, -en, -en er, -en ing, -ened.

Hȧr'le ian (-yan).

har'le quin (-kĭn *or* -kwĭn), -ade', -quin ize, -ized, -ī'zing, har'le quin-flow'er, h. duck.

har′lot, -lot ry.
harm, -er, -ing, -ful, -ful ly,
-ful ness, -less, -less ly, -less-
ness, harmed.
har′ma la, -red.
har mat′tan.
har mon′ic, -al, -al ly, -mon′i ca,
-i con, -ics, -i chord, -i cism, -mon′-
o grăph.
har mŏ′ni ous, -ly, -ness, -ni um.
har′mo nize, -nized, -nī′zer, -nī′-
zing, -nĭ zā′tion, -mo ny, -mo-
nom′e ter.
har′ness, -er, -ing, -nessed, har′-
ness-bell, -board, -căsk, -clamp,
-hook, -lĕath′er, -māk′er,
-mount′ing, -pad, -plate, -room,
-sad′dle, -snap, -tub, -weav′er.
Hă′rod, *Bib.*
harp, -er, -ing, -ist, harped.
harp′-lute, -ped′al, -play er,
-seal, -shell, -shil ling, -string,
-style, -trĕad′le.
har pōōn′, -er, -ing, -pooned′,
har poon′-ar′row, -fork, -gun,
-rock′et, -shut′tle.
harp′si chord (-kord), -gra′ces.
har′py, *pl.* -pĭes, har′py-ea′gle,
-foot′ed.
hăr′ri dan.
har′rŏw, -ing, -ing ly, -er, -rŏwed.
hăr′ry, -ing, -ri er, -rĭed, -ri-
ment, har′ry-gad, -gaud.
harsh, -ly, -ness.
hart, -beest, -ber′ry, -wort, -crop,
harts′horn, harts′horn-plan′taĭn.
hart′s′-clo′ver, -thorn, -tongue,
-tre′foil, -truf′fles (-troof′-).
hăr′um-scăr′um.
ha rus′pex *or* -rus′pĭce, *pl.*
-pi ces (-sĕz), -pi cy, -pi cā′tion.
har′vest, -ed, -er, -ing, -ry, -man,
a man; a spider.
har′vest-ap ple, -bells, -bug,
-doll, -feast, -field, -fish, -fly,
-goose, -home, -la dy, -lord,
-louse, -mite, -month, -moon,
-mouse, -queen, -spi′der, -tick,
har′vest ing-ma chine′.
Här′wĭch, vil. Mass.—(hăr′rij), t.
Eng.
has′-been (-bin).
hash, -ing, hashed.

Hash băd′a na, *Bib.*
hăsh′ish (-eesh) *or* -eesh.
hăsk′wort.
hăsp, -ing, hasped, hasp-lock.
Has′se na′ah, *Bib.*
Hăs′shub (hăsh′ŭb) *or* Hā′shub, *Bib.*
hăs′sock, -fill′er, -grăss.
hăs′tate, -ly.
hăste, hāst′ed, -ing, hāst′ing-
ap ple, -peâr.
hăs′ten (-n), -ing, -er, -tened.
hăs′ty, -ti ly, -ti ness, hăs′ty-
foot ed, -wit′ted, h. pud′ding.
Hä sŭ′pha, *Bib.*
hat, -ter, -ted, -less, -band, -pin.
hat′-block, -bod′y, -box, -brush,
-case, -die, -em boss′ing, -fin′-
ish ing, -fit ting, -form ing,
-full ing, -har den ing, -i ron-
ing, -mak er, -meas ure, -mold,
-mon ey, -nap′ping, -piece,
-plank′ing, -plant, -press, -rack,
-rail, -roll′er, -stand, -store,
-stretch ing, -swĕat, -tip, -tree,
-ven′ti la tor, -weav ing, -wor-
ship.
Hă′tach (-tak), *Bib.*
hatch, -er, -er y, -ing, -way,
hatched, hatch′-bar, -boat, -lad-
der, hatch′ing-box, -jar, -trough.
hatch′el, -eled *or* -elled, -el ing
or -ling, -er *or* -ler.
hatch′et, -bolt, -face, -faced,
-stake, -vetch.
hate, -ful, -ful ly, -ful ness, -less,
ha′tred, hāt′ed, -ing, -er.
Hat′i pha (*or* ha tī′-), *Bib.*
Hăt′i ta (*or* ha tī′-), *Bib.*
Hat tă′a vah, *Bib.*
hau′ber geon (-jun), hau′berk.
Hauch, von (fon houk), Danish
poet.
Hauck (houk), Ger. -Amer. singer.
hăugh′ty, -ti ly, -ti ness.
hăul, -age, -er, -ing, hauled,
haul′-seine, haul′age-clip.
häunch, -ing, haunched, haunch′-
bone.
häunt, -ed, -er, -ing.
Haupt (houpt), Ger. philol.
hausse (hōs), -col, -pouch.
Hauss mann′ (ōss′män′), Fr. admr.
haut′boy (hō′-), -ist.

haute'-de-barde (hōt'dê bärd), *-piece*,
-lisse' (-lēs').
Haute feuille', de (dĕ ōt'fêl'), Fr.
mech.
hau'teur' (hō'têr').
haut gout' (hō'gōō').
hăve, hăv'ing, had.
have'lock (hăv'lok).
hă'ven, -age, -măs'ter.
hav'er sack.
Ha'vet' (ä'vä'), Fr. litt.
Hăv'i lah (*or* ha vī'-), *Bib.*
hav'il dar (*or* -dar').
hav'oc.
hąw, -ing, hawed, haw'buck, a
person, -finch, -thorn, hąwthorn-
grōs'beak, -thorn-tree.
Hä wai'i (-wī'ē), isl. Pacific,
-wai'ian (-wī'yan).
Haweis (hois), Eng. author.
hąwk, -er, -ing, -ish, hawked,
hawk'hill, a turtle, -bit, a plant,
-nut, a tuber; a plant, -weed,
Hawk'eye.
hąwk'-bell, -billed, -boy, -ea gle,
-fly, -moth, -owl, -par'rot,
-swal'low, hawk's'-beard, -bill,
-eye.
hąwse (haz), -bag, -block, -bol-
ster, -buc'kler, -hole, -hook,
-piece, -pipe, -plug, -tim ber,
-wood.
hąw'ser (-zer), hawṡ'ing, ing-
i ron, -mal let.
hay, -ey, -ing, -cock, -maid en, a
plant, -maids, a plant, -māk er,
-mow, -rake, -rick, -seed, a
plant; a person, -stack, -stack'er,
-suck'er, a bird, -thorn.
hay'-asth'ma, -ba cil'lus, -band,
-bird, -cap, -car, -cart, -cold,
-cut'ter, -el'e va tor, -fe ver,
-field, -fork, -hook, -jack,
-knife, -load er, -loft, -mar ket,
-plant, -press, -rack, -scent,
-seed, seed of hay, -sprĕad er,
-tea, -ted'der, -un load'er,
-wag on.
Hay'nau *or* Hai'nau (hī'now), t.
Prus.
Hay'ti *or* Hai'ti (hā'tĭ), isl. West
Indies, -tĭ an.
Hăz'a el (*or* hä'zā el), *Bib.*

Ha zā'iah, *Bib.*
haz'ard, -ed, -ing, -er, -a ble, -ous,
-ous ly, -ous ness, haz'ard-ta'ble.
haze, hazed, hāz'ing, -er, -less,
haz'el nut, -wort.
hăz'el-crot'tles, -earth, -grouse,
-hen, -oil, -rag, -raw, -tree.
Haze brock' (äz'brōōk'), t. Fr.
Ha zĕ'rim, *Bib.*
Ha zĕ'roth, *Bib.*
hă'zy, -zi ly, -zi ness.
hĕad, -ed, -er, -ing, -ful, -y, -i ly,
-i ness, -less, -long, -most, -ship,
-first', -fore'most.
hĕad'ache, head'board, -boom,
-bor'ough, -cheese, -făst, -fish,
-land, -ledge, -light, -quar'ters,
-race, -shake, -spring, -stone,
-strong, -wa'ters, -way, heads'-
man.
head'-band, -bay, -block, -case,
-cell, -chair, -chute (-shōōt),
-cloth, -coal, -court, -crack er,
-crin gle, -dress, -ear'ing,
-frame, -gate, -gear, -guide,
-house, -hunt er, -ker'chĭef,
-kid ney, -knee, -knot, -line,
-lin'ing, -louse, -marl, -mold,
-mold ing, -mon ey, -net ting,
-note, -oil, -pen ny, -piece,
-plate, -pōst, -pump, -rail,
-reach, -rest, -ring, -rope, -sails,
-sheets, -shield, -sill, -sil ver,
-skin, -spade, -stall, -sta tion,
-stick, -stock, -stool, -sword,
-ta'bling, -tim ber, -tire, -tone,
-turn'er, -valve, -veil, -voice,
-wark, -word, -work, -yard.
hĕad'ache-tree, -weed, head-and-
head, head man, h. măs'ter.
hĕad'ing-chis'el, -cir'cler, -course,
-joint, -knife, -ma chine', -tool.
hĕal, -er, -ing, -a ble, healed,
heal'all, a plant, heal-dog,
heal'ing-herb, -pyx.
hĕalth, -ful, -ful ly, -ful ness, -y,
-i ly, -i ness, -less, -less ness,
health-guard, -lift, h. of'fi cer.
heap, -er, -ing, -y, heaped,
heap'-cloud, -keep'er.
hĕar, -er, -ing, hĕard, hĕar'say,
hear'ing-trum pet.
hĕarse, -cloth, -like.

---

nŏt, nôr, ūse, ŭp, ûrn, etüde, fōōd, fŏŏt, aņger, boṅmot, thus, Bach.

22

heärt, -ed, -ed ness, -en, -en er, -en ing, -ened, -y, -i ly, -i ness, -less, -less ly, -less ness, -some.

heärt′ache, heart′break, -break′ing, -brō′ken, -burn, -burn′ing, -felt, -leaf, a plant, -quake, -rend′ing, -seed, a plant, -shake, -wort, hearts′ease, a plant.

heart′-beat, -bird, -block, -blood, -bond, -cam, -clot, -clo ver, -coc kle, -dis ease, -ease, -eas- ing, -eat ing, -fail ure, -free, -hĕav i ness, -heav y, -liv er- leaf, -net, -pea, -rob bing, -rot, -scald, -seine, -serv′ice, -shaped, -shell, -sick, -sick′en ing, -sink′- ing, -snake root, -sore, -spoon, -steel, -stir ring, -struck, -swell- ing, -throb, -tre′foil, -ur′chin, -wheel, -whole, -wood, -yarn, heart-of-the-earth, a plant, heart′s ease, ease of the heart.

heärth, -stĕad, -stone, -broom, -brush, -cin′der, -crick′et, -ends, -mon ey, -pen ny, -plate, -rug, -tax.

heat, -ed, -ing, -er, -less, heat′- ap′o plex y, -e con′o mi zer, -en′- gine, -fac tor, -fe ver, -fo′cus, -pim′ple, -po ten′tial, -reg′u la- tor, -spec′trum, -spot, -u nit.

heat′er-car, -plate, -shaped, heat′- ing-ap pa ra′tus, -back, -chām′- ber, -ov en, -pan, -stove, -sur′- face, -tube.

hĕath, -ber′ry, -cup, a plant, -bell, a flower, -bird, -clad, -cock, -corn, -cy′press, -egg′er, -fowl, -grăss, -hen, -hon ey suc kle, -pea, -peat, -pŏult, -pout, -snail, -thros tle.

hēa′then (-ŧhn), pl. -thens, in- dividually, -then, collectively, -dom, -ish, -ish ly, -ish ness, -ism, -ize, -ized, -ī′zing, -ness, -ry.

hĕath′er, -y, heath′er-bell, -blĕat, -bleat er, -clạw, -grăss, -lin tic, -peep er, -wool.

heaume (hōm).

hĕave, heaved, hĕav′ing, -er, heave′-of′fer ing, -shoul′der, hĕav′- ing-days, -line.

hĕav′en (-n), -ly, -li ness, -ward, hĕav′en-born, -bright, -built, -di rect′ed, -kiss′ing, -tree, hĕav′en ly-mīnd′ed, -mīnd′ed- ness.

hĕav′y, hĕav′i er, -i est, -i ly, -i ness, hĕav′y weight, a person, hĕav′y-armed, -hand′ed, -head′ed, -heart′ed, -lād′en, -pine, -spar, -stone.

hĕb′do mad, -dom′a dal, -dal ly, -da ry.

Hĕ′bĕ, Myth.

hĕb′e tude, -tū′di nous.

He′brew, -brā′ic, -ic al, -al ly, -i cize, -cized, -cī′zing, -brā ist, -is′tic, -tic al, -al ly, -brā ize, -ized, -ī′zing, -Y zā′tion.

Hĕ′bron, Bib.

Hĕc′a te, Myth., -tē′an.

hĕc′a tomb (-tōōm or -tŏm).

heck, -ber′ry, -box.

hec′kle, -kled, -kling, -kler, hec′- kle-cell.

Hĕc′la or Hĕk′la, volc. Iceland.

hec′târe.

hĕc′tic, -al, -al ly.

hĕc′to gram or -grămme, -to- graph, -graph′ic, -to li ter or -tre (-lē′ter), -to mē′ter, -to- stēre.

hĕc′tor, -ing, -ly, -tored.

Hĕc′u ba, Myth.

hĕd′dle, -dled, -dling, hed′dle-eye, -hook, -yarn.

hĕdge, hedged, hĕdg′ing, -er, hedge′bells, a plant, -ber′ry, -hog, -maids, a plant.

hĕdge′-ac cent′or, -bed′straw, -bill, -bīnd′ing, -bīnd′weed, -bird, -born, -bote, -car′pen ter, -chā′fer, -chănt er, -chick′ĕn, -clip per, -gar′lic, -hys′sop (-hĭs′-), -jug, -knife, -lạu rel, -mar riage, -mike, -mush room, -mus tard, -net tle, -pars ley, -par son, -pĕak, -pink, -plant, -plant er, -priest, -rhyme, -row, -school, -school′măs ter, -scis′- sors, -shrew, -spăr row, -speak, -spick, -ta per, -thorn, -vine, -vi o let, -war bler.

hĕdg′ing-bill, -glove, -tools.

hedge'hog-cac'tus, -fruit, -grass,
-pars'ley, -plant, -rat, -this'tle.
hě don'ic, -al, -ics, hed'on ism,
-on ist, -o nis'tic.
heed, -ed, -ing, -er, -ful, -ful ly,
-ful ness, -less, -less ly, -less-
ness.
heel, -er, -ing, heeled, heel'piece,
v., -tap, v.
heel'-ball, -blank, -block, -bone,
-breast'ing, -bur'nish ing, -calk,
-chain, -cut ter, -i ron, -jig'ger,
-joint, -knee, -lift, -ma chine',
-pad, -päth, -piece, n., -plate,
-post, -ring, -rope, -seat,
-shave, -tap, n., -tip, -tool,
-tree, -trim'mer, heel'ing-ĕr'ror.
hĕft, -y.
Hĕ'ge (-gē), Bib.
He'gel (hā'-), Ger. philos., Hē-
gē'lĭ an (or hā gē'- or hā gä'-),
-an ism, -gel ism.
hĕ'ge mŏ ny (or -jem'o ny); -mon ic,
-ic al.
heg'ĭ ra (or hē jĭ'ra), a flight;
Heg'i ra, the flight of Mohammed.
heif'er (hĕf'-).
heigh (hī), -hō.
height (hīt) or hight, -en, -en-
ing, -en er, ened, height'-
board, -staff.
Heil bronn' (hīl'brōn'), t. Ger.
Hei'li gen stadt (hī'lĭ gen stät'),
t. Prus.; t. Aust.
hei'min (hā'-).
Hei'ne (hī'ně), Ger. writer.
hei'nous (hā'nus), -ly, -ness.
heir (âir), -dom, -ess, -less,
-loom, -ship, heir-ap pâr'en cy,
-land, h. ap pâr'ent.
hei'-te'ki (hī'-tē'kĭ).
he'-jäl'ap.
hĕj'ĭ ra (or hē jĭ'ra). See hegira.
Hel chĭ'ah (-kĭ'-), Bib.
hel'coid, hel co'sis.
Hĕl'dăi (or hĕl'dā ĭ), Bib.
Hĕl'e na, c. Ark.; c. Mont.
hĕ'li ac, -lĭ'a cal, -cal ly.
hĕ'li o chrome (-krōm), -chrō'-
mic, -chrō'mo scope, -mo type,
-li och'ro my (-ŏk'-').
Hĕ lĭ o dō'rus, Bib.
hĕ'lĭ o-e lec'tric, -en grav'ing.

hĕ'li o grȧph, -graph'ic, -ic al,
-og'ra pher, -ra phy, -ol'a try,
-a ter, -a trous, -om'e ter,
-e try, -o met'ric, -ric al, -al ly,
-o scope, -scop'ic, -o stat.
Hĕ'lĭ ŏs, Myth.
hĕ'lĭ o trope, -trōp'er, -trŏp'ic,
-ic al, -al ly, -ŏt'ro pism.
hĕ'lĭ o type, -typed, -typ'ing (-tĭp'),
-ty'py (-tĭ'-). -typ'ic (-tĭp'-).
hĕ'lix, pl. hĕ'lix es or hĕl'i ces
(-sēz).
Hĕl'kăi (or -kā ĭ), Bib.
hĕll, -ish, -ish ly, -ish ness, -ben'-
der, -ward, -bent, -black, -born,
-brood, -broth, -cat, -dīv'er,
-doomed, -drīv'er, -fire, -gate,
-hag, -häunt ed, -hound, -kite,
-rake.
hĕl'le bore, -bo rism, -bo rize,
-rized, -rī'zing.
Hel'lēne, a Greek, Hel lē'ni an,
-lĕn'ic, -ic al ly, -len'i cism,
-len ism, -len ist, -le nis'tic,
-tic al, -al ly, -len ize, -ized,
-ī'zer, -ī'zing, -ĭ zā'tion.
hel lo'. See halloo.
helm, -ing, -less, helmed, helm'ĕd,
a., helms'man, helm-bar,
-cloud, -guard, -port.
hĕl'met, -ed, hĕl'met-bee'tle,
-bird, -cock a too', -crab, -crest,
-flow'er, a plant, -quail, -shaped,
-shell.
Hé lo ise' (ā lō ēz'), Fr. abbess.
Hĕ'lon, Bib.
Hĕ'lot (or hĕl'ot), -age, -ism, -ry.
help, -ing, -er, -ful, -ful ly, -ful-
ness, -less, -less ly, -less ness,
helped, help'mate, -meet,
-worth'y, -ale.
hĕl'ter-skĕl'ter.
hĕlve, helved, helv'ing, helve'-
ham'mer.
Hĕl ve'tian (-shạn), -vet'ic.
Hĕl vĕ'ti us (-shĭ us), Fr. philos.
hem, -ming, -mer, hemmed.
hĕ'mal, he mat'ic, -ics.
Hĕm'ans, Eng. poetess.
hĕm'a tīte, -tĭt'ic, -toid, -tose,
-tō'sis.
hem a tom'e ter, -e try.
hem au'to grȧph, -tog'ra phy.

hĕm′i sphere, -sphĕr′ic, -ic al.
hĕm′i stich (-stĭk), -al (or he-
mis′-).
hĕm′lock, -drop wort, -pars ley,
-pitch, -spruce.
hem′ol, he mol′y sin.
hem o pho′bia.
hĕm′or rhage (-rāj), -rhag′ic
(-răj′-), -or rhoid, pl. -rhoids,
-rhoid′al.
hemp, -en, -y, -weed, -wort.
hemp′-ag′ri mo ny, -brake, -bray,
-bush, -har′vest er, -net′tle,
-pälm, -plant, -res′in (-rĕz′-),
-seed, -tree.
hĕm′stitch, -ing, -er, -stitched.
hen, -ner y, -ny, hen′bane, -bill,
a bird, -bit, a plant, -fish, -peck,
-pecked, -ware, -wife, -wom′an.
hen′-billed, -blīnd′ness, -clam,
-coil, -coop, -cur′lew, -hawk,
-house, -huz′zy, -mold, -plant,
-roost.
hen-and-chick ens, a plant,
hen's-bill, -foot.
Hé nault′ (ā′nō′), Fr. hist.
Hen′gist (-gist), Jutish chief.
Hĕn′ne pin, Fr. explorer.
Henne quin′ (ĕn′kăn′), Fr. auth.
he no′sis.
Hen ri′ci (-rĭt′sē), Ger. math.
hĕ pat′i ca, -pat′ic, -ic al.
Hē phæs′tus (-fĕs′-), Myth.,
-phæs′ti an.
Hē′pher, Bib.
Heph′zĭ bäh (hĕf′-), Bib.
hĕp′ta gon, -tag′o nal, -tam′e ter,
-tan′gu lar.
Hep′tă plả.
hĕp′tar chy, -tarch (-tark), -tar′-
chic (-kĭk), -tar chist (-kĭst).
hêr, -self′, hers.
Hē′ra or Hē′rē, Myth.
Hĕr a clĕ′an or -clĕ′ian, Hĕr′a cles
(-klēz), Gr. form of Hercules.
Hĕr a clī′tus, Gr. philos., -clī tē′-
an, -an ism, -clĭt′ic.
hĕr′ad.
hĕr′ald, -ed, -ing, -er, -ry, -ship,
he ral′dic, -dic al ly, hĕr′ald-
crab, -moth.
Her ät′, c. Afghan.
He rault′ (ā′rō′), dept. Fr.

herb (êrb or hêrb), -age, -aged,
-al, a., herb′al, n. (hêrb′-),
-al ism, -al ist, her bă′ri um, pl.
-ri ums or -ri a, her′ba ry,
-bes′cent, -bif′er ous, herb′ist,
herb′let, -less, -ous, -y, her bōse′.
herb′wom′an, -bane, -bar′ba ra,
-ben net, -car′pen ter, -chris′-
to pher, -doc′tor, -frank′in-
cense, -ger′ard, -grace, -i vy,
-lil y, -lou i′sa, -mar′ga ret,
-par′is, -pe ter, -re pent′ance,
-rob ert, -so phi′a, -trin′i ty,
-true′love, -two′pence, -wil′liam,
herb′age-plant, herb-of-grace, a
plant.
Her cu lā′ne um, anc. Rom. city,
-ne an, -nĕn′si an.
Hêr′cũ les (-lēz), Myth., -cu′le an,
Her′cu les′-bee′tle, Her′cu les′-
club.
hêrd, -ed, -er, -ing, -boy, herds′-
man, herds′wom an, herd-book,
-grăss, herd′ing-ground, herd′s-
grăss.
hêr′dic.
hêre, -a bout′, -a bouts′, -ăft′er,
-ăt′, -a wāy′, -by′ (-bī′), -from′,
-in′, -in ăft′er, -in be fore′,
-in′to, -of′ (-ov′), -on′, -to′,
-to fore′, -un′der, -un′to (or
-to′), -up on′, -with′ (or -with′).
hē rĕd′i ty, -i ta ry, -ta ri ly, -ri-
ness, hĕr ē dĭt′a ment.
Hē′res (-rēz), Bib.
hĕr′e si arch (-ark or hē rē′zĭ-
ark), -si og′ra phy, -ra pher, -si-
ol′o gy, -o gist.
hĕr′e sy, -e tic, he ret′ic al, -al ly.
hĕr′it age, -it a ble, -a bil′i ty.
hĕr′ling or hir′-.
her mä′nō, pl. -nōs.
hĕr maph′ro dīte, -dit′ic, -ic al,
-al ly, -dit ism.
Hĕr′mes (-mēz), Myth.; Bib.,
-met′ic, -ic al, -al ly, her met′ics.
Hĕr′mĕs, Ger. theol., -mē′si an,
-an ism.
Her mī′o ne, Shak. Winter's Tale.
hĕr′mit, -age, -a ry, -ess, -mit′-
ic al.
hĕr′mit-bird, -crab, -crow,
-thrush, -war bler.

---

fāte, făt, fär, fall, fâre, fåst, sofå, mēte, mĕt, hêr, īce, ĭn, nōte,

Her mog'e nes (-mǒj'e nēz), *Bib.*,
-mo gē'ne an.

Her na'ni *or* Er- (âr nä'nē),
Hugo's tragedy; Verdi's opera.

her'ni a, -ni al, -ni a ted, -ni oid,
-ni ol'o gy, -ot'o my.

hē'ro, -ro'ic, -ic al, -al ly, -ro i-
com'ic, hēr'o īne, -o ism, he'ro-
wor ship, -wor ship er.

Hěr'od, King of the Jews, He rō'-
di an.

Hě rō'di as, *Bib.*

He rōd'o tus, Gr. hist., -o tē'an.

he rō'in *or* -īne, *Chem.*

hěr'on, -ry, her'on's-bill.

hêr pe tol'o gy, -o gist, -to log'ic,
-ic al, -al ly, her'pe toid, -tot'-
o my, -o mist.

Hěrr, a Ger. title equivalent to Mr.

hěr'ring, -er, hěr'ring-bank,
-bone, -buss, -cobs, -cod,
-cūr'er, -drīv'er, -fish er y, -gull,
-hake, -hog, -king, -pike,
-pond, -spink, -work, h. moun'-
tain.

Herrn'hüt'ěr.

Her'schel, Eng. astron., -schěl'-
i an.

Her vé' (ěr'vä'), Fr. journalist.

her'vi de'ro (-dä'-).

Her ze go vi'na (hěrt'se gō vē'nä),
prov. Tur.

Hě'sī od, Gr. poet, od'ic.

Hě sī'o ne, *Myth.;* a genus of
insects.

hěs'i tate (hěz'- *or* hěs'-), -ta ted,
-ta ting, -ting ly, -ta tive, -ta tor,
-tant, -tant ly, -tan cy, -tā'tion.

Hěs'per, -per id, -*pe rus*, -pē'ri an,
Hes pěr'i des (-dēz), *Myth.*,
-pe rid'i an.

Hesse'-Nas'sau (hěs'-näs'sou),
prov. Prus.

Hes'sian (hěsh'an).

hět'er o dox, -ly, -ness, -al,
-dox y.

het'er o gē'ne ous, -ous ly, -ous-
ness, -ge'ne al, -ge ne'i ty, -ge-
net'ic.

het'er o lith.

hět'man, -man ate, -man ship.

Heug'lin, von (fǒn hoig'lin), Ger.
trav.

Heus'de (hês'deh), Dutch auth.

Heu zey' (ê'zā'), Fr. archæol.

hew (hū), -er, -ing, hewed, hew'-
hole, a bird.

hex'a gon, -ag'o nal, -nal ly.

hex am'e ter, -e tral, -e trist,
-a met'ric, -ric al.

hex'a seme, -se'mic.

hey (hā), -day.

Hěz'rā ī (*or* -rāi), *Bib.*

hī a'tus, *pl.* -tus *or* -tus es.

Hī'a wą'tha, Longfellow's poem.

hī'ber nate, -nā'ted, -nā'ting,
-ber'nal, -nā'tion.

Hī bêr'nī a, Ireland, -ni an, -an-
ism, -ni cism, -ni cize, -cized,
-cī'zing, -nol'o gy, -o gist, Hī-
bêr'no-Cel'tic.

hic a tee'.

hic'cup *or* -cough (hǐk'up), -ing,
-er, -cupped *or* -coughed
(-kǔpt).

hǐc' ja'cet.

hǐck'o ry, -head, a duck, -a ca'-
cia, -elm, -eu ca lyp'tus, -gir-
dler, -nut, -pine, -shad, h.
shirt.

Hicks'īte.

hī dǎl'go, -dal'gism (-jǐzm).

Hǐd'dāi (*or* -dā ī), *Bib.*

hīde, hǐd, hǐd'den, -den ly, -den-
ness, hīd'er, -ing, hide'bound,
-blown, -han'dler, -mill, -rope,
-scrāp'er, -shav'ing, -stretch'er,
-work'er, hide-and-seek, hīd'ing-
place, hid'den-eyed.

hīd'e ous, -ly, -ness.

hīe, hīed, hy'ing (hī'-) *or* hīe'ing.

hiěl'a man, -tree.

hī'e mate, -mā'ted, -mā'ting,
-mal, -mā'tion, hī'ems.

hien (hēn *or* hyen).

hī'er arch (-ark), -al, -arch'ism,
-arch'y, -arch'ic, -ic al, -al ly.

Hī ěr'e el, *Bib.*

Hī ěr'e mŏth, *Bib.*

Hī er'ī ē'lus, *Bib.*

Hī ěr'mas, *Bib.*

hī'er o glyph, -ic, -ic al, -al ly,
-og'ly phist, -ly phize, -phized,
-phī'zing.

hī'er o gram, -gram'mat, -mat'ic,
-ic al, -gram'ma tist.

hī er ol′o gy,   -o gist,   -o log′ic, -ic al, -ol′a try.

Hī′ě rŏn′y mus, *Bib*.

hī ěr′o phant (*or* hī′er-), -phan′tic.

Hig gā′ion, *Bib*.

hĭg′gle,   -gled,   -gler,   -gler y, -gling.

hig′gle dy-pig′gle dy.

high (hī), -er, -er most, -est, -ly, -ness, -bīnd′er, -hold′er, a bird, -hole, a bird, -land, -road, -way, -way man, High′land man.

high′-backed,   -blood′ed,   -boy, -cock a lo′rum,   -cross,   -day, -fli′er, -flown, -go, -hook, -line, a fisherman, -low, -mal′low, -pres′sure, -priest′hood, -priest′-ly, -priest′ship, -proof, -reach-ing,   -sound′ing,   -step′per, -street, -ta per, -top, an apple, High′-church,   -church ism, -church man, high-low-jack, h. priest.

hī lā′ri ous (*or* hĭ-), -ly, -lăr′i ty.

hill, -er, -ing, -y, -i ness, -ock, hilled, hill′ber′ry, -man, -side, -top, -wort.

hill′-ant, -bird, -coun′try, -dig′-ger, -fe′ver, -folk, -fort, -oat, -par′tridge, -plov′er, -site, -spar′row, -star, -tit, hill′ock-tree, hill′side-plow.

hilt, -ed.

hī′lum.

him, -self′.

Hī mä′la ya   (*or*   hĭm a lā′ya), mts. in Asia, -la yan.

hin.

hĭnd, -er, -most, -er most, -ber′ry, -brain, -hand, -head, -sight, -ward, hĭnd′-fore′most.

hĭn′der, -er, -ing, -dered, -drance *or* -der ance.

Hĭn′du (-dōō) *or* -dōō, *pl*. -dus *or* -dōōs, -du ism, -du ize, -ized, -ī′zing, -du stǎn′i (-ē).

hĭnge, -less, hinged, hĭn′gĭng, hinge′-band, -joint, -line, -pil′-lar, -pin, -tooth, hĭn′ging-post.

hĭn′ny, -ing, -nĭed, hin′ny, n., *pl*. -nies.

hint, -ed, -er, -ing, -ing ly.

hin′ter land (-länt).

hip,   n.,   hip′ber′ry,   -brī er,   a plant, -rose, a plant, -wort, -bäth, -belt, -bone, -gir′dle, -gout, -hop, -joint, -knob, -lock, -mold′ing, -răft er, -roof, -shot, -strap, -tile, -tree, -tub.

hip, v., -ping, hipped.

hipe, hiped, hīp′ing.

hip po cam′pus.

Hip poc′ra tes (-tēz), Gr. physi-cian, -ra tism, -po crat′ic.

Hĭp′po crēne, *Myth*.

hĭp′po drōme.

hip pol′o gy, -o gist, -poph′a gy, -a gous, -a gist (-jĭst), -a gī, hĭp′-po phile.

Hip pŏl′y ta (-ĭ-), Shak. *Mid-summer Night′s Dream*.

Hip pol′y tus, *Myth*.

hip po pot′a mus, *pl*. -mus es *or* -mī.

hir cär′ra.

hire, -less, -ling, hired, hīr′ing.

Hi ro shi′ma   (hē′rō shē′mä),   c. Japan.

hir sute′ (her-), -ness.

His pā′ni a, Spain, -pan′ic, -pan′-i cism, -pan′i cize, -cized, -cī′-zing, -pan′i o late, -lā′ted, -lā′-ting, -pan′i o lize, -lized, -lĭ′-zing. His pan′o-Gal′li can.

hĭs′pid, -pi da′ting, -pid′i ty, -pid′-u lous.

hiss, -ing, -er, hissed.

hist.

his tol′o gy,   -o gist,   -to log′ic, -ic al, -al ly, -tol′y sis, -to lyt′ic.

his tŏ′ri an, -tŏr′ic, -ic al, -al ly, -al ness, -to ri og′ra pher, -ra-phy, -o graph′ic, -ic al, -ri ol′-o gy, his′to ry, -to ric′i ty, -paint′-ing, -piece.

his trī on′ic, -al, -al ly, -on′i cism.

hit, -ting, -ter, hit′-off, hit-or-miss.

hitch, -er, -ing, -y, -i ly, -i ness, hitched, hitch′ing-bar, -clamp, -post.

hith′er, -most, -to′ (*or* hith′-), -ward.

hī′ty-tī′ty.

hĭve, hived, hīv′ing, -er, hive-bee, -nest, -vine.

HĪ′vīte, *Bib.*
hŏ.
hoar, -y, -i ness, -stone, h. frost.
hoar′hound *or* hore′hoúnd.
hoard, -ed, -er, -ing.
hoarse, -ly, -li ness.
hoax, -er, -ing, hoaxed.
hob, -like, -thrush, -nail, hob′-
nail-lĭv′er, hob′thrush-louse.
Hŏ bā′iah, *Bib.*
hob′ble, -bled, -bling, -bling ly.
hob′ble de hoy′, -ish.
Hobbs (hŏbz), Eng. philos.
hŏb′by, -ist, hob′by-horse, -owl.
hob gob′lin.
hob′nob′ (*or* -nob′), -bing,
-nobbed′.
hŏ′bo, *pl.* -bos *or* -boes (-bōz).
Hoche (ŏsh), Fr. gen.
hock *or* hough (hŏk), -er, -ing,
hocked, hock′-cart, -glăss.
hock′ey, -cake, -load.
hŏ′cus, -cused (-küst) *or* -cussed,
-ing *or* -sing, hŏ′cus-pŏ′cus.
hod, -ded, -ding, -ful, -man,
hod′-car′ri er, -el′e va tor.
Hŏ dā′iah (*or* hŏd′ā i′ah), *Bib.*
hod′den, -gray.
Hŏ dē′vah, *Bib.*
hodge, -podge, -pud′dlng.
ho dom′e ter, hod o met′ric al.
hŏe, -ing, ho′er, hoed, hoe′-cake,
-down, -plow, hoe′ing-ma chinc′.
hŏ′ey.
hog, -ging, hogged, hog′ger,
-ger y, -gish, -gish ly, -gish ness.
hog′back, a fish, -chŏk′er, a fish,
-fish, -herd, -mol ly, -nut, -skin,
-sty (-stī), -suck′er, a fish, -wash,
-weed, -wort.
hog′-ape, -ap′ple, -back *or*
-backed, shaped like the back
of a hog, -bean, -bed, -brace,
-cat′er pil lar, -chain, -cher′ry,
-chol′er a, -colt, -cote, -deer,
-el′e va tor, -fen nel, -fleece,
-frame, -gum, -hook, -louse,
-mace, -mane, -meat, -mon ey,
-moṇ′key, -mul′let, -pea nut,
-pen, -plum, -rat, -reeve, -ring,
-ring′er, -rub ber, -scald′ing,
-score, -shear′ing, -snake, -suc′-
co ry, -wal′low.

hog's′-back, -bane, -bean, -bread,
-fen′nel, -gar′lic, -haw, -pud′-
ding, hog′ger-pipe, hog′ging-
frame, hog′-in-ar′mor, hog′-
nose-snake.
hogs′head.
Hŏ′hen lo he (hŏ′en lŏ′ĕh), a
Ger. family.
Hŏ′hen zol lern (hŏ′en tsŏl lĕrn),
a Ger. family.
hoi′den *or* hoy′-, -hood, -den ish,
-den ism.
hoist, -ed, -er, -ing, -way, -bridge.
hoist′ing-ap pa rā′tus, -crab, -en′-
gine, -jack, -ma chine′, -tac′kle.
hoi′ty toi′ty.
Hŏl′brook, Amer. naturalist.
hold, -er, -ing, held, hold′back,
-fast, -beam, -gang, hold′er-
forth, hold′ing-ground.
hole, holed, hŏl′ing, hŏl′er, holc′-
wort, -board, -dove, -stitch,
hŏl′ing-ax, -pick.
Hol guin′ (hŏl gēn′), t. Cuba.
hŏl′i day.
Hŏl′land, the Netherlands, -er,
-ish.
hŏl′land, linen imported from the
Netherlands.
Hol′lan daise (-daz′), H. sauce.
hŏl′lands, gin made in Holland.
hŏl′lĭc-point, -stitch.
hŏl lō′, *interj.*, hŏl′lō, *v.*, -ing,
-lōed. See *halloo.*
hŏl′lōw, -ing, -ly, -ness, -lowed,
hŏl′low head, a bird, -root, a
plant, -stock, a plant, -wort,
-billed, -horn, a disease, -plane,
hol′low ing-knife, -plane.
hŏl′ly, -fern, -lau rel, -oak, -rose,
-tree.
hŏl′ly hock, -rose, -tree.
hŏlm (*or* hōm), -cock, -oak,
-screech, -thrush.
hŏl′o caust.
Hŏl′o fēr′nes (-nēz), *Bib.*
hŏl′o grăph, -ic, -ic al.
hŏ lŏm′e ter.
Hŏl′steĭn, Prus.; a breed of cattle.
hŏl′ster, -stered, -ster-pipe.
hŏlt.
hŏ′ly, -li er, -li est, -li ly, -li ness.
hŏ′ly stone, -stoned, -stōn ing.

hŏ'ly-cru'el, -hay, -herb.
Holy Ghost, Holy-Ghost pear,
Holy-Ghost plant.
Hŏl'yoke, Amer. reformer.
hŏm'age,   -a ble,   hom'a ger,
hŏm'age-ju'ry.
hŏme, -less, -like, -like ness, -ly,
-li ly,   -li ness,   -bound,   -come,
-sick,   -spun,   -stall,   -stĕad,
-ward, -ward ly, -wort, homed,
hōm'ing.
home'-born,   -brew,   -com'ing,
-keep'ing,   -rūl'er,   home'ward-
bound, hōm'ing-mill, home rule.
hŏm'i cide, -ci'dal, -dal ly.
hŏm i let'ic, -al, -let'ics.
hom'i ly,   -i list.
hŏm'i ny.
hŏ mŏ gē'ne ous, -ly, -ness, -ge-
nē'i ty, -ge nĕt'ic.
hŏ mŏg'e nize (-moj'-),   -nized,
-nī'zing, -e nous, -e ny.
hŏ'mo grȧph, -graph'ic,   -mog'-
ra phy.
hŏ mŏl'o gous,   -o gize,   -gized,
-gī'zing,   -mo log'ic al,   -al ly,
-mo logue (or hŏm'-), -mol'o gy.
hŏ'mo nym (or hŏm'-), -mon'y-
my, -y mous, -mous ly.
hŏ'mo phone (or hŏm'-), -phŏn'ic,
-mŏph'o nous,   -o ny.
hŏ'mo type (or hŏm'-), hŏ'mo-
ty'py (-tī'-), -typ'ic (-tĭp'-),
-ic al.
Hon du'ras (-dōō'-), rep. Cen.
Amer.
hŏne, -stone, -wort, honed, hōn'-
ing.
hon'est (ŏn'-), -ly, -es ty, hon'est-
heärt'ed.
hŏn'ey (hŭn'-), -eyed (-ĭd),
-eyed ness,   -ey less,   hon'ey-
ber'ry, -bread, a tree, -comb,
-dew, -moon, -stone, -suc'kle,
-sweet, a plant, -ware, a plant,
-wort.
hon'ey-ȧnt, -bad'ger, -bag, -bälm,
-bȧs ket, -beȧr, -bear'er, -bee,
-bird, -blob, -bloom, -brown,
-buz zard, -cell, -creep'er, -crock,
-eat er, -flow er, -gar'lic, -guide,
-lo cust, -lo tus, -mes quit' (-mĕs-
kēt'),   -moth,   -mouthed,   -pod,

-pot, -stalk, -stom'ach, -strain'-
er, -suck er, -su gar, -sweet, a.,
-tube.
hon'ey suc kle-ap ple,   -clō'ver,
-tree.
Hon fleur' (ŏṅ'flêr'), t. Fr.
honk, -er, -ing.
hon'or (ŏn'or), -ing, -a ble, -a ble-
ness, -a bly, -a ry, -o rā'ri um,
-er, -if'ic, -less.
hon'or-court, -man, -point.
hon'or if'i cả bil'ĭ tu din'i ty.
ho no'ris cau'sa (-zà).
hōō'chĭ nōō.
hōōd, -ed, -ing, -er, -less, -lum,
-wort.
hōōd'-cap, -cov'er, -end, -gas'tru-
la, -jel ly, -mold, -mold'ing,
-shēaf,   -shy,   hood'ing-end,
hood'man-blīnd, hood top.
hōōd'ie-crow.
hōōd'wink, -ing, -winked.
hōōf,   -y, hoofed,   hōōf'-bound,
-cush'ion, -mark, -pad, -pâr'ing,
-pick, -sprĕad'er, hoof'ing-place.
hōōk, -ing, -er, -ed, a., -ed ness,
-let, -y, hooked, hook'bill, a
fish, -heal, -tip, a moth, -weed.
hōōk'-beaked,   -bill,   -billed,
-block, -bolt, -bone, -climb'er,
-lad'der, -land, -mon'ey, -mo'-
tion, -net, -pin, -plate, -rope,
-scarf, -squid, -suck'er, -swiv'el,
-tool,   -wrench,   hook'ing-frame,
hook and eye.
hōō'ka or -kah, -stand.
hōō'lee.
hōōn'dee.
hōōp (or hōōp), -ing, -er, hooped.
hōōp'-ash (or hōōp'-), -bee,
-bend'ing,   -coil'ing,   -cramp,
-crimp ing, -cut ting, -dress ing,
-drĭv'er,   -lock,   -net,   -pine,
-plān'ing,   -pole,   -punch ing,
-rack ing,   -rĭv'ing,   -saw'ing,
-shāv'ing, -shell, -skirt, -snake,
-split ting, -tree, -wĭthe, hoop'-
koop-plant, hoop' i'ron.
hōō'pŏe or -pōō.
hōōse.
Hōō'sier (-zher).
hōōt, -ed, -ing, -er, hoot'-owl,
-toot, hoot'ing-owl.

hōōve, hoov'en.
hop, -ping, -per, -bine, hopped, hop'per dŏz'er.
hop'-back, -bŏr'er, -bush, -clo'ver, -cush ion, -dog, -dri'er, -fac'tor, -feed'er, -flea, -fly, -frame, -frog'fly, -froth'fly, -gar den, -horn'beam, -jack, -kiln, -mar'jo ram, -mer'chant, -mil'- dew, -oil, -pest, -pick er, -pock- et, -pole, -press, -rais'ing, -sack- ing, -scotch, -set ter, -tree, -tre'- foil, -vine, -yard.
hop'per-boy, -cake, -cock, -hood, h. car, h. clos'et, hop'ping-dick, -john, hop-o'-my-thumb, hop' pil'low.
hŏp'ple, -pled, -pling.
hŏp'po.
Hŏr'ace, Latin poet, Ho rā'tian (-shan).
hŏ'ral, -ra ry.
horde, hord'ed, hord'ing.
hor de a'ceous.
hor de'i form.
hore'hound. See hoarhound.
hŏ rī'zon, -glăss.
hŏr i zŏn'tal, -ly, -tal'i ty, -ĭ zā'- tion.
horn, -ĭng, -er, -ful, -ist, -less, -less ness, -let, -y, -blende, horned.
horn'beak, a fish, -beam, a tree, -bill, a bird, -book, -finch, -fish, -pie, a bird, -pipe, -plant, -snake, -stone, -tail, an insect, -weed, -work, -wort, -wrack, horns'man, an adder.
horn'-band, -bar, -beech, -blow'- er, -bug, -card, -coot, -core, -cui rass', -dis tem'per, -drum, -eel, -foot'ed, -grăss, -lĕad, -ma- chine', -mad, -mad'ness, -māk'er, -mer'cu ry, -mul let, -nut, -ore, -owl, -pike, -pith, -plate, -play- er, -pock, -pop py, -pout, -pox, -press, -press'er, -quick'sil ver, -shăv'ings, -shōōt, -sil'ver, -tip, -of-plenty, a plant.
horn mail, h. of plen ty, a cornucopia, h. swĭv'el.
horn'y head, a fish, -y wink, a bird, -y-fist ed, -hōō let.

hŏr'net, -clear wing, -fly, -moth.
hŏr'o grăph, ho rog'ra pher, -ra- phy.
hŏr'o lŏge (-lŏj), -lŏg'ic al, -lŏ'- gĭ og'ra pher, -ra phy, -gi o- graph'ic, ho rol'o ger, -o gist, -o gy.
ho rom'e ter, -e try, hor'o met'- ric al.
ho'ro pi'to (-pē'-).
hŏr'o scope, -sco'per, ho rŏs'co- py, -co pist.
hŏr'ri ble, -ness, -bly, -rid, -rid- ness, -rent, hor rib'i le dic'tu.
hŏr'ri fy, -ing, -fied, -rif'ic, -ri- fi cā'tion.
hŏr'ror, -strick'en, -struck.
hors de com bat' (hŏr' dĕ kôn bä'), hors'-d'œuvre' (hŏr'-dêvr').
horse, hors'y, -i ness, horse'back, -bane, -bri'er, a plant, -finch, fish, flow'er, -foot, a plant; a crab, -hair, -head, a fish; a duck, -heal, a plant, -hoof, a plant, -leek, -less, -man, -măs'ter, -mint, -pox, -rad'ish, -shoe, -tail, -tongue, a plant, -way, -weed, -whip, -wom'an, -wood, a tree.
horse'-ăl'oes, -ănt, -arm, -ar'- mor, -ar til'ler y, -balm, -bean, -beech, -blob, -block, -boat, -box, -boy, -bram'ble, -break'er, -brush, -cad'ger, -cane, -cap'per, -car, -cas'sia (-kăsh'a or -ya), -chănt'er, -chest'nut, -clip'per, -cloth, -col'lar, -crab, -dai'sy, -deal'er, -doc'tor, -drench, -el- der, -em'met, -eye, -faced, -fair, -fet'tler, -flesh, -fly, -fur'- ni ture, -gear, -gen'tian, -gin, -gin'seng, -gogs, -gram, -guards, -hạl'ter, -hitch'ing, -hoe, -hold'- er, -hook, -i'ron, -jock'ey.
horse'-knack'er, -knop, -lat'i- tudes, -läugh, -leech, -lit ter, -load, -lot, -mack'er el, -ma rine', -match, -mill, -mus sel, -nail, -net, -net tle, -pars'ley, -păth, -pick, -piece, -pile, -pipe, -pis'tol, -play, -plum, -pond, -pop py, -post, -pow'er, -purs- lane, -race, -ra'cing, -rack,

-rail'road, -rake, -rough, -run,
-sense, -shov'el, -sol'dier, -sŏr'-
rel, -sponge, -steal'ing, -sting'er,
-su'gar, -thief, -this'tle, -thrush,
-thyme (-tīm), -tick, -train'er,
-tree, -trick, -vetch, -vi'o let,
-whim, -win'kle, -worm, -wraṇ'-
gler.

horse'flea-weed, horse'fly-weed,
horse'foot-snipe, h. crab, horse'-
hair-li'chen, -worm, horse'rǎd-
ish-tree, horse'tail-tree, h.
li'chen, horse'well-grǎss, hors'-
ing-block, -i'ron.

horse'shoe'ing, -sho'er (-shōō'-).

horse'shoe-an'vil, -blank, -head,
-kid ney, -ma chine', -nail, h.
bat, h. crab, h. mag'net, h.
vetch.

hors'te.

hor'ta to ry, -ta tive, -tā'tion.

hor'ti cul'ture, -cul'tur al, -tur ist.

Hŏ'rus, *Myth.*

hŏ san'na (-zǎn'-), *pl.* -nas (-nǎz).

hose (hōz), -man, -net, hŏ'sier
(-zher), -sier y.

hose-bib, -bridge, -car'riage, -car'-
ri er, -cart, -clamp, -coŭp'ling,
-fit tings, -hook, -jump'er, -nip'-
ple, -pipe, -pro tect'or, -reel,
-screw, -shiëld, -ūn'ion, -wrench,
hose'-in-hose', hose' com'pa ny.

Hŏ se'a (-zē'-), *Bib.*

Hŏ shā'iah (*or* hŏsh'ā i'ah), *Bib.*

Hŏsh'a ma, *Bib.*

Hŏ shē'a, *Bib.*

hŏs'pi ta ble, -ness, -ta bly, -tal'-
i ty, -*pi'ti um* (-pish'i um),
hos'pice.

hŏs'pi tal, -er, -tal ism, hos'pi tal-
fe'ver, h. ship.

hŏst, -ess, -ess ship, -plant.

hŏs'tage.

hŏs'tel, -er, -ry.

hŏs'tĭle, -ly, -til'i ty.

hŏs'tler (hŏs'ler *or* ŏs'-).

hot, -ly, -ness, -bed, -foot, *adv.*,
-head, a person, -house, -skull,
a person, -spur, a person.

hot'-air, *a.*, -blood'ed, -chis'el,
-flue, -plate, -pot, -press, -saw,
-short, -shot, a person, -wall,
-well, hot-and-hot.

hotch, -pot, -potch.

ho tĕl', -car.

Hŏth'am, t. Austral.

Hŏt'ten tot, -ism, -tot'ic.

hou'dah. See *howdah.*

Hou din' (ōō'dǎṅ'), Fr. conjurer.

Hou don' (ōō'dôṅ'), Fr. sculp.

Hough (hŭf), Amer. writer; hough
(hŏk), to hamstring, -er.

hough'ite (hŏf'-).

Hough'ton (hō'ton), Amer. publisher.

hou guette' (hōō get').

hound, -ed, -er, -ing, -fish,
-plate, -shark, hound's'-ber'ry,
-tongue, -tree.

hour (our), -ly, hour-bell, -cir'cle,
-glǎss, -hand, -line, -plate.

house, -ful, -less, house'breǎk'er,
-fa ther, -hold, -hold er, -keep-
er, -leek, -maid, -mate, -mon'-
ger, -moth er, -stĕad, -top,
-warm'ing, -wife, -wright.

house'-a'gent, -ball, -bell, -boat,
-car, -crick'et, -dog, -du ty,
-en'gine, -fac'tor, -finch, -flag,
-fly, -fuṇ'gus, -line, -lot, -mar-
tin, -mǎs'ter, -mov'er, -paint'er,
-pi'geon, -place, -proud, -rais'-
ing, -room, -shrew, -snake,
-spǎr'row, -spi'der, -swal'low,
-tax, -urn.

house' phy si'cian, h. stew'ard,
h. sur'geon, house'leek-tree.

house (houz), *v.*, housed, hous'-
ing, hous'ing-box, -cloth, -frame.

Hous'sain (hōōs'sǎn), *Arabian
Nights.*

Hous saye' (ōō'sā'), Fr. auth.

Hous'ton (hūs'-), co. Ga.; co.
Minn.; co. Tenn.; c. Tex.; t.
Va.; Amer. statesman.

hout'berg.

hou va ri' (hōō va rē').

Hŏ'va.

hŏv'el, -eled *or* -elled, -el ing *or*
-el ling, -el er.

hov'er (hŭv'er *or* hŏv'-), -er, -ing,
-ing ly, -ered, hov'er-hawk.

how, -ev'er, -so ev'er.

how adj'Ĭ.

how'dah *or* hou'dah.

how'itz er.

howl, -er, -ing, howled.
hoy'den. See *hoiden*.
hua'ca (wä'ka), -cal.
hua ra'cho (wå rä'chō), pl. *-chōs*.
Hua raz' (wä räs'), t. Peru.
Hua ri' (wä rē'), t. Peru.
hub, -bub, hub'-bor'er, -cen'ter-ing, -lāthe, -mor'tis ing, -turn'-ing.
huck, -ber'ry.
huc'kle, -backed, -ber'ry, -bone.
huck'ster, -age, -er, -ing.
hud'dle, -dled, -dler, -dling.
hud dup'.
Hu'dǐ bras, *Fiction*, -bras'tic.
Hu é' (hōō a'), c. Annam.
hûe, -less, hûed, hū'er.
Huel'va (wěl'vä), prov. Sp.
huff, -ing, -ish, -ish ly, -ish ness, -er, -y, huffed.
hug, -ging, -ger, hugged.
huge, -ly, -ness.
Hu ger' (yōō jē'), Amer. Rev. gen.; Confed. gen.
hug'ger-mug'ger.
Hughes (hūz), Eng. auth.
Hū'go, Fr. writer.—(ōō'go), Ger. jurist.
Hu'gue not (-gē nǒt), -ism.
Hui'et (hū'et), tp. S. C.
hui sä'che (hwĕ-).
hŭlk, -y.
hŭll, -er, -ing, hulled, hull'-gull, hull'er-gin, hull'ing-ma chine'.
hŭl'la ba lōō' *or* hal'-.
hŭl lō'. See *halloo*.
hum, -ming, -mer, hummed, hum'dug'geon, hum-cup, hum'-ming-bird, -stick.
hū'man, -kind, -ly, -ness, -ism, -ist, -is'tic, -tic al ly, -man'i ty, hu'man-heart'ed ness.
hū māne', -ly, -ness.
hu man'ǐ tā'ri an, -ism.
hū'man ize, -ized, -i'zer, -i'zing, -ǐ zā'tion.
hŭm'ble, -bled, -bling, -bling ly, -bler, -blest, -bly, hum'ble bee, hum'ble-mouthed, -pie, -plant.
hŭm'bug, -ging, -ger, -ger y, -bugged.
hum'drum, -ming, -drummed.
hū'me fy, -ing, -fīed.

hu'me rus, pl. *-rī*, -me ral.
hŭm'hum.
hū'mid, -ness, -mid'i ty, -mid'or.
hū mǐl'i ate, -a ted, -a ting, -i ty, -i ā'tion.
hŭm'mock, -y, -mocked.
hū'mor (*or* ū'mor), -ing, -ist, -is'tic, -less, -ous, -ous ly, -ous-ness, -some, -some ly, -some-ness.
hump, -ing, -less, -y, humped, hump'back, -back-grunt, -white'-fish.
humph (hŭmf).
hump'ty-dump'ty.
hū'mus, hū'mous, hū'mic, hū'-mus-plant.
hunch, -ing, -back, -backed, hunched.
hun'drěd, -fold, -weight, -dredth, hun'dred-court, -eyes, -legs.
Huŋ'ga ry, -gā'ri an.
huŋ'ger, -er, -ing, -ful, -gered, -gry, -gri ly, huŋ'ger weed, -bit'ten, -flow'er, -grāss, -rot.
huŋk.
huŋ'ker, *v.*, -ing, -kered.
Huŋ'ker, *n.*, hun'ker, *a.*, -ism.
huŋks.
hunt, -ed, -er, -ing, -a ble, -ress, hunts'man, *pl.* -men, -man ship, hunt'ser'geant.
hunt'ing-box, -cap, -case, -coat, -cog, -crop, -dog, -field, -ground, -horn, -jug, -knife, -lěop'ard, -seat, -shirt, -skiff, -song, -spi'der, -sword, -tide, -watch, -whip, hunts'man's-cup, -horn, hunt's-up.
hū'on-pine.
Hū'rāi (*or* -rä ǐ), *Bib.*
hur'dle, -man, -dled, -dler, -dling, hur'dle-nail, -race.
hur'dy-gur'dy.
hurl, -ing, -er, -bone, hurled.
hur'ly-bur'ly, -hack'et, -house.
Hū'ron, -rons, -rō'ni an, Hū'ron-Ir'o quois' (-kwoi').
hur rah' *or* -ra' (hōō rä' *or* hŏŏ-), -ing, -rähed' *or* -räed'.
hŭr'ri cane, -deck.
hŭr'ry, -ing, -ri er, -rǐed, -ried ly, -ried ness.

hŭr'ry-skŭr'ry.
hûrse'-skin.
hûrst, -beech.
hûrt, -er, -ing, -ful, -ful ly,
 -ful ness, -less, -less ly.
hûr'tle, -tled, -tling, -ber'ry.
hus'band (hŭz'-), -ed, -er, -ing,
 -age, -less, -ry, -man.
hŭsh, -ing, hushed, hush'a by'
 (-bĭ'), hush'-mon'ey.
Hŭ'shāi (or -shā ī), Bib.
hu'si (hōō'sē).
husk, -er, -ing, -y, -i ly, -i ness,
 husked, husk'-hack'ler, husk'ing-
 bee, -glove, -peg, -pin.
hus sar' (hŭz zär' or hŏŏz-).
hŭs'sy (hŭz'zy).
hŭs'tings.
hŭs'tle, -tled, -tler, -tling, -tle-
 ment, -tle-cap.
hut, -ted, -ter, -ting, hut-urn.
hŭtch, -ing, hŭtched.
hut'ton, -ing.
hŭz zä' (or hŏŏz-).
hy'a cinth, -cin'thi an, -cin'thĭne.
Hy a cinthe', Père (pâr ē'ä'săṅt'
 or yä'săṅt'), Fr. orator.
hy'a lĭne, -a līte.
hy ăl'o grâph (hī-), -a log'ra phy.
hy al'o plasm (hī al'o plazm).
hy'brid (or hĭb'-), -ism, -ist, -ize,
 -ī'zer, -ī'zing, -ous, -ist, -brid'-
 i ty, -ĭ zā'tion.
Hy dăs'pes (hī das'pēz), Bib.
hy'dra, pl. -dras or -drae, Myth.,
 -hĕad'ed, Hy'dra, Astron.
hy dran'ge a (hī dran'jē a), a
 plant. Hy dran'ge a, a genus of
 plants.
hy'drant.
hy'drate, -drā'tion.
hy drau'lic (hī-), -al, -al ly, -li-
 cian (-lish'an), -lic'i ty, -drau'-
 lics, -list.
hy'dro ce ram'ic.
hy'drŏ dy nam'ic, -al, -ics, -dy-
 na mom'e ter.
hy'dro-e lec'tric.
hy'dro gen, -ize, -ized, -ī'zing,
 -dro gen ate, -ā'ted, -ā'ting,
 -ge nā'tion, -drog'e nous (-drŏj'-).
hy drŏg'ra phy (hī-), -ra pher,
 -dro graph'ic, -ic al.

hy'dro kĭ net'ics.
hy drol'o gy (hī-), -o gist, -dro-
 log'ic, -ic al, -drol'y sis, -dro-
 lyt'ic, -dro man cy, -man'tic.
hy drom'e ter (hī-), -e try, -dro-
 met'ric, -dro mo'tor.
hy'drŏ păth, -path'ic, -ic al,
 -drop'a thist, -a thy.
hy drŏ phŏ'bĭ a (hī-), -phŏ'bic
 (or -fŏb'-).
hy'dro phone (hī'-).
hy'dro phyt'ic.
hy'dro scope.
hy'dro stat, -stat'ic, -ic al, -al ly
 -ics, -sta ti'cian (-tĭsh'an).
hy'drŏ sŭl'phu ret'ed, -phu'ric,
 -sul'phur ous.
hy'dro tech'ny (hī'dro tek'-),
 -tech nol'o gy.
hy'dro thĕr'a py, -a peū'tic, -tics,
 -thĕr'mal, -dro tim'e ter.
hy'drŏ zō'al, -zō'an, -zŏ'ic, -zo'-
 on, pl. -zo'ons or -zo'a.
hy'dru re'sis.
hy ē'na (hī-), pl. -nas, -en'ic,
 -en'i form, -ē'nĭne, -ē'noid,
 hy e'na-dog.
hy'e tal, -e to graph, -graph'ic,
 -ic al, -tog'ra phy, -tol'o gy, -to-
 log'ic al, -tom'e ter.
Hy gē'ia (hī jē'ya), Myth., -gē'-
 ian.
hy'gĭ ĕne, -en'al, -en'ic, -ic al ly,
 -en'ics, -en ism, -en ist.
hy'gro grâph, -grom'e ter, -e try,
 -gro met'ric, -ric al.
hy'gro scope, -scop'ic, -ic al,
 -gro stat'ics.
Hy'men, Myth., hy'men, Anat.,
 hy me ne'al, -nē'an, -mĕn'ic.
Hy'mĕ ne'us, Bib.
hymn (hĭm), -ing (or -ning),
 hymned (hĭmd), hym'nal, -nic,
 -nist, -nō dy, -no dist, -nog'ra-
 pher, -ra phy, -nol'o gist, -o gy.
hymn'-book, -sing'ing, -tune,
 -writ'er.
hy'o glos'sus, -glos'sal.
hy'oid, -e al, -e an.
Hy pa'ti a (hī pā'shĭ a), of
 Alexandria.
hy per'ba ton (hī-), -bat'ic, -ic-
 al ly.

hy per'bo la (hī-), -bo lē, -bŏl'ic,
-ic al, -al ly, -bŏl'i form, -bo-
lism, -bo list, -bo lize, -lized,
-lī'zing.

hy'per bŏ're an.

hy'per crit'ic al, -ly, -i cize,
-cized, -cī'zing, -cism.

hy'per cy ē'sis.

hy per gen'e sis.

hy'per met'a mor'phic, -mor'-
phism, -mor'pho sis, -met a-
phŏr'ic al.

hy'per sen'si tive, -ness.

hy per'tro phy (hī-), -tro phous,
-troph'ic, -ic al, -tro phied (-fĭd),
-phy'ing (-fī'-).

hy'phen, -ate, -ā'ted, -ā'ting,
-ā'tion.

hyp'no tism, -no tist, -tize, -tized,
-tī'zer, -tī'zing, -tĭ zā'tion, -not'ic,
-ic al ly, hyp'nic, -no dy.

hyp o chon'dri a (hĭp'ŏ kŏn'drĭ a
or hī pō-), -dri ac, -ac al,
-al ly, -dri al, -drĭ'a sis, -chon'-
drĭ asm, -dri ast.

hyp'o crĭte, -crĭt'ic al, -al ly,
hy poc'ri sy (hī-).

hyp'o der'ma (*or* hī'po-), -der'mic,
-mic al, -al ly, *-der'mis.*

hyp'o gene (-jēn), -ge'al, -gē'an,
hyp o gē'um, hy pog'e nous (hī-
poj'-).

hy pos'ta sis (hī-), *pl.* -ses (-sēz),
-ta sy, -po stat'ic, -ic al, -al ly.

hy pŏs'ta tize (hī-), -tized, -tī'-
zing, -tĭ zā'tion.

hy pŏt'e nuse *or* -poth'- (hī-),
-nū'sal.

hy poth'e cate (hī-), -cā'ted,
-cā'ting, -cā'tor, -tŏ'ry, -ca ry,
-cā'tion.

hy poth'e sis (hī-), -e sist, -e size,
-sized, -sī'zing, -po thet'ic,
-ic al, -al ly.

hyp som'e ter, -e try, -so met'-
ric, -ric al, -al ly.

hy'son (-sn).

hys'sop (-sup).

hys tĕ'ri a, -tĕr'ic, -ic al, -al ly,
-i form.

I

I beam, I ĭ'ron (ī'urn), I rail.

I ac'chus (i ăk'kus), *Myth.*, -ac'-
chic (-ăk'kĭk).

Iach'i mo (yăk'ĭ mō), Shak.
Cymbeline.

I a'go (ē ä'gō), Shak. *Othello.*

I ăm'bic, -al ly, -am'bus, *pl.*
-bus es (-ĕz) *or* -bī, -am'bist.

I an'thĭne.

I bē'ri an, -ism.

I'bex, *pl.* -bex es *or* Ĭb'i ces
(-sēz).

I bĭ'dem.

I'bis.

Ib nē'iah (-ya), *Bib.*

I cā'ri an (ī kā'-), -ism.

Ic'a rus (ĭk'-), *Myth.*

ice, iced, i'cer, -cing, -cy, -ci ly,
-ci ness, ice'berg, -leaf, a plant,
-man, -work.

ice'-an'chor, -a'pron, -au ger,
-ax, -bag, -ban'ner, -beam,
-bear'er, -belt, -bird, -blink,
-boat, -bone, -bound, -box,

-break'er, -brook, -built, -calk,
-cal o rim'e ter, -ca noe', -cap,
-car'riage, -chair, -chest,
-chis'el, -claw, -clos et, -cold,
-cream, -creep'er, -crush'er,
-cut'ter, -drift, -drops, -el'e-
va tor -es cape', -fall, -fĕath'-
ers, -fern, -field, -fish ing,
-float, -floe, -foot, -fork, -fox.

ice'-glăss, -gorge, -gull, -hill, -hook,
-house, -ledge, -lev'el er, -lo-
co mo'tive, -loon, -ma chine',
-māk ing, -mal let, -mark,
-mark'er, -măs ter, -moun'taĭn,
-pack, -pail, -pa per, -pick,
-pit, -pitch'er, -plane, -plant,
-plow, -pōul'tice, -pre serv'er,
-quake, -riv'er, -safe, -san dal,
-saw, -scrāp'er, -screw, -sheet,
-ship, -spade, -spar, -stream,
-ta ble, -tongs, -tools, -wag'on,
-wall, -wa'ter, -whale, -wool,
-worm, -yacht, -yacht'ing,
-yachts'man.

---

nŏt, nôr, ūse, ŭp, ûrn, etüde, fōōd, fŏŏt, aṅger, boṅmot, thus, Baċh.

Ice'land, -er, -lan'dic, Ice'land
fal'con, I. gull, I. moss, I. spar.
ich neu'mon (Ĭk nū'mon), -fly.
ich'nŏ grăph (Ĭk'-), -graph'ĭc,
-ic al, -nog'ra phy.
ich'no lĬte (Ĭk'-), -lĬt'ic, -li thol'-
o gy, -no lith'o log'ic al, -nol'o-
gy, -no log'ic al, ich'nĬte.
ich'no man'cy (Ĭk'-).
Ĭ'chor (-kôr), -ous, Ĭ'cho rose.
ich'thy og'ra phy (Ĭk'thĬ-), -o-
graph'ic, -ol'a try, -a trous,
-ol o gy, -o gist, -o log'ic, -ic al,
-al ly, -o man'cy, -man tic.
ich thy oph'a gus (Ĭk'thĬ ŏf'-), n.,
a gous, a., -a gist (-jist), -a gy.
ich'thy op'o lism (Ĭk'thĬ op'o lizm).
ich'thy o saur' (Ĭk'thĬ ō sạr'), -sau'-
ri an, -sau'rus.
ich'thys (Ĭk'thiss).
Ic'i ca (Ĭs'-), ic'i can.
Ĭ'cĬ cle, -cled.
Ĭ'con, pl. -cons or -co nes (-ko-
nēz), i con'ic, -ic al.
i con'o clasm, -o clast, -clas'tic.
Ĭ con'o grăph, -graph'ic, -ic al,
-co nog'ra pher, -nog'ra phy, -co-
nol'a ter, -a try, -nol'o gist,
-o gy, -nom'e ter, -e try, -no-
met'ric, -ric al, -al ly.
Ĭ cŏ nom'a chy (-ky), -a chist
(-kĬst), -con o mat'ic, -mat'i-
cism.
ic'ter ode.
ic'tus.
Ĭ da'lah (Ĭ dā'-), Bib.
Ĭ dal'i a.
Ĭ dē'a, i dē'al, -al ly, -al ism,
-de'a less, -de'al ist, -is tic,
-al'i ty, i dē'al ize, -ized, -ĭ'zer,
-ĭ'zing, -Ĭ zā'tion, ĭ de'ate,
-a'tion, -tion al, -de'a tive,
i dē'al-re al, -re'al ism.
Ĭ'dem.
Ĭ den'tic al, -ly, -ness.
Ĭ den'ti fy, -ing, -fĭed, -fi'er,
-fi'a ble, -fĬ cā'tion, i den'ti ty,
-den'tist.
Ĭ'dĕ o grăph (or Ĭ dē'-), -graph'ic,
-ic al, -al ly, -graph'ics, -og'ra-
phy, -ol'o gy, -o gist, -o gism,
-o gize, -o log'ic, -ic al, -o glyph,
-ol'a try.

Ĭ'de o phone, -oph'o nous, -o-
pho-net'ics.
Ĭdes (īdz).
Ĭd'i o grăph, -graph'ic.
Ĭd'i om, -o mat'ic, -ic al, -al ly.
Ĭd'Ĭ ŏ syn'crā sy.
Ĭd'i ot, -i o cy, -ot'ic, -ic al ly.
Ĭ'dle, -ness, -dled, -dling, -dler,
i'dle-ness, -wheel.
Ĭ'dol, -ize, -ized, -ĭ'zer, -ĭ'zing,
-Ĭ za'tion, -dol'a ter, -a tress,
-a trous, -trous ly, -a try, -o clas'-
tic, -o ma'ni a, Ĭ'dol-fire, -shell,
-wor'ship.
Id u mē'a, Bib.
Ĭ'dyl (-dĬl), -ism, -ize or -līze, -ist,
-dyl'lic, -lic al.
Ĭ er'nē, Ireland.
Ĭ e'si (ē ā'sē), t. It.
Ig'dra syl. See Ygdrasyl.
Ĭ ger'na (Ĭ gêr'na), Legendary.
Ĭ gle'si as (ē glä'sē äs), Mex.
statesman.
Ĭg nä'ti ĕff, Russ. dipl.
ig'ne ous, ig'ni fy, -fy'ing, -fied,
-ni form, -nes'cent.
ig'nis jăt'ū us, pl. ig'nes jat'u i
(Ĭg'nēz făt'ū ī).
Ĭg nĬte', -nĬt'ed, -ing, -i ble, -or,
-ni'tion (-nish'-).
ig no'ble, -ness, -bly, -bil'i ty.
ig'no min y, -min'i ous, -ous ly.
ig'no rant, -ly, -rance, -rā'mus.
ig nore', -nored', -nor'ing, -no-
rā'tion.
Ig'or rŏ'te (-tä or ē gor-).
Ĭ guä'na, -guä'ni an, -nid.
ih ram' (Ĭ räm').
i i'wi (ē ē'wē).
Ĭ'lai (i'lä), Bib.
Il'i ad, -ist, -ad'ic, -i ac, -i an.
ill, -ness, il'ly, worse, worst, ill'-
ad vis'ed, -bred, -breed'ing,
-con di'tioned, -dis posed', -făt'ed,
-fa'vored, -got'ten, -hu'mored,
-judged, -look'ing, -man'nered,
-matched, -na'tured, -o'mened,
-sort'ed, -starred, -tem'pered,
-timed, -treat, -treat'ed, -willed,
ill treat ment, ill will.
il lē'gal, -ly, -ness, -gal'i ty.
il lĕg'i ble (-lej'-), -ness, -bly,
-bil'i ty.

---

fāte, făt, fär, fạll, fâre, fâst, sofȧ, mēte, mĕt, hêr, īce, Ĭn, nōte,

il le git'i mate, -ly, -ma cy, -ma-
tize, -tized, -tī'zing.
il lib'er al, -ly, -ness, -al'i ty.
il lic'it, -ly, -ness.
Il li ma'ni (ēl yē mä'nē), mt.
Bolivia.
il lim'i ta ble, -ness, -bly, -bil'-
i ty.
Il lī nois' (-noi' or -noiz'), state
U. S., -nois'an or -i an (-noi'an
or -zĭ an), Il li nois'-nut.
il lit'er ate, -ly, -ness, -a cy.
il log'ic al (-loj'-), -ly, -ness.
il lū'mi nate, -nā'ted, -nā'ting,
-nȧ ble, -nant, -nâ'ry, -nā'tive,
-nā'tor, -na'tist, -nā'tion.
il lū'mĭne, -mĭned, -min ing,
-min ism.
il lu'sion (-zhun), -ism, -ist, -lu'-
sive, -sive ly, -sive ness, -so ry.
il lus'trate, -trā'ted, -trā'ting,
-trā'tive, -tive ly, -trā'tor, -tō'ry,
-trā'tion.
il lus'trī ous, -ly, -ness.
I lo ca'no (ē'lō kä'nō).
I lo i'lo (ē'lō ē'lo), prov. P. I.
im'age, -age less, -age ry, -aged,
-a ging, -a ge'ri al, im'age-breāk'-
er, -mug, -wor'ship.
im ag'ine (-aj'-), -ĭned, -in er,
-in ing, -i nȧ ble, -ble ness,
-bly, -bil'i ty, -nâ'ry, -ri ly,
-ri ness, -na'tion, -tion al, -al-
ism, -nâ'tive, -tive ly, -tive ness.
ĭ mäm', -ate.
ĭ mä'ret (or ĭm'-).
im'be cĭle, -cil'i ty.
im'bed', -ded, -ding.
im bĭbe', -bĭb'er, -ing, -bibed,
-bĭ bi'tion (-bĭ bĭsh'un).
ĭm bit'ter. See embitter.
ĭm'brex, pl. -brĭ ces (-cēz).
im'brĭ cate, -ly, -cā'ted, -cā'ting,
-ca'tion.
im brogl'io (-brōl'yō).
im brue', -ment, -brued', -bru'ing.
im bue', -ment, -bued', -bu'ing.
im'i tate, -tā'ted, -tā'ting, -tȧ-
ble, -ble ness, -bil'i ty, -tā tive,
-tive ly, -tive ness, -tā'tor, -tor-
ship, -tā'tion.
im măc'u late, -ly, -ness, -la cy.
im măl'le a ble.

im'ma nent, -ma nence, -nen cy.
im ma tē'ri al, -ism, -ist, -ri ally, -al ness, -al ize, -ized,
-ī'zing, -al'i ty.
im ma ture', -ly, -ness, -tured',
-tu'ri ty.
im meas'ur a ble (-mĕzh'-), -ness,
-bly, -bil'i ty.
im mē'di ate, -ly, -ness, -di a cy.
im'mē mō'ri al, -ly.
im mense', -ly, -ness, -men'si ty,
-men'su ra ble (-shu-), -ra bil'-
i ty.
im merge', -merged', -mer'ging,
-mer'gence.
im merse', -mersed', -mers'a ble
or -i ble, -ing, -mer'sion, -sion-
ist, im mer'sion-lens.
ĭm'mĭ grate, -grā'ted, -grā'ting,
-grant, -gra'tion.
ĭm'mi nent, -ly, -nence.
im mis'ci ble, -ci bil'i ty.
im mit', -ted, -ting, -mis'sion.
im mit'i gȧ ble, -gȧ bly.
im mō'bĭle, -bil'i ty, -mo'bil ize
(or -mŏb'-), -ized, -ī'zing,
-ĭ zā'tion.
im mod'er ate, -ly, -ness, -ā'tion.
im mod'est, -ly, -es ty.
im'mo late, -lȧ'ted, -la'ting, -lȧ'-
tor, -lā'tion.
im mŏr'al, -al ly, -mo ral'i ty.
im mŏr'tal, -ly, -ism, -ist, -tal'i ty,
-tal ize, -ized, -ī'zing, -ĭ zā'tion,
im'môr tĕlle'.
im mov'a ble (-mōōv'-), -ness,
-a bly, -a bil'i ty.
im mūne', -mu'ni ty, -mu'nize,
-nized, -nī zing, -nĭ zā'tion.
im mure', -ment, -mured', -mur'-
ing.
im mū'ta ble, -ness, -bly, -bil'i ty.
Ĭm'o gen, Shak. Cymbeline.
imp, -ish, -ish ly, imp'-pole.
im pact', -ed, -ing, -pac'tion.
im pâir', -er, -ing, -ment, -pâired'.
im pale' or em pale', -ment,
-paled', -pāl'ing.
im păl'pa ble, -pa bly, -pa bil'-
i ty.
im pal'u dism.
im păn'el, -ment, -eled or -elled,
-el ing or -el ling.

im păr'a dise (-dĭs), -dised, -dīs-ing.

im păr'ĭ syl lab'ic.

im park', -ing, -parked'.

im part', -ed, -er, -ing, -i ble, -i bil'i ty, -ment, -par tā'tion.

im par'tial, -ly, -ness, -ti al'i ty (-shĭ-).

im pass'a ble, not passable, -ness, -bly.

im'passe' (ĭm păs' *or* ăṅ'päs').

im pas'si ble, incapable of suffer-ing, -ness, -bil'i ty.

im pas'sion (-pash'un), -a ble, -ate, -sioned.

im pas'sive, -sive ly, -sive ness, -siv'i ty.

im pāste', -pāst'ed, -pāst'ing, -păs tā'tion, im păs'to.

im pa'tient, -ly, -tience.

im pēach', -a ble, -er, -ment, -ing, -pēached'.

im pêarl', -ing, -pearled'.

im pec'ca ble, -ca bil'i ty, -cance, -can cy, -cant.

im pe cū'ni ous, -ni os'i ty.

im pede', -pēd'ed, -ing, -ance, -pĕd'i ment, -men'tal, *-men'ta,* -pĕd'i tive, -pe'di ent.

im pel', -ling, -lent, -ler, -pelled'.

im pen', -ning, -penned'.

im pend', -ed, -ing, -ence, -en cy, -ent.

im pen'e tra ble, -ness, -bly, -bil'i ty, -pen'e trate, -tra'ted, -tra'ting, -tra'tion.

im pen'i tent, -ly, -i tence, -ten-cy.

im pĕr'a tive, -ly, -ness, -tī'val.

im'pe rā'tor (*or* im'pē- *or* -per ā'-tor), -pĕr'a to ry, -to'ri al.

im per cep'ti ble, -ness, -bly, -bil'i ty, -cep'tion, -tive, -cip'i-ent.

im pêr'di ble.

im per'fect, -ly, -ness, -fec'ti ble, -ti bil'i ty, -tion.

im pē'ri al, -ism, -ist, -is tic, -ly, -al'i ty, -pē'ri al ize, -ized, -ī'zing, -ĭ zā'tion, -ri ous, -ous-ly, -ous ness, *-ri um,* pl. *-ri a.*

im pĕr'il, -ing *or* -ling, -ment, -iled *or* -illed.

im pĕr'ish a ble, -ness, -bly, -bil'-i ty.

im pêr'mē a ble, -ness, -bly, -bil'-i ty, -me a tor.

im'per script'i ble.

im per'son al, -ly, -al'i ty.

im per'son ate, -ā'ted, -ā'ting, -ā'tor, -á tive, -ā'tion.

im pêr'ti nent, -ly, -nence, -nen cy.

im pêr turb'a ble, -a bly, -a bil'-i ty.

im pêr'vi ous, -ly, -ness.

im' pē tī'go.

im pet'u ous, -ly, -ness, -u os'i ty.

im'pe tus.

im'phee (-fē).

imp'ing, -nee'dle.

im pinge' (-pĭnj'), -ment, -pinged', -pin'ging, -pin'gent.

im'pi ous, -ly, -ness, -pī'e ty.

im plā'ca ble, -ness, -bly, -bil'i ty.

im plant', -ed, -ing, -plan tā'tion.

im plau'si ble (-zĭ-), -ness, -bly, -bil'i ty.

im plēad', -ed, -ing, -a ble, -er.

im'ple ment, -men'tal.

im'pli cate, -cā ted, -ting, -tive, -tive ly, -cā'tion.

im plĭc'it (-plĭs'-), -ly, -ness.

im plōre', -plored', -plor'ing, -ing ly, -er, -a tō'ry.

im plū'vi um, pl. *-vi a.*

im ply' (-plī'), -ing, -plied', -pli'ed ly.

im pol'i cy.

im po lite', -ly, -ness.

im pŏl'i tic, -ly, -ness.

im pon'der a ble, -ness, -bil'i ty.

im pō'rous.

im port', -ed, -er, -ing, -a ble, -por tā'tion, im'port, *n.*

im por'tant, -ly, -tance.

im por'tu nate, -ly, -ness, -nā'cy.

im'por tune', -tuned', -tūn'ing, -tūn'er, -tu'ni ty.

im pose' (-pōz'), -posed', -pōs'-a ble, -ble ness, -er, -ing, -ing ly, -ing ness, -po si'tion (-zish'un), im pos'ing-stone, -ta'ble.

im pŏs'si ble, -si bly, -bil'i ty.

im pos'tor, -ship, -pos'ture, -tūr-ous.

im pŏ'ta ble.

im'po tent, -ly, -tence, -ten cy.
im pound', -age, -ed, -er, -ing.
im pŏv'er ish, -ing, -er, -ment,
-ished.
im prac'ti ca ble, -ness, -bly,
-bil'i ty.
im'pre cate, -cā'ted, -cā'ting,
-ca tŏ'ry, -cā'tion.
im preg'nate, -nā'ted, -nā'ting,
-nȧ ble, -ble ness, -nȧ bly, -nȧ-
bil'i ty, -nȧ tŏ'ry, -nā'tion.
im'pre sa'ri o (ĕm'prä sä'rē ō), pl.
-ri os (-ōz).
im pre scrip'ti ble, -ti bly, -bil'i ty.
im press', -ing, -i ble, -ble ness,
-bly, -i bil'i ty, -ive, -ive ly,
-ive ness, -ment, -or, -pres'sion,
-sion a ble, -a ble ness, -a bil'-
i ty, -sion ism, -ist, -is'tic.
im prē vis'i ble (-vĭz'-), -i bil'i ty,
-vis'ion (-vĭzh'un).
im'prĭ mä'tur.
im print', -ed, -ing, im'print, *n.*
im pris'on (-prĭz'n), -ing, -ment.
im prŏb'a ble, -a bly, -a bil'i ty.
im prŏb'i ty.
im promp'tu.
im prŏp'er, -ly, -prō pri'e ty.
im prove' (-prō͞ov'), -ment,
-prov'a ble, -ble ness, -a bly,
-a bil'i ty, -prov'er, -ing, -ing ly,
-proved'.
im prŏv'i dent, -ly, -dence.
im prŏ vise' (-vīz'), -vised',
-vīs'ing, -vīs'er, -prŏv'i sate,
-sa'tor, -tŏ'ry (*or* -prō viz'-), -tŏ'-
ri al.
im'prov vi'sa to're (ĕm'prŏv vē'zȧ-
tŏ'rä), pl. *-to'ri* (-rē), fem.
im prov vi sa tri'ce (ĕm'prŏv vē'-
zȧ trē'chä), pl. *-tri'ci* (-trē chē).
im pru'dent, -ly, -dence.
im'pu dent, -ly, -dence.
im pugn' (-pūn'), -a ble, -er,
-ing, -ment, -pugned'.
im'pŭlse, -pul'sion, -sive, -sive ly,
-sive ness.
im pū'ni ty.
im pūre', -ly, -ness, -pū'ri ty.
im pute', -pūt'a ble, -ble ness,
-bly, -bil'i ty, -pūt'a tive, -tive-
ly, -pūt'ed, -er, -ing, -pu tā'-
tion.

i mu' (ē mō͞o').
in a bil'i ty.
in ac cess'i ble, -ness, -i bly,
-i bil'i ty.
in ac'cu rate, -ly, -ra cy.
in ac'tive, -ly, -tiv'i ty, -ac'tion.
in ad'e quate, -ly, -ness, -quā'cy.
in ad mis'si ble, -si bly, -si bil'-
i ty.
in ad vert'ence, -en cy, -ent,
-ent ly.
in ad vis'a ble (-vīz'-), -a bil'i ty.
in āl'ien a ble (-yĕn-), -ness, -bly,
-bil'i ty.
in a mo ra'to (ĕn ä'mō rä'tō), pl.
-tos (-tōz), fem. *-rä'tȧ.*
in āne', -ly, -an'i ty.
in ăn'i mate, -ness, -mā'ted,
-mā'tion.
in'a ni'tion (-nish'un).
in ap'pe tence, -ten cy.
in ap'pli ca ble, ness, bly, bil'-
i ty.
in ăp'po site (-zĭt), -ly.
in ap pre'ci a ble (-shĭ-), -ȧ tive,
-ȧ'tion.
in ap pre hen'sive, -si ble, -sion.
in ap proach'a ble, -a bly.
in ap prŏ'pri ate, -ly, -ness.
in apt', -ly, -i tude, -ness.
in ăr'a ble.
in ar tic'u late, -ly, -ness, -la-
ted, -lā'tion.
in ar tis'tic, -al, -al ly.
in'as much'.
in at ten'tion, -ten'tive, -tive ly,
-tive ness.
in au'di ble, -ness, -bly, -bil'i ty,
-di phone.
in au'gu ral, -gu rate, -rä'ted,
-rä'ting, -rä'tor, -to'ry, -rä'tion.
in aus pi'cious (-pish'us), -ly,
-ness.
in'born.
in brēathe', -brēathed', -brēath'-
ing.
in breed', -ing, -brĕd', in'bred, *a.*
in'ca, a chief, -bone.
Iṇ'ca, an ancient emperor of Peru;
In cä'ri al.
in cal'cu la ble, -ness, -bly, -bil'-
i ty.
in ca les'cent, -cence, -cen cy.

---

nŏt, nôr, ūse, ŭp, ûrn, etüde, fō͞od, fŏ͝ot, aṇger, boṅmot, thus, Bach.

23

in cam'e ra.
in can desce', -desced' (-dest), -des'cing, -cence, -cen cy, -cent.
in can ta'tion, -can'ta tō'ry.
in cǎ'pa ble, -ness, -bly, -bil'i ty.
in ca pā'cious, -ness.
in ca pac'i ty (-pǎs'-), -pac'i tate, -tā'ted, -tā'ting, -tā'tion.
in cap'su late.
in car'cer ate, -ā'ted, -ā'ting, -ā'tor, -ā'tion.
in car'di nate, -nā'ted, -nā'ting.
in car'na dǐne, -dǐned, -din ing.
in car'nate, -nā'ted, -nā'ting, -nā'tion, -tion ist.
in case' *or* en case', -ment, -cased', -cās'ing.
in cau'tious, -ly, -ness, -tion.
in caved', -cā'vate, -vā'ted (*or* in'ca-), -vā'tion.
in cä'vŏ.
in cen'di a ry, -a rism.
in cense', -ment, -censed', -cen'sing, -cen'ser *or* -sor, -so ry, -sive.
in'cense, *n.*, -boat, -brĕath'ing, -burn'er, -ce dar, -cup, -tree.
in cen'tive, -ly.
in'ce ra tive (*or* in cĕr'-), -rā'tion (*or* -cer a'tion).
in cer'ti tude.
in ces'sant, -ly, -ness.
in'cest, -ces'tu ous, -ous ly, -ous-nèss.
inch, -worm, -meas'ure, -pound, -rule, -tape, inch board, i. stuff.
in'cho ate (-kō-), -ly, -cho ant, -chō'a tive, -ā'tion.
in'ci dence, -dent, -dent less, -den'tal, -tal ly.
in cin'er ate, -ā'ted, -ā'ting, -ā'tor, -ā'tion.
in cip'i ent, -ly, -i ence, -en cy.
in cir'cum spect, -ly, -spec'tion.
in cise' (-sīz'), -cīsed', -cīs'ing, -ci'sion (-sǐzh'un), -cis'ure (-sǐzh'ur).
in cī'sive (-sǐv), -ly, -ness, -cise-ly.
in cī'sor, -so ry, -so'ri al.
in cīte', -ment, -cīt'ed, -ing, -ing ly, -er, -ant, -cī tā'tion.
in clem'ent, -ly, -en cy.

in cline', -clined', -clīn'ing, -a ble, -ble ness, -clǐ nā'tion, -clǐn'a-tō'ry, -tō'ri ly.
in close' *or* en close', -closed', -clōs'ing, -er, -clo'sure (-zhur).
in clude', -clūd'ed, -ing, -i ble, -clu'sive (-sǐv), -sive ly, -sion (-zhun).
in cog'i tant (-kǒj'-), -ly, -i tā'tive, -i tà ble, -tà bil'i ty, -i tance, -tan cy.
in cog'ni to, *fem.* -ni ta, -ni zant, -ni zance, -ni za ble, -za bil'i ty, in cog'.
in cog nos'ci ble, -ci bil'i ty.
in co hĕr'ence, -en cy, -ent, -ent ly, -ent ness, -he'sion (-zhun).
in co in'ci dent, -ci dence.
in com bus'ti ble, -ness, -bly, -bil'i ty.
in'come (-kum), -com er, -com ing.
in com men'su ra ble (-shŏŏ-), -ness, -bly, -bil'i ty, -su rate, -rate ly, -rate ness.
in com mode', -mōd'ed, -ing.
in com mō'di ous, -ly, -ness.
in com mū'ni ca ble, -ness, -bly, -bil'i ty, -cà tive, -tive ly, -tive-ness.
in com mūt'a ble, -ness, -bly, -mu'ta bil'i ty.
in com'pa ra ble, -ness, -bly, -bil'i ty.
in com pǎt'i ble, -ness, -bly, -bil'i ty.
in com'pe tent, -ly, -tence, -ten-cy.
in cŏm plete', -ly, -ness, -plēt'ed, -plē'tion.
in com plex' (*or* -com'-), -ly.
in com pre hen'si ble, -ness, -bly, -bil'i ty, -hen'sive, -sive ly, -sive-ness, -hen'sion.
in com press'i ble, -ness, -bil'i ty.
in con cĕiv'a ble, -ness, -bly, -bil'i ty.
in con'gru ence, -ent, -ous, -ous-ly, -ous ness, -con gru'i ty.
in con'se quent, -ly, -ness, -quence, -quen'tial, -tial ly.
in con sid'er a ble, -ness, -bly.

in con sid′er ate, -ly, -ness, -ā′tion.

in con sist′ent, -ly, -en cy.

in con sŏl′a ble, -ness, -bly.

in con′so nance, -nan cy.

in con spic′u ous, -ly, -ness.

in con′stan cy, -stant, -stant ly.

in con tam′i nā ble.

in con test′a ble, -ble ness, -bly, -bil′i ty.

in con tig′u ous, -ly.

in con′tin ent, -ly, -nence, -nen cy.

in con tro vert′i ble, -ness, -bly, -bil′i ty.

in con vĕn′ience (-yens), -ien cy, -ient, -ient ly.

in con vert′i ble, -ness, -bly, -bil′i ty.

in cŏr′pŏ rate, -rā′ted, -rā′ting, -rà tive, -rā′tor, -rā′tion.

in cŏr pŏ′re al, -ism, -ist, -ly, -rē′i ty, -re al′i ty.

in cor rect′, -ly, -ness.

in cŏr′ri gi ble, -ness, -bly, -bil′i ty.

in cor rŏd′i ble.

in cor rupt′, -ly, -ness, -ive, -i ble, -ble ness, -bly, -bil′i ty, -rup′tion.

in cras′sate, -sā′ted, -sà tive, -sā′tion.

in crease′, -creased′, -creas′ing, -ing ly, -a ble, -a ble ness, -er, in′crease, n., in crĕs′cent, -cres cence.

in cred′i ble, -ness, -bly, -bil′i ty.

in cred′u lous, -ly, -ness, -cre dū′li ty.

in′crĕ ment, -men′tal.

in crim′i nate, -nā′ted, -nā′ting, -nà tō′ry, -nā′tion.

in crust′, -ed, -ing, -ment, -crus ta′tion.

in′cu bate, -bā′ted, -bā′ting, -bā′tive, -bā′tor, -cu′bà to ry, -bā′tion, -tion al.

iŋ′cu bus, n., pl. -bus es or -bī, iŋ′cu boŭs, a.

in cul′cate, -cā′ted, -ca′ting, -ca′tor, -to′ry, -cā′tion.

in cul′pate, -pā′ted, -pā′ting, -to′ry, -pà ble, -ble ness, -bly, -pà tive, -pā′tion.

in cum′bent, -ly, -ben cy.

in cur′, -ring, -curred′.

in cŭr′a ble, -ness, -bly, -a bil′i ty.

in cŭ′ri ous, -ly, -ness.

in cur′sion (-shun), -sive.

in curve′, -curved′, -curv′ing, -ate, a., -a ture, -cur′vate, v., -vā′ted, -vā′ting, -vā′tion.

in′cut.

in dä′ba.

In′da pur (-pōor), t. Bombay.

in debt′ed (-dĕt′-), -ness.

in dē′cent, -ly, -cen cy.

in de ci′pher a ble.

in de cī′sive (-sīv), -ly, -ness, -ci′sion (-sĭzh′un).

in′de cŏ′rous (or -dek′-), -ly, -ness, -cŏ′rum.

in de făt′i ga ble, -ness, -bly, -bil′i ty.

in de fea′si ble, -ness, -bly, -bil′i ty.

in de fen′sĭ ble, -ness, -bly, -bil′i ty.

in de fīn′a ble, -a bly.

in dĕf′i nĭte, -ly, -ness.

in dĕl′i ble, -ness, -bly, -bil′i ty.

in dĕl′i cate, -ly, -i cà cy.

in dem′ni fỹ, -ing, -fīed, -ni ty, -ni tor, -ni tee′.

in de mon′stra ble, -ble ness, -bil′i ty.

in dent′, -ed, -ed ly, -ing, -den′tion, -ture, n., -tā′tion.

in den′ture, v., -tūred, -tūr ing.

in de pend′ent, -ly, -ence, -en cy.

in′de scrīb′a ble, -a bly.

in de struc′ti ble, -ness, -bly, -bil′i ty.

in de ter′mi na ble, -ness, -na bly.

in de ter′mi nate, -ly, -ness, -nā′tion, -ter′mĭned, -min ism, -min ist.

in′dex, n., pl. -dex es or -dĭ ces (-sēz), -dex less, -dex′ic al, in′dex cor rec′tion, -dig′it (-dĭj′-), -ĕr′ror, -fiŋ ger, -gāge, -glăss, -law, -ma chine′.

in′dex, v., -ing, -dexed.

In′dĭ a, -di an, -an ist, -di a man, -dic, -an ol′o gist, In′dies (-dĭz).

In′di an-ăr′row, a plant, -cup, a plant, -dye, -eye, a plant, -heart, a plant, -pipe, a plant, -poke, a plant, -root, a plant, -săl _or_ -sạul, a plant, -shoe, a plant, -shot, a plant, In di an's- dream, a plant.

In′di an ar′row, I. balm, I. bark, I. ber′ry, I. dart, I. hemp, I. meal, I. pud′ding, I. rice, I. sum′mer, I. tur′nip.

in′di a-rub′ber.

in′di cate, -cā′ted, -cā′ting, -cā′- tor, -to′ry, -cant, -dic′a tive, -tive ly, -di cā′tion, in′di ca tor- dī′a gram, -card.

in dic′o līte.

in dict′ (-dīt′), -ed, -er, -ing, -a ble, -ment, -or, -ee′, -dic′- tion, -tion al.

in di enne′ (aṅ dĭ ĕn′).

in dif′fer ence, -en cy, -ent, -ent ism, -ist, -ly.

in′di gence, -gen cy, -gent, -gent ly.

in dig′e nous (-dĭj′-), -ly.

in di gest′i ble, -ness, -bly, -bil′- i ty, -gest′ed, -ed ness, -ges′tive, -ges′tion (-chun).

in dig′nant, -ly, -nā′tion.

in dig′ni ty.

ĭn′di go, -ber′ry, -bird, -broom, -cop′per, -finch, -mill, -plant, -snake, -weed.

in′di go blue, i. brown, i. car′- mĭne, i. ex′tract, i. red, i. white.

in dĭ rect′, -ly, -ness, -rec′tion.

in dis cern′i ble (-dĭz zêrn′-), -ness, -bly.

in dis creet′, not prudent, -ly, -ness, -cre′tion (-krĕsh′un).

in dis crete′, not separated.

in dis crim′i nate, -ly, -nā′ting, -ting ly, -nå tive, -nā′tion.

in dis pen′sa ble, -ness, -bly, -bil′i ty.

in′dis pose′ (-pōz′), -posed′, -pos′- ed ness, in dis′po si′tion (-zish′- un).

in dis′pu ta′ble, -ness, -bly, -dis′- pu ta bil′i ty.

in dis′so lū ble, -ness, -bly, -dis′- so lū bil′i ty.

in dis tinct′, -ly, -ness, -tinç′tive, -tive ly, -tive ness, -tinc′tion.

in dis tin′guish a ble, -ness, -bly.

in dite′, -ment, -dīt′ed, -er, -ing.

in di vid′u al, -ism, -ist, -is tic, -ize, -ized, -ī′zer, -ī′zing, -ĭ zā′- tion, -al ly, -vid′u ate, -ā′ted, -ā′ting, -ā′tor, -ā′tion.

in dĭ vis′i ble (-vĭz′-), -ness, -bly, -bil′i ty.

In′do-Ar′yan (-är′-), -Brit′on, -Chi nese′, -Eu ro pe′an, -Ger- man′ic, -I ran′ic, -Pa cif′ic.

in′dō lent, -ly, -lence, -len cy.

In dol′o gy, -do lo′gi an.

in dŏm′i ta ble.

in′door, -doors.

In′do phile, -dō′phil ist, -phil- ism.

in dorse′, -ment, -dorsed′, -dors′- ing, -a ble, -er; in law, -or, -dor see′.

in′do tint.

In′drä, _Hindu Myth._

in′drâft _or_ -draught.

in dū′bi ta ble, -ness, -bly.

in duce′, -ment, -duced′, -du′- cing, -cer, -ci ble.

in duct′, -ed, -er, -ing, -ive, -ive ly, -duc tiv′i ty, -duc′tion.

in duc′te ous, -duc′tĭle, -til′i ty, -duc to′ri um, _pl._ -ri ums _or_ -ri a, -duc′tric, -tric al, -to- scope, -tom′e ter, -duct′or.

in duc′tion-bal′ance, -bridge, -coil, -ma chine′, -mo′tor, -pipe, -port, -valve, in duct′-pipe.

in dūe′, -ment, -dued′, -du′ing.

in dulge′, -dulged′, -dul′ging (-jĭng), -dul′gence, -gen cy, -gent, -gent ly, -ger.

In′du nä′.

in′dŭ rate, -rā′ted, -rā′ting, -ra- tive, -rā′tion.

in dū′si um, _pl._ -si a (-zĭ-), -si- form.

in dus′tri al, -ism, -ist, -ly, -ize, -ized, -ī′zing, -tri ous, -ous ly, -ous ness, in′dus try.

in′dwell′ing.

in ē′brĭ ate, -ā′ted, -ā′ting, -ant, -bri ism, -bri ous, -brī′e ty, -bri- ā′tion.

---

fāte, făt, fär, fạll, fâre, fåst, sofå, mēte, mĕt, hêr, īce, ĭn, nōte,

in ĕd'i ble, -bil'i ty.
in ed'i ta, -i ted.
in ef'fa ble, -ness, -bly, -bil'i ty.
in ef face'a ble, -a bly.
in ef fect'ive, -ly, -ness, -fec'tu al,
   -al ness, -al ly, -al'i ty.
in ef fi că'cious, -ly, -ness, -ef'-
   fi ca cy.
in ef fi'cient   (-fĭsh'ent),   -ly,
   .-cien cy.
in e lâs'tic, -tic'i ty.
in el'e gant, -ly, -gance, -gan cy.
in el'i gi ble, -bly, -bil'i ty.
in el'o quent, -ly, -quence.
in ept', -ly, -ness, -i tude.
in e qual'i ty (-kwŏl'-).
in eq'ui ta ble   (-ĕk'wĭ-),   -ta bly,
   -ĕq'ui ty.
in e răd'i ca ble, -ca bly.
in ĕr'ra ble, -ncss, -bly, -bil'i ty,
   -rant, -ran cy.
in ert', -ly, -ness, -er'ti a (-shĭ a),
   -er'tial.
in es'ti ma ble, -ma bly.
in ev'i ta ble, -ness, -bly, -bil'-
   i ty.
in ex act' (-egz ăkt'), -ly, -ness,
   -i tude.
in ex cus'a ble (-eks kūz'-), -ness,
   -bly, -bil'i ty.
in ex haust'i ble   (-ĕgz aust'-),
   -ness, -bly, -bil'i ty, -haust'ed,
   -ed ly, -ive.
in ex'o ra ble, -ness, -bly, -bil'-
   i ty.
in ex pē'di ent, -ly, -ence, -en cy.
in ex pen'sĭve, -ly, -ness.
in ex pē'ri ence, -enced.
in ex pert', -ness.
in ex'pĭ a ble, -ness, -bly.
in ex plâin'a ble, -a bly.
in ex'plĭ ca ble, -ness, -bly, -bil'-
   i ty
in ex plic'it (-plĭs'it).
in ex press'i ble,   -i bly,   -ive,
   -ive ness.
in ex pug'na ble (or -pūn'a-), -na-
   bly.
in ex tin'guish a ble, -a bly.
in ex tre͞'mis.
in ex'trĭ ca ble, -ness, -bly.
in fa ci e cu ri æ (ĭn fā'shĭ ē
   kū rĭ ē).

in făl'li ble, -ness, -bly, -bil ism,
   -bil ist, -bil'i ty.
in'fa mo͝us, -ly, -ness, -fà my.
in'fan cy,   -fant,   -fant ho͝od,
   -fan'ti cide,   -cĭ'dal,   -fan tĭle
   (or -tĭl)   or   -tĭne   (or -tĭn),
   in făn'ta,   masc.,   -fan te   (-tā),
   in'fant-class, -school.
in fan'try, -man.
in'fâre.
in făt'u ate, -ā'ted, -ā'ting, -ā'tion.
in fea'si ble, -ble ness.
in fect', -ed, -ed ness, -er, -ing,
   -i ble, -ive, -ive ness, -fec tiv'-
   i ty, -fec'tion, -tious, -tious ly,
   -tious ness.
in fe cun'di ty.
in fe lic'i ty (-lĭs'-), -i to͝us.
in fer', -ring, -ferred', -fer'a ble
   or -ri ble.
in'fer ence, -en'tial,   -tial ly.
in fē'ri or, -ly, -ŏr'i ty.
in fer'nal, -ize, -ized, ĭ'zing, -ly,
   -nal'i ty, in fer'no.
in fĕr'ri ble. See infer.
in fest', -ed, -er, -ing, -ive,
   -fes tā'tion.
in'fi del, -ize, -ized, ĭ'zing, -del'i ty.
in'field, a., in'-field, n.
in fĭl'e rĭ.
in fil'trate,   -trā'ted,   -trā'ting,
   -trā'tion.
in'fin ite, -ly, -ness, -i tes'i mal,
   -mal ism, -mal ly, -fin'i tive, -tive-
   ly, -i tude, -i ty, in fĭ ni'to (-nē'-).
in firm', -ly, -ness, -a ry, -i ty,
   -fir ma'ri an.
in flame',   -flamed',   -flăm'er,
   -ing,   -flăm'ma ble,   -ble ness,
   -bly, -bil'i ty, -ma tive, -ma-
   tŏ'ry, -mā'tion.
in flate', -flāt'ed, -er, -ing, -ing ly,
   -flā'tion, -tion ist, in flā'tus.
in flect', -ed, -ing, -ive, -flec'tion,
   -tion al, -tion less, -flec'tor.
in flex'i ble, -ness, -bly, -bil'i ty.
in flict', -ed, -er, -ing, -ive,
   -flic'tion.
in flŏ res'cence, -cent.
in'flŭ ence,   -enced,   -en cing,   -en-
   cer,   -en'tial,   -tial ly,   in'flu ence-
   ma chine͞'.
in flu en'za.

in'flux, -flux'ion (-flŭk'shŭn),
-ion ism, -ion ist.
in form', -al, -al ly, -ant, -a tive,
-er, -ing, -ing ly, -formed',
-for mal'i ty, -mā'tion.
in frac'tion, -tor.
in fran'gi ble, -ness, -bil'i ty.
in fre'quent, -ly, -quen cy.
in fringe', -ment, -fringed',
-frin'ging (-jing), -frin ger.
in fruc'tu ous, -ly.
in fū'ri ate, -ā'ted, -ā'ting.
in fuse' (-fūz'), -fused', -fūs'ing,
-er, -i ble, -i ble ness, -i bil'i ty,
-fu'sive (-sĭv), -fū'sion (-zhŭn),
-fu'sor (-zor).
in'găth'er ing.
In'ge low (ĭn'jē lō), Eng. poetess.
in gē'ni ō.
in gē'ni ous, -ly, -ness, -ge nū'-
i ty.
in'gë'nue' (ăṅ'zhā'nŏŏ').
in gĕn'u ous (-jĕn'-), -ly, -ness.
iṇ'gle, -side, -cheek, -nŏŏk.
in glō'ri ous, -ly, -ness.
iṇ'got, -i'ron, -mold.
in grăft', -ed, -er, -ing, -ment.
in grain', *v.,* -ing, -grained', in'-
grain, *n.* and *a.*
in'grate.
in grā'ti ate (-shĭ-), -ā'ted, -ā'ting,
-à to'ry.
in grat'i tude.
in grē'di ent.
Ingres (ăṅgr), Fr. painter.
in'gress, -gress'ive, -gres'sion
(-gresh'un).
in grŏŏve', -grooved', -groov'ing.
in'grown.
in gur'gi tate (-jĭ-), -tā'ted, -tā'-
ting, -tā'tion.
in hăb'it, -ed, -ing, -a ble, -ance,
-an cy, -ant, -er, -ive, -i tā'-
tion.
in hāle', -haled', -hāl'ant *or* -ent,
-er, -ing, -hà lā'tion.
in har mō'ni ous, -ly, -ness,
-mon'ic, -ic al.
in hēre', -hered', -hēr'ing, -ence,
-en cy, -ent, -ent ly.
in hĕr'it, -ed, -er, -ing, -a ble,
-a bly, -a bil'i ty, -ance, -or,
-ress *or* -rix.

in hĭb'it, -ed, -er, -ing, -i tor,
-tō'ry, -hi bi'tion (-bish'un).
in hoc.
in hos'pĭ ta ble, -ness, -bly, -pi-
tal'i ty.
in hu'man, -ly, -man'i ty.
in hu mane'.
in hume', -humed', -hūm'ing,
-hu mā'tion.
in im'i cal, -ly, -cal'i ty.
in im'i ta ble, -ness, -bly, -bil'-
i ty.
in iq'ui tous (-ĭk'wĭ tus), -ly, -ui ty.
in ĭ'tial (-ĭsh'al), -ly, -ize, -ized,
-ĭ'zing.
in i'ti ate (-ĭsh'ĭ-), -ti à tive,
-ā'tor, -tō'ry, -ā'tion.
in ject', -ed, -ing, -or, -jec'tion,
in jec'tion-cock, -con dens'er,
-en'gine, -pipe, -syr'ĭnge (-sĭr'-),
-valve, -wa ter, in ject'or-valve.
in ju di'ci o (-dĭsh'i o).
in ju di'cious (-dĭsh'us), -ly, -ness.
in juṇc'tion, -junc'tive, -tive ly.
in'jure (-jŏŏr), -jured, -jur er,
-jur ing, -ju'ri ous, -ous ly,
-ous ness, in'ju ry.
in jus'tice (-tis).
iṇk, -er, -ing, -y, -ish, -i ness,
inked, iṇk'bĕr'ry, -fish, -hold'er,
-horn, -nut, -root, -shed,
-stand, -stone, -wood.
iṇk'-bag, -ball, -bench, -block,
-bot'tle, -bray'er, -cap, -cup, -cyl'-
in der, -duct, -e rās'er, -foun'-
taĭn, -gland, -knife, -mush'-
room, -pad, -pen cil, -plant,
-pow der, -roll er, -sac, -slice,
-sling'er, -sur'face, -ta'ble,
-well, -writ'er.
iṇk'ing-ap pa ra'tus, -ball, -pad,
-roll er, -ta ble, -trough, ink'-
ber'ry-weed.
Ink er män', t. Russ.
iṇ'kle, -kled, -kling, suspecting,
ink'ling, *n.,* a hint.
in knit' (-nĭt'), -ted, -ter, -ting.
in'land, -er.
in lay', -er, -ing, -laid'.
in'let, *n.*
*in līm'i nē, in lō'co, in lō'co
pa ren'tis.*
in'mate.

in mĕ'dĭ as res (rēz), *in mĕ mō'-
rĭ am.*
in'mŏst.
inn, a dwelling, -hold'er, -keep'er.
in'nate', -ly, -ness, -nas'ci ble.
ĭn'ner, -most.
in ner'vate,   -vā'ted,   -vā'ting,
-vā'tion.
in nerve', -nerved', -nerv'ing.
ĭn'ning.
in'no cent, -ly, -cence, -cen cy.
in noc'u ous, -ly, -ness.
in'no vate,   -vā'ted,   -va'ting,
-va'tive, -va'tor, -va'to ry, -vā'-
tion, -tion ist.
in nox'ious (-nŏk'shus), -ly, -ness.
Inns'bruck (-prŏŏk), c. Aust.
in nŭ'cē.
in'nŭ en'dŏ, *pl.* -does (-dōz).
in nū'mer a ble, -ness, -bly, -bil'-
i ty.
in nū'trĭ tive, -trĭ'tious (-trĭsh'us),
-trĭ'tion.
in oc'u late, -lā'ted, -lā'ting, -là-
tive, -lā'tor, -lā'tion.
in ŏ'dor ous, -ness.
in of fen'sive, -ly, -ness.
in'ŏf fĭ'cial (-fĭsh'al), -ly, -cious,
-cious ly.
in op'er a tive.
in op'por tūne', -ly, -ness.
in or'di nate, -ly, ness, -di na cy.
in or găn'ic, al, al ly.
*in per pet'ŭ um, in per sō'nam,
in prō'prĭ a per sō'na.*
in'quest.
in'quĭ lĭne.
in quĭre',   -quir'a ble,   -quir'er,
-ing, -ing ly, -y.
in quĭ si'tion (-zĭsh'un), -al, -a ry.
in quis'i tive (-kwĭz'-), -ly, -ness,
-i tor, -to'ri al, -al ly, -in quis'-
i tor-gen'er al.
in rē.
in'rigged.
in'rŏad.
in sa lŭ'bri ous, -brĭ ty.
in sāne', -ly, -ness, -san'i ty.
in san'i ta ry, -i tā'tion.
in sā'tia ble (-sā'shà- *or* -sāsh'-
yà-), -ness, -bly, -bil'i ty,
-sā'ti ate (-shĭ-), -ate ly, -ate-
ness.

in scrĭbe', -scribed', -scrĭb'a ble,
-ble ness, -er, -ing, -scrĭp'tĭve,
-ti ble, -tion, -tion ist.
in scru'ta ble, -ness, -bly, -bil'-
i ty.
in sculpt'.
in'sect, -sec ta'ry, -ta'rĭ um, *pl.*
-ums *or* -a, -sec'ti cĭde, -tĭ cĭ'-
dal, -sec'ti form, -ti fuge (-fūj),
-tif'er ous, in'sec tĭle.
in'sect-de stroy'er, -fun'gi (-jĭ),
-gun, -net, -pow der, -trap.
in se cure', -ly, -ness, -cu'ri ty.
in sen'sate, -ness.
in sen'si ble, -ness, -bly, -bil'i ty,
-si tive, -tive ness, -sen'tient
(-shent).
in sep'a ra ble, -ness, -bly, -bil'-
-i ty.
in sert', -ed, -ing, -ser'tion.
in ses'sor.
in'set.
in'shŏre, *a.,* in'shŏre', *adv.*
in'sĭde, *n.,* in'sĭde', *adv.,* -sĭd'er.
in sĭd'i ous, -ly, -ness.
in'sĭght.
in sig'ni a.
in sig nĭf'i cant,   -ly,   -cance,
-can cy, -cà tive.
in sin cere', -ly, -cĕr'i ty.
in sin'u ate,   -ā'ted,   -ā'ting,
-ting ly, -à tive, -ā'tor, -tō'ry,
-ā'tion.
in sip'id, -ly, -ness, -si pid'i ty.
in sist', -ed, -ence, -ent, -ent ly,
-ing, -ing ly.
in sĭ'tŭ.
in snare'.   See *ensnare.*
in sŏ brĭ'e ty.
in'so late, -lā'ted, -lā'ting, -lā'-
tion.
in'-sŏle.
in'so lent, -ly, -lence.
in sŏl'u ble, -ness, -bil'i ty.
in sŏl'vent, -ven cy.
in sŏm'nĭ a, -ni ous.
in'sŏ much'.
in'sou'ciance' (ăn'sŏŏ'syäns'), -ciant'
(-syän').
in spect', -ed, -ing, -ing ly, -ive,
-or, -or ate, -or ship, -spec'tion,
-tion al, in spec'tion-car, -gen'-
er al.

in spīre', -spired', -spīr'er, -ing,
-ing ly, in'spǐ rate, -rā'ted, -rā'-
ting, -rā'tor, -spīr'a tŏ'ry, -spī-
rā'tion, -tion al, -tion ist, -tion-
ism, -spi rom'e ter.
in spǐr'it, -ed, -ing.
in spǐs'sate, -sā'ted, -sā'ting, -sant,
-sā'tion.
in'-square.
in sta bil'i ty.
in stall', -ing, -stalled', -stăl lā'-
tion, -stal'ment or -stall'-.
in'stance, -stanced, -stan cing.
in'stant, -ly, -stan'ta'ne ous, -ous ly,
-ne'i ty, -stan'ter.
in stā'tŭ quo.
in stĕad'.
in'step.
in'stǐ gate, -gā'ted, -gā'ting, -ting-
ly, -gā'tor, -gā'tion.
in stil' or -still', -stilled', -stil'-
ling, -ler, -ment, -lā'tion.
in'stǐnct, n., -stǐnct', a., -stǐnc'-
tǐve, -tive ly.
in'stǐ tūte, -tū'ted, -tū'ting, -tū'-
tive, -tive ly, -tū'tor, -tu'tion,
-tion al, -al ism, -al ist, -tion a ry.
in'stroke.
in struct', -ed, -ing, -ive, -ive ly,
-ive ness, -or, -ress, -struc'tion,
-tion al.
in'stru ment, -men'tal, -tal ist,
-tal ly, -tal'i ty, -tā'tion, -men'-
tist.
in sub jec'tion.
in sŭb or'di nate, -nā'tion.
in sub stan'tial (-shal), -ti al'i ty
(-shǐ-).
in suf'fer a ble, -a bly.
in suf fi'cient (-fǐsh'ent), -cien cy,
-cient ly.
in'sū lar, -ize', -ized', -ī'zing, -ism,
-ly, -lär'i ty.
in'su late, -lā'ted, -lā'ting, -lā'-
tor, -lā'tion.
in'sult, n., in sult', v., -ed, -er,
-ing, -ing ly.
in sū'per a ble, -ness, -bly, -bil'-
i ty.
in sup port'a ble, -ness, -bly.
in sup press'i ble, -i bly.
in sure' (-shōōr'), -sured', -sūr'er,
-ing, -a ble, -ance, -ee'.

in sur'gent, -gen cy.
in sur mount'a ble, -ness, -bly,
-bil'i ty.
in sur rec'tion, -al, -a ry, -ist.
in sus cep'ti ble, -ti bly, -ti bil'-
i ty.
in tact', -ness, -tac'ti ble or -ta-
ble.
in tagl'io (-tăl'yō), pl. -ios (-yōz),
-io type.
in'take, -tak'er, in'take-hol'der.
in tăn'gi ble (-jǐ-), -ness, -bly,
-bil'i ty.
ǐn'te ger, -te gral, -gral ism, -gral-
ly, -grà ble, -bil'i ty.
in'te grate, -grā'ted, -grā'ting,
-grà tive, -grā'tor, -grant, -grā'-
tion.
in teg'ri ty.
in teg'u ment, -men'tal, -ta ry,
-tā'tion.
in'tel lect, -lec'ti ble, -tion, -tive,
-tive ly, -tu al, -al ism, -al ist,
-al ly, -al ness, -al is'tic, -al'i ty,
-al ize, -ized, -ī'zing, -ǐ zā'tion.
in tĕl'li gent, -ly, -gence, -gen'cer,
-gen'tial, -gi ble, -ble ness,
-bly, -bil'i ty.
in tem'per ate, -ly, -ness, -per-
ance.
in tem'pō.
in tend', -ance, -an cy, -ant, -ed,
-ed ly, -er, -ing.
in tense', -ly, -ness, -ten'sion,
-sive, -sive ness, -si ty, -si ty-cur'-
rent.
in ten'si fy, -ing, -fīed, -fī er,
-fī cā'tion.
in tent', -ly, -ness, -ten'tion,
-tion al, -al ly, -al'i ty, -tioned.
in têr', -ring, -ment, -terred'.
in ter act', -ăc'tion, -ac'tive.
in'ter ā'lǐ a.
in'ter cā'dence, -ca'dent.
in ter'ca lar, -là ry, -ca late, -là-
tive, -lā'ting, -lā'tion.
in ter cede', -cēd'ed, -er, -ing,
-cĕs'sor, -so ry, -sō'ri al, -cĕs'-
sion.
in ter cept', -ed, -er, -ing, -ive,
-cep'tion.
in ter chănge', -a ble, -ble ness,
-a bly, -a bil'i ty, -changed',

-chăn'ging, -chăn'ger, in'ter-
change, *n.*
in'ter col lē'gĭ ate, -co lō'ni al,
-al ly, -co lum'nar, -lum ni a'-
tion, -cos'tal.
in'ter cŏurse.
in'ter cul'tŭr al.
in'ter dĕ pend'ent, -ence, -en cy.
in ter dict', -ed, -ing, -ive, -o ry,
-dic'tion.
in'ter est, -ed, -ed ly, -ed ness,
-ing, -ing ly, -ing ness.
in ter fēre', -fered', -fēr'ence,
-fēr'er, -fēr'ing, -ing ly, in ter-
fēr'ing-strap.
in'ter im.
in tē'ri or, -ly.
in'ter jac'u la to'ry.
in ter ject', -ed, -ing, -jec'tion,
-tion al, -al ly, -tion a ry.
in ter lāce', -ment, -lāced',
-lā'cing.
In ter lăk'en *or* -läch en, vil.
Switz.
in ter lap', -ping, -lapped'.
in ter lard', -ed, -er, -ing, -ment.
in'ter leaf, *pl.* -lēaves, -lēave', *v.*,
-leaved', -lēav'ing.
in ter līne', -lined', -līn'ing,
-līn'e ar, -e ate, -â ry, -är ly, -â ri-
ly, -ā'tion.
in ter lock', -ing, -locked'.
in ter lŏc'u tor, -tō'ry, -u tive, -lo-
cū'tion.
in'ter lo'per, -lope', -loped',
-lōp'ing.
in'ter lūde, -lu'ded, -lu'der, -lu'-
di al.
in ter lū'nar.
in ter măr'ry, -ing, -rĭed, -rĭage.
in ter mĕd'dle, -dled, -dler,
-dling, -dle some, -some ness.
in ter mē'di ate, -ly, -di a cy,
-di al, -di a ry, -di a tor, -di ā'-
tion, -di et'to, *in'ter mez'zo*
(-mĕd'zō).
in ter'mi nà ble, -ness, -bly.
in ter min'gle, -gled, -gling.
in ter mit', -ted, -tence, -ten cy,
-tent, -tent ly, -ting, -ting ly,
-mis'sion.
in ter mix', -ed ly, -ing, -ture,
-mixed'.

in ter mon'tāne, -mun'dane,
-mū'ral.
in ter'nal, -ly, -nal'i ty.
in ter na'tion al (-năsh'un-), -ist,
-ly, -ize, -ized, -ī'zing.
in terne' (-têrn').
in'ter nē'cĭne, -ne'cive.
in'ter nōs.
in'ter pel'late, -la tor, -pel'lant,
-lā'tion.
in ter plēad', -er, -ing.
in'ter pŏc'u la.
in ter'po late, -lā'ted, -la'ting,
-lā'tor, -lā'tive, -tive ly, -lā'tion,
-là ble, -lar, -lâ ry.
in ter pose' (-pōz'), -posed',
-pōs'er, -ing, -po si'tion (-zish'-
un).
in ter'pret, -ed, -er, -ing, -à ble,
-pre tā'tive, -tive ly, -tā'tion.
in ter reg'num, *pl.* -nums.
in tĕr'ro gate, -gā'ted, -gā'ting,
-gā'tor, -gā tee', -gā'tion, -rog'-
a tive, -tive ly, -tō'ry.
in ter rupt', -ed, -ed ly, -er, -ing,
-ive, -ive ly, -rup'tion.
in ter sect', -ed, -ing, -sec'tion,
-tion al.
in ter sperse', -spersed' spers'-
ing, -sper'sion.
in'ter state.
in'ter stice (-stĭs *or* -ter'stis),
-sticed (-stĭst), -sti tial (-stĭsh'al),
-tial ly.
in ter twīne', -twined', -twīn'ing,
-ing ly.
in'ter ur'ban.
in'ter val.
in ter vene', -vened', -vēn'er, -vēn'-
ing, -vĕn'tion, -tion ist.
in'ter view (-vū), -er, -ing,
-viewed.
in'ter vo lute'.
in ter wēave', -weav'ing, -wove',
-wōv'en (-n).
in tes'tate, -tes'ta ble, -ta cy.
in tes'tīne, -tĭ nal.
in'ti mate, -ly, -mā'ted, -mā'-
ting, -mà cy, -mā'tion.
in tĭm'i date, -dā'ted, -dā'ting,
-da tō'ry, -dā'tion.
in'to.
in'toed.

---

nŏt, nôr, ūse, ŭp, ûrn, etüde, fōōd, fŏŏt, aŋger, boṅmot, thus, Bach.

in tol′er a ble, -ness, -bly, -bil′-
i ty, -ance, -an cy, -ant, -ant ly.
in tō′nä cō or *-ni co* (-nē kō).
in′to nate, -nä′ted, -nä′ting,
-nä′tor, -nä′tion, in tone′,
-toned′, -tōn′ing.
in tox′i cate, -cā′ted, -cā′ting, -cā′-
tive, -cant, -cā′tion.
in tract′a ble, -ness, -bly, -bil′-
i ty.
in tra mun′dane, -mu′ral.
in tran′si tive, -tive ly.
in tran′sĭ tū.
in′tra-state′.
in trench′, -er, -ing, -ment,
-trenched′.
in trĕp′id, -ly, -trē pĭd′i ty.
in′tri cate, -ly, -ness, -ca cy.
in trigue′ (-trēg′), -trigued′,
-trigu′er, -er y, -ing, -ing ly,
in′tri gant, *fem. -gante′.*
in trin′sic (-sĭk), -al, -al ly, -al-
ness, -si cal′i ty.
in tro duce′, -duced′, -dū′cer,
-cing, -duc′tive, -tive ly, -to ry,
-to ri ly, -duc′tion.
in trŏ′it.
in′tro mis′si ble, -sive, -si bil′i ty.
in trorse′, -ly, -tror sal.
in tro spect′, -ed, -ing, -spec′-
tive, -tion, -tion ist.
in trude′, -trŭd′ed, -er, -ing,
-ing ly, -tru′sive, -sive ly, -sive-
ness, -sion (-zhun), -sion ist.
in trust′ *or* en trust′, -ed, -ing.
in′tu bate, -bā′ted, -bā′ting.
in′tu ent.
in tu i′tion (-ish′un), -al, -al ism,
-al ist, -ism, -ist, -tū′i tive,
-tive ly, -tive ism, -tive ist.
in twine′. See *entwine.*
in un′date, -da′ted, -da′ting,
-dā′tion.
in ūre′, -ment, -ured′, -ūr′ing.
in urn′, -ing, -urned′.
in vāde′, -vād′ed, -ing, -er,
-va′sĭve, -vä′sion (-zhun).
in′va lid, *n.,* -ism, -lid′i ty, in′-
va lid-bed, -chair.
in văl′id, *a.,* -ly.
in văl′i date, *v.,* -da′ted, -da′ting,
-dā′tion.
in văl′u a ble, -ness, -bly.

in vä′ri a ble, -ness, -bly, -bil′-
i ty, in vä′ri ant.
in vec′tive, -ly.
in veigh′ (-vā′), -er, -ing,
-veighed′.
in vei′gle (-vĕ′-), -ment, -gled,
-gler, -gling.
in vent′, -ed, -er, -ing, -i ble,
-ble ness, -ive, -ive ness, -or,
-ven′tion.
in ven tä′ri o.
in′ven to′ry, -ing, -to′rĭed, -to′-
ri al, -al ly.
In ver ness′, co. Scot. in′ver-
ness, a garment.
in verse′, -ly, -ver′sive.
in vert′, -ed, -ed ly, -ing, -i ble,
-or, -ver′sion (-shun), in′vert-
su′gar.
in vest′, -ed, -ing, -ment, -or,
-i ture.
in ves′ti gate, -gā′ted, -gā′ting,
-gä′tive, -gä′tor, -gä′tion.
in vet′er ate, -ly, -ness, -a cy.
in vid′i ous, -ly, -ness.
in vig′or ate, -ā′ted, -ā′ting, -ant,
-ā′tion.
in vin′ci ble, -ness, -bly, -bil′i ty.
in vī′o la ble, -ness, -bly, -bil′i ty,
-late, -late ly, -late ness.
in vis′i ble (-vĭz′-), -ness, -bly,
-bil′i ty.
in vīte′, -vīt′ed, -er, -ing, -ing ly,
-ing ness, -vī′ta to′ry, -vī tä′-
tion, in′vī tant, -vī tee′.
in′voice, -volced, -voi′cing, in′-
voice-book.
in voke′, -voked′, -vŏk′er, -ing,
-vŏc′à tive, -tō′ry, -vo cä′tion.
in′vō lū′cre (-ker), -cred (-kerd),
-lū′cret.
in vŏl′un ta ry, -ta ri ly, -ri ness.
in′vo lute, -lū′ted, -lū′tant, -lū′-
tion.
in vŏlve′, -ment, -vŏlved′, -vŏlv′-
ing, -volv′ed ness.
in vul′ner a ble, -ness, -bly,
-bil′i ty.
in′-wale.
in wall′, -walled′.
in′ward, -ly, -ness.
in wĕave′, -wĕav′ing, -wove′,
-wov′en (-n).

in work', -ing, -worked' or
-wrought'.
in yä'la.
ĭ'ŏ, an exclamation; a moth; a bird.
 I'o (ĭ'ō), Myth.; Astron.; Entom.
i'o did (ĭ'ō dĭd) or -dĭde (or -dĭd),
 -o dĭn or -dĭne.
I'o dĭze, -dized, -dī'zing, -dī'zer.
ĭ'ŏ dŏ met'ric, -do ther'a py, -do-
 thy'rin (-thī'-).
ĭ'ŏ lĭte.
I'on, ĭ'on ize, -ized, -ĭ za'tion.
I ŏ'ni a, -ni an, -on'ic, -on'i cize,
 -cized, -cī'zing, I'o nism,
 -o nist, -on'i cism.
I ŏ'ta, -cism, -ta cist.
I'o wȧ, state U. S., -o wan.
ĭp'e cac, -cac u an'ha.
Iph'e de'iah (ĭf'e dē'ya), Bib.
Iph'ĭ gē nī'a, Myth.
i'pil (ē'pĭl),
ĭp'se dĭx'it, ĭp sis'si ma ver'ba,
 ĭp'sŏ fac'to.
I qui'que (ē kē'kä), t. Chile.
i'ra cun'di ty.
I ran' (ē'rän'), Persia, I ra'ni an
 (ī rä'-), I răn'ic.
i ras'ci ble, -ness, -ci bly, -bil'-
 i ty.
Ire, -ful, -ful ly, -ful ness, ĭ rāte'.
Ir e næ'us (ĭr ē nē'us), Bishop of
 Lyons.
I rene' (ī rēn'), Chr. name,
 I re'ne (ī rē'nĕ), Empress of
 Constantinople; Astron.; Zoöl.
 genus.
ĭ rĕn'ic, -ic al, -i con, pl. -i ca.
Ĭr I des'cent, -cence, -cen cy.
I rid'i um.
Ĭr'i dize, -dized, -dī'zing, -dĭ zā'-
 tion.
ĭ'ris, pl. -ris es or -rĭ des (-dēz),
 Anat.; the rainbow, ĭ'ris a'ted,
 ĭ'rĭ scope, ĭ'rised (-rist), ĭ'ris-
 di'a phragm, -rōōt, -swal'low.
 I'ris, Myth.; Astron.; Bot. genus.
I'rish, -ize, -ized, -ī'zing, -ly, -ism,
 -man, -wom'an, -A mer'i can.
irk'some, -ly, -ness.
Ir kutsk' (ĭr kōōtsk'), c. Sib.
i'ron (ĭ'ûrn), -roned (-ûrnd),
 -ron'ing, -y, a.

i'ron bark, a tree, -clad, n.,
 -head, a duck, -heads, a plant,
 -man, -măs'ter, -mon'ger, -sides,
 a person, -smith, -stone, -ware,
 -weed, -wood, a tree, -work,
 -wort.
i'ron-al'um, -black, -bound,
 -chăm'ber, -clad, a., -clay,
 -cloth, -flint, -found'er, -found'-
 ry, -fur'nace, -glănce, -grăss,
 -gray, -gum tree, -ĭ'o dĭd,
 -line, -liq'uor, -mold, -oak,
 -o'chre (-ō'ker), -red, -rust,
 -sand, -saw, -scale, -shrub,
 -sick, -stain, -strap, -tree,
 -work'er, -works, -yel'low.
i'ron age, i. ce ment', i. cross,
 i. crown, i. horse, i. lac'quer.
i'ron ing-board, -box, -cloth,
 -lăthe, -ma chine', i'ron bark-
 tree.
I'ron y (-rŭn-), n.
Ir'o quois' (ĭr'ō kwoi'), -quoi'an.
Ir'pe el (ĭr'pē ĕl), Bib.
Ĭr ră'di ate, -ā'ted, -ā'ting, -ance,
 -an cy, -à tive, -ā'tion.
Ĭr ra'tion al (-rash'un-), -ly, -ism,
 -ist, -ness, -al'i ty.
ir're cep'tive.
Ĭr re clāim'a ble, -ness, -a bly.
Ĭr rec'og nī'za ble.
Ĭr rec'on cī'la ble, -ness, -bly,
 -bil'i ty, -cile'ment, -cĭl'i ā'tion.
Ĭr re cov'er a ble (-kŭv'-), -ness,
 -bly.
Ĭr're deem'a ble, -ness, -bly,
 -bil'i ty.
Ĭr re dū'ci ble, -ness, -bly, -bil'-
 i ty.
Ĭr ref'ra ga ble, -ness, -bly, -bil'-
 i ty.
Ĭr re fran'gi ble, -ness, -bly,
 -bil'i ty.
Ĭr're fūt'a ble, -ness, -bly, -bil'-
 i ty.
Ĭr reg'u lar, -ly, -lăr'i ty.
Ĭr rĕl'a tive, -ly, -re lā'tion.
Ĭr rel'e vant, -ly, -vance, -van cy.
Ĭr re li'gion (-lĭj'un), -ist, -gious,
 -gious ly, -gious ness.
Ĭr rĕ mē'dĭ a ble, -ness, -bly.
Ĭr re mĭs'si ble, -ness, -bly, -sive,
 -sion (-mĭsh'un).

nŏt, nôr, ūse, ŭp, ûrn, etüde, fōōd, fŏŏt, aŋger, boṅmot, ṫhus, Bach.

Ĭr re mov′a ble (-mōōv′-), -ness, -a bly, -a bil′i ty.

Ĭr rep′a ra ble, -ness, -bly, -bil′-i ty.

Ĭr rep re hen′si ble, -ness, -bly.

Ĭr re press′i ble, -ness, -i bly.

Ĭr re prŏach′a ble, -ness, -bly.

Ĭr re sist′i ble (-zĭst′-), -ness, -bly, -bil′i ty.

Ĭr res′o lŭ ble (-rĕz′-), -ness.

Ĭr res′o lute (-rĕz′-), -ly, -ness, -lu′tion.

Ĭr re sŏlv′a ble (-zŏlv′-), -ness, -bil′i ty.

Ĭr re spec′tive, -ly.

Ĭr re spon′si ble, -bly, -bil′i ty.

Ĭr re spon′sive, -ness.

Ĭr re străin′a ble.

Ĭr re trăce′a ble.

Ĭr re triĕv′a ble, -ness, -bly, -bil′i ty.

Ĭr rev′er ent, -ly, -ence.

Ĭr rĕ vers′i ble, -ness, -bly, -bil′-i ty.

Ĭr rĕv′o ca ble, -ness, -bly, -bil′-i ty.

Ĭr′rĭ gate, -gā′ted, -gā′ting, -gà-ble, -gā′tive, -gā′tor, -gā′tion, -tion ist.

Ĭr′rĭ ta ble, -ness, -bly, -bil′i ty.

Ĭr′ri tate, -ta′ted, -ta′ting, -ting ly, -ta′tive, -tant, -tan′cy, -tā′tion.

Ĭr rup′tion, -rup′tive.

I′saac (ī′zăk), a bird. I′saac, a Chr. name.

is′a bel or -belle (ĭz′a bĕl), a color. Is′a bel, a proper name. is′a bel-yel low.

is a bel′la (ĭz-), -bĕl′ite, -bel′lĭne, is a bel′la-wood.

Ĭ sa gog′ic (-gŏj′-), -ic al, -gog′ics.

I sa′iah (ī zā′yà or -zä′yà), I sa ian′ic (ī zā yăn′ik).

Is′chi a (ĭss′kē ä), isl. It.

is′chi al′gic (-kĭ-), -gĭ a.

is′chi or rho′gic (-kĭ or -rŏ′jik).

I′sen grin (ē′zĕn grēn), a legend-ary wolf.

I′ser (ē′zer), r. Aust.

I sère′ (ē′zār′), dept. Fr.

Ish′mĕ rài, Bib.

Ish′u ăi, Bib.

I′sin glåss (-zĭn-), -stone.

I′sis (ī′sis), Myth., I′sĭ ac.

Is′lam (iss′läm or ĭz lâm or iss lăm), -ism, -ite, -it′ic, -ize, -ized, -i zing, -lam′ic.

is′land (ī′-), -er.

Is′lay (ī′lä) or Is′la (ī′là), isl. Hebrides.

isle (īl), is′let (ī′let), -let ed.

I′slip (ī′slip), vil. N. Y.

Is mă′iah (-yà or Ĭs ma ī′ah), Bib.

Is ma il′ (ēs mä ēl′), t. Russ.

Is ma il′ (ĭs mă ēl′), -ma ĭl′i an or -maē′li an, -ma il īte or -ma-ĕl ite, -ma i lĭt′ic or -ma el it′ic, Is ma il′ Pa sha′ (ĭss mä ēl′ pä shä′).

Is ma il′ia (ēs′mä ēl′yä), t. Egypt.

isn′t, contraction of is not.

I′so bar, -ism, -bär′ic, -băr′o-met′ric, -so băth′i therm, -ther′-mal, -ther′mic.

I soch′rŏ nal (-sŏk′-), -ly, -ro-nism, -ro non, -ro nous, -nous-ly, -ro us, -so chron′ic.

I′so clīne, -cli′nal, -clĭn′ic.

I sog′ra phy, -so graph′ic, -ic al-ly.

Is′o late (ĭs′- or ī′so-), -lā′ted, -ted ly, -lā′ting, -lā′tor, -lā′tion.

I solde′ (I sŏld′), Round Table, spelled also Isolt, Isoud, Ysolde, Ysoude, Yseult. I sol′de (I sul′dĕ), Wagnerian opera.

I sŏ mĕr′ic, -ic al, -al ly, -som′-er ism.

I sŏ mĕt′ric, -ric al.

I′sŏ morph, -mor′phic, -mor′-phism, -mor′phous.

I sŏn′o my, -sŏ nŏ′mi a, -nom′ic.

I sŏs′ce les (-lēz).

I sos′ta sy, -tat′ic.

I′sŏ therm, -ther′mal.

I′sŏ trope, -sŏt′ro py, -ro pous, -ro pism, -so trŏp′ic.

Is′ra el (ĭz′rā el or -rà-), -īte, -ī′tish, -ĭt′ic.

is′sue (ĭsh′ōō), -less, -su à ble, -à bly, -ance, -ant, -er, -ing, is′sue-pēa.

isth′mus (ĭss′- or ĭst′-), -mi an, -mic.

Is′trĭ a, pen. Adriatic, -trĭ an.

Ĭ tăl'i cize, -cized, -cī'zing, -cĭ-
za'tion, Ĭ tal'ic, a printer's type.
It'a ly, Ĭ tal'ian (Ĭ tăl'yan), -ism,
-ian ize, -īzed, -i'zing, -Ĭ zā'tion,
-tal'ic, -Ĭ cism, -ian esque', It'a-
lo-By zăn'tĭne (-bĭ-).
itch, -ing, -less, -y, -i ness,
itched, itch'weed, -in'sect,
-mite, itch'ing-ber'ry.
Ĭ'tem, -ize, -ized, -i'zer, -i'zing,
-Ĭ zā'tion.
Ĭt'er ate, -ā'ted, -ā'ting, -å tive',
-tive'ly, -ant, -å ble, -an'cy,
-ate ly, -ā'tion.
Ith'a ca, c. N. Y.; vil. Mich.;
isl. Mediterranean.
I'thai (ī'thä or Ĭth'a ī), Bib.
I tho'me (ē thō'mā), mt. Gr.
Ĭ tĭn'er a cy, -an cy, -ant, -ant ly,
-a ry, -er ate, -ā'ted, -ā'ting.
Ĭts, pos. pro.; it's, contraction of
it is; it self'.
It'tăi (or it'ta ī), Bib.

I tur bi'de, de (dä ē tōōr bē'dä),
Emp. of Mex.
i vaar'īte (ē vär'-).
I van' I van'o vitch (ē vän'
ē vän'ō vĭch).
I'vi son (ī'vĭ son), Amer. pub.
I'vŏ ry, -bill, a bird, -nut, -type,
-wood, -billed, -black, -brown,
-gull, -gum, -pälm, -pa'per,
-paste, -porce'laĭn, -shell, -tree,
-white, -yel'low, ī'vŏ ry lines, i.
spä'ces.
I'vy, ī'vĭed, ī'vy wort, -bĭnd'weed,
-bush, -gum, -leaf, -man'tled,
-owl, -tree.
i wa'na (ē wä'-).
Ix Ĭ'on, Myth.
Ixt lil xo'chitl (ĭxt lēl hō'chĕtl),
Mex. hist.
I'yar (ē'är) or Iy'yar' (ē'yär').
I'ynx (ī'inks).
iz'ar.
Iz'ard (ĭz'-), Amer. statesman.

J

Jå'a kan, Bib.
Jå'a kŏ'bah, Bib.
Jå å'la, Bib.
jå'al-goat.
Jå å'sĭ el, Bib.
jab, -ber, -bing, jabbed, -ber er,
-ber ing, jab'ber ing crow.
Jăb'nē ĕl or -nēl, Bib.
jăb'ot (jăb'o or zhä bō')
ja bul (hä bōōl' or hå vōōl').
ja cal' (hå kål').
jå'cinth.
jack', -a dan'dy, -a nape, -a-
napes, -daw, -fish, -man, -smith,
-stone, -straw, -weight, -y.
jack'-ad'ams, a fool, -ape,
-arch, -back, -bāk'er, -bird,
-block, -boot, -chain, -cross'tree,
-cur lew, -en'gine, -fish'ing,
-flag, -frame, -fri'ar, -fruit,
-hare, -hern, -hole, -hunt ing,
-knife, -lad der, -lamp, -lan-
tern, -light, -oak, -pin, -pit,
-plane, -pot, -pud ding, -rab-
bit, -råft'er, -rib, -roll, -sal'-

mon, -saw, -screw, -sink er,
-snipe, -span iard, -spin ner,
-stäff, -stay, -tim ber, -tow el,
-tree, -wood.
jack'-at-the-hedge, a plant, -in-
a-bot tle, -in-a-box, -in-the-
bush, -in-the-pul pit, -jump-
a bout.
Jack'-a-green, -a-Lent, -o'-lan-
tern, -o'-Lent.
jack'al, -buz'zard, jack'alṣ-kŏst.
jack'a rōō'.
jack'ass, -brig, -deer, -fish, -pen'-
guin, -rab'bit.
jack'et, -ed, -ing.
jăck'ŏ.
jack'y-win'ter.
jå'cob, a bird.
Jac'o bĭn, -ism, -bin'ic, -ic al,
-al ly, -bin ize, -ized, -i'zing.
Jac'ŏ bīte, -bĭt ism, -bĭt'ic, -ic al,
-al ly.
Jå'cob's-chăr'i ot, -lad der, -rod,
-stäff, -sword.
jăc'o net.

Jac'quand' (zhä'kŏń'), Fr. painter.
Jac quard' (zhä kär'), Fr. inventor.
Jac quard' (jăk kärd'), J. loom.
Jacque mart' (zhäk'mär'), Fr. auth.
Jacque'mi not (jăk'mĭ nō).
Jacque mont' (zhäk'mŏń'), Fr. naturalist.
Jacque'rie' (zhäk'rē').
jade, jād'ed, -ed ly, -ing, -er y, -ish, -y.
Ja'ĕl, Bib.
jag, -ger, -ging, jagged, jag'ged, -ged ness, -gy, jag'ger y-pälm, jag'ging-board, -i ron.
ja guär' (or jăg'wär), jä guå rŏn'-dĭ, jag'uar ete'.
Jah (jä or yä), -veh, -vism, -vist, -vis'tic.
Ja hăl'e lel, Bib.
Jäh'dăi (or -dä ī), Bib.
Jäh'lĕ ĕl, Bib.
Jäh'măi (or -mä ī), Bib.
Jahn (yän), Ger. philol.
jahr'zeit (yar'tsīt).
ja i'ba (hä ē'ba).
jäil, -er, -ing, jailed, jail'bird, a person, -de liv'er y, -fe ver, -house, -keep'er.
Jai'pur (jī'pōōr), India.
Jä'ir, Bib.
Jä'ĭ rus, Old Test. Jä ī'rus, New Test.
jăl'ap, -plant.
Ja la'pa (hä lä'pä), c. Mex.
ja'lee or ja'li (jä'lē).
ja le'o (hä lä'o).
ja let' (zhå lä').
Ja lis'co (hä lēs'kō), state Mex.
ja lou sie' (zhå lōō zē').
jam, -mer, -ming, jammed, jam'-nut, -weld.
jä'ma.
Ja mai'ca (-mä'ka), isl. W. I.; t. N. Y., -mai'can, Ja mai'ca bark, J. bil'ber ry, J. birch, J. buck'thorn, J. chĕr'ry.
jamb, Arch., -lĭn'ing, -post, -shäft, -stone.
jambe (jămb), armor, jam bi eres' (zhŏń bē âr').
jăm bŏ ree'.

Jăm'bres (-brēz), Bib.
jăm'e war.
Jä'mĭe son, Scotch lexicog.
Jăm'nĭ a (or -nī'a), Bib.
jä'mŏń'.
jăm'pan, -pa nee'.
jam'rach (-răk).
jăn'a pum.
Ja'nau schek (yä'nou shĕk), Bohem. actress.
Ja net' (zhä'nä'), Fr. auth.
jan gä'da.
jaŋ'gle, -gled, -gler, -gling, -gly.
jăn'i tor, -i tress.
jăn'i za ry, -za'ri an.
Jăn'nes (-nēz), Bib.
Jan'sen, -ism, -sen ist.
Jăn'u a ry.
Jä'nus, Myth., -cloth, -cord, -faced, -head'ed.
Ja păn', -ism, -ĭ zä'tion, Jap a-nese' (or -nēz'), -a nesque', Japan' all'spice, J. black, J. color, J. earth, J. work.
ja păn', v., -ner, -ning, -panned'.
Jä'pheth, Bib., -ite, -phet'ic, -phet'i an.
Japh'lĕ tī (or -lē'tī), Bib.
ja pon'i ca.
Ja'ques (jăk'wĕs), Shak. As You Like It.
jaq'ui ma (jăk'ĭ ma).
jar, -ring, -ry, jarred, jar'nut, -bird, -fly, -owl.
järde.
jar di nière' (zhär dē nyâr').
jar'gon, -ist, -ize, -ized, -ĭ'zing, -gon'ic.
jar go nelle'.
Järn'dyce (-dĭs), Dickens Bleak House.
jar'ret' (zhä rä').
jä'sey (-zy).
jăs'mĭne, -tree.
jaspe (jăsp).
jas'pé (jăs'pā).
jas'per, -ä'ted, -per ize, -ized, -ĭ'zing, -per y, jas pid'e an, -pid'-e ous, jas'pure, jas'pered, jas'-per-dip, -o pal, -ware, -wash.
Jau bert' (zhō'bêr'), Fr. orient.
jäun'dĭce, -dĭced, -dĭ cing, jaun'-dice-ber'ry, -tree.

jäunt, -ed, -ing, jäun'ty, -ti ly,
-ti ness, jaunt'ing-car.
Jä'va, isl. East Indies, -van,
Jav a nese' (or -nēz'), Ja'va
al'monds, J. cat, J. spar'row.
jä'va, a breed of fowls, *ja va li'na*
(hä'va lē'na).
Jä'van, *Bib.*
jave'lin (jăv'lin), -bat, -man,
-snake.
Ja vert' (zhä'vâr'), Hugo *Les
Miserables.*
jaw, -ing, -less, jawed, jaw'fall,
-fall en, -smith.
jaw'-bit, -bolt, -bone, -box,
-break'er, -chuck, -foot, -foot-
ed, -hole, -jerk, -lev er,
-mouthed, -rope, -spring, -tac-
kle, -tooth, -wedge, jaw'ing-
tac kle.
jay, -hawk'er, -weed, -bird,
-cuck'oo, -pie, -teal, -thrush.
jĕal'ous, -ly, -ness, -y.
Jeames (jēmz).
jean (jān), jean ette' (jä nĕt'), a
kind of cloth, Jea nette' *or*
Jēan nĕtte' (jē nĕt'), Chr. name.
Jean Jacques (zhäṅ zhăk),
Rousseau.
Jĕan Pạul (*or* zhäṅ poul), Ger.
writer.
Jeanne d'Arc (zhän dark), Joan
of Arc (jōn *or* jō an').
Jeb'u site (-zīt), -sit'ic (-zĭt'ĭk).
Jĕ dä'iah (-yä), *Bib.*
Jĕd'dart jus tice, J. stäff.
jed'ding-ax.
Jĕ dĕ'iah (-yä), *Bib.*
Jĕ dĕ'us, *Bib.*
jĕdge.
Jĕ dī'a el, *Bib.*
Jĕ dī'dah (*or* jĕd'-), *Bib.*
Jĕ dū'thun (*or* jĕd'-), *Bib.*
Jed'wood ax, J. jus'tice.
Jĕ ē'lī, *Bib.*
jeer, -er, -ing, -ing ly, jeered.
Jĕ ē'zer, *Bib.*
Jef'fer son, Pres. U. S., -sō'ni an,
-an ism, jef'fer son īte.
Jĕ ha lē'lĕ ĕl (*or* jē hăl'ĕ lĕl),
Bib.
Jĕ hoi'a kĭm, *Bib.*
Je ho'vah, -ho'vist, -vis'tic.

Jĕ'hū.
Jĕ hŭ'dī, *Bib.*
Jĕ'hū dī'jah, *Bib.*
Jĕ ĭ'ĕl, *Bib.*
je jūne', -ly, -ness, -jū'nal.
je'lick (jä'-).
jĕl'ly, -lĭed, -li fy, -fy ing, -fied,
jel'ly fish, -bag, -leaf, -li'chen,
-plant.
jem'i dar.
Jĕ mī'ma, *Bib.*
Jĕm'ū el (*or* jē mū'el), *Bib.*
jen'net, a horse.
jen'net ing, an apple.
jĕn'ny, -spin'ner.
Jen'ny ass, J. crŭd'le (-l), J.
wren.
jeop'ard (jĕp'-), -ed, -er, -ing,
-y, -ize, -ized, -ī'zing.
Jeph'thah (jĕf'tha), *Bib.*
jer'bŏ a (*or* -bō'-), -mouse.
Jĕr'e chus (-kŭȝ), *Bib.*
jĕr eed' *or* -id' (jĕr ĕd').
Jĕr'e mäi, *Bib.*
Jĕr ĕ mī'ah, -mī an'ic, jer e mī'ad.
jer'fal con (-fạ'kn). See *gerfalcon.*
Jĕr'i bäi, *Bib.*
jerk, -er, -ing, -ing ly, -y, -i ness,
jerked.
jer'kĭ net.
jer'kin-hĕad.
Jĕr ō bō'am, *Bib.* jĕr ō bō'am, a
metal bowl.
Jĕ rō'ham (*or* jĕr'-), *Bib.*
jĕr'ry, -build'er, -build'ing, -built,
-shop.
Jer'sey (-zy), isl. Eng. Channel;
co. Ill.; a breed of cattle, -man.
Jer'sey light'ning, J. cloth, J. cud-
weed, J. flan'nel, J. live'long,
mates, J. match, J. pine, J. tea,
J. team, J. this'tle.
jer'sey (-zy), woolen yarn; a
garment.
Jĕ rŭb'ba ăl (*or* jĕr'ŭb bā'ăl),
Bib.
Jĕr'ū el (*or* jē ru'el), *Bib.*
Je ru'sa lĕm, t. Syria; twp. N. Y.
J. ar'ti choke, J. cher'ry, J.
cow'slip, J. had'dock, J. oak,
J. po'ny.
Jĕsh'i mon (*or* jē shī'-), *Bib.*
Jĕ shī'shäi (*or* jē shĭsh'a ī), *Bib.*

Jĕsh′u run (*or* jē shū′run), *Bib.*
jess, jessed.
Jes′sē, Chr. name, *masc.* Jĕs′sie,
Chr. name, *fem.*, diminutive of
Jess.
jest, -ed, -er, -ing, -ing ly, -word,
jest′-book, -moŋ′ger, jest′ing-
beam, -stock.
Jes′ū it (jĕz′-), -u it ism, -it ry,
-u it′ic.
jes u it′ic al, crafty, -ly.
Jĕs′u run (*or* jē sū′-), *Bib.*
jet, -ted, -ting, -ty, -ti ness, jet-
ant, -black, -breāk, -glăss,
-pump.
jet d′eau′ (zhā′ dō′).
Jĕ′thrŏ (*or* jĕth′-), *Bib.*
jet′sam, jet′tage.
jette (jĕt).
jet′ti son, -ing, -soned.
jet′ty, -ing, -tïed, jet′ty head.
jeu d′es prit′ (zhĕ dĕs prē′).
Jĕ′ū ĕl (*or* jeū′-), *Bib.*
jeune pre mier′ (jên prê myā′).
Jĕv′ons, Eng. philos.
Jew, -dom, -ess, -ish, -ish ly,
-ish ness, -ry, Jew-bait′er, -crow.
Jews′-ap′ple, -mal′low, -man′na,
-myr′tle, -stone, -thorn, -trump,
Jew's-ear, a plant.
jew, *v.*, -ing, -fish, jewed, jew′-
bush, jew's-harp.
jew′el, -eled *or* -elled, -el ing *or*
-el ling, -el er *or* -el ler, -el ry,
-el y *or* -el ly, -weed.
jew′el-block, -case, -draw′er,
-house, -like, -of fice, -set ter,
-stand.
Jĕz′e bel, *Bib.;* a vicious woman.
jez′iah (jāz′yä).
Jĕ′zǐ el, *Bib.*
Jē zŏ′ar (*or* jĕz′-), *Bib.*
jhil (jĕl).
jhou (jow).
jib, -bing, -ber, jibbed.
jib′bä′.
jib′-boom, -door, -frame, -hank,
-head, -i ron, -lot, -net′ting,
-sheet, -stay, -top sail, jib-o′-
jib.
jībe, jibed, jīb′ing.
ji′bi (jĕ′bǐ).
jif′fy.

jig, -ging, -ger, -gered, -gish,
jigged.
jig-clog, -giv′en, -māk′er, -mold,
-pin, -saw, jig′ging-ma chine′,
jig′ger-knife, -māst, -pump.
jil gue′ro (hēl gā′rō).
jĭlt, -ed, -er, -ing.
jim′ber-jaw, -jawed.
jim′-crow, a tool, Jim Crow, a
minstrel, Jim-crow car, Jim′-
crow's-nose, a plant.
jim′my.
jim′son, -weed.
jin′gāl.
jin′gle, -gled, -gler, -gling, -glet,
jin′gle-jan gle, -shell.
Jin′go ism.
jiŋk, -game.
jink′er, -ers.
jǐnn.
jin rik′i shä.
ji′va (jē′va).
Jŏ′a chim (-kǐm), *Bib.*
Jo′a chim (yō′a chim), Ger.
violinist.
Jŏ ăn′ of Arc (*or* jŏn′), The Maid
of Orleans, Fr. heroine.
jŏb, -ber, -bing, jobbed, job′-
mās′ter, -of fice, -print′er, -type,
-watch, -work, job′bing-man.
Jŏb, *Bib.,* Job's-tears, Job's com′-
fort er, J. news, J. post.
jŏck′ey, -ing, -ism, -ship, -eyed
(-ǐd).
jŏck′ey-box, -club, -gear, -grăss,
-pad, -pul′ley, -sleeve, -stick,
-wheel, -whip.
jŏck′ŏ.
jŏ cose′ (-kōs′), -ly, -ness, -cŏs′-
i ty.
jo cu′ (hō kōō′).
jŏc′u lar, -ly, -lā′tor, -lä tō′ry,
-lăr′i ty, jŏc′und, -und ly, -und-
ness, jŏ cun′di ty.
jo′del (yō′del). See *yodel.*
jog, -ger, -ging, jogged, jog-trot,
jog′ging-cart.
jog′gle, -gled, -gling, -gly, jog′gle
work.
jog′gle-beam, -joint, -piece, -post,
-truss, jog′gling-ta ble.
John, *Bib.;* Chr. name, Jŏ hän′-
ne an, -hăn′nǐne, -nīte.

---

fāte, făt, fär, fạll, fâre, făst, sofȧ, mēte, mĕt, hêr, īce, ǐn, nōte,

John-Bull'ism, -crow, a bird, -crow's-nose, a plant, -do ry, -go-to-bed-at-noon, a plant.
John Bar ley corn, J. Bull, J. Chi'na man, J. Com'pa ny, J. Crow beans.
john'-ap ple, -paw, a fish, -to-whit.
john'ny, -cake, -cranes.
John'ny-jump-up, a plant, -verde, a fish, John's-wood, -wort.
Joi'a da, Bib.
Joi'a kim, Bib.
join, -er, -er y, -ing, joined.
joint, -ed, -ed ly, -er, -ing, -less, -ly, -weed, -worm.
joint-chair, -coǔp ling, -end, -e vil, -file, -fir, -gråss, -hinge, -oil, -pipe, -pli ers, -rack ing, -ring, -rod, -saw, -snake, -splice, -stock, -stool, -strip, -test, -wire.
joint'er-plane, joint'ing-ma chine', -plane, -rule.
join'ture, -ture less, -tured, -tūr ing.
joist.
Jǒk'de am, Bib.
joke, joked, jōk'er, -ing, -ing ly, -ish, -y.
Jo li et' (zhō'lē ā'), Fr. explorer. Jō'lǐ ĕt, c. Ill.
Jo li ette' (zhō'lē ĕt'), co. Que.
jǒl'ly, -li ly, -li ness, -li ty, -li fi cā'tion, jol'ly-boat, j. bal'ance.
jǒlt, -ed, -ing, -ing ly, -head, a person, -head, a head.
Jo ly' (zhō'lē'), Fr. actress.
Jǒ'nah.
Jon'a than, Chr. name, Broth er Jon'a than, jon'a than, a cigar lighter.
jong (yǒng).
jonk'herr (yǒnk'-).
jǒn'quil.
Jǒ'räi (or jō'ra ĭ), Bib.
Jor'dan, r. Palestine, J. al mond, jor'dan, a bottle.
jo'ree.
jor na'da (hōr nä'thä).
jǒ'rŏ bä'dŏ (hŏ'-).
Jo rul'lo (hŏ rōōl'yō), vol. Mex.

Jo'seph (-zĕf), Chr. name, Jō'seph-and-Ma ry, a plant, Jo'seph's-coat, a plant, -flow'er, jō'seph, a garment.
jǒss, -block, -house, -pa per, -pid gin, -stick, joss'ing-block.
Jost (yōst), Ger. hist.
jǒs'tle, -tled, -tling.
jot, -ted, -ter, -ting.
jo'ta (hŏ'tä).
Jǒ'tham, Bib.
Jou bert' (zhōō'bêr'), Fr. gen.
joule (joul), -me'ter, Joule's e quiv'a lent.
jounce, jounced, joun'cing.
joûr'nal, -naled or -nalled, -nal ing or -nal ling, -nal ism, -ist, -is'tic, -ize, -ized, -ī'zing, -ese' (-ēz').
jour'nal-beâr'ing, -book, -box, -bråss, -pack ing.
joûr'ney, -er, -ing, -neyed (-nǐd), jour'ney man, -ring, -weight, -work.
joust (just). See just.
Jǒve, Jo'vi al, -vi an, -vin'i an ist, Jove's-fruit, -nuts.
jō'vi al, -ize, -ized, -ī'zing, -al ly, -al ness, -al'i ty.
jowl (jŏl or joul), n., -er.
joy, -ing, -ful, -ful ly, -ful ness, -less, -less ly, -less ness, -ous, -ous ly, -ous ness, -some.
Joy euse' (zhwȧ'yêz'), the sword of Charlemagne.
Ju a'rez (hōō ä'res), Pres. Mex.
jŭ'ba, pl. -bæ, Zoöl.; Bot. jū'ba, a dance, ju'ba (hōō'vä), a snake. jū'ba-pat ting.
jū'bate.
jub'bah or jubh'a (jŭb'bȧ).
ju'bē (or zhōō'bä').
jū'bi lant, -ly, -lance, -late, -lā'ted, -lā'ting, -lā'tion, -bi lee, -le'an, -bil ize, -ized, -ī'zing, -bil ist, Ju bǐ lā'tē (or -lä'te).
ju'bō (hōō'-).
juch'ten (yōōch'-).
Ju dä'ic, -al, -al ly, Ju'dä ist, -dä is'tic, -tic al ly, -dä ize, -ized, -ī'zer, -ī'zing, -ī zā'tion.
Jū'das, -col'ored, -cup, -ear, -light, -tree, jū'das-hole.

---

nǒt, nôr, ūse, ǔp, ûrn, etüde, fōōd, fǒǒt, aɳger, boɳmot, thus, Bach.
24

judge, -ship, judged, judg'ing, -er, -ment, judge'-ad'vo cate.

judg'ment-cap, -day, -hall, -note, -seat.

jŭ'dĭ cȧ ture', -cȧ ble, -cā'tive, -ca'tor, -cȧ tō'ry, -ca to'ri al, -ca'tion.

jŭ dĭ'cial (-dĭsh'al), -ly, -di'ci a- ry (-dĭsh'ĭ a ry), -di'cious (-dĭsh'us), -cious ly, -cious ness.

Ju'dith.

ju'ey (hōō'ā).

jug, -ger *or* -gar, -ful, -ging, -fish, jugged, jug-fish'ing.

jŭ'gate, -gā'ted.

Jug'ger nȧut.

jug'gle, -gled, -gler, -gler y, -gling, -gling ly.

jŭ'gu lar, -lā'tion.

juice, -ful, -less, jui'cy, -ci ness.

ju'ju (jōō'jōō).

jŭ'jŭbe.

jŭ'lep.

Jŭl'ian (-yan), -ist, Jul'ian cal'- en dar, J. ep'och, J. e'ra, J. pe'ri od.

ju li enne'.

jum'ble, -bled, -bler, -bling, -bling ly, jum'ble-bēad.

jum'bo.

ju melle' (zhŏŏ mĕl').

jump, -er, -ing, -a ble, -y, jumped, jump'a bout, a plant, jump'- coŭp'ling, -joint, -ring, -rocks, -seat, -weld.

jump'ing-bet'ty, j. bean, j. bug, j. deer, j. hare, j. mouse, j. mul let, j. rat, j. seed, j. shrew, j. spi der.

juṇ'cŏ, juṇ'cal.

juṇc'tion, junc'ture, juṇc'tion-box, -plate, -rails.

June, -ap'ple, -ber'ry, -bug, -grȧss.

Ju neau' (zhü'nō'), Amer. pioneer.

Ju neau' (jŭ'nō'), t. Alas.; co. Wis.

Jung'frau (yŏŏng'frou), mt. Switz.

juṇ'gle, -gled, -gly.

juṇ'gle-bear, -ben'dy, -cat, -cock, -fe ver, -fowl, -nail, -ox, -sheep.

Jŭ'nĭ ăt'a, co. and r. Pa.

jūn'ior (-yor), -ship, -iŏr'i ty.

jŭ'ni per, -oil, -res'in (-rez'-).

Jun'ius (jūn'- *or* jŭ'nĭ ŭs), Eng. writer.

juṇk, -man, -bot tle, -deal er, -ring, -shop, -strap, -vat, -wad.

juṇ'ket, -ed, -er, -ing.

Jŭ'no, -no'ni an, Jū'no's-rose, -tears.

jun'ta, -to.

Jŭ'pi ter, Ju'pi ter's-beard, -dis'- tȧff, -eye, -flow er, -nut, -stȧff.

ju pon' (*or* jŭ'-).

Jŭ'ra, -ras'sic.

jŭ'ral, -ly.

Ju'ra men tä'dō (hōō'-), *ju ra- men'tō* (hōō'-).

jŭ'rat, -ra tō'ry.

ju're dĭ vĭ'no.

ju rid'ic, -al, -al ly.

ju ris dic'tion.

ju ris pru'dence, -dent, -den'tial.

ju'rist, -ris'tic, -tic al ly.

jŭ'ry, -man, jŭ'ror, ju'ry-box, -du- ty, -leg, -list, -mȧst, -proc'ess (-prŏs'-), -rig, -rigged, -room, -rud der.

just, -ly, -ness, jŭs'tĭce, -ship, jus'ti fy, -ing, -fied, -fi er, -fi'- a ble, -ble ness, -bly, -fĭ cȧ'tion, -ca'tor, -tif'i ca tive', -i ca tō'ry, jus'ti fy ing-stick.

jŭst *or* joust (jŭst *or* jōōst), -er, -ing, just'ing-hel'met.

Juste (zhüst), Bel. hist.

Jus'ti (yŏŏs'tē), Ger. auth.

jut, -ted, -ting, -ting ly, -ty, jut'-win dow.

Jute, a Ger. tribe, *pl.* Jutes, jūte, a plant, jūte'-fi ber.

Ju've nal, Rom. poet, -nā'li an.

ju ve nes'cent, -nes'cence.

ju've nĭle, -nĭl'i ty.

jux ta pose', -posed', -po'sing, -po sĭ'tion (-zish'un), -tion al.

K

Kaa'ba or Caa'ba (kä'bä or kä'-
a bä or kä'a ba or kå ä'ba).
Ka byle' (-bīl').
Kä'desh-bar'ne a, Bib.
kä'di (or kä'-). See cadi.
kä di-kä'ne.
Käf'ir or Kaf'fir, Käf'ir-boom,
-brĕad, -corn, -tea, Käf'ir's-tree.
ka go (kăg'ō or kä'go).
kä'gu (-gōō).
kä hu'na (-hōō'-).
kai (kī).
kai'ak or kay'- (kī'- or kä'-), -er.
kä i'ka (-ē'-).
kail, a game.
kä'ĭl, a tree.
kai'ma kam' (kī'-).
kain-fowl, -hen.
kai'ser (kī'zer), -ship.
ka jä'wah.
kä'kĭ, a fruit.
Kä la kow'a, King of Hawaiian
Isl.
kale, a plant, kale'stock, -wife,
-bell, -blade, -brose (-brōz),
-pot, -runt, -tur nip, -worm.
ka lcī'do grăph, -do phone, -do-
scope, -scōp'ic, -ic al.
kä'lĭ, a plant, kä'li (-lē), Hind.
Myth.
Kal'lāi (or -lä ī), Bib.
Käl'muck or Cal'-, a Mongolian,
kăl'muck, a kind of cloth.
kăl'pa.
kal'pis.
kal'so mīne. See calcimine.
Käm chät'ka or Kamt chat'ka,
Russia, -chat'kan.
Kä mĕ hä'mĕ hä, King of Hawaiian Isl.
kä'mĭ.
ka mis' (ka mēs').
käm ly'ka.
kä'na.
Kä năk'a (or -nä'ka).
ka nä'rĭ, -oil.
kå näĭ'.
kăng.
kaṇ'ga rōō', -ap ple, -bear, -bee-
tle, -dog, -grape, -grăss, -hare,

-hound, -mouse, -rat, -thorn,
-vine.
kaṇ'ke.
kăn'na.
Kan'sas, state U. S., -Ne bras'ka
Bill.
Kănt, Ger. metaphys., Kăn'ti an,
-an ism, Kant'ism, -ist; känt,
lace.
Ka nuck'. See Canuck.
ka nun' (ka nōōn').
kä'o lin, -ite, -ize, -ized, -ĭ'zing,
-ĭ zā'tion, -lin'ic.
ka pel'le (-lä), ka pell'meĭs'ter.
kăpp.
kapp'land (käp'länt).
Kärls kro'na (-krōō'-), t. Sweden.
Karls'ruhe or Carls- (kärlz'rōō),
dist. Ger.
Kar'na im (or -nä'-), Bib.
kä'rob (or kär'ob).
kä roo' or kär rōō', pl. -rōōs'
(-rōōz').
ka rŏss'.
kär'ree.
kar'tel.
kar'wats.
Kas'chau (käsh'ou) or Kas'sa
(kŏsh'shō), c. Hung.
Kăsh'mir' (-mĕr'), India.
Käst'ner (kest'ner), Ger. poet.
kä'tän'dä'.
kat'chung (-chōōng).
Kä'ti pu'an (-pōō'-).
kä'ty did.
kau'ri (kou'rĭ), -gum, -pine, -res'in.
kay'ak. See kaiak.
kä zä'.
Kaz'in czy (kŏz'in tsē), Hung.
auth.
ka zoo'.
kĕ'a.
Kear'ney (kär'ny), co. Neb.; tp.
Mo.; Keär'ny, co. Kan.; Keär'-
ny, Amer. gen.
Kĕ'ble, Eng. poet.
kec'kle, -kled, -kling.
kĕd'dah.
kedge, kedged, kedg'ing, -er, -y,
kedge'-aṇ'chor, -rope.

Kĕ'dron, brook Palestine.
keek, -er, -house.
keel, -age, -er, -ing, -less, keeled,
keel'haul, -man, -rake, -vat,
-block, -com pel'ling, -line,
-mold'ing, -pet'als, -shaped, keel'-
er-tub.
keel'son (kĕl'sun).
keen, -er, -ly, -ness, -wit'ted.
kee'na, -nut, -oil.
keep, -er, -ing, kept, keep'sake,
-wor thy, keep'ing-room, keep'-
er less, -er ship.
kĕf'ĭt eh.
keg.
Kĕ hä'ma, a Hindu rajah.
Kehl (kāl), t. Ger.
Keigh'ley (kēth'ly), t. Eng.
Keight'ley (kīt'ly), Eng. auth.
Kĕi'lah (*or* keī'-), *Bib.*
keir *or* kier (kēr).
Kĕ lā'iah (-ya), *Bib.*
Kĕl ät'. See *Khelat.*
kel'ly, -ing, -lied.
kelp, -wort, -fish, -goose, -pi'-
geon, -whāl'ing.
Kĕ'nai (-nī).
ken'dal, a cloth, Ken'dal green,
Ken'dall's case.
Kĕ'nĕz īte (*or* kĕn'-), *Bib.*
Ken'il worth i'vy.
Kĕ'nīte (*or* kĕn'-), *Bib.*
ken'ne beck'er.
ken'nel, -neled *or* -nelled, -nel-
ing *or* -ling.
kĕ'nŏ.
kĕ nŏ'sis, -not'ic, -ism, -not'i cism.
Kĕn'u el (*or* kĕ nu'el), *Bib.*
Kĕ'o kuk, co. Ia.
kep, -ball.
kĕph'ir.
kĕp'ĭ.
ker au'no pho'bi a.
ker'chĭef, -ing, -chĭefed.
kerf, kerfed, kerf'ing-ma chine'.
ker'mes (-mēz), -ber'ry, -in sect,
-min er al, -oak.
kern, -ba'by, -cut, -dol'lie, -stone.
ker'nel, -neled *or* -nelled, -nel ing
or -ling, -nel y *or* -nel ly, ker'-
nel wort, -sub'stance.
kĕr'o sene, -o se lene'.
ker'sey (kêr'zy), -mere, -nette'.

ke ryg'ma, -rys'tic.
Kes'wick (kĕz'ĭk), t. Eng.
Keszt hely' (kĕst'hĕl'), t. Hung.
ketch.
ketch'up. See *catchup.*
ke thib' (ke thĕv').
ke tose (-tōs).
ket'tle, -drum, an entertainment,
-man.
ket'tle-bail, -case, -dock, -drum,
a drum, -drum'mer, -hole, -mo-
raine', -pin, -smock, -stitch.
Kĕ tū'rah, *Bib.*
Ke un'jhar (kĕ ōōn'jar), India.
kĕv'el, -head.
kĕy, -ing, keyed, key'board, -hole,
-stone, -way.
key'-ac tion, -bås'ket, -bed, -bolt,
-bone, -bu'gle, -chain, -chord,
-col'or, -coŭp'ler, -desk, -drop,
-fas'ten er, -file, -fruit, -groov'-
ing, -guard, -harp, -head, -note,
-pat tern, -piece, -pin, -pipe,
-plate, -point, -ring, -seat,
-sig'na ture, -stop, -tail, -tone,
-trum pet, -valve, -word.
key'hole-guard, -lim pet, -pro-
tect'or, -saw.
Keys, a parliament.
Key'ser (kī'zer), tp. Ind.; t. W.
Va.
Kĕ zī'a, *Bib.*
Kha'i bar Pass (kä'ē bär), India.
khä'kĭ, a kind of cloth.
khäl'sa.
khăm'sĭn.
khän, -ate, -jar, -jee.
khän'sa män.
kha num' (kä nōōm').
Khar tum' (kär'tōōm'), t. Afr.
khe dive' (kä'dēv').
Khel at' (kĕl ät'), t. Baluchistan.
khi'no (kē'-)
khir'kah.
kĭ ăck'.
ki'a o'ra (kē'-)
kib'ble, -bled, -bler, -bling, -ble-
chain.
kĭbe, kibed, kīb'y.
kick, -a ble, -er, -ing, kicked,
kick'-a bout', -off.
kid, -ded, -der, -ding, -ling, kid's-
man.

---

fāte, făt, fär, fạll, fâre, fåst, sofå, mēte, mĕt, hêr, īce, ĭn, nōte,

kid'dle, -dled, -dling.
kid'nap, -ping, -per, -napped.
kid'ney, -root, -wort, -bean, -cotton, -form, -link, -paved, -shaped, -stone, -vetch, -worm, kid'ney ore, k. po ta'to.
kiĕf, -e kil or kĕf'fe kil.
Kiel (kēl), t. Prus.
Ki el'ce (kē ĕlt'sā), t. Pol.
kiĕr. See keir.
Ki ev' (kē ĕf'), c. Russia.
ki'kar (kē'-).
Ki lau e'a (kē' lou ā'ä), volc. Hawaii.
kil'der kin.
kil'erg.
kī'ley, pl. -leys (-līz).
kill, -er, -ing, -ing ly, killed, kill'buck, -calf, -cow, -dev il, -hog, -joy, -man.
kill'dee or -deer.
kil'ma gore.
kiln (kĭl), -man, -dried, -hole, -house.
kil'o dyne (-dīn).
kĭl'o gram or -grämme, -o gram'e ter, -o li'ter (-lē'-), -o mē'ter, -o stēre (or -stâre).
ki'lon go'si (kē'-).
kil'ŏ watt-hour.
kilt, -ed, -er, -ing.
kĭ mō'nŏ.
kin, -dred, -less, -ship, kins'folk, kins'man, -wom'an, -peo'ple.
kin'a kĭ.
kin'cob.
kĭnd, -ly, -li ness, -ness, kind'heärt'ed, -heärt'ed ness, -spo'ken, -tem'pered.
kĭn'der gar'ten, -gart'ner.
kin'dle, -dled, -dler, -dling, kin'dling-coal, -wood.
kin e mat'ic, -al, -ics, kin'e ograph'.
kin'e sal'gi a.
kĭ nĕt'ic, -al, -ics.
kĭ ne'to gen'e sis (or kĭ-), -ne'tograph, -to mat'o graph, -to pho'nograph, -ne'to scope, -to scop'ic.
king, -ly, -li ness, -less, -let, -bird, -crâft, -cup, -fish, -fish er, a bird, -hunt er, a bird, -mâk'er, -nut, -ship, -wood.

king'-ap ple, -auk, -bird, -bolt, -crab, -crow, -dev il, -duck, -eī'der, -fern, -gut ter, -hake, -kill'er, -mul let, -or'to lan, -pen'guin, -piece, -pin, -pine, -plant, -post, -rail, -rod, -roller, -sal mon, -snake, -ta ble, -truss, -ty rant, -vul ture.
king's-clo ver, -cush'ion, -fĕath-er, -fish er, -flow er, -hood, -piece, -spear, king-at-arms.
King of Yve tot' (ēv'tō'), Beranger's model potentate.
kĭn'ĭt.
kiŋk, -ing, -y, kinked.
kin'nĭ kĭ nic'.
ki'no (kē'no or ki'no), -no'ic.
kĭ osk'.
Kī'ŏ wa, co. Col.; co. Kan.
kip, -skin.
kip'per.
kir'bĕh.
Kĭr'ĭ â thâ'im, Bib.
Kĭr'jâth-jĕ'a rĭm, Bib.
kĭrsch'was'ser (-vŏs'-).
kir'tle, -tled, -tling.
kis'met.
kiss, -er, -ing, kissed, kiss'ing-bug, -com'fĭt, -crust, -dânce, -gate, -hand, -kind, -mus cle.
kit, -ted, -ting.
kit'-cat, -dress'ing, -drill, -had'-dock.
kit'cat-roll.
kitch'ĕn, -dom, -er, kitch'en-fare, -fee, -gar den, -knave, -maid, -mid'den, -mort, -phys'ic, -stuff.
kite, kīt'ed, -ing, -ish, kite'foot, -bal loon', -ea'gle, -fal'con (-fạ'kn), -fly ing, -key, -pho'tograph, -stick, -string, -tail, -tailed, -wind.
kith.
kit'tel (-l), a coat or tunic.
kĭt'ten (-tn), -hood, -ish, kit'ty, kit'ten-shark.
kit'tle, -tled, -tling.
kit'tly, -bend'ers.
kit'ty-coot, -cor'nered, -key, -need'y, -witch.
Kiu shiu' (kyoo shoo'), isl. Japan.
ki'va (kē'va).
Klä'math, co. Ore.

---

nŏt, nôr, ūse, ŭp, ûrn, etüde, food, foot, aŋger, bonmot, thus, Bach.

kläng, -*jär'be*.
klepht, -ic.
klep'to mä'ni a. See *cleptomania*. -ni ac.
klink'er.
klip'hŏk.
klo͞otch'man.
klop, -klop.
Klŏp'stŏck, Ger. poet.
knack (năk), -er, -er y, -ing, knacked.
knag, -gy, -gi ness, knagged (nagd *or* năg'ged).
knăp, -ping, -per, -py, knapped, knap'sack, -weed, knap'ping-ham'mer, -ma chine'.
Knäpp, Ger. theolog.; Ger. chemist; Knăpp, Amer. revivalist.
knär.
knăve, knäv'er y, knäv'ish, -ish-ly, -ish ness, knave's-mus'tard, knave' bairn.
knead (nēd), -a ble, -er, -ed, -ing, knead'ing-ma chine', -trough.
kneck (něk).
knee, kneed, knee'cap, the knee-pan, -hol'ly, a plant, -holm, a plant, -hul ver, a plant, -pan, -stĕad, -string.
knee'-bone, -boss, -breech'es, -brush, -cap, a protection to the knee, -cop, -cords, -crooking, -deep, -guard, -gus set, -high, -i ron, -jerk, -joint, -joint ed, -kick, -piece, -pine, -plate, -răft'er, -re'flex, -stop, -strap, -swell, -tim ber, -trib ute, -wor-ship, k. roof.
kneel, -er, -ing, knelt *or* kneeled.
knell, -ing, knelled.
knib'ber.
knick'er.
Knick'er bock er, a New Yorker of Dutch descent. knick'er-bock er, a garment; a stout fabric of wool and linen.
knick'knack (nĭk'năk), -er, -er y.
knife (nīf), knifed, knīf'ing, knife-bar, -băs ket, -bay o net, -blade, -board, -box, -boy, -clean er, -dag ger, -edge, -edged, -file, -grăss, grīnd er, -guard, -han dle, -lan yard,

-mon ey, -pol'ish er, -rest, -sharp'en er, -tool, -tray.
knight, -age, -hood, -ly, -li ness, knight'-er'rant ry, -head, -ser-vice, knight's-spur, -wort, knight er rant, knight'hood er rant.
knit, -ted, -ter, -ting, -ta ble.
knit'ting-burr, -case, -gage, -ma-chine', -nee dle, -pin, -sheath, -stick, -work.
knit'tle.
knob, -bing, -by, -bi ness, -ber, knobbed, knob'stick, -weed, -wood, a shrub, -front'ed (-frŭnt'-), -latch.
knock, -er, -ing, knocked, knock'-a bout', -out, *n.*, -stone, -down, -kneed, -off, -out, *a.*, -tree, knock'er-off, knock'ing-buck'er, -trough.
knŏll, -ing, -er, -y, knŏlled.
knop, -per, knop'weed.
knot, -ted, -ter, -ting, -ty, -ti-ness, knot'horn, -weed, -work, -wort, -grăss, -wood, knot'ting-nee'dle.
knout, -ed, -ing, -ber'ry.
know, -a ble, -ble ness, -er, -ing, -ing ly, -ing ness, knew, known, know'-all, -noth'ing, Know'-noth'ing ism.
knowl'edge (nŏl'ĕj).
knuc'kle, -kled, -kling, -kly, knuc'kle-bone, -bŏw, -dust er, -end, -guard, -joint, -kneed, -shield, -thread, -tim ber.
knurl, -y, knurled, knur, -ry.
Knyp'hau sen, von (fŏn knĭp'-hou zen), Ger. gen.
kob.
Ko'be (kō'bā), c. Japan.
kŏ'bird.
Kŏch, Ger. naturalist.
Koek'koek (ko͞ok'ko͞ok), Dutch painter.
kŏff.
Kŏ'fu (-fo͞o), t. Japan.
kŏhl.
Kŏh'ler *or* Koeh'ler (kê'ler), Ger. writer.
ko'ko.
Kŏ lä'iah (*or* kŏl'a ï'ah), *Bib*.
Kŏl'bĕ, Ger. chem.

---

fāte, făt, fär, fạll, fâre, fȧst, sofȧ, mēte, mĕt, hêr, īce, ĭn, nŏte,

ko le'a (-lä'-).
ko lŏ'a.
kŏm'mers.
Kö'nig (kê'nicͪh), Ger. inventor.
Kö'nigs berg (kê'nĭgs bĕrg), c. Prussia.
kŏn'ĭ scŏpe.
Koord, -ish. See *Kurd.*
kŏp, a mountain, *kŏp'je* (kŏp'ĭ or -yē), a hillock.
kŏ räd'jĭ.
Ko'ran (*or* kō rän'), -ran'ic.
Kor do fän', dist. Afr.
Kŏ're, *Bib.*
Kör'ner (kêr'-), Ger. poet.
kŏr rē'ro.
Kos ci us'ko (kŏs sĭ ŭs'kō), Pol. patriot.
kŏ'sher.
Kŏs suth' (-sōͦth'), co. Ia.; tp. Wis.—(kŏsh'ōͦt), Hung. patriot.
kŏ'tō, a musical instrument.
kŏ tow' (-tou'), an act of worship.
kou'miss *or* -mys. See *kumiss.*
krä'ken (*or* krä'-).
krall (kräl *or* krạl).
Kra szew'ski (krä shĕv'skē), Pol. auth.
Kraus (krouss), Ger. economist.
Krau'se (krou'zĕ), Ger. philos.
krem'lin, a citadel. Krem'lin, the citadel of Moscow.
Kreut'zer (kroit'scr), Ger. composer.
kreut'zer *or* creut'zer (kroit'ser).
Kreuz'nach (kroits'näcͪh), t. Prus.
Krish'na, Myth.
Kriss Krin̦'gle.
krŏ'ne, pl. *-ner.*

Krŏn'os, *Myth.*
Krŏn'stadt (-stät), c. Hung.
Krōͦ, -man, *pl.* -men.
Kro to szyn' (krō tō shēn'), t. Prus. Republic.
Kru'ger (krōͦ'ger), Pres. S. Afr.
Krupp (krŏͦp), Ger. mfr., Krupp'-ize, -ized, -ĭ' zing, Krupp' proc'-ess.
krup'sis, -tist.
kry om'e ter (krī-).
Ku'ba (kōͦ'bä), t. Russ.
Kuen-Lun' (kwĕn lōͦn'), mts. Asia.
Kuhn (kōͦn), Ger. philol.
Kŭ'klŭx (*or* -klŭx'), -ism, K. klan.
ku'miss (kōͦ'-) *or* kou'miss *or* -mys.
Kun chin'jun'ga (kŏͦn chĭn'jŏͦn̦'-gä), mt. Asia.
kun'ner.
ku'phar (kōͦ'-).
Kurd (kōͦrd) *or* Kōͦrd, -ish.
Kur dis tan' (kōͦr dĭs tän'), Asia.
Ku ro shi'wo, or *Ku'ro-Si'wŏ* (kōͦ-rō shē'wō), or *ku'ro si'o* (-sē ō).
kur'saal (kōͦr'säl).
kur'sĭ.
kur vey'or (kōͦr-).
Kū shä'iah (-ya), *Bib.*
kus'tĭ.
kut'tar.
ky'an ize (kĭ'-), -ized, -ĭ'zĭng.
ky bosh' (kī-).
kyl (kĭl).
kyle (kil).
ky'ma tol'o gy (kĭ'-)
Kyr'ĭ ē (kĭr'-), K. e lei son (ē lĭ'-son *or* ē lä'ĭ son).

L

ʟaa'ba (lä'-)
Lä'a dah, *Bib.*
laa'ger (lä'-), an encampment.
Lăb'a na, *Bib.*
lab'a rum.
La bat' (lä'bä'), Fr. missionary.
La bé' (lä bā'), Fr. poetess.
lä'bĕl, -bĕled *or* -bĕlled, -bel ing *or* -bel ling, -bel er *or* -bel ler,

lä'bel-ma chine', lä'bel ing-ma-chine'.
lä'bi al, -ism, -ize, -ized, -ĭ'zing, -ĭ zā'tion, -bi ate, -ā'ted.
La biche (lä'bēsh'), Fr. auth.
lä'bor, -er, -ing, -ing ly, -bored, -bō'ri ous, -ous ly, -ous ness, la'bor-säv'ing, -time, -un ion, -yard, l. mar'ket.

lăb'or a tŏ' ry, -to'ri al, -ri an,
l. forge, l. fur'nace.
La bou chère' (lä'bōō'shâr'), Eng.
statesman.
La bou laye' (lä'bōō'lä'), Fr. jurist.
lä'bret.
la bur'num.
lăb'y rinth, -rin'thal, -rin'thi an
or -the an, -rin'thĭne.
lac, a resin; a great sum; milk;
lac'-dye, -in'sect, -lake, -paint'-
ed, -work.
lace, -ry, laced, la'cing, -cer, -cy,
lace'bark, a tree, -bor der, a
moth, -man, -wood.
lace'-boot, -bor der, on lace,
-cŏr'al, -em boss'ing, -fern, -fly,
-frame, -lĕath'er, -liz'ard, -māk'-
ing, -mend'er, -pa per, -piece,
-pil low, -run ner, -tree, -winged,
-wom'an, lace'bark-pine, lac'ing-
cut'ter, lace bor der, made of
lace.
lac'er ate (lăs'-), -ly, -à ble, -ā'-
ted, -ā'ting, -ā'tive, -ā'tion.
lach'es (-ĕz).
Lach'e sis (lăk'-), Myth.
Lä'chish (-kish), Bib.
lach'ry mal (lăk'rĭ-), -mà ble,
-mā'tion, -ma'ry, -ma to'ry, -mose
(-mōs), -mose ly.
lack, -age, -ing, -er, lacked, lack'-
all, -beard, -brain, -Lat'in, -lin-
en, -lus ter, -thought.
lack'a day, -dai'sy, -dai'sic al
(-dā'zik al), -al ly.
lăck'ey, -ing, -eyed (-ĭd), lack'ey-
moth.
La cŏ'ni a, Greece; t. N. H.;
-cŏ'ni an, -cŏn'ic.
la cŏn'ic, -al, -al ly, -con'i cism,
lăc'o nism, -o nize, -nized, -nĭ'-
zing.
la con'i cum, pl. -ca.
lac'quer (lăk'er), -er, -ing, -quered
(-erd), lac'quer-tree, -ware, lac'-
quer ing-stove.
La croix' (lä'krwä'), Fr. auth.
la crosse' (-krŏs'), -stick.
lac'tate, -tā'ted, -tā'tion, lac'te al,
-al ly, -te an, -te in, -te ous,
-ous ly, -tes'cence, -cent, lac'tic,
-tĭd, -tif'er ous, -tif'ic, -tif'lu ous,

-tiv o rous, -ti fuge, -tom'e ter,
-to scope.
la cus'tri an, -trĭne.
lad, -dĭe.
lad'der, -man, -way, -brăid, -car'-
riage, -cells, -dredge, -shell, -sol-
lar, -stitch, -work.
lade, lād'ed, -en, -ing, lade'man,
-pail, lad'ing-hole.
lä'dle, -dled, -dler, -dling, lä'dle-
ful, -dle wood, a tree, -board,
-fur'nace, -shell.
Lăd'o ga, l. Russ.
lä'dy, Lä'dy, a title, la'dy like,
-ship, -bird, an insect; a duck,
-bug, an insect, -clock, an insect, -cow, an insect, -fĭn ger, a
plant, -fish, -fly, an insect.
lä'dy-cat, a fish, -chair, -coc kle,
-court, -crab, -fern, -fluke, -hen,
-key, -kill'er, -love, Lä'dy-day.
la'dy's-bed'straw, a plant, -bow-
er, -comb, -cush ion, -de light,
a plant, -ear drops, a plant,
-glove, a plant, -gown, -hair, a
plant, -maid, -man tle, a plant,
-seal, a plant, -slip per, a plant,
-smock, a plant, -this tle,
-thumb, a plant, -tress es, a
plant.
Lae'ken (lä'-), vil. Belg.
Lä'el, Bib.
laen (lān).
læ'na (lē'-), pl. -næ (lē'nē).
La fa yette', de (dĕ lä'fä'yĕt'),
Fr. patriot. la fä yette', a fish.
La Flèche' (lä' flăsh'), t. Fr.
La fourche' (lä' fōōrsh'), t. La.
lag, -gard, -ger, -ging, -ging ly,
lagged, lag'-goose, -last, -link,
-machine, -screw.
lä'ger, -beer'.
Lä'ges (-zhĕs), t. Braz.
lagn appe' (lăn yăp').
La'go Mag gio're (lä'gō mäd jō'-
rä), l. It.
la gōōn', l. whāl'ing.
la gŏ'tic.
La grange (lä'grŏnzh'), Fr. astron.
lä'gre (-gr)
lag ri man'do, -ri mo'so.
Läg'thing (-tĭng).
la gu'na (-gōō'-).

La hāi'roi, _Bib._
Läh'mĭ, _Bib._
Lä hore', India, L. cloth.
lâir.
lâird, -ship.
Lä'ish, _Bib._
lä'i ty, lä'ic, -ic al, -al ly, -i cize,
-cized, -ci zing, -cĭ zä'tion.
Lä'i us (_or_ lä'yus), _Myth._
lake, -let, -weed, -carp, -dwell'er,
-fever, -fly, -her ring, -land, -law-
yer, -shad, -stur geon, -trout,
-whīt'ing.
Lake Mä rä cai'bo (-kī'bō), Venez.
Lake Nĭp'is sing, Can.
Laksh'mi (-mē), _Myth._
lal lä'tion, la lop'a thy.
lam, -ming, lammed.
lä'ma, a priest, lä'mä ic, -ma se-
ry.
Lä'ma ism, -ma ist, -is'tic, -ma īte.
lamb (lăm), -like, -ling, -kin,
-kill, a plant, -skin, -ale.
lamb's-let'tuce (-let'tĭs), -quar-
ters, -tongue, -wool, a drink,
lamb's wool.
lam balle' (-băl').
lamb'da (lăm'-), -da cism, -da'ic,
-doid.
lam'bel.
läm'bent, -ben cy.
Lăm'bert, Brit. gen.
Läm'hert, Ger physicist.
Lam bert' (lôṅ'bêr'), Fr reformer.
läm'bick.
läm'bre quin (-bêr kĭn).
lame, -ly, -ness, läm'ing, lamed.
Lä'mech (-mĕk), _Bib._
la mĕl'la, _pl._ -las _or_ -læ, lăm'el-
lar, -lar ly, -late, -lä'ted, lăm'-
el lar-stĕl'late.
la ment', -ed, -er, -ing, -ing ly,
lam'en tå ble, -ble ness, -bly,
-tä'tion, Lam en tä'tions, _Bib._
la mĕt'ta.
Lä'mĭ a (_or_ lä'-), Keats.
lăm'i na, _pl._ -nas _or_ -næ, -nar,
-na ry, -nate, -nä'ted, -nä'ting,
-nä'tion, -nå ble, -bil'i ty, lăm'-
i nĭ form, -i nif'er ous, lam'i nä'-
ting-ma chine', -roll'er.
Lam'mer moor', Bride of, Scott.
lăm'my _or_ -mĭe.

lamp, -black, -flow'er, -light,
-light er, -wick, a plant.
lamp'-brack et, -burn er, -can'o-
py, -case, -ce ment', -chim ney,
-cone, -el'e va tor, -fly, -fur-
nace, -glåss, -globe, -hang er,
-head, -hold er, -hole, -hoop,
-i ron, -jack, -māk'ing, -pend-
ant, -plug, -post, -pro tect'or,
-prün'er, -shade, -shell, -stand,
-store, -stove, -wick, lamp'-
black-fur'nace.
lam'per-eel.
lam pōōn', -er, -ing, -ry, -pōōned'.
lăm'prey, -eel.
lăm'pro type.
lä'nate, -nä'ted.
Lan'cas ter, Eng. navigator; co.
Neb.; co. and c. Pa.; co. Va.;
t. Ky.; t. Mass.; t. N. H.; t.
N. Y.; c. Ohio; c. Wis., -cas-
tē'ri an, -cas'tri an.
lánce, lănced, lan'cing, -cer,
lånce'pod, a plant, -wood, a
tree, -buck et, -cor po ral, -fly,
-head, -hook, -leafed, -lĭn'e ar,
-o val, -plate, -rest, -ser geant,
-shaped, -snake, -throw.
Lance lot' (lôṅss'lŏ'), Fr gram.
lan'ce o lar, -o late, -o lä'ted,
-late ly, -lä'tion.
lan cé-stitch (lăn sä').
lân'cet (_or_ lăn'-), -arch, -fish,
-point'ed, l. win'dow.
län'cha.
lan'ci nate, -nä'ting, -nä'tion.
Lan ci'si (län chē'sē), It. schol.
lănd, -ed, -er, -ing, -less, -ward,
-fall, -hold'er, -la'dy, -locked,
-lo per, -man, -mark, -own er,
-reeve, -shut, -slide, -slip,
-work'er, lands'man.
land'-bank, -bee tle, -blink,
-breeze, -bug, -car riage, -cod,
-com pass, -crab, -crake, -cress,
-croc o dile, -daw, -dog, -drain-
age, -drake, -flŏe, -flood, -grab-
ber, -huṇ ger, -huṇ gry, -ice,
-job ber, -lea'guer, -leech,
-mark er, -meas ure, -meas ur-
er, -of fice, -ot ter, -own ing,
-pâr er, -pike, -pi lot, -pi rate,
-plås ter, -poor, -rail, -rent,

-roll, -roll er, -scrip, -scur v̇y,
-shark, -shell, -sick, -side,
-slāt′er, -snail, -spout, -spring,
-stew ard, -tax, -ten ure, -tie,
-tor toise, -turn, -tur tle, -ur-
chin, -wait er, -war rant, -wash,
-wind.
land′ing-bar, -net, -place, -stage,
-strake, -sur vey′or, -wait er.
lăn′dau, -dau let′.
land′grāve, -gra vine (-vĕn), -grā′-
vi ate.
länd′ler (lĕnd′ler), a dance.
land′lord, -ism.
land′scape, -gar′den ing, -mir ror,
-paint er.
Lands′thing (läns′ting).
land′sturm (länt′stōōrm).
Land′tag (länt′tach).
land′wehr (länt′vâr).
lane, -route (-rōōt).
la ne te (lä nä′tä).
Lan frey′ (lŏṅ′frā′), Fr. hist.
Lăng, Eng. essayist.
Lang′e (läng′ĕ), Ger. theol.
laṇ′get.
Lan glois′ (lŏṅ′glwä′), Fr. orientalist.
Langres (lŏṅgr), t. Fr.
lang′shan.
lang′spiĕl.
lang′syne (-sīn).
laṇ′guage, -less, -guaged, laṇ′-
guage-les son, -mäs′ter.
Laṇ′gue doc, prov. Fr.; a wine,
-dō′cian.
langue d′oc′ (läṇg dŏk′), *l. d′oui′*
(-dwē′), *l. d′oil′* (-dwĕl′).
laṇ guette′.
laṇ′guid, -ly, -ness, -guor (-gûr *or*
-gwûr), -gour ous.
laṇ′guish, -er, -ing, -ing ly
-ment, -guished.
Lăn′Ï er, Amer. poet.
la nis′ta.
lank, -ly, -ness, -y.
lans′downe, a silk and wool fabric.
lan tā′na, lan′ta nĭn.
lăn′tern, -ing, -terned, lăn′tern-
flow′er.
lăn′tern-bel lows, -car′ri er, -fish,
-fly, -gur nard, -jack, -jawed,
-jaws, -keg, -light, -pin ion,

-pump, -shell, -sprat, -tow er,
-wheel.
lăn′tun.
lăn u gin′ic (-jin′-), lă nu′gi nous,
-gi nose.
lanx, *pl.* lan′ces (-sēz).
lan′yard.
Lă ŏc′ŏ ŏn, *Myth.; Sculp.*
Lă od′a mī′a, *Myth.*
Lă ŏd′i cě′a, *Bib.* -cě′an, -an ism.
lap, -ful, -per, -ping, lapped,
lap′streak, -weld, *v.*, -wing, a
bird, -work.
lap′-band er, -board, -dog, -dove′-
tail, -eared, -frame, -joint, -ma-
chine′, -plate, -ring, -roll er,
-scale, -shăv′er, -sīd′ed, -stone,
-ta ble, -tea, -weld, *n.*, lap′ping-
en′gine, -ma chine′.
lap a rot′o my, -o mist, -o mize,
-mized, -mi zing, -ro tŏm′ic, -ros′-
co py.
Lä Paz′ (päth′), dept. Bolivia.
la pĕl′, -pelled′.
lap′i da ry, -dā′rist, -dā′tion,
-i dif′ic, -ic al, la pid′i fi cā′tion.
Lap′i thæ (-thē), Myth.
La place′ (lä′pläss′), Fr. astron.,
-plä′ci an.
Lap′land, -er, -ish, Lapp, Lapp′-
ish, lapp′-owl.
lăp′pet, -ed, -ing, lap′pet-end,
-frame, -head, -moth, -wĕav′-
ing.
lapse (lăps), lapsed, laps′i ble,
-ing.
lap′sus, *l. cal′a mi,* *l. liṇ′guæ.*
lar′board, lar′bo lins.
lar′ce ny, -ce ner, -ce nist, -ce-
nous, -nous ly.
larch, -bark, -scales, -tree.
lard, -y, -stone, -boil′er, -but ter,
-cheese, -cool er, -oil, -press,
-ren′der er, -tank, lard′ing-
ba′con, -nee dle, -pin.
lard′er, -er, lard′er-bee′tle.
large, -ly, -ness, large′-a′cred
(-kerd), -hand′ed, -heart′ed,
-heart′ed ness, -mind′ed, -mind′-
ed ness.
lar′get (-jĕt).
lar ghet′to (-gĕt′to), *lar′go.*
lăr′Ï at.

---

fāte, făt, fär, fạll, fâre, fåst, sofà, mēte, mĕt, hêr, īce, ĭn, nōte,

lä ri' go (-rē'-).

lark, -spur, -bunt ing, -finch,
-heeled, -plov er (-plŭv'-), -spar-
row, -worm, lark's-heel, a plant.

larme (lärm), lar'mi er.

La Roche fou cauld', de (dĕ lä
rōsh'foo'kō'), Fr. writer.

La rousse' (lä'roos'), Fr. lexicog.

lär'rup, -rŭped or -rupped, -rup-
ing or -ping.

lär'um.

lar'va, *pl.* -vas or -væ, -val, -væ-
form, -va'ri um, -vate, -vä ted.

la ryn'go scope, -go scŏp'ic, -ic al,
-al ly, -gos'co pist, -co py, -ryŋ'-
go tome, -tom'ic, -got'o my.

lär'ynx, *pl.* la ryn'ges (-jēz), -gal,
-ryn'ge al (or lär'yn jē'-) -ge an,
-gic, -gĭt'ic, -gī'tis, -gŏl'o gy,
-goph'o ny.

lä sä'gne (-nyä).

Lä Salle (säl'), Fr. priest; Fr.
explorer.

La salle' or La Salle' (là săl' or
-säl'), co. Ill.; co. Tex.

las car', -ca ree'.

Las Cases (läs' käz'), Fr. writer.

las civ'i ous, -ly, -ness.

lash, -er, -ing, lashed, lash'-comb,
-lorn, -rail, lash'ing-eye, -ring,
-string.

lask or lasque.

las'ket.

Lä Spe'zi a (spĕd'zē ä), t. It.

lâss, lăs'sĭe, lass-lorn.

las'si tude.

lăs'so, -so ing, -sōed, las'so-cell,
-har ness.

lâst, -age, -ed, -er, -ing, -ing ly,
-ing ness, -ly, lâst'-court, -fin'-
ish ing, -hold er, -lâthe, -mâk'-
ing, -turn ing.

lâst'ing-awl, -jack, -ma chine',
-pin cers, -tool.

Lăs'the nes (-nēz), *Bib.*

Läs Ve'gas (vä'gäs), c. N. Mex.

lä'tä'.

Lä'tä'né' (-nä'), Amer. bishop.

latch, -et, -ing, latched, latch'-
clōs'er, -key, -lift er, -lock,
-o'pen er, -pan, -string.

late, -ly, -ness, lāt'er, -est.

la teen', -er.

lä'tent, -ly, -tence, -ten cy, -tes'-
cent.

lä'ter, pl. *lăt'e res* (-rēz).

lăt'er al, -ly, -al'i ty.

Lăt'er an.

lat'er ite, -er it'ic.

lâth, -ing, -y, -work, -brick,
-coop, -cut'ter, -ham'mer, -mill,
-nail, -pot, -saw'ing, lâth'ing-
clamp, -ham mer, -saw, -stâff.

Lä'tham, Eng. ornith.

lâthe, lâth'ing, lâthed, lâthe'-
bear'er, -bed, -car'ri er, -cen-
ter, -chuck, -cords, -dog, -head,
-hoist, -saw, -tool, l. drill.

lâth'er, -ing, -ered.

Lä ti ä'nŏ, t. It.

lat'i go, -hạl'ter, -strap.

Lăt'ĭn, -er, -ism, -ist, -ize, -ized,
-ĭ'zing, -ĭ zā'tion, -is'tic, -ĭn i-
tăs'ter, La tin'i ty.

lăt'i tude, tu'di nal, -di nous,
-di nā'ri an, -an ism.

La tō'na.

La tour' d'Au vergne' (lä'toor'
dō'vârn'), Fr. soldier.

La treille' (lä'trāl'), Fr. entom.

la trine' (-trēn').

la trōbe'.

lăt'ten, -er, lat'ten-brăss.

lăt'ter, -ly, -math, -day, a., -kin,
-mint, Lat'ter-day Saints.

lăt'tice (-tĭs), -tĭced, -tĭ cing,
lăt'tĭce leaf, a plant, -work,
-moss, -plant, l. blind, l. braid,
l. bridge, l. gird'er, l. truss, l.
win'dow.

lat ti ci'ni o (lăt tē chē'nĭ ō).

Lau'be (lou'bĕ), Ger. poet.

laud, -a ble, -ble ness, -bly, -bil'-
i ty, -a tive, -a to'ry, -er, -ist,
lau dā'tion.

Laud, Archbishop, Laud'ism, -ist.

lauf (louf).

laugh (läf), -a ble, -ble ness, -bly,
-er, -ing, -ing ly, -ter, -ter less,
laughed, laugh'wor'thy.

laugh'ing-bird (läf'-), -gas, -jack-
ass, -mus cle, -stock, laugh'ing
crow, l. dove, l. goose, l. gull,
l. hy e'na, l. thrush.

Lau gier' (lōzh'yä'), Fr. astron.

laun, a sieve.

---

läunch, -er, -ing, launched, launch'-
ways, -en gine, läunch'ing-tube,
-ways.
läun'der, -er, -ing, -dered or
dried, -dress, -dry, läun'dry-
maid, -man, -stove.
lau're ate, -ship, -ā'ted, -ā'ting,
-ā'tion.
lau'rel, -rĕled or -relled, lau'rel-
bot tle, -cher ry, -oak, -oil,
-shrub, -tree, -wa ter.
Lau sanne' (lō'zän'), c. Switz.
lau'wine (lou'vēn).
lä'va (or lā'va), -vat'ic, la'va-
streak.
La va'ter (lä fä'ter or -vä ter'),
Swiss physiog.
lăve, lāved, lāv'ing, -age, lăv'a tory, lăve'-eared, -lugged, lä'ver-
wort, -bread, -pot.
Lave leye' (läv'lä'), Belg. economist.
lăv'en der, -cot ton, -drop, -oil,
-thrift, -wa ter.
lăv'en tĭne.
lăv'ish, -er, -ing, -ly, -ment, -ness,
-ished.
La voi sier' (lä'vwä'zyā'), Fr.
chem.
law, -ful, -ful ly, -ful ness, -less,
-less ly, -less ness, -yer ly, law'-
breāk' er, -breāk'ing, -giv' er,
-māk'er, -mon̡'ger, -suit.
law'-a bĭd'ing, -bīnd'ing, -blank,
-book, -bur rows, -cälf, -court,
-day, -list, -lord, -of'fi cer,
-piece, -sheep, -sta'tion er,
-wor'thy, -wrīt'er.
law'yer, -cane, -palm, -vine.
lawk, -a-day.
lawn, -y, lawn'-meet, -mōw'er,
-par'ty, -roll'er, -sĭeve, -sprin'-
kler, -ten nis.
lax, -a tive, -tive ness, -ly, -ism,
-i ty.
lay, -er, -ing, laid, lain, lay'man,
-out, -cap, -day, -fig ure, -race,
-rod.
lay'er-board, -board'ing, -on,
-out, -o ver, -up.
lay'ing-down, -hook, -house, -in,
-ma chine', -on, -press, -tool, -top,
-trow'el.

lä'zar, -man, -haunt, -house, -like.
lăz a rĕt'to.
Lăz'a rus, Amer. poet.—(lät'sä-
rōͦos), Ger. philos.
laz'u lĭ, -u līte, -lĭt'ic, -u līne.
lā'zy, -zi ly, -zi ness, lā'zy back,
-board, -bones, a person, -boots,
a person, -bed, -jack, -pin'ion,
-scis'sors, -tongs.
lăz za rŏ'nĕ, pl. -rŏ'nĭ.
lēa, -rod.
lēach, -er, -ing, -y, lēached,
lēach'-line, -trough, -tub, lēach'-
ing-vat.
lēad, v., -ing, -ing ly, led, lēad'-
mule, -screw, -sink'ers.
lēad'er, -ette', -ship, -boy, -fŭr-
row, -hook, -writ'er, lēad'ing-
block, -hose, -screw, -spring,
-stăff, -strings, -wheel, -wire.
lĕad, n., -ed, -en, lĕad'back, a
bird, -wort, -arm'ing, -ash, -băth,
-col ic, -col or, -col ored, -cut-
ter, -eat er, -fur nace, -glănce,
-glāze, -gray, -lap, -line, -lus'-
ter, -mill, -nail, -o cher, -pa-
ral'y sis, -pen cil, -plant, -poi-
son ing, -pot, -spar, -tra'cer y,
-tree, -vit'ri ol, -wa ter, -works,
lĕad'plăs'ter, l. soap.
lĕad'en-gray, lĕad'ing-in, -rod.
lēaf, pl. lēaves, lēaf'age, -ing, lēafed,
leaved, lēaf'y, -i ness, -less,
-less ness, -let, lēaf'cup, a plant,
-nose, a bat, -stalk, -work.
lēaf'-beâr'ing, -bee tle, -blade,
-blight, -bridge, -bud, -bug,
-but ter fly, -car'ri er, -climb er,
-comb, -crum'pler, -cut ter,
-feed er, -finch, -fold er, -foot-
ed, -gild'ing, -hop per, -in sect,
-li'chen, -louse, -min er, -mold,
-net ting, -roll er, -rust, -sheath,
-sight, -sil ver ing, -spot, -spring,
-stalk, -tī'er, -trace, -turn er,
-valve.
lēaf' gold, l. lard, l. met al, l.
sil ver, l. to bac'co.
lēague, lēagued, lēa'guing, -guer.
Lē'ah, Bib.
lēak, -age, -ing, -y, -i ness,
lēaked, leak'-a larm', -in'di cator, -sig'nal.

lēal, lēal'ly.
lēa'land.
Leam'ing ton (lĕm'-), t. Eng.
lēan, a., -er, -est, -ly, -ness,
lēan'-faced, -wit'ted, lēan'ing-
knife.
lēan, v., -ing, lēaned, lēan'-to,
lēan'ing-note.
Lē ăn'noth, Bib.
lēap, -er, -ing, lēaped, lēap'-frog,
-ore, -year, lēap'ing-fish, -head,
leap'ing cu'cum ber, l. spi'der.
lēarn, -a ble, -ed, -ed ly, -ed ness,
-er, -ing, lēarned.
lease (lēs), -hold, -hold er, -mon-
ger, leased, leas'er, -ing, les see',
-see'ship, les sor', lease-band,
-pin, -rod, leas'ing-corn.
lēash, -ing, leashed.
lēast, -ways, -wise, -dart'er.
lēath'er, -ing, -ered, -et or -ette',
-oid, -y, -ern.
lēath'er back, a turtle; a duck,
-coat, an apple, -flow'er, -head,
a bird; a person, -leaf, -side,
a fish, -wood, a shrub.
lēath'er-awl, -backed, -bee tle,
-board, -board'ing, -brown,
-buf fing, -carp, -cloth, -cor'ru
ga ting, -creas'ing, -cut ting,
-di cing, -dress er, -em boss'ing,
-fin ish ing, -flesh ing, -flūt'ing,
-glâss'ing, -glu ing, -gouge,
-grain'ing, -grind er, -ham mer-
ing, -jack, -jack et, -knife.
lēath'er-lap, -pa per, -plant, -pol-
ish er, -press ing, -punch, -punch-
ing, -quilt ing, -rais ing, -re du'-
cing, -roll ing, -round ing, -scal-
lop ing, -scarf'ing, -scour'ing,
-seat, -skin, -slit ting, -sof'ten er,
-sort ing, -split ting, -stamp,
-stretch er, -strīp'ing, -strip-
ping, -stuff er, -ta per ing, -tur-
tle.
Leathes (lēths), Eng. theol.
lēave, left, lēav'ing, lēave'-breāk'er,
-lŏŏk'er, -tāk'ing, leav'ing-shop.
lēav'en, -ing, -ened.
Leb bæ'us or -bē'us, Bib.
Lē beau' (-bō'), Fr. poet.
Le bœuf' (lê bŭf'), Fr. gen.
Lē bŏ'nah, Bib.

lĕch'er, -ous, -ous ly, -ous ness, -y.
leck'-stone.
Le clerc' or Le Clerc' (lê klâr'),
Swiss theol.
Le cocq' (lê kŏk'), Fr. musician.
Le Conte (lē kŏnt), Amer. physicist; Amer. entom.; Amer.
geol.
Le conte' de Lisle' (lê kŏnt' dê
lēl'), Fr. poet.
Le coq' (lê kŏk'), Fr. naturalist.
Le cou vreur' (lê kōō vrêr'), Fr.
actress.
lĕc'tern.
lĕc'tion, -a ry.
lĕc'ture, -ship, -tūred, -tūr ing,
-tūr er, -tūr ess, lec'tress, -trĭce,
lĕc'ture-day, -room.
Lē'da, Myth., -clay.
lĕdge, -ment, lĕdged, ledg'y.
lĕd'ger, -bait, -blade, -book.
lee, -way, -ward, -ward ly, -ward
ness, -board, -bow (-bou), v.,
-bowed, -clue, -gāge.
leech, -er, -ing, -crâft, -dom,
-eat'er, a bird, -fee, -gait ers,
-glâss, -line, -rope.
lee'fang.
leek, -green.
leer, -ing, leered, leer-pan.
lees (lēz).
leet, -man.
Leeu'wen hoek, van (vän lê'wen-
hŏŏk), Dutch naturalist.
Le febre' (lê fävr'), Fr. marshal.
left, -ness, -ward, -hand'ed,
-hand'er, -hand ed ness, -off.
leg, -ging, -less, -let, legged, leg'-
bail, -band, -bone, -boot, -by,
-har ness, -ill, -i ron, -lock, -muff,
-rest, -shiĕld, legged or leg'ged, a.
lĕg'a cy, -a tee', -a tor, lĕg'a cy-
hunt'er, -hunt'ing.
lē'gal, -ly, -ness, -ism, -ist, -ize,
-ized, -ī'zing, -ĭ zā'tion, -gal'i ty,
lē'gal-ten'der.
Le garé' (lê grē'), Amer. statesman.
lĕg'ate, -ship, -a tĭne, -a ta'ry,
-a to'ri al.
le gā'tion.
le ga'to (lä gä'tō), le ga tis'si mo
(lä gä tēs'sē mō).

nŏt, nôr, ūse, ŭp, ûrn, etüde, fōōd, fŏŏt, anger, bonmot, thus, Bach.

lĕg'end (lĕj'-), -ed, -en da'ry, -en-
dist, -en dize, -dized, -di'zing,
le gen'da.
Le gendre' (lê zhŏndr'), Fr. geom.
lĕg'er (lĕj'-).
lĕg'er de măin' (lĕj'-), -ist.
Lĕg'horn (or -horn'), prov. It.;
a breed of fowls; pertaining to
Leghorn. lĕg'horn, a hat.
lĕg'i ble (lĕj'-), -ness, -bly, -bil'-
i ty.
lĕ'gion (-jun), -a ry, -ize, -ized,
-ĭ'zing.
lĕg'is late (lĕj'-), -lā'ted, -lā'tive,
-tive ly, -lā'ting, -lā'tor, -tor-
ship, -tŏ'ri al, -lā'ture, -lā'tion.
lĕ'gist.
lĕ git'i mate, -ly, -ness, -ma cy,
-mā'tion, -git'i ma tize, -tized,
-tī'zing, -tist, -git'i mism, -i-
mist, -mize, -mized, -mi zā'tion,
lĕg'i tĭme (lĕj'-).
Le gou vé' (lê gōō'vä'), Fr.
dram.; Fr. poet.
Le grand' (lê grŏṅ'), Fr. architect.
Le gros' (lê grō'), Fr. artist.
lĕg'ume (or lĕ gūme'), le gŭ'mĭ-
nose (-nōs), -mi nous.
Lĕ'ha bim (or -hä'-), Bib.
Leh'mann (lā'män), Ger. miner-
alogist.
Leib'nitz, von (fŏn lĭp'nĭts), Ger.
philos., -nitz'i an, -an ism.
Leices'ter (lĕs'ter), Eng. Earl.
Lei'dy (lī'dy), Amer. naturalist.
Leigh (lē), Eng. theol.
Leigh'ton (lā'ton), Eng. painter.
Leip'sic (līp'sĭk), c. Ger.
lei'sure (lē'zhŭr or -zhûr), -ly,
-li ness, -sured.
Lei'trim (lē'-), co. Ire.
Le jeune' (lē jūn'), Eng. painter;
—(lê zhên'), Fr. gen.
Lĕ'land, Amer. auth.
Lĕl'and, Eng. linguist.
Lel ew'el (lĕl ĕv'el), Pol. hist.
Lé lie' (lā'lē'), Molière.
Le mais'tre (lê mā'tr), Fr. writer.
Le mai'tre (lê mā'tr), Fr. actor.
le man'tin.
Le mer cier' (lê mĕr'syä'), Fr. dram.
lem'ming, -mouse.
Le Moine', Can. auth.

Le moine' (lê mwän'), Fr. publicist.
lĕm'on, -ade', -weed, -balm,
-bird, -cad'mĭ um, -col or, -col-
ored, -drop, -fish, -grăss,
-juice, -sole, -squash, -squeez'er,
-wal'nut, -wood, -yel low, l.
thyme (tīm), l. ver be'na.
Le Mon nier' (lê mōn'yā'), Fr.
astron.
Le Moyne' (lê mwän'), Can.
colonizer; colonial gov. of La.
Lĕm priere' (-preer'), Eng. schol.
Lĕm'u res (-rēz), Le mū'ri a, -ri-
an.
L'En clos' (lŏṅ'klō'), a noted Fr.
woman.
lend, -a ble, -er, -ing, lent.
Len fant' (lŏṅ'fŏṅ'), Fr. hist.
length, -en (-n), -ened, -ways,
-wise, -y, -i ly, -i ness.
length'en ing-bar, -piece, -rod.
lĕ'nĭ ent (or lēn'yent), -ly, -ence,
-en cy, len'i tive, -tive ness, -i ty.
lĕ'no.
lens (lĕnz), pl. lens es, lens-cap,
-hold er, -shaped.
Lens (lŏṅ), t. Fr.
Lent, lent'en or Lent'en, Lent'-
lil y, -rose, lent'en crab.
lĕn'tĭl, -tic'u lar, lĕn'til-shell.
Lĕ'ŏ, Astron.
Leo min ster (lĕm'in ster), t.
Mass.—(lĕm'ster), t. Eng.
Lĕ'on, co. Fla.; co. Tex.; t. Ia.;
—(lā ōn'), prov. Sp.; prov.
Ecuador; t. Mex.; t. Nicaragua.
Le'o nese' (-nēs' or -nēz').
Lĕ'ŏ nid, pl. -ŏn'i des (-dēz),
Astron.
lĕ'ŏ nĭne (or -nīn), -ly.
Lĕ ŏ now'ens (-nou'enz), Amer.
auth.
leop'ard (lĕp'-), -wood, a tree,
-cat, -fish, -flow'er, -frog, -lil y,
-moth, -seal, -tor toise, leop'-
ard's-bane.
Le o par'di (lā ō par'dē), It. poet.
Le Pays' (lê pā'ē'), Fr. poet.
lĕp'er, lĕp'rous, -rous ly, -rous-
ness, -rose, -ro sĭed, -ro sy, le-
prŏs'i ty, lep rol'o gy, -o gist.
Lĕp'si us (-sē ŏŏs), Ger. Egyptol.

Le roux' (lĕ rōō'), Fr. writer.
Le Sage' (lê säzh'), Fr. novelist.
lese-maj'es ty (lēz-măj'es ty).
lē'sion (-zhun).
Les que reux' (lā'kê rê'),   Swiss
    paleontol.
less, -er, least.
les see', -ship, les sor'.
les'sen (-sn), -ing, -sĕned.
Les'seps, de (dê lĕs'ĕps or dê
    lā'sep'), Fr. engineer.
les'sive.
les'son (-sn).
lest.
les'te (lās'tā).
L'Es trange' (lĕs trānj'),   Eng.
    writer.
Le su eur' (lê soo'êr'), Fr. painter.
Le Su eur' (lê soo'êr'), Fr. com-
    poser.
let, -ting, let'-a lone, -off, -up.
lĕth'ar gy, -ar gize, -gized, -gī'-
    zing, le thar'gic, -gic al, -al ly,
    -al ness.
Le'thĕ, Myth., -thē'an, le'thal.
Lē'to, Myth.
let'ter, -ing, -less, -tered, let'ter-
    leaf, a plant, -press, printed
    matter, -wood, a tree.
let'ter-bal ance, -board, -book,
    -box, -căr'ri er, -case, -clip,
    -cut ter, -drop, -file, -found'er,
    -found'ry, -hĕad, -hĕad ing, -li-
    chen (-ker.), -lock, -name, -of fice,
    -or na ment, -pa per, -per fect,
    -plant, -press, a press to copy
    letters, -punch, -rack, -scale,
    -stamp, -winged, -writ'er, -wor'-
    ship.
let'ter ing-box, -tool.
Letts, Lithuanians, Let'tic, -tish.
let'tuce (-tĭs), -bird, -o pi um,
    -sax'ĭ frage.
leu (lā), pl. lei (lē).
leu co'sis (lū kō'-), leu'cous.
Leutsch', von (fŏn loich'), Ger.
    schol.
Leut'ze (loit'sĕ), Amer. painter.
le vä'da.
Lĕ vant', the eastern Mediterra-
    nean, -ĭne.
lev'ant, a spring of water, le vant'-
    er, a gale of wind; one who

absconds. le vant', v., -ed, -ing,
    le vant'ĭne, a silk fabric.
lĕv ee' (or lĕv'-).
lĕv'ĕl, -ing or -ling, -eled or
    -elled, -er or -ler, -ly, -ness,
    lĕv'ĕl-dye ing, -hĕad'ed.
lĕv'ĕl ing-block,   -in stru ment,
    -plow, -pole, -rod, -screw,
    -stăff, -stand.
lĕv'er (or lē'ver), -age, -wood, a
    plant.
lĕv'er-board, -brace, -com press'-
    or, -drill, -en gine, -es cape-
    ment, -fau cet, -frame, -hoist,
    -jack, -press, -punch, -valve.
Lē'ver, Irish novelist.
lĕv'er et, -skin.
Le ver'ri er (lē vĕr'i er or lê vâr-
    yā'), Fr. astron.
Lé vesque' (lā'văk'), Fr. hist.
lē vī'a than.
lĕv'i gate, -gà ble, -gā'ted, -gā'-
    ting, -gā'tion, lev'i gā'ting-ma-
    chine, -mill.
lĕv'i rate, -rat'ic, -ic al, -rā'tion.
lĕv'i tate, -tā'ted, -tā'ting, -tā'-
    tor, -tā'tion.
Le'vīte, -vīt ism, -vit'ic, -ic al,
    -al ly, -vit'i cus.
lĕv'i ty.
lĕv'y, -ing, -i à ble, -i er, -ied.
lewd, -ly, -ness.
Lew'es (lū'ĭs), Eng. writer.
Lew'is (lōō'is), Chr. name, Fr.
    Lou'is, lew'is, Mech.
lew'is-bolt, -hole.
lex i cog'ra pher, -ra phist, -ra-
    phy, -co graph'ic al, -al ly.
lex i col'o gy, -o gist, -co log'ic al
    (-lŏj'-), lex'i con.
lex i phan'ic, -i cism.
ley (lā), -pew'ter.
Ley'den (lī'-), Scotch poet; Dutch
    painter; c. Holland; L. jar, L.
    vi al.
Leys (līs or lā), Belg. painter.
Le'y te (lā'ē tā), isl. Philippines.
Ley'ton (lē'-), t. Eng.
Le zig nan' (lā'zēn'yŏñ'), t. Fr.
L'ho pi tal' (lō'pē'tăl'), Fr. chan-
    cellor.
lī'a ble, -ness, -bly, -bil'i ty.
li ai son' (lē ā zŏñ').

lĭ ăn'a *or* lī āne'.
liang (lyăng).
lī'ar.
lī'ard.
lī'bate, -bā'ted, -bā'ting, -bà tō'-
ry, -bā'tion.
lī'bĕl, -bĕled *or* -bĕlled, -bel ing
or -ling, -bel er *or* -ler, -ous,
-ous ly, -ant.
lĭ bel'la.
lĭb'er al, -ly, -ism, -ist, -is'tic,
-er al'i ty, -al ize, -ized, -ī'zer,
-ī'zing, -ĭ zā'tion.
Lib'er al-Un'ion ism (-ūn'yŭn-),
-Un'ion ist.
lĭb'er ate, -ā'ted, -ā'ting, -ā'tor,
-ā'tion, -tion ism, -tion ist.
Li'be ri (lē'bā rē), It. painter.
Lĭ bĕ'ri a, Afr., -bĕ'rĭ an.
lĭb'er tĭne, -tin age, -tin ism.
lĭb'er ty, -book, -cap, -day, -man,
-pole, -tick'et.
lĭ bĭd'i noŭs, -ly, -ness, -nos'i ty.
Lĭ'bra, Astron., *li'bra* (lē'-), a
weight, lī'bral, li'brate, -brā'ted,
-brā'ting, -brà tō'ry, -brā'tion.
lī'bra ry, -bra'ri an, -an ship, lī'-
bra ry-keep er.
lĭ brĕt'to, -bret'tist.
Lib'y a (-Ɪ à), Afr., -y an, Lib'y-
an des ert, L. Sea.
lī'cense, -censed, -cens er, -ing,
-a ble, -cen sure, -cen see', lī'-
cense-tax.
lĭ cen'ti ate (-shĭ-), -ship, -ti ā'-
tion.
lĭ cen'tious (-shus), -ly, -ness.
lī'cet.
li'chen (lī'kĕn), -ism, -ist, -ous,
-ose, -a'ceous, -chen'ic, -i form,
-chen og'ra pher, -ra phy, -o-
graph'ic, -ic al, -chen ol'o gy,
-o gist, -o log'ic al, -chē'ni an,
-chĕned, li'chen-starch.
lĭch'road, lich'way, -work, -fowl,
-gate, -owl.
Lich'ten steĭn, t. Ger.
lick, -ing, -er, licked, lick'pen ny,
-plat ter, -spit tle, lick'er-in, -up.
lick'et y-cut, -split.
lic'o rice (lĭk'ō rĭs), -weed, -mass,
-paste, -vetch.
lic'tor.

lid, -ded, -less, -cells, -clōs'er
(-klōz'-), -flow'er.
Lĭd'dell, Scotch math.; Eng.
schol.
līe, lay, lain, ly'ing, līe'-a-bed.
līe, līed, ly'ing.
Lie'ber kühn, Ger. physician.
Lie'big (lē'bich), Ger. chem.
Lieb'knecht (lēp'knĕcht), Ger.
socialist.
lied (lēt), pl. *liē'der, liē'der tä fel.*
lie'der kranz (lē'der kränts).
lie-de-vin (lē'-dè-văn').
liĕf.
liege (lēj), -dom, -less, -man.
Li ége' (lē äzh'), prov. Belg.
Lieg'nitz (lēg'nĭts), dist. Prus.
li'en (lē'en *or* lēn *or* lī'en),
-hold'er.
lī'en ter'y.
Li erre' (lē är'), t. Belg.
lieu (lū).
lieū ten'ant, -ship, -ten'an cy, lieu-
ten'ant-colo nel, -com mand'er,
-gen'er al, -gov'ern or, -gov'ern or-
ship.
Lié vin' (lyā văn'), t. Fr.
life, *pl.* lives, life'less, -less ly,
-less ness, -like, -like ness, -long,
-root, a plant, -spring, -string,
-time.
life'-ar row, -belt, -blood, -boat,
-breath, -buoy, -car, -cord,
-cy cle (-sī'-), -drop, -es tate, -ev-
er lảst'ing, a plant; -giv'ing,
-guard, -his to ry, hold, -in-
sur'ance, -in ter est, -land,
-line, -mor tar, -of fice, -peer,
-peer age, -plant, -pre serv'er,
-rảft, -rate, -ren'der ing, -rent,
-rent er, -rock et, -root, -sav ing,
-shot, -sig nal, -size, -spot, -ta-
ble, -ten ant, -wea ry, -work,
life's-blood.
lift, -ed, -er, -ing, -a ble.
lift'-bridge, -gate, -ham mer,
-latch, -lock, -pump, -ten'ter,
-wall.
lift'ing-ap pa rā'tus, -bar, -blade,
-bridge, -day, -dog, -gate,
-gear, -hitch, -jack, -ma chine,
-piece, -pump, -rod, -screw,
-set, -tongs, -wire.

lig'a ment, -men'tal, -men'tous, -tous ly, -ta ry.

li'gan.

li'gate, -gā'ted, -gā'tor, -gā'tion.

lig'a ture, -tured, -tūr ing, lig'a-ture-căr'ri er.

lig'ger.

light (līt), -ed, -er, -ing, -a ble, -less, -ly, -ness, -some, -some ly, -some ness, light'brain, a person, -house, -house man, -spir it ed, -struck, -weight, -wood.

light'-a pos'tro phe, -armed, -ball, -bar rel, -boat, -box, -course, -dues, dues paid for light, -e las tic'i ty, -e qua tion, -fin gered, -foot, -foot ed, -hand ed, -head ed, -head ed-ness, -heart ed, -heart ed ly, -heart ed ness, -heeled, -horse, -horse man, -i ron, -keep er, -leg ged, -mak'er, -mind ed, -mind ed ness, -mod er a tor, -mon ey, -or gan, -room, -ship, -tight, -ves sel, -wave, -weight, a person, -winged, -wit ted.

light'en, -ing, -ened.

light'er, -age, -man, -screw, -ståff.

light'ning, -ăr rest'er, -bug, -con-duct or, -dis charg'er, -print, -proof, -pro tect or, -rod, -tube.

lig näl'oes (-ōz).

lig'ne ous, -nĭ fy, -fy ĭng, -fied, -nin, -nīte, -nĭt'ic, -ni tif'er ous, -ni tize, -tized, -tī'zing, -nose, -num, lig'num-vi'tæ (-tē).

Lig ny' (lēn'yē'), vil. Belg.; t. Fr.

Lĭg ō nier' (-neer'), Eng. marshal; t. Ind.; t. Pa.

Li Hung Chang (lē hŏŏng chăng), Chinese statesman.

like, liked, lik'ing, lik'a ble or like'-, -ble ness, like'li hood, -li-ness, -ly, -ness, -wise, like'-mind'ed, like'-as-we-lie'.

li'kin' (lē'kēn').

lī'lăc, li lā'ceous (-shus), lĭ'lă-cĭne, li'lac throat, a bird, -gray, -mil dew, -rust.

Lille or Lisle (lēl), c. Fr.

Lil lers' (lē'yā'), t. Fr.

Lil'lĭ put, Gulliver, -pū'tian (-pū'shan).

lĭl'y, lil'lĭed, -i ā'ceous (-shus), lĭl'y liv er, a person, -wort.

lĭl'y-bee'tle, -en'cri nīte, -faced, -hy a cinth, -i ron, -liv ered, -pad, -star, -white, lĭl'y-of-the-val ley.

Lĭ'ma, t. N. Y.; c. O.; tp. Wis.; —(lē'ma), t. Peru.

limb, limbed, limb'-beâr'ing, -gir dle, -guard, -root.

lim'ber, -bēred, -ber ing, -ber-ness, lim'ber-board, -box, -chain, -chest, -hole, -strake.

lim'bō.

Lim bourg' (lăn'bōōr'), prov. Belg.

Lĭm'burg (-bŭrg), prov. Neth.

Lim'burg'er cheese.

lime, limed, lim'ing, -y, lime'ball, -stone, -twig, v., -wash, v.

lime'-boil, -burn er, -bush, -catch er, -crack er, -feld'spar, -floor, -juice, -kiln, -light, -ma chine, -pit, -pow der, -rod, -sink, -sour, -spread'er, -tree, -twig, n., -vi al, -wash, n., lime'ball-light, lime'stone-me-ter, lime' oint ment, l. punch.

lĭm'it, -ed, -ed ly, -ed ness, -er, -ing, -a ble, -less, -i ta ry, -ta tive, -i tā'tion, lim'it-gäge, -point.

limn (lĭm), limned (lĭmd), lĭm'-ning, -ner.

Li mo'e i ro (lē mō'ā ē rō), t. Braz.

Li moges' (lē'mōzh'), t. Fr.

Li mou sin' (lē'mōō'zăn'), prov. Fr.

Li moux' (lē'mōō'), t. Fr.

limp, -er, -ing, -ing ly, -ly, -ness, limped.

lĭm'pet.

lĭm'pid, -ly, -ness, -pid'i ty.

Li na'res (lē nä'rĕs), t. Sp.

linch, -pin, -hoop.

lin'den, -tree.

lĭnd'er.

line, līned, lin'er, lin'ing, lin'y, line'let, -man, lines'man.

line'-conch (-konk), -co or'di-nate, -den si ty, -en grāv'ing, -e qua tion, -fish, -fish er man,

nŏt, nôr, ūse, ŭp, ûrn, etūde, fōōd, fŏŏt, aŋger, boṅmot, thus, Bach.

25

-fish ing, -in'te gral, -pin, -rīd'-
ing, -rock'et, -squall, -storm,
-wire, line'-and-line.
lĭn'e age.
lĭn'e al, -ly, -e ar, -ar ly, -ăr'i ty,
-e ate, -ā'ted, -ā'tion.
lĭn'e a ment.
lĭn'e ar-a cute', -en'sate, -lan'ce-
o late, -ob long.
lĭn'en, -drăp'er, -mus lin, -pan el,
-prov er (-proōv'-), -scroll.
lĭn'e o grăph, -o late, -lā'ted.
ling, -y, ling'ber'ry, -thorn, a
fish, -bird, -pink.
Ling, Sw. poet, ling'ism.
lin'ger, -ing, -ing ly, -er, -gered.
lin ge rie' (lăṇ zhê rē').
lin'go.
lin'got.
lin'gual, -ly, -gui form, -guist,
-guis try, -guis'tic, -tic al, -al ly,
-tics, -gua nā'sal.
lĭn'i ment.
lĭn'ing-brush, -felt, -nail, -pa-
per, -strip.
link, -age, -er, -ing, linked, link'-
boy, -man, -work, -block, -lĕv'-
er, -mo'tion, -room'ing.
Lin næ'us (-nē'-) or Lin né, von
(fŏn lĭn'nä), Sw. bot., Lin næ'-
an or -ne'an.
lin'net, -finch, -hole.
lĭ nō'le um.
lĭn'o type.
lĭn'seed, -cake, -meal, -mill, -oil.
lĭn'sey (-sĭ), -wool'sey.
lint, -white, a bird, -doc'tor,
-white, a.
lin'tel.
lin'ter.
lĭ'on, -el, -ess, -et, -ize, -ized,
-ī'zing, -ism, -heart, a person.
lĭ'on-ant, -dog, -drag on, -hearted,
-hunt er, -lĕop ard, -like, -liz ard,
-mon key, -tailed, -toothed.
lĭ'on's-ear, -foot, -heart, -leaf,
-mouth, -tail, -tooth, -tur nip.
lip, lipped, lip'ping, -py, lip'-bit,
-born, -cell, -com fort, -com-
fort er, -de vo'tion, -fern, -fish,
-good, -head, -hom age, -hook,
-la bor, -la bo'ri ous, -lan-
guage, -or na ment, -plate,

-pro tect'or, -read'ing, -right'-
eous ness, -salve (-säv), -serv'ice,
-spine, -tooth, -wis dom, -wise,
-work, -work ing.
lĭp'a ri (-rē), isl. Medit. sea.
lĭp'pe, r. Ger.
lī'quate, -quā'ted, -quā'ting, -quā'-
tion, lĭq'ua ble, liq ue fā'cient,
-făc'tion, -fac'tive, lī quā'tion-
fur nace, -heärth.
liq'ue fy (-fī), -ing, -fīed, -fī'a-
ble, lī ques'cent, -cence, -cen cy.
lĭ queur' (lĭ kêr'), -ing, li queur'-
cup, -glass.
liq'uid (lĭk'wĭd), -à ble, -ly, -ness,
li quid'i ty.
liq'ui date, -dā'ted, -dā'ting, -dā'-
tor, -dā'tion.
liq'uor (lĭk'ur), -bot tle, -cock,
-deal er, -gāge, -pump, -sa-
loon', -sell er, -store, -thief.
lĭ'ra (lē'ra), pl. lĭ're (lē'rā).
lĭre, a rare cloth; brawn.
Lisle (lēl), c. Fr.; t. N. Y., L.
glove, L. stock ing, L. thread.
L'Ĭs let' (lē'lä'), co. Que.
lisp, -er, -ing, -ing ly, lisped.
lis'sang.
lisse (lēs).
lis'sens (snz), strands of a rope.
lĭs'some, -ness.
Lĭs sō'ne (-nā), t. It.
list, -ed, -ful, -ing, -less, -less ly,
-less ness, -work, -mill, -pan,
-pot, -wheel, list'ing-plow.
lis'ten (-n), -er, -ing, -tened (-nd).
lis'ter ine (-ĭn).
lit'a ny, -desk, -stool.
li'ter or -tre (lē'tr).
lit'er al, -ism, -ist, -al ize, -ized,
-ī'zing, -ī'zer, -ĭ zā'tion, -al ly,
-al ness, -al'i ty.
lit'er a ry, -a cy, -a ri an, -ate,
-ā'tor, -à ture, -tured, lit te ra-
teur' (-têr').
lit e ra'tus, pl. -rā'tĭ, -rā'tim.
lith'arge.
lĭttle, -ness, -some, -some ness.
lith'i a, lith'ic, -i um.
lith'o graph, -graph'ic, -ic al, -al-
ly, lĭ thog'ra pher, -ra phy.
lĭ thŏl'o gy, -o gist, lith o log'ic,
-ic al, -al ly.

lith'o tome, -tom'ic, -ic al, li-
thot'o mize, -mized, -mĭ'zing,
-o mist, -o my.
lith'o type, -typed, -typ ing (-tĭp'-),
-ty'py (-tī'-), -typ'ic (-tĭp'-).
lit'i gate, -gā'ted, -gā'ting, -gȧ-
ble, -gant, -gā'tor, -gā'tion.
lĭ tĭg'ious (lĭ tĭj'us), -ly, -ness,
-i os'i ty.
lit'mus.
li'tre (lē'tr), a measure, a term
in heraldry.
lĭt'rĕ, a tree.
lit'ter, -ing, -er, -y, -tered.
lit'tle, -ness, -beak, an animal,
-ease, -en'di an, -neck, -worth.
lit'to ral.
Lit trĕ' (lē'trā'), Fr. philol.
lĭ tur'gic, -al, -al ly, -gics, -gi ol'o-
gy, -o gist, lit'ur gy, -gist.
lĭve, v., lĭved, lĭv'ing, -ing ly, -ing-
ness, -er, a blc, lĭvc'long, -for-
ev'er, a plant, lĭv'ing-chām ber,
-room.
lĭve, a., -ly, -li ly, -li ness, -li-
hood, lĭved, lĭve'-box, -cen ter,
-hĕad, -oak, -well.
lĭv'er, -ered, liv'er leaf, a plant,
-stone, -wort.
lĭv'er-col'or, -col ored, -com-
plaint', -fluke, -ore, -py rī'tes
(-tēz), -spots, -wing.
lĭv'er y, -er Ied, lĭv'er y man,
-coat, -col lar, -col ors, -cup-
board, -fish, -gown, -of fice,
-serv ant, -sta ble, l. com'pa ny.
lĭv'id, -ness, lĭ vid'i ty.
li'vre (lē'vr).
lix iv'i ate, -ā'ted, -a'ting, -i al,
-i ous, -i ā'tion.
liz'ard, -tail, a plant, -bait, -fish,
-seek er, -stone, -tailed, liz'ard's-
tail, -tongue.
llä'ma.
llä'nŏ, pl. -nos (-nōz), lla ne'ro
(lyȧ nā'rō).
Lla'no Es tä cä'dŏ (lyä'nō),
plateau, Texas.
Llew el'lyn (lōō ĕl'in), Prince of
Wales.
Lloyd's.
lōad, -ed, -er, -ing, load'-line,
-pen ny.

load'ing-bar, -fun nel, -ma chine',
-plug, -tongs, -tray.
lōaf, pl. loaves, loaf'er, -er ish,
-ing, loafed, loaf' su'gar.
loam, -y, loam'-beat'er, -board,
-cake, -mold, -mold ing, -plate,
-work.
loan, -a ble, -ing, loaned, loan'-
of'fice, -word.
lōath or lōth, a., unwilling.
lōathe, v., lōathed, lōath'er, -ful,
-ing, -ing ly, -ly, -li ness, -some,
-some ly, -some ness.
lŏb, lŏbbed, lob'bing, lob'worm.
lō'bate, -ly, -bā'ted, -bā'ting,
-bā'tion.
lŏb'by, -ing, -ist, -bĭed, lob'by-
mem'ber.
lōbe, -let, lōbed, lō'bose, lōbe'-
foot, a bird, -ber ry, -foot ed,
-plate.
lŏb'lol ly, -bay, -boy, -pine,
-sweet wood, -tree.
lob'ster, -ing, -man, -car, -chum,
-claw, -claws, -crawl, -louse,
-moth, -pot, -tail, -tailed, lob'-
ster's-claw.
lob'-stick.
lŏb'ule, -u lar, -u late, -lā'ted,
-lā'tion.
lō'cal, -ism, -ly, -ize, -ized, -ī'zer,
-ī'zing, -ī'za ble, -l zā'tion, -cal-
ĭs'tĭc, -cal'i ty, lo'cale' (-käl').
lō'cate, -cā'ted, -cā'ting, -cā'tor,
-cā'tion.
Loch a ber ax (lŏk'- or -ä'bêr).
Loch'ee (lŏch'ē), t. Scot.
Loches (lōsh), t. Fr.
Loch'in var' (lŏk'-), Scott.
lock, -age, -ing, -er, -et, locked,
lock'fast, -jaw, -man, -out,
-rand, -smith, -up, -work,
locks'man.
lock'-band, -bay, -bolt, -bond,
-box, -chain, -chăm'ber, -cock,
-cramp, -down, -fau cet, -gate,
-hatch, -hole, -hook, -house,
-keep er, -lan yard, -nail, -nut,
-pad dle, -piece, -plate, -pul ley,
-rail, -saw, -sill, -spit, -spit-
ting, -step, -stitch, -string,
-tool, -tor toise, -weir.
lock'er-up, lock'ing-pal let, -plate.

Locke (lŏk), Eng. metaphys.,
Lock'i an, -an ism.
lo'co, -dis ease', -plant, -weed.
lo co fō'co, a cigar; a match.
Lo co fo'co, a political term.
lo co mō'tive, -mō'tion, -mō'tor,
-mo'to ry, -mo'bĭle (or -bĕl), lo-
co mō'tive-bal ance, -pump, l.
car.
lŏ'cust, -bean, -ber ry, -bird,
-bor'er, -eat er, -shrimp, -tree.
loc'u to ry, lo cu'tion.
lode, -star, -stone, -stuff.
Lŏ'-dē'bar (or lō'de-), Bib.
lŏdge, lŏdged, lŏdg'er, -ing, -ment,
lodge'-gate, lodg'ing-car, -house,
-knee, -mon'ey.
lodh'-bark (lōd'-).
loft, -er, -y, -i ly, -i ness, -ing-
i'ron.
log, -ging, -ger, logged, log'fish,
-hĕad, a person, -man, -roll,
-wood.
log'-beam, -board, -book, -but-
ter, -chip, -cock, -frame, -glăss,
-head'ed, -line, -meas'ur er,
-perch, -reel, -roll er, -roll ing,
-scale, -slate, -turn er, -up.
log cab'in, l. house, l. rail'way.
log'ging-ax, -bee, -camp, -head,
l. rock.
lŏg'a rithm (or -rĭthm), -rĭth'-
mic, -mic al, -al ly, -met'ic al.
log'ger hĕad, -ed.
log'ger hĕat.
log'ic (lŏj'-), -al, -al ly, -al ness,
lō gi'cian (-jish'an), lo gis'tic,
-tic al, -tics, log'ic-chop ping.
log'o gram, -o graph, -graph'ic,
-ic al, -al ly, lō gog'ra phy, -ra-
pher, log'agriph, lo gom'a chist
(-kist), -a chy (-ky), log o mā'-
ni a, -o lept.
lo gom'e ter, log o met'ric, -ric al.
Lo'hen grin (lō'ĕn-), Wagner.
loin, -cloth.
Loir (lwär), a small r. Fr.
Loire (lwär), largest r. in Fr.
Lŏ'is, Bib.
loi'ter, -er, -ing, -ing ly.
Lŏ'la Mŏn'tĕz (or -tēz), Countess
of Landsfeld.
lŏll, -ing, -ing ly, lŏl lard.

Lol'lard, a monastic society, -lard-
ist, -lard ism, -lard y.
lŏl ly pop or -li pop.
Lo maz'zo (lō mät'so), It. painter.
Lom'bard (lŏm'bard or lŏn bär'),
It. theol.
Lŏm'bar dy, a prov. It., L. pop'-
lar, Lom'bard, -bar'dic.
lŏ'mĭ lŏ'mĭ.
Lon'don (lŭn'dŭn), c. Eng., -er,
-ese, -ism, -ize, -ized, -ĭ'zing.
Lon'don-pride, a plant, -rock et,
a plant, -tuft, a plant, L. paste,
L. smoke, L. sprat, L. white.
lōne, -ly, -li er, -li ness, lone'-
ness, lone'some, -some ly, -some-
ness.
long, lon'ger, -gest, longed
(longd), long'ing, -ing ly, long'-
beak, a bird, -beard, a man,
-bill, a bird, -bōw, -hand, -horn,
an insect, -neck, a duck, -nose,
a fish, -shanks, a bird; a
person, -shore, -shore man,
-spur, a bird, -stop, v., -tail,
an animal, -tongue, a bird; a
person, -worm.
long'-arc, a., -boat, -brĕathed,
-de scend'ed, -drawn, -eared,
-ears, a donkey, -faced, -field,
a person, -glăss, -head'ed,
-horned, -legs, an insect,
-legged (or -leg'ged), -līved,
-moss, -off, -on, -pur ples,
-range, a., -rest, in music,
-ruff er, -run, -set tled, -short,
-sight ed, -sight ed ness, -slip, a
person, -spun, -sta ple, a.,
-stitch, -stop, a person, -suf'fer-
ance, -suf'fer ing, -tail, a.,
-tailed, -take, -tongued, -vis-
aged, -wall, a., -waist ed,
-wind ed.
long' coats, l. prim er, l. shawl,
l. slide.
lon gĕv'i ty (-jev'-), -ge'val.
Lon gī'nus (-jī'-), Gr. philos.
lon'gi tude, -tu'di nal, -nal ly.
Long pé ri er' (lŏn'pā'rē ā'), Fr.
archæol.
Longue ville' (lŏng'vēl'), Fr.
agitator.
lōō, -măsk, -ta'ble.

---

lŏŏk, -er, -ing, -out, lŏŏked, look'-
down, a fish, look'er-on, look'-
ing-for, -glåss, look'out-bås ket.

lōōm, -ing, lōōmed, loom'-card,
-comb, -fig ured, -har ness,
-pic ture, -sheet ing.

lōōn, -ing, -y.

loon'ghee (lōōn'gĕ).

lōōp, -er, -ing, looped, loop'hole,
-light, -work, -worm.

loop'-bolt, -head, -hold er, -test,
-yoke, loop'ing-snail, -worm.

Loos (lōs), t. Fr.—(lōōs), prov.
Baluchistan.

lōōse, -ly, -ness, loosed, loos'ing,
-en er, loose'strife, a plant.

loose'-bŏd'ïed, -box, -house, -kir-
tle, -work, loos'en ing-bar.

lōōt, -ed, -er, -ing, -y.

lop, -ping, lopped, lop'seed, a
plant, -sīd'ed, -tail, v., lop'-
eared, -wood, lop'ping-ax,
-shears.

lŏpe, lōped, lōp'er, -ing.

Lo'pez (lō'pĕs), Pres. Para.

lŏ quā'cious (-shus), -ly, -ness,
-quăc'i ty, lŏq'ui tur.

lo'ranth.

lord, -ed, -ing, -less, -like, -ly,
-li ness, ship, -wood, a tree.

lord'-lieu ten'ant, -lieu ten'an cy,
lords-and-la dies, a plant; a
duck.

lŏre.

Lŏ're lei (lō'rā lī'), Ger. legend.

lor gnette' (lôrn yĕt'), lor'gnon
(lôrn'yŏn).

lŏrn.

Los An'ge les (lŏs ăn'jĕ lĕs or
-lēz), c. Cal.

lose (lōōz), los'ing, -ing ly, -er,
loss, lost.

lot.

lŏte, -bush, -fruit, -tree.

lŏ'tion.

lŏt'ter y.

lŏt'to.

lŏ'tus, -ber'ry, -eat er, -tree.

Lou bet' (lōō'ba'), Pres. Fr.

loud, -ly, -ness, loud'-mouthed.

lough (lŏch).

Lough (lŭf), Eng. sculp.

Lough Neagh' (loch nā'), l. Ire.

Lou'is, Chr. name, Lou is-Qua-
torze (lōō'ï-kå tôrz'), -Quinze
(-kănz'), -Seize (-sāz'), -Treize
(-trāz').

lou'is (lōō'ï) or lou'is d'or (lōō'ï
dôr'), a coin.

lou i sette' (lōō ï zĕt').

Lou i si an'a (lōō ē'zï ăn'a), -ăn'-
i an.

lou i sine' (lōō ï zēn').

Lou'is ville (lōō'ïs vïl or lōō'ï-),
t. Ky.; tp. N. Y.; vil. O.

Lou'lé (lōō'lä), t. Port.

lounge, lounged, loun'ger, -ging,
loun'ging-room.

loup (lōōp), a mask; to leap.

loupe (lōōp), a mass of hot iron.

Lourdes (lōōrd), t. Fr.

loure (lōōr).

Lou ren'ço Mar ques' (lō rĕn'sō
mär kĕs'), prov. Afr.

louse, pl. lice, lous'y (louz'-), -i ly,
-i ness, louse'ber'ry, a tree, -wort,
louse'-bur, -fly, -herb, lous'y-
bill, a bird.

lout, -ish, -ish ly, -ish ness.

lou tre (lōō'tr).

lou'trin (lōō'-).

Lou vain' (lōō'văn'), c. Belg.

luu'ver (lōō'-), -vered, lou'ver-
board, -win dow.

L'Ou ver ture' (lōō'vĕr'tür'),
Negro patriot.

Lou viers' (lōō'vyä'), t. Fr.

lou'vre (lōō'-), a palace; a dance.

love (luv), -less, -ly, -li ly, -li-
ness, -ling, -some, -some ly,
lov'a ble, -ble ness, -bil'i ty, -er,
-ing, -ing ly, -ing ness, love'-
flow er, a plant, -man, -wor thy.

love'-af fair, -ap ple, -bird,
-bro ker, -charm, -child, -dart,
-fa vor, -feast, -gråss, -knot,
-let ter, -lock, -lorn, -lorn ness,
-māk'ing, -match, -par'ra keet,
-par rot, -plant, -po tion, -rib bon,
-scene, -set, -shåft, -sick, -song,
-spell, -suit, -tap, -to ken, -tree,
-trout, -vine, -worth, lov'ing-cup,
-kind'ness.

love'-in-a-mist, a plant, -in-a-
puz zle, a plant, -in-i dle ness,
a plant, -lies-bleed ing, a plant.

---

nŏt, nôr, ūse, ŭp, ûrn, etüde, fōōd, fŏŏt, anger, bonmot, thus, Bach.

lŏw, -er, -er most, -ness, -ing,
-ly, -li ly, -li ness, low'land,
Low'land er.
lŏw'-boy, -day, -di lu'tion ist,
-down, *a.*, -down er, -line,
-līved, -mīnd'ed, -necked, -pres-
sure, *a.*, -spir it ed, -stud ded,
-warp, *a.*, -worm.
lŏw'er-case, *a.*
lŏw'-Church, -church'ism, -church'-
man, -Ger'man.
low'bell (lou'-), -ing, -belled.
Lö'we (lê'vê), Ger. composer;
Ger. trav.; Ger. singer.
Lowe (lō), Brit. gen.
Lö'wen berg (lê'ven bĕrg), t. Prus.
Lö'wen thal (lê'vĕn täl), famous
chess player.
low'er (lou'-), -ing, -ing ly, -ered.
Lŏw er Al sace' (äl'säs'), prov.
Ger.
low'rie (lou'-), a fox.
low'ry (lou'-), a car; a plant.
lox'ic, lox'o dŏnt.
loy'al, -ism, -ist, -ize, -ized,
-ī'zing, -al ly, -al ness, -al ty.
Loy ŏ'la, Sp. divine.
Loy son' (lwä'zŏn'), Fr. orator.
lŏz'enge, -enged, -en gy, lŏz'enge-
coach, -fret, -goad, -grãv'er,
-ma chine, -mold ing, -shaped,
-spur, -tool.
Lŏ'zier (-zher), Amer. physician.
Lreux (lrōō), The Round Table.
lu'au (lōō'ou).
lub'ber, -ly, -li ness, -head, a
person, -wort, -cock, -grãss'-
hop per, -hole, -line.
Lüb'ke (lüp'kê) Ger. hist.
lu'bra (lōō'-).
lū'brĭ cate, -cã'ted, -cã'ting, -cã'-
tive, -cã'tor, -cant, -cã'tion,
lu'brĭ cous, -bri fac'tion, -bric'-
i ty (-bris'-), lu'bri cã'ting-oil,
lu'bri cant-test'er.
Lū'cas, Eng. painter.—(lü'kä'),
Fr. reformer.
Luc'ca (lŭk'ka *or* lŏŏk'a), Ger.
vocalist.—(lōōk'ka), c. It.
lū'cent, -cu lent, -lent ly.
Lu cerne', Switz., lū'cern, a lamp;
an animal; a plant, -cer'na, -nal.
lū'cid, -ly, -ness, -cid'i ty.

Lū'ci fer, *Astron.; Bib.,* lū'ci fer,
a match.
lū cim'e ter.
Lū'ci us (-shĭ-), *Bib.*
luck, -less, -less ly, -less ness, -y,
-i ly, -i ness.
luck'-pen'ny, luck'y-bag, -hands,
-min nie, -proach, a fish, -stone.
Luc'ke (lük'kê), Ger. theol.
Lŭck'now (-nou), Brit. India.
lū'cre, -crà tive, -tive ly.
Lu crē'ti us (-shĭ us), Roman
poet.
lū'cũ brate, -brã'ted, -brã'ting,
-brã'tor, -to'ry, -brã'tion.
lū'di crous, -ly, -ness.
luff, -ing, luffed, luff'-hook, -tac-
kle, luf'fer-board, -board'ing.
Lufft (lŏŏft), Ger. printer.
lug, -ging, -ger, lugged, lug'bait,
a worm, -worm, -bolt, -fore-
sail, -mark, -perch, -sail.
lŭg'gage, -sad dle, -van.
lū gū'brĭ ous, -ly, -ness, -os'i ty.
Luke, *Bib.*, luke, tepid, luke'-
warm, -warm ly, -warm ness.
lull, -ing, -ing ly, -er, -a by (-bĭ),
-by ing (-bĭ-), -bīed.
lum, -head.
lŭm bã'go, -bag'i nous (-baj'-).
lŭm'bar, -bal.
lum'ber, -er, -ly, -ing, -bered,
lum'ber man, -car, -dri er, -kiln,
-meas ure, -port, -room, -wag-
on, -yard.
lum'ber dar.
lum'brĭ cĭde, -bri cĭne.
lū'mi na ry, -na'rist, -nant, -nif'-
er ous, -nol'o gist, -nous, -nous-
ly, -nous ness, -nos'i ty.
lump, -ing, -er, -y, -i ness, -ish,
-ish ly, -ish ness, lumped, lump'-
fish, -suck er, l. su gar, lump'y-
jaw.
lū'na, -nar, -nar ist, -na'ri an,
-nate, -nã'ted, -nate ly, -ni-
form, -nis tĭce, -ni sõ'lar, -ni-
ti'dal, -nã'tion, -na tel'lus, *pl.*
-tel'lī, lū'na-moth, -silk worm.
lū'nà cy (-nà tic, *n.* and *a.*, lū'-
noid.
lunch, -ing, -eon (-un), lunched,
lunch'-count er, lunch'eon-bar.

Lū nel'.
lū nette'.
lung, -less, lunged (lungd), lung'-
flow'er, -wort.
lung'-fish, -grown, -li chen (-ken),
-moss, -strong gle, -test er, -worm.
lunge, lunged, lun'ging, -ger.
lü'nu la, pl. *-læ,* -nu lar, -nu late,
-lā'ted, -nule, -nu let.
Lu per'cus, *Myth.,* Lū'per cal (*or*
-per'-), *-ca'li a,* *-cā'li an.*
lū'pine (*or* -pīn).
lŭp'pa.
lurch, -er, -ing, lurched, lurch'-
line.
lūre, lūred, lūr'er, -ing.
lū'rid, -ly.
lurk, -er, -ing, lurked, lurk'ing-
place.
lus'cious (lŭsh'us), -ly, -ness.
lust, -ed, -er, -ing, -ful, ful ly,
-ful ness, -y, -i ly, -i ness,
-brĕathed.
lus'ter *or* -tre, -tered *or* -tred,
-ter ing *or* -tring, -ter less, lus'-
ter-ware, -wash.
lus'trate, -trā'ted, -trā'ting, -tral,
-tri cal, -trous, -trous ly, -trum,
pl. -trums *or* -tra, -trā'tion.
lū'sus na tū'ræ.
lute, lūt'ed, -ing, lū'ta nist, lū'-
tist, lute'string.
lū'te ous, -tosc, -tes'cent.
Lū'ther an, -ism, -ther ism, -ther-
ist.
Lüt'kĕ, Russ. trav.
Lux em bourg' (lüks'ŏn'bōōr'),
prov. Belg.; Fr. marshal.
Lŭx'ĕm burg, grand duchy.
lux u'ri ance (lug zhōō'- *or* -zū'-),
-an cy, -ri ant, -ant ly, -ri ate,

-ā'ted, -ā'ting, -ā'tion, -ri ous,
-ous ly, -ous ness, -u ry (lŭk'-
shŏŏ ry).
Lu ynes' (lü'ēn'), Fr. archæol.
Lu zon' (lōō zōn'), isl. P. I.
Lyc a ŏ'ni a (lĭk-), *Bib.*
ly cē'um (lī-), *ly'cée'* (lē'sā').
Ly'ci a (lĭsh'i a), *Bib.*
Lyc'i das (lĭs'-), Virgil.
lydd'ite (lĭd'ĭt).
lye (lī), lyed.
ly'ing, being prostrate; falsifying,
ly'ing-down, -in, l. to. See *lie.*
lymph, -y, lym phat'ic.
lymph'-cell, -chan nel, -cor'pus-
cle, -heart, -sac, -sĭ'nus, -space,
-ves sel.
lynch, -ing, -er, lynched, lynch'-
law.
lynx, lyn ce'an, lynx'-eyed.
Ly on nais' (lē'ōn'nā'), prov. Fr.,
ly on naisc' (lē'ō'nāz'), cookery.
Ly'ons (lī'-), c. Fr., -on nese'
(-nēs' *or* -nēz').
lyre (līr), ly'rate (lī'-), -rate ly, -rā'-
ted, -ra wise, lyr'ist (līr'-),
lyre'man, an insect, -tail, a
bird, -bat, -bird, -pheas ant,
-tailed, -tur tle.
lyr'ic (lĭr'-), -ic al, -i chord,
-i cism, -i cist.
Lys (lēs), r. Fr.
Ly san'der, Spartan gen.
Ly sā'ni as (lī-), *Bib.*
Ly'si as (lĭsh'i as *or* lĭs'-), *Bib.*
Lys'i as (lĭs'-), Athenian orator.
Ly sim'a chus (lī sĭm'a kus), Gr.
gen.; *Bib.*
ly sim'e ter (lī-).
ly'sin.
lys'sic.

M

M pa per, M roof, M teeth.
mä, ma'am (mäm).
Mā'a cah, *Bib.*
Maad (mäd), t. Hung.
Mā ăd'ăi (*or* mā'a dä), *Bib.*
Mā ā'i (*or* mā'ā), *Bib.*

maar (mär), pl. *maa're* (mä're)
or *maars* (märz).
Mā'a sĕ'iah, *Bib.*
Mā ăs'ĭ ăi, *Bib.*
Mā'a sī'as, *Bib.*
Mā'ath, *Bib.*

nŏt, nôr, ūse, ŭp, ûrn, etüde, fōōd, fŏŏt, anger, bonmot, thus, Bach.

Măb′da ĭ (or -dāi), Bib.
ma cä′co (or -cä′-), -worm.
mac ad′am ize, -ized, -ī′zing,
-ĭ zā′tion.
mä′can.
Mä cä′ŏ, t. China.
mac′a rŏ′nĭ, pl. -nis or -nies
(-nĭz), -rŏ′ni an, -ron′ic.
mac a rōōn′.
Ma cas′sar oil.
ma casse′ (-kăs′).
Ma cau′lay (-kaw′ly), Eng. hist.
ma cäw′, -bush, -palm, -tree.
Mac′ca bees, -ca bē′an.
Mac Cheyne′ (măk shān′), Scot.
divine.
măc′co.
mace, ma′cer, mace′-ale, -bear er,
-cup, -reed, Mace Mon′day.
Mac e dŏ′ni a (mas-), -ni an,
-an ism.
mac′er ate (mas′-), -ā′ted, -ā′ter,
-ā′ting, -ā′tion.
Mac Geoghe′gan (măk gē′găn),
Irish hist.
Mach′ba nai (măk′-), Bib.
Măch′bē nah (or -bē′-), Bib.
ma che′te (ma chā′tä).
Ma che′tes (-kē′tēz), Ornith.
genus.
Mă′chĭ (-kĭ), Bib.
Ma chĭ′as (-chĭ′-), t. Me.
Mach′i a vel′li (măk′ē ä vĕl′lē) or
Măc′chĭ-, Florentine statesman,
-vĕl′li an or -vēl′ian, -an ism.
mach′i nate (măk′-), -nā′ted,
-nā′tor, -nā′ting, -nā′tion.
ma chine′ (-shēn′), -chined′,
-chin′ing, -chin′er y, -chin′ist,
-chin′īze, -ized, -ĭ′zing.
ma chine′-bolt, -boy, -head,
-made, -man, -mind′er, -ov en,
-shop, -twist, -work.
ma chine′ gun, m. rul er, m.
tool.
Mă′chir ĭtes (-ker-), Bib.
Mach′na dē′bai (or -năd′-), Bib.
Mach pē′lah, Bib.
ma ci′gno (ma chē′nyŏ).
Mac kay′ (măk kī′ or -kā′), Scot.
poet.
mack′er el, -ing or -ling, -er or
-ler.

mack′er el-bait, -boat, -bob,
-cock, -găff, -guide, -gull, -latch,
-midge, -mint, -pike, -plow,
-scad, -scales, -scout, -shark,
m. sky.
Mack′i nac (-i năw), strait and
co. Mich.
Mack′i naw, r. Ill., M. blaṅ′ket,
M. boat, M. trout.
Mack′in tosh, Brit. statesman.
mack′in tosh, a garment; rub-
ber cloth.
mac′kle (-kl), a blemish in printing, -kled (-kld), -kling.
mac′le (măk′l), Mineral.; Her.
Mac Lean′ (măk lān′), Amer.
jurist.
Mac leod′ (măk loud′), Henry
Dunning, Scot. polit. writer,—
Norman, Scot. divine.
Mac Ma hon′ (măk′ mä′ōṅ′), Pres.
Fr. Rep.
Ma comb′ (-kōōm′ or -kōm′),
Amer. gen.
Ma′con, co. Ala.; co. Ga.; co.
Ill.; co. N. Mex.; co. N. C.;
co. Tenn.; c. Ga.; t. Miss.
Ma con′ (mä′kôṅ′), t. Fr.
Mac rea′dy (măk rē′dy), Eng.
trag.
mac ro coc′cus (-kŏk′-), pl. -coc cĭ.
mac′ro cosm (-kŏzm), -cos′mic.
ma crom′e ter.
mac′ron (or mä′kron).
mac′ro pod, -pŏ′di an, ma crop′o-
dal, -o dous.
mac′ro scŏp′ic, -ic al, -al ly.
mac′u la, -læ, -lar, -late, -lä′-
ted, -lä′ting, -la to′ry, -lose,
-lous, -lä′tion.
mad, -der, -dest, -den (-dn),
-dĕned, -den ing, -ding, -ding ly,
-ly, -ness.
mad′brain, -cap, -house, -man,
-nep, -pash, -stone, -weed, -wort,
-ap′ple, -brained, -doc′tor.
Măd′a ĭ (or mä′dāi), Bib.
mad′am, pl. mad′ams or mes′-
dames (mĕz′damz).
ma′dame′, pl. mes dames′ (mä′-
dăm′).
măd′der, a plant, -dered, -der-
ing, mad′der wort.

măd′der-bloom, -print, m. brown, m. car mine, m. red.
Ma dei′ra (má dā′ra *or* -dē′-), isl.; a wine, -dei′ran, Ma dei′-ra-nut, -vine, -wood, M. ma-hog′a ny.
măd′el-pa rōō′wa.
mă′dĕm oi′selle′ (-wŏ zĕl′ *or* măd-mwŏ zĕl′), *pl. mes de moi selles,* (măd mwŏ zĕl′).
madge.
Mă′di an, *Bib.*
măd is tē′rĭ um, pl. *-ri a.*
ma dŏn′na, madam; the Ma-dŏn′na, the Virgin Mary.
măd′o qua.
Ma drăs′, c. Brit. India, M. ging-ham, M. hemp, M. lace, M. work, ma drăs′, a handkerchief.
ma dras′a, *or* Ma dras′a.
mad′rē gal, a fish.
măd′rē pore, a coral, -pŏr′ic.
Ma drĭd′, prov. Sp.—(măd′rĭd), tp. N. Y.
măd′ri gal, a song, -ga let′to, -gä′li an.
mael′strom (māl′strum *or* mäl′-).
Mă ē′lus, *Bib.*
mæ′mad (mē′-).
Maes′tricht (mäs′-), t. Neth.
mä ĕs′trō, -es tō′so (-zo).
Mä′/ĭ a or *Mäf′/ĭ a, -/ĭ ō′sō.*
Mä′gä gua dä vic′ (-gwä dä vĕk′), r. Can.
Ma gal la′nes (mä gä yä′nĕz), Chile.
măg a zine′ (-zĕn′), -dress, -screen, m. bat ter y, m. gun, m. ri fle, m. stove.
mag′da lĕn *or* -lēne, a reformed woman, Mag′da lē′ne (*or* mag′-da lēne), Mary, *Bib.*
Măg′dĕ burg (-bŏŏrg), Prus.
Ma gel′lan (-jĕl′-), Port. nav.
Ma gen die′ (mä′zhŏń′dē′), Fr. physiol.
ma gen′ta (-jen′ta).
magged.
Mag′gi (măd′jē), It. poet.
mag gio re (măd jō′rä).
mag′got, -y, -i ness, -ish, mag′-got-eat′er, -snipe.
Mä′gĭ, -gĭ an, -an ism.

mag′ic, -al, -al ly, ma gi′cian (-jĭsh′an).
Ma gĭd′do, *Bib.*
Ma gio′ne (mä jō′nă), t. It.
mag′is tē′ri al, -ly, -ness, -al′i ty, -ri um, pl. -ri a.
mag is trand′.
mag′is trate, -is tral, -tral ly, -tral′i ty, -is trat′ic, -ic al.
Mag′na Char′ta (kär′ta).
Mag nan′ (män′yŏń′), Fr. marshal.
mag nan′i mous, -ly, -na nim′i-ty.
mag′nate.
Mag nē′si a (-shĭ a), an ancient city, -si an.
mag nē′si a (-shĭ a *or* -sha *or* -zhĭ a), -nē′sian (-shan), -si um (-shĭ um), mag nē′si um-lamp, -light.
·**mag′net,** -net′ic, -ic al, -al ly, -al ness, -ics, -ne ti′cian, -ne-tĭne, -net ism, -net ist.
mag′net ize, -ized, -ī′zing, -ī′zer, -i zee′, -īz′a ble, -a bil′i ty.
mag′net o-bell, -e lec′tric, -e lec-tric′i ty, -ma chine′, -print′er, -tel′e graph, -tel e phone, -trans-mit ter.
mag net′o gram, -o graph, -ol′-o gy, -om e ter, -om e try, -o met′ric, -o mō′tive, -net′o-phone, -net′o scope, -o thĕr′a py.
mag nif′i cent, -ly, -i cence, -nif′ic, -ic al, -al ly, Mag nif′i cat.
mag′ni fy, -ing, -fied, -fī er, -fī-a ble, -fī cā′tion, mag′ni fy′ing-glăss, -lens.
mag nil′o quent, -ly, -quence.
mag′ni tude.
Mag nō′lĭ a, *Bot. genus,* mag nō′-lĭ a, a plant.
mag′num, a wine bottle; a bone, -bō′num, a large barrel-pen.
măg′ot, an ape; a Chinese figure.
măg′pie, -div er, -finch, -mä′kĭ, -moth, -rob in, -shrike.
ma guä′rĭ (*or* -gwä rē′).
ma guey′ (-gwä′).
Mă′gus, *pl.* -gī (-jī).
Măg′yär (*or* mä jär′ *or* mŏd′-yŏr′ *or* măd′yär), a race; a lan-guage.

Mag'yar (mŏd'yor), Hung. trav.
Ma hä de'va (-dā'va).
Ma hä'lah (*or* mä'-), *Bib.*
Ma hä'la lĕ'el (*or* ma hăl'a leel),
  Bib.
Ma hä'lĕ ĕl, *Bib.*
Mä'ha noy, t. Pa.
Ma här'a ī (*or* mä'ha rāi), *Bib.*
Ma'hä rä'jä or *-jah.*
mä hät'ma.
Mäh'di (-dĕ), -di an, -dism *or*
  -di ism, -dist.
Mäh'lītes, *Bib.*
Mäh'lon, *Bib.*—(mä'lon), a man's
  name.
mähl'stĭck *or* maul'-.
Mah mud' (mä mōōd'), Sultan of
  Turk.
mä'hŏe.
ma hog'a ny, -a nize, -nized, -nĭ'-
  zing.
ma hog'a ny-birch, -brown, -col-
  or, -gum, -snap'per, -tree.
Ma hom'ed *or* -et. See *Mohammed.*
ma hŏne'.
Ma hŏ'pac, v. N. Y.
ma hout' (*or* -hōōt').
Mäi än'e äs (*or* -ä'ne as), *Bib.*
maid, -hood, -pale, -of-the-
  mead ow, a plant, m. child, m.
  serv ant.
mai'dan (mĭ'-).
maid'en, -head, -hood, -ly, -li ness,
  -like, -meek, *a.*, -nut, -pink,
  -plum, -skate, -tongued, maid'-
  en's-blush, -hon es ty.
maid'en hair, a fern; -hair-gråss,
  -tree, mai'den name, m. race, m.
  speech.
mail, -ing, -er, -a ble, mailed.
mail'-bag, -box, -car, -căr ri er,
  -cart, -catch er, -cheeked, -clad,
  -coach, -coif, -guard, -hood,
  -hose, -mås ter, -mat ter, -net,
  -poućh, -quilt, -route (-rōōt),
  -sack, -shell, -stage, -train, mail'-
  ing-ma chine', -ta'ble.
maim, -ing, -ed ly, -ed ness,
  maimed.
main, -ly, -land, -måst, -måst'-
  man, -roy al, -roy'al måst, -sail,
  -spring, -stay, -stay'sail, -top,

-top gal'lant måst', -top'måst',
  -top'sail'.
main'-beam, -boom, -brace,
  -chocks, -cou ple, -hatch, -hold,
  -link, -pend'ant, -pin, -post,
  -rig ging, -sheet, -tack, -wales,
  -yard, main'top'sail'-yard'.
main tāin', -ing, -er, -or [in law],
  -a ble, -tained', -te nance.
Main te non' (mănt nŏň'), wife
  of Louis XIV.
Mainz (mīnts) *or* May'ence'
  (mä'yŏńs'), c. Ger.
Mai son neuve' (mä zŏ nêv'), Fr.
  surgeon.
Mais tre (mä tr), It. statesman;
  Fr. novelist.
mais'tri (mäs'trē).
mai'tre (mä'tr), *-trise'* (-trēz').
Mai'va (mĭ'-), t. It.
mäize, -bird, -eat er, a bird, -oil,
  -smut, -thief, a bird.
ma ja' (mä hä').
ma jĕs'tic, -al ly, -al ness, măj'-
  es ty.
mä'jŏe-bit'ter.
ma jŏl'i ca.
mä'jor, -dō'mō, -jor ship, -jŏr'i ty,
  ma'jor-gen'er al, -gen'er al ship.
mä'jo rä'no (-yō-).
Ma jo'ri (mä yŏ'rē), t. It.
Mä'jor ism, -ist, -is'tic.
Maj'sa (mĭ'shŏ), vil. Hung.
mä kä tŏ'.
make, made, mäk'er, mäk'ing,
  make'bate, a person; a plant,
  -game, a person, -shirt, -weight.
make'-be lieve, -hawk, -read y,
  n., -up, mäk'er-up, mäk'ing-
  felt, -i ron, -off, -up, make-
  and-break.
mäk'wä.
Măl'a bar', dist. India, M. cat'-
  mint, M. night'shade, M. nut,
  M. plum, M. rose.
Măl'a chi (-kī), *Bib.*
măl'a chite (-kīt), -green.
mal a droit', -ly, -ness.
măl'a dy.
mä'la jĭ'de.
mä lä ju' (-fōō').
măl'a pert, -ly, -ness.
măl ä'prŏ pos' (-pŏ' *or* -ăp'rŏ pŏ').

---

fāte, făt, fär, fạll, fåre, fåst, sofå, mēte, mĕt, hêr, īce, ĭn, nōte,

mă lä′rĭ a, -ri al, -al ist, -ri ous.

măl′ax age, -ax ate, -ä′ted, -ä′-
ting, -ä′tor, -ä′tion.

Ma läy′, -sĭ an, -lay′an, Ma läy′o-
Pap′u an, -Pol′y nē′sian (-shan).

Măl′chi shu′a (-kĭ- or -kĭsh′u a),
Bib.

mal′con tent, -ed, -tent′ed ly,
-ed ness, -tent′ly, -tent′ment.

măl dĕ mer (mâr).

male, -fern, -spir′it ed.

Ma le bol′ge (mă lä bōl′jä), Dante,
Inferno.

Male branche′ (mäl′brŏnsh′), Fr.
philos.

măl e dic′tion, -dic′to ry.

mal′e fac′tor (or mal′-), -fac′tion.

ma lef′i cent, -i cence.

Ma lĕ′le el (or măl′e leel), Bib.

male′tolt or -tote.

ma lev′o lent, -ly, -o lence.

mal fēa′sance (-zans).

mal formed′, -for ma′tion.

mal′ĭce, ma li′cious (-lĭsh′us), -ly,
-ness.

ma lign′ (-lĭn′), -ing, -er, -ligned′,
-lig′nant, -nant ly, -nance, -nan-
cy, -ni ty.

ma lin′ger, -gered, -ger er, -ger y.

mal′kin (maw′kin or mal′-).

mall, a hammer; a game.

mall (măl or mĕl), a public walk;
a street.

măll, a court of justice; a place
of meeting.

măl′lard.

măl′le a ble, -ness, -bil′i ty, -le ate,
-ä′ted, -ä′ting, -ä′tion.

măl′let, -flow′er.

măl′lŏw, -wort, -rose.

malm (mäm), -y, malm′stone.

Mal′mai′son′ (mäl mā′zŏn′), chateau Fr.

Malmes′bur y (mämz′bĕr y), Eng.
statesman.

malm′sey (mäm′zy).

mal ŏ′dor, -ous, -ous ness.

mal prac′tĭce, -ti′tion er (-tĭsh′-
un er).

malt, -ed, -ing, -er, -ster, -y,
malt′man, -mäs ter.

malt′-barn, -dri er, -dust, -ex′-
tract, -floor, -horse, -house, -kiln,

-mad, -mill, -rake, -screen, -sur′-
ro gate, -turn er, m. tea.

Mal tese′ (-tēs′ or -tēz′), M.
cross.

Mal thū′sĭ an (or -zhan), -ism.

măl trĕat′, -ment.

Măl′vern, t. Ark.—(maw′vern), t.
Eng.

măl ver sä′tion.

Mal vo′lĭ o, Shaks. Twelfth Night.

ma ma or mam ma (mà mä′ or
mä′mà).

Ma mä′ias (-yas), Bib.

Mâm bri′nŏ (-brē′-), Cervantes.

mam bri′no (-brē′-).

măm′e lū′co.

măm′e lūke.

Mä mi ä′ni (-mē ä′nē), It. philos.

măm′mal, -mä′li an, -mal′o gy,
-o gist, -ma log′ic al.

mam mee′, a tree, -ap ple, -sa-
pŏ′ta.

mam mil′la, pl. -læ, măm′mil lar,
-la ry, -lä′ted, -la′tion.

Măm′mon, a personification of
wealth, mam′mon, material
wealth, măm′mon ish, -ism, -ist,
-ite, -ize, -ized, -ĭ′zing, -ĭ zā′-
tion.

măm′moth.

măm′my, mother; a colored
nurse.

Mä mŏ re′ (-rä′), r. Bolivia.

ma moul′ (-mōōl′).

Măm′rē, Bib.

man, pl. men, man′ful, -ful ly,
-ful ness, -less, -like, -ly, -li ly,
-li ness, -nish, -nish ly, -nish-
ness, -ning, manned, man′han′-
dle, -hole, -jack, a tree, -kind,
-root, a plant, -slaugh′ter, -slay-
er, -steal er, -way, -wor′thy.

man′-ape, -bound, -car, -cat er,
-en′gine, -fun′gus, -hät′er,
-made, -or chis (-kis), -plēas′er,
-pow er, -rope, -sty, -trap,
-wor ship.

man′ child, m. mil′li ner, m.
serv′ant, man-at-arms, man-of-
the-earth, a plant, man-of-war,
man′-of-war′s′-man.

mä′na.

man′a cle, -a cled, -a cling.

mâ nä′da.

Măn′ä ĕn (or ma nä′en), Bib.

man′age, -a ble, -ble ness, -bly, -bil′i ty, -ment, -á ging, -á ger, -ger ship, -aged, -a ge′ri al.

Măn′a hath (or ma nä′-), Bib.

Ma nä′heth Ites, Bib.

măn a tee′.

man can′do (măn căn′dō).

măn chette′ (-shĕt′).

Man chu′ or -chōō′, a race of people; a language, pl. Man-chūs′, the people of Manchuria.

man chu′ (-chōō′), a boat.

man dä′mus, -ing, -mŭsed.

măn′da rin′ (-rēn′ or măn′da-rĭn), a Chinese official; a duck; a dye; a fruit, -rin ate, -rin ism. Man da rin, the official language of China.

man′date, -da to′ry, -dä′tor, man′date-bread.

măn′di ble, -dib′u lar, -la ry, -late, -la ted.

man′do lin or -lĭne, -ist.

man′drake.

man′drel, a bar or spindle; a rod; a miner's pick.

man′drel-col lar, -frame, -lāthe, -nose, -screw.

man′drill, a baboon.

man′du cate, -cä′ted, -cà ble, -cä′ting, -cà to′ry, -cä′tion.

mane, -less, māned, mane′-comb, -sheet.

ma nege′ (ma nāzh′).

mä′nĕh (or măn′ĕ).

mä′nes (-nēz).

Măn′ē thō, Egypt. hist.

ma neu′ver (-nū′-) or -nœu′vre (-nōō′ver), ma neu′vêred, -ver-er, -ver ing.

man′ga nese′ (-nēs′ or -nēz′), -nĕ′-sĭ an, -nĕ′sious (-shus), maŋ ga-net′ic, man′ga nese′-glaze.

mänge, măn′gy, -gi ness, mange′-in′sect, -mite.

man′gel, -wur′zel.

măn′ger, -board.

man′gle, -gled, -gler, -gling, maŋ′gle-bark, -rack, -wheel.

man′go, -bird, -fish, -hum mer, -tree.

---

maŋ′grove, -bark, -cuck′oo, -hen, -snap per, a fish.

Maŋ′gy ans (-gĭ-).

man′hole, -cov er, -pa per, -writ′-er.

mä′ni (-nē).

mä′ni a, -ni ac, -nĭ′a cal, -cal ly.

măn′i cure, -cured, -cūr′ing.

man′ĭ fest, -ed, -er, -ing, -a ble or -i ble, -ly, -ness, -fes tä′tion, -fes′to.

măn′i fold, -ed, -er, -ing, -ly, -ness, -i form.

măn′i kin.

Ma nĭl′a, c. P. I.; a cheroot, M. cŏ′pal, M. hemp, M. pa per, M. rope.

ma nil′la, a ring; a coin; a game.

ma nille′ (-nĭl′ or -nĕl′), a bracelet.

ma nille′ (-nēl′), highest card in the game of omber.

măn′i nose (-nōz).

măn′i oc (or mä′-), a plant, -oc′-ca.

ma nip′u late, -lä′ted, -lä′ting, -là tive, -lä′tor, -to′ry, -lar, -lä′tion.

Man is tee′, co. Mich.

măn′i tŏ or -tou (-tōō).

Man′i tŏ bä′, prov. Can.

Măn′i tou′lin (-tōō′-), isls. Lake Huron.

man′jack.

man′kind′.

Maŋks. See Manx.

măn′na, man nif′er ous, man′na-ash, -croup, -grăss, -gum tree, -lĭ′-chen (-ken), -seeds.

măn′ner, -ism, -ist, -less, -ly, -li ness, -nêred.

Ma nŏ′ah, Bib.

ma nœu′vre. See maneuver.

ma nom′e ter, măn o met′ric, -ric-al.

măn′or, ma no′ri al, man′or-house, -seat.

Man′sard roof or man′sard roof.

manse.

man′sion, -house.

Man te gaz′za (män′tä gät′sä), It. schol.

Man te′gna (män tän′yä), It. painter.

---

măn'tel (-tl), -board, -piece, -tree, -clock, -set, -shelf.

man'tel et, -tel let'ta.

Măn'teuf fel (-toi fel), Prus. field-marshal.

man til'la.

man'tle, -tled, -tler, -tling, man'-tle-an i mal, -brēath'ing, -cell.

man'tu a, a cloak, -māk'er.

Man'tu a, t. It., -tu an.

Mä'nu (-nōō or -nū), Myth.

măn'u al, -ly, -al'i ter, man'u al-key.

man'ū fac'ture, -tured, -tūr er, -tūr ing, -tūr al, -to ry.

man u mit', -ted, -ter, -ting, -mis'sion.

man'u mo'tor (or -mō'-).

ma nūre', -nūred', -nūr'er, -nūr'-ing, -nūr'a ble, -nū'ri al, -al ly, ma nure'-dis trib'u ter, -drag, -drill, -fork, -hook, -load'er, -spread er.

man'u script.

Manx, -man, -wom an, Manx cat, M. puf fin.

ma'ny (měn'y), -plies, -root, -wise, -fold ed, -hěad'ed, -mīnd'-ed, -sīd ed, -sid'ed ness.

man za nil'la.

Măn za nil'lo (-thä nēl'yō), t. Cuba.

man za ni'ta (-nč'-).

Măn zŏ'ni (-nē), It. writer.

Mä'ŏ rǐ, a people; a language; -land, -land er, -head, -hen, M. chief.

map, -per y, -ping, -pist, mapped, map'-draw ing, -hold er, -li chen (-ken), -measur er, -mount er, -pro jec'tion, -stud y, -tur tle.

mä'ple, -bor'er, -cup, -dis ease, -hon ey, -mo las ses, -su gar, -syr up, -tree.

mä quå hui'tl (-wē'tl).

Ma quo'ke ta (-kŏ'-), c. Ia.

mar, -ring, marred.

Mä'ra, Hindu myth.; Norse myth. Mä'ra, Bib.

mä'ra, an animal.

măr'a bou (-bōō' or -bōō'), -fěath'ers, -stork.

Măr'a bout (-bōōt).

Mä rä cai'bŏ (-kǐ'-), c. Venez., M. bark.

mä'rah, bitter water. Mä'rah, Bib.

ma rai' (-rī').

mar'a năth'a. Măr'a năth'a, Bib.

ma ras'mus (-răz'-), -ras'mic (-răz'-).

Ma rat' (mä'rä'), Fr. revolutionist.

ma rạud', -ed, -er, -ing.

mar'ble, -bled, -bler, -bling, -bly, -ble ize, -ized, -ī'zing, mar'ble-head, a bird, -wood, a tree.

mar'ble-brĕast ed, -con stant, -cut-ter, -fish, -hand saw, -paste, -pol-ish er, -rub ber, -saw, -scour er, -thrush, -work er, m. silk.

märc (märk).

mar căn'dō, -cä'to.

march, -er, -ing, marched, march'-land, -man, -line, -move ment, -time, -trea son, -ward.

March, a month, -mad.

mär che'sa (-kä'za), pl. -che'se (-kä'zā).

mar'cid, -cid'i ty.

Mar co'ni, It. inventor. M. sys'-tem, mar co'nǐ gram.

Mar'di gras (mär'dē grä).

mare, mare's-tail, mare's nest.

Ma ré chal' (mä'rä'shäl'), Fr. painter.

mä'rē claụu'sum.

Mar'ga ret, Chr. name, mar'ga-ret, a bird.

mar'ga rǐn, -gär'ic.

mar'gin, -al, -al ly, -ate, -ā'ted, -gin ing, -gǐned, mar'gin-drăft, -line, -tailed.

mar'grāve, -gra văte, -gra'vǐ ate, -gra vine (-vēn).

mar'gue rite (-gě rēt), a flower.

Ma ri'a de' Mé'di ci (mä rē'ä dä mä'dē chē) or Ma rie' de Mé di cis' (mä rē' dê mä dē-sēs'), wife of Henry IV.

Mä'rǐ an, pertaining to Caius Marius; pertaining to the Virgin Mary, -an ism, Măr'ǐ on, Fr. form of Mary, măr'i an, a fish.

Ma rie' An toi nette' (mä'rē' ŏń'twä'nět'), wife of Louis XVI.

măr'i gold, -finch, m. win'dow.
măr'i graph, -graph'ic.
ma rine' (-rēn'), măr'i ner, mar'-
i tĭme.
Ma ri'ni (mä rē'nē), It. poet, -ri'-
nism, -ri'nist, a follower of Ma-
rini, măr in'ist (-ēn'-), a believer
in certain marine forces.
Mä'ri o (-rē ō), It. singer.
măr'ĭ ŏ nette'.
Măr'i pŏ'sa, riv. and co. Cal., M.
lil y, măr'i po'sa, a fish, -pŏ'sīte.
Măr'i sa, *Bib.*
măr'i tal.
Mä'rĭ us, Roman gen.
mar'jŏ ram.
mark, -er, -ing, -ed ly, marked,
mark'mote, -wor thy, marks'-
man, marks'man ship, marks'-
wom an.
mark'-boot, -tooth, mark'ing-
cur'rent, -gage, -iṇk, -i ron, -ma-
chine, -nut, -plow.
mar'ket, -a ble, -ble ness, -bil'i ty,
-er, -ing, mar'ket man.
mar'ket-bȧs ket, -bell, -court,
-cross, -day, -fish, -gar den,
-gar'den er, -hours, -house,
-Jew, a bird, -lĕad, -maid,
-mȧs ter, -place, -pot, -town,
-wag on, -wom an.
marl, a soil, marl'ing, -ite, -y,
marled, mar lā'ceous, -lit'ic,
marl'stone, marl'-grȧss, -pit,
-slate, m. brick, m. stock.
marl, *v.*, to wind, as a rope, -ing,
marled, marl'ing-hitch.
marl, *n.*, a fiber of feathers.
marl'bor ough-wheel.
mar'lin, a bird.
mar'lĭne, a nautical term, -lĭned,
-lĭn'ing, -lĭne spike.
mar'lŏtte.
mar'ma lade, -plum, -tree.
mar'ma la-wa ter.
mar'mose (-mōs), -mo set (-zet).
mar'mot, -squir'rel.
Mä rō ni' (-nē'), r. S. Amer.
ma rōōn', -er, -ing, -rōōned'.
Mar os' (mŏr ōsh'), r. Hung.—
(mä'rōs), Celebes isl.
Mä rot' (-rō'), Fr. auth.
Mä'roth, *Bib.*

mar'plot.
marque (mark).
mar quee' (-kē').
Mar que'sas (-kä'säs), isls. Pacific
ocean.
mar'quet ry (-ket-).
Mar quette' (-kĕt'), co. Mich.;
co. Wis.
Mar quez' (-kās'), Mex. gen.
mar'quis, -al, -ate, -quise' (-kēz').
măr'rĭage, -a ble, -a ble ness,
mar'ry, -rĭed, -ri er, -ry ing.
măr'rŏw, -ish, -less, -y, -fat, a
pea, -bone, -cells, -spoon, m.
pud ding, m. squash.
Mars, Mar'tial, -tian.
Mar sä'la.
Mar'seil'lais' (mar sä lyä') *or*
-laise' (-lyāz' *or* -sel läz').
mar seilles' (-sälz'), a fabric.
Mär seilles' (-sälz'), c. Ill.,—
(mär'säl'), c. Fr.
Mar'se na, *Bib.*
marsh, -y, -i ness, marsh'buṇ'ker,
-fish, -mal'low, -wort.
marsh'-bee tle, -bell'flow er, -black-
bird, -but ter cup, -ciṇque foil,
-cross, -dĭv er, -eld er, -fern,
-fe ver, -five fiṇ ger, -flow er, -gas,
-goose, -grȧss, -hȧr ri er, -hawk,
-hen, -land, -măr'i gold, -mī as'-
ma, -nut, -pars ley, -peep, -pen-
ny wort, -pes tle, -plov er, -pul let,
-quail, -ring let, -rob in, -rose-
ma ry, -sam phire, -shrew, -snipe,
-tack ey, -tea, -tern, -tit, -tre-
foil, -wa ter cress, -wren.
mar sū'pĭ a, -pi al, -pi ate, *pi um*,
pl., -*pi a*.
mart.
Mar tel', Charles, often called
"The Hammer." mar'tel, a war-
hammer.
mar'ten, a quadruped.
mar'tial (-shal), -ism, -ist, -ly.
Mar tigues' (-tēg'), t. Fr.
mar'tin, a bird, -snipe, -swal'-
low.
Mar'tĭ neau, Harriet (-tĭ nō),
Eng. writer.
mar ti net', -ism.
Mar ti'nez Cam'pos (mar tē'nĕth
käm'pōs), Span. gen.

mar'tin gale.
Mär ti'ni (-tē'nē), Giovanni Battista, It. mus. composer; Johann Paul Ægidus, Ger. mus. composer; Vicente, Span. mus. composer.
Mar'tĭ nique' (-nēk'), isl. W. I.
mar'tyr, -ing, -dom, -ize, -ized, -ĭ'zing, -ĭ zā'tion, -ol o gy, -ol o gist, -o log'ic al, -ship, -y, -tyred.
Mar've jols' (-zhōl), t. Fr.
mar'vel, -veled or -velled, -vel ing or -ling, -vel ous or -lous, -ous ly, -ous ness, mar'vel-moŋ'ger, -of-Pe ru', a plant.
mar'ver.
Mă'ry lĕ bone (or mär'ē bŭn), bor. Eng.
Mä say'a (-sī'-), t. Nicaragua.
mas'cot.
Mas cou'tah (-kow'-), c. Ill.
mas'cu lĭne, ly, -nc₃₃, -lin'i ty.
mash, -er, -ing, mashed, mash'-cool er, -ma chine', -pulp er, -tub, -tun, -vat, -wort, mash'-ing-tub.
Ma sī'as or Mas sī'as, Bib.
mâsk, -er, -ing, mâsked, mas-kĕtte', mâsk'flow er, -ball, -crab, mâsk'ing-piece.
mâs'kĭ nŏnge or mâs'ka lŏnge.
mä'son (-sn), -er, -ry, -rĭed, -son'ic, mä'son work, -bee, -shell, -spi der, -swal low, -wasp.
ma soo'la-boat.
mas'quer ăde' (-ker-), -ăd'ed, -ăd'er, -ăd'ing.
Mas're kah (or -rē'-), Bib.
mâss, -ing, -ive, -ive ly, -ive ness, -y, -i ness, mâssed.
mass'-bell, -book, -cen ter, -day, -house, -meet ing, -pen ny, -priest, -vec'tor, -ve loc'i ty, mâss'ing- chăl'Ice.
mas'sa cre (-ker), -cred (-kerd), -cring.
mas'sage (or mâs säzh'), n.
mas sage (mâs säzh' or mâs'-sage), v., -saged, -sa'ging, mâs-sêur', masc.; -sêuse' (-sêz'), fem.; mas sé (mâs sā'), v., -séed (-sād'), -sé ing (-sā'ing).
Mâs'sa soit', Indian chief.

mas sé' (-sā'), a stroke in billiards, -shot.
Mas'se na, t. N. Y.
mas sif' (mâs sēf').
Mâs'sil lon' (or mä'sē'yōn'), Fr. pulpit orator; (mâs'sil lon), c. O.
mâst, -ed, -less, mâst'head, -man, -bâss, -car lĭne, -coat, -hoop, -house, -mäk'er, -pock et, -prop, -rope, -scrăp er, -step, -tac kle, -tree, -trunk.
mâs'ter, -ing, -dom, -ful, -ful ly, -ful ness, -hood, -less, -less ness, -ly, -li ness, -ship, -y, mâs'ter-piece, -sing er, -work, -wort.
mâs'ter-joint, -key, -lode, -sin ew, -spring, -stroke, -touch, -wheel, -at-arms, m. car pen-ter, m. print er.
mâs'tic, -ce ment', -cloth, -herb, -tree.
mâs'ti cate, -cå ble, -cā'ted, -cā'-ting, -cā'tor, -to'ry, -cā'tion.
mâs'tiff, -bat.
mâs'to don, -to dŏnt, -don'tic, -don'tĭne.
mâs'ty.
mat, -ted, -ter, -ting, mat'hook, -weed, -work, -boat, -braid, -grâss.
Măt a bĕle'land (or mä tä bā'lĕ land).
mat a dôr' (or mat'-).
Mä tä rŏ', c. Sp.
match, -a ble, -ble ness, -er, -ing, -less, -less ly, -less ness, matched.
match'lock, a gun, -lock man, -board, -board ing, -box, -cord, -dip ping. -gear ing, -hook, -joint, -linc, -lock, a lock, -mäk ing, -pipe, -plane, -plăn'-ing, -plate, -play, -pot, -ri fle, -ri-fling, -safe, -shoot ing, -split, -stâff, -terms, -tub, -wheel, -wood.
match'er-head, match'ing-ma-chine, -plane.
mate, -less, mât'ed, -ing, māt'ing-time.
ma'te (mä'tā), a kind of tea.
mate las sé' (măt'lăs sā' or -lăs'sā).
mat'e lŏte, a dish.
mat'e lŏtte, a dance.

---

nŏt, nôr, ūse, ŭp, ûrn, etüde, fōōd, fŏŏt, aŋger, boṅmot, ᵺus, Bach.

mā′ter.

ma tē′ri al, -ism, -ist, -ist′ic,
-tic al, -ri al ly, -al ness, -al′i ty,
-al ize, -ized, -ī′zing, -ĭ zā′tion.
ma tē′ri a med′i ca.

ma ter′nal, -ly, -nal′i ty, -ter′-
ni ty.

math e mat′ic, -al, -al ly, -ma-
ti cian (-tish′an), -mat′ics.

mä′ti (-tē), a sedge.

mä′tĭe (*or* mä′-), a herring.

mǎt′in, -al, mat′i née′ (-ĭ nä′).

mǎt′rass (*or* mä trǎss′), *Chem.*

mat′ri cĭde, -ci′dal.

ma tric′ŭ late, -lā′ted, -lā′ting,
-lā′tor, -lant, -lā′tion, -*u la,* pl.
-*læ.*

mat′ri mō ny, -ni al, -al ly, mat′-
ri mō ny-vine.

ma′trix, *pl.* mǎt′rĭ ces (-sēz).

mä′tron (*or* mǎt′ron), -age, -al,
-hood, -ize, -ized, -ĭ′zing, -like, -ly,
-li ness, -ship, mat′ro nym ic.

mat′su.

Mǎt′ta nah, *Bib.*

Mat′ta pŏ ny′ (-nī′), r. Va.

Mǎt′ta tha, *Bib.*

matte (mǎt).

Mat′te a wän′, t. N. Y.

Mǎt′tĕ nä′i (*or* -nāi′), *Bib.*

mat′ter, -ful, -less, -tered, mat′-
ter-of-course′, mat′ter-of-fact′.

Mat ter′ (mǎt′têr′), Fr. hist.

Mǎt′ter horn, Switz.

Mat te′uc ci (mät tä′ōōt chē), It.
scientist.

Mǎt′than, *Bib.*

Mat thē′las, *Bib.*

Mǎt′thew (mǎth′ū), *Bib.*

Mat thī′as (mǎ thī′as *or* mat thī′-),
Bib.

mat′ting, -boat, -loom, -punch,
-tool.

mat′tock.

mat′tress, a bed, -boat.

Mä′tu rä (-tōō-), dist. Ceylon.

ma ture′, -ly, -ness, -tured′, -tūr′-
a ble, -a tive, -ing, -tu′ri ty.

Mä tu rin′ (-tōō rēn′), t. Venez.

Mǎt′u rin, Irish preacher.

ma tū′ti nal (*or* mǎt′u tǐ′nal).

Mǎtz′ner (mĕts′ner), Ger. philol.

Mau beuge′ (mō bêzh′), t. Fr.

Maud, a girl's name; maud, a
garment.

maud′lin, -ism, -drunk, -fair.

Mau′i (mou′ē), isl. Hawaii.

maul, -ing, mauled, maul′stick,
-oak, -in-goal′.

Mau′le (mou′lä), r. Chile.

Maul main′ (-mīn′), t. Burma.

Mau′na Ke′a (mou′na kä′ä), mt.
Hawaii.

maun′der, -er, -ing, -dered.

Mau pas sant′ (mō′pä′sŏn′), Fr.
novelist.

Mau per tuis′ (mō′per twē′), Fr.
astron.

Maure pas′ (mōr′pä′), Fr. statesman.

Mau′rice (maw′rĭs), Ger. gen.;
Prince of Orange; Eng. auth.;
—(mō′rēs′), Fr. theol.

Mau ri ti us (-rĭsh′ĭ us), isl. Indian oc.

Mau′ry, Amer. scientist;—(mō′-
rē′), Fr. orator; Fr. archæol.

mau′ser (mou′zer), a rifle.

mau′so lē′um, *pl.* -ums *or* -a,
-lē′an.

Mau vaises′ Terres (mō vāz′
tär′), S. Dak.

Mau van′ (mou bän′), t. Luzon.

mauve (mōv).

mav′er ick.

mä′vis, -skate.

ma vour′neen (-vōōr′-).

maw, -mouth, a fish, -seed, -skin,
-worm.

mawk′ish, -ish ly, -ish ness, -y.

max.

max il′la, pl. -*læ,* max′il lar, -lâ-
ry.

max′im, -mon ger, Max′im gun.

Max′i mil′ian, Emp. Mex.; a
coin.

max′i mize, -mized, -mī′zing, -mĭ-
zā′tion, -i mal, -mal ly, -i mum.

may, might, may′ing, may′be,
-cock, a bird, -hap, -weed,
-wort, -drink, -pop, a plant,
-skate, -suck er, a fish, may′-
cock-fluke.

May, a month, -duke, -fish,
-flow er, -ap ple, -bee tle, -bird,
-blob, -bloom, -blos som, -bug,

-bush, -cha'fer, -cher ry, -cur-
lew, -day, -dew, -fly, -fowl,
-game, -gar land, -haw, -hill,
-la dy, -lil y, -lord, -morn,
-pole, -time, M. queen.
May a guez' (mī ä gwäth' *or*
-hwĕs'), t. P. R.
May'en (mī'en), t. Prus.
May enne' (mī'en'), r. and t. Fr.
Mä'yenne' (-yĕn'), Fr. gen.
May'er (mā'er), Amer. physicist.
—(mī'er), Ger. astron.; Ger.
physicist; Ger. mus.
may'hem.
Mayn'wa ring (măn'a ring), Eng.
writer.
May o' (mā ō'), co. Ire.—(mā'ō),
tp. N. C.—(mī'ō), r. Mex.; isl.
Cape Verde; isl. Malay Arch.
May'o (mā'ō), Amer. educationist.
may'on naise' *or* mä'yŏn naise'
(-nāz').
may'or, -al, -al ty, -ess, -ship.
May pu' (mī pōō'), r. and volc.
Chile.
Măz a rin' (-rēn'), Prime minister
of Louis XIV, -hood, M.
Bi ble.
măz a rine' (-rēn'), -blue.
Mä zat lan' (-sät län'), t. Mex.
maze, mazed, māz'ing, ma'zy,
-zi ly, -zi ness.
ma zur'ka (-zōōr'-).
Maz zi'ni (mät sē'nē), It. patriot.
Mc Crea' (-krā'), Jane, slain by
Indians.
Mc Dou'gall (măk dōō'gal), Amer.
gen.
Mc Leod' (măk loud'), Alexander,
Amer. divine,—Xavier Donald,
Amer. auth.
mĕad.
mĕad'ow, -er, -y, mead'ow sweet,
-wort.
mĕad'ow-beau ty, -bird, -bright,
-brown, -cam pi on, -clap per,
-clo ver, -crake, -cress, -drake,
-fern, -fox tail, -grăss, -hen,
-land, -lark, -mouse, -mus sel,
-ore, -pars nip, -pea, -pine,
-pink, -pip it, -queen, -rue,
-saf fron, -sage, -sax i frage,
-snipe, -tit ling.

mĕa'ger *or* -gre, -ly, -ness.
Mea'gher (mē'ger), co. Mon.
Mea'gher (mä'her), Irish rev.
and Amer. gen.
mĕal, -y, -i ness, meal'ber ry,
-man, -mon̨ ger.
meal'-arc, -bee tle, -cool er,
-moth, -mouthed, -of fer ing,
-time, -tub, -worm, m. bread.
meal'ie-field, meal'ing-stone,
meal y-bird, -mouthed, -tree.
mĕan, -ing, -ing ful, -ing less,
-less ly, -less ness, -ing ly, -ing-
ness, -ly, -ness, mĕant, mĕan'-
time, -while, -spir it ed.
Me ä'nĭ, *Bib.*
Mĕ ä'rah, *Bib.*
mea'sles (mē'zlz), -sled (-zld),
-sly (-zlĭ).
meas'ure (mĕzh'-), -less, -less-
ness, -mcnt, -ur a ble, -ble ness,
-a bly, -ured, -urcd ly, -ur er,
-ur ing, meas'ure-moth.
meas'ur ing-chain, -fau cet, -fun-
nel, -glăss, -line, -ma chine,
-pump, -tape, -wheel, -worm.
meat, -less, -y, -i ness, -rife, *a.*
meat'-chop per, -crush er, -earth,
-fly, -ham mer, -hunt er, -mag-
got, -man̨ gler, -of fer ing, -safe,
-saw, -screen, -spit, -tea, -tub,
m. pie.
mĕ ä'tus, pl. -tus es, -a'tal, me ä'-
tus-knife.
Meaux (mō), t. Fr.
Mĕ bŭn'nâi, *Bib.*
me cä'te (mä kä'tä).
me chan'ic (-kan'-), -al, -al ize,
-al ly, -al ness, -i cize, -cized,
-ci'zing, mech a ni'cian (mĕk'a-
nĭsh'an), -a nism, -a nist, -nis'-
tic, -a nize, -nized, -nī'zer, -nī'-
zing.
mĕ chan'o graph (-kăn'-), mech'-
a nog'ra phy, -ra phist, -no-
graph'ic.
Mĕ chĕ'rath ĭte (-kē'-) *or* Mĕch'-
e rath ĭte (mĕk'-), *Bib.*
Mech'lin (mĕk'-), c. Belg.
Meck'len burg, co. N. C.; co. Va.
Meck len burg-Schwe rin' (-bŏŏrg
shvä rēn'), -Stre'litz (-strä'lits),
Ger.

Mĕd'a ba, *Bib.*
mĕd'al, -ist, mē dal'lic, mĕd'al-
cup, -ma chine, -tank'ard.
me dal'lion (-dăl'yun), -lioned,
me dal'lion car pet, m. pat tern.
me'da nŏ (mā'då nō).
med'dle, -some, -some ness, -dled,
-dler, -dling, -dling ly.
Me'de (mā'dā), t. It.
Mĕ dĕ'a, heroine in Euripides'
tragedy.
Mĕd'e ba, *Bib.*
Me del lin' (mā dĕl yēn'), t. Colom.
Mĕd'gyes (-yĕsh'), t. Hung.
Mĕ'di a, *Bib.*, -di an, Mede,
Mĕ'dic.
mĕ'di al, -ly.
mĕ'di an, -ly, -di ant.
me'di ate, -ā'ted, -ā'ting, -ā'tor,
-to'ry, -to'ri al, -al ly, -tor ship,
-ā'tion, -ate ly, -ate ness, -à tive,
-a tize, -tized, -tī'zing, -tĭ zā'-
tion, -a'trix.
med'ic al, -ly, -i cå ble, -cå ment,
-men'tal, -cas ter.
med'i cate, -cā'ted, -cā'ting, -cå-
tive, -cā'tion.
Med'i ci (mĕd'e chē *or* mā'de-
chē), a notable Italian family.
med'i cĭne, me dic'i nal, -nal ly.
med'i cĭne-bag, -chest, -man,
-pan ni er, -seal, -spoon, -stamp,
-stone, -tree.
med'i cis (-i sē), a garment.
med'i co chi rur'gic al (-kō kĭ-
rur'jĭk al), -co le'gal.
me di e'val, -ism, -ist, -ly, -ize,
-ized, -ĭ'zing.
Me dī'na, co. Tex.; vil. N. Y.;
co. O.—(mā dē'na), c. Arabia;
t. Afr.
mĕ'dĭne.
mĕ'dĭ ŏ cre (-ker), -o cral, -o-
crist, -oc'ri ty.
med'i tate, -tā'ted, -tā'ting, -tā'-
tive, -tive ly, -tive ness, -tā'tion.
mĕ'di um, *pl.* -di ums *or* -di a,
-um ship, -um is'tic, mĕ'di um-
sized.
Mĕd jid je' (-jēd'jā'), t. Roum.
med'lar, -tree, -wood.
med'ley.
Me doc' (mā dok').

Me dŏ'ro (mā-), Ariosto.
me dul'la, -dul'lar, med'ul la ry,
-lā'ted.
Me dū'sa, Myth.; Zoöl. genus; pl.
-*sæ*, me dū'sa, a jelly fish, -sal,
-san, me dū'sa-bell, -bud, Me-
du'sa's-head.
meed.
Mĕ ē'da, *Bib.*
meek, -ly, -ness, -eyed.
meer'schaum.
meet, -ing, -ly, -ness, met, meet'-
ing-house, -post, -seed.
meg'a dyne (-dīn), -a erg, -a-
fär'ad, -a fog, -a ty'py.
meg'a lo grȧph, -log'ra phy.
meg'a phone, -a scope, -scop'ic,
-ic al, -al ly.
meg'a vŏlt, -a we ber (-vā'ber),
meg'ōhm.
Mĕ gĭd'do, *Bib.*
mĕ'grim.
Mĕ hŏ'lath ĭte (*or* -hŏl'-), *Bib.*
Meigs (mĕgz), Amer. gen.; co. O.;
co. Tenn.
Meil hac' (mā'läk'), Fr. auth.
Meï'ning en, t. Ger.
Meiss'ner (mīs'-), Ger. poet.
Meis so nier' (mā sō nyā'), Fr.
painter.
meïs'ter säng'er (-sĕng'er), *-sing er.*
Me ji'a (mā hē'ä), Mex. soldier.
Mĕj'maa' (-mä'), t. Arab.
Me kŏ'nah (*or* mĕk'o-), *Bib.*
me la'då or *-la'dō* (mā lä'-).
mel'an chol y (-kŏl-), -chol'ic,
-chol'i ly, -i ness, mel'an chol y-
this tle.
Mĕ lanch'thon (-lănk'-), Ger.
reformer.
mê lange' (mā'lŏnzh').
Mel'bourne (-burn), Eng. states-
man; c. Austral.
Mel chi'ah (-kī'-), *Bib.*
Mĕl'chi el (-kĭ-), *Bib.*
Mel chis'e dec *or* Mel chĭz'e dek
(mĕl kĭz'e dĕk), *Bib.*
Mĕl chĭ shu'a (-kĭ shōō'- *or* -kish'-
u a), *Bib.*
Mĕ'le a, *Bib.*
Mĕl e ā'ger (-jer), *Myth.*
Mĕ'lech (-lĕk), *Bib.*
mê lée' (mā'lā').

Me len'dez-Val'dez (mā lĕn'deth-
väl'dĕth), Span. poet.
Mĕ lī'a dus, a Knight of the
Round Table.
Mĕl'i cū, *Bib.*
mĕl'i nīte, an explosive.
mĕl'io rate (-yō-), -rā'ted, -rā'-
ting, -rā'tor *or* -ter, -rā'tion,
-io rism, -rist, -ris'tic.
Mĕl'i ta, *Bib.*
mĕ lī'tis.
Me li to'pol (mā lē tō'pŏl), t.
Russ.
mel'lic, -lif'ic, -li fi cā'tion.
mcl lif'lu ent, -ly, -ence, -ous,
-ous ly, -liv'o rous.
mel'lōw, -ly, -ness, -y, -ing, -lōwed.
me lŏ'de on, -di a.
mel o drä'ma, -dra mat'ic, -ic al,
-al ly, -dram'a tist.
mel'o dy, -o dist, -o dize, -dized,
-dī'zing, me lod'ic, -ic al ly, -ics,
-lo'di ous.
mel'o grâph.
mel o ma'ni a, -ni ac.
mel'on, -blub ber, -cac tus, -cat-
er pil lar, -hole, -oil, -seed,
-shaped, -shell, -thick, -this tle,
-tree, -worm.
mĕl'o nīte, a mineral.
mel'o phone, -phō'nist, -phon'ic.
Mel pom'e ne, *Myth.*
mel'rose, Mel rose', abbey Scot.;
tp. Ill.; tp. Mass.
melt, -a ble, -ed, -er, -ing, -ing ly,
melt'ing-cham ber, -fur nace,
-pan, -point, -pot.
mel'ton.
mem'ber, -less, -ship, -bered.
mem'brane, -less, -bra nous, mem'-
brane-bone, -su ture, -winged.
mĕ men'tŏ, *mĕ men'lō mŏ'ri.*
Mem'min ger (-jer), Ger.-Amer.
polit.
Mem'non, *Myth.*, -nō'ni an, -nō'-
ni um.
mĕm'oir (-wŏr), -ism, -ist.
mem'o ra ble, -ness, -bly, -bil'-
i ty, *-bil'i a.*
mem o ran'dum, *pl.* -dums *or*
-da, -book.
me mŏ'ri al, -ist, -ize, -ized,
-ī'zing, me mŏ'ri al-stone.

mem'o rize, -rized, -rī'zer, -rī'-
zing, -rī'za ble, -o ry, -rī zā'tion,
me mŏr'i ter.
Mem'phis, ancient city Egypt; t.
Mo.; c. Tenn., -phi an, -phite,
-phit'ic.
mem'-sä'hib (-ib).
Me mū'can, *Bib.*
men'āce, -ment, -aced, -à cing,
-cing ly, -a cer.
Mé nage' (mā'näzh'), Fr. writer.
me nage' (mā'năzh'), a household.
men ag'er ie (mĕn ăj'er y *or*
mĕn ăzh'-).
Men'a hem, *Bib.*
Mé nard' (mā'när'), Fr. painter.
Men'ci us (-shǐ us), Chinese
philos.
mend, -a ble, -ed, -er, -ing.
men dā'cious, -ly, -ness, -dac'i ty.
Mende (mŏnd), t. Fr.
Mĕn'dels sohn (dĕls sōn), Ger.
philos.
Men'dels sohn-Bar thol'dy (-bar-
tōl'dē), Ger. mus. composer.
Men dès (mŏn'dā'), Fr. novelist.
men'di cant, -can cy, -dic'i ty.
Men dŏ'za (-thä), prov. Argen.
Rep.
Mĕ'nĕ, *Bib.*
Mĕn'e lā'us, *Bib.*; Homer's *Iliad.*
Me nes' (mā'nĕsh'), t. Hung.
Mĕ nĕs'theûs (*or* nĕs'the us), *Bib.*
men'gīte.
men hā'den (-dn), -fish'er y.
men'hǐr.
mĕ'ni al.
Mĕ nin' (-năn'), t. Belg.
mĕn ǐn gī'tis (-jī'-), -git'ic.
me nis'cus, *pl.* -cus es *or* -nis'cī.
Men'no, relig. leader, Men non ist,
-non īte.
mĕ nol'o gy.
men'ses (-sēz).
men'stru ate, -ā'ted, -ā'ting, -ant,
-ous, -a'tion.
men'stru um, *pl.* -ums *or* -a.
men'su ra ble (-shoͻ-), -ness, -bil'-
i ty, -su ral, -su rà tive, -su rā'tion.
men'tal, -ly, -tal'i ty.
men'thol.
men'tion, -a ble, -ing, -tioned.
Men ton' (mŏn tōn'), t. Fr.

men'tor, -to'ri al.
Mē ŏn'e nim, *Bib.*
Mē ŏn'o thāi, *Bib.*
Meph'ā ăth, *Bib.*
Mē phĭb'o shĕth, *Bib.*
Meph'is toph'e les (mĕf'is tŏf'e-
    lēz), Goethe's *Faust,* -to phē'-
    li an.
mē phī'tis, -phit'ic, -ic al, -al ly,
    me phī'tism (*or* meph'i tism).
Mē rā'iah (*or* mĕr'ā ī'ah), *Bib.*
Me ran' (mā rän'), t. Aust.
Mē rā'rī (*or* mĕr'a rī), *Bib.*
Mē rā'rītes (*or* mĕr' a), *Bib.*
mer'can tĭle, -til ism, -til ist, -is-
    tic.
Mêr ced' (-sād'), co. and r. Cal.
Mĕr ce des (-sā'dĕs), t. Urug.
mer'ce na ry, -na ri ly, -ri ness.
mer'cer, -ship, -y, -ize, -ized,
    -ī'zing, -ī zā'tion.
mer'chan dise (-dīz), -dised, -dī'ser,
    -dī'sing, -dī'sa ble.
mer'chant, -á ble, -ry, -hood,
    -man.
mĕr'cu ry, -cu'ri al, -al ist, -al-
    ize, -ized, -ī'zing, -al ly, -cu'-
    ric, -ri fy, -fy ing, -fied, -fī cā'-
    tion, mer'cu ry-cup, -fur nace,
    -gath er er, -goose foot, -hold er.
Mĕr'cu ry, *Myth.,* Mer'cu ry's-
    vi'o let.
Mer cu'ti o (-shī ō), Shaks. *Romeo
    and Juliet.*
mêr'cy, -ci ful, -ful ly, -ful ness,
    -ci less, -less ly, -less ness,
    mêr'cy-seat, -stroke.
mēre, -ly, -stead, -stone, -stake.
Mĕr'e dith, Owen, Lord Lytton.
mere'goutte (mâr'gōōt).
Mĕ'res (-rēz), *Bib.*
mĕr ē tri'cious (-trish'us), -ly,
    -ness, -tri'cian.
mer gan'ser.
mĕrge, merged, mer'ger, -ging.
Mĕr gui' (-gē'), t. Burma.
Mĕr'i bah, *Bib.*
Mĕr'Ĭ da, c. Sp.; c. Yucatan; t.
    Venez.
mē rĭd'i an, -i o nal, -nal ly, -nal'-
    i ty, me rid'i an-cir cle, -mark.
mĕr'i hē'dric.
me'ringue' (mē'răng').

me ri'no (mē rē'nō).
mĕr'it, -ed, -ed ly, -ing, -i to'ri-
    ous, -ous ly, -ous ness.
mêrle *or* mêrl.
Mer'lin, Tennyson, *Idylls of the
    King.*
mêr'lin.
mer'li on.
mêr' măid, -en, mer'man, -peo ple,
    -wom an, mer'maid-fish.
mêr'maid's-egg, -glove, -hair,
    -head, -purse.
Mē rŏ'dach (-dăk *or* mĕr'o-), *Bib.*
Mĕr'ŏ ē, isl. Nile.
me rol'o gy.
Mē ron'o thīte (*or* -rō'nō-), *Bib.*
mĕr'ry, -ri ly, -ri ment, -ri ness,
    -ry make, -māk'ing, mer'ry-
    thought, -wing, a duck.
mĕr'ry-an drew, -night, -go-
    down, -go-round.
mêrse, mêrsed, mêr'sion.
Mĕr'se burg (-bŏŏrg), t. Prus.
Mĕr'sey (-zy), r. Eng.
Mĕr'u (-ōō), *Myth.*
Mé ry' (mā'rē'), Fr. auth.
me'sa (mā'sà).
Me sa'gne (mā sän'yā), t. It.
mé sal li ance' (mā'zà'lē'ŏns').
mes cal'.
mes'en tĕr y (*or* mĕz'-), -tĕr'ic,
    -tē'ri al.
mesh, -ing, -y, meshed, mesh'-
    work, mesh'-stick, mesh'ing-net,
    mesh' struc'ture.
Mē'shach (-shăk), *Bib.*
Mĕsh'chovsk' (-kŏvsk'), t. Russ.
mĕs'i al (*or* mĕz'- *or* mē'zi al *or*
    -zhal), -al ly, -al ward.
mes'mer ism (mez'-), -mer ize,
    -ized, -ī'zer, -ī'zing, -ī zā'tion,
    -mĕr'ic, -ic al, -al ly, -mĕr ist,
    -mer o mā'ni a, -ni ac.
mesne (mēn), mes'nal ty (mē'-
    nal-), -nal'i ty.
Mē sŏ'bā īte (*or* mĕs'o bā'īte),
    Bib.
mē sŏl'o gy, mes o log'ic al.
mes quit (-kēt' *or* mes'-) *or*
    -quite' (-kēt' *or* -kē'tā), mes quit-
    bean, -grăss, -gum, -tree.
mess, -ing, -y, messed, mess'-
    māk'ing, -mate.

mess'-chest, -cloth, -deck, -gear,
-ket tle, -kit, -lock er, -ta ble,
-traps, mess'mate-gum, -tree.
mes'sage.
mes'sen ger, -at-arms.
Měs sī'ah, *Bib.*, -ship, -sĭ an'ic.
Mes si'na (-sē'-), prov. It.
mes'suage (měs'wāj).
mes tee', -ti'zo (-tē'zo), *pl.* -zos
(-zōz), *fem.* -ti za (-tē'zȧ), -ti'no,
pl. -nos (-nōz), mes ti'zo wool.
Měs'tre (-trā), t. It.
mē tab'a sis, -tab'o la, -o lism,
-o līte, met a bat'ic, -a bo'li an,
-a bŏl'ic.
met a car'pus, *pl.* -pī.
mět'al, -aled *or* -alled, -al ing *or*
-ling, -al ĭne, -al ist *or* -list,
-al lĭc'i ty, -al li fac'ture, -al-
lif'er ous, -al lĭne, -al lize, -lized,
-lī zing, -lĭ zā'tion, -al lo chrome,
-chro'my, -log'ra phy, -ra phist,
-lo graph'ic, -al loid, -loid'al,
-al lo sco'py, -scŏp'ic, -al lur gy,
-lur gist, -lur'gic, -gic al, -al ly.
mět'al-bäth, -bend ing, -cȧst ing,
-gage, -plane, -saw, -wheel,
-work, m. cast ing, a plate of
metal cast into shape.
mē tăl'lic, -al ly, -li form, -li fy,
-fy ing, -fied, -lo phone.
met a mŏr'phic, -mor'phism,
-phize, -phized, -phi zing,
-phose (-fōz *or* -fōs), -phosed,
-pho sing, -pho ser, -pho sis, *pl.*
-ses (-sēz).
met'a phor, -ist, -phŏr'ic, -ic al,
-al ly, -al ness.
met'a phragm (-fram), -phrag'-
mal.
met'a phrase (-frāz), -phrased,
-phrast, -phras'tic, -tic al, me-
taph'ra sis.
met'a phys'ic (-fĭz'ĭk), -al, -al ly,
-ics, -phys'i cist, -phy si'cian
(-zĭsh'an), -phys'i o log'ic al.
mē tăth'e sis, met a thet'ic, -ic al.
mē tā'yāge (*or* mā'tā'yäzh'), *mē-
tā'yer* (*or* mā'tā'yä').
měte, mět'ed, -ing, mete'stick,
-wand.
me temp'sy chose   (-sĭ kōz   *or*
-kōs), -cho'sis.

mē'te or, -ŏr'ic, -ic al,   -ôr ism,
-or īte,   -ĭt'ic,   -or ize,   -ized,
-ī'zing,   -or o graph,   -graph'ic,
-or og'ra phy,   -ol'o gy,   -o gist,
-o log'ic, -ic al, -o man cy, -om'-
e ter, mē'te or-cloud, -dust.
mē'ter *or* -tre, -ter ing, -tered, me'-
ter age, me'ter-prov er, -wheel.
Mē tē'rus, *Bib.*
Mē'thĕg ăm'mah, *Bib.*
mē thĕg'lin.
me thinks', me thought'.
mĕth'od, -ism, -o dist, -o dis'tic,
-tic al,   -al ly,   -od ize,   -ized,
-ī'zer, -ī'zing, -ĭ zā'tion, -ol'o gy,
-o log'ic al,   me thŏd'ic,   -ic al,
-al ly, -ics.
Mĕth'o dist, -o dis'tic, -tic al, -o-
dism.
Mē thū'en, t. Mass.
Mē thū'sĕ lah, *Bib.*
mĕth'yl, -blue, -sal i cyl'ic, -vi o-
let.
mĕth'y lēne, -blue.
mé tif' (mā'tēf'), *mé tive'* (mā'-
tēv'), *mé tis'* (mā'tēs'), *mé tisse'*
(mā'tēs').
Mē'tis, *Myth.*
met'o chy (-kĭ).
met'ol.
me tŏn'y my, mět o nym'ic, -ic-
al, -al ly.
met o pos'co py, -co pist, -po-
scŏp'ic, -ic al.
mĕt'ric, -al, -al ly, -ri cist, -rics,
mē'trist, -tri cian (-trish'an).
mĕt'ro chrome, -ro graph.
me troc'ra cy.
me trol'o gy, -o gist, met ro log'-
ic al.
met ro mā'ni a, -ni ac.
met'ro nome, -nom'ic, -ron'o my,
-ro nym'ic.
me trop'o lis,   met ro pol'i tan,
-tan ate,   -tan ism,   -tan ize,
-ized, -ī'zing, -pol'i tic, -po lit'-
ic al.
mĕt'tle, -tled, -tle some, -some ly,
-some ness.
Mē ū'nim, *Bib.*
Meuse (mūz *or* mēz), r. Fr.
mew (mu), -ing, -er, mewed,
mew'-gull.

Me'we (mā'vĕ), t. Prus.
mewl, -er, -ing, mewled.
mews.
Mĕx'ĭ a (*or* mā hē'a), t. Tex.
mez za-ma jŏl'i ca (mĕd'za-),
  mez'za vǒ'ce (mĕd'za vǒ'cha).
mez'zo (mĕd'zo), -rē liĕ'vo, m.
  for'te, m. pi a no, m. so pra'no,
  m. stac ca'to.
Mez'zo fan'ti (mĕt'so fän'tē), It.
  linguist.
mĕz'zo tint, -tint'er, -tin'to.
mho (mō), mhom'e ter (mŏm'-).
mi (mē).
Mī'a min, *Bib.*
mĭ aou'lĭ (-ou'-).
mī'asm, -as ma (-ăz'ma), -as'-
  mal, -as mat'ic, -ic al, -ma tist,
  -ma tous, -mol'o gy, -as'mous.
mī'ca, -pow der, -schist (-shist),
  -slate.
Mĭ cā'iah (-yah), *Bib.*
Mī'cha el (*or* -kĕl), *Bib.*
Mi chael an'ge lo (mē kĕl än'jā-
  lō), It. painter, -gel esque (-jĕl-
  ĕsk' *or* mī'kĕl ăn'-), -gel ism.
Mi cha e'lis (mē kä ā'lis), Ger.
  Bib. critic.
Mich'ael mas (mĭk'el-).
Mĭ chā'iah (-kā'yah), *Bib.*
Mi chaud' (mē'shō'), Fr. hist.
Mi chaux' (mē'shō'), Fr. bot.
miche (mitch), mich'ing.
Mĭ chē'as (-kē'-), *Bib.*
Mi chel (mē'shĕl'), Fr. revolutionist; Fr. archæol.
Mi che let' (mē'shĕ lā'), Ger.
  philos.
Miche let' (mēsh lā'), Fr. hist.
Mich'mas *or* -mash (mĭk'-), *Bib.*
Mic kie'wicz (mĭts kyā'vĭch), Pol.
  poet.
mi'co (mē'ko).
mī'crŏbe, -crŏ'bi an, -crŏb'ic,
  -i cide, -cro bī'o log'ic al, -bi ol'-
  o gist, -o gy.
mī'cro cosm, -cos'mic (-kŏz'-),
  -mic al, -cos mog'ra phy, -mol'-
  o gy, -cos'mos.
mī'cro graph, -ic, -crog'ra pher,
  -ra phist, -ra phy.
mĭ crohm'.
mi crol'o gy, -cro log'ic al, -al ly.

mi crom'e ter, -crō met'ric, -ric-
  al, -al ly, -crom'e try, -cro mil'-
  li me'ter, mi crom'e ter-bal ance,
  -screw.
mĭ crō min er al'o gy, -a log'ic al.
mī'cron.
mī'cro-or gan'ic, -or'gan ism.
mĭ cro pa thol'o gy, -o gist, -path'-
  o log'ic al.
mī'cro phone, -pho'ny (*or* mī-
  krŏf'-), -phŏn'ic, -ics, -pho'nograph, -croph'o nous.
mĭ crō'pi a.
mī'cro scope, -scŏp'ic, -ic al, -al-
  ly, -sco'pist (*or* -cros'co pist),
  -sco'py (*or* -crŏs'co py), mī'cro-
  scope-lamp.
mi cro seïs'mic, -al, -mo graph,
  -mom'e try.
mī'cro tome, -crot'o my, -o mist,
  -cro tom'ic, -ic al.
mī'cro vŏlt.
mid, -bod'y, -brain, -day, -dy,
  -fĕath'er, -land, -lay er, -leg,
  -night, -rib, -ship, -ship man,
  -ship mite, -ships, -stream,
  -sum mer, -vein, -way, -wick et,
  -wife, -win ter, midst.
mid'-cou'ples, -heav en, -hour,
  -im ped'i ment, -main, -morn,
  -mor row, -noon, -o cean, -off,
  -on, -pâr ent, -pâr ent age, -sea,
  -styled, -su per ior, -watch,
  Mid-Lent, mid'day-flow er, mid'-
  sum mer-men, a plant.
mid'dle, -man, -most, -weight,
  -dler, -dling, -dling ly, -dling-
  most, -dlings, mid'dle-aged,
  -clåss, *a.,* -rate, -sized, -spear,
  -stead, mid'dlings-pu ri fi er.
Mi ed zyr'zyc (mē ĕd zĕr'zĭts), t.
  Pol.
mien (mēn).
mĭff, miffed.
might, -y, -i ly, -i ness, -less.
Migne (mēn), Fr. editor.
Mig net' (mēn'yā'), Fr. hist.
Mi gnon' (mē'nyŏń'), Goethe.
mĭ gnon ette' (mĭn'yŭn ĕt').
mī'grate, -grā ted, -grā ting, -grant,
  -grå to'ry, -grā'tion, -tion ist, mi-
  grā'tion-wave, m. sta'tion.

Mi guel' (mē gĕl'), Port. prince.
mǐ kä'dō.
Mǐk'lō sich (-sich), Slavic philol.
Mǐk nē'iah, *Bib.*
mil, a unit of measure.
mǐ lä'dy or *mi lä'di* (mē lä'dē).
Mǐl'a lä'ǐ (*or* mǐ lä'la ǐ *or* mǐl'a-
   läi), *Bib.*
Mǐl'an (*or* mǐ lan'), c. It., Mi'lan,
   t. Mo.; tp. O.; c. Tenn., Mǐ'-
   lan ese (-ēse *or* -ēze).
milch, -er, -y, -wom'an, m. cow.
mǐld, -er, -est, -ly, -ness, mild'-
   spo'ken.
mil'dew, -y, -dewed, mil'dew-
   brŏnze.
mǐle, -age, mile'-post, -stone.
Mǐ lē'tus, anc. c. Asia Minor,
   -lē'sian (-shan *or* -zhan).
mǐl'i tant, -ly, -tan cy.
mǐl'i ta ry, -ta rist, -ta ri ly, -rism.
mǐl'i tate, -ta ted, -ta ting, -tä'-
   tion.
mǐ lǐ'tia (-lǐsh'a), -man.
milk, -er, -ing, -ful, -y, -i ly,
   -i ness, -less, milked, milk'fish,
   -maid, -man, -sop, -stone, -weed,
   -wom an, -wood, a tree, -wort.
milk'-ab scess, -blotch, -can,
   -car, -cool er, -crust, -cure,
   -den ti'tion, -duct, -fac to ry,
   -fe ver, -gāge, -glǎss, -glob ule,
   -hedge, -house, -kin ship, -leg,
   -liv ered, -meat, -mǐr ror, -mite,
   -mo lar, -nurse, -pail, -pan,
   -pars ley, -pea, -por ridge,
   -pump, -quartz, -rack, -scab,
   -sick, -sick ness, -snake, -su gar,
   -test er, -this tle, -thrush, -tie,
   -tooth, -tree, -tube, -vat, -ves-
   sel, -vetch, -walk, -warm,
   -white, -wood, milk-and-wa ter,
   a., milk punch, m. shake.
milk'ing-shield, -stool, -time,
   -tube, milk'y-tailed, Milk'y Way.
mill, -er, -ing, milled, mill'board,
   -man, -stone, -weir, -wright.
mill'-bar, -cake, -cin der, -dam,
   -driv er, -eye, -feed er, -fire,
   -fur nace, -gang, -hand, -head,
   -holm, -hop per, -horse, -jade,
   -mon ey, -own er, -pick, -pond,
   -pool, -post, -race, -ream,

-rine, -rolls, -round, -rynd
(-rīnd), -saw, -scale, -skate,
-spin dle, -tail, -ward, -wheel,
-work.
mill'board-cut ter, mil'ler's-dog,
-thumb, mill'-hop per a larm,
mill'ing-cut ter, -ma chine, -tool.
mill'stone-bal ance, -bridge, -curb,
-dress, -dress er, -drǐv er, -feed,
-ham mer, -pick, -reg u la tor,
-spin dle, -ven ti la tor, mill'stone
grit.
Mǐl lais' (-lā'), Eng. painter.
Mille Lacs' (mēl lǎk'), co. Minn.
mil len'i al, -ist, -i um, -le nä'-
ri an, -an ism, -le na'ry, -les'i-
mal.
mǐl'le ped.
mil'let, -grǎss.
mil'li am pere' (-pâr').
mil'liard.
mil li ä'rō, a mile, -li a ry.
mil'lǐ âre, a unit of surface.
mil lier' (mēl yä').
mil'li gram *or* -grǎmme, -lǐ li'-
ter (-lē'ter), -li mē'ter.
mil'li ner, -ner y.
mil'li net.
mil'lion (-yun), -aire', -lion ism,
-ist, -ize, -lionth, -li stere (-stâr).
Milnes (mǐlnz), Eng. statesman.
Mǐ'lō, tp. N. Y.—(mē'lō), isl. Gr.
mǐl'reis (-ıēs).
milt, -er, milt'waste, a plant.
Mil tǐ'a des (-dēz), Athenian general.
Mil'ton, Eng. poet, -tō'ni an,
-ton'ic.
mime, mǐm'e o graph, mǐ met'ic,
-ic al, -al ly, mǐm'e tism.
mim'ic, -icked, -ick ing, -ick er,
-ic ry, mim'ic-bee tle, -thrush.
mim'-mouthed.
mǐ mō'sa, -sa'ceous.
mi'na, -bird.
mǐn'a ret.
mǐn'a to ry, -to ri ly, -to'ri al, -al ly,
-al'i ty.
mince, minced, min'cing, -cer,
-cing ly, mince'-meat, m. pie.
min'cing-horse, -knife, -spade.
mind, -ed, -ed ness, -er, -ing,
-ful, -ful ly, -ful ness, -less.

mind'-cure, -cur er, -day, -heal-
er, -read er, -stuff, -trans'fer-
ence, mind'ing-school.
Min dä nä'ō (mēn-), isl. Philippines.
Min dŏ'rō (mēn-), isl. Philippines.
mine, mined, mīn'ing, mīn'er,
-y, mine'-cap tain, -chäm ber,
-dī al, mīn'ing-camp, -dis trict,
-ma chine, -re gion, -tool.
Mi ne'o (mē nä'ō), t. It.
mĭn'er al, -ist, min'er al-dress er,
-hold er.
min'er al ize, -ized, -ī'zing, -ī'za-
ble, -ī'zer, -I zā'tion.
mĭn er al'o gy, -a log'ic, -ic al,
-al ly, -al'o gist, -o gize, -gized,
-gī'zing.
mĭ nette'.
miṇ'gle, -gled, -gled ly, -gler,
-gle ment, miṇ'gle-maṇ gle.
Mĭn'ho (mēn'yō), r. Sp.
Mĭn'i a min (*or* mĭ nī'-), *Bib.*
mĭn'i a ture (*or* -i ture), -tur ist.
mĭn'i bus.
Min'ie (mĭn'ĭ), M. ball, M. ri fle.
Mi'niē' (mē nyä' *or* mē nē ā'), Fr.
inventor.
mĭn'i fy, -ing, -fïed.
mĭn'im, -i mal, min'im rest.
mĭn'i mize, -mized, -mī'zing,
-mĭ zā'tion, -i mum.
min'ion (-yun) -ship, min'ion-
like.
min'ish, -ing, -ished.
min'is ter, -is tē'ri al, -al ly, -al-
ist, -ter ing, -tē'ri um, -is trant,
-is tra'tive, -is try, -is trā'tion.
min'i ver.
miṇk, -er y.
Min ne hä'hä, Longfellow; co. S.
Dak.
min'ne sing er, -ne lied (-lēt),
-ne po'let ry, -ne-drink'ing.
mĭn'nŏw, -har ness.
mi'no (mē'nō).
mĭ'nor, -ship, mĭ nŏr'i ty.
mi'no rät (mē'-).
Min'o taur, *Myth.*
min'ster.
min'strel, -sy, min'strel-squire.
mint, -ed, -er, -ing, -age, mint'-
bush, -mäs ter, -drop, -ju'lep,

-mark, -stick, -tree, -war den,
m. sauce.
mĭn'u end.
mĭn'u et.
Mĭn'u it, Gov. of New Neth.
mī'nus, mĭ nus'cule.
mĭ nute', *a.,* -ly, -ness, *-nu'ti a*
(-shĭ a), pl. *-ti æ* (-shĭ ē), -ti-
ose (-shĭ ōs).
mĭn'ute (-ĭt), *n.,* -ute man, -ute-
book, -clock, -hand, -glåss,
-jack, -jump er, -watch, -wheel.
min u te'ri a.
miṇx, -ot ter.
Mi que lon' (mē'kĕ lōň'), isl. off
Newfoundland.
mir (mēr).
Mi ra beau' (mē rä bō'), Fr. rev.
mi rab'i le dic'tū, m. vī'sū.
mĭr'a cle, mĭ rac'u lous, -ly, -ness,
mir'a cle-moṇ ger, -play, -work er.
mĭr a dōr'.
mi rage' (mē'räzh').
Mĭr'a mĭ chi' (-shē'), r. Can.
Mire (mēr), t. Fr.
mīre, mired, mīr'ing, mīr'y,
-i ness, -ish, mire'-crow, -drum,
-duck.
Mi rim' (mē rēň'), l. S. Amer.
Mir'pur' (mēr pōōr'), t. India.
mĭr'ror, -ing, -rored, mĭr'ror-
black, -carp, -gal van om'e ter,
-script, -writ'er.
mirth, -ful, -ful ly, -ful ness, -less,
-less ness.
mis ad ven'ture, -tur ous.
mis ad vise', -vised', -vis'ed ly,
-ed ness.
Mĭs'a el (*or* mĭ'sa el), *Bib.*
mis al lege' (-lĕj'), -leged.
mis al lī'ance, -al līed'.
mis'an thrōpe, -thrŏp'ic, -ic al,
-al ly, -an'thro pist, -thro py.
mis ap ply', -ing, -plïed', -pli cä'-
tion.
mis ap pre'ci ate, -ā'ted, -à tive,
-ā'tion.
mis ap pre hend', -ed, -ing, -hen'-
sive, -sive ly, -sion.
mis ap pro'pri ate, -ā'ted, -ā'ting,
-ā'tion.
mis ăr rănge', -ment, -rănged',
-răn'ging.

---

mis be have', -haved, -hāv'ing, -hāv'ior.

mis cal'cu late, -lā'ted, -lā'ting, -lā'tion.

mis call', -ing, -called'.

mis căr'ry, -ing, -rĭed, -rĭage.

mis cel lā'ne ous, -ly, -ness, -la'- ny, -la'nist.

mis cen'sure (-shŏor), -sured, -sur ing.

mis chânce', -chânced', -chăn'- cing.

mis charge', -charged', -char'- ging.

mis'chĭef, -chĭev ous, -ous ly, -ous- ness, mis'chief-māk'er, -night.

mis'ci ble.

mis cīte', -cīt'ed, -ing, -cī tā'tion.

mis con cēive', -ceived', -ceiv'er, -ceiv'ing, -con cep'tion.

mis con'duct, n., -duct', v., -ed, ing.

mis con struct', -ed, -ing, -struc'- tion.

mis con'strue, -strued, -stru ing, -stru er.

mis'cre ant, -an cy.

mis date', -dāt'ed, -ing.

mis dĕal', -ing, -dĕalt'.

mis deed'.

mis deem', -ing, -deemed'.

mis de mean'or, -mean'ant.

mis dĭ rect', -ed, -ing, -rec'tion.

misc en scène (mēz ŏn sān).

mis em ploy', -ing, -ment, -ployed'.

mī'ser (-zer), -ly, -li ness, mĭs'- er y (mĭz'-).

mis'er a ble (mĭz'-), -ness, -bly.

mis e re're (mĭz'ē rē'rē).

mis ē rĭ cor'dĭ a (mĭz-).

mis fĕa'sance (-zans), -sant, -sor.

mis fĭt', -ted, -ting.

mis for'tŭne.

mis giv'ing.

mis gov'ern, -ing, -ment, -erned.

mis guide', -guid'ance, -ed, -ing.

mis hap'.

mis in form', -er, -ing, -ant, -formed, -for mā'tion.

mis in ter'pret, -a ble, -er, -pre- tā'tion.

mis join', -ing, -joined', -join'der.

mis judge', -judg'ing, -ment, -judged'.

mis'kạl.

mis lay', -ing, -er, -laid'.

mis lĕad', -ing, -ing ly, -er, -lĕd'.

mis man'age, -ment, -aged, -a ging.

mis match', -ing, -ment, -matched.

mis mate', -māt'ed, -ing.

mis meas'ure (-mezh'-), -ment, -ured, -ur ing.

mis name', -nāmed', -nām'ing.

mis nō'mer.

mĭ sŏg'a my, -a mist.

mĭ sog'y ny (-sŏj'-), -y nous, -y nist, -nis'tic al.

mĭ sol'o gy, -o gist, mis'o logue.

mis place', -ment, -placed', -plā'- cing.

mis plĕad', -ing, -ed.

mis print', -ed, -ing.

mis prize', -prized', -prĭz'ing, -pris'ion (-prizh'un).

mis pro nounce', -ment, -nounced', -noun'cing, -nun'ci a'tion.

mis pro por'tion, -tioned.

mis quote', -quŏt'ed, -ing, -quo- tā'tion.

mis rĕad', ing, -rĕad'.

mis rep re sent' (-zent'), -ed, -er, -ing, -sen tā'tion.

mis rule', -ruled', -rŭl'ing.

miss, -ĭsh, -ĭsh ness, -ing, -y, missed.

mis'sal.

mis shape', -shaped', -shāp'en (-n), -en ly, -en ness.

mis'sĭle.

mis'sion, -a ry, -er, mis'sion- rooms, m. school, mis'sion ary bish'op.

Mis'sis sip'pĭ, r. and state, -pi an.

mis'sĭve.

Mis sou'la (mĭz zōō'la), c. Mont.

Mis sou'ri (-sōō'rĭ or miz zōō'-), r. and state U. S., -ri an, Mis sou'ri com'pro mise, M. cŭr'rant, M. hy'a cinth, M. suck er.

mis spĕak', -spoke', -spo'ken.

mis spell', -ing, -spelled'.

mis spend', -ing, -spent'.

mis state', -ment, -stāt'ed, -ing.

---

nŏt, nôr, ūse, ŭp, ûrn, etüde, fōod, fŏŏt, aṇger, boṅmot, thus, Bach.

mis step', -ping, -stepped'.
mist, -ful, -y, -i ly, -i ness, -like,
mist'flow'er, mist'-bōw, -col'-
ored, -rick, -tree.
mis take', -tăk'a ble, -tăk'en,
-en ly, -took'.
mis tēach', -ing, -taught'.
mis'ti co.
mis'tle thrush (-l-), -tle toe
(mĭz'l tō or mĭs'-).
Mis'tral' (mēs'träl'), Provençal
poet.
mis'tral.
mis'tress.
mis trī'al.
mis trust', -ed, -er, -ing, -ful,
-ful ly, -ful ness, -less.
mis un der stand', -ing, -stood'.
mis use' (-ūz'), v., -used', -ūs'-
ing, -ūs'er, -ūs'age, mis use'
(-ūs'), n.
mis write', -wrote', -wrĭt'ten,
-wrīt'ing.
mīte, mīt'y.
mī'ter or -tre, -tered or -tred,
-ter ing or -tring, -tral, mī'ter-
flow'er, -wort.
mī'ter-block, -board, -box, -cut,
-dove tail, -drain, -gāge, -i ron,
-jack, -joint, -mush room,
-plane, -post, -shaped, -shell,
-sill, -square, -valve, -wheel,
mī'ter ing-ma chine.
Mith rĭ dā'tes (-tēz), King of
Pontus, -dat'ic.
mit'i gate, -gā'ted, -ted ly, -gā'-
ting, -gā'tive, -gā'tor, -ga to'ry,
-gā'tion.
mī'tis, -căst ing, -green.
mi traille' (mē'träl'), -trail leur'
(-träl yêr'), -trail leuse' (-träl-
yēz').
Mĭt'rō wicz (-rō vĭts), t. Hung.
mitt, mit'ten (-tn), -tened (-tnd).
Mĭt y lē'nē, isl. Ægean sea.
mix, -a ble, mixed, mix'ed ly,
-er, -ing, -tion (-chun), -ture,
mix'ing-ma chine, -sĭeve, mix'-
ture-stop.
Mix i a'na (mĭsh ĭ ä'nä), isl. Braz.
Mix te că păn' (mēks tä-), table-
land Mex.
Mi zhi ritch' (mē jē rĭch'), t. Russ.

Mĭz'ra ĭm (or -rä'-), Bib.
miz'zen (-zn), -măst, -sail, miz'-
zen-rig ging.
miz'zle, -zled, -zling, -zly.
Mnā'son (nä'-), Bib.
mnē mŏn'ic, -ic al, -ics, -mo nist,
-mo ni'cian (-nĭsh'an), -mo tech'-
nic (-tĕk'nik), -nics, -ny,
Mne mos'y nē, Myth.
Mŏ'ab, Bib., -īte, -ĭ'tish, -ī'tess.
mŏan, -ing, mōaned.
mŏat, -ed, -ing, moat'-hen.
mob, -bing, -bish, mobbed, mob-
oc'ra cy, -o crat, -crat'ic, mobs'-
man, mob-law, -măs ter, -sto ry.
mŏ'bee.
mŏ'bĭle, -bil'i ty, mō'bil ize (or
mŏb'-), -ized, -ĭ'zing, -ĭ zā'tion.
Mŏ bile' (-bēl'), c. Ala., -bil'i an.
moc'ca sin, -sined, moc'ca sin-
flow er, -plant, -snake.
mŏ'cha (-ka), a coffee; a weight;
a moth; a cat.
Mŏ'cha (-kȧ), c. Arabia; M. peb'-
ble, M. sen'na, M. stone.
moche (mōsh).
Moch'mur (mŏk'-), Bib.
mŏck, -er, -er y, -ing, -ing ly,
-ish, mocked.
mock'-ap ple, -bird, -he ro'ic,
-or ange, -shad ow, -thrush,
-tur tle, -vel vet, mock'er nut,
mock'ing-bird, -wren.
mŏc'māin.
mŏ cŭd'dum.
mode, mŏ'dal, -dal ism, -dal ist,
-dal ly, -is'tic, -dal'i ty, mōd'ish,
-ish ly, -ish ness, -ist, mo diste'
(-dēst'), mŏ'dus, mode'-book.
mŏd'el, -eled or -elled, -el ing or
-ling, -el er or -ler, mŏd'el-wood.
mŏd'el ing-board, -clay, -loft,
-plane, -stand, -tools.
Mŏd'e na (-ā nä), prov. It.,
Mŏ dē nēse' (or -nēz').
mŏd'er ate, -ly, -ness, -ā'ted,
-ā'ting, -ā'tist, -ā'tor, -tor ship,
-ā'tion, mod'er a tor-lamp.
mŏd'ern, -er, -ism, -ist, -ize,
-ized, -ĭ'zer, -ĭ'zing, -ness,
-ĭ zā'tion.
mŏd'est, -ly, -es ty.
mŏd'i cum.

mod′i fy, -ing, -fīed, -fī′er, -fī′a-
ble, -ble ness, -bil′i ty, -fī ca′-
tive, -ca′tor, -cā′to ry, -cā′tion.
mō′di us, pl. *-dĭ ī.*
Mŏd jĕs′ka, Pol. actress.
Mŏ′doc, -docs, Mŏ′doc whis′tle.
mŏ′dō et jor′ma.
mod′u late, -lā′ted, -lā′ting, -lā′-
tor, -to′ry, -lar, -lā′tion.
mō′dus vĭ vĕn′dĭ, m. op e ran′dĭ.
mo fus′sil.
mog′i graph′i a (mŏj′-), *-i lā′li a.*
Mo gŭl′.
Mŏ′hacs′ (-häch′), t. Hung.
mō′hâir, -shell, m. braid, m.
lus′ter.
Mo ham′med *or* Ma hŏm′et,
-med an, -an ism, -med ism,
-an ize, -ized, -ī′zing.
Mŏ′hawk.
Mo hi′can (-hē′-) *or* -hē′gan.
mohr (mōr).
mō′hur.
moi′dŏre.
moi′e ty.
Moig no′ (mwän yō′), Fr. math.
moil, -ing, moiled.
moi′neau (-nō).
Mŏ i′ra, tp. N. Y.;—(Moi′ra), co.
Austral.
moire (mwŭr).
moi ré (mwŏ rā′), *m. an tique′.*
moist, -en (mois′n), -en er, -en-
ing, -ened, moist′ful, -less,
-ness, mois′ture, -ture less.
Moivre (mwävr), Fr. math.
mō′kō.
mo′kuk.
Mŏl′a dah (*or* mō′la-), *Bib.*
mō′lar, -lar y, -lăr′i form, -la-
rim′e ter.
mŏ las′ses (-sez).
mŏld *or* mōuld, -ed, -er, -ing,
-a ble, -a bil′i ty, -y, -i ness.
mŏld′-black ing, -board, -box,
-can dle, -cis tern, -fa cing, -loft,
-stone, -turn er.
mŏld′ing-ap pa ra′t u s, -bed,
-board, -box, -crane, -cut ter,
-file, -flăsk, -frame, -hole,
-loam, -ma chine, -mill, -plane,
-plow, -sand, -saw, -ta ble,
mold′y-hill, -rat.

mŏle, -skin, -bat, -but, -căst,
-catch er, -crick et, -eyed, -hill,
-hole, -plant, -plow, -rat,
-shrew, -spade, -track, -tree.
mŏl′e cule, mō lec′u lar, -lar ly,
-la′ri um, -lăr′i ty.
mŏ lest′, -ed, -er, -ing, -ful,
mŏl es tā′tion (*or* mō′les-).
Mo lière′ (mŏl yâr′), Fr. dram.
mŏl′le ton.
mŏl′li fy, -ing, -fīed, -fī′er, -fī′-
a ble, -fī cā′tion, -li ent, -ent ly.
mŏl′lusk.
Mŏ′loch (-lŏk), *Bib.*
mŏlt *or* mōult, -ed, -er, -ing.
mŏl′ten (-tn), -ly.
Mŏlt′kĕ, Ger. field-marshal.
mŏl′tō.
Mŏ lŭc′cas (-kăz), isls. Malay
arch., Mo luc′ca balm, M. bean,
M. deer.
mome.
mō′ment, -ly, -men ta′ry, -ta ri-
ly, -ri ness, -men′tous, -tous ly,
-tous ness.
mŏ men′tum, *pl.* -tums *or* -ta.
Mŏ′mus, *Myth.*
Mŏn′ä cō, principality Europe.
mŏn′ad, -ism, -ol′o gy, mō nad′ic,
-ic al, -al ly, -i form, mŏn′ad-
deme.
mŏn a del′phic, -del′phous.
mŏn′arch (-ark), -ism, -ist, -ize,
-ized, -ī′zing, -ī′zer, -y, mō nar′-
chal (-kal), -chi al, -chi an,
-chic (-kĭk), -chic al.
mŏn′as ter y, -tc′ri al, -al ly,
mō nas′tic, -tic al, -al ly, -ti-
cism, -ti con.
mŏn a tom′ic.
mŏn au′ral, -ax′i al, -ax′on, -ax-
o′ni al, -on′ic.
Mŏn creiff′ (-krēf′), Scot. divinc.
Mon′day (mŭn′-).
moṅde (mŏṅd *or* mŏṅd).
mon′ey (mŭn′y), *pl.* -eys, -e tary, -e tize, -tized, -ti zing, -tī-
zā′tion, -eyed (-ĭd), -ey er,
-ey less, mon′ey bags, a person,
-flow′er, -wort.
mon′ey-bag, -bill, -box, -brŏ′ker,
-chăn ger, -corn, -deal er,
-draw er, -drop per, -grub ber,

---

nŏt, nôr, ūse, ŭp, ûrn, etüde, fōōd, fŏŏt, aṇger, boṅmot, thus, Bach.

-job ber, -land, -lend er, -mãk'-
er, -moṇ ger, -moṇ ger ing, -or-
der, -pot, -scriv en er, -spi der,
-spin ner, -tãk er, m. mar'ket,
m. mat'ter, mon'ey's worth.
Monge (mõṅzh), Fr. math.
moṇ'ger (mŭṇ'ger), -ing.
Mon gŏ'lï a, Chinese empire, -li-
an, Moṇ'gol, -gol'ic, -go loid.
moṇ'gōōs, *pl.* -gōōs es (-ĕz).
moṇ'grel (mung'-), -ism, -ize,
-ized, -ĭ'zing, moṇ'grel-skate.
mŏn'ism, -ist, mo nis'tic.
mon'i tor, -to'ri al, -al ly, -to'ry,
-tress, -trix, -i tive, mon'i tor-
-liz ard, -roof.
moṇk (munk), -er y, -hood, -ish,
-ish ness, moṇk'fish, -bat, -bird,
-seal, -seam.
moṇk's-gun, -har que bus, -hood,
-rhu barb, -seam.
moṇ'key (muṇ'ky), -ing, -ism,
-keyed (-kĭd), moṇ'key flow'er,
-tail, a lever; a rope.
moṇ'key-ap ple, -bag, -block,
-board, -boat, -bread, -cup,
-drift, -en gine, -gaff, -grãss,
-ham mer, -jack et, -pot, -press,
-pump, -puz zle, -rail, -shine,
-spar, -tail, tail of a monkey,
-wheel, -wrench, mon key's-
face.
Mŏn'moŭth, co. Eng.; co. N. J.;
c. Ill., M. cock, M. hat, mŏn'-
moŭth, a cap.
Mon nier' (mŏn yã'), Fr. writer.
mŏn'o chord (-kord).
mŏn'o chrome (-krōm), -chro'ic,
-chro mat'ic, -chro'mic al, -chro'-
my.
mŏn'o cle, mo noc'u lar, -lar ly,
-noc'u lous.
mŏn o cot y lĕ'don, -lĕd'o nous.
mŏn'o crat, mo noc'ra cy.
mŏn o drä'ma, -dra mat'ic.
mŏn'o dy, -o dist, mo nŏd'ic, -ic-
al, -al ly.
mo nog'a my, -a mous, -a mist,
-mis'tic, mon o gã'mi an, -gãm'-
ic.
mon o gen'e sis, -ge net'ic.
mŏ nog'e ny (-nŏj'-), -e nism,
-e nist, -e nous, mon'o ge nis'tic.

mon'o glot.
mo nog'o ny, mon o gon'ic.
mon'o gram, -mat'ic, mon'o-
gram-ma chine.
mŏn'o grâph, -ing, -graphed,
-graph'ic al, -al ly, mo nog'ra-
pher, -ra phist, -ra phous, -ra-
phy.
mo nog'y ny (-noj'i ni), -y nist,
-y nous, mon o gyn'i an.
mŏn'o lith, -lith al, -lith'ic.
mŏn'o lŏgue, mō nol'o gist, -o gy.
mon o mã'ni a, -ni ac, -nï'a cal.
mon o met'al list, -al lism, -me-
tal'lic.
mo nom'e ter, mon o met'ric, -ric-
al.
mŏ nŏ'mi al.
mon'o pho'ny (*or* mo nŏph'-),
-pho'nous (*or* mo noph'-), -phon'ic.
mŏn'oph thong, -thoṇ'gal.
mo nop'o ly, -o list, -o lis'tic,
-o lize, -lized, -lï'zer, -lï'zing,
-lï zä'tion.
mŏn'o rïme *or* -rhyme.
mŏn'o stich (-stĭk), mo nos'ti-
chous (-kus).
mo nos'trŏ phe, mon o stroph'ic.
mon'o syl la ble, -lab'ic, -ic al ly,
-syl'la ble.
mon o tel'e phone, -phon'ic.
mon'o the ism, -the ist, -is'tic.
mon'o tone, -toned, -tōn ing,
-tŏn'ic, -ic al, -al ly, mo not'o-
nist, -o nous, -nous ly, -nous-
ness, -o ny.
mon'o type, -ty'pal (-tï'-), -typ'ic
(-tĭp'-), -ic al.
Mons (mōṅs), t. Belg.
mon seig neur' (mŏṅ sã nyêr').
Mŏn se li'ce (-sã lã'chã), t. It.
Mŏn sĕr rät', mt. Sp.
mon sieur' (mŏ'syê'), pl. *mes-
sieurs'* (mã'syê').
mon sig'nor (mŏṅ sē'nyor).
mon sōōn'.
mŏn'ster, -ship, -strous, -strous-
ly, -strous ness, -stros'i ty.
Mŏn'ta gu, Basil, Eng. lawyer;
Charles, Eng. statesman; Edward, Eng. statesman; Elizabeth, Eng. authoress; Lady
Mary Wortley, Eng. authoress.

---

fãte, fãt, fär, fạll, fâre, fãst, sofà, mēte, mĕt, hêr, īce, ĭn, nōte,

Mon′ta gūe, Shak.; co. Tex.; vil. Mass.; vil. Mich.
Mon taig lon′ (mŏn′tăl′yŏn′), Fr. bibliog.
Mŏn tä jo′ne (-yō′nä), t. It.
Mŏn täl bän′, t. Venez.
Mon ta len bert′ (mŏn′tä′lŏn′-bâr′), Fr. statesman.
mŏn′tane, -tan′ic.
Mon taud′ (mŏn′tō′), t. Fr.
Mont Blanc (mŏn blŏn), mt. Fr.
Mŏnt blanch′ (-blänk′), t. Sp.
Mont Ce nis′ (mŏn′ sĕ nĕ′), Alps.
mŏn′te (-tä).
Mon te Cär′lŏ (mŏn′tä), t. Monaco.
Mon te fi o′re (mŏn tē fē ō′re), Eng. philanthropist.
mon tĕith′, a punch-bowl; a handkerchief.
Mon te le′pre (mŏn′tä lä′prä), t It.
Mon′te Mag gio′re (mŏn′tä mäd jō′rä), t. It.
Mon te ne′gro (mŏn tä nä′grō), principality Europe, -neg′rin (mŏn tē nĕg′rin), mon te neg′rin, a garment.
Mŏn′te pul cia′no (-pōōl chä′nō), t. It.; a wine.
mon te′ro (-ta′-), -cap.
Mŏn te′se (-tä′sä), t. It.
Mŏn′tĕs quieu′ (-kū′), Fr. jurist.
Mon te zu′ma (zōō′-), Aztec emperor.
Mont Ge ne′vre (mŏn zhĕ nä′vr), mt. Fr.
mont gol′fi er, a balloon.
month (mŭnth), -ling, -ly.
Mŏn ti′jo (-tē′hō), t. Sp.
Mŏn til la (-tĕl′yä), t. Sp.
Mon ti vil liers′ (mŏn′tĕ′vĕ′yä′), t. Fr.
Mont lu çon′ (mŏn′lü sŏn′), t. Fr.
Mont mar′tre (mŏn′mär′tr), t. Fr.
Mŏnt′mŏ ren cy, co. Mich.;— (-rĕn′cy), r. Can.;—(mŏn′mō′-rŏn′sē′), vil. Fr.
Mŏnt o gŏl′fi er, Fr. scientist.
mon′toir′ (mŏn′twŏr′).
mŏn′ton.
Mont Pe lee′.
Mŏnt pē′li̇ er, t. Vt.;—(mŏn′pĕl′-yä′), c. Fr.

Mont pen sier′ (mŏn′pŏn′syä′), Fr. prince.
mŏn′tre (-ter).
Mont rouge′ (mŏn′rōōzh′), t. Fr.
mon′u ment, -men′tal, -tal ly.
Mŏn zon′ (-thōn′), t. Sp.
mon′zo nīte.
mōō, -ing, -er, mōōed.
mōōd, -y, -i ly, -i ness, -ish, -ish ly, mood′y-heart ed.
moon, -et, -ish, -less, -y, moon′-beam, -bill, a duck, -eye, a fish, -fish, -flaw, -flow er, -glade, -light, -lit, -rise, -seed, a plant, -set, -shine, -shīn y, -stone, -strick en, -struck, -wort.
moon′-blast ed, -blind, -blink, -box, -calf, -creep er, -cul mi-na ting, -cul mi na tions, -dai sy, -di al, -eye, an eye, -face, -fern, knife, -mad ness, -month, -pen-ny, -plant, -rāk′er, -sail, -tre-foil, -year.
moon′shee.
mōōr, -ing, -age, -ish, -y, moor′-band, -ber ry, -land, -pan, -stone, -wort.
mōōr′-ball, -black bird, -bread, -buz zard, -coal, -cock, -root, -fowl, -game, -grass, -hawk, -heath, -hen, -ill, -monkey, -peat, -tit, -whin.
moor′ing-bend, -bits, -block, -bri dle, -chocks, -pall, -post, -shack le, -stump, -swiv el.
Mōōr, -ish, -man, M. dånce.
mōōse, -wood, a tree, moose′-bird, -call, -deer, -elm, -yard.
Mŏ′ŏ sī′as, Bib.
mōōt, -ed, -ing, -a ble, -er, moot′-hill.
mop, -ping, mopped, mop′board, -head, a person, -stick, -fair, -head, a frowzy head, -head ed, -nail, -wring er.
mŏpe, moped, mōp′ing, -ing ly, -ish, -ish ly, -ish ness, -ful, -eyed.
mŏps.
mŏ′pus.
mŏ quette′ (-kĕt′).
mo ra′ceous.
mŏ räine′, -rain′ic, -rain′al.

mŏr′al, -ist, -is′tic, -al ize, -ized,
-i zing, -i zer, -ĭ zā′tion, -al ly,
mo ral′i ty, *mŏ′rale′* (-rål′).
mŏ râss′, -y, -weed.
mŏ′rat.
Mor′ay (mŭr′ĭ), Eng. statesman.
mor′bid, -ly, -ness, -bid′i ty,
-bif′ic, -ic al, -al ly.
mor′ceau′ (-sō′).
mor dā′cious, -ly, -dac′i ty.
mor′dant, -ly.
Mor′de căi, *Bib.*
more, -o′ver, more′-pork′.
mo reen′.
mŏr′el, mō rĕlle′.
mo rel′lo.
mŏ′rē ma jŏ′rum.
Mŏ resque′ (-rĕsk′), Mŏ ris′co.
Mŏ′rez′ (-rā′), t. Fr.
mor′ga nat′ic, -al, -al ly.
morgue.
mŏr′i bund.
Mor′mon, -dom, -ism, -ist, -īte.
morn, the morning, -ward.
morne, head of a lance, morned.
mor nē′ (mor′nā′), Her.
morn′ing, morn, morn′ing flow′-
er.
morn′ing-cap, -gift, -glo′ry,
-gown, -land, -room, -sphinx,
-star, a weapon, -tide.
mŏ′ro, a bird, Mŏ′ro, *pl.* -ros
(-rōz), a tribe in P. I.
mo roc′co, a leather, -head, -jaw,
Mo roc′co, Afr., M. gum.
mŏ rose′ (-rōs′), -ly, -ness.
Mor′pheus (-fûs *or* -fe us), -phe-
an.
mor′phĭne, -phin ism, -phi o mā′-
ni a, -ni ac, -o met′ric.
mor phog′e ny (fŏj′-), -pho-
gen′ic, -gen′e sis, -ge net′ic.
mor phog′ra phy, -ra pher, -pho-
graph′ic al, -phol′o gy, -o gist,
-o log′ic, -ic al, -al ly.
mor phom′e try, -pho met′ric al,
-phon′o my, -pho nom′ic.
mŏr′ris, -dance, -dan cer, -dan-
cing, Mor′ris-chair.
mŏr′rŏw.
mor′sel (-sl).
mor′sing-horn.
Mŏr′tagne′ (-tän′), t. Fr.

mor′tal, -ize, -ized, -i zing, -tal-
ly, -tal ness, -tal′i ty.
mor′tar, -bat ter y, -bed, -board,
-boat, -car riage, -mill, -ves sel,
-wag on.
mort′gage (mor′gāj), -gaged,
-gà ging, -gà gor (-jor), -gà gee′,
mort′gage-deed.
mor′ti fy, -ing, -fi er, -fīed, -fī-
cā′tion.
mor′tĭse, -tĭsed, -tis ing, mor′-
tise-block, -bolt, -chis el, -cor-
ner, -gāge, -joint, -lock, -wheel.
mor′tis ing-ma chine.
mort′mâin.
mor′tu a ry.
mŏ sā′ic (-zā′-), inlaid work,
-ic al, -al ly, -sa′i cist.
Mos′by (mōz′by), Confed. officer.
Mŏsch′el ĕs, Ger. pianist.
Mŏ selle′ (-zĕl′), a river; a wine.
Mŏ sē′rŏth, *Bib.*
Mŏ′ses (-zĕs), Mo sa′ic (-zā′-),
-ic al, -sa ism, mo′ses, a boat.
Mos′lem, -ism.
mos′lings (mŏz′-).
mŏsque.
mŏs qui′tŏ (-kē′-), -bar, -can o-
py, -cur tain, -hạwk, -net,
-net ting.
mŏss, -y, -i ness, moss′back, a
fish; a person, -ber ry, -bun ker,
-head, a duck, -wort.
mŏss′-ag ate, -al co hol, -an i-
mal, -an i mal′cule, -bass, -box,
-cam pi on, -capped, -cheep er,
-cor al, -crops, -duck, -hags,
-lo cust, -owl, -piṇk, -pol yp,
-rake, -rose, -rush, -starch, -troop-
er, -wood.
mŏst, -ly.
mŏt.
mŏte, -less, -ling, mōt′ed.
mŏt′er.
mŏ tet′, -tē′tus, -tet′tist, *mot tet′-
to.*
mŏth, -y, moth′-blight, -ci ca′da,
-eat en, -gnat, -hawk, -hunt er,
-mul leĭn, -or chid, -patch,
-plant, -sphinx, -trap.
moth′er (mŭth′-), -ing, -hood,
-less, -ly, -li ness, -er y, -ered,
moth′er land, -wort.

moth′er-câsk, -cell, -cloves, -liq uor, -lode, -love, -lye, -maid, -spot, -ves sel, -wa ter, -wit.

moth′er-in-law, -of-coal, -of pearl, -of-thou sands, a plant, -of-thyme, -of-vin e gar.

moth′er coun try, m. queen, m. tongue, Moth′er Hub·bard.

mŏ′tif (*or* -tēf′), -tĭf′ic.

mŏ′tĭle, -til′i ty.

mŏ′tion, -al, -less, -ing, -tioned, mŏ′tion-bar, -dis tor′tion, -in′ di ca tor.

mo′ti vate, -vā′ted, -vā′ting, -vā′ tion.

mŏ′tĭve, -less, -less ness, -tĭv′i ty.

mŏt′ley, -mĭnd′ed.

mŏ′tō

mŏ′tŏ cy′cle (-sī′kl).

mŏ′to graph, -graph′ic, -to phone.

mŏ′tor, -to′ri al, -*ri um,* pl. -*ri a,* -to ry, mŏ′tor-car, m. ā′re a, m. point.

motte (mŏt).

mot′tle, -tled, -tling, mot′tle faced.

mot′to, *pl.* -toes *or* -tos, -tŏed, mot′to-kiss.

mou chard′ (mōō′shär′).

mou′choir′ (mōō′shwŏr′).

mouil la′tion (mōōl yä′shun), *mouil′ lĕ′* (mōōl′yä′).

mou lin′ (mōō lâṅ′).

mou′lin age (mōō′-).

mou′li net (mōō′-).

Mou lins′ (mōō′lâṅ′), t. Fr.

Moul′trie (mōl′try), fort S. C.;— (mōō′try *or* mōōl′-), Amer. Rev. gen.;—(mōō′try *or* mōl′try), co. Ill.

mound, -ed, -ing, mound′-bird, -bŭild′er, -māk′er.

Mou nier′ (mōō nyä′), Fr. states man.

mount, -a ble, -ed, -er, -ing, -ing ly, -ant, mount′-nee dle work, mount′ing-block, -stand.

moun′tain, -tained, -tain eer′, -ous, -ous ness, -ward.

moun′tain-ar til′ler y, -ash, -ăv′ ens, -balm, -beau ty, -bea ver, -black bird, -blue, -bram ble, -cat, -chain, -cock, -cork, -cow slip, -crab, -cran ber ry,

-cross, -cu ras′sōw, -dam son, -deer, -dew, -eb o ny, -fern, -fe ver, -finch, -flax, -fringe, -grape, -green, -guä′va.

moun′tain-hare, -her ring, -hol ly, -how itz er, -lau rel, -lĕath er, -lic o rice, -lin net, -li on, -lov er, -mag no li a, -ma hoe, -ma hog a ny, -man, -maṇ go, -ma ple, -meal, -milk, -mint, -pars ley, -pep per, -pine, -plum, -pride, -rhu barb, -rice, -rose, -sand wort, -sheep, -soap, -sor rel, -spăr row, -spin ach (-āj), -sweet, -tal low, -tea, -to bac co, -trout, -witch, -wood.

mount′e baṇk, -ing, -ish, -ism, -er y.

mŏurn, -er, -ful, -ful ly, -ful ness, -ing, -ing ly, mŏurn′ful-wid ow, a plant, mŏurn′ing-bride, a plant, -dove, -piece, -wid ow, a plant.

mŏurn′ing brŏoch, m. cloak, m. coach, m. liv er y, m. ring, m. stuff.

mouse, *pl.* mice, mouse (mouz), *v.,* moused, mous′ing, -er, -er y, -y, mouse′fish, tail, a plant.

mouse′-bar ley, -bird, -bur, -but tock, -chop, -col or, -col ored, -deer, -dun, -ear, -grăss, -hawk, -hole, -hound, -hunt, -le mur, -mill, -owl, -pea, -piece, -roll er, -sight, -thorn, -trap, mouse′tail-grăss, mous′ ing-hook (mouz′-).

mous que taire′ (mōōs′ke târ′), a collar; a glove; a cloak; a musketeer

mous se line′ (mōō′sĕ lēn′), *-de laine′* (-dĕ-lān′), *-de-soie′* (-dĕ swŏ′).

mouth, *n.,* -ful, -less, -piece, -root, mouth′-arm, -blow er, -case, -fill ing, -foot, -foot ed, -friend, -gage, -glăss, -glue, -hon or, -made, -or gan, -part, -pipe, -ring, -spec u lum.

mouth, *v.,* -er, -ing, -a ble, mouthed, mouth′ing-ma chine.

mou ton′ (mōō-).

mou′zah (mōō′-).

move (mōōv), -less, -ment, mov'-
a ble, -ble ness, -bly, -bil'i ty,
-er, -ing, -ing ly, -ing ness,
move'ment-cure, mov'ing-plant.
mŏw, to cut grass, -er, -ing,
mōwed, mōwn, mōw'-lot, mōw'-
ing-ma chine.
mow (mou), to store in a barn,
-er, -ing, mowed, mow'burn,
-yard.
mŏw, *n.*, a grimace, mŏw, *v.*, to
make faces, mōw'ing.
mow (mou *or* mōō), a Chinese
land-measure.
mox'a, mox i bus'tion (-chun).
moy'a.
Mo zam bique' (-bēk'), Afr.,
-zam bi'can (-bē'kan).
Mo zart' (*or* mŏ'-), Ger. mus.
composer.
mo zet'ta (*or* -tsĕt'ta).
much, -ness.
mŭ'cid, -ness.
mŭ'ci lage, -lag'i nous (-laj'-),
-nous ness, -cig'e nous (-sĭj'-),
mŭ'ci lage-bot tle, -brush, -ca-
nal', -cell, -res'er voir, -slit.
mŭ cip'a rous.
mŭ'ci vore, -civ'o rous.
muck, -er, -ing, -y, -i ness,
mucked, muck'worm, a person.
muck'-bar, -fork, -heap, -hill,
-pit, -rake, -rolls, -swĕat,
-thrift, -worm, a worm.
muc'kle, -ham mer.
mŭ'cus, *n.*, -cous, *a.*, -cous ness,
-cose, -cos'i ty.
mud, -dy, -di er, -di est, -di ly,
-di ness, -dĭed, -dy ing, mud'-
fish, -sill, -stone, -weed, -wort.
mud'-bank, -bằss, -bằth, -bit,
-boat, -bur'row er, -cat, -cock,
-cone, -coot, -crab, -daub er,
-dev il, -dip per, -drag, -dredg-
er, -drum, -eel, -flat, -frog,
-goose, -hen, -hole, -hook, -laff,
-lam prey, -lark, -lä'va, -min-
now, -pat tens, -plan tain,
-plov er, -plug, -pup py, -rake,
-scow, -shad, -snail, -snipe,
-suck er, -swal low, -teal, -ter ra-
pin, -tor toise, -tur tle, -valve, -vol-
ca no, -walled, -wasp, -worm.

mu ez'zin.
muff, -ing, -et, muffed, muff'-
dog, -glăss.
muf'fin, -eer', muf'fin-cap, -man,
-ring.
muf'fle, -fled, -fler, -fling, muf'-
fle jaw, a fish, -fur nace, -paint-
ing.
muf'tĭ, Moham. officer, *pl.* -tĭs
(-tĭz).
muf'ty, a bird.
mug, -weed, -wort, -wump, -house,
-hunt'er.
mu'ga (mōō'-).
mug'gar, a crocodile.
mug'gard, *a.*, sullen.
mug'gins.
mug'gy.
Mühl'bach (mül'bäch), t. Hung.;
Ger. novelist.
Muh'len berg (mū'len-), Amer.
divine.
Mühl hau'sen (mül hou'zn), t.
Prus.
Muil rea' (mŭl'rā'), mt. Ireland.
Mŭir, Scot. auth.
muk'luk.
mu lat'to, -lat'tress.
mul'ber ry, -faced, -germ, -juice,
-măss, -rash, -silk worm, -tree.
mulch, -ing, mulched.
mulct, -ed, -ing, mulc'tà ry *or*
-tu â'ry.
mule, mu le teer', mŭl'ish, -ish-
ly, -ish ness, mule'kill er, an
insect, -wort.
mule'-ar ma dil'lo, -chair, -deer,
-doub ler, -drĭv er, -jen ny, -skin-
ner, -spin ner, -twist.
mu'ley (mū'-), -ax le, -head,
-saw.
mŭ'li er, -li eb'ri ty.
mŭll, -ing, -er, mŭlled, mull'-
head, -mad der, -mus lin.
mul'lein (-lĕn *or* -lĭn), -pink,
-shark.
Mül ler' (mü'ler'), Fr. painter;—
(mü'ler), Ger. schol.
mul'let, -hawk, -smelt, suck er.
mul'li ga taw'ny.
mul'li grubs.
mul'lion, -ing, -lioned.
mulse.

---

fāte, făt, fär, fạll, fâre, fặst, sofả, mēte, mĕt, hêr, īce, ĭn, nōte,

mulsh.
mult.
mul tan′gu lar, -ly, -ness.
mul ti den′tate, -ti dig′i tate (-dǐj′),
  -ti faced,   -ti fa′ri ous,   -ous ly,
  -ous ness, -tif′er ous, -ti flō′rous.
mul′ti form, -form′i ty,   -ti lat′-
  er al,   -ti lin′e al,   -lin′e ar,   -ti-
  lō′bate,   -til′o quence,   -o quence,
  -ti par′tīte,   -tip′a rous,   -ti ped,
  -ti ple.
mul′ti ply,   -ing,   -ti pli′a ble,
  -ble ness,   -pli ca ble,   -pli cand′,
  -pli cate,   -ca′tive,   -ca′tor,   -cā′-
  tion, -pli er,   -ti plic′i ty.
mul′ti ply ing-lens,   -ma chine,
  -wheel.
mul ti pō′lar, -ti pres′ent,   -pres′-
  ence,   -ti spī′ral.
mul′ti tude, -tū′di nous, -nous ly,
  -nous ness,   -tiv′a lent,   -a lence,
  -ti valve,   -val′vu lar.
mum.
mum′ble,   -bled,   -bler,   -bling,
  -bling ly, mum′ble-the-peg.
mum′bo-jum′bo.
mum′mer, -y, mum′ming.
mum′my,   -mi fy,   -fy ing,   -fied,
  -mi form,   -mi fi cā′tion,   -my-
  ing,   -mĭed,   mum′my-case,
  -cloth, -wheat.
mump, -ish, -ish ly, -ish ness.
mumps.
munch, -er, -ing, munched.
Mǔn chau′sen   (-chạw′zen   *or*
  münch′ou zen), Ger. soldier.
mun′dane, -ly, -dan′i ty.
mun′di fy,   -fi er,   -fied,   -dif′i-
  cant, -i cā′tion.
Mundt (moͦont), Ger. auth.
Mū′nich (-nich), c. Bav.
mu nic′i pal (-nis′-), -ly, -ize, -ized,
  -i′zing, -ism, -pal i zā′tion, -pal′-
  i ty.
mu nif′i cent, -ly, -cence, -cen cy.
mu′ni ment, -house, -room.
mu ni′tion (-nĭsh′un).
Mun kacs′ (moͦon′käch′), t. Hung.
Mun kac′sy (moͦon kä′chē), Hung.
  painter.
mun′nion (-yŭn).
Müntz (münts), Fr. art hist.
mū′ral, -ly, -rǎled, -rage.

Mü rǎt′ (*or* mü′rä′), Fr. marshal.
Mur′chi son (-kǐ son), Brit. geol.
Mur′ci a (-shǐ a), prov. Sp.
mur′der, -er, -ing, -ous, -ous ly.
mū′ri ate, -a ted, -a ting, -at′ic.
mu′ri cate, -cā′ted.
Mū ril′lō   (*or*   moͦo rēl′yō),   Sp.
  painter.
murk, -y, -i ly, -i ness.
mur′mur, -er, -ing, -ing ly, -ous,
  -ous ly, -mured.
mǔr′raĭn.
mǔr′rey.
mur′shid (moͦor′shēd).
mu ru′mu ru-pǎlm   (moͦo roͦo′-
  moͦo roͦo-päm).
mus ca din′ (moͦos ka dǎn′), a fop.
mus′ca dǐne, a grape.
mus′cat.
mus′ca tel.
mus′cle, -cled, -cling (-ling), -cu-
  lar,   -lar ly,   -lǎr′i ty,   -lar ize,
  -ized, -i zing, -cu lous, *a.*, mus′-
  cle bill, a duck.
mus′cle-band,   -case,   -cas′ket,
  -cell,   -clot,   -col umn,   -com-
  part ment,   -cor′pus cle,   -cur-
  rent,   -nu cle us,   -plasm,   -plate,
  -plum,   -prism,   -rēad′ing,   -rod,
  -se rum, -sound, -su gar.
mus col′o gy,   -o gist,   -co log′-
  ic al, -cos′i ty.
mus co vā′do.
Mus′co vīte, a Russian, -vǐt′ic,
  mus′co vīte, a mineral; a rat.
muse (mūz), -ful, -ful ly, -less,
  mused,   mǔs′er,   -ing.   Muse,
  Myth.
mu sette′ (-zět′).
mu se′um   (-zē′-),   -se og′ra pher,
  -ra phist,   -ra phy,   -se ol′o gy,
  -o gist.
mush, -ing, -y, -i ness, mushed.
Mū′shǐ, *Bib.*
Mū′shītes, *Bib.*
mush′room,   -hitch es,   -spawn,
  -stone, -strain er, -su gar.
mush′ru (-roͦo).
mū′sic (-zǐk), -al, -al ly, -al ness,
  -si cal′i ty,   *mu si cale*   (mū′zǐ′-
  käl′),   -si cian (-zǐsh′an),   -si co-
  dra mat′ic,   -si cog′ra phy,   -co-
  mā′ni a.

---

nŏt, nôr, ūse, ŭp, ûrn, etüde, foͦod, foͦot, aŋger, boɴmot, th͡us, Bac͡h.

mu'sic-book, -box, -cab'i net,
-case, -chair, -clamp, -club,
-de my' (-mĭ'), -desk, -en-
grăv'er, -fol io, -hall, -hold er,
-house, -loft, -mad, -măs ter,
-mis tress, -pa per, -pen, -print-
ing, -rack, -re cord er, -roll,
-school, -shell, -smith, -stand,
-stool, -type, -wire, -wrĭt'er.
musk, -y, -i ness, musk'flow'er,
-mal low, -mel on, -rat, -root,
a plant, -wood, a tree.
musk'-bag, -ball, -bea ver, -bee-
tle, -cake, -cat, -cat tle, -ca vy,
-deer, -duck, -gland, -hy a-
cinth, -mole, -o kra, -or chis,
-ox, -peâr, -plant, -plum, -root,
a root, -rose, -seed, -sheep,
-shrew, -this tle, -tor toise, -tree,
-tur tle, -wea sel, musk'y-mole.
mus'kal longe. See maskinonge.
mus'keg.
mus'ket, -eer', -oon', -ry, mus'-
ket-lock, -proof, -rest, -shot.
mus'lin (mŭz'-), -lĭned, -lin et',
mus'lin-glâss, -kale, -de-laine.
mus'nud.
mus'role (mŭz'-).
muss, -ing, -y, -i ness, mussed.
mus sạl', a torch, -sạl'chee.
mus'sel, a mollusk, mus'sel-band,
-bed, -bĭnd, -dig ger, -duck,
-eat er, -peck er, -shell.
Mus set' (mü'sā'), Fr. poet.
mus'suck.
Mus'sul man, pl. -mans, -man ish,
-man ism, -man ly, -man'ic.
must, -y, -i ly, -i ness.
mus tâche', pl. -tâch es (-ĕz),
-tached', -tach'ial (-yal), mus-
tache'-cup.
mus'tang, -er.
Mŭs'tä phä, t. Algiers.
mus'tard (-têrd), -tard er, mus'-
tard-leaf, -pa per, -pot, -seed,
-shrub, -spoon, -to ken, m.
plas ter, m. pōul tĭce.
mus'ter, -ing, -tered, mus'ter-
book, -day, -file, -măs ter, -roll.
mū'ta ble, -ness, -bly, -bil'i ty.
mū'tage.
mū'tate, -tā'ted, -tā'ting, -tā-
tive, -ta to'ry, -tant, -tā'tion,

mu tan'dum, pl. -da, mū tā'-
tion-stop.
mu tā'tis mu tan'dis.
mute, -ly, -ness, mūt'ism.
mū'ti late, -lā'ted, -lā'ting, -lā'-
tor, -lā'tion.
mū'ti ny, -ing, -nĭed, -ti neer',
-ti nous, -nous ly, -nous ness.
mu'to scope.
Mut'su hi'to (mōŏt's͞oŏ hē'tō),
Emperor of Japan.
mut'ter, -er, -ing, -ing ly, -tered.
mut'ton (-tn), -y, mut'ton head,
a person.
mut'ton-bird, -chop, -fish, -fist,
-ham, -head ed, -leg ger,
-thump er.
mū'tu al, -ism, -ist, -is tic, -al ly,
-al'i ty.
mu zhik' (mōō-).
Mu zi a'no (mōōt sē ä'nō), It.
painter.
muz'zle, -zled, -zling.
muz'zle-bag, -cap, -en er gy,
-lash ing, -load er, -sight,
-strap, -ve loc'i ty.
muz'zy, -zi ness.
My ce'næ (mī sē'nē), c. Gr.
my col'o gy, -o gist, -co log'ic,
-ic al, -al ly, -coph'a gy, -a gist.
my co'sis (mī-), -cŏt'ic.
my ol'o gy (mī-), -o gist, -o log'-
ic, -ic al.
my'o man cy (mī'-), -man'tic.
my ŏ'pi a (mī-), -op'ic, my'ope
(mī'-).
my'o scope (mī'-), -o tome, -o-
tom'ic, -o ton'ic, -ot'o my.
myr'i ad (mĭr'-), -mĭnd'ed.
myr'i a gram (mĭr'-) or -gramme,
-a li ter or -li tre (-lē'ter), -a-
me'ter or -tre.
myr'i a pod, -i ap'o dan, -o dous.
myr'i arch (mĭr'i ark), -i âre.
myr'i o rä'ma (mĭr'-), -o scope.
Myr'mĭ don, a follower of Achil-
les, -dŏ'ni an, myr'mĭ don, an
unscrupulous follower.
myrrh (mêr), myr'rhic (mĭr'rĭk),
-rhine (-rĭn), myrrh'y (mêr'-),
myrrh'-oil, -plas ter, -seed.
myr'tle, -ber'ry, -bird, -green,
-wax.

myr'tŏl, an oil.
my self' (mī-).
My'si a (mĭsh'i a *or* mĭzh'-), *Bib.*
My sŏre' (mī-), state India.
mys'ter y, -te'ri ous, -ous ly, -ous ness.
mys'tic, -tic al, -al ly, -al ness, -ti cism, -ti fy, -fy ing, -fīed, -fĭ cā'tor, -cā'tion.
myth, -ic, -ic al, -al ly, -ist,

my thog'ra pher, -ra phy, myth'-his to ry.
my thol'o gy (mĭ-), -o ger, myth'o lō'gi an, -log'ic, -ic al, -al ly, -thol'o gist, -o gize, -gized, -gī'zer, -gi zing.
myth o pe'ic, -pe'ist, -o plasm.
Mzc zo'now (mshā zō'nŏv), t. Russ.
Mzensk (mtsĕnsk), t. Russ.

N

N-way, N pa per.
Nă'am, *Bib.*
Nă'a mah, *Bib.*
Nă'a măn, *Bib.*
Nă ash'on (*or* nā'à shon), *Bib.*
Nă ăs'son, *Bib.*
nab, -bing, nabbed.
Năb'a the'ans, *Bib.*
Nă'bath ītes, *Bib.*
nă'bob.
nac'a rat.
Nă'chor (-kor), *Bib.*
Nach'ti gal (năch'tē găl'), Ger. trav.
nack'et.
Nac og do'ches (năk'ō dō'chĕz), co. Tex.
nă'cre (-kcr), *n.*, mother-of-pearl, nă'crĕ ous.
nac rḗ' (nă'krā'), *a.*
Nă dăb'a tha, *Bib.*
nă'dir, -ba'sin (-sn).
Na dud var' (nŏ'dō͞od'vär'), t. Hung.
nǽ'vus, pl. *-vī*, -void, -vose, -vous.
nag, -ger, -ging, nagged, nag'-tailed.
Nä gà sä'kĭ, c. Japan.
Nä'ge li (nä'gĕ lē), Ger. bot.
Năg'ge, *Bib.*
nă'gor.
Năg'pur' (-pō͞or'), div. Brit. India.
Nagy A bony (nŏdj ŏ'băn'), t. Hung.
Na hă'li el, *Bib.*
Na hăl'lal, *Bib.*

Nă'ha lŏl, *Bib.*
Na hăm'a nĭ (*or* nā'ha ma'ni), *Bib.*
Nă'iad (-yad), *Myth.; Bo . genus,* Nā'ia des (-ya dēz), nā'iad, a plant.
na'if (nä'ēf).
Naĭ hă'ti (-tē), t. Brit. India.
nä'ik.
năil, -er, -er y, -ing, nailed, nail'wort.
năil'-ball, -bone, -brush, -drĭv'er, -ex tract or, -fĭd dle, -file, -hammer, -head, -head ed, -ma-chine', -māk'er, -plate, -rod, -roll ing, -scis sors, -se lect or, nail'ing-ma chinc'.
nail'bourne (-bō͞orn).
năin'sō͞ ok.
na'īve (nä'ēv'), -ly, -ty, *na'īve'tē'* (nä'ēv'tä').
nă'kĕd, -ly, -ness, nă'kĕd wood, -eyed.
nam'by-pam'by.
name, named, nām'a ble, -er, -ing, name'less, -less ly, -less-ness, -ly, name'sake.
name'-board, -day, -fa ther, -plate, -saint, -son.
năm'măd.
nam'nism, -ni zā'tion.
Nä'nä Sä'hib, leader of Sepoy mutiny.
nan'cy-pret'ty (-prĭt'-), a plant.
nă'nism, na'noid, nā'nĭ zā'tion.
nan keen', -bird, -crane, -hawk.
nan'ny, -ber ry, -goat.

Nän'sen, Nor. explor.
Nantes (nănts), c. Fr.
Nant'wich (-Ich), t. Eng.
nap, -less, -per, -ping, -py, -pi-
ness, napped, nap'-me ter,
-warp, nap-at-noon, a plant,
nap'ping-ma chine.
Nä'pä, co. and c. Cal.
nāpe, nāped, nāp'ing, nāpe'-
crest.
nä'per y.
nä'pha-wa ter.
naph'tha (or nap'-), -lene, -lin,
-len'ic, -thal'ic, -thal'i dIne,
-tha lize, -lized, -li zing.
Nä'pĭ er, Brit. admiral; Brit. gen.;
Scot. inventor; tp. Pa.; t. N.
Zeal., Nä piē'ri an, Nä'pĭ er's
a nal'o gies, N. bones, N. rods.
nä'piēr-cloth.
nap'kin, -ring.
Nä'ples (-plz), tp. N. Y.; c. It.,
Ne ap'o lis, Nē a pŏl'i tan, pertaining to Naples.
Na pŏ'le on, Fr. gen., -on ist,
-on ism, -on'ic, Na pŏ'le on
blue, N. gun.
na pŏ'le on, a coin, -īte, a rock.
nappe (nap).
Nä'quet' (-kā'), Fr. polit.
N ǎr'ȧ kȧ.
Nar bonne' (-bŏn'), c. Fr.
nar cis'sus, -cis'sīne.
nar'co mä'ni a.
nar cot'ic, -al, -al ly, -al ness, -cŏ'-
sis, -co tize, -tized, -ti'zing,
-tism.
nard, nar'dĭne.
nâre, nä'ri al, nǎr'i corn, -i form.
Nâres, Eng. explor.; Eng. critic.
Nä'rew (-rĕv), r. Pol.
nǎr'ra.
nǎr rāte', -ra'ted, -ra ting, -ra'-
tion, -ra'tor, -to'ry, nǎr'ra tive,
-tive ly.
nǎr'rŏw, -er, -ing, -ing ly, -ly,
-ness, nǎr'rŏw-gāge, -mīnd'ed,
-mind ed ness, -souled, -work.
Na rus ze'vitch (nä rōō shĕ'vich),
Pol. hist.
Nar vä'ez (-ĕth), Sp. warrior; Sp.
statesman.
nar'whal.

nä'sal (-zăl), -ly, -sal'i ty (-zăl'-),
-sal ize, -ized, -i zing, -ĭ zä'tion,
na sol'o gy (-zŏl'-).
Nas'by, Petroleum V. (năz'by),
Amer. humorist.
nas'cent, -cen cy.
nase'ber ry (nāz'-), -bat.
Nase'by (nāz'-), battlefield Eng.
Nä'smyth (-smĭth), Scot. painter;
Brit. inventor.
nas tur'tion, a plant, Nas tur'ti-
um (-shI um), a genus of plants.
nâs'ty, -ti ly, -ti ness.
nä sute', -ness, -su'ti form.
Nä täl', Brit. col. Afr.; t. Braz.
nä'tal, -tal'i ty, -ta li'tial (-lIsh'-
al), -ta li'tious (-lIsh'us).
nä ta tŏ'ri um, pl. *-ums* or *-a*,
-to'ry, -tŏ'ri al.
Nätch'Ĭ tŏch'ĕs (or năk'Ĭ tŏsh'),
par. La.
Nä'tick, vil. Mass.
nä'tion, -al (năsh'un al), -al ly,
-al ism', -al ist', -al ize, -ized,
-ĭ'zer, -ĭ'zing, -Ĭ zä'tion, -al ness,
-al'i ty.
nä'tive, -ness, -tiv ism, -tiv ist,
-ti vis'tic, -tiv'i ty, nä'tive-born.
nat'ter jack, -toad.
nattes (nāts).
Nät'tur' (-tōōr'), t. Brit. India.
nät'ty, -ti ly, -ti ness, năt'ty-
box es.
nat'u ral, -ize, -ized, -ĭ'zing,
-Ĭ zä'tion, -al ist, -is'tic, -al ly,
-al ness, nat'u ral-born.
nä'ture, -tured, -tūr ism, -ist.
nä'ture-de i ty, -god, -myth,
-print, -print ing, -spir it,
-wor ship.
Nau'det' (nŏ'dā'), Fr. hist.
naught (nᾳwt).
naugh'ty, -ti ly, -ti ness.
nᾳu'ma chy (-ky).
Nau'männ (nou'-), Ger. composer.
nᾳu'se a (-shē a), -se ant, -se ate,
-a ted, -a ting, -a tive', -ä'tion,
nau'seous (-shŭs), -seous ly,
-seous ness.
Nᾳu sic'a a (nᾳw sĭk'ā ȧ), Homer
Odyssey.
nᾳutch, -girl.

---

fāte, făt, fär, fᾳll, fâre, fȧst, sofȧ, mēte, mĕt, hêr, īce, Ĭn, nōte,

nạu'tic al, -ly.
nạu'ti lus, *pl.* -lus es *or* -lī,
 nạu'ti lus-cup.
na vä'ja (-hå), a knife.
Nä'vä jo (-hō), *pl.* -joes (-hōz).
nä'val, -ly.
Nä vär'rä, prov. Sp.
Ná vär'rō, co. Tex.
nave, -box, -hold, -shaped.
nä'vel, -veled *or* -velled, nä'vel-
 wort.
nä'vel-gall, -hole, -hood, -hill.
Nä'vez' (-vä'), Belg. painter.
nav'i gate, -gā'ted, -gā'ting, -gȧ-
 ble, -ble ness, -bly, -bil'i ty,
 -gā'tor, -gā'tion, -tion al.
nä'vy, -a gent, -bill, -list, -reg-
 is ter, -yard.
nay.
Naz a rēne', -rēn'ism.
Naz'a rite, -ship, -rī tism, -rĭt'ic.
näze.
Näze, The, headland Eng.—
 (nä'zĕ), cape Norw.
na zir' (-zēr').
Nē æ'ra (-ē'ra), Virgil, a sweetheart.
nēap, nēaped.
Nē a pŏl'i tan. See *Naples.*
nĕaɪ, -ly, -ness, near'-by, -dwell-
 er, -hand, -point, -sight ed,
 -sight ed ness, n. horse, n.
 side.
neat, -ly, -ness, neat'-hand ed,
 -land, neat's-foot, -foot oil.
nĕat'herd, -herd ess.
neb.
nĕb'el.
nĕb'ris.
nĕb'u la, *pl.* -læ, -u lar, -lif'er-
 ous, -u list, -u lose, -u lous,
 -lous ness, -u lize, -lized, -lī'-
 zer, -lī'zing.
nec'es sa ry, -sa ri ly, -ri ness,
 -sä'ri an, -ri an ism.
ne ces'si tate, -tā'ted, -tā'ting,
 -ta'ri an, -an ism, -tā'tion, -si-
 tīed, -si tous, -tous ly, -tous-
 ness, -si ty.
neck, -ing, necked, neck'er chĭef,
 neck'laced, -let, -tie, -wear,
 -weed.
neck'-band, -bear ing, -beef,

-bone, -breäk, -cell, -chain,
-cloth, -guard, -hac kle, -hand-
ker chĭef, -mold, -mold ing,
-piece, -ring, -strap, -twine,
-yoke.
neck'lace, -moss, -pop lar,
-shaped, -tree.
nĕc rol'o gy (*or* nē crŏl'-), -o-
gist, -ro log'ic, -rol'a try.
nec'ro man cy, -man cer, -man-
cing, -man'tic, -man'tic al ly,
-ro pho'bi a, -roph'o rous, -rop'-
o lis (*or* nē crop'-), -ro sco'py,
-scop'ic, -ic al.
nec ro'sis (*or* nē cro'-), -rot'ic,
-rose, -rosed, -rot'o my, -ro-
tom'ic, -ro type, -typ'ic.
nec'tar, -tared, -ta rīed, -ta're al,
-re an, -re ous, -ous ly, -ous-
ness, -ri al, -tar if'er ous, -tar-
Ine, -tar ous, -ta ry, nec'tar-
bird, -gland, -guide.
née (nā).
need, -ed, -er, -ing, -ful, -ful ly,
-ful ness, -y, -i ly, -i ness, -less,
-less ly, needs, need'fire, need'-
be.
nee'dle, -dled, -dler, -dling, -dle-
ful, nee'dle man, -tail, a bird,
-wom an, -work.
nee'dle-an nun'ci a tor, -bar,
-beam, -bear er, -board, -book,
-bug, -car rĭ er, -case, -clerk,
-file, -fish, -for ceps, -gun,
-hold er, -hook, -house, -in-
stru ment, -loom, -māk ing,
-ore, -pa per ing, -point ed,
-set ter, -sharp en er, -shell,
-spar, -stone, -tel e graph,
-thrĕad er, -wov en, -wrap per,
-ze o lĭte, n. test.
ne'er (nâr), -do-good, -do-well.
neeze'wort.
nef.
ne fä'ri ous, -ly, -ness.
ne gä'tion, -ist, neg'a tive, -tive-
ly, -tive ness, -tive ism, -tived,
-tiv'ing, -tiv'i ty, ne gä'tor,
neg'a tive-bäth, -clåsp, -rack.
Neg ạu'nee, t. Mich.
neg lect', -ed, -ed ness, -er, -ing,
-ing ly, -a ble, -ful, -ful ly,
-ful ness.

neg'li gent, -ly, -gence, -gi ble,
-gi bly.
ne go'ti ate (-shĭ-), -ā'ted, -ā'-
ting, -ā'tor, -to'ry, -a ble, -a bil'-
i ty, -ant, -ā'tion.
nĕ'gro, -ism, -groid, -gress, Ne-
gri'to (nā grē'-), -gril lo (-grĕl'-
yō), ne'gro-bug, -fish, -head.
nĕ'gus, a mild punch, *Ne'gus,*
King of Abyssinia.
Neh tour' (nā towr'), t. Brit.
India.
neigh (nā), -ing, neighed.
neigh'bor (nā'-), -er, -ing, -ly,
-li ness, -hood, -bored.
Neil'son (nēl'-), Eng. actress.
Neis'se (nĭ'sĕ), r. and t. Ger.
nēi'ther (*or* nī'-).
Neï'thrŏp, t. Eng.
Ne'me an (*or* -mē'-).
Nem'e sis, *Myth.,* Ne mĕs'ic.
nem'o ral, -o rose (-rōs), -o rous.
Ne'nagh (nā'na), t. Ire.
nĕ'o cene.
ne o-Chris'tian, -Chris ti an'i ty,
-Kan'ti an, -Lat'in.
Nĕ'ŏ dĕ shä', c. Kan.
Ne o grad' (nā'ō grät'), co. Hung.
ne ol'o gy, -o lō'gi an, -log'ic,
-ic al, -al ly, -ol'o gist, -o gism,
-o gis'tic, -tic al, -o gize, -gized,
-gī'zing.
ne on tol'o gy, -o gist.
nĕ'o nym, -on'y my.
ne o pa'gan ize, -ized, -ī'zing,
-ism.
ne o pho'bi a.
ne'o phyte, -phyt ism (-fīt-).
ne o tĕr'ic, -al, -ot'er ism, -er ist,
-is'tic, -er ize, -ized, -ī'zing.
Ne pal' (nā päl'), king. India.
nĕ pĕn'thĕ, -thes (-thēz).
neph'a lism, -a list.
Neph'e lŏ'cŏc cyg'i a (-kŏk sĭj'-
ĭ a), a town built in the clouds.
neph'ew (nĕf'ū *or* nĕv'-).
Nĕph'in, mt. Ireland.
neph'o graph, -o gram.
ne phol'o gy, neph o log'ic al, -o-
scope.
neph rit'ic (*or* ne frĭt'-), -al,
-ri'tis, -rol'o gy, -o gist, -rol'y sis.
nē plus ul'tra.

nep'o tism, -o tist, -o tal, ne-
pot'ic, -pō'tious.
Nep'tune, *Myth.,* -tu nist, -tu'-
ni an.
Né rac' (nä'räk'), t. Fr.
Ner'cha, r. Sib.
Nĕ'rĕ id.
Ner is'sa, Shak. *Merchant of
Venice.*
ne rit'ic, -rit'id, nĕr'i toid.
nerve, -less, -less ness, nerved,
nerv'al, -ate, -a ture, -ĭne, -ing,
-ous, -ous ly, -ous ness, -ure,
-y, ner vā'tion, -vose', -vos'i ty.
nerve'-au ra, -broach, -ca nal',
-cap ping, -cell, -cen ter, -col-
lar, -cord, -cor pus cle, -drill,
-end ing, -fi ber, -force, -hill,
-mo tion, -nee dle, -paste,
-päth, -pen'ta gon, -plate,
-ring, -shak en, -storm, -stretch-
ing, -sub stance, -tire, -tis sue,
-track, -tube, -tuft, -tu nic,
-twig, -wave, -winged.
nes'cience (nĕsh'-), -cient, -cious.
Nĕs quē hŏ'ning, t. Pa.
nest, -ed, -er, -ful, -ing, -ler,
-ling, nest'-egg, -pan, -spring.
nes'tle (-l), -tled, -tling.
Nes'tor, -to'ri an, -an ism, nes'-
tor Ine.
net, -ted, -ter, -ting, -ty, net'-
work.
net'-berth, -braid er, -fern, -fish,
-fish er man, -fish er y, -fish-
ing, -loom, -mack er el, -māk'er,
-ma son ry, -mend er, -veined,
-winged, n. struc'ture, net'ted-
car pet, a moth, -veined, net'-
ting-ma chine, -nee dle.
neth'er, -most, -ward, -formed,
-vert.
Neth'er lands, Holland, -land er,
-land ish.
net'su ke (-kā).
net'tle, -tled, -tler, -tling, net'-
tle wort.
net'tle-bird, -blight, -but'ter fly,
-cell, -cloth, -creep er, -fe ver,
-fish, -ge ra'ni um, -leaf, -mon-
ger, -rash, -springe, -stuff, -tap,
-thread, -tree.
Neu'burg (noi'bŏŏrg), t. Ger.

Neu cha tel' *or* Neuf cha tel'
(nê shä tĕl'), t. Switz.
Neu'mann (noi'-), Ger. orient.;
Ger. math.
neûme, neū mat'ic, neū'mic.
Ne u'quen (nä ōō'kĕn), Arg. Rep.
neû'ral, -ist, -ral'gi a, -gic, -gi-
form.
neū ras'thē nĭ a, -then'ic, -ic al ly.
neū rec'ta sy, *-ta sis,* -to my.
neū re'mi a, -re'mic.
neū rĭ'tis, -rĭt'ic, neū'ric, -ric'i ty.
Neu'ro de (noi'rō'dĕ), t. Prus.
neū rog'ra phy -rol'o gy, -o gist,
-ro log'ic al.
neū rop'a thy, -ro path'ic, -ic al,
-al ly, -path o log'ic al, -pa-
thol'o gist, -o gy, -ro phys'i o-
log'ic al, -ol'o gy, neū rot'ic,
-rot'o my.
Neu'satz (noi'säts), t. Hung.
Neuse (nūs), r. N. C.
Neuss (noiss), t. Prus.
Neûs'tri an.
neū'ter, -tral, -tral ly, -tral ist,
-tral ize, -ized, -ĭ'zer, -ĭ'zing,
-tral'i ty, -ĭ zā'tion.
Neu'ville' (nê'vĕl'), Fr. painter.
Neu'wied (noi'vēt), t. Prus.
Ne'va (nä'và *or* nē'-), r. Russ.
Ne vä'da, state U. S.; co. Ark.;
co. Cal.; t. Ia.; c. Mo.
Nève (näv), Belg. orient.
né vé' (nä'vä').
nev'er, -more, -the less'.
Ne vers' (nĕ vâr'), c. Fr.
Nĕv'is, Leeward isl., Brit. W. I.
new (nū), -ish, -ly, -ness, new'-
com er, -fan gle, -gled, -gled-
ness.
new'-born, -come, -cre'ate, -fash-
ion, -fash ioned, -fledged, -mod-
el, *v.,* -sad.
New-En gland er, N.-light, N.-
Mex i can, N.-year, N.-York er.
New'found land (nū'fund land'),
isl. Brit. Amer., -er.
New mar'ket, t. Eng.; a coat,
New' Mar'ket, t. N. H., new'-
mar'ket, a game of cards.
news (nūz), -less, -boy, -man,
-mon ger, -pa per, -pa per dom,
-room, -y.

news'-a gent, -house, -ink, -pam-
phlet, -stand, -vend er, -writ'er,
-yacht, news'pa per-clamp, -file.
next, -ness, -ways.
nex'us.
Ney (nä), Marshal of Fr.
Nĕzh'in (-ēn), t. Russ.
Nez Per ces' (nä pĕr'sä'), co. Ida.
Ngä'mi (-mē), l. Afr.
Ngän'hwei' (-hwī'), prov. China.
Nĭ ăg'a ra, r. and Falls; co.
N. Y.
nib, -bing, nibbed.
nib'ble, -bled, -bler, -bling,
-bling ly.
Nĭ'bel ung (nē'bĕl ŏong), Myth.,
-ung'en lied' (-lēt').
nib'lick.
ni'bu (nē'bōō).
NĬ căn'der, Swed. poet.
Ni că ră'guạ (nē-), rep. Cent.
Amer., -guan.
Nic co li'ni (nĕk kō lē'nē), It.
poet.
Nice (nēs), c. Fr.
nice, -ly, -ness, ni'cer y, -ce ty.
Nĭ'cene.
nĭche.
nĭck, -ing, nicked, nick'name,
-named, Nick, Satan.
nick'-eared, -stick, nick'ing-file,
-saw.
nick'ĕl, -ĕled *or* -ĕlled, -ĕl ing *or*
-ling, -age, -Ine, -ize, -ized,
-ĭ'zing, -ous.
nick'ĕl-bloom, -glance, -green,
-o cher, -plāt ed, -plāt ing,
-sil ver.
nick'er, -ing, -ered, nick'er-nuts,
-peck er, -tree.
Nĭ'co lai (nē'kō lī), Ger. auth.;
Ger. composer.
Nic o lä'i tan.
Ni cole' (nē'kōl'), Molière's comedy.
Nic o let' (nĭk'ō'lä'), co. Que.
Nic'ol let (nĭk'-), co. Minn.
nic'o lo.
Nĭ'cot' (nē'kō'), Fr. schol.
nic'o tine, -o tĭned, -tin ism, -tin-
ize, -ized, -ĭ'zing, -tī'na.
nic'tate, -tā'ted, -tā'ting, -tā'tion.
nidge, nidged, nidg'ing.
Nid'högg (nēd'hêg), *Myth.*

---

nŏt, nôr, ūse, ŭp, ûrn, etüde, fōōd, fŏŏt, aṇger, boṅmot, thus, Bach.

nid′i fi cate, -cā′ted, -cā′ting,
-cant, -cā′tion, nid′i fy, -ing,
-fīed, nid′u late, -lā′ted, -lā′-
ting, -la′tion.
nid′nod, -ded, -ding.
ni dol′o gy, -o gist.
nī′dor, -ose, -ous, -do ros′i ty,
nī′dose.
Nie′buhr (nē′bōͦr), Ger. philol.;
Ger. trav.
niece (nēs).
Ni el′ (nē ĕl′), Marshal of Fr.
nĭ el′lo, -el′lure, nĭ el′lo-work.
Niem ce′wicz (nyĕm tsĕ′vĭch), Pol.
auth.
Ni e′mes (nē ā′mĕs), t. Aust.
Ni epce′ (nē ĕps′), Fr. chem.
Niēr′steīn er.
Nieu′we-Diep (nyü′vĕ-dēp), vil.
Holland.
Nieuw′poort (nyüv′pōrt), t. Belg.
Ni′evre′ (nē′āvr′ or nyāvr), dept.
Fr.
niff′naff y.
Nifl′heim, *Myth.*
nig′gard, -ly, -li ness, -ness.
nig′ger, -dom, -ish, -ling, -hair,
a plant, -head, a rock; tobacco;
nig′ger-chub, -fish, -goose, -head,
a mussel, -kill er.
nig′gle, -gled, -gler, -gling.
nigh (nī).
night (nīt), -ed, -ish, -less, -ly,
-y, night′churr, -clothes, -fall,
-flow er, -gown, -jar, -mare,
-shade, -shirt, -ward.
night′-ape, -bat, -bell, -bird,
-blind ness, -bloom ing, -bolt,
-born, -brawl er, -breeze, -but-
ter fly, -cart, -chair, -charm,
-cloud, -com er, -crow, -dew,
-doc tor, -dog, -dress, -eyed,
-far ing, -feed er, -fire, -fish,
-fish er y, -fli er, -fly, -foe,
-foun′dered, -glåss, -hawk,
-her on, -house, -key, -lamp,
-latch, -light, -line, -līn er,
-long.
night′-mag′is trate, -man, -mon-
key, -moth, -owl, -pal sy, -par-
rot, -par tridge, -peck, -piece,
-por ter, -ra ven, -robe, -school,
-sea son, -shoot, -side, -sight,

-sing er, -soil, -spar row, -spell,
-steed, -stool, -swal low, -swĕat,
-ta per, -ter rors, -time, -trip-
ping, -wāk′er, -walk, -walk er,
-wan der er, -war bling, -watch,
-watch er, -watch man, -witch,
-work, -yard.
night′in gale.
ni gres′cent, -cence.
Ni gri′ti a (-grĭsh′-), -gri′tian
(-grish′an), -grit′ic.
nĭ′hil, -ism, -ist, -is′tic, -hil′i ty.
Nij me′gen (nē mā′gĕn) or Nĭm-
e′guen (-ā′gĕn), t. Neth.
Nĭj′ni Nov gŏ′rŏd (or -rŏd′), c.
Russ.
Nĭj′ni tä ghilsk′ (-gĭlsk′), t. Russ.
Nĭ′ke, *Myth.*
Ni ki tine′ (nē kĕ tēn′), Russ.
auth.
nĭl des per an′dum.
Nile, r. Egypt, Nĭ′lo scope, -lom′-
e ter, -lot′ic.
Nĭls′son, Swed. singer; Swed.
naturalist.
nim′ble, -ness, -bly, nim′ble-fiṇ-
gered, -Will, a plant.
nim′bus, nimb, nimbed, nim-
bif′er ous.
Nimes or Nismes (nēm), t. Fr.
niṇ′com poop.
nine, -teen, -teenth, -ti eth, -ty,
nīnth, ninth′ly.
nine′bark, a plant, -pegs, -pence,
-pins, -eyed, -eyes, a fish,
-holes, a game, -kill′er, a bird,
-mur der, nine′ty-knot.
Nĭn′e veh, *Bib.*, -e vīte, -vĭt′ic al.
nĭn′ny, -ham′mer, ham′mer ing.
Ni non′ de L′En clos′ (nē′nŏn′
dê lŏṅ′klō′), Fr. adventuress.
Nĭ′o be, *Myth.*, -o bid, -o bīte,
-o bē′an.
ni ŏ′bi um, -ob′ic.
nĭ ŏ′po-snuff, -tree.
nip, -ping, -ping ly, -per, -py,
nipped, nip′cheese, a person.
Nĭp′ä ni′ (-nē′), t. Brit. India.
nippe (nĭp).
nip′per, -ing, -kin, -pered, nip′-
per-crab, -gäge, -men, nip′ping-
claws.
nip′ple, -less, -wort, -pled, -pling.

---

fāte, făt, fär, fạll, fâre, fåst, sofå, mēte, mĕt, hêr, īce, ĭn, nōte,

nip'ple-cac tus, -line, -piece, -pin, -seat, -shield, -wrench.
Nĭp pŏn' *or* Niph on' *or* Nip on', Japan.
nip'ter.
Nĭ'quée' (nē'kā'), romance of *Amadis de Gaul.*
Nir vä'na.
Nĭ'san *or* Nĭ'son, *Bib.*
nĭ'sĭ prĭ'us.
nis'try.
nĭ'sus, effort. Nĭ'sus, a genus of hawks.
nĭt, -ty, nit'-grȧss.
nĭ'ter, -tri a ry, nĭ'trĭde, nĭ'ter-bush, -cake.
nĭ'trate, -trā'ted, -tra tĭne, -trā'-tion.
nĭ'tri fy, -er, -ing, -fied, -fi'a ble, -fĭ cā'tion, nĭ'tric, -trĭne, -trīte, -trŏŭs.
nĭ'tro gen, gen'ic, trog'e nous (-trŏj'-), -e nize, -nized, -nĭ'zing.
nĭ'val, -ve ous.
Ni vose' (nē vōz').
nix, nix'ie.
nĭ zam'.
nō, *pl.* noes (nōz), no'how, -way, -ways, -where, -whĭth er, -wise, no'-ac count.
Nō'ah, *Bib.*, -ȧ'chi an (-kĭ-), -ach'ic (-ăk'-), Nō'ah's ark, N. bot tle, N. gourd.
No ailles' (nō'äl'), Fr. statesman.
nob'ble, -bled, -bler, -bling.
nŏb'by.
nō'ble, -bil'i tate, -tā'ted, -tā'ting, -tā'tion, -bil'i ty, -ble ness, -bly, no'ble man, -wom an, -end ing, -finch, -mīnd'ed.
nō'bod y.
Nō ce'tŏ (-chā'-), t. It.
Nō'ci (-chē), t. It.
nock, nock'ing-point.
noc tam'bu list, -bu lism, -bu-lā'tion.
noc'ti flō'rous.
noc tĭ lū'cent, -lu'cid, -tiv'a gant, -a gous, -tiv'a gā'tion.
noc'turn, -tur'nal, -nal ly, -tur'-no graph, -turne'.
nod, -ded, -der, -ding, -ding ly, -dy.
nod'dle, -dled, -dling.

nŏde, nōd'al, nŏd'ic al, nō dif'er-ous, nō'di form, nō'dōse (*or* -dose'), -dŏs'i ty.
nŏde'-cou ple, -cusp, -plane, -trip let, node'-and-flec'node, node'-and-spī'nŏde.
nŏd'ūle, -uled, -u lar, -u la'ri ous, -u lā'ted, -u lā'tion, nŏ'dus, pl. -dī, nod'u lus, pl. -lī, -u lōse.
Nō'el, Eng. divine.—(nō'ĕl'), Fr. grammarian.
nŏ ē mat'ic, -al, -al ly.
Nō'eux' (-ê'), vil. Fr.
nog, -ging, -ger, nogged.
Nō'gent' (-zhŏṅ'), t. Fr.
nog'gin.
noil, -yarn.
Noi re' (nwä rä'), Ger. philos.
noise, -less, -less ly, -less ness, noised, nois'ing, -y, -i ly, -i ness.
noi sette' (-zĕt' *or* nwŏ zĕt').
noi'some, -ly, -ness.
nō'lens vo'lens, nŏl'lē pros'e quĭ, nō'lō con ten'de re.
nom (nôṅ), *nom de guerre'* (nôṅ' dê gâr'), *nom' de plume'* (plüm').
nŏm'ad, -ism, -ize, -ized, -i zing, nō mad'ic, -ic al ly.
no'mä mä hay' (-hī').
nom'arch, -y.
nŏme.
nŏ'men clȧ ture, -tu ral, -clȧ'-tive, -clā'tor, -to'ry, -to'ri al.
nŏm'ic, customary, Nŏm'ic.
nŏm'i nal, -ism, -ist, -is'tic, -i nal ly.
nom'i nate, -nā'ted, -na ting, -nate ly, -nȧ tive', -tive ly, -na'-tor, -i nor, -i nee', -nā'tion.
nŏ mog'e ny (-mŏj'-), -e nist, -mog'ra phy, -ra pher, -mol'o-gy, -o gist, nom o log'ic al.
non-ac cept'ance, -ac quaint'ance, -ap pear'ance, -ap point'ment, -ar riv al, -at tend'ance, -at ten'-tion, -com mis'sioned, -com-mit'tal, -com ple'tion, -compli ance, -con cŭr'rence, -con-duct'ŏr, -con form'ist, -con-form'i ty, -con ta'gious, -con-trib'u to ry, -de liv'er y, -de vel'-op ment, -dis cov'er y, -e las'tic,

-es sen'tial, -ex ist'ence, -ful-
fil'ment, -im por ta'tion, -in-
hab'it ant, -in ter ven'tion, -ob-
serv'ance, -pay'ment, -per form'-
ance, -prep a ra'tion, -pres en-
ta'tion, -pro duc'tive, -pro-
fes'sion al, -pro fi'cien cy, -re-
cŭr'ring, -res'i dent, -re sist'-
ance, -so lu'tion, -so'nant,
-sub mis'sion, -sub mis'sive.
non'age, legal infancy, -aged.
nŏ'nage, one-ninth part.
nŏn'a ge nä'ri an, -a ges'i mal.
nŏn'a gon.
nŏnce, -word.
non'cha'länce' (-läns'), -cha länt',
-länt'ly.
*nŏn cŏm'pŏs mĕn'tis, non pŏs'sū-
mus, non prō seq'ui ter* (-sĕk'-
wĭ-).
nŏn'de script.
none (nŭn), -such.
nŏn en'ti ty.
nŏnes.
nŏ net', *nŏ net'to.*
non'i den'tist.
nŏ nĭl'lion.
non'ju ror, non'suit', non'suit'ed,
non fea'sance (-zans), non'plus,
non'plŭsed *or* -plussed, non'-
plus ing *or* -plus sing, non sub-
stan'tial ism, -tial ist.
nŏn pa reil' (-rĕl').
non'plus, -plused *or* plussed.
non'sense, -sen'si cal, -cal ly,
-cal ness, non'sense-vers'es.
nōō'dle, -dom, nōō'dle-soup
(-sōōp).
Noodt (nōt), Dutch jurist.
nōŏk, -y.
no ol'o gy, -o gist, -o log'ic al.
nōōn, -ing, -day, -flow'er, -stĕad,
-tide, -mark.
Noort, van (vän nōrt'), Flemish
painter.
noose, noosed, noos'ing.
Nor'den skjold (nôr'dĕn shêld),
Sw. explorer.
Nôrd'hŏff, Amer. auth.
nŏ'ri a.
norm, nor'ma, -mal, -mal ly,
-mal ize, -ized, -ī'zing, -ĭ zā'-
tion, -mal'i ty, ma tive.

Nor'man, -ize, -ized, -ī'zing,
-man dy.
Norn, *Myth.*
Norse, -man.
north, direction, north'most, -ness;
the North, a region; North-
Căr ō lĭn'i an.
norfh'er, -er ly, -li ness, -ern,
-ern er, -ern most, north'ing (*or*
norfh'-).
north east', -er, -er ly, -ern,
-ward, -ward ly, north-north-
east'.
North'man, *pl.* -men, -um'bri an.
north'ward, -ly, -wards, -west',
-west'er, -er ly, -west'ern, -ward,
-ward ly, the North west', north-
-north west'.
Nor'way, N. crow, N. ger'fal con,
N. had dock, N. lem ming, N.
lob ster, N. ma ple, N. spruce,
Nor we'gi an.
Nor'wich, c. Ct.; vil. N. Y.;—
(nor'rĭj), c. Eng.
nose (nōz), -less, nosed, nōs'ing,
-y, no sŏl'o gy, -o gist, nŏs'o-
log'ic al, nose'bleed, -burn, a
tree, -fish, -gay.
nose'-ape, -bag, -band, -bit,
-brain, -flute, -fly, -glăss es,
-hole, -horn, -key, -leaf, -led,
-or na ment, -piece, -pipe,
-ring, nose'gay-tree, nŏs'ing-
mo tion, -plane.
nos tal'gi a, -tal'gic, -tal'gy.
nos tol'o gy, -to log'ic.
nos'tril, -trĭled *or* -trilled.
nos'trum, *pl.* -trums.
nŏ'ta bĕ'ne.
nŏ'ta ble, -ness, -bly, -bil'i ty,
no'ta bil'i a.
No tä'li a, -li an.
no'ta ry, -ta'ri al, -al ly.
nŏ ta'tion.
notch, -ing, notched, notch'weed,
-wing, a moth.
notch'-block, -board, -eared,
notch'ing-adz, -ma chine'.
nŏte, -less, -less ness, -wor fhy,
-fhi ly, -fhi ness, nōt'ed, -ed-
ness, -ing, -er, note-book, -pa-
per.
noth'ing (nŭth'-), -ness.

---

fāte, făt, fär, fạll, fâre, fạst, sofà, mēte, mĕt, hêr, īce, ĭn, nōte,

nŏ'tĭce, -a ble, -a bly, -tĭced, -tĭ-
cing, -ti cer, nŏ'tice-board.
nŏ'ti fy, -ing, -fī a ble, -fīed,
-fī er, -fī cā'tion.
nŏ'tion, -al, -al ly.
nŏ tō'ri ous, -ous ly, -ous ness,
-rī'e ty.
not witħ stand'ing.
Noue, de la (dê lä nōō), Fr.
commander.
nou gat' (nōō'gä').
nou'ille (nōō'y), *pl.* -illes (nōō'y).
noŭr'ish, -a ble, -er, -ing, -ment,
-ished.
nou veau' riche (nōō vō' rēsh).
Nŏ vä kŏ'vitch, Servian polit.
Nŏ vä'lis, Ger. poet.
nŏv'el, -ist, -is'tic, -ism, -ize,
-ized, -ī'zing, -el ly, -el ty, -el-
ette'.
No vem'ber, -ish.
nŏ vēne', -*vē'na*, -věn'ni al, nŏv'-
e na ry.
no ver'cal.
nŏv'ĭce, -ship.
nŏ vi'ti ate (-vĭsh'-).
now, -a days.
nŏw'el.
nox'ious (nŏk'shŭs), -ly, -ness.
no yade' (nwŏ'yȧd').
noy'au' (nwŏ'yō').
Noyes, Amer. Bib. schol.; Amer.
communist.
noz'zle, -block, -clock, -mouth,
-plate.
nu'ance' (nōō'ŏns').
nub, -by, -bly.
Nū'bi a, Afr., -bi an, nu'bi a, a
garment.
nū'bĭle, -bil'i ty.
nū'bi lous.
nū'cle us, *pl.* -us es *or* -i, -cle ar,
-cle ate, -ā'ted, -ā'ting.
nude, -ly, -ness, nū'di ty.
nudge, nudged, nudg'ing.
Nue'ces (nwā'sĕs), r. and co.
Tex.
Nue'va Viz cay'a (nwā'vä vēth-
kī'ä), prov. Luzon Isl.
nū'ga to ry.
nug'gar.
nug'get, -y.
nūi'sance.

Nuit ter' (nwē'tä'), Fr. dramatist.
nŭll, -ing, null'-line.
nŭl'lah.
nul'la-nul'la.
nŭl'li fy, -ing, -fied, -fī er, -fī-
cā'tion, -li ty.
nul lip'a rous.
numb (nŭm), -ing, -ness, numbed
(nŭmd), numb'fish.
num'ber, -ing, -less, -bered,
Num'bers, *Bib.*, num'ber ing-
ma chine', -press, -stamp.
nū'mer al, -ly, -a ry, -a ble, -ant,
-ate, -ā'ted, -ā'ting, -ā'tor,
-a tive, -ā'tion.
nū'mer ous, -ly, -ness, -měr'ic,
-ic al, -al ly, -os'i ty.
nū'mis mat'ic (*or* -miz-), -al,
-al ly, -ics, -mis'ma tist, -ma-
tog'ra phy, -tol'o gy, -o gist.
num'ma ry, num'mu lar, -lȧ ry,
-mu lĭne, -lā'tion.
num'skull, -skulled.
num'ud.
nun, -ning, -ner y, -nish, -nish-
ness, nunned, nun'-bird, -buoy.
nun's'-cloth, -col lar, -cot ton,
-thread, -veil ing.
nunc, nunch.
Nunc Di mit'tis.
nun'cheon *or* -chion.
nun'ci ate (-shī-), -ci a ture, -ci o,
pl., -ci os, *nun'ci us* (-shī-).
nuṇ cu'pa tive (*or* nŭn'cu pā'-),
-pa to'ry.
nun'di nal, -di na ry.
Nu'nez (nōō'nĕs), Pres. Colombia.
Nu'nez (nōōn'yĕth), Sp. explor.
Nu'nez (nōō'nĕz), Port. math.
nun na'tion.
nup'tial, -ly, -tial'i ty.
nur, nur'-and-spell'.
nu rang' (nōō-).
nurl, -ing, nurl'ing-tool.
nurse, nursed, nurs'ing, -er, -er y,
-er y man, -ling.
nurse'-child, -frog, -hound,
-keep er, -maid, -name, -pond,
-shark, nur'ser y-maid, nurs'-
ing-bot tle, -lamp.
nur'ture, -tured, -tur ing.
nut, -let, -ted, -ter, -ty, -ti ness,
-ting, nut'breāk'er, a bird,

---

nŏt, nôr, ūse, ŭp, ûrn, etüde, fōōd, fŏŏt, aŋger, boñmot, ŧhus, Baĉh.

-cake, -crack er, a bird, -gall,
-grăss, -hack er, a bird, -hatch,
a bird, -job ber, a bird, -meal,
-peck er, a bird, -shell.
nut'-bone, -brown, -crack'er, a
tool, -fas ten ing, -hole, -hook,
-lock, -ma chine', -oil, -pick,
-pine, -plăn er, -roast er, -rush,
-sedge, -tap per, -top per, -tree,
-wee vil, -wrench, n. coal.
nut'meg, -gy, -megged.
nut'meg-bird, -but ter, -flow er,
-grăt'er, -hick o ry, -liv er,
-oil, -pi geon, -tree, -wood.

nŭ'tri ment, -men'tal, -tri ent,
-tri fy, -fy ing, -fied, -tri'tion
(-trĭsh'un), -tion al, -al ly, -tri'-
tious (-trĭsh'us), -ous ly, -ous-
ness, -trĭ tive, -tive ly, -tive-
ness, -to'ry, -tri tŏ'ri al.
nut'ta-tree.
nux vom'i ca.
nuz'zer.
nuz'zle, -zled, -zling.
Ny amtz' (nē ämts'), t. Roum.
Ny äs'sä (nē-), l. Afr.
nymph, -al, -ic, -ic al, -ish, -like,
nym pho'sis.

O

O, Oh, oh.
ŏaf, -ish, -ish ness.
O ä'hu (-hōō), Hawaii isl.
ŏak, -en, -ling, -y.
oak'-ap ple, -bark, -bar ren,
-beau ty, -bee tle, -chest'nut,
-feed ing, -fern, -fig, -frog,
-găll, -hook tip, -lap pet,
-lĕath er, -lungs, -o'pen ing,
-pa'per, -pest, -plum, -po ta'to,
-spaŋ'gle, -taŋ'gle, -tanned,
-tree, -wart, -web.
ŏak'um.
Oam'a ru' (wäm a rōō'), t. New
Zealand, -stone.
ŏar, -fish, -laps, -less, oared,
oars'man, -man ship.
ŏar'-foot'ed, -hole, -lock, -peg,
-port, -pro pel'ler, -swiv'el.
ŏ'a sis (*or* -ā'sis), *pl.* -ses (-sēz),
ō'a sal.
ŏast, -house.
ŏat, -en, oat'meal, ōat'-cake,
-flight, -fowl, -grăss, -malt,
-mill, -moth, ōat'seed-bird.
ŏath, *pl.* oaths (ōthz), oath'-
bound, -breăk ing, -rite.
Oa xa'ca (wä hä'kä), Mex.
ŏ bang'.
ob bli gä'tō. Less correctly, *ob li-
gä'to.*
ob'dū rate, -ly, -ness, -ra cy, -rā'-
tion.
O'bed-ē'dom, *Bib.*

o bĕ'dĭ ent, -ly, -ence.
O beid' (-bād'), t. Afr.
o bĕi'sance (*or* o bā'-).
ŏb'e lisk, -lis cal, -e lize, -lized,
-li zing.
ō'ber haus (-hous).
Ob'er on, *Myth.*
O'ber pfalz (-pfälts'), dist. Bav.
ŏ bese' (-bēs'), -ness, -bĕs'i ty.
ŏ bey' (-bā'), -er, -ing, -ing ly,
-beyed'.
ob fus'cate, -cā'ted, -cā'ting,
-cā'tion.
O'bi (ō'be), r. Sib.; *o'bĭ,* a sash;
ō'bĭ, sorcery, -wom'an.
ŏ'bit (*or* ŏb'-), ō bit'u al.
ŏb'i ter.
ŏ bit'u a ry, -à rist, -ā'ri ly.
ŏb'ject, *n.,* -less, ob'ject-find'er,
-glăss, -les'son, -soul, -stăff,
-teach'ing.
ob ject', *v.,* -ed, -ing, -or, -jec'-
tion, -tion à ble, -à bly, -jec'-
ti vate, -ti vā'tion, -tive, -tive ly,
-tive ness, -tiv ism, -tiv'i ty.
ob jure', -ju rā'tion.
ob jur'gate, -gā'ted, -gā'ting,
-ga to'ry, -gā'tion.
ob late', -ness, -lā'ted, -lā'ting,
-lā'tion, -tion al, -tion a ry.
ob'li gate, -gā'ted, -gā'ting, -gà-
tive, -tive ness, -gà ble, -gant,
-ga to'ry, -to'ri ly, -to'ri ness,
-gā'tion, -tion al.

ŏ blige', -ment, -bliged', -blī'-
ging, -ging ly, -ging ness, -blī'-
ger, ob li gor', -li gee' (-jē').
ob lique' (-lēk' or -līk'), -ly,
-ness, -liq'ui ty (-lĭk'wĭ ty), -lĭ-
quā'tion, ob lī'quus (-kwŭs),
pl. -quī, ob lique'-aŋ gled.
ob lit'er ate, -ā'ted, -ā'ting, -ȧ-
tive, -ā'tion.
ob liv'i on, -i ous, -ous ly, -ous-
ness.
ob'long, -ish, -ly, -ness, ob'loŋ-
gā'ta, ob'long-el lip'soid, -lan'-
ce o late, -o'vate.
ob'lo quy.
ob nox'ious (-nŏk'shŭs), -ly, -ness.
ŏ'bŏ ē, -bo ist.
ŏb'ol, a weight; a Greek coin,
pl. -ols or -o lī, -o la ry.
ŏb'ole, a Fr. coin.
ŏb'o lo, a copper coin.
ob'o lus, a coin; a weight; pl.
-lī.
ŏb ŏ'vate, -ly, -ŏ'val, -ŏ'void,
ob ŏ'vate-clā'vate, -cu'ne ate,
-ob'long.
ob scene', -ly, -ness, -scĕn'i ty.
ob scure', -ly, -ment, -ness,
-scūr'ant, -ant ism, -ant ist,
-scu ra'tion, -scu'ri ty, -scured',
-scūr'ing.
ob sē'qui ous, -ly, -ness, -qui-
ence.
ŏb'se quy, -sc'qui al.
ob serve' (-zerv'), -served', -serv'-
a ble, -a ble ness, -a bly, -ance,
-ant, -ant ly, -a tive, -a to'ry,
-er, -er ship, -ing, -ing ly, -ser-
vā'tion, -tion al, -al ly, ob-
ser vā'tion-car.
ob'so lete, -ly, -ness, -so lesce'
(-lĕs'), -les'cence, -les'cent,
-lĕt ism, -lē'tion.
ob'sta cle, -race.
ob stet'ric, -al, -rics, -rist, -rix,
-ste tri'cian (-trĭsh'an), -tri'-
cious (-trish'us).
ob'sti nate, -ly, -ness, -sti nā'cy.
ob strep'er ous, -ly, -ness.
ob struct', -ed, -er, -ing, -ive,
-ive ly, -ive ness, -or, -struc'-
tion, -tion ism, -tion ist, ob'-
stru ent.

ob tain', -ā ble, -er, -ing, -ment,
-tained'.
ob trude' (-trōōd'), -trud'ed, -ing,
-er, -tru'sive (-sĭv), -sive ly,
-sive ness, -sion (-zhŭn), -sion-
ist.
ob'tu rate, -rā'ted, -rā'ting, -ra'-
tor, -rā'tion.
ob tuse' (-tūs'), -ly, -ness, ob-
tuse'-aŋ'gled, -aŋ'gu lar, -el-
lip'soid.
ob verse', a., -ly, ob'verse, n.
ob vert', -ed, -ing, -ver'sion.
ob'vi ate, -a ted, -a ting, -ā'tion.
ob'vi ous, -ly, -ness.
ob'vo lūte, -lū'ted.
O'Cal'la ghan (-kăl'a hăn), Irish
hist.
oc ca'sion, -al, -al ism, -al ist,
-al ly, -er.
oc'ci dent, den'tal, -ly, -tals,
-tal ism, -tal ist, -tal ize, -ized,
-ī'zing, -tal'i ty.
oc cip'i tal, -tal ly.
oc cult', -ing, -ism, -ist, -ly,
-ness, -cul tā'tion.
oc'cu py, -ing, -cu pant, -pan cy,
-pā'tive, -cu pīed, -pi er, -pā'-
tion, -tion al.
oc cur', -rence, -rng, -curred'.
ŏ'cean (-shăn), -ce ăn'ic (-shē-),
o'ce an og'ra pher, -ra phy, -o-
graph'ic, -ic al, -al ly, -ol'o gy,
o'ccan-grey'hound.
O ce ä'na (or -ä'-), Utopia;—
(ŏ'shē ä'na), co. Mich.
O cē'a na, Harrington's model
commonwealth.
O ce ä'ni a (-shē-), a geographical division, -ăn'i an, -ăn'ī ca,
-i can.
o'ce lot.
ŏ'cher or ŏ'chre (ŏ'ker), -cher-
ous, -cher y, -cher ing, -chered.
O chĭ'el (-kĭ'- or ŏ'kĭ el), Bib.
Och'il tree, E'die (ŏk'il trē),
Scott The Antiquary.
och loc'ra cy (ok lŏk'-), -lo crat'ic,
-ic al.
O cī'na (or ŏs'i na), Bib.
o'clock.
Oc mul'gee (-ge), r. Ga.
O cŏ'nee, co. Ga.; co. S. C.

O'Cŏn'nor, Irish Chartist.
Oc'o nŏm'o wŏc, c. Wis.
O'Con'or, Amer. lawyer.
oc'ta chord.
oc'ta gon, -tag'o nal, -nal ly,
-tag'y nous (-tăj'-).
oc ta hē'dron, -he'dral, -he'drīte.
oc tam'e ter.
oc taṇ'gu lar, -ness.
oc'tave, -taved, -tăv'a lent, oc-
tă'vo, pl. -vos (-vōz), oc'tave-
flute, -stop, oc tă'vo-post.
oc ten'ni al, -ly.
oc tet'.
oc til'lion.
oc'to-băss.
Oc tŏ'ber.
oc'to ge nă'ri an, -tog'e na ry (-tŏj'-).
oc'to pod.
oc'to pus, -to'pe an.
oc to rōōn'.
oc'tu ple, -tu plex.
oc'u lar, -lår y, -late, -lā'ted,
-li form, -u list, oc'u lus, pl. -lī.
ŏd, a kind of force, -force,
o'dism.
o'da lisk or -lisque'.
odd, singular, -ly, -ness, -i ty,
odds, odd'-look'ing, -mark,
-pin nate, Odd'-Fel'low.
ŏde, -let, ŏd'ist, ode'-fac tor,
ŏ'dic, -dic al ly.
O'din, Myth., -ism, -din'ic.
o'di ous, -ly, -ness.
ŏ'di um.
ŏ'do grâph.
O dŏ iev' (-yĕv'), t. Russ.
o dom'e ter, -e try, -e trous, -do-
met'ric al.
o don tal'gi a, -tal'gic, -tal'gy, -don'-
tic, -to gen'ic, -tog'e ny (-tŏj'-).
o dŏn'to grâph, -graph'ic, -tog'-
ra phy, -don'toid, -don'to līte,
-to lith, -tol'o gist, -o gy, -to log'-
ic al.
o'dor, -dored, -dor ant, -dor a-
ting, -dor if'er ous, -ous ly,
-ous ness, -dor less, -dor ous,
-ous ly, -ous ness, -dor scope.
Od'ys sey, Homer's epic.
Œc'o lăm pă'dĭ us (ĕk'-), Ger.
reformer.
Œd'Ĭ pus (ĕd'-), King of Thebes.

Oeh'len schlä ger (ê'lĕn shlä'ger),
Danish poet.
œ nol'o gy, -no log'ic al, œ'no-
man cy, -no mel, -nom'e ter,
-no mä'ni a.
Œ nŏ'ne (ē-), Myth.
œ soph'a gus. See esophagus.
Œ'ta (ē'-), mts. Gr.
o'er (ŏr), -come, -lay.
oer'sted (êr'-).
of (ŏv), prep.
ŏff, adv. and prep., off'cåst, -cut,
-hand, -hand ed, -ish, -let, -print,
-sad dle, -scour'ing, -scum, -set,
-shoot, -shore, a., -shore', adv.,
-spring, -take.
off'-bear, -bear er, -come, -corn,
-flow, -reck on ing, -side, adv.,
off-and-on, a., off horse, o.
side.
ŏf'fal.
Of'fen bäch, t. Ger.
of fend', -ed, -er, -ing, -fence',
-fence'less, -less ly, -fen'sive,
-sive ly, -sive ness.
ŏf'fer, -a ble, -er, -ing, -fêred,
of'fer ing-sheet.
of'fer to ry, -to'ri um, pl. -ri a,
-toire' (-twŏr').
ŏf'fice, -bear'er, -book, -hold'er,
-seek'er.
of fi'cial (-fĭsh'al), -dom, -ism,
-ize, -ized, -ĭ'zing, -cial ly,
-cial ty, -ci al'i ty (-fish'Ĭ al'-).
of fi'ci ate (-fĭsh'Ĭ-), -ā'ted, -ā'-
ting, -ā'tor, -fic'i nal (-fĭs'-),
-fi'cious (-fish'us), -cious ly,
-cious ness.
ŏff'ing.
off'set-glåss, -pipe, -sheet, -ståff,
off'set ting-blaṇ'ket.
oft, oft'times.
ŏf'ten (-n), -ness, -times.
ŏ gee' (-jē'), -plane.
O'gil vĭe (ŏ'gl vĭ), Scot. poet.
ŏ'gle, -gled, -gler, -gling.
Ogl io (ōl'yō), r. It.
O go vé (ŏ'gŏ'vă'), r. Afr.
ŏ'gre, -gre ish (-ger-), -gre ism,
-gress, -gril'lon (-yon).
O'Groat' (ō grawt'), John O'-
Groat's House.

O gyg'i a   (-jĭj'-),   Homer   *The Odyssey.*
Öhl'mül ler (ĕl'mü ler), Ger. arch.
Ohm (ōm), Ger. elect.
ōhm,   ohm'ad,   ohm'age,   ohm'ic, ohm'me'ter, ohm'-am'e ter.
O ho mu'ra (-mōō'-), t. Japan.
oil,   -er,   -er y,   -ing,   -y,   -i ly, -i ness,   -less,   -cloth,   -man, -skin, -stone, -way.
oil'-bag,   -bee tle,   -bird,   -bot tle, -box,   -bush,   -cake,   -can,   -car, -cel lar,   -cock,   -col lar,   -cup, -der rick,   -dis trib'u ter,   -dregs, -dried,   -drop,   -ex tract'ing, -fac to ry,   -fil ter,   -fu el,   -gāge, -gas, -gild ing, -gland, -green.
oil-hole,   -jack,   -mill,   -nut,   -paint-ing,   -palm,   -plant,   -press, -pump,   -re fin'ing,   -ring,   -rub-ber,   -safe,   -sand,   -seed,   -shale, -shark,   -smell er,   -spring,   -still, -stock,   -stove,   -tank,   -taw ing, -tem per,   -tem pered,   -tem per-ing,   -test er,   -tight,   -tree,   -tube, -well,   oil'stone-pow der,   -slips, oil'y-grain.
oint'ment, -syr'inge.
Oise (wäz), r. Fr.
o jan'co (o han'kō).
O je'da (ō hä'dä), Sp. advent.
o kä'pĭ.
oke, a weight.
O ke cho'bē (-chō'-), l. Fla.
O khotsk (ō kōtsk'), arm of the north Pac. Ocean.
ōl'a ca'ceous (-shŭs).
old,   -en (-n),   -ish,   -ness,   -ster, old'wife, a duck; a fish.
old'-ewe,   a fish,   -faced,   -fash-ioned   (-ŭnd),   -fo'gy ish,   (-gĭ-) -fo gy ism,   -gen tle man ly,   -grain, -light,   -line,   -maid, a plant; a clam,   -maid hood,   -maid ish, -maid ism,   -man, a tree,   -school, *a.,*   -sight'ed ness,   -squaw, a duck, -time,   *a.,*   -tīm'er,   -wom an ish, -world, old maid.
old-man's-beard,   a plant,   -man's-eye brow, a plant,   -man's-head, a plant,   old-wom an's-bit ter, a plant,   old-witch grǎss,   -field birch,   -field lark, -field pine.

Old'ham (-am), Eng. poet; old'-ham (-am), a cloth, -ham īte, a mineral.
o le ag'i nous (-ăj'-),   -ness,   *o lē-ā'men.*
o le an'der,   -an'drĭne,   o le an'der-fern.
ō'le in,   -le fīne,   -le ic,   -le o graph, -graph'ic,   -og'ra phy,   -le ose, -le ous.
ō'le o, an oil.
o'lē o mar'ga rĭn   *or*   -rĭne (-ga-).
o le om'e ter.
ol er a'ceous   (-shŭs),   -er i cul'-ture, -tur al ly.
ol fac'to ry,   -fac tom'e ter.
ol'i garch (-gark),   -gar'chy,   -gar'-chist (-kĭst),   -gar'chism,   -gar'-chal (-kal),   -gar'chic, -chic al.
ōl'io (ōl'yo   *or*   ō'lĭ ō), a medley.
ōl'ĭve,   -i va ry,   -ived,   -ive ness, ol'ive back,   a thrush,   -wort.
ōl'ĭve-backed,   -branch,   -green, -nut,   -oil,   -ore,   -plum,   -shell, -tree, -ty'rant, -wood, -yard.
ol'i ver, a hammer.
Ol'i vet,   *Bib.,*   -an;   ol'i vet,   a pearl.
O liv'i a, Shak. *Twelfth Night.*
O li vi er' (ō'lē'vē ā'), Fr. entom.
ol'la.
Ol li vi er' (ō'lē'vē ā'), Fr. polit.
Ol o za'ga   (ōl ō thä'gä),   Sp. statesman.
Ols'hau sen (ōls'how zen),   Ger. theol.; Ger. orient.
O lym'pus,   -pi ad,   -ad'ic,   -pi an, -pic, -pi on'ic.
Om (ōm), r. Sib.
Om'a ē'rus, *Bib*
O'ma ha (ō'ma hạ), c. Neb.
om'ber, a game.
ŏm'brant.
om'bre, a fish, *om'brē'* (ōm'brā'), a silk print.
om'brŏ grăph,   -brol'o gy,   -bro-log'ic al.
om brom'e ter.
O'Mea'ra (ō mā'ra), Irish surgeon.
O mē'ga   (*or*   ō'-),   *Bib.*
ō mē'ga, the last; the end.
om'e let.
ō'men, -ing, -mĕned.

ŏm'i nous, -ly, -ness.
Om'ish.
o mit', -ted, -ter, -ting, -tance,
o mis'sive, -si ble, -mis'sion
(-mĭsh'un).
om'ni bus.
om nif'ic, -nif'er ous, -ni fā'ri ous.
om nip'o tence, -ten cy, -tent,
-tent ly.
om nĭ pres'ent (-prĕz'-), -pres'-
ence.
om nis'cience (-nĭsh'ens), -cien-
cy, -cient, -cient ly.
om niv'o rous, -ness.
Om'pha lē, Myth.
ŏn, -come, -fall, -go'ing, -lay,
-look'er, -set, -shore, adv.,
-slaught, -stĕad, on'-com'ing,
-hang er, on dit (ôṅ dē).
once (wŭns).
one (wŭn), -ness, one'-bĕr'ry,
-blade, a plant, -cross, -eyed,
-hand ed, -horse, a., -i dē'aed,
-leaf, a plant, -sīd'ed, -sid ed-
ly, -sid ed ness, one's self.
ō neĭ'rō dyn'i a, -rŏl'o gy, -ro-
man'cy, -ros'co py, -co pist.
ŏn'er ous, -ly, -ness.
On'e sĭph'o rus, Bib.
O nī'a res (-rēz or -nĭ ā'-), Bib.
O nī'as, Bib.
on'ion (ŭn'yŭn), -y, on'ion-
couch, -eyed, -fish, -fly, -grăss,
-mag got, -shell, -skin, -smut.
ŏn'ly, -be got'ten.
ŏn ō mat o pœ'ia (-pē'ya), -pœ'-
ic, -pō ē'sis, -pō et'ic, -ic al ly,
on'o ma tope'.
ŏn'to (-tōō).
ō'nus.
ŏn'ward, -ness, -wards.
ŏ'nyx (or ŏn'ĭks).
ŏ'ŏ, a bird, ō'ŏ ä'ä, a bird.
ŏ'ŏ līte, -lit'ic, -li tif'er ous.
ŏ ŏl'o gy, -o gist, -o log'ic (-lŏj'-),
-ic al, -al ly.
ōō'long.
ŏ ŏm'e ter, -e try, -ō met'ric.
ōō'mĭ ak.
ōō'păk.
Oost, van (vän ōst), Flemish
painter.
ōō'trum.

ōōze, ōōzed, ōōz'ing, ōōz'y.
ŏ'păl, -păled, -pa lĕsce', -lĕsced',
-les'cing, -les'cence, -cent, -pal-
ĭne, -ize, -ized, -i zing, o'pal-
blūe, -jas'per.
ŏ paque', -ly, -ness, ō pac'i ty
(-păs'-).
ŏ peĭ'dŏ scope.
ŏ'pen (-pn), -a ble, -er, -ing, -ly,
-ness, -bill, a stork, -work,
-pened.
o'pen-air, -brĕast'ed, -căst,
-doored, -dot, -eyed, -hand'ed,
-hand ed ness, -heart ed, -heart-
ed ness, -mind ed, -mind ed-
ness, -mouthed (or moutht), -ses'-
a me, -steek, -tide, o. door, o. sea.
o'pen ing-bit, -knife, -ma chine'.
op'er a, -er at'ic, -ic al, -al ly,
op er et'ta, op'er a-cloak, -dan'-
cer, -girls, -glăss, -hat, -house,
-sea'son, -sing'er, -troupe.
op'er ate, -ā'ted, -ā'ting, -à ble,
-am'e ter, -er ā'tion, op'er ant,
-à tive, -tive ly, -tive ness, -tiv'-
i ty, -tor.
op'er ose.
O phē'li a, Shak. Hamlet.
oph i og'ra phy, -ol'a ter, -a-
trous, -a try, -ol'o gy, -o gist,
-o log'ic, -ic al, oph'i o man'cy.
Oph'rah, Bib.
oph thal'mi a, -thal'mic, -mist,
-mīte, -mit'ic, -mī'tis, -mog'ra-
phy, -mol'o gy, -mo log'ic, -ic-
al, -mom'e ter, -e try.
oph thal'mo scope, -scop'ic, -ic-
al, -al ly, -mos'co py (or -mo-
sco'py).
ŏ'pĭ ate, -ā'ted.
O'pie (ŏ'pē), Eng. authoress;
Eng. painter.
ŏ pīne', -pīned', -pīn'er, -pīn'ing.
o pĭn'ion, -a ble, -ā'ted, -à tive',
-tive'ly, -tive'ness, -ion ist,
-ioned.
ŏ'pi um, -eat er, -hab it, -pop py,
o. lin'i ment, o. plas'ter.
ŏp ŏ del'doc.
o pop'a nax.
o pŏs'sum, -mouse, -shrew,
-shrimp, -tree.
op pō'nent.

op por tune′, -ly, -ness, -tuned′,
-tūn′ism, -ist, -tu ni ty.
op pose′ (-pōz′), -less, -posed′,
-pōs′er, -pos′ing, -pos′a ble,
-a bil′i ty.
op′po site (-zĭt), -ly, -ness, -si′-
tion (-zĭsh′un), -tion al, -tion-
ist, -pos′i tive.
op press′, -ing, -ive, -ive ly, -ive-
ness, -or, -pressed′, -pres′sion.
op pro′bri ous, -ly, -ness, -bri um.
op pugn′ (-pūn′), -ing, -er,
-pugned′, -pug′nant, -nan cy.
op′ta tive, -ly.
ŏp′tic, -tic al, -al ly, -ti′cian
(-tĭsh′an), -ti cist, -tics, -ti-
graph.
op′ti mism (-mĭzm), -mist, -mis′-
tic, -tic al ly, -ti mize, -mized,
-mĭ′zing.
op′tion, -al, -al ly.
op tom′e ter, -e try.
op′to type.
op′u lence, -len cy, -lent, -lent ly.
ō′pus, pl. ŏp′e ra, o pus′cule,
o pus′cu lum, pl. -la, ō′pus-
num ber.
o quăs′sa.
ŏr′a cle, o rac′u lar, lar ly, lar-
ness, -lăr′i ty.
ō′ral, -ly, -ism, -ist.
ō rā′lĕ.
ŏr′ange (-ĕnj), -ade′, -an geat′
(-zhăt′), -an ger, -an ger y, ŏr′-
ange leaf, a plant, -root, a plant,
-tip, a butterfly.
or′ange-bird, -blos som, -but ter,
-col ored, -crowned, -dog,
-flow′er, -grăss, -juice, -legged,
-lil y, -list, -musk, -oil, -pea,
-peel, -pē′kōe, -pip′pin, -scale,
-seed, -skin, -spoon, -taw ny,
-thorn, -wife, -wom an.
Or′ange, co. Cal.; co. Fla.; co.
Ind.; co. N. Y.; co. Tex.; c.
N. J.; dist. Fr.;—founder of
the Dutch Rep., Or′ange ism,
-ange man.
ō răng′-ou tăng′ (-ōō-).
o rā′ri on, pl. -ri a.
ō′rate, -rā′ted, -rā′ting, -rā′tion.
ŏr′a tor, -to′ry, -tō′ri al, -al ly,
-tŏr′ic, -ic al, -al ly, -tō′rĭ ō.

orb, -y, orbed, or bic′u lar, -lar-
ly, -lar ness, -bic′u late, -lā′ted,
-late ly, -lā′tion, orb′fish, orb′-
like, -weav′er.
Or′bi gny′, d′ (dor′bēn′yē′), Fr.
naturalist.
or′bit, -al, -a ry.
or′chard, -ing, -ist, or′chard-
clam, -grăss, -house, -o′ri ole.
or chä′ta.
or che′sis (-kē′-), -che sog′ra-
phy, -ches′tic (-kĕs′-).
or′ches tra (-kĕs-), -tral, -trate,
-trā′ted, -trā′ting, -trā′tion,
-ches′tric, -tri on.
or′chid (-kĭd), -chid′e al, -e an,
-e ous, -ol′o′gist, -o gy, or′chis
(-kis).
or dāin′, -a ble, -er, -ment, -ing,
-dained′, -di nä′tion.
or′dĕ al, -root, -tree.
or′der, -a ble, -er, -ing, -less, -ly,
-li ness, -dered, or′der-book,
-clăss.
or dĭ nâire′.
or′di nal, -ism.
or′di nance, -di nant.
or′di na ry, -na ri ly, -ry ship.
ord′nance, cannon, ord′nance office, o. of fi cer, o. ser′geant.
or′don nance, order of arrangement, -don nant.
or′dure, -du rous.
ore, a mineral, ore′weed, -wood.
ore′-con′cen tra tor, -crush er,
-de pos it, -hearth, -roast ing,
-scp′a ra tor, -smelt ing, -stamp,
-wash′er.
ō′re (ê′rĕ), a coin.
ō′re ad.
o rec′tic.
o re jon′ (ō′rä hōn′).
O res′tes (-tēz), Myth., -res tē′an.
or′gan, -gan′ic, -ic al, -al ly, -al-
ness, -i cism, -i fy, -fy ing,
-fīed, -fī er, -ga nif′ic, -gan ism,
-gan ist, -gan is′mal (-ĭz′-), -is′-
tic (-ĭs′-), -is′trum.
or′gan-al bū′min, -bench, -blow′-
er, -build′er, -coup′ler, -fish,
-grind′er, -har mo′ni um, -ling,
-loft, -pi a′no, -pipe, -play′er,
-point, -rest, -screen, -seat, -stop.

nŏt, nôr, ūse, ŭp, ûrn, etüde, fōōd, fŏŏt, aŋger, boṅmot, thus, Bach.
28

or'gan ize, -ized, -i zer, -i zing,
-i'za ble, -i'za bil'i ty, -ĭ zā'tion.
or gan'o gen, -gen'e sis.
or'geat (ôr'zhăt).
or'gies (-jĭz), -gi as'tic.
Or go'glio (-gŏl'yo), Spenser
Faërie Queene.
or'gui nette' (-gĭ nĕt').
ŏ'ri ĕl.
ŏ'ri ent, -en'tal, -tal ly, -tal ism,
-tal ist, -tal ize, -ized, -ĭ'zing,
-tal'i ty, -en'tate (or ŏ'ri en-),
-ta'ted, -ta ting, -ta tor, -tā'tion;
the O'ri ent.
ŏr'i fĭce, -i form.
ŏr'i flămme.
Or'i gen (ŏr-), early Christian
writer, -ism, -ist, -is'tic.
ŏr'i gin, ō rig'i nal, -nal ly, -nal-
ness, -nal'i ty, -nå ble, -nant,
-nâ'ry.
o rig'i nate (-rĭj'-), -nā'ted, -nā'-
ting, -nå tive, -tive ly, -nā'tor,
-nā'tion.
o ril'lon.
ŏ'rĭ ŏle, -tan'a ger.
O rī'on, Astron.
ŏr'i son (-zŭn).
O ri za'ba (ō rē thä'bä), volc. Mex.
Or lan'do, Shak. As You Like It.
Or'le ans, parish La.; co. N. Y.;
co. Vt.—(ŏr'lā'ŏṅ'), c. Fr.
or'mŏ lu (-lōō or -lōō'), -var'-
nish.
Or'muzd.
or'na ment, -er, -men'tal, -tal ly,
-tā'tion.
or nate', -ly, -ness.
or nĭ thol'o gy, -o gist, -tho log'ic,
-ic al, -al ly, or'nĭ tho man cy (or
-nĭth'ō-), -man'tic, -tho sco py
(or -nĭth'ō-), -sco'pist, -thot'o my,
-o mist, -tho tom'ic al.
o rol'o gy, -o gist, -o log'ic al.
O rŏn'tes (-tēz), r. Syr.
ŏ'ro tund, -tun'di ty.
or'phan, -phan ing, -age, -hood,
-phăned, or'phan a sy'lum (-sĭ'-).
Or'phĕ us (or or'fūs), Myth.,
-phe'an (or or'-), -phic, -phism,
-phize.
ŏr're ry.
ŏr'ris, -pea, -root.

Or si'ni (-sē'nē), noted Italian
family.
Or si'no (-sē'-), Shak. Twelfth
Night.
Or'thez' (-tā'), t. Fr.
or'tho dox, -ly, -ness, -y, -dox'-
ic al.
or'thŏ ĕ py, -e pist, -pis'tic, -tho-
ep'ic, -ic al, -al ly.
or thog'na thism, -na thous.
oı thog'ra phy, -ra pher, -ra-
phist, -ra phize, -phized, -phi-
zing, -tho graph'ic, -ic al, -al ly.
or thom'e try, -tho met'ric.
or tho pē'di a or -thop'e dy, -pē'-
dic (or -pĕd'ic), -pē'dist (or
-thop'e dist).
or'thŏ phŏ ny (or -thŏph'o ny).
Or'thŏ sī'as (or -thŏ'sĭ-), Bib.
or'tŏ lan.
ŏr'yx.
O sä'ias (-zā'yas), Bib.
O sä'kä (-zä'kä), c. Japan.
ŏs'cil late, -lā'ted, -lā'ting, -lā'-
tor, -to ry, -lā'tion, -lan cy,
ŏs'cil lō graph, -lom'e ter.
os'cĭ tate, -ta ted, -ta ting, -tant,
-tant ly, -tan cy, -tā'tion.
os'cu late, -la ted, -la ting, -lant,
-lar, -la to'ry, -lā'tion.
O'Shaugh'nes sy (ō sha̤w'nes sy),
Brit. poet.; Irish electr.
O'Shea' (ō shā'), Irish soldier.
ŏ'sier (-zhêr), -y, -siered (-zhêrd),
o'sier-ait, -bed, -holt, -peel'er.
Os'i mo (ŏs'ē mō), t. It.
O sī'ris, Myth., -sī'ri an (or
-sĭr'i an).
Os män'-Dig'ma, Afr. adventurer.
ŏs'mo gene, -mom'e ter, -e try,
-mo met'ric, os'mose (-mŏs),
-mō'sis, -mŏt'ic, -ic al, -al ly,
-mō sĭt'ic.
ŏs'prey (-prā).
os sä'ri um, pl. -ri a, os'se an,
-se ous, -ous ly.
Os'sian (ŏsh'an), legendary bard,
-si an'ic (ŏs'sĭ-).
ŏs'si fy, -ing, -fīed, -si form,
-su a ry, -si fi cā'tion, os'te al,
-tē ĭ'tis, -te it'ic.
Os tend', t. Flanders.
os ten'si ble, -si bly, -si bil'i ty.

os ten tā'tion, -ta'tious, -tious ly,
-tious ness.

os tĕ ŏl'o gy, -o gist, -o log'ic,
-ic al, -al ly, -te om'e try, -o-
met'ric al.

os'tĕ op'a thy, -ō path'ic, -ic al,
-al ly.

os'ti ole, -ti o late'.

os'tra cize, -cized, -cī'zing, -cism.

os'tre Ĭ cul'ture, -tūr ist, -tre oph'a-
gist (-jĬst), -trĬf'er ous.

ŏs'trich, -board, -eggs, -farm,
-farm'ing, -fĕath'er, -fern,
-plume.

Os'trow (-trŏv), t. Pol.

Os'wes try (ŏz'es try), t. Eng.

ŏ tal'gi a, -tal'gy, -tal'gic.

O te'ro (-tā'-), co. Col.

oth'er (ŭth'er), -ways, -where,
-while, -whiles, -wise.

Oth män' or **Os män',** founder
of Ottoman Empire.

Oth'o nī'as, Bib.

ŏ'tĬ ose (-shĬ ōs), -ŏs'i ty.

O'toe (-tō), co. Neb.

ŏ tŏl'o gy, -o gist, -to log'ic al,
-top'a thy, ō'to phone, -to scope,
-scŏp'ic, -ic al, -to sco'py (or
-tŏs'-), -tō'sis.

ŏt'ter, -ca noe', -dog, -hound,
-pike, -shell, -shrew, -spear.

Ot'ter beĬn, founder of the United
Brethren sect.

Ot'to man, pl. -mans, a Turk;
ot'to man, pl. -mans, a stool.

Ouach'i ta (wŏsh'i ta), co. Ark.;
parish La.

Ouar'glä (wär'-) or **War'glä,** t. Afr.

Ouche (ōōsh), r. Fr.

ou de narde' (ōō dĕn ärd').

Oudh (oud), prov. India.

Ou di not' (ōō'dĕ'nŏ'), Fr. marshal.

Ou dry' (ōō'drē'), Fr. painter.

ought (awt).

Oui'da (wē'da), pen name of
Louise de la Ramé.

oui'ga (wē'ja), -board.

ounce, o. land.

our, ours, our self', pl. -selves'.

Ou ray' (ōō-), co. Col.

Ourcq (ōōrk), r. Fr.

Ouse (ōōz), r. Eng.

oust, -ed, -er, -ing.

out. Most words compounded with
out are written without the
hyphen. Nouns and adjectives,
as a rule, take the accent on the
first syllable, as: out'break, out'-
burst, out'door, out'er most;
verbs, upon the second syllable,
or upon the accented syllable of
the word compounded with *out,*
as: out bar', out bid', out-
bal'ance, out dis'tance.
Words in common use beginning with *out* and not coming
within the scope of this note are
here given.

out, -er, -er most, -ing, -land'ish,
-ish ly, -ish ness, -let, -ness,
-ward, a. and adv., -wards,
-ward ly, -ward ness.

out bid', -bid'der, out dis'tance,
-flank, -gen'er al, -grow', -live',
-num'ber, play', reach', ride',
-run', -stretch', -strip', -wear',
-weigh', -work', v.

out'board, -break, -build'ing,
-burst, -cåst, rejected, -cåste,
expelled from caste, -come,
-cri'er, -crop, -cry, -door, a.,
-doors', adv., -field, -fit, -fit'ter,
-flow, -go, -go'ing, -growth,
-house, -land, -law, n., -law'ry,
-lay, -line, -look, -ly'ing, -part,
-port, -post, -pour'ing, -put,
-rid'er, -rig'ger, -set, -spo'ken,
-work, n.

out'side, n. and a., -side', adv.,
-sĬd'er.

out'-bound, -court, -cut, -edge,
-field, a term used in games
of ball, -field'er, -Hĕr'od,
-lodg'ing, -nook, -ov en, -par-
ish, -pa'tient, -pen'sion er,
-pick'et, -sale, -serv ant, -set'-
tle ment, -street, -talk, -tongue,
-top, -trav el, -turn, -ward, an
outlying ward.

out-and-out, -at-el bows, -of-
doors, -of-fash ion, a., -of-the-
way, a., out'side-car, a jaunting
car, out'ward-bound, -saint ed.

Ou'ta găn ie (ōō'-), co. Wis.

Ou'tran (ōō'-), Eng. gen.

ou tré' (ōō'trā').

---

nŏt, nôr, ūse, ŭp, ûrn, etüde, fōōd, fŏŏt, aŋger, boṅmot, thus, Bach.

ou'zel *or* -sel (ōō'zl).

ŏ'val, -ly, -ness, -val'i form, -va-
les'cent.

O väl'le (-yä), t. S. Amer.

ŏ'va ry, -va'ri al, -ri an, -ri ot'o-
my, -o mist.

o'vate.

o va'tion.

ov'en (ŭv'n), -bird, -build'er,
-cake, -coke, -tit, -wood.

ŏ'ver. See remark after *out*, which
for the most part applies to *over*.

ŏ'ver ly, -much', -plus.

ŏ'ver all, -bear'ing, -bear'ing ly,
-bear'ing ness, -board, -bold',
-bus y, -coat, -coat ing, -drăft,
-due', -flow, *n.*, -hand', *a.* and
adv., -hand'ed, -hang, *n.*, -hās'-
ty, -is'sue, *n.*, -laid, *a.*, -land',
n., -land', *adv.*, -lay', *n.*, -lord',
-match', -neat', -nice', -nice ly,
-pay'ment, -pow'er ing ly, -ripe,
-seer', -seer'ship, -sight', -strung',
-throw', *n.* defeat, -tone', -ween'-
ing, -ing ly, -ing ness, -weight',
-work', *n.*, -wrought'.

o ver arch', -bal'ance, -bur'den,
-cloud,' -come', -draw', -flow',
v., -hand', *v.*, -hang', *v.*, -hạul',
-hear', *v.*, -is'sue, *v.*, -lāde', *v.*,
-lay', *v.*, -look', *v.*, -măs'ter,
-per suade', -pow'er, -ride',
-rule', -run', -set', -shad'ow,
-sprěad', -take', -throw', *v.*,
-weigh', -whelm', -work', *v.*

o ver-anx i'e ty, -anx'ious, -anx'-
ious ly, -brimmed', -chord',
-cloth', -con'fi dence, -con'fi-
dent, -con'fi dent ly, -cu'ri ous,
-de vel'op ment, -dil'i gent, -dis-
charge', -en treat', -ex er'tion,
-ex po'sure, -ex'qui sĭte, -fired',
-fond', -fond'ly, -force', -for'-
ward, -fruit'ful, -gaze', -hair',
-has'ti ly, -has'ti ness, -hours',
-kind', -king', -learn'ed ness,
-learn'ing, -mod'est, -plate',
-pro duce', -pro duc'tion, -pur'-
chase, -re fine', -re fine'ment,
-right'eous, -scru'pu lous, -scru'-
pu lous ness, -soul', -vi'o lent.

o'ver cup-oak, o'ver draw-check,
o'ver flow-ba sin, -bug, -găge,

o'ver flow meet ing, o ver heat-
ing-pipe, o ver load-mag net,
-switch.

ŏ'vert, -ly.

ŏ'ver ture, -tured, -tūr ing.

O'ver yssche' (-ēsh'), vil. Belg.

Ov'id (ŏv'-), Roman poet; vil.
Mich.; vil. N. Y.

O vi e'do (ō vē ā'dō), prov. Sp.

ŏ'vule, o vip'a rous, o'void, -vu-
late, -lā'tion, -*vum*, pl. -*vums*
or -*va*, o'vum-cy'cle, -prod'uct.

owe (ō), owed, ōw'er, ow'ing.

owl, -er y, -et, -ing, -ish, -ish-
ness, -ism, -y.

owl'-but ter fly, -eyed, -fly, -gnat,
-head, -light, -moṇ key, -moth,
-par rot, -swal low, -train, owl'-
et-moth.

own (ōn), -er, -ing, -ness, owned,
own'er less, -er ship, own'-form,
-root.

O wy'hee (-wī'hē), co. Idaho.

ox, *pl.* -en, -ber'ry, -bīt'er, a
bird, -eye, a plant, -heal, a
plant, -heart, a cherry, -hoof,
a leaf, -lip, a flower, -man,
-peck er, a bird, -tongue, a
plant.

ox'-ac id, -an'te lope, -bälm,
-bōw, -brake, -cheek, -eyed,
-fence, -fly, -foot, -gall, -goad,
-head, -hide, -horn, -mush'-
room, -ray, -reīm (*or* -rēm),
-shoe, -sole, -stall, -tail, -team,
-tongue, a tongue, -yoke.

ox al'ic, o. ac'id.

ŏx'a lis, a plant, Ox'a lis, a
genus of plants.

ŏx'y gen, -gen ate, -ā'tor, -ā'tion,
-gen'ic, -gen ize, -ized, -ī'zer,
-ī'zing, -ize ment, -yg'e nous (-Ij'-).

ŏ'yer.

ŏ'yĕs *or* o'yĕz.

oys'ter, -er, -ing, -ling, oys'ter-
man.

oys'ter-baṇk, -bar, -bay, -bed,
-bird, -boat, -bot tom, -brood,
-catch er, -crab, -crack er, -cul-
ture, -cul tur ist, -dredge,
-farm, -farm ing, -field, -fish,
-fish er y, -fish ing, -fork, -găge,
-grăss, -green, -ham mer, -keg,

---

fāte, făt, fär, fạll, fâre, făst, sofå, mēte, mĕt, hêr, īce, ĭn, nōte,

-knife, -mush room, -o pen er,
-park, =plant, -plov er, -rake,
-reef, -rock, -shell, -shop, -sign,
-tongs, -wife, -wom an, o. pie,
o. stew.
O zärk', co. Mo.; vil. Ala.; tp.
Mo.
O zī'as, *Bib.*
O'zĭ el, *Bib.*

O zi e'ri (ŏd zē ā'rē), t. It.
ŏ'zone, -zo nā'tion, -zŏn'ic, -zo-
nize, -nī'zer, -nized, -nī'zing,
-nĭ zā'tion, -zō'ni fy, -fy ing,
-fied, -fĭ cā'tion, -zo nif'er ous,
-zō'no graph, -zo nog'ra pher,
-nom'e ter, -e try, -no met'ric,
-zo'no scope, -scop'ic.
O zŏr'kow (-kŏv), t. Pol.

P

pä.
Pä'a răi, *Bib.*
pab'u lum, -u lar.
pace, a step, paced, pa'cing, -cer,
pace'-aisle, -board, -eggs, -māk'-
er.
pä'cē, by your leave.
Pa ce'co (pä chā'kō), t. It.
Pä chä cä mä', vil. Peru.
Pä che'co (-chā'-), t. Sp.
pa chi'si (-chē'zĭ) or *par chi'si*
(pär chē'zĭ).
pach'y derm (păk'-), -der'mal,
-der'ma tous,   pa chym'e ter
(-kĭm'-).
pa ci'ʃĭ cō (på cē'-).
pac'i fy, -ing, -fĭ cr, -fi'a ble, -fied,
pa cif'ic, -cif'ic al ly, -cif'i cate,
-cā ted, -cā tor, -to'ry, -ĭ cā'
tion.
Pä ci'ni (-chē'nē), Sicilian comp.
Pa cio'li (-chō'lē), It. math.
pack, -age, -a ging, -er, -et, -ing,
packed, pack'all, a basket,
-horse, -man, -moth, -nee dle,
-sheet, -stăff, -thread, -ware,
-wax, -way.
pack'-an'i mal, -cinch, -cloth,
-duck, -house, -ice, -load,
-mule, -rat, -road, -sad'dle,
-train, -wall, pack'a ging-ma-
chine'.
pack'et-boat, -day, -note, -ship,
-ves sel.
pack'ing-awl, -block, -bolt, -box,
-case, -cell, -crib, -ex pand'er,
-gland, -lĕath'er, -nee dle, -nut,
-of'fi cer, -pa per, -press, -ring,
-shed, -sheet, -stick.

pä'cŏ (*or* pä'-).
pac'tion, -al, pact.
Pac tō'lus, an ancient river noted
for its golden sands; vil. N. C.,
-tō'li an.
pä'cu (-kōō *or* păk'-).
pad, -ded, -der, -ding, pad'lock.
pad'-brack'et, -clink'ing, -cloth,
-crimp, -el'e phant, -hook, -nag,
-sad'dle, -screw, -top, -trace,
-tree, pad'ding-flue, -ken, -ma-
chine.
Pä'dan-ä'ram, *Bib.*
pad'dle, -dled, -dler, -dling, pad'-
dle cock, -wood, a tree.
pad'dle-beam, -board, -boat,
-box, -crab, -end, -fish, -hole,
-row, -shăft, -sleep, -stăff,
-tum'ble, -wheel, pad'dling-crab.
păd'dock, -stool, a plant, pad'-
dock-pipe, -rud, -stone.
păd'dy, a duck; rice. Pad'dy, an
Irishman.
pad'dy whack, pad'dy-bird, -field,
-mel'on, -pound'er.
păd'lette.
pad'lock, -ing, -locked.
păd'ou (-ōō).
pä'dre (-drä).
Pä drŏn', t. Sp.
på drō'ne (-nä), pl. *-ni* (-nē).
Păd'ŭ a, c. It.
pæ'an (pē'-), a song, -ism.
Pae jae'ne (pä yä'ne), l. Russ.
pæ'on (pē'-), a foot in prosody,
-on'ic.
Pä ez' (-ĕth'), Span. mission.
pä'gan, -dom, -ish, -ism, -ize,
-ized, -ī'zing.

---

nŏt, nôr, ūse, ŭp, ûrn, etüde, fōōd, fŏŏt, aŋger, boṅmot, thus, Bach.

Pä ga ni′ni (-nē′nē), It. violinist.

page, -hood, paged, pä′ging, pag′i nal (păj′-), -i nate, -nä′- ted, -nä′ting, -i nä′tion, page′- cord, -gäge, pä′ging-ma chine′.

pag′eant (păj′ant or -ĕnt or pä′-), -ry.

Pag′et (păj′-), Eng. diplomat; Eng. surgeon.

Pä′gĭ el, *Bib.*

Pä′gŏ, isl. Adriatic sea.

pa gŏ′da, -stone, -tree.

päh, an exclamation of disgust. *păh,* an intrenchment.

Pä′ĭ, *Bib.*

päil, -ful, pail′-brush, -han′dle, -läthe, -ma chine′, -nail, -stake.

pail lasse′ (păl yăs′).

Pail let′ (pä yä′), Fr. advocate. *pail lette′* (păl yet′).

pail lon′ (păl′yôn′).

Pain (păṅ), Fr. publicist.

päin, -ful, -ful ly, -ful ness, -less, -less ly, -less ness, pained.

pains′täk′er, -tak′ing, -ing ly, pains′wor′thy (-wur′thy).

paint, -ed, -er, -ing, -a ble, -less, -y, -i ness, paint′root, -work.

paint′-box, -bridge, -brush, -burn′er, -can, -frame, -mill, -mix er, -re mov′er, -room, -strake.

paint′ed-cup, a plant, -la dy, a plant; a butterfly; paint′er- stain′er.

pâir, -ing, pâired, pair′wise, pair′-tōed, pair′ing-time.

pä′i sä′nō.

pa jä′mas (-màz).

pa′ke ha (pä′kä hå).

Päk racz′ (-räts′), t. Hung.

Paks (pŏksh), t. Hung.

păl′ăce, pa lä′tial, pal′ace-car, -court.

Pal′a mon, Chaucer *Canterbury Tales.*

păl′am pore′.

pal′an quin′ (-kēn′).

păl′ate, pal′ä tä ble, -ble ness, -bly, -bil′i ty, -à tal, -tal ize, -ized, . -ĭ′zing, -ĭ zä′tion, pa lăt′ic

Pa lăt′i nate, div. Ger.

păl′a tĭne, pa lăt′i nate.

Păl′a tĭne, pertaining to the vil- lage of Pallet. Păl′a tīne, t. Ill.; tp. N. Y.

pa lä′ver (*or* -lăv′-), -er, -ing, -vered.

Pä lä wän′, isl. P. I.

pale, -ly, -ness, paled, päl′ing, -ish, pale′brĕast, a bird, -buck, an antelope, -face, a man, pale′-eyed, -faced, -heart′ed.

Pa lē′mon, Falconer *The Ship- wreck.*

Pä lĕn′que (-kä), vil. Mex

pä′le o graph′, -graph′ic, -ic al, -og′ra pher, -ra phy.

pä′le o lith, -lith′ic, -ic al, -le- ol′o gy, -o gist.

pä′le on tog′ra phy, -to graph′ic- al, -tol′o gy, -o gist, -to log′ic al, -al ly.

Pal′es tĭne, Syria; c. Tex., -tĭn′- i an.

pa les′tra, *pl.* -tras *or* -træ, -tral, -tri an, -tric, -tric al.

Pä lĕs tri′na (-trē′-), c. It. *păl′e tot* (-tŏ), păl′ette (-ĕt), -knife.

Pal′frey (pawl′frĭ), Amer. divine.

pal′frey (pawl′frĭ), -freyed (-frĭd).

Päl′ghät′, t. India.

Pä′li (-lē), t. India; a language, *pä′lī,* parts of the coral.

păl′imp sest.

pal′in drome, -drom′ic, -ic al, pa lin′drŏ mist.

päl′ing, -board.

păl′i säde′, -säd′ed, -säd′ing, păl- i sade′-cell, -tis sue, -worm. *pal is sée′* (-sä′).

Păl′is ser, Brit. inventor.

Pa lis sy′ (pä′lē′sē′), Fr. potter, Päl′is sy ware. *pä li′tō* (-lē′-).

pall, -ing, palled, pall′-bear′er. *păl′la,* pl. -læ.

pal lä′di um, *pl.* -di a, -di um ize, -ized, -ĭ′zing.

Pal′las, *Myth.,* -lä′di an, -an ism.

pal les′cence, -les′cent.

pal′let, -ing, pal′let-ar bor, -box, -eye, -lĕath er, -mold ing, -tail.

pal′li ate, -a ted, -a ting, -a tive, -a to ry, -ā′tion.

Päl′lice (-lēs), t. Ireland.

păl′lid,' -ly, -ness, -lid′i ty, păl′lor.
pal′li um, pl. *-ums* or *-a*.
pall-mall′ (pĕl-mĕl′), a game.
Pall-Mall (pĕl-mĕl′), a street in London.
pal′lo met′ric.
palm (päm), -er, -er y, -ing, -y, palmed, păl mā′ceous, -mar, -mà ry, -mate, -mä ted, -mate-ly, -mif′er ous.
palm′-bar′ley, -bird, -but ter, -cab bage, -cat, -col or, -crab, -cross, -fi ber, -hon ey, -house, -kale, -leaf, -lil y, -mar ten, -oil, -su gar, -tree, -veined, -vi′per, -war′bler, -wasp, -wax, -worm, p. wine, Palm′ Sun′day, palm′bark-tree, palm′er-worm.
Päl′mä del Ri′o (rē′ō), t. Sp.
Päl′mä Nuo′vä (nwō′-), t. It.
păl met′to.
păl′mis try, -mist.
Păl my′ra (-mī′-), ancient city Syr.; tp. Kan.; c. Mo.; t. N. J.; vil. N. Y.; vil. N. C., -my rēne′, -myr′i an (-mĭr′-). păl my′ra (-mī′-), a palm.
Pä′lo Al′tō (äl′-), co. Ia.; t. Pa.; battlefield Tex.
Pŭ′lōs, t. Sp.
pal′pa ble, -ness, -bly, -bil′i ty.
păl′pate, -pä′ted, -pä′ting, -pä′-tion.
păl′pi tate, -tä′ted, -ting, -tant, -tä′tion.
pals′grave (pạwlz′-), -gra vine′ (-vēn′).
pal′sy (pạwl′zy), -ing, -sied (-zĭd), -sy wort.
păl′try, -tri ly, -tri ness.
Pa mi ers′ (pȧ′mē ā′), t. Fr.
Päm pän′ga, prov. P. I.
păm′pas (-pạz), -cat, -deer, -grăss, -rice.
pam′per, -ing, -er, -ize, -ized, -i zing, -pered.
păm pe′rō (-pä′-), pl. *-ros* (-rōz).
pam′phlet, -a ry, -eer′.
Pan, Myth., -de an, Pan-pipe.
păn, -ful, -ning, panned.
păn, a sheet of water.
pan′cake, -fish, the king-crab, Pan′han′dle, a strip of land.

pan′-cov er, -fish, a fish, -han-dle, -ice, -man, -pud ding, -rock, Pan′-pipe, pan′cake-turn′er, pan′ning-ma chine′.
Pan-A mer′i can, -An′gli can, -Pres by te′ri an, Pan hel′len ism *or* pan-Hel′len ism, -len-ist, -le′ni on, -ni um, -len′ic, Pan is lam′ic, Pan-I on′ic, Pan-slav′ism, -slav′ist, -slav′ic, -sla-vist′ic, -sla von′ic.
pan a ce′a, -ce′an.
pȧ nâche′.
pa nä′da (*or* -nä′-).
pȧ näl′.
Păn a mä′, isth. and t. Cent. Amer., P. Canal′, P. fe ver, P. hat.
Pä nay′ (-nī′), isl. P. I.
pan′cre as, -cre at′ic.
pan′da.
Pan′da rus, Shak. *Troilus and Cressida.*
pan′dect.
pan de′mi a, -dĕm′ic.
pan de mō′ni um, -ni ac.
pan′der, -ing, -er, -age, -ism, -ly, -ize, -ized, -i′zing, -dered.
pan dic′u la ted, -lä′tion.
Pan dō′ra, *Myth.* pan dō′ra, a bivalve; a fish; an insect.
pan′dy, -ing, -died; Pan′dy, a Hindu.
pane, paned, pan′ing.
pan e gyr′ic, -al, -al ly, -gyr′ist, -gy rize, -rized, -ri′zing.
pan′el, -eled *or* -elled, -el ing *or* -ling.
pan′el-fur ring, -game, -house, -pic ture, -plane, -plăn′er, -rail, -rāis′er, -saw, -strip, -thief, -truss, -wheel, -work′ing, p. door.
Păn′e la, title of a novel.
pang, -ful, -less.
Pän gä sĭ nän′, prov. P. I.
pan gram′ma tist.
păn′ic, -ick y, pan′ic-grăss, -moṇ′-ger, -strick′en, -struck.
pan′i cle, -cled, pa nic′u late, -lä′-ted, -late ly.
pan i con′o grăph, -graph′ic, -co-nog′ra phy.
pan′jam.

Păn jim' (-zhĕn'), t. India.
pånne.
pan'nier (-yer *or* -nĭ er), -niered,
pan'nier-man.
păn'nŏse.
pan'o ply, -o plist, -o plĭed.
pan o rä'ma, -răm'ic, -ic al, -al ly.
pan'sy (-zĭ), -sied (-zĭd).
pânt, -ed, -ing, -ing ly.·
Pan tag'ru el, Rabelais' satire.
pan ta loon', -loons'.
pan tel'e graph, -e phon'ic.
pan'the ism, -ist, -is'tic, -tic al,
-al ly, -the ol'o gy, -o gist.
Pan'the on, a temple; pan'the on,
a shrine.
pan'ther, -ess, -ine, pan'ther-
lil y, -moth, -wood.
pan'tĭle, -tĭl ing, pan'tĭle-lāthe,
-shop.
pan'to graph, -graph'ic, -ic al,
-al ly, -tog'ra phy, -tol'o gy,
-o gist, -to log'ic al, -tom'e ter,
-e try, -to met'ric.
pan'to mĭme, -mĭ'mist, -mĭm'ic,
-ic al, -al ly.
pan'to scope, -scop'ic.
pan'try.
păp, -ping, papped.
på pä (*or* pä'på), pä'pa, a bird;
a baboon.
på'pa cy, på'pal, -pal ism, -pal-
ist, -pal ly, -pal ize, -ized,
-i zing.
pa'pas, a priest.
pa păw', -tree.
Pa pé i'ti (pä pä ĕ'tē), t. Society
Isl.
på'per, -er, -ing, -y, -pered, pä'-
per bark, a tree.
på'per-birch, -box, to hold paper,
-case, -chase, -clamp, -clip,
-cloth, -coal, -col'or ing, -cut-
ter, -day, -en am'el, -en am'-
el ling, -faced, -feed er, -file,
-fold er, -gåge, -gloss er, -hang-
er, -hold er, -hor net, -knife,
-ma chine', -măk'er, -mar'bler,
-mill, -mold ing, -mul ber ry,
-mus lin, -nau'ti lus, -of'fice,
-per'fo ra ting, -pol'ish ing,
-pulp, -punch, -reed, -rŭl'er,
-rush, -sail or, -shell, -size,

-spar, -split ting, -stain er,
-stock, -test er, -tree, -wash ing,
-weight, p. box, made of paper,
pa'per bark-tree.
pa'pe terie' (pä'pe trĕ').
Pä'phos, *Bib.*
pa pier'-ma che' (på'pyä'-mä'shä').
pa pil'la, *pl.* -læ, pap'il lar, -la-
ry, -late, -lā'ted, -lā'ting, -pil'-
li form.
Pa pil lon' (pä'pē'yŏn'), Fr.
physiol.
pap'il lote.
pa'pist, -pis'tic, -tic al, -al ly,
-pist ry, pa'pish.
pa pōōse', -root.
Păp'u a (-ōō a), isl. Malay Arch.
pa pyr'o graph (-pĭr'-), pap'y-
rog'ra phy, -ro graph'ic.
pa py'rus (-pī'-), *pl.* -rī.
Pä rä', r. S. Amer., Pä rä'-
gräss, -nut. *på rä',* a coin.
păr'a ble, -bled, -bling.
pa rab'o la, *pl.* -las, a curve,
-a bol'ic, -ic al, -al ly.
pa rab'o lĕ, a simile.
Păr'a cel'sus, Swiss physician,
-cel'sĭ an, -cel'sist.
păr'a chute (-shōōt), -chūt ist,
par'a chute-light.
Pä'rä'clet' (-klä'), t. Fr.
păr'a clēte.
pa räde', -rād'ed, -rād'ing, -rād'-
er, pa rade'-ground, -rest, -wall.
păr'a digm (-dĭm), -dig mat'ic,
-ic al, -al ly, -dig'ma tize, -tized,
-tī'zing.
Păr'a dīse, *Bib.*
păr'a dise (-dīs), -a dĭs'i ac, -di-
sī'a cal, -dĭs'i al, -dĭs'i an, par'-
a dise-bird, -duck, -nut, -stock,
-tree.
păr'a dos, *pl.* -dŏs es.
păr'a dox, *pl.* -dox es, -dox'ic al,
-al ly, -al ness, -dox'er, -dox'ist,
-dox ol'o gy.
păr'af fin, -ize, -ized, -ī'zing,
par'af fin-but'ter, -oil, -scales.
păr'a gŏ'ge, -gog'ic (-gŏj'-), -ic al.
păr'a gon.
păr'a gram, -gram'ma tist.
păr'a graph, -er, -ist, -graph'ic,
-ic al, -al ly.

Pä rä guay' (-gwī' or pä'rä gwä), rep. and r. S. Amer., **Păr'aguäy'an,** Păr'a guäy tea.

Pä'rah, *Bib.*

păr a lä'lĭ a.

păr'al lax, -al lac'tic, -tic al.

păr'al lel, -ism, -is'tic, -leled *or* -lelled, -lel ing *or* -ling, -lel'ogram, -gram mat'ic, -ic al, -lel'o pī'ped, -o pĭp'e don.

pa ral'o gism, -o gize, -gized, -gizing, -ral'o gy.

pa răl'y sis, par'a lyt'ic, -ic al, -al ly, păr'a lyze, -lyzed, -lyzing, -ly zā'tion.

Păr a măr'i bō, c. Dutch Guiana.

păr'a mim'i a.

păr'a mount, -ly.

păr'a mour (-mōōr).

Pä rä nä', r. S. Amer.; state Braz.; t. Arg. Rep.

păr'ang.

pa ran'gon.

pä rä'o, a boat.

păr'a pet, -ed.

păr'aph, -ing, -aphed.

păr'a phā'si a (-zhĭ a), *-phō'ni a, -phrä'si a* (-zhĭ a).

păr a pher nä'li a.

păr'a phrase (-frāz), -phrased, -phrā'sing, -ser, -phrast, -phras'tic, -tic al, -al ly.

par'a ple gy, *-ple'gi a,* -ple'gic.

păr'a sīte, -sĭt'ic, -ic al, -al ly, -al ness, -sit'i cīde, -sī'tism, -sītol'o gy, -o gist, -to log'ic al.

păr'a sōl, -sōled *or* -solled, -soling *or* -ling, păr'a sol-ant, -fir, -han dle.

Pä rä ti' (-tē'), t. Braz.

par'bake, -boil, -boiled, -buc kle, -kled, -kling.

par'cel, -celed *or* -celled, -cel ing *or* -ling, -cel lā'tion.

par'cel-lift, -māk'er, -of fice, -paper, -post, -van, par'cel ingma chine'.

par'ce ner, -ce na ry.

parch, -er, -ing, -ed ness, parched.

par chi'si (-chē'zĭ). See *pachisi.*

parch'ment, -y, parch'mentbea'ver, -lace, -skin.

par'do, a coin.

par'don (-dn), -a ble, -a ble ness, -a bly, -er, -ing, -doned.

par'don-bell, -chair, -screen, -stall.

pâre, pared, pâr'er, -ing, pâr'ingchis'el, -i'ron, -knife, -ma chine', -plow, -scis sors, -spade.

păr'e gŏr'ic.

pa ren'chy ma (-kĭ-), -chy mal, -mat'ic, -chym'a tous (-kĭm'-).

pâr'ent, -age, -hood, -less, på ren'tal, -tal ly, -tal'i ty.

pâr'ent-cell, -form, -ker'nel.

păr'en tä'li a.

pa ren'the sis, *pl.* -ses (-sēz), -the size, -sized, -sī'zing, -thet'ic, -ic al, -al ly.

păr'e sis, pa ret'ic.

par ex cel lence' (ek'sĕ lŏns').

pär fleche' (-flĕsh').

par hē'lĭ on, *pl.* -li a.

Pä'ri ah (*or* pä'-).

pä'ri es (-ēz), -rī'e tal.

pä'rĭ păs'su.

Păr'is, -rĭs'i an (-rĭz'- *or* -rĭzh'Ĭ an *or* -rĭzh'an), *Pa ri si enne'* (på'rĕ'zē'ĕn').

Păr'is red, P. vi o let, P. white, P. ycl low.

păr'ish, pa rish'ion al (-ŏn al), -ion er.

păr'i ty.

park, -ing, -ish, -way, parked, park'leaves, a plant, -keep'er.

par'ka, a coat; a fossil.

par'lance.

par län'do.

par'ley, -ing, -leyed (-lĭd).

par'lia ment (-lĭ-), -men'tä ry, -tä ri ly, -ta rism, tä'ri an, par'lia ment-cake, p. hinge, P. röll.

par'lor, -board'er, -car, -or gan, -skate.

Par'ma, t. It., Par mē san' (-zăn'), -mēse' (*or* -mēz'), parme san' cheese.

Par'mē nas, *Bib.*

Par nas'sus, *Myth.*, -nas'sian (-năs'yan *or* -năsh'an).

Par'nell, Irish statesman; Brit. poet, -ism, -ite.

pa rō'chĭ al (-kĭ-), -ism, -al ly.

pär'o dy, -o dist, pa rŏd'ic, -ic al.
pa role', -roled', -rōl'ing, pa-
role'-ar rest'.
Pa rŏl'lĕs, Shak. *All's Well That
Ends Well.*
pär'o nō mä'si a (-zhĬ a), -no mas'-
tic, -tic al, -nom'a sy.
pär'o nym, -nym'ic, pa ron'y-
mize, -mized, -mĭ'zing, -mĬ zä'-
tion, -ron'y my.
Pä'rŏs, isl. Ægean sea, Pä'ri an.
Pä'rŏsh, *Bib.*
pa ros'mĭ a (-rŏz'-).
pa rŏt'ic, -rŏt'id.
pär'ox ysm, -ys'mal, (-Ĭz'-), -mal-
ly, -ys'mic.
par quet' (-kĕt' *or* -kä'), -quet'ed
(-kĕt'-), -quet'ting, par'quet age,
-quet ry, *-quet e rie'* (-kĕt e rē').
parr, a fish, -marks.
pär'ra.
pär'ra keet.
pär'rel, -rope, -truck.
Par rhä'si us (-rä'shĬ-), Gr. painter.
pär rhe'si a (-zhĬ a).
pär'ri cĬde, -cĬ'dal.
pär'rot, -er, -ry, par'rot beak, a
plant, -weed.
pär'rot-bill, -bull finch, -coal,
-cross bill, -finch, -fish, -flow er,
-green, -green finch, -law yer,
-wrasse, par rot's-bill.
Par'rott gun.
pär'ry, -ing, -rĬed.
parse, parsed, pars'ing, -er.
Par'see, -ism.
Par shan'da tha (*or* -dä'-), *Bib.*
par'sĬ mo ny, -si mō'ni ous, -ly,
-ness.
pars'ley, -cam phor, -fern, -haw,
-piert.
pars'nip, -cher'vil.
par'son (-sn), -age, -ish, -ize, -ized,
-ĭ'zing, -soned, -son'ic, -ic al,
-al ly.
par'son-bird, -gull, -in-the-pul'-
pit.
part, -ed, -ing, -a ble, -er, -ly,
part'-mu'sic, -own'er, -sing'ing,
-song, -writ'ing.
part'ing-cup, -glåss, -line, -rail,
-sand, -shard, -strip, -tool.

par take', -took', -täk'ing, -en, -er.
par terre' (-târ').
Par'the non.
Par'thĬ an, P. är'row.
par'tial (-shăl), -ly, -ism, -ist, -ize,
-ized, -ĭ'zing, -ti al'i ty (-shĬ-
äl'-).
part'i ble, -i bil'i ty.
par'ti ceps crĬm'i nis.
par tic'i pate, -pä'ted, -ting, -tor,
-pant, -pant ly, -pä'tive, -pä'-
tion.
par'ti ci ple, -cip'i al, -al ly.
par'ti cle.
par'tĬ-col ored. See *party-colored.*
par tic'u lar, -ly, -ness, -ism, -ist,
-is'tic, -ize, -ized, -ĭ'zing, -Ĭ zä'-
tion, -lär'i ty.
par'tĬ zan *or* -san (-zăn), -ship.
part'ner, -ship.
par'tridge, -ber'ry, -hawk, -pea,
-wood.
par tu ri'tion (-rĬsh'un), -tū'ri ent,
-ri en cy.
par'ty, -ism, par'ty-coat'ed, -col'-
ored, -gold, -ju'ry, -list, p. man,
p. wall. *Parti-* is frequently, but
less correctly, used in some of the
hyphenated compounds in this
group.
Pa ru'ah (*or* pär'u-), *Bib.*
par've nū'.
pas (pä).
pä'sa.
Pas a de'na, c. Cal.
Pas ca gou'la (-gōō'-), r. Miss.
pas'chal (-kăl), -ist, pasch'-egg
(päsk'-).
Päs coag' (-kōg'), vil. R. I.
på se'ō (-sä'-).
pa shä' (*or* päsh'a̤), -shä'lic.
Päsh'ur (*or* pä'-), *Bib.*
Pä sig' (-sēg'), t. P. I.
pa sig'ra phy, pas'i graph'ic, -ic al.
pasque' flow er.
păs'quin, -ade', -äd'er.
pâss, -a ble, -a ble ness, -a bly,
-ing, -er, passed, pass'man, -mås-
ter, -port, -word, -wort, Pass'o-
ver.
pâss'-book, -box, -by, -check,
-guard, -hold'er, -key, -pa role',
-shoot'ing, -tick'et, pass er-by'.

---

fāte, făt, fär, fa̤ll, fâre, få̤st, sofà, mēte, mĕt, hêr, īce, Ĭn, nŏte,

pas'sa cä'glia (päs'så käl'ya).

pås såde' *or* pas sä'do.

pås'sage, -saged, -sä ging, pas'-sage way, pas'sage-board, -mon'-ey.

Pas sa'glia (päs säl'yä), It. theol.

Pas sa vant' (pä'sä'võn'), Ger. art hist.

passe men'terie (pås mĕn'trĭ).

pas'sen ger, -car, -el'e va tor, -en'gine, -lo co mo'tive, -pi'-geon, -ship, -train.

passe-par tout' (päs-pär tōō'), -ing, -touted' (-tōōd').

pass'i ble, capable of feeling, -ness, -bil'i ty.

pass'ing-bell, -braid, -dis'cord, mĕas'ure, -note, -place, -tone.

pas'sion (påsh'un), -al, -a ry, -ate, -ate ly, -ate ness, -ing, -less, -sioned.

pas'sion-flow er, -mu sic, -or a-tō'rĭ o, -play, -vine, Pas'sion-tide.

pås'sive, -ly, -ness, -siv'i ty.

påst, -per fect.

påste, påst'ed, -er, -ing, pås'ty, paste'board.

påste'-down, -eel, -måk'er, -point, -pot, -rock, -wash, paste'board-cut'ter.

pås'tel, -ist.

pås'tern, -bone, -joint.

Pås'teur' (-ter'), Fr. chem., -ism, -ize, -ized, -ĭ zä'tion.

pas tic'ci o (päs tēt'chē ō).

pås'tĭl *or* -tille' (-tēl'), -til lage, pas'til-pa per.

pås'time.

pås'tor, -al, -al ism, -al ist, -al ly, -ate, -less, -ship, -al ize, *pås tō-rä'le* (-lä).

pas tou relle' (-tōō rĕl').

pås'try, -cook, -man.

pås'ture, -less, -tured, -tūr å ble, -a bil'i ty, -age, -er, -ing.

pås'ty, *pl.* -ties, a pie.

Pasz'tŏ (päss'-), t. Hung.

påt, -ted, -ting, pat-a-cake, pat'ty-cake, -pan.

Påt, an abbreviation of Patrick; pät, a plant.

pa tä'ō.

Påt'a ra, *Bib.*

påtch, -a ble, -er, -er y, -ing, -ing ly, -y, -i ness, patch'head, -work, -bolt, -box, -pŏlled.

pa tchou'lĭ (-chōō'-).

påte, the top of a head, påt'ed.

pate (pät), a decoration of fine enamel.

pa té (pä tä'), a fortification.

påt'e la, a boat.

pa tel'la, pl. -læ, a dish or vase; the knee-pan; a limpet.

påt'en, a dish or bowl.

påt'ent, *n.*, letters patent, påt'ent, *v.*, -ed, -a ble, -a bil'i ty, -or, -ee', pat'ent-right, -rolls.

påt'ent (*or* pä'tent), *a.*, evident, manifest, -ly, -en cy.

pa'ter ja mĭl'ĭ as, pl. *på tres-* (-trēz-).

pa ter'nal, -ism, -ly, -ter'ni ty.

på'ter nŏs'ter, -pump, -wheel.

pa te'lĭ cō (på tä'-).

påth, -less, -way, -find er, -måk'-er.

pa thet'ic, -al, -al ly, -al ness, pä'thos.

Pa thē'us, *Bib.*

pa thog'e ny (-thŏj'-), påth'o-gen'ic, -gen'e sis, -ge net'ic.

pa thol'o gy, -o gist, -o log'ic, -ic al, -al ly.

Påth'ros, *Bib.*

på'tient, -ly, -tience.

på'tĭ o (-tē-).

Påt'mo *or* Påt'mŏs, isl. Asia Minor.

på'tois' (-twŏ').

Pä träs', t. Gr.

Pä tri' (-trē'), t. India.

på'tri arch (-ark), -ism, -ship, -arch'y, -ar'chal, -chal ism, -chal ly, -ar'chate, -ar'chic (-kĭk).

pa tri'cian (-trĭsh'an), -ism, -hood.

påt'ri cĭde, -ci'dal.

påt'ri mŏ'ny, -mo'ni al, -al ly.

på'tri ot, -ot'ic, -ic al ly, -ot ism.

Pa trŏ'clus, Homer *Iliad.*—(*or* påt'ro-), *Bib.*

pa trŏl', -trŏlled', -trŏl'ling, -man, -wag'on.

på'tron (*or* påt'ron), -age (påt'-ron age *or* pä'-), -ess, -ize, -ized, -ĭ'zer, -ĭ'zing, -ĭ'zing ly, -ĭ zä'tion, -less.

păt rŏ nym'ic, -al, -ro nom a tol'-
o gy.
pa troon', -ship.
pat'ten, a clog, -tened.
pat'ter, -er, -ing, -tered, pat'ter-
song.
păt'tern, -ing, -terned.
pat'tern-book, -box, -card, -chain,
-cyl'in der, -draw'er, -māk'er,
-mold'er, -read'er, -shop, -wheel.
Pät'ti (-tē), c. It., Păt'ti (-tē),
operatic singer.
Pau (pō), t. Fr.
Pä'u or Pä'i, Bib.
pau'ci ty.
Paul, Bib., -ist, -īte. Paul'īne, -in-
ism, -in ist, -in ize.
Pau lï'na, Shak. Winter's Tale.
Pau line' (-lēn'), Bulwer Lady
of Lyons.
Pau'lus, Rom. gen., Pau'lus (pow'-
lŏŏs), Ger. theol.
päunch, -y, -i ness, paunch'-mat.
pau'per, -ism, -ize, -ized, -ī'zing,
-ī zä'tion.
Pau sä'nĭ us, Gr. traveler.
pause, -less, -less ly, paused,
paus'ing, -ing ly, -er.
Pau thi er' (pō'tē ä'), Fr. scholar.
Pauw (pow), Dutch scholar.
pave, -ment, paved, pāv'ing, -er,
pāv'ing-bee'tle, -ma chine, -stone,
-tile, pave'ment-pipe, -ram'mer.
pa vil'ion (-yŭn), -ioned.
Päv'lŏv', t. Russ.
pa vŏ'ni an, păv'o nīne.
paw, -er, -ing, pawed.
pawl, pawled, pawl'-bitt, -press,
-rim.
pawn, -a ble, -er or -or, -ee', -ing,
pawned, pawn'bro'ker, -cock,
-shop, -pro mo'tion, -tick'et.
paw'nee, water.
Paw nee', co. Kan.; co. Neb.; a
tribe of Indians.
pay, -a ble, -a bly, -er, -ee', -ing,
-ment, paid, pay'mȧs ter, -mis-
tress.
pay'-bill, -board, -car, -clerk,
-corps, -day, -di rect'or, -in-
spect'or, -list, -of'fice, -roll.
Pay'er (pī'er), Aust. explorer.
păy'nim.

pāy'nize, -nized, -nī'zing.
pĕa, pl. individually, peas; collectively, pease, pea'ber'ry, -bird,
-flow'er, a plant, -lip, a fish,
-stone.
pea'-bean, -bee tle, -bluff, -bone,
-bug, -bush, -chā fer, -chick,
-chick'en, -clam, -coat, -cod,
-comb, -crab, -dove, -drop per,
-finch, -flow er, a flower, -green,
-grit, -gun, -jack'et, -mag got,
-mea sle, -moth, -ore, -pheas'-
ant, -pod, -rake, -rï'fle, -rise,
-roe, -shell, -shell'er, -shoot'er,
-spawn, -tree, -vine, -wee vil,
pea coal, p. soup.
pease'weep, a bird, pease'-crow,
-hook, -meal, pease' por'ridge,
p. pudding, p. soup, pease'cod-
doub'let.
peace, -a ble, -ble ness, -a bly,
-ful, -ful ly, -ful ness, -less,
-less ness, peace'-breāk' er,
-māk'er, -of'fer ing, -of'fi cer,
-pipe, p. par ty.
peach, -er y, -y, peach'blow, a
potato, -wort.
peach'-black, -blight, -blis ter,
-blos som, -bor er, -brake, -col-
or, -col ored, -down, -house,
-myr tle, -oak, -palm, -pâr er,
-stone, -stōn'er, -tree, -wa ter,
-wood, -worm, -yel lows, peach'
bran'dy.
peach'ka.
pea'cock, pea'fowl, pea'hen, pea'-
cock-bit'tern, -blue, -but ter fly,
-fish, -flow er, -hat ter, -i ris,
-pheas ant, pea cock's-tail.
peag.
peak, -ed, -ing, -ish, -y, peaked,
peak'-arch, -cleat, -crest,
-down'haul, -hal'yards, -pur'-
chase.
peal, -ing, pealed, peal'-ring er,
-ring ing.
pĕa'nut, -dig ger, -pick er.
pear (pâr), -i form, pear'mon ger,
-main, peâr'-blight, -en'cri nite,
-louse, -shaped, -shell, -slug,
-tree, -wïthe.
pearl (pêrl), -a'ceous, -ing, -y,
-i ness, pearled.

pĕarl′ash, -side, a fish, -stone, -weed, -wort.

pĕarl′-bar′ley, -bear′ing, -bĕr′ry, -bird, -blue, -bush, -dis ease′, -dīv′er, -edge, -eye, -eyed, -fish′er y, -fish′ing, -fruit, -grain, -grăss, -gray, -hen, -lash′ing, -mī′ca, -moss, -moth, -mus′sel, -nau′ti lus, -o′pal, -oys′ter, -plant, -pow′der, -purl, -sa′go, -shell, -sin′ter, -skip per, -spar, -stitch, -tea, -tie, -tumor, -white, -win ning.

peas′ant (pĕz′-), -ly, -ry.

pĕat, -y, peat′-bed, -bog, -burn′ing, -char′coal, -coal, -coke, -cut ter, -gas, -ma chine′, -moor, -moss, -reek, -soil, -spade.

peau d′o range′ (pō dō rŏnzh′).

pĕa′vey.

peb′ble, -bled, -bling, -bly, peb′-ble ware.

peb′ble-dash ing, -lĕath er, -pāv-ing, -pow der, -stone, peb′-bling-ma chine′.

pe căn′, -nut.

pec′ca ble (pĕk′-), -can cy, -cant, -cant ly.

pec ca dil′lo.

pec′ca ry.

Pec′ci (pĕt′chĕ), Pope Leo XIII.

Pec′cio li (pĕt′chō lē), t. It.

Po-chi-li′ (pä′-chē′-lē′), gulf China.

pe′cite.

peck, -er, -ing, pecked, peck′ing-bag.

Pe′cos (pä′kōs), co. Tex.

pec′to ral, -ly, -to rā′lis, -to ril′o-quy.

pĕc′u late, -lā′ted, -lā′ting, -lā′-tor, -lā′tion.

pe cūl′iar, -ly, -ness, -cu ll ăr′i ty (*or* -kūl yăr′-).

pĕ cū′nī a ry (*or* -kūn′yā-).

ped′a gŏgue, -gog′ic (-gŏj′-), -ic-al, -al ly, -ics, -gŏg ism, -gō gy.

Pĕ däh′zur (*or* pĕd′-), *Bib.*

Pe dä′iah (-ya), *Bib.*

pĕd′al, -aled *or* -alled, -al ing *or* -ling, -al ist, -a liĕr, ped′al-point.

pĕd′ant, -ry, pe dan′tic, -tic al, -al ly, -ti cism.

pĕd′dle, -dled, -dler *or* ped′ler, -dler ism, -dler y, -dling, ped′-dler′s-bas′ket, -pack.

pĕd′es tal, -tăled *or* -tălled, -tal-ing *or* -ling, ped′es tal-box, -cov er.

pĕ des′tri an, -ism, -ize, -ized, -ī′zing, -tri al, -al ly.

ped′i cel, -cĕled, ped′i cel-cell.

ped′i gree.

pĕd′i māne, pe dim′a nous.

ped′i ment, -ed, -men′tal.

ped′lar, -ler. See *peddle.*

pĕ dō bap′tist, -bap′tism.

ped′o man cy.

pĕ dŏm′e ter, pĕd o met′ric, -ric al.

pĕd o mō′tor, -mō′tive.

Pĕ′drō (*or* pä′-), Emp. of Braz., Pĕ′dro Xim′e nes (zĭm′e nĕz), a wine, pĕ′dro, a game.

pe′dum, pl. *-da.*

pĕ dun′cle, -cled, -cu lar, -cu late.

peek, -ing, peeked, peek′a bōō.

peel, -er, -ing, peeled, peel′-ax, -end, -house, -tow er, peel′ing-ax, -i ron.

peen, -ham′mer.

peep, -er, -ing, peep′-bō, -eye, -hole, -show, -sight.

peer, -age, -ess, -less, -less ly, -less ness, -ing, -y, peered.

pee′vish, -ly, -ness.

peg, -ger, -ging, -gy, pegged.

peg′-cut ter, -fiched, -float, -joint, -lad′der, -leg, -strik′er, -strip, -tank′ard, -top.

peg′ging-awl, -jack, -ma chine′, -ram′mer, peg′gy-chaw, -cut′-throat.

Peg′a sus, *Myth.*

pĕ gŏl′o gy.

peh′-tsai′ (pä′-tsī′).

peig noir′ (pēn wor′).

Pei′-Ho′ (pä′-hō′), r. China.

Pei′ne (pī′-), t. Prus.

peine (pän).

Peint (pänt), state India.

peĭ ram′e ter.

Pĕk′a hī′ah, *Bib.*

Pē′kin, c. Ill.

pĕ kin′ (pä′kăn′), a civilian.

Pē′king′, c. China.

pĕ lä′gi an, marine, -lag′ic.

Pe lă′gĭ us, a monk, -gi an, -an ism.
Pe′lä gō (pä′-), t. It.
Pe lā′iah (*or* pĕl′ā ï′ah), *Bib.*
Pĕl′a tī′ah, *Bib.*
Pĕ′le's-hair.
Pe les tri′ na (pā lĕs trē′-), isl. It.
Pĕl′e thītes (*or* pē′-), *Bib.*
pelf.
Pĕ lī′as, *Bib.*
pĕl′i can, -can ry, pel′i can-fish, -flow′er, pel′i can's-foot, -head.
Pe-Ling′, mts. China.
pe lisse′ (-lēs′).
Pe lis si er′ (pä′lē′sē′ā′), Fr. marshal.
pĕl′let, -pow der.
Pelle tan′ (pĕl′tŏṅ′), Fr. auth.
Pelle ti er′ (pĕl′tē ä′), Fr. chem.
pĕl′li cle, -lic′u lar, -u late.
Pel lis si er′ (pä′lē′sē′ā′), Fr. writer.
pell′-mell′.
pel lū′cid, -ly, -ness, -cid′i ty.
pel mat′o gram.
Pel′o pon ne′sus, -ne′sĭ an.
pe lō′rus, *Naut.*
pelt, -er, -ed, -ing, -ry, -moṇ ger, pelt′-rot, -wool.
pel′tate, -ly.
pel′vic, -vis, -vi form.
Pē mä′tes (-tēz), Rom. Antiq.
Pem′bi na (-bē-); co. N. Dak.
pem′mi can.
pen, -ner, -ning, penned *or* pent, pen′fish, -fold, -hold er, -man, -wom an.
pen′-case, -cut ter, -drīv er, -fĕath er, -gos sip, -gun, -holding, -māk er, -mȧs′ter, -name, -rack, -sack, -tray, -trough, -wīp′er, pen-and-ink, *a.*
pĕ′nal, -ize, -ized, -ī′zing, -nal ly, pen′al ty.
pen′ance, -less, -anced, -an cing, -an cer.
pence, -ta ble.
pen chant′ (pŏṅ′shŏṅ′).
pen′chute (-shōōt).
pen′cil, -cĭled, -cil ing, -cĭl′i form.
pen′cil-blue, -case, -ce dar, -compass, -draw ing, -flow er, -māk′ing, -sharp′en er, -sketch, -tree, -vase.

pend, -ed, -ing.
pend′ant, *n.*, -bow, -tac kle.
pend′ent, *a.*, -ly, -ence, -en cy.
pen′du lum, *pl.* -lums, -du lous, -lous ly, -lous ness, -lent, -let, -līne, -los′i ty.
pen′du lum-lev′el, -pump, -spin′dle, -wheel, -wire.
Pe nel′o pē, *Myth.*, -o pize, -pized, -pī′zing.
pĕ′ne plain.
pen′e trate, -trā ted, -trā ting, -ting ly, -trā′tive, -tive ly, -tiveness, -trȧ ble, -ble ness, -bly, -bil′i ty, -trance, -tran cy, -trā′tion.
pen′guin, -er y, pen′guin-duck, -rook′er y.
Pĕ nï′el, *Bib.*
pen in′su la, -su lar, -lăr′i ty.
pe′nis, *pl.* -nes (-nēz).
pen′i tent, -ly, -tence, -ten′tial, -tial ly.
pen ï ten′tia ry (-shȧ ry), -ship.
pen′lops.
pen′nant.
pen′nate, -nā ted, -ni form.
pen′nill.
pen′non, -noned.
pen′ny, *pl.* pen′nĭes, coins; pence, amount or value, -ni less, -lessness, pen′ny rot, a plant, -roy al, -weight, -wort, -worth.
pen′ny-bird, -cress, -dog, -fee, -flow er, -gaff, -grȧss, -land, -mail, -pies, -purse, -rent, -room, -wis dom, -wise, pen ny-a-lîn er, -a-lîn er ism.
pĕ nol′o gy, -o gist, -no log′ic al.
pen′sĭle, -ness, -sil′i ty.
pen′sion, -ȧ ble, -ȧ ry, -er, -ing, -sioned, pen′sion-writ, pen′sion ing war′rant.
pen′sive, -ly, -ness, *pen sō′sō.*
pen′stock.
pen′sum.
pent, -house.
pen′ta gon, -tag′o nal, -nal ly, -o nous.
pen′ta gram, -gram mat′ic.
pen tal′o gy, -ta log′ic.
pen tăm′e ter.
pen′tar chy (-ky).

pen'ta stich (-stĭk), -tas'ti chous (-kŭs).
Pen'ta teuch (-tūk), -al.
Pen'te cost, pen te cos'tal (or pen'-).
pĕ'nuc kle (-nŭk l). See *pinocle.*
Pe nū'el, *Bib.*
pĕ'nult (*or* -nult'), -nul'ti ma, -ti mate.
pĕ num'bra, -bral, -brous.
pĕn'u ry, pe nū'ri ous, -ly, -ness.
pĕ'on, a foot soldier, -age, -ism.
pĕ'o ny.
pĕo'ple, -pled, -pling.
pep'e ri'nō (-rē'-).
Pĕp'in, King of France.
pe pi'no (pā pē'nō).
pe pi'ta (pā pē'-).
pep'per, -er, -ing, -y, -pered, pep'per corn, -grăss, -mint, -root, -wood, -wort.
pep'per-bot'tle, -box, -bush, -cake, -căst'er, -cress, -crop, -dulse, -elder, -gin ger bread, -mill, -moth, -plant, -pod, -pot, -rod, -sauce, -sax'i frage, -shrub, -tree, -vine, -wa ter, -wood.
pep'per-and-salt, a plant, pep'per-mint-cam phor, -drop, -tree.
pep'sin, -ate, pep'sis, -sic.
pep'tic, -al, -tics, -tic'i ty.
pep'tŏne, -to nize, -nized, -ni zing, -ton ĭ zā'tion, -ton'ic, -to noid, -tog'e ny (-tŏj'-).
Pĕpys (pĕps *or* pĕp'is), Eng. polit.
per ad ven'ture.
per am'bu late, -lā'ted, -lā'ting, -lā'tor, -to'ry, -lā'tion.
per cale' (-kăl' *or* -kāl'), per'ca lĭne.
per ceive', -ceived,' -ceiv'ing, -er, -a ble, -a bly, -cep'tion, per'-cept.
per cent'age, -cent'ĭle.
per cept'i ble, -ness, -i bly, -bil'-i ty, -cep'tion al, -cep'tive, -tive ness, -tiv'i ty, -cep'tu al.
pĕrch, -er, -ing, -ant, perched.
pĕrch'-backed, -i ron, -lōōp, -pest, -plate, -pole, -stay.
per chânce'.
Perche (persh), tp. Mo.
Per'che ron (-she- *or* -rôn').

per cip'i ence, -en cy, -ent.
per'co late, -lā'ted, -lā'ting, -lā'-tor, -lā'tion.
per con'tra.
per cuss', -ing, -ant, -ive, -ive ly, -or, -cussed', -cus'sion.
per cus'sion-bull'et, -cap, -fuse, -grīnd'er, -gun, -ham mer, -lock, -match, -pow der, -prīm'er, -stop, -ta'ble.
pĕr den'do (-dān'dō).
Per'dĭ ta, Shak. *Winter's Tale.*
per di'tion (-dĭsh'un).
per due' *or* -du', *a.*
per dure', -dured', -dūr'a ble, -a bly, -a bil'i ty, -ance, -ing, -du rā'tion.
père (pâr).
pĕr'e grĭ nate', -na'ted, -na'ting, -na'tor, -nă'tion, -e grĭne, -grĭn'-i ty.
pe rei'ra (-rā'ra).
Pe re'i ra (pā rā'ē rä), Sp. in struct. of deaf mutes.
Pe rei'ra (pā rē'ra), Eng. phar macologist.
Pe reire' (pa râr'), Fr. financier.
pĕr'emp to ry, -to ri ly, -ri ness.
per en'ni al, -ly, -stemmed.
Pe'rez (pā'rĕs), Pres. Chile.
per'fect, *a.,* per'fect (*or* -fect') *v.,* -fect er, -fect'i ble, -ive, -ive ly, -fect ly, -ness, -fec'tion, -tion ism, -tion ist, per'fect ing ma chine', p. press.
per fid'i ous, -ly, -ness, -fi dy.
per fŏ'li ate.
per'fo rate, -rā'ted, -rā'ting, -ra ble, -rā'tive, -rā'tor, -rant, -rā'-tion, per'fo ra ting-ma chine'.
per force'.
per form', -a ble, -ance, -er, -ing, -formed'.
per'fume (*or* -fume') *n.,* per fume' (*or* per'-) *v.,* -fūm'er, -er y, per'fu my, per'fume-burn er, -foun tain, -set.
per func'to ry, -ri ly, -ri ness.
per fuse' (-fūz'), -fused', -fū'sing, -fū'sive (-sĭv), -fū'sion (-zhŭn).
per haps'.
pĕ'rĭ, *pl.* -ris (-rĭz), *Myth.*
pe ri' (pā rē'), Her.

pĕr'ĭ ä'gua.

pĕr'i anth.

pĕr i car'dĭ um, -di al, -di an, -dit'ic, -dĭ'tis.

pĕr'i carp, -car'pĭ al, -car'pic.

Pĕr'i cles (-klēz), Athenian states-man, -clē'an.

pĕr'ĭ crā'ni um, pl. -ni a, -ni al.

Pē rĭ'da, Bib.

Pé ri er' (pā'rē ā'), Fr. politician.

pĕr'i gee (-jē), -ge'an.

pĕr i glot'tis, -glot'tic.

Pe ri gueux' (pā'rē'gê'), t. Fr.

pĕr'i hē'li on, -oned (-ŭnd).

pĕr'il, -iled or -illed, -il ing or -ling, -ous, -ous ly, -ous ness.

pĕr im'e ter, -e try, -ĭ met'ric, -ric al.

pĕ'rĭ od, -od'ic, -ic al, -al ly, -al-ness, -al ist, -o dic'i ty.

pĕr'ĭ ŏs'te um, -te al, -os tĭ'tis, -os-tit'ic, -os te ot'o my.

pĕr'i pa tet'ic, itinerant, -ic al, Pĕr'i pa tet'ic, a follower of Aristotle, -tet'i cism.

pĕ rĭph'er y, -er al, -al ly, pĕr' ĭ-phĕr'ic, -ic al.

pĕr'i phrase (-frāz), -phrased, -phrās'ing, -phrăs'tic, -tic al, -al ly, pĕ rĭph'ra sis, pl. -ra ses (-sēz).

pĕ rique' (-rēk').

pĕr'i scope, -scŏp'ic, -ic al.

pĕr'ish, -a ble, -ble ness, -a bly, -a bil'i ty.

pĕr'i style, -sty'lar (-stĭ'-).

pe rit'o my.

pĕr i tŏ nē'um, -nē'al, -to nĭ'tis, -nit'ic.

pĕr'i wig, -ging, -wigged, per'i-wig-pāt ed.

pĕr'i win̦'kle.

per'jure, -jured, -jured ly, -jūr er, -jur ing, -ju ry.

perk, -y, -i ly, -i ness, -ing, perked.

per'ma nent, -ly, -nence, -nen cy.

per'me a ble, -a bly, -a bil'i ty, -ance, -ant, -ate, -ā'ted, -ā'ting, -à tive, -ā'tion.

per me am'e ter.

Per'me nas, Bib.

per mit, v., -ted, -ting, -ter, -mis'-si ble, -si bly, -si bil'i ty, -sive,

-sive ly, -mis'sion (-mĭsh'un), per'mit (or -mit'), n.

per mŭt'a ble, -ble ness, -bly, -bil'i ty, -mū tā'tion, per mu tā'-tion-lock.

Per näm bu'co (-bōō'kō), state Braz.

per nĕt'ĭ.

per ni'cious (-nĭsh'us), -ly, -ness.

per nick'et y.

pĕr'o rate, -rā'ted, -rā'ting, -rā'-tion.

per ox'id, -i dize, -dized, -dĭ'zing, -dā'tion.

per pen dic'u lar, -ly, -lăr'i ty.

per'pe trate, -trā'ted, -trā'ting, -trā'tor, -trà ble, -trā'tion.

per pet'u ate, -ā'ted, -ā'ting, -à-ble, -al, -al ly, -ance, -ant, -ā'-tor, -ā'tion, -pe tū'i ty.

per plex', -ed ly, -ed ness, -ing, -ing ly, -i ty, -plexed'.

pĕr'quĭ site (-zĭt), -quis'i tor, -qui si'tion (-kwĭ zĭsh'un).

Per ɹault' (pā'rō'), Fr. auth.; Fr. architect.

Per rens' (pā'rŏn̊), Fr. hist.

Per rin' (pā'răn̊'), writer of Fr. operas.

Per ro'ne (pĕr rō'nā), It. theol.

Per ro net' (pā'rō'nā'), Fr. engi-neer.

pĕr'ro tĭne.

pĕr'ry, a drink.

per sē'.

per'se cute, -cū'ted, -cū'ting, -cū'-tor, -to ry, -cū'tion.

Per'se ŭs (or -sūs), Myth.

per se vere', -vered', -vēr'ing, -ing ly, -ance.

Per'si a (-shĭ a), kingdom Asia, -sian, (-shan), -sic, per sĭ ā'na.

per sĭ ĕnne', a muslin, per si ennes' (-sĭ ĕn'), window-blinds.

per'sĭ flage (-fläzh), -si fleur' (-sē'-flêr').

per sim'mon.

per sist', -ed, -ing, -ing ly, -ive, -ence, -en cy, -ent, -ent ly.

per son (-sn), -a ble, -ble ness, -age, -al, -al ly, -al'i ty, -al ism, -al ist, -al ize, -ized, -ĭ'zing, -ĭ zā'tion, -al ty, -ate, -a ted,

-a ting, -a tor, -ā'tion, *per so'na
grā'ta.*
per son'i fy, -ing, -fīed, -i fi ca'-
tor, -ca'tive, -cā'tion, *per son-
nel'.*
per spec'tive, -ly, per spec'tive-
glǎss, -in'stru ment.
per spĭ cǎ'cious, -ly, -ness, -cac'-
i ty (-kas'-), per'spi ca ble.
per spĭ cū'i ty, -spic'u ous, -ous-
ly, -ous ness.
per spĭre', -spired', -spĭr'ing, -a-
ble, -a bil'i ty, -a tive, -a to'ry,
-spĭ rā'tion.
per suade' (-swād'), -suad'ed,
-ed ness, -er, -ing, -a ble, -a ble-
ness, -a bly, -sua'si ble, -ble-
ness, -bil'i ty, -sive, -sive ly,
-sive ness, -so ry, -sua'sion
(-swā'zhŭn).
pêrt, -ly, -ness.
per tāin', -ing, -tained'.
Per'thes (pěr'těs), Ger. publish.
per tĭ nā'cious (-shŭs), -ly, -ness,
-nac'i ty (-năs'-).
per'ti nent, -ly, -ness, -nence,
-nen cy.
per turb', -ance, -ant, -er, -ing,
-ed ly, -å ble, -å bil'i ty, -å to'-
ry, -turbed', -tur bā'tion, -tion-
al, per'tur bā'tive, -bā'tor.
per tuse' (-tūs'), -tused, -tū'sion
(zhŭn).
Pe ru' (-rōō'), rep. S. Amer.; c.
Ill.; c. Ind.; vil. N. Y., -ru'vi-
an, Pe ru'vi an bạl'sam, P.
bark.
Pĕ ru'da, *Bib.*
Pe ru'gia (pā rōō'jä), prov. It.
Pe ru gi'no (pā rōō jē'nō), It.
painter.
pěr'uke (-ōōk *or* -ōōk').
pě ruse' (-rōōz'), -rūs'al, -er, -ing.
Pe ruz'zi (pā rōōt'sē), It. architect.
per vade', -vād'ed, -vād'ing, -vā'-
sive (-sĭv), -vā'sion (-zhŭn).
per verse', -ly, -ness, -ver'si ty,
-ver'sive.
per vert', *v.*, -ed, -er, -ing, -i ble,
-ver'sion, per'vert, *n.*
per'vi ous, -ness.
pes (pēz), pl. *pe'des* (pē'dēz).

pe sāde'.
pes'ăge (*or* pě zäzh').
pe san'te (pā zǎn'tä).
pes'ca dōr'.
Pěs chi e'ra (-kē ā'ra), t. It
Pes'cia (pěsh'a), t. It.
Pe sci'na (pā shē'na), t. It.
pe se'ta (pā sā'ta).
Pe sha'wur (pā shou'er), div. India.
pes'ky, -ki ly.
pe'so (pā'sō), *pe'so du'ro* (dōō'rō).
pěs'si mism, -si mist, -mis'tic,
-tic al, -si mize, -mized, -mĭ'zing.
pest, -ful, pes tif'er ous, -ous ly,
pest'-house.
Pěs tä loz'zi (-lŏt'sē), Swiss edu-
cator, -zi an, -an ism.
pes'ter, -er, -ing, -ing ly, -ment.
pes'ti lent, -ly, -ness, -ti lence,
-len'tial, pes'ti lence-weed, -wort.
pes'tle (pěs'l), -tled, -tling, pes'-
tle-pie.
pet, -ted, -ting.
pět'al, -aled, -al if'er ous, -al ĭne,
-al ism.
pe tard', pet'ar deer' *or* -dier'.
pe tä'te (pā tä'tä).
petch'a ry.
Pet cho'ra, r. Russ.
pe'ter, a term in cards; to diminish,
-tered, -ter ing, pe'ter-boat, Pě'-
ter-pence, Pe'ter's bird, P. cress,
P. fish, P. pence.
pe'ter sham.
Peth'a hī'ah, *Bib.*
Pe thu'el, *Bib.*
pět'i ole, -oled, -o'lar, -lā'ry,
-o late, -la'ted.
pet'it (pět'ĭ), -baume (-bōm)
pet'it con'sta ble, p. ju'ry, p.
trea'son, *pet it' māl* (pet ē').
pe tite' (pā tēt').
pe ti'tion (-tĭsh'un), -a ry, -er,
-ing, -ist, -tioned.
pět'rěl.
pe tres'cence, -cent.
pět'ri fy, -ing, -fīed, -fĭ'a ble, -ri
fac'tion, -fac'tive, pě trĭf'ic.
Pe'trin ism, -ist, -ize.
pet rog'ra phy (*or* pe trog'-), -ra-
pher, -ro graph'ic, -ic al, -al ly.
pě trō'lĕ um, *pé tro leur'* (pä'tro'-
lêr'), fem. *pé tro leuse'* (-lêz').

---

nŏt, nôr, ūse, ŭp, ûrn, etüde, fōōd, fŏŏt, ạnger, boṅmot, thus, Bach.
29

pe trŏ'le um-burn'er, -car, -e'-
ther, -fil'ter, -fur'nace, -still,
-stove.
pĕ trol'o gy, -o gist, pet'ro log'ic,
-ic al, -al ly.
Pĕ tru'chĭ o, Shak. *Taming of
the Shrew.*
pĕt'ti cŏat, -ed, pet'ti coat-af fair',
-breech'es, -gov'ern ment, -pen'-
sion er, -pipe, -trou'sers.
pet'ti fog, -ger, -ger y, -ging,
-fogged.
pet'to.
pet'ty, -ti ly, -ti ness, -tish, -tish-
ly, -tish ness.
pet'u lant, -ly, -lance, -lan cy.
pe tune' (*or* pĕt'-) -tuned', -tūn'ing.
Pĕ ŭl'thăi, *Bib.*
pew (pū), -hold'er, -chair, -gaff,
-o'pen er, -rent.
pĕ'wee.
pe'weep.
pĕ'wit.
pew'ter, -er, -y, -wort, pew'ter-
mill.
pey'ŏth (pā'-).
pey'ton (pā'tun).
Peze'nas (pāz'nä), t. Fr.
Pfaff (pfäf), Ger. theol.
Pfalz (pfälts), the Palatinate, Ger.
Pfeif'fer (pfī'fer), Ger. trav.
pfen'nig.
Pforz'heim (pfŏrts'-), t. Ger.
Phæ'dra, *Myth.*
Phă'e thon, *Myth.*
phă'e ton, -tŏn'ic.
Phāi'sur, *Bib.*
phă'lanx (*or* făl'-), *pl.* pha lan'-
ges (fa lăn'jēz) *or* phă'lanx es.
In *Anat.* and *Bot.* only phalanges.
Phăl'a ris, a tyrant of Sic.
Phal dā'ius, *Bib.*
Pha lĕ'as, *Bib.*
phan'tasm (fan'tăzm), -tas'ma-
go'ri a, -ri al, -gŏr'ic, -tas'-
mal, -mal ly, -mal'i ty, -mat'ic,
-ic al, -tas'mo grăph.
phan'tom.
Pha nū'el (*or* făn'-), *Bib.*
Pha'raoh (fā'rō *or* fā'rā ō), *Bib.*
Phăr'ā on'ic.
Pha'res (-rēz), *Bib.*
Pha'rĕz, *Bib.*

Phăr'i see, phăr'i sā'ic, -ic al, -al-
ly, -al ness, -sa'ism, -see'ism.
phar ma ceu'tic (-sū'tĭk), -tic al,
-al ly, -tics, -tist, phar'ma cist,
phar'mic.
phar ma col'o gy, -o gist, -co log'-
ic al.
phar'ma co pœ'ia   (-kō pē'ya),
-pœ'ial (-pē'yal), -cŏp'o list.
phă'ros, a lighthouse, Phā'ros,
isl. Medit.
phăr'ynx, *pl.* pha ryn'ges (fā-
rĭn'jēz), -ryn'ge al, -gī'tis (-jĭ'-),
-gĭt'ic (-jit'-), phar yn gol'o gy,
-go log'ic al,   pha ryŋ'go scōpe,
-go sco'py, -got'o my.
phase (fāz), -less, phās'er, phās'-
ing, phase-split'ter.
Pha sĕ'ah (*or* phā'-), *Bib.*
phȧ sĕ'lin, -se'o lin.
phȧ'sĭ a nīne'.
pheas'ant (fĕz'-), -ry, pheas'ant-
cuck'oo, -duck, -finch, -shell,
-tail, -wood, pheas'ant's-eye.
Phé'dre (fā'dr), Racine's tragedy.
Phĕ nĭ'ce (*or* phē'nĭce), *Bib.*
phe'nix *or* phœ'nix, a sacred
bird; a moth.   phe'nix-stone.
Phœnix, Bot. genus.
phe'nol.
phe nol'o gy, -o gist, -no log'ic al.
phe nom'e non, *pl.* -na, -nal,
-nal ism,   -nal ist,   -e nal'i ty,
-nal ize, -ized, -i'zing, -e nal ly,
-e nism, -e nist, -e nize, -nized,
-ni zing,   -e nol'o gy,   -no log'-
ic al.
phē'nyl, -nyl'ic.
Phĭ bĕ'seth (*or* phĭb'-), *Bib.*
Phid'i as, Athenian sculpt., -i an.
phi lan'der, -er, -der ing.
Phi lante'   (fē'lăṅt'),   Molière's
comedy.
phil'an thrŏpe, -throp'ic, -ic al,
-al ly,   -throp'i nism,   -i nist,
phĭ lan'thro pism, -thrō pist, -thro-
py, -pis'tic.
phĭ lăt'e ly, -e list, phil a tel'ic.
Phĭ lĕ'mon, *Myth.; Bib.*
Phĭ lĕ'tus, *Bib.*
phil har mon'ic.
Phĭl'ip, Chr. name; phil'ip, a
sparrow.

Phĭ lĭp′pĭ, ancient city, -lip′pi an, -lip′pic, an oration of Demosthenes, phĭ lip′pic, any acrimonious declamation.

Phi lip po teaux′ (fē′lē′pō′tō′), Fr. painter.

Phil′i sĭdes (or -lĭs′ĭ dēz), Sir Philip Sidney.

Phĭ lis′tĭne, Bib.

phĭ log′y ny, -y nist.

phĭ lŏl′o gy, -o gist, -o gize, -gized, -gī′zing, phil′o logue, -log′ic, -ic al, -al ly.

phĭl′o math, -ic, -ic al, phi lom′- a thy.

phĭl′o mel, Phĭl o mē′la, Myth.

phĭl o pē′na.

phil′o pro gen′i tive ness, -pro ge- nē′i ty.

phĭ los′o pher, -o phy, -o phist, -o phize, -phized, -phī′zer, -phī′- zing, phil o soph′ic, -ic al, -al- ly, -al ness.

phil o tech′nic (-tĕk′nĭk), -al.

phil ox′e ny.

phil′ter, -ing, -tered.

phil′y drous or -hy′drous.

phle bŏt′o my, -o mist, -o mize, mized, -mī′ zing.

Phleg′e thon (flĕj′- or flĕg′-), Myth.

phlegm (flĕm), -y, phleg măt′ic (flĕg-), -ic al, -al ly.

Phlē′gon, Bib.

phle oph′a gous.

phlŏ gis′ton, -gis′ti an, -gis′tic.

phlox, -worm.

Pho′ci on (fō′shĭ on), Athenian gen.

Phō′cis, ancient state, -cian (-shan).

Phœ′be (fē′-), the moon-goddess, -be′an, phœ′be, a bird.

Phœ′bus, Apollo.

Phœnix, Bot. genus; phœ′nix. See phenix.

phŏ nas′cus, pl. -ci, -nas cet′ics.

phŏ′nate, -nā′ted, -nā′ting, -nȧ- to′ry, -nā′tion, -nau′to gram, -to grȧph, -graph′ic, -ic al ly.

phone (fōn), phoned, phōn′ing, phō neī′do scope, -scŏp′ic.

pho nĕt′ic, -al, -al ly, -net′i cism, -i cist, -i cize, -cized, -cī′zing, -net′ics, -ne ti′cian (-tĭsh′an),

-ne tism, -ne tist, -ne tize, -tized, -tī′zing, -tĭ zā′tion, phon′- ic, -ics, pho ne′sis.

pho no camp′tic, -tics.

phŏ′no gram, -no grȧph, -graph′- ic, -ic al, -al ly, -nog′ra pher, -ra phist, -ra phy.

pho nol′o gy, -o gist, -no log′ic, -ic al, -al ly.

pho nom′e ter, pho no mō′tor, -no phore, -noph′o rous, -no- plex, -no scope, -no te lem′e ter.

pho′no type, -typ′ic (-tĭp′-), -ic al, -al ly, -no ty′pist (-tī′-), -ty′py.

phŏr′o scope.

phos′phate, -phā′ted, -phȧ tize, -tized, -tĭ zing, -tĭ zā′tion, -phat′ic, -phĭte.

phos′pho rate, -rā ted, -rā ting, phos′phor-bronze, -cop′per.

phos pho resce′, ′-resced′ (-rest′), -res′cing, -res′cence, -cent, -phŏr′- ic, -ic al.

phos′phŏ rize, -rized, -rī zing, -phor ous, a.

phos′pho rus, n., -box.

Pho′ti us (fō′shĭ us), Patriarch of Constantinople.

pho to chem′is try (-kĕm′-), -chem′- ist, -chem′ic al.

phŏ′to chro′my (or -tŏk′-), -chrō′- mo type, -mo lĭth′o graph, -chro- mat′ic.

phŏ′to chrŏn′o graph, -o graph′ic, -chro nog′ra phy.

pho to cray′on.

pho′to e lec′tric, -tric al, -tric′- i ty, -lec′tro grȧph, -tro type.

pho′to en grave′, -grāv′ing, -to- etch′ing.

phŏ′to gene, -gĕn′ic, -tog′e nous (-tŏj′-), -e ny.

pho tog′ly phy, -to glyph′ic.

pho′tŏ gram, -gram′me ter, -me try, -met′ric, -to neph′o grȧph.

pho′to grȧph, -tog′ra pher, -ra phy, -to grȧph′ic, -ic al, -al ly, -graph om′e ter, -to gra vūre′.

pho to hē′lĭ o grȧph, -grăph′ic.

pho to lith′o grȧph, -li thog′ra- pher, -ra phy, -lith o graph′ic.

pho tŏl′o gist, -o gy, -to log′ic, -ic al.

pho tom′e ter, -e try, -e trist, -to-
mĕt′ric, -ric al, -al ly.
pho to mĭ′cro grȧph, -mĭ crog′ra-
pher, -ra phy, -cro graph′ic.
pho′to neph′o grȧph (-nef′-).
phŏ′to phone, -phŏ′ny (or -tŏf′o-
ny), -to phon′ic.
pho′to phore.
pho′to phos′pho res′cent.
phŏ′to-proc′ess (-prŏs′-), -re liēf′.
phŏ′to scope, -to sphere, -sphĕr′ic,
-to type, -typed, -typ′ing (-tĭp′-),
-ty′py (-tĭ′- or -tot′y py), -typ′-
ic (-tĭp′-), -ty po graph′ic.
pho′tō tax′is, -to tac′tic.
pho′to te leg′ra phy, -to thĕr′a py.
pho′to to pog′ra phy, -to po-
graph′ic, -ic al, -al ly.
pho to xy log′ra phy (-zī lŏg′-).
pho to zin′co grȧph, -zin cog′ra-
phy, -co graph′ic, -to zin′co-
type, -ty′py (-tĭ′-).
phrase (frāz), phrased, phrās′ing,
-al, phra′se o grȧph (-zē o-), -o-
gram, -og′ra phy, -ol′o gy,
-o gist, -o log′ic, -ic al, -al ly,
phrase′man, -mon′ger, phrase′-
book, -mark.
phre nē′sis, -net′ic, -ic al, -al ly.
phrĕn′ic, phre nĭ′tis, -nĭt′ic.
phre nol′o gy, -o gist, -o ger,
phren o log′ic, -ic al, -al ly.
phre no mag′net ism, -mag net′ic.
Phryg′i a (frĭj′-), Bib.
phthis′ic (tĭz′ĭk), -ic al, -ick y,
phthis i ol′o gy, phthī′sis (tī′-).
phul ka′ri (fo͝ol kä′rē).
Phy gel′lus (fĭ-), Bib.
phy lac′ter y (fĭ-), -tered, -tĕr′ic,
-ic al.
phy′le (fī′le).
phyl′lŏx ē′ra.
phys′ic (fĭz′-), -icked, -ick ing,
-ick y, -ic al, -al ly, -al ness,
-i cist, -ics, phy sique′ (fĭ zēk′).
phy si′cian (fĭ zĭsh′an), -ly, -cian-
ship.
phys i og′e ny (fĭz ĭ ŏj′-), -o gen′-
ic, -gen′e sis, -ge net′ic.
phys i og′no my, -no mist, -nom′-
ic, -ic al, -al ly, -ics, -no mon′ic.
phys i og′ra phy, -ra pher, -o-
graph′ic, -ic al, -al ly, -ol′a try.

phys i ol′o gy (fĭz-), -ol′o gist,
-o gize, -gized, -gī′zing, -o log′-
ic, -ic al, -al ly.
phy to gen′e sis (fī-), -ge net′ic,
-ic al, -tog′e ny (-tŏj′-).
phy′to ge og′ra phy (fī′-), -ra-
pher, -o graph′ic, -ic al.
phy tŏg′ly phy (fĭ tŏg′lĭ fĭ), -to-
glyph′ic (-glĭf′-).
phy tog′ra phy (fĭ-), -ra pher,
-to graph′ic, -ic al.
pĭ, jumbled type, pīed, pīe′ing.
pĭ′a, Anat., pĭ′a mā′ter.
pi′a (pē′a), a plant.
pĭ ăffe′.
pĭ ăn′ō (or pĭ ăn′ō), n., pl. -os
(-ōz), -for′te (-tä), -o graph,
pi a′no (pe ä′nō or pyä′nō),
adv., pi a′no (pe ä′nō), a story
of a house, pl. pi a′ni (-nē),
pĭ a nĭs′sĭ mō, pi a ni′no (pē′-
ȧ nē′nō), pĭ ăn′ist, pĭ ȧ nō′la.
pi an′o-case, -cov er, -mȧk′er,
-mu sic, -play er, -school, -stool,
-tūn′er, -vi o lin′.
pĭ as′ter.
pĭ ăz′za, pl. -zas (-zȧz), -zi an.
Pĭ bē′seth (or pĭb′-), Bib.
pi′broch (pē′brŏch or -brŏk).
pĭ′ca, a bird; a craving for what
is unfit to eat; a catalogue of
names; a size of printing-type.
Pī′ca, Ornith. genus.
pic a dor′ (pĕk′ȧ dōr′).
pic′a lil′lĭ.
Pi card′ (pē′kär′), Fr. auth.
pĭc′ard.
pic a rōōn′.
pic a yune′.
pic′ca dil ly.
pic′ca nin′ny or pick′a-.
pic che tä′to (pĭk kē-).
pic′co lo.
Pic co lo′mi ni (pĭk kō lō′mē nē),
It. philos.; Aust. gen.
pĭce.
Piche gru′ (pēsh′grü′), Fr. gen.
pĭ′cĭne.
pick, -er, -ing, picked.
pick′ax, pick cheese, a bird; a
fruit, -man, -maw, a gull, -mire,
a bird, -pock et, a person, -purse,
a person, -tooth, a plant, -wick,

pick-mat tock, -mirk, -o ver, -point ed, -rake, -up.
pick'er-bar, -bend, -mo tion, -staff, pick'ing-peg, -stick.
pick'a back.
pick'er el, -weed.
pick'et, -ed, -er, -ing, pick'et tail, a duck.
pick'et-clamp, -guard, -line, -machine', -pin, -point'er, -rope, p. fence.
pick'le (-l), -led (-ld), -ler, -ling, pick'le-cured, -her'ring, -worm.
Pick'wick, Dickens' hero, -wick'-i an.
pic'nic, -nicked, -nick er, -nicking.
Pi cot' (pē'kō'), Fr. philol.; Fr. writer.
pi cot' (pē'kō'), -rib bon.
pic'o tīte.
pic qué-work (pē kā'-).
pic'ra (*or* pī'-), pic'ric (*or* pī'-).
Pi cro chole' (pē'krō'kōl'), Rabelais' satire.
pic'to gràph, -tog'ra phy, -to-graph'ic.
Pic tou' (-tōō'), co. N. S.
pic'ture, -tured, -tūr ing, -tūr er, -to'ri al, -al ly, -tur al, -tur a ble, -tur esque' (-ĕsk'), -esque'ly, -ness.
pic'ture-board, -book, -frame, -gal'ler y, -lens, -mold'ing, -mosa'ic (-zā'-), -nail, -plane, -rod, -writ'ing.
pid gin-Eŋ'glish.
pīe, -man, -pie-bāk'er, -crust, -eat'er, -finch, -mag, -māk ing, -nan ny, -plant.
pie (pyā *or* pē ā'), a measure.
pīe'bald.
piĕce, -less, -meal, pieced, piĕ'-cing, -cer.
piece'-bro ker, -dyed, -goods, -liq uor, -mås ter, -mold, -work, -work'er, *pièce de ré sis tance'* (pyās dê rā'zēs'tŏns'), *pièce mon tée'* (mŏn tā').
pīed, -ness, pied'-billed, -fort, -winged.
Pie di mon'te (pyā dē mŏn'tā), t. It.

pié douche' (pyā'dōōsh'), *pie droit'* (-drwŏ').
piel (pĕl).
pi e'na (pē ā'na).
piĕnd, -cheek, -råft er.
piĕr, -arch, -glåss, -ta ble.
piĕrce, -a ble, pierced, piĕr'cer, -cing, -cing ly, -cing ness, piĕr'-cing-drill, -file, -saw.
piĕr ĕlle'.
Pī ĕr'ĭ des (-dēz), the Muses.
Pi erre' (pē âr' *or* peer), c. S. Dak.
pierre per due' (pyâr pĕr dü').
Pi erre' Per tuis' (pē âr' pĕr-twē'), tunnel Switz.
Pierre'pŏnt (pēr'-), tp. N. Y.
Pie ter mar'itz burg (pē ter mâr'-Its bōōrg), t. S. Afr.
Pī'e tirm, -e tist, -e tis'tic, -tic al.
Pi e'to le (pē ā'tō lā), vil. It.
pi e'tra du'ra (pē ā'tra dōō'ra).
pī'e ty.
pī'ē zŏm'e ter.
pij'je ro (pēf'fā rō).
pif'fle, -fled, -fler, -fling.
pig, ging, gish, -gish ly, -gish-ness, -gy, -ger y, pigged, pig'-fish, -foot, a fish, -nut, -root, -skin, -sty, -tail, -tailed, -weed.
pig'-bed, -boll ing, -cote, -dee r, -eyed, -head ed, -head ed ness, -hole, -pen, -rat, -stick er, pig's-face, -wash, -wrack, pig' i ron, p. lĕad.
pi'geon (pĭj'un), -ry, -ber'ry, -foot, a plant, -gram, -hole, -holed, -tail, a duck, -wing, -wood, tree.
pi'geon-brĕast, -brĕast ed, -cher ry, -ex press', -fan'ci er, -goose, -gråss, -hawk, -heart'ed, -house, -liv ered, -match, -pair, -pea, -plum, -post, -toed, -tre'mex, -wing, a wing, -wood peck er, pig'eon's-blood, -grass.
pig'gin.
pig'gle.
pigh'tle (pī'tl) *or* -tel.
pig'ment, -less, -men'tal, -ta ry, -tā'tion.

---

pig'ment-cell, -gran ule, -mol e-
cule, -print ing, -spot.
pi'gnon (pĭn'yon).
pig'no rate, -rā'ted, -rā'ting, -rā'-
tion.
pig'nus, pl. *-nŏ'ra.*
pĭk.
pĭ'ka, a quadruped, -squir'rel.
pike, -let, pike'head, a fish, -man,
-stăff, -tail, a duck.
pike'-fork, -head, head of a pike,
-head ed, -keep er, -perch, -pole,
-suck'er.
pĭ'la, a mortar, pĭ'la (pē'-), a
font.
pĭ'lar, -la ry, pĭ'lē ous, -lif'er ous,
-lig'er ous (-lĭj'-), pĭ'lose, -lŏs'-
i ty, -lous (-lŭs).
pĭ las'ter, -tered.
pĭ lau'.
pil'chard.
pĭ' le (pē'lā), a nut.
pile, piled, pĭl'ing, -er, pile'work,
-wort.
pile'-beam, -build er, -cap,
-clamp, -drĭv'er, -en gine, -hoop,
-plank, -saw, -shoe, -start,
-warp, -weav'ing, -wire, -worm,
-worn, pile' bridge, p. dam,
p. dwell ing, p. pier, pil'ing-
i ron.
Pĭ lē'ser (-zer), *Bib.*
pĭ'le us, *-le'o lus,* pl. *-o lĭ.*
pil'fer, -er, -ing, -ing ly, -fered.
pil'grim, -age, -er, -ize, -ized,
-ī'zing, pil'grim-bot tle.
pill, -corn, -wort, -bee'tle, -box,
-bug, -coat er, -mil'le ped, -tile,
-wil let, -worm.
pil'lage, -laged, -lā ging, -lā ger.
pil'lar, -et, -ing, -ist, -lared.
pil'lar-block, -box, -brick, -com'-
pass es, -file, -lip, -plait, -saint.
pil'lion (-yŭn), -lioned.
pil'lo ry, -ing, -rĭed.
pil'lŏw, -y.
pil'low-bar, -beâr, -beer, -block,
-case, -cup, -lace, -lin'en, -pipe,
-sham, -slip, -word.
pi lon' (pē lŏn').
pĭ'lot, -ed, -ing, -age, -weed.
pĭ'lot-bird, -boat, -bread, -cloth,
-en'gine, -fish, -flag, -house,

-jack, -jack et, -light, -snake,
-whale, p. bal loon.
Pĭl'tāi, *Bib.*
pĭ'lum, pl. *-la.*
pi'lus, pl. *-lĭ.*
pĭ men'to, -walk.
Pim'lĭ co, a suburb of London,
Eng.; pim'li co, a bird.
pimp, -ing, pimped, pimp'ship,
-like.
pim'per nel.
pim'ple, -pled, -pling, -ply, pim'-
ple-met'al, -mite.
pin, -ner, -ning, pinned, pin'-
bor er, a beetle, -case, -cush-
ion, -dust, -fish, -fold, -hold,
-hole, -patch, a plant, -tail, *n.,*
a duck; a grouse, -wheel, -work,
-worm.
pin'-block, -bush, -cher ry, -clov-
er, -con nec tion, -cop, -drill,
-eyed, -fĕath er, -fĕath ered,
-fire, -flat, -foot ed, -grăss,
-head, -head'ed, -joint, -lock,
-ma chine, -māk'er, -mark,
-mill, -mon ey, -necked, -oak,
-pil low, -point, -pool, -pop pet,
-rack, -rail, -rib, -rod, -switch,
-tail, *a.,* -tongs, -tool, -vise,
-winged.
pi' na (pēn'ya), -cloth.
pin'a fore.
pĭ nas'ter.
pince'-nez' (păńs'-nā').
pin'cers *or* pinch'ers, *pin cette'*
(păń sĕt').
pinch, -ing, -ing ly, -er, pinched,
pinch'back, a person, -beck,
-fist, a person, -pen ny, a
person.
pinch'-bar, -cock, -plane, -point,
-spot ted.
pinch'ing-bar, -bug, -nut, -pin,
-tongs.
pinc'-pinc (pink'-).
Pĭn'czow (-chŏv), t. Pol.
pĭnd.
pĭn'dal.
Pin'dar, Gr. poet, -dar ism, -dar-
ist, -dăr'ic, -ic al.
pin dăr'ee.
pind'ja jap (pĭn'-).
pine, *v.,* pined, pĭn'ing, -ing ly.

pine, *n.*, pīn'e al (*or* pī'ne-),
pīn'er y, pīn'y, *or* -ey, *pi nē'-*
tum, pī'nic, -nĭc'o lĭne, -o lous,
-ni form, pine'ap'ple, -maw, a
bird, -weed.

pine'-bar'ren, -beau ty, -bee tle,
-blight, -bull'finch, -car pet, a
moth, -chä'fer, a beetle, -clad,
-cloth, -cone, -drops, -finch,
-grŏs'bēak, -grouse, -gum,
-house, -ker nel, -knot, -lin net,
-liz ard, -mar ten, -măst,
-mouse, -nee dle, -nut, -oil,
-sap, -sis kin, -snake, -stove,
-this tle, -tree, -war bler, -wee-
vil, -wool, -worm, pine'ap ple-
cloth, -flow er.

ping, -ing, pinged (pingd).

ping'ler.

ping'-pong.

pin'ion (-yŭn), -ing, -ioned,
pin'ion-bone, -file, -gäge, -jack,
-wire.

pink, -ing, -er, -ish, -y, -i ness,
pinked, pink'cheek, a fish, -eye,
a disease, -root, a plant, -weed,
-wood, a tree.

pink'-eyed, -nee dle, -sau cer,
-stern, pink'ing-i ron, pink'ster-
flow'er, pink'y-bullt.

pin'nace.

pin'na cle, -cled, -cling, pin'na-
cle-work.

pin'nate, -ly, -nä'ted, -nat'i fid,
-i ped.

pĭn'na-wool.

pin'o cle.

pĭ nŏ'lē (*or* -nole').

pin'on (pēn'yŏn).

pīnt, -pot, a person; pīnt pot, a
pot; p. stoup.

pin ta'do (pēn tä'dō), spotted;
pìn tä'dō, a fish.

pin tä'no.

Pin'to (pēn'tō), Port. adventurer.

Pin zon' (pēn thōn'), Sp. navigator.

pī o neer', -ing, -neered'.

pī'ous, -ly, pī'e ty, pī'ous-mīnd'ed.

pip, -ping, pipped.

pīpe, piped, pīp'ing, -age, -er,
pipe'fish, -mouth, a fish, -wood,
a tree, -work, -wort.

pipe-bend er, -box, -case, -clamp,
-clay, -clear er, -con nec'tion,
-coup'ling, -cov'er ing, -cut'ter,
-dănce, -die, -drīv er, -fit ter,
-fit'tings, -foot, -grab, -grip,
-joint, -key, -lay'er, -lee, -line,
-loop, -met al, -mold ing,
-mouthed, -of fice, -or gan,
-ov en, -plug, -prov er, -rack,
-re duc'er, -roll, -screw'ing,
-slot'ting, -sock'et ting, -sta-
ple, -stay, -stem, -stick, -stone,
-stop, -thread'ing, -tongs, -tree,
-twist er, -un ion, -vein, -vine,
-vise, -wine, -wrench.

pīp'ing-i ron, p. crow, p. guan
(gwän), p. hare, p. plov er,
pi'per-ur chin.

pip'kin.

pĭp'pin, -face, -faced.

pip sis'se wa.

Pĭq'ua (pĭk'wa), c. O.

pi'quant (pē'kant *or* pĭ'-), -ly,
-quan cy.

pique (pēk), piqued (pēkt),
piqu'ing (pēk'-).

pi qué' (pē kā'), a cotton fabric,
-work.

pi quet' (pē kĕt'), a game.

pi quette' (pē kĕt'), a drink,

pi'qui a-oil (pē'kĭ a-).

pĭ'ra cy, -rate, -rä ted, -rä ting,
-rat'ĭc, -ĭc al, -al ly, pi'rate-
fish, -perch.

pirn.

pĭ rogue' (-rōg'), -rig.

pir ou ette' (-ōō ĕt'), -et'ted, -et'-
ting.

Pi'sa (pē'za), prov. It.

pis'ca to ry, -to'ri al, -tol'o gy.

pis'ci cul'ture, -tu ral, -tur ist,
-ci form, -civ'or ous.

pi sé' (pē zā').

pish.

pĭ shaug'.

pish'-pash.

Pĭ sĭs'tra tus, Athenian tyrant.

pis tä'chio (-shō), -green, -nut,
-tree.

Pis tic'ci (pēs tē'chē), t. It.

pis'til, -til late, -la ry, -lĭne, -lif'-
er ous, -la'ceous.

pis'tol, -tŏled, -tol'ing, -to leer'.

---

nŏt, nôr, ūse, ŭp, ûrn, etüde, fōōd, fŏŏt, aŋger, boǹmot, thus, Bach.

pis′tol-cane, -car bīne, -crack,
-grip, -pipe, -rout er, -shaped,
-shot, -splint.
pis′ton, -bel′lows, -head, -knob,
-pack′ing, -pump, -rod, -sleeve,
-spring, -valve, -wheel, -whis′-
tle.
pit, -ted, -ter, -ting, pit′fall, -hole,
-man, -pan.
pit′-bot tom, -coal, -cock, -cra′-
ter, -eye, -fish, -frame, -game,
-guide, -head, -head ed, -kiln,
-mar′tin, -mirk, -saw, -saw′yer,
-specked, -vi′per, -wood, -work.
pi′ta (pē′-), -*fi′ber*, -flax, -hemp,
-thread.
pi tä hä′yä (pē- *or* pĭt a hä′ya).
pit′a pat.
pitch, -er, -ing, -y, -i ness,
pitched, pitch′fork, -stone.
pitch′-black, -blende, -block,
-board, -boat, -chain, -cir cle,
-coal, -dark, -faced, -far thing,
-ket tle, -ket tled, -la dle, -line,
-min′er al, -o pal, -ore, -pine,
-pipe, -plås ter, -point, -pol′-
ish er, -pot, -tank ard, -tree,
-wheel, -work, pitch-and-toss,
pitch′-back wheel.
pitch′er, -mold, -mold′ing, -nose,
-plant, -shaped, -vase.
pitch′ ing-ma chine′, -pence,
-piece, -sta′ble, -tem′per a ture,
-tool, -yeast.
pĭt′e ous, -ly, -ness.
pĭth, -y, -i ly, -i ness, -less, -some,
pith′-pa′per, -tree, -work.
Pī′thon, *Bib.*
pit′man-box, -coup′ling, -head,
-press.
pi ton′ (pē′tôn′).
pit′ta cal.
pit′tance, -tan cer.
pit u ī′ta, -ī′tal, -ī′tous, pit′u i ta ry
(*or* pĭ tū′-).
pĭt′y, -ing, -ing ly, pit′i a ble,
-ble ness, -bly, -ied, -i er, -i ful,
-ful ly, -ful ness, -i less, -less ly,
-less ness.
piu (pū).
pĭv′ot, -al, -al ly, -ing.
piv′ot-bolt, -bridge. -broach,
-drill, -file, -gear′ing, -gun,

-joint, -lāthe, -man, -pin, -pol′-
ish er, -span, -tooth.
pĭ war′rie (-wŏr′rĭ).
pix′y, *pl.* pix′ies, pix′y-led, -puff,
-purse, -seat, -stool, -wheel.
Pi y Mar′gall (pē ē mär′gäl), Sp.
politician.
piz zi ca′to (pēt′sē kä′tō).
Piz′zo (pēt′sō), c. It.
plaat (plät).
plä′ca ble, -ness, -bly, -bil′i ty.
plăc′ard (*or* plà kärd′), *n.*, plà-
card′ (*or* plăk′-) *v.*, -ed, -er, -ing.
plä′cate, *v.*, -cä′ted, -cä′ting, -cà-
to′ry.
plăc′cate, *n.*
place, -less, -ment, plä′cing, -cer,
placed, place′man, -mon ger.
place′-brick, -bro ker, ~ -hunt er,
-name, -proud.
pla cen′ta, *pl.* -tas *or* -tæ, -cen′-
tal, -cen′ta ry, -cen′tate, plăc en-
ta′tion (plăs′-).
Plä′cer, co. Cal.
plac′er (plăs′er), a mineral deposit.
plä′cet.
plac′id (plăs′-), -ness, -id ly, pla-
cid′i ty.
plack′et, -hole.
plac′u lăr, -u late.
plä′gi a rize′ (*or* -jà rize), -rized′,
-rī′zing, -rist, -rism.
plague (plāg), -ful, -less, plagued,
pla′guing (-gĭng), -guer (-ger),
-guy (-gĭ), -gui ly (-gĭ ly).
plague′-mark, -sore, -spot.
plăice.
plaid (plăd), checkered, -ed, -ing,
plāid, a Highland garment.
plāin, -ing, -ing ly, -ly, -ness,
plāin′backs, plains′man.
plain′-chânt, -clay, -deal′er, -edge,
a., -heärt′ed, -pug, -sing ing,
-song, -speak ing, -spo ken,
-wan′der er, -wave, -work.
plăint, -ful, -ive, -ive ly, -ive-
ness, -less.
plâin′tiff.
plăit, -ed, -er, -ing, plait′-work,
pläit′ing-ma chine′.
plăn, -less, -ner, -ning, plănned.
Planche (plŏñsh), Fr. critic.
Plan ché′ (plŏñ shā′), Eng. dram.

planch′et, a coin-blank.

plăn chette′ (-shĕt′), a circumferentor.

plăne, -ness, planed, plăn′ing, -er, -nar.

plăne′-bit, -guide, -i ron, -plane, *a.,* -po′lar ized, -sail′ing, -stock, -ta ble, -ta bler, -tree.

plăn′er-bar, -cen′ter, -chuck, -head, -tree, -vise, plăn′ing-ma chine, -mill.

plăn′et, -a ry, -oid, -oid′al, -e tă′-ri um, *pl.* -ri ums *or* -ri a, pla-net′ic, -ic al.

plan′et - gear ing, -strick en, -struck, -wheel.

plă nĕ′ta.

pla nim′e ter, -e try, plan i met′-ric, -ric al.

plăn′ish, -ing, -er, -ished.

plăn′i sphere, -sphĕr′ic.

plank, -ing, planked, plank′-hook, -sheer, plank′ing-clamp, -ma-chine′, -screw.

plă′nŏ-con′cave, -con′ic al, -con′-vex, -spi′ral.

pla nom′e ter, -e try.

plant, -ed, -er, -ing, -a ble, -i cle, -less, -let, -iv′o rous.

plant′-an i mal, -bug, -cane, -cut ter, -dis ease′, -eat′ing, -feed′er, -food, -louse, -mark er, -move′ment, -or gan, plant-of-glut′ton y, plant′ing-ground.

plăn′tāin (*or* -tĭn), -cut ter, -eat-er, -lil y, -tree.

plan tā′tion, -mill.

plan′tĭ grade.

plăp, -ping, plapped.

plaque (plăk), plaqu′age (plăk′-), plaqu′et (plăk′-), *pla quette′* (-kĕt′).

Plaque mine′ (plăk′mēn′), vil. La.

Plaque mines′ (plăk′mēn′), par. La.

plash, -ing, -y, plashed, plash′-wheel, plash′ing-tool.

plas′ma (plăs′- *or* plăz′-), plas′mic.

plăs′ter, -er, -er y, -ing, -tered, plas′ter bill, a duck, plas′ter-mill, -spat′u la, -stone, plas′ter-ing-ma chine′.

plas′tic, -ti cal ly, -tic′i ty.

plăt, -ted, -ter, -ting, plat′band.

plate, -ful, -let, plăt′ed, -er, -ing.

plate′-bås ket, -bend er, -black, -bone, -box, -brăss, -bulb, -cul-ture, -en grăv′ing, -frame, -găge, -hat, -hoist, -hold er, -key, -lay er, -lĕath er, -ma-chine, -mark, -mill, -pa per, -piece, -plăn ing, -pow der, -press, -print er, -print ing, -rack, -rail, -rail way, -roll er, -shears, -tra′cer y, -vise, -warm-er, -wheel, plăt′ing-ham mer.

plate′ ar′mor, p. gird er, p. glåss, p. i′ron, p. mail, p. mat ter, p. met al.

plă teau′ (-tō′), *pl.* -teaus *or* -teaux (-tōz).

plăt′en.

plat′form, p. bridge, p. car, p. car-riage, p. crane, p. scales, p. spring.

pla ti′na (-tē′- *or* plăt′-), plăt′i-nize, -nized, -nī′zing, -nĭ ză′-tion, -I nate, -i num, -i nous, plat′i num-black, -lamp.

plăt′i no type.

plăt′i tude, -tu′di nize, -nized, -nī′zing, -nous, -nous ness, -nă′-ri an.

Plă′to, Gr. philos., -tŏn′ic, -ic al, -al ly, -to nism, -to nist, -nize, -nized, -ni zer, -ni zing.

pla tom′e ter, -e try.

pla tōōn′.

plăt′ten, -ten ing.

pla tym′e ter.

plăt′y note, -no′tal, -y ope, -y ŏp′ic, -y phyl′lous, -y pod.

plau′dit, -di to ry, plău′sive.

Plau′en (plow′-), t. Ger.

plau′si ble, -ness, -bly, -bil′i ty.

play, -a ble, -er, -ful, -ful ly, -ful-ness, -some, -some ness, -ing, played.

play′bill, -fel low, -game, -go′er, -ground, -house, -mate, -room, -thing, -time, -wright.

play′-act ing, -ac′tor, -book, -club, -day, -măk′er, -right, -writ′er.

plă′za, *pla′zu e′la* (plä′thōō ä′la).

plĕach, -er, -ing, plĕached.

plĕad, -ed (*or* plĕad), -er, -ing, -ing-ly, -a ble, plĕa, plĕad′ing-place.

---

pleas'ant (plĕz'-), -ly, -ness, -ant-
ry, -ance, pleas'ant-spir'it ed.
please (plēz), pleased, plēas'ed ly,
-er, -ing, -ing ly, -ing ness.
pleas'ure (plĕzh'-), -ūr a ble,
-ble ness, -bly, -ured, -ūr ing,
-ūr er, -ure less, pleas'ure-ground,
-house, -train, -trip.
plĕbe, plĕb, *plĕbs*, plĕb'i fy, -fy-
ing, -fīed, -fī cā'tion.
plĕ bē'ian (-an *or* -yan), -ism,
-ian ize, -ized, -i'zing.
plĕb'i scĭte (-sĭt), plĕ bis'ci ta ry,
pleb'is cī'tum (*or* plĕ'-).
plec'trum, pl. *-trums* or *-tra.*
plĕdge, plĕdged, pledg'ing, -ee', -er,
[in law] pledg'or (*or* -or'), pledge'-
cup, -ring.
Plē'iad (-yăd *or* pleï'ad), *pl.* Plē'-
iads (*or* pleï'-) *or* -a des (-dēz).
plē'na ry, -nå ri ly, -ri ness, -nar ty.
ple nip'o tent, -tence, -ten cy.
plen'i po ten'ti a'ry (-shĭ-).
plen'ish, -ing, plen'i tude, -tu'di-
na ry, plē'nist.
plen'ty, -te ous , -ous ly, -ous ness,
-ti ful, -ful ly, -ful ness.
plĕ'o nasm, -o nast, -nas'tic, -tic-
al, -al ly.
Plĕs che ie'vo (-chä yä'vō), l.
Russ.
Ples sé' (plās'sä'), t. Fr.
pleth'o ra, ple thor'ic (*or* plĕth'-),
-ic al, -al ly.
plĕth'ron.
pleu'ra, *pl.* -ras *or* -ræ, -ral'gi a,
-ral'gic, pleu'ric, -ri sy, -rit'ic,
-ic al, *-rī'tis*, pleu'ro pneu mo'-
ni a (-nū mō'-), pleu'ri sy-root.
plex'us, *pl.* -us es (-ĕz) *or* plex'-
us, plexed, plex al, -i form, -or,
-ure.
Pley'dell (plā'-), Scott *Guy Man-
nering.*
Pley'el (plī'el), Ger. mus. composer.
plī'a ble, -ness, -a bly, -a bil'i ty,
-ant, -an cy, -ant ly, -ant ness.
plī'cate, -ly, -cā'ted, -cā'tion.
plī'er.
plight (plīt), -ed, -er, -ing.
plĭnth.
Plĭn'y, Rom. auth.

plissé (-sä').
ploc.
plŏ'cē.
plod, -ded, -der, -ding, -ding ly.
Plŏ e meur' (-ä'mêr'), t. Fr.
plŏnge, plonged, plon'ging, *plon-
gée'* (plôṅ zhä').
Plon-Plon' (plôṅ-plôṅ'), nickname
of Prince Napoleon Bonaparte.
plot, -ted, -ter, -ting, -ting ly,
plot'ting-ma chine', -scale.
Plou hi nec' (plōō'ē'nĕk'), vil. Fr.
Plou i gneau' (plōō'ēn'yō'), vil. Fr.
plou'ter, -ing, -tered.
plov'er (plŭv'-), -quail, -snipe.
plow *or* plough (plou), -a ble,
-er, -ing, plowed, plow'boy, -land,
-man, -share, -wright.
plow'-beam, -bolt, -bote, -clev'is,
-gang, -gate, -han dle, -head,
-i ron, -knife, -point, -press,
-serv'ice, -shoe, -sil ver, -sock,
-stăff, -star, -stilt, -swain, -tail,
-team, -tree, -truck, -wise,
-witch er, plow'ing-ma chine',
plow'share-bone.
ploy, -ment.
pluck, -er, -ing, -y, -i ly, -i ness,
-less, plucked.
plug, -ging, -ger, plugged, plug'-
board, a switch-board.
plug'-arbor, -ba'sin, -bay'o net,
-cock, -fin'ish er, -hole, -jog'-
gle, -ma chine', -rod, -switch,
-tap, -tree, -ug ly, -valve,
plug'ging-for'ceps, plug hat.
plum, a fruit, -bird, -broth,
-but ter, -cake, -col or, -col ored,
-cur cu'li o, -fir, -gou'ger,
-juice, -ju'ni per, -loaf, -moth,
-pig, -pit, -pud ding er, -tree,
-wee vil.
plum' duff, p. por'ridge, p. pud'-
ding.
plū'mage, -maged, -mage ry,
-mate, *plū'ma*, pl. *-mæ*, *plu mas-
sier'* (plōō mås sêr').
plumb (plŭm), vertical, -ing,
plumbed, plumb'-bob, -joint,
-lev el, -line, -rule.
plum bā'go, -bag'i nous (-băj'-).
plŭm'be an, -be ous, -bic, -bif'-
er ous.

---

fāte, făt, fär, fạll, fâre, fȧst, sofȧ, mēte, mĕt, hêr, īce, ĭn, nōte,

plumb'er (plŭm'-), -er y, -ing, -less, plumb'er-block.

plŭme, -less, -let, plūm'er y, plu-mig'er ous (-mĭj'-), plŭ'mi ped, -mist, -mose (-mōs), -mos'i ty.

plŭme'-al'um, -bird, -hold'er, -māk'er, -moth, -nut'meg, -plucked.

plŭm'met.

plump, -er, -ing, -ly, -ness, -y, plumped, plump'-face.

Plŭmp'trē, Eng. clergyman.

plŭ'mŭle, -mu la, pl. -las or -læ, -mu la'ceous (-shŭs), -mu lar, -mu late, -mu lose (-lōs), plŭm'y.

plun'der, -age, -er, -ous, -ing, -dered.

plunge, plun'ger, -ging, plunged.

plunge'-bäth, -bat'ter y, -pole.

plun'ger-buck'et, -case, -lift, -pis'ton, -pump, plun'ging-si'-phon.

plu'per'fect.

plu'ral, -ism, -ist, -is'tic, -ize, -ized, -ī'zer, -ī'zing, -ral ly, -ral'i ty.

plus.

plush, -y, plush'-cop per, -stitch, p. vel'vet, p. vel vet een'.

Plŭ'to, Myth., -nism, -nist, -tö'-ni an, -tŏn'ic.

plŭ'to crat, -crat'ic, -toc'ra cў, -tol'o gy, -o gist, -to mā'ni a.

Plu'tus, Myth.

plu'vi al, -vi o graph, -vi om'e ter, -e try, -o met'ric, -ric al, -al ly, -vi o scope, -vi ous.

Plŭ'vi ose', a calendar month.

ply, -ing, plied, pli'er.

Plym'outh (plĭm'ŭth), t. Eng.; co. and t. Mass.; vil. Ct.; c. Ind., P. Breth ren, P. Rock, Plym'outh ism, -ist, -īte.

pnē'o dy nam'ics (nē'o dĭ-), -o-gas'ter, -gas'tric, -o graph, -o scope, -om'e ter, -e try.

pneu mat'ic (nū-), -ic al, -al ly, -ma tize, -tized, -tī'zing, -tic'-i ty, -mat'ics, -ma tog'ra phy, -to graph'ic, -ma tol'o gy, -o gist, -to log'ic al, -tom'e ter, -e try.

pneu mo gas'tric (nū-), -mo-gram, -mo graph, -graph'ic,

-mog'ra phy, -mol'o gy, -mo-log'ic al, -mom'e ter, -e try.

pneu mŏ'ni a (nū-), -mon'ic, -mo nit'ic, -mo nī'tis.

Pnŏm penh' (-pĕn'), t. Indo-China.

Pnyx (nix).

pŏach, -er, -ing, -y, -i ness, pŏached.

pŏak, tanner's-waste.

pŏ'chard.

Poch'e reth (pŏk'-), Bib.

pŏck, -y, -i ness, pocked, pock'-wood, -bro'ken, -house, -mark, -marked, -pit'ted, -pud'ding.

pŏck'et, -ed, -ing, -ful, -y, pock'-et book, a purse.

pock'et-book, a book, -di'al, -drop, -flap, -go'pher, -ham'-mer, -hand'ker chief, -judg'-ment, -knife, -lid, -mon'ey, -mouse, -net, -piece, -pis tol, -rat, -re lay', -shĕr'iff, p. e di'-tion.

pŏ'co.

pŏc'u lĭ form.

pod, -ded, -ding, pod'-au ger, -bit, -fern, -gäp'er, -lov er, -pep per, -shell, -shrimp, -this-tle, -ware.

pod'a gra (or po dag'-), pod'a-gral, -a grous, po dag'ric, -ric-al.

po dal'gi a, -dal'ic.

pod'dy.

pŏ der'.

po des tä' (or -des'-), -des'ter ate.

pŏdge, podged, podg'ing, -y.

po dol'o gy, -dom'e ter.

pŏ'ĕ, -bird.

pŏ'ĕm, -et, -et ess, -et'ic, -ic al, -al ly, -ics, -et'i cule, -et ize, -ized, -ī'zing, -I zā'tion, -et ry, -e sy, -et as'ter, -et ship, po'et-mu si'cian.

pŏ eph'a gous.

pŏ'gy, -catch er, -gull.

pŏ'ĭ.

poign'ant, -ly, -an cy.

poin sĕt'ti a.

point, -a ble, -ed, -ed ly, -ed ness, -er, -ing, -less, -y, point'blank', points'man.

point'-cir'cle, -co or'di nate, -e-
qua'tion (-shŭn), -find'er, -hole,
-lace, -pair, -pa'per, -rail,
-sphere, -tool, point'ing-ma-
chine', -stock, point'er dog.
Point de Galle' (point dê gäl'),
t. Ceylon.
pointe (pwănt), a shawl, *poin té'*
(pwăn tä'), Her.
Pointe à Pitre' (pwănt' ä pêtr'),
t. Fr. W. I.
Pointe aux' Vaches' (ŏ' vȧsh'),
headland Can.
poise (poiz), -less, poised, pois'-
ing, -er.
poi'son (-zn), -a ble, -er, -ing,
-ous, -ous ly, -ous ness, poi'son-
ber'ry, -bulb, -wood.
poi'son-ash, -bag, -bay, -cup,
-dog'wood, -el'der, -fang,
-gland, -hem'lock, -i'vy, -nut,
-oak, -or'gan, -pea, -plant, -sac,
-su'mac, -tooth, -tow'er, -tree,
-vine.
Pois sy' (pwȧs'sē'), t. Fr.
Poi ti ers' *or* Poic ti ers' (pwȧ'-
tĭ ä'), t. Fr.
Poi tou' (pwȧ tōō'), prov. Fr.
poi'tre, -trĭne.
pŏ käl'.
poke, poked, pōk'er, -ing, -ing ly,
-y, poke'ber'ry, -root, -weed.
poke'-bag, -milk'weed, -net,
-stick, p. bon net.
pŏk'er, -ish, -ish ly, pok'er-paint'-
ing, -pic'ture, -play'er.
po lac'ca.
pō'lar, -im'e ter, -e try, -lăr'i-
scope, -scŏp'ic, -lär is'co py,
-is'tic, -lăr'i ty, -lär īze, -īzed,
-ī zer, -ī zing, -ī'za ble, -ī zā'-
tion, *Pō lä'ris,* po'lar-bī loc'u-
lar, -plant, po lar i zā'tion-
mi'cro scope.
pŏl'der, -land.
pole, -less, -ward, poled, pōl'ing,
pole'ax, -cat, -wig, a fish.
pole'-bean, -brack'ets, -burn,
-chain, -chän'ger, -crab, -dab,
-foot, -ham mer, -head, -hook,
-horse, -lāthe, -măst, -net,
-pad, -piece, -plate, -prop,
-rack, -rush, -sling, -stȧff, -star,

-strap, -tip, -tor pe'do, -vault,
-vault'ing, pole'cat-weed.
pŏl'e march (-mark).
po lĕm'ic, -al, -al ly, -ics, -lem'-
i cist.
po lĕm'o scope (*or* pŏl'em o-).
po lĕn'ta.
pŏl'hōde.
Pŏl'ĭ an'thes (-thēz), *n.,* -an'thous.
. **po lice'** (-lēs'), -man, po lice'
nip'pers.
pŏl'i cy, -book, -hold'er, -shop,
-slip.
Po li gna'no (pō lēn yä'nō), t. It.
Po li gny' (pŏ'lēn'yē'), t. Fr.
Pŏ lil'lo (-lēl'yō), isl. P. I.
pol'ish, -a ble, -er, -ing, -ings,
-ment, -ished, pol'ish-pow der.
pŏl'ish ing-bed, -block, -căsk,
-disk, -ham mer, -i ron, -jack,
-ma chine', -mill, -paste, -pow-
der, -slate, -snake, -stone, -tin,
-wheel.
po lis soir' (pŏl is swȯr').
po lis'ta.
po līte', -ly, -ness, *pŏl'ĭ tesse'*
(-tĕs').
pŏl'i tic, -i tics, po lit'i cal, -cal-
ism, -cal ly, -cas'ter, pol'i ti'-
cian (-tĭsh'an).
pŏl'i ty.
Po lix ène' (pŏ'lēk'sän'), Molière's
comedy.
Po lix'e nes (-nēz), Shak. *Winter's Tale.*
Pŏ liz'zi (-lēt'sē), t. It.
pŏl'ka, -dot, -jack'et, p. gauze.
pŏll, -ing, -age, polled, poll'man.
pŏll'-adze, -book, -clerk, -e vil,
-mad, -pick, -suf'frage, -tax,
poll'ing-booth, -place, -sher iff,
-sta tion.
pŏll, a parrot; a student.
pŏl'lan, a fish.
pŏl'lard,
pŏl'len, a dust, -ize, -ized, -ī'zing,
-ī zā'tion.
pŏl'len-brush, -ca tarrh', -cell,
-cham'ber, -fe ver, -gland,
-grain, -măss, -paste, -sac,
-spore, -tube.
pŏl'lex, pl. *-lĭ ces* (-sēz), Anat.
pŏl'li wog.

pol lūte', -lūt'ed, -ed ly, -ed ness,
-er, -ing, -ing ly, -lū'tion.
pŏl'lux, a mineral; Pŏl'lux, a star.
pō'lŏ, a game; a gypsy dance.
pō lŏ naise' (-nāz').
Po lŏ'nĭ us, Shak. *Hamlet.*
pō lŏ'ny.
pŏl'ska.
pŏl trōōn', -ish, -er y.
pŏl y an'drous, -an'dry, -an'-
drist, -an'thus, *a.,* -an'thus, *n.,*
-ar'chist (-kĭst), -ar'chy, -car'-
pus.
pŏl'y chrome (-krōm), -chro my,
-chro'mic, -chro mat'ic.
Pŏl y clē'tus, Gr. sculp., -clē'tan.
pŏl'y cŏt'y lē'don, -lĕd'on ous,
-on a ry.
pō lyg'a my (-lĭg'-), -a mist, -a-
mous, -a mize, -mized, -mĭ'zing.
pŏl'y glot, -glot'tic.
pŏl'y gon, -go na'ceous, po lyg'o
nal, -o nate.
pol'y go nom'e try, -gon'o met'-
ric.
pŏl'y graph, -graph'ic, -ic al, po-
lyg'ra phy.
po lyg'y ny (-lĭj'-), -y nous, pol-
y hē'dral, -hē'dric, -dric al, -he-
drom'e try, -dro met'ric, -hē'-
dron, -hē'drous.
pŏl'y math, -math'ic, po lym'a-
thist (-lĭm'-), -a thy.
pō lym'e ter, pŏl y mĭ'cro scope,
-y mor'phic, -mor'phism, -mor'-
phous, -mor'phy.
Pŏl'y nē'si a (-shĭ a), isls. Pac.
Oc., -ne'sian (-shăn).
pŏl y nŏ'mi al, -al ism, -al ist.
pŏl'yp, pō lyp'e an, -lyph'a gous,
-a gy (-jĭ), pŏl y phā'gi a,
-phag'ic (-făj'-).
pol'yp-col'o ny, -stem, -stock.
pŏl'y pĕt'a lous.
pŏl y phē'mus, a cyclops; the
king-crab, Pŏl y phē'mus, *Zoöl.
genus;* Homer *Odyssey.* pol-
y phē'mous, one-eyed.
pol'y phone, -phō'ni a, -ni an,
-phŏn'ic, po lyph'o nism, -o nist,
-o nous, -o ny.
pŏl'y phŏte, -phō'tal.
pŏl'y phyl'lous.

pŏl'y pod, po lyp'o da.
pŏl'y pus, *n., pl.* -y pus es (-ĕz)
or -pī, pŏl'y pous, *a.*
pŏl'y scope, -y sperm, -sper'my,
-sper'mal, -sper'mous.
pŏl y syl'la ble, -lăb'ic, -ic al,
-lăb'i cism.
pŏl y syl'lo gism, -lo gis'tic, -y-
syn'de ton, -y syn'the sis, -the-
tism, -thet'ic, -ic al, -al ly,
-thet'i cism.
pŏl y tech'nic (-tĕk'-), -al, -nics.
pol'y the'ism, -the'ist, -is'tic,
-tic al, -al ly, -the'ize, -ized,
-ī zing.
pŏl'y type, -typed, -typ ing (-tīp'-),
-typ'ic al (-tĭp'-).
pom'ace (pŭm'-), crushed fruit;
fish refuse, po mā'ceous, pom'ace-
fly.
pō māde', -mād'ed, -mā'tum,
man'der, po man'der-ball.
Pŏ mard' (-mär'), a kind of wine.
pŏm'be.
pŏme, po-mif'er ous, pō'mi form.
pŏme'gran ate (*or* pŭm'-).
pŏme'roy.
pŏ'mĭ cul'ture, -mĭ form.
Po mi'no (-mē'-).
pom mā'do.
pom'mel (pŭm'-), -ing *or* -ling,
-meled *or* -melled, -mel er.
Po mō'la, *Myth.*
po mol'o gy, -o gist, -mo log'i cal.
pŏmp.
pom'pa dour (-dōōr).
pom pä'no, -shell.
Pom pe'ii (-pā'yē), ancient city,
-pē'ian (-yăn).
pom'pom, a gun; pom'-pom', a
dance.
pom'pon.
pom'pous, -ly, -ness, -pŏs'i ty,
-pō'sō.
Pŏn'ce (-thā), t. P. R.
pon ceau' (-sō').
Pon'ce de Le on' (pōn'thā dā
lā ōn' *or* pŏns dē lē'on), Sp.
discoverer.
Ponce let' (pōns'lā'), Fr. engineer.
pon'chŏ.
pŏnd, -age, pond'weed.

---

nŏt, nôr, ūse, ŭp, ûrn, etüde, fōōd, fŏŏt, anger, bonmot, thus, Bach.

pond'-ap'ple, -carp, -dog'wood, -fish, -hen, -lil y, -mul let, -mus sel, -perch, -pick'er el, -pine, -scum, -shrimp, -snail, -spice, -tur tle.

pon'der, -a ble, -ble ness, -a bil'-i ty, -er, -ing, -ing ly.

pon'der ous, -ly, -ness, -os'i ty, -o mo'tive.

Pŏn dĭ cher'ry (-shĕr'-), t. E. Indies.

pŏne, corn bread.

pŏ'nĕ, a writt; a game.

pon gee'.

poṇ'go.

pon'iard (-yard).

Po ni a tow'ski (pō nē ä tŏv'skĕ), Pol. prince.

Po noc'ra tes (-tēz), Rabelais' romance.

pŏnt.

Pon'tacq (-tăk), a wine.

pŏn'tage.

Pont char train' (pŏn'shar'trăn'), Fr. Minister of State.

pŏn'tiff, -tĭf'ic, -ic al, -al ly, -tif'-i cate, -cā'ted, -cā'ting, -ti fex.

pŏn'til, an iron rod.

pŏn'tĭle, -ti nal.

Pŏn'tĭne.

Pŏn'ti us Pī'late (pŏn'shĭ us), *Bib.*

pŏn toon', -ing, -to niĕr', pon toon'-train, p. bridge.

pŏ'ny, -saw, -truck, p. en'gine.

poo͞od.

poo͞o'dle.

pooh (poo͞o *or* pŏo͞), -pooh.

pŏo͞o'jä or -jäh.

poo͞ol, -er, -ing, pooled, pool'-ball, -play'er, -room, -rush, -sell er, -snipe, -tick'et.

poo͞o'na-wood.

poo͞on'dy-oil.

poo͞oṇ'ga-oil.

poo͞op, -cab'in, -lan'tern.

poo͞or, -ly, -li ness, -ness, poo͞or'-house, -măs ter, -will, a bird.

poor'-box, -farm, -lights, -rate, -spir'it ed.

pop, -per, -ping, popped, pop'-corn, -dock, -eyed, -eyes, -gun, -shop, pop'ping-crease.

Pŏ pay an' (-pī än'), c. Colombia.

pope, -dom, -hood, -kin, -ling, -ship, pōp'er y, -ish, -ish ly.

pope-joan' (-jōn'), pope's-eye, -head, -nose.

pŏp'in jay.

pŏp'lar, -lâred, pop'lar-birch, -bor er, -buds, -dag'ger, a moth, -gir'dler, a beetle, -gray, -kit-ten, -leaf, -lute'string, -root, -spin ner, -tree, -twig.

pŏp'lin.

Pŏp'o crat.

Pŏ pŏ vec' (-vĕts'), t. Hung.

pŏp'pet, -hĕad, -valve.

pop'ple, -pled, -pling.

pop'py, -pĭed, pop'py cock, pop'-py-bed, -bee, -bud, -flow'er, -head, -leaf, -mal'low, -oil, -seed, -stem.

pop'u lar, -ly, -ness, -ize, -ized, -i'zer, -i'zing, -ĭ zā'tion, -lär'i ty.

pop'u late, -lā'ted, -lā'ting, -lā'-tor, -lā'tion, -lace, -lous, -lous-ly, -lous ness.

Pŏp'u lism, p. u list.

Pŏr'a tha (*or* pō rä'-), *Bib.*

por'cate, -cā'ted.

porce'lāin (*or* -lĭn *or* por'cē lĭn), -ist, -lain īte, -lain ized, por'-ce lā'ne ous.

porce'lāin-ce ment', -clay, -col'-or, -crab, -fur'nace, -gild'ing, -jas'per, -lace, -ov'en, -pa'per.

por'ce lāne, shell money.

porch.

por'cĭne (*or* -sīn).

Por'ci us (-shĭ us), *Bib.*

por'cu pīne, -crab, -dis ease', -fish, -grăss, -quill, -wood.

pore, pored, pōr'ing, pōr'al, po-rif'er al, -er an, -er ous, po'-rose, -roŭs, -rous ly, -rous ness, -ros'i ty.

por'gee, a coarse silk.

por'gy, *pl.* -gies (-gĭz), a fish.

po'ri cī'dal, po rif'er ous.

pork, -er, -ling, -y, pork'wood.

pork'-butch'er, -chop, -eat'er, -pit, p. pie, p. sau'sage.

por noc'ra cy.

por'no grăph, -graph'ic, -nog'ra-pher, -ra phy.

por'phy rīte, -rĭt'ic, -ic al ly,
-rize, -rized, rī zing, -rĭ zā'tion,
-phy ry, por'phy ry-moth, -shell.
por'phy ro gene', -ro gen'i tus.
por'poise (-pŭs), -oil, -skin.
pŏr'ridge.
pŏr'rin ger.
port, -ed, -ing, -er, -a ble, -a ble-
ness, -a bil'i ty, -age, por'ta,
por'tal, -ta tive.
port'last, port'man, -reeve, -way,
-fōl'io (or -fō'lĭ ō).
port'-bar, -bit, -caus tic, -cray on,
-e lec'tric, a., -face, -fire, -flange,
-hole, -hook, -lan yard, -lid,
-lift er, -mote, -pend'ant, -rope,
-rule, -sale, -sash, -sill, -stop'-
per, -tac kle, -town, port'man-
note, port-tac kle man, port
wine.
Por tage' des Sioux' (por täzh'
dā ѕoo'), vil. Mo.
por ta men'to.
Port au Prince' (ō prăńs'), t.
Haiti.
port cul'lis, -ing, -lised.
Port de Paix' (dê pā'), t. Haiti.
Porte, the Turkish court.
porte'-ac id, -bon heur' (-bŏn-
ner'), -co chère' (-kō shãr'), -dra-
peau' (-pō'), -mon naie' (-nā').
por tend', -ed, -ing, -tent', -tent'-
ous, -ous ly, -ous ness.
por'ter, -age, -ess, por'ter-house, a
house, por'ter house steak.
Por'ti a (-shĭ a), Shak. Merchant
of Venice.
por'ti co, pl. -coes or -cos (-kōz),
-cōed.
por'tière' (port yãr').
por'tion, -a ble, -er, -ing, -ist,
-less, -tioned.
port'ly, -li ness.
port man'teau (-tō).
por'trait, -ist, -trai ture, por'-
trait-lens, -paint'er, -stone.
por tray', -al, -er, -ing, -trayed'.
Port Sa id' (sä ēd'), t. Egypt.
Por'tu gal, Geog., -tu guese (-gēs
or -gēz).
por tu lä'ca (or -lăk'a), a plant;
Por tu la ca, Bot. genus.
po sä'da.

pō sau'ne (-zou'nĕ).
pose (pōz), posed, pōs'ing, -er.
po sé (pō zā').
Po seī'don, Myth., -do'ni an,
-seī'dē on, a Gr. month.
pŏ'ser (-zer).
po si'tion (-zĭsh'un).
pos'i tive (pŏz'-), -ly, -ness, -tĭv-
ism, -tiv'i ty, -ti vis'tic, Pos'i-
tiv ist.
pos'net.
pos'sē, p. com i tā'tus.
pos sess' (pŏz zĕs'), -sessed', -ses'-
sion (-zĕsh'un), -sion al, -sive,
-sive ly, -sor, -so ry.
pos'set, -ale, -cup, -pot.
pŏs'sĭ ble, -si bly, -si bil'i ty.
pos sum, -oak.
pŏst, n., a piece of timber, -bird,
-butt, -ce dar, -drill, -drĭv er,
-hole, -jack, -line, -mill, -oak,
-pock et, -wĭnd'lass.
post, v., to bring to public notice,
-ed, -er, post'-bill.
post, a station, -ad'ju tant, -cap'-
tain, -chaise, -coach, -hold er.
post, the mail; to mail, -age, -al, -ed,
-ing, -boy, -man, -mark, -marked,
-mās'ter, mās'ter ship, -mis'-
tress,
post'-bag, -book, -box, -card, -day,
-free, -hack'ney, -haste, -horn,
-horse, -house, -mon'ey, -note,
-of'fice, -paid, -rĭd'er, -road,
-stamp, -time, -town, -trād'er,
-wag'on, post'age-stamp, post'-
ing-house, -inn, post'al card,
pŏste res tänte'.
post, adv., after, -clas'sic, -sic al,
-date, -dāt'ed, -dāt'ing, -dĭ lū'-
vi al, -vi an, -fact, -fac'tor,
-grad'u ate, -lude, -me rid'i an,
-rid'i on al, -mil len'ni al, al ism,
-al ist, -nā'tal, -pran'di al.
post'-com mūn'ion, -dis sēi'zin,
-dis sēi'zor, -en'try, -ex il'i an,
-ex is'tence, -ex is'tent, -morn'-
ing, -mor'tem, -Nī'cene, -night,
-nup'tial.
post'mās ter-gen'er al, -gen'er al-
ship.
pŏs tĕ'rĭ or, -or ly, -or'i ty.
pos tĕr'i ty.

pŏs'tern, -door, -gate.
pŏst'hu mous, -ly.
pŏs tĭl'ion, -bȧsque, -belt.
post na'tus, pl. *-tī.*
post pone', -ment, -poned', -pōn'-
a ble, -er, -ing.
post'script.
pŏs'tu late, -lā'ted, -lā'ting, -lant.
pŏs'ture, -tūred, -tūr ing, -tūr al,
-tūr er, -tūr ist.
pō'sy (-zĭ), -ring.
pot, -ful, -ted, -ter, -ting, pot'-
bel ly, a fish; a person, -hĕad,
a person, -hook, a character, -pie,
-rack, -shell, -sherd, -stone, -work,
pot'ting-cask, -house, -stick.
pot'-bar'ley, -bel'lied, *a.,* -bel'ly,
a belly, -boil'er, -boil'ing, -boy,
-cake, -celt, -cheese, -claw, -clep,
-com pan'ion, -eye, -fish, -fish'-
er, -fish'er man, -hang'er, -hat,
-hel met, -herb, -hole, -hook, a
hook, -house, -hunt er, -knight,
-lace, -lĕad, -lid, -liq uor,
-luck, -man, -mar'i gold, -met-
al, -mi ser, -pa per, -plant,
-plate, -roast, -set ting, -shop,
-shot, -stick, -still, -tree, -val-
iant, -wab bler, -wal ler, -wal-
lop er, -wheel, -works, -wres-
tler.
pō'ta ble, -ness, -tā'tion, po tā'-
tion-pen ny.
Po tage', Jean (zhäṅ pō'tȧzh'),
a buffoon in Fr. literature.
pot'a mog'ra phy, -mol'o gy, -mo-
-log'ic al.
pŏt'ash, po tas'sa, -tas'sic, -tas'-
si um.
po tä'to, *pl.* -toes (-tōz).
pŏ tä'tŏ-bee tle, -bing, -blight,
-bread, -bug, -dig'ger, -dis-
ease', -eel, -fern, -fuṇ'gus,
-grant, -hook, -mash'er, -mold,
-mur'raĭn, -oat, -oil, -on ion,
-pen, -peel er, -plant, -plant er,
-rot, -scoop, -sep'a ra tor, -skin,
-spir it, -starch, -su gar, -vine,
-wash er.
pot-au-jeu' (pō'tō'fê').
potch, -er, -ing, potch'er-en gine,
· potch'ing-en gine, -ma chine'.
pŏ teen'.

po'ten cy, -tence, -tent, -ten tate,
-ten'tial, -tial ly, -ti al'i ty (-shĭ-
ăl'-), -tial ize, -ized, -ĭ'zing,
-ti ate (-shĭ ate), -ā'ted, -ā'ting,
-a ry, -ā'tion, -ti om'e ter (-shĭ-
om'-), -ten tize, -tized, -tī'zing,
-tent ly, -tent ncss.
poth'er.
po tiche' (-tēsh').
pō'tion.
Pŏt'i phar, *Bib.*
Pŏ tiph'e rah (*or* pŏt'i phĕ'-), *Bib.*
pŏ tŏm'e ter.
pot pour ri' (pō'pōō'rē').
po tre'ro (-trä'-).
pŏt'tage.
Pot'ta wat'to mies (-wŏt'-), tribe
of Indians; -wat'ta mie, co. Ia.;
-wat'o mie, co. Kan.; co. Okla.
pot'ter, -er, -y, pot'ter-wasp, pot'-
ter y-gȧge, -kiln, -paint ing,
-print ing, -tis sue, -tree, -ware.
pot'tle, -bel'lied, -bod'ied, -deep,
-drȧft *or* -draught.
pouch, -er, -ing, -less, pouched,
pouch'gill, a fish, -bone, -gilled,
-hook, -māk'er, -mouse, -toad.
Pou chet' (pōō'shā'), Fr. naturalist.
pou drĕtte' (pōō-).
pouf (pōōf), a head-dress.
pouffe (pōōf), rounded and soft.
Pough keep'sie (pō kĭp'sĭ), c. N. Y.
Pou gin' (pōō'zhäṅ'), Fr. art critic.
Pouil let' (pōō'yā'), Fr. physicist.
Pou jou lat' (pōō'zhōō'lä'), Fr. hist.
pou lāine' (pōō-).
pou lard' (pōō-).
poule (pōōl).
pou let' (pōō lä').
poulp *or* poulpe (pōōlp).
pŏult, pŏul'ter er.
poult-de-soie' (pōō-dê-swŏ').
pŏult'-foot.
pŏul'tĭce, -tĭced, -tĭc'ing, poul'-
tice-boot, -shoe.
pŏul'try, -farm, -feed'er, -house,
-yard.
pounce, pounced, poun'cer, -cing.
pounce'-bag, -box, -pa'per, -tree,
poun'cing-ma chine'.
pound, -age, -al, -ed, -er, -ing,
pound'man, -mȧs ter, -wort.

---

fāte, făt, fär, fạll, fâre, fȧst, sofȧ, mēte, mĕt, hêr, īce, ĭn, nōte,

pound-boat, -breach, -cake, -fool'ish, -keep'er, -net, -rate, -scoop, pound'ing-bar rel, -ma-chine', pound' weight.

pŏur, -er, -ing, pŏured, pour'ing-gate, -hole, -stick.

pour'boire' (pōor bwŏr').

Pour ceau gnac' (pōor'sŏn'yäk'), Molière's comedy.

pou'rie (pōo'rĭ).

pour'par'ler' (pōor'pär'lā').

pour'point (pōor'-), -*poin te rie'* (-pwăṅ tĕ rē').

pousse'-ca fé' (pōos'-kȧ fā').

pous sĕtte' (pōos-), -set'ted, -set'-ting.

pou stō (pōo).

pout, -ed, -er, -ing, -ing ly, pout'-net.

pŏv'er ty, -grȧss, -plant, -strick-en, -struck, -weed.

pow'der, -er, -ing, -y, -i ness, -dered.

pow'der-blow'er, -box, -cart, -chăm'ber, -chest, -di vi'sion, -down, -flag, -flȧsk, -gun, -horn, -hose, -mag a zine', -man, -mill, -mine, -mix er, -mon key, -pa-per, -post, -prov er, -puff, -room, -scut tle, -skoot, pow'-der ing-gown, -mill, -tub.

pow'er, -ful, -ful ly, -ful ness, -less, -less ly, -less ness, -ered.

pow'er-cap'stan, -ham mer, -house, -lāthe, -loom, -ma-chine', -press, -ūs'er.

Pow'ha tăn', co. Va.; Indian chief.

pow'wow, -ing, -er, -wowed.

pox, -stone.

poy'net.

Poz so ny' (pŏzh'ō nĕ'), t. Hung.

poz'zo (pŏt'sō).

poz zu o la'na (pŏt'sōo ō lä'nȧ), -lăn'ic.

Poz zu o'li (pŏt sōo ō'lē), t. It.

prăc'tice, *n.*, -ti cal, -cal ly, -cal ness, -cal'i ty, -cȧ ble, -ble ness, -bly, -bil'i ty, prac'tice-ship.

prăc'ti co (-tē kō).

prăc'tise *or* -tĭce, *v.*, -tised, -tis-ing, -tis er, -ti'tion er (-tish'un-).

Prä di er' (-dē ā'), Fr. sculptor.

Praed (prād), Eng. poet.

Prä ĕ vä'li (-lē), vil. Aust.

prag mat'ic, -ic al, -al ly, -al ness, -ma tism, -tist, -tize, -tized, -tī'zer, -tī zing.

prăi'rĭe, -rĭed, prai'rie-al li ga tor, -ap ple, -bean, -bird, -bit ters, -brant, -bur dock, -chick'en, -clo ver, -cock tail, -dock, -dog, -fȧl con, -fly, -fox, -goose, -grȧss, -hawk, -hen, -mar mot, -mole, -oys ter, -pĭ geon, -plov-er, -plow, -rat tler, -rat tle-snake, -rose, -schoon er, -snipe, -squir rel, -tur nip, -war bler, -wolf.

Prai'rie du Chien' (prä'rē du shēn'), c. Wis.

praise, -ful, -less, -wor thy, -thi ly, -thi ness, praised, prais'ing, -er, praise'-meet ing.

prā' line (or -lēn').

pram.

prănce, pran'cer, -cing, -cing ly, pranced.

pran'di al.

prank, -er, -ing, -ing ly, -ish, -some.

prase (prāz), pra'soid, pras'i nous.

prate, prāt'ed, -er, -ing, -ing ly.

prăt'ique (-ēk).

prat'tle, -tled, -tler, -tling, prat'-tle box, a person.

prawn.

prax'is.

Prax it'e les (-lēz), Gr. sculp., -it e lē'an.

pray, -er, -ing, -ing ly, prayed.

pray'ing-desk, -in'sect, -ma chine', -man'tis, -wheel.

pray'a (prī'a), a walk or drive.

Prăy'a, *Zoöl. genus.*

prayer (prâr), -ful, -ful ly, -ful-ness, -less, -less ly, -less ness.

prayer'-bead, -book, -car pet, -cure, -meet ing, -mill, -mon-ger, -rug, -stick, -thong, -wheel.

prĕach, -er, -er ship, -ing, -ment, -y, preach'ing-cross.

pre ac quaint'ance.

pre act', -ed, -ing, -ac'tion.

pre ăd'ăm īte, -ĭt'ic, -ic al, -a-dam'ic.

nŏt, nôr, ūse, ŭp, ûrn, etüde, fōod, fŏŏt, aṇger, boṅmot, thus, Bach.

30

prĕ'am ble, -am'bu lar, -lâ'ry.
prĕb'end, -en dâ'ry, -ry ship, -en-
dal (*or* pre ben'dal).
prĕ că'ri ous, -ly, -ness.
prec'a tǐve, -a to'ry.
prē cau'tion, -al, -a ry, -cau'tious,
-tious ly.
pre cede', -cēd'ed, -ence, -en cy,
-ent, *a*., -ent ly, -er, -ing, -ces'-
sion, -sion al, prec'e dent
(pres'-), *n*.
pre cen'tor, -ship.
pre'cept, -cep'tive, -tor, -tō'ri al,
-cep'to ry, -tress.
prē'ces (-sēz).
Pre cheur' (prä'sher'), t. Martinique, W. I.
prē'ci'euse' (prä'sē'ĕz').
prĕ'cinct.
pre'cious (prĕsh'us), -ly, -ness.
prec'i pǐce (prĕs'-), pre cip'i tous,
-tous ly, -tous ness.
pre cip'i ent.
pre cip'i tate, -tā'ted, -tā'ting,
-tā'tive, -tā'tor, -tā'tion, -i tance,
-tan cy, -tant, -tant ly, -tant-
ness, -tā ble, -tā bǐl'i ty, -i tate-
ly, -tate ness.
prē'cis' (prä'sē').
pre cise' (-sīs'), -ly, -ness, -cis'-
ian (-sǐzh'an), -an ism, -an ist,
-cis'ion (-sǐzh'un), -on ist, -on-
ize, -ized, -i zing, -cī'sive, *pre-
ci'so* (prä chē'sō).
prē clūde', -clūd'ed, -ing, -clu'-
sive, -sive ly, -sion (-zhŭn).
pre cō'cious (-shŭs), -ly, -ness,
-coc'i ty (-kŏs'-).
pre cog nǐ'tion (-nish'un).
pre-Co lum'bi an.
pre con ceive', -ceived', -ceiv'ing,
-ceit', -cep'tion.
pre con cert', *v*., -ed, -ed ly, -ed-
ness, -cer'tion, prē con'cert, *n*.
pre cur'sor, -so ry, -sive.
prē dā'ceous (-shŭs), -dā'ce an.
pre dăte', -dāt'ed, -dāt'ing.
prĕd'a to ry, -to'ri ly, -ri ness,
-dā'tion.
pred'e ces'sor (*or* pred'-).
prē des'tǐne, -tǐned, -tin ing, -ti nā'-
tive, -nā'tor, -nā'ri an, -an ism,
-ti nate, -nā'ted, -nā'ting, -nā'tion.

pre de ter'mǐne, -mǐned, -mǐn-
ing, -mi nate, -nā'tion.
prē'dǐ al.
pred'i cate, -ca'ted, -ca'ting, -cà-
ble, -cà bǐl'i ty, -cā'tive, -tive ly,
-cà tō'ry, -cant, -cā'tion.
pre dict', -ed, -ing, -à ble, -ive,
-ive ly, -or, -o ry, -dic'tion,
-tion al.
prē dǐ lect', -ed, -ing, -lec'tion.
pre dis pose', -posed', -pōs'ing,
-pō'nent, -po si'tion (-zǐsh'un).
pre dom'i nant, -ly, -nance, -nan-
cy, -nate, -nā'ted, -nā'ting,
-ting ly, -nā'tion.
prē'dy.
pre em'i nent, -ly, -nence, -nen cy.
pre empt', -or, -o ry, -emp'tion,
-tion er, -emp'tive.
Pre'ez (prä'ĕts), t. Prus.
prĕf'ace, -aced, -ā cing, -ā cer,
-à to ry, -to'ri al, -ri ly.
pre'fect, -fec'to ral, -to'ri al, -fec-
ture, -fec'tu ral.
pre fêr', -er, -ment, -ring, -fêrred',
prĕf'er a ble, -ble ness, -bly, -a-
bil'i ty, -er ence, -en'tial, -tial ly.
prē'fet' (prä'fā').
pre fig'ure, -ment, -ured, -ûr ing,
-ûr a tive, -û rā'tion.
pre fix', *v*., -ing, -fixed', pre'fix, *n*.
pre hen'sǐle, -si ble, -sor, -so ry,
-sion.
pre his tŏr'ic, -al, -al ly.
Preig nac' (prän yăk').
pre judge', -judged', -judg'ing,
-ment.
pre ju'di cate, -cā'ted, -cā'ting,
-cal, -ca'tive, -cā'tion.
prĕj'u dǐce, -diced, -dǐ'cing, -dǐ'-
cial (-dǐsh'al), -cial ly, -cial ness.
prĕl'ate, -ship, prel'à cy, -a tism,
-a tist, -a tize, -tized, -ti'zing,
-a ture, -ture ship, pre la'tial,
-lăt'ic, -ic al, -al ly.
pre lect', -ed, -ing, -lec'tor, -lec'-
tion.
pre lim'i na ry, -na ri ly.
prē'lude (*or* prĕl'-), *n*., pre lude',
v., -lūd'ed, -lūd'ing, -lūd'er (*or*
prē'- *or* prĕl'-), pre lū'sive,
-sive ly, -so ry, -so ri ly.
prē ma ture', -ly, -ness, -tu'ri ty.

pre med'i tate, -tā'ted, -ted ly,
-ted ness, -tā'ting, -tate ly, -tā'-
tive, -tā'tion.
prĕ'mĭ er, *a.* and *n.*, -ship, *pre-
mière'* (prĕm yâr').
prĕm'ĭse, *n.*, prē mise' (-mīz'),
v., -mised, -mīs'ing.
prĕ'mĭ um, *pl.* -ums.
prē mŏn'ish, -ished, -ish ing,
-i tive, -i tor, -to'ry, -ri ly.
prē mū'ni to ry, -nĭ'tion (-nĭsh'un).
prē nā'tal, -tal ly.
prē oc'cu py, -ing, -pĭed, -pan cy,
-pant, -pā'tion.
prē or dāin', -ing, -dained', -or'-
di nance, -di nā'tion.
prē pare', -pared', -pâr'ed ly, -ed-
ness, -par'ing, -păr'a tive, -tive-
ly, -tor, -to ry, -to ri ly, prĕp'-
a rā'tion.
prē pay', -ing, -ment, -pāid'.
prē pense', -ly, -pen'sive.
pre pon'der ant, -ly, -ance, -an-
cy, -ate, -ā'ted, -ā'ting, -ting ly,
-der ous, -der ā'tion.
prep o si'tion (-zĭsh'un), -al, -al ly.
prē pos sess' (-pŏz zĕs'), -sess'ing,
-ing ly, -or, -ses'sion (-zĕsh'un).
prē pŏs'ter ous, -ly, -ness.
prē rĕq'uĭ sĭte (-rĕk'wĭ zĭt).
prē rog'a tive, -ly.
prĕs'age (*or* prē'-), *n.*, prē sage',
v., -ment, -saged', -sā'ging, -sā'ger.
Pre-Saint-Ger vas' (prā'-săń'-
zhĕr'vä'), suburb Paris.
pres'by ter (*or* prĕz'-), -byt'er al,
(-bĭt'-), -byt'er ate (-bĭt'-), -by-
te'ri al, -al ly, -tē'rĭ um, -ter-
ship, -ter y.
Pres by tē'ri an, -ism, -an ly, -an-
ize, -ized, -i zing.
prē'sci ence (-shĭ ens *or* -shĕns),
-sci ent, -ent ly.
pre scribe', -scribed', -scrĭb'ing,
-er, pre'script, -scrip'ti ble, -bil'i-
ty, -scrip'tive, -tion, -tion ist, pre-
scrip'tion-glăss.
pres'ence (prĕz'-), -ent, *n.* or *a.*,
-ly, prē sent' (-zĕnt'), *v.*, -ed,
-er, -ing, -a ble, -a tive, -ment,
pres'en tā'tion (prĕz'-), pres'-
ence-chām'ber, -room, pres'ent·
per fect.

pre sen'ti ment, -ti men'tal, -sen'-
tient (-shĕnt).
pre sent'ment.
pre serve' (-zerv'), -serv'a ble,
-a bil'i ty, -à tive, -à to ry, -er,
-ing, -served', pres'er vā'tion
(prĕz'-), pre serve'-jar.
pre side' (-zīd'), -sid'ed, -sid'er,
-sid'ing, pres'i den cy (prĕz'-),
-dent, -dent ship, -den'tial, pre-
sĭd'i al, -sĭd'i a ry, *pre si'di o*
(prä sē'dē ō), a military post,
Pre si'di o (prä sē'dē ō), co. Tex.
pre'sō (prä'-).
Presque Isle (prĕsk ēl), co.
Mich.; tp. Me.
press, -er, -ing, -ing ly, -or,
pressed, pres'sion, press'man,
-room, -work.
press'-a'gent, -beam, -bed, -blaŋ-
ket, -blocks, -boards, -boy,
-cake, -gang, -girth'ing, -key,
-mark, -măs ter, -mon ey,
-pack, -pile, -pin, -plate,
-print'ing, -proof, -stone, -yeast.
press'el.
press'er-bar, -fly'er, -foot, -frame.
press'ing-bag, -board, -i'ron,
-plate, -roll'er.
Prĕs sen sé' (prä'sŏn sā'), Fr. theol.
pres'sure (prĕsh-), -bar, -blow'er,
-fig'ure, -fil'ter, -for'ging,
-frame, -gāge, -note, -reg'is ter,
-screw, -spot, -tone.
pres tez'za (präs tāt'sa).
pres'tĭ dig'i tā'tor (-dĭj'-), -i tā'-
tion, pres tig'i ā tor (-tĭj'-).
pres'tige (-tĭj *or* -tēzh').
prĕs'tŏ, *pres tis'si mo.*
Prĕst'wich, vil. Eng.
pre sūme' (-zūm'), -sūm'à ble,
-à bly, -ed ly, -er, -ing, -ing ly,
-sumed', -sump'tion, -sump'tive,
-tive ly, -tu ous, -ous ly, -ous-
ness.
pre sup pose', -posed', -pōs'al,
-pōs'ing, -po sĭ'tion (-zĭsh'un),
-tion less.
pre tend', -ed, -ed ly, -er, -er-
ship, -ing, -ing ly.
pre tense' *or* -tence', -less, -ten'-
sion, -ten'tious (-shŭs), -tious-
ly, -tious ness.

prĕt′er it *or* -ĭte, -it ness, prē tĕr′i-
tive.

pre ter nǎt′u ral, -ism, -ral ly,
-ness.

prē′text.

pre ton′ic.

prē′tor, -ship, -to′ri al, -ri an,
-an ism, *-ri um*, pl. *-ri a*.

pret′ty (prĭt′-), -ti ly, -ti ness,
pret′ty pret′ty, pret′ty-grǎss, a
plant, -spo ken.

prĕt′zel (-sĕl).

Preuss (prois), Ger. hist.

pre vǎil′, -ing, -ing ly, -vailed′,
prĕv′a lent, -ly, -lence, -len cy.

prē vǎr′i cate, -cā′ted, -cā′ting,
-cā′tor, -cā′tion.

prē vēn′i ent.

pre vent′, -a ble, -a bil′i ty, -a-
tive, -ed, -er, -ing, -ive, -ive ly,
-ive ness, -ven′tion.

Pre′ve sa (prā′vä sä), t. Turk.,
Europe.

prē′vĭ ous, -ly, -ness.

prē vise′ (-vīz′), -vised′, -vīs′ing,
-vi′sion (-vĭsh′un).

Pre vost′ (prē vō′), Eng. gen.

Pré vost′ (prā′vō′), Fr. geol.;
Swiss philos.; Fr. auth.

prey (prā), -er, -ing, preyed.

Prī′an, Homer *Iliad*.

Prī ā′pus, Myth., -a pē′an.

Pri bi lof′ Is lands (prē bē lŏv′),
Behring sea.

prīce, -less, -less ly, priced, prī′-
cing, price′-cŭr′rent, -list, -tag.

prick, -ing, -er, -et, pricked,
prick′fish, -foot, -shot, -tim ber, a
tree, -wood, a tree, prick′-eared,
-post, -punch, -spur, -wheel,
-me-dain ty, prick′ing-note,
-wheel.

pric′kle, -kled, -kling, prick′ly,
-li ness.

pric′kle back, a fish, pric′kle-
-cell, -fish, -lay er, -yel low.

prick′ly back, a fish, prick′ly-
ash, -broom, -ce dar, -grǎss,
-peǎr, -pole, -spined, -withe.

pride, -ful, -ful ly, -ful ness, -less,
prīd′ed, -ing.

pride′-gav′el, -of-Bar bā′dos, a
plant, -of-Chi′na, a plant, -of-

Co lum′bi a, a plant, -of-In′-
di a, a plant, -of-Lon′don, a
plant, -of-O hi′o, a plant.
prie-dieu′ (prē′-dyē′).

prī′er.

Priess′nitz (prēs′nĭts), Ger.
originator of the water-cure.

priĕst, -ess, -hood, -like, -ly, -li-
ness, priest′craft, -fish, -rid′den.

priĕst′-cap, -ill, -monk, priest′s-
crown.

prig, -ger y, -gish, -gish ly, -gish-
ness.

Prim (prēm), Sp. statesman.

prim, -ly, -ming, -ness, primmed.

pri′ma (prē′-), *p. dŏn′na*, pl.
-dŏn′nas (-nåz), *prī′ma ja′ci e*
(-shĭ ē).

prī′ma cy, -mal, -mal′i ty.

prī′mage.

pri′ma ry, -ri ly, -ri ness, -mā′-
ri an.

prī′mate, -ship, -mā′tial, -mat′ic,
-ic al.

prime, -ly, -ness, prīmed, prīm′-
ing, prīm′er, prime′-stǎff.

prīm′er, a first book; a kind of
type.

prīm′er-pouch, -sĕi′zin.

prī mē′val, -ly.

prī mĭ cē′rĭ on or *-um*.

prīm′ing-horn, -i′ron, -ma chine′,
-pow′der, -tube, -wire.

prim′i tive, -tive ly, -tive ness,
-tiv′i ty.

pri′mō (prē′-).

prī mŏ gen′i tal, -i ta ry, -i tive,
-i tor, -i ture, -ture ship.

prī mor′di al, -ism, -al ly, -an,
-al′i ty.

prīmp, -ing, primped.

prim′rose, -rosed, prim′rose-peer′-
less, -wil′low.

prīnce, -dom, -hood, -kin, -less,
-let, -like, -ling, -ly, -li ness,
-wood, prince′s-fĕath′er, -pine.

Prince-Al′bert, a coat.

prin′cess, -like, prin cesse′, a
dress.

prin′ci pal, chief, -ly, -ness, -ship,
-pal′i ty.

prin cip′i a.

prīn′ci ple, -pled, -pling.

prin'gle, -gled, -gling.
prink, -er, -ing, prinked.
print, -ed, -er, -ing, -less.
print'-bro ker, -cloth, -cut ter,
-field, -hold er, -room, -sell'er,
-shop, -works.
print'ing-bod'y, -frame, -house,
-ink, -ma chine', -of'fice, -pa'-
per, -press, -tel'e graph, -type,
-wheel.
prī'or, -ate, -or ess, -or ship, -o ry,
-or'i ty.
prism (prĭzm), pris mat'ic, -ic al,
-al ly, -moid, -moid'al, -my,
prism'-train.
pris'on (prĭz'n), -on er.
pris'on-bars, -base, -breach,
-breāk'ing, -fe'ver, -van, p. ship.
prĭs'tĭne.
prĭth'ee.
prī'vate, -ly, -ness, -va cy.
prī'va teer', -ing, -teers'man.
prī vā'tion, prĭv'a tive, -tive ness.
prĭv'et, -moth, p. hawk-moth.
prĭv'i lĕge.
prĭv'y, -i ly, -i ty, priv'y-fly.
prix (prē).
prīze, prized, prīz'ing, -er, -a ble,
prize'man.
prize'-bolt, -court, -fight, -fight'er,
-list, -mās'ter, -mon ey, -ring.
Prje väl'ski (przhā väl'shē), Russ.
explorer.
prŏb'a ble, -a bly, -a bil'i ty,
-a bil ism, -a bil ist.
prō'bate, -ba tive, -ba to ry, -bā'-
tion, -tion al, -tion a ry, -tion er,
-er ship, -tion ism, -tion ist, prō'-
bate-du ty.
prōbe, probed, prōb'ing, probe'-
point'ed, -scis'sors, -syr'inge,
prōb'ing-awl.
prŏb'i ty.
prob'lem, -at'ic, -ic al, -al ly.
prō bō'nō pub'li co.
prō bos'cis (-sĭs), pl. -ci des
(-dēz), -cid'e an, -cid'e ous,
-cid'i al, -i an, -i form, pro bos'-
cis-mon'key, -rat.
pro ceed', -ed, -er, -ing, -cē'dure,
-ces'sion (-sĕsh'un), -sion al, -al-
ist, -al ly, -a ry, -er, -ing, -ist,
-ces'sive, pro ces'sion-flow'er.

proc'ess (prŏs'-), prō cès ver bal'
(prō'sä vâr'bål'), proc'ess-serv'er.
Proch'o rus (prŏk'-), Bib.
prō clāim', -ant, -er, -ing,
-clāimed', prŏc la mā'tion.
prō clĭv'i ty, -clī'vous, -vous ness.
Proc'ne (prŏk'-), Myth.
pro con'sul, -su lar, -lâ ry, -late,
-sul ship.
pro cras'ti nate, -na ted, -na ting,
-na tive, -na tor, -to ry, -nā'-
tion.
prō'cre ate, -ā'ted, -ā'ting, -ā'tive,
-tive ness, -ā'tor, -ā'tion.
Pro crus'tes (-tēz), Myth., -tē an,
pro crus'te an ize, -ized, -ī'zing.
pro cryp'tic.
prŏc'tor, -age, -ship, -to'ri al.
pro cum'bent.
prŏc'u rā'tor, -ship, -to'ry, -tō'ri al,
-ra'cy, -rā'tion.
prō cure', -ment, -cured', -cūr'er,
-ing, -a ble.
pro'cu'reur' (prō'ko͞o'rêr').
prō cur'sive.
prō cur va'tion.
Prō'cy on (-sĭ-), Astron.
prod, -ded, -ding.
prŏd'i gal, -ly, -gal ize, -ized,
-ī'zing, -i gate, -gā'ted, -gā'ting,
-gal'i ty.
prod'i gy, pro dig'ious (-dĭj'ŭs),
-ious ly, -ious ness.
pro duce', v., -duced', -dū'cing,
-cer, -cent, -ci ble, -ble ness,
-bil'i ty, -duc'tĭle, -duc'tive,
-tive ly, -tive ness, -duc tiv'i ty,
-duc'tion, prŏd'uce, n., -uct, n.
prŏd'uce-bro'ker, -mer'chant, p.
ex change'.
prō'em, -ē'mi al.
prō fāne', -ly, -ness, -faned',
-fān'er, -ing, -făn'i ty, -fan'a to ry,
prŏf'a nā'tion.
pro fess', -ing, -ing ly, -ed ly,
-fes'sion (-fĕsh'un), -sion al, -al-
ism, -al ly, -fess'or, -or ship, -fes-
so'ri al, -so'ri ate, -fessed'.
prŏf'fer, -er, -fer ing.
prō fi'cient (-fĭsh'ent), -ly, -fi'-
cience, -cien cy.
prō'file (-fēl or -fĭl), -filed, -fil-
ing, -fĭl ist, -fĭl'o grăph.

prŏ′file-board (-fĕl-), -cut′ter, -pa′-
per, -piece, pro′fil ing-ma chine′.
prŏf′it, -a ble, -ble ness, -a bly,
-ed, -er, -ing, -less, -less ly,
prof′it-shar′ing.
prof′li gate, -ly, -ness, -gă cy.
pro found′, -ly, -ness, -fun′di ty.
prŏ fuse′ (-fūs′), -ly, -ness, -fū′-
sion (-zhŭn).
prog, -ger, -ging, progged.
prog′e ny (prŏj′-), prŏ gen′i tor,
-to′ri al.
prŏg nŏ′sis, -nos′tic, -nos′ti cate,
-cā′ted, -cȧ′ble, -cā′ting, -cȧ-
tive, -cā′tor, -cā′tion.
prŏ′grăm or -gramme, -gram-
mer, -grăm′ma, pl. -ma ta.
prŏg′ress, n., -ress ist, prŏ gress′,
v., -ing, -ive, -ive ly, -ive ness,
-gres′sion (-grĕsh′un), -sion al,
-sion ist.
prŏ′gym nä′si um (-zĭ um).
prŏ hĭb′it, -ed, -er, -ing, -ive,
-or, -o ry, -hi bĭ′tion (-bĭsh′un),
-tion ist, Prŏ hi bĭ′tion ist, -tion-
ism.
prŏj′ect, n., prŏ ject′, v., -ed,
-ing, -ing ly, -ĭle, -or, -jec′tion,
-jec′ture.
prŏ jet′ (-zhä′).
pro′le gŏm′e non (or prŏl′-), pl.
-e na, -e na ry, -e nous.
prŏ′les (-lēz).
pro le taire′ (prŏ′lä′târ′), prol e ta′-
ri an, -an ism, -an ize, -ized,
-ĭ′zing, -tä′ri at.
prŏ lĭf′ic, -al, -al ly, -ic ness, -i ca-
cy, -cā′tion, -li fy, -ing, -fīed,
-lig′er ous (-lĭj′-).
prŏ′lix (or -lix′), -ly, -ness, -lix′-
i ty.
prŏ loc′u tor (or prŏl′o cū′-), -ship.
prŏ′lŏgue or -log, -log ist (or prŏl′-
o gist), -log ize (or prol′o gize),
-ized.
pro long′, -a ble, -er, -ing, -ment,
-longed′, -loṇ gā′tion.
pro lŏnge′.
prŏm′e näde′, -näd′ed, -er, -ing.
Pro mē′the us (or -mē′thŭs),
Myth., -mē′thē an, pro mē′the a,
a moth, -the an, a glass tube;
a lucifer maṭch.

prŏm′i nent, -ly, -nence, -nen cy.
prŏ mis′cu ous, -ly, -ness -cū′i ty.
prŏm′ĭse, -ised, -is ing, -ing ly,
-er, -or, -ee′, -is so ry, -so′ri ly,
prŏm′ ise - breach, -breāk′ er,
-crammed.
prom ne′si a.
prŏm′on to ry, -tŏ′ri ous, -ri um.
prŏ′morph, -mor phol′o gy, -o-
gist, -pho log′ic al, -al ly.
prŏ mote′, -mōt′ed, -er, -ing,
-mo′tive, -mō′tion.
prŏmpt, -ed, -er, -ing, -ly, -ness,
-i tude, -u å′ry.
prompt′-book, -cen′ter, -note,
-side.
pro mul′gate, -gä′ted, -gä′ting,
pro′mul gä′tor, -gä′tion.
prŏ′nate, -nä′tor, -nä′tion.
prone, -ly, -ness.
prŏng, -buck, -doe, -horn, prong′-
chuck, -hoe.
prŏ′nôn′cē′ (-sä′).
prŏ′noun, -nom′i nal, -nal ly.
pro nounce′, -a ble, -ment,
-nounced′, -noun′ced ly, -cing,
-cer, pro nun′cial, -ci å tive
(-shĭ-), -ā′tor, -to′ry, -ci ā′tion,
-ci a men′to.
pro′nymph.
prŏ œ′mĭ um, -mi ac.
prŏŏf, -less, -less ly.
proof′-ar mor, -gal ley, -glåss,
-house, -leaf, -mark, -pa per,
-plane, -press, -print, -print er,
-read er, -read ing, -sheet,
-spĭr′it, -ståff, -stick, -text.
prop, -page, -ping, propped, prop′-
joint, -leg, -stay, -wood.
prŏp′a gand, -gan′da, -gan′dic,
-gan′dism, -dist.
prop′a gate, -gä′ted, -ga′ting,
-tive, -tor, -to′ry, -ga tŏ′ri um,
-gä′tion.
prop′a ga′ting-bench, -box, -glåss,
-house.
prŏ pel′, -ling, -lant, -lent, -ler,
-ment, -pelled′.
pro pel′ ler-en gine, -mow′ er,
-pump, -shåft, -well, -wheel.
prŏ pense′, -ly, -ness, -pen′sion,
-pen′si ty.
prŏp′er, -ly, prŏ prī′e ty.

fāte, făt, fär, fạll, fâre, fåst, sofȧ, mēte, mĕt, hêr, ice, Iṇ, nōte,

prŏp′er ty, -man, -măs ter, -plot,
-room, p. tax.

proph′e cy, *n.*, proph′e sy (-sī),
v., -sy′ing, -sī′er, -sīed, proph′-
e cy-moṇ′ger.

proph′et, -ess, -hood, -ism, -flow′-
er, -ship, pro phĕt′ic, -ic al,
-al ly.

prŏph′y lac′tic (prŏf′Ĭ- *or* prŏ′fĬ-),
-al, -*lax′is*, -lax′y.

prŏ pīne′, -pīned′, -pīn′ing, prŏp-
i nă′tion.

prŏ pĭṇ′quĭ ty.
prŏ′pio (-pyō).

prŏ pi′ti ate (-pĭsh′i ate), -ā′ted,
-a ting, -a tor, -to′ry, -to′ri ly,
-ti á ble (-pĭsh′Ĭ-), -ā′tion.

prŏ ponĕ′, -poned′, -pōn′ing, -pŏ′-
nent.

prŏ por′tion, -á ble, -ble ness,
-a bly, -al, -al ly, -al′i ty, -ate,
-ate ly, -ate ness, -ment, -tioned.

prŏ pose′, -pōs′al (-pŏz′-), -er,
-ing, -posed′, prop o sĭ′tion
(-zĭsh′un), -tion al, -al ly, -tion-
ize, -ized, -ĭ′zing.

prŏ pound′, -ed, -er, -ing.

prŏ prī′e tá′ry, -e tor, -tor ship,
-to′ri al.

prŏ pul′sion, -pul′sive, -so ry.

prŏ rate′, -rāt′ed, -rāt′ing, -a ble,
pro rā′ta.

prŏ rogue′ (-rōg′), rogued′,
-rogu′ing, -ro gā′tion.

prŏ sce′ni um, *pl.* -ni a, -arch,
-box, -grooves.

prŏ scribe′, -scribed′, -scrĭb er, -ing,
prŏ′script, -scrip′tion, -tion al,
-tion ist, -scrip′tive, -tive ly.

prose (prōz), prŏ′sy, -si ly, -si-
ness, prōs′ing, -ing ly, prŏ sa′ic
(-zā′-), -ic al, -al ly, -ic ness,
-i cism, prŏ′sa ism (-zā-), -sa ist,
prose′-man, -wrīt′er.

prŏs′e cute, -cū′ted, -cū′ting, -tor,
-cu′tion.

prŏs′e lyte, -ly′ted (-lī′-), -ting,
-ting ly, -ly tize′ (-lĭ-), -tized, -tī′-
zing, -ti′zer, -tism, -tist.

Prŏs′er pīne, *Myth.*, Pro ser′-
pĬ na, *Myth.; Astron.*
pro′sit.

pro slāv′er y.

Pros′na (prŏsh′-), r. Pol.

pros o det′ic.

prŏs′o dy, -o dist, pro sō′di ac, -di-
al, -di an, -sŏd′ic, -ic al, -al ly.

pros′o pŏ pē′ia (-ya).

pros′pect, *n.* and *v.*, -ing, -less,
-or, pro spec′tion, -tive, -tive ly,
-tive ness, -tus.

pros′per, -ing, -ous, -ous ly, -ous-
ness, -pĕr′i ty.

Prŏs′pē ro, Shak. *Tempest.*
pros′the sis, -thet′ic.

pros′ti tute, -tū′ted, -tū′ting, -tor,
-tū′tion.

pro slŏ′ma, -sto′mi um, pl. -mi a,
-mi al.

pros′trate, -trā′ted, -trā′ting, -tor,
-trā′tion.

Prŏ tăg′o ras, Gr. philos.
prŏ tan′to.

prŏ tect′, -ed, -er, -ing, -ing ly,
-tec′tion, -tion al, ism, -ist,
-to ry, -tect′ive, -ive ly, -ive-
ness, -or, -or al, -or ate, -or-
less, -or ship, -tec tŏ′ri al.

pro té gé′ (prŏ′tā′zhā′), fem. -*gée′*
(-zhā′).

pro′te id, -te in.

prŏ tend′, -ed, -er, -ing, -ten′-
sion, -si ty, -sive.

Pro tes′i lă′us, *Myth.*

prŏ test′, *v.*, -ed, -er, -ing, -ing-
ly, prŏt′es tā′tion, -ta′tor, -es-
tant, prŏ′test, *n.*

Prŏt′es tant, -ism, -ize, -ized,
-i zing, -tan cy.

Prŏ′tĕ us (*or* -tūs), *Myth.*, -te an,
-an ly.

prŏ thŏn′o ta ry, -ship.

prŏ′to cŏl, -ist, -ize, -ized, -ĭ′zing,
pro′to col-book.

Prŏ′tŏ dŏr′ic, -to hel len′ic, -to ī-
on′ic, -to se mĭt′ic, *or* Pro′to-
Dŏr′ic, -Hel len′ic, -I on′ic,
-Se mĭt′ic.

Prŏ tog′e nes (-tŏj′e nēz), painter
of Rhodes.

prŏ to gen′e sis, -gen′ic, -ge net′ic.

prŏ′tŏ his tŏr′ic, -to psy′che (-sī′-),
pro to-com pound.

prŏ′to plasm, -to plast, -plas′tic,
-plas′mic (-plăz′-).

prŏ′to type, -typ′ic al (-tĭp′-).

prŏ tract', -ed, -ed ly, -er, -ĭle,
-ing, -ive, -or, -trac'tion, pro-
tract' ing-bev el.

prō trude', -trŭd'ed, -ing, -a ble,
-tru'sĭle, -sive, -sive ly, -sive-
ness, -sion (-zhŭn).

pro tu'ber ant, -ly, -ance, -an cy,
-ate, -ā'ted, -ā'ting, -ā'tion.

proud, -ly, -ness, -ish, -ling, proud'-
heart'ed.

Proud hon' (prōō'dŏn'), Fr. jurist; Fr. socialist.

prove (prōōv), proved, prov'a ble,
-ble ness, -bly, -ing, -en, -er,
prōōf.

pro vel'i ger (-jer).

prov'ing-ground, -hut, -ma chine',
-press, -pump.

Pro'ven'çal' (-vŏn'säl'), -ven'cial.

Prŏv'ence oil, P. rose.

Prō vence' (-vŏns'), province Fr.,
Pro vin'cial.

prŏv'en der, -ing, -dered.

pro vĕn'ience (-yens).

prŏv'erb, pro ver'bi al, -al ism,
-al ist, -al ize, -ized, -ĭ'zing,
-al ly, Prŏv'erbs, Bib.

prō vīde', -vīd'a ble, -ed, -er, -ing.

prŏv'i dence, -dent, -dent ly,
-dent ness, -den'tial, -tial ly,
Prŏv'i dence.

prŏv'ĭnce, pro vin'cial, -cial ism,
-ist, -ize, -ized, -ĭ'zing, -cial ly,
-cial ship, -ci al'i ty (-shĭ al'-).

Prō vins' (-văn'), t. Fr.

prō vī'sion, -al, -al ly, -a ry, -er,
-ing, -sioned.

pro vi'sion-car, -deal'er, -mer'-
chant.

pro vī'so (-zō), -vī'sor, -so ry,
-so ri ly.

prō vōke', -voked', -vōk'er, -à ble,
-ing, -ing ly, -vo'ca tive, -tive-
ness, -to'ry, prŏv'o cā'tion.

prŏv'ost (-ŭst), -ship, -ry, prov'ost
marshal. As applied to a military officer, the word is pronounced prŏv'ost or prō'vo or
prō vō'.

prow.

prow'ess.

prowl, -er, -ing, -ing ly, prowled.

prox.

prŏx'i mal, -ly, -mate, -mate ly,
-im'i ty.

prox'i mo.

prox'y, -ship, prox'y-wed'ded.

prude, prūd'er y, prūd'ish, -ish-
ly, -ish ness.

pru'dent, -ly, -dence, -den'tial,
-tial ist, -tial ly, -ti al'i ty (-shi-
al-).

Prud homme' (prĕ'dŏm'), Fr.
poet.

prud homme' (prü dŏm').

prune, -let, pruned, prūn'ing, -er.

prune'-pur'ple, -tree, prūn'ing-
chis'el, -hook, -knife, -saw,
-shears, -tools.

pru nell', a heavy cashmere.

pru nel'la, a disease of the throat.

pru nel'la, or -nel'lo, a strong
woolen cloth.

Pru nel'la, Bot. genus; Ornith.
genus.

pru nelle', a small acid prune.

pru nel'lo, a superior dried prune.

pru'ri ent, -ly, -en cy.

pru rī'go, -rig'i nous (-rĭj'-), -rī'-
tus.

Prus'sian (prŭsh'an or prōō'-),
-sian ize, -ized, -i zing.

prŭs'si ate, -sic.

pry, -ing, -ing ly, prīed, prī'er.

Przem'ysl (pzhĕm'ĭsl), t. Aust.

Przhed'borz (pzhĕd'bŏrsh), t. Pol.

Przi'bräm (pzhē'-), t. Bohem.

psalm (säm), -ist, -ist ry, psal'mo-
dy (săl'- or säm'o-), -mŏd'ic, -ic al,
-mō dist, -mo dize, -dized, -dī'-
zing, -mo graph, -mog'ra pher,
-ra phist, -ra phy, Psalms
(säms), Bib.

psalm'-book, -me lod'i con, -sing-
ing, -tone.

psal'ter (sąwl'-), psąl tē'ri al, -ri an,
-ri on, -ri um, pl. -ri a, -ter y.

psel'lism (sĕl'-), -lis'mus.

pseu'do-Christ, -Chris ti an'i ty,
-Chris tol'o gy.

pseŭ'do nym, (sū'-) -dŏn'y mal,
-y mous, -mous ly, -do nym'i ty.

pshaw (shąw).

psi (psē or sī).

Psi ŏl' (psē-), r. Rus.

pso'as (sō'-), pso at'ic.

psō rī'a sis (so-), pso'ric, -rous.
Psy'che (sī'kē), *Myth.; Astron.; Zoöl.; Conch.,* psy'che, the soul; a mirror, psy'chal (-kăl), -chian, -chic (-kĭk), -chic al, -chics, -chism.
psy chŏ gen'e sis (sī kō jen'-), -genet'ic al, -al ly.
psy chog'e ny (sī kŏj'-), -chogon'ic, -ic al, -chog'o ny (-kŏg'-).
psy'cho grăph (sī'kō-), -graph'ic, -chog'ra phy (-kŏg'-).
psy chol'o gy (-sī kŏl'-), -o gist, -o gize, -gized, -gī'zing, -cholog'ic, -ic al, -al ly, -ics.
psy'cho man cy (sī'kō-), -man'tic.
psy chom'e try, -e trize, -trized, -trī'zing, -cho mĕt'ric, -ric al.
psy chon'o my (sī kŏn'-).
psy chop'a thy (sī kŏp'-), -a thist, -cho path'ic.
psy chŏ'sis (sī kō'-), -chos'o phy (-kŏs'-), -cho stat'ic, -ic al, -al ly, -ics.
psy chrom'e ter, -e try, -chromet'ric, -ic al.
psyl'lid, -loid.
Ptah (ptä), *Myth.*
ptar'mi gan (tär'-).
Ptchals'kŏ (pŭchăls'-), l. Sĭberĭa.
pter'o dac'tyl (tĕr'-), -ous, -tyl'i an.
pte rog'ra pher (tē-), -ra phy, pter o graph'ic, -ic al.
ptis'an (tĭz'-).
Ptitch (ptĭch), r. Russ.
Ptŏl'ē mā'is, *Bib.*
Ptŏl'e mē'us, *Bib.*
Ptol'e my (tŏl'-), ruler Egypt, -e mā'ic, -mā'ist.
pto'ma in *or* -ine (tō'-).
ptŏ'sis (tō'-), pto'tic.
pty' a lin (tī'-), -a lize, -a lized, -a lism, -a lose (-lōs).
pū ber' ty, -bes'cence, -cen cy, -cent.
pub'lic, -ly, -ness, -li can, -li cā'tion, -li cist, -lic'i ty, pub'licheärt'ed, -mind'ed, -mind'edness, -spir'it ed.
pub'lish, -a ble, -er, -ing, -ment, -ished.
pu che'ro (pōō chā'rō).

Pu-ching-hi en' (pōō'-chĭng'-hēĕn'), t. China.
puck, an elf; a goatsucker; puck'ish. Puck, a chief of the fairies.
puck'er, -er, -ing, -y, -ered.
pŭd'der, -ing, -dered.
pud'ding (pŏŏd'-), -head, a person, -bag, -cloth, -faced, -fish, -grăss, -pīe, -sleeve, -stone, -time, -wife.
pŭd'dle, -dled, -dler, -dling, -dly.
pŭd'dle-ball, -bar, -duck, -po'et, -rolls, pud'dling-fur'nace, -machine', -rolls.
pŭdg'y.
pū dic'i ty.
pueb'lo (pwĕb'lō), Pueb'lo, c. Colo., Pueb'la, state Mex.
pū'er ile, -ly, -ness, -il'i ty.
pu er'per al, -al ly, -per ous, -per y.
Puer'to Prin ci'pe (pwĕr'tō prēn'sē pä), t. Cuba.
Puer'to Rī'co (rē'kō), isl. W. I.
Puer'to vi e'jo (-vē ā'hō), t. Ecuador, S. A.
puff, -er, -er y, -y, -i ness, -ing, -ing ly, puff'ball, -leg.
puff'-ad'der, -bird, -box, -fish, -net'ting, -paste, puff'er-pipe, puff'ing-pig, p. ad'der, p. grub'by.
puf'fin.
pug, -ging, pugged, pug'nose, an eel.
pug'-dog, -faced, -mill, -nose, a nose, -nosed, -piles, -pīl'ing.
Pū'get (-jet), a sound on the coast of Wash.
Pu get' (pü'zhā'), Fr. sculptor.
pugh (pōō *or* pŏŏ).
Pughe (pū), Welsh philol.
pu'gil ism, -gil ist, -is'tic, -tic al, -al ly.
pug nā'cious, -ly, -ness, -nac'i ty.
pŭg'ree.
puis'ne (pū'nĭ).
pū'is sant, -ly, -ness, -sance.
Pu jol' (pü'zhŏl'), Fr. painter.
puke, puked, pūk'er, -ing, puke'weed, pūk'ing-fe'ver.
Pū lăs'kĭ, co. Ark.; co. Ga.; co. Ill.; co. Ind.; co. Ky.; co. Mo.; co. Va.; Polish-Amer. gen.

---

nŏt, nôr, ūse, ŭp, ûrn, etüde, fōōd, fŏŏt, aŋger, boṅmot, thus, Bach.

pŭl'chrĭ tude.
pūle, puled, pūl'ing, -ing ly, -er.
Pū lĭt'zer, Amer. journalist.
pŭl'kha (-ka).
pull (po͝ol), -ing, -er, pulled,
  pull'back.
pull'=cock, -dev'il, -down, -i'ron,
  -off, -o'ver, -piece, -pipes, -to,
  pull'ing-jack, -out.
pul'let (po͝ol'-).
pul'ley (po͝ol'-), *pl.* -leys.
pul'ley-block, -box, -check,
  -clutch, -drum, -frame, -mor'-
  tĭse, -shēave, -shell, -stand,
  -stone, -wheel.
pŭl'lu late, -lā'ted, -lā'ting, -lā'-
  tion.
pul'mo nâ ry, -mo nate, -nā'ted,
  -mŏn'ic.
pulp, -er, -ing, -y, -i ness, -less,
  -ous, -ous ness, -i fy, -fy ing,
  -fied, pulped.
pulp'-boil'er, -cav'i ty, -col'ors,
  -di gest'er, -dress'er, -en'gine,
  -grind'er, -ma chine', -me'ter,
  -mill, -strain'er, -wash'er, pulp'-
  ing-ma chine'.
pul'pit (po͝ol'-), -eer', -ish, -ry.
pul'que (po͝ol'kā), p. bran'dy.
pŭl'sate, -sā'ted, -sā'ting, -sâ tile,
  -sâ tive, -sa'tor, -sâ to'ry, -sā'tion.
pŭlse, -less, -less ness, pulsed,
  puls'ing, pul sil'o gy, -sim'e ter,
  -som'e ter.
pŭlse'-beat, -curve, -glǎss, -rate,
  -warm'er, -wave.
Pŭlte'ney, Eng. statesman.
pu'lu (po͞o'lo͞o).
pŭl'ver ize, -ized, -ī zing, -ī zer,
  -ī'za ble, -ī zā'tion, -ver ous,
  -vĕr'u lence, -u lent.
pŭl vī'nar, -vĭ nate, -nā'ted,
  -nate ly.
pul'za-oil (po͝ol'-).
pū'ma.
pŭm'ĭce, a volcanic stone, -ĭced,
  -i cing, -i cose (-kōs), pu mi'-
  ceous (-mĭsh'us), -mic'i form
  (-mĭs'-), pum'ĭce-stone.
pŭmp, -age, -er, -ing, pumped.
pŭmp'-bǎr'rel, -bit, -bob, -bolt,
  -box, -brake, -cart, -chain,
  -cis'tern, -coat, -dale, -gear,

-han'dle, -head, -hood, -house,
-ket'tle, -lug, -pis'ton, -plun'ger,
-room, -scrǎp'er, -spear, -stǎff,
-stock, -stop'per, -thun'der,
-well, pump'ing-en'gine, -haft.
pun, -ner, -ning, -ster, punned.
pu'na (po͞o'-), -wĭnd, *pu'no*, a cold
  trade-wind.
punch, -er, -ing, punched; Punch,
  a puppet.
punch'-bowl, -check, -cut'ter,
  -glǎss, -house, -jug, -la'dle,
  -pli'ers, -prop, punch'ing-bag,
  -bear, -ma chine', -press.
punch'eon (-ŭn).
Pun chĭ nel'lo.
punc'tate, -tā'ted, -tā'tor, -tā'tion,
  punc'ti form.
punc til'io (-yō), *pl.* -ios (-yōz),
  -til'ious, -ious ly, -ious ness.
punc'tu al, -ly, -al ist, -al ness,
  -al'i ty.
punc'tu ate, -ā'ted, -ā'ting, -â-
  tive, -ā'tor, -ā'tion.
punc'ture, -less, -tured, -tūr ing,
  -tu rā'tion.
pun'dit.
pun'gent, -ly, -gence, -gen cy.
Pungh (pŭnj), dist. India.
pun'gi (po͞ong'gē), a flute.
pŭng'y, a boat.
pŭn'ish, -a ble, -ble ness, -bil'i ty,
  -er, -ment, -ing, -ished.
pu'ni tive, -ni to ry.
Pun jäb' (po͝on-), prov. India.
pŭnk, -oak.
pun'ka.
punt, -ed, -er, -ing, punts'man,
  punt'-fish'ing, -gun, punt'y-rod.
pun til'la.
pŭn'to.
pū'ny.
pū'pa, *pl.* -pas *or* -pæ, -pal, -pǎ'-
  ri al, -ri um, -pate, -pā'tion.
pū pē'lo (*or* pū'-).
pū'pil, -age, pu'pil-teach'er.
pŭp'pet, -ish, -man, -ry.
pup'pet-head, -mǎs'ter, -play,
  -play'er, -show, -valve.
pŭp'py, *pl.* -pĭes, -py ism, -hood,
  pup'py-dog, -fish, -head'ed.
Pu rä'cé (po͞o rä'sā), vol. Colombia, S. A.

---

fāte, fǎt, fär, fạll, fâre, fǎst, sofâ, mēte, mĕt, hêr, īce, ĭn, nōte,

pur'blind, -ly, -ness.
Pur'cell, Eng. mus. composer.
pur'chase, -chās a ble, -chās er,
  -ing, -chased.
pur'chase-block, -fall, -mon'ey,
  p. sys'tem.
pur'dah, -dahed (-dȧd).
pure, -ly, -ness, pŭr'ism, -ist, pu-
  ris'tic, -tic al, pū'ri ty.
pu rée' (pọ̄ rā').
pur'fle, -fled (-fld), -fling, -fly.
purge, purged, pur'ging, -ger,
  -ger y, -ga tive, -tive ly, -gȧ to'ry,
  -tō'ri al, -ri an, -gā'tion.
purge'-cock, pur'ging-ăg'a ric,
  -cas'sia (-căsh'ȧ), -cock, -flax,
  -nut.
pū'ri fy, -ing, -fī'er, -fīed, -fi ca'-
  tive, -ca'tor, -cā'tion, pu rif'i cȧ-
  to'ry, pu ri fi cā'tion-flow'er.
pū'ri tan, -tan'ic, -ic al, -al ly,
  -tan ism, -ize, -ized, -ī'zing,
  Pū'ri tan, one of a religious sect.
purl, -ing, purled, purl'man,
  purl'-goods, -house.
pur'lieŭ.
pur'lin, -post.
pur loin', -er, -ing, -loined'.
pur'ple, _n._ and _v._, -pled, -pling,
  pur'ple heart, a tree, -lip, a
  plant, -wood, a tree, -wort.
pur'ple-egg, a sea-urchin, -fish,
  -mar'bled, -wreath, a plant.
pur'port, _n._ and _v._, -less.
pur'pose (-pŭs), -posed, -pos ing,
  -posed ly (-pŭst-), -pos er, -pose-
  ful, -ful ly, -ful ness, -less,
  -less ly, -less ness, -like, -ly.
purr, -ing, -er, purred.
purre (pur), a bird.
pŭr'ree.
purse, -ful, pursed, purs'ing,
  pur'sy, -si ness.
purse'-bear'er, -boat, -clȧsp,
  -crab, -crew, -cut'ter, -dȧv'it,
  -gang, -gill, -gilled, -leech, -line,
  -mouth, -net, -pride, -proud,
  -ring, -rope, -seine, -sein'er,
  -silk, -snap, -spi'der, -strings,
  -tak'ing, -twist, -weight, purs'-
  ing-block, -gear, -line, purse'-
  net-fish.
purs'er, -ship.

purs'lane, -tree, -worm.
pur sue', -sū'a ble, -sū'ance, -ant,
  -ant ly, -sued', -sū'ing, -su'er,
  -suit', -sui vant (-swǐ-).
pur'te nance.
pū'ru lent (-rọ̄-), -ly, -lence,
  -len cy.
pur vey' (-vā'), -ance, -or, -ing,
  -veyed'.
pur'view.
pŭs.
push (pọ̄sh), -ing, -ing ly, -er,
  . pushed.
push'-but ton, -car, -hoe, -hold,
  -pick, -pin, push'ing-jack.
pŭsh mi'na (-mē'-).
pŭsh'tǐ.
Pŭsh'tu (-tọ̄).
pŭsh'um.
pu sil lan'i mous, -ly, -ness, -la-
  nim'i ty.
puss (pọ̄s), -y, puss'tail, a grass.
puss'-clo'ver, -gen'tle man, -moth,
  puss'y-cat, -wil'low.
pŭs'tule, -tu lant, -lar, -late, -la-
  ted, -lous, -lā'tion.
put (pọ̄t), -ter, -ting, put'log,
  -off, -pin, -up, put'log-hole.
pū'ta tive, -tā'tion.
pŭt'e lǐ.
Pū tĕ'ŏ lǐ, _Bib._
Pŭt'nam, Amer. Rev. gen.; Amer.
  publish.
pu tois' (pọ̄ twŏ').
pŭt'ọ̄.
pū'tre fy, -ing, -fī'er, -fīed, -fā'-
  cient, -fac'tion, -fac'tive, -tive-
  ness, pu tres'cence, -cent, -ci-
  ble, pū'trid, -trid ness, -trid'i ty,
  -tred'i nous.
pŭtt, in golf-playing, pŭt'ting-
  green, -stone.
pŭt tee'.
pŭt'ti (pọ̄t'tē).
pŭt'tọ̄.
pŭt'ty, -ing, -tǐed, -ti er, -ty root,
  a plant.
pŭt'ty-eye, -faced, -knife, -pow'-
  der, -work.
puy (pwē).
_pu'ya_ (pọ̄'ya).
pŭz'zle, -zled, -zling, -zling ly,
  -zler, puz'zle head, a person.

nŏt, nôr, ūse, ŭp, ûrn, etüde, fọ̄od, fọ̄t, aŋger, boṅmot, thus, Bach.

puz'zle-cup, -head'ed, -jug, -lock,
-mon'key, -peg, -ring.
pyc nom'e ter.
py e'mi a (pī-), -e'mic.
Pyg mā'lǐ on, *Myth.*
pyg'my, *pl.* -mǐes, -me'an, pyg'-
my-weed.
Pyl'a des (-dēz *or* pī lā'-), Gr.
legend.
py lō'rus, pl. *-rǐ,* -lŏr'ic.
Pynch'eon (-ŭn), Hawthorne,
House of Seven Gables.
Pyn'chon (pǐn'-), Eng. theol.
py'o scope (pī'-).
pyr (pīr), a unit of light intensity.
pyr'a mid (pǐr'-), -mid'ic, -ic al,
-al ly, -al ness, -mid'ist, py-
ram'i dal (pī-), -dal ism, -dal ist,
-dal ly, pyr'a mid-shell (pǐr'-).
Pyr'a mus (pǐr'-), hero of a classic
legend.
pyre (pīr), py'ral (pī'-).
Pyr go pol i nī'ces (-sēz), Plautus'
comedy.
py rī'tes (-tēz), -rǐt'ic, -ic al,
pyr'i tize (pǐr'-), -tized, -ti zing,
-tǐ zā'tion.
py ro ē lec'tric (pī-), -tric'i ty.
py rŏ gen'e sis (pī-), -gen'ic,
-ge net'ic, -rog'e nous (-rŏj'-).
py rog'ra phy.

py rŏl'a try (pī-) -rŏl'o gy, -o-
gist, -rŏl'e ter, *-rol'y sis,* pyr o-
lyt'ic (pǐr-), -ro man'cy, -mā'-
ni a, -ma'ni ac.
py rŏm'e ter (pī-), -e try, -ro-
met'ric al, -al ly.
py'ro scope (pī'-), -ro stat, -ro-
stěr'e o type.
py'ro tech ny (pī'ro těk-), -tech'-
nic, -nic al, -nics, -nist, -ni'-
cian (-tek nǐsh'an).
Pyr'rha (pǐr'ra), Gr. legend.
pyr'rhic (pǐr'ǐk), *Pros.,* -rhi cist.
Pyr'rho (pǐr'-), Gr. philos., -rho-
nism, -rho nist, -rhon'ic.
pyr'rhous (pǐr'ŭs), reddish.
Pyr'rhus (pǐr'-), King of Epirus,
Pyr'rhic.
Py thag'o ras, Gr. philos., -o rē'-
an, -an ism, -an ize, -ized,
-i zing, -o rism, -rize, -rized,
-ri zing, Pyth a gor'ic, -ic al.
Pyth'i a (pǐth'-), Priestess of
Apollo, -i an.
Pyth'i as, the friend of Damon.
py thō gen'e sis (pī-), -gen'ic.
Py'thon (pī'-), *Antiq.; Bib.,* py'-
thon (pī'-), a serpent, pyth'o-
ness (pǐth'-), py thon'ic.
pyx, a sacred vessel, -cloth, -ker'-
chief, -veil.

Q

qe ri (kē rē' *or* krē).
Qo hěl'eth (kō-).
quā (*or* kwä), quä'-bird.
quä'chil' (*or* -chēl').
quack, -er y, -ish, -ism, quack'-
grass.
quad (kwŏd), -ded, -ding.
Quad ra ges'i ma (-jěs'-), quad ra-
ges'i mal.
quad'ran'gle (kwŏd'-), -ran'gu-
lar, -lar ly, *-rans,* -rant, -ran'-
tal, -rat, -rate, -ra ted, -răt'ic,
-ic al ly, -ra ture, quad'rant-
com'pass.
quad ren'ni al (kwŏd-), -ly, -ni-
ate, *-ni um.*

quad ri lat'er al (kwŏd-), -al ness,
-ri lit'er al.
qua drille' (kwä-), -drilled', *qua-
dril lě'* (kä drěl yä').
quad ril'lion (kwŏd-).
quad'rǐ lobed (kwŏd'-), -ri lŏ'-
bate, -ri nŏ'mi al, -nom'ic al,
-nom'i nal.
quad ri syl'la ble (kwŏd-), -syl-
lab'ic, -ic al.
quad roon' (kwŏd-).
quad ru'ma nous (kwŏd-).
quad'ru ped, -ru'pe dal.
quad'ru ple, -pled, -pling, -plot,
-plex, -ru ply.
quæs'ta (kwěs'-), pl. *-tæ.*

quâff, -ing, quâffed, quâff′ing-pot.
quăg, -gy, -mire.
quăg′ga.
quạ′hŏg or -hạug.
quâil, -ing, quailed.
quâil′-call, -dove, -mut′ton, -pi′-
geon, -pipe, -snipe.
quâint, -ly, -ness.
quâke, quaked, quāk′ing, -ing ly,
-y, -i ness, quāke′tail, a bird.
quâke′-grâss, quāk′ing-grăss.
Quăk′er, -dom, -ish, -ism, -ly,
Quak′er-col′or.
quăk′er-bird, -grăss, -moth.
qual′i fy (kwŏl′-), -ing, -fīed,
-fīed ly, -fied ness, -fī a ble, -I fi-
că′tive, -că′tor, -că′tion.
qual′i ty, -i ta′tive, -tive ly, qual′-
i ty-bīnd′ing.
qualm (kwäm), -ish, -ish ly, -ish-
ness.
quạ măsh′, -rat.
quan′dong (kwŏn′-).
quan′da ry (kwŏn′-) -ing, -da rĭed.
quăn′net (or kwŏn′-).
Quan tin′ (kŏn′tăn′), Fr. pub.
quan′ti ta tive (kwŏn′-), -tive ly,
or -ti tive ly, -ta tive ness.
quan′ti ty, -cul′ture, -fuse.
quan tĭv′a lence, -a len cy, -a lent.
quar′an tinc (kwŏr′an tēn), -tined,
-tin′ing, -tin′a ble.
quarl, fire-clay.
quar′rel (kwŏr′-), -ing or -ling,
-er or -ler, -reled or -relled,
-rel some, -some ly, -some ness,
quar′rel-pane, -pick′er.
quar′ry (kwŏr′-), -ing, -rĭed, -ri
a ble, -ri er, quar′ry man.
quar′ry-faced, -hawk, -slave,
-stone, -wa ter, quar′ry ing-ma-
chine′.
quạrt, -let.
quarte (kärt).
quạr′ter, -ing, -age, -foil, -ly,
quạr′ter land, -man, -tered.
quar′ter-ạn gled, -as pect, -back,
-badge, -bend, -bill, -bitts,
-blạn ket, -blocks, -board, -boat,
-boot, -boys, -bred, -căsk,
-câst, -cloth, -day, -deck,
-deck er, -e vil, -face, -făst,
-fish es, -franc, -gal ler y, -grain,

-guard, -gun ner, -hol low,
-horse, -ill, -i ron, -light, -line.
quar′ter-net′ting, -no′ble, -pace,
-par ti′tion, -pie′ces, -point, -rail,
-round, -săv′er, -seal, -sec′tion,
-ses′sions, -sights, -sling,
-square, -stâff, -stan′chion,
-stuff, -tac kle, -tim ber, -tone,
-trap, -turn, -un du la′tion,
-vine, -wait er, -watch, -wĭnd,
-yard, quar′ter note, q. plate,
q. rest.
quar′ter ing-belt, -block, -ham′-
mer, -ma chine′.
quar′ter măs ter, -gen′er al, -ser′-
geant.
quar′tern, -loaf.
quạr tet′ or -tette′.
quar′tic.
quạr′to, *pl.* -tos (-tŏz).
quạrtz, -if′er ous, -īte, -it′ic, -y.
quạrtz′-crush′er, -li q′uc fī er,
-mill, -por′phy ry, -reef, -rock,
-sin′ter, -vein.
quash (kwŏsh), -ing, -er, -ey,
quashed.
quash′ee (kwŏsh′ē), a negro.
quâ′sī, -nor′mal, -pe ri od′ic, -ra′-
di ate, -ten′ant, -trus tee′.
Quạ′si mŏ′do (kä′zē-), Hugo,
Notre Dame de Paris.
quas′si a (kwŏsh′Ĭ a or kwăsh′-
ya), -tree.
quâ′tern, qua ter′na ry, -ter′nate,
-ni on, -ni ty.
qua torze′ (kạ torz′).
quat′rāin (kwŏt′-).
qua′tre (kä′tr), -foil.
Quatre Bras (kâtr brä′), vil. Belg.
Quatre fages′ de Brẻ au′ (kätr′-
fäzh′ dẻ brä′ŏ′), Fr. naturalist.
Quatre mère′ de Quin cy′ (kätr′
mâr′ dẻ kăṅ′sẻ′), Fr. art critic.
quät tri′no (-trẻ′-).
quät trō cen′tō (-chĕn′-), *-cen′tist.*
qua′ver, -ing, -ing ly, -y, -er,
-vered, qua′ver rest.
quay (kē), -age, quay′-berth.
quẽan, a low woman.
quẽa′sy, -si ly, -si ness.
Quẽ bĕc′, c. and prov. Can.
que brä′da (kē- or kä brä′tha).
Que′da (kä′dä), state Malay Pen.

queen, -ing, -dom, -ite, -less, -let, -like, -ly, -li ness, -ship, -cråft, -fish, -hood.
queen'-ap'ple, -cell, -conch (-kŏnk), -gold, -lil y, -post, -stitch, -truss, Queen'-day, queen-of-the-mead ows, a plant, -of-the-prai rie, a plant, queen bee, q. dow'a ger, q. moth'er.
queen's'-arm, -de light', -flow'-er, -lil'y, -met'al, -pi'geon, -root, -ware, -yel'low.
queer, -ly, -ness.
Que'i ros, de (dā kā'ē rōs), Port. navigator.
que'lis (kā'lēs).
quĕll, -er, -ing, quĕlled.
quelque'chose (kĕlk'shōz).
quench, -a ble, -er, -ing, -less, -less ly, -less ness, quenched, quench'ing-tub.
que nelle' (kē nĕl').
Que quay' (kā kwī'), r. Uruguay.
quer'cit ron, -bark, -oak.
Que ré'ta ro (kā rā'tä rō), state Mex.
quĕr i mo'ni ous, -ly, -ness.
Que ri'ni (kwä rē'nē), It. schol.
querl, -ing, querled.
quern, -stone.
quĕr'u lous, -ly, -ness.
quē'ry, -ing, que'ried, -rist.
Que sa'da (kā sä'thä), Conquerer of New Granada; Cuban gen.
Ques nay' (kā'nā'), Fr. economist.
quest, -er, -ful, -ing.
ques'tion (-chŭn), -er, -ing, -ing ly, -a ble, -a ble ness, -a bly, -a ry, -ist, -less, -tioned.
ques'tor, -ship.
ques'tus.
quet (kĕt).
Que telet' (kā'tlā'), Belg. statistician.
queue (kū), queued (kūd), queu'-ing.
quib'ble, -bled, -bler, -blet, -bling, -bling ly.
Qui beron' (kē'brŏn'), pen. Fr.
Quiche rat' (kēsh'rä'), Fr. archæol; Fr. lex.
quick, -en (-n), -ened, -en er, -en ing, -er, -ling, -ly, -ness, quick'-

hatch, -lime, -sand, -set, -step, -wood.
quick'-beam, -eyed, -gråss, -hedge, -lunch, -march, -match, -wit'ted, -wit'ted ness, -work, part of a ship, quick'-in-hand.
quick'sil ver, -ing, -vered, quick'-sil ver-fur nace.
quid, -ded, -ding.
quī'dam.
quĭd'da ny.
quĭd'di ty, -di ta tive.
quĭd'dle, -dled, -dler, -dling.
quid'nunc.
quid pro quo.
quien sa'be (kyĕn sä'bĕ).
qui es'cent, -ly, -cence, -cen cy, -esce', -esced', -es'cing.
quī'et, -ed, -er, -ing, -ism, -ist, -is'tic, -ive, -ize, -ized, -ī'zing, -et ly, -ness, -e tude, -ē'tus, quī'et ing-chaṁ'ber.
quī'-hī'.
Quĭ i'na.
quī'ler.
quill, -ing, -er, -y, quilled, quill'-back, a fish, -tail, a duck, -wort.
quill'-bit, -cov'erts, -drīv'er, -fĕath'er, -turn, -work, quill nib, q. pen.
quil lai' (kē li'), -bark.
quĭl'let.
quil lon' (kĕl yŏṅ').
quilt, -ed, -er, -ing, quilt'ing-bee, -cot'ton, -frame.
quin.
qui'na ry, -nā'ri an, -nā'ri us.
Qui nault' (kē'nō'), Fr. poet.
quince, -es'sence, -juice, -seed, -tree, q. wine.
quin cen'te na ry, quin'cunx, -cun'cial (-shăl), -cial ly, quin dec'a gon, -de cem'vir, -vi rate.
Quĭn'cy, c. Ill.; c. Mass.; tp. Ia.; tp. Mich.; tp. Pa.
quĭn'īne (*or* quī'nīne *or* quĭ nīne' *or* quĭn'in), quĭ nĭn'ic, -nin ism.
quin'o līne.
quin'qua gĕ nä'ri an, -qua ges'i ma (-jes'-), -quaṇ'gu lar.
quin'que den'tate, -que fō'li ate, -que lō'bate, -que nerved.
quin quen'ni al, -ly, -ni um.

---

quin'que reme, -que sect, -sec' tion, -que syl'la ble, -syl lăb'ic, -que val'vu lar.
quin'qui no (kĭn'kĭ nō).
quin'sy (-zĭ), -wort, -ber'ry.
quint.
quin'ta (kēn'ta).
quin ta dē'na.
quin'tăin.
quin'tal.
Quin tard', Amer. Bishop.
quin tes'sence, -sen'tial.
quin tet' *or* -tette', -tet'to.
Quin tĭl'i an, Rom. rhet.
quin trōōn'.
quin'tu ple, -pled, -pling, -plet, -tu'pli cate, -cā'ted, -cā'ting, -cā'tion, quin'tu ple-nerved.
quĭnze (kwĭnz) *or quinze* (kănz).
quip, -ping, -pish, quipped.
qui'pu (kē'pōō *or* kwĭp'ōō), pl. *-pus* (-pōōz).
qui'qui hatch (kwē'kwē-).
quire, quired, quīr'ing.
Quĭ rĭ'nal, a palace in Rome.
Quĭ rĭ'nus, *Myth.*, *Quĭr i nā'lĭ a.*
quirk, -float, quirk'ing-plane.
Quir pon' (keer pŏn'), isl. off Newfoundland.
quirt, -ed, -ing.
Qui sä'da (kē-), Don Quixote.
qui'sutsch (kē'sŭch).
quit, -ted, -ter, -ting, ta ble,

-tance, quit'claim, -claim ance, quit'-rent.
qui tam.
quitch, -grăss.
quite.
Quit'ta (kē'ta), t. Upper Guinea.
quiv'er, -ing, -ing ly, -ish, -ered, quiv'er-tree.
qui vive (kē vēv).
Quĭx'ŏte, Cervantes' hero, quix'-ote, to act like Don Quixote, quix ot'ic, -ic al ly, -ot ism, -ot-ly.
quiz, -zing, -zi ness, -zer, -zer y, -zic al, -al ly, -zĭ cal'i ty, -zi fy, -fy ing, -fĭed, quiz'-clăss, -măs'-ter, quiz'zing-glăss.
quŏd'li bet, -bet al, -bet'ic, -ic al -al ly, -be tā'ri an.
quŏd vĭ'de.
quoin (or koin), -post.
quoit, -play'er.
quō jū're, quō mĭ'nus.
quŏn'dam.
quō'rum.
quō'ta.
quote, -less, -wor thy, quŏt'ed, -er, -ing, -a ble, -a ble ness, -a bly, -a bil'i ty, quo tā'tion, -tion ist, -al, quo tā'tion-mark.
quŏ tĭd'i an.
quŏ'tient (-shĕnt).
quo war ran'tō.

R

Rä, Myth.
raad (räd), the electric catfish. *Raad* (rạwt *or* räd), a legislative assem-bly. *raad'zaal* (rạwt'sạwl'), a parliament building.
Rā'a mah, *Bib.*
Rā'a mĭ'ah, *Bib.*
Ra ăm'ses (-sēz), *Bib.*
ra băt' (*or* -bä'), a collar; a neck-band.
răb'at, a polishing material.
răb'bet, -ed, -ing.
răb'bet-joint, -plane, -saw, rab'-bet ing-ma chine'.

răb'bĭ (*or* -bī), -bin ate, -bin ism, -ist, -ite, -bin'ic, -ic al, -al ly.
rab'bit, -er, -ry, rab'bit ber'ry, -ear an oyster, -mouth, a fish, -root, a plant.
rab'bit-brush, -eared, -fish, -hutch, -moth, -mouthed, -rat, -spout, -squir'rel, -war'ren.
rab'ble, -ment, -bled, -bler, -bling, rab'ble-fish.
rab bō'nĭ (or -nī).
Rab e lais' (räb'ĕ lā' *or* rä blā'), Fr. philos.
răb'ĭ.

răb′id, -ly, -ness, *rä′bĭ es* (-ēz),
-bi ate, -bi et′ic, -bif′ic.

Räb nä′bäd′, isl. India.

răb′ot (*or* rä′-).

Rä′bus son′ (-bü′sôṅ′), Fr. novelist.

Rā′ca, *Bib.*

rä′ca (*or* rä′-).

răc′ca hout (-hōot *or* rå kå ōō′).

răc′con tän′dō.

răc coon′, -ber′ry, -dog, -oys′ter,
-perch.

răce, raced, rā′cing, -cer, race′way.

race′-card, -cloth, -course, -cup,
-gin′ger, -ground, -horse, -knife,
-meet′ing, -plate, -sad′dle, -track,
rā′cing-bell, -bit, -cal′en dar.

ra cê′ (ra sä′).

ra cĕme′, -cemed′, -cĕm′ic, -cĕm′-
i form, rac e mif′er ous (răs′-),
-e mose, -mose ly, -e mous,
-e mule.

Rā′chal (-kăl), *Bib.*

Rā′chĕl, Chr. name,—(rä′shĕl′),
Fr. actress,—(rä′c̓hel), Ger.
poet.

rä′chis (-kĭs), pl. *-chis es* or *-chi-
des* (-kĭ dēz), rā′chĭ al (-kĭ-),
-chit′ic (-kĭt′-).

rā′cial (-shăl), -ly.

rack, -ing, -er, racked, rack′a-
bones, a person or animal,
-a pelt, a person, rack′work.

rack′-bar, -block, -cal′i pers,
-car, -com′pass, -hook, -pin,
-rail, -rail′way, -rent, -rent′er,
-saw, -stick, -tail.

rack′et, -ed, -er, -ing, -y, rack′et-
tail, a bird.

rack′et-court, -ground, -tailed.

rack′ing-cán, -cock, -crook, -fau-
cet, -pump, -ta ble.

ra con teur′ (rä′kôṅ têr′).

rā′cy, -ci ly, -ci ness.

Racz-Ke′ve (räts-kä′vä′), isl. and
t. Hung.

Rä′dautz (-douts), t. Austria.

rad′dle, -dled, -dling, rad′dle-hedge.

ra deau′ (-dō′), pl. *-deaux′* (-dōz′).

rā′di al, -al ly, -al′i ty, -al ize,
-ized, -i zing, -ĭ zā′tion.

rā′di ance, -an cy, -ant, -ant ly.

rā′di ate, -ā′ted, -ā′ting, -ting ly,

-ate ly, -ate ness, -ā′tive, -ā′tor,
-to′ry, -ā′tion.

răd′i cal, -ism, -ness, -ly, -căl′-
i ty, -cal ize, -ized, -ĭ′zing.

răd′i cate, -cā′ted, -cā′ting, -cā′-
tion, -cant, -i cel, a minute rootlet,
-i cle, a rootlet, -i cose, ra dic′-
o lous.

ra′dĭ o grăph, -di og′ra phy.

rä dĭ ŏm′e ter, -o met′ric, -o mi-
crom′e ter, -o phone -o phon′ic,
-ics.

răd′ish, -fly.

rä′dĭ um.

rä′di us, *pl.* -us es *or* -ī, rä′di us-
bar, -rod, -saw.

rä′dix, *pl.* -dix es *or* -di ces (-sēz).

ra doub′ (-dōōb′).

Rä′dŏ witz (-vĭts), Prus. statesman.

råff, -ish, raff′-mer′chant.

raffe (răf).

răf′fle, -fled, -fling, răf′fle-net,
-fling-net.

råft, -ed, -er, -ing, råfts′man.

råft′-brĕast′ed, -dog, -duck, -like,
-mer′chant, -port, -rope, råft′ing-
dog.

råf′ter, -ing, -tered, raf′ter-bird.

răg, -ging, ragged, rag′ged, -ged-
ly, -ged ness, rag′man, -pick er,
-shag, -stone, -weed, -worm,
-wort.

rag′-bolt, -bush, -cut′ting, -dust,
-dust′er, -en′gine, -fair, -fish,
-knife, -loop′er, -shop, -sort′er,
-tag, -time, -turn′sŏl, -wheel,
-wool, -work, rag ba′by, r. car′-
pet, r. mon′ey, rag′weed fe ver.

rag′ged-la′dy, a plant, -rob′in, a
plant, -sail′or, a plant, -school,
-stăff, rag′ging-frame, -ham′mer.

răg′a muf fin, -a bash.

rage, -ful, raged, rā′giṅg, -ging ly.

rag′gle, -gled, -gling.

rag′lan.

ra gout′ (-gōō′).

Ra gŭ′el (*or* răg′-), *Bib.*

Rai a te a (rī ä tā′ä), isl. Pac.

råid, -ed, -er, -ing.

Rai garh′ (rī′gär′), state India.

råil, -er, -ing, -ing ly.

rail′-bend′er, -bird, -bit′tern,
-board, -bor′er, -brace, -chair,

-clamp, -coup'ling, -drill'ing,
-guard, -jack, -joint, -key, -post,
-punch, -saw, -snipe, -split'ter,
-straight'en ing, rail'ing-post.
rail'ler y (*or* răl'-), *rail'leur'* (rå-
lyêr').
rail'road, -ed, -er, -ing, rail'road-
car, -cross'ing, -frog, -i'ron,
-switch, -train, -worm, r. com'-
pa ny.
rail'way, -car, -car'riage, -chair,
-cross'ing, -frog, -slide, -stitch,
-switch, -tie, -train, r. com'pa ny,
r. cross'ing.
răi'ment.
răin, -ing, -less, -y, -i ness, rain'-
ball, -band, -bird, -fall, -pour.
rain'bird, -box, -cham'ber, -chan-
nel, -chart, -cloud, -crow, -doc'-
tor, -door, -drop, -fowl, -gäge,
-goose, -māk'er, -map, -pad'dock,
-pie, -print, -proof, -quail, -storm,
-tight, -tree, -wash, -wa'ter,
-wind, rain'fall-chart.
rain'bow, -bōwed, rain'bow-ag'ate,
-fish, -her'ring, -hued, -tint'ed,
-trout, -worm, -wrasse, r. quartz,
r. style.
Rai pur' (rī'poor'), dist. India.
raise (raz), raised, rais'er, -ing.
rai'si née' (rå'ze nä').
rais'ing-bee, -board, -gig, -ham'-
mer, -knife, -piece, -plate.
rai'sin (rā'zn), -seed, -tree, r. wine.
Raismes (räm), t. Fr.
rai son' d'être (rä zŏn' dä'tr).
rai son né' (rä'zō'nä').
räj.
rä'jä *or* -jäh, -ship.
Räj ä pur' (-poor'), t. India.
Räj'put' *or* -poot' (räj'poot').
rake, raked, rāk'ing, -er, -ish, ish-
ly, -ish ness, rake'hell.
rake'-dredge, -head, -vein, rāk'-
ing-piece.
răk'i or -*ee* (-ē).
Rä'koc zy (-kō tsē), Hung. patriot.
Ra̧'leigh (-lǐ'), Eng. statesman.
răl ly, -ing, -lĭed, -li er, ral'ly ing-
point.
Ralph (rălf), Chr. name, ralph, a
printer's spirit of evil.

răm, -mer, -ming, -mish, -mish-
ness, -my, rammed, ram'skin.
răm'-bow, -cat, -goat, -head,
-head'ed, -line, -rīd'ing, -stag,
-stam, ram's-head, -horn.
Rä'ma *or* -mah, *Bib.*, Rä'ma, *Myth.*
Rä'math ā'im (*or* răm'a thā'im),
Bib.
Răm a zăn'.
ram'ble, -bled, -bler, -bling,
-bling ly.
Ram bouil let' (rŏṅ'boo'yä'), Fr.
leader of society.
Rä'mé' (-mä'), Fr. archæol., *rå mĕ'*
(rå ma') a term in heraldry.
Rä mée' (-mā'), Fr. architect; ramée (rå mä'), a plant.
ram'e kin.
Răm'e ses (-sēz *or* ra mē'-), *Bib.*
rä'mĭ.
Ra mĭ'ah, *Bib.*
răm'iĕ, -fi'ber, -plant.
ra mier' (rå myä').
răm'i fy, -ing, -fied, -fī că'tion.
Răm'i liĕ.
Ra mil lies' (rå mē yē'), t. Belg.
Rä mi'rez (-mē'rĕs), Mex. philos.
ram'mel.
rä'mose (-mōs *or* -mōs'), -ly, ra'-
mous.
rămp, -ing, ramped.
ram'page, ram pa'geous, -geous-
ness, ram'pant, -pant ly, -pan cy.
ram'part, -ed, -ing, ram'part-gren-
ade', -slope.
ramps'man.
Răm'pur (-poor), t. India.
ram'rod, -rod dy, ram'rod-bay'-
o net.
ram'shac kle, -kled, -kly.
Rance (rŏṅs), r. Fr.
rănce.
rånch, -er, -ing, ranched, *răn-
che ri'a* (-chä rē'ä), a dwelling,
-*che'ro* (-chä'rō), a herdsman,
răn'cho, a rude hut; a grazing
farm, pl. -*chos* (-chōz), ranch'-
man, ranch'-house.
răn'cid, -ly, -ness, -cid'i ty.
răn̈'cor, -ous, -ous ly.
rand, rand'ing-ma chine', -tool.
ran'dan, -gig.
ran'dom (-dŭm), -ly.

---

nŏt, nôr, ūse, ŭp, ûrn, etüde, food, foot, anger, boṅmot, thus, Bach.

31

ra'nga ti ra (rä'ngå tĕ'rå or răṇ'-
gà tī'rà).
rănge, rănged, răn'ger, -ging, -gy.
range'-find'er, -heads, -horse,
-lights, -plate, -stove, -ta'ble,
răn'ging-rod.
rä'nĭ or răn'ee.
raṇk, -er, -ing, -ly, -ness, ranked.
rank'-ax'is, -curve, -plane, -point,
-ra'di ant, -scent'ed, -sur'face.
raṇ'kle, -kled, -kling.
ran'sack, -ing, -sacked.
ran'som (-sŭm), -a ble, -er, -ing,
-less, -somed, ran'som-bill, -free.
rănt, -ed, -er, -ing, -ing ly, -ism.
ranz des vaches' (rŏṅs' dä' våsh').
răp, -ping, -per, rapped, rap'-full.
ra pä'cious, -cious ly, -cious ness,
-pac'i ty (-pas'-).
răp a du'ra (-dōō'-).
rape, raped, răp'ing, rape-but'ter-
fly, -cake, -oil, -seed, -wine.
Răph'a el, Italian painter, -el-
esque', -el ism, -el īte; Rä'phä-
el (or răf'-), Bib.
Răph'ä ĭm (or ra fä'-), Bib.
Rä'phon, Bib.
răp'id, -ly, -ness, ra pid'i ty, răp'-
i dō, ra pi da men'te (rå pē dä-
mĕn'tä).
Rap i dan', r. Va.
Răp ides' (-ēd'), par. La.
rä'pi er, -ered, ra'pi er-fish.
ra' pin' (rå'påṅ).
răp'ĭne.
răp pee'.
rap pel'.
răp'pen.
rap port'.
răp proche'ment (-prōsh'mŏṅ).
rap scăl'lion, -lion ry.
rapt, exalted; transported.
răp'ture, -tured, -tūr ous, -ous ly.
rä'rä, a bird.
rä'ra ä'vis, a wonder.
rare, -ly, -ness, răr'i ty, răr'e fy,
-fy'ing, -fied, -fi'a ble, -fac'tion,
râre'bit, -ripe, răr'ee-show.
răs (or räs), a cape; a chief minister.
ras (rä), a fabric of wool or silk.
răs'cal, -dom, -ism, -ly, -cal'lion,
-cal'i ty, ras'cal-like.
rase (räz). See raze.

rås gä'dō.
răsh, -ly, -ness.
răsh'er.
rä'sing (-zing), -i'ron, -knife.
ra sŏ'rĭ al.
râsp, -er, -ing, -ing ly, -y, -i ness,
-a to ry.
rasp'-house, -palm, -pod, -punch,
rasp'ing-ma chine', -mill.
rasp'ber ry (răz'-), -bor'er, -bush,
-slug, r. vin'e gar.
rasse (răs).
Räs'tätt, t. Ger.
ras'trum, pl. -tra.
rat, -ted, -ter, -ter y, -tish, -ting,
rat'fish, -tail, a fish; a horse; a
plant; rats'bane.
rat'-catch'er, -goose, -hare, -hole,
-kaṇ ga roo', -mole, -pit, -poi-
son, -snake, -tail, a tail, -tailed,
-tĕr'ri er, -trap, rat's-tail.
rät'a fi'a (-fē'-).
ra tan'. See rattan.
rä'tå plan' (-plŏṅ').
răt'-a-tat'.
rătch, -ment, ratched.
rătch'et, -y, ratch'et-brace, -burn'-
er, -coup'ling, -drill, -jack, -lĕv'-
er, -ped'al, -post, -punch, -ri'-
fling, -wheel, -wrench.
rate, rät'ed, -ing, -er, rate'pay er,
rate'-book, -tithe, răt'ing-in'-
stru ment.
răth, a mound.
rath (rät), a temple; a Burmese carriage.
răth'er.
raths'kel'ler (räts-).
Ra thū'mus (or răth'-), Bib.
răt'i fy, -ing, -fīed, -fī er, -fī că'-
tion.
rä'ti o (-shĭ ō or răsh'yō).
ra ti oc'i nate (răsh'ĭ ŏs'ĭ nate),
-nä ted, -nä ting, -nä tive, -nant,
-nà to'ry, -nä'tion.
rä'tion (or răsh'ŭn), -mon ey.
ra'tion al (răsh'un al), -ism, -ist,
-is'tic, -tic al, -al ly, -tion a ble,
-a bil'i-ty, -al ize, -ized, -ī'zing,
-ĭ zä'tion, -al ly, -al ness.
Răt'is bon, t. Ger.
răt'lĭnes, răt'lĭne-stuff.
Răt'nä gi'ri (-gē'rē), dist. India.

ra tōōn'.
răt tan', r. cane.
răt'ta nas.
Rät taz'zi (-tät'sē), Fr. auth.
răt teen'.
rat'ten, -tened.
rat'tle, -tled, -tler, -tling, rat'tle-
bags, a plant, -box, a plant,
-brain, a person, -bush, a plant,
-cap, a person, -head, a person,
-pate, a person, -skull, -trap, a
vehicle, -weed, -wing, a duck,
-wort.
rat'tle snake, -fern, -gråss, -herb,
-mås ter, -plan'taÏn, -root,
-weed, r. flag.
rat'wa.
Rät'ze burg (-sĕ bŏŏrg), princ. Ger.
Rau (row), Ger. archæol.
rau'coŭs, -ly, rau'cid, -ci ty.
Raud'nitz (roud'nÏts), t. Aust.
Rau'mer (rou'mer), Ger. hist.
Rau san' (rŏ zŏń'), a wine.
Rau wŏl'fÏ a.
răv'age, -aged, -å ger, -å ging.
rave, raved, råv'er, -ing, -ing ly,
rave'-hook.
råv'el (-l), -eled or -elled, -el er
or -ler, -el ing or -ling, -el ly,
-el ment, råv'el ing-en'gine.
rave'lin (răv'-).
rä'ven (-vn), n., -ry, ra'ven-
stone, ra'ven-cock a too', ra ven's-
duck.
răv'en (-ṇ), v., -ened, -en ing,
-ing ly, -en er, -en ous, -ous ly,
-ous ness.
Rav'en så'ra.
Rä'vens burg' (-bŏŏrg'), t. Ger.
Rä'vens wŏŏd, t. N. Y.
ra vine' (-vēn'), -deer.
råv'ish, -er, -ing, -ing ly, -ment,
-ished.
raw, -ish, -ly, -ness, raw'head,
-hide, raw'-boned, -port, -pot.
Rä'witsch (-vÏch), t. Prus.
rax.
ray, -ey, -ing, -less, rayed, ray'-
on nant.
ray'-flo'ret, -flow'er, -fun'gus,
-gråss, -oil, -pod, -point, -print.
rä'ya (or rä'-) or Ra'ya, a Turk
who is not a Mohammedan.

raze or rase (rāz), razed, råz'ing,
rä'sure (-zhŭr).
ra zee', v., -zeed', -zee'ing, ra-
zee', n.
rä'zor, -back, a fish; a hog; -bill,
a bird; -blade, an oyster.
ra'zor-backed, -blade, a blade,
-clam, -fish, -gråss, -grÏnd'er,
-hone, -pa'per, -paste, -shell,
-stone, -strop.
raz'zi a (răt'sÏ a or rä'zē a).
reach, -a ble, -er, -ing, -less,
reached, reach'ing-post, reach-
me-down, a.
rē act', -ed, -ing, -ive, -ive ly,
-ive ness, -ac'tion, -tion a ry,
-tion ist, re ac'tion-pe'ri od, -rim,
-time, -wheel.
read, -a ble, -a ble ness, -a bly,
-a bil'i ty, -er, -er ship, -ing,
read. .
read'ing-book, -boy, -desk, -glåss,
-lamp, -mat'ter, -pew, -room,
-stand, -ta'ble.
read'y, -i ly, -i ness, read'y-made,
-man, -pole, -reck'on er, -wit'ted,
r. mon'ey.
rē å'gent, -gen cy.
Rē å'ia (-å'ya or rē'å Ï'a), Bib.
re al' (ra al'), a coin, pl. re a'les
(rä ä'les).
rē'al, -ism, -ist, -is'tic, -tic al ly,
-al'i ty, -al ness, -al ty, rē'al-
school.
rē'al ize, -ized, -i'zing, -i'za ble,
-i za bil'i ty, -zer, -Ï zā'tion.
rēalm.
rēam, -er, -ing, -y, -i ness,
ream'-kit, ream'er-bit, ream'-
ing-i'ron.
rēap, -er, -ing, reaped, reap'-
hook, reap'ing-hook, -ma chine'.
rēar, a., -horse, -most, -ward,
-ward ly, rear'-ad'mi ral, -guard.
rēar, v., -ing, -er, reared, rear'-
ing-bit, -box.
rēa'son (-zn), -a ble, -a ble ness,
-a bly, -er, -ing, -less, -soned,
rea'son-piece.
re a'ta (rä ä'ta).
Ré au mur' (rä'ŏ'mür'), Fr. philos.
rē båte', n., rē bate', v., -ment,
-båt'ed, -ing.

---

nŏt, nôr, ūse, ŭp, ûrn, etüde, fōōd, fŏŏt, aṇger, boṅmot, thus, Bach.

rĕb'el, *n.,* rē bel', *v.,* -belled', -bel'ling, -bel'lion, -lious, -lious-ly, -lious ness.
rĕ boise' (-bwäz'), -ment, -bois'ing, -boised'.
rĕ bound', -ed, -er, -ing.
re bō'zo (rā bō'thō).
re buff', *n.* and *v.,* -ing, -buffed'.
rĕ build', -er, -ing, -built'.
rĕ būke', -ful, -ful ly, -būked', -būk'er, -ing, -ing ly.
rĕ'bus.
re bŭt', -tal, -ta ble, -ted, -ter, -ting.
re cal'ci trate, -trā'ted, -trā'ting, -trant, -trā'tion.
rĕ cà lesce' (-lĕs'), -les'cence.
re call', -a ble, -ment, -ing, -called'.
Rĕ ca mi er' (rā'kä'mē ā'), Fr. leader of society.
re cănt', -ed, -er, -ing, -can'ta-tion.
re ca pit'u late, -lā'ted, -lā'ting, -là tive, -lā'tor, -là to'ry, -lā'-tion, -tion ist.
re cap'ture, -tured, -tūr ing, -tor, -tion.
re cede', -cēd'ed, -ing, -ces'sion, -sion al, -ces'sive, -sive ly.
rĕ ceipt' (-sēt'), -a ble, -ed, -er -ing, -ment, -or, re ceipt'-book.
re cĕive', -cĕiv'a ble, -a ble ness, -a bil'i ty, -er, -ing, -ed ness, -ceived', -er ship, -er-gen'er al.
re cĕiv'ing-house, -ap pa rā'tus, -in'stru ment, -mag'net, -of'fice, -ship, -tomb, -vault.
re cen'sion, -sion ist.
rĕ'cent, -ly, -ness, re'cen cy.
re cĕp'ta cle, -tăc'u lar, -cep'ti-ble, -ti bil'i ty, -cep'tion, -tive, -tive ness, -tiv'i ty, re cep'tion-room.
re cĕss', -ing, -cessed'.
Rĕ'chăb (-kăb), *Bib.*
Rĕ'chab ite (-kăb-) *or* Rech'a-bīte (rĕk'-), *Bib.,* -bī'tism.
rē chauf fé' (rā'shō'fā').
re cher chē' (rĕ shär shā').
Re ci'fe (rā sē'fā), state Brazil.
rec'i pe (rĕs'-), *pl.* -pes (-pēz).
re cip'i ent, -i ence, -i en cy.

re cip'ro cal, -ly, -ness, -cant, -cal'i ty.
re cip'ro cate, -cā'ted, -cà tive, -cà to'ry, -cant, -cant ive, -cā'-tion, rec i proc'i ty (-prŏs'-).
rĕ ci'sion (-sĭzh'un).
rĕ cīte', -cīt'ed, -er, -ing, -al, rec i tā'tion (rĕs'-), -tion ist, -ta tive' (-tēv'), *n.,* -ta tĭve', *a.,* -tĭve'ly. *re ci tän'do* (rā'chē-), *rec'i tä ti'vo* (-tē'vō), re cit'ing-note, rec'i tā'tion-room.
reck, -ing, recked.
reck'less, -ly, -ness, reck'ling.
reck'on (-n), -er, -ing, reck'on-ing-book, -pen ny.
rĕ clāim', -a ble, -a bly, -er, -ing, -less, -clāimed', rec la mā'-tion, rec la ma'tion-plow.
ré'clame' (rā'kläm').
re clīne', -clined', -clīn'er, -ing, -ant, rec'li nate, -nā'tion, re-clin'ing-board, -chair.
rec'li vate.
Rĕ clus' (-klü'), Fr. geog.
rĕ clūse', -ly, -ness, -clu'sive, -so ry, -sion (-zhun).
rec'og nize, -nized, -nī'zing, -nĭ'-tion (-nĭsh'un), -nī'za ble, -za-bly, -za bil'i ty, re cog'ni tive, -ni to ry, -ni zant (*or* -kŏn'ĭ-), -cog'nĭ zee' (*or* -kŏn'ĭ-), -cog'-ni zor' (*or* -kŏn'ĭ-), -cog'ni-zance (*or* -kŏn'ĭ-).
re coil, -er, -ing, -ment, -coiled'.
re coil'-check, -es cape'ment, -pal'-let, -spring, -wave.
rĕ coin', -age, -er, -ing, -coined'.
rec'ol lect', to remember, -ed, -ed ness, -ive, -lec'tion.
rĕ'col lect', to collect again, -ed, -ing.
Rec'ŏl lĕt *or* -lect, a friar.
rec om mend', -a ble, -a ble ness, -a bly, -à tive, -a to'ry, -er, -ing, -men dā'tion.
rec'om pense, -pensed, -pen sing, -ser, -sive.
re con'cen trä'do (rā-).
rec'on cīle, -ment, -ciled, -cī'la-ble, -ble ness, -bly, -cī'ling, -ler, -cĭl'i a to ry, -ĭ ā'tion.
rĕc'on dīte (*or* rē kŏn'dĭt), -ness.

re cŏn'nais sance *or* -nois sance
(-kŏn'nĭs säns).

rĕc'on noi'ter, -ing, -tered.

re con sĭd'er, -ing, -ered, -er ā'-tion.

re con struct', -ed, -ing, -ive, -struc'tion, -tion ist.

rĕc'ord, *n.*, rē cord', *v.*, -a ble, -ed, -er, -er ship, -ing, rec'ord-of'fice.

re count', -ed, -ing.

rē coup' (-kōop'), -er, -ment, -couped'.

rē côurse'.

re cov'er (-kŭv'-), -ing, -er, -a ble, -a ble ness, -a bil'i ty, -y, -ered.

rec're ant, -ly, -ance, -an cy.

rĕc're ate, to divert or amuse, -ā'tcd, -ā'ting, -ā'tive, -tive ly, -tive ness, -ā'tion, rec re ā'tion-ground.

rē crē ate', to create anew, -a'tcd, -a'ting, -ā'tion.

rec're ment, -men'tal, -men ti'-tial (-tĭsh'al), -ti'tious.

re crim'i nate, -nā'ted, -nā'ting, -nȧ tive, -nā'tor, -to'ry, -nā'tion.

rē cru desce' (-dĕs'), -desced' (-dĕst'), -des'cing, -cence, -cen cy, -cent.

re cruit', -ed, -er, -ing, -ment, re cruit'ing-ground, -par'ty, -ser'-geant.

rec'tan gle, -gled, -tan'gu lar, -lar ly, -lar ness, -lăr'i ty.

rec'ti fy, -ing, -fi'a ble, -fied, -fi-er, -fĭ cā'tion.

rec tĭ lĭn'e al, -ly, -lin'e ar, -ar ly, -ar ness, -ăr'i ty.

rec'ti tude.

rec'to.

rĕc'tor, -age, -al, -ate, -ess, -ship, -to ry, -to'ri al.

rec'u bant.

rē cŭm'bent, -ly, -bence, -ben cy.

re cū'per ate, -ā'ted, -ā'ting, -ȧ tive, -ȧ ble, -a bil'i ty, -a'tor, -to'ry, -ā'tion.

re cur', -rence, -ren cy, -rent, -rent ly, -ring, -curred'.

re curve', -curved', -curv'ing, -cur vā'tion.

rĕc'u sant (rĕk'u zant *or* rē kū'-), -sance, -san cy, -sā'tion.

re'cuse.

re cus'sion (-kŭsh'un).

red, -ded, -ding, -der, -dest, -dish -dish ness, -ly, -ness.

red'back, a bird, -beard, a sponge, -bel'ly, a terrapin, -ber'ry, -bird, -breast, a bird, -buck, an antelope, -bud, a tree, -bug, -cap, a bird, -coat, a person, -edge, a mollusk, -eye, a fish, -fin, a fish, -fish, -head, a duck, -horn, an insect, -knees, a plant, -legs, a bird, -man, a fish, -mouth, a fish, -pŏll, a bird, -rib'bon, a fish, -root, -sear, *v.*, -seed, crustaceans, -shank, a bird, -shanks, a plant, -share, *v.*, -sides, a fish, -skin, a person, -start, a bird, -streak, an apple, -tail, a bird, -top, a grass, -warc, a seaweed, -weed, -wing, a bird, -wood, a tree.

red'-backed, -car'pet, a moth, -chest'nut, a moth, -crest'ed, -cross, *a.*, -dog, a flour, -eyed, -faced, -fig'ured, -foot'ed, -green, *a.*, -gum, a tree; a disease, -hand, -hand'ed, -head'ed, -horse, a fish, -hot, -lac, a tree, -legged, -let'ter, *a.*, -mo roc'co, a plant, -mouth, *a.*, -necked, -nosed, -pai'dle, -pŏlled, -rob'in, a fungus, -shãfl'ed, -short, -short'ness, -stãff, -tail, *a.*, -tape, *a.*, -tăp'-er y, -tăp'ism, -tăp'ist, -throat'-ed, -tipped, -tubs, a gurnard, -wat, *a.*, -wa ter, a disease, -whelk, -whis'kered, -winged, -withe.

red bãss, r. bat, r. ce'dar, r. cod, r. cusk, r. dace, r. deer, r. drum, r. fend'er, r. fight'er, r. met'al, r. oak, r. spi'der, r. squir'rel, r. thrush, Red Book, R. Crag.

re dact', -ed, -ing, -dac'tor, -to'-ri al, *ré dac teur'* (rã'dãk'ter') -dac'tion.

re dăn'.

red'den, -ing, -dened.

re deem', -a ble, -a ble ness, -a-bil'i ty, -er, -ing, -less, -deemed', -demp ti'ble, -demp'tion, -tion a ry,

-tion ist, -tive, -to ry, Re deem′er,
Re demp′tor ist.
red′in gŏte.
re din′te grate, -grā′ted -grā′-
ting, -grā′tion.
red′i vī′vus.
rĕd′o lence, -len cy, -lent, -lent ly.
re doū′ble, -bled, -bling.
re doubt′a ble (-dout′-).
re dound′, -ed, -ing.
re dout′ *or* -doubt′ a fortification.
rĕd′ŏw a.
re dress′, -al, -er, -i ble, -ive,
-less, -ment.
re dūce′, -ment, -duced′, -dū′cent,
-cer, -ci ble, -ci ble ness, -bly,
-ci bil′i ty, -cing, -dŭc′tion,
-tive, -tive ly, -ti bil′i ty.
re dū′cing-coup′ling, -fur′nace,
-press, -scale, -T, -valve, re-
duc′tion-com′pass es, -for′mu la,
-ma chine′, -works.
ré duc teur′ (rā′dook têr′).
re dun′dant, -dant ly, -dance,
-dan cy.
reed, -er, -y, -i ness, -less, -ling,
reed′bird, -buck.
reed′-bunt′ing, -grăss, -in′stru-
ment, -knife, -mace, -mote, -moth,
-mo′tion, -or′gan, -pälm, -phĕas′-
ant, -pipe, -pit, -plane, -spar′row,
-stop, -thrush, -tus′sock, -wain′-
scot, -war′bler, -work, -wren.
reef, -er, -ing, reefed, reef′ing-
beck′ets, -jack′et, -point.
reef′-band, -build′er, -crin′gle,
-ear′ing, -goose, -jig, -jig′ger,
-knot, -line, -oys′ter, -pend′ant,
-point, -sponge, -squid, -tac′kle.
reek, -ing, -y, reeked.
reel, -able, -er, -ing, reeled, reel′-
ing-ma chine′.
reel′-band, -bed, -check, -click,
-cot′ton, -hold′er, -keep′er, -line,
-ov′en, -plate, -seat, -stand.
Rĕ′el ā′iah (-ya), *Bib.*
Rĕ ĕl′i ŭs (*or* -ē′li-), *Bib.*
rĕ en force′ *or* -ĭn force′, -ment,
-for′cer, -for′ci ble, -forced′, re-
en force′-band, -rings.
Rĕ′e sā′i as (-yas *or* ree sā′-),
Bib.

reeve, reeved, reev′ing.
re fait′ (rê fā′).
re fec′tion, -tion er, -tive, -to ry.
re fer′, -ment, -ring, -ferred′, rĕf′-
er a ble *or* re fer′ri ble, -er ence,
-er ee, -er en′da ry, *-er en′dum,*
-er en′tial, -tial ly.
re fer ment′, to ferment again.
rĕ fine′, -ment, -fīned′, -fīn′ed ly,
-ed ness, -er, -er y, -ing, re fīn′-
ing-fur′nace, -heärth.
rĕ fit′, -ted, -ter, -ting, -ment.
re flect′, -ed, -i ble, -ing, -ing ly,
-ive, -ive ly, -ive ness, -or,
-flec′tion, -tion ist.
re flet′ (rê flā′).
rĕ flex′, *v.,* -flexed′, -flex′i ble,
-i bil′i ty, -ive, -ive ly, -ive ness,
-ly, rĕ′flex, *a.* and *n.*
ref′lu ent, -ence, -en cy.
rĕ′flux, -valve.
rĕ för′est, -ed, -ing, -es tā′tion.
re form′, -a ble, -er, -ing, -a tory, -ist, -formed′, re′for mā′-
tion, forming anew, ref′or mā′-
tion, correction of life or manners,
The Ref′or mā′tion.
re fract′, -a ble, -ed, -ing, -ive,
-ive ness, -or, -frac′tion, -to ry,
-to ri ly, -to ri ness, -ture,
-tured, -tom′e ter.
rĕf′ra ga ble, -ga bil′i ty.
re fräin′, -er, -ing, -ment,
-fräined′.
ref′ra nā′tion.
re fran′gi ble, -ness, -bil′i ty.
re fres′co (rā frās′kō), a drink.
re fresh′, -er, -ing, -ing ly, -ing-
ness, -ful, -ful ly, -ment,
-freshed′.
re frig′er ate (-frĭj′-), -ā′ted,
-ā′ting, -ā′tive, -ā′tor, -to′ry,
-ant, -ā′tion.
re frig′er a ting-cham′ber, -ma-
chine′, re frig′er a tor-car.
rĕf′uge, -u gee′, -gee′ism.
re fūl′gent, -ly, -gence, -gen cy.
re fund′, -ed, -er, -ing, -ment.
re fuse′ (-fūz′), *v.,* -fūs′al, -er,
-ing, -fūsed′, rĕf′use (-ūs), *n.*
re fute′, -fūt′a ble, -a bil′i ty, -al,
-a to′ry, -er, -ing, rĕf u tā′tion.
rĕ gāin′, -er, -ing, -gained′.

---

fāte, făt, fär, fạll, fâre, fȧst, sofȧ, mēte, mĕt, hêr, īce, ĭn, nōte,

rē′gal, -ism, -ly, -gal′i ty.
rē gale′, -ment, -galed′, -gāl′ing,
-er.
re gā′li a, -li an.
rē gā′lo.
re gard′, -a ble, -ant, -ed, -er,
-ing, -ful, -ful ly, -less, -less ly,
-less ness, re gard′-ring.
re găt′ta, *pl.* -tas.
rē′gē late (-jē), -lā′ted, -lā′ting,
-lā′tion.
Rē′gĕm-mē′lech (-gĕm-me′lĕk),
Bib.
re gen′er ate, -ā′ted, -ā′ting,
-à tive, -tive ly, -ā′tor, -to′ry,
-ā′tion, re gen′er a tor-fur nace.
re gen′e sis.
rē′gent, -ship, -gen cy, re′gent-
bird, -o′ri ole.
Reg′gio di Ca la′bri a (rād′jō
dē kä lä′brē a), prov. It.
Reg gio′lo (rād jō′lō), vil. It.
reg′i cide (rĕj′), -ci′dal.
re gi dor′ (rä′hē thŏr′).
rē gime′ (rä zhēm′).
reg′i men (rĕj′-), *pl.* -mens *or*
re gim′i na, re gim′i nal (-jĭm′-).
reg′i ment (rĕj′-), -men′tal, -tal-
ly, -tals, -tā′tion.
rē′gion (-jŭn), -al, -al ly, -a ry.
reg′is ter (rĕj′-), -ing, -ship,
-a ble, -tered, reg′is trà ble,
-trar, -trar ship, -trā′ry, -trate,
-trā′ted, -trā′ting, -trā′tion,
-trā′tion al, -try.
reg′is ter-grate, -of′fice, -plate,
-point, reg′is trar-gen′er al.
rē′gi um do′num, rē′gi us pro fes′-
sor.
rĕg′let, -plane.
reg′nan cy, -nant, *reg′num.*
Reg nault′ (rē nō′), Fr. painter.
re gress′, *v.,* -ing, -ive, -ive ly,
-gressed′, -gres′sion, rē′gress, *n.*
re gret′, -ted, -ting, -ful, -ful ly,
-ta ble, -ta bly.
rĕg′u lar, -lar ly, -lar ness, -lär′-
i ty.
rĕg′u late, -lā′ted, -lā′ting, -lā′-
tive, -lā′tor, -to ry, -lā′tion.
reg′u la ting-screw, -valve, reg′-
u la tor-box, -cock, -cov′er,
-lev′er, -shåft.

re gur′gi tate, -tā′ted, -tā′ting,
-tant, -tā′tion.
re ha bil′i tate, -tā′ted, -tā′ting,
-tā′tion.
re hêarse′, -hêars′al, -er, -ing,
-hêarsed′ (-hêrst′).
Rē′ho bō′am, *Bib.*
Rē hŏ′bŏth, bay Del.; *Bib.*
Reich′en au (rīch′en ou), isl. Ger.
Reich′en bach (rīch′en bäch), r.
Switz.; t. Prus.; t. Sax.
reichs′land (-länt).
Reichs′rath (rīchs′rät), *Reichs′stadt*
(-stät), *Reichs′tag* (-täch), reichs′-
tha′ler (-tä′ler).
reign (rān), -ing, reigned.
Reī′kī a vīk, t. Iceland.
rē ĭm burse′, -ment, -burs′a ble,
-er, -bursed′.
Reims (rēmz), c. Fr., Rhe′mish.
rein (rān), -ing, -less, reined, reins′-
man.
rein′-hold′er (rān′-), -hook, -or′-
chis (-kis), -slide, -snap.
rei′na (rä′-).
rein′deer (rān′-), -li′chen, -moss.
reīn′īte.
rē in state′, -ment, -stāt′ed, -ing.
re′is (rä′is *or* rās *or* rēz), a coin.
reis (rīs), an overseer.
rē it′er ate, -ā′ted, -ted ly, -à tive,
-ā′tion.
rēive.
rē ject′, -a ble, -ed, -er, -ing,
-ive, -ment, -jec′tion.
re joice′, -joiced′, -joi′cer, -cing,
-cing ly.
re join′, -ing, joined′, -join′der.
re jū′ve nate, -nā′ted, -nā′ting,
-nā′tor, -nā′ tion, -nesce′,
-nesced′ (-nĕst′), -nes′cing, -nes′-
cence, -cent, -ve nize, -nized,
-ni′zing.
re lais′ (rē lä′).
re lăpse′, -laps′er, -ing, -a ble,
-lăpsed′.
re late′, -lāt′ed, -ed ness, -er,
-ing, -lā′tion, -tion al, -al′i ty,
-tion ism, -ist, -ship.
rĕl′a tive, -ly, -ness, -tĭv′i ty.
re lax′, -a ble, -ant, -a tive, -ing,
-laxed′, -ā′tion.
re lay′, *n.,* re lay′, *v.,* -ing, -lāid′.

re lĕase', -ment, -leas'er, mechan.,
-or, law, -ing, re lease'-spring.
rĕl'e gate, -gā'ted, -gā'ting, -gā'-
tion.
re lent', -ed, -ing, -less, -less ly,
-less ness, -ment.
rĕl'e vance, -van cy, -vant, -vant ly.
re lī'a ble, -ness, -bly, -bil'i ty,
-lī'ance, -ant.
rĕl'ic, -knife, -moṇ'ger.
rĕl'ict.
rē lĭef', -en grav'ing, -map, -per-
spec'tive, -valve, -work.
rē lĭēve', -lieved', -liēv'a ble, -er,
-ing, re liēv'ing-tac'kle.
re li'gion (-lĭj'un), -ism, -ist,
-ize, -ized, -ī'zing, -less, -lĭ'-
gious (-lĭj'us), -gious ly, -gious-
ness, re li gi eux' (rĕ lē'zhē'ê');
fem. re li gi euse' (rĕ lē'zhē'êz'),
re li gio'so (rā'lē jō'sō).
re liṇ'quish, -er, -ing, -ment,
-quished'.
rĕl'i qua ry.
re liq'ui an (-lĭk'wĭ-).
rĕl'ish, -a ble, -ing, -ished', rel'-
ish ing-ma chine'.
re luc'tance, -tan cy, -tant, -tant-
ly.
rĕl'uc tiv'i ty.
rē ly', -ing, -lied'.
re māin', -ing, -mained', -main'-
der, re main'der-man.
Rĕm'a lī'ah, Bib.
re mānd', -ed, -ing, -ment.
re mark', -ing, -a ble, -a ble-
ness, -a bly, -er, -marked'.
rem blai' (rŏṅ'blā').
Re me'di os (rā mā'dē ōs), t. Cuba.
rĕm'e dy, -ing, -dĭed, rem'e di-
less (or rē mĕd'-), -less ly, -less-
ness, re mē'di al, -al ly, -di ā-
ble, -ā ble ness, -a bly.
re mem'ber, -a ble, -a bly, -er,
-ing, -bered, -brance, -bran cer.
rĕm'i grate (or rē mī'-), -grā'ted,
-grā'ting, -grā'tion.
re mīnd', -ed, -er, -ing, -ful.
rem'i nĭs'cence, -cent, -cen'tial,
-tial ly.
re mise' (-mīz'), -mised', -mīs'ing.
rē mĭss', -ful, -ly, -ness, -sive.
re mit', -ted, -ter, -ting, -ta ble,

-tal, -tance, -tan cer, -tent,
-ment, -mis'si ble, -si bil'i ty,
-so ry, -sion (-mĭsh'un).
rĕm'nant, -al.
ré mo lade' (rā'mō'lȧd') or -mou-
lade' (-mōō'-).
re mon'strate, -stra'ted, -strā'-
ting, -strȧ tive, -tive ly, -stra'-
tor, -strant, -strant ly, -strā'-
tion.
re'mon tä'dō.
re mon'toir (rē mŏn'twŏr or rĕ-
mŏṅ twŏr').
rem'o ra.
re morse', -ful, -ful ly, -ful ness,
-less, -less ly, -less ness.
re mōte', -ly, -ness.
re mount', -ed, -ing.
re move' (-mōōv'), -mov'a ble,
-a bly, -a bil'i ty, -al, -ed ness,
-er, -ing, -moved'.
rē mū'ner ate, -ā'ted, -ā'ting,
-ȧ tive, -tive ly, -tive ness, -a-
to'ry, -a ble, -a bil'i ty, -ā'tion.
Ré mu sat' (rā'mü'zä'), Fr.
orient.; Fr. statesman; Fr. auth.
Re nais sance (rĕ nā'sŏṅs' or rē-
nā'säns), Rē nāis'sant, re nȧs'-
cence, -cen cy, -cent, -ci ble.
Re naix' (rĕ nā'), t. Belg.
Re nan' (rĕ nŏṅ'), Fr. critic.
ren coun'ter, -ing, -tered.
rend, -ing, -er, rent.
rĕn'der, -ing, -a ble, -er, -dered,
ren di'tion (-dĭsh'un), ren'der-
ing-pan, -tank.
ren'dez vous (rĕn'dĕ vōō or rŏṅ'-
dä vōō), -voused (-vōōd), -vous-
ing (-vōō-).
ren'e gade, -gā'do.
re nēw' (-nū'), -a ble, -a bil'i ty,
-al, -ed ly, -ed ness, -er, -ing,
-newed'.
re nī'tence (or rĕn'-), -ten cy, -tent.
Rennes (rĕn), c. Fr.
ren'net, -ed, -ing, ren'net-bag, -fer'-
ment, -whey, -wine.
re nounce', -ment, -noun'cer,
-cing, -nounced', re nun'ci a-
to'ry (-shĭ-), -ci ā'tion (or -shĭ-).
rĕn'o vate, -vā'ted, -tor or -ter,
-ting, -vā'tion, -tion ist.
re nown', -er, -ed ly, -nowned'.

Rens'se laer (rĕn'sel er), co. N. Y.; t. Ind.

rent, -a ble, -al, -er, -ed, -ing, *rente* (rŏnt), *ren'tier'* (rŏn'tyā').

rent'-ar rēar', -charge, -day, -free, -roll, -seck, -serv'ice, rent'-er-war'den.

ren'ter, *v.*, to sew, -ing, -er, -tered.

rĕp *or* repp, repped (rĕpt).

rē pair', -a ble, -er, -ing, -ment, -pâired', rĕp'a ra ble, -ra bly, -ra bil'i ty, -rā'tion, re pār'a-tive, re pair'-shop.

rĕp ar tee'.

re *par ti mi en'to* (rā'par tē'mē ān'-tō).

re pâst'.

rē pā'tri ate, -ā'ted, -ā'ting, -ā'tion.

re pay', -a ble, -ing, -ment, -pāid'.

re pēal', -a ble, -a ble ness, -a bil'-i ty, -er, -ing, -ment, -pēaled'.

re peat', -ed, -ed ly, -er, -ing, rĕp e ti'tion (-tĭsh'un).

re pĕl', -pelled', -pel'ling, -lence, -len cy, -lent, -ler.

re pĕnt', -ance, -ant, -ant ly, -ed, -er, -ing, -ing ly, -less.

re pēo'ple, -pled, -pling.

rē per cep'tion.

re per cŭss', -cussed', -cus'sing, -sive, -sion (-kŭsh'un).

rep'er toire' (-twŏr'), rep'er tō'ry, *-to'ri um.*

rĕp'ē tĕnd' (*or* -tĕnd').

rĕp ē tent', rep'e ti'tor (*or* re pĕt'ĭ-).

rĕp'e ti'tion (-tĭsh'un), -al, -a ry, -er, -tious, -tious ly, -tious ness, re pĕt'i tive, rē pē ti'tion (-tĭsh'-un), to petition again.

Rē'phă el (*or* rĕf'-), *Bib.*

Rē phā'iah (-ya *or* rĕf'ā i'ah), *Bib.*

Rĕph'ă ĭm (*or* rē fā'im), *Bib.*

rē pīne', -pīned', -pīn'er, -ing, -ing ly.

re pique' (-pēk').

re plăce', -a ble, -ment, -plā'cer, -cing, -placed', re plā'cing-switch.

re plen'ish, -er, -ing, -ment, -ished.

rē plēte', -ness, -plĕt'ed, -ing, -plē'-tive, -tive ly, -to ry, -plē'tion.

rē plĕv'in, -ĭned, -plĕv'ish, -y, -ĭed, -i sor.

rĕp'li ca, rĕ pliche' (-plēsh').

rep'li cate, -cā'ted, -cā'ting, -ca'-tive, -cā'tion.

rep'lum.

re ply', -ing, -plīed', -plī'er, rĕp'-li cant.

re port', -a ble, -age, -ed, -er, -ing, -ing ly, -por to'ri al.

re pose' (-pōz'), -ful, -pōs'al, -ed-ly, -ed ness, -er, -ing.

rē pŏs'i tor, -to ry.

re pous'sage (rê pōō'såzh), *re-pous sé'* (rê pōō'sā').

rĕp rē hend', -ed, -er, -ing, -hen-si ble, -ble ness, -bly, -bil'i ty, -hen'sion, -sive, -sive ly, -so ry.

rĕp rē sent' (-zĕnt'), -ed, -er, -ing, -a ble, -a bil'i ty, -ant, -a tive, -tive ly, -tive ness, -sen-tā'tion, -tā'tion al, -tion ism, -tion ist.

re press', -er, -i ble, -i bly, -ive, -ive ly, -ing, -or, -pressed'.

rē priēve', -prieved', -priēv'ing.

rĕp'ri mand', *n.*, -mand' (*or* rĕp'-), *v.*, -ed, -er, -ing.

rē prĭm'er.

re prĭnt', -ed, -ing.

rē prīse' (-prīz'), prīs'al.

re prōach', -a ble, -a ble ness, -a bly, -er, -ful, -ful ly, -ful-ness, -ing, -less, -proached'.

rĕp'ro bate, -ness, -bā'ted, -bā'-ting, -bā'ter, -bā'tion, -bā'-tion er, -bā'tive, -ba'tor, -to ry.

rē prō dūce', -duced', -dū'cer, -cing, -ci ble, -duc'tive, -tive-ness, -to ry, -tion, -tiv'i ty.

re prove' (-prōōv'), -prov'a ble, -a ble ness, -a bly, -al, -er, -ing, -ing ly, -proved', -proof'.

rĕp'tĭle, -tĭl'i an, -tĭl'i um, *pl.* -ums.

re pub'lic, -lic an, -an ism, -an-ize, -ized, -ī'zing, Re pub'lic an, U. S. politics.

rē pub'lish, -er, -ing, -lished.

rē pū'dĭ ate, -ā'ted, -ā'ting, -à ble, -ā'tor, -ā'tion, -tion ist.

re pugn' (-pūn'), -pugned', -pugn'er, -pŭg'nance, -nan cy, -nant, -nant ly, -na to'ri al.

re pŭlse', -pulsed', -pŭls'er, -ing,

-pul'sion, -sive, -sive ly, -sive-
ness, -so ry.

rĕp'u ta ble, -ble ness, -bly, -tā'-
tion, rē pūte', -less, -pūt'ed,
-ed ly.

re quest', -ed, -er, -ing, re quest'-
note, r. pro'gram.

rĕ'quī em, -măss, -shark.

req ui es'cat in pa'ce (rĕk wĭ es'-
kat in pā'sē).

re quire', -ment, -quīr'a ble, -er,
-ing, -quired'.

req'ui site (rĕk'wĭ zĭt), -ly, -ness,
-si'tion   (-zĭsh'un),   -tion ed,
-quis'i tor, -to ry.

re quīte', -quīt a ble, -al, -ed, -er,
-ing.

rēre'brăce, rēre'-brake.

rēre'dŏs.

Re sa'ca de la Päl'ma (rā sä'-
kä dä lä), co. Tex.

rē scĭnd', -ed, -ing, -a ble, -ment.

re scis'sion (-sĭzh'un), -scis'so ry
(-sĭs'-).

rē'script, -scrip'tive, -scrip'tion.

rĕs'cue,   -cued,   -cu er,   -cu ing,
res'cue-grăss.

res cus'sor, -cus see'.

re sêarch',   -er,   -ing,   -ful,
-sêarched'.

re sêat', -ed, -ing.

ré seau' (rā zō').

rē sect', -ed, -ing, -sĕc'tion, -tion-
al.

rē sem'ble (-zĕm'-), -bled, -bler,
-bling, -bling ly, -blance.

rē sent' (-zĕnt), -ed, -er, -ing,
-ing ly, -ful, -ful ly, -ive, -ment,
rē sĕnt', sent again.

rē serve' (-zêrv'), -served', -serv'-
ing, -a tive, -a to'ry, -serv'ed ly,
-ed ness,   -er,   res'er vä'tion
(rĕz'-).

rĕs'er voir (rĕz'er vwôr').

rē side' (-zīd'), -sīd'ed, -er, ing
res'i dence   (rĕz'-),   -den cer,
-den cy, -dent, -den'tial, -den'-
tia ry (-sha ry), -dent ship.

re sid'u al (-zĭd'-), -u a ry, -u ate,
-ā'ted, -ā'ting, -u ent, -u ous,
-ū um,   -u ā'tion,   res'i due
(rĕz'-).

rē sign' (-zīn'), -ed ly, -er, -ment,

-signed',   res ig nā'tion   (rĕz'-),
res ign ee' (rĕz'ĭ nē').

rē sil'i ence (-zĭl'-), -en cy, -ent.

res'in (rĕz'-), -i na'ceous, -i nate,
-nā'ted, -nā'ting, -in if'er ous,
-in i form, -i fy, -fy ing, -fied,
-in ous, -in ous ly, -ous ness,
-in ize, -ized, -i'zing, -in y.

res'in-bush, -cell, -duct, -flux,
-gland, -pas'sage, -tube, res' i-
no-e lec'tric.

res'i nä'ta (rĕz'-).

res'i pis'cent (rĕs'-).

rē sist' (-zĭst'), -ed, -er, -ing,
-ing ly, -ance, -ant, -ful, -i ble,
-i ble ness,   -i bly,   -i bil'i ty,
-ive, -ive ly, -sist'less, -less ly,
-less ness, -sis tiv'i ty (-zĭs-).

re sist'-work (-zĭst'-), re sist'ance-
box, -coil.

res'o lute (rĕz'-), -ly, -ness, -o-
lū'ble, -lu'tion, -tion ist.

re solve' (-zŏlv'), -solved', -sŏlv'-
ed ly, -ed ness, -end, -ent, -er,
-ing.

res'o nance (rĕz'-), -nant, -nant-
ly, -nate, -na'tor, res'o nance-
box.

re sort' (-zort'), -ed, -er, -ing.

re sound' (-zound'), to reverber-
ate, -ed, -er, -ing, re sound',
to sound again.

rē sŏurce' (-sōrs'), -ful, -ful ness,
-less.

rē spect', -ed, -er, -ing, -a ble,
-a ble ness,   -a bly,   -a bil'i ty,
-less, -ful, -ful ly, -ful ness,
-spec'tive, -tive ly.

rē spīre', -spīred', -spīr'ing, -spīr'-
a ble, -a ble ness,   -a bil'i ty,
-spīr'a to'ry, -a tive, rĕs pĭ rā'-
tion, -tion al, -pĭ rom'e ter.

rĕs'pĭte, -less, -pĭt ed, -pĭt ing.

re splen'dence,   -den cy,   -dent,
-dent ly.

re spŏnd', -ed, -ing, -ence, -en cy,
-ent, re spŏnse'.

re spŏn'si ble, -ness, -bly, '-bil'i ty,
-sive, -sive ly, -sive ness, -so ry,
-sō'ri al.

res'sa la.

res'sal dar.

res sąut'.

rest, -ed, -ing, -ful, -ful ly, -ful-
ness, -ive, -ive ly, -ive ness,
-less, -less ly, -less ness.
rest'-cure, -har row, -house,
rest'ing-cell, -place, -spore, -stage,
-state.
res taur'.
res'tạu rant, -car, re stau ra teur'
(rä'stǒ'rà têr').
Rěs'tǐ gouche' (-gōōsh'), r. Can.
res'ti o na'ceous.
res tǐ tu'tion, res'tǐ tu tive.
rě store', -stored', -stōr'ing, -stor'-
a ble, -ble ness, -a tive, -a tively, -er, rěs to rā'tion, -tion ism,
-tion ist.
rě strāin', -a ble, -ed ly, -er, -ing,
-ment, -strāined', -strāint'.
re strī'all.
rě strict', -ed, -ed ly, -ive, -ive ly,
-ive ness, -stric'tion, -tion a ry,
-tion ist.
rě strin'gend, -strin'gent.
rě sub lime', -lǐ mä'tion.
re sū dā'tion.
re sult' (-zŭlt'), -ed, -ing, -ance,
-ant, -ful, -less, -less ness.
re sume' (-zūm'), -sumed', -sūm'-
a ble, -ing, -sump'tion, -tive,
ré su mé' (rä'zū'mä').
res ur rect' (rěz'-), -a ble, -rec'-
tion, -tion a ry, -tion ist, res-
ur rec'tion-man, -plant.
re sus'ci tate, -tā'ted, -tà ble,
-tā'ting, -tā'tive, -tā'tor, -tant,
-tā'tion.
ret, -ted, -ting.
re tā'ble, n.
rě'tail, n. and a., rě tail', v., -ing,
-er, -ment, -tailed',
rě tāin', -a ble, -er, -ing, -ment,
-tained', -ten'tion, re tain-wall.
rě tăl'i ate, -ā'ted, -ā'ting, -à-
tive, -a to'ry, -ā'tion.
re tard', -ed, -er, -ing, -ment,
-a tive, -a to'ry, re tar dā'tion.
retch, -ing, retched.
rě ten'tion, -ten'tive, -tive ly,
-tive ness, -tǐv'i ty.
Re thel' (rě těl'), t. Fr.
rě'ti a ry (-shǐ-).
rět'i cence, -cen cy, -cent.
rě tic'u lar, -ly, -u lose, -late,

-late ly, -lā'ted, -lā'ting, -lā'-
ri an, -lā'tion, re tic'u late-
veined.
rět'i cule, rě tic'u lum, pl. -la.
rět'i na, -i nal, -i nī'tis.
rět'i nūe.
rě tīre', -tīred', -tired'ly or -tīr'-
ed ly, -tired'ness or -ed ness,
-er, -ing, -tire'ment.
rě tort', n. and v., -ed, -er, -ing,
-tor'sion, re tort'-hold'er, -house,
-scāl'er.
rě touch', -er, -ing, -ment,
-touched'.
re touch'ing-desk, -ea'sel, -frame,
-ta'ble.
rě trāce', -a ble, -traced', -trā'-
cing.
rě tract', -tract'a ble or -i ble,
-bil'i ty, -tract'ive, -ive ly, -or,
-ed, -ing, -īle, -trac'tion, -trac til'-
i ty.
rě trēat', -ed, -er, -ing.
rě tree'.
rě trench', -ing, -ment, -trenched'.
rě trǐb'u tive, -u tor or -ter,
-to ry, rět rǐ bū'tion.
rě triěve', -ment, -trieved', -triěv'-
a ble, -a ble ness, -a bly, -al,
-ing, -er.
rě trǒ act' (or rět'ro-), -act'ive,
-ive ly, -ac'tion.
rě tro cede' (or re'- or rět'-),
-cēd'ent, -ces'sion, -sion al.
rět'ro grade (or rě'-), -grā'ded,
-ding, -ding ly, -grà dā'tion,
-gres'sion, -sion al, -gres'sive,
-sive ly.
rě trorse', -ly.
rět'ro spect (or rě'-), -spec'tion,
-spec'tive, -tive ly.
re trous sage' (rě trōō'sàzh').
re trous sé' (rě trōō sā').
rě trǒ vert' (or rě'tro- or rět'ro-),
-ed, -ing, -ver'sion.
rě turn', -a ble, -a bil'i ty, -er,
-ing, -less, -turned'.
rě turn'-al'ka li, -ball, -bēad,
-bend, -crease, -day, -piece,
-shock, -valve, re turn'ing-
board, -of'fi cer.
re turn' car'go, r. check, r.
match, r. tag, r. tick'et.

nǒt, nôr, ūse, ŭp, ûrn, etüde, fōōd, fǒǒt, aṅger, boṅmot, thus, Bach.

Rĕ′u (*or* rōō), *Bib.*
Reu′el (rōō′- *or* rē ū′el), *Bib.*
rē ū′nĭ fy (-fĭ), -ing, -fĭed, -fĭ cā′-
tion.
rē ū nĭte′, -nĭt′ed, -ed ly, -ing.
Re′us (rā′ōōs), t. Sp.
Reuss (rois), r. Switz.; Fr. theol.
Reuss-Schleiz′ (rois-shlītz′), prin.
Ger.
Reu′ter (roi′ter), Ger. poet; Ger.
teleg. agency.
rev′a len′ta.
rē vamp′, -ing, -vamped′.
rē vēal′, -a ble, -ble ness, -er,
-ing, -vēaled′.
re veil′le (rĕv ĕl lē′ *or* rĕ văl′yä).
rĕv′ĕl, -ĕled *or* -ĕlled, -ĕl ing *or*
-ling, -er *or* -ler, -el ment, -el-
ry, rev′el-mǎs′ter.
rĕv e lā′tion, -tion al, Rev e lā′-
tions, *Bib.*
rev′e nant.
re venge′, *n.* and *v.*, -a ble, -ful,
-ful ly, -ful ness, -ven′ger, -ging,
-ging ly, -venged′.
rĕv′e nūe, -nūed, rĕv′e nue-of′fi-
cer.
rē ver′ber ate, -ā′ted, -ā′ting,
-à tive, -ā′tor, -to′ry, -ant,
-ā′tion.
rē vere′, -vered′, -vēr′ing, -vēr′-
a ble.
rĕv′er ence, -enced, -en cer, -en-
cing, -end, -ent, -ent ly, -en′-
tial, -tial ly.
rĕv′er ie *or* -er y, -er ist.
re vers′ (rĕ vâr′).
re verse′, -ly, -versed′, -ver′sal,
-sa tĭle, -vers′i ble, -i bly, -i bil′-
i ty, -ing, -er, -or, -ver′sion,
-sion a ry, -sion er.
re vers′ ing-cyl′in der, -gear,
-lay′er, -lev er, -ma chine′,
-mo′tion, -shǎft, -valve.
re ver′so.
re vert′, -ed, -er, -ing, -ant,
-i ble, -ive, -ive ly.
re vest′, -ed, -ing.
rē vet′, -ted, -ting, -ment.
re view′ (-vū′), -a ble, -al, -er,
-ing, -viewed′.
rē vīle′, -ment, -vīled′, -vīl′er,
-ing, -ing ly.

re vin′di cate, -cā′ted, -cā′ting,
-cā′tion.
re vise′ (-vīz′), -vised′, -vīs′er,
-ing, -o ry, -vi′sion (-vĭzh′un),
-sion al, -sion a ry, -sion ist.
re vis′it (-vĭz′-), -ed, -ing, -ant,
-vis i tā′tion.
re vive′, -ment, -vived′, -vīv′al,
-al ism, -al ist, -is′tic, -a ble,
-a bil′i ty, -er, in law -or, -ing,
-ing ly.
re vĭv′i fy, -fy ing, -fĭed, -i fĭ cā′-
tion, rĕv′i vis′cence, -cen cy,
-cent.
re vŏke′, -ment, rĕv′o ca ble, -ble-
ness, -bly, -bil′i ty, -cā′tion,
-ca to′ry.
rē vŏlt′, -ed, -er, -ing, -ing ly.
rĕv o lū′tion, -â ry, -er, -ist, -ize,
-ized, -ī′zing, rev′o lute, -lu-
tive.
re vŏlve′, -ment, -volved′, -vŏlv′-
er, -ing.
re vŭl′sion, -vul′sent, -sive, -sor.
re ward′, -ed, -er, -ing, -a ble,
-a ble ness, -a bly, -less.
rey′nard (rā- *or* rĕn′-), Rey′nard,
Fiction.
rez′-de-chaus′sèe′ (rā′-dĕ-shŏ′sā′).
Rē zī′a, *Bib.*
rhap′so dy (răp′-), -sod′ic, -ic al,
-so dist, -dis′tic, -so dize, -dized,
-di zing, -do man′cy.
Rhe′a (rē′-), *Myth.*,—(rā), co.
Tenn., rhē′a, an ostrich; a satel-
lite; a fiber plant; rhē′a-fi′ber,
-grǎss.
Rhē′gi ŭm (rē′jĭ-), *Bib.*
Rheims (rēmz). See *Reims.*
rhē′o chord, rhe om′e ter, -om′e try,
-o met′ric, -o mo′tor, -o phore,
-o scope, -o scŏp′ic, -o stat,
-stǎt′ic, -ics, -o tome, -o trope,
-trŏp′ic, -ot′ro pism.
rhĕt′o ric, -ri′cian (-rĭsh′an), -o-
rize, -rized, rhe tŏr′ic al, -al ly.
rheum (rōōm), a catarrhal affec-
tion, -y, Rhe′ŭm, *Bot. genus.*
rheu′ma tism (rōō′-), -mǎt′ic,
-ic al.
Rheydt (rīt), t. Prus.
rhī′nal, -nal′gi a.
Rhine (rīn), r. Ger., Rhĕn′ish.

---

fāte, fǎt, fär, fạll, fâre, fǎst, sofȧ, mēte, mĕt, hêr, īce, ĭn, nōte,

rhine'stone.
rhī noc'e rŏs (-nŏs'-), -e rŏt'ic,
rhi noc'e ros-auk, -bee'tle, -bird,
-bush, -cha me'le on, -horn'-
bill, -tick.
rhi nŏl'o gy, -o gist, -no log'ic al.
rhi'no scope, -scŏp'ic, -nos'cō py.
rhĭp'i date.
Rhœ'cus (rē'kŭs), *Myth.*
rhŏmb (*or* rŏm), rhom'bic, -bic-
al, -boid, -boid'al, -bus, *pl.* -bī,
rhomb'-sol'id, -spar.
rhü'barb, -y, rhu'barb-root.
rhumb *or* rumb (rŭm *or* rŭmb),
rhumb'-line, -sail'ing.
rhyme. See *rime*.
rhyn'chote (ring'kōt), -chō'tous.
rhyne (rīn).
rhythm (rĭthm *or* rĭthm), -less,
rhyth'mic, -mic al, -al ly, -al'i ty,
-mics, -mist, -mize, -mized, -mī'-
zing, -mom'e ter, -mus.
ri (rē).
rĭ'ant, -an cy.
rib, -bing, rib'less, -let, ribbed, rib'-
wort.
rib'-band, -baste, -bone, -faced,
-grass, -like, -nosed, -piece, -roast,
-roast'er, -stitch, -vault'ing, rib'-
bing-nail.
Rĭ'bai (-bä), *Bib.*
rĭb'ald, -ish, -ry.
ri bat tu'ta (rē bŭt tōō'tä).
rib'ble-rab'ble.
rib'bon, -ing, -boned (-bŭnd), rib'-
bon weed, -wood, a tree, -worm.
rĭb'bon-bor'der ing, -brake, -fish,
-grass, -line, -loom, -map, -pat'-
tern, -reg'is ter, -saw, -seal,
-snake, -stamp, -tree, -wave,
-wire, r. gur'nard, r. i'ron.
Rĭb'bon ism, -bon man.
Ric'ci (rēt'chē), It. reformer.
Ric'cia (rēt'chä), t. It.
Ric'cio (rēt'chō), It. painter.
Ric cio'li (rēt chō'lē), It. astron.
rice, -flow'er.
rice'-bird, -bun'ting, -corn, -drill,
-dust, -em broid'er y, -field,
-flour, -glue, -grain, -hen, -hull-
er, -meal, -milk, -mill, -pa per,
-plan ta'tion, -plant er, -pound-
er, -rat, -shell, -sow er, -stitch,

-stone, -su gar, -ten'rec, -troop'-
i al, -wa'ter, -wee vil, r. pudding, r. soup, r. wine.
rich, -es, -ly, -ness, -weed.
Ri che lieu' (rē shē lōō'), co. and
r. Que.;—(rĭsh'ĕ lōō *or* rēsh-
lyê'), Fr. cardinal.
Rich'ter, Ger. polit.; Ger. mus.;
Ger. auth.
rick, -er, -ers, rick'yard, -stand.
rick'ets, -et y, -et i ness.
rick-rack.
ric'o chet' (rĭk'ō shä' *or* -shĕt'),
-chet'ted, -chet'ting.
rid, -ded, -ding, -dance, -der.
rid'dle, -dled, -dling, -dling ly,
-dlings, -dler.
ride, rode, rĭd'den, rīd'a ble,
rīd'er, -er less.
ride'-of'fi cer, rīd'er-roll, rīd'ing-
bitts, -boot, -day, -glove, -hab'it,
-hood, -light, -mas'ter, -robe,
-rod, -sail, -school, -skirt, -suit,
-whip.
ri'deau' (rē dō'), pl., *-deaux* (-dōz).
ridge, ridged, ridg'ing, -ing ly, -y.
ridge'-band, -beam, -drill, -fil-
let, -har'row, -hoe, -piece, -plate,
-plow, -pole, -roof, -rope, -stay,
-tile, ridg'ing-grass, -plow.
rĭd'i cule, -culed, -cūl'ing, -cul-
er, rĭ dic'u lous, -lous ly, -lous-
ness, -los'i ty.
ri dot'to (rē dŏt'tō).
riem (rēm).
Riĕs'ling, a wine.
rīfe, -ly, -ness.
riff.
rĭf'fle, -fler, rif'fle-bars.
riff'raff.
rī'fle, -fled, -fling, -fler, ri'fle man.
rī'fle-ball, -bird, -corps, -fish, -pit,
-range, -shell, -shot, -ri'fling-ma-
chine', -tool, ri'fle man-bird.
rĭft, -ed, -ing.
rig, -ger, -ging, -gish, rigged,
rig'-out, rig'ging-cut'ter, -loft,
-screws, -tree.
Rĭ'ga, tp. Mich.; tp. N. Y.,—
(rē'ga), c. Russ., Rĭ'ga bal'sam
(rē'ga), R. fir, R. pine.
rĭg a doon'.
right (rīt), -ed, -er, -ful, -ful ly,

-ful ness, -less, -ly, -ness, -ing,
-eous (rī'chŭs), -eous ly, -ness.
right'-a bout', -aṅ'gled, -drawn,
-edge, -hand, *a.*, -hand'er,
-whāl'er.
Ri'gi (rē'gē), mt. Switz.
rig'id (rĭj'-), -id ly, -id ness,
ri gid'i ty.
rig leen'.
rĭg'ma rŏle.
Rig na'no (rēn yä'nō), vil. It.
rig o lette'.
rig'or, -ism, -ist, -ous, -ous ly,
-ous ness.
ri gō rō'sō (rē'-).
Rĭgs'dåg or *Riks'-*.
rĭgs'dä'ler.
Rig-Ve'da (-vä'-).
rig wĭd'die.
Riis (rēs), Amer. writer.
ri lie'vo (rē lyä'vō).
rĭll, -et, rill'-mark.
rim, -less, -mer, -ming, rimmed.
rim'-fire, -line, -lock, -plān'er,
-rock, -saw, -stock.
rime, white frost; a round of a
ladder, rĭm'y, rime-frost,
-frost'ed.
rĭme *or* rhyme, rimed, rĭm'ing,
rime'less, -ster, rime'-let'ter.
rĭ'mose (-mōs), -ly, -mous,
-mŏs'i ty.
rim'ple, -pled, -pling.
rin.
Ri näl'dŏ (rē-), *Fiction.*
rĭnd, -ed, -less, -y, rĭnd'-gąll,
-grȧft'ing, -lay er.
Rinde (rīnd), r. India.
rĭn'der pest.
rin for zan'do (-tsän'dō), . *rin
for za'to* (-tsä'tō).
ring, -er, -ing, -ing ly, -ster,
-wise, -y', rang, rung, ringed,
ring'bill, a duck, -bone, a
disease, -fish, -lēad'er, -man,
-mȧs'ter, -neck, a plover; a
duck, -sail, -tail, a bird, -toss,
-work, -worm.
ring'-band'ed, -bark, -bark'er,
-bird, -bit, -black'bird, -bolt,
-bone, -boot, -brŏoch, -bun'ting,
-bush, -ca nal', -car ri er,
-chuck, -cross, -di al, -dog,

-dot'ter el, -dove, -drop per,
-fĭṅ ger, -foot ed, -formed,
-fowl, -frame, -gage, -han dle,
head, -hedge, -joint, -keep er,
-lock, -lock'et, -mal let, -mon-
ey, -mule, -necked, -net,
-ou'zel, -par rot, -perch, -plain,
-plov er, -rope, -saw, -shaped,
-small, -snake, -spar row,
-spin ner, -stand, -stop per,
-streaked, -tailed. -thros tle,
-thrush, -time, -tongue, -top,
-vor tex, -wad, -wall, ringed'-
arm, -car'pet, a moth, ring'ing-
en gine, ring'worm-root, -shrub.
ring' ar'ma ture, r. ar'mor, r.
fence, r. mail, r. tum bler, r.
valve, ring'ing out.
rĭng'let, -ed.
ring'ster.
Rĭ nous ki' (rē'nōōs kē'), co. Que.
rinse, rinsed, rĭns'er, -ing, rĭns'-
ing-ma chine'.
Ri'ŏ, a coffee, *ri o'* (rē ō'), a
weight.
Ri'o de Ja nei'ro (rē'ō dä zhä-
nā'rō), c. and state Braz.
Ri'o de la Pla'ta (lä plä'tä),
r. S. Amer.
Ri'o Gran'de (rē'ō grän'dā), r.
Afr.; r. N. Amer.; r. Braz.; co.
Colo.; c. Tex.
Ri'o Grände do Sul' (dō sōōl'),
state Braz.
Ri om' (rē'ŏṅ'), t. Fr.
Ri'os (rē'ōs), prov. Ecuador.
Ri'o Sä lä'dŏ, r. Arg. Rep.
rĭ'ot, -ed, -er, -ing, -ous, -ous ly,
-ous ness, -ry.
rip, -per, -ping, ripped, rip'sack,
rip'-fish'ing, -saw.
rip'ping-bed, -chis el, -i ron, -saw.
rĭ på'rĭ an (*or* rĭ pä'-), -al, -ri ous.
rĭpe, -ly, -ness, rĭp'en, -ened,
-en ing.
ri pie'no (rĭ pyä'nō *or* rē pē ā'nō),
-pie nist.
rĭ post'.
rip'ple, -pled, -pling, -pler,
-plet, -ply.
rip'ple-bȧr'rel, -gråss, -mark,
-marked.
rip'rap, -rapped.

rise (rīs *or* rīz), *n.*, rise'-bush
(rīs'-), -dike, -wood.

rise (rīz) *v.*, rose (rōz), rīs'en
(rīz -), rīs'er, -ing.

rīs'ing-an vil, -line, -main,
-rod, -seat, -square, -wood.

rīs'I ble (rīz'-), -ble ness, -bly,
-bil'i ty.

risk, -er, -ing, -ful, -y, -i ness,
risked.

ri so lu'to (rē zō lōō'tō).

rī sŏ'rī al, *-rī us,* pl. *-rī ī.*

ri sot'to (rē zŏt'tō).

risp.

ris qué (rēs'kā').

ris'sole (rīs'sōl *or* rē'sōl').

Ris to'ri (rēs tō'rē), It. actress,
rīs tō'rī, a jacket.

ri tar'do (rē tar'dō),   *ri tar dan'-
do* (-dän'dō).

rite.

rītĥe, a vine.

ri tor nelle' (rē tor nĕl'), *-nĕl'lō.*

rit'u al, -ism, -al ist, -is'tic, -al ly.

rīv'age.

rī'val, -ry, -văled *or* -valled,
-val ing *or* -ling.

rive, rived *or* rīv'en, rīv'ing,
rīv'er, rīv'ing-knife, -ma chine'.

rīv'er, -ăin, -ine, -ish, -y, rīv'er-
head, -side, -weed.

rīv'er-bank, -băss, -bed, -birch,
-bot tom, -bull'head, -carp,
-chub, -crab, -crăft, -craw'-
fish, -dol phin, -drag on,
-drīv er, -duck, -flat, -god,
-hog, -horse, -jack, -lam prey,
-lim pet, -man, -mĕad ow,
-mus sel, -ot ter, -perch, -pie,
-plain, -shrew, -snail, -swal'low,
-tĕr'race, -tor toise, -tur tle,
-wall, -wa ter, -weight, -wolf.

Rive'saltes (rēv'sălt), a wine.

rīv'et, -et ed *or* -ted, -et ing *or*
-ting, -et er.

rīv'et-clip'per, -cut ter, -heärth,
-joint, -knob, -ma chine'.

riv'et ing-bur, -forge, -ham'-
mer, -ma chine', -plates, -set,
-tools.

ri vière' (rē vyâr').

Ri vi ère'   **Pi lote'**   (rē'vē'âr'
pē'lōt'), t. Martinique.

Ri vi ères'   **du**   **Sud'**   (rē'vē'âr'
dü süd'), Fr. colony W. Afr.

Ri'vo li (rē'vō lē), t. It.

riv'u let, -tree.

rix'-dol lar.

rŏach, -backed, -dace.

rŏad, -er, -ing, -man, -ster,
-side, -stĕad, -way, -weed,
-wor thy, roads'man.

rŏad'-a gent, -bed, -book, car,
-drift, -har row, -lev el, -lev el-
er, -lo co mo'tive, -ma chine',
-māk'er, -meas'ur er, -met al,
-plow, -roll er, -run ner, -scrāp'-
er, -steam er, -sul'ky, -sur -
vey'or, -work.

rŏam, -er, -ing, roamed.

rŏan, -tree.

Rŏ'a noke', co., and c. Va.; tp.
N. C., rō'a noke', shell-money.

rŏar, -er, -ing, -ing ly, roared.

rŏast, -ed, -er, -ing, roast'-bit ter,
-stall, roast'er-slag.

rŏast'ing-bed, -cyl'in der, -ear,
-fur nace, -jack, -kiln, -ov en.

rŏb, -ber, -ber y, -bing, robbed,
rob'-al tar, rob'ber-crab, -fly,
-gull.

rŏb'bin, rope-yarn; a carriage-
spring; a chest.

rŏbe, robed, rŏb'ing, robe'-māk'er,
rŏb'ing-room,   *robe-de-cham'bre*
(rōb'-dĕ-shŏn'br).

Rŏ'bĕs pierre' (-peer'), Fr. revolutionist.

rŏb'in, a bird, -et, rŏb'in-ac cent'or,
-breast, -dip per, -sand'pi per,
-snipe, -wheat, rŏb'in's-plan'-
tain, -rye, rŏb'in-run-in-the-
hedge, a plant, rŏb'in red-
breast, r. rud'dock.

Rŏ bŏ'am (*or* rŏb'-), *Bib.*

rŏb'o rant.

rŏ bust', -ly, -ness.

rŏc.

Rŏ chä', dept. Uruguay.

Rŏ'cham'beau' (-shŏn'bō'), Amer.
gen.

Rŏch'dale, t. and bor. Eng.

Roche fort' (rōsh'fōr'), t. Fr.

Rŏ chelle', **La** (-shĕl'), c. Fr.,
Ro chelle', c. Ill., Ro chelle'
pow der, R. salt.

---

nŏt, nôr, ūse, ŭp, ûrn, etüde, fōōd, fŏŏt, aṅger, boṅmot, thus, Bacĥ.

roches' mou ton nées' (rōsh'mōō'tō'-nā').

rŏch'et.

rŏch'ing-câsk.

Roch'litz (rŏk'lĭts), t. Ger.

Ro ci nan'te (rŏ'sē nän'tä), Don Quixote's steed.

rock, -er, -ered, -er y, -ing, -y, -i ness, -less, -let, -ling, rocked, rock'fish, -weed, -work.

rock'-a lys'sum, -bad ger, -bar'-na cle, -ba sin, -båss, -beau ty, -bird, -black bird, -bor er, -bot'-tom, -bound, -brake, -breāk er, -but ter, -can dy, -cā'vy, -cist, -cod, -cook, -cork, -crab, -cress, -crowned, -crush er, -crys tal, -de mon, -dol phin, -dove, -drill, -drill ing, -duck, -eel, -elm, -fal con, -fe ver, -fire, -flint, -flour, -gas, -goat, -goose, -grouse, -hair, a lichen, -har-mon'i con, -hawk, -head, -hop-per, -kan ga roo', -kelp, -knot'-weed.

rock'-lark, -leath'er, -lev er, -lil y, -lim pet, -lin tie, -lob ster, -man i kin, -ma ple, -meal, -milk, -moss, -mouse, -nōs'ing, -oil, -ou'zel, -oys'ter, -par'ra keet, -pi geon, -pip it, -plant, -plov-er, -ptar mi gan, -pul'ver i zer, -punch, -rab bit, -rat, -rose, -rub'ble, -ru by, -sal mon, -sam'-phire, -scor pi on, -seal, -ser pent, -shâft, -shell, -shrike, -slåt er, -snipe, -soap, -spar row, -ståff, -star ling, -stur geon, -suck er, -swal low, -swift, -tar, -tem ple, -thrush, -tools, -tripe, -trout, -tur'quoise, -vi'o let, -war bler, -wa ter, -win kle, -wood, -wren, rock' al um, r. salt, Rock day.

rock'a way, a carriage.

rock'er-cam, -shâft, -sleeve.

rŏck'et, -er, rock'et-bird, -case, -drift, -har poon', -lark'spur.

rock'ing-bar, -beam, -chair, -horse, -tree, r. pier, r. shâft.

Rock'y Moun tain blue'bird, R. M. gar rot, R. M. goat, R. M. lo cust, R. M. pī'ka, R. M. rat, R. M. sheep.

rod, -ded, -ding, -let, -ster, rod'-man, -wood, a tree, rods'man.

rod'-bac te'ri um, -bay'o net, -chis'el, -coup'ling, -end, -fish, -fish'er, -fish'ing, -fruc ti fi ca'-tion, -gran'ule, -hold er, -i ron, -line, -ma chine', -plān'er, -ring.

rŏ'dent.

rō de'o (-dā'ō).

Rŏd e ri'go (-rē'go), Shak., *Othello.*

rŏd'o mel.

Rŏd'ō mŏnt or Rō'dō mōn'te (-tä), *Fiction.*

rŏd'o mont, -mon tāde', -tā'dor.

Rŏ'drigues' (-drēg'), isl. Indian Oc.

Rŏ dri'guez (-drē'gĕth), Sp. auth.

roe (rō), rōed, roe'buck, roe'-deer, -fish, -stone, roe'buck-ber'ry.

Roeb'ling (rêb'ling), Amer. en-gineer.

Roent'gen (rûnt'gen), Ger. in-ventor, R. pho'to gram, R. pho'-to grȧph, R. rays.

ro gā'tion, rŏg'a to ry, ro gā'tion-flow'er.

Rŏ'ge lim (or -gē'-), *Bib.*

Rŏ'get' (-zhā'), Eng. auth.

rŏgue, rōgued, rogu'ing, rogu'-er y, rogu'ish, -ish ly, -ish ness, rouge'ship, rogue'-house.

rŏ'ĭ.

roil, -er, -ing, -y, roiled.

Rŏ'i mŭs, *Bib.*

rois'ter, -ing, -ter ly, -ous, -er, -tered.

rōke, -age, rōk'ee, rōk'y.

rŏk'e lay.

rôle (rōl).

rōll, -er, -ing, -a ble, -ey, rōlled, roll'way.

rŏll'-a bout, -boil ing, -box, -call, -cu'mu lus, -joint, -lâthe, -mold ing, -top, -train, -up.

rŏll'er-bar, -băr row, -bear ing, -bird, -board, -bowl, -box, -com po si'tion, -die, -flag, -forks, -gin, -grip, -lift, -mill, -mold, -skate, -stock, -stop, -tow el.

roll'ing-bar rel, -chock, -clēat, -dam, -frame, -ma chine', -mill, -pin, -plant, -press, -rope, -stock, -tac'kle.

---

fāte, făt, fär, fạll, fâre, fåst, sofâ, mēte, mĕt, hêr, īce, ĭn, nōte,

rŏl'lick *or* -lic, -licked, -lick ing.
rŏ'ly-pŏ'ly.
Rŏm, a gypsy, Rŏm'a ny *or* -ma ny.
rō mä'ĭ ka.
rō mäl'.
Rō'män, dist. and c. Roum.
Rō'man, -esque', -man'ic, -man ize, -ized, -ĭ'zer, -ĭ'zing, -ĭ zä'- tion, rō'man, a letter or type, ro man es'ca, a dance, Rō'- man ō-Byz'an tĭne (-bĭz'-).
rō mănce', *n.*, *a.*, and *v.*, -manced', -măn'cing, -cer, -cist.
Ro'man ism, -ish, -ist, Rōm'ish.
Rō mä'nŏff, Czar of Russ.
Rō măns, *Bib.*—(rō'mŏn'), t. Fr.
rō man'tic, -tic al ly, -ti cism, -ti cist, -tic ness.
rom bō nĕl'lĭ.
Rŏm'e o, Shak.
Rŏ'meyn (-mĭn), Amer. theol.
Rŏm'il ly, Eng. statesman.
Rŏ'mo la, *Fiction.*
rŏmp, -ing, -ing ly, -ish, -ish ly, -ish ness, rŏmped.
rŏṇ ca dor'.
Ron cigl io'ne (rŏn chēl yō'nā), t. It.
rŏn dache' (-dăsh').
rŏnde.
rŏn'deau (-dō), -del, a poem, -del et, rŏn'do, music, -do let'to, -di'- no (dē'nō).
rŏn delle', something round, -dle.
Rönt'gen (rĕnt'gĕn). See *Roentgen.*
rōōd, -y, rood'hout, rōōd'-al tar, -arch, -beam, -free, -loft, -screen, -spire, -stee'ple, -tow'er, Rood'-day.
rōōf, -er, -ing, -less, -let, -y, rōōfed, roof'tree.
rōōf'-cell, -gar den, -gra da'tion, -guard, -like, -nu'cle us, -plate, -rat, -shaped, -sta'ging, -stay, -truss.
rōōf'ing-felt, -ma chine', -pa per, -slate.
rōōk, -ing, -y, -er y.
rōōm, -age, -er, -ful, -y, -i ly, -i ness, -less, -stĕad, -mate, roomed, room'-keep'er, -pa'per -rid'den.

rōōp, -y.
rōōr'back.
Roo'se vĕlt (rō'zĕ-), Pres. of U. S. roosh.
rōōst, -ed, -ing, -er, roost'-cock.
rōōt, -ed, -ed ly, -ed ness, -er, -er y, -ing, -less, -let, -y, root'fåst, -stock.
root'-al'co hol, -bark, -bar na cle, -book, -bor er, -bound, -breāk'er, -bruis'er, -built, -cap, -cel lar, -drop, -dig ger, -eat er, -fi'bril, -foot ed, -for ceps, -form, -grăft'ing, -grīnd er, -hair, -house, to store roots, -knot, -leaf, -loop, -louse, păr'- a site, -pres sure, -pulp er, -sheath, -tree, -vole, -wash er, -wood, -zone, r. beer, r. house, made of roots.
rōpe, roped, rōp'ing, -er, -er y, -y, -i ly, ish, rope'bark, a shrub, -walk, -way, -work.
rōpe-band, -clamp, -clutch, -cord, -dan cer, -drill ing, -el'e va tor, -end, -grăss, -house, -ma chine', -māk'er, -pat tern, -por ter, -pull, -pull ing, -pump, -rail way, -ripe, -roll, -run ner, -shaped, -sock et, -spin ner, -stitch, -trick, -walk er, -winch, -yarn, rope's-end, rōp'ing-nee dle, -palm, -pole.
Roque fort' (rōk'fôr' *or* -fort'), t. Fr., R. cheese.
Rŏ'que Gui nart' (rō'kä gē- närt'), Cervantes, *Don Quixote.*
rŏq'ue laure (rŏk'ē lōr).
rō quet' (-kā'), a game, -quet'- ing (-kā'-), -queted' (-kād'), ro quet'-cro quet' (rō kā'-krō kä'), *v.*, r. cro quet', *n.*
rŏ'quet (-kĕt), a lizard.
rŏ'ric, rō rif'er ous, rŏs'cid.
ror'qual.
ro'ru lent.
Ros'a lĭnd (rŏz'-), Shak., *As You Like It.*
ro'sa ry (-zä-), -plant, -shell.
rose (rōz), ros'i ness, ro sa'ceous, ro sa'ri um (-zā'-), *pl.* -ri ums *or* -ri a, -ri an, rōs'e ry, a rose garden, rō'så ry (-za-), a string

nŏt, nôr, ūse, ŭp, ûrn, etüde, fōōd, fŏŏt, aṇger, boṅmot, thus, Bach.

32

of beads, ro'se ate, ros'y, ro'-
sied (-zĭd), ros'i ly, ro sière'
(rō zyâr').
rose'ber'ry, -bone, a fish, -bud,
-fish, -let, -root, -wood, -wort.
rose'-a ca'cia, -an'i līne, -ā'phis,
-ap ple, -back, -bay, -bee tle,
-bit, -blaṇ ket, -box, -brĕasted,
-bug, -bush, -cam phor, -cam'-
pi on, -car na'tion, -ca tarrh',
-chā fer, -cheeked, -cold, -col-
or, -col ored, -comb, -cop per,
-cross, -cut, -drop, -ear, -en'-
cri nite, -en'gine, -fes'ti val,
-fe ver, -fly, -fly'catch er, -gall,
-ge ra'ni um, -haw, -house, -hued.
rose-knot, -lash'ing, -lāthe, -leaf,
-lip, -mal low, -mal oes, -mon ey,
-nail, -no ble, -oil, -ou'zel, -par'-
ra keet, -pink, -point, -quartz,
-rash, -red, -ringed, -row el, -ry'al,
-saw'fly, -slug, -steel, -tan'a gar,
-taṇ gle, -to paz, -tree, -vin e gar,
-wa ter, -wil low, -worm, -yard.
rose' burn'er, r. mold ing, r.
win dow.
rose'ma ry, -moor'wort, -pine,
rose-of-hĕaven, a plant, rose'-
wood-oil.
ros'y-bo'so med (rōz'-), -col ored,
-crowned, -drop, a disease, -fin-
gered, -foot'man, a moth, -kin'-
dled, -mar'bled, -marsh, a moth,
-rus'tic, a moth, -tint'ed, -wave,
a moth.
Rŏ'se crans (-zĕ krăns), Amer. gen.
ro sel'la (-zĕl'-), -fi ber.
ro selle' (-zĕl').
Rŏ'sĕn kranz (-kränts), Ger.
philos.
Ro set'ta stone (-zĕt'-), ro set'ta-
wood.
ro sette' (-zĕt'), -set'ted, ro sette'-
cell, -cop per, -cut ter, -plate,
r. burn er.
ros'in (rŏz'-), -ined, -ĭn y, ros'in-
weed, ros'in-oil, -plant, -tin, r.
soap.
Ro si'ni (-sē'nē), It. auth.
Ros'i phele, Gower, *Confessio
Amantis.*
Ros ny' dĕ (rŏ'nē'), Fr. orient.
ro sŏ'lio (-zŏ'lyō).

rŏss, -ing, rossed, ross'ing-ma-
chine'.
Rŏs sĕt'ti (-tē), Eng. poetess;
Eng. painter; Eng. critic.
rŏs'si gnol (-nyŏl).
ros'trum, *pl.* -trums *or* -tra.
rŏt, -ted, -ting, -ten ly, -ten ness,
-ten stone, rot'-grăss, -steep.
rō'ta, a court; a political club, ro'ta,
Mus.
rŏ'tate, -tā ted, -tā ting, -tà ry,
-tā tive, -tive ly, -tā'tion, -tion-
al, -tā'tor, -tà to'ry, -to'ri al.
rŏ'tate-plane, rŏ'tā ting-ring, ro-
tā'tion-a're a.
rŏte, -song.
Rothe'say (rŏth'sā), bor. Scot.
Rothes'chĭld (rŏs'-), Eng. banker.
rŏ tŏnde'.
rŏ ton'do.
rŏ tŭnd', -tund'ate, -i ty, -ness,
ro tund'-o'vate, -point'ed.
rŏ tun'da.
Rou baix' (rōō'bā'), t. Fr.
rou'ble. See *ruble.*
rou'cou (rōō'kōō).
rou é' (rōō'ā'), a debauchee, rou'-
e riē.
rou elle'-guard (rōō ĕl'-).
Rou en' (rōō'ŏn'), c. Fr., R.
cross, R. duck, R. pot'ter y.
rou et' (rōō'ā'), a wheel.
rouge (rōōzh), rouged (rōōzhd),
rou'ging (rōō'zhĭng).
rouge'-berry, -dish, -plant, -pot,
-pow der, *rouge-et-noir'* (-ā-
nwŏr').
rou get' (rōō zhā').
rough (rŭf), -age, -ing, -en, -ened,
-er, -ly, -ness, -shod, -head, a
lizard; a fish, -leg, a hawk, -tail,
a snake, -wing, a moth; a bird.
rough'-backed, -billed, -bore, -cåst,
v., -cåst er, -clad, -cull, *v.*, -dab,
v., -drăft, *v.*, -draw, *v.*, -dry,
-foot'ed, -grind, -hew, -hew er,
-hound, -legged, -necked, -per'-
fect, -rid'er, -scuff, -set ter, -slant,
v., -spun, -string, *v.*, -tailed, -tree,
-winged, -work, *v.*, r. stuff.
rough'ing-drill, -hole, -lāthe, -mill,
-rolls.
rou lade' (rōō'låd').

fāte, făt, fär, fạll, fâre, fåst, sofà, mēte, mĕt, hêr, īce, ĭn, nōte,

rou leau' (rōō'lō'),   pl.   *-leaus'*
or *-leaux* (-lōz').
Rou lers' (rōō'lā'),   t. Belg.
rou lette' (rōō lĕt').
rounce, -han dle.
round, -ed, -er, -ing, -a bout,
-ish, -ish ness, -let, -ly, -ness,
round'fish, -hand, -house, -mouth,
a fish, -stone, a cobblestone,
-worm, rounds'man, Round'head,
a Puritan, round'head, a fish.
round'-all, -arched, -arm, *a.*, -bend,
a., -faced, -head'ed, -i ron,
-leaved, -mouthed, -nosed, -ridge,
-rob in, -shoul'dered, -tailed, -up,
-winged.
round'ing-adz, -gage, -jack, -ma
chine', -out, -plane, -tool.
roun'de lay.
roup (rōōp).
rouse (rouz), roused, rous'er, -ing,
-ing ly.
Rous seau' (rōō'sō'),   Fr. poet;
Fr. philos.; Fr. painter, -seau'-
ism, -seau'ist, -seau'īte.
Rous set' (rōō'sā'), Fr. hist.
rous sette' (rōō sĕt').
roust, -ed, -er, -ing, -y, -a bout.
rout, -ed, -er, -ing, rout'-cake,
rout'er-gage, -out, -plane, -saw,
rout'ing-ma chine', -tool.
route (rōōt), rout'ed, -ing, route-
march, -step.
rou tier' (rōō'tyā').
rou tine' (rōō tēn'), -tī neer', -ti'-
nist (-tē'-).
Routt (rout), co. Col.
roux (rōō).
rove, roved, rōv'er, -ing, -ing ly,
-ing ness.
rove'-bee'tle, rōv'er-bee'tle, rōv'-
ing-frame, -head, -ma chine',
-plate, -reel.
rō ves'cio (-vĕsh'ō).
rŏw, *v.*, -er, -ing, rōwed, row'boat,
-lock, -cloth, -mark er, -port,
row'ing-fĕath er, -gear, -ma chine'.
row (rou), -er, -ing.
Rŏw'an, Amer. Admiral, Row-
ăn', co. Ken.; co. N. C.
row'an (rō'-), a tree; a fruit,
-ber'ry, -tree.
row'dy (rou'-), -ish, -ism.

row'el (rou'ĕl), -eled *or* -elled, -el-
ing *or* -ling, row'el-head, -spur,
row'el ing-nee'dle, -scis'sors.
row'en (rou'-), a stubble field.
Row e'na (rō ē'-), Scott, *Ivanhoe.*
row'et (rou'-), -work.
Rox'burgh (rŏks'bŭr ō), co. Scot.,
rox'burghe (-bŭr ō), a book
binding.
roy'al, -ism, -ist, -ize, -ized,
-ī'zing, -ly, -ty, -măst, roy'al-
yard.
Rshĕv *or* Rjev (rzhĕv), t. Russ.
rub, -ber, -bing, rubbed, rub'stone,
rub'-i ron.
rub'bing-bat ten, -bed, -block,
-ma chine, -pănch, -post, -stone.
rub'a dub.
rub'ber, -ide, -ite, -oid, rub'bers,
rub'ber-file, -gage, -knife, -mold,
-saw, -tree, -vine.
rŭb'bish, -ing, -y, rub'bish-heap,
-pul'ley.
rub'ble, rub'bly, rub'ble work,
-ice, -stone, -wall'ing.
ru be fā'cient, -fac'tion.
ru bel'la.
ru bes'cence, -cent.
ru'bi can, flecked with gray.
Ru'bi con, a river.
ru'bĭ cund.
ru bĭ'go,   -bĭg'i nose   (-bĭj'i nōs),
-ĭ nous.
Ru'bin steIn, Russ. pianist.
ru'ble, a Russian coin.
ru'bric,   -bricked,   -brick ing,
-bric al, -al ly, -bri cal'i ty, -cate,
-cā'ted, -ca'ting, -cā'tor, -cā'-
tion, -brĭ'cian (-brĭsh'an), -bri-
cist, -bric'i ty.
ru'by, -bĭed, -bi fy, -fy ing, -fied,
-bi fac'tion, -bi fĭ cā'tion, -bi-
form, -bif'ic, ru'by tail, a wasp,
-wood.
ru'by-blende, -cop per, -crowned,
-mī ca, -tailed, -throat ed, -ti ger,
a moth.
ruche (rōōsh), ruch'ing (rōōsh'-).
ruck, -ing, rucked.
ruc tā'tion.
rŭd'der,   -less,   rud'der-band,
-brace, -brake, -case, -chain,
-chock, -coat, -duck, -fĕath'er,

---

nŏt, nôr, ūse, ŭp, ûrn, etüde, fōōd, fŏŏt, aṅger, boṅmot, thus, Bach.

-fish, -hanger, -head, -hole, -iron, -nail, -pendant, -perch, -port, -post, -stock, -tac'kle, -trunk, -wheel.

rud'dle, -dled, -dling, -dle man.

rud'dock.

rud'dy, -dĭed, -di ly, -di ness, rud'dy-rud der.

rude (rōōd), -ly, -ness, rude'-grow'ing.

rudge'-wash.

ru'di ment, -men'tal, -men'ta ry, -ta'ri ly.

rue (rōō), rued, rū'er, -ing, rue'-ful, -ful ly, -ful ness, rue'wort, rue'-a nem'o ne, -bar gain, -fern.

Ru eil' (ru'āl'), vil. Fr.

rŭff, -ing, -er, ruffed, ruff'-band, -cuff, -wheel.

ruf'fian (-yan), -age, -ish, -ism, -like, -ly, -hood.

ruf'fle, -fled, -fler, -fling, -fle less, -fle ment.

ruf'fy-tuf'fy.

Ru'fus, a Chr. name, ru'fous, of a red color, ru'fu lous.

rug, -ging, -gy, rug'-gowned, -head'ed.

ru'ga, pl. *-gæ* (-gē), -gate.

rŭg'ged, -ly, -ness.

Rug gie'ro (rōōd jā'rō), *Orlando Furioso.*

ru'gose (-gōs), -ly, -goŭs, -gu-lōse, -gos'i ty.

Ru hä'mah (*or* rōō'-), *Bib.*

Ruhr (rōōr), r. Prus.

ru'ĭn, -er, -ing, -a ble, -ous, -ous-ly, -ous ness, -ĭned, -in ā'tion, ru'in-ag'ate, -mar'ble.

rule (rōōl), -less, -less ness, rūl'-a ble, -er, -ing, -ing ly, ruled.

rule'-case, -cut ter, -drill'er, -joint, -stăff, -work, rul'ing-en gine, -ma chine', -pen.

rŭl'lion (-yŭn).

rum, -mer, -my, rum'cel lar, -shop, -swiz zle, -barge, -blos'-som, -booze, -bud, -cher'ry, -hole, r. shrub.

ru'mal (rōō'-).

rum'ble, -bled, -bler, -bling, -bling ly.

ru'men, pl. *-mi na.*

ru'mi nant, -ly, -nate, -nā'ted, -nā'ting, -ting ly, -nā'tive, -nā'-tor, -nā'tion.

rum'mage, -maged, -mā ging, -mā ger, rum'mage-sale.

ru'mor, -ing, -mored.

rump, -er, -y, rump'-bone, -fed, -post, -steăk.

rum'ple, -pled, -pling, -ply.

rum'pus.

run, -ner, -nel, -ning, -ning ly, ran, run'a bout, -a way, -rig, -way.

run'-fish, -lace, -man, -out, -up.

run'ner-ball, -stick, -tac'kle.

run'ning-gear, -rein, -roll, -string, -thrush, -trap.

runch, -balls.

run'del, a moat.

run'dle, a rung of a ladder.

rund'let.

rune (rōōn), runed, rūn'er, ru-nol'o gist, -o gy, rune'crăft, -smith, -stone.

rŭng, -head.

runn, a bog.

runt, -y.

ru pee', -pa'per.

rup'ture, -tured, -tūr'ing, -ture-wort.

ru'ral, -ism, -ist, -ize, -ized, -ĭ'zing, -ly, -ness.

ru'sa-oil.

ruse (rōōz).

ru'set-of'fal.

rŭsh, -er, -ing, -y, -i ness, rushed, rush'light.

rŭsh'-bear'ing, -bot'tomed, -broom, -daf'fo dil, -grăss, -grown, -hold er, -like, -lil y, -line, -nut, -stand, -stick, -toad, rush'y-fringed.

rusk.

rusk'ie.

rŭs'sel-cord.

rŭs'set, -y.

Rus'sia (rŭsh'a), Rus'sian, -ism, -sian ize, -ized, -ĭ'zing, -si fy, -fy ing, -fĭed, -fĭ cā'tion, Rus'-so phĭle, -phĭl ism, -phĭl ist, -so-phobe, -phō'bi a, -phō'bist (*or* -sŏph'o-), Rŭs'so-Byz'an tĭne (-bĭz'- *or* -bĭ zăn'-), -Greek'.

Rus'sia braid, R. duck, R. lĕath'er, R. mat ting.
rus'sud.
rust, -ed, -ing, -ful, -y, -less, -i ly, -i ness.
rust'-ball, -col'ored, -fun gus, -joint, -mite, -proof, -red, rust'y back, - a fern, rust'y-crowned.
Rust chuk' (roost chook'), c. Bulgaria.
rŭs'tic, -al ly, -al ness, -ti cate, -cā'ted, -cā'ting, -cā'tion, -ti cize, -cized, -cī'zing, -tic'i ty, -tic ly.
rus'tle (-l), -tled (-ld), -tling, -tling ly, -tler.

rut, -ted, -ter, -ting, -tish, -tish-ness, -ty, rut'-time, rut'ting-time.
ru ta bā'ga.
Rŭt'gers (-gerz), Amer. philanthropist.
ruth (rooth), sorrow, grief, -ful, -ful ly, -less, -less ly, -less ness.
Rŭth'er ford, Scot. physician.
rut'ton-root.
ry'al (rī'-), a coin.
rye (rī), -grăss, -moth, -straw, -wolf, -worm, r. whis'ky.
rynd (rĭnd).
ry'ot (rī'-), a farmer.
rype (*or* rē'pā), a bird.
Rzesz'ow (zhĕsh'ŏv), t. Aust.

S

S brake, S chis'el, S joint, S wrench.
Saa'lĕ (sä'-), r. Ger.
Saar (sär), r. Ger.
Sá bach'thà nī (*or* sä'băk tha'nī), *Bib.*
sab'a lo.
Săb'a ŏth (*or* sá bā'-), *Bib.*
Săb'a tē'as, *Bib.*
Săb'bath, -less, -bat'ic, -ic al, -al ly, -ba tā'ıi an, -an ism, Sab'bath-breāk'er, -school.
Sab bē'us, *Bib.*
sa'be (sä'bā).
sa'bel īne (*or* -ine).
sä'ber, -ing, -bered, *sä'bre tache* (-tăsh), sa'ber bill, a bird, -tooth, a fish, -wing, a bird, -billed, -fish.
Sä'bī, *Bib.*
săb'i cu (-koo *or* -koo'), -wood.
Sä'bĭ ē, *Bib.*
Sá bine' (-bēn'), par. La.; co. and r. Tex., Sä'bine, pertaining to the ancient Sabines; mts. Europe, Sä'bīne, Amer. auth., Săb'īne, Brit. astron.
sa bi'no.
Sä'blĕ' (-blā'), t. Fr.
sä'ble, -bled, -bling, sa'ble-fish, -stoled, -vest'ed.

Sä'ble Is land, N. S.
săb lĭ ère' (-âr').
sa bot' (să'bō'), *-bo tier'* (-tyā').
sa'bŏ'tière' (-tyâr').
sa brī'na-work.
sab'u lous, -losc, -lŏs'i ty.
Sac (săk), r. Mo.; co. Ia.
sac, a pouch, *pl.* sacs, sac'ci-form, -cif'er ous, -cu lar, -cu-latē, -lā'ted, -la'tion, Sac, one of a tribe of Indians.
sac cade'.
sac cha rim'e ter, -e try, -ri met'-ric al.
sac'cha rin, *n.,* -rine, *a.,* -rĭn'ic, -rin'i ty, -rize, -rized, -rī'zing.
sac er dō'tal (săs-), -ism, -tal ist, -tal ly, -tal ize, -ized, -i'zing.
sä'chem, -dom, -ship.
sa'chet' (sá'shā'), -pow'der.
Sachs (säks), Ger. poet.
sack, -ing, -er, -ful, -less, sacked, sack'but, -pipe.
sack'-bar'row, -bear er, -cloth, -coat, -doo dle, -emp'ti er, -fil'-ter, -hoist, -hold er, -lift er, -moth, -pack er, -pos'set, -pot, -race, -tree, -winged, sack'ing-bot'tomed.
Sạ'cŏ, c. Me.

săc'ra ment, -men'tal, -tal ism, -tal ist, -tal ly, -tā'ri an, -an- ism, -men'ta ry.

să'cred, -ly, -ness.

săc'ri fice (or -fīz), n., (-fīz or -fīs), v., -ficed, -fī cing, -fī cer, -fi'cial (-fīsh'al), -cial ly, sa- crīf'ic, -ic al, -i cant, -i ca to'ry.

săc'ri lege (-lĕj), -lē'gious (-jŭs), -gious ly, -gious ness.

să'crist, sac'ris tan, -ris ty.

să'crum, pl. -cra or -crums.

săd, -den, -den ing, -dened, -ly, -ness, sad-col ored, -eyed, -faced, -heärt'ed, -i ron, -tree.

Sad dē'us, Bib.

sad'dle, -dled, -dler, -dler y, -dling, sad'dle back, -rock, an oyster, -seal'ing, -tree, frame of a saddle; a plant.

sad'dle-backed, -bag, -bar, -billed, blanket, -bōw, -brack et, -clip, -cloth, -fåst, -fĕath'ers, -flap, -gall, -girth, -gråft, -hac kle, -har ness, -hill, -hook, -horse, -joint, -leaf, -lĕath er, -nail, -nosed, -plate, -quern, -rail, -reed, -ring, -roof, -rug, -seal, -seal'ing, -shaped, -shell, -sick, -stone, sad'dler-cor'por al, -ser'- geant.

Sad'du cee, -ism, -cē'an, -du cize, -cized, -ci zing.

saeng'er bund (sĕng'er bŏŏnt), -fest.

safe, -ly, -ness, safe'-a larm', -con'duct, -de pos'it, -edged, -keep ing, -lock, -pledge.

safe'guard, -ed, -ing.

safe'ty, -arch, -beam, -belt, -bolt, -bri dle, -buoy, -cage, -car, -catch, -chain, -disk, -door, -fun nel, -fuse, -grate, -hang er, -hatch, -hoist, -hook, -ink, -lamp, -latch, -link, -lin tel, -lock, -loop, -match, -nut, -pa per, -pin, -plug, -rail, -ra zor, -rein, -stop, -strap, -strip, -switch, -tac kle, -tank, -tint, -tube, -valve, s. bī'- cy cle, s. touch-down.

săf'fi an.

săf'fron, -y, -fron wood, a tree, -cro cus, -this tle.

sag, -ging, sagged.

să'ga (or sā'-), pl. -gas (-gȧz), -man.

să gā'cious, -ly, -ness, -gac'i ty.

Săg'a da hŏc', co. Me.

sa gä'mi té' (-mē tä').

săg'a more.

sage, -ly, -ness, sā'gy, sage'wood.

sage'-ap ple, -brush, -bush, -cock, -green, -grouse, -hare, -hen, -rab- bit, -rose, -spar row, -thrash er, -tree, -wil low.

sa gĕne'.

săg'gar or -ger, săg'gar-house.

sa gil'ta, sag'it tal (săj'-), -tal ly, -tä'ry, -tate, -tä'ted.

Sag'it tä'ri us, Astron.

să'go, -palm, -plant, -spleen.

Sa gauche' (sa gwătch'), co. Col.

Sä'gua lä Grän'de (-dä), t. Cuba.

Săg'uĕ năy', r. Quebec.

să'gum, pl. -ga.

Så hä'ra, N. Afr.

să'hib (-ĭb or -hĭb or -hēb).

sä'ic.

said (sĕd).

Saï'dä, t. Syria.

sai'er (sī'er).

săi'ga, -an'te lope.

Sä'i gon (-ē-), c. China.

sail, -less, -ing, -er, a ship, -or, a mariner, sailed, sail'boat, -fish, -māk'er.

sail'-borne, -broad, -bur ton, -cloth, -clutch, -cov er, -fluke, -gang, -hook, -hoop, -liz'ard, -loft, -nee'dle, -room, -trim'mer, -wheel, -yard.

sail'ing-di rec'tions, -fish, -gang, -ice, -mås'ter, -or'ders.

sail'or man, sail'or-fish, -plant, sail'or's-choice, -purse.

säint, -dom, -ed, -ish, -ism, -like, -ly, -li ly, -li ness, -hood, -ship, saint'-seem'ing.

Saint-Bri euc' (săṅ'-brĕ'ê'), t Fr.

Saint Claude' (săṅ klōd'), t. Fr.

Såint Cloud', c. Minn.

Saint-Cloud' (săṅ'-klōō'), t. Fr.

Saint-Cyr' (săṅ'-sēr'), vil. Fr.; Fr. marshal.

Saint-Denis (săṅ'-dnē' or -dê nē'), t. Fr.; t. Réunion Isl.

Sainte-Croix' (săṅt-krwä'), vil. Switz.

---

fāte, făt, fär, fall, fâre, fåst, sofȧ, mēte, mĕt, hêr, īce, ĭn, nōte,

Sāinte Gen e vieve′ (jĕn′e vēv′), co. and tp. Mo.
Sāint Fran′çois (frän′sis), co. and tp. Mo
Saint-Fran çois′ (săṅ′-fräṅ′swä′), t. W. I.
Saint-Gau dens′ (săṅ′-gō′dŏṅ′), t. Fr.
Saint-Ger main′ (săṅ′-zhĕr′măṅ′), t. Fr.
Saint Giles′ (sĕnt jīlz′), dist. London.
Saint-Gilles′ (săṅ′-zhēl′), t. Belg.; t. Fr.
Saint Go thard′ (săṅ gō′tär′), mts. Switz.
Saint Hĕ lē′na (sĕnt), par. La.; t. Cal.; tp. S. C.; isl. Atlantic Ocean.
Saint Hy′a cinthe (sĕnt hī′a-sĭnth), c. and co. Que.
Saint Ig nace′ (sĕnt ĭg näs′), c. and tp. Mich.
Saint Jean Bap tiste′ de Mon-tre al′ (săṅ′ zhŏṅ′ bȧp′tēst′ dê mōṅ′trā′ȧl′), vil. Que.
Saint-Jean-d′An gé ly′ (săṅ′-zhŏṅ′-dŏṅ′zhā′lē′), t. Fr.
Saint-Jo a chim′ (săṅ′-zhō′ȧ′-kăṅ′), vil. Fr.
Sāint Lou′is (lōō′ĭs *or* -ĭ), co. Minn.; co. and c. Mo.; vil. Mich.; isl. S. Amer.—(săṅ′lōō′ē′), isl. and t. W. Afr.
Sāint Lu ci′a (lōō sē′a), isl. Brit. W. Indies.
Saint-Pi erre′ (săṅ′-pē′âr′), isl. Switz.; isl. off Newfoundland; ruined t. Martinique isl.; isl. Indian O.; t. Réunion isl.
sais (sīs).
saith (sĕth), from the verb *say;* sāith, a fish.
Saī′va, Sai′vism.
sä′jou (-jōō *or* -jōō′).
sä′ka.
sake.
săk′e, a liquor.
sa keen′.
sā′ker.
sāk′i eh.
Săk′ta.
sal.
sa läam′ or *-läm′.*
sa lā′cious, -ly, -ness, -lac′i ty.
săl′ad, -bur net, -fork, -oil, -plate, -rock et, -spoon, s. days.
sä lä grä′ma.
săl′al-ber ry.
Săl a măṇ′ca, tp. and vil. N. Y. —(sä lä mäṇ′kä), prov. Sp.; t. Mex.
săl′a man′der, -man′drīne, -man′-droid.
Săl′a mĭs, *Bib.*
săl′a ry, -a rĭed.
Sȧ lā′thĭ el, *Bib.*
săl′-dam′mar.
sale, -work, sāl′a ble (*or* sale′-), -ble ness, -a bly, -a bil′i ty, sales′man, -room, -wom an.
sa lee′tah.
săl′e rā′tus.
Săl′ic.
Săl′ĭ da, c. Col.
sā′li ent, -ly, -ence, -en cy.
sa′lière′ (sȧ′lyâr′).
săl′i fy, -ing, -fīed, -fī a ble, -fĭ-cā′tion.
Sa li′na (-lē′-), c. Kan.; tp. N. Y.; isl. Medit.
sā′līne (*or* sȧ līn′), -lin′i ty, sal i-nif′er ous, -i nom′e ter, -e try.
Salis′bur y (sạlz′bĕr ĭ), tp. Conn.; tp. and vil. Mass.; tp. and vil. Mo.; tp. and c. N. C.; tp. O.; tp. Pa.; c. Eng.
Salis′bur y (sạlz′bĕr ĭ), Amer. philol.; Eng. statesman.
sa lī′va, -e ject′or, -pump.
săl′i vate, -vā′ted, -vā′ting, -vȧ′-ry, -vā′tion.
Săl′lāi (*or* -lā ī), *Bib.*
săl′lee-man *or* **săl′ly-man.**
săl′lōw, -ness, -y, sal′low-kit ten, -moth, -thorn.
săl′ly, -ing, -lĭed, -ly man, -pick′-er, a bird, -port, -lunn, -wood.
salm (säm).
săl′ma gun′di.
sal′mi or *-mis* (săl′mē).
Săl′mŏn, *Bib.*
sălm′on (săm′ŭn), -et, -ing, sal-mon′ic.
salm′on-bel′ly, -ber ry, -col or, -col′ored, -dis ease′, -fish′er y,

-fish ing, -fly, -fry, -kill'er, -lad-
der, -leap, -louse, -peal *or* -peel,
-pink, -pool, -spear, -spring,
-stair, -tac'kle, -trout, -twine,
-weir.

Săl mŏ'nē, *Bib.*

Sà lŏme' (*or* -lŏ'mē), *Bib.*

så lŏn'.

Sä lŏ ni'cä *or* -kä (-nē'), vilayet
Europ. Tur.; gulf Ægean sea; c.
Macedonia.

sa lōōn', -ist, sa loon'-car, -keep er.

sa loop', -lŏ'pi an, sa loop'-bush.

sälse.

săl'si fy (-fī).

săl-sŏ'da.

sạlt, -ed, -er, -ing, -y, -i ness,
-less, -ish, -ish ly, -ish ness,
-cel'lar, -măs'ter, -wort.

sạlt'-bar row, -bear er, -block,
-box, -burned, -bush, -cake,
-cat, -cote, -du ty, -foot, -fur-
nace, -gāge, -gar den, -glaze,
-grăss, -group, -hold er, -horse,
-lick, -marsh, -mill, -mine,
-mon ey, -pan, -pit, -răk'er,
-rheum, -ris ing, -sliv ered,
-spoon, -spring, -stand, -tree,
-wa ter, *a.*, -works, salt'ing-box,
-house, -point, Salt River, s.
bot'tom, s. group, s. junk, s.
vein.

săl'tant, -tate, -tā'ted, -tā'tion,
-tà to'ry, -to'ri al, săl'to, *-tä'to.*

sạlt'ĭe, a fish.

săl tier'ra (-tyĕr'-).

Säl til'lo (-tĕl'yō), t. Mex.

sạlt pe'ter, -ing, -trous.

sa lū'bri ous, -ly, -ness, -bri ty.

săl'u ta ry, -ta ri ly, -ri ness.

sa lūte', -lūt'ed, -ing, -lu'ta to'ry,
-to ri ly, -tŏ'ri an, sal u tā'tion.

Säl'vä'dŏr', Fr. hist.

Säl'vä dŏr', rep. Cen. Amer.

săl vä'tion, Săl vä'tion ist, -tion-
ism.

săl'vē, an exclamation.

salve (säv), an ointment, salved,
salv'er, -ing, -y, salve'-bug.

salve (sălv), to save, sălved, sal'-
ving, -vage, -va ble, -ble ness,
-bly, -bil'i ty, -vor.

săl'ver, a tray, -shaped.

Säl vi'ni (-vē'nē), It. actor.

săl'vo, *pl.* -vos (-vōz), a salute;
an excuse.

Salz'burg (sälts'bŏŏrg), duchy
and c. Aust.

så mädh'.

Sà mä'ias (-yas), *Bib.*

Sä mä nä', pen. Santo Domingo.

Sa mä'ri a, -mär'i tan, -tan ism,
Sa mar'i tan co'dex, S. ver'sion.

Säm'ar känd', govt. cen. Asia.

Sä ma ve'da (-vä'-).

săme, -ness.

Sà mē'ius (-yŭs), *Bib.*

sä'mi el.

Sä'mis, *Bib.*

sam'i sen.

săm'ĭte (*or* -īt).

săm'my, -ing, -mĭed, -mi er.

Sä mŏ'ä, isl. Polynesia, -mo'an.

Sä'mŏs, island, Sä'mi an.

Săm'o thrā'ci a (-shĭ a), *Bib.*

săm'o var.

samp.

săm'pan.

săm'phĭre (*or* -fêr).

săm'ple, -pled, -pler, -pling.

sam'ple-card, -cut ter, -room,
-scale, -spig ot, sam'pling-tube.

sam'shu (-shōō) *or* -shōō.

săm'son-post.

săn'a tive, -ness, -a to ry, -to'ri-
um *or* -ĭ tā'ri um, săn'a ble, -ble-
ness, -a bil'i ty.

Sän Bue'na ven tu'ra (bwä'nä-
vĕn tōō'rä), c. Cal.

san'cho (-kō), an instrument.

Saṇ'cho (-kō), a game, S-Pē'drō.

saṇc'ti fy, -ing, -ing ly, -fīed,
-fī'ed ly, -fi er, -fĭ cā'tion, -ta-
nim'i ty.

saṇc'ti mo ny, -mŏ'ni ous, -ous ly,
-ous ness.

saṇc'tion, -ing, -a ble, -a ry,
-tioned.

saṇc'ti ty, -ti tude, -tu a ry.

saṇc'tum, *s.* saṇc tŏ'rum, saṇc'-
tus.

sand, -ed, -ing, -y, -i ness, sand'-
bag, *v.*, -fish, -hop per, an
insect, -man, -neck er, a fish,
-pa per, -peep, a bird, -pi per,
a bird, -rock, -run'ner, a bird,

---

fāte, făt, fär, fạll, fâre, fâst, sofà, mēte, mĕt, hêr, īce, ĭn, nōte,

-screw, -spout, -stay, -stone, -suck'er, a fish, -weed, -weld, -wich, -wood, -worm, -wort.

sand'-bad'ger, -bag, -ball, -band, -bank, -bäth, -bear, -bear'ings, -bed, -bee tle, -bel lows, -bird, -black'ber ry, -blåst, -blind, -blow er, -board, -box, -brake, -bug, -bur, -burned, -cå nal', -cher ry, -clam, -club, -cock, -col lar, -corn, -crab, -crack, -crick et, -crush er, -cusk, -dab, -dart, -dart er, -dīv'er, -dol lar, -dri er, -drift, -dune, -eel, -e ject'or, -fence, -flag, -flaw, -flea, -flood, -floun'der, -fluke, -fly, -gall, -gäp'er, -glåss, -gråss, -grouse, -guard, -heat, -hill, -hill er, -hold er, -hor net.

sand'-jack, -jet, -lance, -lark, -leek, -liz ard, -lot, -mar tin, -ma son, -mole, -mon'i tor, -mouse, -myr tle, -nat ter, -oys- ter, -par'tridge, -perch, -pic ture, -pi'geon, -pike, -pil lar, -pine, -pipe, -pit, -plov er, -prey, -pride, -pul'ver i zer, -pump, -rat, -reed, -reel, -ridge, -sau- cer, -scoop, -screen, -shark, -shot, -shrimp, -sift er, -skink, -skip per, -smelt, -snake, -snipe, -sole, -spur ry, -star, -storm, -swal low, -throw er, -trap, -tube, -vi per, -wash er, -wasp, -whirl, -wind.

sand'ing-plate, sand'pa per-tree, sand'wich-man, sand'y-car'pet, a moth.

sån'dal, -dåled, -dal'i form, san'- dal wood, san'dal-tree, san'dal- wood-bark.

San dål'phon, an angel in Jewish Angelology.

Sän Di e'gŏ (dē ā'-), co. and c. Cal.; t. Tex.

Sän dŏ väl' (or -dŏ'-), Sp. hist.

San'dy, a Scotsman.

sane, -ly, -ness, sån'i ty.

Sän Fe li'ce (fä lē'chä), vil. It.

Sän Fe li'pe (fä lē'pä), t. Venez.; t. Chile.

sång, did sing; sang (sŏṅ); sang (sŭng), a musical instrument.

Sãṇ'ga mŏn, co. and r. Ill.
saṇ'ga ree'.
sang-froid' (sŏṅ-frwŏ').
sän'gley.
saṇ'guĭ fy (-fĭ), -ing, -fied, -fĭ er, -fĭ cā'tion, -guic'o lous, -guif'- er ous.
saṇ'guine (-gwĭn), -less, -ly, -ness, -gui na ry, -na ri ly, -ri- ness, -guin'e ous, -guin'i ty.
San'he drin or -drim.
sån'i ta ry, -ta ri ly, -ta rist, -tä'- ri um, -tä'tion.
Sän Jo a quin' (hō ä kēn'), r. and co. Cal.
Sän Jo sé' (hō sä'), tp. and c. Cal.; isl., Gulf of Panama; isl. Gulf of Cal.; t. Cen. Amer.; dept. Uruguay.
Sän Ju an' (hōō än'), co. Col.; co. N. Mex.; co. Wash.; tp. Cal.; r. Bolivia; r. Mex.; r. Colombia; prov. Arg. Rep.; t. Puerto Rico.
sank'ha.
säṅkh'yä (sänk'yä).
Sän Lu is' Po to si' (lōō ēs' pō- tō sē'), state and c. Mex.
Sän Mä te'ŏ (-tä'-), co. and t. Cal.; mt. pass. S. Amer.
Sän Mi guel' (mē gĕl'), co. and t. Col.; co. N. Mex.; gulf of Colombia; t. and vol. Cen. Amer.; t. P. I.; Sp. gen.
sån'nup.
Sän Pē'drŏ, bay and inlet Cal.; t. Paraguay.
Sän Rä fä ĕl', tp. and t. Cal.
Sän Rŏ'que (-kä), c. Sp.
sans (sŏṅ or sänz), *sans' sou'ci'* (sŏṅ'sōō'sē').
sans'cu'lotte' (sŏṅ'kōō'lŏt' or sänz'- kū lŏt'), -lŏt'tic, -lŏt'tism, -lŏt'- tist.
Sån'skrit, -skrĭt'ic.
Sän tä Fé' (fä'), co. and t. N. Mex.; prov. and isl. Arg. Rep.
sån'tal, a plant.
Sän tän der' (-där'), prov. and c. Sp.; dept. Colombia.
sån'tee, a measure, Sän tee', r. S. C.
San te not' (sŏṅ tĕ nō').

Sän ti ä′gŏ (-tē-), r. Ecuador; isl. Cape Verde; prov. and c. Chile.

Sän ti ä′gŏ de Cu′ba (-tē- dä kōō′bä), c. Cuba.

săn′tir or -tur.

Sän′tŏ An tŏ′ni ŏ (än tŏ′nĕ-), isl. Cape Verde.

Sän′tŏ Dŏ min′gŏ (-mēn′-), east part of Haiti.

săn′tol, a tree and its fruit.

săn′ton.

Saône (sōn), r. Fr.

Sao Pau′lo (sowń pow′lō), state and c. Brazil.

sap, -less, -per, -ping, -py, -piness, sapped, sap′hĕad, a person, -skull, -suck er.

sap′-ball, -bee tle, -boil er, -bucket, -cav′i ty, -col or, -fag ot, -fork, -green, -head ed, -pine, -roll er, -rot, -shield, -spile, -spout, -suck′ing, -tube, -wood, sap′ping-ma chine′.

sa pan′-wood or săp pan′-.

Să′phir (or săf′-), *Bib.*

săp′id, -less, -ness, sa pid′i ty.

sä′pi ent, -ly, -ence, -en′tial

săp′ling, -cup, -tank′ard.

sä′pō, a toadfish. *sä′pō,* soap.

săp o nă′ceous, -nac′i ty (-năs′-), -o nä′ry

sa pŏn′i fy, -ing, -fīed, -fī′a ble, -fī cä′tion.

săp′o rous, -o ros′i ty, -o rif′ic.

Sap′phic (săf′ik).

Sap phī′ra (saf fī′-), *Bib.*

sap′phire (săf′ĭr), -phī rĭne, sap′phire wing, a bird.

Sap′pho (săf′ō), Gr. poetess, sap′pho, a bird.

săp′rŏ gen′ic, sa prŏg′e nous (-prŏj′-).

sap′sä′go.

sap′u că′ia (or -kä′ya or -kī′a), -nut, -oil.

săr′a bănd.

Săr′a cen, -ism, -cen′ic, -ic al.

Sa rä′ia (or săr′ä ī′a), *Bib.*

săr′an gous′ty (-gōōs′-).

Săr a to′ga, a trunk; a mineral water; t. N. Y.

săr′casm, -cas′tic, -tic al ly.

sär coph′a gus (-kŏf′-), *n., pl.* -gi (-jī) or -gŭs′es, -a gous, *a.,* -a gal, -a gan, -a gy (-jĭ).

sard, sar′dĭne, a precious stone sar′di us, sar′do nyx.

Sar da na pä′lus, King of Assyria; hero of Byron's tragedy.

sar dine′ (-dēn′), a fish, -tongs.

Sar dĭn′i a, isl. Medit., -din′i an.

Sar′dis, an ancient city, -di an.

sar dŏn′ic, -ic al ly.

Sar′dou′ (-dōō′), Fr. dram.

Sà re′a (or sä′-), *Bib.*

Sär gäs′sŏ, part of Atl. Oc.

sar gäs′so, gulf-weed.

sä′rĭ.

sa rigue′ (-rēg′).

sark.

sä′rŏng (or -rong′).

Sa′ros (shä′rŏsh′), co. Hung.

Sà rŏ′thĭ é (or -thĭe), *Bib.*

sar′sa pa rĭl′la.

Sar′se chim (-kĭm or -sĕ′-), *Bib.*

sarse′net.

şärt, -age.

sar′tor, -to′ri al.

sä′rus.

sash, -ing, -er y, sashed.

sash′-bar, -bor ing, -căs′ing, -chisel, -clamp, -door, -fas ten er, -fil lis ter, -frame, -gate, -lift, -line, -lock, -mold ing, -mor tising, -plăn ing, -pul ley, -rail -saw, -sluice, -stick ing, -support′er, -ten on ing, -tool, -window.

Săs katch′e wän (-kăch′-), r. and dist. Can.

sas′sa fras, -bark, -nut, -oil, -pith, -root.

sas′sy-bark.

Sä′tan, sä′tan ism, -ist, -tan′ic, -ic al, -al ly, -al ness, sä′tanshrimp.

satch′el.

săte, săt′ed, -ing.

săt een′.

săt′el lite, -de pres′sion, -line, -moth, -point, -sphinx, s. vein.

Săth′ra bū′za nĕs (-nēz or -ză′-), *Bib.*

sä′ti ate (-shĭ ate), -ā′ted, -ā′ting, -ā′tion, -tī′e ty.

săt'ĭn, -y, sat'in flow'er, -leaf, a plant, -wood, a tree.

sat'in-bird, -bush, -car pet, a moth, -cloth, -dam ask, -fin ish, -fou lard', -grac'kle, -lisse, -loom, -moth, -pa per, -sheet ing, -spar, -spar'row, -stitch, -stone, -strïped, -wave, a moth, -weave, sat'in-de-laine', sat'in ing-ma chine', săt'ĭn fĭg'ure, s. sul tan, s. Su rah, s. Turk.

sat i nē' (-nä'), a wood.

sat i net', -loom.

sat'ïre, -ï rist, -ï rism, -ï rize, -rïzed, -rï'zing, sa tïr'ic, -ic al, -al ly, -al ness.

sat'is fy, -ing, -ing ly, -fïed, -fï a ble, · -is fac'tion, -fac'to ry, -ri ly, -ri ness.

să'tive.

să'trap (or săt'-), -al, -ess, -y, să'trap-crowned.

sat'u rate, -rā'ted, -rā'ter, -rā'ting, -rå ble, -rant, -rā'tion, sat u rā'tion-e quiv'a lent, -pres'sure.

Sat'ur day.

Sat'urn, Astron., -ur nïne (or -nĭn), pertaining to the god or the planet Saturn; sat'ur nine, morose, dull; -ur nist.

Sat ur nā'li a, a Roman festival, -nä'li an.

Sa tur'ni an, Myth.

săt'yr (or să'tyr), sa tyr'ic (-tĭr'-), -ic al, sat'yr-pug.

sạu'ba-ånt.

sạuce, sauced, sau'cing, sauce'box, a person, -pan.

sauce'-a lone, a plant, -boat, -cray on, -dish, -tu reen', sauce'pan-fish.

sạu'cer, -eye, -eyed.

sau cisse' (sō'sēs'), -cis son' (-sē sŏn').

sạu'cy, -ci ly, -ci ness, sau'cy-bark.

sauer'kraut' (sour'krout').

Sạu'ger ties' (-tēz'), tp. and vil. N. Y.

Sault Sainte Ma'rie (sōō' sént mä'rĭ), tp. and c. Mich.

Sau'mur' (sō'mōōr'), t. Fr.

säun'ter, -er, -ing, -ing ly, -tered.

sạu'rel.

sạu'sage, -cut ter, -fill er, -grïnd er, -ma chine', -meat, -poi son ing, -roll, -stuff'er.

sau'ter' (sō'tä').

sau te relle' (sō'tĕ rĕl').

Sau'terne' (sō'tärn'), a wine.

săv'age, -dom, -ly, -ness, -ry, -a gism.

Sä vai'ĭ (-vï'ē), Samoan Isl.

Sa văn'na, c. Ill.; sa văn'na, a treeless plain, -black'bird, -finch, -flow'er, -spar'row, -wat'tle.

Sa van'nah, r. N. C.; c. Ga.; t. Mo.; t. Tenn.

sa vant' (sä'vŏn').

săve, saved, săv'er, -ing, -ing ly, -ing ness, săv'a ble, save'-all, săv'ings-bank.

săv'e loy.

Sä vï as (or sä'vï äs), Bib.

Sä vig ny' (-vĕn'yē'), Ger. jurist.

Sa vig'ny (-vēn'ĭ), a wine.

Săv'ior or -iour, săv'ior.

Sä vŏ nä rŏ'lä, It. reformer.

să'vor, -ing, -y, -i ly, -i ness, -less, -vored.

Sa voy', dept Fr., -voy'ard, an voy', a cabbage.

saw, -ing, -yer or -er, sawed or sawn, saw'back, a larva, -bel ly, a fish, -bill, a bird, -bones, a person, -buck, -dust, -fish, -horn, an insect, -log, -mill, -wort.

saw'-ar bor, -back, a gage, -backed, -bear ing, -bench, -block, -clamp, -doc tor, -file, -fïl ing, -fly, -frame, -gage, -gate, -gin, -grăss, -grïnd ing, -guide, -gum mer, -han dle, -hang ing, -horse, -joint er, -jump er, -likc, -man drel, -pad, -pal met'to, -pit, -sash, -set, -set ting, -sharp en er, -spin dle, -swage, -ta ble, -tem per ing, -tooth, -tooth ing, -up set'ter, -vise, -whet, -whet ter, -wrack, -wrest.

saw'dust-car'ri er, saw'ing-block, -ma chine' saw'mill-gate.

să'wä.

sax.

Saxe (săks), Fr. marshal; Amer.
poet; saxe, photograph paper.
Săxe-Co′burg-Gô′tha (-kō′burg-
gō′tä), duchy Ger.
Săxe-Mei′ning en (-mī′-), duchy
Ger.
sax′horn, sax′-tū′ba, -valve.
sax′i frăge.
Sax′on, -dom, -on′ic, -ic al, -on-
ism, -on ist, -on ize, -ized,
-ī′zing.
sax′on y, a wool, Sax′on y, Ger.,
S. blue, S. green, S. lace, S. yarn.
sax′o phone, -pho nist, -o trom′-
ba.
say, -er, -ing, said (sĕd), say′-so.
sä′ya.
săy ette′.
săy′id.
săy′nay.
săy′on.
sbir′rŏ, *pl.* -ri (-rē).
scab, -bed, -bed ness, -bing, -by,
-bi ly, -bi ness, scabbed, sca′-
bi ous, *sca′bi es* (-ēz), scab′-
wort, -fuṇ′gus, -mite.
scăb′bard, -fish, -plane.
scab′ble, -bled, -bler, -bling, scab′-
bling-ham′mer.
scă′brous, -ness.
Scä′er′ (-âr′), t. Fr.
scăf.
scăff′-net, -raff.
scăf′fold, -age, -ing, scaf′fold-
brack et, scaf′fold ing-pole.
scagl′ia (skăl′ya), -io′la (-yō′la).
sca lăr′i form.
scăl′a wag.
scạld, -ed, -er, -ing, scald′ber ry,
-fish, -weed, -head.
scăld *or* skăld (*or* skạld *or* shäld),
a Scandinavian poet, -ic.
scal di′no (skăl‾dē′nŏ).
scale, -less, scăl′a ble, -er, -ing,
-y, -i ness, scaled, scale′back, a
worm, -fish, -foot, a fish, -tail, an
animal, -work, -worm.
scale′-backed, -bĕam, -beâr er,
-board, -bor er, -bug, -carp,
-de gree′, -dove, -drake, -duck,
-fĕath′er, -fern, -fish,‾ -ground,
-hair, -in sect, -louse, -mī-
crom′e ter, -moss, -pat′tern, *a.*

-pĭ pette′, -quail, -shell, -stone,
-winged, s. ar mor, s. pat tern, *n.*
scăl′ing-bar, -fur nace, -ham mer,
-knife, -lad der, -ma chine′,
scăl y-winged.
scâ lĕne′, -le′nous, -le′num.
scạll, scalled.
scăl′lion (-yŭn).
scal′lop (skŏl′lup), -loped, -lop er,
-ing.
scal′lop-crab, -moth, -net, -shell,
scal′loped-ha zel,   a   moth,
-hook tip, a moth, -oak, a moth,
scal′lop ing-tool.
scălp, -er, -ing, -less, scalped,
scalp′-lock, scalp′ing-ī′ron, -knife,
-tuft.
scăl′pel, -pel′li form.
scal pel′lum, -pel′lar.
scam′mo ny.
scămp, -ish, -y.
scăm‾pä vi′a (-vĕ′a).
scăm′per, -er, -ing, -pered.
scan, -ning, -sion, scanned.
scăn′dal, -ize, -ized, -ī′zer, -I zā′-
tion, -ous, -ous ly, -ous ness,
scan′dal-bear′er, -moṇ′ger.
scăn′dent, scan so′ri al.
Scăn′dĭ nă′vi a,   Sweden   and
Norway, -vi an, Scan di an.
scan′di um, -dic.
scănt, -ed, -ing, -y, -i ly, -i ness,
-ly, -ness.
scant′ling.
scape, -less, -ment, scape′gal-
lows, a person, -goat, a person,
-grace, a person, -wheel.
Sca pin′ (skă păṅ′), a ballet in
Molière's comedy.
scap′net.
scap′pling-ham mer.
scap′u la, *pl.* -læ *or* -las, -lar,
-lâ′ry.
scar, -less, -ring, -ry, scarred, scar′-
lime′stone.
Scăr′a mouch *or* scar′.
Scär′bor ough (-bŭr rŏ), t. Eng.
scârce, -ly, -ment, -ness, scâr′-
ci ty.
scare, scared, scâr′ing, -y, scare′-
babe, -crow.
scarf, *pl.* scarfs, scarfed, scarf′ing,
scarf′wise.

scarf'-bolt, -joint, -loom, -pin, -ring, -skin, -weld, scarf'ing-frame, -ma chine'.

scăr'i fy, -ing, -fïed, -fï cā'tor, -cā'tion.

scar la ti'na (-tē'-), -ti'nal, -ti'-ni form, -ti'noid, -ti'nous.

scar'let, -seed, a tree, -let-faced, -ti ger, a moth, s. sage, a flower.

scarp, scarped, scar'pĭnes.

Scärpe, r. Fr.

Scär rŏń', Fr. comic writer.

scăt, -ted, -ting.

scatch.

scāťhe, -less, scāth'ing, -ing ly, scāthed.

scat'ter, -er, -ing, -ing ly, -tered, -tered ly, -ter y, -ter ā'tion, scat'ter brain, a person, -good, a person, -brained.

scąup, -duck.

scaup'er.

scaur'le or -y.

scăv'age, -ry, -a ging, -enge, -enged, -en ging, -en ger, -ger-ing, -ger ism, scav'en ger-bee'-tle, -crab, -roll.

sceat (skēt).

scelp (skĕlp).

sce măn'dŏ (shĕ-).

sce'na (sē'na or shā'-).

see na'ri o (shā nä'rē ō).

scene, scēn'er y, scĕn'ic (or sē'-), -ic al, -al ly, scĕn'o grăph, -graph'ic, -ic al, -al ly, scē nog'-ra phy.

scene'-dock, -man, -paint er, -plot, -shift'er, scen'er y-groove.

scent, -ed, -ing, -ful, -less, scent'-wood.

scent'-bag, -bot tle, -box, -gland, -hold er, -or gan, -pore, -vase, -ves'i cle.

scep'ter (sĕp'ter), -less, -tered, -tral.

scep'tic (skĕp'-). See skeptic.

Scē'va (sē'-), Bib.

Schäaf, Ger. orient.

schab'zie'ger (shäp'tsē'ger), a cheese.

Schaff hau'sen (shäf how'zĕn), canton Switz.

Schaght'i coke (skăt'ĭ kŏŏk), vil. N. Y.

schäl.

schăn'zĕs.

schäp'ska.

Schar'lăch ber'ger, a wine.

Scharz'ber ger (shärts'-), a wine, Scharz'hŏf ber'ger, a wine.

Schäss'burg (shĕs'bŏŏrg), t. Hung.

schät'chen (shet'shĕn or -chen).

Schaum'burg-Lĭp'pĕ (shoum'-bŏŏrg-), prin. Ger.

Schaum'-earth (shoum'-).

Schäv'li (-lē), t. Russ.

sched'ule (skĕd'-), -uled, -ūl ing.

Sche he re zä'de, Queen (shä-hă'rā zä'dä), a marvelous story-teller.

Scheï'dĕck, mt. Switz.

Scheldt (skĕlt), r. Holland.

schel'ly (shĕl'-), a fish.

scheme (skēm), -ful, schemed, schem'ing, -ing ly, -er, -ist, -y, sche mat'ic, -ic al ly, -ma tism, -ma tist, -ma tize, -tized, -tī'-zing.

Schem'nitz (shĕm'-), t. Hung.

Schenck (skĕnk), Amer. states-man.

schene (skēn).

Sche nĕc'ta dy (ske-), co. and c. N. Y.

Schenk'el (shĕnk'el), Ger. theol.

sche'pen (skä'-).

Schĕ rer', Fr. critic.

Scher'zer (shĕrt'ser), Ger. trav.

scher'zo (skĕr'tsō), scher zan'do (-tsän'dō).

sche'sis (skē'-), schĕt'ic (skĕt'-).

Sche'vĕn ĭn'gen (skä'-), watering place, Holland.

schia vo'ne (skyä vō'nĕ).

Schie'däm' (skē'-), t. Holland; a kind of gin.

Schie'vel bein (shē'fĕl bīn'), t. Prus.

Schil'ler (shĭl'-), Ger. poet.

schil'ler (shĭl'-), -ite, -ler ize, -ized, -ī'zing, -ī zā'tion, schil'-ler-spar.

Schi'ŏ (skē'-), t. It.

schism (sĭzm), schis mat'ic (sĭz-), -ic al, -al ly, -al ness.

schis'ma (skĭs'- or skĭz'-), pl. -mȧ tä, schis'tic (skĭs'-).

schist (shĭst), -ic, -ous, schis-tōse', -tos'i ty.
schis'to scope (skĭs'-).
Schklov (shklŏv), t. Russ.
schlä'ger (shlä'-).
Schlan (shlän), t. Bohem.
Schlä'we (shlä'vĕ), t. Prus.
Schle'gĕl (shlä'-), Ger. critic.
Schlei'er mach'er (shlī'er mach'-er), Ger. theol. and philos.
Schleiz (shlīts), t. Ger.
Schles'wĭg (shlĕs'-), t. Wis.
Schley (shlĭ), co. Ga.
Schliĕ'männ, Ger. archæol.
schmel'ze (shmĕl'tsĕ).
schnapps (shnăps *or* shnäps).
Schnee'bĕrg (shnä'-), t. Ger.
Schnei'de mühl' (shnī'dĕ mül'), t. Prus.
schnŏr'rer.
Scho däck' (skō-), tp. N. Y.
Scho här'Ie (skō-), co. and tp. N. Y.
schŏl'ar, -ly, -ship, schō las'tic, -tic al ly, -ti cism.
schŏ'li um, *pl.* -li a *or* -li ums, -li ast, -as'tic.
Schöm'bĕrg (shêm'berch), t. Aust.
Schön'beIn (shên'-), Ger. chem.
Schön'brunn (shên'broŏn), pal. Vienna.
Schö'ne feld (shĕ'nĕ fĕlt'), vil. and commune Ger.
Schön'heI dĕ (shên'-), vil. Ger.
Schö'nĭng en (shĕ'-), t. Ger.
school (skoōl), -a ble, -ing, schooled, school'boy, -cräft, -fel'-low, -girl, -house, -ma'am, -maid, -man, -mås ter, -mate, -mis'tress, -room, a room.
school'-book, -bred, -dame, -days, -fee, -fish, -fund, -in spect'or, -miss, -mon'ey, -name, -pence, -ship, -taught, -teach er, -time, -whale.
school' board, s. com mis'sion er, s. com mit'tee, s. dis trict, s. doc tor, s. the ol'o gy.
schoon'er (skoōn'-), -rigged, -smack, -yacht.
schorl, -ous, -y.
Scho'ter land (skō'ter länt), tp. Neth.

schot tische' (-tĕsh' *or* shŏt'-tĕsh).
Schou'ler (skoō'-), Amer. hist.
schout (skout).
Schou'wen (skou'ven), isl. off Neth.
Schrĕck'horn, mt. Switz.
Schroep'pel (skroō'-), tp. N. Y.
Schroon Lake (skroōn), N. Y.
Schu'ja (shoō'yä), t. Russ.
Schultz (shoŏlts), tp. S. C.
Schul'ze (shoŏlt'sĕ), Ger. poet.
Schu'mach er (shoō'mäch er), Danish astron.
Schu'männ (shoō'-), Ger. com-poser.
Schurz (shoŏrts), Ger.-Amer. statesman.
Schut'ten hŏ'fen (shoōt'-), t. Aust.
Schuy'ler (skī'-), co. Ill.; co. Mo.; co. N. Y.; c. Neb.; Amer. dipl.; Amer. gen.
Schuyl'kill (skoōl'-), co. and r. Pa.
Schwab (shväp), Ger. poet.
Schwalm (shvälm), r. Ger.
Schwartz (shvarts), Swed. novelist.
Schwarz (shvarts), Ger. monk.
Schwat'ka (shwŏt'), Amer. ex-plorer.
Schwein'furth (shvīn'foŏrt), Ger. trav.
Schwei'nitz, von (fon shwī'nits), Amer. botanist.
Schwenk'feld (shvĕnk'fĕlt), Sile-sian reform., -feld'er, -feld'i an.
Schwe rin' (shvä rēn'), t. Ger.
Schwyz (shvīts), canton Switz.
Schyll (shēl), r. Hung.
Sciac'ca (shäk'kä), t. It.
scī'a grâph (sī'-), -graph'ic, -ic al, -al ly, -ag'ra pher, -ra phy.
scī a ther'ic, -al, -al ly.
scī ăt'ic, -al, -al ly, -i ca.
scĭb'i le.
Scic'li (shĕk'lē), t. It.
scī'ence, -en'tial, -en ti'cian (-tĭsh'an), -en tif'ic, -ic al ly, -en tism, -en tist, -tis'tic, -en'-to lism.
Scigl'io (shēl'yō), headland Sic.
Scil'la (sĭl'-).

scĭm′i tar. See *simitar*.
Sci na′ (shē nä′), Sicilian math.
scin til′la, scin′til lant, -til late,
-lä′ted, -lä′ting, -lä′tion, -lom′-
e ter, -*lan′te* (shĕn′til lăn′tä).
Scĭ′ŏ (sĭ′-), tp. Mich.;—(sĭ′ŏ *or*
shē′ō) isl. Ægean sea.
sci o grăph (skĭ′-). See *skiagraph*.
scĭ′ŏ lĭsm, (sĭ′-), -o list, -listic,
-o lous.
sciol′tō (shŏl′-).
scĭ′o man cy, -man′tic.
sci′on (sĭ′-).
Sci op′pi us (stsē ŏp′pē ŏŏs), Ger.
schol.
scĭ ŏp′tic (sĭ-), -tics, -tric, -ti con.
sci′o the ism′.
Scĭ ŏ′tŏ (sĭ-), r. and co. O.
Scip′Ĭ ŏ (sĭp′-), tp. N. Y.
scĭ′rē fā′ci as (-shĭ as).
sci ren′ga.
scir′rhus (sĭr′rŭs *or* skĭr′-), *n.*,
-rhoŭs, *a.*, -rhoid.
scis′sel (sĭs′-), scis′si ble, scis′-
sĭle, scis′sion (sĭsh′un).
scis′sor (sĭz′zur), -ing, -sored,
-sors, -sor wise.
scis′sor bill, a bird, -tail, a bird,
-bird, -tailed, -tooth, -sors-
grīnd′er.
scis′sure (sĭsh′-).
Scit′u ate (sĭt′-), vil. Mass.
sclăff.
sclĕ′ra (sklĕ′-), -ral, -*rĭ′a sis*,
-*rĭ′tis*, -*rō′sis*, -rō′tal, -rŏt′ic,
-rŏt′o my.
scobs.
scŏff, -er, -er y, -ing, -ing ly,
scoffed.
scŏld, -ed, -er, -ing, -ing ly.
scō′lĭ on, pl. -*li a*.
scŏnce, sconced, scon′cing, -cheon
(-shŭn).
scŏne.
Scone (skōōn), parish Scot.
scoop, -er, -ing, scooped, scoop′-
net, -shov′el, -wheel.
scoot (skōōt), -ed, -er, -ing.
scŏ′pa, pl. -*pæ*.
scōpe, -less.
scō pe tin′ (-tăn′).
scŏp′tic.
scor bū′tus, -bū′tic, -tic al, -al ly.

scorch, -er, -ing, -ing ly, -ing-
ness, scorched, scorched′-car-
pet, a moth, -wing, a moth.
scor dä′to, -dä tu′ra (-tōō′-).
Scor di′a (-dē′-), t. Sic.
score, scored, scor′er, -ing, scor′-
ing-en gine, -ma chine′, -sheet.
scō′ri a, pl. -*æ*, -ā′ceous, -ri fy,
-fy ing, -fīed, -fī er, -fī cā′tion.
scorn, -er, -ing, -ful, -ful ly,
-ful ness, scorned.
scor′per.
scor′pi on, -wort.
scor′pi on-broom, -bug, -dag-
ger, -fish, -fly, -grăss, -lob-
ster, -oil, -plant, -sen na,
-shell, -spi′der, -thorn, scor′-
pi on′s-tail.
Scotch, -man, Scot′tish, -ti cism,
-ti cize, -cized, -cĭ′zing, -ti fy,
-fy ing, -fīed, -fī cā′tion, Scots′-
man.
Scotch′-am′u let, a moth, -cap,
a berry, -and-Eŋ glish, a game.
scotch, a scratch; a prop; to
notch; to check, scotched,
scotch′ing, -man, a wrapping
as a protection, scotch′-col′lops,
-hop, Scotch-I′rish.
scōte.
scot-free.
Scŏ′ti a (-shĭ-), a poetic name
of Scotland, *scō′ti a*, a molding.
scot′o grăph, *scō tō′ma*, scŏt′o my.
scoun′drel, -dom, -ism, -ly.
scour, -age, -er, -ing, scoured.
scour′ing-ball, -bar rel, -ba sin,
-drops, -ma chine′, -rush,
-stock, -ta′ble.
scourge (skurj), scourged, scoûr′-
ging, scourge′-stick.
scout, -ed, -er, -ing, -ing ly,
scout′măs′ter.
scove, scoved, scŏv′ing.
scov′el (skŭv′l).
scow, -house.
scowl, -ing, -ing ly, scowled.
scrab′ble, -bled, -bler, -bling.
scrag, -ged, -ged ness, -gy, -gi ly,
-gi ness, -gly, scrag′-necked,
-whale.
scram′ble, -bled, -bler, -bling,
-bling ly.

scrap, -per, -py, -pi ness, -ping, scrapped.

scrap'-book, -cake, -cheese, -cinders, -for ging, -heap, -house, -i ron, -met al, scrap'ping-machine.

scrape, scraped, scrăp'er, -ing, -ing ly.

scrape'-good, -pen ny, scrăp'er-bar, -ma chine', scrăp'ing-ground, -plane.

scrap'ire.

scrap'ple.

scratch, -er, -ing, -ing ly, -y, scratched, scratch'back, -weed, -work, s. shot.

scratch'-awl, -brush, -coat, -com ma, -cra dle, -fig ure, -fin ish, -gage, -grăss, -pan, -play'er, -wig, scratch'er-up.

scrawl, -er, -ing, -y, scrawled.

scraw'ny, -ni ness.

screak (skrēk), -ing, screaked.

scrĕam, -er, -ing, -ing ly, screamed.

screech, -er, -ing, -y, screeched.

screech'-cock, -hawk, -mar tin, -owl, -thrush.

screed (skrēd), -coat.

screen, -er, -ing, -ings, screened, screen'ing-ma chine'.

Screv'en (skrĭv'-), co. Ga.

screw (skrōō), -a ble, -er, -ing, -y, screwed, screw'man, -stone.

screw'-al ley, -au ger, -bean, -bell, -blank, -blast, -bolt, -box, -burn er, -cal i per, -cap, -clamp, -col lar, -coup ling, -cut, -cut ter, -cut'ting, -die, -dock, -dog, -dol lar, -drĭv'er, -el'e va tor, -eye, -feed, -fish, -for ceps, -găge, -gear, -head, -hoist, -hook, -jack, -joint, -key.

screw-lock, -ma chine, -mak ing, -man drel, -med al, -mold ing, -nail, -neck, -pile, -pil lar, -pin, -pine, -plate, -pod, -post, -press, -punch, -quoin, -rod, -shac kle, -shell, -spike, -stem, -stock, -ta ble, -tap, -thread, -thread'ing, -tool, -tree, -tunnel, -valve, -ven'ti la tor, -well, -wheel, -wire, -worm, -wrench, screwed'-work.

screw'ing-en'gine, -ma chine', -stock, -ta ble.

screw' pro pel'ler, s. rud der, s. stair, s. steam'er, s. ven'ti la tor.

Scrĭ'ba, vil. N. Y.

scrib'ble, -bled, -bler, -bling, -bling ly, -blage.

scrib'ble-scrab ble, scrib'bling-en'gine, -ma chine'.

Scribe (skrēb), Fr. dram.

scrībe, scribed, scrīb'er, -ing, -ism, scribe'-awl.

scrĭb'ing-awl, -block, -com pass, -i ron.

scrim.

scrīme, scrimed, scrīm'ing.

scrim'mage.

scrimp, -ing, -ing ly, -ness, -ly, -y, scrimped, scrimp'-rail, scrimp'-ing-bar.

scrip, -com'pa ny, -hold'er.

scrip'ee.

script, scrip'tion, -ti'tious (-tĭsh'-us), -tor, -to ry, -tō'ri um, *pl.* -ri ums *or* -ri a.

scrip'ture, -tūr al, -al ism, -al-ist, -al ly, -al ness, -ist, -ture-wort. The Scrip'tures. Scrip'-ture-read'er.

scrī vel'lo.

scrĭv'en er (*or* skrĭv'ner), -ship.

scrod, -ded, -ding, scrod'gill.

scrōf'u la, -u lit'ic, -u lous, -lous-ly, -lous ness.

scrŏg, -gy.

scrōll, -ing, scroll'work, scrolled.

scrōll'-bone, -chuck, -fī'nis, -gear, -head, -lăthe, -saw, -seal, -wheel.

scrō'tum, pl. *-ta,* -tal, -ti form, -to-cele.

scrouge, scrouged, scrou'ger, -ging.

scrow (*or* skrō).

scrub, -bed, -ber, -bing, -by, scrubbed, scrub'stone, -wood, a tree.

scrub'-bird, -box wood, -broom, -cat tle, -gang, -grăss, -oak, -pine, -rĭd'er, -rob in, -tur key.

scrub'bing-board, -brush, -machine'.

scru'ple, -pled, -pler, -pling.

scru'pu lous, -ly, -ness, -los'i ty.
scru'tin' de liste' (skrōō'tăn' dê
lēst').
scru'ti nize, -nized, -nī'zer, -nī'-
zing, -nous, -nous ly, -ny,
-neer', scru tā'tor.
scud, -ded, -der, -ding, scud'-
ding-stone.
scu'do (skōō'-), a coin, *pl. -di* (-dē).
scuff, -ing, -y, scuffed.
scuf'fle, -fled, -fling, -fler, scuf'-
fle-har row, -hoe.
scull, -er, -ing, sculled.
Scul la bogue' (skŏŏl a bōg'), vil.
Ireland.
scul'ler y.
scul'lion (-yŭn).
sculp, *n.*, sculp'ing-knife.
sculp'sit.
sculp'tor, -tress, -ture, -tūr al,
-tūr ing, -tūr esque', -tured,
ture-cop'i er.
scum, -mer, -ming, -my, scummed.
scum'ble, -bled, -bling.
scun, -ner, -ning, scunned.
scup, -ping, scupped.
scŭp paug'.
scŭp'per, -hole, -hose, -lĕath er,
-nail, -plug, -shoot, -tube, -valve.
Scŭp'per nŏng', tp. N. C.
scup'per nong, a grape.
scûrf, -er, -y, -i ness.
scŭr'ril ous, -ly, -ness, -ril *or*
-rīle, -ril'i ty.
scŭr'ry, -ing, -rīed.
scûr'vy, -vi ly, -vi ness, scur'vy-
grăss.
scŭ'tage.
Scu'tä ri (skōō'tä rē), t. Turk.
scutch, -er, -ing, scutched,
scutch-blade, -grăss.
scutch'ing-ma chine', -mill,
-shâft, -stock, -sword.
scutch'eon (-ŭn), -eoned (-und).
scûte.
scŭ tĕl'lum, pl. *-la,* scŭ'tel lar,
-tel līne, -ti form, -tif'er ous.
scut'tle, -tled, -tler, -tling, scut'-
tle fish, -tle-butt, -căsk.
scŭ'tum, pl. *-ta,* -tu lum.
Scyl'la, *Myth.*
scyph'u la (sĭf'-).
scy'tal (sī'-), scyt'a līne (sĭt'-).

scythe (sīth), -man, scythe'-fas'-
ten ing, -snăth, -stone, -whet.
Scyth'i a (sĭth'-), ancient kingdom,
-i an, -ic.
sde gno'so (sdä nyō'sō).
sea, -ber ry, -board, -coast,
-fâr'er, -fâr'ing, -go ing, -man,
-port, -scape, -shore, -sick,
-sick ness, -side, -ward, -ware,
-way, -weed, -wor thy, -wor'-
thi ness.
sea'-a corn, -ad der, -an chor,
-a nem'o ne, -ăn gel, -ape, -ap-
ple, -a pron, -ăr row, -ash,
-as păr'a gus, -bank, -bar, -bar-
ley, -bar row, -băs ket, -băss,
-bat, -bean, -beâr, -beard,
-beast, -beat en, -bea ver, -beet,
-bells, -belt, -bent, -bīnd weed,
-bird, -bis cuit, -blub ber,
-boat, -bor der ing, -born,
-borne, -bot tle, -bound, -bōw,
-brant, -brēach, -brēam, -breeze,
-brièf, -bris tle, -buck'thorn,
-bug, -built, -bum'ble bee, -bun,
-bur dock, -but ter fly.
sea'-cab bage, -cac tus, -călf,
-ca na'ry, -cap, -cap taĭn, -car-
na'tion, -cat, -cat'er pil lar, -cat-
fish, -cau'li flow er, -cen'ti ped,
-change, -chart, -chest nut,
-chick'weed, -clam, -cloth, -cob,
-cock, -cock roach, -co'coa nut,
-col'an der, -cole'wort, -com-
pass, -cook, -coot, -cor'mo rant,
-corn, -cow, -crab, -crăft,
-craw fish, -crawl er, -crow,
-cu'cum ber, -cud weed, -cun-
ny, -cush ion.
sea'-dace, -daf'fo dil, -dai sy,
-dev'il, -dog, -dot ter el, -dove,
-drag on, -drake, -duck, -ea gle,
-ear, -eel, -egg, -el e phant,
-e riŋ'go, -fan, -fĕath'er, -fen-
nel, -fern, -fight, -fir, -fire,
-fish, -flea, -flī er, -flow er,
-foam, -fog, -folk, -fowl, -fox,
-front, -froth, -fur'be low, -gâge,
-gas ket, -gates, -gher kin
(-ger'-), -gil'li flow er (-jil'-),
-gin ger, -gir dle, -girt, -god,
-god dess, -goose, -goose foot,
-gōurd, -gown, -grape, -grăss,

nŏt, nôr, ūse, ŭp, ûrn, etüde, fōōd, fŏŏt, aŋger, boṅmot, thus, Bach.

33

-green, -gud'geon, -gull, -hair, -hang'er, -hare, -hawk, -heath, -hedge hog, -hen, -hog, -hol'ly, -hōlm (*or* -hōm), -hon'ey comb, -horse, -hound, -is land, -jel ly.

sea'-kale, -kelp, -kemp, -kid ney, -king, -kit tie, -lace, -lam'- prey, -lark, -lav en der, -law yer, -leech, -legs, -lem on, -len'til, -lĕop ard, -let ter, -let tuce, -lev el, -light, -lil y, -line, -li on, -liz'ard, -long'worm, -louse, -luce, -lungs, -lung'- wort, -mag'pie, -măll, -mal low, -man tis, -marge, -mark, -mat, -mat'weed, -mel on, -mew, -mile, -milk'wort, -mink, -monk, -mon ster, -mouse, -mud, -mus sel.

sea'-neck'lace, -nee dle, -nest, -net tle, -nurse, -nymph, -oak, -on ion, -ooze, -or ange, -orb, -ot ter, -owl, -ox, -ox'eye, -packed, -pad, -pan ther, -par- rot, -pars nip, -par tridge, -păss, -pay, -pea, -peach, -peâr, -pen, -perch, -pert, -pheas'ant, -pie, -piece, -pig, -pi'geon, -pike, -pi lot, -pim'- per nel, -pin cush ion, -pink, -plant, -plan taĭn, -plov er, -poach er, -pŏk er, -pool, -pop py, -por'cu pine, -pork, -po ta'to, -pud ding, -pump kin, -purse, -purs lane, -pye, -quail.

sea'-rad ish, -rag wort, -rat, -ra ven, -reach, -reed, -reeve, -risk, -rob ber, -rob in, -rock et, -rod, -roll, -room, -rose, -rose'ma ry, -rŏv er, -ruff, -ruf fle, -run, -run ning, -sălm'- on, -salt, -sand wort, -saُu'ri an, -scor'pi on, -scurf, -sedge, -ser'- pent, -serv ice, -shark, -shell, -shrimp, -shrub, -skim mer, -slāt'er, -sleeve, -slug, -snail, -snake, -snipe, -spi der, -spleen'- wort, -squid, -squirt, -stăff, -star, -star wort, -stick, -stic kle back, -stock, -straw ber ry, -sun flow er, -sur geon, -swal low, -swine.

sea'-tang, -taŋ'gle, -tench, -term,

-thong, -thorn, -thrift, -tit'- ling, -toad, -tor toise, -tossed, -trout, -trum'pet, -turn, -tur tle, -um brel'la, -u'ni corn, -ur'chin, -vam pire, -view, -wall, -wand, -wa ter, -wax, -whip, -whip cord, -whip lash, -whis tle, -wife, -wil low, -wĭnd, -wing, -with'wĭnd, -wōld, -wolf, -wood'cock, -wood'louse, -worm, -worm'- wood, -worn, -wrack.

sea'man, -ly, -ship, sea'man gun'ner.

sē'ah.

sĕal, -er, -ing, sealed, seal'wort, seal'-bag, -en grāv'ing, -flow er, -hook, -lock, -pipe, -press, -ring, seal'ing-press, -wax.

sĕal, a marine animal, -er, -er y, -ing, seal'skin, -bird, -brown, -club, -fish'er y, -lance, -rook'- er y.

seam, to unite with a seam, -er, -less, -y, seamed, seam'stress.

seam'-blast, -ham'mer, -lace, -press'er, -rent, -roll'er, -rub'- ber, -set, seam'ing-lace, -ma chine', -tool.

sé ance' (sā'ŏns').

sean'na chie (sĕn'na shĭ *or* -chē *or* -kĭ).

sĕar, -er, -ing, -ness, seared, seared'ness, sear'-spring, sear'- ing-i ron.

sĕarch, -a ble, -a ble ness, -er, -er ship, -ing, -ing ly, -ing ness, -less, searched, search'-light, -par ty, -war rant.

Sĕar'cy, co. and t. Ark.

sĕa'son (-zn), -a ble, -a ble ness, -a bly, -al, -al ly, -er, -ing, -less, -soned, sea'son ing-tub.

seat, -ed, -er, -ing, seat'-back, -earth, -fas'ten er, -lock, -rail, -stand, -stone, -worm.

Sĕ ăt'tle, c. Wash.

sĕave.

sĕ bā'ceous, se bip'a rous, -bif'er ous.

Sĕb'as tō'pŏl (*or* sĕ băs'-) *or* Sĕv'as tō'pŏl, t. Russ.

sĕ'cant, -can cy.

Sec'chi (sĕk'kē), It. astron.
Sĕc'chi a (sĕk'kē ä), r. It.
sē cede', -cēd'ed, -er, -ing.
se ces'sion, -ism, -ist.
Sĕch'e nī'as (sĕk'-), Bib.
sĕck'el.
sē clūde', -clūd'ed, -ed ly, -ed-
ness, -clu'sion (-zhŭn), -sion-
ist, -sive (-sĭv).
sec'ohm (sĕk'ōm), -ohm me'ter.
sĕc'ond (-ŭnd), -ed, -er, -ing,
-â'ry, -a ri ly, -a ri ness, -ly,
se conde' (sĕk ŏnd'), sē cŏn'do.
sĕc'ond-ad'vent ist, -clăss, a.,
-cut, -hand, -mark, -rate, a.,
-sight'ed, sec'onds-pen'du lum.
sē'cret, -age, -ly, -ness, sē'cre cy,
se crē'ta.
sĕc're tâ'ry, -ship, -tâire', -tā'ri-
al, -ri ate, sec're ta ry-bird.
sē crēte', -crēt'ed, -ing, -ive, -ive-
ly, -ive ness, cre'tion, crc'tor,
-to ry.
sect, sec tā'ri al, -tā'ri an, -an-
ism, -an ize, -ized, -ī'zing, -ta ry.
sec'tant.
sĕc'tĭle, -til'i ty.
sec'tion, -al, -al ism, -al ist,
-al ly, -al ize, -ized, -ī'zing,
-ī zā'tion, sec'tion ize, -ized,
-ī'zing.
sec'tion-beam, -cut ter, -līn'er,
-plane.
sec'tor, -tor al, -tō'ri al, sec'tor-
cyl'in der, -gear, -wheel.
sĕc'u lar, -ism, -ist, -ly, -ness,
-ize, -ized, -ī'zing, -ī zā'tion,
-lăr'i ty.
sec'u lum, pl. -la.
se cure', -ly, -ment, -ness, -cured',
-cūr'a ble, -ance, -er, -ing, -cu'-
ri ty.
sed.
Sĕ dan' (-dŏn'), t. Fr.
sē dăn', -chair.
sē dâte', -ly, -ness, -dā'tion,
sĕd'a tive.
Sĕd'e cī'as (-sī'-), Bib.
sed'en ta ry, -ta ri ly, -ri ness,
sē'dent.
sĕdge, sedged, sedg'y, sedge-bird,
-flat, -hen, -ma rine', -war bler,
-wren.

sē dī'lē, pl. -dĭl'i a.
sĕd'i ment, -men'tal, -men'ta ry,
-tā'tion, sed'i ment-col lect'or.
sē di'tion (-dĭsh'un), -â'ry, -tious,
-tious ly, -tious ness.
sē duce', -ment, -duced', -du'cer,
-dū'ci ble or -duce'a ble, -du'-
cing, -cing ly, -duc'tion, -tive,
-tive ly, -tive ness.
sed'u lous, -ness, sē dū'li ty.
see, -a ble, -ing, saw, seen, see'-
catch, -cawk, see'-bright.
seed, -ed, -er, -ing, -ful, -y,
-i ness, -less, -ling, seeds'man.
seed'-bag, -băs'ket, -bed, -bird,
-box, -bud, -cake, -coat, -ccd,
-cŏ ral, -corn, -crush er, -down,
-drill, -eat er, -em broid'er y,
-field, -finch, -fish, -gall, -gar-
den, -grain, -lac, -leaf, -leap,
-lip, -lobe, -oil, -oys ter, -pearl,
-plant er, -plat, -plot, -sheet,
-sōw er, -stalk, -tick, -time, -ves-
sel, -wee vil, -wool, seed' ing-
ma chine', -plow, seed'y-toe.
seek, -er, -ing, sought, seek'-no-
fur'ther, an apple.
seel, to blind; to lean, -ing, seeled.
seem, -er, -ing, -ing ly, -ing ness,
-ly, -li ly, -li ness.
seen.
seep, -age, -ing, -y, seeped.
seer, a prophet, -ess, -ship, sē'er,
one who sees.
seer, sure; a weight.
seer'fish, -paw, -suck'er.
see'saw, -ing, -sawed.
seethe, seethed, seeth'er, -ing.
see'tul pŭt'ty, a mat.
Seez (sā), t. Fr.
seg'ment, -al (or -men'tal), -al ly,
-â'ry, -ed, -men tā'tion.
seg'ment-gear, -rack, -saw, -shell,
-valve, -wheel.
se'gno (sān'yō).
Se'gre (sā'grā), r. Sp.
seg're gate, -gā'ted, -gā'ting, -gā'-
tive, -gā'tion.
se'gue (sā'gwā), seg ui dil'la (sĕg-
ĭ dēl'ya).
Se guin' (sà gĕn'), t. Tex.;—
(sē găn'), Fr. physician—(sā'-
gwĭn), Eng. singer.

seiche or *seiches* (sāsh).
se'id (sā'ĭd *or* sēd).
Seid'litz pow'der (sĕd'lĭts).
seign'ior (sēn'yur), -age, -al ty,
-y, -io'ri al.
Sei'länd, isl. off Norway.
Seim (sām) *or* Sĕm, r. Russ.
Seine (sān), r. Fr.
seine (sān *or* sēn), seined, sein'er,
-ing.
seine'-boat, -cap tain, -crew, -en-
gine, -fish er, -gang, -ground,
-haul er, -man, -nee dle, -roll-
er, sein'ing-ground.
Sē'ir (-êr), *Bib.*
Sē'ĭ răth (*or* sē ĭ'-), *Bib.*
seis'mal (sīs'-), seis'mic *or* -mot'ic,
-mic al, -mism, -mo gram, -mo-
grăph, -mog'ra pher, -ra phy,
-mo graph'ic, -ic al, -mŏl'o gy,
-o gist, -mo logue, -mo log'ic al,
-al ly, -mom'e ter, -e try, -mo-
met'ric, -ric al, -mo scope, -scŏp'-
ic.
Seis'tän' (sās'-), region Persia.
sĕize, seized, sĕiz'a ble, -er, -ing,
-or, sēi'zure (sē'zhûr *or* -zhŏŏr),
seiz'ing-stuff, sēi'zin *or* -sin (-zĭn),
sēi'zor The last two are law
terms.
Sē'la ham mäh'lĕ kŏth (*or* -lĕ'-),
Bib.
Se län'gän' (sā'-), t. P. I.
sel'dom (-dŭm).
sĕ lect', -ed, -ed ly, -ing, -ive,
-ive ly, -ness, -or, -lec'tion, select'man.
Sĕ lĕ'nĕ, *Myth.*
sĕ lĕ'nŏ grăph, -graph ic, -ic al,
-nog'ra pher, -ra phist, -ra phy,
-nŏl'o gy, -o gist, -no log'ic al.
Se leŭ'ci a (-shi a), *Bib.*
self, -ish, -ish ly, -ish ness, -less,
-less ness, -hood, -same, -same-
ness. Most words beginning with
self are written as hyphenated
compounds. The above are the
principal exceptions.
sell, -a ble, -er, -ing, sold.
Selles-sur-Cher' (sĕl'-sür-shâr'), t.
Fr.
sĕl'văge *or* -vĕdge, -vaged, -va-
ging, -va gee'.

Sĕ mā'iah (-ya *or* sĕm'ă ĭ'ah), *Bib.*
sĕm'a phore, -phŏr'ist, -phŏr'ic,
-ic al, -al ly.
sĕ mă sĭ ol'o gy, -o log'ic al.
sĕm'a sphere.
se măt'ic.
sĕm a tol'o gy.
sĕm'a trŏpe.
sem'blance, -blant.
se mĕ' (sĕ mā').
Sĕm'ē lē, *Myth.*
se mĕs'ter, -mes'tral.
sem'i. Most words beginning with
semi are written without the hyphen. The principal exceptions
are here given: Sem'i-Au'-
gus tin'i an ism, -A'ri an, -A'ri
an ism, -Pe lā'gi an, -Pe lā'gi-
an ism, -Qui'et ist, -Qui'et ism,
-Sax'on, -Chris'tian ized.
sem'i co lon-but'ter fly.
sĕm'i nal, -ly, -nal'i ty, -nā'tion,
-nif'er ous, -nif'ic, -i nist.
sĕm'i na ry, -na'rist, -nā'ri an.
Sĕm'i noles.
sĕ mĭ ŏl'o gy, -o log'ic, -ic al,
-mi og'ra phy, -mi ot'ic, -ics.
Se mĭr'a mis, wife of Ninus.
Sometimes applied to Margaret,
Queen of Denmark, and to Cath-
arine II, Empress of Russia.
sĕ'mis.
sĕm'ĭte, -i tism, -i tist, -i tize,
-tized, -tĭ'zing, -tĭ zā'tion, sĕ-
mĭt'ic.
Sĕm'li ki (-lĕ kĕ'), r. Afr.
Semmes (sĕmz), Confederate naval
officer.
sĕm'per ĭ'dem.
sĕm pi ter'nal, -ter'ni ty.
sĕm pli'ce (-plĕ'chä).
sĕn, a coin.
Sĕ nā'ah (*or* sĕn'-), *Bib.*
se nal' (sā nyäl').
se nă ri us, pl. *-rĭ ĭ.*
sen'ate, -a tor, -tor ship, -tō'ri al,
-al ly, -tō'ri an, sen'ate-cham'-
ber, -house.
send, -er, -ing, sent, send'-off.
sen'dä (sän'-).
Sĕn'e ca, -oil, -ca's mi'cro scope,
sĕn'e ca-grass.
Sĕn'e găl', r. Afr.

se nes'cence, -nes'cent.
sen'e schăl (-e shăl *or* -es shăl *or* -es kăl), -schal ship.
Se nhor'. See *Señor.*
sĕ'nĭle (*or* -nĭl), -nĭl'i ty.
sĕn'ior (-yur), -ior'i ty.
Sĕn'jen (-yĕn), isl. off Norway.
Sen lis' (sŏń'lēs'), t. Fr.
senn, a herdsman.
sĕn'na, -tree.
Sen năch'e rĭb (-năk' *or* -kē'-), *Bib.*
sĕn'net, a fish.
sĕn'night (-nĭt), a week.
sĕn'nĭt, plaited cordage or grass.
Se ñor' (sā nyôr'), Spanish for Mr. or Sir; fem. *Se ño'ra* (sā nyō'-ra); *Se ño ri'ta* (sā nyō rē'ta), equivalent for Miss. In Portuguese, *Se nhor'* (sā nyôr'), fem. *-nhō'ra* (-nyō'ra). In Italian, *Si gnor'* (sē nyôr'), fem. *Si-gnō'ra* (sē nyō'rä); for Miss, *si-gno ri'na* (-rē'na). These words are capitalized only when used as a title.
se ño ri'ta (sā nyō rē'ta), a fish.
sĕn'sate, -sā'tion, -tion al, -al-ism, -al ist, -is'tic, -al ly, -a ry, -tion ism.
sense, -less, -less ly, -less ness.
sense'-bod y, -cap'sule, -cav'i ty, -cell, -cen ter, -el'e ment, -ep-i thē'li um, -fil'a ment, -im-pres'sion, -or gan, -per cep'tion, -rhythm, -se ta, -skel'e ton.
sen'si ble, -ness, -bly, -bil'i ty, -sif'er ous, -sif'ic, -sif'i ca to'ry.
sen'si tive, -ly, -ness, -tiv'i ty, sen'sĭle, sen'sion, sens'ism, -ist, sen'si tive-plant.
sen'si tize, -tized, -tī'zer, -tī'-zing, -si to'ry, -si tom'e ter, -tĭ-zā'tion.
sen'sor, -so ri mo'tor, -so'ri al, -rī'o-lum, -ri um, *pl.* -ri ums *or* -ri a, -ry.
sen'su al (-shōō-), -ism, -al ist, -is'tic, -al'i ty, -al ize, -ized, -ī'zing, -ĭ zā'tion, -al ly, -al-ness, -su ous, -ous ly, -ous-ness, -su os'i ty.
sen'tence, -tenced, -ten cer, -cing, -ten'tial, -tial ly, -ten'tious, -tious-

ly, -tious ness, -ten'ti a ry (-shĭ-), -ti ā'ri an.
sen'ti ence (-shĭ ens *or* -shēns), -ti ent (-shĭ-), -ent ly.
sen'ti ment, -men'tal, -tal ism, -tal ist, -tal ize, -ized, -ī'zer, -ī'zing, -tal ly, -tal'i ty.
sĕn'ti nel, -neled *or* -nelled, -nel ing *or* -ling, sen'ti nel-crab.
sĕn'try, -board, -box, -go.
Sĕ nū'ah (*or* sĕn'-), *Bib.*
Sĕ ō'rim, *Bib.*
Se oul' (sā ōōl'), c. Korea.
sep'al (*or* sē'-), sep'aled, -al ĭne, -al o'dy (*or* se păl'-), -a lous.
sep'a rate, -ly, -ness, -ra'ted, -ra'ting, -rā ble, -ble ness, -bly, -bil'i ty, -rā'tion, -tion ist, -rā-tism, -ra'tist, -ra'tive, -ra'tor, -to'ry, -ra'trix, -ră'tum, *pl.* -ta.
sep'a ra'ting-disk, -fun nel, -sieve, -weir.
Se'phar, *Bib.*
Sĕph'a răd, *Bib.*
Sĕph'ar vă'im, *Bib.*
Sĕ'phar vītes (*or* -fär'-), *Bib.*
Sĕ phē'la, *Bib.*
sĕ'pi a, sĕ'pic.
sĕ'poy.
sĕp'sis, sep'tic, -tic al, -al ly, -ti-ce'mi a, -cē'mic.
sept, a clan, sep'tal.
sep'tan.
sep'tan gle, -tan'gu lar.
Sep tem'ber, -ism, -bral, -brist.
sep tem'vir, *pl.* -virs *or* -vĭ rī, -vĭ-rate.
sep'te nă'ry, -te nate, *Bot.,* having seven parts. -ten'nate, seven years, -ten'ni al, -al ly, -ten'ni um.
sep ten'trĭ on al, -ly, -al'i ty.
sep tet'.
sep til'lion (-yŭn).
sep'time (-tēm).
Sept-Isles' (sĕt'-ēl'), isls. Fr.
sep tŭ ag'e na ry (-ăj'-), -e nā'-ri an.
sep'tŭ a ges'i ma (-jes'-), -i mal.
Sep'tŭ a gint, -gin'tal.
sĕp'tum, pl. *-ta.*
sep'tu ple, -pled, -pling, -plet.
sep'ul cher (-ker), -ing, -chered,

se pul'chral, -pul'tu ral, sep'ul-
ture.
sĕ quä'cious (-shŭs), -ly, -ness,
-quac'i ty (-kwăs'-).
sē'quel.
sē'quence, -quent, -quen'tial,
-tial ly, -ti al'i ty (-shĬ-), *quen'-*
ti a.
se ques'ter, -ing, -tered, -tral,
-tra ble, -trate, -trä'ted, -trä'-
ting, -ques trot'o my, seq'ues-
trä'tor (sĕk'wes-), -trä'tion, *se-*
ques'trum, pl. -tra.
Se quil'lo (sä kēl'yō), r. Sp.
sĕr, a weight.
sé rac' (sä răk').
se ragl'io (sē räl'yō *or* sä räl'yō).
sĕ rä'ĭ.
Sĕ rä'iah (-ya *or* sĕr'ä ĭ'), *Bib.*
sē răng'.
se rä'pe (sä rä'pä).
sĕr'aph, Eng. *pl.* ser'aphs; Heb.,
sĕr'a phim, se raph'ic, -ic al,
-al ly, -al ness, sĕr'a phim-moth.
Sē rä'pis, Myth., -rä'pic.
se ras'kier, -at *or* -ate.
Se reg'no (sä rĕn'yō), t. It.
se rein' (sĕ răń').
sĕr'e nä̆de', -nä̆d'ed, -nä̆d'er,
-nä̆d'ing, -nä̆'ta.
sĕ rēne', -ly, -ness, -ren'i tude,
-i ty.
Sē rē'nō a.
Sĕr'ĕs, t. Turk.
Se'reth' (sä'rĕt'), r. Roum.; ' t.
Aust.
sĕrf, -age, -dom, -hood, -ism.
sĕrge, ser gette', serge'-blue.
ser'geant (sär'jĕnt), -cy, -ry,
-ship, ser'geant-fish, -ma jor,
-at-arms.
Sĕr ghi ĕvsk' (-gē-), t. Russ.
Ser gi'pe (sär zhē'pä), state Braz.
sĕ'ri al, -ly, -al'i ty, -ate, -ate ly,
-ä'tim, -ä'tion.
Sĕr'ic.
se ri'ceous (-rĬsh'us), sĕr'i cul'-
ture, -tūr ist, -tūr al.
sē'ries (-rēz *or* -rĭ ēz).
sĕr'if. See *ceriph.*
sĕr'in, -i nette', sĕr'in-finch.
sē'rĭ ŏ-cŏm'ic, -cŏm'ic al, -cŏm'-
ic al ly.

se rĭ'o la.
sē'ri ous, -ly, -ness, *-ri ŏ'sō.*
ser moc i nä'tion (-mŏs'-).
ser'mon, -er, -eer', -et', -ist, -ize,
-ized, -ĭ'zer, -ĭ'zing.
se roon'.
ser'o ther'a py (*or* sē'rō-).
se'roŭs, -ros'i ty.
ser'pent, -pen tĬne (*or* -tĬn),
-tine ly, -tĬn'ic, -tin ize', -ized,
-ĭ'zing, ser'pent fence, s. wood.
ser'pent-boat, -charm er, -cu'-
cum ber, -de'i ty, -ea gle, -eat-
er, -fish, -god, -grăss, -like,
-liz ard, -moss, -poi'son, -star,
-stone, -tur tle, -wĭthe, -ser'-
pent's-tongue, Ser'pent-bear'er.
ser pette'.
Sĕr pu khov' (-pōō kŏv'), t. Russ.
ser'ra, pl. -rœ.
ser rä'no (*or* -rä'-).
sĕr'rate, -rä'ted, -rä'tion.
Ser rä vez'za (sär rä vĕt'sä), t. It.
sĕr'rĭed.
se'rum.
serv'ant, -girl, -maid, -man,
serv'ant's call.
serve, served, serv'er, -ing, -Ĭce,
-ice able, -ble ness, -a bly, -a-
bil'i ty.
serv'ice-ber'ry, -book, -box,
-clean er, -cock, -line, -mag a-
zine', -pipe, -stop, -tree.
serv'ing-board, -maid, -mal let,
-man.
Ser ve'tian.
serv'Ĭle, -ly, -ness, -i tor, -tor-
ship, -i tude, ser vil'i ty.
ser'vo-mo'tor.
sĕs'a mĕ, -a mĬne, -a moid,
-moid'al, ses'a me-oil.
Sĕs'el ĭ.
se'si (sä'sē).
Sē sŏs'tris, King of Egypt.
ses'quĭ cen ten'ni al.
ses'qui pĕ dä'li an, -ism, -dal'-
i ty.
sĕs'sĬle, -eyed.
ses'sion (sĕsh'un), -al, ses'sion-
clerk.
ses'terce, *pl.* -ter ces (-sēz),
-ter'ti us (-shĬ us), pl. *-ter'tĭ ĭ*
(-shĬ ĭ), *-ti um,* pl. *-ti a.*

fāte, fă̆t, fär, fa̧ll, fâre, fȧst, sofȧ, mēte, mĕt, hêr, īce, Ĭn, nōte,

ses'tet (*or* -tet'), -*tet'to*, -ti'na
(-tĕ'-).
Set or *Seth*, Myth.
set, -ness, -ter, -ting, set'back.
set'-bolt, -down, -fair, -foil,
-gun, -ham mer, -in, -net, -off,
-out, -pin, -pot, -ring, -screw,
-stitched, -to, -trap, -up, -work.
set'ter, -wort, -grǎss.
set'ting-back, -board, -box,
-cir cle, -coat, -dog, -fid, -gage,
-ma chine', -nee dle, -pole,
-punch, -rule, -stick, -sun, a
mollusk.
sĕ'ta, pl. -*tæ*, -tā'ceous (-shŭs),
-ceous ly, se'tal, -tā'ri ous, -tif'-
er ous, -ti form, -tose.
Sĕt'e bos, Shak., *The Tempest.*
sĕ'ton, -nee dle.
set tee'.
set'tle, -ment, tled, -tlcd ncss,
-tler, -tling, set'tle-bed, set'-
tling-day.
sev'en (-n), -teen', -teenth', -en-
ty, -ti eth, sev'en eyes, -fold,
-gills a shark, -holes, a fish,
-night, sev'en-gilled, -point,
-shoot er, -spot ted, -thir ty,
-up, sev'enth-chord.
sĕv'er, -a ble, -ance, -er, -ing,
-ered.
sev'er al, -ly, -al ty.
sĕ vēre', -ly, -ness, -vĕr'i ty.
Sĕ vĕ'rus, Roman emperor.
Sĕ viĕr', co. Ark.; co. Tenn.;
co. Utah.—(sē-), Amer. pioneer.
Sĕ vig nĕ' (sā'vēn'yā'), Fr. writer.
Sĕv'ĭlle (*or* sĕ vĭl'), prov. and c.
Sp.
Sèvres (sāvr), t. Fr.
sew (sō), -er, -ing, sewed.
sew'ing-bench (sō'ing-), -bird,
-cir cle, -clamp, -cot ton, -horse,
-ma chine', -ma te'ri als, -nee-
dle, -press, -school, -silk,
-ta ble.
sew'age (sū'-), -aged, -a ging,
-er, -er age, -er man.
sew'age-fuṇ gus, -grǎss, sew'er-
ba sin, -gas, -hunt'er, -rat,
-trap.
Sew'ard (sū'-), co. Kan.; co. and
c. Neb.

Sew'ard (sū'-), Amer. statesman;
Eng. authoress.
Se wick'ley, t. Pa.
sex, -less, -less ness, sexed.
sex ag'e na ry (-ăj'-), -nā'ri an.
sex'a gene (-jēn), -a ges'i mal,
-mal ly, -a gesm.
Sex a ges'i ma.
sex'aṇ'gle, -gled, -aṇ'gu lar, -lar-
ly.
sex cen'te na ry.
sex en'ni al, -ly.
sex par'tite.
sex'tan.
sex'tans, a coin, *Sex'tans*, Astron.
sex'tant, -al.
sex ten'ni al.
sex tet'.
sex til'lion (-yŭn).
sex'tŏ, -to dec'i mo.
sex'ton, -ship, sex'ton-bee'tle.
sex'tu ple, -pled, -plct, -plex,
-pling.
sex'u al, -ly, -al ist, -al ize, -ized,
-ī'zing, -ĭ zā'tion, -al'i ty.
Sey chelles' (sā'shĕl'), isls.
Indian Oc.
Sey'mour (sē'mur), c. Ind.; vil.
Ct.—(sē'mōr), Jane, Queen of
Henry VIII; Horatio, Amer.
statesman.
Seyne (sān), t. Fr.
Sĕ zanne' (sā'zăn'), t. Fr.
Sĕz'za (sĕt'sä), t. It.
sfor zan'do (sfôr tsän'dō), -zä'to.
sfre gaz'zi (sfrĕ gät'sĭ), sfu mä'tō
(sfoo-), sgräf fi'to (-fē'tō).
Sgă'nă'relle (răl'), hero in
Molière's comedy.
Sgj ĕrsht' (sgĕ ĕrsht'), t. Pol.
Shă'a ră'im, *Bib.*
Shăb'be thăi (*or* -bĕth'ā ĭ), *Bib.*
shab'by, -bi ly, -bi ness, shab'by-
gen teel'.
shab'rack.
Shă chī'a (-kĭ'- *or* shăk'ĭ a), *Bib.*
shack, -ing, shacked, shack'bag,
a person.
shack'-bait, -bolt, -fish'er man,
-fish ing, -lock.
shac'kle, -kled, -kling, -kly.
shac'kle-bar, -bolt, -bone, -crow,
-flap, -jack, -joint, -pin, -punch.

shad, -Ine (*or* -ēn), shad'bel'ly,
-bird, -bush, a plant.
shad'-bel lied, -blos som, -fly,
.-frog, -hatch er, -salm on,
-seine, -spir it, -splash, -trout,
-wait er, -wash, -work ing.
Shăd'dăi (*or* -dā ī), *Bib.*
shade, -ful, -less, shăd'ed, -ing,
-y, -i ly, -i ness, shade'fish,
-hook, -tree, shăd'ing-pen.
sha dooſ'.
shăd'ŏw, -ing, -ish, -less, -y,
-grăph, -owed.
shăd'ow-bird, -fig ure, -stitch,
-test, -vane.
Shā'drach (-drăk), *Bib.*
shâft, -ed, -ing.
shâft'-al ley, -bear ing, -bend er,
-coup'ling, -drill, -eye, -fur-
nace, -horse, -jack, -line, -loop,
-mon'ture, -pipe, -spot,
-straight'en er, -stripe, -tac kle,
-tip, -tug, -tun nel, shaft'ing-
box, -hang er.
shag, -ged, -ged ness, -ging, -gy,
-gi ly, -gi ness, -ling, shag'-
bark, a tree, shag'-dog, -eared,
-haired.
shag a nap'py.
Shā'ge (-gē), *Bib.*
sha green', a leather, -greened'.
shah (shä).
sha heen'.
shä'hi.
Shah'ja han pur' (shä'jä hän-
pōōr'), dist. India.
Shäh'pur' (-pōōr'), dist. India.
shâirl.
shaī'län or *sheī'-.*
shake, shook, shāk'en, shāk'er,
-ing, -y, -i ly, -i ness.
shake'-bag, -down, -fork, -up,
-wil ly.
shāk'ing-frame, -ma chine', -shoe,
-ta ble.
Shāk'er, -er ess, -er ism, Shāk'-
ing-Quāk'er.
shăk'ŏ.
Shāk'speare *or* Shake'-, -spear'-
i an, -an ism, -spear ize, -ized,
-ī'zing, -I ā'na.
shăk'u dŏ'.
shäl, a fish.

shale, shaled, shāl'ing, -y, shale'-
oil.·
shăll, should, shalt.
shăl'lĪ. See *challis.*
shal loon'.
shal'lop.
shal'lŏw, -ing, -ling, -ly, -ness,
-lowed, shal'low-brained, -heart-
ed, -păt'ed, -waist'ed.
Shăl'măi (*or* -mā ī), *Bib.*
Shăl ma nĕ'ser (-zer), *Bib.*
sha lot'.
sham, -mer, -ming, shammed.
sham'ble, -bled, -bling.
shame, -ful, -ful ness, -less, -less-
ly, -less ness, shăm'er, -ing,
shamed, shame'faced, -faced ly,
-faced ness, -flow'er, shame'-
proof, -reel.
Shā'med, *Bib.*
Shăm'măi (*or* -mā ī), *Bib.*
sham'my. See *chamois.*
shăm'oy (-oi *or* -my), to dress as
leather.
shăm pōō', -er, -ing, -pooed'.
sham'rock, -pea.
Shăm'she răi (*or* -rā'ī), *Bib.*
shăn'dry, -dry dan, -da ra dan.
shăn'dy gaff.
Shăng hä'Ī (*or* -hī'), c. China,
shang haī', a fowl, -haī'ing,
-haied'.
Shäng'-I-Yu en' (-ē-yōō'ĕn'), t.
China.
Shäng'tung (-tōōng'), prov. China.
shănk, -er, -ing, shanked.
shank'-cut ter, -i ron, -last'er,
-paint'er, -shell, -spring, -wheel.
sha'n't, shall not.
shăn'ty, -man.
shape, -less, -less ness, -ly, -li
ness, shāp'a ble, -er, -ing,
shaped, shape'smith.
shăp'er-plate, -vise, shăp'ing-
ma chine'.
shăps.
Shā'răi (*or* shăr'ā ī), *Bib.*
Shà rā'im (*or* shăr'à Ĭm), *Bib.*
shard, -ed, -y, shard'-bee'tle.
shâre, shared, shâr'er, -ing, share'-
hold er, -wort, shares'man.
share'-beam, -bone, -bro'ker, -line,
-list.

---

shark, -er, -ing, shark'-moth,
-mouthed, -oil, -ray, shark's-
mouth.
Shâr'on, vil. Ct.; tp. N. Y.; tp.
N. C.; tp. O.; bor. Pa.
sharp, -er, -ling, -ly, -ness, -y, -en
(-n), -ened, -en er, -en ing,
sharp'fin, a fish, -nails, a fish,
-shoot er, -tail, a bird, sharp'-
ce dar, -cut, -eyed, -ground,
-head ed, -look'ing, -nosed,
-saw, a saw sharpener, -shinned,
-shod, -sight ed, -tailed, -vis-
aged, -wit ted.
Shā'shāi (or shăsh'ā i), Bib.
Shäs'tä, mt. and co. Cal.
shas'ter or -tra.
shăt'ter, -ing, -y, -tered, shat'ter-
brain, a person, -brained, -păt'ed.
Shā'ul (or shaul), Bib.
Shā'ul ītes (or shaul'), Bib.
shä'u ri' (-ōō rē').
shave, -ling, shaved, shāv'er, -ing,
-en, shave'weed, shave'-grass,
-hook.
shāv'ing-ba sin, -brush, -cup,
-horse, -ma chine, -tub, shav'-
ings-con duc'tor.
shąw, -fowl.
Shä wą'nō, co. Wis.
shąwl, -loom, -man tle, -ma te'-
ri al, -pat tern, -pin, -strap,
-waist'coat.
shawm.
shă'yăk.
shā'ya-root.
she, -oak, -pine, -sole.
shē'a, -but ter, -tree.
shēad'ing.
shēaf, pl. sheaves, sheaf'y, sheaf'-
bind'er.
Shē'al, Bib.
Shē ăl'tǐ el, Bib.
shēar, -er, -ing, -ling, sheared,
shorn, shear'bill, a bird, -hog, a
sheep, -man, -tail, a bird; a moth,
-wa ter, a bird.
shēar'-grass, -hooks, -legs, -steel,
-struc'ture, shear'ing-ma chine',
-stress, -ta ble.
Shē'a rī'ah, Bib.
Shē'ar-jā'shub, Bib.
shears, -moth.

shēat, -fish.
shēath, -y, sheath'bill, a bird, -claw,
a lizard, -fish, sheath'-billed,
-knife, -winged.
shēathe, sheathed, shēath'er, -ing,
sheath'ing-nail, -pa'per.
shēave, sheaved, shēav'ing, sheave'-
hole.
shē bang'.
shĕb'bel.
shē been'.
She boy'gan, co. Wis.
Shē'chem (-kĕm), Bib., -ītes.
shed, -der, -ding, shed'-line, -roof,
shed'ding-mo'tion.
Shee chail'lin (-kā'-), mt. Scot.
sheen, -y.
sheep, -ish, -ish ly, -ish ness, -y,
shep'py.
sheep'ber ry, a tree, -fold, -head,
a fish, -man, -măs ter, -skin,
-walk, sheeps'head, a person; a
fish, sheeps'wool, a sponge.
sheep'-backs, -bīt'ing, -bot, -cote,
-dip, -dip ping, -dog, -faced,
-farm er, -head ed, -hold er,
-hook, -lau rel, -louse, -mar-
ket, -pen, -pest, -pick, -plant,
-poi son, -pox, -rack, -range,
-rot, -run, -shank, -shear'er,
-shears, -sil ver, -sor rel, -split,
-sta tion, -steal er, -tick, -walk-
er, -wash, -whis tling, -worn.
sheep's-bane, -beard, -bit, -eye,
-fes'cue, -foot, -pars ley, -sil-
ver.
sheer, -ing, -ly, sheered, sheers, a
hoisting apparatus.
sheer'-bat ten, -hooks, -hulk,
-lash ing, -leg, -mold, -pole,
-strake, Sheer Thurs'day.
Sheer nĕss', t. Eng.
shee'shĕh.
sheet, -ed, -ing.
sheet'-an̓chor, -bend, -ca ble,
-cal'en der, -de liv'er y, -met al,
a., -min'er al, -pile, -work,
sheet'ing-ma chine', -pile.
sheet' cop'per, s. glass, s. i'ron, s.
lead, s. light'ning, s. met al, n.
shēik.
shĕk'ĕl.
Shē kī'nah or -chī'-, -kī'nal.

sheld, -ap'ple, a bird, sheld'-fowl.
shel'drake, shel'duck.
shĕlf, *pl.* shelves, shelf'y.
Shĕl'iff' (-ēf'), r. Alg.
She'li kŏf (shā'lē-), strait Alas.
shell, *v.*, -er, -ing, shelled.
shell, *n.*, -y, shell'back, a sailor,
-bark, a tree, -flow er, a plant,
-head, an insect, -man, -work.
shell'-ap ple, -au ger, -bank,
-bit, -blow, -board, -boat, -box,
-crack'er, -crest, -dove, -eat'er,
-fire, -fish, -flow'er, made of
shells; -fol'li cle, -gage, -gland,
-grīnd'er, -gun, -heap, -hook,
-i'bis, -ice, -jack'et, -less, -lime,
-lime'stone, -mar ble, -marl,
-meat, -mound, -or'na ment,
-par'ra keet, -par'rot, -proof.
-pump, -quail, -re du'cer, -room,
-sac, -sand, -snail, -worm, s.
but'ton, s. cam'e o, s. keep, s.
road.
shel'lac (*or* -lac'), -lacked, -lack-
ing.
Shĕl'ley, Eng. poet.
shel'ter, -er, -ing, -less, -tered,
shel'ter tent.
shelve, shelved, shelv'er, -ing, -y.
Shem, -īte, -Ĭ tish, -Ĭ tism, -Ĭt'ic.
shĕ mä'.
Shē mä'ah (*or* shĕm'ä ah), *Bib.*
Shē mä'iah (-ya *or* shĕm'ä ĭ'ah),
Bib.
Shĕm ē'ber (*or* shĕm'-), *Bib.*
Shē'mer, *Bib.*
Shē mĭr'a mŏth, *Bib.*
Shĕm'ŭ el (*or* shē mū'-), *Bib.*
Shē nä'zar, *Bib.*
Shē'ōl, she o'lic.
shĕp'herd (-erd), -ed, -ing, -ess,
-ish.
shep'herd-bird, -dog, -spi'der.
shep'herd's-bag, -club, -cress, -joy,
-knot, -myr'tle, -nee'dle, -pouch,
-purse, -rod, -stäff.
sher'bet, -bet lee, -bet zīde.
shĕr if' (-ēf' *or* shĕr'Ĭf) *or* shĕr'-
eef *or* cher if' (shĕr ēf'), a descendant from Mohammed.
shĕr'Ĭff, an officer, -al ty, -dom,
-hood, -ship, -wick, sher'iff-clerk,
-of'fi cer.

she ris'ta där'.
sher'ry, -val'lies, s. cob'bler.
Shē'shāi, *Bib.*
Shesh bäz'zar, *Bib.*
shē'sōle.
Shē'thar-bŏz'nāi (*or* -bŏz'nā ĭ),
Bib.
Shet'land, isls. N. Atlantic, S. lace,
S. po'ny, S. wool.
Shey enne' (shī ĕn'), r. N. Dak.
Shi'ah (shē'ä).
Shĭ'a was'see (-wŏs'-), r. and co.
Mich.
shĭb'bo leth.
Shĭc'ron (*or* shĭ'-), *Bib.*
shiēld, -ed, -er, -ing, -less, -less-
ly, -less ness, shield'tail, a
snake.
shield'-an i mal'cule, -backed,
-bear ing, -bee tle, -belt, -bone,
-brooch, -bud ding, -bug, -cen'-
ti ped, -crab, -dag ger, -drake,
-duck, -fern, -gilled, -head ed,
-lan tern, -louse, -plate, -rep-
tile, -shaped, -ship, -slāt'er, -toad,
-ur chin.
shī'er, -est. See *shy.*
shift, -a ble, -ed, -er, -ing, -ing-
ly, -y, -i ness, -less, -less ly,
-less ness, shift-joint, shift'er-bar,
shift'ing-boards, shift'ing back'-
stay, s. bar, s. cen'ter, s. clause.
Shig gā'ion (-yon), *Bib.*
Shĭg'Ĭ ŏ'nŏth (*or* shĭ gī'-), *Bib.*
shi'ism (shē'-).
shĭ kär', shĭk'rḍ.
shĭ kä'ree or -kä'ri (-rē).
shĭk'ō.
shĭl lä'lah.
shĭl'ling.
shĭl'ly-shal'ly.
Shī'lōh, tp. S. C.
Shī'lō nīte (*or* shĭ lō'-). *Bib.*
shĭm, a wedge; a plow; to wedge,
-ming, shimmed, shim'-plow.
shĭm'mer, -ing.
Shī'mon, *Bib.*
Shĭm'shāi (*or* -shā ĭ), *Bib.*
shin, -ning, shinned, shin'dig, shin'-
leaf, a plant, -plas ter, shin'-
bone, -boot, -piece, -tan'gle.
Shī'nar, *Bib.*
shin'dy.

---

fāte, făt, fär, fạll, fâre, fâst, sofá, mēte, mĕt, hêr, īce, Ĭn, nōte,

shine, shōne (*or* shŏn), shīn′er, -ing, -y.

shǐng.

shǐn′gle, -gled, -gler, -gling, -gly, shin′gle wood, a tree.

shǐn′ gle-joint′ing, -ma chine′, -mill, -nail, -oak, -plăn′ing, -rĭv′-ing, -roofed, -saw, -trap, -tree.

shǐn′gling-brack′et, -gage, -ham′-mer, -hatch′et, -mill, -tongs.

Shin′to, -ism, -ist.

shin′ty an *or* -ti yan.

ship, -fŭl, -per, -ping, -less, -ment, -shape, shipped, ship′-board, -man, -măs ter, -mate, -way, -wreck, -wrecked, -wreck-ing, -wright, -yard.

ship′-bis cuit, -board, a plank, -boat, -bor er, -borne, -boy, -break er, -bro′ker, -build er, -ca nal, -cap tain, -car′pen ter, -carv′er, -chan dler, -chan′-dler y, -de liv′er er, -fe ver, -hold er, -jack, -keep er, -let-ter, -load, -mon ey, -own er, -pen′du lum, -plate, -pound, -pro pel′ler, -rail way, -rigged, -scrăp er, -stay′er, -stores, -sur′-vey, -worm, -writ, S. Com mis′-sion er.

ship′ping-a gent, -ar′ti cles, -bill, -clerk, -măs′ter, -note, -of′fice.

Shī′phī (*or* ʒhĭf′ī), *Bib.*

ship pō′.

Shī′räz (shē′-), c. Persia.—(-räz′ *or* shē′-), a wine.

Shī′ré (shē′rā), r. Afr.

shire (shēr *or* shīr), -man, shire′-clerk, -day, -ground, -host, -land, -moot, -town.

shirk, -er, -ing, -y, shirked.

shirr, -ing, shirred, shirr′ing-string.

shirt, -ing, -less, shirt′but ton, a plant, -tail.

shirt′-bos′om, -but ton, a button, -col lar, -frame, -frill, -front, -măk er, -sleeve, -store, -waist.

Shī′shăk, *Bib.*

shit′tim-wood.

shiv′er, -ing, -ing y, -y, -ered, shiv′er-spar.

shi zō′ku (shē zō′kŏŏ).

shōal, -er, -ing, -y, -i ness, -wise, -brain, shoaled, shoal′-a larm′, -duck, -in′di ca tor, -mark.

Shŏ′băi (*or* -bā ī), *Bib.*

shŏck, -er, -ing, -ing ly, -ing-ness, shocked, shock′-dog, -head, -head′ed.

shŏd. See *shoe.*

shŏd′dy, -ism, shod′dy-ma chine′, -mill.

shōde, shŏd′ed, -er, -ing, shode′-pit, -stone.

shō′der.

shoe (shōō), -less, shoe′ing, sho′er, shod.

shoe′beak, a bird, -bill, a bird, -black, -flow er, -măk′er, -măk′-ing, -pack.

shoe′-billed, -black′ing, -block, -bolt, -boy, -brush, -buc kle, -but ton, -dis tend′er, -em boss′-ing, -eye′let ting, -fas′ten er, -ham mer, -heel, -horn, -jack, -key, -knife, -lace, -latch et, -lĕath′er, -pad, -peg, -pock′et, -rose, -sew ing, -shave, -sole, -stir rup, -stone, -strap, -stretch′-er, -string, -thread, -tie, -valve, -work er.

shoe′black-plant, shoe′ing-ham-mer, -horn, shoe′măk er′s-bark, shoes-and-stock ings, a plant.

sho′gun, -al, -ate.

shole.

shōlt.

shōne. See *shine.*

shōō, -ing, shooed.

shōōd, chaff; husks.

shōōk. See *shake.*

shōōt, -er, -ing, -a ble, shot, shoot′-board, shoot′er-sun.

shoot′ing-board, -box, -coat, -gal′ler y, -i ron, -jack′et, -nee-dle, -plane, -range, -star, a plant, -stick, s. star, a star.

shŏp, -like, -per, -ping, -pish, -py, -oc′ra cy, shopped.

shop′hold er, -keep er, -lift er, -lift ing, -maid, -man, -mate.

shop′-bell, -bill, -board, -book, -boy, -girl, -thief, -walk er, -win′dow, -wom an, -worn.

shŏ′phär.

---

nŏt, nôr, ūse, ŭp, ûrn, etüde, fōōd, fŏŏt, aŋger, boṅmot, thus, Bach.

shore, -less, -ward, shored, shor'-
ing, shor'er, -age, shore'man,
-weed, shores'man.
shore'-aŋ chor, -bee tle, -bird,
-cliff, -crab, -gråss, -hop per,
-jump er, -land, -lark, -line,
-oil, -pip it, -plov er, -serv ice,
-shoot ing, -snipe, -tee'tan,
-wain scot, -whāl'ing.
shor'ling.
shorn. See *shear.*
short, -age, -er, -en, -en er, -en-
ing, -ened, -ly, -ness.
short'cake, -hand, -head, a
whale, -horn, a cow, -neck, a
bird, -tail, a snake, -wing.
short'-armed, -ax, -bread, -cir-
cuit, -coarse, a wool, -com ing,
-heeled, -horned, -līved, -shipped,
-sight ed, -sight ed ly, -sight ed-
ness, -spo ken, -sta ple, a.,
-stop, -tailed, -tem pered, -toed,
-tongued, -waist ed, -wind ed,
-wind ed ness, -winged, -wit ted.
Shŏ shŏ'ne, co. Ida.
Shŏ shŏng', t. Afr.
shot, -ted, -ting, -ty.
shot'-belt, -bor er, -box, -bush,
-car tridge, -com press'or, -corn,
-cross bŏw, -flag on, -free,
-gage, -gar land, -glåss, -gun,
-hole, -ice, -line, -lock er,
-met al, -pep per, -plug, -pouch,
-proof, -prop, -rack, -sort er,
-star, -ta ble, -tow er, -win dow.
shŏtt, the bed of a lake.
should (shŏŏd). See *shall.*
shŏul'der, -ing, -dered.
shoul'der-aŋ gle, -belt, -blade,
-block, -bone, -brace, -brōoch,
-cal los'i ty, -cap, -cov er, -gir-
dle, -guard, -hit ter, -joint,
-knot, -knot ted, -lobe, -mŏth,
-note, -pegged, -piece, -pole,
-screw, -shiēld, -slip, -slipped,
-strap, -tip pet, -wash er,
-wrench, shoul'der ing-file.
shout, -ed, -er, -ing.
Shou vä'lŏff (shōō-), Russ. dipl.
shove (shŭv), shoved, shov'er, -ing.
shov'el (shŭv'l), -eled *or* -elled,
-el ing *or* -ling, -el er *or* -ler,
-el ful.

shov'el bill, a duck, -board, a
game, -head, a fish, -nose, a
shark.
shov'el-fish, -foot'ed, -hat, -head'-
ed, -plow, shov'el ing-flat.
shŏw, -er, -ing, -y, -i ly, -i ness,
shŏwed, shŏwn, shŏw'bread,
-man, -room, a room for showing goods.
shŏw'-bill, -box, -card, -case,
-end, -glåss, -place, -room, a
showy room, -stone, -up, -win'-
dow, -yard, show'ing off.
show'er (shou'-), -ing, -y, -i ness,
-less, show'er-bath.
shrăb.
shrăg.
shrăp'nel.
shrĕd, -ded, -der, -ding, -dy,
shred'-cock, -pie, shred'ding-
knife.
shrew (shrōō), -ish, -ish ly, -ish-
ness, shrew'-ash, -foot ed,
-mole, -mouse, -struck.
shrewd (shrōōd), -ly, -ness.
shriĕk, -er, -ing, shriēked, shriek'-
owl.
shriĕv'al, -al ty.
shrĭft, -fa'ther.
shrīke, -crow.
shrill, -ing, -y, -ness, shrill'-
edged, -gorged, -tongued,
-voiced.
shrimp, -er, -ing, shrimped,
shrimp'-chaff, -net.
shrīne, shrined, shrīn'ing.
shrĭŋk, -a ble, -er, -ing, -ing ly,
shrank, shrunk, shrunk'en,
shrink'ing-head.
shriŋk'age, -crack, -rule.
shrīve, shrīved *or* shrŏve, shrĭv'-
en *or* shrīved, shrīv'er, -ing.
shriv'el, -ing *or* -ling, -eled *or*
-elled.
shroff, -age.
shroud, -ed, -ing, -less, -like.
shroud'-bri dle, -knot, -laid,
-plate, -rope, -stop per, -truck,
shroud'ing-gear.
shrove, -cake, shrŏv'ing-time,
Shrove'tide, Shrove'-day, Shrove
Sun day, S. Mon day, S. Tues-
day.

shrub, -by, -bi ness, -less, -ber y, shrub'-nail, -shil'ling, -yel low-root.

shrŭff.

shrug, -ging, shrugged.

Shtshig'ri (shchĭg'rē) *or* Tchig'ri (chēg'rē), t. Russ.

shŭck, -ing, -er, shucked, shuck'-bot tom, -bot'tomed.

shud'der, -ing, -ing ly, shud'dered.

shuf'fle, -fled, -fler, -fling, -fling-ly, shuf'fle board, a game, -wing, a bird, shuf'fle-cap, -scale, shuf'fling-plates.

shun, -ner, -ning, shunned.

Shun shä'bäd' (sho͞on-), t. India.

shunt, -er, -ed, -ing, shunt'-gun, -off, -out, shunt'ing-en'gine.

shut, -ting, shut'-down, *n.*, -in, -off, *n.*, shut'ting-post.

shute (sho͞ot), twisted silk. As a trough or tube, *chute* is preferred.

shŭt'ter, -tered, -ter less.

shŭt'ter-dam, -eye, -fas'ten ing, -hook, -lift, -lock, -screw.

shŭt'tle, -tled, -tling, -tle wise, -tle cock.

shut'tle-bind'er, -board, -box, -check, -crab, -lēv'er, -mo tion, -race, -shaped, -shell, -train, -wind'er, -wit.

Shwe.gyin' (shwā gyēn'), dist. and t. Burma.

shy, *a.,* -er *or* shi'er, shy'est *or* shi'est, shy'ly, -ness.

shy, *v.,* shīed, shy'ing (shī'-).

shy'ster (shī'-).

si (sē), a musical syllable.

Sī'à hà, *Bib.*

Si al'kot (sē äl'kōt), dist. India.

Sĭ ăm' (*or* sē äm'), coun. Asia, -a mese' (*or* -mēz').

Si ä tis'tä (sē'ä tēs'-), t. Turk.

Sī'ba, *Bib.*

sĭb'i lance, -lan cy, -lant, -late, -lā'ted, -lā'ting, -la to'ry, -lā'-tion.

Sib rä'im (*or* sĭb'-), *Bib.*

sĭb'yl, -ist, -līne.

sic'ca.

sic'cate, -cā'ted, -cā'ting, -cà-tive, -cā'tion.

sīce (*or* sīz), a game.

Sic'i ly, isl. Medit., Si cil'i an, *sĭ cĭ lĭ ä'nō* (*or* sē chē'lē ä'nō), a dance, *si cil i enne'*, a textile fabric.

sick, -en, -en ing, -ing ly, -er, -ish, -ish ly, -ish ness, -ly, -li ly, -li ness, -ness.

sick'-bay, -bed, -berth, -brained, -call, -flag, -head'ache, -leave, -list, -list ed, -re port', -room.

sic'kle, -kled, -kler.

sic'kle bill, a bird, -heal, a plant, -man, -pod, -weed, -wort, sic'-kle-billed, -fĕath'er, -head, -shaped.

sĭc'săc.

Si'cy on (sĭsh'ĭ on), *Bib.*

Sī'dĕ, *Bib.*

sīde, -less, sīd'ed, -er, -ing, sīde'-ling, -long, -track, *v.,* -tracked, -ward, -way, -ways, -wise, sides'man.

side'board, -līn er, a snake, -walk, -wind er, a snake, -wĭp'er, a snake.

side'-arms, -ax, -bar, -beam, -bone, -box, -boy, -chain, -chăp el, -check, -comb, -cous in, -cov er, -cut ting, -dish, -drum, -file, -fin, -flap, -fly, -guide, -hatch et, -head, -hill, -hook, -hunt, -keel son, -light, -līne, -lock, -mark, -meat, -note, -piece, -pier cing, -pipe, -plane, -plate, -pond, -post, -rail, -re-flect'or, -rib, -rod, -round, -sad dle, -screw, -scrip tion, -seat, -show, -slip, -snipe, -space, -split ting, -step, -stick, -stitch, -strap, -stroke, -ta ble, -tak ing, -tool, -track, *n.,* -tran sit, -tree, -walk er, -wheel, -wheel er, -whisk er, -winch, -wind, -wings, -wipe.

side'sad dle-flow er, sīd'ing-hook, -ma chine, -tile, side' view.

sī'dle, -dled, -dling.

Sid'ro phel, a character in Butler's *Hudibras.*

Sĭe'bĕn gĕ bĭr'gĕ, mts. Prus.

Siĕdl'cĕ, t. Pol.

siēge, siēged, siē'ging.

si**ĕge′-bas ket,** -bat ter y, -cap, -gun, -piece, -train, -works.

Siĕg′friĕd, hero of Norse legends.

Siĕ′mens, Ger. inventor.

sĭ en′na.

Sĭ′en nese′ (*or* -nēz′).

Sierpc (syĕrps), t. Pol.

si ĕr′ra (sē-), a chain of mts. Si er′ra Ne vä′da.

Sĭ ĕr′ra Lē ō′nĕ, West Afr.

Sĭ ĕr′ra Mä′dre (-drä), mts. Cal.

si ĕs′ta (sē-).

sieur (syêr).

sieve (sĭv), sĭeved, sĭev′ing, sieve′beaks, -ducks.

sieve′-beaked, -cell, -disk, -hypha, -like, -plate, -pore, -tissue, -tube, -ves sel.

Si ĕvsk′ (sē-), t. Russ.

sĭft, -ed, -er, -ing, sift′ing-machine′.

Si′gel (sē′-), Ger.-Amer. gen.

sigh (sī), -er, -ing, -ing ly, sighed.

sight, -ed, -en, -en ing, -ful, -less, -less ly, -less ness, -ly, -li ness, sight′see ing, -wor thy, sights′-man.

sight′-bar, -drăft, -feed, -hole, -o′pen ing, -pouch, -proof, -read er, -seek er, -shot, -sing′ing, -vane, sight′ing-notch, -shot.

sĭg′il, -la ry, -late, -lā′ted, -lā′-tion, -log′ra phy, *sig′la.*

Sig′is mŭnd (sĭj′-), Emp. of Ger.

sig′ma, -mate, -ma tism, -mat′ic, -mā′tion, sig′moid, -moid′al, -al ly.

sign (sīn), -er, -ing, signed, sign′-board, · -lan′guage, -paint er, -post, -read′ing, -sym bol, s. man′u al.

Sig′na (sēn′yä), vil. It.

Sĭg′näk′, t. Russ.

sĭg′nal, -naled *or* -nalled, -nal-ing *or* -ling, -nal er *or* -ler, -nal ize, -ized, -ī′zing, -ist, -nal ly, sig′nal man.

sig′nal-ap pa ră′tus, -book, -box, -chest, -code, -corps (-kōr), -fire, -flag, -gun, -hal yard, -lamp, -lantern, -light, -of′fi cer, -or der, -post, -rock et, -serv ice, -tow er.

sig′na ture, -na to′ry, -nā′tion, sig′na ture-line, -mark.

sig′net, -ed, -ing, sig′net-ring.

sig nif′i cance, -can cy, -cant, -cant ly.

sig′ni fy, -ing, -fīed, -fī a ble, -fī er, -fī cā′tion, -nif′i cà tive, -tive ly, -tive ness, -ca′tor, -to′-ry.

si gnor′ (sē nyor′), -gno′ri al. See *Señor.*

Sig′oûr ney, Amer. authoress.

Si hun′ (sē hōōn′), r. Asia Minor.

Si kän dä rä′bäd′ (sē-), t. India.

Sikh (sēk), -ism.

sil, yellow earth.

sĭ′lage, -laged, -lā′ging.

si′lence, -lenced, -len cing, si′-lent, -lent ly, -lent ness.

Sĭ lē′nus, *Myth.;* a monkey.

Sĭ lē′si a (-shĭ a), prov. Prus., -le′sian (-shan *or* -sĭ an), sĭ le′-sia (-sha), a textile fabric.

Sil hou ette′ (sĕ′lōō′ĕt′), Fr. financier.

sil hou ette′ (-ōō ĕt′), -et′ted, -et′ting, -et′tist.

sil′i ca, -i cate, -cā′ted, si li′cious (-lĭsh′us), -lic′i fy, -fy ing, -fīed, -fī cā′tion.

silk, -en, -y, -i ness, silk′flow er, a tree, -man, -tail, -weed, -wood, a moss; a shrub, -worm.

silk′-bun ting, a bird, -clean ing, -cot ton, -cul ture, -dou bling, -dress er, -fac to ry, -fig ured, -fowl, -gel′a tine, -gland, -glue, -grăss, -grow er, -hen, -loom, -man u fac′ture, -mer cer, -mill, -moth, -print ing, -reel, -shag, -sĭz ing, -sort ing, -spi der, -spin ner, -stock ing, a man, -stretch ing, -throw er, -tree, -twist ing, -vine, -weav er, -wĭnd er, silk′worm-cul ture, silk′y-wain scot, a moth, -wave, a moth.

sill, -dress ing, -step.

sil′la dar.

sĭl′lĭ bub *or* -la bub.

sĭl′ly, sil′li ly, -li ness.

sĭ′lō.

Sĭ lō′ah (*or* sĭl′-), *Bib.*

Sĭ lŏ'am (or sĭl'-), Bib.
Sĭ lŏ'ĕ (or sĭl'-), Bib.
silt, -ed, -ing, -y, silt'-grăss.
Sĭl vä'nus, Bib.; Myth.
sil'ver, -er, -ette', -ing, -y, -i ness,
-ite, -ize, -ized, -ĭ'zing, -less,
-ling, -vern, -vered.
sil'ver back, a bird, -bell, a tree,
-bel ly, a fish, -ber ry, -bill, a
bird, -bil ly, a fish, -bush,
-chain, a tree, -eye, a bird,
-fin, a minnow, -fish, -head, a
plant, -leaf, a plant, -rod, a
plant, -sides, a fish, -smith,
-spot, a butterfly, -tail, a fish,
-tip, -tongue, a sparrow, -ware,
-weed, -wood, a tree, -work.
sil'ver-barred, -bath, -beat er,
-black, -boom, -bracts, -cloud,
a moth, -cres'cent, -eel, -fern,
-foil, -gilt, -glance, -grain,
-grăss, -gray, -ground, a., -haired,
-head'ed, -king, -leafed, -mill,
-moth, -owl, -pa per, -plăt'ed,
-plăt'er, -print ing, -shăft'ed,
-shell, -skinned, -sol der, -sprig,
a rabbit's skin, -stick, a person,
-this tle, -tongued, -top, a disease of grass, -tree, -vine,
-washed, -white, -witch, sil'ver-
bell-tree, sil'ver băss, s. ce dar,
s. chick'weed, s. chub, s. duck'-
wing, s. fir, s. fox, s. gar, s.
grebe, s. hake, s. plate, s. plover, s. rain, s. sand, s. skin, s.
string.
Sĭ'mal cū'ē, Bib.
sim'bil.
sĭ'mĕn, a fish.
sim'i an.
sim'i lar, -ly, -lar'i ty, si mĭl'i-
tude, -tu'di na ry.
sim'i lĕ, -mark.
sĭm'i tar or scim'i tar or scim'i-
ter, -tared, sim'i tar-pod,
-shaped, -tree.
sĭm'mel.
sim'mer, -ing, -mered.
Sĭ mŏn'ĭ des (-dēz), Greek poet.
sĭ'mon-pure'.
sim'o ny, -o nĭ'a cal, -cal ly, -cal-
ness, si mō'ni ac.
sĭ mōōl'.

sĭ moom' or -moon.
sĭm'per, -er, -ing, -ing ly, -pered.
sim'ple, -ness, -ton, -pler, -plest,
-plism, -plist, -ply, -plic'i ty,
sim'pli fy, -fy ing, -fī er, -fīed,
-fī cā'tion.
sim'ple-faced, -heart ed, -mind-
ed, -mind ed ness, -toothed,
-winged.
sim'u late, -lā'ted, -lā'ting, -lant,
-lā'tor, -to'ry, -lā'tion.
sĭm'ul tā'ne ous (or sī'mul-), -ly
-ness, -ta nē'i ty.
sĭ mung'.
sĭ murg' (-mōōrg').
sin, -ful, -ful ly, -ful ness, -less,
-less ly, -less ness, -ning, -ner,
sinned.
sin'-born, -bred, -of'fer ing, -sick.
si'na (sē'-), a silkworm.
Sī'naĭ (or -nā ĭ), Bib., -nā ĭt'ic.
si'nä may' (sē'-).
since.
sin cere', -ly, -ness, -cer'i ty.
Sĭn'clâir, Scot. authoress; Scot.
statistician.
sĭnd'i (-ē).
sīne, -com'plē ment, -in'te gral.
sī'nē, without, sī'nē di'ē, sī'nē
qua non.
sī'ne cure, -cu'ral, -cu rism', -cu-
rist'.
sĭn'ew, -ing, -y, -i ness, -less,
-ewed, sin'ew-shrunk.
sing, -er, -ing, -ing ly, sang or
sung, sing'song, -spiēl, sing'-
sing, an antelope.
sing'ing-book, -gal ler y, -glăss,
-hin ny, -măs ter, -mus cle,
-school, sing'ing bird, s. fal'con,
s. flame, s. hawk, s. man, s.
voice, s. wom an.
Sin'ga pōre', isl. Malay pen.
singe (sĭnj), singe'ing, -ing ly,
singe'ing-lamp, -ma chine'.
Sin gha lese'. See Cingalese.
sin̄'gle, -ness, -gled, -glet, -gling,
-gly, sin̄'gle thorn, a fish, -ton,
-tree, a swingletree.
sin̄'gle-act ing, -banked, -bar,
-breast ed, -brood ed, -cut,
-dot ted, -eyed, -fire, a., -foot,
a gait of horses, -foot er,

-hand ed, -hearted, -heart ed ly,
-hung, -load er, -lunged, -mind-
ed, -mind ed ness, -phase', phās'-
er, -seed'ed, -soled, -stick, -tax-
ism, -touch, s. court, s. en'try,
s. flow'er, s. mor'dent, s. oys'-
ter, s. tax.
sin'glŏ.
Sing'-Sing, t. and prison N. Y.
sin'gu lar, -ly, -lăr'i ty.
Si ni gag'lia (sē nē gäl'yä), t. It.
sin'is ter, -ly, -ness, -is trous,
-trous ly, si nis'tra mä'no.
sin'is trad, -tral, -tral ly, -tral'-
i ty, -trä'tion.
Sī'nīte (or sĭn'-), Bib.
Si nj' (sē nē'), t. Aust.
sink, -a ble, -er, -ing, sank,
sunk, sink'field.
sink'-dirt, -hole, -pipe, -plug,
-room, -stone, -trap, sink'er-
bar, -wheel.
sink'ing-fund, -head, -pump,
-ripe.
sin'na ker.
sĭ nol'ŏ gy, -o gist, sin'o logue,
-o log'ic al.
sĭ nŏ'pis, sin'o ple.
sin'ter.
sĭn'u ate, -ā'ted, -ā'ting, -ā'tion,
-u ose, -ose ly, -ous, -ous ly, -ous-
ness, -ŏs'i ty.
Sioux (sōō), Indian tribe ; Siou'an.
Sioux (sōō), co. Ia.; co. Neb.
sip, -per, -ping, sipped.
sĭ'phŏn, -age, -al, -less, -phŏned,
-phon'ic.
sĭ'phon-bot tle, -cup, -fill ing,
-gage, -mouthed, -shell, -slide,
-tube, -worm.
sĭ'phon ba rom'e ter, s. con-
dens'er, s. pipe, s. pump, s.
re cord'er.
Sĭp'pāi, Bib.
sir (ser).
Sir'am pur' (sĕr'äm pōōr'), t. India.
sir dar', -bear er.
sīre, -less.
sī'ren, -ize, -ized, -ī'zing, -ren'-
ic al. Sī'ren, Zool. genus.
sĭr'itch.
Sĭr'i us, Astron.
sir'loin.

sĭ rŏc'co.
sĭr'rah.
sĭr'up or syr'-, -y, sĭr'up-gage.
sĭs'al (or sĭ säl'), Sĭs'al grăss, S.
hemp.
Sĭs'a mãi (or sĭ săm'ā ī), Bib.
sis'co, a fish.
Sĭs'e ra, Bib.
Sĭ sĭn'nĕs (-nēz), Bib.
sis'si fy, -ing, -fied.
sĭs'ter, -hood, -less, -ly, sis'ter-
block, -hook, sis'ter-in-law,
sis'ter ship.
Sis'tĭne.
sĭs'trum.
Sĭs'y phus, Myth., -y phe'an.
sit, -ter, -ting, sat, sit-sick er,
sit'ting-room.
Si'ta (sē'-), Myth., Sĭt'ta, Ornith.
Si tä'pur (sē'tä'pōōr), div. India.
sĭte.
sĭt'u ate, -ā'ted, -ā'ting, -ā'tion.
Si'va (sē'-), Myth., -va is'tic, -va-
ite, si'va-snake (sē'-).
Sī'van, Bib.
sĭ'wash (-wŏsh).
six, -er, -fold, -teen, -teen mo,
-teenth, sixth, sixth'ly, six'ty,
-ti eth, six'pence, -pen ny.
six'-band ed, -belt'ed, -cor'nered,
-foot er, -hand'ed, -hour, -point,
-shoot er, -spot, six ty-fourth,
six teenth note, s. rest, six'ty-
fourth note.
sī'zar, -ship.
size, dimension, sized, sĭz'a ble,
-er, -ing, size'-cue, -roll, -stick,
sĭz'ing-chis el, -ma chine.
size, a viscus fluid, sized, sĭz'-
ing, sĭz'y, -i ness.
sizz, -ing.
siz'zard.
siz'zle, -zled, -zling.
sjam'bŏk (shăm'-).
Skăg'er Răck, arm of the sea
off Norw.
Skăn e ăte'lĕs, vil. and l. N. Y.
skăt (or skät), a game.
skate, skăt'ed, -er, -ing, skate'-
bar row, -grind er, -suck er,
skăt'ing-rink.
skąw.
skēan, -dhu (-dōō).

ske dad'dle, -dled, -dling.
skee, -race, -run ner.
skeel, -duck, -goose.
skee'sicks (-zĭx).
skeet, a fish.
skĕg'shore.
skein (skān), -screw, -set ter.
skĕl'e ton, -less, -wise, -e tal,
-e tog'e nous (-tŏj'-), -tog'e ny
(-tŏj'-), -tog'ra phy, -tŏl'o gy,
-ton ize, -ized, -ĭ'zer, -ĭ'zing.
skel'e ton-face, -fi ber, -screw,
-shrimp, -spic ule.
skel'ly.
skep.
skep'tic or scep'tic, -tic al, -al ly,
-al ness, -ti cize, -cized, -cĭ'-
zing, -cism.
sketch, -a ble, -a bil'i ty, -er,
-ing, -y, -i ly, -i ness, sketched.
sketch'-block, -book, -map,
sketch'ing-block.
skew (skū), -ing, skewed, skew'-
back, -bald, -cor'bel, -fil'let,
-gear'ing, -gee, -sym met'ric al,
-ta'ble, -wheel.
skew'er, -ing, -ered, skew'er-
ma chine', -wood.
skĭ'a graph or sci'o graph (skĭ'o-).
ski'a scope, -as'co py (or skĭ'a-
sco'py).
skid, -ded, -der, -ding, skid'way.
skĭ'der.
skiff, -hand ed.
skil, a fish.
skill, skil'ful or skill'-, -ful ly,
-ful ness, -less, skilled.
skĭl'let.
skilts.
skim, -mer, -ming, -ming ly,
skimmed, skim'back, a fish,
skim'-col ter, -milk, -net, skim'-
ming-dish, -gate.
skīme.
-i ness, skimped.
skimp, -ing, -ing ly, -ings, ry,
skin, -ful, -less, -ner, -ning, -ny,
-ni ness, skinned, skin'flint, a
person.
skin'-a're a, -bone, -bound, -coat,
-deep, -eat er, -fric tion, -gråft,
-gråft'ing, -house, -mer chant,
-moth, -plant ing, -sen so ry,

-tight, -tis sue, -wool, skin'ning-
ap pa rā'tus, -ta ble, skin' boat,
s. game.
skip, -per, -per y, -ping, -ping ly,
skipped, skip'jack, a person; a
fish, skip'per ship.
skip'-mack er el, -rope, -shåft,
-wheel, skip'per-bird, skip-
ping-rope, -stone, -teach.
skip'pet.
skir'mish, -er, -ing, -mished,
. skir'mish-drill, -line.
skirt, -ed, -er, -ing, -less, skirt-
braid, -dan cing, -fur row,
skirt'ing-board.
skit, -ted, -ting.
skit'ter, -ing, skit'ter-brained,
-wit.
skit'tish, -ly, -ness.
skit'tle, -tled, -tling.
skit'tle-al ley, -ball, -dog,
-frame, -ground, -pin, -pot.
skive, skived, skĭv'er, -ing, skĭv'-
er-wood, skĭv'ing-knife, -ma-
chine'.
skŏ'li on, pl. -li a.
Skow hē'gan, vil. Me.
skrabe (or skrä'bĕ).
Skraĕl'ling.
skry'er (skrī'-).
skŭg.
skŭlk, -er, -ing, -ing ly, skulked,
skulk'ing-place.
skull, skulled, skull'cap, a plant;
cap of a skull.
skull'-cap, a cap for the head,
-fish, -roof, -shell.
skunk, -ish, -er y, skunk'bill, a
duck, -head, a duck, -top, a
duck, -weed.
skunk'-bird, -black bird, -cab-
bage, -farm, -por poise.
Skvi'rä (skvē'-), t. Russ.
sky, pl. skies, sky'er, -ey, sky'-
lark, -less, -ward, -flow'er, a
plant, -light, -sail, -scape.
sky'-blue, -born, -clad, -col or,
-col ored, -drain, -dyed, -gāz er,
-high, -line, -par lor, -pip it,
-rock et, -scråp er.
Skye (skī), a dog.
skyr (skêr).
slab, -bing, slabbed, slab'board,

---

nŏt, nôr, ūse, ŭp, ûrn, etüde, fōōd, fŏŏt, aŋger, boṅmot, thus, Bach.

-grind er, -line, -sīd ed, -stone, slab'bing-gang, -ma chine', -saw.

slab'ber, -ing, -er, -er y.

slăb'by, -bi ness.

slack, -ly, -ness, -en, -en ing, -ened, slack'-backed, -bake, *v.*, -jaw, -wa ter, *a.*

slade.

slag, -ging, -gy, slagged.

slag'-brick, -bug'gy, -car, -dump, -fur nace, -heärth, -pot, -shiŋ gle, -wool.

Slä'gĕl sĕ, t. Den.

slāin. See *slay.*

slake, -less, slaked, slāk'ing, slake'-kale, -trough.

slam, -ming, slammed, slam'- bang.

slan'der, -er, -ing, -ous, -ous ly, -ous ness, -dered.

slang, -y, -i ly, -i ness, slang'- whang'er.

slănt, -ed, -ing, -ing ly, -ly, -wise.

slap, -ping, slapped, slap'jack, a cake.

slap'-bang, -dash, -sīd ed, -up. *slar gän'do.*

slăsh, -er, -ing, -y, slashed, slash'-pine.

slat, -ted, -ting, slat'-bar, -crimp er, -i ron, -ma chine, -plane, -seat.

slate, slāt'ed, -er, -ing, -y.

slate'-ax, -bev'el ing, -black, -blue, -clay, -coal, -col ored, -cut ter, -frame, -gray, -māk'- ing, -peg, -pen cil, -saw, -spar, -tint'ed, -trim ming, s. globe.

slat'ter, -tered, -tern, -tern ly, -li ness, -ter y.

slaugh'ter, -er, -ing, -ous, -ous ly, -tered, slaugh'ter-house, -pen, -weap on.

Slăv, -dom, -ic, -ism, Sla vō'- ni an, -an ize, -ized, -i zing, -vŏn'ic, -von'i cize, -cized, -ci zing, Slăv'o nize, -nized, -ni zing, -o phil, -phil ism, -o phō bist.

slăve, slāved, slāv'er, -er y, -ing, -ing ly, -ish, -ish ly, -ish ness, -o crat, -oc'ra cy, slave'hōld'er.

slave'-bǎr on, -born, -cof fle,

-drīv er, -fork, -hunt er, -māk ing, -ship, -trade, -trăd er, s. state, S. Coast.

slaw.

slay, -er, -ing, slew, slain.

sleave, sleaved, slēav'ing, sleave'- silk.

slēa'zy (*or* slā'zy), -zi ness.

sled, -ded, -der, -ding, sled'man, sled'-brake, -knee, -run ner.

slĕdge, sledged, sledg'ing, sledge'- chair, -dog, -ham mer.

sleek, -er, -ing, -ly, -ness, -y, sleeked, sleek'-head ed, sleek'- ing-glåss.

sleep, -er, -ing, -y, -i ly, -i ness, -less, -less ly, -less ness, slept, sleep'wort, sleep'y head, a per son; a duck.

sleep'-drunk, *a.,* -wāk'er, -walk'- er, sleep'er-shark, sleep'y-seeds, sleep-at-noon, a plant.

sleep'ing-bag, -car, -car riage, -draught (drȧft), -drop sy, -room, -sick ness, -ta ble.

sleet, -y, -i ness, sleet'bush, -squash.

sleeve, -less, sleev'ing, sleeved, sleeve'fish.

sleeve'-ax le, -board, -but ton, -coup ling, -knot, -link, -nut, -waist'coat, -weight.

sleigh (slā), -er, -ing, sleigh'- bell, -ride.

sleīght, cunning; craft.

Sleip'nir (slāp'nĕr), *Myth.*

slen'der, -ly, -ness, slen'der- beaked, -billed, -grăss, -rayed, -tongued.

Slĕs'wĭck-Hŏl'steīn, prov. Prus.

sleūth, -dog, -hound.

slew (slo͞o). See *slay.*

slīce, sliced, sli'cer, -cing, slice'- bar, -gal ley, sli'cing-ma chine'.

slick, -en, -ens, -en sides, -er, -ing, -ness, slick-chis el.

slīde, slīd'a ble, -er, -ing, -ing ness, slĭd, slide'way.

slide'-ac tion, -bar, -box, -case, -cul ture, -head, -knife, -knot, -lāthe, -rail, -rest, -rod, -rule, -trom bone, -trum pet, -valve, slīd'er-bin, -pump.

---

fāte, făt, fär, fạll, fâre, fȧst, sofȧ, mēte, mĕt, hêr, īce, ĭn, nōte,

slīd'ing-balk, -band, -box, -gage, -gun ter, -nip pers, -plank, -rel ish, s. keel, s. scale.

Slī dĕll', Confed. polit.

slī dom'e ter.

slight (slīt), -ed, -er, -ing, -ing ly, -ly, -ness.

slim, -ly, -mish, -ness.

slīme, slimed, slīm'ing, -y, -i ly, -i ness.

slīme'-eel, -fuṇ gus, -gland, -mold, -pit, -sep'a ra tor, -sponge.

sling, -er, -ing, slung.

sling'-band, -bone, -bul let, -cart, -dog, -fruit, -piece, -shot, -stay, -stone, -trot, -wag on.

sliṇk, -ing, -y, slunk, slink'- butch er, -skin.

slip, -per, -per y, -per i ness, -i ly, -ping, -py, -pi ness, -page, slipped, slip'shod, -slop, -way, slip'per y back, a lizard, slip'- per y-Dick, -Jack.

slip'-board, -car riage, -chase, -clēav age, -cov er, -dec o ra'- tion, -dock, -gal ley, -hook, -house, -kiln, -knot, -link, -rails, -rope, -shac kle, -shave, -stitch, -stop per, -strain er, slip'per y-elm, slip'ping-piece, -plane.

slip'per, -pered, slip'per wort.

slip'per-bäth, -drag, -flow er, a plant, -lim pet, -plant, -shell, -spurge.

slirt, -ed, -ing.

slit, -ter, -ting, -tered, slit'-shell.

slit'ting-disk, -file, -gage, -ma chine', -mill, -plane, -roll er, -saw, -shears.

slĭv'er, -ing, -ered, sliv'er-box, sliv'er ing-knife, -ma chine'.

slŏb'ber, -er, -ing, -y, -bered.

Slŏb ŏds koi', t. Russ.

slōe, pl. sloes.

slog, -ging, slogged.

slō'gan.

sloid or sloyd.

slōōp, -rigged, -smack, -yacht.

slop, -ping, -py, -pi ness, slopped, slop'sell er.

slop'-ba sin, -book, -bowl, -buck et, -chest, -dash, -hop per, -jar,

-mold ing, -pail, -room, -shop, -work, -work er.

slōpe, -ly, -ness, -wise, slōped, slōp'ing, -ing ly, -ing ness, -y, slope'-lev el.

slŏsh, -ing, -y, sloshed, slosh'- wheel.

slot, -ted, -ting, slot'-ma chine'.

slŏth (or slōth), -ful, -ful ly, -ful ness.

slŏth'-an i mal'cule, -bear, -mon key.

slŏt'ter, -tered, -ter ing.

slŏt'ting, -au ger, -ma chine'.

slouch, -ing, -y, -i ly, -i ness, slouched, slouch'-hat.

Slough (slou), vil. Eng.

slough (slou), a mire, -y.

slough (slŭf), -ing, -y, sloughed.

slov'en (slŭv'n), -ly, -li ness, -ry, slov'en wood, a tree.

Slŏ vēne', -vē'ni an, -vē'nish, Slō vǎk'.

slŏw, -ing, -ly, -ness, slowed, slow'back, a person, -worm.

slow'-gäit'ed, -hound, -match, -paced, -sight ed, -sure, -up, -winged, -wit ted.

sloyd. See sloid.

slub, -ber, -bing, slubbed, slub'- bing-bil ly, -ma chine'.

sludge, sludg'er, -ing, -y, sludge'- door, -hole.

slūe (or slōō), slued, slu'er, -ing, slue'-rope.

slug, -ger, -ging, slugged, slug'a- bed.

slug'-cat'er pil lar, -fly, -horn, -shaped, -snail, -worm, slug'- ging-match.

slug'gard, -gish, -gish ly, -gish- ness.

slūice, sluiced, slui'cing, -cy, sluice'way, sluice'-fork, -gate, -valve.

slum, -mer, -ming, slummed.

slum'ber, -er, -ing, -ing ly, -less, -ous, -ous ly, -y, -brous, slum'- ber land.

slump, -ing, -y, slumped, slump'- work.

slung, -shot.

sluṇk.

slur, -ring, -ry, slurred, slur'-bar, -bōw.

slush, -ing, -y, slushed.

slush'-bar rel, -buck et, -fund, -horn, -lamp, -pot.

slut, -tish, -tish ly, -tish ness, -ter y.

sly, -ly, -ness, slī'er *or* sly'er, slī'est *or* sly'est, sly'-boots, -bream.

Smạa le ne'ne (-lā nä'nä), prov. Norw.

smack, -er, -ing, smacked, smack'man, smacks'man, smack'-boat, -fish er man, -smooth.

smạll, -age, -ish, -ish ly, -ness, small'fish, -mouth, a fish, -pox.

small'-clōthes, -dot, lace, -head-ed, -mouthed, s. arms, s. beer, s. fry, s. let'ter, s. pi ca, s. piece, s. stuff, s. talk, s. wares.

smạlt, -Ine, -īte, smalt'-blue.

smart, -ing, -ly, -ness, -y, smart'-weed, smart'-grạss, -mon ey, -tick et.

smash, -er, -ing, smashed, smash'-up, smash'ing-ma chine', -press.

smat'ter, -er, -ing, -ing ly.

smẹar, -ing, -y, -i ness, smeared, smear'-case, -dab.

smĕg'ma, -mặt'ic.

smell, -a ble, -er, -ing, smelled *or* smelt.

smell'-feast, -less, -trap, smell'-ing-bot tle, -sạlts.

smelt, -ed, -er, -er y, -ing, smelt'ing-fur nace,   -house, -works.

smĭd'dum-tails.

smī'lax, a plant, Smi'lax, *Bot. genus.*

smile, -ful, -less, smiled, smīl'er, -ing, -ing ly, -ing ness, smil'ing-mus cle.

smirch, -ing, smirched.

smirk, -ing, -y, smirked.

smīte, smīt'er, -ing, smōte, smĭt'ten.

smith, -ing, -y *or* -er y, -work, smith'y-coal.

smĭth'ers, -er eens'.

Smith sŏ'ni an.

smock, -ing, -less, smock'-faced, -frock, -lin ên, -mill, -race, -ra cing.

smōke, -less, -less ly, -less ness, smōk'er, -ing, -ing ly, -y, -i ly, -i ness, smoked, smoke'wood, a plant.

smoke'-arch, -ball, -bell, -black, -board, -box, -brown, -bush, -con-dens'er,   -con sụm'er,   -dry, -gray, -house, -jack, -mon ey, -paint ed, -paint ing, -pen ny, -pipe, -plant, -quartz, -rock et, -sail, -shade, -sil ver, -stack, -stone, -tight, -tree, -wash er.

smōk'ing-cap, -car, -car riage, -duck, -jack et, -lamp, -pipe, -room, -to bac co, smoke'less pow'der.

smōl'der, -ing, -dered.

Smō lĕnsk', c. Russ.

smōlt.

smōōth, -er, -ing, -ly, -ness, smoothed, smooth'bore, a gun, -sides, a fish.

smōōth'-bore, *a.,* -bored, -browed, -chinned, -dab, -faced, -grained, -paced, -say er, -scaled, -shod, -spo ken, -tongued, -winged, smooth mus'cle, s. snake, s. sole.

smōōth'ing-box, -i ron, -mill, -plane, -stone.

smō ren'dō, smor zän'dō (-tsän'-).

smoth'er (smǔth'-), -ered, -er y, -er i ness, -er ing, -ing ly, -a'tion, smoth'er-fly, -kiln.

smudge, smudged, smudg'er, -ing, -y.

smug, -ly, -ness, -ging, smugged, smug'-boat, -faced.

smug'gle, -gled, -gler, -gling.

smut, -ted, -ting, -ty, -ti ly, -ti-ness, smut-ball, -fụn gus, -ma-chine', -mill, smut'ty-nosed.

smutch, -ing, -y, smutched.

Smyth (smith), co. Va.

snab'ble, -bled, -bling.

snack.

snaf'fle, -fled, -fling, snaf'fle-bit.

snag, -ger, -ging, -gy, snagged, snag'bush, snag'-boat, -chặm'-ber, -tooth.

---

fāte, fặt, fär, fạll, fâre, fạst, sofà, mēte, mĕt, hêr, īce, ĭn, nōte,

snag'gle, -gled, -gling, snag'gle-
tooth, -toothed.
snail, -ing, -er y, -y, snailed,
snail'bore, -fish, -flow er.
snail'-bor er, -clo ver, -like,
-pace, -paced, -park, -plant,
-shell, -slow, -track, -tre foil,
-wa ter, -wheel.
snail'ey, a bullock.
snake, -let, snāk'ing, -ish, -ish ly,
-y, snaked.
snake'fish, -head, a plant, -like,
-mouth, a plant, -neck, a bird,
-nut, a tree, -pipe, a plant, -root,
a plant, -skin, -stone, -weed,
-wood, -worm.
snake'-bird, -boat, -box, -buz-
zard, -cane, -charm er, -cor'alline, -crane, -cu'cum ber, -doc-
tor, -cat er, -eel, -feed er,
-fence, -fern, -fly, -gourd,
-head ed, -kill er, -leaves, -line,
-liz ard, -locked, -moss, -piece,
-rat, -shell, snake' nut-tree,
snake'skin-snail, snāk'y-head ed.
snake's-beard, -egg, -head, -mouth,
-tail, -tongue.
snap, -per, -ping, -pish, -pish ly,
-pish ness, -py, snapped, snap'-
drag on, -weed, -wort.
snap'-ac tion, -ap ple, -back,
-bee tle, -block, -bolt, -bug,
-cap, -crack er, -flask, -head,
-hook, -jack, -link, -lock, -ma-
chine, -mack er el, -shoot er,
-tool, snap'per-back, snap'ping-
tongs, -tool.
snap'ping bee tle, s. bug, s.
mack er el, s. turtle.
snape, snaped, snāp'ing.
snâre, snared, snâr'er, -ing, snare'-
drum, -head.
snarl, -er, -ing, -y, snarled, snarl'-
knot, snarl'ing-i ron, -mus cle,
-tool.
snash.
snatch, -er, -ing, -ing ly, -y,
snatched, snatch'-block, -cleat,
snatch'ing-roll er.
snáthe, snáthed, snáth'ing.
snéad, -ed, -ing.
snĕak, -er, -ing, -ing ly, -ing-
ness, -y, -i ly, -i ness, sneaked,

sneak'-boat, -box, -shoot ing,
-thief.
sneck, -ing, snecked, sneck'-band,
-drawer, -drawn, -pos set.
sneer, -er, -ing, -ing ly, sneered,
sneer'ing-match, -mus cle.
sneeze, sneez'er, -ing, sneezed,
sneeze'weed, -wood, -wort,
sneeze'-horn, sneez'ing-pow'der.
snell, -loop.
Sni ä'tin (snē ä'tēn), t. Aust.
snick, -er, -ing, snicked.
snick'er, -er, -ing, -ered.
sniff, -ing, sniffed.
snif'fle, -fled, -fling, -fler, -fles.
snift'ing-valve.
snig'gle, -gled, -gling.
snip, -per, -ping, -py, snipped,
snips, snip'per-snap per.
snipe, snīp'y, snipe'fish, snipe'-bill,
-eel, -fly, -hawk, -like, -nosed,
snipe's-head.
sniv'el (-l), -eled, or -elled, -el ing
or -ling, -el er or -ler, -el y or
-ly, sniv'el-nose.
snob, -ber y, -bish, -bish ly,
-bish ness, -bism, -by, -ling,
-oc'ra cy, -og'ra pher, -ra phy.
Snŏ hŏ'mĭsh, co. Wash.
snŏod, -ed, -ing.
snook, -ing, snooked.
snoop, -er, -ing, snooped.
snooze, snoozed, snooz'er, -ing.
snore, snored, snōr'er, -ing, snore'-
hole, -piece.
snort, -ed, -er, -ing.
snout, -ed, -er, -ing, -y.
snout'-bee tle, -but ter fly, -mite,
-moth, -ring.
snow, -ing, -y, -i ly, -i ness, -ish,
-less, -like, snowed.
snow'ball, -bank, -ber ry, -bird,
-break, a thaw, -bush, -cap, a
bird, -drop, a plant, -fall, -flake,
-fleck, -flight, -flow er, -fowl,
-slide, -slip.
snow'-ap ple, -blind, -blind ness,
-blink, -boot, -bound, -box, -broth,
-bun ting, -capped, -chü'kor,
-clad, -cloud, -cock, -cov'ered,
-crowned, -decked, -drift, -eat er,
-eyes, -fed, -field, -finch, -flange,
-flea, -flood, -fly, -gage, -gem,

---

nŏt, nôr, ūse, ŭp, ûrn, etüde, fōod, fŏot, aŋger, boṅmot, thus, Bach.

-glory, -gnat, -gog gle, -goose, -grouse, -ice, -in sect, -knife.

snow'-lĕop'ard, -light, -lim'it, -line, -man'tled, -mouse, -owl, -par tridge, -pear, -pheas ant, -pi geon, -plăn'er, -plant, -plow, -probe, -scrăp'er, -shed, -shoe, -sho er, -shov el, -skate, -snake, -spar row, -squall, -storm, -sweep er, -tipped, -track, -wa ter, -white, -wreath, snow blaŋ'-ket, s. cor'nĭce, s. hut.

snow'ball-tree, snow'drop-tree, snow-in-har vest, a plant, snow-in-sum mer, a plant, snow-on-the-moun tain, a plant, snow'y e gret, s. her on, s. lem ming, s. owl, s. plov er.

snowl (snoul).

snub, -ber, -bing, -bish, -by, snubbed, snub'nose.

snub'-cube, -nosed, -post, snub'-bing-line, -post.

snuff, -er, -ers, -ing, -ing ly, -y, -i ness, snuffed, snuff'man.

snuff'-bot tle, -box, -col or, -dip-per, -dish, -head ed, -māk'er, -mill, -rasp, -spoon, -tāk'er.

snuff'er-dish, -pan, -tray, snuff'ing pig.

snuf'fle, -fled, -fler, -fling, -fling ly.

snug, -ging, -ger, -ger y, -ly, -ness, snugged.

snug'gle, -gled, -gling.

snuz'zle, -zled, -zling.

sny, -ing.

so, sō be it *or* sō bē'it, so'-called, so-and-so.

sŏak, -age, -er, -ing, -ing ly, -y, soaked, sōak'-bar rel, -hole, sōak'ing-pit.

soal, a pond.

sŏam.

sŏap, -er, -less, -ing, -y, -i ness, soap'bark, -ber ry, -bush, -fish, -nut, a plant, -root, -stone, -weed, -wood, -wort.

sōap'-ap ple, -ash es, -balls, -bar ring, -beck, -boil er, -bub-ble, -bulb, -cĕ'rate, -coil, -crutch, -crutch ing, -cut ting, -earth, -en gine, -fat, -frame, -glue, -house, -ket tle, -lock, -māk'er,

-mill, -pan, -plant, -pod, -pow'-der, -slab'bing, -suds, -tree, -works, soap film, s. lin'i ment.

soap'bark-tree, soap'wort-gen'tian, soap' lin'i ment, soap' plas'ter.

soar, -ing, -ing ly, soared.

sob, -bing, -bing ly, sobbed.

sŏ'ber, -ly, -ness, -ing, -bered, sō-bri'e ty, so'ber sides, so'ber-blood'ed, -mind'ed, -mind'ed-ness, -suit'ed.

Sō brän'je (-brĕ'kä' *or* -yä).

sŏ'bri'quet' (-brĕ'kä'), or *sou'* - (sōō'-).

sŏc'age (sŏk'-), -a ger, soc'man, -man ry.

Sō cha'czew (-kä'chĕv), t. Pol.

so'cia ble (-sha-), -ness, -bly, -bil'i ty, -cial (-shăl), -cial-ism, -ist, -is'tic, -tic al ly, -ize, -ized, -ĭ'zing, -ĭ zā'tion, -cial ly, -cial ness, -ci al'i ty (-shĭ-).

sŏ cī'e ty, -e ta ry, -tā'rĭ an, *so ci-e taire'* (so'ce'ä'târ').

Sō cin'i an, -ism, -an ize, -ized, -ĭ'zing.

Sō cī'nus, Ital. reform.

so ci ŏl'o gy (-shĭ-), -o gist, -o-lŏg'ic, -ic al, -al ly, -og'e ny (-ŏj'-), -og'ra phy, -ŏn'o my.

sŏ'ci us (-shĭ-), pl. *-ci ĭ.*

sock, -less, -ing, socked, sock-dol'a ger, sock'head, a person.

sŏck'et, -ed, -ing.

sock'et-bay o net, -bolt, -cast'er, -celt, -chis el, -drill, -joint, -pipe, -pole, -screw, -tile, -wash-er, -wrench.

Sō cŏr'rŏ, co. N. Mex.

Sŏc'ra tes (-tēz), Athenian philos., So crăt'ic, -ic al, -al ly, -i cism, Soc'ra tize, -tized, -tī'zing, -tism, -tist.

sod, -ded, -ding, -dy, sod'-burn-ing, -cut ter, -oil, -plow, -worm, sod'ding-im'ple ments, -mal let, -spade.

sŏ'da, -dā'ic.

sŏ'da-al um, -ap pa ra'tus, -ash, -ball, -bis cuit, -crack'er, -feld'-spar, -foun tain, -fur nace, -lime, -lye, -mes'o type, -mint, -pa per, -plant, -pow'der, -prai'rie, -sąlt, -waste, -wa ter, so'da lake.

sŏ dăl'i ty.

sod'den (-dn), -ness, sod'den-wit-
ted.

sŏ'di um, sō'dic, sō'dic-cha lyb'-
e ate (-kà lib'-).

Sŏd'om, *Bib.*, -om īte, sŏd'om y,
-om it'ic al, -al ly.

soe, a wooden pail.

Soe'pä (sōō'-), state Malay Arch.

Soe ra bay'a (sōō'rä bī'ä), Java.

Soest (sêst), t. Pruss.

sŏ'fa, -arm, -back, -bed, -bed-
stĕad, -cov er, -cush'ion, -leg,
-pil low.

sŏf'fit.

Sŏ fi'a (-fē'-), c. Turk.

soft, -ly, -ness, sŏf'ten (sŏf'n),
-tened, -ten er, -ten ing, soft'-
horn, -soap, *v.*, -soaped, -wood, a
tree.

soft'-bod ied, -eyed, -finned,
-grass, -hand ed, -head ed,
-heart ed, -heart ed ness, -rayed,
-saw der, -shell, -shelled,
-skinned, -sol id, -spo ken,
-tack, soft clam, s. crab, s.
snap, s. wĕath'er, sof'ten ing-
i ron, -ma chine.

sog, -gy.

sog get'to (sŏd jĕt'tō).

sŏ hŏ'.

Soh'rau (sō'rou), t. Prus.

soi-di'sant' (swŭ-dē'zŏn').

soil, -ing, -less, -ure, soiled.

soil'-bound, -branch, -cap, -cup,
-pipe, -pul'ver i zer.

soi rée' (swŏ'rā').

Sois sons', (swås sŏn'), t. Fr.

sŏ'joûrn, *n.*, so'journ (*or* -jurn'), *v.*,
-er, -ing, -ment, -journed.

Sŏ kŏ tŏ', region Afr.

Sŏ kŏ'trä, isl. Indian Oc.

sŏl, a Fr. coin; a tincture. Sŏl, the
sun.

sŏl, a note in music; a coin of Peru.

sŏ lä', a cry or call, sŏ'lä, a
swamp-plant.

sol'ace, -ment, -aced, -a cing.

sō lä'nŏ.

sŏ'lar, -ism, -ist, -ize, -ized,
-ī'zing, -ī zā'tion.

sŏl dä'do (-thō).

sol'der (sŏd'er *or* sŏl'der), -er, -ing.

sol'der-cast ing (sŏd'er-), -ma-
chine, -mold.

sol'der ing-block (sŏd'er-), -bolt,
-frame, -fur nace, -i ron, -ma-
chine', -nip ple, -pot, -tongs,
-tool, -ūn ion.

sŏl'dier (-jer), -ing, -like, -ly, -ship,
-y, sol'dier wood.

sŏl'dier-ant (-jer-), -bee tle, -bug,
-bush, -crab, -fish, -fly, -moth,
-or chis (-kis), sol dier's-herb.

sŏl'dō (*or* sŏl'-), pl. *-dĭ.*

sŏle, -ly, soled, sŏl'ing, sole'fish.

sŏle'-beat ing, -chan nel, -chan'-
nel ling, -cut ting, -fin'ish ing,
-fleūk, -lĕath er, -mold ing,
-piece, -plate, -rē'flex, -round-
ing, -tile.

sŏ'lē a.

sŏl'e cism, -e cist, -cis'tic, -tic al,
-al ly.

sŏl'emn (-ĕm), -ly, -em ness *or*
-emn ness, -em nize, -nized, -nī'-
zer, -nī'zing, -nĭ zā'tion, so-
lĕm'ni ty.

so'len.

sō lĕn'ne men'te (-nä mĕn'tä).

Sŏ'lesmes' (-lăm'), t. Fr.

Sŏ'leure' (-lêr'), canton Switz.

sŏl'-fä', -fä'ing, -ist, -fäed', sŏl fä-
mĭ zā'tion.

sŏl fa nä'ri a.

sŏl fä tä'ra.

sŏl feg'gio (-fĕd'jō), *-feg gia're*
(-jä'rä).

Sŏl'fer i'no (-ē'-), vil. It.

sŏl'fe ri'no (-fä rē'nō), a color.

sŏ lic'it, -ed, -ing, -or, -ant, -ous,
-ous ly, -ous ness, -i tude, -i tā'-
tion, so lic'it or-gen'er al.

sŏl'id, -ly, -ness, -ism, -ist, -is'tic,
sŏ lid'i ty, so lid'i fy, -fy ing,
-fied, sol'id-drawn, -hoofed,
-horned.

sŏl'i dâ ry, -dăr'i ty.

sŏl i fīd'i an, -an ism.

sŏ lil'o quize, -quized, -quī'zing,
-quy.

sŏl i tâire'.

sŏl'i ta ry, -ta ri ly, -ri ness, -ta-
ri'e ty, -i tude.

so'lĭ tĭ'dal.

Sŏl ler' (-yâr'), t. Balearic isls.

sŏl'mi zate, -zā'ted, -zā'ting, -zā'-tion.

sō'lŏ, *pl.* -los (-lōz), -lo ist.

sŏl'o graph.

Sŏl'o mon, *Bib.*, -o mŏn'ic, Sol'-o mon's-seal, Sol'o mon's hys-sop, S. Porch, S. serv ants, S. Song.

Sō'lon, Athenian lawgiver, -lō'-ni an, -lŏn'ic, Sō'lon por ce'lain.

sŏl'stĭce, -sti'tial (-stĭsh'al).

sol'u ble, -ness, -bil'i ty, sō lu'-tion.

sō'lus, fem. sō'la.

sŏlve, solved, sŏlv'a ble, -a ble-ness, -a bil'i ty, -en cy, -ent, -er, -ing.

sō'ma, -plant.

Sō mäj'.

Sō mä'li (-lē), Afr.

sō ma tol'o gy, -to log'ic, -ic al, -al ly.

sŏm'ber, -ly, -ness, -brous, -brous-ly, -brous ness.

som bre'rō (-brä'-).

some (sŭm), -body y, -how, -thing, -time, *adv.*, -times, -way, *adv.*, -what, -when, -where, -while, -whitħ er.

som'er sạult *or* som'er set (sŭm'-).

sŏm nam'bu lant, -lance, -bu-lar, -bu late, -lā'ted, -lā'ting, -lā'tor, -lā'tion, -nam'bule, -bu-lic, -bu lism, -bu list, -bu lis'-tic, -bu lous.

som nĭ fā'cient (-shĕnt), -nif'er-ous, -nif'ic, -nif'u gous.

sŏm nĭl'o quence, -quism, -quist, -quous (-kwŭs), -quy.

som'no lence, -len cy, -lent, -lent-ly, -no lism, -les'cent.

Sŏm'nus, *Myth.*

son (sŭn), -less, -ny, -ship, son-in-law.

sō'nant, -nan cy.

sō nä'ta, *-nä ti'na* (-tē'-).

sŏn'de li (-dä lē).

sŏn'er ĭ.

song, -ful, -less, -ster, -stress, -craft, -man.

song'-bird, -book, -mus cle, -mu-sic, -spar row, -thrush, s. form.

sŏn'i fer, sō nif'er ous.

sŏn'net, -net eer', -net ize, -ized, -ĭ'zing, son'net-writ'er.

sō nŏ'roŭs, -ly, -ness, -nom'e ter, -no res'cence, -res'cent, -no rif'-ic, -no'ro phone, so nor'i ty.

Sŏn'tăg (*or* zōn'täg), Ger. vocalist.

sŏn'tâg, a cape.

sōon.

sōot (*or* sōot), -y, -i ly, -i ness, -ish, -less, soot'-can'cer, -dew, -flake, -wart.

sōoth, -fast, -say, -say er, -say-ing.

sōothe, soothed, sōoth'er, -ing, -ing ly.

sop, -ping, -py, sopped.

Sŏp'a ter, *Bib.*

Sŏph'e rĕth, *Bib.*

sŏph'ism, -ist, -ist ry, so phis'tic, -tic al, -al ly, -al ness, -phis'-ti cate, -cā'ted, -cā'ting, -cā'-tor, -cā'tion.

Soph'o cles (-klēz), Athenian poet, -clē'an.

sŏph'o more, -mŏr'ic, -ic al.

sō phros'y nē (-frŏs ĭ nē).

sō'pi ent, sō'pite, sō'por, sŏp o-rif'er ous, -ous ly, -ous ness, -o rĭf'ic, -o rose, -o rous.

sō prä'nŏ, -nist.

Sor bŏnne', -bŏn'ic al, -bon ist.

sor'cer er, -cer ess, -cer ous, -cer y.

sor'did, -ly, -ness, *sor'des* (-dēz).

sor di'no (-dē'-), *sor'do*, *-dō'no.*

sore, -ly, -ness, sore'head, a per-son, sore'-eyed, -fal con.

Sō rĕl', t. Can.

sor'ghum, -mill, -strip'per.

sō rō'ral, -rŏr'i cide.

sō rō'sis, *pl.* -ses (-sēz).

sŏr'rel, -tree, -vine.

sŏr'rŏw, -er, -ful, -ful ly, -ful-ness, -less, -ing, -ing ly, sor'ry, -ri ly, -ri ness, -rowed.

sort, -a ble, -ed, -er, -ing, sort'-ing-box.

sor'tes (-tēz), -ti lĕge.

sortiē.

sō'shĭ.

Sō'si a (-shĭ-), servant of Amphit-ryon.

Sō sĭp'a ter, *Bib.*

sos te lu'to (-ta loo'tō).
Sŏs thē nēs (-nēz), *Bib.*
Sŏs'trȧ tŭs, *Bib.*
sŏt, -ted, -ting, -tish, -tish ly, -tish ness.
Sŏ'tȧi (*or* -tā ĭ), *Bib.*
sŏ tĕ rĭ ol'o gy, -o log'ic al.
Soth'ern (sŭth'-), Amer. actor.
sot'ni a.
sŏt'to, sŏt'to vō'ce (-chä).
sou (soo), *pl.* sous (sooz *or* soo), a coin.
sou ä'rĭ, -nut.
sou'brette'.
sou bri quet' (soo'brĕ'kä'). See *sobriquet.*
sou chong' (soo shŏng').
Sou dän' (soo'-). See *Sudan.*
souf'fle (soo'fl), *Med.*
souf'flĕ (soo'flä), *Cookery* and *Ceramics.*
souf fler' (soo flêr'), a prompter.
sou frière'-bird (soo frȧyr'-).
sough (sŭf *or* sou), -ing, soughed, sough'ing-tile.
sought (sawt).
sŏul, -ful, -ful ly, -ful ness, -less, -less ness.
sŏul'-blind, -blind ness, -dĕaf, -fear ing, -kill ing, -sick, -sleep er, -stuff, -vexed.
Sou langes' (soo'lŏnzh'), co. Que.
Sou lĕ' (soo lä'), Amer. polit.
Sou louque' (soo look'), Emp. of Haiti.
Soult (soolt), Marshal of Fr.
sound, -a ble, -ed, -er, -ing, -less, -ly, -ness, sound'board.
sound'-board ing, -bod y, a box, -bone, a fish-bone, -bow, of a bell, -box, -chest, -dĕaf ness, -fig ures, -hole, -lens, -line, -post, -proof, -ra di om'e ter, -reg'is ter, -shad ow, -wave, sound'er mag net.
sound'ing-ap pa ra'tus, -board, -bot tle, -lĕad, -line, -ma chine, -post, -rod.
soup (soop), -y, soup'-bone, -kitch ĕn, -māi'gre, -meat, -plate, -stock, -tick'et.
soup çon' (soop sôṅ').
sou'ple (soo'-).

sour, -ing, -ly, -ness, soured, sour'wood, a tree.
sour'-eyed, -gourd, a tree, -grȧss, -gum, a tree, -mash, -sop, -tree, sour'ing-ves sel.
sŏurce.
sour'crout'. See *sauerkraut.*
sour dine' (soor dĕn').
souse, soused, sous'ing.
sou tache' (soo tȧsh').
sou tane' (soo'tȧn').
south, -land, -ly, -most, -ward, -ward ly, -wards, south'er, south'ing, south'-seek ing, the South.
south east', -east'er, -er ly, -ern, -east'ward, -ward ly.
south west', -west'er, -er ly, -ern, -west'ward, -ward ly, sou' west'er.
South'down, South-Af'ri can.
south'ern (sŭth'-), -ern er, -ern ism, -ern ize, -ized, -i'zing, -ern most *or* -er most, -er ing, -er land, -er ly, -li ness, -ern wood.
South'ey (*or* sŭth'ĭ), Eng. poet.
sou ve nir' (soo'vĕ nêr' *or* soov'nēr).
sov'er eign (sŭv'er ĭn *or* -ĕn), -ly, -ty.
So vi cil'le (sō vĕ chē'lä), vil. It.
sŏw, -er, -ing, sŏwed, sŏwn, sŏw'ing-ma chine'.
sow (sou), -back, a ridge of sand, -bane, a plant, -bread, a plant, sow'-bean, -bug, -drunk, -fen nel, -pea, -this tle, sow'ar (sou'-).
Sŏw'er, Ger. printer in Amer.
soy, -bean, -pea.
soz'zle, zly.
Spa (*or* spä), a watering place Belg.
spä, a mineral spring.
space, -ful, -less, spaced, spä'cer, -cing, spä'tial, -tial ly, -ti al'i ty.
space'-box, -co or'di nate, -curv'a ture, -ho mol'o gy, -line, -mark, -per cep'tion, -re la'tion, -rule, -writ'ing, spä'cing-lace.
spä'cious (-shŭs), -ly, -ness.
spa das sin' (spä'dȧ'sȧṅ' *or* spȧd'ȧs sĭn).

spade, -ful, spād′ed, -er, -ing, spade′fish, -foot, a toad.

spade′-bay o net, -farm, -foot, *a.*, -foot ed, -grȧft, -guin ea, -gun, -han dle, -hus′band ry, -i ron, -rack, spād′ing-ma chine.

spā′dix, *pl.* -dix es *or* spa dī′ces (-cēz).

spȧ ghet′ti (-gĕt′tē).

spake′net.

spȧld, -er, spȧld′ing-knife.

spale.

spȧll, a chip or splinter; to split or chip, spȧll′ing-floor, -ham- mer.

spȧl′peen.

span, -less, -ning, spanned, span′- worm.

span′-beam, -block, -dogs, -lash- ing, -long, -new, -piece, -roof, -saw, -shac kle.

spăn′drel, -wall.

span′gle, -gled, -gler, -gling, -gly, span′gling-ma chine.

Spăn′iard (-yard), Span′ish.

spăn′iel (-yĕl).

spănk, -er, -ing, spanked.

spank′er-boom, -eel, -gȧff, -mȧst.

spar, -rer, -ring, -ry, sparred, spar′hawk, spar′-buoy, -deck, -dust, -māk′er, -tor pe′do.

spâre, -ly, -ness, spared, spâr′er, -ing, -ing ly, -ing ness, spare′rib, spare′-built.

sparge, sparged, spar′ger, -ging.

spark, -er, -ish, -ing, sparked.

spark′-ar rest′er, -coil, -con- dens′er, -con sum′er, -gap, -net- ting, sparked′-back.

spar′kle, -kled, -kler, -kling, -kling ly, -kling ness, spar′kle- ber′ry.

spar′ling, -fowl.

spăr′rōw, -tail, shaped like a sparrow's tail, -wort.

spar′row-bill, -grȧss, -hawk, -owl, -tail, a sparrow's tail.

sparse, -ly, -ness, spars′i ty.

Spär′ta, an ancient kingdom, -tan, -tan ism.

spär′ter iĕ.

spasm (spăzm), spas mod′ic (spăz-), -ic al, -al ly.

spat, -ted, -ter, -ting.

spāthe, spāthed, spāthe′bill.

spat′ter, -ing, -tered, spat′ter- dash, -work, spat′ter-dock.

spat′tle, spat′tling-ma chine′.

spăt′u la, -u late, -u lar, -ule, -u lĭ form, -u lā′tion.

spăv′in, -ined.

spawl, saliva; to eject saliva; -ing, spawled.

spȧwn, -er, -ing, spawned.

spawn′-brick, -eat er, -fuṇ gus, -hatch er, -ris ing.

spawn′ing-bed, -ground, -screen, -sea son.

spay, -ing, spayed.

spēak, -a ble, -er, -er ship, -ing, -ing ly, spoke, spo ken.

speak′ing-ma chine′, -trum pet, -tube, s. voice.

spear, -er, -ing, speared, spear′- fish, -flow er, -man, -mint, -wood, a tree, -wort.

spear′-billed, -dog, -foot, -grȧss, -hand, -head, -hook, -jăve′lin, -leafed, -lil y, -nail, -plate, -this tle, -wid geon.

spe′cial (spĕsh′al), -ist, -ism, -ize, -ized, -ī′zing, -ly, -ty *or* spe ci- al′i ty (spĕsh′ĭ ăl′-).

spē′cie (-shĭ), coin; money.

spē′ci e (-shĭ ē), in kind.

spē′cies (-shēz), -cov er, -cy cle, -mon ger, -pa per, -sheet.

spē cĭf′ic, -al ly, -al ness, -ic ness.

spec′i fy, -ing, -fi a ble, -fied, -fi er, -fĭ cā′tion.

spec′i men.

spē′cious (-shŭs), -ly, -ness.

speck, -ing, -less, -y, specked, speck′-block, -fall, -moth.

spec′kle, -kled, -kled ness, -kling, spec′kle bel ly, a goose; a duck; a trout, spec′kle-bel lied, -tailed, spec′kled-bill, spec′kled beau′ty, s. bird, s. brant, s. foot′man, s. In′dian, s. trout, s. wood.

spec′ta cle, -cled, -cles, -tac′u lar, -lar ly, -lăr′i ty.

spec′ta cle-fur nace, -gage, -glȧss, -māk er, -or na ment.

spec ta′tor, -ship, -tant.

spec′ter *or* -tre, -tral, -tral ly.

spec'ter-bar, -can dle, -crab, -in-
sect, -le mur, -shrimp.
spec'tro graph, -graph'ic, -trog'-
ra phy, -trol'o gy, -tro log'ic al,
-trom'e ter, -tro met'ric, -tro-
mī'cro scop'ic al, -tro phone,
-phon'ic, -tro pho tom'e ter, -e-
try, -pho to met'ric, -tro po lăr'-
i scope, -tro py rom'e ter.
spec'tro scope, -scop'ic, -ic al,
-al ly, -tro scŏ'py (or -trŏs'co-),
-tro scŏ'pist (or -trŏs'co-), spec'-
trum, pl. -tra, spec'u lar.
spec'u late, -la ted, -la ting, -la-
tist, -lå tive, -tive ly, -tive ness,
-lā tor, -lå'to'ry, -la ble, -lā'-
tion.
spec'u lum, pl. -la or -lums,
spec'u lum-for ceps, -met al.
speech, -less, -less ly, -less ness,
speech'māk'er, -māk ing, speech'-
cen ter, -cri er, -day, -read ing.
speed, -ed, -er, -ing, -ful, -ful ly,
-less, -y, -i ly, -i ness, speed'-
way, -well.
speed'-cone, -gage, -in di ca tor,
-meas ur er, -mul'ti pli er, -pul-
ley, -re cord'er, -rig gers, -sight,
speed'y-cut.
speiss.
spĕk'-bōōm.
spē'le ol'o gy, -le'an.
spell, a ble, er, ing, spelled or
spelt, spell'bīnd, v., -bīnd er,
-bound, spell'-bone, -stopped,
-work, spell'ing-bee, -book,
-match.
spĕl'ter.
spĕn'cer, -gaff, -måst.
Spen'cer, Eng. philos., -ce'ri an,
-an ism.
spend, -er, -ing, spent, spend'-
thrift, spend'-all, spend'ing-
mon ey.
Spen'ser, Eng. poet, -se'ri an.
sperm, -ol'o gy, -o gist, -o log'-
ic al, sperm'-ball, -blas'to derm,
-blas'tu la, -cell, -ker nel, -mor'-
u la, -nu cle us, -oil, -rope,
-whale.
sper'ma cĕ'tĭ, -oil, -whale.
spetch.
spew (spū), -er, -ing, -y, spewed.

Spey (spā), r. Scot.
Spey'er or Spei'er (spī'er or spīr),
c. Bav.
Spe'zi a (spä'dzē ä), t. It.
Spez'zi a (spĕt'sē ä), isl. and gulf,
Greece.
sphe'noid, -noid'al.
sphēre, -less, sphĕr'al, sphĕr'ic,
-ic al, -al ly, -al ness, sphē ric'-
i ty, -roid, -roid'al, -al ly,
sphere'-crys tals, -yeast.
sphĕr'ule (sfĕr'ōōl or -ūl), -u lar,
-u late, -u līte, -lĭt'ic.
sphinc'ter (sfĭnk'-), -ter al, -ter-
ate, -tĕr'ic, -tĕ'ri al.
sphinx, pl. sphinx'es or sphin'ges
(-jĕz), Sphinx, Myth., sphinx'-
moth.
spice, -ful, spiced, spī'cer, -cer y,
-ci ly, -ci ness, -cing, -cy,
spice'ber ry, -bush, -wood.
spice'-ap ple, -box, -cake, -mill,
-nut, -shop, -tree.
spick, -and-span.
spī'cose, -coŭs, -cŏs'i ty, -ci form,
spī cif'er ous.
spĭc'ule (spĭk'-), -u lar, -u late,
-u lous, spic'ule-sheath.
spī'der, -y, spi'der flow er, -work,
-wort.
spī'der-ant, -band, -bug, -catch-
er, -cells, -cot, -crab, -dīv'er,
-eat er, -fly, -hel met, -hunt er,
-legs, -line, -mite, -moɳ key,
-net, -or chis, -shell, -stitch,
-wasp, -web, -wheel.
Spiē'gel, Ger. orient.
spiē'gel, -gel ei'sen (-zĕn), -gel-
erz (-erts), spie'gel-i ron.
spiē'ler.
Spiĕl'hä gen, Ger. novelist.
Spiĕss, Ger. painter.
spĭg'ot, -joint, -pot.
spīke, -let, -nard (or spĭk'nard),
spīk'er, -ing, -y, spiked, spike'-
bill, a duck, -fish, -horn, a
deer, -nose, a fish, -tail, a
duck, -worm.
spike'-ex tract or, -grass, -horn,
a horn, -lav en der, -ma chine,
-nail, -oil, -plank, -rush, -shell,
-tac kle, -tailed, -team, spike'-
nard-tree.

spile, spiled, spīl'ing, spile'-
bor er, -hole.

spill, -er, -ing, spilled *or* spilt,
spill'way.

spill'-case, -chan nel, -stream,
-trough, spill'ing-line.

spin, -ner, -ner et, -ner ule, -ner y,
-ning, -stress, spun.

spin'ning-frame, -head, -jack,
-jen ny, -ma chine, -mill, -mite,
-or gan, -roll er, -spi der, -wheel,
-wort.

spĭn'ach *or* -age (-āj *or* -ĕj).

Spi naz'zō la (spē nät'sō lä), t. It.

spin'dle, -dled, -dling, -dly, spin'-
dle legs, a person, -shanks, a
person, -tail, a duck, -worm.

spin'dle-cat'a ract, -cell, -celled,
-lāthe, -legs, slender, -legged,
-shanked, -shanks, legs, -shaped,
-shell, -step, -strŏmb, -tree, -valve,
-whorl.

spin'drift.

spine, -less, spined, spī'nal, -nate,
-nes'cent, spīn'y, -i ness, spine'-
back, a fish, -bel ly, a fish,
-bill, a bird, -foot, a lizard, -tail,
a bird, spine'-armed, -bear er,
spīn y-eel, -finned, -skinned.

spĭn'na ker, -boom.

spin'ney *or* -ny.

spī'nōde, -nose, -nose ly, -nous,
-nŏs'i ty, spī'node-curve, -torse.

Spi nō'za (spē-), Dutch philos.,
-nō'zism, -zist, -zis'tic.

spin'ster, -dom, -hood, -ship.

spĭr'a cle (*or* spīr'-), spī răc'u lar,
-u late.

spī ræ'a, Spī ræ'a, *Bot. genus.*

spī'rant, -rā'tion.

spire, *n.*, spired, spī'ral, -ral ly,
-răl'i ty, spīr'y, spī'ral tail, a
bird, spire'-bear er, -light, -stee-
ple.

spire, *v.*, spired, spīr'ing.

spĭr'it, -ed, -ed ly, -ed ness, -ing,
-ism, -ist, -is'tic, -less, -less ly,
-less ness, -ous, -ous ness, *spi-
ri tō'so* (spē'rē tō'sō), spir'it leaf,
a plant, -weed.

spir'it-back, -blue, -brown, -but-
ter fly, -duck, -gum, -lamp,
-lev el, -mer chant, -me ter,

-rap per, -rap'ping, -room, -stir-
ring, -world.

spĭr'it u al, -ism, -ist, -is'tic, -al-
ly, -al'i ty, -al ize, -ized, -ī'zer,
-ī'zing, -ī zā'tion, -al ness, -it u-
ous, -ous ness, *spir it u elle'*
(spē'rē'tŏŏ ĕl').

spi'ro grăph.

spī rom'e ter, -e try, -ro met'ric,
-ro phore.

spit, -ter, -ting, spit'ball, -box, -fire.

spit'-bug, -curl, -deep, -poi son,
-rack, -stick er, -ven'om, spit'-
ting-snake.

spite, -ful, -ful ly, -ful ness, spīt'-
ed, -ing, -toon'.

spit'tle, -tly, spit'tle-fly, -in sect,
-of-the-stars, a plant.

spitz, -flute -käs ten, spitz-dog.

splanch'nic (splănk'nĭk), splanch-
nog'ra pher, -ra phy, -no graph'-
ic al, -nol'o gy, -o gist, -no log'-
ic al.

splash, -er, -ing, -y, splashed,
splash'-board, -dam, -wing.

splat'ter, -ing, -tered, splat'ter-
dash, splat'ter-faced.

splay, -er, -ing, splayed, splay'foot,
a person, splay'-foot, a foot,
-footed, -mouth, -mouthed.

spleen, -ful, -ful ly, -ish, -ish ly,
-ish ness, -less, -y, *splē nal'gi a,*
-nal'gic, spleen'wort, spleen'-pulp,
-stone.

splen'dent, -did, -did ly, -did-
ness, -dor, -dor ous.

splĕ nĕt'ic (*or* splĕn'e tic), -ic al,
-al ly, splĕn'ic.
splē nī'tis, -nĭt'ic.

splice, spliced, splī'cer, -cing,
splice'-grăft'ing, -piece, splī'cing-
fid, -ham mer, -shac'kle.

spline, splined, splīn'ing-ma-
chine.

splint, -age, splint'-bone, -bot-
tomed, -box, -coal, -ma chine,
-plane, s. ar mor, s. band'age.

splin'ter, -ing, -y, -tered, splin'ter-
bar, -bone, -net ting, -proof.

split, -ful, -ter, -ting, split'beak, a
bird, -feet, animals, -foot, Satan,
-mouth, a fish, -tail, a duck; a
fish.

split'-back, *a.,* -bot tomed, -brilliant, -har ness, -new, -tongued, split'ting -knife, -ma chine, -saw, split dy'na mom'e ter, s. in fin'-i tive, s. phase, s. staves, s. stuff.

splotch, -y.

splurge, splurg'y, -ing, splurged.

splut'ter, -er, -ing, -tered.

spoil, -a ble, -age, -er, -ing, spoiled *or* spoilt, spoils'man, -mon ger, s. sys'tem, spoil'-bank, -five, -pa per, -sport.

spoke, *v.,* spo'ken, spokes'man.

spoke, *n.,* -au ger, -bone, -drīv'-ing, -gage, -lāthe, -plān'ing, -point er, -pol ish ing, -set ter, -shave, -siz'ing, -ten on ing, -throat ing, -trim mer, -turn ing, spōk'ing-ma chine.

spō'li ate, -ā'ted, -ā'ting, -ā'tive, -ā'tor, -to'ry, -å ry, -ā'tion.

spǒn'dee, -dā'ic, -ic al.

spǒn'dyl.

sponge (spŭnj), sponged, spon'ger, -ging, -gi form, -gy, -gi ness, sponge'wood, a plant.

sponge'-an i mal'cule, -bar, -cake, -cov er, -crab, -cu cum ber, -cup, -dīv'ing, -farm er, -fish er, -fish-er y, -glăss, -gourd, -hook, -moth, -spic ule, -tongs,-tree, spon'ging-house, spon'gy-pu bes'cent, -vil-lous.

spǒn gǒl'o gy, -o gist, -go log'ic al.

spǒn'sion, -al.

spǒn'son.

spǒn'sor, -ship, -so'ri al.

spon ta'ne ous, -ous ly, -ous ness, -ta nē'i ty.

spo͞ok, -ish, -y.

spo͞ol, -stand, spool'-cot ton, -hold er, -la bel ing, spool'ing-ma chine, -wheel.

spo͞on, -ful, -y, -i ly, -i ness, -ing, spooned.

spoon'beak, a bird, -bill, a bird, -flow er, a plant, -tail, a crustacean, -wood, a tree, -worm, -wort.

spoon'-bait, -billed, -bit, -chis el, -drift, -fash ion, -gouge, -hold-er, -hook, -man, -meat, -net, -oar, -saw, -shaped, -vict uals.

spo͞or, -er, -ing, spoored.

spǒ rad'ic, -ic al, -al ly, -al ness, spǒ'ral.

spore, spor'ous, spǒr'ule, -u lar, -u late, -u lā'tion, spore'-capsule, -case, -cell, -for ma'tion, -group, -plasm, -sac.

sport, -er, -ful, -ful ly, -ful ness, -ing, -ing ly, -ive, -ive ly, -ive-ness, -less, -ling, sports'man, sports'man like, -man ship, sports'wom an, sport'ing-book, -house.

spot, -ted, -ted ness, -ter, -ting, -ty, -ti ness, -less, -less ly, -less-ness, spot'neck, a bird, -rump, a bird, spot'-ball, -lens, -stitch, spot'ted-tree, spot'ted bǎss.

spouse (spouz), -less, spous'al.

spout, -ed, -er, -ing, -less, spout'-fish, spout'-hole, -shell.

sprag, -ging, spragged, sprag'-road.

sprain, -ing, sprained.

sprat, -ted, -ter, -ting, sprat'-bar-ley, -bōr er, -day, -loon, -mew.

sprawl, -er, -ing, sprawled.

spray, -er, -ing, -ey, sprayed.

spray'-board, -drain, -in stru-ment, -noz zle, spray'ing-ma-chine.

sprĕad, -er, -ing, -ing ly, spread'-ea gle, -ea gle ism.

spread'ing-ad der, -board, -frame, -fur nace, -ham mer, -ma chine, -ov en, -plate.

sprec'kled.

Spree (sprāy), r. Ger.

spree, -ing, spreed.

sprew (spro͞o).

sprig, -ging, -gy, sprigged, sprig'-tail, a duck, sprig'-bolt, -crys-tal, -tailed.

sprīght'ly, -li ness.

spring, -er, -ing, -less, -let, -like, -y, -i ness, sprang *or* sprung, sprung, *p. p.*

spring'bok, a gazel, -tail, an insect, -tide, a season, -time, -worm, -wort.

spring'-back, -band, -bar, -beam, -beau ty, -bee tle, -bell, -block, -board, -box, -buck, -flood, -fly, -fore lock, -gun, -häas, -hạlt,

-ham mer, -hang er, -hĕad, -hook, -house, -jack, -latch, -lig- a ment, -line, -lock, -net, -oys- ter, -pad lock, -pawl, -plank, -pole, -shac kle, -stay, -stud, -tailed, -tide, a tide, -wa ter, -wĕir.

spring′ bal ance, s. bed, s. car- riage, s. cart, s. cress, s. cro′cus, s. fe′ver, s. mat tress, s. punch, s. search er, s. tool, s. trap, s. valve, s. wag on.

spring′ing-bee tle, -course, -hairs, -line, -tool, -wall.

springe, springed, springe′ing, sprin′gle.

sprin′kle, -kled, -kler, -kling.

sprint, -ed, -er, -ing, sprint′-race, -run ner.

sprit, -ty, sprit′sail, -tail, a duck.

sprite, sprīt′ish ly.

sprŏck′et, -wheel.

sprout, -ed, -ing, sprout′-cell, -chain, -gem′ma (-jem′-), -ger- mi nā′tion.

spruce, -ly, -ness, spruced, spru′- cing.

spruce′-duff, -fir, -grouse, -gum, -o cher, -par tridge, -pine, s. beer.

sprue, -hole.

spruit (sproit).

spry, -er, -est.

spud, -ded, -ding, -dy.

spud′dle, -dled, -dling.

spume, spumed, spūm′ing, -y, -i ness, -ous, spu mes′cent, -cence, -mif′er ous, -mose′.

spun, -out, *a.*, -yarn, s. silk, s. sil′ver.

spunk, -y.

spur, -rer, -ri er, -ring, -ry, -less, spurred, spur′flow er, -way, -wing, a bird, -wort.

spur′-bun ting, -fowl, -gall, -gall y, -gear ing, -hawk, -heeled, -lĕath er, -legged, -pep- per, -prŭn′ing, -roy al, -shell, -shore, -track, -tree, -wheel, -winged.

spurge, -wort, -creep er, -flax, -lau rel, -net tle, -ol ive.

spū′ri ous, -ly, -ness.

spur′ling-line.

spurn, -er, -ing, spurned, spurn′- wa ter.

spurt, -ed, -er, -ing.

Spurz′heĭm (spōŏrts′-), Ger. phrenologist.

sputch′eon.

sput′ter, -er, -ing, -tered.

spū′tum, pl. *-ta.*

spy, -ing, -ism, spīed, spy′boat, -crâft, spy′-glass, -hole, -mon- ey.

squab (skwŏb), -bing, -bish, -by, squabbed, squab′-chick, squab- pie.

squab′ble, -bled, -bler, -bling.

squăc′co.

squad (skwŏd), -ded, -ding.

squad′ron, -ing, -roned.

squail, -er, -ing, squailed.

Squā′li.

squal′id (skwŏl′-), -ly, -ness, squa lid′i ty, squal′or (skwŏl′- *or* squā′lor).

squall, -er, -y, squalled.

squam (skwŏm), -duck.

squā′ma, -mate, -mā′tion, -mous.

squan′der (skwŏn′-), -er, -ing, -ing ly, -dered.

square, -ly, -ness, squared, squâr′er, -ing, square′head, a person, -man, one who uses a square, -sail, -spot, a moth.

square′-built, -flip per, a seal, -leg, -spot, *a.*, -stern, a boat, -toes, a person, squâr′ing- boards, -plow, -shears, square coûp ling, s. end, s. knot, s. man, an upright man, s. meas′ure, s. num′ber, s.′ root, s. rule.

squash (skwŏsh), -er, -ing, -y, -i ness.

squash′-bee tle, -bōr er, -bug, -gourd, -mel on, -vine.

squat (skwŏt), -tage, -ted, -ter, -ting, -ty, squat′-snipe, -tag, squat′ting-pill.

squaw, -fish, -root, a plant, -weed.

squaw′-ber ry, -duck, -huc′kle- ber ry, -man, -mint, -vine.

squawk, -er, -ing, squawked, squawk′-duck, squawk′ing- thrush.

squĕak, -er, -ing, -ing ly, -y, -i ly,
-let, squeaked.
squĕal, -er, -ing, squealed.
squĕam'ish, -ish ly, -ish ness.
squee'gee, -ing.
squeeze, squeez'a ble, -a bil'i ty,
-er, -ing, squeezed, squeez'ing-
box.
squelch, -ing, squelched.
squĕ tĕague'.
squib, -bing, -bish, squibbed.
squid, -ded, -ding, squid'-fork,
-hound, -jig, -jig ger, -throw er.
Squier (skwīr), Amer. archæol.
squig'gle, -gled, -gling.
squil'gee, -ing, -geed, squil'gee-
tog gle.
squill, -fish.
squint, -ed, -er, -ing, -ing ly,
squint'-eyed, -mind ed.
squire, -hood, -ling, -ly, squired,
squir'ing, squire'arch (-ark),
-arch al, -arch y.
squirm, -ing, squirmed.
squir'rĕl (skwêr'- or skwĭr'- or
skwŭr'-), -cup, a plant, -tail, a
grass.
squir'rel-bot, -corn, -fish, -grass,
-hake, -hawk, -le mur, -lock,
-mon key, -mouse, -pe tau'rist,
-pha lan'ger, -shrew.
squirt (skwêrt), -ed, -er, -ing,
squirt'-gun.
Sri'nä gär' (srē'-), dist. India.
stab, -ber, -bing, -bing ly, -wort,
stabbed, stab'bing-ma chine,
-press.
Stā'bat Mā'ter.
stăb'il ize, -ized, -i' zing, -ĭ zā'-
tion, stā'ble, -ble ness, -bly,
-bil'i ty.
stā'ble, -bled, -bler, -bling, stā'-
ble man.
stā'ble-boy, -call, -fly, -room,
-stand.
stăc cä'tō, -ca tis'si mo.
stā'chis (-kĭs).
Stā'chys (-kĭs), *Bib.*
stack, -age, -er, -ing, stacked.
stack'-bŏr er, -fun nel, -guard,
-room, -stand, -yard.
stack'ing-band, -belt, -dĕr rick,
-stage.

stad'dle, -dled, -dling, stad'dle-
roof, -stand.
Stä'dĕ, c. Prus.
stade, a furlong; a wharf.
stăd'hold'er or stadt'- (stăt'-),
-er ate, -er ship.
stä'di um, pl. *-di a*, stā dĭ om'e ter.
stăff, *pl.* stāves (*or* stävz), a pole
or cane; a character in music;
stăffs, military officers; a body
of assistants. stăffed.
stăff'-an gle, -bead, -cap tain,
-com mand'er, -de gree, -du ty,
-herd ing, -hole, -man, -no tā'-
tion, -of fi cer, -ser geant,
-stone, -sur geon, -tree, -vine.
stag, -ging, stagged, stag'bush, a
plant, -hound.
stag'-bee tle, -dance, -e vil,
-head ed, -horn, -par ty, -stick,
-tick, -worm, stag's-horn.
stage, staged, stā'ging, -ger, -gy,
stage'wright.
stage'-box, -car riage, -coach,
-crăft, -drīv'er, -fe ver, -for ceps,
-hand, -house, -man'a ger, -mi-
crom'e ter, -plate, -play, -play er,
-set ter, -struck, -wag on.
stage' di rec'tion, s. door, s.
ef fect, s. fright, s. right, s.
wait, s. whis per.
stag'ger, -er, -ing, -ing ly, -gered,
stag'ger bush, a plant, -wort,
stag'ger-grăss.
Stăg'I rīte (stăj'-), name applied
to Aristotle.
stăg'nant, -ly, -nan cy, -nate,
-nā'ted, -nā'ting, -nā'tion.
stähl'spiēl.
staid, sober; grave, -ly, -ness.
stāin, -a ble, -er, -ing, -less, -less-
ly, stained.
stāir, -beak, a bird, -case, -way,
stair'-foot, -head, -rod, -wire,
stair'case-shell.
stake, staked, stāk'er, -ing, stake'-
hold er.
stake'-boat, -drīv'er, -head, -hook,
-i ron, -net, -net ter, -pock et,
-pull er, -rest.
sta lac'tīte, -tī'ted, -tic, -tic al,
-ti form, stăl ac tĭt'ic, -ic al,
-tit'i form.

---

nŏt, nôr, ūse, ŭp, ûrn, etüde, fōōd, fŏŏt, aṅger, boṅmot, ṫhus, Baċh.

sta lag′mīte, stal ag mit′ic, -ic al,
-al ly, -ag mom′e ter.

stale, -ly, -ness, stale′mate, -ma-
ted, -ma ting.

stalk (stǎwk), -er, -ing, -less, -let,
-y, stalked.

stalk′-bŏr er, -cut ter, -eyed,
-pull er, stalk′ing-horse.

stạll, -age, -er, -ing, stalled,
stall′man.

stạll′-board, -fed, -feed, -plate,
-read er.

stăl′lion (-yŭn).

stạl′wart, -ism, -ly, -ness.

stă′men, *pl.* stă′mens, *Bot.*,
stăm′i na, threads, stăm′i nal,
-nate, -nā′ted, -nā′ting, sta-
min′e ous.

stam′mer, -er, -ing, -ing ly,
-mered.

stamp, -age, -er, -ing, stamped.

stamp′-af fix er, -al bum, -bat-
ter y, -block, -book, -can cel-
ler, -col lect ing, -dis trib′u ter,
-du ty, -ham mer, -head, -ma-
chine, -mill, -mois′ten er, -note,
-of fice, stamp′ing-ground, -ma-
chine, -mill, -press.

stăm pēde′, -pēd′ed, -ing.

stặnch *or* stäunch, -er, -ing, -ly,
-less, -ness, stanched.

stăn′chion (-shŭn), -gun.

stand, -er, -ing, -ish, stood,
stand′by, -point, -still.

stand′-gall, -off, -off ish, -pipe,
-rest, -up.

stand′ing-cy press, -ground, -press,
-room, -stool.

stand′ard, -ize, -ized, -ī′zer, -ī′zing,
-ī zā′tion, stand′ard wing, a
bird.

stand′ard-bear er, -bread, -grăss,
-knee.

stand′er, -by, -grăss, -wort.

Stän ĭs lau′ (-lou′), t. Aust.

Stän ĭs laus′ (-lou′), co. Cal.

stăn′za, *pl.* -zas (-záz), -zaed,
-zā′ic.

stā′ple, -pled, -pler, -pling, stā′-
ple-house, -punch, -right.

star, -less, -let, -like, -lit, -ring,
-ry, -ri ness, starred.

star′beam, -blind, -board, -bush,

-crăft, -finch, -fish, -flow er,
-fruit, -light, -nose, a mole,
-shine, -tail, a bird, -throat, a
bird, -ward, -wort.

star′-an i mal, -an ise, -ap ple,
-bear er, -blăst ing, -bright, *a.*,
-buz zard, -cap si cum, -cat a-
logue, -chăm′ber, -clus ter,
-crossed, -di a mond, -drift,
-dust, -făc et, -gage, -gaze,
-gāz′er, -gāz′ing, -goose ber ry,
-grăss, -head, -hy a cinth, -liz-
ard, -map, -mold ing, -mouthed,
-net ting, -nosed, -pep per, -pile,
-pine, -proof, -reed, -row el,
-ru by, -sap phire, -sax i frage,
-scaled, -shake, -shell, -shoot,
-shot, -slough (-slŭf), -spạn′-
gled, -spot ted, -stone, -this tle,
-trap, -worm, star′fish-flow er,
star-of-Beth le hem, a plant,
-of-night, a plant, -of-the-earth,
a plant.

star′ fort, s. pa go′da, s. wheel.

starch, -er, -ing, -ly, -ness, -ed-
ly, -ed ness, -y, -i ness, starched,
starch′root, a plant.

starch′-cel lu lose, -gum, -hy a-
cinth, -ma chine, -star, -su gar.

stare, stared, stâr′ing, -ing ly, -er.

stark, -ly, -ness, stark′ na ked.

star′ling.

stăr′ost, -os ty.

start, -ed, -er, -ing.

start′ing-bar, -bolt, -en gine,
-place, -point, -post, -valve,
-wheel.

star′tle, -tled, start′ler, -ling,
-ling ly.

starve, -ling, starv′er, -ing,
starved, starve-a cre, a plant.

state, -less, -ly, -li ly, -li ness,
-ment, stăt′ed, -ed ly, -ing,
state′crăft, -hood, -room, states′-
man, -man like, -man ly, -man-
ship, -wom an, state-house,
-mọn ger, -so cial ism, -so cial-
ist, states-gen er al.

Stăt′en Is′land, isl. N. Y.

stath′mŏ grăph.

stăt′ic, -al, -al ly, -ics.

stā′tion, -al, -â ry, -â ri ness, -ing,
-tioned.

---

fāte, făt, fär, fạll, fâre, făst, sọfâ, mēte, mĕt, hêr, īce, ĭn, nōte,

stā′tion-bill, -cal en dar, -er′ror,
-house, -in di ca tor, -măs ter,
-me ter, -point er, -pole, -stăff.
stā′tion er, -er y.
sta tis′tic, -al, -al ly, -tics, stăt′-
is ti′cian (-tĭsh′an), -is tol′o gy.
stăt′or.
stăt′ūe, -u å ry, -ūed, -u ing,
-u esque′, -esque′ly, -esque′ness,
-u ette′, stat′u a ry-brass, -căst-
ing, stăt′ūe dress.
stăt′ure, -ured.
stā′tus, stā′tus in quō′, stā′tus
quō′.
stăt′ūte, -u tå ble, -tå bly, -u to′-
ry, stat′ute-book, -fair, -roll.
stave, n., pl. staves; stave, v.,
staved or stōve, stăv′er, -ing,
stave′wood, a tree.
stave′-bend er, -bil ging, -cham-
fer ing, -crōz ing, -cut ter,
-dress ing, -how el ling, -joint-
er, -plăn′ing, -rime, -riv ing,
-saw ing, -set ter, -tank ard.
stăv′er, -ers, -er wort.
stay, -er, -ing, -less, stayed or
staid, stay′busk, -cord, -lace,
-māk′er, -sail.
stay′-bar, -bolt, -chain, -end,
-foot, -gage, -hole, -hook, -light,
-pile, -plow, -rod, -tac kle,
-wedge, stay-at-home, a person.
stĕad.
stĕad′fast or sted′-, -ly, -ness.
stĕad′y, -ing, -i ly, -i ness, -i er,
stĕad′y-go ing.
steăk, -crush′er, -mash er.
stĕal, -er, -ing, -ing ly, stole, stō′-
len (-ln), stĕalth, -y, -i ly,
-i ness.
stĕam, -er, -ing, -y, -i ness,
steamed, steam′boat ing, steam′-
ship.
steam′-at′om i zer, -blow er,
-boil er, -box, -brake, -car,
-car riage, -case, -chăm ber,
-chest, -chim ney, -cock, -coil,
-col or, -crane, -cut ter, -cyl′-
in der, -dome, -dredg er, -en-
gine, -ex′ca va tor, -foun tain,
-gage, -gas, -gen′er a tor, -gov-
ern or, -gun, -ham mer, -heat,
-hoist, -house, -jack et, -jet,

-joint, -ket tle, -kitch en,
-läunch, -mo tor, -nav i ga′tion,
-na vy, -or gan, -ov en, -pack-
et, -pan, -pipe, -plow, -port,
-pow er, -press, -print ing, -pro-
pel′ler, -pump, -ra′di a tor,
-ram, -reg′u la tor, -room,
-space, -ta ble, -tank, -tight,
-toe, -trap, -tug, -valve, -ves sel,
-wag on, -wheel, -whis tle,
-winch, -worm, -yacht, steam′er-
cap, -duck.
steam′boat, -bug, -coal, -rolls,
-screen.
stē′a rin, -a rate, -ăr′ic, stē′a rin-
press.
stē′a tīte, -tĭt′ic.
steed, -less.
steel, -ing, -y, -i ness, -i fy, -fy-
ing, -fīed, -fī cā′tion, steeled.
steel′boy, -head, a duck; a trout,
-măs ter, -ware, -work, -yard.
steel′-blue, -bow, a., -clad, -en-
grav ing, -finch, -mill, -ore,
-press, -saw, -work er, -works.
steen, -bok, -kirk.
steep, -en, -er, -ing, -ly, -ness,
steeped, steep′weed, -wort, steep′-
down, -grăss, -to, -tub, -up,
-wa ter.
stee′ple, -pled, stee′ple bush, a
plant, -chase, -chās′er, -top, a
whale.
stee′ple-crowned, -en gine, -hunt-
ing, -jack, s. hat.
steer, -a ble, -age, -age way, -er,
-ing, steers′man, -man ship.
steer′ing-ap pa ra′tus, -com pass,
-gear, -sail, -wheel.
steeve, steeved, steev′ing.
Stein′ber ger, a wine.
stein′bok or -bock. See steenbok.
stē′lē, ste′lar.
stel′la, -lar, -lå ry, -late, -late ly,
-lå ted, -lu lar, -lu late.
stel′ler, the sea-cow.
stem, -mer, -mer y, -ming, -less,
-let, -son, stemmed.
stem′-char ac ter, -clăsp ing,
-clīmb er, -eel worm, -head,
-knee, -leaf, -piece, -sick ness,
-stitch, -wīnd er, s. end.
stench, -y, stench′-pipe, -trap.

nŏt, nôr, ūse, ŭp, ûrn, etüde, fōōd, fŏŏt, aṅger, boṅmot, thus, Bach.

35

sten'cil, -cĭled *or* -cilled, -cil ing
or -ling, -cil er *or* -ler.
sten'cil-cut ter, -pen, -plate.
sten'o grăph, -grăph'ic, -ic al,
-al ly, stē nog'ra pher, -phist,
-phy.
sten'o pa'ic.
stĕn'o type, -ty'py, -typ'ic (-tĭp'-),
-o te lĕg'ra phy.
sten'ter, a machine.
sten'tor, a person with a loud voice;
a howling monkey; a species of
Infusoria. sten tō'ri an.
step, -per, -ping, stepped.
step'bairn, -broth er, -child,
-daugh ter, -fa'ther, -moth er,
-moth er ly, -sis ter, -son.
step'-back, *a.*, -bit, -box, -coun-
try, -cov er, -cut, -dame,
-dance, -fault, -gage, -grate, -lad-
der, -par ent, -stone, -vein,
step'ping-point, -stone.
Stĕph'a năs, *Bib.*
stĕph'a nē, a head-dress, *-a nos.*
Steph'a no (stĕf'-), Shak., *Tempest.*
Stĕ'phen (-vn), *Bib.*
steppe (stĕp), a level treeless plain.
stĕre (*or* stâr).
stĕr'ĕ ŏ gram, -o grăph, -grăph'-
ic, -ic al, -al ly, -og'ra phy,
-om'e ter, -e try, -o met'ric al,
-al ly.
stĕr'ĕ ŏ scope (*or* stē'rē-), -scŏp'-
ic, -ic al, -al ly, -scŏ'pist (*or*
-ŏs'co pist), -scō'py (*or* -ŏs'copy), -ŏp'ti con.
stĕr'ĕ ŏ type (*or* stē'-), -typed,
-ty'per, -per y, -ty'ping, -pist,
-py, -pog'ra pher, -ra phy.
stĕr'ĕ ŏ type-block, -found'ry,
-met al, s. plate.
stĕr'ĭle, -il ize, -ized, -ĭ'zing,
-ĭ zā'tion, ste rĭl'i ty.
ster'ling.
stern, -ly, -most, -ness, stern'way,
-ward.
stern'-board, -cap, -chase, -chās-
er, -fåst, -frame, -gal ler y,
-hook, -knee, -port, -post, -sheets,
-wheel'er.
ster'num, *pl.* ster'na *or* -nums,
-nal.

stĕr'tor, -ous *or* -tō'ri ous, -tor-
ous ly *or* -to'ri ous ly, -ous ness
br -to'ri ous ness.
stet, -ted, -ting.
stĕth'o grăph, -grăph'ic, -o scope,
-scŏp'ic, -ic al, -al ly, -o scō'py
(*or* stē thŏs'-), -o scō'pist (*or*
stē thŏs'-), stē thom'e ter.
Stĕt tin' (-tēn'), c. Prus.
stĕ'vĕ dore.
stew (stū), -ing, stewed, stew'-pan,
-pond, -pot.
stew'ard (stū'-), -ess, -ly, -ship.
sthē nĭ'a, sthĕn'ic, sthĕn'o chire
(-kĭr).
stich (stĭk), a verse; a line in the
Scriptures; a rank or row, -ic,
-o man cy, -o met'ric, -ric al,
stĭ chom'e try (-kŏm'-).
sti cha'ri on (-kā'-), pl. *-ri a.*
stick, -er, -ing, -y, -i ness, stuck,
stick'seed, a plant, -tail, a duck,
-tight, a weed.
stick'-bait, -bug, -cul ture, -han-
dle, -hel met, -in sect, -lac,
-play, stick'ing-place, -plas ter,
-point.
stic'kle, -kled, -kler, -kling, -kly,
stic'kle back, a fish, -bag.
stiff, -en, -ened, -en er, -en ing,
-ly, -ness, stiff'tail, a duck, stiff'-
borne, -heart ed, -necked,
-necked ness, -tailed, stiff'en-
ing-ma chine, stiff bit, s. joints,
s. neck, s. or der.
stĭ'fle, -fled, -fler, -fling, stĭ'fle-bone,
-joint, -shoe.
stĭg'ma, *pl.* -mas *or* *-mà tà,*
-mal, -ma tal, -măt'ic, -ic al,
-al ly, -ma tist, stig'ma-disk.
stĭg'ma tize, -tized, -tĭ'zing, -tĭ'-
zer, -tĭ zā'tion.
stile, steps; a framework.
stĭ lĕt'tŏ, *pl.* -tos, -tōed, -tō ing.
still, -er, -ing, -ness, -y, stilled.
still'-birth, -born, -burn, -fish,
-fish ing, -house, -hunt, -hunt er,
-liq uor, -room, -stand, -watch-
er, s. life.
Stĭl'lĕ, Amer. physician; Amer. hist.
stilt, -ed, -ed ness, -ing, -y.
stilt'-bird, -pet rel, -plov er,
-sand'pĭp er, -walk er.

stim'u lant, -u late, -la ted, -la-
ting, -lā tive, -la tor, -lā'tion,
-u lus, pl. -lī.
sting, -er, -ing, -ing ly, -less, -y,
stung, sting'fish, -tail, a fish.
sting'-bull, -moth, -ray, -win kle,
sting'ing-bush, a plant, -cell.
stin'gy (-jy), -gi ly, -gi ness.
stink, -ing, -ing ly, -er, stunk or
stank, stink'horn, a plant, -pot,
-stone, -weed, -wood, a tree.
stink'-a live, -ball, -bird, -bug,
-bush, -rat, -shad, -trap, -tur tle,
stink'ing-weed, -wood.
stint, -ed, -ed ness, -er, -ing, -ing-
ly, -less.
sti'pend, -pen'di a ry, -a'ri an.
stip'ple, -pled, -pler, -pling, stip'-
ple-en grav'ing, -en grav'er, -ma-
chine'.
stip'u late, -la ted, -la ting, -la-
tor, -lā'tion.
stip'ule, -uled, -u li form.
stir (stēr), -rer, -ring, stirred.
stir'rup (or stēr'-), -bar, -bone,
-cup, -hose, -i ron, -lan tern,
-lĕath er, -mus cle, -oil, -piece.
stitch, -er, -er y, -ing, stitched,
stitch'work, -wort.
stitch'-fall en, -reg'u la tor, -rip-
per, -wheel, stitch'ing-clamp,
-horse, -ma chine.
stive.
sti'ver, a coin.
stō'a.
stōat.
stock, -er, -ing, -ish, -less, -y,
stocked, stock'hold er, -man,
-work.
stock'-ac count', -beer, -blind,
-board, -book, -bōw, -breed er,
-bro ker, -brush, -buc kle, -car,
-cer tif'i cate, -dove, -duck,
-farm, -farm er, -feed er, -fish,
-gang, -gil ly flow er, -hawk,
-horse, -in'di ca tor, -job ber,
-job ber y, -list, -mar ket, -mŏr'el,
-owl, -pot, -print er, -pump,
-pun ished, -purse, -rais er,
-ranch, -range, -rīd er, -room,
-sad dle, -sta tion, -still, -stone,
-tac kle, -tāk ing, -train, -whaup,
-yard, s. com'pa ny, s. ex change'.

stock ade', -ād'ed, -ād'ing.
stock i net'.
stock'ing, -er, stock'ing-frame,
-loom, -ma chine, -māk'er, -yarn.
stoep (stoop).
stō'gy.
stō'ic, -ic al, -al ly, -al ness, -i cism.
stoke, stoked, stōk'er, -ing, stoke'-
hole.
stōle, n., a garment, stō'la, pl. -læ;
stole, v. See steal.
stŏl'id, -id ly, sto lĭd'i ty.
stō'ma, pl. -ma ta.
stom'ach (stŭm'ak), -al, -er, -ing,
-less, -y, sto măch'ic (-măk'-),
-ic al.
stom'ach-ache, -brush, -cough,
-grief, -piece, -plas ter, -pump,
-qualmed, -sick, -stag gers,
-sweet bread, -tim ber, -tooth,
-tube, -worm.
stōne, stoned, stōn'ing, -y, -i ly,
-i ness.
stone'break, a plant, -buck, an antelope, -cat, a fish, -chack er, a
bird, -chat, a bird, -chat ter, a
bird, -clink, a bird, -crop, a plant,
fish, -hatch, a bird, -man, -peck-
er, a bird, -root, -seed, a plant,
-smic kle, a bird, -ware, -weed,
-wood, -work, -wort.
stone'-ax, v., to cut stone, -bas'il,
-bass, -bird, -bit'er, -blind, -blue,
-boat, -boil ers, -boil ing, -bōr-
er, -bōw, -bram ble, -brash,
-break er, -bruise, -but ter, -ca-
nal', -căst, -cen'ti ped, -climb-
er, -clo ver, -coal, -cold, -col or,
-col ored, -cŏr al, -crab, -craw'-
fish, -cray, -crick et, -crush,
-crush er, -cur lew, -cut ter,
-dĕad, -dĕaf, -dev il, -dress er,
-drill ing, -dumb, -eat er, -en-
grav ing.
stone'-fā cing, -fal con, -fence,
-fern, -fly, -fruit, -gall, -gath-
er er, -gray, -grig, -grind ing,
-ham mer, -hard, -har mon'i con,
-hawk, -head, the bed-rock, -leek,
-li chen, -lil y, -lob ster, -lug-
ger, a fish, -mar ten, -ma son,
-mer chant, -mill, -mint, -mold-
ing, -mor tar, -oak, -oil, -owl,

-pars ley, -pine, -pit, -pitch, -plăn'ing, -plov er, -pock, -polish ing.

stone'-quar ry, -quar ry ing, -rag, -raw, -roll er, a fish, -rue, -run ner, a bird, -saw, -saw ing, -sep'a ra tor, -shot, -show er, -snipe, -sort ing, -sponge, -squar er, -still, -stur'geon, -suck er, a fish, -thrush, -tōt'er, a fish, -wall ing, -work ing, -works, -yard, stōn'y-heart ed, stone age, s. ax, an ax, s. cir'cles, stone's cast.

stōŏd. See *stand.*

stōŏk, -er, -ing, stooked.

stōōl, -ing, stooled, stool'-ball, -end, -pi geon.

stōōp, -er, -ing, -ing ly, stooped, stoop'-shoul dered.

stōōp, *n.,* a porch; stōōp *or* stoup (stōōp), a drinking-cup.

stop, -per, -ping, stopped, stop'wa ter.

stop'-cock, -col lar, -cyl'in der, -drill, -fin ger, -gap, -gate, -hound, -knob, -mo tion, -net, -off, -or der, -o ver, -plank, -plate, -ridge, -rod, -seine, -shăft, -ship, -thrust, -valve, -watch, -wheel, -work.

stop'per-bolt, -hole, -knot, stop'ping-brush, -coat, -knife.

stŏpe, stoped, stŏp'ing.

stŏp'ple, -pled, -pling.

store, stōr'a ble, -age, -er, -ing, stored.

store'house, -keep er, -man, -măs ter, -room, store'-cit y, -farm, -farm er, -ship.

stor'age-bat'ter y, -bel'lows, -res'er voir, -ware'house.

stork, storks'bill, stork'-billed.

storm, -er, -ful, -ful ness, -y, -i ly, -i ness, -less, -ward.

storm'-a're a, -ax'is, -beat, -beaten, -belt, -bird, -bound, -card, -cen ter, -cir cle, -cloud, -coat, -cock, -com pass, -cone, -cur rent, -door, -drum, -finch, -flag, -glăss, -house, -jib, -kite, -pane, -păth, -pave ment, -pet rel, -proof, -sail, -sig nal, -stay,

-stayed, -stone, -tossed, -track, -wave, -wind, -win dow, -zone, storm'ing par'ty.

stor nel'lō, *pl.* -lĭ.

Stor'thing (-tĭng).

stō'ry, -rĭed, stō'ry-book, -post, -rod, -tell er, -wrĭt'er.

Stough'ton (stō'-), vil. Mass.; c. Wis.

Stour'bridge (stûr'-), t. Eng.

stout, -ly, -ness, stout'-dart, -heart ed.

stove, stoved, stŏv'ing, stove'pipe.

stove'-coal, -cov er, -drum, -glăss, -hearth, -house, -jack, -plate, -pol ish, -truck, s. plant.

stow, -er, -ing, -age, stowed, stow'a way, -down, stow'-wood.

stra bis'mus (*or* -bĭz'-), -bis mal, -mic, -mic al.

străd'dle, -dled, -dling, strad'dlebug, -legged, -pipe, -plow.

Străd ĭ vă'rĭ ŭs, Ital. violin maker.

străg'gle, -gled, -gler, -gling, -gling ly, -gly, strag'gle-tooth, strag'gling-mon ey.

straight (strāt), not crooked, -en, -ened, -en er, -en ing, -ly, -ness, straight'a way, *a.,* -for ward, -horn, -way, *adv.,* straight'billed, -edge, -joint, *a.,* -lined, -out, *a.,* straight'en ing-block, -ma chine, straight ends, s. face.

strain, -er, -ing, -a ble, strained, strain'-nor'mal, -sheet, -type, strain'er-vine.

strain'ing-beam, -fork, -lĕath er, -piece, -reel, -sill.

străit, narrow, -en, -ened, -ening, -ly, -ness, strait'-heart ed, -jack et, -laced, -waist coat.

stra mō'ni um.

strand, -ed, -ing, strand'-bird, -my cele', -plov er, -rat, -wolf, strand'ing-ma chine.

strange, -ly, -ness, străn'ger.

stran'gle, -gled, -gler, -gling, stran'gle weed, stran'gle-tare.

stran'gu late, -lā'ted, -lā'ting, -lā'tion.

strap, -per, -ping, -ping ly, strapped, strap'work, -worm, -wort.

---

fāte, făt, fär, fạll, fâre, fạst, sofà, mēte, mĕt, hêr, ice, ĭn, nōte,

strap'-bolt, -clamp, -game, -head, -hinge, -joint, -laid, -loop, -mounts, -oil, -oys ter, -rail, -shaped, -skein, -wire, strap'-ping-plate.
străp pä'dŏ, *pl.* -does (-dōz), -dōed, -dō ing.
Stras'burg (străz'-), bor. Pa.— Străs'burg *or* Sträss'burg (-bŏŏrg), c. Ger.
străt'a gem, stra teg'ic (-tĕj'- *or* -tē'gic), -ic al, -al ly, -ics, străt'e gist, -e gy, stra tē'gŏs.
Strat'ford-up on-A'von (-ā'von), t, Eng.
străt'i fy, -ing, -fīed, -form.
stra tig'ra phy, strat'i graph'ic, -ic al, -al ly.
stra to-cir'rus, -cu'mu lus.
stra tog'ra phy, -to graph'ic, -ic al, -al ly.
strä'tum, *pl.* -tums *or* -ta, -tus.
Strauss (strous), Ger. theol.; Viennese mus. composer.
straw, -y, straw'board, -small, a bird, -smēar, a bird.
straw'-boil er, -buff, -built, -car ri er, -cat, -coat, -col or, -col ored, -cot ton, -cut ter, -drain, -em broid'er y, -fid dle, -house, -necked, -nee dle, -ride, -stem, -stone, -un'der wing, a moth, -wine, -worm, -yard, -yel low, s. bail, s. bed, s. bid, s. hat, s. vote.
straw'ber ry, -bed, -blite, -bor er, -bush, -clo ver, -comb, -crab, -finch, -ge ra'ni um, -leaf, -mark, -moth, -pear, -plant, -roan, -shrub, -to ma'to, -tree, -vine, -worm, straw'ber ry băss, s. blond, s. perch, s. tongue.
stray, -er, -ing, -ling, strayed, stray'-line, -mark.
streak, -ed, -ing, -y, -i ly, -i ness, streaked.
stream, -er, -ing, -ful, -less, -let, -ling, -y, -i ness, streamed, stream'way, -wort.
stream'-an chor, -ca ble, -clock, -cur rent, -gold, -ice, -line, -tin, -wheel, -works.
street, -ed, -ling, -ward, -way.

street'-car, -door, -lo co mo'tive, -or der ly, -rail road, -sprin kler, -sweep er, -walk er, -wash'er.
Streh'len (strä'-), t. Prus.
strength, -ful, -ful ness, -less, -en, -en er, -en ing, -ened.
strĕn'ŭ ous, -ly, -ness, -ŏs'i ty.
stress, -ful, -less, stress'-di a gram, -sheet.
stretch, -er, -ing, -y, stretched, stretch'-hal ter.
stretch'er-bond, -fly, -mule, stretch'ing-frame, -i ron, -ma chine, -piece.
strew (strōō), -er, -ing, -ment, strewed, strewn.
strī'ate, -ly, -ā'ted, -ā'ting, -ā'tion, strī'ate-plī cate, -punc tate, -sul cate.
strick'en (-n). See *strike.*
stric'kle, -kler, -kled.
strict, -ly, -ness, stric'ture, -tured.
strīde, strīd'ing, strode, strīd'den.
strī'dent, -ly.
strīd'u late, -lā'ted, -lā'ting, -la tor, -to'ry, -lant, -lous, -lā'-tion, strid'u la ting-or gan.
strife, -ful.
strig'il, -i lose.
strike, struck, strick'en, strīk'er, -ing, -ing ly, -ing ness.
strike'-block, -fault, -pan, -pay, -plate, strike'-a-light, a flint, strike-or-si lent.
strīk'er-arm, -boat, -out, -plate, strīk'ing-beam, -knife, -plate, -so lu'tion, s. dis'tance.
string, -ing, -less, -y, -i ness, stringed, *a.*, strung, string'wood, a tree.
string'-bark, -bean, -block, -board, -course, -gage, -halt, -line, -min strel, -or gan, -pea, -piece, -plate, string'y-bark, string' band, s. or'ches tra.
strin'gent, -ly, -ness, -gen cy.
strip, -ling, -per, -ping, stripped, strip'-lēaf, -lights, strip'ping-knife, -plate, strip ar mor.
strīpe, strīped, strīp'ing, stripe'-tail, a bird, striped băss, s. go'-pher, s. skunk, s. snake, s. squir'rel.

strīve, strīv'er, -ing, -ing ly, strove, strĭv'en (-n).
stroke, stroked, strŏk'er, -ing, strokes'man, stroke'-gear, -hole, -oar, -oars man.
strŏll, -er, -ing, strolled.
Strŏm'bŏ li (-lē), isl. and vol. Medit.
strong, -ly, strong'bark, a tree, -hold.
strong'-back, n., -hand'ed, -knit, -mīnd'ed, strong'man's-weed.
stron'ti a (-shĭ a), -ti an, -an īte, -ti um (-shĭ um), stron'tic, -tit'ic.
strŏp, -ping, stropped.
strŏ'phe, pl. -phes (-fēz), strŏph'ic, -ic al.
stroud, -ing.
struc'ture, -less, -tured, -tūr al, -al ly, struc'tūr al i'ron, s. plain, s. steel.
strug'gle, -gled, -gler, -gling.
strum, -mer, -ming, strummed.
strum'pet.
strut, -ted, -ter, -ting, -ting ly, strut'ting-piece.
Stry (strē), r. Aust.
strych'nīne or -nin, -nic.
stub, -bed, -bed ness, -by, -bi-ness, -bing, stubbed, stub'wort.
stub'-book, -dam ask, -end, -fĕath er, -i ron, -mor tise, -nail, -short, -shot, -ten on, -twist, stub pen.
stub'ble, -bled, -bly, stub'ble-field, -goose, -land, -plow, -rake, -turn er.
stŭb'born (-burn), -ly, -ness, stub'born-shăft ed.
stŭc'co, pl. -coes or -cos (-kōz), -co ing, -co er, -cōed, stuc'co-work.
stuck. See stick. stuck'-up.
stud, -ded, -ding, stud'fĭsh, -flow er, stud'ding sail, stud'-bolt, -book, -farm, -groom, -horse, stud'ding sail-bōōm.
stŭ'dent, -ry, -ship, stu'dent-lamp, -pars nip.
stŭd'y, -ing, -ĭed, -ĭed ly, stŭ'di-ous, -ous ly, -ous ness, stŭ'dĭ o.
stu'fa (stōō'-).
stuff, -er, -ing, -y, -i ness, stuffed,

stuff'-chest, -en gine, -gowns-man.
stuff'ing-box, -brush, -ma chine, -wheel.
stŭll.
stŭl'ti fy, -ing, -fĭed, -fĭ er, -fĭ cā'tion, -til'o quent, -quent-ly, -quence.
stum, -ming, stummed.
stum'ble, -bled, -bler, -bling, -bling ly, stum'bling-block, -stone.
stump, -age, -er, -ing, -y, -i ness, stumped, stump'foot.
stump'-ex tract'or, -joint, -ma chine', -pull er, -tailed, -tree, stump speaker, s. speech, s. or'a tor, s. tra cer y.
stun, -ner, -ning, -ning ly, stunned, stun'sail.
stunt, -ed, -ed ness, -ing.
stupe, a piece of flannel or other cloth, stuped, stūp'ing.
stu'pe fy, -ing, -fĭed, -fĭed ness, -fĭ er, -fā'cient, -fac'tive, -fac'-tion.
stŭ pĕn'doŭs, -ly, -ness.
stŭ'pid, -ly, -ness, -pid'i ty, -por.
stur'dy, -di ly, -di ness.
stur'geon (-jŭn).
Sturm (stōōrm), Swiss math.; Ger. clas. schol.
stŭt'ter, -er, -ing, -ing ly, -tered.
Stuy've sant (stī'-), Dutch Gov. of N. Y.
sty (stī), pl. stĭes.
style (stīl), sty'lar, -let, styl'ish (stīl'-), -ish ly, -ish ness, -ist, styled, style'wort, style'-branch, -curve.
sty'lŏ graph (stī'-), -graph'ic, -ic al, -al ly, -log'ra phy, -lom'-e ter.
sty'lus (stī'-), pl. -lĭ.
sty'mĭe (stī'-).
styp'tic (stĭp'-), -al, -tic'i ty, styp'tic weed, styp'tic-bur.
Styx, Myth., Styg'i an (stĭj'-).
Suä'kin, t. N. Afr.
suave (swäv or swäv), -ly, suav'i ty (swăv'-).
sub a'gent, -gen cy.
su'bah (sōō'bä), -dar (or -dar'), -där'y, -bah ship.

Sū'bāi (*or* -bā ī), *Bib.*
sub ạl'tern, -ăl ter'nant, -ter'-
  nate, -al'ter na ting, -ăl ter nā'-
  tion.
sub con'scious (-shŭs), -ly, -ness.
sŭb'dĕa'con (-kn), -ry, -ship.
sub dĭ vīde', -vīd'ed, -ing, -vis'-
  i ble (-vĭz'-), -vi'sion (-vĭzh'un),
  -sion al, -vī'sive.
sub dūce', -duced', -du'cing,
  -duct', -duct'ed, -duct'ing, -duc'-
  tion.
sŭb dūe', -dued', -dū'er, -dū'ing.
sŭb'făm'i ly (*or* -făm'-).
sŭb'gĕ nus (*or* -gē'-), *pl.* -gen e ra.
sub jā'cent, -cen cy.
sŭb'ject, *a.* and *n.*, -less, -ness,
  sub ject', *v.*, -ed, -ing, -jec'tive,
  -tive ly, -tive ness, -tiv ism,
  -tiv ist, -ti vis'tic, -tic al ly,
  -tiv'i ty, -tion, sub'ject-mat ter,
  -no tion, -ob ject, -word.
sub join', -ing, -joined'.
sub jū'dĭ cē.
sub'ju gate, -gā'ted, -gā'ting,
  -gā'tor, -gā'tion.
sub junc'tive, -junc'tion.
sub lēase', -leased', -lēas'ing,
  -let', -let'ting.
sub'li mate, -mā'ted, -mā'ting,
  -mȧ to'ry, -mā'tion.
sub lime', -ly, -ness, -limed,
  -līm'ing, -er, -līm'i ty.
sub lin'gual.
sŭb'lu na'ry.
sub ma rine' (-rēn').
sub merge', -merged', -mer'ging,
  -ger, -gence, -mersed', -mer'sion.
sub mit', -ted, -ter, -ting, -mis'-
  sive, -sive ly, -sive ness, -mis'-
  sion (-mĭsh'un).
sub nas'cent.
sub or'di nate, -ly, -ness, -di nȧ-
  cy, -nȧ tive, -nā'tion, -tion ism.
sŭb orn', -er, -ing, -orned', -or-
  nā'tion.
sub pœ'na *or* -pē'-, -nȧed, -nȧ ing,
  -nal.
sub'ro gate, -gā'ted, -gā'ting,
  -gā'tion.
sub rō'sa (-za).
sub scrībe', -scribed', -scrīb'er,
  -ing, -scrip'tive, -tive ly, -tion.

sub'se quent, -ly, -quence, -quen-
  cy.
sub serve', -served', -serv'ing,
  -serv'i ent, -ent ly, -ence, -en cy.
sub side', -sīd'ed, -ing, -si'dence.
sub sid'i a ry.
sub'si dize, -dized, -di zing, -dy.
sub sist', -ed, -ing, -ence, -en cy,
  -ent.
sub'soil, -soiled, -soil ing, -er,
  sub'soil-plow.
sŭb'stance, -less, -stan'tial (-shăl),
  -tial ism, -ist, -tial ize, -ized,
  -ĭ'zing, -tial ly, -ness, -ti al'i ty
  (-shĭ ăl'-).
sub stan'ti ate (-shĭ āte), -ā'ted,
  -ā'ting, -ā'tion.
sub'stan tīve, -ly, -ness, -tī'val
  (*or* -tĭv'al), -al ly.
sub'sti tute, -tu ted, -tu ting,
  -tū'tion, -tion al, -al ly, -ȧ ry.
sub strā'tum, *pl.* -strā'ta.
sub struc'ture (*or* sub'-), -tu ral.
sub'style.
sub tend', -ed, -ing, -tense'.
sub'ter fuge (-fûj).
sub ter rā'ne an, -ne ous, -ous ly.
sub'tĭle (*or* sŭt'ĭl *or* sŭt'l), tenuous;
  rarefied, -ly, -ness, -til ism, -til'-
  i ty, -til ize, -ized, -ĭ'zer, -ĭ'zing,
  -ĭ zā'tion.
sub'ti'tle.
sub'tle (sŭt'l), sly; artful; cunning,
  -ness, -ty, sub'tly (sŭt'ly), sub'-
  tle-wit'ted.
sub tŏn'ic.
sub tract', -ed, -er, -ing, -trac'tive,
  -tion, -tra hend.
sub treas'ur y, -ur er.
sŭb'urb, -urbed, -ur'ban, -ban-
  ism.
sub vene', -vened', -vēn'ing,
  -vĕn'tion.
sub vert', -ed, -ing, -er, -i ble,
  -ver'sive, -ver'sion, -sion a ry.
sub vō'cē.
sub'way.
suc ceed', -er, -ed, -ing, -cess',
  -cess'ful, -ful ly, -ful ness, -ces'-
  sion (-sĕsh'un), -sion al, -al ly,
  -sion ist, -ces'sive, -sive ly, -sive-
  ness, -cess'less, -less ly, -less-
  ness, -ces'sor, -sor ship, -so ry.

---

nŏt, nôr, ūse, ŭp, ûrn, etüde, fō͞od, fŏͦt, aɴger, boɴmot, thus, Baċh.

suc cinct' (sŭk sĭnkt'), -ly, -ness, -cinc'to ry.

sŭc'cor, -a ble, -er, -ing, -less, -cored.

suc'co ry, a plant.

sŭc'co tash.

sŭc'cu lent, -ly, -lence, -len cy.

sŭc cumb' (-kŭm'), -ing, -cumbed'.

such.

suck, -er, -ing, sucked, suck'fish, -stone, a fish, suck'-in, n.

suck'er-fish, -foot, -mouthed, -rod, -tube.

suck'ing-bot tle, -disk, -fish, -pump, -stom ach.

suck'et.

suc'kle, -kled, -kler, -kling, p. p., suck'ling, n.

su'cre (sōō'kra), a coin. Su'cre (sōō'krĕ), c. Bolivia.

suc'tion, -an e mŏm'e ter, -box, -chăm ber, -fan, -pipe, -plate, -prīm'er, -pump, -valve.

Su cza'wa (sōō chä'vä), r. Aust.

sud, a young oyster, -oil.

Su dän' or Sou- (sōō'-), region Cent. Afr., -dan ēse' (or -ĕz').

sū'da to ry, -to'ri um, pl. -ri a, -dā'tion.

sudd, a floating island.

sud'den (-dn), -ly, -ness.

sū'dor, -do ral, -do rif'er ous, -rif'ic.

Su'drä (sōō'-).

suds.

sūe, sūed, sū'ing.

suède (swād).

suer'te (swâr'tä).

sū'et, -y.

Sue tō'nĭ us (swē-), Rom. hist.

Su ez' (sōō ĕz'), prov., t., and canal Egypt.

sŭf'fer, -a ble, -a ble ness, -a bly, -ance, -er, -ing, -fered.

suf fīce' (or -fīz'), -ficed', -fi'cing, -cing ly, -cing ness, -fi'cient (-fĭsh'ent), -cient ly, -cien cy.

sŭf'fix, n., suf fix', v., -ing, -fixed' (-fĭxt'), -fix'ion (-fĭk'shŭn).

sŭf'fo cate, -cā'ted, -cā'ting, -ting ly, -tive, -cā'tion.

sŭf'fra gan, -ship.

sŭf'frage, -fraged, -frā'ging, -gist.

suf fuse' (-fūz'), -fused', -fūs'ing, -fū'sion (-zhŭn), -fū'sive (-sĭv).

su'fi (sōō'fē), -fic, -fism, -fis'tic.

su'gar (shŏŏg'ar or -er), -ing, -less, -y, -i ness, -gared, su'gar ber-ry, -loaf, a hat; a hill.

su'gar-ap ple, -bar rel, -bean, -beet, -bird, -bowl, -bush, -camp, -cane, -clăr i fi'er, -coat ed, -cut ting, -drain er, -e vap'o ra-tor, -fil ter, -fur nace, -gran'u-la tor, -grăss, -gum, -house, -huc kle ber ry, -ket tle, -loaf, -louse.

su'gar-ma chin'er y, -māk ing, -ma ple, -meat, -mill, -mil let, -mite, -mole, -nip pers, -or-chard, -pack er, -pan, -pea, -pine, -plan tā'tion, -plant er, -plum, -press, -re fīn'er, -re-fin'er y, -sift er, -sĭr'up, -squir'-rel, -syr'up, -tēat, -tongs, -tree, -vin'e gar, -wa'ter, s. can'dy.

su'gent.

sug gest' (or sŭ jĕst'), -ed, -ed-ness, -er, -ing, -i ble, -ive, -ive-ly, -ive ness, -ges'tion (-jes'-chun).

sū'i cide, -cī'dal, -dal ly.

sū'ĭ gen'ē ris, sū'ĭ jū'ris.

sū'ĭne.

Sui'o-Goth'ic (swē'ō-).

sui ri'ri (swī rē'rĭ).

sūit, -a ble, -a ble ness, -a bly, -a bil'i ty, -ed, -ing, -or, suit'-case, -shape.

suite (swēt), a series; a retinue.

sui vez' (swē vä').

su'jee (sōō'jē) or -ji (-jē).

Sū'la.

sŭl'cate, -cā'ted, -cā'tion.

su'lē a (sōō'-).

Su lei män' (sōō lā-), Mosque, Constantinople.

Su li män' (sōō lē-) or -lei or -lai- (sōō lā män'), mts. Afghan-istan.

sulk, -ing, sulked, sŭl'ky, a., -ki ly, -ki ness.

sul'ky, n., s. cul'ti va tor, s. hăr'row, s. plow, s. rake, s. scrăp'er.

sul'lĕn, -ly, -ness.

sul'phate *or* sul'fate, -phā'ted, -ting, -tīte, -phăt'ic.

sŭl'phĭd *or* -phīde *or* -fĭd, -phīte *or* -fīte.

sul'phur *or* -fur, -phu rā'tion, -phu're ous, -ous ly, -ous ness, -phu rĕt'ed, -phū'ric, -phûr ize, -ized, -ĭ'zing, sul'phur root, a plant, -weed, -wort.

sul'phur-bot tom, -con crete, -ore, -rain, -salt, -spring, -wa ters, -whale, -yel low.

sul'tan, *fem.*, sul tā'na (*or* -tä'-), -tan ate, -ry, -ship, -tăn'ic, sul'-tan-flow er, sul tā'na-bird.

sul'try, -tri ly, -tri ness.

sum, -less, -ming, summed, sum'-cal'cu lus.

su'mac *or* -mach (sōō'măk *or* shōō'-), su'mac-bee tle.

Su mä'trä (sōō-), isl. Malay Ar-chi., -mä'tran, Su ma'tra cam'-phor, S. or'ange, S. pep'per, su mä'trä, a sudden squall.

sŭm'bul, -root.

sŭm'ma rize, -rized, -rī'zing, -ma ry, -ri ly, -ri ness, -rist, -mā'tion, -tion al.

sum'mer, -ing, -less, -ly, -li ness, -y, -mered, sum'mer tide, -ward.

sum'mer-bird, -dried, -fal low, -house, -like, -ripe, -seem'ing, -shine, -stir, -stone, -time, -tree, s. ca tarrh, s. com plaint, s. day, s. fe ver, s. finch, s. quar-ters, s. war bler, s. wĕath er.

sum'mer sault. See *somersault.*

sum'mit, -less, -lev'el, -line.

sum'mon, -er, -ing, -moned.

sum'mons, *pl.* -mons es.

sum'mum bō'num.

sump, -fuse, -plank, -pump, -shăft, -shot.

sump'ter, a pack-horse; a porter; a burden.

sump'ter-cloth, -horse, -mule, -po ny.

sump'tu ous, -ly, -ness, -tu â ry, -tu ŏs'i ty.

sun, -less, -less ness, -like, -lit, -ny, -ni er, -ni est, -ni ness, -ning, -ward, -wise, sunned.

sun'beam, -bird, -bon net, -bŏw, -burn, -burned, -burnt, -burst, -dew, -down, -down er, -drops, a plant, -fish, -flow er, -light, -rise, -ris ing, -set, -set ting, -shade, -shine, -shīn'y, -stĕad, -stone, -stroke, -struck, -up.

sun'-ăn gel, -an i mal'cule, -bâth, -bear, -beat, -beat en, -bee tle, -bit tern, -blink, -bright, -broad, -burn er, -case, -crack, -cress, -dance, -dart, -dawn, -di al, -dog, -dried, -fern, -fe ver, -fig ure, -fruit.

sun'-gem, -glăss, -glimpse, -glow, -god, -gold, -grebe, -hat, -myth, -o pal, -perch, -pic ture, -plane, -plant, -proof, -ray, -rose, -scald, -smit ten, -snake, -south ing, -spot, -spurge, -squall, -star, -strick en, -tree, -trout, -try, -wake, -wheel, -wor ship, -wor-ship er, -year, -yel low, sun'-flow er-oil, sun'set-shell, sun'-shine-re cord er.

sun'dang (sōōn'däng).

Sun'day, -school.

sun'der, -ing, -dered.

sun'dry, -dries, sun'dry-man.

sunk, -en. See *sink.*

sunn.

Sun'na, -ni ah, -nīte.

sup, -ping, supped.

Su pai wa'si (sōō pī wä'sē), mt. Bolivia.

sû'per.

sû'per a ble, -ble ness, -bly.

sû'per a bound', -ed, -ing, -a bun'-dance, -dant, -dant ly.

su per an'nu ate, -ā'ted, -ā'ting, -ā'tion.

sû perb', -ly, -ness.

su per cal'en dered.

su per car'go.

sû per cil'i ous, -ly, -ness.

sû per ĕr'o gate, -gā'ted, -gā'ting, -gā'tion, -e rog'a tive, -a to ry.

su per ex'cel lent, -lence.

su per fi'cial (-fĭsh'al), -cial ist, -cial ly, -cial ness, -fi ci al'i ty (-fĭsh ĭ ăl'-), -fi'ci a ry (-fĭsh'ĭ-), -fi'cies (-fĭsh'ēz *or* -fĭsh'ĭ ēz).

sû'per fine (*or* -fine'), -fine ness.

sû pĕr'flu ous, -ly, -ness, -flu'i ty.

sū per hu′man, -ly.

su per im pose′, -posed′, -pos′-ing, -po si′tion (-zĭsh′un).

sū′per in cum′bent, -bence, -ben-cy.

sū′per in duce′, -ment, -duced′, -du′cing.

su per in tend′, -ed, -ing, -ence, -en cy, -ent, -ent ship.

sū pĕ′ri or, -ly, -ness, -or′i ty.

su per′la tive, -tive ly, -tive ness.

su per′nal.

su per na′tant, -na tā′tion.

su per nat′u ral, -ly, -ness, -ism, -ist, -is′tic, -ral′i ty, -ral ize, -ized, -ī′zing.

su per nū′mer a ry.

sū per pose′, -posed′, -pōs′ing, -pōs′a ble, -po si′tion (-zĭsh′un).

su per scribe′, -scribed′, -scrīb′-ing, -scrip′tion.

su per sede′, -sēd′ed, -ing, -er, -ses′sion (-sĕsh′un), su per se′-de as, su per se dē′rē.

su per sen′si tive, -ness.

su per sti′tion (-stĭsh′un), -sti′-tious, -tious ly, -tious ness.

su per stra′tum, pl. -ta.

su per struc′ture (or sū′-), -tūr al.

sū per vene′, -vened′, -vēn′ing, -vēn′ient, -vĕn′tion.

su per vise′ (-vīz′), -vised′, -vīs′ing, -vīs′or, -or ship, -vī′so ry, -vī′-sion (-vĭzh′un).

sū pīne′, a., -ly, -ness, sū′pīne, n.

sŭp′per, -less, sup′per-board, -ta-ble, -time.

sup plant′, -ed, -er, -ing, -plan-tā′tion.

sup′ple, -ness, -pled, -pling, sup′-ple-jack.

sŭp′plē ment, -men′tal, -tȧ ry, -tȧ ri ly, -tā′tion, -ple to′ry.

sŭp′pli ant, -ly, -ness, -ance.

sŭp′pli cate, -cā′ted, -cā′ting, -ting ly, -cant, -cant ly, -ca′tor, -to′ry, -cā′tion.

sup ply′, -ing, -plīed′, -plī′er, sup ply′-roll er, -train.

sup port′, -a ble, -a ble ness, -a bly, -ed, -er, -ing, -less.

sup pose′, -posed′, -pōs′a ble, -a ble ness, -a bly, -al, -er, -ing,

-po si′tion (-zĭsh′un), -tion al, -pos′i tive, -tive ly, -i ti′tious (-tĭsh′ŭs), -tious ly, -tious ness.

sup press′, -ed ly, -er or -or, -i ble, -ing, -ive, -pressed′, -pres′sion, -sion ist.

sup′pu rate, -rȧ tive, -rā′tion.

sū prême′, -ly, -ness, -prĕm′a cy, -prĕm′i ty.

su′ra (soo′-), a chapter of the Koran.

su′ra (soo′-), fermented sap or milk.

su′rah (soo′-), twilled silk.

Su rät′ (soo-), dist. Brit. India.

su răt′ (soo-), a cotton cloth.

sur′base, n., -ment, -based′, v., sur′based, a.

sur bed′, -ded, -ding.

sur cēase′, -ceased′, -cēas′ing.

sur charge′, -charged′, -char′ging.

sur′cin gle, -gled, -gling.

sur′cōat.

surd, -al.

sure (shoor), -ly, -ness, -ty, -ty-ship, sure-e nough, a., -foot ed, -foot ed ly, -foot ed ness.

su′res (soo′rās).

Sü resnes′ (-rān′), vil. Fr.

surf, -er, -y, surf′man, surf′-bäth-ing, -bird, -boat, -boat man, -clam, -duck, -fish ing, -scō′ter, -smelt, -whĭt′ing, -worn.

sur′face, -faced, -fa cer, -cing, sur′face man.

sur′face-car, -chuck, -col or, -con-dens er, -cŭr′rent, -en am el, -fish, -gage, -ge ol′o gy, -glaze, -grub, -in te gral, -joint, -mĭn-ing, -mo tion, -plane, -print ing, -rĭb, -road, -roll er, -ten sion, -tōw ing, -ve loc′i ty, -wa ter, -work ing, -worm, sur′fa cing-ma chine, -plane.

sur′fĕlt, -ed, -er, -ing, sur′feit-swelled, -wa ter.

surge, -ful, -less, surged, sur′ging, sur′gent, -gy.

sur′geon (-jŭn), -cy, -ship, sur′-ger y, -gi cal, -cal ly.

sur′geon-a poth′e ca ry, -au rist, -den tist, -fish, -gen′er al, -gen′-er al ship.

sur′ly, -li ly, -li ness, sur′ly-boots.

sur'mark.
sur mise' (-mīz'), -mised', -mīs'-
a ble, -er, -ing.
sur mount', -a ble, -a ble ness,
-ed, -er, -ing.
sur'name, *n.*, sur'name (*or* -name'),
v., -named', -nām er, -ing.
sur pâss', -a ble, -ing, -ing ly,
-ing ness, -passed'.
sur'plĭce, -plĭced, sur'plice-fee.
sur'plus, -age.
sur prise', -prised', -prĭs'al, -er,
-ing, -ing ly, -ing ness, surprise'-cup, -par ty.
sŭr'ra or *-rah* (*or* sōō'ra), a disease
of horses.
sur ren'der, -er, -ing, -dered; [in
Law] sur ren'der or, -der ee'.
sŭr'rep ti'tious (-tĭsh'us), -ly.
sŭr'rey, a light vehicle, Sŭr'rey, co.
Eng.
sŭr'ro gate, -ship.
sur round', -ed, -ing.
Sŭr'ry, co. N. C.; co. Va.
sur tout' (-tōōt').
sur veil'lance (-vāl'yans), -lant
(-yant).
sur vey' (-vā' *or* sur'-), *n.*, sur-
vey', *v.*, -a ble, -ance, -ing, -or,
-or ship, sur vey'ing-ves sel, sur-
vey or-gen er al.
sur vīve', -vīved', -vīv'al, -a bil'-
i ty, -ing, or, or ship.
Sur'ya (sōōr'-).
Sū'san chĭtes (-kītes), *Bib.*
sus cep'ti ble, -ness, -ti bly, -bil'-
i ty.
sus cep'tive, -ness, -tiv'i ty.
Sū'sĭ, *Bib.*
su'sĭ (sōō'-), a cotton fabric.
sus pect', *n.*, *a.*, and *v.*, -ed,
-ed ly, -ed ness, -er, -ing.
sus pend,' -ed, -er, -ing, -pense',
-pen'si ble, -si bil'i ty, -sive,
-sive ly, -sor, -sō'ri al, -so ry,
-pen sā'tion, -pen'sion.
sus pen'sion-bridge, s. drill, s.
rail way.
sus pi'cion (-pĭsh'un), -al, -cious,
-cious ly, -cious ness.
sus pīre', -pired', -pīr'al, -pĭ rā'-
tion.
sus tāin', -a ble, -er, -ing, -ment,

-tained', sus'te nance, -ten'ta-
tive, -ten tā'tion.
sū sŭr'rus, -rā'tion.
sŭt'ler, -ship, -y, sut'tling.
sū'tor.
su'tra (sōō'-), pl. *-tras.*
sut tee', -ism.
sū'tūre, -tūr al, -al ly, -a ted,
-rā'tion, -tured, su'ture-nee dle.
sū'ze rāin, -ty.
Svi e ci a'ny (svē ĕt sē ä'nē), t.
Russ.
swab (swŏb), -ber, -bing, swabbed,
swab'-pot, -stick.
swab'ble (swŏb'-), -bled, -bling.
Swä'bĭ a or Suä'-, dist. Bav.,
-bi an.
swad (swŏd), -dy.
swad'dle (swŏd'-), -dled, -dler,
-dling, swad'dling-band, -clothes,
-clout.
swag, -ging, swagged, swag'man,
swag'-shop.
swäge, swäged, swä'ging, swage'-
block, swä'ging-ma chine, -mal-
let.
swăg'ger, -er, -ing, -ing ly, -gered.
swäin.
swäle, swaled, swäl'ing.
swal'lōw (swŏl'-), -er, -ing,
-lōwed, swal'low tail, a coat; a
bird, -wort.
swal'low-day, -fish, -fly catch er,
-hawk, -hole, -peâr, -plov er,
-roll er, -shrike, -stone, -struck,
-tailed, -wing, swal'low's-nest.
swamp (swŏmp), -er, -ing, -y,
-i ness, swamped, swamp'weed,
-wood.
swamp'-ap ple, -ash, -beg gar-
ticks, -black ber ry, -black-
bird, -blue ber ry, -broom,
-cab bage, -cot ton wood, -crake,
-cy press, -deer, -dock, -dog-
wood, -elm, -fe ver, -gum,
-hare, -hel le bore, -hen, -hick-
o ry, -hon ey suc kle, -land,
-lau rel, -lil y, -lo cust, -loose-
strife, -lov er.
swamp'-mag no'li a, -ma hog'-
a ny, -ma ple, -marl, -milk weed,
-moss, -muck, -oak, -ore, -owl,
-par tridge, -pine, -pink, -quail,

---

nŏt, nôr, ūse, ŭp, ûrn, etüde, fōōd, fŏŏt, aŋger, boṅmot, thus, Bach.

-rob in, -rose, -sas sa fras,
-sax i frage, -spar row, -su mac,
-this tle, -war bler, -wil low.

swan (swŏn), -ner y, -ny, swan'-
flow'er, -herd, -neck, a plant;
the end of a pipe, -skin, -wort.

swan'-an i mal'cule, -coat, -down,
-goose, -hop ping, -maid en,
-mark, -mark ing, -mus sel,
-shot, -song, -up ping, swan's-
down.

swănk, -y.

Swan'sea (swŏn'sē), t. Wales.

swap (swŏp), -ping, swapped.

swape, -well.

swạrd, -y, swạrd'-cut ter.

swärf, -mon ey.

swạrm, -ing, swarmed, swarm'-
cell, -spore.

swạrt, -back, a bird, swart'-
rut ter, -star, -vis aged.

swạrth'y, -i ly, -i ness.

swash (swŏsh), -er, -ing, -y,
swashed, swash'way.

swash'-bank, -buck'et, -buc'-
kler, -let'ters, -plate, -work.

Swa tä'ra, tp. Pa.

swạth, -er.

swäthe, swathed, swäth'ing, -y.

Swä'tow' (-tou'), t. China.

sway, -ing, swayed, sway'-backed,
-bar, -bra cing.

swĕal, -ing, swealed.

sweâr, -er, -ing, swore, sworn,
swear'-word.

swĕat, -ed, -er, -ing, -y, -i ly,
-i ness, -less.

swĕat'-band, -box, -ca nal, -cen-
ter, -cloth, -duct, -fi ber,
-gland, -house, -lĕath er, -lodge,
-shop, -stock.

swĕat'ing-bäth, -cloth, -fe ver,
-house, -i ron, -pit, -room,
-sick ness, -tub, s. sys'tem.

Swē'den, kingdom Europe; tp.
N. Y., Swēde, Swēd'ish.

Swē'den borg, Swedish philos.,
-bor'gi an, -an ism.

swee'ny, a disease of horses.

sweep, -er, -ing, -ing ly, -ing-
ness, -y, swept, sweep'stake,
-stakes.

sweep'-bar, -net, -piece, -rake,

-saw, -seine, -sein'ing, -wash er,
-wash ings, sweep'ing-car, -day.

sweet, -en, -ened, -en er, -en ing,
-ly, -ness, sweet'bread, -bri er,
-heart, -leaf, a tree, -lips, a
fish, -meat, -root, a plant,
-suck'er, a fish, -weed, -wood,
a tree, -wort.

sweet'-ap ple, a tree, -bay, -box,
-brĕathed, -fern, -flag, -gale,
-grăss, -gum, -john, a flower,
-nan cy, a flower, -oil, -reed,
-rush, -scent ed, -sop, -tan gle,
-tem pered, -wa ter, -wil liam,
a flower, -wil low, sweet'bri er-
sponge, sweet cal a mus, s. cane,
s. herbs, s. mash, s. po ta'to, s.
wa'ter.

sweīn'mŏte.

swell, -dom, -ing, -ish, -y,
swelled, swŏll'en, swell'fish.

swell'-blīnd, -box, -key'board,
-mob, -mobs'man, -or gan,
-ped al, -rule, -shark, -toad.

swĕl'ter, -ing, -tered, -try.

swerve, swerved, swerv'ing.

swift, -er, -est, -let, -ly, -ness,
swift'foot, a bird, swift'-boat,
-foot ed, -hand ed, -heeled,
-moth, -winged.

swig, -ging, swigged.

swill, -er, -ing, swilled, swill'-
bowl, -milk, -pail, -trough, -tub.

swim, -mer, -mer et, -ming,
-ming ly, -ming ness, swam,
swum, swim'-blad der.

swim'ming-ap pa ra'tus, -bäth,
-bell, -belt, -blad der, -fin,
-foot, -plate, -pond, -school,
-stone, -tub, s. crab, s. spi der.

Swīn'burne, Eng. poet.

swin'dle, -dled, -dler, -dler y,
-dling.

swīne, swīn'er y, -ish, -ish ly,
-ish ness, swine'bread, a plant,
-fish, -herd, -stone, -sty, -ward.

swine'-chopped, -cress, -fĕath'er,
-flesh, -grăss, -oat, -pen ny,
-plague, -pox, -this tle,

swine's'-bane, -cress, -fĕath'er,
-grăss, -snout, -suc co ry.

swing, -er, -ing, -ing ly, swung,
swing'tree.

---

fāte, făt, fär, fạll, fâre, fȧst, sofȧ, mēte, mĕt, hêr, īce, ĭn, nōte,

swing'-back, -beam, -boat, -bol'-
ster, -bridge, -churn, -dev'il,
-han dle, -jack, -knife, -mo-
tion, -pan, -plow, -press, -saw,
-shelf, -stock, -swang, -ta ble,
-tool, -trot, -wheel.
swing'ing-block, -post, s. boom,
s. saw, s. valve.
swinge, swinged, swinge'ing,
-ing ly, swĭn'ger (-jer), swinge'-
buc'kler.
swiŋ'gle, -gled, -gling, swiŋ'gle-
tail, a shark, -tree, swiŋ'gle-bar,
-stȧff, -wand.
swiŋ'gling-knife, -ma chine',
-stȧff, -tōw.
swĭpe, swiped, swĭp'ing, -er,
swipe'-beam.
swirl, -ing, -y, swirled.
swish, -ing, -cr, swished, swish'-
broom, -swash.
Swiss, S. cam'bric, S. em broid'-
er y, S. mus lin.
swiss'ing, calendering.
switch, -er, -ing, -y, switched,
switch'back, -board, -man.
switch'-bar, -gear, -grȧss, -lan tern,
-lĕv er, -mo tion, -sig nal, -sor-
rel, -stand, -ta ble, -tend er,
-tow'er, switch'er-gear.
switch'ing-bill, -en gine, -eye,
-ground, -lo co mo'tive, -neck,
-plug.
switch'el.
switḥ'er, -ing, -ered.
Swit'zer land, Rep. Europe; co.
Ind., Swit'zer (-ser).
swiv'ĕl, -ĕled or -ĕlled, -ĕl ing
or -ling, -ĕl er or -ler.
swĭv'ĕl-bridge, -eye, -eyed, -gun,
-hang er, -hook, -joint, -keep er,
-loom, -mus ket, -plow, -sink-
er, -ta ble.
swiz'zle, -zled, -zling, swiz'zle-
stick.
swŏll'en (-n).
swo͞on, -ing, -ing ly, swooned.
swo͞op, -ing, swo͞oped.
sword (sōrd), -ed, -ing, -less,
sword'bill, a bird, -crȧft, -fish,
-fish er y, -fish ing, -man, -tail,
a bug, swords'man, -man ship.
sword'-arm, -bay o net, -bean,

-bear er, -belt, -blade, -break-
er, -cane, -car riage, -cut, -cut-
ler, -dȧnce, -dol lar, -fight,
-flag, -flight ed, -gäunt let,
-grȧss, -guard, -hand, -hilt,
-knot, -law, -lil y, -mat, -play,
-play er, -pom mel, -proof,
-rack, -sedge, -shaped, -shrimp,
-stick, -tailed, -thrust.
swore, sworn. See swear.
swum. See swim.
swung. See swing.
Syb'a rĭte, -rĭt ism, -rĭt'ic, -ic al.
sy'bot ism (sī'-), -bot'ic.
syc'a more, -dis ease', -fig, -ma-
ple, -moth.
syce (sīs), a groom.
sy cee' (sī-), silver coin, sy cee'-
sil ver.
Sy'char (sī'kar), Bib.
Sy'chem (sī'kem), Bib.
syc'o phan cy, -o phant, phan'-
tic, -tic al, -phant'ish, -ish ly,
-ism, -ize, -ized, -i zing.
Sy e'lus (sī-), Bib.
Sy e'nē (sī-), Bib.
sy'e nĭte (sī'-), -nĭt'ic.
syl'la ble, -lăb'ic, -ic al, -al ly,
-lab'i cate, -cā'ted, -cā'ting,
-cā'tion, -lab'i fy ing, -fied,
-fĭ cā'tion, -la bism, -la bist,
-la bize, -bized, -bī'zing, -la-
bled, -la bling, syl'la ble-stum-
bling, s. name.
syl'la bus, pl. -bus es or -bī.
syl lep'sis, -lep'tic, -tic al, -al ly.
syl'lo gism, -gis'tic, -tic al, -al-
ly, -gize, -gized, -gi zer, -zing,
-zā'tion.
sylph (sĭlf), -ĭne, -ish, sylph'-
like.
syl'va, pl. -vas or -væ, -van,
-vage, -vi cul ture, -cul'tūr al,
-tūr ist.
syl ves'tral, -tri an, pertaining to
the woods, Syl ves'tri an, a
monk.
sym'bol, -ism, -ist, -is'tic, -tic al,
-ize, -ized, -ī'zer, -ī'zing, -ĭ zā'-
tion, -bŏled or -bŏlled, -bŏl ing
or -ling, -bŏl'ic, -ic al, -al ly,
-al ness, -ics, -bŏl'o gy, -o gist,
-bō log'ic al, sym'bŏl-print ing.

sym'me try, -me tral, -me trist, -me trize, -trized, -tri zing, -trĭ-zā'tion, -met'ri an, -met'ric, -ric al, -al ly, -al ness, -me tri'-cian (-trĭsh'an).

Sym'onds (sĭm'-), Eng. auth.

sym pa thet'ic, -al, -al ly, -i cism, -pa thist, -thize, -thized, -thi-zing, -thi zer, -thy.

sym'pho ny, -nist.

Sym plĕg'a des (sĭm plĕg'a dēz), two rocks at the entrance of the Euxine Sea.

sym pŏ'si um (-zĭ-), *pl.* -si a.

symp'tom (sĭmp'-), -to mat'ic, -ic al, -al ly, -ma tize', -tized, -ti zing, -ma tol'o gy, -mat'o log'-ic al, -al ly, -to mol'o gy.

syn'a gogue, -gog'ic al (-gŏj'-).

syn ar thrŏ'sis, pl. *-ses* (-sēz).

syn'chrŏ nal, -chron'ic al, -ic al-ly, -chrŏ nism, -chrŏ nis'tic, -tic al ly, -chrŏ nize, -nized, -ni'zer, -ni'zing, -nĭ zā'tion, -nol'o gy, -chrŏ noŭs, -noŭs ly, -noŭs ness, -chrŏ ny.

syn'co pate, -pā'ted, -pā'ting, -pā'tion, -co pe, -cŏp'ic, -cŏp'-tic, -co pist, -pize, -pized, -pi zing.

syn'di cate, -cā'ted, -cā'ting, -cā'-tor, -cā'tion.

syn ec'dŏ chē (-kē), -doch'ic al (-dŏk'-), -al ly.

syn'od (sĭn'-), -od al, -od'ic, -ic-al, -al ly, -od ist.

syn'o nym (sĭn'-), -nym'ic, -ic al, -nym'i ty, sy non'y mist, -y mize, -mized, -mĭ'zing, -non'y mous, -mous ly, -y my.

syn op'sis -op'tic, -tic al, -al ly, -tist, -tis'tic.

syn'tax, -tăc'tic, -tic al, -al ly.

syn'the sis, *pl.* -ses (-sēz), -sist, -size, -sized, -sĭ'zing, -thĕt'ic,

-ic al, -al ly, -i cism, -the tist, -tize, -tized, -tī'zing.

Syn'tĭ chē (sĭn'tĭ kē), *Bib.*

syn'to ny, -to nize, -nized, -ton'ic.

sy'pher-joint, a lap joint in car-pentry.

syph'i lis (sĭf'-), -i lize, -lized, -li za'tion, -i lit'ic, -ic al ly, syph'i lo derm, -der'ma tous, -i-loid, -i lous, -i lol'o gist, -o gy, -i lo'ma, -lo ma'ni a, -lom'a tous.

Syr'a cuse (-kūs), *Bib.;* c. N. Y.; vil. O.; c. It.

Syr'i a (sĭr'-), div. Turk., -i ac, -a cism, -i an, -an ism.

sy riŋ'ga (sĭ-).

syr'inge (sĭr'-), -inged, -in ging sy rin'ge al, syr'inge-gun, -valve.

syr'inx (sĭr'-), *pl.* syr'in ges (-jēz) *or* sĭ rin'jĕz *or* -jēz).

Sy'rŏ phē nĭ'cian (sī'rŏ fē nĭsh'-an), *Bib.*

syr'tis, pl. *-tes* (-tēz).

syr'up (sĭr'-). See *sirup.*

sys'tem, -less, -at'ic, -ic al, -al ly, -a tize, -tized, -tī'zer, -tī'zing, -tist, -tism, -tĭ zā'tion, -tem a-tol'o gy, -tem'ic, -tem ize, -ized, -i zer, -i zing, -ĭ zā'tion, sys'-tem-māk'er, -mon'ger.

sys'tŏ lē, -tŏl'ic.

sys'tyle

syz'y gy (sĭz'ĭ jy).

Szé'chen yi (sā'kĕn yē), Hung. statesman.

Sze chu en' (zā'chōō'ĕn'), prov. China.

Szeg ed in' (sĕg'ĕd'ēn'), t. Hung.

Szen tes' (sĕn'tĕsh'), t. Hung.

Szi'geth' (sē'gĕt'), t. Hung.

Szi'vacz (sē'väts'), vil. Hung.

szo pel'ka (tsō-).

Szta ni csics (stä'nē'chĭch'), t. Hung.

---

fāte, făt, fär, fạll, fâre, făst, sofà, mēte, mĕt, hêr, īce, ĭn, nōte,

T

T band age, T bar, T beard, T bolt, T bone, T branch, T bulb, T cart, · T cloth, T cross, T fit'ting, T head, T hinge, T i ron, T joint, T pan el, T pipe, T plate, T rail, T square.
T-like, -shaped.
taal (tạl *or* täl).
taa weesh' (tä-).
tăb'ard, -er.
tăb'a ret.
ta bas'co sauce.
tä bä'ua (-wä).
tăb'bi net.
tăb'by, -ing, tab'bĭed, tab'by-cat.
ta bel'la.
tăb'er nâ cle, -cled, -cling, -nac'-u lar, tab'er na cle-work.
tä'bes (-bēz), -bes'cence, -cent, -bet'ic, tab'ic, tab'id, -id ly, -id-ness, ta bif'ic.
Tăb'i tha, *Bib.*
tăb'la ture.
tä'ble, -ful, -bled, -bling, ta'ble-man, -spoon, -spoon'ful, -tree, -ware, -wise.
tä'ble-an'vil, -bit, -board, -book, -car pet, -clamp, -cloth, -cloth-ing, -cov er, -cut, -cut ter, -flap, -knife, -land, -läthe, -leaf, -lift ing, -line, -lin en, -mon ey, -mov ing, -mu sic, -plane, -rap-ping, -rent, -saw, -serv'ice, -shore, -song, -spar, -sport, -talk, -talk er, -tip ping, -tomb, -topped, -turn ing, -work, t. di'a mond, t. grind'er.
tä'ble d'hote (tä'bl dōt).
ta bleau' (tä blō' *or* tăb'lō), *pl.* -*bleaux'* (-blōz'), *t. vi'vant'* (vē'-vŏń').
tăb'let, -ted, -ting.
tab'lette, a coping stone in fortifications.
ta blier' (tä blyä').
tab'loid.
ta bōō' *or* ta bu' (-bōō'), -ing, -booed'.

tä'bor, -er, tăb'ō ret *or* -ou ret (-ōō-) *or* tăb'ret, tăb'ō rĭne *or* -ou rine (*or* -rēn).
tăb'u lar, -ly, -lar ize, -ized, -ĭ'zing, -ĭ zä'tion.
tab'u late, -lā'tor, -lä'ting, -lä'-ted, -lä'tion.
tac'a ma hac'.
tac'-au-tac'.
tä'cē.
tä'cet.
tache (tăsh), a spot or freckle.
tache (tatch), a sugar-pan.
ta chom'e ter (-kŏm'-), -e try, tach'o grăph (tăk'-).
ta chyg'ra phy (-kĭg'-), -ra pher, tach y graph'ic (tăk'ĭ-), -ic al.
ta chym'e ter (-kĭm'-).
tac'it (tăs'-), -ly, -i turn, -turn ly, -tur'ni ty.
tack, -er, -ing, -y, -i ness, tacked, tacks'man.
tack'-block, -claw, -comb, -drĭv'-er, -du ty, -free, -ham mer, -head, -lash ing, -lift er, -mold, -pin, -pull er, -riv et, -tac kle.
tac'kle, -kled, -kling, -kler, -kle-man.
tac'kle-block, -board, -fall, -hook, -post.
tac'nŏde, -cusp.
tact, -ful, -less, -less ness.
tac'tic, -tic al, -al ly, -tics, -tĭle, -tion, -tor, -tu al, -al ly, -tus, -ti'cian, -tom'e ter, tac'tic al u'nit.
tad'pŏle, -fish, -hake.
tael (tāl).
tæ'nĭ a, -ni ate, -ni cĭde, -ni form, -ni fuge.
tăf'fe ta.
taff'rail.
tăf'fy, -ing, -fĭed.
tăft.
tăg, -ger, -ging, -let, tagged, tag'tail.
tag'-al der, -belt, -boat, -end, -fas ten er, -hold er, -lock, -ma-chine, -nee dle, -rag, -sore, -wool.

---

nŏt, nôr, ūse, ŭp, ûrn, etüde, fōōd, fŏŏt, aŋger, boṅmot, thus, Bach.

Ta gäl' (*or* tä'-), -gä'la, -gä'log, -gäls'.

tag bä'nuas (-nwȧs).

tagl'ia (tȧl'ya).

Tagl ia men'to (täl yä-), r. It.

Tagl io'ni (täl yō'nē), Swed. opera dancer.

tagl io'ni (tȧl yō'nĭ), an overcoat.

Tä hi'ti (-hē'tē), isl. Pacific, -hi'-ti an (-hē'tē-), T. chest'nut.

täh'lĭ.

tä hŏ'na.

täh sil där' (-sēl-).

tä'i (-ē).

tail, -ing, -less, tailed, tail'flow-er, -wort.

tail'-bay, -block, -board, -bone, -coat, -corn, -cov erts, -crab, -drain, -end, -fĕath er, -fin, -fly, -gate, -grape, -hook, -lamp, -lobe, -mus cle, -piece, -pin, -pipe, -race, -rope, -screw, -stock, -switch ing, -tac kle, -trim mer, -valve, -vise, -wa-ter, tails-com mon.

taille (tāl), form; build; make.

tail lë' (täl yä'), *Her.*

tail leur' (tȧ lyêr').

tail loir' (tȧ'lwŏr').

tai'lor, -ess, -ing, -lored, tai'lor-bird, -made, -mus cle, -war-bler, tai'lor ing-ma chine, tai'lors' chair, t. cramp, t. spasm, t. twist.

täin.

Täine, Fr. auth.

täint, -ed, -ing, -less, -less ly, taint'-worm.

Tai'ping' (tĭ'-).

tai'po (tĭ'pŏ).

täj.

tä'jo (-hō).

take, took, tāk'en (-n), -er, -ing, -ing ly, -ing ness.

take'-heed, *n.*, -in, -off, -up, tāk'er-off.

Tal'bot, co. Ga.; co. Md.

tălc, -ous, tal'cīte, -cōse, -cum, talck'y, talc'-schist.

Täl'chir' (-kēr'), state India.

tāle, -ful, -bear'er, -tell'er, -wise, tale-book, -pi et.

tăl'ent, -ed.

tä'les (-lēz), tales'man.

Tal'fourd (tạwl'furd), Eng. poet.

tä'li (-lē).

Tal'ia ferro (tŏl'ĭ ver), co. Ga.; Amer. Rev. officer.

tä'li on, -on'ic.

tăl'i pes (-pēz), -i ped.

tăl'i pot, -palm.

tăl'is man (*or* -ĭz-), -măn'ic.

Tȧ lĭ'tha-cū'mĭ (*or* tăl'ĭ-), *Bib.*

talk (tạwk), -a tive, -tive ly, -tive ness, -er, -ing, talked, talk'ing-ma chine', -to.

tạll, -ness, -boy.

Tăl'la hătch'ie, co. and r. Miss.

tăl'lĭth.

Tăll'madge (-mĭj *or* -mäj), Amer. jurist and statesman.

tăl'lōw, -er, -ish, -y, tal'low-ber'ry, -face, a person, -nut, a tree, -wood.

tal'low-can, -chan dler, -chan'-dler y, -cup, -drop, -faced, -gourd, -keech, -nut meg, -oil, -shrub, -top, -tree, t. can dle, t. dip.

tăl'ly, -ing, -lĭed, -li er, tal'ly-man, -mȧs ter, -wom an.

tal'ly-book, -ho, -mark, -pot, -sheet, -shop, -stick, t. sys'tem, t. trade.

Tăl'ma (*or* täl'mä'), Fr. tragedian.

tăl'ma, a cape.

Tăl'mage (-mĭj *or* -mäj), Amer. divine and auth.

Tăl'măi, *Bib.*

Tăl'mud, -ist, -mud'ic, -ic al, -is'tic.

tăl'on, -oned.

ta luk' *or* -look' (-lo͞ok'), -dar.

Tä'lus, Spenser, *Faerie Queene.*

tä'lus, pl. -*lĭ,* the ankle.

tä'lus, a bastion; loose rocks and gravel.

Tä'mar, *Bib.*

tăm'a rack, -pine.

tăm'a rĭnd, -fish, -plum.

tăm'a risk.

Tä mä tä've (-vä), port Mada-gascar.

Tä mau li'päs (-mou lē'-), state Mex.

tăm'bor, -oil.

tăm′bour (-bōōr), -ing, -boured,
-*bour′gy* (-boor′jĭ), -bour ine′
(-ēn′), tam′bour-cot ton, -em
broid′er y, -frame, -lace, -nee
dle, -stitch, -stitch er, -work.

tame, -less, -less ness, -ly, -ness,
tamed, tăm′a ble, -ble ness,
-a bil′i ty, -er, -ing, tame′-
poi′son.

Tăm′er lăne′, Asiatic conqueror.

tam′i dĭne.

Tä mil′ (-mēl′), race in India.

Tä mise′ (-mēz′), t. Belg.

ta mise′ (-mēz′), a woolen fabric.

Täm′luk′ (-lōōk′), t. India.

tam′-o′-shan′ter, a cap.

tamp, -ing, tamped, tamp′-work.

tamp′ing-bar, -i ron, -ma chine,
-plug.

tam′per, -er, -ing, -pered.

tăm′pi on.

tăm′pon, -ade, -age, -ing, -ment,
-poned.

tam′-tam′ *or* tom′-tom.

tä mu′re (-mōō′rä).

tan, tan′na ble, -nage, -ner, -ner y,
-ning, tanned.

tan′-balls, -bark, -băth, -bay,
-bed, -col ored, -ex tract′or,
-house, -liq uor, -mill, -ooze,
-pic kle, -pit, -press, -ride,
-spud, -stove, -turf, -vat,
-yard.

tan′ning-ap pa ră′tus, -cyl in der,
-ma te ri als.

tăn′a ger, -a grine, -a groid.

Tä nä′nä ri vŏ′ (-rē-), t. Mada
gascar.

Tän′dä *or* -däh, t. India.

tan′dem.

Ta′ney (tạw′nĭ), Amer. jurist; co.
Mo.

tăng, -ing, -y, tanged, tang′-
tool, -whaup.

taṇ′ga lung.

Tän gän yi′kä (-yē′-), l. Afr.

tăn′gent, -gence, -gen cy, -gen′-
tial (-shăl), -tial ly, -ti al′i ty
(-shĭ ăl′-).

tan′gi ble, -ness, -bly, -bil′i ty,
tan gib′i lē (-jĭb′-).

Tän giĕr′ *or* -giĕrs′, t. Morocco,
Afr., -ge rine′, pertaining to

Tangier; tăn ge rine′ (-rēn′), a
fruit.

tan′gle, -gled, -gling, -gling ly,
-gly, tan′gle ber ry, -foot, a
liquor.

tan′gle-fish, -pick er, -swab,
-wrack, t. tent.

tä′ni wha (*or* tăn′ĭ wä).

tank, -age, -ing, tank′-car, -en
gine, -fur nace, -i ron, -lo co
mo′tive, -pump, -run′ner, -sta′-
tion, -tog′gle, -ves sel, -wa′ter,
-worm.

tan′ka-boat.

tank′ard, -bear′er, -shaped, -tur
nip.

Tänn′häu ser (-hoi zer), German
lyric poet; opera by Wagner.

tan′nin, -nic, -nif′er ous, -nom′-
e ter, tan′nin-plate.

tăn′sy (-zy).

tan′ta lize, -lized, -lī′zer, -lī′zing,
-zing ly, -zing ness, -lĭ zä′tion.

Tăn′ta lus, *Myth.*, T. cup *or*
-lus′s cup.

tăn′ta mount.

tan-tan, -met al.

tăn tăr′a.

tăn tĭv′y, -ing, -tĭv′ĭed.

tăn′tra, -tric, -trism, -trist.

tăn′trum.

tăn′ty, a Hindu loom. *pl.* -ties.

tăn′zĭ mat.

Tä′o ism (*or* tou′-), -o ist, -is′tic.

tä′ō-tai′ (-tī′), a Chinese officer.

tap, -ster, -ling, -net, -per, -ping,
tapped, taps′man.

tap′-bar, -bolt, -bor er, -cin der,
-hole, -house, -pic′kle, -plate,
-riv et, -room, -root, -root ed,
-screw, -shac kled, -wrench.

tap a de′ra *or* -rŏ (-dä′-).

tä pä′que (-kä).

tape, taped, tăp′ing, tape′work,
-worm.

tape′-car′ri er, -grăss, -nee′dle, t.
line, t. meas′ure, t. prīm′er,
tape′worm-plant.

tä′per, -ing, -ing ly, -ness, -wise,
-pered, ta′per-can′dle stick, -fuse,
-point ed, -stand, -vise.

tăp′es try, -ing, -trĭed, tap′es try-
cloth, -moth, -paint ing, -stitch.

---

nŏt, nôr, ūse, ŭp, ûrn, etüde, fōōd, fŏŏt, aṇger, boṅmot, thus, Bačh.

tap'e tal.
Tăph'nes (-nēz), *Bib*
tăp i ŏ'ca.
tă'pir, a quadruped.
tă'pis (*or* tă pē'), a carpet or cover; *tä'pis* (-pēs), a sash or belt.
ta pŏ'a.
tăp'pet, -loom, -mo tion, -ring, -rod, -wheel.
tap'ping, -ap pa ra'tus, -bar, -cock, -drill, -gouge, -hole, -machine, -tool.
tar, -ring, -ry, tarred, tar'weed.
tar'-board, -box, -brush, -kiln, -lamp, -oil, -put ty, -vetch, -wa ter, -well.
tä ra gui'ra (-gē'-).
tär an tăss'.
tär'an tel'la, tar'ant ism.
ta ran'tu la, *pl.* -las *or* -læ, -tu lar, -la ted, ta ran'tu la-dănce, -kill er.
Tarbes (tärb), t. Fr.
tar boosh'.
tar'dy, -di ly, -di ness, *tar'dō*, tar'dy-gait'ed, -ris ing.
tare.
targe, -man, targed, tar'ging.
tar'get, -eer', tar'get-card, -fīr'-ing, -lamp, -prac'tice, -range.
Tä ri'fä (-rē'-), t. Sp.
tär'iff, -rid den.
tar'la tan.
tarn.
tar'nish, -a ble, -er, -ing, -nished.
tä'rŏ, a plant, tä rō', a coin.
tar'pan, a horse.
tar pau'lin.
Tar pē'ia (-ya), a Roman maiden. -pe'ian, noting a rock.
tar'pon, a fish.
tär'ry, -ing, -ri er, -rïed.
tärt, -ly, -ness.
tär'tan, t. vel'vet.
tar tä'na, a vehicle.
tär'tar, a chemical substance, -tär'ic, -ta rïne, -rize, -rized, -ri-zing, -rï zā'tion, -rous.
Tär'tar, -us, -tä're an.
Tar tŭffe', Molière.
Tasche reau' (täsh'rō'), Fr. biog. and editor.

tăsh.
ta sim'e ter, tas i met'ric.
tăsk, -er, -ing, tăsked, tăsk'-mäs ter, -mis tress, task'-work.
Tas mä'nï a (tăz-), isl. S. Pac. Oc.
tas sä'go.
tas'sel, -seled *or* -selled, -sel ing *or* -ling, tas'sel flow'er.
tas'sel-grăss, -hy'a cinth, -stitch, -tree, -worm.
tas'set, a piece of armor.
tas sette', a term in cookery.
tăste, -ful, -ful ly, -ful ness, -less, -less ly, -less ness, tăst'a ble, -ed, -er, -ing, -y, -i ly.
taste'-a re a, -bud, -bulb, -center, -cor'pus cle.
tä'ta, an African dwelling.
tä'ta, a shrub.
tä'-tä', farewell.
tä tä'o, a bird.
Tăt'năi (*or* -nä ï), *Bib.*
tăt'ter, -ing, -y, -tered, tat'ter-de măl'ion (*or* -măl'yŭn), tat'-ter wal'lop.
tăt'ting, -shut tle.
tăt'tle, -tled, -tler, -tler y, -tling, -tling ly.
tăt tōō', *pl.* -tōōs' (-tōōz'), -er, -ing, -tōōed', tăt tōō'ing-nee dle.
tăt'ty.
tạu, -bone, tau cross, t. cru ci fix, t. stăff.
Tauch'nitz (toućh'nĭts), Ger. publisher.
tạught. See *teach.*
Tau'ler (tow'-), Ger. mystic.
tăunt, -ed, -er, -ing, -ing ly.
tau'pie *or* taw'-.
tạut, tight; tense, -en, -ly, -ness.
tau'ted.
tạu tog', *or* -taug'.
tạu tol'o gy, -to log'ic, -ic al, -al-ly, -tol'o gism, -o gist, -o gous, -o gize, -gized, -gī'zing.
tăv'ern, -er, tav'ern-bush, -haunt-er, -keep er, -to'ken.
Tä'vĕr'ni er' (-nē ā'), Fr. trav.
taw, -er, -er y, -ing.
tä'wa.
Tạ'was, tp. and v. Mich.
taw'dry, -dri ly, -dri ness.
tạw'ny, -ni ness.

---

fāte, făt, fär, fạll, fâre, fạst, sofä, mēte, mĕt, hêr, īce, ĭn, nŏte,

tax, -a ble, -ble ness, -a bly, -a bil′i ty, -ā′tion, -er, -ing, -less, -man, taxed, tax′pay er.

tax′-cart, -col lect′or, -dodg er, -free, -gath er er, -list, -roll, taxing-dis trict, -mȧs ter, tax bond, t. cer tif′i cate, t. com mis′sioner, t. deed, t. du′pli cate, t. lev′y, t. li′en, t. sale, t. ti′tle.

tăx′i der my, -der mal, -der′mic, -der′mist, -der mize, -mized. ·

tax ŏl′o gy, -on′o mer, -on′o mist, -on′o my, -o nŏm′ic, -ic al, -al ly.

tay′saam (tī′säm).

Tăze′well, co. Ill.; co. Va.

tăz′za (tät′sa).

tchä păn′.

tchick (chĭk).

Tchir′păn (chĕr′-), t. Turk.

tĕa, -ber ry, -cup, -cup ful, -ket′tle, -pot, -poy, -spoon, -spoon′ful, -wort.

tĕa′-bis cuit, -board, -bread, -bug, -cad dy, -cake, -can ister, -case, -chest, -clam, -clipper, -cloth, -deal er, -drink er, -drunk ard, -fight, -gar den, -gown, -house, -lĕad, -leaf, -oil, -par ty, -plant, -room, -rose, -scent, -scrub, -serv ice, -set, -shrub, -stick, -ta ble, -tȧst er, -things, -tray, -tree, -urn, -ware.

tĕach, -a ble, -a ble ness, -a bil′i ty, -er, -ing.

tĕak, -tree, -wood.

tĕal, -duck.

team, -ing, -ster, -wise, teamed, team′-shov′el, -work.

teâr, -er, -ing, tore, torn, teâr′thumb, -up, teâr′ing-ma chine′.

tĕar, -ful, -ful ly, -ful ness, -less, -y, tĕar′-bag, -drop, -duct, -fall ing, -gland, -pit, -pump, -sac, -shaped, -stained.

tease (tēz), teased, teas′er, -ing, -ing ly, tĕas′ing-nee′dle.

tĕat, -ed, -like, -fish.

teaze-hole, -ten′on.

tĕa′zel *or* -sel, -zeled *or* -zelled, -zel ing *or* -ling, -zel er *or* -ler, tea′zel wort, tea′zel-card, -frame, tea′zel ing-ma chine′.

---

teb′bad.

Teche, Bay′ou (bī′o͞o tĕsh), stream La.

tech′nic (tĕk′-), -al, -al ly, -alness, -nĭ cal′i ty, -ni′cian (-nĭsh′an), -ni cist, -nics, -nique′ (-nēk′), -nism, -nol′o gy, -o gist, -no log′ic, -ic al.

tĕc nŏl′o gy, a treatise on children.

ted, -ded, -der, -ding.

Te des′co (tā-).

Te Dē′um.

tĕ′dĭ ous (*or* tēd′yŭs), -ly, -ness, -di um.

tee, -ing, teed.

teel, -seed.

teem, -er, -ing, -less, teem′inghole, -punch.

teens.

teer, -er.

tee′ter, -ing, -tered, -ter tail.

teeth. See *tooth.*

teethe, teethed, teeth′ing.

tee′tŏ′tal, -er, -ism, -tal ly.

tee′-tŏ′tum.

Te gu ci gäl′pä (tā go͞o sē-), t. Cent. Amer.

tĕg′u ment, -men′tal, -tȧ ry, -tum.

tĕ hee′, -heed′, -hee′ing.

Tĕ hĕ rän′, c. Pers.

Te huan te pĕc′ (tā wän tā-), t. Mex.

Teign′mouth (tĭn′mŭth), Eng. gov. gen. of India.

tĕil.

Tĕ kă′mah, tp. Neb.

tĕk non′y my, -y mous.

tĕ′la, -lar, -la′ri an, tĕl′a ry.

Tĕ lā′im (*or* tĕl′-), *Bib.*

tĕ lau′to grȧph (*or* tĕl-) -togram.

te le′ga (-lā′-).

tĕl′e gram, -gram′mic.

tĕl′e grȧph, -ing, -grȧphed, -graph′ic, -ic al, -al ly, -graph′er (*or* tĕ lĕg′ra pher), -graph′ist (*or* tĕ lĕg′-), -graph′y (*or* tĕlĕg′-), -graph′o phone.

tĕl′e grȧph-board, -ca ble, -carriage, -clock, -cock, -di al, -key, -line, -op e ra′tor, -plant, -pole, -post, -reel, -reg is ter, -wire.

---

nŏt, nôr, ūse, ŭp, ûrn, etüde, fo͞od, fo͝ot, aṇger, boṇmot, thus, Bach.

tel'e kĭ nē'sis,   -net'ic,   te lel'o-
grăph,   tel'e ma nom'e ter,   -e-
mē'te or o grăph,   -graph'ic.
tel'e lec'tro scope.
Tĕ lem'a chus   (-kŭs),   Homer's
Odyssey.
Te le maque'   (tā lā måk'),   Féne-
lon's Romance.
tĕ lĕm'e ter,   -e try,   tel e met'ric,
-mo'tor,   te lĕn'gi scope   (-jĭ-).
te lĕp'a thy,   -a thist,   tel e path'-
ic,   -ic al ly.
tĕl'e phone,   -phoned,   -phōn er,
-ing,   -ist,   -phŏn'ic,   -ic al ly,
-phŏ'no grăph,   -graph'ic,   -phŏ'-
ny   (or   tĕ lef'-),   tel'e phone-
booth,   -harp,   -line.
tel'e phŏte,   -phŏ'to graph,   -tog'-
ra phy.
tĕl'ē phŏ'tŏs.
tel'e scope,   -scoped,   -scōp'ing,
-scŏp'ic,   -ic al,   -al ly,   -scŏ'py
(or   te lĕs'-),   -scŏ'pist   (or   tĕ-
les'-),   -scrip'tor.
tĕl'e scope-bag,   -carp,   -chim'ney,
-drĭv'er,   -eye,   -fish,   -fly,   -joint,
-shell,   -sight,   -ta ble,   -word.
tel ē spec'tro scope,   -e stĕr'ē ō-
scope,   -e ther'mo grăph,   -ther-
mom'e ter,   -e try,   tel'e tō pom'-
e ter.
Tĕl'ford,   Scotch   engineer;   inventor   of   Telford   pave ment,
tel'ford ize,   -ized,   -ī'zing.
tell,   -a ble,   -er,   -er ship,   -ing,
-ing ly,   told,   tell'tale,   a person,
tell'ing-house,   tell-bill-wil ly,   a
bird.
tel lŭ'ri an,   -lŭ'ric.
tĕl'pher,   -age,   -way.
Tĕm'a nĭ   (or   tĕ'-),   Bib
tĕ mĕr'i ty.
Tĕm'es'   (-ĕsh'),   r. Hung.
tĕm'i ak.
tĕm'per,   -a ble,   -a ment   -a men'-
tal,   -tal ly,   -pered,   -pered ly,
-per er,   -per ing,   tem'per-
screw.
tem'per ing-fur'nace,   -ma chine',
-ov'en,   -wheel.
tem'per ance,   -per ate,   -ate lý,
-ate ness,   -a tive.
tem'per a ture,   -a larm,   -curve.

tĕm'pest,   -pes'tu ous,   -ous ly,   -ous-
ness,   tem'pest-beat en,   -tossed.
Tĕm'plar,   Knights   Tem'plars.
tĕm'ple,   -pled,   -pling.
tem'plet.
tĕm'po,   Mus.
tĕm'po,   a coin.
tĕm'po ral,   -ly,   -ness,   -ral ty,
-rā'le.
tĕm'po ra ry,   -ra ri ly,   -ri ness,
-rā'ne ous.
tĕm'po rize,   -rized,   -rī'zer,   -rī'-
zing,   -zing ly,   -rĭ zā'tion.
temps   (tŏñ).
tempt   (tĕmt),   -a ble,   -a ble ness,
-a bil'i ty,   -ed,   -er,   -ing,   -ing ly,
-ing ness,   -ress,   temp tā'tion,
-tion al,   -tion less.
tĕm'pus.
temse,   -bread,   -loaf.
ten,   -fiŋ'gers,   a   starfish,   -fold,
-pence,   -pen ny,   -pins,   tenth,
tenth'ly,   ten'-fôr'ties   (-tĭz),
-pound er   -strike,   ten-o'-clock,
a plant
tĕn'a ble,   -ness,   -a bil'i ty.
tĕn'ace.
tĕ nā'cious,   -ly,   -ness,   -nac'i ty
(-năs'-).
tĕ năil'   or   -nāille',   -nail'lon   (-nāl'-
yŭn).
tĕn'ant,   -a ble,   -a ble ness,   -cy,
-ed,   -ing,   -less,   -ry,   ten'ant-
farm er,   -right.
tend,   -ance,   -ed,   -er,   -ing.
tĕn'den cy.
ten'der,   a.,   -er,   -ly,   -foot,   -ling,
-loin,   -ness,   ten'der-dy ing,
-eyed,   -foot ed,   -heart ed,
-heart ed ly,   -heart ed ness,
-mind ed,   -sīd'ed.
tĕn'der,   v.,   -der er,   -der ing,   -der-
ee'.
tĕn'don,   -don ous.
ten'dre   (tän'dr).
ten'dril,   -driled   or   -drilled,   ten'-
dril-climb er.
tĕn'e bræ,   -hêarse.
te ne brŏ'si   (tā'nā brč'sĕ).
tĕn'e broŭs,   -ness,   -brŏs'i ty.
tĕn'e ment,   -men'tal,   -men'tā ry,
ten'e ment-house.
ten'ent,   clinging.

Tĕn'er ĭffe' *or* -Ife, one of the Canary isls.; a wine.
tĕn'et.

Ten nes see', State U. S., -see'an.

Tĕn niel' (-neel'), Eng. artist.

ten'nis, -arm, -ball, -court, -elbow, -play er.

ten'nŏ (*or* -nŏ').

tĕn'on, -oned, -on er, -on ing.

ten'on-au ger, -saw, -tru'ing, ten'on ing-chis el, -ma chine.

tĕn'or, -ist, *-o ri'no* (-rē'nō), *pl.* *-ri'ni* (-rē'nē).

tense, -less, -less ness, -ly, -ness.

ten'si ble, -si bil'i ty.

ten'sĭle, -sĭled, -sion, -sion al, -si ty, -sil'i ty.

ten'sion-bar, -beam, -brace, -bridge, -fuse, -mem ber, -rod, -roll er, -spĭc ule, -spring.

tent, -age, -ed, -er, -ing, -ĭ form, -less, tent'wise, -wort.

tent'-bed, -bed stĕad, -cat er pillar, -cloth, -fly, -guy, -māk er, -peg, -peg ging, -pin, -pole, -rope, -stitch, -tree, -wine, -work.

tĕn'ta cle, -cled, ten tac'u late, -lā'ted.

tĕn'ta tive, -ly.

tĕn'ter, a machine, -bar, -ground, -hook, ten'ter ing-ma chine'.

tĕn'u ous, -ness, te nū'i ty.

tĕn'ure, -horn, -sword.

te nu'tō (tä nōō'-), -mark.

tĕ ŏ cal'li, *pl.* -lis (-lĭz).

tĕp ee' (*or* tē'pē).

tĕp'e fy, -ing, -fĭed, -fac'tion.

tĕp'id, -ly, -ness, *-ĭ dä'ri um*, pl. *-ri a*, tĕp'or (*or* tē'-) te pid'i ty.

tĕr a tol'o gy, -o gist, -to log'ic, -ic al.

ter cen'te na ry, -ten'ni al.

ter'cet.

ter'gi ver sate, -sa tor, -sā'tion.

Ter hūne', Amer. authoress.

term, -er, -ing, -less, -ly, termed, term'-day, -fee, -piece.

ter'ma gant, -ly, -gan cy.

ter'mi nate, -nā'ted -nā'ting, -nà ble, -ble ness, -nal, -nal ly, -nā'tion, -tion al, -nā'tive, -tively, -nā'tor, -to'ry.

ter'mi nism, -mi nist.

ter mi nol'o gy, -no log'ic al, -ally.

ter'mi nus, *pl.* -nī, Ter'mi nus, *Myth.*

tern, a bird; a ship; a prize, -er y.

ter'nal, -nà ry, -nate, -nate ly.

Tĕr'naux' (-nō'), Fr. auth.

terne, roofing-tin, -plate.

Terp sich'ŏ rĕ (-sĭk'-), *Myth.*, -rē'an.

tĕr'ra cul'ture, -cul tūr al, tĕr'ra cot'ta, t. Ja pon'i ca.

tĕr'ra al'ba, t. firm'a, t. in cog'nĭ ta.

tĕr'race, -raced, -rā cing.

tĕr'rage, tĕr rāin', tĕr ra mä'rä, ter ra'ne an.

tĕr'ra pin, -farm, -paws.

tĕr rä'que ous.

tĕr rä'ri um, *pl.* -ri ums *or* -ri a.

Tĕrre'bŏnne', par. La.

Tĕr'rĕ Haute (hōt), c. Ind.

tĕr rēne', earthy, mundane, -rĕn'i ty.

terre'plein' (târ'plān').

ter res'tri al, -ly, -ness.

tĕr'ret.

tĕr'ri ble, -ness, -bly.

tĕr ric'o lous, -o lĭne.

tĕr'ri er.

tĕr'ri fy, -ing, -fĭed, -fĭed ly, -rif'ic, -ic al ly.

ter rig'e nous (-rĭj'-).

tĕr rine' (-rēn'), an earthen jar.

tĕr'ri to ry, -rĭed, -tō'ri al, -al ly, -al ism, -al'i ty, -al ize, -ized, -ĭ'zing.

tĕr'ror, -ism, -ist, -ĭs'tĭc, -ize, -ized, -ĭ'zer, -ĭ'zing, -less.

tĕr'ror-brĕatĥ ing, -fraught, -giv'ing, -haunt ed, -smit ten, -stricken.

tĕr'ry.

terse, -ly, -ness.

ter'tial, -tian, -ti â ry.

ter tu'li a (târ tōō'lē á).

Te ru ĕl' (tā rōō-), prov. Sp.

ter zet'tō (ter tsĕt'-), *ter'za-ri'ma* (ter'tsä-rē'mä).

tĕs'sel late, -lā'ted, -lā'ting, -lā'tion.

test, -ed, -er, -ing, -a ble.

test'-box, -glăss, -meal, -me ter,

---

nŏt, nôr, ūse, ŭp, ûrn, etüde, fōōd, fŏŏt, aŋger, boṅmot, tħus, Bacħ.

-mix er, -ob ject, -pa per,
-plate, -pump, -ring, -spoon,
-tube, -types, t. case, t. oath.
test′ing-box, -clause, -găge,
-hole, -ma chine, -slab.
tes′ta ment, -men′tal, -tå ry,
-ri ly.
test′ar, a fish.
tes′tate, -ta′tor, -ta′trix, -tā′tion.
tes′ter, a canopy, -cloth.
tes′ti cle, -tic′u lar, -u late, -lā′-
ted.
tes′ti fy, -ing, -fīed, -fi er, -fĭ cator, -cā′tion.
tes′ti mo ny, -mō′ni al.
tes′tis, pl. *-tes* (-tēz).
tes′ty, -ti ly, -ti ness.
tĕt′a nus, -a nize, -nized, -ni-
zing, -nĭ zā′tion, te tăn′ic.
tête′-à-tête′ (tāt′-a-tāt′), *tête′-de-
mou′ton* (tāt′-dê mo͞o′tôṅ), *tête′-
de pont′* (tāt′-dê pôṅ′).
teth′er, -ing, -ered, teth′er-ball,
-stick.
tĕt ra hē′dron, *pl.* -drons *or*
-dra, -hē′dral, -dral ly, -drīte,
-droid.
tĕt ra hex a hē′dron, -hē′dral.
te tram′e ter, -tram′er ous.
tĕt′ra pod, te trap′o dous, -o dy.
tĕt′rarch (-rark *or* tē′trark),
-rarch ate, -rarch y, -rarch′ic al.
tet′ter, -ous, -wort, tet′ter-ber ry.
Tĕt u än′ (-o͞o-), t. Morocco.
Teuf′fel (toi′fĕl), Ger. philol.
Teuf′fen (toif′-), t. Switz.
Teû′ton, -ton′ic, -ton′i cism, -ton-
ism, -ize, -ized, -i zing, -ĭ zā′-
tion.
tĕ whĭt′.
tew′ing-bee tle.
Tex ar kăn′a, c. Ark.
tex′as, the top of a grain-elevator.
text, tex′tu al, -al ist, -al ly, -à-
rist, -â ry.
text′-book, -hand, -man, -pen,
-writ er, tex′tus-case.
tex′tĭle.
tex′ture, -less, -tured, -tūr al.
Thal′bĕrg (täl′-), Swiss pianist.
thä′ler (tä′-).
Thä′les (-lēz), Gr. philos.
Thä lĭ′a, *Myth.,* -lĭ′an.

thal′weg′ (täl′vāg′).
Thames (tĕmz), r. Eng.; r. Can.;
t. New Zealand;—(thämz), r.
Ct.
than.
tha′na (tä′-), *-na dar.*
thăn a tol′o gy, -a top′sis.
thane, -dom, -hood, -ship, thān′-
age, thane′-land.
thank, -ful, -ful ly, -ful ness, -ing,
-less, -less ly, -less ness, -wor-
thy, -wor thi ness, thanked,
thanks′giv er, -giv ing, thank′-
of fer ing, thank-you-ma′am, a
watercourse.
that, *pl.* those.
thătch, -er, -ing, -y, thatched,
thatch′wo͝od, -cloak, -grăss,
-palm, -rake, -spar row, -tree,
thatch′ing-fork, -spade, thatch′-
wood-work.
thau′ma turge, -tur′gic, -gic al,
-gics, -gism, -gist, -gus, -tur′gy.
thaw, -ing, -less, -y, thawed,
thaw′-drop.
Thä yet may′o (-mĭ′-) dist.
Burma.
the. Pronounced *thē* when emphatic; *thĭ* when unemphatic before a vowel; *thê* or *thŭ* when
unemphatic before a consonant.
thē′a ter *or* -tre, -ăt′ric, -ric al,
-al ly, -al ness, -al ism, -rics,
-ri cal′i ty, the′a ter go er, the′-
a ter-par ty, -seat.
Thebes, ancient c. Egypt; t. Gr.
Thē cŏ′ĕ, *Bib.*
thee. See *thou.*
thĕft.
thē′ic, -i form, -ĭne.
their, theirs. See *they.*
thē′ism, -ist, -is′tic, -tic al.
Theiss (tīs), r. Hung.
Thē lä′sar, *Bib.*
Thé lème′ (tā lām′), Voltaire.
thĕm. See *they.*
thē′ma, pl. *-ma ta,* -mat′ic, -ic al,
-al ly, -ma tist, theme.
Thē′mis, *Myth.*
The mis′to cles (-klēz), Athenian
statesman.
them selves′.
then.

---

thence, -forth, -for'ward.
Thĕ'ō bạld (or tĭb'bạld), Eng.
play-writer.
the oc'ra cy, direct government
by Jehovah, -o crat, -crat'ic,
-ic al, -oc'ra tist.
the oc'ra sy, the intimate union
of the soul with God.
The oc'ri tus, Gr. poet. -ri tē'an.
thĕ od'o līte, -o lĭt'ic.
Thĕ ŏ dō'rus, Gr. philos.
Thĕ ŏ dō'si us (-shī us), Roman
Emp.
thĕ og'o ny, -o nism, -o nist,
-o gon'ic.
thĕ ŏl'o gy, -ol'o gize, -gī'zing,
-gī'zer, -o lō'gi an, -o log'ic,
-ic al, -al ly, -o lŏgue.
thĕ om'a chy (-ky), -a chist.
thē'o man cy, -o ma'ni a, -ni ac,
-man'tic, -o mor'phic, -mor'-
phism.
thĕ oph'a ny, -o phan'ic.
The o phras'tus, Gr. philos.
thē'o rem, -re mat'ic, -ic al, -rem'-
a tist, -rem'ic.
thē'o ry, -o ret'ic, -ic al, -al ly,
-ret'ics, -re ti'cian (-tĭsh'an),
-o rist, -o rize, -rized, -rī'zer,
-rī'zing, -rī zā'tion.
thē'o sŏph, -soph'ic, -ic al, -al ly,
-os'o pher, -o phism, -o phist,
-phis'tic al, -os'o phy, -o phize,
-phized, -phi zing.
thē'o tech ny (-tĕk-), -tech'nic.
thĕr a peū'tic, -tics, -tic al ly, -tist.
there (thâr), -a bout, -a bouts,
-âf ter, -a gainst, -a mong, -at,
-be fore, -by, -for', -fore (thâr'-
or thêr'fore), -from', -in', -in-
to' (or -in'to), -of' (or -ŏv), -on',
-to', -to fore', -un'der, -un to'
(or -un'to), -up on', -with', -with-
ạl'.
the rese' (tē rĕs'), a kerchief.
ther'mŏ ā'que ous, -mō ba rom'-
e ter, -mo chem'ic (-kem'-), -mo-
chem'is try, -mo dy nam'ic, -ic al,
-nam'i cist, -nam'ics, -mo e lec'-
tric, -tric al ly, -tric'i ty, -mo e-
lec'trom'e ter, -lec'tro mō'tive,
-lec'tro scope, -mo gen'e sis,
-gen'ic, -ge net'ic, -mo gram,

-mo grạph, -mog'ra phy, -mo-
in hib'i to ry, -mo kĭn'e mat'e-
sis, -mo mag net'ic, -mag'ne-
tism, -mo po'di um, -mo sys-
tal'tic, -mo tax'is, -tax'ic, -tac'-
tic, -mo ten'sīle, -mo tē'ri on,
-mo trop'ic, -mo type, -mo ty'-
py (-tī'-), -mo vol tā'ic.
ther'mŏ-bat'ter y, -call', -cou'-
ple, -cŭr'rent, -el'e ment, -junc'-
tion, -mul'ti pli'er, -pair, -reg'-
u la'tor, -tel'e phone, -ten'sion.
ther mŏl'y sis, -mo lyt'ic.
ther mŏm'e ter, -e try, -mo met'-.
ric, -ric al, -al ly, -met'ro grạph.
ther'mo phone, -mo pile, -mo-
scope, -scŏp'ic, -ic al, -mo sī'-
phon.
ther'mo stat, -stat'ic, -ic al ly,
-ics, -mŏt'ic, -ic al, -ics.
Ther sī'tes (-tēz), Shak., Troilus
and Cressida.
the sạu'rus, pl. -rī.
these. See this.
Thĕ'sē us (or -sūs), Myth.; Shak.
thĕ'sis, pl. -ses (-sēz).
Thĕs'pis, Gr. poet. -pi an.
Thĕs'sa lŏ nī'ca, Bib., -lō'ni an,
-ni ans.
Thes'sa ly, a dist. S. E. Europe,
-sā'li an.
The'tis, Myth.
Theū'das, Bib.
thĕ'ur gy, -ur gist, -ur'gic, -gic al.
thew, -less, -y, thewed.
they (thā), poss. their, attrib.
theirs, obj. them.
Thi än'-Shän (tē-), mts. China.
Thi'bau'deau' (tē'bō'dō'), Fr.
revolutionist.
Thi'baut' (tē'bō'), Fr. troubadour.
Thi bĕt' (tĭ- or tĭb'-). See Tibet.
Thib o deaux' (tēb'ō dō'), par. La.
thick, -ly, -ness, thick'back, a
fish, -bill, a bird, -head, a
person; a bird, -knee, a bird,
-leaf, a plant, -lips, a person,
-set, a thicket; a fabric, -skin,
a person, -skull, a person.
thick'-brained, -eyed, -head ed,
-kneed, -leaved, -leg ged (or
-legged), -lipped, -pleached,
-set, a., -sight ed, -skinned,

-skulled, -stā men, a plant, -tongued, -wĭnd, -wĭnd′ed, -wit ted, thick′-and-thin′, a., t. reg′is ter, t. stuff.

thick′en (-n), -ened, -en er, -en ing.

thick′et, -ed, -y.

thiĕf, pl. thiēves, thiēve, thiēved, thiēv′er y, thiĕv′ish, -ish ly, -ish ness, -ing.

thiĕf′-catch er, -lead er, -sto len, -tāk′er, -tube.

Thiel (tēl), t. Netherlands.

Thi ers′ (tē âr′), t. Fr.; Fr. statesman.

thigh (thī), thighed, thigh′-bone, -guard, -joint, -puff.

thĭll, -er, thill′-coup ling, -horse, -jack, -tug.

thĭm′ble, -ful, -ber ry, -man, -rig, -rigged, -rig ger, -rig ging, -weed.

thim′ble-case, -eye, -eyed, -joint, -lil y, -pie, -skein, t. coup′ling.

Thĭm′na thah, Bib.

thin, -ly, -ner, -ness, -nish, -ning, thinned, thin′-blood ed, -faced, -lipped, -shelled, -skinned, -skinned ness.

thine. See thou.

thing, -y.

thing (thĭng), an assembly or parliament, -man.

thĭnk, -ing, -ing ly, -a ble, -er, thought.

third, -ing, -ly, third′pen ny, thirds′man, third′-bor ough, -class, -rate, -rail, a., t. rail, n.

thirst, -er, -ing, -y, -i ly, -i ness, -less.

thir′teen, -teenth, -teenth ly, -teen′er, thir′teen-lined.

thir′ty, -fold, -ti eth, thir′ty-one, -sec ond, -sec ond note, thir′ty- two-mō.

this, pl. these (thēz).

This′bē (thĭz′-), clas. legend.

this′bē (thĭz′-), a moth.

this′tle (-l), -tly (-ly).

this′tle-bird, -but ter fly, -cock, -crop per, -crown, -dig ger, -dol lar, -down, -finch, -merk, -plume, -tube.

thĭth′er, -ward, -wards, -to′.

thōle.

Tho′luck (tō′lo͞ok), Ger. theol.

Thŏ′mism (tō′-), -mist, -mis′tic, -tic al.

thŏng, -y, thong′-seal.

Thŏr, Myth.

thŏ′rax, pl. -rā′ces (-sēz), -rac′ic (-răs′ik), -ral.

Thŏ′reau (-rō), Amer. philos.

thorn, -less, -y, thorned, thorn′- back, a fish; a plant, -bill, a bird, -stone, -tail, a bird.

thorn′-ap ple, -bird, -broom, -bush, -dev il, -head ed, -hop- per, -house, -oys ter, -swine, -tailed, thorn′back-ray.

thor′ough (thŭr′ō), -ly, -ness, thor′ough bred, -fare, -foot, -go ing, -wax, a plant, -wort.

thor′ough-băss, -bolt, -brace, -braced, -joint, -paced, -pin, -shot, -stem.

thorp, thorps′man.

Thor′wạld sen (tôr′-), Danish sculp.

those (thōz). See that.

Thoth (tōt or thŏth), Myth.

Thou, de (dē to͞o), Fr. statesman.

thou, poss. thy, attrib. thine, obj. thee.

though (thō).

thought (thạwt), -ed, -ful, -ful- ly, -ful ness, -less, -less ly, -less ness, -some, -some ness, thought′sick.

thought-ex′e cu ting, -read er, -read ing, -trans fer, -trans fer′- ence, -trans fer en′tial, -wave.

thou′sand (-zand), -fold, -sandth, thou′sand-legs.

Thouve nĕl′ (to͞ov′-), Fr. dipl.

Thrace, S. E. Europe, Thra′cian.

thrall, -ful, thral′dom, thrall′-less, -like.

thrăp.

Thrā sĕ′as, Bib.

thrăsh, -er, -ing, thrashed, thrash′er-shark, -whale, thrash′- ing-floor, -ma chine, -mill, -place.

Thrăs y bū′lus (-I-), Gr. patriot.

thrĕad, -ed, -er, -ing, -y, -i ness,

thread'bare, -fin, a fish, -fish, -flow er, -foot, a plant, -worm.

thrĕad'-an i mal'cule, -car ri er, -cell, -cut ter, -fĕath er, -finish er, -frame, -gage, -guide, -hĕr ring, -lēaved, -mark, -moss, -nee dle, -oil er, -pa per, -plant, -wax er, -wīnd er, thread-the-nee dle, a game, t. lace.

thrĕat, -less, -en, -en er, -en ing, -ing ly, -ened.

three, -ness, -fold, -pence, -penny, -score.

three'-aged, -awned, -beard ed, -birds, -cōat, -cor nered, -deck-er, -foot, -foot ed, -hand ed, -hooped, -leaved, -light, -lobed, -man, -mast ed, -mǎst er, -nerved, -out, -part ed, -ply, -quar ter, -quar ters, -ribbed, -square, -valved, -way, three-per-cents, three'pen ny piece.

thren'o dy, -o dist, thrē nĕt'ic, -ic al, -node, -nō'di al, -nŏd'ic.

threw. See *throw*.

thrice.

thrift, -less, -less ly, -less ness, -y, -i ly, -i ness, thrift'-box.

thrill, -ing, -ing ly, -ing ness, -smith, thrilled.

thrīve, thrīv'ing, -ing ly, -ing-ness, thrōve *or* thrived, thrīv'en *or* thrīved.

thrōat, -ed, -er, -ing, -y, -i ness, throat'root, a plant, -work.

throat'-band, -bolt, -brail, -chain, -hal yard, -jaws, -latch, -piece, -pipe, -sĕiz ing, -strap, -sweet bread.

thrŏb, -bing, -bing ly, -less, throbbed.

thrōe.

thrōne, -less, throned, thrōn'al.

thrŏng, -ing, thronged.

thrŏs'tle (-l), -cock, -frame.

throt'tle, -tled, -tler, -tling, throt'tle-damp'er, -lĕv er, -valve.

through (thrōō), -out', through-stone.

thrōw, -er, -ing, -ster, threw, thrōwn, throw'back, throw'-bait, -crank, -crook, -lāthe, -off, -stick.

throw'ing-balls, -clay, -en gine, -house, -mill, -stick, -ta ble, -wheel.

thrŭm, -ming, -my, -wort, thrummed, thrum'-cap, -eyed.

thrŭsh, -bab bler, -black bird, -fun gus, -li chen, -night in gale, -paste, -tit.

thrust, -er, -ing, thrust'-bear ing, -box, -fault, -hōe, -plane, thrust'-ing-screw.

Thu cyd'ĭ des (-dēz), Athenian hist.

thŭd, -ded, -ding.

thug, -gee, (-gē), -gee ism, -ger, -ger y, -gism.

Thü'lē, Ul ti ma thü lē.

thumb (thŭm), -ing, -kin, -less, thumbed, thumb'screw, an instrument of torture.

thumb'-band, -bird, -blue, -cleat, -cock, -latch, -mark, -nut, -pad, -piece, -pin, -po si'tion, -pot, -ring, -screw, a screw, -stall, -tack.

thump, -er, -ing, thumped.

thŭn'der, -er, -ing, -ing ly, -less, -ous, -ous ly, -y, thun'der beat, -bolt, -burst, -clap, -flow er, -smith, -strike, -struck.

thun'der-ax, -bird, -blǎst, -car-riage, -cloud, -crack, -dart er, -dirt, -drop, -fish, -fit, -fly, -gust, -ham mer, -head, -head ed, -house, -peal, -pick, -plant, -plump, -proof, -pump, -pump er, -rod, -show er, -snake, -stone, -storm, -tube, -worm, thun-der-and-light ning, thun'der bolt-bee tle.

thŭ'ri fy (-fī), -rĭ fer, -rif'er ous, -rif'i cate, -ca'tion.

thurm.

Thurs'day.

thus.

thwack, -er, -ing, thwacked, thwack'ing-frame, -knife.

thwart, -ed, -er, -ing, -ing ly, -ly, -ness, -ship, -ships, thwart'-hawse (-hạwz).

thy (thī), thy self'. See *thou*.

Thy'a tĭ'ra (thī'-), *Bib*.

Thy ĕs'tes (thī ĕs'tēz), *Myth*.

thyme (tīm), thym′y (tīm′-).
Thyr′sis (thêr′-), Virgil.
thyr′sus, pl. -*sī*.
ti (tē), a plant, -palm, -plant, -tree.
tĭ ä′ra, -rǎed.
Tĭ bĕt′ (*or* tĭb′-) *or* Thi bĕt′ (tĭ-*or* tĭb′-), country China.
tĭb′i a, pl. -*æ or -as*, -i al.
tĭc′-dou′lou reux′ (-dōō′lōō rōō′).
Ti ci′nŏ (tē chē′-), r. Switz.
tick, -er, -ing, ticked, tick′seed, a plant, -weed.
tick′-bean, -eat er, -hole, -tack, -tock, -tre foil, tick′er-in, tick′-ing-work.
tick′et, -ed, -ing, tick′et-day, -hold er, -night, -por ter, -punch, -scǎlp′er, -sell er, -tǎk er, -writ er.
tic′kle, -kled, -kler, -kling, -klish, -klish ly, -klish ness, -kly, tic′kle-grǎss.
Tĭ con′der ŏ′ga, vil. N. Y.
tĭd′dle dy winks′ *or* -dly winks.
tide, -less, -wait er, -way, tīd′al, -al ly, tīd′ed, -ing, tīd ol′o gy, tides′man, tide′way.
tide′-ball, -crack, -cur rent, -day, -di al, -gage, -gate, -har bor, -land, -lock, -mark, -marsh, -in di ca tor, -me ter, -mill, -mo′tor, -net, -pole, -pool, -pre-dict′or, -rips, -rock, -rode, -run ner, -ta ble, -wa ter, -wave, -wheel, tīd′ing-well.
tī′ding, news; intelligence, -dings.
Tĭd ĭ oute (-ōōt′), t. Pa.
tī′dy, -di ly, -di ness, tī′dy tips, a plant.
tĭe, tĭed, tī′er, ty′ing (tī′-), tie′-boy.
tĭe′-bar, -beam, -block, -bolt, -chain, -plate, -rod, -strap, -ties, -up, -wig.
Tieck (tēk), Ger. poet.
ti en′da (tē än′-).
Ti en′-tsin (tē ĕn-tsēn), c. China.
tiĕr, -er, tier′-pole, -rod, -saw, -shot.
tiĕrce.
Tĭ ĕr′rä dĕl Fue′go (fwä′-), isls. So. Pac.
ti er′ras (tē ĕr′rǎs).

Ti e′te (tē ä′tä), r. Braz.
tĭff.
tĭf′fa ny, a gauzy fabric.
Tĭf lis′ (-lēs′), c. Russ.
tĭg.
tige (tēzh), -arm.
tĭ gĕlle′ (-jĕl′), -gel′la, -gel′lous, tig′el late (tĭj′-).
tī′ger, -ish, -ism, -kin, -gress, -grĭne, ti′ger flow′er.
ti′ger-bee tle, -bit tern, -cat, -chop, -cow ry, -eye, -foot ed, -frog, -grǎss, -lil y, -moth, -shark, -shell, -wolf, -wood.
ti′ger′s-claw, -eye, -foot, -milk.
Tighe (tī), Irish poetess.
tight (tīt), -er, -ly, -ness, tights.
tight′en (tīt′n), -en er, -en ing, -ened, tight′en ing-pul ley.
ti je′ra (tē hä′).
tĭke.
til, -wood, til′-oil, -seed, -tree.
tĭl′bu ry.
til′de (tĭl′dĕ *or* -dä *or* tĕl′dä).
tĭle, tiled, til′ing, til′er, -er y, tile′fish, -root, a plant, -seed, a tree, -stone.
tĭle′-cop per, -creas ing, -drain, -earth, -field, -kiln, -lay ing, -ma chine, -mǎk ing, -ore, -ov en, -pin, -red, -tea, -tree, -works, t. tea.
Tilgh′man (tĭl′-), Amer. jurist.
tĭll, -a ble, -age, -er, -ing, tilled, till′-a larm, -lock.
till′er-chain, -head, -rope.
Tĭl′lŏt son, Eng. theol.
tĭl′päh.
tĭlt, -ed, -er, -ing, tilt′-boat, -ham mer, -mill, -roof, -ta′ble, -up, -yard.
tilt′ing-fil let, -gäunt let, -ham mer, -hel met, -lance, -shield, -spear, -tar get.
tĭm′bal.
tim bale′ (tǎn bǎl′).
tĭm′ber, -er, -ing, -ling, -bered, tim′ber doo dle, a bird, -man.
tim′ber-bee tle, -brick, -cart, -frame, -grouse, -head, -hitch, -line, -lōde, -mer chant, -scribe, -tree, -wolf -work, -worm, -yard.

---

fāte, fǎt, fär, fạll, fâre, fǎst, sofà, mēte, mĕt, hêr, īce, ĭn, nōte, tim'bre (tĭm'ber *or* tăṅ'br), -bred (-berd).

tĭm'brĕl.

tim brŏl'o gy.

Tim buk'tu (-bŏŏk'tōō *or* -bŭc'-tōō), c. Afr.

time, -ful, -less, -less ly, -ly, -li ness, tĭm'er, -ing, -ist, timed, time'keep er, -piece.

time' -a larm, -at tack, -ball, -bar gaĭn, -be guĭl'ing, -bill, -book, -can dle, -card, -check, -clause, -clock, -con stant, -course, -de tect or, -fuse, -glăss, -globe, -gun, -hon'ored, -in'di ca tor, -in'te gral, -lock, -me'ter, -pleas er, -săv'ing, -sense, -serv er, -serv ing, -sight, -sig nal, -sig na ture, -ta ble, -thrust, -tick'et, -train, -val'ue, -work, time'ly part ed, tĭm'ing-ap pa ra'tus.

tĭ men'o guy (-gĭ).

tĭm'ĭd, -ly, -ness, tĭ mĭd'i ty.

tĭ moc'ra cy, -mo crat'ic.

tĭm'o rous, -ly, -ness, tĭm ō rō'ōs.

TĬ mō'thē ŭs, *Bib.*

tĭm'o thy, a grass; Tĭm'o thy, *Bib.*

Ti mour' *or* Ti mur' (tē mōōr'), a Tartar conqueror.

tĭm'pȧ nō, pl. *-nĭ.*

tin, -ner, -ning, -ny, tinned, tin'clad, a gunboat, -man, -mouth, a fish, -plate, *v.,* -smith, -smith ing, -stone, -type, -ware, tins'man.

tin'-băth, -bound, -floor, -foil, -glăss, -glaze, -ground, -liq uor, -mor dant, -pen ny, -plate, *n.,* tin in plates, as a material, -pot, -pulp, -put ty, -saw, -scrap, -shop, -stream ing, -stuff, -witts, -works, tin'ning-met al, tin' pĭnt.

ti nä'ja (tē nä'ha).

tinc'ture, -tured, -tūr ing, -tō'ri al, -tu rā'tion, tinc'ture-press.

tin'der, -y, tin'der-box, -fuṇ gus, -like, -ore.

tĭne, tĭned, tine'-grăss, -stock.

ting, ting'-a-ling'.

tĭnge, tinged, tinge'ing, tin'gi ble.

tin'gi (tĭng'gĭ *or* -gĭ).

tiṇ'gle, -gled, -gling.

tiṇk.

tiṇk'er, -ly, -ing, -ered, -er man, -er shire, tiṇ'ker's dam, Tiṇ'ker's-weed.

tiṇ'kle, -kled, -kler, -kling.

tin'sel, -seled *or* -selled, -sel ing *or* -ling, -sel y *or* -ly, -sel ry, tin'sel-em broid'er y.

tint, -ed, -er, -ing, -less, -y, -i ness, tint'-block, -draw ing, -tool.

tin'tin nab'u lā'tion, -nab'u lar, -u lous, *-u lum,* pl. *-la,* -u la ry.

tī'ny.

tip, -per, -ping, -ster, tipped, tip'stăff, *pl.* -stăves (*or* -stävz), -toe, -tōed, -tōe ing.

tip'-car, -cart, -cat, -cheese, -foot, -pa per, -sled, -stock, -stretch er, -tilt ed, tip'-top', -up, -wag on, -worm, tip'ping-wag on.

Ti pä'ra (tē-), dist. Bengal.

ti pi'ti (tē pē'tē).

Tĭp'pe cȧ noe' (-nōō'), c. and r. Ind.; vil. O.

tĭp'pet, -grebe, -grouse.

tip'ple, -pled, -pler, -pling, tip'-pling-house.

tip'sy, -si ly, -si ness, tip'sy-cake, -key.

tĭ rȧde'.

ti rail leur' (tē'răl'yêr').

tĭ rasse'.

tĭre, tīred, tīr'ing, tired'ness, tire'less, -less ly, -less ness, -some, -some ly, -some ness, -man, -smith, -wom an.

tire'-bend er, -bolt, -drill, -glăss, -heat er, -meas'ur er, -press, -roll er, -room, -set ter, -shrink er, tir'ing-room.

Tir'ha kah (têr'-), *Bib.*

Tir'ha nah (têr'-), *Bib.*

tirl, -mill, tir'lĭe-whir'lie.

Tir shä'tha (*or* têr'-), *Bib.*

Tisch'en dorf (tĭsh'-), Ger. critic.

TĬ sĭph'ŏ nĕ.

Tis sot' (tē sō'), Fr. jour.; Fr. painter.

tis'sue (tĭsh'ōō), -sued, -su ing, tis'sue-pa per, -se cre'tion.

Tis'za (tē'sŏ), Hung. statesman.
Tī'tan, *Myth*., -ess, -esque', -tā'ni a,
tī tā'ni an, -tăn'ic.
tī'tan, -ite, tī tā'nĭ um.
Tĭ tā'ni a, Shak.
ti'tar (tē'ter).
tit'bit *or* tid'-, tit'ling, a bird,
tit'lark, -man -mouse, tit'-war-
bler.
tit'-for-tat'.
tīthe, -less tīth'a ble, -er, -ing,
tīthed.
tīthe'-free, -gath er er, -own er,
-pay er, -pig, -proc'tor, -steal-
er, tīth'ing-man, tithe' com mis'-
sion er.
Tĭ thŏ'nus, *Myth*.
tīth'y mal.
ti'ti (tē'tē).
Ti'tian (tĭsh'an), a Venetian
painter, -esque'.
Ti ti cä'cä (tē tē-), l. S. Amer.
Tit'iens *or* Tit'jens (tēt'yence),
Ger. vocalist.
tĭt'il late, -lā'ted, -lā'ting, -lā'-
tive, -lā'tion.
tī'tle, -less, -tled, -tling, ti'tle-
deed, -leaf, -let ter, -page,
-scroll, -sheet, -type.
tĭt'ling.
tĭt'rate (*or* tī'-), -rā'ted, -rā'ting,
tĭ trā'tion.
tĭt'-tăt-tŏ', a game.
tĭt'ter, -er, -ing, -tered.
tĭt'tle, -bat, a fish, tit'tle-tat'tle.
tĭt u bā'tion.
tit'u lar, -ly, -lâ ry, -lăr'i ty.
Tĭt'y rus, *Virgil*.
tĭv'er, -ered.
Tĭv'o lĭ, vil. N. Y.; t. It.
tiv'y.
Tiw (tē'ōō), *Myth*.
Tlax cä'lä (tläs-), state Mex.
Tlĭn'kĭt.
tmē'ma, *pl*. -ma ta.
tmē'sis (*or* mē'-).
to (tōō), to-day' *or* to day', to-
mor'row *or* to mor'row, to-
night' *or* to night', to-do', to-
and-frō.
tŏ, a liquid measure.
tŏad, -ish, -let, -ling, -y, -y ing,
-y ish, -y ism, -ĭed.

toad'back, a potato, -fish, -flow-
er, a plant, -head, a bird,
-rock, -stone, -stool, toads'eye.
toad'-back, *a*., -eat er, -flax,
-lil y, -liz ard, -or chis, -pipe,
-rush, -snatch er, -spit, -spot'-
ted, toad's-cap, -hat, -meat.
toast, -ed, -er, -ing, toast'-mås-
ter, -rack, -wa ter, toast'ing-
fork, -glåss, -i ron.
toat, a curved handle.
tŏ băc'co, -nist, -nize, -nized,
-nī'zing.
to bac'co-bee'tle, -box, -chew'er,
-cūr ing, -cut ter, -dove, -grāt'er,
-heart, -knife, -man, -pack ing,
-pipe, -plant, -pouch, -press,
-roll ing, -root, -stem ming,
-stick, -stop per, -strip per,
-tongs, -wheel, -worm.
tŏ bŏg'gan, -er, -ing, -ist, to bog'-
gan-shoot, -slide.
Tŏ bŏlsk', dist. Sib.
tŏc cä'lä, *-ca tel'lä*, *-ca ti'na* (-tē'-).
Tocque'ville, dê (tŏk'-), Fr. statesman.
tŏc'sin.
tŏd, -boat, -stove, tod's-tail.
tod'dle, -dled, -dler, -dling.
tŏd'dy, -man, tod'dy-bird, -blos-
som, -draw er, -la dle, -palm,
-stick.
Tŏd'hun ter, Eng. math.
Tod'le bĕn (tŏt'lā-), Russ. engineer.
tŏ'dy, a bird.
tŏe, -ing, -less, tŏed.
toe'-bĭt'er, -cap, -drop, -nail,
-piece, -ring, -tights, -weight.
Toeb'bĕ (tĕb'-), Gr. bishop.
tog, -ger y, togs.
tŏ'ga, pl. *-gas* or *-gæ* (-jē), -gäed,
-gä ted.
to gethʹer.
tog'gle, -gled, -gling.
tog'gle-bolt, -chain, -har poon',
-hole, -i ron, -joint, -lan yard,
-press.
tŏgue.
Tŏ'ĭ, *Bib*.
toil, -er, -ing, -ful, -less, -some
(-sum), -some ly, -some ness,
toiled, toil'-worn.

toile (twäl), cloth.

toi lé' (twä lä'), lace pattern.

toi'let, -ed, toi'let-cap, -cloth, -cov er, -cup, -glåss, -pa per, -quilt, -room, -serv ice, -set, -soap, -sponge, -ta ble.

Tois'nŏt (tŏs'-), tp. N. C.

toi'son (-zon).

tŏ'ka, a war-club.

To kåy, a grape; a wine.

to'ken (-kn), -ing, -less, -kened, to'ken-mon'ey, -sheet.

tŏ kŏ-pǎt'.

To ku shi'ma   (-kōō shē'-),   c. Japan.

Tŏ'ky ŏ *or* -kĭ-, c. Japan.

tŏ'la, a weight; a burial-mound.

tŏ'laı̈.

Tŏl'ba nĕs (-nēz), *Bib.*

Tŏ lĕ'dŏ, t. Ia.; c. O.; c. Sp.; a sword-blade.

tŏl'er a ble, -a ble ness, -a bly, -ance, -ant, -ant ly, -ate, -ā'ted, -ā'ting, -ā'tor, -ā'tion.

tŏll, -a ble, -age, -er, -ing, tolled, toll'booth, -house.

toll'-båit, -bar, -book, -bridge, -col lect'or, -corn, -dish, -free, -gate, -gath'er er, -man, toll'-ing-lĕv er.

Tŏl'stoi, Russ. novelist.

Tŏl'tec, -te can.

tom'a hawk, -hawked.

tŏ män'.

tŏ mä'tŏ (*or* -mä'-), *pl.* -toes, to ma'to-gall, -plant, -sauce, -sphinx, -worm.

tomb (tōōm), -ic, -less, tomb'-stone, tomb'-bat, -house.

tom'bo la.

tom'boy, -cod, -fool, -fool er y, -tit, tom'-cat, -hur ry, -nod dy, -nor ry, -noup, -pud ding, -tom, -trot, -tur key, Tom'-pi per, -pok er, tom'my-nod dy, -shop.

tŏme, -let.

Tŏm mä se'ŏ (-sä'-), Ital. states-man.

ton (tŭn), -nage, -naged, -na-ging, ton'nage-deck, -du'ty.

Tŏn a wan'da (-wŏn'-), t. N. Y.

tŏn'dŏ (*or* tōn'-), pl. *-di* (-dē), *-di'no* (-dē'-), pl. *-di'ni* (-dē'nē).

tŏne, -less, -less ness, toned, tŏn'ing, tŏn'al, -al ly, to nǎl'i ty, -nic'i ty, tŏn'ous, tŏn'ic, -al ly.

tone'-col or, -mǎs ter, -meas ur-er, -paint ing, -re la'tion ship, -syl la ble.

tŏ ne lä'da (-nä lä'tha).

tŏng, -er, -ing, -man, tongs.

tŏn'ga, a light vehicle; Tŏn'ga, one of the Friendly Isls., Tŏn'-ga land, E. Afr.

ton'go, a plant.

Tongres (tŏngr), t. Belg.

tongue (tŭng), -less, -let, tongu'-ey, -ing, tongued, tongue'fish, -flow er.

tongue'-bang, -bang er, -bat-ter y, -bird, -bit, -bone, -case, -chain, -com press or, -de-press or, -dough ty, -fence, -grǎft ing, -grǎss, -hold er, -hound, -joint, -lash ing, -mem-brane, -shaped, -shell, -shot, -spat u la, -sup port, -test, -tie, -tooth, -tree, -val iant, -vi o let, -war rior, -work, -worm.

tŏn'ic. See *tone.*

tŏn'jŏn.

tŏn'ka-bean wood, ton'ka bean *or* Tŏn'ka bean.

ton neau' (tŏ nō').

Tŏn nerre' (-nâr'), a wine.

tŏn'o gram.

tŏ nom'e ter, -e try.

to'no phant.

Tŏn quin' (-kēn'), Fr. dist. in China, -quin ese' (*or* -ēz').

tŏn'sil, -lar, -lå ry, -lit'ic, *-sil ĭ'-tis* or *-lĭ'tis,* -sil'lo tome, -lŏt'o-my.

tŏn'sı̈le, capable of being clipped.

tŏn sŏ'ri al, tŏn'sure, -sured, -sūr-ing, ton'sure-plate.

ton tine' (-tēn').

tōō.

tŏŏk. See *take.*

tōōl, -er, -ing, tool'-box, -car, -chest, -coup ling, -ex tract'or, -gage, -hold er, -mark, -mark ing, -post, -rest, -stack, -stay, -stock, -stone.

tōōt, -ed, -er, -ing, tōōt'hill, toot'-plant, -poi son.

---

tooth, *pl.* teeth, -ful, -less, -let,
-let ed, -some, -some ly, -some-
ness.

tooth′ache, -back, a moth, -bill,
a pigeon, -edge, -flow er, -pick,
-pick er, -wort.

tooth′-backed, -bear er, -brush,
-car pen ter, -cress, -draw ing,
-fill ing, -key, -like, -net, -or-
na ment, -paste, -plug ger,
-pow der, -pulp, -rash, -rib bon,
-sac, -saw, -shell, -vi o let,
-wash, -wound.

tooth′ache-gràss, -tree, tooth′-
brush tree, tooth′ing-plane.

tōō′tle, -tled, -tling.

top, -per, -ping, -ping ly, -less,
-loft y, -loft i ness, -most.

top′knot, top′man, -màst, -sail,
-side, -tail, *v.*, tops′man.

top′-ar mor, -beam, -block,
-boot, -boot ed, -card, -chain,
-cloth, -coat, -cross, -drain,
-drain ing, -dress, -dress ing,
-flat, -full er, -grain ing, -ham-
pered, -heav y, -lan tern, -light,
-lin ing, -log, -min now, -mi nor,
-pend ant, -rail, -rim, -rope,
-saw, -saw yer, -shaped, -shell,
-soil, -soil ing, -stone, -tac kle,
-tim ber, -tool.

top′mast-head, -shrouds, top′-
sail-yard.

tŏ′parch (-park), -parch y.

tŏ′paz, -rock.

tŏpe, toped, tōp′ing.

top′gal′lant, -màst, -sail, top′-
gal′lant-bul warks, -fore cas tle,
-shrouds.

tŏ pha′ceous (-fā′shŭs), tō′phus.

Tŏ′phet, *Bib.*

tŏ′pi a, -pi â ry, -ā′ri an.

tŏp′ic, -ic al, -al ly.

tŏ pŏg′ra phy, -ra pher, -ra phist,
-po grăph′ic, -ic al, -al ly.

to pŏl′a try.

tŏ pŏl′o gy.

top′ple, -pled, -pling.

top′sy tur′vy, -vi ness, -vi ly.

toque (tōk).

torch, -ing, -less, -light, -wood,
a tree, -wort.

torch′-bear er, -dance, -fish ing,

-lil y, -pine, -race, -stàff,
-this tle, -wood, a wood.

tor chère′ (-shâr′).

tor′chon board (-shŏn), t. lace,
t. mat, t. pa per.

tōre. See *teâr.*

to′re a dor′ (tō′rā ä dōr′ *or* tor′-
ē ä dôr′).

tor′ment, *n.*, -ment′, *v.*, -ed, -ing,
-ing ly, -ing ness, -or.

tor nä′do, *pl.* -does, -năd′ic.

tor pē′do, *pl.* -does; Tor pe′do,
Ornith. genus.

tor pe′do-aŋ chor, -boat, -boom,
-catch er, -cruis′er, -drag, -fuse,
-net, -net ting, -of fi cer, -ràft,
-school, -spar, -tube.

tor′pid, -ly, -ness, -pid′i ty, -pi fy,
-fy ing, -fïed, -por, -po rif′ic.

Tor quay′ (-kē′), t. Eng.

torque, torqued.

tŏr′re fy, -ing, -fïed, -fac′tion.

Tŏr′re jon cil′lo (-rä hōn thēl′yō),
t. Sp.

tor′rent, -ren′tial, -tial ly, tor′-
rent-bōw, -duck.

Tŏr ri cel′li (-rē chĕl′lē), Ital.
physicist.

tor′rid, -ness, -rid′i ty.

tŏr ron′tĕs.

tor sàde′.

torse, tor′sal, tor′sion, -sion al,
-al ly, -sion less, -sive, -si bil′-
i ty, tor′tive, *tor til lé* (-tēl yä′).

tor′sel.

tor′shent.

tort.

tor′tïle, -til′i ty.

tor til′la (-tēl′yä).

tor′toise (-tĭs *or* -tŭs), -flow er.

tor′toise-bee tle, -head ed, -plant,
-ro′ti fer, -shell, -wood.

tor′tū ous, -ly, -ness, -tu lous,
-tu ōse, -ŏs′i ty.

tor′ture, -tured, -tûr er, -tûr ing,
-ing ly, -ous, -a ble, -a ble ness.

tŏr′up.

tŏ′ry, -ism. Polit. Tŏ′ry, -ism.

tŏss, -er, -ing, -ment, -y, tossed,
toss′-pot, -up.

tŏt.

tŏ′tal, -taled *or* -talled, -tal ing
or -ling, -tal ize, -ized, -ī′zer,

---

fāte, făt, fär, fạll, fâre, fàst, sofà, mēte, mĕt, hêr, īce, ĭn, nōte,

-i′zing, -I zā′tion, -tal ly, -ness, -tal′i ty.
tote, tōt′ed, -er, -ing, tote′-lōad, -road, -team, -wag′on.
tŏ′tĕm, -ism, -ist, -is′tic, -tem′ic.
tŏt′i tive.
tot′ter, -er, -ing, -ing ly, -y, tot′ter-grăss.
Tŏ′ŭ, *Bib.*
tou căn′ (tōō- *or* tōō′-), -ca nĕt′.
touch (tŭtch), -a ble, -ble ness, -er, -ing, -ing ly, -ing ness, -less, -y, -i ly, -i ness, touch′-box, -piece, -stone, -wood.
touch′-back, -bod′y, -cor pus cle, -down, -hole, -line, -nee dle, -pan, -pa per, touch′ing-stuff, touch′-and-go′, touch′-me-not, a plant.
tough (tŭf), -en, -ened, -en ing, -ly, -ness, tough′bark, a tree, -head, a duck, tough′-cake.
Tou′louse′ (tōō′lōōz′), c. Fr.
toup (tōōp).
tou pee′ (tōō-).
tou pet′ (too pā′).
tour (tōōr), -ing, -ist, toured, *tour dê force, tour dê māi′tre.*
Tour′coing′ (tōōr′kwăń′), t. Fr.
Tour géc′ (tōōr ɀhā′), Amer. novelist.
tour′ma lĭn *or* -lĭne, -gran ite.
tour′na ment (tōōr′-)
Tour nay′ *or* -nai′ (tōōr′nā′), t. Belg.
tour′nay (tōōr′-), a worsted fabric.
tour nette′ (tōōr-).
tour′ney (tōōr′-), a combat, -helm.
tour′ni quet (tōōr′nĭ kĕt).
tour nure′ (tōōr-).
Tours (tōōr), c. Fr.
touse (touz), toused, tous′er, -ing.
tou′sle (-zl), -sled, -sling.
tous-les-mois′ (tōō-lä-mwŏ′).
Tous saint′ L′Ou ver ture′ (tōō′-săń′ lōō′vĕr′tür′), Haytian negro gen. and liberator.
tou′sy (-zy).
tout, -er, -ing.
tout en sem′ble (tōō′ tän′säń′bl).

tŏw, -age, -er, -ing, -y, towed, tow′boat, tow′-car, -cock, -hook, -i ron, -line, -net, -păth, -rope.
tŏw′ing-bitts, -bri dle, -hooks, -net, -path, -post, -rope, -tim ber.
tŏ′ward, -ly, -li ness, -ness, -wards.
tow′el, -eled *or* -elled, -el ing *or* -ling.
tow′el-gŏurd, -horse, -rack, -roll er.
tow′er, -ing, -y, -ered, tow′er-wort.
tow′er-clock, -cress, -mill, -mus tard, -owl, -shell.
tŏw′head, a person, tow′-head′ed.
town, -ish, -less, -let, -y, town′-folk, -land, -ship, -ward, towns′folk, -man, -peo′ple.
town′-ad ju tant, -ball, -coun cil lor, -cress, -hus band, -ma jor.
town clerk, t. col lect′or, t. coun′-cil, t. cri′er, t. gate, t. hall, t. house, t. land, t. line, t. meet′-ing, t. of′fi cers, t. plot, t. pound, t. rec ords, t. site, t. talk, t. tax, t. top, t. wall.
Town′shend (-zĕnd), Eng. states-man.
tox i col′o gy, -o gist, -co log′ic-al, -al ly, -co mā′ni a, tŏx′ĭn *or* -ĭne.
toy, -er, -ful, -ing, -ing ly, -ish, -ish ly, -some, toyed, toy′man, a maker of toys, -wort, toy′-block, -box, -mutch, -shop, toy man, a toy.
To yä′mä′, c. Japan.
trace, -a ble, -a ble ness, -a bly, -a bil′i ty, -less, -less ly, traced, trā′cer, -cing.
trace′-buc kle, -chain, -fas ten er, -hook, -horse, -loop, -mate.
trā′cing-cloth, -in stru ment, -lin en, -lines, -ma chine, -pa per, -thread, -wheel.
tra′cer y, -cer ied.
trā′che a (*or* -kē′a), -al, -ā′lis, -che an, -ate, -a ted.
trā chē ŏs′co py, -os′co pist, -o scŏp′ic.
tra chē′o tome, -che ot′o my, -o mist, -o mize, -mized, -mi zing.
Trăch′o nī′tis (trăk′-), *Bib.*

---

track, -age, -er, -ing, -less, -less-
ly, -less ness, tracked, track'-
man, -mås ter, -way.

track'-boat, -chart, -clear er,
-edge, -har ness, -hound, -in-
di ca'tor, -lay er, -pot, -rais er,
-road, -scale, -scout, -sweep'er,
-walk er.

tract, -a ble, -a ble ness, -a bly,
-a bil'i ty.

tract'ïle, -ive, -or, -o ry, trac-
til'i ty, -tion, -to rā'tion.

trac'tion-an'eu rism, -en gine,
-gear ing, -wheel.

trăde, -ful, trăd'ed, -er, -ing,
trade'mås ter, trades'folk, -man,
-peo ple, -wom an.

trade'-hall, -mark, -name, -un-
ion, -un ion ism, -un ion ist,
-wind, t. dol'lar, t. name, t.
price, t. sale.

tra di'tion (-dïsh'un), -al, -al-
ism, -al ist, -is'tic, -al ly, -â ry,
-â ri ly, -er, -ist.

tra dûce', -ment, -duced', -du'-
cer, -du'cing, -cing ly, -ci ble,
-duc'tive, -tion.

Tra făl'gar, kind of type.

trăf'fic, -less, -ficked, -fick ing,
-er, traf'fic-man a ger, -re turn.

trag'a canth.

trä ga zon' (-sŏn' *or* -gä'zŏn).

trag'e dy (trăj'-), *pl.* -e dies,
tra gē'di an, *tra gé dienne'* (trå'-
zhā'dyĕn' *or* tra jĕ'dĭ ĕn').

trag'ic, -ic al, -al ly, -al ness,
trag i com'e dy, -com'ic, -ic al,
-al ly.

trăil, -er, -ing, -y, trailed.

trail'-board, -bridge, -car, -eye,
-hand spike, -net, -plate, trail'-
ing-spring, -wheel.

trăin, -a ble, -er, -ing, -less,
trained, train'man, -way.

train'-band, -bear er, -bolt, -boy,
-car, -hand, -mile, -oil, -road,
-rob ber, -rope, -tac kle, -wreck er.

train'ing-bit, -day, -gear, -hal ter,
-lev el, -pen du lum, -school,
-ship, -wall.

trăit.

trāï'têur', keeper of an eating-
house.

trai'tor, -ous, -ous ly, -ous ness,
trai'tress.

Trā'jan, Roman Emperor.

tra jec'to ry, -jec'tion.

trăm, -pot, -rail, -road, -way.

tram'-car, -line, -plate, -stăff,
-wheel, tram'way-car.

tram'mel, -meled *or* -melled,
-mel er *or* -ler, -mel ing *or*
-ling, tram'mel-net, -wheel.

trăm'mer, -ming.

tra mŏn'tāne, -tä'na.

tramp, -er, -ing, tramped,
tramp'-pick.

tram'ple, -pled, -pler, -pling.

trănce, tranced, tran'ced ly, -cing.

trank.

tran'ka, an acrobat's box.

tran'kĕh, a large boat.

tran'quil, -ize, -ized, -ï'zer,
-ï'zing, -zing ly, -quil ly, -ness,
-quil'li ty.

trans act', -ed, -ing, -or, -ac'tion.

trans ăl'pïne, -an'dïne, -ap pa-
lā'chi an, -at lan'tic.

trans ca'lent, -len cy.

tran scend', -ed, -ing, -ence,
-en cy, -ent, -ent ly, -ent ness,
-scen den'tal, -tal ism, -tal ist,
-tal ly, -tal'i ty.

trans con ti nen'tal.

tran scribe', -scribed', -scrïb'er,
-ing, tran'script, -scrip'tion,
-tion al, -tive, -tive ly.

tran'sept, -sept'al, tran'sept-aisle.

tran'sĕ unt.

trans'fer, *n.*, -fer', *v.*, -ferred',
-fĕr'ring, -fer'a ble *or* -ri ble,
-a bil'i ty, -fer'rer, -fer ee', -fer'-
ence.

trans'fer-book, -day, -el'e va tor,
-gild ing, -ink, -pa per, -press,
-print ing, -re sist'ance, -ta'ble,
-work, trans fĕr'ring-ma chine.

trans fig'ure, -ured, -ūr ing, -u-
rā'tion.

trans fix', -ing, -fixed', -fix'ion.

trans form', -a ble, -er, -ing,
-a tive, -ism, -ist, -for mā'tion,
trans for mā'tion-scene.

trans fuse', -fused', -fūs'er, -fu'-
si ble, -sive, -sive ly, -sion,
trans fu'sion-ap pa ra'tus.

---

fāte, făt, fär, fạll, fâre, fåst, sofà, mēte, mĕt, hêr, ïce, ïn, nōte,

trans gress', -ive, -ive ly, -or, -gres'sion, -sion al.

tran ship', -ping, -ment, -shipped'.

tran'sient (-shĕnt), -ly, -ness, -sience, -sien cy.

trăn'sit, -cir cle, -com pass, -du ty, -in'stru ment, -trade.

tran si'tion (-zĭsh'un or -sĭsh'- or -sĭzh'-), -al, -al ly, -â ry, -si tive, -tive ly, -tiv'i ty.

tran'si to ry, -to ri ly, -ri ness.

trans late', -lāt'ed, -lāt'ing, -lāt'- a ble, -a ble ness, -lā'tion, -tion al, -tive, -tor, trans lāt'ing-screw.

trans lit'er ate, -a tor, -er ā'tion.

trans lo'cate, -cā'ted, -cā'ting, -cā'tion.

trans lu'cent, -ly, -cence, -cen cy, -lū'cid.

trans'mi grate, -grā'ted, -ting, -tor, -mĭ'gra to'ry, -grā'tion.

trans mit', -ted, -ting, -ta ble, -tal, -tance, -ter, -ti ble, -mis'si ble, -si bil'i ty, -sive, -sion.

trans mute', -mūt'ed, -er, -ing, -a ble, -a ble ness, -a bly, -a bil'- i ty, -ant, -a tive, -mu tā'tion, -tion ist.

trăn'som (-sŭm), -somed, tran'- som-knee, -win dow.

trans pâr'ent, -ly, -ness, -ence, -en cy, trans pâr'en cy-paint'ing.

tran spire', -spīred', -spīr'ing, -a ble, -a to'ry, -spi rā'tion.

trans plant', -ed, -er, -ing, -a ble, -plan tā'tion.

tran splen'dent, -ly, -den cy.

trans'port, n., -port', v., -ed, -ed ness, -er, -ing, -ing ly, -a ble, -a bil'i ty, -al, -por tā'tion, trans'port-rĭd'er, -ship, -ves sel.

trans pose', -posed', -pŏs'a ble, -al, -er, -ing, -pŏs'i tive, -tive ly, -i tor, -pô si'tion, -tion al.

tran sub stan'ti ate (-s hĭ-), -ā'ted, -ā'ting, -ā'tion.

tran sude', -sūd'ed, -ing, -su'da to'ry, -su dā'tion.

Trăns văal', state S. Afr.

trans verse', a. and v., -ly, -versed', -ver'sal, -sal ly, -ver'sion, trans'- verse (or -verse'), n., transverse'- cu bi tal,-me di al, -quad'rate.

trap, -per, -ping, trapped, trap'- fall.

trap'-ball, -bat, -bit tle, -bril liant, -cel lar, -cut, -door, -fish er, -hole, -hook, -net, -rock, -seine, -shoot'ing, -stair, -stick, -tree, -tuff, -valve, -wĕir, trap'- ping-at tach'ment.

trăpe, trāped, trāp'ing, trāpes.

tra pĕze', -pē'zi form.

tra pĕ'zi um, pl. -zi ums or -zi a, trap'e zoid, -zoid'al, -zoid'ĭ form.

trá pĭ'che (-pē'chā).

Trap'pist, -Ine.

trash, -er y, -y, -i ly, -i ness, trash'-house, -ice.

trăss.

trät tō rĭ'a (-rē'-).

Trau (trow), t. Aust.

trav'ăil, -ing, -ailed.

tra vail' (trá vā' or -vä'Ĭ), an Indian sledge, pl. tra vaux' (-vō').

tra vale', a sound in tambourine playing.

trave.

trăv'ĕl, -eled or -elled, -el ing or -ling, -el er or -ler.

trav'el-soiled, -stained, -worm, trav'el ing-bag, -cab'i net, -cap, -car riage, -chest, -cou vert, -dress, trav'el er's-joy, -tree.

trav'erse, -ersed, -ers ing, -er.

trav'erse-board, -cir cle, -drill, -ju'ry, -saw, -ta ble.

trăv'es ty, -ing, -tĭed.

trá vois' (-vwä').

trawl, -er, -ing, trawled, trawl'er man.

trawl'-an chor, -beam, -boat, -fish, -fish er man, -head, -keg, -line, -net, -roll er, -warp.

tray, -ful, tray'-cloth.

trĕach'er ous, -ly, -ness, -er y.

trĕa'cle, -cly, trĕa'cle-mus tard, -sleep, -wag, -wa ter, -worm'- seed.

trĕad, -er, -ing, trod, trod'den, tread'mill, -wheel, tread'-be hind, -board, -soft ly, a plant.

trea'dle (trĕd'l), -dler, -dling, trea'dle-ma chine, -press.

trĕa'son (-zn), -a ble, -ble ness, -a bly, trea'son-fel'o ny.

nŏt, nôr, ūse, ŭp, ûrn, etüde, fōōd, fŏŏt, aṇger, boṅmot, tħus, Baсh.

37

treas'ure (trĕzh' ûr *or* -ūre), -ured,
-ur ing, -ur er, -ur y, treas'ure
flow'er.
treas'ure-chest, -cit y, -house,
-trove.
trĕat, -ed, -er, -ing, -ment, -y.
trĕa'tĭse.
Tre big'ne (trä bēn'yā) t. Austro-
Hung.
Tre'bitsch (trä'bĕch), t. Aust.
Trĕb'i zŏnd, vil. Asia Minor. ·
trĕb'le, -ness, -led, -ling, -let, -ly,
treb'le tree, treb'le-bar, -cours'ing,
-dāt'ed, t. clef.
tre cen'to (trä chĕn'tō), -cen'tist
(-chĕn'-).
trĕ chom'e ter (-kŏm'-).
tre cor'de (trä kor'dĕ).
tre dille'.
tree, -less, -less ness, tree'fish,
-hop per, -nail. ·
tree'-ag ate, -al oe, -asp, -a za'-
le a, -bear, -beard, -bee tle,
-bo'a, -box, -bug, -cab bage, -cac-
tus, -calf, -cat, -cel an dine,
-climb er, -clip per, -clo ver,
-cof fin, -co pal, -cor al, -cot-
ton, -coup ling, -crab, -creep er,
-crick et, -crow, -cuck oo, -dig-
ger, -dove, -duck, -fern, -finch,
-fly, -frog, -fuch sia, -ger man-
der, -gol den rod, -goose, -hair,
-heath, -hoop oe, -house leek,
-i ron, -job ber, -kaŋ ga roo,
-lark, -lil y, -liz ard, -lob ster,
-lo tus, -louse, -lung wort, -lu-
pine.
tree'-mal low, -mar bling, -med-
ic, -mig non ette, -milk, -moss,
-mouse, -net tle, -nymph, -oil,
-on ion, -or chis, -oys ter, -par-
tridge, -pe o ny, -pie, -pi geon,
-pip it, -poke, -pop py, -por-
cu pine, -prim rose, -pro tect-
or, -prun er, -rat, -re mov er,
-scape, -scrap er, -ser pent,
-shrew, -shrike, -snake, -sor-
rel, -soul, -spar row, -squir rel,
-swal low, -swift, -ti ger, -toad,
-to ma to, -top, -vi o let, -war-
bler, -wax, -wool, -worm wood,
-wor ship, -wor ship er.
trĕf'le (-l), a mine in fortifications.

tré'flé' (-flä'), a term in heraldry,
trĕf lee'.
trĕ'foil, -wise, -foiled.
tre hä'lä, tre'hä lose.
treille (trĕl), treil'lage (trĕl'-).
Tre in'ta y Trĕs' (trä ēn'tä ē trĕs),
dept. Uruguay.
trĕk, -ker, *trek'schuit* (-skoit),
trek'-ox en, -rope, -tōw.
trĕ law'ny.
trel'lis, -lised, trel'lis work.
trem'ble, -bled, -bler, -bling,
-bling ly, -bly, trem'bling-jock,
-jock ey.
tre men'doŭs, -ly, -ness.
trĕm'o lo, -o län'dō, -o lant.
trĕm'or (*or* trē'mor), -less, -u lant,
-u lous, -lous ly, -lous ness, -lā'-
tion.
trench, -er, -ing, -ant, -ant ly,
-an cy, trenched, trench'er man.
trench'-cart, -cav a lier', -plow.
trench'er-cap, -coat, -crit ic,
-friend, -knight, -law, -mate,
-plate.
trend, -er.
trente'-et-qua rante' (trŏńt'-ā-kà-
rŏńt'), a game.
trĕ păn', -ner, -ning, -panned',
trĕp a nā'tion, tre pan'ning-el'-
e va tor.
trĕ phĭne', (*or* -fēn'), -phined',
-phĭn'ing, tre phine'-saw.
trep'id, -i dā'tion, tre pid'i ty.
trĕs'pass, -er, -ing, -passed, tres'-
pass-of'fer ing.
tress, -er, -ing, -y, tressed.
trĕs'tle (-l), -tling, tres'tle tree,
-work, tres'tle-board, t. bridge.
tret.
Treu'en (troi'-), t. Sax.
trĕv'at (*or* trē'vat), a cutting instrument.
Trĕves, govt. Prus.
trĕv'et, a three-legged stool.
Tre vig'lio (trä vēl'yō), t. Lom-
bardy.
Trĕv'or ton, t. Pa.
trey, a card.
trī'ad, -ist, -ad'ic, trī'ad-deme.
trī'age.
trī'al, -a ble, -ble ness.
trī'al-case, -day, -fire, -glass es,

-ground, -jar, -piece, -plate, -proof, -sight, -square, tri′al heat, t. trip.

trī′a logue.

trī′aṇ gle, -gled, -aṇ′gu lar, -lar ly, -lăr′i ty, -aṇ′gu late, -late ly, -lā′ted, -lā′ting, -lā′tor, -lā′tion.

trĭb′ble, -pa′per.

tribe, trīb′al *or* trĭb′u al *or* trĭb′ u lar, trīb′al ism, -al ly, tribes′ man.

trĭb′let, -tubes.

trī′brach (-brăk), -brā′chi al, -brach′ic.

trĭb u lā′tion.

trĭb′ûne, -ship, -u nâ′ry, -u nate, -u ni′cial, *or* -tial -ni′cian *or* -tian, trī bu′nal.

trĭb′ûte, -u ted, -u ter, -u ting, -u tâ′ry, -ta ri ly, -ri ness, trib′ ute-mon ey, -pitch, -work.

Tri cä′ri cŏ (trē kä′rē-), t. It.

trīce, triced, trī′cing.

trī cen′ni al, -cen′te nâ′ry, -cen ten′ni al.

trī′ceps.

trĭ chi′a sis (-kĭ′-).

trĭch′i nize (trĭk′-), -nized, -nī′ zing, -nĭ zā′tion, *-nī′a sis*, -i nosed (-nōzd), -i nō′sis, -i not′ic, -ĭ nous, trĭ chī′no scope.

tri chī′tis (-kĭ′-), *-cho′sis* (-kō′-).

Tri chŏ ni′a (trē kŏ nē′a), dist. Gr.

trick, -er, -er y, -ing, -ish, -ish ly, -ish ness, -y, -i ly, -i ness, -sy, -si ness, -ster, tricked, trick′ măk′er.

trick′-dag ger, -line, -lock, -scene, -sword, -track, -wig, trick′er lock.

tric′kle, -kled, -kling, -klet.

trī′col or, -ored.

tri′cot (trē′kō *or* -kō′), -stitch.

trī cus′pid, -al, -ate, -pi da′ted.

trī′cy cle (-sĭ-), -cy clist.

trī′dent, -den′tate, -den′tā ted.

trī en′ni al, -al ly.

trī′er arch (-ark), -arch′al, -arch′y.

Tri ĕst′ (trē-) *or* Tri ĕs′tē (trē-), c. Aust.

trī′fle, -fled, -fler, -fling, -fling ly, -fling ness.

trī fŏ′li ate, -ā′ted.

trī fur′cate, -cā′ted, -cā′ting, -cā′ tion.

trig, -ness, -ger, -ging, trigged.

trĭg′a my, -a mist, -a mous.

trig′ger, -gered, trig′ger-fiṇ ger, -fish, -guard, -hair, -line, -plant.

Trig gia′nŏ (trē jä′-), t. It.

trī′glyph, -al, -glyph′ic, -ic al.

trĭg o nom′e try, -no met′ric, -ric al, -al ly.

trī′grâph.

trī lin′e ar.

trī lin′gual, -guar.

trill, -ing, trilled.

trĭl′lion (-yŭn), -lionth.

trī′lōbed, -lō′bate, -bā′ted.

trī′lo bite, -bĭt′ic.

trĭl′o gy.

trim, -ly, -ness, -mer, -ming, -ming ly, trimmed, trim′ming board, -joist, -ma chine, -shear.

trī mes′ter, -mes′tral, -mes′tri al.

trĭm′e ter, trī met′ric, -ric al.

trin′i ty, a triad; a trio. Trin′ i ty, the Godhead, Trin i tā′ ri an, -an ism.

trin′ket, -er, -ry.

Trĭn o ma li′ (-lē′), t. India.

trī no′mi al, -al ism, -al ist, -al ly, -al′i ty, -nom′i nal.

tri′o (trē′- *or* trī′-), tri′ole (trē′-), -o let (trē′- *or* trī′-).

trip, per, ping, -ping ly, -ping ness, tripped, trip′mad am, a plant.

trip′-book, -cord, -gear, -ham mer, -shâft, -skin, -slip, trip′ ping-line, -valve.

trĭp′ar tīte (*or* trī par′-), -tīte ly, -ti′tion.

Trĭp a tur′ (-tōōr′), t. India.

tripe, trĭp′er y, tripe′man, tripe′ stone, -vis′aged.

Trĭp′et tĭ, t. India.

triph′thong (trĭf′- *or* trĭp′-), -thoṇ′gal.

trī′ple, -pled, -pling, trip′ly, trī′ ple tail, a fish, trī′ple-awned, -crowned, -ex pan′sion, -grained, -grâss, -head ed, -ribbed, -screw, t. crown, t. meas′ure, t. pro gres′sion, t. ra′ti o, t. salt, t. screw, t. star, t. tree.

---

nŏt, nôr, ūse, ŭp, ûrn, etüde, fōōd, fŏŏt, aṇger, boṅmot, thus, Bach.

trip′let, -lil y.
trī′plex, -plic′i ty, trip′li cate, -cā′ted, -cä′ting, -ca ture, -cā′-tion.
trī′pod, trĭp′o dal, -o dy, trī′pod-jack.
Trĭp′o lĭ, coun. N. Afr.; t. Syr., Trip′o lĭne, Trĭ pol′i tan, trĭp′-o lĭ, a mineral, -o lite.
Tri pŏ′lĭs (trē-), t. Gr.
trĭp′pet.
trĭp′tych (-tĭk).
trī′rēme.
trĭ sect′, -ed, -ing, -sec′tion.
Tris′so tin′ (trēs′sŏ′tăň′), Molière.
Tris tän′ dä Cun′ha (kōōn′yä), isl. S. Atlantic.
trĭ syl′la ble, -lab′ic, -ic al, -al ly.
trīte, -ly, -ness.
trī′the ism, -ist, -is′tic, -tic al.
Trī′ton, Myth., Trī′ton′s-horn.
trī′tŏne.
trĭt′u rate, -rā′ted, -rȧ ble, -rä′-ting, -rä′tor, -rȧ ture, -rä′tion.
trī′umph, -er, -ing, -ing ly, -umphed, -um′phal, -phant, -phant ly.
trī um′vir, pl. -virs or -vĭ rī, -vi ral, -vi rate.
trī′ūne, -u′ni ty.
trī′valve, -valved, -val′vu lar.
trĭv′et, -ta ble.
trĭv′i al, -ism, -ize, -ized, -ĭ′zing, -al ly, -al ness, -al′i ty.
trĭ week′ly.
trŏat.
trŏ′cha (-chȧ).
trŏ′che (-kē or trŏch or trŏk), a lozenge, trŏ′chal (-kăl).
trŏ′chee (-kē), a foot of two syllables, -chä′ic, -ic al.
Trŏ′chu′ (-shü′), Fr. gen.
trŏd, trod′den (-dn). See tread.
trog′lo dyte, -dyt′ic (-dĭt′-), -ic al, -dyt′ism (-dĭt′-).
Trŏ gyl′li ŭm (-jĭl′-), Bib.
troi′ka.
Trŏ′ĭ lus, Myth.; Shak.
Trŏ′jan, Trŏ′ic, pertaining to ancient Troy or Troas.
trŏll, -er, -ing, trolled, troll′-flow er, trŏll′-plate.
trŏll′ing-bait, -hook, -rod, -spoon.

trŏl′ley, -car, -hook, -lace, -line, -pole, -thread, -wheel.
trŏl′lŏl, -lol′ling, -lolled.
trŏl′lop, -ing, -ish, -y.
Trŏl′lope (-lŭp), Eng. writer
trŏm′bŏne, -bōn ist.
trŏ mom′e ter, trŏm o met′ric.
trŏmpe, trŏm pille′ (-pēl′).
troop, -er, -ing, trooped, troop′-bird, -fowl, -horse, -ship.
trōō′pi al.
trŏpe, trŏp′ist, trō pol′o gy, trŏp′-o log′ic, -ic al, -al ly.
Trŏph′i mŭs, Bib.
trŏ′phy, -phĭed, trō′phy wort, trō′phy-cress, -lock, -mon ey, -tax, -wort.
trŏp′ic, -al, -al ly, trop′ic-bird.
trop′po.
trot, -ted, -ter, -ting, trot′-line, trot′ter-boil er, -oil, trot′ting-horse, -sul′ky.
trŏth (or trōth), -plight, -plight ed, -ring.
trŏt′toir (or -wŏr′).
trou′ba dour (trōō′bȧ dōōr′).
trou′ble (trŭb′l), -some, -some-ness, -bled, -bler, -bling, -blous. trou′ble-hunt′er, -mirth.
trough (trȧwf or trŏf), -bat ter y, -fault, -gut ter, -room, -shell.
trounce, trounced, troun′cing.
troupe (trōōp).
trous′-de-loup′ (trōō′-dê -lōō′).
trou′sers (-zerz), -ser ing.
trousse (trōōs).
Trous′seau′ (trōō′sŏ′), Fr. physi-cian.
trous seau′ (trōō sŏ′).
trout, -let, -y.
trout′-bȧs ket, -bird, -col ored, -farm, -hole, -hook, -line, -louse, -net, -perch, -pick er el, -pond, -rod, -shad, -spoon, -stream, -tac kle.
trŏ′ver.
trŏw, to think; suppose; believe; a boat.
Trŏw′bridge, t. Eng.; Amer. novelist.
trow′ĕl, -eled or -elled, -el ing or -ling, trow′el beak, a bird, trow′el-bay o net.

fāte, făt, fär, fạll, fâre, fȧst, sofȧ, mēte, mĕt, hêr, īce, ĭn, nōte,

Troyes (trwä), c. Fr.
troy weight.
tru'ant, -ly, -ship, -an cy.
Trü'bau (-bou), t. Bohemia.
truce, -less, truce'-break'er.
truck, -age, -er, -ing, truck'man,
-mås ter.
truck'-bol ster, -farm, -farm er,
-gar'den, -house, -jack, -patch,
-pot, -shop, -store, -wind'lass,
t. sys'tem, truck'ing-house.
Trŭc kee', t. and r. Cal.
truc'kle, -kled, -kler, -kling,
truc'kle-bed, -cheese.
tru'cu lent (trōō'-), -ly, -lence,
-len cy.
trudge, trudged, trudg'ing.
true, -ness, tru'er, -est, -ish,
-ism, -ly, true'love, a plant,
-pen ny, a person.
true'-blue, -born, -bred, -heart ed,
-heart ed ness, -love, -stitch,
tru'ing-tool.
truf'fle (trōō'fl or truf'-), -fled,
truf'fle-dog, -worm.
Tru jil'lo or Tru xil'lo (trōō hēl'-
yō), t. Honduras; c. Sp.; t. Peru;
t. Venez.
trump, -ing, trumped, trump'-
card, trumped-up.
trump'er y.
trump'et, -ed, -er, -ing, trump'et-
flow er, leaf, -weed, -wood, a
tree.
trump'et-an i mal'cule, -ash, -ban-
ner, -bird, -call, -conch, -creep-
er, -fish, -fly, -gall, -gourd,
-hon ey suc kle, -jas mine, -keck,
-lamp, -lil y, -ma jor, -milk'-
weed, -reed, -shaped, -shell,
-tone, -tongued, -tree, -vine.
trun'cate, -ly, -cā'ted, -cā'ting,
-cā'tion.
trun'cheon (-chŭn), -cheoned.
trun'dle, -dled, -dling, trun'dle-
tail, a dog.
trun'dle-bed, -head, -shot, -tail,
a tail.
trunk, -ing, -less, trunked, trunk'-
back, a turtle, -fish, -nose.
trunk'-a larm, -bear er, -brace,
-breech es, -cab in, -case, -en-
gine, -hose, -light, -mak'er,

-mail, -nail, -roll er, -sleeve,
-stay, -store, -tur tle, trunk' line,
t. road.
trun'nion (-yŭn), -nioned, trun'-
nion-band, -lāthe, -ledge, -plate,
-ring, -sight, -valve.
tru'queur' (trü'kêr').
truss, -er, -ing, trussed.
truss'-beam, -block, -bridge,
-gird er, -hoop, -piece, -plank,
-rod, -tac kle, truss'ing-ma chine.
trust, -ed, -er, -ing, -ing ly, -ful,
-ful ly, -ful ness, -less, -less-
ness, -y, -i ly, -i ness, -wor thy,
-wor thi ness.
trus tee', -ship.
truth (trōōth), -ful, -ful ly, -ful-
ness, -less, -less ness, truth'-
lov er, -tell er.
try (trī), -ing, trīed, try'sail,
try'-cock, -house, -pot, -square,
-works, try'ing-plane, -square.
try'pa (trī'pa), tryp'i ate.
Try phē'na (tri-), *Bib.*
Try phō'sa (trī-), *Bib.*
tryst (trīst), -er, -ing, tryst'ing-
day, -place, -time.
tsăm'ba.
tsar. See *czar.*
Tsä rit syn' (-rēt sēn'), t. Russ.
Tschem kĕnd' (chĕm-), t. Russ.
tsĕt'sĕ, -fly.
tsu'ba (tsōō'-).
Tsung'-li Yä'mĕn (tsŏŏng'-lē).
tub, -bing, -bish, -by, tubbed,
tub'fish, -man.
tub'-fake, -gig, -oar, -oars'man,
-preach er, -race, -saw, -size,
-su gar, -thump er, -wheel.
tū'ba, *pl.* -bas or -bæ.
tŭb'beck.
tub'ber.
tub'bing, -wedge.
tūbe, tubed, tūb'al, -ate, -ing,
-u lar, -lar ly, -lar'i ty, -u late,
-lā'ted, -lā'ting, -lā'tion, -ule,
-u lose, -u lous, tube'flow er.
tūbe'-bear ing, -board, -breath-
er, -brush, -casts, -clamp,
-clean er, -clip, -cock, -col ors,
-com pass, -cor al, -cut ter,
-door, -draw ing, -ex pand er,
-fas ten er, -fer rule, -fil ter,

---

nŏt, nôr, ūse, ŭp, ûrn, etüde, fōōd, fŏŏt, aŋger, boṅmot, thus, Bach.

-flue, -foot, -form, -ger mi na'-
tion, -heart ed, -ma chine, -nosed,
-pack ing, -plate, -plug, -pouch,
-re tort, -scal er, -scrāp er,
-shell, -spin ner, -stop per,
-valve, -vise, - weav er, -well,
-worm, -wrench.

tū'ber, -cle, -cule, -ose, -os'i ty,
-ous, -ous ly, -ous ness, -ber'cu-
lar, -lar ly, -cu late, -lā'ted,
-lā'tion, -cu li form.

tu ber cu lō'sis, -ber'cu lose, -losed,
-lous, -*lum,* pl. -*la.*

tū'be rose' (-rōs' *or* tūb'rōz), a
fragrant white flower.

Tü'bing en, t. Ger.

tu'bu late, -lā'ted, -la'ting, -la'tion.

tuck, -er, -ing, tucked.

tuck'-creas er, -fold er, -in,
-joint, -mark er, -net, -out,
-seine, -shop, tuck'er-in, tuck'-
ing-gage.

tuck'et.

Tuc sŏn' (tū- *or* tuk'-), t. Ariz.

Tues'day (tūz'-).

tū'fa (*or* tōo'-), -fā'ceous.

tuff, volcanic rock, -cone.

tuft, -ed, -er, -ing, -y, tuft'gill,
a fish, tuft'-gilled, -hunt er,
tuft'ing-but ton.

tug, -ger, -ging, -ging ly, tugged,
tug'boat, -man, -mut ton.

tug'-car'ri er, -chain, -hook, -i ron,
-slide, -spring.

tuille (twēl *or* twĭl), tuil lette'.

tū ĭ'tion (-ĭsh'un), -al, -a ry.

Tu lä'rē (*or* -lâre'), c. and l. Cal.

Tu'lē, t. Cal.

tu'lē (tōo'-), -wren.

tū'lip, -ear, -eared, -pop lar,
-root, -shell, -tree, -wood.

Tülle, t. Fr.

tulle (tōol).

tum'ble, -bled, -bler, -bling, -bly,
tum'ble bug, -weed.

tum'ble-car, -down, *a.,* -home.

tum'bler-brush, -cart, -dog,
-drum, -glass, -hold er, -lock,
-punch, -stand, -tank, -wash er.

tum'bling-bar rel, -bay, -bob,
-box, -net, -shăft, -trough,
-wheel.

tum'brel.

tu'mĕ fy (-fĭ), -ing, -fĭed, -fā'-
cient, -făc'tion, tu mes'cent,
-cence, tu'mid, -ly, -ness, -mid'-
i ty.

tu'mor, -like.

tŭmp, -y, tump'-line.

tum-tum.

tū'mult, -mul'tu ous, -ous ly,
-ous ness.

tu'mu lus, -mu lar, -la ry, -late,
-la ted, -la ting, -lose, -lous.

tun, a cask; to put into casks,
-ning, tunned, tun'hoof, a plant,
tun'-bel ly, -moot, -shell, tun'-
ning-cask, -dish.

tun'dra (tōon'-).

tūne, -ful, -ful ly, -less, tuned,
tūn'er, -ing, -a ble, -a ble ness,
-a bly.

tūn'ing-cone, -crook, -fork,
-ham mer, -horn, -key, -knife,
-lĕv er, -peg, -pin, -slide, -wire.

tū'nic, -ni cate, -ni cle.

tŭn'nel, -ing *or* -ling, -neled *or*
-nelled.

tun'nel-bor er, -dis ease, -head,
-hole, -kiln, -net, -pit, -shăft,
-vault, -weav er, -worm.

Tuol'um nē (twŏl'-), co. and r.
Cal.

tup, -ping, tupped, tup'see, tup'-
man.

tūque.

tur (tōor).

tur'ban, -băned, tur'ban-shell,
-stone, -top.

tur'bid, -ly, -ness, -bid'i ty.

tur'bĭne, -dy na mom'e ter, -pump.

tur'bit, -bit teen'.

tur'bot.

tur'bu lence, -len cy, -lent, -lent ly.

Tur'co *or* -kŏ, a soldier; tur'co, a
bird.

tu reen'.

turf, *pl.* turfs, -y, -i ness, -ing,
turfed, turf'man.

turf'-ant, -bound, -char coal,
-cut ter, -drain, -knife, -moss,
-plow, -spade, -worm, turf'ing-
i ron, -spade.

tur'gent, -ges'cence, -cen cy, -cent,
-ci ble.

tur'gid, -ly, -ness, -gid'i ty.

---

fāte, făt, fär, fạll, fâre, fåst, sofå, mēte, mĕt, hêr, īce, ĭn, nōte,

Tur′kes tän′ *or* -kis- (to͞or′-), region Cent. Asia.
Tur′key, S. E. Europe, Turk, Turk′man, Tur′key car pet, T. gum, T. hone, T. myrrh, T. red, T. slate, T. stone, Turk′s-cap, -head, -tur ban.
tur′key, -back, a bird, -beard, a plant, -ber ry.
tur′key-bird, -blos som, -buz-zard, -call, -cock, -corn, -gnat, -gob bler, -grass, -hen, -lĕath er, -louse, -pea, -pen, -poult, -shoot, -vul ture, tur′key ber ry-tree.
tur′mer ic, -oil, -pa per, -plant, -root, -tree.
tur′moil.
turn, -er, -er y, -ing, turned.
turn′a bout, -back, -buc kle, -cap, -coat, a person, -cock, a person, -key, -out, -o ver, -pike, -plate, -sick, -side, -spit, -stile, -stone, -ta ble.
turn′-bench, -bridge, -down, -file, -pin, -poke, -row, -screw, -un der, -up, -wrest, turned′-shells.
turn′er-harp, -hood, turn′pike-man, -stair, turn′sole-blue, turn′-stile-reg is ter.
turn′ing-bridge, -car ri er, -chis el, -en gine, -gagc′, -gouge, -lathe, -ma chine, -mill, -piece, -place, -point, -rest, -saw, -steel, -stool.
tur′nip, -wood, a tree, tur′nip-äph′id, -cab bage, -cut ter, -flea, -fly, -mag got, -pars nip, -pest, -pull er, -pulp er, -rad ish, -root ed, -shaped, -shell, -tailed.
turn′ve rein′ (to͞orn′fĕ rīn′).
tur′pen tǐne, -tin′ic, tur′pen tine-hack, -moth, -oil, -still, -tree.
tur′pi tude.
Tur qui′nô (to͞or kĕ′-), mt. Cuba.
tur quoise′ (-koiz′ *or* -kēz′), -ber′ry, -green.
tŭr′rĕl.
tŭr′ret, -ed, tur′ret-gun, -head, -lathe, -shǐp, -spi′der.
tŭr ric′u la, *pl.* -læ, -late, -lā′ted.
tur′tle, -tled, -tler, -tling, tur′tle-back, a vessel.
tur′tle-cow′ry, -crawl, -deck,

-dove *or* -dove, -egg ing, -foot-ed, -grass, -head, -peg, -run, -shell, -stone, tur′tle soup.
Tus′ca ny, dept. It., Tus′can.
Tŭs′ca ra̤′wȧs, co. and r. O.
Tus′cŏ la, co. Mich.; c. Ill.
tush, tushed.
tusk, -er, -y, tusked, tusk′-shell, -ten on, -worm.
Tŭs kē′gee, t. Ala.
tŭs′sal, relating to cough, -sic′u lar.
tus′ser, -silk, -worm.
tus′sle, -sled, -sler, -sling.
tus′sock, -y, tus′sock-cat′er pil lar, -grass, -moth, -sedge.
tŭ′te lage, -te lar, -lā′ry.
tu′te nag.
Tŭ′tǐ vil′lus, a demon.
tŭ′tor, -age, -ess, -ing, -ship, -y, -tored, -tō′ri al, -al ly.
tut′ti (to͞ot′tē), *tut′ta* (to͞ot′-), tut′ti-frut′ti (-fro͞ot′tē).
tu-whit′ (to͞o-), -who͞o′.
tux e′ do.
Tux pän′ (to͞os-), t. Mex.
twad′dle (twŏd′l), -dled, -dler, -dling, -dly.
twäin, -cloud.
twäng, -er, -ing, twanged.
twan′gle, -gled, -gler, -gling.
twat′tle (twŏt′l), -tled, -tler, -tling.
twĕak, -ing, tweaked.
tweed.
twee′dle, -dled, -dler, -dling.
twee′zer, -zers, twee′zer-case.
Twelfth′-cake, -day, -night, -tide.
twelve, -mo, -month, -pence, -pen ny, twelfth, twelve′-score.
twĕn′ty, -mo, -ti eth, twen′ty four-mo, twen′ty-fold, -sec ond.
twǐce, -stabbed, -told.
twid′dle, -dled, -dler, -dling, twid′dling-line.
twig, -ger, -ging, -gy, twigged.
twig′-blight, -bor er, -bug, -gir-dler, -in sect, -prün er, -rush.
twī′lǐght.
twǐll, -ing, twilled.
twǐn, -ling, -ning, twinned, twin′-flow er, -leaf, -ship, the relation of twins.

twin'-born, -cyl in der, -like,
-screw, -shell, -spot, -stock, t.
boat, t. e qua to'ri al, t. pair, t.
ships, t. steam'er, t. valve.
twin'ning-ax is, -ma chine, -plane,
-saw.
twĭne, twined, twĭn'er, -ing,
twine'-cut ter, -hold er, -ma-
chine, -reel er.
twinge, twinged, twin'ging.
twin'kle, -kled, -kler, -kling.
twirl, -er, -ing, twirled.
twist, -a ble, -ed, -er, -ing, -ing-
ly, -y.
twist'-joint, -ma chine', -stitch,
-ve loc'i ty, twist' to bac'co.
twist'ed-flow er, -horn, a plant,
-stalk, -stick, a plant, t. col'-
umn, t. pine, t. sur'face.
twist'ing-crook, -for'ceps, -ma-
chine, -mill.
twĭt, -ted, -ter, -ting, -ting ly,
twit'-lark, -twat (-twŏt).
twitch, -er, -ing, -et y, twitched,
twitch-grass.
twĭt'ter, -er, -ing, -ing ly, -tered,
twit'ter-bit, -bone, -boned.
two (tōō), *pl.* twos (tōōz), -fold,
-pence, -pen ny.
two'-blåd'ed, -cleft, -deck'er,
-eared, -edged, -eyes, -faced,
-flow ered, -forked, -hand ed,
-head ed, -horse, *a.*, -leaved,
-legged, -lipped, -måst ed, -part-
ed, -pet aled, -ply, -pronged,
-ranked, -seed ed, -sĭd'ed, -spot,
-step, -stringed, -throw, -tongued,
-toothed, -valved.
Tyb'ălt (tĭb'-), Shak., *Romeo and
Juliet.*
Ty'che (tī'kē), *Myth.*
Tych'i cus (tĭk'i kus), *Bib.*
Ty'cho Brahe (tī'kō brä *or* brä),
Ty chon'ic (tī kŏn'-).
ty coon' (tī-), -ate.
tye, ty'ing, tyed, tye-block.
ty'ee.
Ty'ghee (tī'gē), mt. pass Idaho.

tymp, -arch, -plate, -stone.
tym'pan, -pa nal, -pa num, *pl.*
-nums *or* -na, -pan'ic.
type (tīpe), typ'al (tĭp'-), -ist,
typ'ic (tĭp'-), -ic al, -al ly,
-al ness, -i cal'i ty, type'set ter,
-write, -wrīt'er, -wrīt'ing, -wrīt'ist.
type'-bar, -block, -case, -cåst ing,
-chart, -cut ter, -cyl in der,
-dress ing, -found er, -found ry,
-gage, -high, -hold er, -life, -ma-
trix, -meas ure, -meas ur er,
-met al, -mold, -punch, -scale,
-wheel.
ty'phoid (tī'-), -al.
Ty'phon (tī'-), *Myth.;* ty'phon, a
bird.
ty phōōn' (tī-), -phon'ic.
ty'phus (tī'-), a fever, -phoŭs, relating to typhus.
typ'i fy (tĭp'-), -ing, -fī'er, -fīed,
-fĭ cā'tion.
Ty pĭn sän' (tī-), isl. off China.
ty'pŏ grâph (tī'-), -graph'ic, -ic-
al, -al ly, -pog'ra pher, -ra phy.
Tyr (ter), *Myth.*
tyr'an nize (tĭr'-), -nized, -nī'-
zing, -nous, -nous ly, -ny, ty-
ran'nic (tī-), -nic al, -al ly, -al-
ness, -ni cide, -cī'dal.
Ty răn'nus (tī-), *Bib.*
ty'rant (tī'-), -bird, -chat, -fly'-
catch er, -shrike, -wren.
Tyre, an ancient city; Tyr'i an,
Tyr'i an pur'ple.
ty'ro (tī'-), *pl.* -ros (-rōz).
Tyr'ol (tĭr'-), prov. Aust., -o lēse'
(*or* -lēz'), Ty rō lĭ' ĕnne' (tĭ'-).
Ty rŏne' (tī- *or* tī'-), co. Ire.; t.
Pa.; tp. N. Y.
Tyr rhene' (tĭr-), -rhe'ni an.
Tys mien i'ca (tĭs myĕn ēt'sä), t.
Aust.
tzar. See *czar.*
Tzig'a ny (tsĭg'-).
Tzin tzou tzän' (tsĭn tsōō tsän'),
t. Mex.
Tzschir'ner (tshĭr'-), Ger. theol.

---

fāte, făt, fär, fạll, fâre, fåst, sofà, mēte, mĕt, hêr, īce, ĭn, nōte,

U

U-shaped, U bolt, U tube.
Ua tu ma′ (wä tōō mä′), r. Braz.
U bä tu′bä (ōō bä tōō′-), t. Braz.
ū′ber ous, -ber ty.
ū bī′e ty.
ū′bĭq′uǐ tous (-bĭk′wǐ tŭs), -ly,
 -ness, -ui ty.
u′da (ōō′da).
ŭd′der, -less, -dered, ud′der-
 cloud.
ū′dŏm′e ter, -dō met′ric, -dŏm′o-
 grăph.
Ue′ber weg (ü′ber vĕg), Ger. philos.
U gän′da, dist. Afr.
ŭg′gur-oil.
ugh (ŏŏ).
ŭg′ly, -li ly, -li ness, -li fy, -fy-
 ing, -fied, -fĭ ca′tion.
U gocs′ (ōō gŏtch′), dist. Hung.
U go li′no (ōō gō lē′nō), immor-
 talized by Dante.
uh′lan (ū′lan *or* ōō′- *or* ōō′län).
Uh′land (ōō′länt), Ger. lyric poet.
U ĭn′ta, co. Utah; co. Wyo.
Uĭ′tĕu hä′gĕ (oi′-), div. Afr.
Uit′länd′er (oit′-).
uit spän′ (oit-).
U j ä′räd (ōō′č-), t. Hung.
U j fä′lu (ōō′ē fä′lōō), t. Hung.
U′j falvy (ōō′ē fŏlv′), Hung. auth.
U j fe jer′to (ōō′ē fē yĕr′tō), t.
 Hung.
u′jǐ (ōō′-).
U ji′ji (ōō jē′jē), coun. Afr.
ū käse′.
U′läi (*or* -lä ĭ), *Bib.*
ŭl′cer, -a blc, -ate, -ā′ted, -ā′ting,
 -ā tive, -ā to′ry, -ous, -ous ly,
 -ā′tion, -cered.
u li′tis.
Ull′männ (ŏŏl′-), Ger. theol.
Ulm (ŏŏlm), t. Ger.
ul′na, pl. *-næ,* -nar.
Ul rī′ca, Scott, *Ivanhoe.*
ŭl′ster, a garment, -ing, -stered.
ŭl tĕ′rǐ or, -ly.
Ul′ti ma Thu′lē.
ŭl′ti mate, -ly, -ness.

ul ti mä′tum, pl. *-tums* or *-ta.*
ŭl′tǐ mŏ, -gen′i ture.
ŭl′tra, -clas′sic al, -fash′ion a ble,
 -ism, -ist, -ma rine′ (-rēn′),
 -mŏn′tane, -ta nism, -ta nist,
 -mun′dane, -red′, -vī′o let.
u′lu (ōō′lōō).
ul′u late, -lā′ted, -lā′ting, -lant,
 -lā′tion.
Ul′va, Ul′van, ul va′ceous.
U lys′ses (-sēz), King of Ithaca.
U ma til′la, co. Ore.
ŭm′bĕl, -bel late, -lā′ted, -let,
 -lif′er ous, -bel′li form, -bel′lu-
 late.
ŭm′ber, -y.
ŭm′brāge, -brā′geous, -geous ly,
 -geous ness.
um brĕl′la, -leaf, -wort.
um brel′la-ant, -bird, -fir, -grăss,
 -man, -palm, -pine, -shell,
 -stand, -tree.
um′iak (ōōm′yăk).
um′laut (ōōm′lout), -ed.
ŭm′pire, -ship, -pǐred, -pǐr age,
 -ing.
un-. The prefix *un-* is used with
 many words, which, for the
 most part, are self-explaining.
 With adjectives, adverbs, and
 nouns, it usually has a negative
 force; as, unclean, unfair, un-
 fairly, unthinkingly, unclean-
 ness, untruth, unwisdom. With
 verbs, the prefix conveys the sense
 of reversal; as unsex, undo, un-
 bend, unfold.
  The divisions and accents of
 the words combined with *un-* are
 the same as when not combined,
 and as these words are found in
 their appropriate alphabetic order,
 it is not deemed necessary to repeat many of them here.
  The prefix *un-* is rarely separated from the rest of the word
 by a hyphen. The principal exceptions are here given.

---

nŏt, nôr, ūse, ŭp, ûrn, etüde, fōōd, fŏŏt, aŋger, boṅmot, ᴛhus, Bac͟h.

un-A mĕr'i can, -A mer'i can ize,
-Ar'yan ize, -Eŋ'glish, -Ho mĕr'-
ic, -Lat'in, -Mo sa'ic, -Quak'-
er like, -Scot'ti fy.
U na dil'la, vil. N. Y.
U nä läs'ka (ōō-), isl. Aleutian Isls.
ŭ năn'i mous, -ly, -ness, -na-
nim'i ty.
un bos'om (-bŏŏz'-), -ing, -omed.
un cĕas'ing, -ly.
un cĕr'e mŏ'ni ous, -ly, -ness.
un cer'taĭn, -ly, -ness, -ty.
un chal'lenge, -a ble, -lenged.
un change', -a ble, -ble ness, -bly,
-bil'i ty, -changed', -chan'ging.
un clâsp', -clasped'.
uŋ'cle, -ship.
un clĕan', -ness, -clĕan'ly, -li ness.
un cŏm'pro mis ing.
un con cern', -ed ly, -ed ness,
-cerned'.
un con di'tion al (-dĭsh'un-), -ly,
-al'i ty, -tioned.
un coŋ'quer a ble, -ness, -bly,
-quered.
un con'scion a ble, -ness, -bly.
un couth' (-kōōth'), -ly, -ness.
un cov'er (-kŭv'-), -er, -ing, -ered.
unc'tion, -tu ous, -ous ly, -ous-
ness.
un däunt'ed, -ed ly, -ed ness.
un de cĕive', -cĕived', -cĕiv'a ble.
ŭn'der, -act', -ac'tion, -a'gent,
-bid', -bill', -bind', -bit'ten,
-brace', -bred', -brush', -burn',
-bush', -câst', -charge', -clothed',
-clothes', -cloth'ing, -croft',
-cur'rent, -curved', -ditch', -do',
-do'er, -done', -dose', -draw',
-es'ti mate, -es ti mā'tion, -feed',
-fill'ing, -floor', v., -flow', -foot',
-fur'nish, -fur'row, -gar'ment,
-gear', -gird', -glaze', -gore',
-gown', -grad'u ate, -grove'.
un der hang', -hew', -hole', -hung',
-lay', n., -lay', v., -lease', -let',
-lie', -line', n., -line', v., -lin'en,
-ling', -lock', -look'er, -ly'ing,
-man', v., -mâst'ed, -men'-
tioned, -mine', -named', -nĕath'
(or -nĕath'), -note', -not'ed,
-part', n., -part', v., -pay', v.,
-peo'pled, -pin', -pin'ning, -play',

-plot', -praise', -prize', -pro-
duc'tion, -proof' (or -proof'),
-prop', -pro por'tioned, -quote'.
un'der rate', n., -rate', v., -reck'-
on, -ripe', -run', -score', -sell',
-set', v., -set', n., -shirt', -shoot',
-shot', a., -shrub', -sign', -sized',
-skirt', -sleeve', -soil', -song',
-sparred', -sphere', -spread',
-state', -state'ment, -stock',
-strap'per, -stra'tum, -stroke',
-stud'y, -suit', -sward'.
un'der timed', -tint', -tone',
-tow', -trump', -vest', -view'er,
-wa'ter, -wear', -wing', a moth,
-winged', -wood', -world'.
un'der-a'gent, -arm, -back, -buy',
-chord', -clay', -clerk, -clerk'ship,
-cliff', -coat', -col'or, -col'ored,
-deal'ing, -de ter mi nant,
-dressed', -driv'en, -ex posed',
-fac'ul ty, -farm er, -fur, -fired',
-grade', -hold, -keep', -kind',
-king', -king'dom, -la'bor er,
-life', -mâs ter, -of'fi cer, -part,
-re'gion, -roof', -scribe', -sec're-
ta ry, -serv'ant, -shĕr'iff, -sky',
-ten'an cy, -ten'ant, -work'man,
u. can vas, u. way.
un'der cut, n., -ter, -cut', v.,
-cut'ting.
un'der drain, n., -age, -drain', v.,
-ing, -drained'.
un der go', -ing, -went', -gone'.
un'der ground, a. and n.,
-ground', v.
un'der growth, n., -grown', a.
un'der hand, -hand'ed, -ed ly,
-ed ness.
un der stand', -ing, -ing ly, -a ble,
-er, -stŏŏd'.
un der take', -tŏŏk', tāk'en, -ing.
un'der tāk'er.
un'der văl'ue, n., -văl'ue, v.,
-ued, -u er, -u ing, -u ā'tion.
un'der work, n., -work'er, -work',
v., -work'ing, -worked'.
un'der wrĭt'er, -wrĭt'ing, -write',
v., -wrōte', -writ'ten.
un dĕ served' (-zervd'), -serv'ed-
ly, -ed ness, -er, -ing, -ing ly.
un de signed' (-zīnd'), -sign'ed ly,
-ed ness, -ing.

fāte, făt, fär, fạll, fâre, fâst, sofà, mēte, mĕt, hêr, īce, ĭn, nōte,

un de sired' (-zīrd'), -sir'a ble, -ble ness, -bly, -sīr'ing, -sīr'ous.

Un dine' *or* un dine' (-dēn'), a water-sprite, -din'al (-dēn'-).

un dis cern'i ble (-dĭz zern'-), -ness, -bly, -cern'ed ly, -ing.

un dis cov'er a ble, -a bly, -cov'-ered.

un dis guis'a ble (-gīz'), -guis'ed ly, -guised'.

un dis mayed'.

un dis turbed', -turb'ed ly, -ed-ness.

un do', -ing, -er, -did', -done'.

un doubt'a ble (-dout'-), -a bly, -ed, -ed ly, -ing, -ing ly.

un dress' *or* un'-, *n.*, -dress', *v.*, -dressed'.

un dūe'.

un'du late, -ly, -lā'ted, -lā'ting, -ting ly, -lant, -lā'tion, -tion ist, -la'to ry.

un dy'ing (-dī'-), -ly, -ing ness.

un êarth', -ing, -ly, -li ness, -earthed'.

un êa'sy, -si ly, -si ness.

un end'ed, -ing, -ing ly, -ing ness.

un en dūr'a ble, -a bly.

un ê'qual, -ly, -ness, -qualed *or* -qualled, -êq'ui ta ble.

un e quiv'o cal, -ly, -ness.

un ex cep'tion al, -ly, -a ble, -ble-ness, -bly.

un ex pect'ed, -ly, -ness.

un fāil'ing, -ly, -ness.

un fătĥ'om a ble, -ness, -bly, -omed.

un feel'ing, -ly, -ness.

un fold', -ed, -er, -ing.

un gāin'ly, -li ness.

un gov'ern a ble, -ness, -bly, -erned.

un gram măt'ic al, -ly.

un grâte'ful, -ly, -ful ness.

un'guent, -guen tâ'ry, -guĭ nous, -guen'tous.

un hĕalth'ful, -ly, -ful ness, -y, -i ly, -i ness.

ū'ni corn, -cor'ne al, -cor'nous, -cor nū'ted.

u'ni corn-bee tle, -bird, -fish, -moth, -plant, -root, -shell, -whale, u'ni corn's-horn.

ū'ni form, -ly, -ness, -form'i ty.

ū'ni fy (-fĭ), -ing, -fĭed, -fĭ'a ble, -fĭ er, -nĭf'ic, -fĭ cā'tion.

u ni gen'e sis, -ge net'ic, -nig'e-nist (-nĭj'-), -ni ge nis'tic.

ūn'ion, -ism, -ist, -is'tic.

un'ion-bŏw, -cord, -grăss, -joint, -pump, -room, u. jack, U. par'ty.

u'ni phase.

u ni pla'nar.

u ni po'lar.

ū nique' (-nēk'), -ly, -ness.

ū'ni rĕme.

ū'ni son (-sŭn), -sō'nal, -nal ly, -so'nance, -nant, -nous (*or* -nĭs'o nal, -nal ly, -nance, -nant, -noŭs).

ū'nit, -ni tâ'ry, -tā'ri an.

U ni tā'ri an, -ize, -ized, -ī'zing, -ism.

U'ni tas Fra'trum.

ū nīte', -nīt'ed, -ed ly, -er, -ing, ū'ni ty.

ū'ni vălve, -valved, -văl'vu lar.

ū nĭ ver'sal, -ly, -ness, -sal ize, -ized, -ī'zing, -Ĭ zā'tion, -săl'i-ty, -ver'si ty.

U ni ver'sal ist, -sal ism.

un lace', -laced', -la'cing.

ŭn lĕss'.

ŭn lŏad', -ed, -er, -ing, un load'-ing-block, -ma chine.

un măn', -ning, -mănned'.

un meas'ured (-mĕzh'-).

un mis tăk'a ble, -a bly.

un mit'i ga ted, -ted ly, -gå ble.

un năt'u ral, -ly, -ness.

un nec'es sâ'ry, -sa ri ly, -ri ness.

un prĕj'u diced, -ly, -ness.

un qual'i fied, -ly, -ness.

un quench'a ble, -ness, -å bly, -a bil'i ty.

un ques'tion a ble, -ness, -a bly, -a bil'i ty, -tioned.

un răv'ĕl, -eled *or* -elled, -el ing *or* -ling, -el er *or* -ler, -el ment.

un re lent'ing, -ly, -ness.

un scru'pu lous, -ly, -ness.

un sêarch'a ble, -ness, -bly, -searched'.

un sêa'son a ble, -ness, -bly, -soned.

un seem'ly, -li ness.

nŏt, nôr, ūse, ŭp, ûrn, etüde, fō͞od, fŏ͝ot, aṅger, boṅmot, tḧus, Baċh.

un so phis'ti cate,   -cā'ted,   -ted-
ness, -cā'tion.
un spâr'ing, -ly, -ness.
un spēak'a ble, -bly.
un stĕad'y, -i ly, -i ness.
un tĭl'.
ŭn'to.
un tŏ'ward, -ly, -li ness, -ness.
un trav'eled or -elled.
un truth', -ful, -ful ly, -ful ness.
un ŭ'su al (-zhōō-),   -al ly,   -al-
ness, -al'i ty.
un ut'ter a ble, -a bly, -tered.
un wă'ry, -ri ly, -ri ness.
un whole'some (-sŭm), -ly, -ness.
un wiĕld'y, -i ly, -i ness.
un wont'ed (-wŭnt'-), -ed ly, -ed-
ness.
un wor'thy, -thi ly, -thi ness.
ŭ'pas, -tree.
up brăid', -ed, -er, -ing, -ing ly.
up'-coun'try,   adv.,   up'-coun'try,
n. and a.
U phar'sin, Bib.
up hĕave', -heaved', -hĕav'al, -ing.
ŭp'hill, a. and n., up'hill', adv.
up hŏld', -er, -ing, -hĕld'.
up hol'ster,   -ster er,   -ster ing,
-ster y, -stered, up hol'ster er-bee.
ŭ'phroe (-frō).
up'land, -er.
ŭp'lift, n., -lift', v., -ed, -er, -ing.
ŭp ŏn'.
ŭp'per,   -most, up'pish,   -pish ly,
-pish ness, up'per cut, -grōwth,
-ten' dom, -wing, up'per-lĕath'er,
-ma chine', -stocks, u. back, u.
case, u. cur'rent, u. key'board,
u. strake, u. works, u. world.
up'right, -ly, -ness.
up rise' (-rīz'), -rīs'ing, -rĭs'en,
-rose'.
ŭp'rŏar, -rōar'i ous, -ous ly, -ous-
ness.
up rōōt', -ed, -er, -ing.
Up sä'lä, prov. Sw.
up'set, n. and a., -set', v., -set'-
ter, -ting.
up'shōōt, n., -shōōt', v.
ŭp'shŏt.
up'-stairs, a. and n., up'-stairs',
adv.
up'start, n. and a., -start', v.

up'-strēam, a., up'-strēam', adv.
up'-to-date'.
up'-town, adv., up'-town', a.
up'ward or -wards, -ward ly.
U'räl, r. and mts. Russ., -rä'li an,
-răl'ic.
U rä'ni a, Myth., -ni an.
u rä'ni on, a musical instrument.
U'ra nus, Myth.; Astron.
ur'ban, -ist, ur bĭc'o lous.
ur bāne', -ly, -băn'i ty.
Ur'ban ist, a follower of Pope
Urban.
ur'ban iste (-ist), a pear.
ur'chin, -fish, -form.
u re'mi a, -re'mic.
u re'thra, pl. -thræ, -thral, -thro-
scope, -sco py, -tome, -tŏm'ic,
-throm'e ter, -throt'o my, u re'ter,
-ter i'tis, -ter or'rha phy.
Ur găn'da (ōōr-), an enchantress
in Spanish fiction.
urge,   urged,   ur'ging,   -gence,
-gent, -gent ly, -gen cy, -ger.
U'rĭ el (or -rī'-), Bib.
u'rine (-rĭn), -ric, -ri nal, -ri na
ry, -ri nate, -nā'ted, -nā'ting,
-nā'tive, -nā'tor, -na'ri um, -na'-
tion, -nal'y sis, -rin e'mi a, -ri-
nif'ic, -ri nol o gy, -ri no met'-
ric, -no scop'ic, -nos'co py (or
u'ri no scŏ'py),   -ri nif'er ous,
-nip'a rous, -no gen'i tal, -ri-
nom'e ter, -e try, ū'ri nose (-nōs),
-ri nous.
urn, -al, -ful, -flow'er, urn'-
shaped.
Ur'quhart (-kwurt), Scot. politician.
ur'sĭne, -si form.
Ur sī'nus, Ital. schol.
Ur'sŭ lĭne.
U ru guay (ōō rōō gwī' or ū'rōō-
gwä), r. and rep. S. Amer.
use (ūs), n., -ful, -ful ly, -ful-
ness, -less, -less ly, -less ness.
use (ūz), v., ūs'a ble (ūz'-), -ble-
ness, -age, -ance, used, ūs'ing, -er.
U shăs' (ōō-), Myth.
ŭsh'er, -dom, -ing, -less, -ship,
-ered.
u sine' (ü zēn').
ū'su al (-zhōō-), -ly, -ness.

---

fāte, făt, fär, fạll, fâre, fạst, sofà, mēte, mĕt, hêr, īce, ĭn, nōte,

ü'su fruct (-zū-), -fruc'tu â ry.
u surp' (-zurp'), -er, -ing, -ing ly,
-surped, -surp'a to'ry, -sur pā'-
tion.
ü'su ry (-zhōō-), -su rer, -su'ri-
ous, -ous ly, -ous ness.
ü'sus.
U'täh, state U. S.
Ute.
u tĕn'sil.
u'te rus, *pl.* -rī, u'ter Ine, -ter al'-
gi a, -ter ī'tis, -ot'o my, -ter o-
vag'i nal (-văj'-).
U'thăi (*or* -thä ī), *Bib.*
U'ther, father of King Arthur.
ü'tĭl'i ty, -i tä'ri an, -an ism,
u til'i ty-man.
ü'til ize, -ized, -ĭ'zing, -ĭ'za ble,
-ĭ'zer, -ĭ zä'tion.
ut'most.

U tŏ'pi a, Sir Thomas More's
imaginary island, -pi an.
ü tŏ'pi a, a place or state of
ideal perfection, -pi an, -an ism,
u'to pist.
U'trecht, prov. Netherlands.
ut'ter, -a ble, -ble ness, -ance,
-er, -ing, -less, -ly, -most, -tered.
u'u ä'u (ōō'ŏō ä'ŏō), a petrel.
ü'vate.
ü'vu la, -vu lar, -lar ly, -la tome.
ŭx ŏ'ri al, -ri ous, -ous ly, -ous-
ness, -ŏr'i cide, -cī'dal.
U'zăi (*or* -zä ī), *Bib.*
Uz'beg.
ü'zē ma.
Uz zī'a, *Bib.*
Uz zī'el (*or* ŭz'zĭ-), *Bib.;* an angel
in *Paradise Lost.*
Uz zī'el Ites, *Bib.*

V

V, *pl.* vees *or* V's *or* Vs. V-moth,
-shaped, V bob, V croze, V gage,
V gear, V gear ing, V hook, V
point, V tool, V tooth, V vat.
Väal, Afr.
vă'can cy, -cant, -cant ly.
vă'cate, cā'ted, -cā'ting, -cā'-
tion, -tion ist, -tion less, *va cā'-
tur.*
vac'cĭne (*or* -sĭn), -ci nate, -na-
ted, -na ting, -nä'tion, -tion ist,
-na'tor, -ci nal, -ci nist, -cig'e-
nous (-sĭj'-), -cin'ic, vac'cĭne-
farm, -point, vac ci na'tion-scar.
vŭ cher' (-shä'), vach'er y (väsh'-).
Vache rot' (väsh'rŏ'), Fr. philos.
văc'il late (văs'-), -lā'ted, -lā'-
ting, -ting ly, -lant, -la to'ry,
-lā'tion.
va cū'i ty, văc'u ist, -u ous, -ous-
ness, -ū um, *pl.* -ums.
văc'ŭ um-brake, -fil ter, -gage,
-line, -pan, -pump, -tube, -valve.
Va cū'na, Myth.
vă'dĕ-mē'cum.
Vä'di us' (-dē'ŏŏs'), Molière's
comedy.

Vä'gä, Russ.
văg'a bŏnd, -age, -ish, -ism, -ize,
-ized, -i zing.
Vä'gai (-gī), r. Sib.
va gă'ry, -ri an, -ri ous, -rish,
-găr'i ty.
va gi'na (-jī'-), *pl.* -næ (-nē),
vag'i nal (văj'-), -i nant, -i nate,
-i nä'ted, -i ner'vose (*or* -vōs'),
-i no pen'nous.
vag'i nä'tĭ (văj-), *-i nic'o la,*
-i nis'mus, -i nĭ'tis.
vă'grant, -ly, -gran cy.
vague (väg), -ly, -ness.
vail.
vain, -ly, -ness, -glŏ'ry, -glo'ri-
ous, -ous ly, -ous ness, văn'i ty.
Vaish'na va, *Myth.*, -na vism.
Vais'ya.
Va jĕz'a tha (*or* văj'ē zā' tha), *Bib.*
va käss'.
Vă lais' (-lā'), canton Switz.
văl'ance, -anced, -an cing.
Väl'dĕs, c. Sp.
văle, a valley.
vä'lē, farewell, văl e dic'tion, -dic'-
to ry, -tō'ri an.

Vä'lĕ, *Myth.*
Vâ'lence' (-lŏns'), t. Fr.
vă'lence, *Chem.*
va lĕn'ci a (-shĭ-), a linen fabric.
 Va len'ci a, prov. and c. Sp.;
 c. Venez.; co. N. Mex.; Va len'-
 ci a rai'sins.
Va len ci ennes' (vå'lŏn'sē ĕn'),
 t. Fr.; Fr. landscape painter;
 V. lace (-lŏn'sĭ ĕnz' *or* -lĕn'-).
Va lĕn'ti a (-shĭ a), t. and isl. Ire.
văl'en tĭne.
Văl'en tĭn'i an, -an ism.
va lē'ri an, a plant. Va lē'ri an,
 pertaining to Valerius.
văl'et (*or* văl'ā).
văl ē tū dĭ nā'ri an, -an ism, -tū'-
 di na ry, -nā'ri um, -ri us.
Val hăl'la, *Myth.*
văl'iant (-yănt), -ly, -ness.
văl'id, -ly, -ness, -i date, -dā'ted,
 -dā'ting, -dā'tion, va lid'i ty.
va lise' (-lēs'), -sad dle.
Val'jean', Jean (zhän văl'zhän'),
 Hugo, *Les Miserables.*
văl'kyr, *Myth., pl.* -kyr'es (-kĭr'-
 ēz), -kyr'i a (-kĭr'-), -i an.
Väl la do lid' (-yä dō lēd'), prov.
 and t. Sp.
Väl le'jo (-yä'hō), c. Cal.
val'ley, *pl.* -leys, val'ley-board,
 -quail, -piece, -råft er.
Vâ'lognes' (-lōn'), t. Fr.
Väl'ois' (-wŏ'), Fr. antiquary.
văl'or, -ous, -ous ly.
Väl pä raī'sŏ, prov. and c. Chile;
 c. Ind.
val'ūe, -less, -less ness, -u a ble,
 -ble ness, -u ā'tion, -a'tor, -ued,
 -u ing, -u er.
valve, valved, vălv'al, -ar, -ule,
 -u lar, -i form, val'vate, -vĭf'er-
 ous.
valve'-buck et, -cham ber, -cock,
 -coup'ler, -file, -gear, -mo tion,
 -key, -line, -pal let, -rod, -seat,
 -stem, -tailed, -view.
Väl ver'de (-vâr'dä), co. Tex.;
 t. Canary Isls.
vamp, -er, -ing, vamped.
vam'pire, -pĭr ism, -pĭr'ic, vam'-
 pire-bat.
van, -ner, -ning, -ward, vanned,

van'-winged, van'ner-hawk, van'-
 ning-ma chine'.
Văn'dal, one of the Germanic race,
 -dal ism, -dăl'ic.
văn'dal, one who wilfully destroys
 or disfigures, -dal ism, -dăl'ic.
Van dyke' (-dīke') *or* -dyck'
 (-dĭck'), a Flemish painter, V.
 beard, V. brown, V. cape, V.
 col lar, V. edge, V. lace, van-
 dyked' (-dīked').
vane, -less, vaned.
Văn Eyck' (-īk'), Flemish painter.
van'guard.
va nĭl'la, -nĭl'lic, -nĭl'lin, -nĭl'-
 lism, -nil'lōes (-lōz), va nil'la-
 bean, -gråss, -plant.
van'ish, -er, -ing, -ing ly, -ment,
 -ished, van'ish ing-line, -point, v.
 stress.
van'i ty.
Vannes (văn), t. Fr.
van'quish, -a ble, -er, -ing,
 -ment, -quished.
Văn Rĕns'se laer (rĕns'se ler),
 Amer. gen.; Amer. statesman.
văn'tage, -ground, -loaf, -point,
 -post, -set.
Vanves (vŏnv), vil. Fr.
văp'id, -ly, -ness, va pĭd'i ty.
vā'por, -a ble, -a bil'i ty, -er,
 -ing, -ing ly, -ish, -ish ness,
 -ize, -ized, -ī'zer, -ī'zing, -ous,
 -ous ness, -os'i ty, -y, -pored,
 -i form (*or* -pŏr'-), -po rif'er-
 ous (*or* văp'-), -po rim'e ter
 (*or* văp'-).
va'por-bâth, -burn er, -den'si ty,
 -douche, -en gine, -in hal er,
 -lamp, -pan, -plane, -pres'sure,
 -spout, -ten sion, va'por er-moth,
 va'por i zing-stove.
vä que'rō (-kä'-), *vaq'ue ri'a*
 (văk'a rē'a).
vä'ra.
vare, a weasel, -head ed, -wid-
 geon.
Va rennes' (-rĕnz'), tp. S. C.
Vä re'se (-rä'sā), t. It.
vā'ri a ble, -ness, -bly, -bil'i ty,
 -ance, -ant, -ate, -ā'ted, -ā'ting,
 -ā'tion, -tional, -a'tor, va ri ā'-
 tion-chart, -com pass.

văr′i cose (-kōs), -cosed, -i co′sis, -cŏs′i ty.

vă′rĭ e gate, -gā′ted, -gā′ting, -gā′tor, -gā′tion.

va rī′e ty, -hy′brid, -plān′er, va ri′-e ty show, v. store, v. the′a ter.

va rī′o la, -o lar.

vă′rĭ o loid, -rī′o lous.

va ri om′e ter.

va′rĭ ō′rum.

vă′ri ous, -ous ly, -ous ness.

var′let, -let ry.

var′nish, -er, -ing, -nished, var′-nish-pol′ish, -tree, -wat tle, var′nish ing-day.

văr′sŏ′vienne′ (-vyĕn′).

Va ru′na, Myth.

var′vels.

va′ry, -ing, -rĭed, -ried ly, -ri er.

Väs′co dä Gä′mä, Port. nav.

văse (or väz), -ful, vase′-clock, -paint′ing, -shaped.

văs′e lĭne.

Văs′quez (-kwä), mt. peak Col.

văs′sal, -age, -săled or -salled, -sal ing or -ling.

văst, -ly, -ness.

văt, -ful, -ting, vat′-blue, -net.

văt′ic, -i cide, va tic′i nal (-tĭs′-), -i nate, -nā′tor, -nā′tion.

Văt′i can, -ism, -can ist.

Vạu, *Bib.*

Vaud (vō), canton Switz.

vaude′ville (vōd′-), -vil list.

Vau dois′ (vō dwŏ′).

Vau dreuil′ (vŏ′drûl′), Governor of Can.; co. Que.

Vaughan (vawn or vạw′an), Eng. auth.; Brit. poet; Brit. gen.; Eng. divine.

vạult, -ed, -er, -ing.

vault′-cov′er, -light, -shell, -work.

vault′ing-cap′i tal, -horse, -pil′-lar, -shăft, -tile.

väunt (or vạwnt), -ed, -er, -ing, -ing ly, -ful.

Vaux (vawks), Amer. philan-thropist;—(vō), marshal of Fr.

Vä′yu, *Myth.*

Vĕ′a dar.

vĕal, -y, veal′-skin.

Ve′da (vă′- or vĕ′-), -dic.

vĕ dette′.

veer, -ing, -ing ly, veered.

veer′y.

Vĕ′ga, *Astron.; ve′ga* (vă′-), a fer-tile plain.

vĕg′e ta ble, -e tal, -tal ĭne, -tal′-i ty, -tā′ri an, -an ism, -e tate, -tā′ted, -tā′ting, -tā′tive, -tive-ly, -tive ness, -tā′tion.

vĕ′he mence, -men cy, -ment, -ment ly.

vĕ′hĭ cle, -cled, -cling.

vehm (făm), *veh′me* (fā′mĕ).

vehm′gĕ richt (făm′gĕ ric͟ht), pl. *-ric͟h′tĕ.*

veil (văl), -er, -ing, -less, veiled, *veil leuse′* (văl yêz′).

Veĭ′lĕ, t. Den.

vein (văn), -age, -ing, -less, -let, -ous, -stone, -ule, -y, vein′-like, -stuff.

Veit (fīt), Ger. painter.

Veitch (vêc͟h), Scot. metaphysi-cian.

Ve las′quez (vä läs′kĕth), Span. painter.

veld or *veldt* (velt or felt), *veld′-schoe′* (-shōō′), pl. *-schoen′* (-shōōn′).

vĕl′lum, -y, vel′lum-form.

ve lŏ′ce (vä lō′chä).

ve loc′i man (-lŏs′-), -i pede, -pe-dist, -pe′de an.

ve loc′i ty (-lŏc′-).

vĕ lours′ (-lōōr′), **vel ou tine′** (-ōō tēn′), vĕl′ūre.

ve lou té′ (vĕ lōō′tä′).

vĕ lŭ′men, pl. *-mi na.*

vĕl′vet, -ed, -ing, -y, -een′, -ver et, vel′vet breast, a duck, -flow′er, a plant, -leaf, -seed, a tree.

vel′vet-bur, -cloth, -ear, -grăss, -loom, -moss, -paint ing, -pa-per, -pile, -sat in, -work.

vĕ′nal, -ly, -nal′i ty.

vĕ năt′ic, -al, -al ly.

vend, -ed, -er, -ing, -i ble, -ble-ness, -bly, -bil′i ty, -or, ven dūe′.

ven dă văl′ (văn′-).

Ven dee′ (vŏn′dā′), dept. Fr.

Ven dé mi aire′ (vŏn dä mē âr′).

vĕn det′ta.

Ven dome′ (vŏn′dōm′), t. Fr.; Fr. gen.

---

nŏt, nôr, ūse, ŭp, ûrn, etüde, fōōd, fŏŏt, aŋger, boŋmot, t͟hus, Bac͟h.

ve nĕer', -ing, -neered', ve neer'-
cut ter, -mill, -moth, -plăn'ing,
-press, -saw, -scrăp'er, -straight'-
en ing, ve neer'ing-ham mer.
vĕn'er a ble, -ness, -a bly.
vĕn'er ate, -ā'ted, -ā'ting, -ā'tor,
-ā'tion, ve nêur'.
vĕn'er y, ve ne're al.
ve ne zo lä'nō (vă'nă'sō-).
Vĕn'e zuĕ'la, rep. S. Amer., -lan.
vĕn'geance (-jăns), venge'ful,
-ful ly, -ful ness.
vĕ'ni al, -ly, -ness, -ăl'i ty.
Vĕn'ĭce, c. It.; tp. O., Ve ne'tian.
vĕn'i son (-ĭ zn or vĕn'zn).
vĕn'om, -ous, -ous ly, -ous ness,
-omed.
ven'om-al bu'min, -duct, -fang,
-gland, -glob u lin, -mouthed,
-pep tone, -sac.
ve'noŭs, -ly, -nōse, -nō'sal, -nŏs'-
i ty.
vent, -age, -ed, -er, -ing, -less.
vent'-bit, -bush ing, -cock, -cov-
er, -fau cet, -fĕath er, -field,
-gage, -gim let, -guide, -hole,
-peg, -piece, -pin, -pipe, -plug,
-punch, -search'er, -stop per,
-tube, -wire.
ven'ta (văn'-).
ven'ter.
vĕn'til.
vĕn'tĭ lä'brum, pl. -bra.
vĕn'tĭ late, -lā'ted, -lā'ting, -lā'-
tive, -lā'tor, -lā'tion.
ven'ti la ting-brick, v. heat er,
v. mill stone, v. saw, ven'ti la-
tor-de flect'or, -hood.
Ven tose' (vŏń tōz').
vĕn'tral, -ly.
ven'tri cle, -tric'u lar, -u lose,
-u lous.
ven tril'o quist, -quis'tic, -quism,
-quy, -o quous (-o kwŭs), -tri-
lŏ'qui al, -al ly.
vĕn'ture, -some, -some ly, -some-
ness, -tured, -tūr er, -tūr ing,
-tūr ous, -ous ly, -ous ness.
vĕn'ŭe.
vĕn'ule, -u la, -u lose, -u lous.
Vĕ'nus, Myth., Ve'nus's-comb,
-ear, -fan, -pride, -shoe, -slip per,
ve nus's fly-trap.

vĕ rā'cious, -ly, -rac'i ty.
Ve'ra Cruz (vā'rä krōōs), state
and t. Mex.
Ve ra'gua (vä rä'gwä), coun. and
t. S. Amer.
vĕ'răn'da.
verb, ver'bal, -bal ism, -ist, -ize,
-ized, -ī'zing, -ĭ zā'tion, -bal ly,
-băl'i ty, -bā'ri an, -bā'ri um,
-ba'tim.
ver be'na, -oil.
ver'bi age, -bose', -bose'ly, -bose'-
ness, -bŏs'i ty.
Vĕr'cheres' (-shär'), co. Que.
ver'dant, -ly, -ness, -dan cy.
Ver'di (vâr'dē), Ital. mus. composer.
ver'dict.
ver'dĭ gris (-grēs), -green.
Vĕr'dŭń', t. Fr.
ver'dure, -less, -dured, -dūr ing.
ve rein' (fĕr īn').
Ve re scha gin' (vä rä shä gēn'),
Russ. painter.
verge, verged, ver'ging, ver'gent,
-ger, -ger ism, -ger ship, verge'-
board, -es cape'ment, -file.
Vĕr gennes' (-jĕnz'), c. Vt.—
(vĕr'zhĕn'), Fr. statesman.
Vĕr'gni aud' (-nyē ō'), Fr. revolutionist.
vĕr'i fy, -ing, -fīed, -fi'a ble, -bil'-
i ty, -fĭ ca'tive, -cā'tion.
vĕr'i ly.
vĕr i sĭm'i lar, -lar ly, -i lous,
-si mĭl'i tude.
vĕr'i ta ble, -ta bly.
vĕr'i tas, -i ty.
ver'juice.
ver'meĭl.
ver mĕ ŏl'o gy, -o gist.
ver mi cĕl'lĭ (or -chĕl'-).
ver'mĭ cĭde, -cī'dal, -mĭc'u lar,
-u late, -lā'ted, -lā'ting, -lā'tion,
-mi cule, -mic'u lose, -u lous, a.,
-u lus, n., pl. -lĭ, -mi form, -mi-
fuge, -mif'u gal.
vĕr migl'ia (-mēl'ya).
Vĕr mi'glo (-mē'lyō), It. theol.
ver mil'ion (-yŭn).
ver'min, -ous, -ous ly, -mi nate,
-nā'tion, -mip'a rous, -miv'o-
rous.

ver năc'u lar, -ism, -ize, -ized,
-ī'zing, -ĭ zā'tion, -lar ly, -lăr'-
i ty.
ver'nal, -ly, ver'nant, -nate, -nā'-
ted, -nā'ting, -nā'tion.
ver nunjt' (fĕr nōōnft').
Ve rŏ'na, prov. It.; vil. N. Y.;
bor. Pa., Vĕr ō nēse' (or -nēz').
Ver plănck', Amer. auth.
Vĕr rä za'nŏ (-tsä'-) or -za'ni
(-tsä'nē) or -raz za'no (-rät sä'-
nŏ), Florentine nav.
vĕr'ru cous, -ru'ci form, -ru'cu-
lose.
Ver sailles' (-sālz'), t. Ky.; t.
Mo.; vil. O.; -(vĕr sälye'), c.
Fr.
ver'sa tĭle, -ly, -ness, -til'i ty.
verse, -let, -man, versed, vers'ing,
ver'si cle, -sic'u lar.
verse'-an them, -col ored, -māk'-
er, -mon ger, -mon ger ing,
-serv ice, verse' tale.
ver'si col or, -ored, -or ous.
ver'si fy, -ing, -fied, -fī er, -fī-
cā'tion.
ver'sion (-shŭn), -al, -sion ist.
verst, a Russian measure.
ver stand' (fĕr stänt').
Ver stĕ'gan, Eng. antiquary.
ver'sus.
ver sute'.
ver'te bra, pl. -bræ, -bral, -bral ly,
-brate, -brā'ted, -brā'tion.
ver'tex, pl. -tex es or -ti ces
(-sēz), -ti cal, -cal ly, -cal ness,
-cal'i ty.
ver tig'i nous (-tĭj'-), -ly, -ness.
ver'tĭ gŏ, pl. -goes.
Ver tum'nus, Myth.
ver'vain, -mal'low, -sage.
verve.
vĕr'y.
Ver ze nay', a kind of wine.
vĕs'i cate, -cā'ted, -cā'ting, -ca-
to'ry, -cā'tion.
ves'i cle, ve sic'u lar, -lar ly, -late,
-lā'tion, -u lose, -u lous.
Ves på'si an (-zhĭ an), Roman
Emp.
ves'per, -tĭne, ves'per-bell, -bird,
-mouse, -spar'row.
vĕs'pi a ry, -pi form, -pĭne.

Vĕs puc'ci (-pōōt'chē), It. nav.
vĕs'sĕl, -ful.
ves'ses.
vest, -ed, -ing, -let, -ment, ves-
ti ture.
Ves'ta, Myth., ves'tal, -ta'li a.
vĕs'ti būle, -buled, -būl ing,
-tĭb'u lar, -tĭb'u late.
ves'tige (-tĭj), -tĭg'i al, -tĭg'i a ry.
vĕs'try, -dom, -man, ves'try-
room, v. board, v. clerk.
vĕs'ture, -tured, -tūr al, -tūr er.
Vĕ su'vĭ us, vol. It., -vi an.
ve tan'da.
vetch, -ling, -y.
vĕt'er an, -ize, -ized, -i zing.
vĕt'er i na ry, -nā'ri an.
vet'i tive.
vĕt'i ver, -oil.
vĕ'tŏ, pl. -tōes, -tōed, -to er, -to-
ist.
vĕt tu'ra (-tōō'-), -tu ri'no (tōō-
rē'-), pl. -ri'ni (-rē'nē).
Veuil lot' (vû yŏ'), Fr. auth.
veuve (vêv).
vex, -er, -ing, -ing ly, -ing ness,
-ed ly, -ed ness, -ā'tion, -ā'tious,
-tious ly, -tious ness, vexed.
Ve'zin (fāt'sin), Ger. actor.
vi (vē), -ap ple.
vi'a (or vē'-), a road, vī am'e ter,
-at'ic.
vī'a (or vē'-), prep., by way of.
vī'a ble, bil'i ty.
vī'a duct.
vi a ja'ca (vē'å hä'kå).
vī'al, -ful.
vī'and.
vī'brate, -brā'ted, -brā'ting, -tive,
-tor, -to ry, -bra tĭle, -til'i ty,
vī'brant, -brā'tion, -tion al, vi-
brä'tō (vē-).
vĭc'ar, -age, -ate, -ess, -ship.
vĭ cā'ri ous, -ly, -ness, -ri al, -ri an.
vĭce, n., vi'ce, prep., in the place of.
vice'ge'rent, -ge'ren cy, -re'gal,
-roy', -roy'al, -roy'ship, -roy'-
al ty.
vice-ad'mi ral, -ad'mi ral ty, -a'-
gent, -bit'ten, -chair'man, -chair'-
man ship, -cham'ber lain, -chan'-
cel lor, -chan'cel lor ship, -con'-
sta ble, -con'sul, -con'sul ship,

-dean, -gov′ern or, -king, -leg′ate,
-pres′i dent,   -pres′i dent ship,
-pres′i den cy,   -prin′ci pal,
-queen′, -rec′tor, -re′gent, -sher′-
iff, -treas′ur er, -war′den.

Vi cen′te (vē sĕn′tä), Port. dram.

vi′ce ver′sa.

Vi chy′ (vē′shē′), t. Fr.

vĭ cĭn′i ty, vĭc′i nage, -i nal.

vĭ′cious (vĭsh′us), -ly, -ness, -ci-
ŏs′i ty.

vĭ cĭs′si tude,   -tu′di na ry,   -di-
nous.

vic′tim, -ize, -ized, -ĭ′zer, -ĭ′zing,
-ĭ zā′tion.

vĭc′tor, -to ry, -tō′ri ous, -ous ly,
-ous ness.

Vic to′ri a, Queen of England; a
planetoid; a genus of water-lilies.
Vic tō′ri an, Vic to′ri a blue, V.
crape, V. cross, V. green, V. lawn,
V. Ny an′za (nĭ än′za), l. Afr.

vic tŏ′ri a, a vehicle; a breed of
pigeons.

vic to rine′ (-rēn′), a fur tippet;
a peach.'

vict′ual (vĭt′l), *pl.* -uals, -ual less,
-ualed *or* -ualled, -ual er *or*
-ler, -ual ing *or* -ling.

vict′ual ing-bill,   -de part′ment,
-house, -note, -of fice, -ship,
-yard.

vĭ cu′gna *or* -cu′na (-kōōn′ya),
-cloth, -wool.

Vi cu′na (vē kōōn′yä),   Chilian
hist.

vide (vēd), *a.*, open.

vi′dē, v., to see, *vi′de an te, v.
in fra, v. post, v. su pra.*

vi dĕl′i cet.

Vi docq′ (vē′dŏk′), Fr. detective.

vĭd′u age, -u ate, -u ā′tion, -u ous,
vĭ du′i ty.

vīe, vied, vy′ing (vī′-), -ing ly.

Vie lé′ (vē lā′), Amer. engineer.

VĬ ĕn′na,   c.   Aust.-Hung.;—(vĭ-
ĕn′na), tp. Mich.; tp. N. Y.;
Vĭ en nēse′ (*or* -nēz′).

Vi enne′ (vē ĕn′), dept., r., and
t. Fr.

vier′kleur′ (fēr′klĕr′).

Vieux temps′ (vyû tŏṅ′),   Belg.
violinist.

view (vū), -er, -ing, -less, -less ly,
-y, -i ness, viewed, view′point,
view′-hal loo′, -tel′e scope.

vig′il   (vĭj′-),   -i lance,   -i lant,
-lant ly, -i län′te (-tä).

*vi gne ron*ᵏ (vē′nyĕ rôṅ′).

vign ette′ (vĭn yet′ *or* vĭn′-), -et′ted,
-et′ter, -et′ting, -et′tist, vign et′-
ting-glass, -mask, -pa per.

Vi′gno la (vēn′yō lä), It. architect;—(-yō′la), t. It.

Vig ny′ (vēn′yē′), Fr. novelist.

Vi′go (vē′- *or* vī′-), co. and tp. Ind.;
—(vē′gō), t. Sp.

vig′or, -less, -ous, -ous ly, -ous-
ness, *vig′ō rō′sō.*

vī′king, -ism.

vi lä yet′ (vē-).

vīle, -ly, -ness.

vĭl′i fy (-fī), -ing, -fīed, -fī er, -fĭ-
cā′tion.

vil′la, -lage, -la ger.

Vil′la Clä′ra (vēl′yä), t. Cuba.

vil′laĭn (*or* -lĕn), -age, -ous, -ous-
ly, -ous ness, -y.

vil′lan age *or* -lĕin- *or* -len-, a
tenure of lands.

Vil la nue′vä (vēl′yä nwä′-),   Sp.
statesman.

Vil la nue′ va de la Se re′na
(vēl′yä nwä′vä dä lä sä rä′nä),
t. Sp.

Vil′la Re al′ (vēl′yä rä äl′),   t.
Sp.;—(vēl′lä rä äl′), dist. and c.
Port.

Vil′la Rŏ′sä (vēl′lä), t. It.

Vil la vi ci o′sa de Odon′ (vēl-
yä vē thē ō′sä dä ō dōn′), t. Sp.

Vil′la Vi ço′sa (vēl′lä vē sō′sä),
t. Braz.

Ville franche′-sur-Saone′   (vēl′-
frôṅsh′-sür′-sōn′), t. Fr.

vĭl leg′gia tu′ra (-lä′jä tōō′ra).

Vil le′nä (vēl yä′nä), t. Sp.

Ville neuve′ (vēl′nûv′), Fr. admiral.

Ville neuve′-sur-Lot′   (vēl′nûv′-
sür-lō′), t. Fr.

Ville roi′ (vēl′rwä′), Fr. marshal.

Vil lers′ (vē′yä′), Fr. philos.

Vĭl′liers (-yerz), Eng. politi.

vim.

vĭ nä′ceous (-shŭs).

vĭn äi grette′, vĭ näi′grous.

vĭ nâi′grĭ er.

Vĭn cennes′ (-sĕnz′), c. Ind.;—
(văṅ′sĕn′), t. Fr.

Vĭn′ci (-chē), Florentine painter.

vin′ci ble, -ness, -ci bil′i ty.

vin′cu lum, pl. *-la* or *-lums*.

vin′-de-fimes′ (văṅ′-dè-fēm′).

vĭn′di cate, -cā′ted, -cā′tive, -cā′-
tor, -to′ry, -cā′tion, -ca bil′i ty.

vin dic′tive, -ly, -ness.

vīne, vīned, vīn′er y, -y, vĭn′ic
(*or* vī′-), vĭn′i cul′ture, -cul′tur-
ist, -i fac têur, vī nif′er ous,
-nŏm′e ter, vī′nous, vīne′wort,
vīne′yard.

vīne′-black, -bor er, -bow er,
-clad, -cul ture, -cur cu′lĭ ŏ,
-dis ease, -dress ing, -feeder,
-for est er, -fret ter, -gall, -grub,
-hop per, -land, -lcck, -louse,
-ma ple, -mil dew, -pest,
-plume, -pull er, -rake, -slug,
-sor′rel, -sphinx, -tie, -wee vil, v.
flea-bee tle, v. gall-louse, v. inch′-
worm, v. leaf-hold er, v. leaf-hop-
per, v. root-bor er, v. saw-fly.

vĭn′e gar, -ish, -y.

vin′e gar-cru et, -eel, -fly, -māk′-
er, -plant, -tree, -yard.

vingt′-et-un′ (vaṅt′-ā-ŭṅ′), a game
of cards, *vingt′-un′*.

vin or di naire′ (văṅ), *vi′no săn′-
tō* (vē′-).

vĭnt′age, -a ger, -a ging, -ner,
-ner y.

vī′ŏl, -ist, *vi ō lŏ′ne* (vē′—nā).

Vī′o la, Bot. genus; Vī′o la, Shak.,
Twelfth Night.

vī′o la (*or* vē ō′-), a musical instrument.

vī′ŏ late, -lā′ted, -lā′ting, -lā′tive,
-lā′tor, -lā′tion.

vī′o lence, -o lent, -lent ly.

vī′o let, -wort, -o les′cent, -o lā′-
ceous, -ceous ly.

vī′o let-blind ness, -blue, -cress,
-ear, a bird, -ears, -pow′der,
-shell, -snail, -tip, -wood.

vī ō lĭn′, -ette′, -ist, -o lī′na, *vi′-
ō li′nō* (vē′ō lĕ′-), vi o lin′-bow,
-pī ăn′o, -play′er.

vī′o līne, a blue precipitate.

violle (vyōl *or* vĭ ol′le).

vi o lon cel′lo (vē′ō lŏn chĕl′lō *or*
vī ō lŏn sĕl′lō), -cel′list.

vī′per, -īne, -ish, -ous, -ous ly.

vī′per-fish, -gourd, vi′per′s-bū′-
gloss, -grăss, -wine.

vĭ rä′gŏ (*or* vĭ- *or* vē rä′gŏ), *pl.*
-goes (-gōz), -rag′i nous (-răj′-),
vir a gin′i an.

Vir′chow (vêr′chou *or* fīr′chō),
Ger. pathol.

vir′gin, -al, -al ly, -hood, -ly,
-gĭn′i ty, vir′gin-born, -knot, vir′-
gin′s-bow′er, vir′gin clay, v.
queen.

Vir′gin, -wor′ship.

Vir gin′i a, -i an.

Vir′go, *Astron*.

vĭr′ĭd, -ness, -i des′cence, -des′-
cent, vi rid′i an, -rid′i ty.

vĭr′ĭle (*or* vī′-), -i les′cence, -les′-
cent, vĭ ril′i ty (*or* vī-).

vĭr tu′ (-tōō′ *or* vêr′tōō).

vir′tūe (vêr′-), -less, -tu al, -al ly,
-al′i ty, -tued, -tu ous, -ous ly,
-ous ness, -os′i ty, vir tu ō′sŏ
(-tōō-), *pl.* -sos (-sōz) *or* -si
(-sē), *fem.* -ō′sä, *pl.* -ō′se (-sā).

vĭr′ū lence (*or* -ŏō-), -lent, -lent ly.

vī′rus, -rōse (-rōs), -rous.

vis.

vi′sa (vē′za) *or* *vi sé′* (vē zā′), *n.*,
an indorsement.

vis′age (vĭz′-), -aged.

vis′-à-vis′ (vēz′-ā-vē′).

Vi sa′yan (vē sä′yan *or* vis ā′-),
pl. -yans (-yanz).

Visch′er (fĭsh′-), Ger. auth.; Ger.
sculptor.

vis′cid, -cid′i ty.

vis′count (vī′kount), -cy, -ess,
-ship.

vis′cous, -ness, -cos′i ty.

vis′cus, pl. *vis′ce ra*, -ce ral.

vise (vīs), -man, vise′-bench, -cap,
-clamp, -press.

vi sé′ (vē zā′), v., *vi séed′* (vē-
zād′), *vi sé′ing* (vē zā′ing).

Vish′nu (-nōō), *Myth*.

vis′i ble (vĭz′-), -ness, -i bly,
-i bil′i ty.

vis′ie (vĭz′ĭ).

vi′sion (vĭzh′un), -al, -al ly, -â′ry,
-â′ri ness, -ist, -less, vi′sioned.

vis'it, -ed, -ing, -a ble, -ant, -or,
-ā'tion, vis'it-day.

vis'it ing-ant, -book, -card, -day.

vī site' (-zēt'), a cloak.

vĭs'ta, *pl.* -tas, -tåed, vis'ta scope.

vis'u al (vĭzh'-), -ize, -ized, -ĭ'zer,
-ĭ'zing, -ĭ zā'tion, -al ly, -al'i ty.

vī'tal, -ism, -ist, -is'tic, -ize
-ized, -ĭ'zer, -ī'zing, -ĭ zā'tion,
-tals, -tal ly, -tal'i ty, vī tā'tive-
ness.

Vi ta'lis (vē tä'lēs), pseudonym
of Erik Sjöberg.

vī'ta scope.

vite (vēt).

VĪ tĕl'lĭ us, Roman Emp.

vī tel'lus, -tel'lĭne, -tel'li cle.

vi'ti ate (vĭsh'i ate), -ā'ted,
-ā'ting, -ā'tor, -ā'tion, -ti os'-
i ty.

vĭt'i cul'ture, -tūr al, -tūr ist.

vĭt're ous, -ness, -os'i ty, -ric,
-rics, vĭ tres'cence, -cent.

vĭt'ri fy, -ing, -fīed, -fi a ble,
-fĭ cā'tion, -fac'tion, -fac'ture.

vĭt'ri ol, -o late, -lā'ted, -lā'ting,
-lā'tion, -ol'ic, -ri o lĭne, -ri ol-
ize, -ized, -ĭ'zing, -i'za ble,
-ĭ zā'tion.

vit'rō-di-tri'na (-dē-trē'-).

vĭt'rō phyre (-fīre).

Vi try'-le-Fran çois' (vē'trē'-l-
frŏn swŏ'), t. Fr.

Vit tŏ'ri a (vēt tŏ're ä), t. It.

vi tu'per ate, -ā'ted, -ā'ting,
-ā'tive, -tive ly, -ā'tor, -à ble,
-ā'tion.

Vi u' (vē ōō'), vil. It.

vi'va (vē'-), *vi va'ce* (vē vä'chä).

vī vā'cious (*or* vĭ-), -ly, -ness,
-văc'i ty, *vi va cis'si mo* (vē vä-
chĭs'sē mŏ).

vi van dière' (vē'vŏn'dyâr').

vĭ vā'rĭ ŭm, pl. *-ums* or *-ri a.*

vī'va vō'ce.

vive (vēv).

vīves.

viv'id, -ly, -ness.

vĭv'i fy, -ing, -fīed, -fĭ er.

vī vip'a rous, -ly, -ness.

vĭv i sect' (*or* vĭv'-), -sec'tion,
-tion al, -tion ist, -tor, -tŏ'ri um.

vi'vō (vē'-), *Mus.*

vĭx'en (-n), -ish, -en ly.

viz., abbreviation of *videlicet;* usually read 'namely.'

vĭ ziĕr' *or* -zir' (-zēr' *or* vĭz'yer),
-ate, -i al, -ship.

vĭz'or *or* vis'- (vĭz'-), -less.

Vlăd'i mir (-mēr), Grand Duke
of Russ.

Vlä di'mir (-dē'mēr), t. Russ.

Vlä di vŏs tŏk' (-dē-), fortified
seaport Sib.

vlei or *vley* (flī).

vly (vlī *or* flī).

vŏ.

vŏ cab'u lå'ry, -u list.

vŏ'cal, -ly, -ness, -ism, -ist, -ize,
-ized, -ĭ'zing, -ĭ zā'tion, -ca ble,
-cal'ic, -cal'i ty.

vŏ cā'tion, -al, -al ly.

voc'a tive.

vŏ'ce (-chä).

vŏ cĭf'er ate, -ā'ted, -ā'ting, -ā'tor,
-ā'tion, -ance, -ant, -er ous,
-ous ly, -ous ness.

Vogt (fōcht), Ger. naturalist.

vŏgue.

voice, -ful, -ful ness, -less, -less-
ness, voiced, voi'cer, -cing,
voice'-part, -thrill.

void, -a ble, -ance, -ed, -er, -ing,
-ly, -ness.

Voigt (foicht), Ger. hist.

vŏ'lant, -piece.

vo lăn'te (-tä), a two-wheeled
vehicle.

Vŏ lä pük', -ist.

vŏl'a tĭle, -ness, -til ize, -ized,
-ĭ'zing, -i'za ble, -ĭ zā'tion, -til'i ty.

vŏ lā'tion, -al, -lā'tor.

vŏl cā'no, *pl.* -noes, -can'ic, -ic-
al ly, -ca nism, -ca nist, -ca-
nol'o gy, -no log'ic al.

vŏle, voled, vŏl'ing.

vol'et (-ä).

vŏ lĭ'tion (-lĭsh'un), -al, -al ly,
-å'ry, -less, vŏl'i tive.

Volk'männ (fōlk'-), Ger. physiol.

volks'lied (fōlks'lēt'), pl. *-lied er,
volks'raad'* (-rät').

vol'ley, *pl.* -leys (-lĭz), -leyed
(-lĭd), *v.*, -ley ing, vol'ley-gun.

Vŏl pō'nĕ, title of a play by Ben
Jonson.

Volsk, t. Russ.
vŏlt, -age, -am'e ter (or vŏl-
tam'-), -a mĕt'ric, volt'-am pere,
-cou lomb, -me ter.
vōl'ta (or vŏl'-), pl. *-te* (-tä), *Mus.*
vŏl'ta e lec'tric, -e lec tric'i ty,
-e lec trom'e ter, -e lec tro mō'-
tive, vŏl'ta ism, -ta plast, -ta-
type, -tag'ra phy.
Vol tâire', Fr. auth., -tâir'i an or
-e an, -an ism, -tâir'ism.
vŏl'ti geur' (or vŏl tĭ zhêr').
vŏl'u ble, -ness, -u bly, -u bĭl'i ty.
vŏl'ûme, -umed, vŏ lŭ'mĭ nous,
-nous ly, -nous ness, -nos'i ty.
vŏl'u mē'ter, -met'ric, -ric al, -al-
ly, -me nom'e ter, -e try, vo-
lu'mi nal.
Vö'lund (vê'lōont), *Myth.*
vŏl'un ta'ry, -ta ri ly, -ta ri ness.
vŏl un teer', -ing, -teered'.
vŏ lŭp'tu ous, -ly, -ness, -tu â'ry.
vŏ lūte', -lūt'ed, -lū'tion, vo lute'-
com pass, -spring, -wheel.
vŏm'it, -ed, -ing, -ing ly, -i tive,
-i to (or vŏ mē'tō), -to ry, *-i tus*,
-i tu ri'tion (-rĭsh'un), vŏm'it-
nut.
vōō'dōō (or -dōō'), -ism.
vŏ rā'cious, -ly, -ness, -rac'i ty
(-răs'-).
Vorst (fōrst), vil. Prus.
vor'tex, *pl.* -tex es or -ti ces
(-sēz), vor'ti cal, -cal ly, -ti cose,
-tic'u lar, -tig'i nous (-tĭj'-).
vor'tex-fil'a ment, -line, -mo tion,
-ring, -sheet, -tube, -wheel.
Vosges (vōzh), mts. Fr.
Vos'si us (vŏsh'Ĭ-), Dutch philos.
vŏ'ta ry, -ta ress, -ta rist.

vŏte, -less, vŏt'ed, -er, -ing,
vote'-re cord'er, vŏt'ing-pa per.
vō'tive, -ly, -ness.
vouch, -er, -ee', -ing.
vouch safe', -ment, -safed',
-sâf'ing.
voulge (vōōzh).
vous soir' (vōō swŏr').
vow, -er, -ing, -less, vowed.
vow'-brĕach, -brĕak, -brĕak'er,
-fel low.
vow'el, -ism, -ist, -ize, -ized,
-i zing, -ly, -eled or -elled, -el-
ing or -ling.
vox, v. an gel'i ca, v. hu ma'na,
v. pop'u lī, v. quin'ta.
voy'age, -a ble, -aged, -a ger,
-a ging, *voy'a'geur'* (vwŏ'yă'-
zhêr').
vue.
vug, -gy.
Vul'can, -ist, -cā'ni an, -căn'ic,
-ca nā'lĭ a.
vul'can ize, -ized, -ĭ'zer, -ĭ'zing,
-ism, -ite, -ĭ'za ble, -ĭ zā'tion,
-ca nic'i ty, -can ol'o gy, -o log'-
ic al.
vul'gar, -ism, -ize, -ized, -ĭ'zing,
-ĭ zā'tion, -gar ly, -ness, -găr'i ty.
Vul'gate, the Latin Scriptures,
vul'gate, common; general.
vŭl'ner a ble, -ble ness, -a bil'i ty.
vul'pĭne, pin ism.
vŭl'ture, -tūr Ĭne, -tūr ish, -tūr
ism, -tūr ous, vul'ture-ra ven.
vul'va, *pl.* -væ, -var, -vi form,
vul vi'tis, vul vo ū'ter ine, -vo-
vag'i nal (-văj-), -vag i nī'tis.
Vyer' nyi' (vyĕr'nyĕ'), t. Turkestan.
vy'ing (vĭ'-). See *vie.*

W

Waa'gen (vä'-), Ger. art critic.
Wä'bä sha', co. Minn.
Wa baun'see, co. Kan.
wab'ble (wŏb'-), -bled, -bler,
-bling, -bly, wab'ble-saw.
Wach'ter (väch'-), Ger. archæol.

Wäch'ter, von (fon vĕch'-), Ger
jurist.
Wą chū'sett, mt. Mass.
Wä'cŏ, c. Tex.
wad (wŏd), -ded, -der, -ding,
wad'set.

wad′-cut ter, -hook, -punch, wad′ding-siz′er.

wad′dle (wŏd′-), -dled, -dler, -dling, -dling ly.

wăd′dy or wad dĭe (or wŏd′-), a war-club.

wăde, wăd′ed, -er, -ing.

Wä dĕ laī′, t. Afr.

Wä dē′na, co. Minn.

wad′i or wad′y (wŏd′ĭ), pl. wad′ies.

wă′fer, -ing, -y, -fered.

wa′fer-ash, -bread, -cake, -i ron, -tongs.

waf′fle (wŏf′-), -i ron.

wăft, -age, -ed, -er, -ing, -ure.

wag, -ging, -ger y, -gish, -gish ly, -gish ness, wagged, wag′-wit.

wăge, waged, wa′ging, wage′-earn er, -fund, -work, -work er, wa′ging-board.

wä′gĕn-bōom.

wä′ger, -ing, -gered, wa′ger-cup.

wä′ges, -fund, -man.

wag′gle, -gled, -gling.

Wag′ner (väg′- or wăg′-), Ger. natur.; Ger. mus. composer, -ner ism, -ist, -nē′ri an, -an ism.

wag′on, -age, -er, -ette′, -ful, wag′on way, -wright.

wag′on-bed, -boil er, -bōw, -box, -brake, -brĕast, -ceil ing, -coup ling, -drag, -ham mer, -hĕad′ed, -hoist, -jack, -load, -lock, -măs ter, -roof, -sheet, -shoe, -tongue, -top, -train, -tree, -vault.

wag′tail, -fly′catch er.

Wä hōō′, vil. Neb., wa hoo′, a tree.

Wạh′pē ton, c. N. Dak.

wăif, -pole.

wăil, -er, -ful, -ing, -ing ly, wailed.

wăin, -age, wain′wright.

wain′-house, -load, -rope, -shil ling.

wăin′scŏt, -scŏt′ed or -ted, -scŏt′ ing or -ting.

wain′scot-chair, -clock, -oak, -pan el.

Waī ping′, t. China.

wăist, -ed, -er, waist′band, -coat.

waist′-aṇ′chor, -belt, -board,

-boat, -boat er, -cloth, -deep, -high, -pan el, -piece, -rail, -torque, -tree.

wăit, -ed, -er, -er age, -er ing, -ing, -ing ly, -ress.

wait′-fee, -serv′ice, -trĕb′le, wait′-ing-maid, -room, -wom′an.

wăive, waived, wăiv′er, waiv′ing.

Wä kä mät′su (-sōō), t. Japan.

wăke, -ful, -ful ly, -ful ness, wăk′er, -ing, waked or woke, wake′-rob in, -time.

wăk′en (-n), -en er, -en ing, -ened.

Wal′de mar (wŏl′- or väl′-), King of Den.

Wal den′ses (wŏl dĕn′sēz), -den′ sian (-shan).

wald′flute (wŏld′-).

wald′grăve (wŏld′-), wald′horn.

Wald′heīm (vält′-), t. Ger.

wăle, waled, wāl′ing, wale′-piece.

wăl′er, a horse.

walk (wạk), -er, -ing, walked, walk′o′ver, -out, walk′-a round′.

walk′ing-beam, -cane, -dress, -fan, -fern, -fish, -foot, -leaf, a plant; an insect, -pa pers, -stăff, -stick, -straw, -sword, -tick et, -twig, an insect, -ty rant, a bird, -wheel, w. gen′tle man, w. la dy, w. sta tion er.

wạll, -er, -ing, walled, wall′-flow er, a plant; a person, -hick, -wort.

wall′-ar cade, -bar ley, -bear ing, -bird, -box, -clamp, -clock, -crane, -creep er, -cress, -desk, -drill, -en gĭne, -eye, -eyed, -fern, -fruit, -geck o, -ger man der, -gil ly flow er, -gre nade′, -hawk′weed, -ink, -knot, -less, -let tuce, -light, -liz ard, -louse.

wall′-moss, -net, -newt, -paint ing, -pa per, -pel li to ry, -pen ny wort, -pep per, -pie, -piece, -plat, -plate, -pock et, -rib, -rock, -rock et, -rue, -salt pe ter, -scrăp′er, -space, -spleen′-wort, -spring, -tent, -tooth, -tow er, -tree, -vase, -wash er, -wasp.

wal′la (wŏl′-), a merchant or agent.

wal'la by (wŏl'-), -la rōō'.
Wal'lach (wŏl'lăk), -lā'chi an
(-kĭ-).
Wäl lă'chi a (-kĭ-), prin. Europe.
Wal'la wal'la (wŏl'-), co. Wash.
Wal'len steĭn (wŏl- *or* väl'-),
Aust. gen.
wal'let (wŏl'-), -ful.
Wal lōōn' (wŏl-), a race; a dialect; wal loon', a disease.
wal'lop (wŏl'-), -er, -ing, -loped.
wal'low (wŏl'-), -er, -ing, -lowed.
Walmes'ley (wŏmz'lĭ), Eng. monk
and schol.
wạl'nut, -moth, -oil, -scale,
-sphinx, -tree.
Wal pur'gĭs night (väl pōōr'-).
wal'rus (wŏl'-), -bird, -i'ron.
Wal'thăm (wŏl'-), c. Mass.
waltz (wạlts), -er, -ing, waltzed.
wam'mi can (wŏm'-).
wăm'mus.
wam'pum (wŏm'-), -pum-pēag,
-snake.
wam sut'ta (wŏm-).
wan (wŏn), -ly, -ness, -ning,
-nish, wanned.
wand (wŏnd), -y.
wan'der (wŏn'-), -er, -ing, -ing-
ly, -dered, wan'der ing-sail'or,
a plant.
wan der ōō' (wŏn-).
wāne, wāned, wān'ing, wān'cy,
wane'-cloud.
wạn'gun.
wạnt, -ed, -ing, -age, want'-hill.
wa'n't (wạnt), was not.
wan'ton (wŏn'tün), -ing, -ly,
-ness, -toned.
wap (wŏp), -ping, wapped.
Wä pä kŏn ĕt'a, vil. O.
wap'ĭ tĭ (wŏp'-), a stag.
wap'pa tŏ (wŏp'-), a plant.
Wap'pin ger (wŏp'pĭn jer), tp.
N. Y.
wạr, -ring, -ri or, warred, war'-
craft, -fare, -like, -wolf.
war'-ax, -cart, -chief, -cloud, -cry,
-dănce, -ea'gle, -fain, -flail, -flame,
-fork, -gear, -god, -ham mer,
-horse, -knife, -man, -of fice,
-paint, -păth, -plume, -proof,
-sad dle, -scythe, -ship, -song,

-thought, -wast ed, -wea rĭed,
-whip, -whoop, -worn, war tax,
war'ri or-ant.
wạr'ble, -bled, -bler, -bling,
-bling ly, war'ble-fly.
wạrd, -ed, -ing, -mote, -robe,
-ship, -wit, wards'man, ward'-
hold ing, -mote, -pen ny, -room,
ward'ing-file.
ward'en (-n), -en ry, -en ship.
wåre, -house, -house man, -room,
ware-goose.
wa re'ga-fly.
Wåre'ham, vil. Mass.
Wår'ing că'ble, Wår'ing's meth'-
od.
wạrm, -er, -ing, -ly, -ness,
warmed, warmth.
warm'-blood ed, -head ed, -heart-
ed, -heart ed ness, -sĭd'ed,
warm'ing-pan, -stone.
wạrn, -er, -ing, -ing ly, warned,
warn'ing-piece, -wheel.
wạrp, -age, -er, -ing, warped.
warp'-beam, -dress er, -dress ing,
-dye ing, -frame, -lace, -land,
-ma chine, -net, -roll er, -stitch,
-thread.
warp'ing-bank, -block, -chock,
-hook, -jack, -ma chine, -mill,
-past, -pen ny.
war'rant (wŏr'-), -a ble, -a ble-
ness, -a bly, -er *or* -or, -ee',
-y, war'rant-of fi cer.
war'ren (wŏr'-), -er.
wạrt, -ed, -less, -let, -y, wart'-
weed, -wort.
wart'-cress, -grăss, -herb, -hog,
-pock, -shaped, -snake, -spurge,
wart'y-faced.
War'wick (wŏr'ĭk), Duke of
Northumberland; Eng. soldier;
co. Eng.
Wạr'wick, co. Va.; tp. N. Y.;
tp. R. I.
wă'ry, -ri ly, -ri ness.
was (wŏz).
Wäs'cŏ, co. Ore.
Wä sĕ'ca, co. Minn.
wash (wŏsh), -a ble, -er, -ing,
-y, washed, wash'dish, -man,
-out, -tail, a bird, wash'er man,
-er wom an.

---

nŏt, nôr, ūse, ŭp, ûrn, etüde, fōōd, fŏŏt, aŋger, boṅmot, thus, Bach.

wash'-back, -ball, -ba sin, -bås-
ket, -bear, -bee tle, -board,
-boil er, -bot tle, -bowl, -brew,
-cloth, -day, -dirt, -draw ing,
-gild ing, -gourd, -grav el,
-house, -lĕaṭh er, -off, -pan,
-pot, -rag, -stand, -stuff, -tub.
wash'er-cut ter, -gage, -hoop.
wash'ing-bear, -crys tals, -drum,
-en gine, -gourd, -house, -hutch,
-ma chine, -pow der, -roll ers,
-shield, -ta ble, -trom mel, -ves-
sel.
wä'shĭ ba.
Wash'oe (wŏsh'ō), co. Nev.
Wash'te naw, co. Mich.
Wasmes (väm), vil. Belg.
wasp (wŏsp), -ish, -ish ly, -ish-
ness, -y.
wasp'-bee, -bee tle, -fly, -grub,
-kite, -waist ed.
was'sail (wŏs'sĕl *or* -sĬl), -er.
was'sail-bout, -bowl, -bread,
-can dle, -cup, -horn.
wăste, -ful, -ful ly, -ful ness, -less,
-ness, -way, wăst'ed, -er, -ing,
-ing ly, -a ble, -age, -y.
waste-bås ket, -board, -book,
-card, -dust er, -gate, -pal let,
-pick er, -pipe, -pre vent er,
-trap, -weir, -well.
Wä tạu'ga, co. N. C.
watch (wŏtch), -er, -ing, -ful,
-ful ly, -ful ness, watched,
watch'māk er, -word, -work.
watch'-bill, -box, -can dle, -case,
-chain, -clock, -dog, -fire,
-glåss, -guard, -gun, -hĕad er,
-house, -jew el, -key, -light,
-mark, -meet ing, -night, -of-
fi cer, -oil, -pa per, -peel,
-pock et, -pole, -rate, -spring,
-stand, -tac kle, -tel e scope,
-tow er, -wise, -work, watch'-
ing-can dle, watch'-case cut ter.
wạ'ter, -age, -er, -ing, -ish, -ish-
ness, -tered.
wa'ter course, -cress, -cup, a
plant, -fall, -flow, -hole, *v.*,
-leaf, a plant, -man, -mel on,
-phone, -proof, *n.*, -scape, -shed,
-side, -spout, -way, -weed, a
plant, -witch, -wort.

wa'ter-ad der, -ag ri mo ny, -al-
oe, -a nal y sis, -aṇ chor, -ante
lope, -ap ple, -a rum, -ash,
-av ens, -back, -bag, -bail iff,
-bal ance, -bar, -ba rom'e ter,
-băr rel, -bar row, -bas il,
-băth, -bat ter y, -bean, -bear,
-bear er, -bed, -beech, -bee tle,
-bel lows, -bells, -bet o ny,
-bird, -bis cuit, -black'bird,
-blåst, -blebs, -blink, -blinks,
-blob, -blue, -board, -boat,
-boat man, -borne, -bot tle,
-bound, -box, -brain, -brash,
-brax y, -breaṭh er, -bridge,
-brose, -buck, -buc kler, -budg-
et, -buf fa lo, -bug, -butt.
wa'ter-cab bage, -cal a mint, -cal-
trop, -can, -can cer, -caṇ ker,
-cap, -car pet, -car riage, -car-
ri er, -cart, -căsk, -cat, -ca vy,
-cel er y, -cell, -cen ti ped,
-char ger, -chat, -check, -chest-
nut, -chick en, -chick weed,
-chiṇ ka pin, -ci ca da, -cis tern,
-clam, -clock, -clos et, -cock,
-col ly, -col or, -col ored, -com-
pa ra tor, -cool er, -core, -cow,
-crack er, -crăft, -crake, -crane,
-crow, -crow'foot, -cure.
wa'ter-deck, -deer, -deer let,
-dev il, -dock, -doc tor, -dog,
-drag on, -drain, -drain age,
-dress ing, -drink er, -drip,
-drop, -drop per, -drop wort,
-dust, -ea gle, -el der, -el e-
phant, -el e va tor, -elm, -en-
gine, -e riṇ go, -er mine, -ex-
tract or, -farm ing, -fĕaṭh er,
-fĕaṭh er foil, -fen nel, -fern,
-fight, -fig wort, -fil ter, -find-
er, -fire, -flag, -flan nel, -flax-
seed, -flea, -float, -flood,
-floun der, -flow ing, -fly, -foot,
-fowl, -frame, -fright, -fringe,
-fur row.
wa'ter-gage, -gall, -gap, -gas, -gate,
-gav el, -ger man der, -gĬld er,
-gil ly flow er, -glad i ole, -glåss,
-god, -gram pus, -gråss, -gru el,
-guard, -gull, -gum, -gut, -hair'-
gråss, -ham mer, -hare, -haze,
-heat er, -hem lock, -hemp,

-hen, -hick o ry, -hoar'hound,
-hog, -hole, *n.*, -horse, -horse-
tail, -hys sop, -ice, -inch, -in-
di ca tor, -in ject or, -jack et,
-joint, -juṇ ket, -kel pie.

wa'ter-lade, -laid, -lav er ock,
-leg, -lem on, -lens, -len til,
-let tuce, -lev el, -lil y, -lime,
-line, -liv er wort, -liz ard, -lo-
be'li a, -lock, -lo cust, -logged,
-lot, -lo tus, -lung, -lute, -main,
-maize, -man tle, -ma ple,
-mar i gold, -mark, -mĕad ow,
-meas ur er, -me ter, -mil foil,
-mill, -mint, -mite, -moc ca sin,
-mole, -mon i tor, -moṇ key,
-moss, -moth, -mo tor, -mouse.

wa'ter-net, -newt, -nix y, -nut,
-nymph, -oak, -oats, -o pos sum,
-oī de al, -or gan, -ou zel, -ov-
en, -ox, -pad da, -pang, -pars-
ley, -pars nip, -part ing, -par-
tridge, -pas sage, -pen ny wort,
-pep per, -per si ca'ri a, -pe-
wit, -pheas ant, -pi et, -pig,
-pil lar, -pim per nel, -pine,
-pipe, -pip it, -pitch er, -plane,
-plant, -plan tain, -plate, -plat-
ter, -plow, -poise, -pore, -post,
-pot, -pow er, -pox, -press,
-prism, -priv i lege, -proof, *a.*,
-pro pel ler, -pump, -pup py,
-pur ple, -purs lane.

wa'ter-qualm, -quin tain, -rab-
bit, -rad ish, -rail, -ram, -ran-
ny, -rat, -rate, -rat tler, -reed,
-rent, -res er voir, -ret, -ret-
ting, -rice, -rob in, -rock et,
-room, -rose, -rot, -route, -sail,
-sal a man der, -sal low, -sap-
phire, -scor pi on, -screw, -seal,
-sen green, -ser pent, -shell,
-shield, -shoot, -shrew, -sil ver-
ing, -sink, -skin, -skip per,
-sky, -slāt'er, -smart weed,
-smoke, -snail, -snake, -soak,
-socks, -sod den, -sol dier, -sor-
rel, -sou chy, -space, -span iel,
-spar row, -speed well, -spi der,
-spike, -spin ner, -sprite,
-stairs, -stand ing, -star, -star-
grăss, -star wort, -stream,
-strīd'er, -sup ply, -sys tem.

wa'ter-tab by, -ta ble, -tank,
-tap, -tar get, -tath, -tel e-
scope, -ther mom e ter, -thief,
-this tle, -thrush, -thyme, -tick,
-ti ger, -tight, -tow er, -trĕad er,
-tree, -tre foil, -trunk, -tube,
-tu pe lo, -tur key, -twist,
-twy'er, -vac u ole, -var nish,
-vas cu lar, -vine, -vi o let, -vi-
per, -vole, -wag tail, -weed,
any weed growing in water,
-wee vil, -wheel, -white, -whorl-
grăss, -wil low, -wing, -withe,
-wood, -work, -work er, -works,
-worm, -worn, -wraith, -yam,
-yar row.

wa'ter ing-bri dle, -buck et, -càll,
-can, -cart, -house, -place, -pot,
-trough.

Wạ'ter vliĕt', tp. N. Y.

watt, -me ter.

Wät teau' (-tō'), W. back, W.
bod'ice, W. cos'tume, W. man'-
tle.

wat'tle (wŏt'-), -tled, -tling,
wat'tle work.

wat'tle-bark, -bird, -crow, -gum,
-jaws, -tree, -tur key.

Watt'wyl (vät'vĭl), vil. Switz.

Wạu kē'gan, c. Ill.

Wạu'kĕ sha, co. Wis.

Wạu kŏn', t. Ia

wạul.

Wạu pä'ca, co. Wis.

Wạu pŭn', c. Wis.

wave, -less, -let, waved, wāv'ing,
wāv'i ly, -i ness, wāv'y, wave'-
son.

wave'-ac tion, -brĕast, -crest,
-front, -goose, -length, -line,
-loaf, -mold ing, -mo tion, -of'-
fer ing, -path, -shell, -sur face,
-trap, -trough, -worn, wāv'ing-
frame, wāv'y-barred.

wă'ver, -er, -ing, -ing ly, -ing-
ness, -y, -ered, wa'ver-drag on,
-roll er.

wă'vey, a goose.

waw'prōos.

wax, -en, -er, -ing, -y, -i ness,
waxed, wax'ber ry, -bill, a bird,
-flow er, -weed, -wing, a bird,
-work, -work er.

---

wax′-bush, -chan dler, -cloth,
-clus ter, -dolls, a plant, -end,
-gourd, -in sect, -light, -mod eling, -moth, -myr tle, -paint ing,
-palm, -pa per, -pine, -pink,
-plant, -pock et, -red, -scale,
-tree, -worm.
wax doll, w. o pal, w. pol ish,
waxed cloth, waxed end.
Wăx′a hăch′iĕ, t. Tex.
wax′ĕ.
way, -board, -bread, a plant,
-bung, a bird, -fare, -fâr′er,
-fâr′ing, -go ing, -goose, -less,
-side, -wode, -worn, -wort.
wä yä′ka.
way′-bar ley, -beat en, -bill, -bit,
-gate, -grăss, -māk′er, -mark,
-post, -shăft, -slĭd ing, -this tle,
-thorn, -war den, -wise, way′-
far ing-tree.
way′ bag gage, w. pas sen ger,
w. sta tion, w. traf′fic, w.
train.
way lay′ (or way′-), -ing, -er,
-laid′.
way′ward, -ly, -ness.
Wa zemmes′ (vå zĕm′), t. Fr.
we.
Wĕ′a, tp. Kan.
wĕak, -en, -en er, -en ing, -ened,
-ling, -ly, -li ness, -ness, -fish.
weak′-built, -eyed, -hand ed,
-head ed, -heart ed, -hinged,
-kneed, -mind ed, -mind edness, -sight ed, -spir it ed.
wĕal.
weald, a wold.
Wĕald, a district in Kent.
wĕalth, -y, -i ly, -i ness.
wĕan, -ing, -ling, weaned.
wĕap′on, -less, -oned, weap′onsmith.
Wĕar, r. Eng.
weâr, -a ble, -er, -ing, wore,
worn, weâr′-i ron, -plate, wear′-
ing-ap par′el.
Wĕare, tp. N. H.
wĕa′ry, -ing, -rĭed, -ri ful, -ful ly,
-less, -ly, -ri ness, -some, -somely, -some ness.
wea′sand (-zand).
wĕa′sel (-zl), -cat, -coot, -duck,

-faced, -fish, -le mur, -snout,
-spi der.
wĕaŧħ′er, -ing, -ly, -li ness, -most,
-cock, -ered.
weaŧħ′er-bĕat′en, -bit, -bit′ten,
-bitt, -board, -board ing, -bow,
-box, -breed er, -căst, -căst er,
-chart, -cloth, -con tact, -cross,
-dog, -eye, -fend, -fish, -fore′-
căst, -gage, -gall, -glăss, -gleam,
-head, -house, -map, -molding, -no ta′tion, -plant, -proof,
-proph et, -re port, -roll, -service, -shore, -sign, -spy, -stain,
-sta tion, -strip, -sym bol, -tile,
-vane, -wăft, -wind, -wise, -work,
-wreck, W. Bu′reau.
wĕave, wĕav′er, -ing, wove or
weaved, wŏv′en (-n) or weaved.
weave′-house, wĕav′er-bird, -finch,
-shell.
web, -bing, -by, webbed.
web′-eye, -eyed, -fin gered, -foot,
-foot ed, -foot ed ness, -saw,
-toed, -wheel, -winged, -work,
-worm, web′ ma chine′, w. press.
Wĕb′er (or vä′br), Ger. Sanscrit
schol.; Ger. painter; Ger. hist.;
von We′ber (fŏn vä′ber), Ger.
mus. composer. Wĕ′ber, co.
and riv. Utah.
wed, -ded, -der, -ding, -lock,
wed′-fee.
wed′ding-cake, -chest, -clothes,
-day, -dow er, -dress, -fa vor,
-feast, -flight, -flow er, -garment, -knife, -knot, -ring, -song.
wedge, -like, -wise, wedged,
wedg′ing, -y, wedge′bill, a bird.
wedge′-bone, -cut ter, -formed,
-mi crom′e ter, -pho tom′e ter,
-play, -press, -shaped, -shell,
-tailed, -valve, wedg′ing-crib.
Wedg′wood scale, W. ware.
Wednes′day (wĕnz′-).
wee.
weed, -ed, -er, -ing, -y, -i ness,
-less.
weed′-grown, -hook, weed′er-
clips.
weed′ing-chis el, -for ceps, -fork,
-hoe, -hook, -i ron, -pin cers,
-rim, -shears, -tongs, -tool.

week, -ly, week'-day, -work.
ween, weened.
weep, -ing, -ing ly, -er, wept, weep'ing-cross, -wid ow, a plant, weep'ing ash, w. birch, w. grăss, w. mon key, w. oak, w. pipe, w. pop lar, w. rock, w. sin ew, w. spring, w. tree, w. wil low.
Weerdt (wärt), t. Netherlands.
wee'ver, a fish, -fish.
wee'vil (-vl), -viled *or* -villed, -vil y *or* -ly.
wĕft, -fork, -hook.
Weh'lau (vä'lou), t. Prus.
We'i (wä'ē), prov. China.
weï gĕ'lĭ a (*or* -jĕ'-) *or* weï'gĕl a.
weigh (wā), -a ble, -age, -er, -er ship, -ing, weigh'man.
weigh'-bank, -beam, -board, -bridge, -can, -house, -lock, -mǎs'ter, -shǎft.
weigh'ing-cage, -house, -ma-chine, -scale, -scoop.
weight (wāt), -ed, -ing, -y, -i ly, -i ness, -less, weight'-nail, -rest.
Wei'mar (vī'mär), c. Ger.
Wêir, c. Kan.
wêir, -fish ing, -ta ble.
wêird, -ly, -ness.
Weiss'kirch en (vīs'kïrch'-), t. Hung.; t. Aust.
wel'come (-kŭm), -comed, com er, -ing.
weld, -a ble, -ed, -er, -ing, -less.
weld'-bore, -i ron, -steel, weld'-ing-heat, -ma chine, -pow der, -swage, -trans form'er.
wel'fare.
wĕl'kin.
well, *a.,* better, best, well, *n.,* well, *v.,* -ing, welled, well'a day, well'a way.
well-ad vised', -bal'anced, -be-haved', -be'ing, -be loved', -be lov'ed, *a.* and *n.,* -bor'er, -born', -brĕathed', -bred', -buck'et, -chain', -con-di'tioned, -con duct ed, -curb', -deck', -deck'er, -dis posed, -do'er, -do'ing, -drain', -dress'-ing, -drill', -earned', -fa'vored, -fed, -flow'er ing, -found'ed,

-graced', -ground'ed, -grǎss', -hĕad', -hole', -house', -in-formed', -in ten'tioned, -judged', -knit', -known', -man'nered, -mean'ing, -meant', -nigh', -off', -or dered, -pack'ing, -pleas'ing, -paint'ed, -pro por'tioned, -rĕad', -reg'u la ted, -room', -round ed, -set', -sink'er, -smack', -sphe-rom'e ter, -spo'ken, -spring', -stair'case, -sweep', -tem'pered, -tim'bered, -timed', -tomb', -trap', -tube', -turned', -wa'ter, -wish'er, -won', -worn', well'-to-do'.
Welles (wĕlz), Sec. of U. S. navy.
Welles'ley (wĕlz'lĭ), Brit. states-man; Amer. fem. college.
Welsh, -man, W. rab bit, W. ware, W. wig, Welsh'man's-breech es, a plant; welsh, *v.,* -er, -ing.
wĕlt, -ed, -ing, welt'-cut ter, -guide, -knife, -lĕath er, -ma-chine, -shoul ders, -trim mer.
wel'ter, -ing, -tered, wel'ter-race, -stakes, -weight.
Wemyss (wēms), par. Scot.;— (wēmz), Eng. politician.
wen, -nish, -ny.
wench, -less, -like.
wend, -ed, -ing.
Wend, a member of the Slavic race, -ic, -ish.
wĕ nõ'na, a serpent.
Wer ni gĕ rŏ'dĕ (vĕr'nĭ-), t. Prus.
Wer'ther (wer'ter *or* ver'-), the hero of Goethe's romance, -ism, -thē'ri an (-tē'-).
wĕr'wolf *or* wēre'-, -ish, -ism.
We'ser (vä'zer), r. Ger.
Wes'ley, -an, -an ism.
west, -er ly, -ern, -ern er, -ern-ism, -ern most, -ing, -most, -ward, -ward ly, -wards, West End, a part of London, the West, a section of country, West-In'dian, -Vir gin'i an, west'-bound, *a.,* west'-north west', west'-south west', West'ern Re-serve', W. States.
West Brom'wich (brŭm'ĭj), bor. Eng.

West'ches ter, co. N. Y.
West Ches'ter, vil. N. Y.; c. Pa.
wet, -ted, -ter, -ting, -tish, -ness.
wet'-bird, -broke, -cup, -cup-
ping, -nurse, -pack, *n.*, -press,
n., -shod, wet'ter-off, wet'ting-
ma chine', -trough, wet bob, w.
goods, w. meth'od, w. plate, w.
pro vis'ions.
weth'er.
Wet'ter horn (vĕt'-), mt. peak
Switz.
Wet tin' (vĕt tēn'), t. Ger.
wey (wā).
Wey'mouth (wā'mŭth), tp. Mass.
whack, -er, -ing, whacked.
whāle, whaled, whāl'er, -er y,
-ing, whale'back, a vessel, -bone,
-man, whal'ing man.
whale'-bar na cle, -bird, -boat,
-brit, -built, -fin, -fisher, -fish-
er y, -flea, -food, -head, -hunt er,
-lance, -line, -louse, -oil, -rīnd,
-shark, -ship, -shot, whale's-food,
-tongue, whale'bone-whale, w.
calf.
whāl'ing-gang, -gun, -man, -mås-
ter, -port, -rock et, -sta tion.
whăng, -ing, -doo'dle, whanged,
whang'-lĕath er.
whä're (-rā).
wharf, *pl.* wharfs *or* wharves,
-age, -ing, -in ger (-jer *or* -ing er),
-man, -mås ter, wharf'-boat, -rat.
what (whŏt), -ev er, -so ev er,
what'-like, -not.
whēal, a pimple; a pustule; a
mine, wheal'-worm.
whēat, -en, wheat'ear, a bird.
wheat'-bird, -brush, -bug, -cat-
er pil lar, -chā fer, -crack er,
-drill, -duck, -ear, ear of wheat,
-eel, -field, -fly, -grād er,
-gråss, -land, -mag got, -midge,
-mil dew, -mite, -moth, -pest,
-rid dle, -rust, -scour er, -scour-
ing, -sep a ra tor, -thief, -thrips,
-wee vil, -worm.
whee'dle, -dled, -dler, -dling.
wheel, -age, -er, -ing, -y, wheeled,
wheel'bar row, -man, -seed, a
plant, -stone, -way, -work,
-wright, wheels'man.

wheel'-an i mal, -an i mal'cule,
-band, -bar, -ba rom'e ter, -base,
-bear er, -bear ing, -bird, -boat,
-box, -bug, -car riage, -case,
-chain, -chair, -col ter, -cross,
-cul ti va tor, -cut, -cut ting,
-drāft, -en grav ing, -fire, -fix-
ing, -guard, -head, -hoe, -horse,
-house, -jack, -joint er, -lāthe,
-lock, -ore, -or gan, -out, -pit,
-plate, -plow, -race, -rib, -rope,
-seat, -shaped, -spic ule, -stitch,
-swarf, -tire, -tooth, -tree,
-ur chin, -worm, wheel win dow.
wheeze, wheezed, wheez'ing, -y,
-i ly, -i ness.
whelk, -y, whelked, whelk'-tin gle.
whelm, -ing, whelmed.
whelp, -ing, -less, whelped.
when, -ev'er, -so ev'er, -e'er.
whence, -so ev'er, whence-ev er.
where (whâr), -a bout, -a bouts,
-as, -at, -by, -fore, -from', -in',
-in'to (*or* -to'), -in so ev'er, -of',
-on', -out', -so, -so e'er', -so-
ev'er, -to', -un'der, -up on',
-with', -with al', wher e'er',
-ev'er.
whĕr'ry, -man.
wherve.
whet, -ted, -ter, -ting, whet'-
stone, whet'-slate, whet'stone-
slate.
wheth'er.
whew (whū), -er, a bird, whew'-
duck.
Whew'ell (hū'el), Eng. philos.
whew'ell īte (whū'- *or* hū'-).
whey (whā), -ish, -ish ness, -ey.
whey'-beard, -cure, -face, -faced,
-whig, -worm.
which, -ev'er, -so ev er.
whĭd'ah, -bird, -finch.
whiff, -ing, whiffed, whĭf'fet,
-fer, whiff'ing-tac'kle.
whif'fle, -fled, -fler, -fler y, -fling.
whif'fle tree. See *whippletree.*
Whig, -ga more, -gar chy (-ky),
-ger y, -gish, -gish ly, -gish-
ness, -gism, -ling.
while, whiled, whil'ing, whīles.
whī'lom (*or* -lōm).
whīlst.

---

fāte, făt, fär, fạll, fâre, fåst, sofå, mēte, mĕt, hêr, ice, ĭn nōte,

whĭm, -my, -si cal, -cal ly, -cal-
ness, -cal'i ty, whim'-gin, -shåft.
whim'per, -er, -ing, -ing ly,
-pered.
whin, -ber ry, -chack er, a bird,
-chat, a bird, -cow, a bush,
-stone, -yard.
whin'-ax, -bruis er, -bush cat,
-gray, -lin net, -lin tie, -rock,
-sill, -spär'row.
whĭne, whined, whīn'er, -ing,
-ing ly.
whĭnge, whinged.
whĭn'ny, -ing, -nĭed.
whip, -per, -ping, -py, -ster,
whipped.
whip'cat, a person, -fish, -jack,
a person, -saw, v., -saw ing,
-snake, -stitch, v., -stitch ing,
-tail, -worm.
whip'-cord, -cord y, -crane, -crop,
-gin, -gråft, -gråss, -hand, -han-
dle, -hang er, -hem, -lash,
-māk er, -māk ing, -net, -ray,
-rod, -roll, -rōw, -saw, n.,
-scor pi on, -shaped, -sock et,
-ståff, -stalk, -stick, -stitch, n.,
-stock, -top.
whip'per-in', -snap'per, whip'-
ping-boy, -hoist, -post, -snap-
ping, -top, whip'-and-der'ry,
whip'sey-der ry, whip'-tom-kel'-
ly, a bird.
whip'ple tree or whif'fle tree.
whip'poor will'.
whir (whêr), -ring, whirred.
whirl, -er, -ing, whirled.
whirl'bat, -blåst, -bone, -i gig,
-pool, -wind.
whirl'-a bout, -pil lar, -worm,
whirl'ing-ta ble, -ma chine.
whish, -ing, whished.
whisk, -ing, whisked.
whisk'er, -ered, -er y, -er less.
whis'ket.
whis'ky or -key, -fris ky, -jack,
-john, -liv er.
whis'per, -er, -ing, -ing ly, -y,
-pered, whis'per ing-gal'ler y.
whist, -play, -play'er.
whis'tle (-l), -tled, -tler, -tling,
whis'tle wing, a duck, -wood, a
tree.

whis'tle-cup, -drunk, -fish, whis'-
tling-shop, whis'tling är'row,
w. buoy, w. coot, w. dick, w.
duck, w. ea'gle, w. mar'mot, w.
plo'ver, w. snipe, w. swan, w.
thrush.
whit, -bee.
Whit-Mon'day, Whit-Tues'day.
whīte, -ness, whīt'ish, -ish ness,
white'back, a duck; a tree,
-bait, a fish, -beam, a tree,
-beard, a man, -bel ly, a bird,
-bill, a bird, -blow, a plant,
-bon net, a person, -bot tle, a
plant, -boy, a person, -bug,
-cap, a person; a bird, -coat, a
seal, -fish, -håuse, a fish, -head,
a bird, -rump, a bird, -scop, a
bird, -side, a duck, -smith,
-spot, a moth, -spur, a person,
-stone, -tail, a bird, a deer,
-throat, a bird; -tip, a bird,
-top, a grass, -wall, -wash,
-washed, -wash er, -wash ing,
-weed, -wing, a bird, -wood, a
tree, -worm, -wort.
white'-armed, -backed, -bāk'er,
a bird, -barred, -beaked,
-beard ed, -bel lied, -billed,
-breast'ed, -brin dled, -browed,
-crest ed, -crowned, -ear, a
mollusk, -eared, -eye, a bird,
-eyed, -faced, -fa vored, -flesh er,
a grouse, -flow ered, -foot ed,
-front ed, -grub, a beetle, -gum,
a disease, -hand ed, -håss,
-hěad ed, -horse, a shrub; a
foam-crested wave, -hot.
white'-leg, a disease, -limed,
-line, a., -lined, -lipped, -list-
ed, -liv ered, -marked, -mouthed,
-necked, -pot, a food, -rib'bon,
a., -rumped, -salt ed, -shåft ed,
-sīd'ed, -spot ted, tailed,
-thighed, -throat ed, -tree,
-wave, a moth, -winged, white'-
beam-tree.
white' al loy, w. båss, w. bråss,
w. bronze, w. ce'dar, w. cop'-
per, w. dai'sy, w. damp, w. gar'-
net, w. gråss, w. gull, w. hake,
w. heath, w. hěr'ring, w. lark,
w. lau'rel, w. mil'ler, w. mouse,

---

nŏt, nôr, ūse, ŭp, ûrn, etüde, fōōd, fŏŏt, aṇger, boûmot, thus, Bach.

w. pud'ding, w. rib'bon, *n.*, w.
vit'ri ol, w. whale, w. wolf.

White'chap'el, suburb of London.

White Fri ar, W. House, W.
Huns, W. Ju ra.

White'fiĕld (whĭt'-), Eng. preacher; vil. Me.; tp. N. H.; t. Eng.

Whīte'ford, tp. Mich.

whĭt'en (-n), -en er, -en ing,
whit'en ing-slick er, -stone.

whith'er, -so ev er.

whĭt'ing, -pol lack, -pout.

whĭt'leăth er.

whĭt'ling, a fish.

whĭt'lōw, -wort, whit'low-grass.

Whĭt'sun, -tide', -sun day, -mon-
day.

Whit'sun-ale, -far things, -la dy,
-Mon day, -Tues day, -week.

whĭt'taw, whit'-taw er.

whĭt'tle, -tled, -tler, -tling, -tlings.

whiz, -zer, -zing, -zing ly, whizzed,
whiz'zing-stick.

who (hōō), *pos.* whose, *obj.*
whom, who ev'er, -sō, -sō ev'er,
whose sō ev'er.

whŏa (hwō).

whole, -ness, -some, -some ly,
-some ness, whōl'ly.

whole'-col ored, -foot ed, -heart'-
ed, -hoofed, -length, -skinned,
-snipe, -souled, whole note, w.
stitch, w. team.

whole'sale, -saled, -sāl'er, -sāl'-
ing.

whom (hōōm), -ev'er, -so ev'er.

whoop (hōōp), -er, -ing, whooped,
whoop'-hymn, -lä, whoop'ing-
cough, w. crane, w. swan.

whorl (whurl), -er, whorled.

whor'tle (whûr'-), -ber ry.

why (whī).

Whyd'ah (wĭd'-), t. Afr.

Wic'cá cá nee', tp. N. C. ◗

Wĭch'i ta, co. and c. Kan.; co.
and r. Tex.

wĭck, -ing, -y, wick'-trim'mer.

wick'ed, -ly, -ness.

wick'en (-n), -tree.

wick'er, -work, -ered.

wick'et, -keep er, -work, wick'et
door, w. gate.

Wĭ'cŏm'i cŏ, co. Md.

Wĭc'o nĭs'cŏ, tp. Pa.

wīde, -ly, -ness, wīd'en (-n),
-ened, -en er, -en ing, wide'gab,
a frog.

wide'-a wake, alert; a person; a
hat; a bird. -chăpped, -eyed,
-gage, *a.*, -mouthed, -spread,
-stretched, -wa tered, -work.

wĭd'geon (-jŭn), -cōōt, -grăss.

Wid'in (vĭd'-), t. Bulgaria.

Wĭd'nĕs, t. Eng.

wĭd'ōw, -hood, -ōwed, -ow er,
-er hood.

wĭd'ōw-bench, -bird, -burn ing,
-duck, -finch, -hunt er, -hunt-
ing, -māk'er, -wail, wid ow's-
cross.

width, -wise.

wiĕld, -a ble, -ed, -er, -ing, -less,
-y, -i ness.

Wie licz'ka (vē lĭch'ka), t. Aust.

Wieprz (vyĕprzh), r. Pol.

Wies bä'den (vēs-), watering
place Prus.

wife, *pl.* wives, wife'hood, -less,
-like, -ly, wife'-bound, -carl,
-rid den.

wig, -less, -ging, wigged, wig'tail,
a bird, wig'-block, -māk er,
-māk ing, -tree, -weav er.

wĭg'an.

wig'gle, -gled, -gler, -gling, -gle-
tail.

wight (wīt), -y.

wĭg'wăg, -ging, -wagged.

wĭg'wam (*or* -wŏm).

wĭld, -ing, -ish, -ly, -ness, wild'-
brain, a person, -cat, *n.* and
a., -grave, wild'-fire, -fly ing,
-wil liams, a plant, -wood,
wild chĕr'ry, *n.*, w. fowl.

wĭlde'beest (*or* wĭl'dĕ bāst).

wil'der, -ing, -ment, -dered,
-dered ly.

wĭl'der ness.

wile, wĭl'y, -i ly, -i ness.

wĭl'ful *or* will'ful, -ly, -ness.

Wil hĕlmj (vĭl hĕl'mē), Ger. violin.

Wil'helms hö he (vĭl'hĕlms hê ĕ),
castle Ger.

Wĭlkes'băr re *or* -Băr're, c. Pa.

Wil ko wisz'ki (vĭl kō vĭsh'kē), t.
Poland.

---

fāte, făt, fär, fạll, fâre, fặst, sofå, mēte, mĕt, hêr, ĭce, ĭn, nōte,

will, -er, -ing, -ing ly, -ing ness, -ful, -ful ly, -ful ness, willed, will'-less, -wor ship, -wor ship er.

Wĭl lä'mĕtte, r. Ore.

wil'let.

wĭl'lie-fish er, -hạwk ie, -muf tie, -man-beard, a fish, wil'lie-waught (-wạcht).

wĭl'li wạw.

Wĭll'mär, vil. Minn.

will'-o'-the-wisp'.

Wĭl'lough by (-lŏ bĭ), vil. O.

wil'low, -ing, -ish, -y, -lowed, wil'low wort.

wil'low-beau ty, -bee, -bee tle, -cac tus, -cat er pil lar, -cim bex, -deer, -dol'er us, -fly, -gall, -gar den, -ground, -grouse, -herb, -lark, -leaf, -ma chine', -moth, -myr tle, -oak, -peel er, -ptar'mi gan, -saw fly, -slug, -spar row, -thorn, -war bler, -weed, -wren.

wĭl'ly-nĭl'ly, wĭl'ly-wăg'tāil.

wilt, -ed, -ing.

wim'ble, -bled, -bling.

Wimp'fen (vĭmp'-), t. Ger.

Wimpf fen' (văṅp'fȧṅ' or -fŏṅ' or vĭmp'fen), Fr. gen.

wĭm'ple, -pled, -pling.

win, -na ble, -ner, -ning, -ning ly, -ning ness, -some, -some ly, -some ness, won (wŭn), win'-bread, win'ning-head way, -post.

win'ber ry.

wĭnce, winced, win'cing, -cer, wince'-pit, -pot, win'cing-ma chine'.

wĭn'cey, a strong cloth.

winch.

wĭnd, -er, -ing, -ing ly, wound, wind'-up.

wĭnd'ing-en gine, -ma chine', -pend ant, -rope, -sheet, -stairs, -sticks, -tac kle, w. up.

wĭnd, -age, -ed, -y, -i ly, -i ness, -ward.

wĭnd'bag, a person, -ball, -ber ry, -break, -fall, -fall en, -fan ner, a hawk, -fish, -flow er, -hawk, -hov er, a hawk, -pipe, -seed, a plant, -stroke, -suck'er, a bird, -thrush, -way.

wĭnd'-band, -beam, -bill, -bore, -bound, -brace, -bro'ken, -chān'ging, -chart, -chest, -col ic, -con tu'sion, -cut ter, -cut ting, -di al, -dog, -drop sy, -egg, -fer til ized, -fur nace, -gage, -gall, -gap, -gun, -gust, -hatch, -herb, -house, -in'stru ment, -mark er, -plant, -pox, -pres sure, -pump, -rec ord, -rode, -rose, -sail, -scale, -scoop, -shȧft, -shake, -shāk'en, -shock, -spout, -stop, -storm, -suck ing, -swept, -swift, -tight, -trunk, -wheel, wind'y-foot ed, wind side.

wĭnd'lass.

win'dle straw, a bird.

wind'mill, -cap, -grȧss, -plant.

wĭn'dŏw, -less, -bar, -blind, -box, -catch, -clean'er, -cur tain, -fas'-ten er, -frame, -gar den ing, -găz er, -glȧss, -jack, -latch, -lĕad, -lift, -mar tin, -mir ror, -o pen er, -oys ter, -pane, -pan'el, -plant, -post, -pull, -sash, -screen, -seat, -sec tor, -shade, -shell, -shut ter, -sill, -stile, -stool.

wĭnd'rŏw, -ing, -rowed.

Wind'sor (wĭn'zur), t. Eng.; co. Vt.; c. Mo.; vil. N. Y.; t. N. C.; W. Cas tle, Eng., W. Locks, vil. Ct., W. Ter race, vil. N. Y., W. bean, W. chair, W. soap, W. Knight.

wĭne, -less, wĭned, wĭn'ing, wĭn'er y, -y, wine'ber ry, -fly, -glass ful.

wĭne'-bag, -bib ber, -bib ber y, -bis cuit, -blue, -bot tle, -bowl, -bush, -car riage, -cȧsk, -cel lar, -col ored, -con ner, -cool er, -fat, -foun tain, -glȧss, -grow er, -grow ing, -marc, -meas ure, -mer chant, -oil, -palm, -par ty, -pier cer, -press, -room, -sap, -skin, -sour, -stone, -tȧst er, -vault, -vin e gar, -war rant.

Wĭne'bren ner, -nĕ'ri an.

wing, -ed, -ed ly, -er, -ing, -less, -less ness, -let, -y, winged, wing'fish, -seed.

wing'-band, -bar, -bay, -beat, -bŏw, -case, -cell, -com pass,

-conch (-koṇk), -cov er, -cov ert,
-fĕath er, -foot ed, -formed,
-gud geon, -hand ed, -leafed,
-mem brane, -nerv ure, -net,
-pad, -pas sage, -pen, -post,
-quill, -rail, -scale, -sheath,
-shell, -shoot ing, -shot, -snail,
-sprĕad, -stop per, -stroke,
-swift, -tip, -tract, -tran som,
-wale, -wall, -wea'ry.

wiṇk, -er, -ing, -ing ly, -less,
winked.

wiṇk'er-lĕath er, -mus cle, -plate,
-strap, wink'ing owl, wink'-a-
peep'.

wiṇ'kel (vĭn'-).

Win'kèl ried (vĭnk'el rēt), Swiss
patriot.

win'kle, -hawk.

Wĭn ne bä'gŏ, co. Ill.; co. Ia.;
co. Wis.; tp. Minn.

win'nel.

Wĭn nĕ mŭc'ca, t. Nev.

Win'ne pe saṇ'kee, l. N. H.

Wĭn'ni pe gŏ'sis, l. Can.

wĭn'nŏw, -er, -ing, -nŏwed.

win'now-sheet, win'now ing-bȧs-
ket, -fan, -ma chine'.

Wĭ nŏ'na, co. Minn.; t. Miss.

Wĭ noōs'kĭ, vil. and r. Vt.

Wĭn'schŏ'ten (-skŏ'-), t. Netherlands.

Wins'lŏw (wĭnz'-), vil. Me.; tp.
N. J.

win'ter, -er, -ing, -ish, -less, -ly,
-tered, -try, -tri ness, win'ter-
ber ry, -green, -weed.

win'ter-bĕat'en (-n), -bloom,
-bon net, a bird, -bound, -cher-
ry, -clad, -clo ver, -crack,
-cress, -flow er, -ground, -kill,
-lodge, part of a plant, -rig,
v., -set tle, -tide, win'ter green-
oil, win'ter gar'den, w. quar ters,
w. sports.

wĭnze.

wipe, wiped, wĭp'er, -ing, wĭp'er-
wheel, wĭp'ing-rod.

wĭre, wired, wĭr'ing, -er, -y, -i ly,
-i ness.

wire'draw, -grub, a worm, -man,
-smith, -way, -weed, -work,
-worm.

wire'-bent, -bird, -cut ter, -dan'-
cer, -edge, -edged, -find er,
-gage, -grȧss, -heel, -mi crom'-
e ter, -pan, -peg ger, -pull er,
-road, -sil ver, -straight en er,
-stretch er, -tram way, -twist,
-works, -work er, -work ing, wīr'-
ing-ma chine, -press.

wire bridge, w. brush, w. car'-
tridge w. cloth, w. net'ting, w.
rod, w. tape.

wis'do m (wĭz'dŭm), -tooth.

wise (wīz), -ly, wīs'er, -est, wise'-
a cre, a person, wise'-heart ed,
-like.

wish, -a ble, -er, -ing, -ful, -ful-
ly, -ful ness, wished.

wish'-bone, -wash, wish'ing-bone,
-cap, -ring, -rod, wish'y-wash'y.

wisp, -y.

wist, knew.

Wis tä'ri a, *Bot. genus,* wis tä'ri a,
a plant.

wist'ful, -ly, -ness, -less.

wit, -less, -less ly, -less ness,
-ling, -ted, -ti cism, -ty, -ti ly,
-ti ness, -ting ly, wit'moṇ ger,
wit'ti cas ter, wit'-starved, -tooth.

witch, -er y, -ing, -ing ly, witched,
witch'crȧft, -wood, a tree.

witch'-al der, -ball, -bells, -chick,
-doc tor, -elm, -grȧss, -hag,
-ha zel, -knot, -meal, -rid den,
-seek er, -stitch, -tree, -wife.

witch'es'-bells, -be som, -broom,
-but ter, -thim ble.

witch'et.

wite.

wĭth, -al', -draw', -draw'al, -er,
-ing, -ment, -drew', -drawn',
-in', -in'side, -out', -stand',
-stand'ing, -stood'.

withe, wĭthed, with'ing, -y,
withe'-rod.

wĭth'er, -ing, -ing ly, -ered,
with'er-band, with'er ing-floor.

wĭth'ers, with'er-wrung.

wĭth hŏld', -er, -ing, -held'.

wĭt'loōf.

wĭt'ness, -er, -ing, -nessed, wit'-
ness-box, -chair, -stand, -tree.

Wit'ten bĕrg (vĕt'-), t. Prus.

wit'wal.

wĭve, wīved, wĭv'ing.
wĭz'ard, -ly, -ry.
wĭz'en (-n), -faced.
Wloc lä'wek (vlōts lä'věk), t. Pol.
wŏad, -ed, woad'wax en, woad'-
mill.
Wo'burn (wōō'-), c. Mass.
Wŏ'den, *Myth.*, -ism.
wŏe *or* wo, -ful *or* wō'ful, -ful ly,
-fulness, -be gone, woe'-wea ried,
-worn.
Wŏ'king, par. Eng.
Wol'cŏtt (wŏŏl'-), vil. N. Y.;
Eng. poet; Gov. of Conn.;
Amer. statesman.
wŏld.
Wolf (vōlf), Ger. critic; Wolff
(vōlf), Ger. sculp.
wolf (wŏŏlf), *pl.* wolves, wolf'er,
-ing, -ish, -ish ly, -kin, -ling,
wolf'ber ry, -hound, -robe, -skin.
wolf'-dog, -eel, -fish, -moth,
-net, -note, -scalp, -spi der,
-tooth, -trap.
wolf's-bane, -claws, -fist, -foot, a
moss, -head, an outlaw, -milk, a
plant.
Wolfe (wŏŏlf), Amer. philan.;
Irish poet; Eng. gen.
wol'ver ene' *or* -ine' (wŏŏl'ver ēn').
wom'an (wŏŏm'-), *pl.* wom'en
(wĭm'ĕn), -ish, -ish ly, -ish ness,
-hood, -kind, -less, -like, -ly,
-li ness, wom'en folk.
wom'an-bod y, -born, -guard,
-hāt'er, -hāt'ing, -quell er, -suf-
frage, -suf fra gist, wom'en's-
tree.
womb (wŏŏm), wombed, womb-
grain, -pas sage, -stone.
won (wŭn). See *win*.
won'der (wŭn'-), -er, -ing, -ing-
ly, -ful, -ful ly, -ful ness, -land,
-ment, won'drous, -drous ly,
-drous ness.
won'der-net, -stone, -strick en,
-work, -work er, -wound ed.
woṇ'ga-woṇ'ga (*or* wong'a-
wong'a).
wont (wŭnt), -ed, -ed ness.
wŏn't (*or* wŭnt), will not.
wōō, -er, -ing, -ing ly, wooed.
wŏŏd, -ed, -en, -en y, -en ness,

-less, -sy (-zy), -ward, -ward-
ship, -y, -i ness.
wood'bine, -bind, -chat, -chuck,
an animal, -cock, -crack er, a
bird, -craft, -cut, -hack, a bird,
job ber, a bird, -knack er, a
bird, -land, -man, -peck er,
-reeve, -ruff, -shock, -suck er,
a bird, -tap per, a bird, -top-
per, a bird, -wale, -wax,
-wax en, -work, wood'en head,
a person, -ware, woods'man.
wood'-ac id, -ag ate, -al co hol,
-al mond, -a nem'o ne, -ănt,
-ap ple, -ash es, -awl, -bab-
oon', -bar ley, -bee tle, -bet-
o ny, -bill, -bird, -block,
-boil er, -bor er, -born, -bound,
-broom, -bug, -cal a mint, a plant,
-carv er, -carv ing, -cell, -char-
coal, -chop per, -chuck, a
chuck in a lathe, -coal, -cop-
per, -corn, -crash, -crick'et,
-cul ver, -cut ter, -cut ting,
-dove, -drill, -drink, -duck.
wood'-eat er, -eat ing, -em boss-
ing, -end, -en gräv'er, -en-
gräv'ing, -e vil, -fell er, -fern,
-fi ber, -fire, -flour, -fran colin, -fret ter, -fret ting, -frog,
-gas, -ger man'der, -girt, -gnat,
-god, -grăss, -grīnd er, -grīnd'-
ing, -grouse, -hack'er, -hag-
ger, -hawk, -hen, -hew er,
-hew ing, -hole, -hon ey, -hōō'-
pōe, -horse, -house, -ĭ'bis, -in-
lay, -king fish er, -lark, -lau-
rel, -lay er, -lěop ard, -lil y,
-liv er wort, -lock, -lot, -louse.
wood'-march, -meas ur er, -meet-
ing, -mill, -mite, -mouse,
-naph tha, -net tle, -night'-
shade, -note, -nut, -nymph,
-oil, -o pal, -owl, -pa per,
-pa ren chy ma (-ren'kĭ-), -par-
tridge, -pea, -peat, -pe wee,
-pie, -pi geon, -pile, -pim per-
nel, -pulp, -quail, -quest, -rab-
bit, -rat, -reed, -rob in, -rock,
-rush.
wood'-sage, -sand pīp er, -san'i-
cle, -saw, -saw yer, -screw,
-shed, -shel drake, -shrike,

nŏt, nôr, ūse, ŭp, ûrn, etüde, fōōd, fŏŏt, aŋger, boṅmot, thus, Bach.

39

-shrimp, -skin, -slave, -snail, -snake, -snipe, -sŏŏt, -sor rel, -sour, -spack, -spir it, -spite, -spurge, -star, -still, -stone, -stork, -stove, -straw ber ry, -swal low, -swift, -tar, -thrush, -tick, -tin, -tit mouse, -tor toise, -turn er, -turn ing, -vetch, -vine, -vin e gar, -vi o let, -wag tail, -walk er, -war bler, -wasp, -wid geon, -wīnd, -wool, -work-er, -worm, -wren, -wroth, -yard.

wood' car pet, made of wood, w. pave ment, w. stamp, wood'-louse mil'le ped.

wood'cock-eye, -fish, -owl, -pi-lot, -shell, -snipe, wood'chat-shrike, wood'en-hĕad ed.

Wood'bu ry type.

wŏŏf, -y.

wŏŏl, -en, -ly, -li ness, -sey (-sĭ), wool en et' *or* -ette', wool'fell, -head, a duck, -mon ger, -pack, -sack, -stock, -work.

wool'-ball, -beâr ing, -burl er, -card er, -clean er, -clip, -comb er, -dry'er, -dust er, -dyed, -ex tract, -fat, -gath er ing, -grăss, -grease, -grow er, -hall, -man, -mer'chant, -mill, -nee dle, -oil, -oil er, -pack er, -pick er, -pow der, -sale, -scrib bler, -shears, -sort er, -sow er, -sponge, -sta ple, -sta pler, -wīnd'er.

wool'en-cord, -dra per, -print er, -print ing, -scrib'bler, wool'ly-but, -haired, -head, a person, -hĕad'ed.

Wŏŏl'wich (-ĭch *or* -ĭj), t. Eng.

wŏŏm, a beaver's fur.

wŏŏn, a governor.

Wŏŏs'ter, c. O.; Amer. gen.

Worces'ter (wŏŏs'-), co. Md.; c. Mass.; tp. N. Y.; Eng. inventor; Amer. lexicographer.

word (wurd), -ed, -ing, -less, -y, -i ly, -i ness.

word'-blind, -book, -bound, -build ing, -catch er, -dĕaf ness, -form, -for mā'tion, -māk ing, -mem'o ry, -paint er, -paint ing, -pic ture, -play, -square, -strife.

wore. See *wear.*

work (wurk), -a ble, -a ble ness, -a bil'i ty, -a day, -er, -ing, -less, -some, worked, work'-fel low, -house, -man, -man-like, -man ly, -man ship, -măs-ter, -mis tress, -room, -shop, -wom an.

work'-bag, -băs ket, -bench, -box, -day, -folk, -folks, -girl, -hold er, -lĕad, -peo ple, -roll er, -stone, -ta ble, -u'nit.

work'er-bob bin, -cell, -comb, -egg, work'er ant, w. bee.

work'ing-beam, -day, -face, -house, -point, -rod, work'ing clăss, w. draw ing, w. man, w. mod'el, w. par ty, w. plan, work'house-sheet ing, w. school.

world (wurld), -ly, -li ness, -ling.

world'-har dened, -lan guage, -old, -wea ríed, -wide, world'ly-mīnd'-ed, -wise.

worm (wurm), -er, -ing, -ling, -y, wormed, worm'seed, -wood.

worm'-bark, -bur row, -căst, -cod, -col ic, -dye, -eat, -eat en, -eat en ness, -eat er, -fe'ver, -fish-er, -gear, -grăss, -hole, -holed, -lar va, -like, -oil, -pipe, -pow-der, -punch, -rack, -safe, -shăft, -shell, -snake, -tea, -track, -wheel, -wire, worm'ing-pot, worm'seed-mus tard, -oil, worm fence, worms' meat.

wŏrn. See *wear.* worn'-out.

wor'ry (wŭr'-), -ing, -ing ly, -ri er, -ri less, -ri ment, -ri some.

worse (wûrs), worst. See *ill.*

wor'ship (wûr'-), -shĭped *or* -shipped, -ship er *or* -per, -ship-ing *or* -ping, -ship a ble, -a-bil'i ty, -ful, -ful ly, -ful ness.

worst (wurst), *v.,* -ed, -ing.

worst'ed (wŏŏst'- *or* wûrst'-), -work.

wort (wûrt), -con dens'er, -cool-er, -fil ter, -re frig'er a tor.

worth (wûrth), -less, -less ly, -less ness, wor'thy, -thi ly, -thi-ness.

Wort'ley (wûrt'-), tp. Eng.

would (wŏŏd), -be.

wound, *v.* See *wīnd.*

fāte, făt, fär, fạll, fâre, fǎst, sofà, mēte, mĕt, hêr, īce, ĭn, nōte,

wound (wo͞ond *or* wound), *n.* and
v., -a ble, -ed, -er, -ing, -less,
wound'wort, wound'-fe ver, -gall.
wou'ra li-plant (wo͞o'rȧ lĭ- *or*
-rä'li-).
wŏve, wŏv'en (-n). See *weave.*
wrack (răk), -grȧss.
wraith (rāth).
wran'gle, -gled, -gler, -gler ship,
-gling, -gle some, -gle-foot'ed.
wrȧp, -page, -per, -ping, wrap'-
ras cal, wrap'ping-pa per, -silk.
wrasse (răs), -fish.
wrȧth, -ful, -ful ly, -ful ness, -less,
-y, -i ly.
wreak (rēk), -er, -ing, wreaked.
wrēath, -less, -y, wreath'-an i mal'-
cule, -shell.
wrēathe, wrēathed, wrēath'er, -en.
wreck (rĕk), -age, -er, -ing, -ful,
wrecked, wreck'fish.
wreck'-car, -chart, -com'pa ny,
-crew, -free, -in'stru ment, -mȧs-
ter, -wood, wreck'ing-car, -pump.
Wrĕk'in, hill Eng.
wren (rĕn), -bab bler, -tit, -war'-
bler.
wrench (rĕnch), -ing, wrenched,
wrench'-ham mer, -han dle.
Wrĕn'tham, tp. Mass.
wrest, -ed, -er, -ing, wrest'-
block, -pin, -plank.
wres'tle (rĕs'l), -tled, -tler, -tling.
wretch, -ed, -ed ly, -ed ness.
Wrĕx'ham, bor. Wales.
wrig'gle (rĭg'l), -gled, -gler, -gling.
wright (rīt).
wring, wrung, wring'er, -ing,
wring'-bolt, -stȧff, wring'ing-ma-
chine', wring'ing wet.
wrin̦'kle, -kled, -kling, -kly,
wrin̦'kle-beaked, wrin̦'kling-ma-
chine.
wrist, -er, -let, wrist'band, -fall.
wrist'-bone, -clŏ'nus, -drop, -guard,
-guide, -joint, -link, -pin, -plate,
-shot, -touch.

writ, wrīte, wrote, wrĭt'ten, wrĭt'-
er, -ing, write-up.
wrīt'ing-book, -box, -cab i net,
-case, -chām bers, -desk, -fōl'io,
-frame, -ink, -ma chine, -mȧs-
ter, -pa per, -reed, -school, -set,
-ta ble, -tel e graph.
wrīthe, wrīthed, wrīth'ing, -ing ly.
Wrŏck'war dīne, vil. Eng.
wrŏng, -er, -ing, -ful, -ful ly,
-ful ness, -less, -ly, -ness,
wronged.
wrong'-do'er, -do'ing, -head,
-head ed, -head ed ly, -head ed-
ness, -heart ed, -heart ed ness,
-mīnd'ed.
wroth (rȧth), -ful.
Wrottes'ley (rŏts'lĭ), Eng. astron.
wrought (rȧwt), -i ron, *a.,*
wrought i ron, *n.*
wrung. See *wring.*
wry (rī), -ly, -ness, wry'bill, a
bird, -mouth, a fish, -neck, a
disease; a bird, wry'-billed,
-mouthed, -necked.
Wu hu' (wo͞o ho͞o'), c. China.
Wu-Ki ang' (wo͞o'-kē äng'), r.
China.
Wulf'rath (vülf'rät), t. Prus.
Wun (wo͞on), dist. India.
Würt'tem bĕrg (vürt'-), king. Ger.
Würz'burg (vürts'bo͝org), t. Bav.
wŭth'er.
Wy'an dŏt' (wī'-), co. O., wy'-
an dŏtte (wī'-), a breed of fowls.
Wy'an dŏtte', a tribe of Indians;
co. Kan.; c. Mich.
Wyc'lif (wĭk'-) *or* -liffe *or* Wick'-
liffe, Eng. reformer, translator
of the Bible, -lif īte, Wyc'liffe,
parish Eng.
wy'lie-coat (wī'-).
Wymond'ham (wĭnd'am), t. Eng.
Wyn'ge ne (wĭn'gä nĕ), vil. Belg.
wynn (wĭn), a wagon.
Wythe (wĭth), co. Va., -ville, t.
Va.

nŏt, nôr, ūse, ŭp, ûrn, etüde, fo͞od, fo͝ot, an̦ger, boṅmot, thus, Bach.

X

X-leg, -rays.
Xa mil te pec' *or* Ja mil- (hä-mēl tā pĕk'), t. Mex.
Xan'a du (zăn'a dōō), Coleridge, *Kubla Khan.*
Xăn'thĭ cŭs (zăn'-), *Bib.*
Xav'i er (zăv'-), Sp. missionary.
Xa'vi er de Me ne'zes (shä'vē-er dā mā nä'zĕs), Port. gen.
xe'bec (zē'bĕk).
Xe'nĭ a (zē-), c. O.
xe'ni al (zē'-).
Xen'o phon (zĕn'-), Athenian gen.
Xe res', de (dā hā rĕth'), Sp. hist.
xe rō'sis (zē-).
Xerx'es (zêrx'ēz), King of Persia.

Xi me'nes (zĭ mē'nēz), Sp. states-man; Sp. explorer.
Xin gu' (shĕn gōō'), r. Brazil.
xi'phoid (zī'foid *or* zĭf'-).
Xir o cho'ri on (zĭr ō kŏ'rē ŏn), eparchy Greece.
Xul'la (zōōl'lä) *or* Su'la (sōō'lä), isls. Malay Arch.
xy'lo grảph (zī'-), -graph'ic, -ic-al, -lŏg'ra pher, -ra phy.
xy'loid (zī'-), -Ine.
xy lŏm'e ter (zī-).
xy'lo phone (zī'-).
xy'lose (zī'lōs).
xy lŏt'o mous (zī-).
xyst (zist).

Y

Y-moth, -shaped, Y branch, Y car'ti lage, Y cross, Y lev el, Y lig a ment, Y track.
yä'bōō *or* -bu (-bōō).
yăc'ca, -tree, -wood.
yacht (yŏt), -ed, -er, -ing, yachts'-man, -man ship, yacht'-built, -club.
Yä'hōō, *Gulliver's Travels.*
yăk (*or* yăk).
Yăk'i ma, co. Wash.
Yăk ŏ'ba, c. Afr.
yăk'sha, *Myth.*
Ya kut' (-kōōt').
Yä kutsk' (-kōōtsk'), prov. Sib.
Yăl'ŏ bush'a (-bŏŏsh'-), co. Miss.
Yä-lu-ki ang' (-lōō-kĭ äng'), r. Korea.
yam, -bean, -root.
Yä'ma (*or* yăm'a), *Myth.*
yä'men.
Yăng-tsĕ-Kĭ äng', r. China.
Yä nit'za (-nēt'sä), t. Turk.
yaṇk, -ing, yanked.
Yaṇ'kee, -dom, -fīed, -ism, -ize, -ized, -i zing, -land, Yaṇ'kee-gang, Yaṇ'kee doo'dle.
Yän te'lĕs (-tä'-), mt. Chile.

yan yēan' (*or* yan'-).
yaourt (yourt *or* yōōrt).
yăp.
Yä qui' (-kē'), r. Mex.
yärd, -age, -ful, -keep, -man, -mås-ter, -stick, yards'man.
yard'-arm, -grảss, -land, -lim it, -rope, -slings, -tac kle, -wand, yard meas ure.
yåre, -ly.
Yar'moŭth, tp. Me.; tp. Mass.; co. N. S.
yärn, -beam, -clear er, -dress er, -me ter, -print er, -reel, -roll, -scale, -spool er, -test er, -wīnd-er.
yar'pha.
yăr'rah, a tree.
yăr'rŏw.
yash'mak or *-mac.*
yăt'a ghan.
yaw, -ing, -ey, yawed.
yawl, -ing, yawled, yawl-rigged.
yawn, -er, -ing, -ing ly, yawned.
yaws.
Yä zōō', co. Miss.
Y bi cuy' (ē bē kwē'), r. S. Amer.
ye *or* you.

fāte, făt, fär, fạll, fâre, fåst, sofȧ, mēte, mĕt, hêr, īce, ĭn, nōte,

yeā.

Yēa'don, t. Eng:

yēan, -ing, -ling, yeaned.

yēar, -ling, -long, -ly, year'-bird, -book.

yêarn, -ing, -ing ly, yearned.

yēast, -y, yeast'-bit ten, -cake, -cell, -fun gus, -plant, -pow der, y. beer.

Ye gŏr yevsk' (yā-), t. Russ.

Ye'ia (yā'yä), r. Russ.

Ye'Ïsk (yä'-), t. Russ.

Ye ka te rin'burg (yā kä tä rēn'-bōorg), t. Russ.

Ye ka te ri no slaf' (yā kä tä rē-nō släv'), t. Russ.

Ye li za vĕt pŏl' (yā lĕ'sä-), t. Russ.

yell, -ing, yelled.

yĕl'lŏw, -ing, -ish, -ish ness, -ness, -y, -lows, -lowed.

yel'low bel ly, a fish, -bill, a duck, -bird, -crown, a bird, -fin, a fish, -fish, -ham, a bird, -ham mer, a bird, -head, a bird, -leg, a bird, -legs, a bird, -poll, a widgeon, -root, a plant, -rump, a bird, -seed, a plant, -shank, a bird, -shanks, a bird, -shell, a moth, -shins, a bird, -tail, a fish, -throat, a bird, -top, a turnip, -weed, -wood, a tree, -wort.

yel'low-backed, -barred, -beak, -billed, -brĕast ed, -browed, -cov ered, -crowned, -duck-wing, a., -eyed, -foot ed, -front ed, -golds, a plant, -gum, a disease, -head ed, -horned, -jack, -jack et, an insect, -leg'-ged, -line, a., -necked, -polled, -ringed, -rock et, a plant, -rumped, -shăft ed, -shoul-dered, -spot ted, -tailed, -throat-ed, -winged, -wrack.

yel'low băss, y. box, y. bun ting, y. cress, y. cy press, y. earth, y. fe'ver, y. flag, a plant, y. i ris, y. jack et, a coat, y. met al, y. perch, y. pike, y. sal ly, y. spot, y. wash, y. wren.

yelp, -er, -ing, yelped.

Yĕm'en, vil. Turk.

yĕn.

Yen i se'i (yĕn'ē sā'ē), r. Sib., -sē'an or -sē'ian (-yăn).

yeŏ'man, -like, -ly, -ry.

Yeot'mäl (yŏt'-), dist. India.

Yeŏ'vil, t. India.

yer'ba, -mä'te.

yes.

yes'ter day, -ter eve, -ter e ven, -ter eve ning, -ter morn, -ter-morn ing, -ter night, yes'ter-year.

yet.

yew (yōō), -en, yew'-pine, -tree.

Yg'dra sil or Ygg'- (ĭg'-), Myth.

YÏd, -dish.

yiĕld, -a ble, -er, -ing, -ing ly, -ing ness.

yŏck'el.

yo'del or -dle, -del er or -dler, -deled or -delled, -del ing or -ling or -dling.

yo'ga, yo'gi (-gē), yo'gism.

yoke, yoked, yŏk'ing, yoke'fel low, -mate.

yoke'-ar bor, -bone, -dev il, -elm, -line, -rope, -toed.

yŏ'kel or yŏch'el or yŏck'el (-kl).

Yŏ kŏ hä'mä, c. Japan, Y. fowls.

yolk (yŏk or yōlk), -y.

yolk'-bag, -clĕav'age, -duct, -gland, -sac, -seg men ta'tion, -skin.

yŏn, yŏn'der.

Yonge (yŭng), Eng. philol.; Eng. novelist.

yŏre.

Yŏ ru'ba, coun. Afr.

Yŏ sĕm'Ï tĕ, valley and fall Cal.

yŏ shÏ wä'ra.

you, your, yours, your self', pl. -selves'.

Youghal (yạwl), t. Ire.

Yough io ghe'ny (yŏ'hŏ gā'nÏ), r. Pa.

yoŭng, -er (-ger), -est (-gest), -ish, -ling, -ness, -ster, young'-eyed.

Yoŭnt, t. Cal.

youse (ūz), a leopard.

youth (yōōth), -ful, -ful ly, -ful-ness, -hood, -like, -wort.

yowl, -ing, yowled.

Y'pres (ē'pr), t. Belg.

Yp sÏ lăn'tÏ, c. Mich.; (Ïp sē-län'tē), Gr. patriot.

Y rē'ka (wĭ-), t. Cal.
Y sa beau' (ē'zä'bō'), Fr. officer.
Ys le'ta (ēs lä'-), t. Tex.
Yss'chĕ (ĭs'-), vil. Belg.
Ys sin geaux' (ēs'sȧn'zhō'), t. Fr.
Ys'täd (ĭs'-), t. Sw.
Y strad'y fo dwg'   (ē străd'ĭ fō-
   dōōg'), t. Wales.
Yu'cä tän', state Mex., -ca tĕc'an.
Yŭc'ca, Bot. genus, yŭc'ca, a
   plant, yuc'ca-bōr'er, -fer til i-
   zer, -moth, -pol len i zer.

Yu'kŏn, r. and c. Alas.
yu'lan, a plant.
Yule (yōōl), -tide, Yule block, Y.
   can dle, Y. clog, Y. log.
Yu'ma, -man.
yurt (yōōrt).
Y vĕr'dŭn' (ē-), t. Switz.
Yves (ēv), Fr. jurist.
Yve tot' (ēv tō'), a model poten-
   tate; t. Fr.
Y-waine' (ĭ-wān'), a Knight of
   the Round Table.

Z

Z bar, Z beam, Z crank, Z i ron.
Zaab (zäb), r. Turk.
Zā'ȧ nȧ'im, *Bib.*
Zā'ȧ năn, *Bib.*
Zaän däm', t. Holland.
Zā'ȧ văn, *Bib.*
Zăb'ȧ dä'ias (-yas), *Bib.*
Za bä rĕl'lä (dzä-), It. theol.
Zăb'bȧi, *Bib.*
Zab dē'us, *Bib.*
Zăb'dĭ el, *Bib.*
Za bor'ze (tsä bôrt'sĕ), t. Prus.
zä'bra.
Zā'bud, *Bib.*
Zä cä'pä (sä-), t. Guatemala.
za ca'te (sȧ kä'tä or thȧ kä'-).
Zä cä te'cas (-tä'-), state and c.
   Mex.
Zăc'căi (or -kä ĭ), *Bib.*
Zac chē'us (-kē'- or zăk'-), *Bib.*
Zach, von (fŏn tsäch), German as-
   tron.
Zā'cher (-ker), *Bib.*
zȧ chun' (-kōōn').
Zăd'kĭ el, the angel of the planet
   Jupiter.
Zä dŏnsk', t. Russ.
zăf'fer, -blue.
Za'frä (thä'-), t. Sp.
Zahn (tsän), Ger. painter.
Zăid pur' (-pōōr'), t. India.
zaim (zīm or zä'ĭm), -et.
Zā'ĭn, *Bib.*
Zā'ir (-êr), *Bib.*
Zai san' (-zän'), l. China.
Zä'los'e (-lŏsh'ä), t. Aust.

Zä lus'ki (-lōōs'kē), Polish bibli-
   ographer.
Za ma co'is (thä'mä kō'ēs), Sp.
   painter.
Zam bä'lĕs (säm-), prov. P. I.
Zäm be'si or -zi (-bä'zē or zăm-
   bē'zē), r. Afr.
Zăm bē'zĭ a, ter. S. Afr.
zam in dar'. See *zemindar*.
Zä moj'ski or -moy'- (-moi'skē),
   Pol. statesman.
Za mŏ'rä (thä-), prov. and c.
   Sp.; state Venez.
Zä'mosz (-mŏsh), t. Pol.
Zän'te (-tä), isl. Gr.
Zan'te, -wood, Zan'te cŭr'rant,
   Z. fus tic.
zä'ny, -ing, -ism, -nĭed.
Za pä'tä (sä-), co. Tex.
za pa te a'do (thä pä tä ä'dō).
za'pa te'ro (sä'pä tä'rō or thä'pȧ-).
Za pŏt'lä (thä-), t. Mex.
Zä'rä, c. Aust.
Zăr'a ces (-sēz), *Bib.*
Zä rä'ias (-yas or zär'ȧ ĭ'as), *Bib.*
Za rand' (zŏ rŏnd'), co. Hung.
zar ce'ta (sar sä'tä or thär thä'-).
Zä're ah, *Bib.*
zȧ rē'ba.
Zär'e phăth, *Bib.*
Zä'reth-shä'har, *Bib.*
zarf.
zȧs tru'ga.
Zăth'ŏ ĕ, *Bib.*
Zä thū'ĭ, *Bib.*
Zä wŏ'ja (-yä), t. Aust.

zax.

Zba'rasz (zbä'räsh), t. Aust.

zĕal, -less, zĕal'ous, -ly, -ness.

zĕal'ot, -ism, -ry.

zē'bra, -brĭne.

zē'bra-cat er pil lar, -o pos'sum,
-par'ra keet, -plant, -poi son,
-shark, -spi der, -swal low tail,
-wolf, -wood, -wood peck er.

Zĕ bu' (-boo'), prov. P. I.

zē'bŭ, -cat tle.

Zech'stein (zech'-).

Zeeb (or zē'ĕb), Bib.

zee'koe (zä'koo).

zeh'ner (tsä'-).

Zei'lah (zä'-), prov. and t. E.
Afr.

Zeist, t. Netherlands.

zeit'geist (tsit'gist).

Zeitz (tsits), t. Prus.

Ze lä'yä (sä-), t. Mex.

Ze'lĕ (zä'-), t. Belg.

Zĕ lŏ'phĕ hăd, Bib.

Zĕ lŏ'tes (-tēz), Bib.

Zĕm'a rä'im, Bib.

zem'in där or zam'- (or -in'- or
-där').

Zĕ mī'ra, Bib.

zĕms'tvo (zĕmst'vō).

zē nä'na.

Zend, -A ves'ta.

zen'dik (-dēk).

zē'nick.

zē'nith, -al, ze'nith-col'li ma tor,
-dis tance, -sec tor, -tel e scope.

Zĕ nŏ'bĭ a, a strong-minded
woman; Queen of Palmyra.

Zen ta' (sĕn'tŏ'), t. Hung.

Zĕph'a thah, Bib.

Zē'phŏn, Milton's Paradise Lost.

zeph'yr (zĕf'er), Zeph'y rus, Myth.

Zĕ rä'iah (-ya or zĕr'ä i'ah), Bib.

Zer bi'nŏ (tsâr bē'-), a famous
warrior.

Zerbst (tsĕrpst), t. Ger.

zer'da.

zē'ro, pl. -ros or -roes.

Zĕ ru'ah, Bib.

Zĕ rŭb'bä bĕl, Bib.

Zĕr'u i'ah (or zē roo'yà), Bib.

zĕst.

zē'ta (or zä'-).

Zē'tham, Bib.

zeūg'mä, -măt'ic.

Zeus (zūs), Myth.

Zhiz'drä (zhĭs'-), t. Russ.

zib'el ĭne.

Zich'rĭ (zĭk'-), Bib.

ziē'ga.

Zie'gĕn häls (tsē'-), t. Prus.

Zieg'ler (tsēg'-), Ger. dram.

Zif.

zĭg'zag, -ging, -gy, -zagged.

zĭl'la, a plant.

zil'lah, a province.

Zĭl'thäi, Bib.

zimb (zĭm).

zĭm'ent-wa'ter.

Zĭm'rĭ, a nickname for the Duke
of Buckingham.

zinc (zĭnk), zincked or zinced
(zĭnkt), zinck'ing or zinc'ing
(zĭnk'-), zinc'ic, -id, -i fy, -fy-
ing, -fied, -ft cä'tion, -if'er ous,
-ite, -o grȧph, -og'ra phy, -og'-
ra pher, zinc'ous, zinck'y.

zinc'-blende', -bloom, -col'ic.

zinc' am in, z. am yl, z. eth yl,
z. meth yl, z. ox id, z. send-
er, z. spar, z. vit ri ol, z. white.

zin'gä rō or -gä rä, pl. -gä ri (-rē).

Zin'gi ber (-jĭ-).

Zin'zen dorf (tsĭn'tsĕn dorf or
zĭn'zĕn-), a religious reformer.

Zip pŏ'rah (or zĭp'-), Bib.

Zips (zĭpsh), co. Hung.

zith'er, -er ist, -ern.

Zit'tau (tsĭt'tou), t. Ger.

zi'zith (zē'-).

Ziz'kŏv (tsĭts'-), t. Bohem.

Zjech'ä now (zhĕch'ä nŏv), c. Pol.

Zlo'czow (zhlŏ'chŏv), t. Aust.

Zna (tsnä), r. Russ.

Znaim, t. Aust.

Zŏ'än, Bib.

Zŏ'ar, Bib.

zŏ'bō.

zŏ'di ac, -dĭ'a cal.

zŏ'ē a, -e al.

Zŏ'hĕ lĕth, Bib.

zŏ'ic, zo ĕt'ic, zo'ism, zo'ist,
-is'tic.

Zŏ'i lus, Gr. critic, -i lism, -i list,
-il'e an.

Zŏ'la (or zŏ'lä'), Fr. novelist.

Zŏl'lĭ cof'fer, Amer. gen.

Zol'li ko'fer (tsŏl'ē kŏ'fer), pulpit orator.

Zöll'nêr (tsêl'-), Ger. physicist, Zöll'ner's lines.

zoll've rein (tsōl'fĕ rīn).

zŏne, -less, zōn'al, -ate, -ule, zoned, zone'-ax is.

Zōō, the Zoölogical Garden.

zŏ'ŏ gē og'ra phy, -ra pher, -o-graph'ic, -ic al.

zŏ og'ra phy, -ra pher, -ra phist, -o graph'ic, -ic al.

zŏ ŏ gy'ro scope (-jī'-).

zŏ ŏl'a ter, -a trous, -a try.

zŏ'ŏ līte, -līt'ic, -līth, -līth'ic.

zŏ ŏl'o gy, -o gist, -o log'ic, -ic al, -al ly.

zŏ ŏm'e try, -ō mĕt'ric.

zŏ'ŏ phyte (-fīt), -phyt'ic (-fĭt'-), -ic al, zŏ'o phyte-trough.

zŏ ŏph'y tŏl'o gy, -o gist, zŏ'ŏ-phy'to log'ic al (-fī'-).

zŏ'ŏ sperm, *-sper'mi um*, -sper-mat'ic.

zŏ'ŏ spŏre, -spo ran'gi al, *-ran'-gi um*, -spŏr'ic.

zŏ ot'o my, -o mist, -o tom'ic, -ic al, -al ly.

Zŏ'phāi, *Bib.*

Zŏ'phĭ ĕl, Milton's *Paradise Lost.*

zop'pō (tsŏp'-).

Zŏ're ah, *Bib.*

Zŏ'rītes, *Bib.*

Zŏ rō ăs'ter, founder of the Persian religion, -as'tri an, -an ism.

Zou ave' (zōō äv' *or* zwäv), -jacket.

zounds.

Zsam bĕk' (säm'-), t. Hung.

Zschok'ke (tshŏk'ĕ), Ger. auth.

Zschop'pau (tshŏp'pou), t. Ger.

Zuc ca rel'li (dzōōk kä rĕl'lē), It. painter.

zuc chet'ta (tsŏŏk kĕt'tä) *or* zu-chet'to (tsōō kĕt'tō *or* zōō-).

Zuck'män'tel (tsŏŏk'-), t. Aust.

zu'jō lō (zōō'- *or* tsōō'-).

Zug (zōōg), canton and c. Switz.

zug (tsōōg).

zui'sin (zoi'zĭn).

Zu lēi'ka, Byron, *The Bride of Abydos.*

Züll'chow (tsül'chŏv), t. Prus.

Zu'lu (zōō'lōō), *pl.* -lus (-lōōz), Zu'lu-Kăf'ir.

zum bōō'rŭk (*or* zŭm'-).

Zumpt (tsŏŏmpt), Ger. philol.

Zu'nĭ (zōō'nyē), *pl.* -nis (-nyēz), -ni an.

zu'pa (zōō'-), zu'pan.

Zü'rĭch (tsü'-), canton and c. Switz.

Zŭ'rĭ ĕl, *Bib.*

Zuy'der Zee (zī'der zē *or* zoi'der zä).

Zwei'brück en (tsvī'brük en), t. Bav.

Zwick'au (tsvĭk'ou), dist. and t. Sax.; t. Bohem.

zwie'bäck (tsvē'-).

Zwing'li (tsvĭng'lē), Swiss reformer, -li an (*or* zwĭng'lĭ an).

zwisch'en spiĕl' (tsvĭsh'-).

Zwit'tau (tsvĭt'tou), t. Aust.

Zwŏl'lĕ, t. Netherlands.

zy'gŏ dŏnt (zī'-).

zy'gon (zī'-), zy'gal (zī'-).

zyme, zym'ic (zĭm'-).

zy'mo gen (zī'- *or* zĭm'o jĕn), -gen'ic, -mog'e nous (-mŏj'-).

zy mŏl'o gy (zī-), -o gist, -mo-log'ic, -ic al.

zy mom'e ter (zī-).

zy'mŏ scōpe (zī'-).

zy mō'sis (zī-), -mŏt'ic, -ic al ly, -mo tech'nic (-tĕk'-), -ni cal, -nics.

zy'mur gy (zī'- *or* zĭm'-).

zy'no scope (zī'-).

zy'thum (zī'-).

zyx om'ma, a dragon-fly.

---

fāte, făt, fär, fạll, fâre, fạst, sofȧ, mēte, mĕt, hêr, īce, ĭn, nōte.

HOMOPHONES

Words of different meanings, resembling each other in sound or appearance, are often misspelled. The following list embraces such homophones and homographs as are most likely to confuse the inexperienced writer. The definitions are brief, being intended simply to differentiate the several words. In the pronunciation of a homophone word, the student must not be governed by the sound of another word in the same group.

A.

aal, a red dye. See *all.*

aam, ahm, aum, *or* **awm,** a measure of liquids. **om** *or* **aum,** a mystic ejaculation; absolute goodness and truth. **ohm,** the unit of electrical resistance.

Abba, father; an invocation; a title. **aba,** an outer garment; an instrument for determining latitude.

abbé, an abbot. **abbey,** a monastery.

able, qualified. **Abel,** a man's name.

aboard, on board; alongside; across. **abord,** arrival; to approach.

absence, being absent. **absents,** remains away.

Acadian, pertaining to or a native of Acadia or Nova Scotia. **Accadian,** an Accad.

accede, agree; assent; to enter upon an office or dignity. See *exceed.*

accept, to agree to receive. **except,** to exclude; unless.

acclamation, a shout of applause. **acclimation,** the state of being acclimated.

acrasia, want of self-control. **acratia,** failure of strength. **acrisia,** inability to judge.

acrimony, sharpness of speech. **agrimony,** a plant.

acts, deeds. **ax** *or* **axe,** a tool for chopping.

adder, one who adds. **adder,** a viper.

addition, an increase. **edition,** copies printed at one time.

adherence, attachment; fidelity. **adherents,** followers.

adieu, farewell. **ado,** trouble; bustle.

adjuster, one who adjusts. **adjustor,** a muscle.

adze, an edged tool. **adds,** does add.

aerie, eyrie, *or* **eyry,** a nest of a bird. **eerie** *or* **eery,** affected with fear.

aes, money or coins. See *ease.*

affect, to influence; to assume. **effect,** result; to bring about.

affluence, a flowing to; an abundant supply. **effluence,** a flowing out; issue; efflux.

affront, an encounter; to confront; to offend. **afront,** face to face; in front of.

agenesis, imperfect development. **agennesis,** impotence; barrenness; mixture of species.

aggressor, the person who first attacks. **egressor,** one who goes out.

617

agnail, a hangnail. **agnel,** a coin.
aigret *or* **aigrette,** the small white
heron; a plume composed of
feathers. See *egret.*
ail, to be ill. **ale,** malt liquor.
air, atmosphere. **aer,** a veil; a gas.
Ayr, a town and river in Scotland.
ayr, an open sea-beach. **ear,**
early. **e'er,** ever. **ere,** before.
eyre, a journey; a court of
judges. **heir,** one who inherits.
aisle, a walk or passage way. **I'll,**
I will. **isle,** an island.
Alaskan, belonging to Alaska.
Alascan, a name given to a
foreign Protestant in England.
alfa, a plant. **alpha,** the first
letter in the Greek alphabet.
alfonsin, a scarlet fish. See *alphonsin.*
alicant, a red wine. **Alicante,** province in Spain.
Alice, Christian name. **allice,** the
European shad.
all, the whole. **aal,** a red dye.
awl, a tool. **al,** a plant. **aul,**
the alder.
Allah, God of the Koran. **alla,** a
musical term.
allegation, an assertion. **alliga-
tion,** an arithmetical term.
alley, a narrow lane. **ally,** a confederate.
alleys, pl. of alley. **allies,** pl. of
ally.
alligator, a large reptile. **allega-
tor,** one who alleges.
allocution, a formal address. **elocution,** utterance by speech.
allowed, permitted. **aloud,** audibly.
allude, to refer to. **illude,** to deceive; to mock. **elude,** to escape.
allure, to entice, to charm. **alure,**
a gallery; a passage.
allusion, a reference. **illusion,**
a deception; a phantom. **elusion,**
an evasion. **elution,** a washing
out.
Almira, a Christian name. **almi-
rah,** a chest of drawers.
almond, the fruit of the almond
tree. **almund,** a Turkish measure.
alphonsin, a three-armed forceps.

Alphonsine, relating to Alphonso.
alfonsin, a scarlet fish.
altar, place of sacrifice. **alter,** to
change.
alum, a double sulphate. **alem,**
a flag or standard.
ama, a large vessel. **amah,** a
nurse; a lady's maid.
ambary, an East Indian plant.
ambari, a covered howdah.
amend, to reform. **amende,** rep-
aration.
amerce, to impose a fine. **immerse,** to put under water.
amice, a friar's hood. **amiss,** out
of order.
Ammon, an Egyptian god. **amun,**
chief rice-crop of Hindustan.
Ammonite, pertaining to Ammon.
ammonite, a fossil. **Ammanite,**
a Mennonite.
amulet, a charm. **amylate,** a compound of starch.
anachronism, out of place. **an-
achorism,** foreign; unsuited.
anaclasis, term in prosody. **anac-
lisis,** medical term.
analogy, resemblance of relations.
enallage, term in rhetoric.
analyst, one who analyzes. **annalist,** a writer of annals.
analyze, to separate; to decompose.
annalize, to record.
anatreptic, overturning. **anatrip-
tic,** pertaining to anatripsis.
anchor, a support. **anker,** a
measure.
anchored, made fast; secure.
ancred, term in heraldry.
anchorite, a hermit. **ankerite,** a
mineral.
anger, to provoke; wrath. **angor,**
extreme anxiety. **Ingres,** a French
painter.
anil, a plant. **anile,** old-woman-
ish; imbecile.
Ann, a Christian name. **ann,** the
first fruits.
Anna, a Christian name. **ana,** a
medical term. **anna,** a skunk;
money.
annalist, a writer of annals. See
analyst.
annumerate, to add. See *enumerate.*

annunciate, to announce. **enunciate,** to utter.

anomalous, deviating from a general rule. **anomalus,** term in anatomy.

answer, to respond; a reply. **ansar,** a helper. **Anser,** a genus of geese; a star.

ant, an insect. **aunt,** a relative.

ante, before. **anti,** against. **antæ,** pl. of anta.

antitype, the original of the type. **antetype,** a prototype.

apophasis, a protuberance; a term used in botany, geology, and architecture. **apophysis,** denial; negation; a term used in rhetoric.

apostasy, desertion of one's religion, principles, or party. **hypostasy,** that which underlies something else.

apostatize, to abandon one's profession or church. **hypostatize,** to attribute substantial existence to.

apostle, one sent forth; a messenger. **apostil** _or_ **apostille,** an annotation.

apostrophe, a term in botany, grammar, and rhetoric. **hypostrophe,** term used in medicine and rhetoric.

apothecary, one who practises pharmacy. **hypothecary,** pertaining to hypothecation or mortgage.

apothesis, term in surgery. **hypothesis,** a supposition; a proposition taken for granted.

appetite, physical craving or desire. **apatite,** a mineral.

appose, to place or bring near; to examine. See _oppose._

apposition, the act of adding; term in grammar. See _opposition._

appressed, pressed closely. See _oppressed._

aps, white poplar wood. **apse,** term in architecture and in astronomy.

arc, part of a circle. **ark,** a boat.

area, a surface. **aria,** a song.

areas, pl. of area. **aries,** a sign of the zodiac.

Arion, a genus of gastropods.

Orion, a constellation; a genus of beetles.

Armenian, pertaining to Armenia. **Arminian,** pertaining to Arminius or to his doctrines.

armor, a defensive covering; to furnish with armor. **armer,** one who arms or supplies with arms.

arrant, notorious. **errant,** wandering.

arrear, backward; into or toward the rear. **arrière,** arrear or rear.

arrow, a missile weapon. **arrha,** a pledge. **arrah,** a common Anglo-Irish expletive.

ascent, an eminence. **assent,** consent.

ascribe, to attribute, impute, or refer. **escribe,** to copy or write out.

Aspasia, mistress of Pericles; a genus of orchids. **Aspatia,** the heroine in "The Maid's Tragedy."

aspirate, to utter with full breath. **asperate,** to sound roughly.

aspiration, a longing. **asperation,** a making rough.

ass, a quadruped. **asse,** a small African fox. **as,** a coin; a weight.

assay, to prove; to attempt. See _essay._

assistance, help. **assistants,** helpers.

aster, a plant. **Aster,** a genus of plants. **Astur** _or_ **Aster,** a genus of hawks.

Ate, a goddess. See _eighty._

ate, past tense of eat. **eight,** a numeral. **ait,** a small island.

atomology, the doctrine of atoms. See _etymology._

atomy, an atom; a mote; a pygmy; an anatomy; a skeleton. **atimy,** disgrace; disfranchisement.

atropos, a genus of insects. **atropous,** erect; not inverted.

attack, to fall upon with force. **atak,** the harp-seal.

attendance, waiting, serving. **attendants,** servants.

atypic, not typical. **attypic,** a term in zoölogy.

auger, a tool. **augur,** to foretell.

aught, anything. **ought,** should.

auk, a bird. **awk,** awkward.

aul, the alder. See *all*.

aune, a French cloth-measure. See *own*.

aunt, a relative. See *ant*.

Austria, a country in Europe. **Ostrya,** a genus of trees.

aversion, a turning away; a change of application. **eversion,** overthrow; destruction.

away, onward; on; along. **aweigh,** a nautical term.

awe, dread; to terrify. **augh,** an exclamation of disgust.

awful, dreadful. **offal,** rubbish.

awheel, on a wheel or wheels. **aweel,** oh, well; very well.

awl, a tool. See *all*.

ax *or* **axe,** a tool for chopping. See *acts*.

axil, a botanical term. **axle,** a connecting bar. **axile,** belonging to an axis or the axis. **axal,** resembling an axle.

axin, the fat of a Mexican cochineal. **axine,** an axine deer.

azure, blue like the sky. **à jour,** a style of decoration.

B.

baa, cry of sheep. **bah,** an exclamation.

bad, vicious. **bade,** past tense of bid.

badger, a mammal; to worry; pester. **badgir,** a wind-tower.

bailer, one who bails; a utensil. **bailor,** law term. **baler,** one who makes up bales or bundles.

bait, a lure; to put meat upon a hook. **bate,** to lessen.

baize, a kind of cloth. **bays,** pl. of bay; the cry of a hound. **beys,** Turkish governors.

bald, without hair. **bawled,** past tense of bawl.

bale, a package of goods; to dip out. **bail,** security; to dip out.

baleen, whale-bone. **baline,** a coarse canvas.

ball, a round body; a dance. **bawl,** to cry aloud.

ballot, to vote; a method of election. **ballet,** an artistic dance.

band, that which binds; a musical company. **banned,** put under ban.

bane, anything pernicious; ruin; destruction. **bain,** direct; near; short.

banket, a bricklayer's bench. **banquet,** a feast; to feast. **banquette,** a raised bank; a sidewalk; a bench.

bar, a rod; a barrier; to fasten; to except. **barr,** to cry as an elephant.

barb, a beard; a horse. **barbe,** a title.

Barbary, region in N. Africa. **barberry,** a shrub.

barbet, a dog; a bird. **barbette,** a mound of earth.

Barcan, pertaining to Barca. **barcon,** a trading vessel.

bard *or* **barde,** a poet. **barred,** hindered.

bare, plain; to uncover. **bear,** an animal; to carry.

Barnaby, a Christian name. **barnaby,** an old dance. **barnabee,** the lady-bird.

baron, a nobleman. **barren,** unfruitful.

baronet, a dignity or degree of honor. **baronette,** a little baroness.

barras, a resin; a coarse linen fabric. **barris,** a chimpanzee.

basalt, a species of marble. **baysalt,** coarse-grained salt.

base, vile; low; abject; to establish; a foundation. **bass,** a fish; a part in music.

based, past tense of base. **baste,** to sew loosely; to beat with a stick; to moisten.

bask, to lie in the sun. **Basque,** a language. **basque,** a skirt-waist.

bathetic, pertaining to bathos. See *pathetic*.

baton, a staff or club. **batten,** grow fat; a strip of wood. **beton,** a concrete.

battle, a general fight. **battel,** to fertilize; single combat.

bawl, a cry; to make a loud noise. See *ball*.

bawled, shouted. See *bald*.

bawling, howling; crying out. **balling,** the act of making into balls.

bay, an inlet of the sea; reddish brown; a berry; to bark. **bey,** a Turkish governor.

bayard, a horse; a self-confident person; a hand-barrow. **byard,** a strap used by miners. **Bayard,** an American statesman.

bays, bodies of water. See *baize.*

bazaar, a fair. **bizarre,** odd; whimsical.

beach, shore. **beech,** a tree.

bead, a prayer; a small perforated ball; to ornament with beads. **bede,** a kind of pickax.

beaker, a cup or goblet. **bekah,** a Hebrew weight. **beker,** a jug.

beat, to strike. **beet,** a vegetable.

beau, a fop. **bow,** a knot; an instrument.

beaver, a rodent. **bever,** a small lunch between meals.

been, from the verb be. **bin,** a receptacle.

beer, a drink. **bier,** a couch for the dead. **bere,** a kind of barley.

beet, a vegetable. See *beat.*

beetle, an insect. **bietle,** a kind of jacket. **betel,** a plant. **bætyl,** a sacred stone.

begin, to commence; a beginning. **biggin,** a cap. **biggen,** to enlarge.

beheaded, past tense of behead. **bee-headed,** crazy, flighty.

bell, a hollow metallic vessel. **belle,** a fair lady. **Bel,** a Babylonian god. **bel,** Bengal quince-tree.

bellows, a machine for producing a strong current of air. **Bellis,** a genus of flowers.

Berlin, city in Prussia. **birlin,** a kind of boat.

bern, berne, a warrior; a hero. **Berne,** canton in Switz. See *burn.*

berried, furnished with berries. See *buried.*

berry, a fruit. **berri,** the Turkish mile. **bury,** to inter. **burry,** full of burs.

berth, a sleeping place; position. **birth,** coming into life.

besa, a measure of capacity. **bisa** *or* **biza,** a coin.

Bess, a nickname. **bise,** a wind. **bes,** a copper coin.

Beton, a concrete. See *baton.*

better, superior. **bettor,** one who bets.

bevel, an angle; slanting; to slope. **bevil** *or* **bevile,** a term in heraldry.

Bey, a Turkish governor. See *bay.*

beys, Turkish governors. See *baize.*

bezel, to grind to a sloping edge; a bevel on the edge of a chisel. **bezzle,** to waste recklessly; to embezzle.

bib, to tipple; a cloth to put under a child's chin. **bibb,** a nautical term.

bier, a couch for the dead. See *beer.*

bietle, a kind of jacket. See *beetle.*

biggen, to enlarge. See *begin.*

bigger, comparative of big; a builder. **bega** *or* **biggah,** a land-measure. **biga,** a two-horse chariot.

biggin, a cap. See *begin.*

bill, the beak of a bird; a billet. **bil,** the coalfish.

bin, a receptacle. See *been.*

binnacle, a stand or case for a ship's compass. **binocle,** a telescope.

birk, to give a tart answer. See *burke.*

birl, to pour out; to move or rotate rapidly. **burl,** a small knot in thread; to pick knots.

birlin, a boat. See *Berlin.*

birn, a stem of dry heather. See *burn.*

birr, to make a whirring noise. See *bur.*

birth, coming into life. See *berth.*

bis, twice. **bisse,** a term in heraldry; an Indian weight.

bisa *or* **biza,** a coin. See *besa.*

bise, a wind. See *Bess.*

bisk *or* **bisque,** a soup; a term in tennis. **bisque,** a kind of porcelain.

bit, part of a bridle. **bitt,** a nautical term.

bite, to seize with the teeth; to grip; to cleave; a morsel of food. bight, a creek; a coil of rope.

bits, pl. of bit. bitts, a nautical term.

bitter, having a harsh taste; grievous. bittor or bittour, the bittern.

bizarre, odd, whimsical. See *bazaar*.

blanket, a covering. blanquette, a fricassee.

blasty, gusty. blastie, a dwarf.

blay, a fish. blae, blue; livid.

blend, to combine. blende, a mineral.

blew, past tense of blow. blue, a color.

blight, mildew; decay; to blast. blite, an herb.

bloat, to swell. blote, to dry by smoke.

blond, fair. blonde, a lady of light complexion.

blot, to stain; a spot; a blur. blat, to bleat.

blue, a color. See *blew*.

bluing, the act of making blue. bluewing, a bird.

blurt, to ejaculate. blirt, a gust of wind and rain.

boar, a male swine. See *bore*.

board, food; to cover with boards. bord, term used in mining. bored, perforated; wearied.

boat, a small vessel or water-craft. bote, compensation; help; aid.

bode, to predict good or ill. bowed, curved.

bold, brave. bowled, past tense of bowl. bolled, formed into a seed vessel.

bolder, more bold. boulder, a rock.

bolk, to belch. boke, to thrust; a term in mining.

bombous, shaped like a bomb; humming; buzzing. bombus, a term in pathology. Bombus, a genus of bees.

bonds, pl. of bond. bonze, a Buddhist monk.

bone, a part of the animal structure. Beaune, city in France; a wine.

boor, a coarse rustic. See *bore*.

boost, to push up; a push from behind. buist, a box; a coffin; to mark, as sheep or cattle.

bootees, children's half-boots. Bootes, a Northern constellation.

boozy, somewhat intoxicated. Bouzy, dist. and town in France; a wine.

border, an edge; a boundary. bordar, a cottier. boarder, one who boards.

bore, to pierce; to tire. boar, male swine. bower, a bow-maker; one who plays with a bow. Boer, a Dutch colonist in South Africa. boor, a coarse rustic.

born, brought forth. borne, carried. bourn or bourne, a boundary; a stream.

borough, a town. burrow, to dig into the ground. borrow, to receive on credit. burro, a donkey.

Bos, a genus of ruminants. bosse, a large glass bottle.

Boston, city in Mass. boston, a game of cards.

botany, the science of plants. bottony, botone, or bottone, a term in heraldry.

bough, branch of a tree. bow, part of a ship; a salutation.

bouquet, a nosegay. buke, the military families of Japan.

bow, a knot; an instrument. See *beau*.

bowl, a basin; a drinking-vessel; a large wooden bowl; to play with bowls. boll, the pod or capsule of a plant; to go to seed. bole, the body or stem of a tree.

bowled, rolled along. See *bold*.

bowman, a man who uses a bow. bollman, a cottager.

boxer, a pugilist; one who packs in boxes. Boxer, a member of a Chinese secret organization.

boy, a male child. buoy, a floating signal.

Brahma, the first of the Hindu-triad. Brama, genus of fishes. brahma, a hen.

braid, a flat cord; to weave. brayed, past tense of bray.

braise, to stew or bake. braze, to solder. brays, noises of an ass.

brake, a thicket; a check on a wheel; a vehicle. See *break*.

branded, past tense of brand. brandied, mingled with brandy.

brass, an alloy; excessive assurance. brasse, a fish.

bray, to make a harsh sound; to grind. brae, a steep ascent.

breach, a fracture. breech, part of a gun.

bread, food made of flour. bred, past tense of breed.

break, to separate violently; a pause. brake, a thicket; a check on a wheel; a vehicle.

breakage, the act of breaking; a break. brakeage, the action or controlling power of a brake.

breezy, blowy; windy. brisé, a term in heraldry.

bret, herring-spawn; the turbot. brett, a carriage.

brew, to boil or seethe; to plot. bruh, a monkey. broo, juice; broth.

brewing, from verb to brew. bruin, a bear.

brews, from verb to brew. bruise, to injure; a contusion.

bridal, pertaining to a bride. bridle, reins of a horse; to control.

bright, brilliant; full of light. brite, to be or become overripe.

bristling, covering with bristles; exciting violently. brisling, a small fish.

broach, to mention; a spit. brooch, an ornament.

broché, woven with a figure. brochet, a fish.

brogue, a stout, coarse shoe; a dialectic pronunciation. brog, a painted instrument; to prod.

brood, to sit upon eggs; to dwell upon gloomily. brewed, did brew.

broom, a plant; an implement for sweeping floors. brume, mist; fog; vapors. brougham, a carriage.

brows, pl. of brow. browse, to pasture.

brute, an animal. bruit, to noise abroad.

buist, a box; a coffin; to mark, as sheep or cattle. See *boost*.

buke, the military families of Japan. See *bouquet*.

bumpkin, an awkward, clumsy rustic. bumkin, a nautical term.

bungle, to act or work in a clumsy manner; to botch. bungall, a coin.

buoy, a signal at sea; to keep afloat. See *boy*.

bur or burr, part of a plant. birr, to make a whirring noise.

buried, past tense of bury. berried, furnished with berries.

burke, to murder by suffocation. birk, to give a tart answer.

burl, a small knot in thread; to pick knots. See *birl*.

burn, to destroy. bern or berne, a warrior; a hero. birn, a stem of dry heather. Berne, canton in Switz.

burral, narrow strips of plowing. burrel, a kind of cloth; a sort of pear. burrhel, a sheep.

burro, a donkey. burrow, to dig into the ground. See *borough*.

bury, to inter. burry, full of burs. See *berry*.

bus, an omnibus. buss, to salute; to dress; a kiss; a fishing vessel; a bush.

buskin, shoe. busking, a sailor's term.

but, except, unless. butt, a cask, a mark; to strike with the head.

buy, to purchase. by, at; near. bye, a dwelling; term used in cricket.

buyer, one who buys. byre, a cow-house.

C.

caama, a fox; an antelope. See *comma*.

cabré, a term in heraldry. *cabrée*, an antelope.

caddy, a box; a ghost. cadie, caddie, or cady, a Scotch errand boy. kadi or cadi, a Moslem judge.

Cæsar, a title; a dictator; a ruling family in ancient Rome. **seizor,** one who seizes.

cæsura, a term in prosody. **scissura,** a term in anatomy.

Cain, brother of Abel. **cane,** a reed or stick; a slender hollow-jointed stem.

calamus, a plant. **callimus,** term in mineralogy. **Callimus,** a genus of insects.

cale, to throw. See *kale.*

calendar, an almanac. **calender,** to smooth by pressing.

calf, the young of the cow. **caph** *or* **kaph,** a Jewish liquid measure.

calin, a Chinese alloy. See *kaolin.*

calk, to close up a seam. **cauk,** chalk, limestone.

calker, one who closes the seams in a boat. **kakar,** a small deer.

call, to cry out; to summon; to arouse; a short visit. **caul,** a membrane; a term in carpentry.

calla, a plant; a cloak. **callow,** unfledged; immature.

called, past tense of call. **cauld,** cold; a dam or weir.

callous, hardened; to make callous. **callus,** thickening; a callosity. **calice,** a calicle; a chalice. **callys,** clay state.

calm, free from disturbance; to bring into repose. **cam,** a piece of machinery.

calumniation, the act of calumniating. **columniation,** a term in architecture.

Cambay, state in India. **cambaye,** a cloth.

came, past tense of come. **kame,** a hill; a fortress or camp.

camel, a quadruped. **camil,** camomile. **chamal,** the Angora goat.

cammaron, a shrimp. **Cameron,** a surname.

campaign, an open field; a connected series of military operations; a canvass. **campane,** a term in heraldry. **campaigne,** a narrow lace.

can, a verb; a vessel. **canne,** a French measure. **Cannes,** a town in France.

canada, a liquid measure. **Canada,** a country.

candid, frank; open; impartial; ingenuous. **candied,** preserved with sugar.

candle, a taper. **kandel,** a tree.

cane, a reed or stick. See *Cain.*

canet, a bamboo-rat. **canette,** a pitcher or jug.

canister, a basket; a box for tea, coffee, spices. **canaster,** a rush basket; a tobacco.

Canna, a genus of plants. **Channa,** a genus of fishes. **kana,** Japanese writing. **kaneh,** a Hebrew measure.

canned, did can. **cand,** fluorite.

cannequin, a cotton cloth. **cannikin,** a drinking-cup.

cannon, a large gun. **canon,** a law or rule. **cañon** *or* **canyon,** a ravine. **canion,** an ornamental roll.

cans, pl. of can. **kans,** a grass.

can't, contraction of cannot. **cant,** hypocritical speech.

canvas, a coarse cloth. **canvass,** to solicit.

cap, a covering for the head; to complete; to crown; to put on a cap. **kapp,** a term in electricity.

caparison, a covering for a horse. See *comparison.*

caphar, a post or station. See *Kafir.*

capital, money invested; principal. **capitol,** public building.

car, a carriage for passengers and for freight. **carr,** a pool.

carat, a weight. **caret,** a sign used in printing. **carrot,** a vegetable. **carotte,** a roll of tobacco.

carcass, a dead body. **corcass,** a salt-marsh. **caucus,** a meeting.

cardinal, a church dignitary. **cardenal,** a fish.

careen, a nautical term. **carene,** a fast; a sweet wine.

Carinthian, belonging to Carinthia. See *Corinthian.*

carnation, a flower. **coronation,** the act of crowning.

carob, a plant. **carrub,** a fish.

carol, a dance; a song; to sing. **carrel,** a fabric; a closet or pew.

caroon, a cherry. **carroon**, a license.

carotte, a roll of tobacco. See *carat*.

carpal, pertaining to the wrist. **carpel**, a pistil; a flower.

carriage, a vehicle; behavior. **carritch**, a catechism.

carry, to bear; to convey. **karri** *or* **kari**, a large gum tree. **karree**, a sumac.

cart, a vehicle. **carte**, a bill of fare; a card. **quart**, a term in card-playing and fencing.

cartel, an agreement in writing; a challenge. **kartel**, a wooden hammock.

carval, a song. **carvel**, a jelly-fish.

cash, ready money. **cache**, a hole in the earth for the preservation of goods. **Cache**, a county in Utah; a river in Arkansas.

casino, a lodge; a club-house; a game of cards. **cassena**, a shrub.

cask, a vessel. **casque**, a helmet.

cast, to throw; to form in a mold. **caste**, class; race.

caster, one who throws. **castor**, a wheel; a bean; a bearer.

cat, a domestic animal. **kat**, Egyptian unit of weight.

caucus, a meeting. See *carcass*.

caudal, relating to the tail of an animal. **caudle**, a drink. **cadelle**, a larval beetle.

cauf, a chest. See *cough*.

cauk, limestone. See *calk*.

caul, a membrane; covering for the head; a term in carpentry. See *call*.

cause, motive; reason. **caws**, noise of a bird.

Cecil, a Christian name. See *scissel*.

cede, to resign. See *seed*.

ceduous, fit to be felled. See *sedulous*.

ceil, to overlay the inner roof. See *seal*.

celery, a vegetable. **salary**, wages.

cell, a small room. **sell**, to barter.

cellar, room under the house. **seller**, one who sells. **cella**, a room or chamber; a cell.

censor, a critic. **censer**, a vessel for incense. **sensor**, sensory.

censual, relating to the census. See *sensual*.

cent, a coin. **sent**, did send. **scent**, odor; to smell.

centless, penniless. **scentless**, without odor.

centnar, a Polish weight. **centner**, a weight.

cents, pl. of cent. **scents**, perfumes. **sense**, perception by the senses. **cense**, to perfume.

cerasin, a gum. **ceresin**, a waxy substance. **cerosin**, a substance found on the sugar-cane.

cercal, pertaining to the tail. See *circle*.

cere, to cover with wax. See *seer*.

cereal, relating to grain. **serial**, forming a series. **cerrial**, pertaining to the cerris.

cereous, wax-like. **cereus**, a plant. See *serious*.

cerge, a large wax candle. See *serge*.

cerin, beeswax; a mineral. See *serene*.

cerise, cherry color. See *series*.

cerous, of the nature of a cere. See *serous*.

cerulean, sky-colored; blue. **cerulein**, a coal-tar color used in dyeing.

cession, a giving up. See *session*.

cetaceous, of the whale species. **setaceous**, resembling a bristle.

cete, a whale. See *seat*.

chagrin, vexation. **shagreen**, skins of animals.

chalky, consisting of chalk. **chaki**, a fabric.

challis, a fabric. **chaly**, a coin.

chamar, a cobbler; a fan; a fly-flap. **chamarre**, a garment for men.

champagne, a sparkling wine. **champaign**, a level country; **Champagne**, an old French province. **Champaign**, a county and city in Illinois; county in Ohio.

chance, a happening. **chants**, hymns of praise, to sing.

chandler, a trader; one who makes or sells candles. **chandla**, an ornament worn by women in India.

Channa, a genus of fishes. See *canna.*

chaos, disorder, confusion; matter unformed and void. **chaus,** a jungle-cat. **Chaos,** the most ancient of the gods in Greek mythology.

chard, part of a plant; a variety of white beet. **charred,** blackened with fire.

charpie, lint for dressing wounds. **sharpie,** a flat-bottom boat.

chasse, a small glass of liquor served at dinner after the coffee; a shrine of a saint. **chassé,** a movement in dancing.

chaste, pure; refined. **chased,** past tense of chase.

chatelaine, an article suspended from a woman's belt. **chatelain,** a keeper of a castle.

chatter, to speak rapidly and foolishly; idle prattle. **chattah** *or* **chatta,** an umbrella.

chau, a unit of weight. See *chow.*

chauffeur, one who drives an automobile. **shophar,** an ancient musical instrument.

cheap, inexpensive. **cheep,** to chirp.

cheat, a fraud; to trick; a game of cards. **cheet,** to chatter or chirrup.

check, to restrain; to mark as a checker-board; an order for money. **cheque,** an order for money. **Czech,** a Slav.

cheeky, impudent. **cheki,** Turkish unit of weight.

chego, a unit of weight. **chigoe,** an insect.

chemise, a garment; a wall. **chimy,** a smock; shift.

Chen, a genus of geese. **ken,** to know; cognizance.

chermany, a game. See *Germany.*

Chermes, a genus of bark-lice. See *kermes.*

chersid, a tortoise. See *cursed.*

chessel, a mold or vat. **chesil,** small pebbles.

chesterfield, a top-coat. **Chesterfield,** an English earl.

cheviot, a woolen cloth. **Cheviot,** a breed of sheep.

chews, from verb to chew. See *choose.*

chic, stylish. **chick,** a chicken; to peep. **Csik,** a country in Hungary. **tchick,** a sound.

chicken, a fowl. **chickeen,** four rupees.

chilly, cold. **chilli,** red pepper. **Chili,** province in China; county in New York. **Chile,** a S. Amer. country.

china, common porcelain ware. **China,** country in Asia.

chinky, full of chinks. **chinche,** the skunk. **chincha,** a rodent. **Chinkie,** a Chinaman.

chintz, a cotton cloth. **chinse,** a nautical term.

chirr, to chirp; to coo as a pigeon. **Chur,** a mountain in India; a town in Switzerland. **churr,** a bird; a rough whirring sound.

chitin, a compound. See *kiting.*

chlak, a Hebrew unit of time. See *clack.*

choil, pertaining to a knife-blade. **choile,** to overreach.

choir, a band of singers. **quire,** twenty-four sheets of paper.

choler, anger. See *collar.*

cholic, pertaining to the bile. See *colic.*

chomer, a Hebrew measure. See *comber.*

choose, to select. **chews,** from verb to chew.

chopping, cutting with quick blows. **chopin** *or* **choppin,** a Scotch liquid measure. **Chopin,** a Polish musical composer. **chopine,** a clog.

choquette, a term in silk-culture. See *coquette.*

chord, a term in music, geometry, and engineering. See *cord.*

chorda, a tendon. **Chorda,** a genus of algæ.

chordal, pertaining to a chord. **chordel,** a plane curve.

chow, to chew; the jowl; a unit of weight. **chau,** a unit of weight.

chrome, a whitish brittle metal. **crome,** a hook.

chronicle, to register; a record. chronical, lingering.

chuff, a coarse, dull fellow; a cheek. chough, a bird.

chute, a trough. See *shoot*.

chyle, a fluid. kyle, a sound; a strait; a lamp.

cibol, a plant. See *sibyl*.

cider, juice of apples. sider, one who takes sides.

cingle, a girth. See *single*.

cingular, circular. See *singular*.

cinque, five in cards. See *sank*.

cion, the uvula. See *scion*.

ciphering, reckoning. syphering, a term used in carpentry.

circle, a ring. cercal, pertaining to the tail.

circulate, to pass from place to place. surculate, to prune; to trim.

circus, a show. cercus, part of an insect.

cirrus, a light fleecy cloud; a tendril. cirrose, *or* cirrhose, *or* cirrous, *or* cirrhous, having a cirrus; resembling tendrils; having a tufted head.

cist, a casket. See *cyst*.

cit, a citizen. See *sit*.

cital, quotation; citation. scytal, a snake.

cite, to summon. See *sight*.

citizen, inhabitant of a city; a private citizen; a freeman. cytisin, an alkaloid.

clack, a sharp sound. claque, hired applause. chlak, a Hebrew unit of time.

claimant, one who claims. clamant, urgent.

clamor, a great outcry. clammer, a forceps.

clarence, a four-wheeled carriage. Clarence, a man's name.

clarendon, a form of printing type. Clarendon, an English earl.

clause, part of a sentence. claws, nails of an animal.

clay, moist earth. claye, a hurdle.

cleft, a crevice; cloven. klepht, a bandit.

click, a sharp sound. clique, a party or faction.

climatic, pertaining to climate.

climactic, of the nature of a climax.

climb, to ascend. clime, climate.

clinker, refuse of burning coal; a scale of oxid of iron; a kind of brick. klinker, a South African biscuit.

close, to shut; the end. clothes, garments.

cluck, a sound made by a hen. cleuch, a steep descent.

cnicin, a term in chemistry. See *Nicene*.

coal, fuel. cole, cabbage. kohl, a variety of cabbage.

coaled, supplied with coal. cold, lacking heat.

coaming *or* combing, raised work around the hatches of a ship. See *combing*.

coarse, not fine. course, direction; career. corse, used poetically for corpse.

coarser, less fine. courser, a horse.

coat, a garment; to cover. cote, a sheepfold. quote, to repeat.

coax, to fondle; cajole; a simpleton. coaks, cinders.

cob, a leader or chief; a haystack; an ear of wheat; a fish; a Spanish dollar; pillar of coal; a horse; a wicker basket; a gull; a breakwater; to strike; to break into small fragments. cobb, a coach used in Australia. kob, an antelope.

cobble, a rounded stone; to mend or patch boots; to put together in a clumsy manner. coble *or* cobble, a flat-bottomed fishing boat.

cobbler, one who cobbles. cobler, a bent rasp.

cobra, a snake. cobbra, the head; skull; top.

cocaine, an alkaloid. Cockaigne *or* Cocagne, the land of cockneys.

coccus, part of a plant; spherical cells of bacteria. Coccus, a genus of insects. coccous, composed of cocci.

cock, a male bird; to tilt. coque, a bow of ribbon.

Cockaigne, the land of cockneys. See *cocaine*.

cockscomb, the comb of a cock. **coxcomb,** a conceited person.

cockspur, a spur; a plant. **cocksper,** salmon-fry.

cocoa or **coco,** a palm. **coca,** dried leaves of a shrub; a measure. **coco,** a bird. **koko,** a plant; a bird.

cocoon, an egg-case. **kokoon,** the gnu.

coda, term in music. **codo,** a measure.

coddling, humoring; pampering; boiling gently. **codling,** a fish; an apple.

cohoes, a fish. **Cohoes,** a city in New York.

coin, money; a wedge. **coigne,** quartering oneself on another. **quoin,** a corner; a wedge. **coign,** a wedge; a coin.

coke, a fuel; to convert into coke. **coak,** a nautical term.

col, a narrow pass. **coll,** to cut off; to embrace.

cole, cabbage. See *coal.*

Coleus, a genus of herbs and shrubs. **Colias,** a genus of butterflies. **Colius,** a genus of birds.

colic, acute pain. **cholic,** pertaining to the bile.

collar, a neckband; to seize by the collar. **choler,** anger.

collared, having a collar. **collard,** a cabbage.

collie, a sheep dog. **colie** or **coly,** a bird.

collin, gelatin. **colin,** a bird. **colline,** a little hill.

collybus, a coin. **collybos,** a cake.

cologne, a kind of perfumed alcohol. **Cologne,** city in Prussia. **colon,** a punctuation mark. **colonne,** part of a roulette-table. **Colon,** city in Panama.

colonel, chief officer of a regiment. **kernel,** the meat of a nut. **cornel,** a tree.

color, hue. **culler,** one who culls.

columbine, a plant; having the characters of a pigeon or dove. **Columbine,** the sweetheart of Harlequin. **columbin,** a nonconducting material used in electric lighting.

column, a pillar; perpendicular section of a page; body of troops. **collum,** the neck.

columniation, a term in architecture. See *calumniation.*

comber, one who combs. **chomer,** a Hebrew measure.

combing, dressing the hair. **coaming** or **combing,** raised work around the hatches of a ship.

comer, one who comes or arrives. **cummer,** a gossip.

comers, those who arrive. **kommers,** festivities among German university students.

comes, does come. **comes,** a book containing the Epistles.

coming, the act of approaching. **cumming,** a vessel.

comma, a punctuation mark; a musical interval. **caama,** a fox; an antelope.

company, fellowship; association; a guest; an assemblage. **compony,** a term in heraldry.

comparison, the act of comparing. **caparison,** a covering for a horse.

compeer, an equal. **compear,** to appear in court.

compilation, the act of compiling; that which is compiled. **compellation,** style of address or salutation.

compliment, courtesy. **complement,** full quantity.

conch, a shell. **conk,** a confidential chat.

conciliary, pertaining to a council. **consiliary,** of the nature of advice.

concourse, an assemblage; a place of meeting. **concours,** a public competition for a prize.

cone, a solid body. **Cosne,** a wine. **chone,** a dome-like cavity.

confectionery, sweetmeats. **confectionary,** pertaining to confectionery; a confectioner; a sweetmeat.

confident, certain. **confidant,** a trusted friend. **confidante,** a female confidant.

congé, permission to depart. **congee,** to make a bow; rice gruel.

congou, a grade of black tea. congo, an eel; **Congo,** a negro dance; a river in Africa.

connaught, a cotton cloth. **Connaught,** a province in Ireland. **Conneaut,** a township in Ohio.

consign, to give, send, or commit. consigne, a special order; a watchword.

consiliary, of the nature of advice. See *conciliary.*

consols, government securities. consuls, representatives of government. consoles, comforts.

consumer, one who or that which consumes. **consumar** *or* **consumah,** in the East Indies, a house steward.

Conté, a French painter. **Conti,** an Italian poet.

conventical, pertaining to a convent. **conventicle,** an assembly.

conventional, established by usage. **conventual,** relating to a convent. **Conventual,** a member of a Franciscan order.

conversable, disposed to converse. conversible, capable of being transformed.

cony *or* coney, a rabbit; a daman; the fur of conics; a term used in heraldry and ichthyology. coni, pl. of conus.

coo, to utter a low, plaintive sound. coup, a sudden stroke.

cookee, a cook. **cooky,** a cake.

cooler, a vessel for cooling liquids. couleur, term in card-playing.

coolly, calmly. cooly *or* coolie, a porter or laborer. **kuli,** hire; wages.

coom, cull; soot; that which exudes from the box of carriage wheels; sawdust; a dry measure. **coomb,** a vat for brewing; a bowl-shaped valley.

coontee, a harrow. **coontie** *or* coonty, a plant.

coop, to cage; an inclosure; a Dutch measure for grain. **coup,** to turn upside down; to trade or bargain; a master-stroke; a fault in a coal-seam; the act of upsetting. **coupe,** a Swiss dry measure; a cup-shaped ornament.

cooper, a maker of barrels. **couper,** a lever. **Cowper,** an English poet.

copenhagen, a drink; a game; a kind of snuff. **Copenhagen,** capital of Denmark.

copies, pl. of copy. **coppice,** a thicket of bushes.

copy, to imitate; to repeat; a reproduction; a single book of a set; manuscript; a law; a transcript; a size of writing paper. **Coppée,** a French poet.

coque, a bow of ribbon. See *cock.*

coquette, a frivolous woman. **choquette,** a term in silk-culture. **coquet,** to flirt.

cora, the Arabian gazel. **Cora,** a girl's name. **corah,** a creamy silk stuff. **Korah,** a Bible name.

coral, a product of the ocean. corral, an inclosure; to capture. corol, a corolla.

coralline, relating to coral. **corylin,** a vegetable globulin. **corallin,** a dyestuff. **corolline,** a botanical term.

corbeil *or* corbeille, a basket of earth on a parapet; a sculptured basket of fruit or flowers. **corbel,** term in architecture and entomology. **corbeil,** term in architecture.

corcass, a salt-marsh. See *carcass.*

cord, a string; a measure of wood. chord, a term used in music, geometry, and engineering.

cordelière, a term in heraldry. Cordelier, a Franciscan monk; a political club of the French Revolution.

cordelle, to tow by hand; a tow-line or rope. **cordel,** a Spanish measure.

core, the inner part. **corps,** a body of soldiers. **khor,** the dry bed of a stream. **coir,** fiber from the husk of the cocoanut.

co-respondent, a term in law. See *correspondent.*

corinne, a gazel; a bird. **Corinne,** the heroine in a novel of that name. **Corinne,** a girl's name.

Corinthian, pertaining to Corinth. Carinthian, belonging to Carinthia.

corm, a stem; a cormus. **corme,** the service-tree.

cornet, a musical instrument. **cornette,** a term in metallurgy.

corollate, resembling a corolla. See *correlate*.

coronation, the act of crowning. See *carnation*.

coronilla, a Spanish dollar. **Coronilla,** a genus of plants. **Coronella,** a genus of snakes.

corporal, an officer. **corporeal,** relating to the body.

correlate, to put in mutual relation; to connect correspondingly; a correlative. **corollate,** resembling a corolla. **corollet,** a floret.

correspondence, fitness; intercourse by letters. **correspondents,** writers.

correspondent, adapted; suitable; one who communicates by means of letters; a commercial agent. **co-respondent,** a legal term.

corse, corpse. See *coarse*.

Coruna, a province in Spain. **Corunna,** city in Michigan.

cosset, a pet lamb; to fondle. **cossette,** beet-root cut up in rectangular prisms.

cote, a sheepfold. See *coat*.

cotter, a cottager. **cotta,** a short surplice; a coarse blanket.

coudé, bent at right angles. **coudée,** a measure; a cubit.

cough, to expel from the throat or lungs. **cauf** *or* **cawf,** a chest for fish. **koff,** a Dutch vessel. **coff,** to purchase; to atone for.

coulé, a musical term. **coulée,** a dry ravine.

couleur, a selected suit in the game of rolo. **coulure,** sterility in plants. **couloir,** a gorge or gully.

council, an assembly. **counsel,** advice; to advise.

coup, a telling blow. See *coo*.

coupé, a carriage. **coupee,** a movement in dancing. **cupie,** a head-dress. **coppé,** a term in heraldry.

couple, a pair; to unite. **cupel,** a shallow cup.

coupon, a commercial instrument; part of a ticket. **cupang,** a tree.

course, direction. See *coarse*.

couril, a fairy. **courol,** a bird. **Kurile,** islands in the North Pacific Ocean.

courts, legal tribunals; woos. **Cortes,** national legislature of Spain or Portugal.

court-marshal, a marshal of a law court. **court-martial,** a court of military or naval officers; to try as a soldier or sailor.

cousin, a relative. **cozen,** to cheat; a cheat. **Cousin,** a French philosopher.

covenanter, one who covenants or agrees. **Covenanter,** one of a Scottish band of Presbyterians. **covenantor,** a law term.

coward, one who lacks courage. **cowered,** past tense of cower. **cowherd,** one who tends cows.

cowl, a monk's hood. **cowle,** a lease.

cows, pl. of cow. **Cowes,** a seaport in the Isle of Wight. **Coues,** an American naturalist.

coxcomb, a conceited person. See *cockscomb*.

Cracovian, pertaining to the city of Cracow. **Cracovienne,** a Polish dance; music written for such a dance.

crape, a thin transparent stuff; to cover with crape; to crimp or frizzle. **crêpe,** a French form of crape.

crate, a large basket or hamper; to put into a crate. **crête,** the crest of a parapet.

crawl, to creep. **kraal,** a Hottentot village.

crawly, creepy. **crawley,** a plant.

crazy, demented, insane. **craisey,** the buttercup.

crease, a mark made by folding; to mark. **creese,** a sword.

cree, to soften by boiling. **Cree,** a tribe of Indians.

creek, a small stream. **creak,** to make a grating sound; a noise. **Creek,** a tribe of Indians.

crêpe, a dress fabric. See *crape*.

cressy, abounding in cresses. **Crecy,** a noted battlefield of France.

crevice, a crack; to make crevices

in. **crevis,** the crawfish. **crev-asse,** a fissure or crack. **crevisse,** a piece of armor.

crew, a company of seamen; a crowd. **creux,** intaglio; a term used in sculpture. **Crewe,** a town in England. **Kroo,** a tribe of negroes.

crews, pl. of crew. See *cruise.*

crewel, yarn. See *cruel.*

crick, a creaking noise; a jack-screw; a teal; a spasmodic action of the muscles. **cric,** part of a lamp.

crier, one who cries. **cryer,** a young goshawk.

critic, one who criticizes. **critique,** a criticism.

criticism, the act of criticizing. **Creticism,** a falsehood; a Cret-ism.

crock, an earthen pot or jar; soot; a small curl; to blacken with soot. **croc,** a hooked rest.

crome, a hook. See *chrome.*

crony, an intimate companion. **krone,** a coin.

crool, to mutter. See *cruel.*

croquet, a game. **croquette,** an article of food.

cross, to intersect; to erase; peevish; an emblem. **crosse,** a lacrosse-stick.

croton, a foliage plant. **Croton,** a genus of plants; a river in New York.

croupier, one who collects the money at a gambling table; an assistant chairman. **croupière,** armor for the croup of a horse.

crower, a fowl that crows. **crore,** the number ten millions.

crows, pl. of crow. **croze,** a cooper's tool.

crozer, a cooper's tool. **crozier** *or* **crosier,** a staff; the Southern Cross.

cruel, inhuman. **crewel,** yarn. **crool,** to mutter.

cruise, a voyage. **cruse,** a jug. **crews,** pl. of crew.

cryptogam, a plant. **cryptogram,** a message or writing; a crypto-graph.

crystal, a symmetrical structure

bounded by plane surfaces; a species of glass; consisting of crystal. **chrysal,** an imperfection in a bow.

cuarta, a long whip. See *quarto.*

cuckold, the husband of an adulter-ess; the cowbird; the cowfish. **cuckhold,** an instrument used in brickmaking.

cuckoo, a bird. **kuku,** a large pigeon.

cucujo, a large firefly. **cucuyo,** a fish.

cud, portion of unchewed food; the first stomach of ruminating animals. **khud,** a ravine.

cue, a hint; a rod used in billiards; the tail. **queue,** a tie of hair; a cue.

culler, one who culls. See *color.*

cummer, a gossip. See *comer.*

cumming, a vessel. See *coming.*

cumulus, a summer cloud. **cumu-lous,** resembling a summer cloud.

cuniculus, an underground pas-sage. **cuniculous,** pertaining to rabbits. **Cuniculus,** a genus of lemmings.

cunner, a fish. **kunner,** a log canoe.

cupel, a shallow cup. See *couple.*

cupper, one who performs cupping. **cuppa,** bowl of a chalice.

cur, a dog. **curr,** to coo, or purr, or hoot.

curassow, a bird. **Curaçao,** an island. **curaçao,** a cordial.

cure, to heal. **curé,** a French priest.

curious, inquisitive, prying. **cu-rios,** bric-a-brac; articles of virtu.

currant, a fruit. **current,** flow of a stream; passing.

cursed, detestable. **chersid,** a tortoise.

curser, one who utters a curse. **cursor,** part of a mathematical instrument.

curtain, a hanging screen. **curtein,** a sword.

curve, crooked; a continuous bend-ing. **kerve,** to carve. **kirve,** a term in coal-mining.

custody, care, guardianship. **cus-todee,** a custodian.

cutter, one who cuts. kuttar, an Indian dagger.

Cyclamen, a genus of plants. cyclamen, a plant. cyclamin, a glucosid. cyclamon, a purplish red.

cygnet, a swan. signet, a seal.

cymbal, a musical instrument. See symbol.

cynical, ill-natured. sinical, relating to a sine.

Cyon, a genus of wild dogs. See scion.

cypress, a tree. Cyprus, an island. cyprus, a thin crape. Cypris, a genus of crustacea; a Cyprian goddess.

cyrus, a crane. Cyrus, a Bible name. syrus, a bird.

cyst, term in medicine, botany, and zoölogy. cist, a casket. sist, a law term.

cystin, a chemical. See Sistine.

cyte, a cell. See sight.

cytisin, an alkaloid. See citizen.

Czech, a Slav. See check.

D.

dab, to strike; a quick blow; a fish. dhabb, dried flesh of the skink.

dado, to groove; term in architecture. dedo, a measure.

dagger, a weapon. daggar, a shark.

dago, slang for an Italian, Spaniard, or Portuguese. degu, a quadruped.

daimen, occasional. daimon, a demon.

daisy, a plant; pretty; charming. dazy, cold; raw.

dally, to loiter, delay. dhalee, an oriental necklace.

dam, an embankment to inclose water. damn, to condemn.

damaskeen or damasken, to embellish; to damask. damaskin, a fine sword.

dan, a title; term in mining. dhan, a weight. Dan, a contraction of Daniel.

dance, to move with measured steps, as with music. danse, term in heraldry.

dandy, a fop; a vessel. dandie, a dog.

Dane, a native of Denmark. See deign.

dart-moth, a noctuid moth. Dartmouth, a town in Massachusetts; a town in England.

dartos, a term used in anatomy. dartars, an ulcer on lambs.

daughter, a female child. darter, one who throws a dart; a fish. dartre, a disease of the skin.

davit, a support for small boats. davite, a sulphate of aluminum.

daw, to become day; a bird. dauw, a zebra.

day, from sunrise to sunset. dey, formerly a governor of Algiers.

days, pl. of day. daze, to stupefy.

dean, a small valley; a title. dein, entirely.

dear, costly; beloved. deer, an animal.

debutant, one who makes a debut. debutante, a female debutant.

decease, death. See disease.

decision, the act of deciding; firmness; positiveness. discission, a cutting asunder.

declivant, declinant. declivent, bent forward.

décolleté, cut low in the neck. decalet, a stanza of ten lines. decollate, to behead. décolletée, having the neck and shoulders bare.

dedalous, marked with intricate windings. Dædalus, in mythology, the builder of the Cretan Labyrinth.

dedimus, a legal term. Didymus, a Bible name.

dedo, a measure. See dado.

deem, to consider, regard, estimate. deme, a territorial division; a term in biology.

deference, respect. See difference.

deferential, expressing deference. differential, indicating difference.

deformity, want of proper form; ugliness. difformity, difference in form.

deign, to condescend. Dane, a native of Denmark.

delate, to carry; convey. See *dilate*.

delegate, a representative. deligate, to ligate.

delegation, persons deputed; act of sending away. deligation, a binding up.

demark, to mark off. demarch, march; a ruler.

demean, to behave. demesne, possessions.

demur, to object; to take exception; a suspension of decision. demure, sober, grave, decorous.

denier, a silver penny. See *dernier*.

dental, pertaining to the teeth; a sound, as that of d, t, or n. dentelle, lace; a lace-like decoration. dentil, or dentel, a term in architecture and heraldry. dentile, a small tooth.

depositary, one entrusted with anything. depository, a place of deposit.

derby, a hat; a tool. Derby, horse-race of England. Derbe, a genus of insects.

derham, an Arabian weight. See *Durham*.

dernier, last, final, ultimate. denier, a silver penny.

derrick, an apparatus for hoisting heavy weights. deric, term in embryology.

descension, a falling or sinking. See *dissension*.

descent, act of descending; lineage. dissent, disagreement.

desert, to forsake; waste land. dessert, last course at dinner.

desman, a small mammal. desmine, a mineral. desmon, a term in medical science.

desperate, reckless; furious. disparate, dissimilar; discordant.

deter, to hinder; to prevent from acting. detur, a prize. detour, a circuitous route.

deva, a Hindu deity. See *diva*.

devil, Satan; an evil spirit. devel, a hard blow.

deviser, one who devises. devisor, one who bequeaths property by will. divisor, the number that divides.

dew, moisture. due, owing. do, to perform.

dey, formerly a governor of Algiers. See *day*.

dhabb, dried flesh of the skink. See *dab*.

dhan, a weight. See *dan*.

dharri, a unit of weight. dhauri, a shrub.

dhole, a dog. See *dole*.

dholl, the pigeon-pea. See *dole*.

diagram, plan or outline; to sketch in outline. digram, consisting of two letters having one sound.

dicast, an Athenian juryman. diecast, a casting of the die.

die, to expire; a stamp. dye, to color.

difference, unlikeness. deference, respect.

different, unlike. deferent, respectful.

differential, indicating difference. See *deferential*.

difformity, difference in form. See *deformity*.

digram, consisting of two letters. See *diagram*.

dilate, to expand; to relate. delate, to carry; convey.

dine, to eat or to give a dinner. dyne, a term in physics.

dingy, of a dusky color. dingey, a small boat.

dire, dreadful. dyer, one who dyes.

disaster, misfortune; to injure. Dysaster, a genus of sea-urchins.

discreet, prudent. discrete, disjoined.

discuss, to debate. discus, a quoit. discous, like a disc.

disease, sickness. disseize, a law term. decease, death.

dissension, disagreement in opinion. descension, a falling or sinking.

dissent, disagreement. See *descent*.

dissimulation, hypocrisy. dissimilation, the act of rendering dissimilar.

distil, to produce by vaporization. distyle, having two columns.

districts, pl. of district. distrix, a disease of the hair.

ditty, a song. dittay, term in Scotch law.

diva, a female singer. deva, a term in Hindu mythology.

divers, different in kind; more than one. diverse, different in kind.

divert, to deflect; to turn aside. divort, a watershed.

divine, godlike; to find out; to surmise. davyne, a mineral.

divisor, the number that divides. See *deviser*.

do, to perform. See *dew*.

doab *or* duab, land between two convergent streams. doob, a kind of grass.

docile, teachable; tractable; easily managed. dossil *or* dossel, a spigot in a cask. dossal *or* dossel, a hanging.

doe, a deer. dough, unbaked paste. do, a syllable in music.

doer, one who performs. douar, a circle of Arab tents.

does, pl. of doe. doze, to sleep.

dole, a part; to deal out grudgingly. dohl, a kind of pea. dhole, a dog. dholl, the pigeon-pea.

dolman, a cloak. dollman, a robe worn by Turks. dolmen, a monument of rough stones.

done, finished; sufficiently cooked. dun, dark; to urge payment of a debt.

donee, a person to whom a gift is made. doni, a boat.

dood, a plant; a camel in military use. See *dude*.

dook, a piece of wood for attaching finishings to. See *duke*.

doon, a tree. See *dune*.

door, gate of a house; entrance. dor *or* dorr, a beetle; a trick; a joker.

dorsal, pertaining to the back. dorsel, a pannier.

dost, past tense of verb do. See *dust*.

doty, decayed, as a tree or log. doti, a measure of four yards. dhotee *or* dhoty, a loin-cloth worn by Hindus.

douzain, a piece of verse. douzaine, a body of men representing a parish.

dowel, a pin or peg; to fasten by dowel pins. dowl, the blade of a feather.

dower, a dowry; to endow. douar *or* dowar, a collection of Arab tents.

dowry, an endowment; a gift. douree, a necklace.

draft, an order; to delineate. draught, act of drinking; to draw.

dram, fraction of an ounce; a glass of liquor. drachm, a weight; a coin.

drier, one who dries; more dry. dreier *or* dreyer, a Silesian money.

droop, to pine away. drupe, a fleshy fruit containing a stone.

dual, double; relating to or composed of two. duel, a combat. Deuel, county in Nebraska.

dualist, a believer in dualism. duelist, a combatant.

dub, to confer a dignity on. dubb, Syrian bear.

duchess, wife of a duke. duchies, pl. of duchy.

ducks, pl. of duck. dux, a leader; a term in music. ducts, pl. of duct.

duct, a tube or canal in bodies or plants. ducked, past tense of duck.

dude, a fop. dood, a plant; a camel in military use.

dudeen, a short-stemmed clay pipe. dudine, a dudish woman.

due, a term in music. Douay, a version of the Bible.

due, owing. See *dew*.

duke, one of the highest order of nobility. douc, a monkey. dook, a piece of wood for attaching finishings to.

dulce, a sweet confection; to sweeten. dulse, a seaweed.

duly, suitably, properly. doolee, a litter or canvas palanquin.

dumb, incapable of speech. dum, a wooden frame.

dun, dark; to urge payment of a debt. See *done*.

dune, a hill of loose sand. doon, a tree.

Dunker, a member of a religious sect. **duncur**, a bird.

dupe, to deceive; to impose upon; one who is misled. **doup**, buttocks; a term in weaving. **doupe**, a carrion-crow.

Durham, one of a breed of cattle. **derham**, an Arabian weight.

dust, fine particles; to brush or wipe off dust. **dost**, past tense of verb do.

dye, to color. See *die*.

dyer, one who dyes. See *dire*.

dying, expiring. **dyeing**, coloring.

dyne, a term in physics. See *dine*.

E.

Eads, an American engineer. **Edes**, Benjamin, an American journalist and patriot. **Edes**, Henry Herbert, American antiquarian.

eager, keenly desirous; ardent. **eger**, a tulip.

ear, early. See *air*.

earing, a nautical term; coming into ear. **ear-ring**, an ornament.

earn, to gain. **urn**, a vase.

ease, to give relief; rest; tranquillity. **aes**, money or coins.

easel, a support for blackboard or portfolio. **easle**, hot ashes or cinders.

east, toward sunrise. **yeast**, leaven.

eau, water. See *O*.

eaves, lower edge of a roof. **Eve's**, possessive of Eve.

edition, copies printed at one time. See *addition*.

e'er, ever. See *air*.

eerie *or* eery, affected with fear. See *aerie*.

effect, result. See *affect*.

effluence, a flowing out; issue; efflux. See *affluence*.

egressor, one who goes out. See *aggressor*.

egret, egrett, *or* egrette, a heron; a heron's plume; bunch of long feathers; a monkey. **aigret** *or* **aigrette**, the small white heron; a plume composed of feathers.

eight, a numeral. See *ate*.

eighty, eight times ten. **Ate**, a goddess.

elapse, to slip away. **Elaps**, a genus of serpents. **illapse**, influx; inspiration.

electrician, one versed in the science of electricity. **electrition**, term in physiology.

elegy, a mournful poem; sad composition in music. **elogy**, a funeral oration.

elicit, to draw out. **illicit**, unlawful.

elision, the cutting off of a vowel. **Elysian**, pertaining to Elysium.

elocution, utterance by speech. See *allocution*.

elogium, a funeral oration. See *eulogium*.

elude, to escape; to evade the pursuit of. See *allude*.

elusion, an evasion. **elution**, a washing out. See *allusion*.

emerge, to come forth; to rise as from a fluid. **immerge**, to put under water.

emersed, term in botany. See *immersed*.

emigrant, one who emigrates. **immigrant**, one who comes into the country.

emigrate, to remove from one's native land. **immigrate**, to move into a country.

eminence, distinction; elevation. **imminence**, impending danger.

eminent, distinguished. **imminent**, threatening. **immanent**, inherent; intrinsic. **emanent**, an algebraic term; flowing from a source.

emission, issue. **immission**, injection.

emit, to send forth. See *omit*.

empress, a ruler. **impress**, a mark; to mark.

emu, a large bird; an Australian wood. **imu**, a pit for roasting meat.

enallage, a term in rhetoric. See *analogy*.

encyst, to inclose in a cyst. See *insist*.

enemy, a foe; an adversary. **enema**, a medical term.

enervate, to render feeble. **innervate,** to supply with nerves.

entomology, science of insects. See *etymology.*

enucleater, one who develops, explains, or discloses. **enucleator,** a surgical instrument.

enumerable, capable of being enumerated. See *innumerable.*

enumerate, to name over. **annumerate,** to add.

enunciate, to utter. See *annunciate.*

equities, pl. of equity. **equites,** a group of butterflies; an ancient order of knights.

eradiation, emission of radiance. See *irradiation.*

ere, before. See *air.*

errant, rambling. See *arrant.*

Erse, belonging to the Celts. **ers,** a species of vetch.

eruption, a bursting forth. **irruption,** a sudden rushing in.

erysipelas, a disease. **erysipelous,** of the nature of erysipelas.

escribe, to copy or write out. See *ascribe.*

essay, a treatise; to attempt. **assay,** to prove; to attempt.

estrayed, past tense of estray. **estrade,** a raised platform.

ethyl, chemistry. **Ethel,** a Christian name.

etymology, derivation of words. **entomology,** science of insects. **atomology,** doctrine of atoms.

eulogium, eulogy. **elogium,** a funeral oration.

euphony, agreeable utterance. **euphone,** an organ stop.

eversion, overthrow; destruction. See *aversion.*

Eve's, possessive of Eve. See *eaves.*

eviction, ejectment. **evection,** term in astronomy.

evil, wicked; wrong. **eval,** relating to an age.

ewe, a sheep. **yew,** a tree. **you,** a pronoun. **yu** *or* **yuh,** jade.

ewer, a jug. **your,** belonging to you. **yore,** long ago.

ewes, sheep. See *use.*

exceed, to go beyond; to surpass.

accede, agree; assent; to enter upon an office or dignity.

except, to object; exclusive of. See *accept.*

executor, one appointed to execute a will. **executer,** one who carries into effect.

exercise, practice; to train. **exorcise,** to expel; conjure up.

exert, to put forth. **exsert,** protruded.

exerted, past tense of exert. **exserted,** standing out.

exertion, the act of exerting. **exsertion,** the state of being exserted.

extent, degree; compass. **extant,** in existence.

eyed, having eyes. **ide,** a fish.

eyelet, a small hole. **islet,** a small island.

eyra, a wild cat. See *Ira.*

eyrie *or* eyry, an eagle's nest. See *aerie.*

F.

facet, a face of a diamond. **fascet,** an iron rod.

fail, to come short of; to prove ineffective. **faille,** an untwilled silk fabric.

fain, gladly. **fane,** a temple. **feign,** to dissemble.

faint, languid. **feint,** a pretense.

fair, just; not cloudy. **fare,** passage money; food.

fakir, a Mohammedan ascetic. **faker,** one who fakes; a thief.

falks, pl. of falk. **falx,** a metal implement.

farrago, a jumble. See *virago.*

fate, destiny. **fête,** a festival.

father, a parent. **farther,** beyond.

faucet, a spigot. **fossette,** a hollow; a dimple.

fawn, to court favor; a deer. **faun,** a woodland deity.

fays, fairies. See *phase.*

fear, dread; to be afraid. **feer,** one who holds a fee.

feat, exploit. **feet,** pl. of foot.

feel, to perceive by the touch; feeling; touch. **fiel,** comfortable; cozy. **feal,** to hide.

fees, pl. of fee. feeze *or* feaze, to drive off; a race; a run.

feign, to dissemble; to imagine; to invent. See *fain*.

feint, a pretense. See *faint*.

fellah, an Egyptian peasant. feller, one who fells; part of a sewing-machine. fellow, an associate. felloe, rim of a wheel.

femoral, pertaining to the thigh. femerell *or* femerel, a lantern or cover placed on a roof.

fen, low wet land; a disease of hops; to forbid, as in a game. foehn, a dry southerly wind.

fendu, slashed as a garment. See *vendue*.

fern, a plant. firn, glacier-snow.

ferrule, a band of metal; a short pipe-coupling; the frame of a slate. ferule, a stick; to punish.

ferry, to carry in a boat; place for ferrying. firry, abounding in firs. furry, covered with fur.

fête, a festival. See *fate*.

few, not many. feu, a tenure of land.

fiel, comfortable; cozy. See *feel*.

figwort, a plant. fig-wart, a term in pathology.

filander, a worm. See *philander*.

file, to reduce or sharpen with a file; an instrument for filing. phial, a small bottle. phyle, a geographical division of ancient Greece.

Filipino, a Philippine Islander. See *philopena*.

fillet, a narrow bandage for the head; a slice of meat; the thread of a screw. filet, a decoration.

fillip, a sharp blow with the finger. Philip, a man's name. philip, a bird.

filter, a strainer; to purify. philter, a charm.

fin, a fish's organ. Finn, a native of Finland.

find, to discover. fined, taxed.

finicking, fussy; exact in trifles. finikin, a pigeon; dainty in dress.

finish, to complete; a last touch. Finnish, pertaining to Finland.

fir, a tree. fur, covering of an animal.

fire-boat, a steamboat for extinguishing fires. fire-bote, a law term.

firm, a partnership; made fast; strong. firme, term in heraldry.

firn, glacier-snow. See *fern*.

firry, abounding in firs. See *ferry*.

first, preceding all others; prior in time; highest in rank. fürst, a German nobleman.

fished, past tense of verb fish. fiched, term in heraldry.

fisher, one who fishes. fissure, a cleft.

fizz, a hissing noise. phiz, the face.

flam, a delusion; to deceive. flamb, to baste, as meat.

flask, a bottle. flasque, term in heraldry.

flea, an insect. flee, to run from.

fleer, one who flees. fleer, to grin in mockery; derision.

flew, did fly. flue, chimney.

flews, a dog's lips. See *flues*.

flies, insects; does fly. flys, light vehicles for passengers.

flight, act of flying or fleeing; flock of birds; stairs. flite, to scold; a noisy quarrel.

flocks, a collection of sheep or birds; gathers in companies. Phlox, a genus of plants. phlox, a plant.

flow, current; to run as water. floe, floating ice.

flower, blossom. flour, meal.

flues, chimneys. flews, the hanging upper lips of certain dogs.

fly, an insect; a vehicle; to move in the air. vlei *or* vly, a valley; a marshy place.

flys, light carriages. See *flies*.

focal, pertaining to a focus. phocal, pertaining to seals.

foes, pl. of foe. foze, to become moldy.

foh, an exclamation of dislike. Foh, a Chinese name for Buddha.

fold, to double; a plait; a pen for animals. foaled, brought forth.

folios, pages of a book. foliose, having the form of a leaf.

fondu, dissolved; blended. fondue, a pudding.

foray, the act of foraging; to ravage. foret, a gimlet or drill.

forbear, to refrain from; desist.
forebear, an ancestor.
forbearing, long-suffering; patient.
fur-bearing, yielding a fur.
forcible, by force; strong. **force-able,** that may be forced.
fore, coming first. **four,** a numeral.
for, a preposition.
foresight, forethought. **forcite,** a compound.
foreway, a highroad. **foreweigh,** to estimate in advance.
forked, shaped like a fork. **fork-head,** an arrow-head.
formally, ceremoniously. **for-merly,** in times past.
fort, a stronghold. **forte,** a peculiar talent.
forte, a musical term. **forty,** a numeral.
forth, forward. **fourth,** next after the third.
forward, onward; in advance; to send or to help forward. **fore-word,** a preface to a literary work.
fossette, a hollow; a dimple. See *faucet.*
foul, gross; impure; to come in collision. **fowl,** a bird.
four, twice two. See *fore.*
fraise, a defense; a small cutter; term in heraldry. See *phrase.*
frank, open, honest. **franc,** a coin. **Frank,** a man's name. **Frank,** a member of a body of Germanic tribes.
frays, quarrels. See *phrase.*
freeze, to congeal by cold. **frieze,** a kind of cloth; a molding. **frees,** sets free. **Friese,** a native of Friesland.
freezer, a refrigerator. **friezer,** one who or that which friezes.
fret, to vex; irritation. **frette,** a coiled ring for a cannon.
friar, a member of a religious order. **frier,** one who fries. **fryer,** one who or that which fries.
frig, to keep in constant motion. **Frigg,** Norse myth.
fro, from. **frow,** a cleaving-knife.
frond, term in botany and zoölogy. **Fronde,** name of a party in France.
fry, to cook in a frying-pan; swarm

of young fishes. **Frey,** Norse myth.
fumet, the dung of deer. **fumette,** scent of meat when kept too long.
funeral, interment. **funereal,** dismal; suited to a funeral.
fungus, a low order of plants. **fungous,** spongy.
fur, covering of an animal. See *fir.*
fur-bearing, yielding a fur. See *forbearing.*
furred, covered with fur; coated.
fyrd, military force.
furry, covered with fur. See *ferry.*
fürst, a German prince. See *first.*
furze, a shrub. **furs,** pl. of fur.
fusel, a kind of oil. **fusil,** that may be melted; a musket.

G.

gabian, a variety of petroleum. **gabion,** a cylinder used in fortification.
gable, term in architecture. **gabel,** a rent; tax.
gage, a pledge; a fruit; to wager. **gage** *or* **gauge,** to measure; a standard.
gain, profit; to acquire. **gaine,** term in sculpture.
gala, festivity; a Scotch fabric. **galah,** an Australian cockatoo.
gale, a strong current of air. **Gael,** a Celt.
gall, bile. **gaul,** a wooden pole used as a lever. **Gaul,** ancient name of France.
galleon, a large ship. **gallein,** a color used in dyeing.
gallop, pace of a horse. **galop,** a dance.
gallows, scaffold for hanging murderers. **Gallus,** a priest of Cybele.
gamble, to play for money. **gambol,** to skip; a frolic.
gammon, to play; to humbug. **gamin,** a neglected street-boy.
gang, a crew; a band. **gangue,** a mineral substance.
gap, a vacant space; a breach; to make an opening. **gape,** to open the mouth wide; to yawn.
garble, to cull so as to mutilate. **garbel,** a plank. **garbill,** a duck.

garden, ground for growing plants and flowers. gardon, a small fish.

gargle, to rinse the throat. gargoyle, a term in architecture. gargil, a distemper in geese. gargol, a distemper in swine.

garret, a watch-tower; a room next the roof. garrot, a duck; a bandage.

garrulous, talkative. Garrulus, genus of jays.

gate, a large door; a passage. gait, manner of walking.

gaud, an ornament. God, the Deity.

gaul, a pole. See gall.

gauntlet, a leather glove. gantlet, a former system of torture; narrowing of two single railroad tracks.

gauzy, thin; like gauze. ghazi, a Mohammedan hero.

gay, merry; showy. guay, term in heraldry. gey, rather.

Geber, an Arabian chemist. See Gheber.

geese, pl. of goose. gies, strong mats.

gelid, cold. See jellied.

genet, a cat. Jeanette, a Christian name. jennet, a small Spanish horse.

genius, inborn faculty. genus, a group; a kind. genys, part of a bird's bill.

german, closely related; a dance. germen, a germ; a shoot; the ovary. germin, to germinate. germon, a fish. German, an inhabitant of Germany.

Germany, a country. chermany, a game.

gey, moderately. See gay.

Gheber, a fire-worshiper. gebur, an old law term. Geber, an Arabian chemist; a Scripture name.

gherkin, a pickle. jerkin, a jacket; a hawk. jerking, a sudden pulling. jerquing, search of a ship.

ghoul, an imaginary evil being. gool, a ditch; a passage. gul, a rose.

gib, to balk. jib, sail of a ship.

gies, strong mats. See geese.

gig (not jig), a chaise; to fish. jig, a light dance.

gild, to cover with gilt. guild, a society.

gilder, one who gilds; a Dutch coin. guilder, a Dutch coin.

gills, organs for breathing. guills, a plant.

gilt, gold leaf. guilt, criminality.

gimp, a kind of braid. guimpe, a chemisette.

gin, a machine; a liquor; a snare. jinn, Mohammedan myth.

girl, a female child. gurl, to growl; grumble.

gizzard, a part of the stomach. guisard, a New Year's harlequin. Guisard, a follower of the Dukes of Guise.

glare, dazzling light; to flare; to stare. glair, white of an egg; a halberd; to cover with glair.

glaucous, sea-green; covered with bluish-white bloom. Glaucus, a genus of fishes; a genus of gastropods. glaucus, a bird.

glaze, to furnish with glass; to incrust with a smooth surface. glaise, a warming at the fire.

glazer, one who or that which applies a glaze. glazier, one who cuts and fits panes of glass.

glean, to gather. glene, socket of the eye.

glede, a bird. gleed, a coal of fire; a flame.

gloom, darkness. glume, husk of a plant.

glossed, rendered smooth and lustrous; passed over lightly. glost, lead glaze used in pottery.

glows, shines with heat. gloze, to flatter; to smooth over; adulation.

gluten, a substance found in grain. glutin, crude gluten.

gnar, to growl or snarl. knar, a knot on a tree.

gnash, to grind the teeth. nash, firm; hard.

gnats, pl. of gnat. nattes, a term in architecture.

gnatter, to grumble. See natter.

gneiss, a mineral. See nice.

gnib, alert. See *nib.*
gnome, a spirit; a misshapen dwarf. **nome,** a province; a term in algebra.
gnu, an animal. See *new.*
goat, an animal. **gote,** a ditch.
gob, a mouthful; term in coal-mining. **gobbe,** a plant.
goblin, a supernatural being. **gobelin,** a kind of tapestry.
goborro, a plant. **goburra,** a king-fisher.
God, the Deity. See *gaud.*
goes, does go. **Goes,** town in the Netherlands.
goliath, a beetle; a bird. **Goliath,** a giant. **golia,** a bracelet.
gool, a ditch; a passage. See *ghoul.*
gopher, an animal. **gofer,** a waffle.
gore, to horn; a clot of blood; an inserted piece of cloth. **goer,** one who goes. **ghor,** a valley.
gored, did gore. **gourd,** a fruit; a dipper; a false die; a coin.
gorilla, an ape. **guerilla,** irregular warfare.
grain, a seed; corn; smallest weight; a particle; fiber. **graine,** the eggs of the silkworm.
granter, one who grants. **grantor,** one by whom a grant is made.
grate, fire-bars; to make a harsh sound. **great,** vast.
grater, a rough instrument. **greater,** larger.
graves, places for the dead; a refuse of lard or tallow. **Graves,** a British admiral.
gray, a color; to become gray. **grès,** grit; sandstone; stoneware.
graze, to scratch; to strike lightly; to feed upon grass or herbage. **grays,** colors.
grazer, an animal that grazes. **grazier,** a person engaged in grazing.
grease, melted fat. **Greece,** a country.
greaved, protected by greaves. See *grieved.*
grenadine, a fabric. **grenadin,** a color.
grès, grit, sandstone. See *gray.*

grieved, moved with grief. **greaved,** protected by greaves.
grieves, laments. **greaves,** armor for the legs.
griff, a term in textile manufacturing; a rocky glen; a dark mulatto. **griffe,** a term in architecture; the refuse of new champagne.
grill, to broil; a gridiron. **grille,** a lattice or grating. **grylle,** a sea-dove.
grip, a hold; to seize. **grippe,** influenza.
grizzly, gray. **grisly,** frightful. **gristly,** like gristle.
groan, a moan; to moan. **grown,** increased in growth.
grocer, a provisioner. **groser,** a gooseberry. **grosser,** more gross.
groom, a servant; a bridegroom; to curry. **grume,** a viscid fluid; a clot.
grot, a cave. **groat,** an English coin. **groot,** a Dutch coin.
group, a cluster; a crowd; to form into groups. **groop,** a trench; a pen for cattle; to form grooves.
grow, to increase; to cultivate. **gros,** decided in tint; a fabric.
guay, term in heraldry. See *gay.*
guerilla, irregular warfare. See *gorilla.*
guernsey, a bird; a knit shirt worn by sailors. **Guernsey,** a breed of cattle.
guest, one entertained. **guessed,** did guess.
guild, a society. See *gild.*
guilder, a Dutch coin. See *gilder.*
guillaume, a carpenter's tool. **Guillaume,** a French painter; the French name for William.
guilt, criminality. See *gilt.*
guimpe, a chemisette. See *gimp.*
guinea, a fowl; an English coin. **Guinea,** a country in Africa.
guisard, a New Year's mummer. See *gizzard.*
guise, to disguise; dress; behavior. **Guise,** French general and statesman.
gundi, a rat. **gundie,** greedy.
gurl, to growl; grumble. See *girl.*
gutter, a water-channel. **guttur,** the throat.

H.

haik, an outside garment of the Arab. **hake,** a hook; a fish; to fish for hake.

hail, to greet; frozen rain. **hale,** healthy; sound.

hair, covering on the head. **hare,** an animal.

hall, a large room. **haul,** to draw; a draught.

handle, to use with the hands; that part of an object by which it is carried. **handel,** mercantile traffic; to trade with. **Handel,** a German musical composer.

hand-made, manufactured by hand. **handmaid,** a female servant.

handsome, beautiful; comely; generous. **hansom,** a carriage.

hart, a stag. **heart,** the source of life.

haws, pl. of haw. **hawse,** part of a vessel; to raise.

hay, grass dried. **hey,** an exclamation; a call.

hazel, a plant; a light-brown color. **hazle,** to make dry; term in coal-mining.

heal, to cure. **heel,** part of the foot. **he'll,** he will. **hele,** cover; shelter.

healer, one who heals. **heeler,** a cock; a hanger-on.

hear, to perceive by the ear. **here,** in this place.

heard, did hear. **herd,** a number of animals.

hearse, a canopy; a bier; a carriage. **herse,** a portcullis for the dead. **Herse,** a genus of moths, birds, crustaceans, and mollusks. **hirse,** the broom corn.

heart, the source of life. See *hart.*

heed, careful attention; to consider. **he'd,** he would.

heigh, an exclamation. See *high.*

heigh-ho, an exclamation. See *highhoe.*

height *or* **hight,** elevation; the summit. **hyte,** mad; crazy.

heir, one who inherits. See *air.*

her, a pronoun. **herr,** a title. **herre,** a lord; master.

herad, a territorial division of Norway. **Herod,** a Bible character.

herds, pl. of herd. **hurds,** the coarse part of flax or hemp.

Hermogenean, pertaining to Hermogenes. **Hermogenian,** pertaining to Hermogenianus.

hew, to cut. **hue,** color; a cry. **Hué,** a city of Anam. **Hugh,** a man's name. **whew,** an exclamation.

hewed, past tense of verb hew. **hued,** having color.

hewer, one who hews. **huer,** one who gives an alarm. **whewer,** the European widgeon.

hey, an exclamation; a call. See *hay.*

hide, to conceal; the skin. **hied,** hurried.

high, lofty; costly. **hie,** to hasten. **heigh** *or* **hi,** an exclamation.

higher, more high. **hire,** wages; to engage for pay.

highhoe, a woodpecker. **heigh-ho,** an exclamation.

him, a pronoun. See *hymn.*

hirse, the broom corn. See *hearse.*

hissed, did hiss. **hist,** hush; be silent.

ho, a cry. **hoe,** an implement; to dig. **whoa,** an exclamation.

hoar, white as with frost. **hoer,** one who hoes. **whore,** a harlot.

hoard, a treasure; to store. **horde,** a migratory tribe. **whored,** practised unchastity.

hoarse, having a rough voice. **horse,** an animal.

hock, a kind of wine. **Hock,** the last card in the box in a game of faro. **hough,** a joint; to hamstring.

hold, to contain; grasp; a prison. **holed,** imprisoned; put into a hole.

hole, a cavity. **holl,** a narrow or dry ditch. **whole,** all.

holy, divine; sacred. **wholly,** entirely.

homage, deference; reverence. **ohmage,** electrical resistance.

home, a dwelling-place. **holm,** low, flat land; an oak. **heaume,** a large helmet.

homer, a homing pigeon; a shark;

a Hebrew measure. **Homer,** a Greek poet.

honorary, honoring; conferring honor. **onerary,** fitted for, or carrying, a burden.

hookah, a pipe. **hooker,** one who hooks; a Dutch vessel.

hoop, a band of wood or metal; to bind with hoops. **whoop,** a shout.

hoose *or* **hooze,** a disease of cattle. See *whose.*

hose, stockings; rubber tube. **hoes,** digs; pl. of hoe.

hour, sixty minutes. **our,** belonging to us.

house-boat, a boat fitted up as a house. **house-bote,** a law term.

hue, color; a cry. See *hew.*

hued, having color. See *hewed.*

huer, one who gives an alarm. See *hewer.*

Hugh, a man's name. See *hew.*

human, pertaining to man. **humin,** humic acid.

humorous, merry. **humerus,** a bone of the arm.

humus, vegetable mold. **humous,** relating to humus.

hurds, the coarse part of flax or hemp. See *herds.*

hussar, a horse-soldier. **huzza,** a shout; to applaud.

hymeneal, pertaining to marriage. **hymenial,** term in anatomy and botany.

hymn, a religious song; to sing praises. **him,** a pronoun.

hyperphysical, higher than the physical. **hypophysical,** term in anatomy.

hypogenous, growing beneath. **hypogynous,** growing from the axil.

hypostasy, that which underlies something else. See *apostasy.*

hypostatize, to attribute substantial existence to. See *apostatize.*

hypostrophe, a term used in medicine and rhetoric. See *apostrophe.*

hypothecary, of or pertaining to hypothecation or mortgage. See *apothecary.*

hypothesis, a supposition. See *apothesis.*

hypothetic, conjectural. **hyperthetic,** showing transposition.

hyte, mad; crazy. See *height.*

I.

ide, a fish. See *eyed.*

idle, unemployed. **idol,** a god. **idyl,** a pastoral poem.

I'll, I will. See *aisle.*

illapse, influx; inspiration. See *elapse.*

illicit, unlawful. See *elicit.*

illude, to deceive; to mock. See *allude.*

illusion, a deception. See *allusion.*

immanent, inherent; intrinsic. See *eminent.*

immerge, to put under water. See *emerge.*

immerse, to put under water. See *amerce.*

immersed, past tense of verb immerse. **emersed,** term in botany.

immigrant, one who comes into the country. See *emigrant.*

immigrate, to move into a country. See *emigrate.*

imminence, a threatening. See *eminence.*

imminent, threatening. See *eminent.*

immission, injection. See *emission.*

immortal, deathless. **immortelle,** a flower.

impassable, not passable. **impassible,** incapable of suffering.

impend, to overhang. **impenned,** past tense of verb impen.

impress, an imprint; a mark; to stamp or print. See *empress.*

imu, a pit for roasting meat. See *emu.*

incense, to enrage; perfume. **insense,** to instruct.

indiscreet, imprudent. **indiscrete,** not discrete or separated.

indite, to write; to compose. **indict,** to accuse.

ingenious, inventive. **ingenuous,** frank; candid.

ingress, access; place of entrance. **Ingres,** a French painter.

inn, a public house. in, within.

innervate, to supply with nerves. See *enervate*.

innumerable, that cannot be counted. enumerable, capable of being enumerated.

insist, to persist; to press. encyst, to inclose in a cyst.

insoul, to endow with soul. insole, an inner sole of a boot.

insulate, to separate; to detach. insolate, to expose to the sun.

intention, aim; purpose. intension, act of making tense.

interpolate, to change, as a book. interpellate, to question imperatively.

Ira, a Christian name. eyra, a wild cat.

irradiation, illumination; surrounding with splendor eradiation, emission of radiance.

irruption, a sudden invasion. See *eruption*.

isle, an island. See *aisle*.

islet, a small island. See *eyelet*.

J.

jam, preserved fruits; to press. jamb, side of a door. jambe, armor for the leg; swift.

Jane, a Christian name. jean, a cotton cloth.

jarred, past tense of verb jar. jarde, a tumor.

Jeanette, a Christian name. See *genet*.

jellied, brought to a jelly. gelid, cold.

jennet, a small Spanish horse. See *genet*.

jerkin, a jacket; a hawk. jerking, a sudden pulling. jerquing, search of a ship. See *gherkin*.

jet, a black substance; a spouting stream; to shoot forward. jette, part of a bridge.

jib, a small sail. See *gib*.

jig, a dance; a tune. See *gig*.

jinn, Mohammedan myth. See *gin*.

joust, a tilting match. See *just*.

jowl, the cheek. joule, an electrical unit.

jubate, fringed with hair. Jewbait, to persecute the Jews.

jury, a committee to pass judgment. Jewry, a Jewish district.

just, actuated by justice; proper; legal. joust, a tilting match between mounted knights

K.

kadi, a Moslem judge. See *caddy*.

Kafir, Kaffir, an unbeliever; one of a S. Afr. race. caphar, a post or station.

kail, a game. See *kale*.

kaki, a fruit. See *khaki*.

kale, a form of cabbage. kail, a game; a tree. cale, to throw; to caper; one's turn. Kehl, a town in Germany.

kame, a hill; a fortress or camp. See *came*.

kana, Japanese writing. See *Canna*.

kandel, a tree. See *candle*.

kans, a grass. See *cans*.

kaolin, a mineral. calin, a Chinese alloy.

kaph, a Jewish liquid measure. See *calf*.

kapp, a term in electricity. See *cap*.

kat, Egyptian unit of weight. See *cat*.

kayak, a boat. kiack, a Buddhist temple.

keach, to dip out, as water. keech, fat rolled into a round lump.

ken, to know; cognizance. See *Chen*.

kermes, a red dyestuff. Chermes, a genus of bark-lice.

kernel, inside of a nut. See *colonel*.

kersey, a cloth. kursi *or* kursy, a low table.

kerve, to carve. See *curve*.

key, an instrument to open a lock. ki, a plant. quay, a wharf. que, a coin.

khaki, dust-colored; a cloth. kaki, a fruit.

kiack, a Buddhist temple. See *kayak*.

kicker, one who or that which kicks; an objector. kikar, a plant.

kill, to deprive of life. **kiln,** an oven. **kyl,** a high silk hat.

kirve, a term in coal-mining. See *curve*.

kisser, one who kisses. **kissar,** a lyre.

kiting, a mode of raising money. **chitin,** a compound.

kittle, to tickle; to puzzle; hard to manage. **kittel,** a long coat worn by Polish Jews.

klepht, a bandit. See *cleft*.

knag, a knot in wood; the prong of an antler. See *nag*.

knap, a knob; to bite. See *nap*.

knape, a framework used in thatching. See *nape*.

knar, a knot on a tree. See *gnar*.

knave, a rogue. **nave,** part of a wheel; body of a church. **Nève,** Belgian orientalist.

knead, to stir. **kneed,** having knees; geniculated; **need,** want.

kneck, a nautical term. See *neck*.

kneel, to fall or to rest on the knees. **neal,** to temper by heat.

knell, sound of a funeral bell; to strike. **Nell,** a girl's name.

knew, did know. See *new*.

knicker, a small ball of baked clay. See *nicker*.

knight, a title of honor. See *night*.

knit, to weave. **nit,** egg of an insect.

knitch, a small bundle; a fagot. See *niche*.

knob, a lump; a rounded hill. **nob,** a nobleman.

knobby, full of knobs. **nobby,** stylish.

knock, to strike or beat; a blow. **nock,** a notch; to notch.

knot, a tie; a hard part of wood. **not,** a negative.

knote, a term in mechanics. See *note*.

knout, a whip or scourge. **knowt,** a shinty-ball.

know, to understand. **no,** a word of refusal.

knows, does know. See *nose*.

kob, an antelope. See *cob*.

koff, a Dutch vessel. See *cough*.

kohl, a variety of cabbage. See *coal*.

koko, a plant; a bird. See *cocoa*.

kokoon, the gnu. See *cocoon*.

kommers, festivities among German University students. See *comers*.

kraal, a Hottentot village. See *crawl*.

krone, a coin. See *crony*.

kuli, hire; wages. See *coolly*.

kuttar, an Indian dagger. See *cutter*.

kyl, a high silk hat. See *kill*.

kyle, a sound; a strait; a lamp. See *chyle*.

L.

lac, a resinous substance; a number.

lack, deficiency; to be in want.

lakh, a gum.

lacquer, a kind of varnish; to varnish. **lacker,** one who lacks.

lager, a kind of beer. **lagar,** a wine press. **laager,** a defensive inclosure formed by wagons. **lagre,** a sheet of perfectly smooth glass.

laid, did lay. **lade,** to load.

lair, home of a beast. **layer,** a stratum.

lama, a celibate priest. **Lama,** a genus of mammals. **llama,** a quadruped.

lamb, a young sheep. **lam,** to thrash; beat.

land, earth; a country; to go on shore. **lande,** an uncultivated plain.

landau, a two-seated carriage. **land-daw,** the carrion-crow.

lane, a narrow street. **lain,** reclined. **Laen,** a province in Sweden.

lap, upper part of the legs when one sits; flap; fold; to lick up. **Lapp,** a native of Lapland.

latches, pl. of latch. **laches,** negligence.

late, after the proper time; recent. **lait,** lightning; to seek.

lath, a thin board. **lathe,** a machine.

latten, fine sheet brass. **Latin,** ancient language. **laten,** to grow later.

laudist, a writer of songs of praise. **Laudist,** a follower of Laud, Archbishop of Canterbury.

laugh, to make the noise caused by mirth. **laff,** a fish. **lauf,** a passage in music.

laughter, a laugh; a mode of expressing mirth. **lafter,** the number of eggs laid by a hen before she sits.

lawn, a grassy space; a fine linen or cambric. **laun,** a fine sieve.

lax, loose. **lacks,** needs. **lacs,** resinous substances.

lay, to place; to bring forth (eggs); a song; relating to the laity. **ley,** yield; produce. **leu,** a silver coin. **lei,** a garland.

lea, a meadow. **lee,** sheltered from the wind. **li,** a Chinese weight and mile. **lei,** pl. of leu.

leach, to strain water through (ashes). **leech,** a worm that sucks blood; a physician.

lead, a guide; a clue; precedence; priority. **leed,** speech, utterance, language.

lead, a metal. **led,** did lead.

leaf, part of a book or plant. **lief,** gladly.

leak, a break. **leek,** an onion.

lean, lacking flesh; to incline. **lien,** a legal claim.

lease, contract renting a house or lands; to let. **lisse,** in tapestry, the threads of the warp taken together. **lis,** a flower; a lawsuit. **Lys,** river in France.

least, smallest. **leased,** rented.

leck, to pour; to leak. **lech,** a crowning stone of an ancient monument.

leed, utterance. See *lead.*

leer, a sinister look; an oven; to look with a leer. **lear,** an archway or oven.

lent, a loan; a term in music. **Lent,** a fast of forty days. **leant,** past tense of lean.

lessen, to diminish. **lesson,** a task.

lesser, inferior. **lessor,** one who leases.

let, to allow; to grant for hire; a hindrance. **Lett,** a member of the Lettic race.

Lethean, pertaining to Lethe. **letheon,** sulphuric ether.

leu, a silver coin. See *lay.*

levy, to assess. **levee,** an assembly; an embankment.

lewd, low; depraved; wicked. **leud,** a servant or vassal.

ley, yield; produce. See *lay.*

li, a Chinese weight and mile. See *lea.*

liar, an untruthful person. **lire,** flesh; brawn; a cloth. **lyre,** a kind of harp. **lyer,** one in a prostrate position.

lie, a falsehood; to recline. **lye,** an alkaline solution.

lief, willingly. See *leaf.*

lien, a legal claim. See *lean.*

lieu, place; room. **loo,** a game of cards.

lightning, an electric flash. **lightening,** to illuminate; to unburden.

limb, part of the body. **limn,** to paint.

limpid, clear; transparent. **limpet,** a small shell fish.

liniment, soft ointment. **linament,** term in surgery. **lineament,** feature; outline.

links, pl. of link. **lynx,** an animal.

lion, a fierce animal. **lien,** a law term.

liquor, any intoxicating drink. **liqueur,** an alcoholic cordial flavored with aromatic substances.

lirk, to jerk; to crease. See *lurk.*

lisse, in tapestry, the threads of the warp taken together. See *lease.*

listen, to hearken. **lissen,** a cleft in a rock. **liston,** a term in heraldry.

literal, not figurative; exact; precise; unimaginative. **littoral,** pertaining to the shore.

liver, one who lives; organ which secretes the bile. **livor,** envy.

lo, behold. **low,** not high; coarse; noise of a cow.

load, a burden; to weigh down. **lode,** a metallic vein. **lowed,** cried, as a cow.

loan, that which is lent. **lone,** solitary.

lock, to fasten; a bolt. **loch,** a lake or bay. **lough,** a lake.

loo, a game. See *lieu.*

loop, a noose; to make a loop.

loup, to leap; a mask. **loupe,** a mass of iron. **lupe,** a pigeon.

loose, unbound; free; lax; to unbind. **luce,** a fish; a rut.

loot, to plunder; booty. **lute,** musical instrument.

lore, learning; the side of the head.

Loir, a short river in France. **Loire,** a long river in France.

lower, more low.

louvre, a dance. **louver,** term in architecture.

lowry, an open box car; the spurge-laurel. **lowrie,** a fox.

loyalist, a partizan supporter. **Loyolist,** a Jesuit.

Lucerne, canton in Switzerland. **lucerne,** a plant. **lucern,** a lamp; a lynx.

lumber, anything cumbersome or useless; timber; to move heavily. **lumbar,** relating to the loins.

lure, enticement; to entice. **loure,** a bagpipe; a slow dance.

lurk, to lie in wait; to hide. **lirk,** to jerk; to crease.

lye, an alkaline solution; a railroad siding. See *lie.*

lynch, to punish by lynch-law. **linch,** a ledge; a projection.

lynx, an animal. See *links.*

lyre, a kind of harp. See *liar.*

M.

mackle, a spot or blemish in printing; to blur or spoil. **macle,** a twin crystal.

macrocosm, the great world. See *microcosm.*

macroscopic, large. See *microscopic.*

madrigal, a pastoral or amorous song. **madregal,** a fish.

maggot, a small grub; a whim. **magot,** an ape; a small grotesque figure.

maid, a girl; a virgin. **made,** past tense of make.

maiden, an unmarried woman; untried; first; a brush used by a blacksmith; an apparatus for washing linen. **maidan,** an open space; a parade ground.

main, chief. **Maine,** a state in U. S.

mane, hair on the neck of an animal.

maize, Indian corn. **maze,** a labyrinth.

mall, a heavy hammer; to beat; a public walk. **maul,** to bruise or beat.

mandrel, a bar of metal. **mandrill,** a large baboon.

mangle, to crush; to iron; a machine. **mangel,** as in mangel-wurzel.

manila, a cheroot; a fibrous material. **manilla,** a piece of ring-money. **Manila,** capital P. I.

manna, a sweet exudation from trees. **manner,** bearing; form. **manor,** residence. **mana,** power; influence.

manteau, a cloak or mantle. **manto,** term in mining.

mantel, a shelf above the fireplace. **mantle,** a cloak; to cover, disguise, or conceal.

Manu, a Hindu sage. See *menu.*

mar, to injure; impair; ruin; blemish; a small lake. **maar,** crater of a volcano. **mahr,** a wedding gift.

mara, the Patagonian cavy. **Mara,** in Hindu mythology, the tempter; the ruling spirit of evil. **maray,** a fish. **Mahra,** district in Arabia.

marc, a coin. **mark,** a coin; a sign; to observe. **marque,** a license of reprisal. **Mark,** a man's name.

mare, female of the horse. **mair,** Scotch form of more. **mayor,** chief magistrate of a city.

marlin, a godwit. **marline,** nautical term.

married, past tense of verb marry. **marid,** an evil spirit.

marshal, a title; to rank in order. **martial,** warlike.

marshalcy, the office of a marshal. **marshalsea,** the court of a marshal.

marten, a weazel. **Martin,** a surname. **martin,** a bird.

mason, one who lays bricks or stones; a bee; to build or construct. **maysin,** a chemical substance.

mast, a pole; fruit of the oak. massed, collected into a mass.

mat, a texture; to twist together. matte, a term in metallurgy.

mate, companion; to match; marry. matie, a herring. mati, a sedge. maté, a tea.

matelote, a stew of fish. matelotte, a sailor's dance.

matrass, a chemical vessel. mattress, a bed. matross, in India, an assistant to a gunner.

maw, stomach or craw. ma, a shorter or childish form of mama.

me, myself. mi, a note in music.

mead, a meadow; a drink. Mede, a native of Media. meed, a reward. Meade, a surname.

mean, base; low; to intend. mien, look; manner. mesne, middle. Migne, French editor.

meat, food. meet, proper; to encounter. mete, to measure.

mechanism, the structure of any mechanical contrivance. meconism, the habit of taking opium.

medal, a reward. meddle, to interfere.

meddler, one who interferes. medlar, a tree and its fruit.

mellow, soft by reason of ripeness; to become mellow. mellah, the Jewish quarter.

melodeon, a small reed-organ; a music hall. melodion, a melodicon.

menu, a bill of fare. Manu, a mythic sage in Hindu mythology.

mere, bare, simple. Mire, a village in France. mir, a Russian commune.

meridian, noon. Meridion, a genus of diatoms.

merlin, a kind of hawk; a pony. merlon, a fortification term.

metal, a hard substance. mettle, spirit. metol, a photographic developer.

meter, a measure. meeter, one who meets.

mewl, cry of a child. mule, an animal.

mews, an inclosure; cries like a cat. muse, to think. Muse, a goddess of poetry and art.

microcosm, a little world or cosmos. macrocosm, the great world.

microscopic, small; minute; pertaining to the microscope. macroscopic, large; visible to the naked eye.

mien, look; manner. See mean.

might, mental, moral, physical, or spiritual power. mite, an insect; a small particle.

mighty, powerful. mity, having mites.

mill, engine for grinding; tenth of a cent; to grind; to stamp. mil, a unit of length.

millinery, articles made or sold by milliners. millenary, pertaining to a thousand.

miner, one who mines. minor, under age; lesser.

mir, a Russian commune. See mere.

missile, a projectile, as an arrow or bullet. missal, a prayer-book. missel, a bird.

missy, characteristic of young misses. misy, a mineral.

mist, fine rain. missed, past tense of miss.

mnemonic, assisting memory. pneumonic, pertaining to the lungs.

moan, to lament; a groan. mown, cut down, as grass.

moat, a trench. mote, a small particle.

mocha, a choice coffee; a weight; a moth; a cat. Mocha, a district in Arabia. mokah, a Turkish doctor of laws. moko, to tattoo; a system of tattooing.

mock, to mimic; to delude; unreal; assumed; a jeer or sneer. mak, domesticated; subdued.

mode, method; fashion. mowed, past tense of mow.

model, anything to be imitated; to plan; to shape. modal, relating to the mode or manner.

mokah, a Turkish scholar. See mocha.

moral, right; just. morale, moral condition. morel, an edible fungus. morelle, the nightshade.

more, greater. **mower,** one who mows. **moor,** to anchor; a heath. **Moor,** a native of Northern Africa. **mohr,** an antelope. **mohur,** an Indian coin. **moire,** a watered appearance; a watered silk.

morn, morning. **mourn,** to grieve. **morne,** part of a lance; a small hill.

morrow, the next day following. **morra,** a large tree. **morro,** a round hill or point of land.

morsel, a small piece. **morsal,** pertaining to the surface of a tooth.

motor, a mover. **moter,** a cotton-gin device.

motto, a principle of action; a rule of life; in heraldry, a phrase accompanying a crest or coat of arms. **moto,** motion; movement.

mountebank, a fakir; a charlatan; to cheat or swindle. **monte-bank,** a gambling place.

mouser, a cat. **mauser,** a magazine rifle.

mow, to cut down with a scythe. **mo** or **moe,** more. **mho,** an electrical term. **Meaux,** a town in France.

much, great in quantity. **mutch,** a cap.

mufti, a Mohammedan officer. **mufty,** a bird.

mule, an animal. See **mewl.**

murrain, a disease of cattle. **murrhine,** a kind of stone. **murrine,** made of murra.

murray, a fish. **murrey,** term in heraldry; a dark red color.

muscadine, a kind of grape. **muscadin,** a dandy, a fop. **muscardine,** a silkworm disease; a dormouse.

muscle, flesh. **mussel,** a mollusk. **mussal,** a torch.

muse, to meditate. See **mews.**

music, science of harmonical sounds. **mucic,** term in chemistry.

mustard, a plant; a spice. **mustered,** enrolled; assembled.

myrrh, a gum. **mur,** a mouse; a catarrh. **murre,** a bird.

myrtle, a tree or shrub. **myrtol,** a chemical substance.

N.

nacre, mother-of-pearl. **Nachor,** a Bible name.

nag, a small horse; to annoy. **knag,** a knot in wood; the prong of an antler.

nap, a short sleep; to doze; woolly surface of plants and cloth. **gnap,** a morsel; to bite. **nappe,** term in geometry. **knap,** a knob; to bite. **Knapp,** American revivalist.

nape, the back of the neck. **knape,** a frame in which to carry the straw used by the thatcher.

narrow, not wide; impoverished; illiberal; niggardly. **narra,** a variety of mahogany.

nash, firm; hard. See **gnash.**

natter, to find fault. **gnatter,** to grumble.

nattes, a term in architecture. See **gnats.**

naval, pertaining to the navy. **navel,** the central part. **nave,** central part of a church. See **knave.**

navy, marine military force of a country. **névé,** the consolidated snow on the summit of a mountain.

nay, no. **neigh,** cry of a horse. **née,** born. **Ney,** marshal of France.

nays, pl. of nay. **naze,** a promontory or headland. **neighs,** makes a noise like a horse.

neal, to temper by heat. See **kneel.**

neck, part between the head and the body. **kneck,** a nautical term.

need, want; to require. See **knead.**

Nell, a girl's name. See **knell.**

neumatic, term in music. See **pneumatic.**

névé, snow on the summit of a mountain. See **navy.**

new, not old. **knew,** did know. **gnu,** an animal.

nib, one of the projecting handles

of a scythe; the point of a pen; the beak of a bird; the growing point of an oyster shell; to furnish with a nib. **gnib**, sprightly; smart.

nice, refined; pure; delicate. **gneiss**, a mineral.

Nicene, pertaining to Nice. **cnicin**, a term in chemistry.

niche, recess in a wall. **knitch**, a small bundle; a fagot.

nickel, a whitish metal; a coin. **nicol**, a nicol prism.

nicker, a water-sprite; to neigh. **knicker**, a small ball of baked clay.

nicks, dents; notches. **nix**, a water spirit; nothing; an exclamation; **Pnyx**, an assembly of Athenians.

niece, daughter of a brother or sister. **Nice**, city in France.

night, period of darkness. **knight**, a champion; a piece used in chess.

nip, to cut; to blast. **nippe**, a wrapping for the foot.

nit, egg of an insect. See *knit*.

no, a word of refusal. See *know*.

nob, a nobleman. See *knob*.

nobby, stylish. See *knobby*.

nock, a notch; to notch. See *knock*.

nocturn, of the night; a midnight prayer-service. **nocturne**, term in painting and music.

nome, a province; a term in algebra. See *gnome*.

none, not any. **nun**, a religious recluse.

nose, organ of smell. **knows**, does know. **noes**, pl. of no.

not, a negative. See *knot*.

note, a mark; short letter; to notice; to jot down. **knote**, a term in mechanics.

O.

O, exclamation of wonder. **oh**, exclamation of pain. **owe**, to be indebted to. **eau**, water.

oak, a tree. **oke**, a Turkish unit of weight.

oar, a long paddle. **o'er**, contraction of over. **or**, either. **ore**, a mineral. **orr**, a globular piece of wood. **ower**, one who owes.

obliger, one who obliges. **obligor**, a law term.

obol, a weight; a Greek coin; passage money paid to Charon. **obole**, an apothecary's weight; a French coin.

obolus, a coin. **obelus**, a mark.

ode, a poem. **owed**, did owe. **od**, a hypothetical force.

odium, hatred; dislike. **odeum**, a kind of theater.

offal, rubbish; refuse. See *awful*.

ohm, the unit of electrical resistance. **om**, a mystic ejaculation; absolute goodness and truth. See *aam*.

ohmage, electrical resistance. See *homage*.

olio, a miscellaneous collection. **oleo**, oleomargarin. **Oglio**, river in Italy.

omber, a game with cards. **ombre**, a cheap grade of silk prints.

omit, to leave out; fail to do. **emit**, to send forth. **immit**, to inject.

one, a unit. **won**, did win.

onerary, fitted for or carrying a burden. See *honorary*.

oppose, to resist; to set up in opposition. **appose**, to place or bring near; to examine.

opposition, the act of opposing or resisting. **apposition**, the act of adding; term in grammar.

oppressed, downtrodden. **appressed**, pressed closely.

orally, in spoken words. **orale**, a white silk veil.

ordinance, a law. **ordnance**, artillery. **ordonnance**, a right arranging of parts.

Oregon, a state in U. S. **origan**, a plant.

origin, a beginning; source. **Origen**, Christian writer of Alexandria.

Orion, a constellation; a genus of beetles. See *Arion*.

Osiris, an Egyptian god. **Osyris**, a genus of herbs.

Ostrya, a genus of trees. See *Austria*.

ottar, oil of roses. otter, an animal.

ought, should. See *aught*.

our, belonging to us. See *hour*.

outcast, an exile; to throw out. outcaste, in India, a person who has forfeited his caste.

overdo, to do too much. overdue, past due.

overlade, to overload. overlaid, spread over.

owe, to. be indebted to. See *O*.

owed, did owe. See *ode*.

own, belonging to; to possess; to confess. aune, a French cloth-measure.

P.

pa, a childish form of papa. pah, an exclamation of disgust; a fortified Maori camp. pas, a dance. paw, foot of a beast.

paced, measured. See *paste*.

packed, pressed together. pact, an agreement.

packs, binds closely. pax, a crucifix.

pæan, a song. peon, a servant. pæon, term in prosody.

pail, a bucket. pale, not ruddy; a pointed stake.

pain, discomfort; to wound. pane, a square of glass. peine, pain or torture. Paine, Thomas, a writer.

pair, a couple. pare, to peel. pear, a fruit. payer, one who pays. père, father.

palace, a splendid mansion. Pallas, a goddess; a planetoid.

palate, roof of the mouth. palette, a painter's tablet. pallet, a small bed. paillette, a bit of metal.

pall, a covering; to satiate; to become insipid. paul, an Italian coin. pawl, a sliding bolt. Paul, a man's name.

pall-mall, a game; an alley. Pall-Mall, a name applied to St. James Park, London, where the game was formerly played. pell-mell, in a confused manner.

pamper, to feed to the full. pampre, term in architecture.

pan, a wide shallow vessel; to obtain gold by using the pan. panne, a fabric resembling velvet. Pan, in Greek mythology, an Arcadian wood-spirit.

panel, part of a door; the jury. pannel, a kind of saddle.

papa, father. papaw, a tree or its fruit.

par, state of equality. parr, a young salmon.

para, a deer; a Turkish coin. parra, a comb-crested jacana. Para, river and state in South America.

paraphrase, explanation in many words; a loose or free translation. periphrase, the use of more words than are necessary.

parasite, a flatterer; a hanger-on. Parisite, a native of Paris. parisite, a mineral.

parquet, lower floor of a theater. parka, a coat; a fossil.

parra, a bird. See *para*.

parthenopian, relating to a genus of crabs. Parthenopean, pertaining to Parthenope.

passable, that may be passed. passible, capable of feeling.

passed, advanced beyond. past, ended.

paste, sticky substance. paced, past tense of pace.

pastel, a crayon; a plant. pastil, a compound for fumigating; a lozenge.

pastoral, relating to a pastor. pastourelle, a quadrille figure.

pat, fit; to tap. patte, term in heraldry.

pate, top of the head; a badger. pâte, a kind of paste. paté, a term in heraldry. pâté, a little pie; a term in military defense.

patela, a flat-bottomed boat. patella, the knee-cap. Patella, a genus of gastropods.

pathetic, full of pathos. bathetic, pertaining to bathos.

patten, a clog or wooden shoe; to walk in pattens. paten, a communion plate.

paume, a French game. See *pome*.

pause, a stop; to halt. **paws,** feet of a beast.

peace, quiet. **piece,** a part.

peak, the top. **peek,** to peep. **pique,** irritation; to nettle. **peeke,** polished shell beads.

peal, a chime of bells. **peel,** skin of fruit; to pare. **piel,** a wedge for piercing stones.

pear, a fruit. See *pair.*

pearl, a jewel. **perle,** a pellet. **purl,** sound of waters; to ripple.

peas, pl. of pea. **pease,** pl. of pea when used collectively. **pes,** the foot.

pease-meal, a flour. See *piece-meal.*

peat, carbonized vegetable substance. **peet,** the lake-trout.

peavey, a lumberman's implement. See *pewee.*

pecan, a kind of nut. **pekan,** an animal.

pectus, the breast. **pectous,** relating to pectine.

pedal, a key or lever. **peddle,** to sell small wares.

peeke, polished beads. See *peak.*

peer, an equal; a nobleman. **pier,** a wharf.

peerage, the rank or body of nobles. **pierage,** toll.

peet, a fish. See *peat.*

pell, a skin or hide; a roll of parchment. **pel,** a stake.

pell-mell, in a confused manner. See *pall-mall.*

pelorus, a nautical instrument. See *pylorus.*

penal, relating to punishment. **pennal,** a student.

pencil, a tool for drawing or writing. **pensile,** hanging; suspended.

pendant, an ear-ring; a long narrow flag. **pendent,** hanging.

people, persons generally; a nation; to stock with inhabitants. **pipul** or **pipal,** the sacred fig-tree.

periphrase, the use of more words than are necessary. See *paraphrase.*

perjury, giving false evidence. **purgery,** part of a sugar house.

permissible, allowable. **permiscible,** capable of being mixed.

pern, to turn to profit; a bird. **pirn,** a small spindle.

peroration, the conclusion of an oration. **pererration,** a wandering or rambling.

per se, essentially. **percée,** term in heraldry. **Parsee,** a Zoroastrian.

perse, a blue color. See *purse.*

persienne, an Eastern cambric. **persiennes,** outside window-shutters.

personal, relating to a person. **personnel,** a body of persons employed in some public service.

pertinence, the quality of being pertinent. **purtenance,** appurtenance; belongings.

pew, an inclosed seat in a church. **più,** more.

pewee, a small bird. **peavey,** a lumberman's cant-hook.

phase, aspect; appearance; to disturb. **fays,** fairies.

phenol, a chemical substance produced from coal-tar by distillation. **phenyl,** the essential residue of benzine forming the basis of many aromatic derivatives.

phial, a small bottle. See *file:*

philander, a lover; a mammal; to make love. **filander,** a worm.

Philip, a man's name. See *fillip.*

philopena, a social game; a forfeit. **Filipino,** a male inhabitant of the Philippine Islands. **Filipina,** a female inhabitant.

philter, a charm. See *filter.*

phiz, the face. See *fizz.*

Phlox, a genus of plants. **phlox,** a plant. See *flocks.*

phocal, pertaining to seals. See *focal.*

phosphorus, a chemical. **phosphorous,** pertaining to phosphorus.

phrase, part of a sentence. **phraise,** to cajole; coax. **fraise,** a defense; a small cutter; term in heraldry. **frays,** quarrels.

physic, a medicine. **physique,** physical structure.

physiogeny, the science of the evolution of vital activities. **physiogony,** the genesis of nature.

Pica, a genus of birds; **pica,** a magpie; a term in medicine and printing. **pika,** a small rodent.

picarel, a fish. See *pickerel*.

pick, a tool; to peck at; to choose. **pic,** a measure of length.

picked, did pick. **pict,** an early inhabitant of Scotland.

pickerel, a pike; the wall-eye. **picarel,** any fish of the family *Menidæ*. **picryl,** the radical of picric acid. **picrol,** a colorless, bitter, crystalline compound.

picket, a sharp stake; a guard; a sentry. **picquet,** a game of cards. **piquette,** a drink.

pickle, brine; thing pickled; to preserve in brine. **picul** *or* **pecul,** a weight.

picks, digs; chooses. **pyx** *or* **pix,** a box for a compass; a case in which the host is reserved.

picryl, a chemical substance. See *pickerel*.

pie, pastry; a magpie; a gossip. **pi,** a mass of type.

piece, a part. See *peace*.

piecemeal, disconnected. **peasemeal,** a flour.

piel, a wedge for piercing stones. See *peal*.

pier, a wharf. See *peer*.

pierage, toll. See *peerage*.

pile, a heap; a timber. **pyle,** a grain of chaff.

pillar, a support. **pillow,** a cushion; to support as with a pillow. **pilau,** a dish used by Mohammedans.

pillory, a frame in which criminals were fastened by the neck. **pilary,** pertaining to hair. **pillery,** robbery; plunder.

pilot, one who steers a ship; guide; to steer. **Pilate,** a Scripture name.

pimento, a tree and spice. **Pimenta,** a genus of trees.

pind, to impound, as cattle. See *pinned*.

pinda, a cake of rice offered to the dead. **pindar,** the peanut. **pinder,** an officer who impounds cattle. **Pindar,** a Greek lyric poet.

pinion, a wing; to bind the arms. **piñon,** a pine and its seed. **pignon,** an edible seed; a gable.

pinned, fastened with a pin. **pind,** to impound, as cattle.

pipul *or* **pipal,** the sacred fig-tree. See *people*.

pique, irritation; to nettle. See *peak*.

piquet, a game of cards; a picket. **piquette,** a coarse, sour wine.

pirn, a small spindle. See *pern*.

pirr, a gentle wind. See *purr*.

pisciform, having the form of a fish. **pisiform,** resembling a pea; a small bone.

pistol, a firearm. **pistole,** a Spanish coin. **pistil,** part of a flower.

pitied, did pity. **pitted,** indented.

più, more. See *pew*.

placate, to appease. **placcate,** a piece of armor.

place, position; to locate. **plaice,** a fish.

placer, one who places; to wash for gold; a place where gold is washed. **Placer,** a county in California.

plaid, a checkered cloth. **played,** did play.

plain, level; homely; distinct. **plane,** a tool; to make smooth.

plainer, more plain. **planer,** one who planes. **planar,** lying in one plane.

plaintiff, one who brings suit. **plaintive,** expressing grief.

plait, to fold or weave. **plate,** a dish; to cover with metal.

planchet, a flat piece of metal. **planchette,** a game.

planing, making smooth. **plaining,** complaint.

plaque, an ornamental plate; a brooch; the plate of a clasp. **plack,** a coin.

plaquet, a term used in medieval armor. **plaquette,** a small plaque or decorative object.

platen, printing term; an alloy. **platten,** term in glass-manufacturing.

playwright, a writer of plays. **play-right,** right of an author.

pleas, pl. of plea. **please,** to gratify.

pledger, one who pledges. **pledgeor,** a term in law.

plot, a secret plan; a piece of ground; to conspire; to locate on a map; to form into cakes by pressure; to scald or parboil. **plaat,** a pond; a school of fish.

plum, a fruit. **plumb,** a weight; vertical.

plural, more than one. **pleural,** relating to the pleura; lateral; a pleurale.

pneumatic, pertaining to air or gas. **neumatic,** term in music.

pneumonic, relating to the lungs. See *mnemonic.*

Pnyx, an assembly of Athenians. See *nicks.*

poe, a bird. **Poe,** an American poet. **Poa,** a genus of grasses. **poh,** an exclamation. **poi** or **poe,** an article of food.

point, sharp end of a thing; a tapering tract of land; a prominent feature; a particular place or position; a mark made by a pointed instrument; to sharpen to a point; to indicate direction. **pointé,** a term in heraldry. **pointe,** the base of the shield.

poke, a thrust; a weed; a dawdler; a bonnet; to thrust; to gape. **poak,** a waste.

pole, a staff; a fishing-rod; a measure of length or of surface; end of the earth's axis; to push or propel. **poll,** the head; to vote. **Pole,** a native of Poland.

polish, a gloss; to make glossy. **Polish,** pertaining to Poland.

pollen, powder in flowers. **pollan,** a fish.

polyanthus or **polyanthos,** a flower. **polyanthous,** bearing many flowers.

polyphemus, a cyclops. **polyphemous,** one-eyed.

polypus, a polyp; a tumor. **polypous,** having many feet or roots.

pomace, fruit crushed by grinding. **pumice,** a volcanic stone.

pome, an apple; a ball or globe. **paume,** a French game.

ponds, pl. of pond. **pons,** term in anatomy.

pongee, a silk. **pungi,** a Hindu pipe.

pontil, an iron rod used in glass-making. **pontile,** pertaining to the pons of the brain.

pony, a small horse. **pone,** a writ.

pool, a small pond. **poule,** a quadrille figure.

porcelain, fine earthenware. **porcelane,** the money-cowry. **purslane,** a plant.

pore, outlet for perspiration; to ponder. **pour,** to discharge in a stream.

port, a harbor; a wine; to turn a ship. **Porte,** the Turkish government.

portion, a share. **potion,** a dose.

postal, relating to the post-office. **postle** or **postel,** an apostle; a preacher. **postil,** any marginal note.

postulate, a position claimed as a basis for argument; to assume as self-evident. **pustulate,** to form into pustules

pouf, part of a head-dress. **pouffe,** anything rounded and soft.

poulet, a familiar note. **Pouillet,** a French physicist.

praise, commendation, to extol. **prays,** petitions. **prase,** a mineral.

pray, to petition. **prey,** to plunder; booty.

praya, a public walk on a river bank. **Praya,** the typical genus of *Prayidœ.*

precede, to go before. **proceed,** to progress.

precious, costly; of great worth. **prescious,** foreknowing.

precision, the quality of being precise. **precisian,** one rigidly precise. **prescission,** the act of prescinding.

premonition, a previous warning. **premunition,** act of fortifying beforehand.

prepense, premeditated. **propense,** a leaning toward.

prescription, direction. **proscription,** condemnation.

presence, state of being present.
presents, gifts; documents.
presentiment, a prophetic apprehension of coming misfortune.
presentment, the act of presenting; a picture, likeness, or representation; in law, a report made by a grand jury.
president, one who presides. precedent, example.
preys, seizes and devours. See *praise*.
pride, haughtiness; to indulge in self-gratulation; to exult. pried, did pry.
primer, first book. primmer, more prim.
principal, chief; highest in rank, character, authority value, or importance. principle, a fundamental truth; a rule of action.
prior, former; preceding in time, order, or importance; head of a convent of monks. prier *or* pryer, one who pries.
prize, a reward; anything of value; to esteem. pries, to force open; to scrutinize curiously.
profit, gain. prophet, one who foretells.
propellant, a propelling agent. propellent, propelling.
prophecy, a foretelling. prophesy, to predict.
proximo, next month. See *ultimo*.
prunell, a heavy cashmere. prunelle, a small French prune.
prunella, a plant; a disease. prunello, a prune. Prunella, a genus of plants and of birds.
psalm, a song of praise. salm, one-fourth of a ton.
Psalter, a book of Psalms. See *salter*.
pschutt, ultra-fashionable. See *shut*.
pshaw, an exclamation. See *shah*.
Psylla, a genus of insects. See *Scylla*.
ptere, term in zoölogy. See *tier*.
pungi, a Hindu pipe. See *pongee*.
puny, small; feeble. puisne, a law term.
pupil, a scholar; apple of the eye. pupal, pertaining to a pupa.

purée, a soup. purree, a coloring matter.
purgery, part of a sugar house. See *perjury*.
puritan, one who is very strict in his religious duties. Puritan, one of a sect of English Protestants; pertaining to or suggestive of the Puritans.
purl, sound of waters; to ripple. See *pearl*.
purr, the low murmuring sound made by a cat; an edible bivalve; a bird; to signify by purring. purre, the sandpiper. pirr, a gentle wind.
purse, a small money-bag; to contract into folds. perse, a blue color.
purslane, a plant. See *porcelain*.
purtenance, appurtenance; belongings. See *pertinence*.
puss, a cat; a hare. pus, a secretion from inflamed tissues.
put, to place; the act of putting. putt, term in golf.
putoo, an article of food. puttoo, a fabric of goat's wool. put-to, a stake for tethering horses and cattle.
putty, a mixture for filling holes or cracks; to fill up cracks with putty. putti, forms of Cupids common in Italian art in the sixteenth century. puttee, a gaiter or bandage worn by sportsmen and soldiers.
puya, a nettlewort. Puya, a genus of plants.
pyle, a grain of chaff. See *pile*.
pylorus, the opening between the stomach and the small intestine. pelorus, a nautical instrument for correcting errors in a ship's compass.
pyre, a funeral pile. pyr, a photometric unit.
pyrrhic, a term in prosody; a martial dance. Pyrrhic, pertaining to Pyrrhus.
pyrrhous, of a reddish color. Pyrrhus, king of Epirus.
pyx *or* pix, a box for a compass; a case in which the host is reserved. See *picks*.

Q.

quadrille, a dance; music for a dance; a game of cards. **quadrel,** artificial stone or brick. **quadrelle,** a square-headed mace or arrow.

quarrel, an angry dispute; a brawl. **quarl,** a piece of fire-clay; a fish.

quarte, a term in fencing. See *cart.*

quarto, a book of large size. **cuarta,** a long whip.

quartos, large books. **cuartas,** whips; **cuartos,** coins; measures.

quartz, a mineral. **quarts,** pl. of quart.

quashey, a pumpkin. **quashee,** a West-Indian Negro.

quay, a wharf. **que,** an old coin. See *key.*

queen, a ruler. **quean,** a worthless woman.

queue, an appendage of hair; a file of persons waiting for admittance; the tail-piece of a violin; the stem of a note in music; a lance-rest. See *cue.*

quire, twenty-four sheets of paper. See *choir.*

quite, completely. **quiet,** at rest; to calm.

quoin, a term in architecture. See *coin.*

R.

raab, a coarse sugar. See *rob.*

raad, a fish. See *rod.*

raad, an assembly. See *wrought.*

rabat, imperfectly baked potter's clay. See *rabbit.*

Rabbi, master; teacher. **rabi,** important cereal crop of India.

rabbit, an animal. **rabbet,** a joint in carpentry. **rabot,** a hard-wood rubber.

raca, a term of contempt. **Raca** and **Racha,** scripture names.

race, a particular breed; a family. contest in running; to run swiftly. **reis,** a Portuguese money; duration of life; swift current of water. **racé,** a term in heraldry.

racer, one who or that which races; part of a braiding-machine; a

snake; a fish; a crab. **raser,** one who destroys or obliterates.

rack, to torture; gait of a horse. **wrack,** a plant; to wreck.

racket, a noise; a tennis bat. **rackett,** a wind instrument. **racquet** *or* **raquette,** a tennis bat.

racks, pl. of rack. **rax,** to stretch. **wracks,** pl. of wrack.

radical, fundamental; extreme. **radicle,** a rootlet.

raff, idle, dissolute; a rabble. **raffe,** a triangular sail.

raid, an invasion; to invade. **rayed,** having rays of lines.

raiment, clothing. **rament,** a scraping.

rain, water from the clouds; to shower. **rein,** part of a bridle; to check. **reign,** rule; to govern.

rainy, characterized by rain. **rani,** *or* **ranee,** the wife of a raja.

raise, to uplift. **raze,** to overthrow; talks loudly; to tear down. **rays,** beams of light.

raised, elevated; leavened, as bread. **rased** *or* **razed,** destroyed; leveled with the ground.

raisonné, logical. **raisinée,** a French confection.

ramé, branched. **ramée,** a plant. **Ramé,** a French archæologist. **Ramée,** a French architect.

rancor, hatred. **ranker,** more rank.

rants, does rant. **rance,** a stone; a prop.

rap, a blow; to strike. **wrap,** a cloak; to envelop.

rapine, plunder; spoliation. **rappen,** a Swiss coin.

rapt, enraptured. **rapped,** did rap. **wrapped,** covered.

ras, a promontory. See *wrasse.*

ras, material of wool or silk. See *raw.*

rased, leveled. See *raised.*

rasse, a cat; a sheep; an eminence. See *wrasse.*

rath, a hill or mound; early; soon. See *wrath.*

rath, a temple. See *wrought.*

rattlings, clattering noises. **ratlines** *or* **ratlins,** ropes on shipboard.

raveling, a raveled thread. **ravelin,** a fortification term.

raven, a bird. **raving,** furious exclamation; mad.

raw, not cooked; unfinished; newly done; inexperienced. **ras,** a smooth material of wool or silk.

ray, a line of light or heat; a fish. **re,** a musical note. **rae,** a roe. **reh,** a salty efflorescence. **wray,** to reveal; disclose.

razor, instrument for shaving. **raiser,** one who lifts up.

ream, twenty quires of paper; to make wide. **riem** or **reim,** a rawhide thong.

reaper, one who reaps; a reaping-machine. **reeper,** a strip of a palmyra-palm used in house-building.

recede, to retreat; to withdraw; to cede back. **reseed,** to seed again.

receipt, an acknowledgment. **reseat,** to seat again.

recision, the act of cutting off. **rescission,** the act of rescinding.

reck, to take heed. See *wreck.*

recks, takes heed. See *wrecks.*

reclaim, to recover; to tame; to restore. **réclame,** advertisement.

recognizer, one who recognizes. **recognizor,** term in law.

red, a color. **read,** perused. **redd,** the nest of a fish.

reed, a hollow stalk. **read,** to peruse.

reek, to smoke; to steam. **wreak,** to revenge.

reel, to stagger; to wind; a frame for winding; a dance. **real,** actual.

reeper, a strip of palmyra-palm. See *reaper.*

reeve, a bailiff, overseer, or steward. **reive,** to take pity; to rob.

reflects, bends or casts back; thinks. **reflex,** turned back.

reis, a Portuguese money. See *race.*

reiter, a soldier. See *writer.*

reive, to take pity. See *reeve.*

relay, a fresh supply. **relais,** term in fortification.

relic, a keepsake. **relict,** a widow.

replete, full; completely filled. **repleat,** to plait or fold again.

reseed, to plant again. See *recede.*

resole, to renew the sole of a shoe. See *rissole.*

rest, to be at peace; the remainder. **wrest,** to twist violently.

retail, to sell in small quantities; to communicate. **retaillé,** a term in heraldry.

retch, to strain. **wretch,** a worthless person.

revere, to venerate; to reverence. **revers,** fold of a garment.

rex, a king. See *wrecks.*

Rhenish, pertaining to the river Rhine. **rennish,** furious.

rheum, thin watery matter. See *room.*

Rhine, river in Europe. **rhyne,** Russian hemp. **rine,** a water-course; to touch. **wrine,** a wrinkle.

rhumb, a term in navigation. See *rum.*

rhyme, similarity in sound. **rime,** hoar-frost.

rice, a grain. **rise,** the act of rising.

rich, wealthy; fertile; fruitful. **ritch,** the Syrian bear.

rick, a heap or pile. **wrick,** to twist.

ridiculous, exciting ridicule. **radicolous,** infesting roots.

riem or **reim,** a rawhide thong. See *ream.*

rig, to dress; nautical term. **wrig,** to wriggle.

riggle, a fish. See *wriggle.*

right, just; proper; to make right; in accordance with right. **rite,** a ceremony. **write,** to express by letter. **wright,** a workman.

righter, one who adjusts. See *writer.*

rigor, stiffness; strictness; severity. **rigger,** one who rigs.

rime, hoar-frost. See *rhyme.*

ring, a circle; to sound as a bell. **wring,** to twist.

riot, to revel; an unlawful tumult. **ryot,** a peasant.

ripe, mature; fully developed. **rype,** a ptarmigan.

risk, to hazard; to endanger; an obligation or contract. **risqué,** verging on impropriety.

risky, fraught with risk. risqué, verging on immorality.

rissole, paste of minced meat or fish. resole, to renew the sole.

rithe, a stream; a potato-stalk. See *writhe*.

road, a highway; a railway; an open place for ships; a roadstead. rode, did ride. rowed, past tense of row. roed, having roe.

roam, to wander. Rome, a city.

roan, a color; grained leather. Rhone, river in Europe. rone, a rain spout; a run of ice.

roar, to bellow; cry of a beast. rower, one who rows.

rob, to plunder or steal; juice of ripe fruit mixed with honey. raab, coarse sugar. Raabe, a German author.

robin, a bird. robbin, a sailyard; a package. robbing, stealing.

rock, a mass of stone. roc, a bird.

rod, a straight piece of wood or iron; a measure of length and surface. raad, the thunder-fish of the Nile; a volksraad.

roll, to cause to revolve; a rounded mass. rôle, part in a play.

rondel, a poem. rondle, step of a ladder; a round. rondelle, a circular disk.

rondo, term in music; a game. rondeau, a poem.

rood, part of an acre. rude, rough; awkward; uncivil. rued, did rue.

room, an apartment. rheum, a mucous discharge.

roosh, a wild sheep. See *ruche*.

root, part of a plant. rute, term in mining. route, direction.

rosary, a string of beads. rosery *or* rosary, a rose-nursery.

rosette, an ornament. roset, a red color.

rote, memory. See *wrote*.

rotund, round; a rotunda. rotonde, a ruff.

roué, a debauchee. rouet, a small wheel.

rough, rugged; uncouth. ruff, a collar.

rougher, more rough. ruffer, a coarse hatchel for flax.

rouse, to awaken; to stir. rows, disturbances.

roux, term in cookery. See *rue*.

row, a rank; to propel with oars. roe, an animal; eggs of fish.

rowan, the rowan-tree or its fruit. rowen, a second cutting of hay.

rows, rank; propels with oars. roes, animals; eggs of fish. rose, a flower.

rubicund, ruddy. rubican, flecked with white or gray. Rubicon, river in Italy.

ruche, a ruffle for the neck or wrist. roosh, a wild sheep.

rude, rough; uncivil. rued, did rue. See *rood*.

rue, to regret. roux, term in cookery.

ruff, a collar. See *rough*.

Rufus, a man's name. rufous, reddish; tawny.

rum, liquor. rhumb, a term in navigation.

run, to move swiftly. runn, a low sandy tract.

rundel, a moat; a streamlet. rundle, a rung of a ladder; the drum of a capstan. rundale, lands held in single holdings.

rung, did ring; step of a ladder. wrung, past tense of wring.

ruse, a trick. rues, regrets. rooze, to scatter; to shed.

rute, term in mining. See *root*.

rye, a grain wry, crooked; distorted.

ryot, a peasant. See *riot*.

rype, a ptarmigan. See *ripe*.

S.

sack, a bag; a wine; to plunder. sac, a membranous receptacle. sack *or* sacque, a garment. Sac, an Indian.

sacks, pl. of sack. sax, a knife; a hammer. saxe, a photograph-paper. sacques, pl. of sacque. Saxe, an American poet; a marshal of France.

sadder, more sad. sadr, the lotebush.

saga, a Scandinavian legend. saiga, an antelope.

42

said, did say. **sed,** a snood.

sail, a ship's canvas; to propel by wind. **sale,** act of selling.

sailor, a seaman. **sailer,** a vessel.

sake, a liquor. **saki,** a monkey.

salable *or* **saleable,** capable of being sold. **sailable,** navigable.

salad, raw herbs; a dish. **sallet,** a helmet.

salary, wages. See *celery.*

sally, to leap or rush out suddenly; a term in architecture; a willow; a wren; a stone-fly. **sallee,** a plant. **Sally,** a familiar name for Sarah.

salm, one-fourth of a ton. See *psalm.*

saloon, a refreshment room. **salon** *or* **saloon,** a drawing-room; a gallery.

salter, more salt. **Psalter,** book of Psalms.

salty, somewhat salt. **saltie,** a fish.

salute, to greet with a bow or kiss; deference shown to rank or nationality. **solute,** to dissolve; loose.

salvage, saving goods from the sea. **selvage** *or* **selvedge,** the edge of cloth.

salver, a tray. **salvor,** one who saves goods.

sand-jack, an American oak. **sanjak,** a Turkish district.

sane, of sound mind. **seine,** a net. **Seine,** a river in France. **Seyne,** town in France. **sain,** to sanctify.

sank, did sink. **cinque,** five in cards.

sapper, a chisel; one who saps. **sappar** *or* **sappare,** a mineral.

sarcel, part of a hawk's wing. **sarcelle,** a duck.

sarcophagus, a stone coffin. **sarcophagous,** flesh-eating.

satiric, pertaining to satire. **satyric,** pertaining to satyrs.

satirical, sarcastic. **satyrical,** burlesque.

saurel, a scad. See *sorrel.*

savor, scent; odor. **saver,** one who saves.

sax, a hammer. See *sacks.*

scaf, term in metal-working. **scaff,** food.

scald, to burn with hot liquid. **scalled,** scabby; base.

scat, to drive off by shouting *scat;* a land-tax. **skat,** a game of cards.

sceat, an ancient coin. See *seat.*

scene, place; part of a play. **seen,** perceived. **seine,** a net.

scent, odor; to smell. See *cent.*

scentless, without odor. See *centless.*

scents, perfumes. See *cents.*

schelly, a fish. See *shelly.*

scilla, a medicinal plant. **Scilla,** a genus of plants. **Scylla,** a seanymph; a dangerous rock.

scion, a shoot or twig; a descendant. **cion,** the uvula. **Cyon,** a genus of wild dogs.

scirrhus, a hard tumor. **scirrhous,** resembling a scirrhus.

scissel, clippings of metals. **scissile,** capable of being cut smoothly. **sessile,** term in botany, anatomy, and zoölogy. **Cecil,** a Christian name.

scissura, a term in anatomy. See *cæsura.*

scoff, to mock; deride; mockery. **skoff,** to gobble up.

scout, a spy; to watch closely; to ridicule. **schout,** a municipal officer.

scripture, a writing. **scriptor,** a writer. **Scripture,** the Bible.

scull, a short oar; to impel a boat. See *skull.*

scur, to graze; to scour. **skyr,** bonnyclabber.

scye, a cutter's term. See *sigh.*

Scylla, a rock. **Psylla,** a genus of insects. **Scilla,** a genus of plants.

scytal, a snake. See *cital.*

sea, the ocean. **see,** to perceive. **se,** a Latin pronoun. **si,** a note in music.

sea-born, born of or produced by the sea. **sea-borne,** carried on the sea.

sea-hair, a polyp. **sea-hare,** a mollusk.

seal, a stamp; an animal; to close. **ceil,** to overlay the inner roof. **seel,** to close the eyes of.

seam, union of edges. **seem,** to appear.

seat, a chair; bench; to sit in or on; mansion. **cete,** a whale. **sceat,** an ancient coin.

seave, a rush. See *sieve.*

second, next to the first; a unit of time. **secund,** term in biology.

sects, pl. of sect. **sex,** the distinction of male and female.

sed, a snood. See *said.*

sedulous, diligent; assiduous. **ceduous,** fit to be felled.

seed, grain. **cede,** to resign. **seid,** a descendant of Fatima.

seek, to look or search for. **Sikh,** member of a religious sect in India.

seeks, does seek. **Sikhs,** members of a religious sect.

seen, perceived. See *scene.*

seer, a prophet. **sear** *or* **sere,** dry; withered. **cere,** to cover with wax.

seine, a net. **Seine,** a river in France. **Seyne,** town in France. See *sane.*

seize, to grasp. **sees,** perceives. **seas,** pl. of sea.

seizing, grasping. **seisin** *or* **seizin,** possession of an estate.

seizor, one who seizes. See *Cæsar.*

sell, to barter. See *cell.*

seller, one who sells. See *cellar.*

selvage *or* **selvedge,** the edge of cloth. See *salvage.*

sen, a Japanese coin. **senn,** Alpine herdsman.

senate, an assembly. **sennet,** a fish. **sennit,** a braided cord or plaited straw. **sennight,** a week.

sense, perception by the senses. See *cents.*

sensible, perceptible; judicious. **sensable,** intelligible.

sensor, sensory. See *censor.*

sensual, affecting the senses. **censual,** pertaining to the census

sent, did send. See *cent.*

septenate, term in botany. **septennate,** a period of seven years.

seraph, a celestial being. **serif,** a hair-line.

serene, calm. **cerin,** beeswax; a mineral.

serf, a slave. See *surf.*

serge, a woolen cloth. **surge,** a wave; to swell. **cerge,** a large wax candle.

sergeant, a military officer. **surgent,** a series of rocks.

serial, forming a series. See *cereal.*

series, a connected succession of things. **cerise,** cherry color.

serious, grave. **cereous,** wax-like. **cereus,** a plant. **Sirius,** a very white star.

serous, pertaining to serum. **cerous,** pertaining to cerium; of the nature of a cere.

serra, a saw or saw-like part. See *sirrah.*

seseli, a plant. See *Sicily.*

sessile, a term in botany. See *scissel.*

session, a court; the act of sitting. **cession,** a giving up.

setaceous, bristly. See *cetaceous.*

sew, to join by threads. See *so.*

sewer, one who sews garments. See *sower.*

sewer, a drain. **suer,** one who sues.

sewing-machine, a machine for sewing or stitching. **sowing-machine,** a seed-planting machine.

sexed, having sex. **sext** *or* **sexte,** term in music; a religious observance.

shagreen, skins of animals. See *chagrin.*

shah, king of Persia. **shaw,** a thicket. **pshaw,** an exclamation.

sharpie, a boat. See *charpie.*

shawl, a covering. **schorl,** a mineral.

shear, to clip. **sheer,** very thin; clear; to turn aside. **shire,** a county.

shears, cutting instrument with two blades. **sheers,** a hoisting apparatus.

sheet, a cloth in a bed; a piece of paper. **sheat,** the shad.

shelled, having a shell. **sheld,** spotted.

shelly, abounding in shells. **schelly,** a fish. **Shelley,** an English poet.

sheriff, a civil officer. **sherif,** a descendant of Mohammed.

shied, past tense of shy. **shide,** a plank.

shiny, glossy; lustrous; bright; clear. **shiney** or **shiny,** a slang term for money.

shirred, puckered or gathered. **sherd,** a potsherd.

shoal, a multitude; shallow. **shole,** a plank.

shoe, covering for the foot. **shoo,** to scare away.

shoer, one who shoes. See *sure*.

shone, did shine. **shown,** past participle of *show*.

shoot, to let fly with force; a young branch. **chute,** a trough. **shute,** a trough; a kind of twisted silk.

shophar, an ancient musical instrument. See *chauffeur*.

shot, did shoot; small globules of lead. **shott,** bed of a lake.

should, imp. of shall. **shood,** husks. **shude,** a fish. **shooed,** did shoo.

showed, did show. **shode** or **shoad,** separation; the top of the head; term in mining.

shown, past participle of show. See *shone*.

shut, to close; to bar out; to exclude; made fast. **pschutt,** extravagant in dress.

si, a note in music. See *sea*.

sibilus, a small flute. **sibilous,** hissing.

sibyl, a prophetess. **cibol,** a plant.

sice, sixpence; the number six at dice; a horseman's attendant. **syce,** a horse-keeper.

Sicily, island in Mediterranean sea. **seseli,** a plant.

sickle, a cutting instrument. **Sikel,** pertaining to the Sicels, who gave name to the island of Sicily. **seckel,** a pear.

side, edge; surface; position. **sighed,** did sigh.

sider, one who takes sides. See *cider*.

sieve, a vessel for sifting. **seave,** a rush.

sigh, to breathe audibly, as in grief.

scye, a cutter's term. **sie** or **sigh,** to sink.

sight, perception by the eye. **site,** situation. **cite,** to summon. **cyte,** a cell.

sign, a token. **sine,** a line in geometry.

signet, a seal. See *cygnet*.

Sikh, member of a religious sect in India. See *seek*.

Sikhs, a religious sect. See *seeks*.

sill, a bottom piece of timber. **sil,** a kind of earth.

Simeon, a man's name. **simian,** like an ape or monkey.

similar, nearly alike. **similor** or **semilor,** an alloy of copper and zinc.

single, not double; unmarried. **cingle,** girth for a horse.

singsing, an African antelope. **Sing Sing,** a village and penitentiary in New York.

singular, single; uncommon; rare. **cingular,** circular.

sinical, pertaining to a sine. See *cynical*.

sire, a father; to beget. **sigher,** one who sighs. **saier,** a religious attendant upon the Mahdi.

sirrah, a word of address. **serra,** a saw or saw-like part.

sist, a law term. See *cyst*.

Sistine, pertaining to Pope Sixtus. **cystin,** a chemical.

sit, to be seated. **cit,** a citizen; a cockney. **Cit,** term used by the Hindu philosophers.

size, bulk; a varnish; to estimate. **sighs,** does sigh; pl. of sigh.

skat, a game. See *scat*.

skeleton, the bones only of an animal, preserved in their natural position. **skeletin,** term in anatomy.

skill, dexterity; efficiency. **skil,** the coal-fish.

skull, cranium. **scull,** a short oar; to impel a boat.

slate, a stone; a thin plate of stone. **slait,** a sheep-run; a familiar haunt.

slay, to kill. **sley,** to separate into threads. **sleigh,** a vehicle.

sleeve, the part of dress that covers

the arm. **sleave,** soft floss or silk used for weaving.
slight, trifling; to neglect. **sleight,** a trick.
sloat, a slat; part of a cart. **slote,** a trap-door.
slow, not quick. **sloe,** a fruit or tree.
slue *or* **slew,** to turn about. **slew,** did slay.
snaily, snail-like. **snailey,** an Australian bullock.
so, in like manner. **sow,** to scatter seed. **sew,** to join by threads. **soe,** a pail or bucket.
soak, to steep. **soke,** term in law.
soal, a dirty pond. See *soul.*
soar, to fly. **sore,** an ulcer; painful.
soared, flew. See *sword.*
solar, pertaining to the sun. **sollar,** term in mining.
sold, did sell. **soled,** fitted with a sole. **souled,** instinct with soul.
Solon, an Athenian lawmaker. **solen,** term in medicine and zoölogy.
solute, to dissolve; loose. See *salute.*
some, a portion. **sum,** the whole.
son, a male child. **sun,** source of light. **sunn,** a plant.
sonny, little son: a familiar address. See *sunny.*
soot, dust of a chimney. See *suit.*
sorrel, a reddish-brown color; an herb. **saurel,** a scad. **Sorel,** town in Quebec.
sorties, pl. of sortie. **sortes,** pl. of *sors.*
soul, the immortal part of man. **sole,** part of a shoe; a fish. **soal,** a pond.
souple, part of a flail. See *supple.*
sour, acid; crabbed. **sowar,** in India, a mounted soldier.
southern, pertaining to the South. **Sothern,** an American actor.
sower, one who sows seed. **sewer,** one who sews garments.
sowing-machine, a seed-planting machine. See *sewing-machine.*
spear, a long, pointed weapon. **speer** *or* **speir,** to search; to pry.
specially, particularly. **spatially,** as regards a space.

spencer, a jacket; nautical term.
Spencer, Herbert, Eng. philos.
Spenser, Edmund, Eng. poet.
spice, an aromatic vegetable to season food. **speiss,** term in metallurgy.
staid, sober; grave. **stayed** *or* **staid,** did stay **stade,** a stadium; a wharf.
stair, a step. **stare,** a fixed look; to gaze intently. **stere,** a cubic meter.
stake, a post; a wager. **steak,** a slice of meat.
stam, to amaze; confusion. **stamm,** part of a game.
star, a luminous celestial body; any star-shaped object; a leading actor. **starr,** a term in old English law.
stationary, fixed. **stationery,** writing materials.
statue, a carved image. **stature,** height.
steal, to take unlawfully. **steel,** refined iron.
steely, like steel. **stelæ,** ancient pillars or milestones. **stele,** an upright slab or tablet of stone.
stele, the wooden part of an arrow. See *steal.*
stellar, pertaining to the stars. **steller,** the sea-cow. **stella,** an aster spicule; a star-shaped bandage.
stentor, one having a powerful voice. **stenter,** a machine.
step, a pace. **steppe,** a desert.
stick, a piece of wood; to adhere to. **stich,** a line in poetry.
sticks, pl. of stick; does adhere. **Styx,** a river in Greek myth.; a genus of butterflies.
stigma, mark of disgrace; top of a pistil. **stigme,** a dot.
stitcher, one who stitches. **sticher,** to catch eels in a particular way.
stolen, acquired by stealth or theft. **stolon,** term in botany and zoölogy.
stoop, to bend; steps of a door; a flagon; to descend from dignity; the act of stooping; a prop or support in mines. **stoup,** a basin; a flagon. **stupe,** a sooth-

ing application. **stoep,** a Dutch
stoop or porch.

straight, correct; not crooked;
correctly kept, as accounts.
strait, a narrow pass.

straightway, immediately; without
delay. **straight-way,** a term in
plumbing.

strewed *or* **strowed,** scattered.
strode, did stride.

style, fashion; a writing instrument. **stile,** steps; a term in
carpentry.

subtle, sly; artful. **subtile,** search-
ing; finely woven. **suttle,** net
weight; to act as a sutler.

succor, relief; to help. **sucker,**
a fish; the piston of a pump.

sud, drift-sand; a scallop. **sudd,**
a floating mass of vegetable
matter.

suds, pl. of sud. **sudds,** pl. of sudd.

sue, to prosecute by law; to en-
treat. **sou,** a French coin. **Sioux,**
a tribe of Indians.

suer, one who sues. See *sewer.*

suit, to please; clothing; a case at
law. **soot,** dust of a chimney.
sutt, a sea-bird.

suite, apartments; retinue. **sweet,**
not sour.

suitor, law term; one who solicits;
a lover. **sutor,** a cobbler; a sirup.

sullen, gloomily angry. **Sullan,**
pertaining to Sulla.

sum, the whole. See *some.*

summary, a comprehensive statement. **summery,** pertaining to
summer.

sun, source of light. **sunn,** a plant.
See *son.*

sunny, like the sun; radiant;
bright. **sonny,** little son; a
familiar address.

super, a supernumerary. **souper,**
a term of contempt.

supple, pliant. **souple,** part of a
flail.

surah, a silk material. **sura,** a
chapter of the Koran; toddy.

surculate, to prune; to trim. See
circulate.

sure, positive. **shoer,** one who
shoes.

surf, broken waves. **serf,** a slave.

surface, the outside; to polish or
give a smooth surface to. **Syr-
phus,** a genus of flies.

surge, a wave; to swell. See
serge.

surgent, a series of rocks. See
sergeant.

surplus, overplus; residue. **surplice,** a clerical garment.

surrey, a light carriage. **Surrey,** a
county in England. **Surry,**
county in North Carolina; county
in Virginia.

susurrus, a gentle murmur; a
whisper; a rustling. **susurrous,**
murmuring; rustling.

sutler, a camp provisioner. **subtler,**
more cunning.

swear, to affirm on oath. **sware,**
archaic form of swore.

Swede, a native of Sweden. **suède,**
undressed kid

sword, a weapon; figuratively, the
power of the sword. **soared,** flew.

syce, a horse-keeper. See *sice.*

symbol, emblem; sign representing
something. **simbil,** a stork.
cymbal, a musical instrument.

syphering, a term in ship carpentry.
See *ciphering.*

syrus, a bird. See *cyrus.*

T.

T, something shaped like the letter
T. See *tea.*

tabaret, a kind of silk. **taboret,**
a stool; an embroidery frame; a
small drum.

tablet, a small flat surface. **tab-
lette,** term in fortification.

tache, term in medicine. **tash,** a
fabric.

tacit, silent; implied. **tacet,** musical term. **tasset,** part of armor.
tassette, a small cone.

tact, touch; nice perception.
tacked, did tack.

tai, a Japanese fish. See *tie.*

tail, the hinder or lower part. **tale,**
a story. **tael,** a coin; a weight.
taille, term in law, music, and
dressmaking.

tailor, a maker of men's garments.
tailleur, a banker or dealer in

certain card games. **tailloir,** an abacus.

taipo, an evil spirit. See *typo.*

taller, more tall. **thaler,** a German coin.

tampan, a tick. **tampon,** term in surgery.

taper, a candle; to narrow to a point. **tapir,** an animal.

tar, a dark liquid pitch; a sailor. **taure,** a Roman head-dress. **Taur,** the sign of the zodiac Taurus.

tare, a weed; an allowance. **tear,** a rent; to rend.

tarpon, a fish. **tarpan,** a wild horse.

tarrier, one who tarries. See *terrier.*

tartar, an acid salt; a hard deposit on the teeth; an ill-tempered person. **Tartar,** a native of Tartary.

Tartarus, a deep abyss. **tartarous,** consisting of tartar. **Tartarous,** of or like a Tartar.

tattoo, to mark by pricking coloring matter into the skin; beat of drum to summon to quarters. **tatou,** an armadillo.

tatty, or **tatta,** a matting made of cuscus-grass. **tata,** a residence of an African chief. **ta-ta,** farewell.

tau, a fish. **taw,** to dress and prepare leather; a game at marbles.

Taurid, one of a shower of meteors. See *torrid.*

taut, not slack; tense; stretched tight. **taught,** did teach.

tax, a charge; a weight. **tacks,** small nails; fastens.

taxis, term in surgery. **Taxus,** a genus of trees.

taxman, a tax-gatherer. **tacksman,** a tenant or lessee.

tchick, a sound. See *chic.*

tea, a drink; a plant. **tee,** a mark; a term in golf. **ti,** a plant. **T,** something shaped like the letter T.

teache, a boiler for sugar-cane. **teach,** to instruct.

teal, a duck; a Welsh dry measure. **teil,** a tree. **teel,** a plant and its seed.

team, several horses or oxen. **teem,** to produce; to multiply.

tear, water from the eye. See *tier.*

tease, to vex; to card wool. **teas,** pl. of tea.

technology, a treatise on the arts. **tecnology,** a treatise on children.

tedium, wearisomeness. **Te Deum,** a hymn; music to this hymn.

teer, to stir. See *tier.*

teeter, to seesaw; a seesaw **titar,** a partridge.

tenant, one who occupies an estate of another. **tenent,** holding.

tennis, a game. **tenace,** a term in whist.

tense, taut; strained; a term in grammar. **tents,** pl. of tent.

tenuous, thin; minute; rare. **tenuis,** term in grammar.

term, a limit; limited time; a word. **turm,** a troop.

tern, a bird; a schooner; term in mathematics. **terne,** sheet iron. See *turn.*

ternary, a triad; formed in groups of three. **ternery,** a breeding-place for terns.

terrace, a level bank with sloping sides; to fashion as a terrace. **terras,** a term in marble-working.

terrene, pertaining to the earth. See *tureen.*

terret or **territ,** part of a harness-pad. See *turret.*

terrier, a dog. **tarrier,** one who tarries.

tester, one who tests. **testar,** a West-Indian fish. **testa,** the outer coat of a seed.

testy, irritable; waspish. **teste,** a law term.

tetanic, term in physiology and medicine. See *Titanic.*

tew, to beat; to scourge; a rope. See *to.*

thaler, a German coin. See *taller.*

their, belonging to them. **there,** in that place.

theocracy, a form of government. **theocrasy,** a form of worship.

thieve, to steal. **theave,** a yearling ewe.

threw, did throw. **through,** from end to end.

throne, a chair of state. **thrown,** hurled.

throw, to hurl; a fling; a cast of dice. **throe,** pain; agony.

thyme, a plant. See *time.*

thyrsus, the wand of Bacchus. **Thyrsis,** a herdsman; a name employed by Theocritus and Virgil.

ti, a plant. See *tea.*

tiar, a tiara. See *tire.*

tick, to beat, as a watch; a parasite. **tic,** neuralgia.

tide, ebb and flow of the sea. **tied,** did tie. **tyed,** separated, as ore.

tie, to bind; a knot. **tye,** term in mining; nautical term. **tai,** a Japanese fish.

tier, a row. **tear,** water from the eye. **teer,** to stir. **ptere,** term in zoölogy.

till, to cultivate, as soil; a money-drawer. **til,** the sesame, or its seed.

timber, building material; to furnish with timber. **timbre,** quality of tone; crest on a coat of arms.

time, measure of duration. **thyme,** a plant.

tinkle, a sharp sound. **tincal,** crude borax.

tire, to weary; band on rim of a wheel. **tier,** one who ties. **Tyre,** a city. **tiar,** a tiara.

Titanic, relating to the Titans. **tetanic,** term in physiology and medicine. **titanic,** term in chemistry.

titar, a partridge. See *teeter.*

to, toward; as far as. **too,** also; likewise. **two,** a number. **tew,** to dress leather.

toad, an animal. **toed,** did toe. **towed,** did tow. **tode,** to haul.

toady, a mean flatterer. **tody,** a bird. **Todi,** a genus of birds.

toat, a handle of a plane. See *tote.*

tode, to haul with a tode; an implement for skidding logs. See *toad.*

toe, part of the foot. **to,** a Japanese measure. **tow,** coarse hemp; to draw a boat.

toes, pl. of toe. **tose,** to pull about or asunder. **tows,** does tow.

tolled, was rung; knelled. **told,** related.

tomb, vault for a dead body. **toom,** to empty; a dumping-ground for rubbish.

ton, a weight. **tun,** a cask.

tongue, fleshy organ in the mouth; language. **tong,** an instrument.

to-night, the present night. **tonite,** an explosive.

tonsil, a gland in the throat. **tonsile,** capable of being clipped.

tool, an instrument. **tulle,** a thin fabric.

toon, a tree. See *tune.*

toot, to sound a horn. **tout,** to follow; to solicit customers; a watcher of races.

tore, did tear. **tor,** a hill.

torrid, burning hot. **Taurid,** one of a shower of meteors.

torsal, pertaining to a torse. **torsel,** a small scroll.

tortil, a heraldic wreath. **tortile,** twisted; curved. **turtle,** a tortoise; a dove.

tote, to carry. **toat,** the handle of a bench-plane.

toucan, a bird. **tucan,** a gopher.

tough, not easily broken. **tuff,** a mineral substance.

tour, to travel about; a journey. **tur,** the urus.

tournay, a material. **tourney,** a mock fight of knights. **tourné,** term in heraldry.

tow, to draw a boat. See *toe.*

toxin *or* **toxine,** a poisonous product. **toxon,** a spicule.

tract, a region of country; a small book. **tracked,** traced.

trail, to drag; a track; anything drawn. **traill,** a bird.

traitor, one who betrays a trust; one who commits treason. **traiteur,** a restaurant-keeper.

tranka, box used by an acrobat. **trankeh,** a boat.

transplanter, one who transplants; a tool. **transplantar,** term in anatomy.

travel, a journey; to journey.

travail, labor; to suffer. travale, term in tambourine-playing.

tray, a waiter; a salver; a wooden trough. trey, three at cards.

treadle, a lever; to work a treadle. tredille or tredrille, a game at cards.

treat, to handle; to discourse on; to settle; to amuse or gratify; an entertainment. treet, a kind of bran.

treatise, a formal essay. treaties, pl. of treaty.

treble, triple; highest part in music. trebble, a frame.

tressed, having tresses. trest, a beam; a trestle.

trevat, a weaver's knife. trivet, a tripod for holding cooking vessels over a fire; a knife for cutting loops of a piled fabric.

triarchy, rule by three persons. triarchie, term in heraldry.

tried, did try; tested. tride, short and swift.

triple, threefold; to treble. tripel, a limestone.

triplet, three of a kind or three united. triblet, a mandrel.

trivet, a tripod. See trevat.

trochal, shaped like a wheel. trochil, the crocodile-bird.

troche, a medicated lozenge. trochee, term in prosody.

trochil, a bird. See trochal.

troop, a company, herd, flock, or swarm; to move rapidly, as a troop of soldiers; to depart hastily. troupe, a company, especially of actors or minstrels.

trophy, a memorial of victory. trophi, term in entomology.

troupe, a company. See troop.

truce, an agreement between belligerents. trousse, a case of small implements, usually fastened to a girdle. truths, facts. trews, trousers.

tryst, a meeting-place. triste, a cattle fair.

tuber, a root. tuba, a trumpet.

tucan, a gopher. See toucan.

tuff, a mineral substance. See tough.

tulle, a thin fabric. See tool.

tumulus, an artificial mound or cairn. tumulous, abounding in mounds or hills.

tun, a cask. See ton.

tune, melodious tones or notes; harmony; to put in tune. toon, a tree.

tur, the urus. See tour.

turbid, muddy; soiled. turbit, a breed of pigeons.

tureen, a covered dish. terrene, pertaining to the earth. terrine, an earthen jar usually sold with its contents.

turm, a troop. See term.

turn, to move round; to change. tern, a bird; a schooner; term in mathematics. terne, sheet iron.

turnip, a plant and its root. turn-up, a disturbance; one who or that which turns up unexpectedly.

turr, a viol. Tyr, the god of war and victory.

turret, a small tower; a monitor-roof. terret or territ, part of a harness-pad.

turtle, a tortoise; a dove. See tortil.

tusky, having tusks. tuskee, a turnip.

tussle, a struggle; to struggle. tussal, relating to or caused by a cough.

twaddle, to babble; idle talk. twaddell, a hydrometer.

twinship, the relation between twins. twin ship, a similar ship of the same line.

two, a number. See to.

tye, term in mining; nautical term. See tie.

tyed, did tye. See tide.

typo, a compositor. taipo, an evil spirit; a theodolite; a vicious dog or horse.

Tyr, the god of war and victory. See turr.

Tyre, a city. See tire.

U.

uhlan or ulan, a mounted soldier. yulan, a Chinese magnolia.

ule, a tree. See Yule.

ultimo, last month. **proximo,** next month. While these words are not homophones, they are sometimes mistaken one for the other.

undue, excessive; not legal. **undo,** to annul; to unfasten.

unlade, to unload. **unlaid,** not laid or placed.

Uranian, pertaining to Uranus. **uranion,** a musical instrument.

urban, belonging to the city. **urbane,** courteous.

urbanist, a resident of a city or town. **urbaniste,** a variety of pear. **Urbanist,** a follower of Pope Urban.

urn, a vase. See *earn.*

ursine, pertaining to a bear. **urson,** a porcupine.

use, to apply; to handle. **yews,** trees. **ewes,** sheep. **youse** *or* **youze,** the chetah.

Utah, a state. **Uta,** a genus of lizards.

V.

vail, a covering for the face; money given to servants. See *vale*.

vain, proud; fruitless. **vane,** a weathercock. **vein,** a blood-vessel.

vair, a kind of fur; term in heraldry. **vare,** a wand or staff of authority.

valance *or* **valence,** a damask; a curtain. **valence,** term in chemistry and biology.

vale, a valley. **veil** *or* **vail,** a covering; to screen.

Valencia, co. N. Mex. **Valentia,** isl. and t. W. coast of Ire.; genus of insects. **valencia,** a linen cloth.

valley, space between hills. **valet,** a male servant.

valor, bravery; courage; prowess. **vallar,** pertaining to a rampart.

varicose, swollen or enlarged veins. **verrucose,** wart-like.

vary, to change. **vairé,** a term in heraldry.

veer, to turn; to shift; to change. **vire,** an arrow; term in heraldry.

vein, a blood-vessel. See *vain.*

velocity, quickness of motion. **villosity,** term in botany and anatomy.

vendue, a public sale. **fendu,** slashed or split, as a garment.

Venus, goddess of love. **venous,** pertaining to the veins.

veracious, truthful. **voracious,** greedy; ravenous.

veracity, truthfulness. **voracity,** greediness; gluttony.

verging, bordering; approaching. See *virgin.*

verrucose, wart-like. See *varicose.*

versed, skilled. **verst,** a Russian measure of length.

vertical, in the zenith; perpendicular. **vortical,** pertaining to a vortex.

vesicle, a little air-bladder. **vesical,** pertaining to a vesica.

vew, the yew. See *view.*

vial, a small bottle. **viol,** a stringed instrument. **vile,** base.

vicarious, acting or suffering for another. **vicarius,** a substitute; a vicar.

vice, a fault; evil conduct. **vise** *or* **vice,** a machine for gripping; to screw.

view, to look at; sight; scene; opinion. **vew,** the yew. **vue,** the sight-opening of a helmet.

villainage, condition of a villain or peasant. **villeinage, villenage,** *or* **villanage,** servitude.

villosity, term in anatomy and botany. See *velocity.*

vindictive, revengeful. **vindicative,** tending to vindicate.

violin, a musical instrument. **violine,** a chemical substance.

virago, a termagant; a vixen. **farrago,** a jumble; a confused mixture.

vire, an arrow; term in heraldry. See *veer.*

virgin, a maiden. **verging,** bordering; approaching.

virtue, moral goodness. **virtu,** artistic excellence; the love of fine art.

virus, contagious or poisonous matter. **virous,** having virus.

viscus, term in anatomy. **viscous,** glutinous.

visit, a call; to make a call. **visite,** a cape or mantle.

viz., to wit; namely. **vis,** physical force; moral power.

vlei, a valley. **vly,** marshy ground. See *fly.*

vo, term in electricity. **voe** *or* **vo,** an inlet or bay.

volcanic, pertaining to a volcano. **Vulcanic,** pertaining to Vulcan.

volition, the act of willing **volation,** flight, as of a bird.

volley, a discharge of many guns. **volet,** a veil; term in painting.

voluble, rolling or turning easily; fluent in speech. **volable,** nimble witted.

voracious, greedy; ravenous. See *veracious.*

voracity, greediness. See *veracity.*

vortical, pertaining to a vortex. See *vertical.*

vue, the sight-opening of a helmet. See *view.*

W.

wacke, a mineral. See *whack.*

wade, to pass through water. **weighed,** did weigh.

wah, the panda. **waw,** a wave; to stir; to cry as a cat. **wha,** who.

wail, to lament. **wale,** a mark or streak; a timber; to mark with stripes. **whale,** a sea animal.

wailer, one who laments. See *whaler.*

waist, part of the body. **waste,** loss; destruction; to spend need-lessly; to impair.

wait, to tarry; a pause. **weight,** heaviness.

waler, a horse. See *whaler.*

wall, side of a building; a defense; to build a wall. **waul,** to cry as a cat. **whall,** wall-eye.

wallow, to roll in mire. **walla** *or* **wallah,** a doer; a worker.

wand, a long slender rod. **wanned,** having become pale or wan.

wander, to ramble; to be delirious. **wonder,** amazement; a marvel; to be amazed.

wane, decrease; to grow less. **wain,** a wagon. **Wayne,** a surname.

want, scarcity; poverty; lack; to be in need. **wa'n't,** an inelegant contraction for *was not* or *were not.*

war, open hostility between nations; to make war. **wore,** did wear.

ward, to watch or guard; a district or division. **warred,** contested; fought.

ware, merchandise. **wear,** carry upon the person. **wair,** a plank.

where, at what place. **weigher,** one who weighs.

warn, to caution. **worn,** from verb wear; used.

warren, a law term; ground kept for rabbits. **warrin,** the Australian blue-bellied lory.

wat, addicted to drinking; a fellow. **Watt,** James, Scotch inventor. **watt,** term in electricity. See *what.*

waul, to cry as a cat. See *wall.*

wave, a billow; to flutter. **waive,** to set aside.

waver, to be unsteady; vacillate. **waiver,** term in law.

wavy, moving like waves. **wavey** *or* **wavy,** a goose.

wax, a thick, tenacious substance; to smear with wax; to grow. **whacks,** pl. of whack.

way, passage; manner; direction. **weigh,** to determine the weight. **wey,** a measure of weight. **whey,** watery part of milk.

ways, pl. of way. **waise,** to guide; direct.

we, a pronoun. **wee,** small.

weak, infirm. **week,** seven days. **weke,** a squealing sound.

weakly, sickly. **weekly,** once a week.

weal, a stripe; welfare; to mark. See *wheel.*

weald, a forest. See *wield.*

wean, drawn away from. **ween,** to imagine. **wheen,** a quantity; a queen.

wear, carry upon the person. See *ware.*

weather, state of the atmosphere.

wether, a sheep. whether, if; which one.

weave, to unite threads so as to form cloth. we've, contraction of *we have*.

weaver, one who weaves; a beetle. weever, a fish.

weel, a whirlpool; a term in heraldry. See *wheel*.

weet, a bird-call. See *wheat*.

weigh, to determine the weight. See *way*.

weighed, did weigh. See *wade*.

weigher, one who weighs. See ware.

weight, heaviness. See *wait*.

weily, nearly. See *wily*.

weir *or* wear, a dam; a fence. we're, contraction of *we are*. weare, term in heraldry.

we'll, contraction of *we will*. See *wheel*.

wen, an encysted tumor. when, at what time.

wert, from verb be. wort, an herb; sweet infusion of malt.

wet, moist; rainy. whet, to sharpen.

wether, a sheep. See *weather*.

wey, a measure of weight. See *way*.

wha, who. See *wah*.

whack, a blow; to strike. wacke, a mineral.

whacks, pl. of whack. See *wax*.

whale, a sea animal. See *wail*.

whaler, a ship or person employed in whale-fishing. wailer, one who laments. waler, a horse; a chastiser.

whall, wall-eye. See *wall*.

what, an interrogative pronoun. watt, term in electricity. wat, addicted to drinking; a fellow. wot, from verb wit. Watt, James, Scotch inventor.

wheat, an important food plant. weet, the imitative call of a bird.

wheel, a circle; to turn about. wheal, a pustule; a mine. weal, a stripe; welfare; to mark. weel, a whirlpool; a term in heraldry. we'll, contraction of we will.

wheeled, did wheel. See *wield*.

wheen, a quantity; a queen. See *wean*.

when, at what time. See *wen*.

where, at what place. See *ware*.

wherry, a boat; a liquor. See *worry*.

whet, to sharpen. See *wet*.

whether, if; which one. See *weather*.

whew, an exclamation. See *hew*.

whewer, the European widgeon. See *hewer*.

whey, watery part of milk. See *way*.

which, a pronoun. witch, a sorceress. wich *or* wych, a salt-pit.

whidah, a bird. See *widow*.

whig, a political party. wig, a covering for the head.

while, space of time; to spend. wile, strategy; deceit.

whiled, did while. See *wild*.

whim, a freak. wim, to winnow grain.

whin, a plant; a rock; a machine for hoisting. See *win*.

whine, to complain. wine, fermented juice of fruits.

whined, did whine. See *wind*.

whir *or* whirr, a sound from rapid whirling; to hum or buzz. wherr, very sour.

whirl, to turn round rapidly. whorl, the fly of a spindle; term in botany and zoölogy.

whirry, to hurry. See *worry*.

whish, to make a whirring sound; silent; hush. See *wish*.

whist, silent; a game at cards. See *wist*.

whit, a small particle. wit, intellect.

white, of the color of snow. wight, a person. wite, to blame; a punishment.

whither, where. wither, to fade.

whoa, a call; to stop. See *ho*.

whoa, an exclamation. See *woe*.

whole, all. See *hole*.

wholly, entirely. See *holy*.

whoop, a call; to shout. See *hoop*.

whortle, the whortleberry. wortle, term in mechanics.

whose, a pronoun. hoose *or* hooze, a disease of cattle.

why, for what cause. **wie** *or* **wye,** a warrior. **wye,** the letter Y; a kind of crotch. **wy,** an African grazing-ground.

whys, reasons. See *wise*.

wich *or* **wych,** a salt-pit. See *which*.

wicked, sinful; vicious. **wicket,** a small gate.

widow, a woman whose husband has died. **whidah,** a bird. **Whydah,** a town in Africa.

wie *or* **wye,** a warrior. See *why*.

wield, to sway or govern. **weald,** a forest. **wheeled,** did wheel.

wig, covering for the head. See *whig*.

wight, a person. See *white*.

wild, not tame or cultivated; violent. **whiled,** did while.

wile, strategy; deceit. See *while*.

wily, cunning, sly, artful. **weily,** nearly; well-nigh.

wim, to winnow grain. See *whim*.

win, to gain. **whin,** a plant; a rock. **wynn,** a truck.

wind, to coil; to move spirally. **whined,** did whine.

windlass, a machine to raise weights. **windless,** having no wind; calm.

windrowed, past tense of windrow. **wind-rode,** nautical term.

winds, pl. of wind. **winze,** term in mining.

wine, fermented juice of fruits. See *whine*.

winkle, a gastropod; vacillating. **winkel,** a shop or store; a canteen.

Winona, a county in Minnesota; a town in Mississippi. **Wenonah,** a town in New Jersey.

wise, sagacious; way. **whys,** reasons.

wish, desire; to crave. **whish,** to make a whirring sound; silent; hush.

wist, knew. **whist,** silent; a game at cards.

wit, intellect; ready perception of unexpected analogies. See *whit*.

witch, a sorceress. See *which*.

wite, to blame; a punishment. See *white*.

with, a preposition. **withe,** a flexible twig; to bind.

wither, to fade. See *whither*.

woad, a plant; a dyestuff. **wode,** mad; wood.

woe, deep grief; sorrow **whoa,** an exclamation.

womb, the uterus. **woom,** beaver-fur.

won, gained. See *one*.

wonder, amazement; a marvel; to be amazed. See *wander*.

wood, timber. **would,** past tense of will.

wore, did wear. See *war*.

worn, from verb wear; used. See *warn*.

worry, to harass; tease. **wherry,** a boat; a liquor. **whirry,** to hurry.

wort, an herb; sweet infusion of malt. See *wert*.

wortle, term in mechanics. See *whortle*.

wot, from verb wit. See *what*.

wrack, a plant; to wreck. See *rack*.

wracks, pl. of wrack. See *racks*.

wrap, to enfold; a covering. See *rap*.

wrapped, covered. See *rapt*.

wrasse, a fish. **ras,** a promontory. **rasse,** a cat; an eminence.

wrath, anger; furious rage. **wroth,** wrathful. **rath,** a hill or mound; early; soon.

wray, to reveal; disclose. See *ray*.

wreak, to revenge. See *reek*.

wreck, a disaster; destruction; to ruin. **reck,** to take heed.

wrecks, pl. of wreck; ruins. **recks,** takes heed. **rex,** a king.

wrest, to twist violently. See *rest*.

wretch, a worthless person. See *retch*.

wrick, to twist. See *rick*.

wrig, to wriggle. See *rig*.

wriggle, to move the body to and fro. **riggle,** a fish.

wright, a workman. **write,** to inscribe. See *right*.

wrine, a wrinkle. See *Rhine*.

wring, to twist. See *ring*.

writer, one who writes. **righter,**

one who adjusts. **reiter,** a soldier.

writhe, to twist, as from pain. **rithe,** a stream; a potato-stalk.

wrote, did write. **rote,** memory.

wrought, performed; worked. **raad,** a legislative assembly. **rath,** a Buddhist rock-temple; a car or chair used in Burma.

wrung, past tense of wring. See *rung.* –

wry, crooked; distorted. See *rye.*

wy, a grazing ground. See *why.*

wych, a salt-pit. See *which.*

wye, the letter Y; a kind of crotch. See *why.*

wynn, a truck. See *win.*

X.

xero, a combining prefix. See *zero.*

Y.

yamma, a llama. **yammer,** to complain peevishly; to whine. **Yama,** the Hindu god who judges the dead.

yarrow, a plant. **yarrah,** the Australian gum-tree.

yeast, leaven; ferment. See *east.*

yew, a tree. See *ewe.*

yews, trees. See *use.*

yo, an exclamation. **yoh,** a Chinese reed.

yoke, a frame of wood; to couple or join together; to mate. **yolk,** part of an egg.

yore, long ago. **your,** belonging to you. See *ewer.*

you, a pronoun. See *ewe.*

youse or **youze,** the chetah. See *use.*

yu or **yuh,** jade. See *ewe.*

yulan, a Chinese magnolia. See *uhlan.*

Yule, Christmas-tide; the feast celebrating Christmas time. **ule,** a tree. **you'll,** contraction of you will.

Z.

zero, naught. **xero,** a combining prefix.

Zillah, a district in India. **zilla,** an herb.